Street by Street

MANCHESTER

BOLTON, BURY, OLDHAM, ROCHDALE, SALFORD, STOCKPORT

Altrincham, Ashton-under-Lyne, Bramhall, Hazel Grove, Hyde, Littleborough, Middleton, Prestwich, Ramsbottom, Sale, Stalybridge, Stretford, Wilmslow

GAZETTEER SYMBOL KEY

☎ - telephone number

📞 - telephone booking service

@ - email address

🖱 - web address

📄 - fax number

⌀ - map page number and grid reference

1st edition published July 2008
© Automobile Association Developments Limited 2008

 This product includes map data licensed from
Ordnance Survey® with the permission of the
Controller of Her Majesty's Stationery Office.
© Crown copyright 2008.
All rights reserved. Licence number 100021153.

The copyright in all PAF is owned by Royal Mail Group plc.

Published by AA Publishing (a trading name of Automobile Association
Developments Limited, whose registered office is Fanum House, Basing View,
Basingstoke, Hampshire RG21 4EA. Registered number 1878835).

Cartography produced by the Mapping Services Department
of The Automobile Association. (A03534)

A CIP Catalogue record for this book is available from the British Library.

Design and management for listings section by ey communications Ltd.
(www.eysite.com). Editorial services by Pam Stagg

Listings data provided by Global DataPoint Limited, London

Printed by Oriental Press in Dubai

The Automobile Association would like to thank the
following photographers, companies and picture libraries
for their assistance in the preparation of this book.

Abbreviations for the picture credits are as follows: (t) top; (b)
bottom; (l) left; (r) right; (AA) AA World Travel Library.
Front Cover Nigel Francis/Robert Harding Travel/Photolibrary;
3 (t) AA/J Mottershaw; 3 (ct) AA/L Whitwam; 3 (cb) AA/J
Mottershaw; 3 (b) AA/L Whitwam; 4 AA/S Day; 5 AA/S Day;
7 AA/C Molyneux; 8 AA/V Greaves; 10 AA/M Taylor;

Every effort has been made to trace the copyright holders, and we
apologise in advance for any accidental errors. We would be happy
to apply the corrections in the following edition of this publication.

Ref: ML43y

Opposite page
Top: Manchester's Central Library
Centre top: Street musicians entertain in St Ann's Square
Centre bottom: Renovated buildings line the canal basin in Manchester
Bottom: Fine architecture on the corner of Market Street

Manchester...

With its theatres, clubs and cafe society Manchester, once one of the most important cities of the industrial revolution, is today a cosmopolitan city with much to offer the visitor. Historical landmarks stand side-by-side with bold, contemporary buildings, and there are plenty of open spaces where you can relax away from the bustling crowds. The shopping here is legendary. You'll find exclusive boutiques and independent shops in the Northern Quarter, designer stores in King Street, and famous department stores in New Cathedral Street, while The Arndale Centre is filled with big high street names. Alternatively, head for the bargains at the city's wide selection of markets.

To help you make the most of your leisure time in Manchester and the surrounding area we have provided a useful listings section covering a range of attractions from stately homes and country parks, outstanding museums and art galleries, to cinemas and grand theatres featuring everything from opera to live music and classical ballet. The city's huge student population guarantees vibrant nightlife and there's an endless choice of cutting-edge designer bars, traditional pubs, chic lounges and comfy watering holes. Entries are listed alphabetically (ignoring The) under each category heading. The map reference at the end of each entry denotes the map page number in the mapping section and the grid square in which the street/road is to be found, not the individual establishments. We have given the street name, town/city name, post code, telephone and fax numbers and, where possible, email and website details.

Please note: the entries in this listings section were provided by a third party and are not in any way recommended or endorsed by the AA.

TOURIST ATTRACTIONS

Bramall Hall

Bramall Hall is a superb example of a Cheshire black and white timber-framed manor house, with origins dating back to medieval England. The property is lovingly cared for and presents the visitor with a marvellous historic record spanning six centuries.

Bramhall Park, Hall Road, Stockport, Greater Manchester SK7 3NX
☎ 0845 833 0974
@ bramall.hall@stockport. gov.uk
🖰 www.bramallhall.org.uk
🖹 0161 486 6959
🕭 Page 183-H3

Brookside Miniature Railway

Macclesfield Road, Poynton, Stockport, Greater Manchester SK12 1BY
☎ 01625 872919, 01625 875088
@ brooksideg.c@tiscali. co.uk
🖹 01625 859119
🕭 Page 195-F1

East Lancashire Railway

East Lancashire Railway was reopened in 1991 and the trip offers an insight into the history of the railway to visitors.

Bolton Street Station, Bolton Street, Bury, Greater Manchester BL9 0EY
☎ 0161 764 7790
@ enquire@east-lancs-railway.co.uk
🖰 www.east-lancs-rly.co.uk
🕭 Page 4-C4

Ellenroad Engine House

Ellenroad Engine House was erected in 1892, and houses 3,000 horse-power steam engines *Victoria* and *Alexandra*, a coal-fired Lancashire boiler and other steam-powered artefacts.

Elizabethan Way, Milnrow, Rochdale, Greater Manchester OL16 4LG
☎ 01706 881952
@ ellenroad@aol.com
🖰 www.ellenroad.org.uk
🕭 Page 44-C1

Etherow Country Park

Etherow Country Park was one of Britain's first country parks. Established in 1968 around an old cotton mill, the park has steadily grown in size and popularity and now attracts over a quarter of a million visitors every year.

George Street, Compstall, Stockport, Greater Manchester SK6 5JD
☎ 0161 427 6937
@ parks@stockport.gov.uk
🖰 www.stockport. gov.uk/contacts/. etherowcountrypark
🖹 0161 427 3643
🕭 Page 163-G4

Fletcher Moss Gardens

The garden has a collection of trees and shrubs together with herbaceous borders and an alpine house. Azaleas, ceanothus, various alpines, wetland plants, junipers and Bhutan Pine adorn the gardens while a puddled-clay pond at the foot of the rockery supports several terrapins and fish.

Wilmslow Road, Didsbury, Greater Manchester M23 2SW
☎ 0161 434 1877
🖰 www.manchester.gov.uk
🕭 Page 157-H5

Heaton Hall

Heaton Hall is an 18th-century neo-classical country house set in 650 acres of rolling parkland. The interiors feature ornate plasterwork, mahogany doors and furniture along with paintings by Italian artist Biagio Rebecca.

Heaton Park, Prestwich, Greater Manchester M25 5SW
☎ 0161 773 1231
🖰 www.manchester galleries.org/our-other-venues/heaton-hall
🖹 0161 235 8805
🕭 Page 86-D1

Heaton Moor Park

Heaton Moor Park was given, in 1894, to the newly formed Heaton Norris District Council by Lord Egerton as a charitable trust for the free use and enjoyment of the public as a public play, pleasure and recreation ground. The park features

Magnificent Bramall Hall, above, dates back to Tudor times

gardens, a toddler play area and bowling greens.

Peel Moat Road, Heaton Moor, Stockport, Greater Manchester SK4 4PH
☎ 0161 474 4512,
   0161 474 4418
@ parks@stockport.gov.uk
⌂ www.stockport.gov.uk/
   content/leisureculture/
   parksrecreation/parks/
   heatonmoorpark
⦿ Page 159-D1

Heaton Park
Heaton Park is a huge family park owned by Manchester City Council, 4 miles north of the city centre. Attractions include an animal centre, children's play areas, an orienteering course, a boating lake and bike hire.

The Farm Centre, Manchester City Council, Manchester, Greater Manchester M25 2SW
☎ 0161 773 1085
@ heatonpark@
   manchester.gov.uk
⌂ www.heatonpark.org.
   uk/HeatonPark/
▤ 0161 798 0107
⦿ Page 86-D2

The Heaton Park Tramway
The Heaton Park Tramway has developed from a restored section of the former siding off the Manchester Corporation Tramways system on Middleton Road just northeast of the city. The park provides relaxation and recreation for families from the inner city areas and the trams provide easy access.

Heaton Park, Tram Depot, Prestwich, Greater Manchester M25 5SW
☎ 0161 740 1919
⌂ www.mtms.org.uk
⦿ Page 86-D2

Heywood Civic Centre
Church Street, Heywood, Greater Manchester OL10 1LW
☎ 01706 368130
☏ 01706 624104
@ heywoodcivic@link4life.
   org
⌂ www.link4life.org/
⦿ Page 41-E4

Manchester Cathedral
Manchester cathedral has a stunning interior with the best late medieval woodwork in the north. The cathedral offers the chance to help children and young people make a stronger connection with the Christian faith. Classical concerts and performances are also put on and the cathedral welcomes visiting choirs. Guided tours available. Visitor centre.

The Cathedral, Manchester, Greater Manchester M3 1SX
☎ 0161 833 2220
@ office@manchester
   cathedral.com
⌂ manchestercathedral.org
▤ 0161 839 6218
⦿ Page 6-E2

Moses Gate Country Park
Moses Gate Country Park covers 750 acres supporting a wide range of wildlife and offers walking, cycling, horse riding, model boating, aircraft flying and fishing facilities.

Rock Hall Visitors Centre, Hall Lane, Bolton, Greater Manchester BL4 7QN
☎ 01204 334343
@ rangers@bolton.gov.uk
⌂ www.bolton.gov.uk
▤ 01204 701330
⦿ Page 66-B2

Lush, green countryside around Bramhall

National Trust: Quarry Bank Mill and Styal Estate
Quarry Bank Mill and Styal Estate once belonged to the wealthy Greg family. The water-powered Georgian mill still produces cotton calico which is sold in the mill shop. Hands-on exhibits and demonstrations show how traditional spinning and weaving was transformed through the ingenuity of early textile engineers. The adjoining garden contains traditional varieties of vegetables, fruit and herbs, as well as geese and hens.

Styal, Wilmslow, Cheshire SK9 4LA
☎ 01625 527468,
   01625 445896
@ quarrybankmill@
   nationaltrust.org.uk
⌂ www.nationaltrust.
   org.uk/main/w-vh/w-
   visits/w-findaplace/w-
   quarrybankmilland
   styalestate
▤ 01625 539267
⦿ Page 190-D5

Platt Fields Park
Platt Fields Park covers 173

acres and features cycle pathways, a Shakespearean garden, orchards, lakes, a labyrinth and picnic areas. The park also hosts the Manchester mela festival, Eid festivals, annual fireworks, bonfire displays and family fun days.

Wilmslow Road, Fallowfield, Manchester, Greater Manchester M14 6LA
☎ 0161 224 2902
⌂ www.manchester.gov.uk
⦿ Page 143-E1

Smithills Hall
The Smithills Hall is set in a 2,000-acre estate dating back to the 14th century and displays medieval, Tudor and Victorian architecture along with collections of furniture and artefacts.

Smithills Dean Road, Bolton, Greater Manchester BL1 7NP
☎ 01204 332377
@ museums@bolton.gov.uk
⌂ www.boltonmuseums.
   org.uk/smithillshall
⦿ Page 33-E2

St Ann's Church
St Ann's church is an elegant, neo-classical

building dating from 1712, and is often ascribed to Sir Christopher Wren or one of his pupils. It is a Grade I listed building of historic and architectural merit.

St Ann Street, Manchester, Greater Manchester M2 7LF
☎ 0161 834 0239
🖰 www.stannsmanchester.com
✐ Page 6-E4

Staircase House

Staircase House is a Grade II listed medieval town house dating back to around 1460. It was originally the home of the Mayor of Stockport, William Dodge, in 1483.

30–31 Market Place, Stockport, Greater Manchester SK1 1ES
☎ 0161 480 1460
@ staircasehouse@stockport.gov.uk
🖰 www.staircasehouse.org.uk
✐ Page 13-G2

Stockport Air Raid Shelters

The Stockport Air Raid Shelters feature a reconstructed labyrinth of tunnels and structures offering an insight into the daily life in 1940s war-torn Britain.

61 Chestergate, Stockport Cheshire SK1 1NE
☎ 0161 474 1940
🖰 www.stockport.gov.uk/content/leisureculture/tourism/placestovisit/airraidshelters/
🖨 0161 474 1942
✐ Page 13-F3

Tameside Hippodrome

Oldham Road, Ashton-under-Lyne, Greater Manchester OL6 7SE

☎ 0161 330 2095
🖰 www.getlive.co.uk/tameside
✐ Page 119-G2

Victoria Baths

The Victoria Baths, near Longsight in Manchester, were designed as a prestigious baths complex by Manchester's first City Architect, Henry Price, and opened by Manchester Corporation in 1906. In their design and construction no expense was spared. The facade has multi-coloured brickwork and teracotta decoration, the main interior public spaces are clad in glazed tiles from floor to ceiling and most of the many windows have decorative stained glass.

Hathersage Road, Chorlton-on-Medlock, Manchester, Greater Manchester M13 0PD
☎ 0161 224 2020, 0161 224 8437
@ info@victoriabaths.org.uk
🖰 www.victoriabaths.org.uk
🖨 0161 224 0707
✐ Page 129-E4

The Wheel of Manchester

With views over one of the fastest changing urban landscapes in Europe, the 60-metre ride in the sky offers a view of Manchester as never seen before. The wheel has 42 capsules which seat up to eight people and each capsule has wheelchair access, air conditioning and heating.

Exchange Square, Manchester, Greater Manchester M3 1BD
☎ 0845 055 6080
🕾 0161 831 9918
@ Manchester@Worldtouristattractions.co.uk

🖰 www.worldtouristattractions.co.uk
✐ Page 6-E3

Wythenshawe Hall

Located in 275 acres of parkland, the Wythenshawe Hall was the home to the Tatton family for over 400 years. The hall features original oak timbers and a painted plaster wall that celebrates the marriage of Robert Tatton and Dorothy Booth in 1539.

Wythenshawe Park, Northenden, Manchester, Greater Manchester M23 0AB
☎ 0161 998 5083
🖰 www.manchestergalleries.org/our-other-venues/wythenshawe-hall
🖨 0161 235 8805
✐ Page 168-A1

MUSEUMS

The Anson Engine Museum

The largest collections of engines in Europe – varying in size from desktop to 100 tons! Among the top attractions are the largest running example of Crossley Atmospheric gas engine; the award-winning, original Gardner L series engine along with EHHS plaque; the oldest diesel engine in the country; a steam engine area with a Stott cross-compound mill engine and a Fowler beam engine; a Heritage Award from IDGTE for the Rattling Monsters Exhibition; a rare Atkinson-cycle engine. Iconic engines are on loan from the museums of London, Birmingham, Bristol, Edinburgh and Delft in Holland. There is a unique collection of photographs, sales leaflets and slides from engine manufacturers.

A free film and video shows on engine development is shown throughout summer. There is also an impressive collection of local history items from the Vernon Estate and the Anson Collieries with changing exhibitions throughout the year.

Anson Road, Poynton, Cheshire SK12 1TD
☎ 01625 874426
@ enquiry@enginemuseum.org
🖰 www.enginemuseum.org
✐ Page 196-B4

CUBE Manchester

CUBE showcase the complex inter-relationships between art, architecture and design through the provision of large-scale exhibitions with an accompanying programme of publications, lectures and seminars.

113–115 Portland Street, Manchester, Greater Manchester M1 6FB
☎ 0161 237 5525
@ info@cube.org.uk
🖰 www.cube.org.uk
🖨 0161 236 5815
✐ Page 7-F6

Fusiliers Museum

The collection includes silver, weapons, costumes, works of art, regimental regalia and personal memorabilia. Fusiliers Museum contains items from all over the world and, most notably, material related to General Wolfe and Napoleon.

Wellington Barracks, Bolton Road, Bury, Greater Manchester BL8 2PL
☎ 0161 764 2208
@ fusilierslancshq@btinternet.com
🖰 www.fusiliersmuseum-lancashire.org.uk
🖨 0161 764 3695
✐ Page 37-G5

Gallery of Costume

The Gallery of Costume is housed in the elegant surroundings of Platt Hall, an 18th-century textile merchant's home. The collection contains clothes worn by men, women and children from the 17th century to the present day. Many of the clothes represent high fashion of the day. Other, much rarer items represent the basic but equally interesting dress of working people, such as the clogs and shawls of Lancashire weavers. The Gallery continues to collect all kinds of clothes worn by people in Britain, including contemporary designer wear, sports and leisure clothes, underwear and the fashions of Manchester's South Asian communities.

Platt Hall, Rusholme, Manchester, Greater Manchester M14 5LL
☎ 0161 224 5217
⌐ www.manchester galleries.org/our-other- venues/platt-hall-gallery- of-costume
🖹 0161 256 3278
◑ Page 143-E1

Greater Manchester Police Museum

The museum contains the original charge office and the cells for the prisoners. Other galleries house examples of police vehicles and displays of uniforms and equipment. There are also rooms devoted to crime and forensic science, forgery and international policing.

Newton Street, Manchester, Greater Manchester M1 1ES
☎ 0161 856 3287
@ police.museum@gmp. police.uk
⌐ www.gmp.police.uk/ mainsite/Pages/history. htm
🖹 0161 856 3286
◑ Page 7-H4

Greater Manchester's Museum of Transport

The museum has historic vehicles ranging from an 1890 Horse bus to a 1994 Ring and Ride accessible minibus as well as archives documenting the transport history of Greater Manchester.

Boyle Street, Cheetham Hill, Manchester, Greater Manchester, M8 8UW
☎ 0161 205 2122
@ email@gmts.co.uk
⌐ www.gmts.co.uk
🖹 0161 202 1110
◑ Page 102-C4

Hall i' th' Wood Museum

Hall i' th' Wood was originally built as a half-timbered hall in the 16th century and was owned by wealthy yeomen and merchants. After 1697 the Hall was rented out to various tenants. It opened as a museum in 1902.

Green Way, Crompton Way, Bolton, Greater Manchester BL1 8UA
☎ 01204 332370
@ hallithwood@bolton. gov.uk
⌐ www.boltonmuseums. org.uk/hall-i-th-wood
◑ Page 34-B2

Hat Works Museum of Hatting

Hat Works is the UKs only museum dedicated solely to the hatting industry, hats and headwear. The museum was developed as a lottery funded regeneration project in Stockport, one of Manchester's leading hatting towns.

Wellington Mill, Wellington Road South, Stockport, Greater Manchester SK3 0EU
☎ 08458 330975
◐ 08458 330991
@ linn.holmstrom@ stockport.gov.uk
⌐ www.hatworks.org.uk
🖹 01614 808735
◑ Page 13-F3

Healey Dell Gallery and Studios

58–59A Healey Hall Mill, Rochdale, Greater Manchester OL12 6BQ
☎ 01706 356348
@ sylvia.oee-wild@ ntlworld.com
◑ Page 18-A5

Imperial War Museum North

The museum is about people and their stories, about how lives have been and still are shaped by war and conflict. The award-winning building by international architect Daniel Libeskind is a symbol of the world torn apart by conflict.

The Quays, Trafford Wharf, Trafford Park, Manchester Greater Manchester M17 1TZ
☎ 0161 836 4000
◐ 0161 836 4007
@ iwmnorth@iwm.org.uk
⌐ www.iwm.org.uk
🖹 0161 836 4012
◑ Page 126-B1

Manchester City Football Museum

Manchester City Football Museum houses

A statue of James Fraser (1818–1885), Bishop of Manchester, stands in Albert Square

memorabilia covering every aspect of the club's story. The stadium tour includes the directors' box, corporate lounge, dressing rooms, players' tunnel, press section and dugouts.

City of Manchester Stadium, SportCity, Manchester, Greater Manchester M11 3FF
☎ 0870 062 1894
@ mcfc@mcfc.co.uk
🖰 www.mcfc.co.uk
📄 0161 438 7999
🐭 Page 116-A3

Manchester Jewish Museum

Manchester Jewish Museum is located in the premises of the former Spanish and Portuguese Synagogue on Cheetham Hill Road. The building, completed in 1874, is a listed building of historical importance. It is, indeed, a beautiful example of Victorian architecture, executed in Moorish style. Particularly noteworthy are the splendid stained-glass windows and the distinctive cast-iron fitments. Since the building became redundant through the movement of the Jewish population away from the area, it has been completely restored, returned to its former glory and listed Grade II. It re-opened as a museum in March 1984.

190 Cheetham Hill Road, Manchester, Greater Manchester M8 8LW
☎ 0161 834 9879
@ don@manchester jewishmuseum.com
🖰 www.manchester jewishmuseum.com
📄 0161 834 9801
🐭 Page 114-D1

Manchester Museum

The museum collections number almost 6 million specimens and objects and encompass archery, archaeology, botany, Egyptology, entomology, ethnography, mineralogy, palaeontology, numismatics and zoology, as well as live specimens in the aquarium and vivarium.

University Of Manchester, Oxford Road, Manchester, Greater Manchester M13 9PL
☎ 0161 275 2630, 0161 275 2634
@ museum@manchester. ac.uk
🖰 www.manchester.ac.uk/ museum
📄 0161 275 2676
🐭 Page 128-C2

Manchester United Museum and Tour Centre

The Museum and Tour Centre is located in the North Stand at Old Trafford. It covers the history of Manchester United in words, pictures, sound and vision, from its inception in 1878 to the present day.

Sir Matt Busby Way, Old Trafford, Manchester, Greater Manchester M16 0RA
☎ 08704 421994
@ tours@manutd.co.uk
🖰 www.manutd.com/
📄 0161 868 8861
🐭 Page 126-C3

Museum of Science and Industry In Manchester

Situated in the oldest passenger railway buildings in the world, the museum tells the story of the history, science and industry of Manchester.

Liverpool Road, Castlefield, Manchester, Greater Manchester M3 4FP
☎ 0161 832 2244
@ collections@msim. org.uk
🖰 www.msim.org.uk
🐭 Page 6-B6

Museum of the Manchester Regiment

The Museum tells the story of the Regiment and its soldiers through 200 years of history, from 1758 until 1958. Follow the Regiment from the colonial wars of the Red Coats in the 18th century through to World War I and II and beyond.

The Aerospace Hall of the Museum of Science and Industry

Enjoy the fine collection of weapons, uniforms and medals, and step inside the World War I trench for an experience of what life was like on the Western Front.

Ashton Town Hall, Market Place, Ashton-under-Lyne, Greater Manchester OL6 6DL
☎ 0161 342 2254
@ museum.manchesters@ tameside.gov.uk
⌂ www.tameside.gov.uk/ museumsgalleries/mom
✐ Page 119-G2

Ordsall Hall Museum

Ordsall Lane, Salford Greater Manchester M5 3AN
☎ 0161 872 0251
@ ordsall.hall@salford. gov.uk
⌂ www.salford.gov. uk/leisure/museums/ ordsallhall.htm
▤ 0161 872 4951
✐ Page 127-E2

The Pankhurst Centre

The Pankhurst Centre provides a women-only space that creates a unique environment in which women can learn together, work on projects and socialise. The centre is of historical significance as it was the home of Emmeline Pankhurst and her daughters Sylvia, Christabel and Adela who were centrally involved in the campaign for votes for women. The Women's Centre includes a workshop and training rooms that run many courses throughout the year on everything from DIY to complementary therapy. There is a resource area with PC's, internet access and lots of useful information. A creche is available on request.

60–62 Nelson Street, Chorlton on Medlock, Manchester Greater Manchester M13 9WP
☎ 0161 273 5673
@ pankhurst@zetnet.co.uk
⌂ www.24hourmuseum. org.uk/manchester/ museum/
▤ 0161 274 4979
✐ Page 128-C3

People's History Museum

The museum is the national centre for the collection, conservation, interpretation and study of material relating to the history of working people in Britain. The museum galleries are housed in the Pump House, a former Edwardian hydraulic pumping station and offers an array of temporary exhibitions on various disciplines.

The Pump House, Bridge Street, Manchester, Greater Manchester M3 3ER
☎ 016 1839 6061
@ info@peoples historymuseum.org.uk
⌂ www.phm.org.uk
▤ 0161 839 6027
✐ Page 6-C4

Portland Basin Museum

Housed within the restored 19th-century Ashton Canal Warehouse, the museum combines a lively modern interior with a peaceful canal side setting. Portland Basin Museum is an exciting family friendly museum, with something for everyone.

1 Portland Place, Ashton-under-Lyne, Greater Manchester OL7 0QA
☎ 016 1343 2878
@ portland.basin@ tameside.gov.uk
⌂ www.tameside.gov.uk/ museumsandgalleries/ portlandbasin.htm

▤ 0161 343 2869
✐ Page 119-F4

Rochdale Pioneers Museum

The aim of the museum is to preserve and maintain the store building and collections relating to the Rochdale Pioneers and the Co-operative movement in general. The educational experience for visitors includes the origins and development of the Rochdale Pioneers Society in the context of 19th-century Rochdale. The musuem promotes an understanding of the motivation and dedication of the Rochdale Pioneers and communicates an understanding of the co-operative alternative and co-operative values and principles as defined by the Pioneers and their contribution and relevance to current times.

31 Toad Lane, Rochdale, Greater Manchester OL12 0NU
☎ 01706 524920
@ museum@co-op.ac.uk
⌂ museum.co-op.ac.uk
✐ Page 10-B5

Saddleworth Museum and Art Gallery

The gallery showcases displays related to history, landscape and inhabitants. There are also displays about domestic life in Saddleworth, the interior of an 18th-century weaver's cottage, a Victorian house, and photographs and memorabilia from two world wars.

High Street, Uppermill, Oldham, Greater Manchester OL3 6HS
☎ 01457 874093
⌂ www.saddleworth museum.co.uk
✐ Page 78-D4

Stockport Museum

The historic building presents original features and historic information about Stockport.

Vernon Park, Turncroft Lane, Offerton, Stockport, Greater Manchester SK1 4AR
☎ 0161 474 4460
⌂ www.stockport.gov.uk/ content/leisureculture/ tourism/placestovisit/ stockportmuseum/
▤ 0161 474 4449
✐ Page 160-C4

Touchstones Rochdale

The Touchstones Rochdale includes four art galleries, a museum, heritage gallery, tourist infomation centre, Local Studies Centre and a cafe.

The Esplanade, Rochdale, Greater Manchester OL16 1AQ
☎ 01706 924492, 01706 864986
@ touchstones@rochdale. gov.uk
⌂ www.rochdale.gov. uk/touchstones
▤ 01706 924944
✐ Page 10-B7

Urbis

Urbis explores urban culture and the cities of today and tomorrow through four floors of exhibitions about city life. Interactive galleries explore the people, place and pulse of the modern city.

Cathedral Gardens, Manchester, Greater Manchester M4 3BG
☎ 0161 605 8200
@ info@urbis.org.uk
⌂ www.urbis.org.uk
▤ 0161 605 8201
✐ Page 6-E2

Wardle Library

448 Birch Road, Wardle, Rochdale, Greater Manchester OL12 9LH
☎ 01706 377476
✆ Page 19-H2

ART GALLERIES AND VISUAL ARTS

Arison Gallery

512 Wilbraham Road, Chorlton, Manchester, Greater Manchester M21 9AW
☎ 0161 881 6734
✆ Page 141-E2

Astley Cheetham Art Gallery

Built as a gift to the town of Stalybridge by John Frederick Cheetham and his wife Beatrice Astley in 1901, the gallery originally opened as a lecture theatre. The space turned into an art gallery to house the Astley Cheetham Art Collection, bequeathed in 1932. This collection has grown with gifts and donations throughout the 20th century and is one of the most interesting small regional collections. Alongside exhibitions of the collection, the gallery also hosts a programme of temporary exhibitions by regional artists.

Trinity Street, Stalybridge, Greater Manchester SK15 2BN
☎ 0161 338 6767
@ astley.cheetham@ tameside.gov.uk
✆ www.tameside.gov.uk/ museumsandgalleries/ astleycheetham.html
✆ Page 120-D4

Bankley Studios Gallery

The studio currently has over 30 artists in residence, working across a range of disciplines including painting, textiles, photography, installation, sculpture and ceramics. The studios are located in Levenshulme, Manchester and were set up in 1992, officially becoming a co-operative in 1998. In addition to the studio spaces there is also an artist-run gallery space, which is curated by the Exhibition Officer, Paul Stanley, and has an exhibition programme of about eight exhibitions each year. There is also an annual Open Studios event.

Bankley House, Bankley Street, Levenshulme, Manchester, Greater Manchester M19 3PP
☎ 0161 256 4143
@ studios@bankley.org.uk
✆ www.bankley.org.uk
✆ Page 144-A2

The Blyth Gallery

Blyth's is a supplier of fine arts, graphics materials and accessories, and also a gallery specialising in quality contemporary art and sculpture.

Amazon House, Brazil Street, Manchester, Greater Manchester M1 3PJ
☎ 0161 236 1004
@ sales@artmanchester. com
✆ www.artmanchester.com
🗎 0161 228 0633
✆ Page 7-G6

Bolton Museum, Art Gallery and Aquarium

Bolton Museum and Art Gallery's displays chart the story of Bolton and the people who have lived here. The fish at the aquarium are freshwater fish, whose natural habitats are streams, rivers or lakes. Each display represents a particular habitat.

Le Mans Crescent, Bolton, Greater Manchester BL1 1SE
☎ 01204 332211
@ museum.customer services@bolton.gov.uk
✆ www.boltonmuseums. org.uk
🗎 01204 398101
✆ Page 2-D5

Bureau Gallery

Bureau Gallery was opened in March 2006 and this gallery has been working with the artists and organisations such as Can Altay, Book Works, Karin de Jong, Tony Garifalakis, Jeroen Jongeleen, Markus Rummens and Jorn de Vries. The Gallery's intention is to promote new work including critical writing, film and video, and publication projects by emerging and established artists, from the UK and internationally.

Ground Floor, Islington Mill, James Street, Salford, Greater Manchester M3 5HW
☎ 07757 956555
@ info@bureaugallery.com
✆ www.bureaugallery.com
✆ Page 114-A4

Castlefield Gallery

The gallery is a resource for contemporary visual artists and their work. It is an essential part of the artistic community in Manchester and the North West, maintaining a close relationship with studio groups.

2 Hewitt Street, Manchester, Greater Manchester M15 4GB
☎ 0161 832 8034
@ info@castlefieldgallery. co.uk
✆ www.castlefieldgallery. co.uk
🗎 0161 819 2295
✆ Page 6-C7

Traditional narrowboats on Manchester's waterways

Central Art Gallery

Central Art Gallery, located above the library on Old Street in Ashton-under-Lyne, hosts a varied programme of temporary exhibitions. There is something to suit most tastes with group and solo shows of artists from the region including paintings, sculpture, installation and textiles.

Old Street, Ashton-under-Lyne, Greater Manchester OL6 7SG

☎ 0161 342 2650

@ central.artgallery@ tameside.gov.uk

🖰 www.tameside.gov.uk/ museumsandgalleries/ centrallibrary.html

✏ Page 119-G3

Chapman Gallery

Chapman Gallery hosts a wide range of modern and contemporary art exhibitions which showcase the work of established and up coming artists and the creative practices of staff and students from the School of Art and Design.

The University of Salford, Peel Park Campus, Salford, Greater Manchester M5 4WT

☎ 0161 295 5223

@ g.parker@salford.ac.uk

🖰 www.arts.salford.ac.uk/ venues.php

✏ Page 113-H3

Colin Jellicoe Gallery

Colin Jellicoe, a Manchester born artist, has painted and exhibited at his own small gallery and elsewhere for over forty years. His website sets out his biography and exhibition record, includes a selection of press reviews and shows a retrospective selection of paintings dating from 1963. The reviews and Colin's narrative explain the

background to the work. A selection of current work available to purchase is also illustrated.

82 Portland Street, Manchester, Greater Manchester M1 4QX

☎ 0161 236 2716

@ webmaster@ colinjellicoe.co.uk

🖰 www.colinjellicoe.co.uk

✏ Page 7-F6

Contact Theatre

Located in the heart of the University of Manchester's student campus, the Contact Theatre hosts a wide variety of cutting edge theatre productions as well as comedy evenings, artwork exhibitions, gigs and student nights. The theatre's Deluxe bar serves Mediterranean inspired lunches with music from live DJs.

Oxford Road, Manchester, Greater Manchester M15 6JA

☎ 0161 274 0600

📞 0161 274 0600

@ bookings@contact-theatre.org

🖰 www.contact-theatre.org

✏ Page 128-C3

Gallery Oldham

Gallery Oldham is a unique and bold new landmark building that opened in February 2002. The gallery forms the first phase of a new Cultural Quarter for Oldham. The building has received an award from the Royal Institute of British Architects.

Oldham Cultural Quarter, Greaves Street, Oldham, Greater Manchester OL1 1AL

☎ 0161 770 4653

@ galleryoldham@oldham. gov.uk

🖰 www.galleryoldham. org.uk

🖹 0161 770 4669

✏ Page 9-H4

The Holden Gallery

With a history dating back over 100 years, the Faculty of Art and Design's gallery offers an ongoing programme of exhibitions that are open free to the public. The gallery is also home to yearly BA and MA Degree Shows and is a major exhibitor of staff and student work.

Manchester Metropolitan University, Grosvenor Building, Cavendish Street, Manchester, Greater Manchester M15 6BR

☎ 0161 247 1705

@ artdes.fac@mmu.ac.uk

🖰 www.holdengallery.mmu. ac.uk

✏ Page 128-B1

Manchester Art Gallery

Manchester Art Gallery houses one of the UKs finest art collections in spectacular surroundings.

Mosley Street, Manchester, Greater Manchester M2 3JL

☎ 0161 235 8888

🖰 www.manchester galleries.org

🖹 0161 235 8899

✏ Page 7-F5

Manchester Craft and Design Centre

Manchester Craft and Design Centre is a unique organisation comprising 18 retail/studio spaces, an excellent cafe and a rolling programme of exhibitions from leading national and international makers of original contemporary craft. Located in Manchester city centre's Northern Quarter, Manchester Craft and Design Centre is at the hub of a growing innovative

and artistic community. It is one of the few places in the UK open to the public where contemporary craft is individually produced and sold on the premises. Formerly the Smithfield Victorian fish market and crowned with a huge glass roof, the Centre now houses two floors of studios ranging from jewellery, ceramics and s to furniture and clothing design.

17 Oak Street, Northern Quarter, Manchester, Greater Manchester M4 5JD

☎ 01618 324274

@ info@craftanddesign. com

🖰 www.craftanddesign.com

🖹 01618 323416

✏ Page 7-G3

Manchester Opera House

Quay Street, Manchester Greater Manchester M3 3HP

☎ 0870 401 9000

🖰 www.manchester operahouse.org.uk

✏ Page 6-C5

Millyard Gallery

Millyard Gallery houses exhibitions of oil paintings, watercolours, etchings and screenprints by artists with a national reputation. Also on display is a wide range of limited edition and fine art prints framed and unframed Saddleworth landscapes in oil, watercolours and pastels.

97 The Square, Uppermill, Saddleworth, Greater Manchester OL3 6BD

☎ 01457 870410

@ sales@millyardgallery. fslife.co.uk

🖰 www.millyard-gallery. co.uk

🖹 01457 870410

✏ Page 79-E4

Oldham Local Studies and Archives

84 Union Street, Oldham, Greater Manchester
OL1 1DN
☎ 0161 911 4654 ;
016170704741
@ archives@oldham.gov.uk
⌂ www.galleryoldham.
  org.uk
✦ Page 9-H4

Philips Art Gallery

Philips Art Gallery began exhibiting and selling a broad range of art work in 1996, with a focus on artists from the UK and Europe.

10a Little Lever Street, Manchester, Greater Manchester M1 1HR
☎ 0161 941 4197
@ philipsartgallery@
  btconnect.com
⌂ www.philipsartgallery.
  com
✦ Page 7-H4

The Portico Library and Gallery

The Portico Library and Gallery opened in 1806 as a Library and Newsroom and still occupies its original site. Its mainly 19th-century collection is accessed by members as well as researchers in the UK and abroad. The Library continues to flourish as a hub of cultural activity and its exhibition gallery sits under the impressive Georgian glass and plaster dome. The Library also hosts a thriving and active programme of events throughout the year, that are open to members and the public generally.

57 Mosley Street, Manchester, Greater Manchester M2 3HY

☎ 0161 236 6785
@ admin@theportico.
  org.uk
⌂ www.theportico.org.uk
🖨 0161 236 6803
✦ Page 7-F5

Richard Goodall Gallery

The new Richard Goodall Gallery is a state of the art gallery facility for viewing the best in contemporary and fine art across all mediums. The gallery has a unique collection of work from the leading artists from around the globe.

103 High Street, Manchester, Greater Manchester M4 1HQ
☎ 0161 834 3330
⌂ www.richardgoodall
  gallery.com
✦ Page 7-G3

Richard Goodall Gallery Underground

The Richard Goodall Gallery exhibits a broad range of artworks consisting of photographs, silk screen prints, contemporary art, posters and designer toys.

59 Thomas Street, Northern Quarter, Manchester, Greater Manchester M4 1NA
☎ 0161 832 3435
@ info@richardgoodall
  gallery.com
⌂ www.richardgoodall
  gallery.com/rggstore/
  index.php
🖨 0161 832 3266
✦ Page 7-G3

Saddleworth Museum and Art Gallery

The gallery showcases displays related to history, landscape and inhabitants. There are also displays about domestic life in Saddleworth, the interior of an 18th-century weaver's cottage, a Victorian house,

and photographs and memorabilia from two world wars.

High Street, Uppermill, Oldham, Greater Manchester OL3 6HS
☎ 01457 874093
⌂ www.saddleworth
  museum.co.uk
✦ Page 78-D4

Salford Museum and Art Gallery

Salford Museum and Art Gallery is an intriguing mix of Victorian and 20th-century architecture. There is a permanent gallery of Victorian art and collections of paintings, sculpture and local and social history. The Art Gallery also hosts a temporary exhibition programme showing work by local, national and international artists.

Peel Park, The Crescent, Salford, Greater Manchester M5 4WU
☎ 0161 778 0800
@ salford.museum@
  salford.gov.uk
⌂ www.salford.gov.
  uk/salfordmuseum
🖨 0161 745 9490
✦ Page 113-H3

Stockport Art Gallery

The gallery shows a rotating selection of works from it's own collection in addition to exhibitions of work by contemporary artists, many from the region.

Wellington Road South, Stockport, Greater Manchester SK3 8AB
☎ 0161 474 4453
@ stockport.artgallery@
  stockport.gov.uk
⌂ www.stockport.gov.
  uk/contacts/artgallery
🖨 0161 480 4960
✦ Page 13-G5

Twenty + 3 Projects

The gallery is run from a converted living room in a terraced house, and has a full programme of changing exhibitions.

23 Bury Avenue, Manchester, Greater Manchester M16 0AT
☎ 07905 944 807
@ h@heidischaefer.net
⌂ www.20plus3.co.uk
✦ Page 141-G1

Urbis

Urbis explores urban culture and the cities of today and tomorrow through four floors of exhibitions about city life. Interactive galleries explore the people, place and pulse of the modern city.

Cathedral Gardens, Manchester, Greater Manchester M4 3BG
☎ 0161 605 8200
@ info@urbis.org.uk
⌂ www.urbis.org.uk
🖨 0161 605 8201
✦ Page 6-E2

Vernon Mill Gallery

Vernon Mill, is an old cotton mill in Stockport, Cheshire and houses over 40 artists' studios in its upper two floors. These artists have joined together to form an artists' collective known as the Vernon Mill Artists (the VMA). Taking into account the large number of artists, operating from within individual studios in this huge building, the VMA is considered to be one of the largest artist-led studio groups in the UK, with one of the largest exhibition spaces open to the general public.

Vernon Mill Artists, 3rd & 4th Floors, Vernon Mill, Mersey Street, Stockport, Greater Manchester SK1 2HX

☎ 07946 477005
@ info@vernon-mill-artists.co.uk
🖳 www.vernon-mill-artists.co.uk
🌐 Page 13-K1

Wendy J Levy Contemporary Art

The Wendy Levy gallery is a select and friendly gallery showing original paintings, drawings and sculpture by well-known artists. We also promote new and talented artists in the North West.

17 Warburton Street, Didsbury, Manchester, Greater Manchester M20 6WA
☎ 0161 446 4880
@ wendy@wendyjlevy-art.com
🖳 www.wendyjlevy-art.com
🌐 Page 157-G3

Wensley Gallery

Wensley Gallery exhibits original work comprising paintings in watercolour, pastel, and oil, also sculpture, ceramics, wood turning and metal work.

Ramsbottom, Bury, Greater Manchester BL0 9HT
☎ 01706 824772
@ staff@wensleygallery.co.uk
🖳 www.wensleygallery.co.uk
📄 0870 162 3999
🌐 Page 16-C1

Whitworth Art Gallery

Internationally famous for its collections of art and design, the gallery is home to a wide range of watercolours, prints, drawings, modern art and sculpture, as well as the largest collections of textiles and wallpapers outside London.

The University of Manchester, Oxford Road, Manchester, Greater Manchester M15 6ER
☎ 0161 275 7450, 0161 275 7452
@ Whitworth@manchester.ac.uk
🖳 www.whitworth.manchester.ac.uk
📄 0161 275 7451
🌐 Page 128-C4

ART CENTRES

Chinese Arts Centre

Chinese Arts Centre aims to develop an infrastructure to allow Chinese arts, and especially British Chinese artists, to flourish. Their work covers exhibitions, education, agency work and advocacy which includes training, conferences and publications.

Market Buildings, Thomas Street, Manchester, Greater Manchester M4 1EU
☎ 0161 832 7271
@ info@chinese-arts-centre.org
🖳 www.chinese-arts-centre.org
📄 0161 832 7513
🌐 Page 7-G3

Cornerhouse

Cornerhouse is Greater Manchester's international centre for contemporary visual arts and film. The centre has three floors of contemporary art galleries, three screens showing the best of independent cinema as well as a bar, café and bookshop. Cornerhouse also operates an international publications service distributing visual arts books and catalogues.

70 Oxford Street, Manchester, Greater Manchester M1 5NH
☎ 0161 228 7621
📞 0161 200 1500
@ info@cornerhouse.org
🖳 www.cornerhouse.org
🌐 Page 7-F1

The Grange Arts Centre

Rochdale Road, Oldham, Greater Manchester OL9 6EA
☎ 0161 785 4239
@ grange.arts@oldham.ac.uk
🖳 www.oldham.tv/grange/index.html
🌐 Page 8-E2

The Lowry

Opened in 2000, The Lowry houses two large theatres, live music, the latest art exhibitions and the largest permanent collection of LS Lowry's paintings. The award-winning building in Salford Quays also offers restaurants, bars, gift shops and conference hire.

Pier 8, Salford Quays, Salford, Greater Manchester M50 3AZ
☎ 0870 787 5780
@ info@thelowry.com
🖳 www.thelowry.com
📄 0161 876 2001
🌐 Page 126-B1

The Met Arts Centre

The Met Arts Centre is a mix of contemporary and classic theatre, music and comedy sourced regionally and touring nationally and internationally. The Met have enjoyed a pre-Partridge Steve Coogan, legendary performances by Joy Division and The Pixies, pre-Elbow Elbow, pre-Hollywood Lee Evans and live music and theatre.

Market Street, Bury, Greater Manchester BL9 0BW
☎ 0161 761 7107
📞 0161 761 2216
@ post@themet.biz
🖳 www.themet.biz
📄 087 0052 0297
🌐 Page 4-D4

Mumbo Arts Centre

86 Princess Street, Manchester, Greater Manchester M60 7AG
☎ 0161 236 3786
🌐 Page 7-F6

Waterside Arts Centre

The Waterside Arts Centre opened in 2004 and the first artistic programme was launched in November 2004. The centre comprises the Robert Bolt Theatre, the Lauriston Gallery, the Chambers, Corridor Community Arts Project and a variety of studios and workshop spaces. Events are often held outside on the plaza.

Sale Waterside, Sale, Greater Manchester M33 7ZF
☎ 0161 912 5899
📞 0161 912 5616
@ watersideartscentre@trafford.gov.uk
🖳 www.watersideartscentre.co.uk
📄 0161 912 1859
🌐 Page 154-C1

Zion Arts Centre

Zion is a unique Edwardian-meets-contemporary building which boasts a wide array of top-class spaces and facilities under one architecturally stunning roof. From Jazz and the Process 06 Festival to numerous workshops, dance classes and music lessons taking place in the building every week, there is something for everyone at Zion.

335 Stretford Road, Hulme, Manchester, Greater Manchester M15 5ZA
☎ 0161 226 1912
@ info@zionarts.com
🖳 www.zionarts.com
🌐 Page 127-H2

DANCE AND PERFORMING ARTS

Albert Halls

The Albert Halls has come a long way since re-opening for business back in 1985. The venue, which had been gutted by fire back in November 1981, spent three and half years undergoing a complete internal rebuild, converting what had been, for the previous 108 years, a single large concert hall into two separate halls. The upper Albert Halls' capacity of 676 in its normal theatre setting is extremely versatile with the option to remove and reconfigure seats depending on the event.

Victoria Square, Bolton, Greater Manchester BL1 1YZ
☎ 01204 334400, 01204 334433
@ info@alberthalls-boltn. co.uk
🖰 www.alberthalls-bolton. co.uk
📖 Page 2-E5

Contact Theatre

Located in the heart of the University of Manchester's student campus, the Contact Theatre hosts a wide variety of cutting edge theatre productions as well as comedy evenings, artwork exhibitions, gigs and student nights. The theatre's Deluxe bar serves Mediterranean inspired lunches with music from live DJs.

Oxford Road, Manchester Greater Manchester M15 6JA
☎ 0161 274 0600
🕓 0161 274 0600
@ bookings@contact-theatre.org
🖰 www.contact-theatre.org
📖 Page 128-C3

The Dancehouse Theatre

10 Oxford Road, Manchester, Greater Manchester M1 5QA
☎ 0161 237 9753
@ admin@thedancehouse. co.uk
🖰 www.thedancehouse. co.uk
📖 0161 237 1408
📖 Page 128-B1

The Forum Theatre

NK Theatre Arts is a Registered Charity which offers weekly workshops in music, dance and drama for anyone aged 5 years to adult. The company produces various theatrical presentations throughout the year and also offers a versatile auditorium for hire, be it for shows, corporate functions or parties etc.

Compstall Road, Romiley, Stockport, Greater Manchester SK6 4EA
☎ 0870 777 8731
@ firstname@ nktheatrearts.org.uk
🖰 www.nktheatrearts. org.uk
📖 0161 406 6782
📖 Page 162-C4

Greenroom

Greenroom was established in 1983 to develop and present local, national and international performance at venues across Manchester.

54–56 Whitworth Street West, Manchester, Greater Manchester M1 5WW
☎ 0161 615 0515
🕓 0161 615 0500
@ info@greenroomarts.org
🖰 www.greenroomarts.org
📖 Page 6-E7

Manchester Evening News Arena (MEN Arena)

Opened in 1995, the Manchester Evening News Arena was originally conceived for Manchester's bid for the Olympics and was built despite the bid's failure. From U2 to Pavarotti, ice hockey to boxing, Disney shows and Motorbike Exhibitions through to blue-chip AGMs, this 21,000 capacity multi-purpose entertainment and sports arena caters for all.

21 Hunts Bank, Victoria Station, Manchester, Greater Manchester M3 1AR
☎ 0870 190 8000
@ enquiries@men-arena. com
🖰 www.men-arena.com
📖 Page 6-E1

Manchester Opera House

Quay Street, Manchester, Greater Manchester M3 3HP
☎ 0870 401 9000
🖰 www.manchester operahouse.org.uk
📖 Page 6-C5

Middleton Civic Hall

Middleton Civic Hall offers comedy, live theatre, music and dance. In addition to the main auditorium there are three other meeting rooms within the complex which provide individual facilities or can be used in conjunction with main hall events.

Fountain Street, Middleton, Manchester, Greater Manchester M24 1AF
☎ 0161 643 2470
🕓 0161 643 2389
@ info@middletoncivic.com
🖰 www.middletoncivic.com
📖 Page 72-C4

Royal Northern College of Music: Bruntwood Theatre

124 Oxford Road, Manchester Greater Manchester M13 9RD
☎ 0161 907 5200
🕓 0161 907 5555
@ info@rncm.ac.uk
🖰 www.rncm.ac.uk
📖 0161 273 7611
📖 Page 128-B2

Royal Northern College of Music: Lecture Theatre

124 Oxford Road, Manchester, Greater Manchester M13 9RD
☎ 0161 907 5200
🕓 0161 907 5555
@ info@rncm.ac.uk
🖰 www.rncm.ac.uk
📖 0161 273 7611
📖 Page 128-B2

Royal Northern College of Music: Lord Rhodes Room

124 Oxford Road, Manchester, Greater Manchester M13 9RD
☎ 0161 907 5200
@ info@rncm.ac.uk
🖰 www.rncm.ac.uk
📖 0161 273 7611
📖 Page 128-B2

Royal Northern College of Music: Studio Theatre

124 Oxford Road, Manchester Greater Manchester M13 9RD
☎ 0161 907 5200
🕓 0161 907 5555
🖰 www.rncm.ac.uk
📖 0161 273 7611
📖 Page 128-B2

LIVE MUSIC VENUES

Albert Halls

The Albert Halls has come a long way since re-opening for business back in 1985. The venue, which had been gutted by fire back in November 1981, spent three and half years undergoing a complete internal rebuild, converting what had been,

for the previous 108 years, a single large concert hall into two separate halls. The upper Albert Halls' capacity of 676 in its normal theatre setting is extremely versatile with the option to remove and reconfigure seats depending on the event.

Victoria Square, Bolton Lancashire BL1 1YZ
- ☏ 01204 334400, 01204 334433
- @ info@alberthalls-boltn. co.uk
- ⌂ www.alberthalls-bolton. co.uk
- ℗ Page 2-E5

Apollo Manchester

Opened in 1930 by the actress Margaret Lockwood, the Manchester Apollo was originally built as an ABC Cinema and variety hall. The venue has a tradition of bringing some of the biggest artists of the day to an intimate venue, as well as bringing through developing acts. Always diverse, the Apollo also caters for comedy shows, be they stand-up or larger scale touring productions.

Ardwick Green, Manchester Greater Manchester M12 6AP
- ☏ 0161 273 6921
- ☏ 0870 401 8000
- ⌂ www.livenation. co.uk/venue/getVenue/ venueId/16155/
- ℗ Page 128-D1

Bakers Vaults

A music venue and pub with live soul, blues, and rock music.

Market Place, Stockport, Greater Manchester SK1 1ES
- ☏ 0161 477 7312
- @ info@bakers-vaults. co.uk

- ⌂ www.bakers-vaults.co.uk
- ℗ Page 13-G2

Band On The Wall

25 Swan Street, Northern Quarter, Manchester, Greater Manchester M4 5JZ
- ☏ 0161 834 1786
- @ development@ bandonthewall.org
- ⌂ www.bandonthewall.org
- ℗ Page 7-G2

The Blue Box Theatre

Nell Lane, Chorlton, Manchester, Greater Manchester M21 7SL
- ☏ 0161 882 1150
- @ boxoffice@ blueboxtheatre.co.uk
- ⌂ www.blueboxtheatre. co.uk
- 🖹 0161 861 8753
- ℗ Page 141-H5

Blue Cat Cafe

Blue Cat is an intimate venue famed for good music, low lighting, decent drinks, eccentricity and experimentation. Based in Heaton Moor, just outside Manchester, it promotes both local and touring bands regularly. International artists from Australia, Boston, New York, Chicago, Germany and Norway have been memorable highlights and include names like Electric Six, Johnny Marr, Haven, Curtis Eller and Viva Stereo.

17 Shaw Road, Heaton Moor, Stockport, Greater Manchester SK4 4AG
- ☏ 0161 432 2117
- @ danny@bluecatcafe. co.uk
- ⌂ www.bluecatcafe.co.uk
- ℗ Page 159-E2

Cafe Saki

A music venue and cafe with resident DJs and live bands.

2 Wilmslow Road, Rusholme,

Rusholme, Greater Manchester M14 5TP
- ☏ 0161 257 0365
- ℗ Page 128-D4

The Castle

The Castle is situated on Union Street, in the heart of the town centre of Oldham. It has been home to Oldham's live rock, alternative and indie music scene for many years. The Castle was the birthplace of the Inspiral Carpets, and has witnessed early performances of Oasis, The Stone Roses, and Northside.

38 Union Street, Oldham, Greater Manchester OL1 1DJ
- ☏ 07969 884868
- @ castle@tokyoindustries. com
- ⌂ www.castleoldham.com
- ℗ Page 9-G4

Castlefield Arena

101 Liverpool Road, Castlefield, Manchester, Greater Manchester M3 4JN
- ℗ Page 6-B6

The Cinnamon Club

The Cinnamon Club is housed in a beautiful Edwardian building called The Bowdon Rooms which were built in 1903. With a fully sprung maple dance floor, and an arched ceiling towering above at over 40 feet, it makes a superb venue for concerts, cabarets, weddings and functions. Situated in leafy South Manchester/Cheshire, The Cinnamon Club is the premier live entertainment venue for music, private parties and corporate entertainment.

The Bowden Rooms, The Firs, Bowdon, Altrincham, Greater Manchester WA14 2TQ

- ☏ 0161 926 8992
- @ information@ thecinnamonclub.net
- ⌂ www.thecinnamonclub. net
- ℗ Page 177-E2

Contact Theatre

Located in the heart of the University of Manchester's student campus, the Contact Theatre hosts a wide variety of cutting edge theatre productions as well as comedy evenings, artwork exhibitions, gigs and student nights. The theatre's Deluxe bar serves Mediterranean inspired lunches with music from live DJs.

Oxford Road, Manchester, Greater Manchester M15 6JA
- ☏ 0161 274 0600
- ☏ 0161 274 0600
- @ bookings@contact- theatre.org
- ⌂ www.contact-theatre.org
- ℗ Page 128-C3

The Dancehouse Theatre

10 Oxford Road, Manchester, Greater Manchester M1 5QA
- ☏ 0161 237 9753
- @ admin@thedancehouse. co.uk
- ⌂ www.thedancehouse. co.uk
- 🖹 0161 237 1408
- ℗ Page 128-B1

Dog and Partridge

For years now the Dog and Partridge has been the spiritual home of thousands of young musicians. A place to perform live in front of a hometown audience before heading off to play gigs across the country, a social gathering to meet like-minded musicians and music fans and their first stop when finding other musicians to form bands.

22 Manor Street, Bolton,
Greater Manchester
BL1 1TU
☎ 01204 388596
🖱 www.thedogpub.co.uk
🔎 Page 3-F4

Dry Bar

Since Dry Bar first opened
its doors, it has been one
of the most well known and
influential venues in the UK.
Initially owned by Factory
Records, Dry Bar opened
on the 25th of July 1989 in
the city's Northern Quarter.
It is one of the places that
gave birth to 'Madchester'
in the early 90s and where
many musicians still hang
out today.

28–30 Oldham Street,
Manchester, Greater
Manchester M1 1JN
☎ 0161 236 9840
@ enquiries@drybar.co.uk
🔎 Page 7-G4

Dunicans Bar

Sedgeborough Road, Moss
Side, Manchester, Greater
Manchester M16 7EZ
☎ 0161 226 2724
🔎 Page 127-H4

Fab Cafe

111 Portland Street,
Manchester, Greater
Manchester M1 4PY
☎ 0161 236 2019
@ info@fabcafe.co.uk
🖱 www.fabcafe.co.uk
🔎 Page 7-F6

The Forum Theatre

NK Theatre Arts is a
Registered Charity which
offers weekly workshops
in music, dance and drama
for anyone aged 5 years
to adult. The company
produces various theatrical
presentations throughout
the year and also offers a
versatile auditorium for hire,
be it for shows, corporate
functions or parties etc.

Compstall Road, Romiley,
Stockport, Greater
Manchester SK6 4EA
☎ 0870 777 8731
@ firstname@
nktheatrearts.org.uk
🖱 www.nktheatrearts.
org.uk
📄 0161 406 6782
🔎 Page 162-C4

Greenroom

Greenroom was established
in 1983 to develop and
present local, national and
international performance at
venues across Manchester.

54–56 Whitworth Street
West, Manchester, Greater
Manchester M1 5WW
☎ 0161 615 0515
🕓 0161 615 0500
@ info@greenroomarts.org
🖱 www.greenroomarts.org
🔎 Page 6-E7

HMV Manchester

90–100 Market Street,
Manchester, Greater
Manchester M1 1PD
☎ 0161 834 8550
🖱 www.hmv.co.uk
🔎 Page 7-F4

Hark To Towler

43 Market Street, Tottington,
Bury, Greater Manchester
BL8 4AA
☎ 01204 883856
@ hark2towler@aol.com
🖱 www.hark2towler.co.uk
🔎 Page 26-A5

Hidden, Manchester

28–34 High Street,
Manchester Greater
Manchester M4 1QB
☎ 0161 834 1392,
07851 731697
@ info@high-st.com
🖱 www.high-st.com
🔎 Page 7-F3

The Hobo's Retreat

Heywood Reform Club, 34
Tower Street, Heywood,
Greater Manchester
OL10 3AA
☎ 01706 622638
🖱 www.folkimages.com/
hobo/
🔎 Page 40-D4

Iguana Bar

A bar that hosts music for
all tastes, with sounds such
as the Country and Eastern
Band's Turkish and Kurdish
music, the Nile Band's
Egyptian sounds, Jazz,
Spanish and Irish music. It
also hosts regular nights like
Open Mic Night, Acoustic
Gig Night, True Poets Society
and World Music Night

115–117 Manchester Road,
Chorlton, Manchester,
Greater Manchester
M21 9PG
☎ 0161 881 9338
@ Iguanabar@gmail.com
🖱 www.iguanabar.co.uk
🔎 Page 141-F1

Irish World Heritage Centre

10 Queens Road, Cheetham
Hill, Manchester, Greater
Manchester M8 8UF
☎ 01942 724166,
01612 054007
@ office@iwhc.com
🖱 www.iwhc.com
📄 01612 059285
🔎 Page 102-C5

Jilly's Rockworld

Jilly's provides a variety of
rock and alternative club
nights, live music and one-
off events.

65a Oxford Street,
Manchester, Greater
Manchester M1 6FQ
☎ 0161 236 9971
@ jillysrockworld@hotmail.
co.uk
🖱 www.jillys.co.uk

📄 0161 236 9972
🔎 Page 7-F7

Joshua Brooks

Joshua Brooks is a great bar
and nightclub situated on
the corner of Charles Street
and Princess Street next
to the BBC. Home to some
of the best club nights in
Manchester, Joshua Brooks
features indie, dance, live
bands, and drum 'n' bass
along with great DJs and
a variety of different club
night and live gigs.

106 Princess Street,
Manchester, Greater
Manchester M1 6NG
☎ 0161 273 7543
@ info@joshuabrooks.
co.uk
🖱 www.joshuabrooks.co.uk
📄 0161 273 7336
🔎 Page 7-F7

Korumba

York Street, Manchester,
Greater Manchester
M1 7HR
☎ 0161 273 4357
@ korumba@hotmail.com
🖱 www.korumba.co.uk
🔎 Page 7-F7

The Lloyds Hotel

617 Wilbraham Road,
Chorlton, Manchester,
Greater Manchester
M21 9AN
☎ 0161 862 6990
🔎 Page 141-E2

Maloneys Bar

Provincial House, 6 Nelson
Square, Bolton, Greater
Manchester BL1 1LH
☎ 01204 366 111
🖱 www.myspace.com/
maloneysrocks
📄 01204 366 111
🔎 Page 3-F5

Manchester Academy 1
The largest of the campus-based gig venues, Manchester Academy 1 show cases popular touring British and international bands.

Oxford Road, Manchester, Greater Manchester M13 9PR
☎ 0161 275 2930
🖱 www.manchester academy.net
📖 Page 128-B4

Manchester Academy 2 + 3 + Club Academy
Manchester Academy 2 (formerly known as the MDH) and Manchester Academy 3 (formerly known The Hop and Grape) provide a stage for touring British and international bands as well as local unsigned talent. In the student union basement, Club Academy hosts various club nights and the Club NME band showcase.

Manchester University Union, Oxford Road, Manchester, Greater Manchester M13 9PR
☎ 0161 275 2930
🖱 www.manchester academy.net
📖 Page 128-B4

Manchester Evening News Arena (MEN Arena)
Opened in 1995, the Manchester Evening News Arena was originally conceived for Manchester's bid for the Olympics and was built despite the bid's failure. From U2 to Pavarotti, ice hockey to boxing, Disney shows and motorbike exhibitions through to blue-chip AGMs, this 21,000 capacity multi-purpose entertainment and sports arena caters for all.

21 Hunts Bank, Victoria Station, Manchester Greater Manchester M3 1AR
☎ 0870 190 8000
@ enquiries@men-arena. com
🖱 www.men-arena.com
📖 Page 6-E1

Manchester Metropolitan University Students Union
99 Oxford Road, Manchester, Greater Manchester M1 7EL
☎ 01612 471162
@ mmunion@mmu.ac.uk
🖱 www.mmunion.co.uk
📄 01612 476314
📖 Page 128-B1

Manchester Opera House
Quay Street, Manchester, Greater Manchester M3 3HP
☎ 0870 401 9000
🖱 www.manchester operahouse.org.uk
📖 Page 6-C5

Manto
Manto opened in December 1990 when Manchester's Canal Street was a run-down back street and the Gay Village was in its infancy. After a two-year break, the groundbreaking bar returned in October 2003 to its original location at 46 Canal Street. Manto is spread over three floors – the Main Arena, a two-floor open space with a dance floor, internet access and food, and the top-floor Lounge, the perfect antidote to Canal Street in every respect.

46 Canal Street, Manchester, Greater Manchester M1 3WD
☎ 0161 236 2667
@ enquires@mantobar.com
🖱 www.mantobar.com
📄 0161 236 3767
📖 Page 7-G6

Matt & Phred's Jazz Club
A live jazz music venue in Manchester with local and international musicians performing six days a week.

64 Tib Street, Northern Quarter, Manchester, Greater Manchester M4 1LW
☎ 0161 831 7002
@ club@mattandphreds. com
🖱 www.mattandphreds.com
📄 0161 831 7003
📖 Page 7-G4

Middleton Civic Hall
Middleton Civic Hall offers comedy, live theatre, music and dance. In addition to the main auditorium there are three other meeting rooms within the complex which provide individual facilities or can be used in conjunction with main hall events.

Fountain Street, Middleton, Manchester, Greater Manchester M24 1AF
☎ 0161 643 2470
🕓 0161 643 2389
@ info@middletoncivic.com
🖱 www.middletoncivic.com
📖 Page 72-C4

Mint Lounge
Mint Lounge has every kind of music from the residents and live gigs from home-grown talent.

46–50 Oldham Street, Manchester, Greater Manchester M4 1LE
☎ 0161 228 1495
@ info@mintlounge.com
🖱 www.mintlounge.com
📖 Page 7-G4

Moho Live
MoHo Live is Manchester's newest independent live music, club and arts space. Based in the heart of the city (just off Piccadilly) and in the exciting and bustling Northern Quarter, MoHo Live is set to be one of the best entertainment venues not only in the North West, but in the country.

Tib Street, Northern Quarter, Manchester, Greater Manchester M4 1SH
☎ 0161 834 8188
@ info@moholive.co.uk
🖱 www.moholive.com
📖 Page 7-G4

The Moses Gate
The Moses Gate Hotel has had various major tribute and cover bands perform this compact and lively venue.

5 Bolton Road, Farnworth, Bolton, Greater Manchester BL4 7JU
☎ 01204 576278
@ info@mosesgate.co.uk
🖱 www.mosesgate.co.uk
📖 Page 65-H2

Music Box
Certified dance venue that hosts underground club nights, such as Electric Chair and Mr Scruff's Keep It Unreal at the weekend. Mid-week it presents up-and-coming live bands.

65 Oxford Street, Manchester, Greater Manchester M1 6QF
☎ 0161 236 9971
🖱 www.jillys.co.uk
📖 Page 7-F7

Night and Day Cafe
Night and Day Cafe is an intimate well-established live music venue offering local and international bands as well as breaking unsigned talent. Food and drink served.

26 Oldham Street, Northern Quarter, Manchester, Greater Manchester M1 1JN

☎ 0161 236 1822
✆ 0161 236 4597
@ jay@nightnday.org
🖰 www.nightnday.org
🔊 Page 7-G4

O'Sheas Irish Bar

80 Princess Street,
Manchester, Greater
Manchester M1 6NF
🔊 Page 7-G7

The Old Brewery

Strangeways, Manchester,
Greater Manchester M3 1LA
☎ 0787 9843224
@ computercontrolled@
btn.com
🔊 Page 114-C1

The Old Pint Pot

Adelphi Street, Salford,
Greater Manchester M3 6EN
✆ 0161 839 1514
🔊 Page 113-H3

Opus

Opus Manchester provides
a variety of entertainment
including club nights, stand-
up comedy and live bands.

The Printworks, Units
21–23, Withy Grove,
Manchester, Greater
Manchester M4 2BS
☎ 0161 834 2414
@ robin@opusmanchester.
com
🖰 www.opusmanchester.
com
🔊 Page 7-F2

Playhouse 2

The home of amateur
theatre company Crompton
Stage Society since
1966, a wide variety of
entertainment, professional
as well as amateur, is
produced each year.

Newtown Street,
Shaw, Oldham, Greater
Manchester OL8 2NX
☎ 01706 847281
@ info@playhouse2.com
🖰 www.playhouse2.com
🔊 Page 60-A3

Railway Inn

Situated in the West Riding
of Yorkshire, The Railway is
the gateway to Greenfield,
literally steps away from
the main Manchester-
Wakefield train link and
Oldham-Uppermill A road.
Surrounded by scenic views,
beautiful hills and pleasant
valleys, it is a hidden gem
of a watering hole and
resting place, providing
it's visitors with quality
live entertainment and the
warmest welcome.

11 Shaw Hall Bank Road,
Greenfield, Saddleworth,
Greater Manchester
OL3 7JZ
☎ 01457 872307
@ info@railway-greenfield.
co.uk
🖰 www.railway-greenfield.
co.uk
🔊 Page 94-D1

The Roadhouse

A live music venue featuring
a wide variety of acts
including punk, rock, indie
and retro music. Regular
club nights.

8 Newton Street, Piccadilly,
Manchester, Greater
Manchester M1 2AN
☎ 0161 832 1111,
0161 237 9789
@ info@theroadhouselive.
co.uk
🖰 www.theroadhouselive.
co.uk
📄 0161 236 9289
🔊 Page 7-H4

Rochdale Transport Club

Baron Street, Rochdale,
Greater Manchester
OL16 1SJ
☎ 01706 632087
@ barryrock@tiscali.co.uk
🖰 www.jlc-rock-promotions.
com
📄 01706 345602
🔊 Page 10-D7

Royal Northern College of Music: Bruntwood Theatre

124 Oxford Road,
Manchester, Greater
Manchester M13 9RD
☎ 0161 907 5200
✆ 0161 907 5555
@ info@rncm.ac.uk
🖰 www.rncm.ac.uk
📄 0161 273 7611
🔊 Page 128-B2

Royal Northern College of Music: Lecture Theatre

124 Oxford Road,
Manchester, Greater
Manchester M13 9RD
☎ 0161 907 5200
✆ 0161 907 5555
@ info@rncm.ac.uk
🖰 www.rncm.ac.uk
📄 0161 273 7611
🔊 Page 128-B2

Royal Northern College of Music: Lord Rhodes Room

124 Oxford Road,
Manchester, Greater
Manchester M13 9RD
☎ 0161 907 5200
@ info@rncm.ac.uk
🖰 www.rncm.ac.uk
📄 0161 273 7611
🔊 Page 128-B2

Royal Northern College of Music: Studio Theatre

124 Oxford Road,
Manchester, Greater
Manchester M13 9RD
☎ 0161 907 5200
✆ 0161 907 5555
🖰 www.rncm.ac.uk
📄 0161 273 7611
🔊 Page 128-B2

Royal Oak

440 Barlow Moor Road,
Chorlton-cum-Hardy,
Manchester, Greater
Manchester M21 0BQ

☎ 0161 860 7438
@ 7953@greeneking.co.uk
🔊 Page 141-F2

The Ruby Lounge

28–34 High Street,
Manchester, Greater
Manchester M4 1QB
☎ 0161 834 1392
@ info@ruby-lounge.co.uk
🖰 www.ruby-lounge.co.uk
🔊 Page 7-F3

Saddleworth Civic Hall

This venue holds regular
wedding receptions,
concerts, dinners and
meetings.

Lee Street, Uppermill,
Oldham, Greater
Manchester OL3 6AE
☎ 01457 876665
@ enquiries@ParishCoun
cil.saddleworth.org.uk
🖰 www.parishcouncil.
saddleworth.org
📄 01457 872929
🔊 Page 79-E4

Solomon Grundy

447–449, Wilmslow Road,
Withington, Manchester,
Greater Manchester
M20 4AN
☎ 0161 374 5861
🖰 www.manchesterad.com
🔊 Page 142-D4

Soundhouse

Ash Street, Bolton, Greater
Manchester BL2 1DG
☎ 01204 389360
✆ 01204 522914
@ soundhouselive@
googlemail.com
🖰 www.soundhouselive.
co.uk
🔊 Page 3-G6

South West Manchester Cricket Club

Ellesmere Road, Chorlton, Manchetser, Greater Manchester M21 0SG
☎ 0161 881 1921
🖰 www.swmanchester.play-cricket.com
⊘ Page 141-G2

The Southern Hotel

Mauldeth Road West, Chorlton, Manchester, Greater Manchester M21 9AT
☎ 0161 881 7048
@ info@thesouthernhotel.co.uk
🖰 www.thesouthernhotel.co.uk
⊘ Page 142-A3

The Star and Garter

A premier live music and weekly club night venue in Manchester.

18–20 Fairfield Street, Manchester Greater Manchester M1 2QF
☎ 0161 273 6726
@ gigdetails@starandgarter.co.uk
🖰 www.starandgarter.co.uk
⊘ Page 7-J7

Thatched House

74 Churchgate, Stockport, Greater Manchester SK1 1YJ
☎ 0161 355 1910
@ thatched-live@ntlworld.com
🖰 www.thatched-live.co.uk
⊘ Page 13-H3

Three Pigeons

587 Blackburn Road, Bolton, Greater Manchester BL1 7AA
☎ 01204 594296
⊘ Page 33-H2

Tribeca and Bed

Tribeca Bar and Bed is a chic and vibrant city centre bar in the heart of Manchester with

a distinct and sophisticated New York air. The bar offers a relaxed atmosphere by day, and a buzzy, vibrant scene by night. A mix of raw tunes and fresh cocktails.

50 Sackville Street, Manchester, Greater Manchester M1 3WF
☎ 0161 236 8300
@ ask@tribeca-bar.co.uk
🖰 www.tribeca-bar.co.uk
📄 0161 236 8244
⊘ Page 7-G6

Trof Northern Quarter

5–8 Thomas Street, Manchester, Greater Manchester M4 1EG
☎ 0161 833 3197
⊘ Page 7-G3

Union Music Lounge

845 Stockport Road, Levenshulme, Manchester, Greater Manchester M19 3PW
☎ 0161 224 1271
🖰 www.levenshulme.com/Union/index.html
⊘ Page 144-A2

The Warehouse Project

Beneath Picadilly Train Station, Manchester, Greater Manchester M1 2GH
☎ 0161 835 3500
@ guestlist@thewarehouseproject.com
🖰 www.thewarehouseproject.com
⊘ Page 7-J6

White Hart

51 Stockport Road, Lydgate, Oldham, Greater Manchester OL4 4JJ
☎ 01457 872566
🖰 www.thewhitehart.co.uk
📄 01457 875190
⊘ Page 93-H2

Willows Variety Centre

Willows Road, Weaste, Salford, Greater Manchester M5 2FQ

☎ 0161 736 8541
@ info@thewillowsonline.co.uk
🖰 www.thewillowsonline.co.uk
📄 0161 743 0488
⊘ Page 112-C3

The Witchwood

152 Old Street, Ashton-under-Lyne, Greater Manchester OL6 7SF
☎ 0161 344 0321
@ witchwood@witchwoodashton.ssbusiness.net
🖰 www.thewitchwood.co.uk
⊘ Page 119-F3

Ye Olde Man and Scythe

6–8 Churchgate, Bolton, Greater Manchester BL1 1HL
☎ 01204 451237
⊘ Page 3-F4

COMEDY CLUBS AND VENUES

Albert Halls

The Albert Halls has come a long way since re-opening for business back in 1985. The venue, which had been gutted by fire back in November 1981, spent three and half years undergoing a complete internal rebuild, converting what had for the previous 108 years been a single large concert hall, into two separate halls. The upper Albert Halls' capacity of 676 in its normal theatre setting is extremely versatile with the option to remove and reconfigure seats depending on the event.

Victoria Square, Bolton, Greater Manchester BL1 1YZ
☎ 01204 334400, 01204 334433
@ info@alberthalls-boltn.co.uk

🖰 www.alberthalls-bolton.co.uk
⊘ Page 2-E5

Apollo Manchester

Opened in 1930 by the actress Margaret Lockwood, the Manchester Apollo was originally built as an ABC Cinema and variety hall. The venue has a tradition of bringing some of the biggest artists of the day to an intimate venue, as well as bringing through developing acts. Always diverse, the Apollo also caters for comedy shows, be they stand-up or larger scale touring productions.

Ardwick Green, Manchester, Greater Manchester M12 6AP
☎ 0161 273 6921
📞 0870 401 8000
🖰 www.livenation.co.uk/venue/getVenue/venueId/16155/
⊘ Page 128-D1

Bar XS

This bar, in the heart of the student area, houses the XS Malarkey stand-up comedy night every Tuesday.

341–343 Wilmslow Road, Fallowfield, Manchester, Greater Manchester M14 6XS
☎ 0161 257 2403
⊘ Page 143-E3

Blue Cat Cafe

Blue Cat is an intimate venue famed for good music, low lighting, decent drinks, eccentricity and experimentation. Based in Heaton Moor, just outside Manchester, it promotes both local and touring bands regularly. International artists from Australia, Boston, New York, Chicago, Germany and Norway have been memorable highlights

and include names like Electric Six, Johnny Marr, Haven, Curtis Eller and Viva Stereo.

17 Shaw Road, Heaton Moor, Stockport, Greater Manchester SK4 4AG
☎ 0161 432 2117
@ danny@bluecatcafe.co.uk
🖰 www.bluecatcafe.co.uk
❂ Page 159-E2

The Comedy Store, Manchester
The Manchester Comedy Store offers a 500 seat theatre-style auditorium, a spacious public bar, a dining area and VIP ward room, all contained within two converted railway arches, costing £14m.

Arches 3 and 4 Deansgate Locks, Whitworth Street West, Manchester, Greater Manchester M1 5LH
☎ 0161 839 9595
🕓 0870 593 2932
@ john@thecomedystore.co.uk
🖰 www.thecomedystore.biz
📄 0161 839 9696
❂ Page 6-D7

Contact Theatre
Located in the heart of the University of Manchester's student campus, the Contact Theatre hosts a wide variety of cutting edge theatre productions as well as comedy evenings, artwork exhibitions, gigs and student nights. The theatre's Deluxe bar serves Mediterranean inspired lunches with music from live DJs.

Oxford Road, Manchester Greater Manchester M15 6JA
☎ 0161 274 0600
🕓 0161 274 0600
@ bookings@contact-theatre.org
🖰 www.contact-theatre.org
❂ Page 128-C3

The Dancehouse Theatre
10 Oxford Road, Manchester, Greater Manchester M1 5QA
☎ 0161 237 9753
@ admin@thedancehouse.co.uk
🖰 www.thedancehouse.co.uk
📄 0161 237 1408
❂ Page 128-B1

The Frog and Bucket Comedy Club
The Frog and Bucket prides itself as developing some of the best comic talents on the circuit.

102 Oldham Street, Manchester, Greater Manchester M4 1LJ
☎ 0161 236 9805
@ info@frogandbucket.com
🖰 www.frogandbucket.com
📄 0161 228 1652
❂ Page 7-H3

Iguana Bar
A bar that holds music for all tastes, with sounds such as the Country and Eastern Band's Turkish and Kurdish music, the Nile Band's Egyptian sounds, jazz, Spanish and Irish music. It also holds regular nights like Open Mic Night, Acoustic Gig Night, True Poets Society and World Music Night

115–117 Manchester Road, Chorlton, Manchester, Greater Manchester M21 9PG
☎ 0161 881 9338
@ Iguanabar@gmail.com
🖰 www.iguanabar.co.uk
❂ Page 141-F1

Manchester Comedy Balloon at The Ape and Apple
Manchester's official underground comedy club is dedicated to developing new comedy talent through the medium of open mic spots.

28 John Dalton Street, Manchester, Greater Manchester M2 6HQ
☎ 0161 839 9624
🖰 www.comedyballoon.co.uk
❂ Page 6-D5

Manchester Evening News Arena (MEN Arena)
Opened in 1995, the Manchester Evening News Arena was originally conceived for Manchester's bid for the Olympics and was built despite the bid's failure. From U2 to Pavarotti, ice hockey to boxing, Disney shows and motorbike exhibitions through to blue-chip AGMs, this 21,000 capacity multi-purpose entertainment and sports arena caters for all.

21 Hunts Bank, Victoria Station, Manchester, Greater Manchester M3 1AR
☎ 0870 190 8000
@ enquiries@men-arena.com
🖰 www.men-arena.com
❂ Page 6-E1

The Melville
Barton Road, Stretford, Manchester, Greater Manchester M32 9RB
❂ Page 125-G5

Middleton Civic Hall
Middleton Civic Hall Offers comedy, live theatre, music and dance. In addition to the main auditorium there are three other meeting rooms within the complex which provide individual facilities or can be used in conjunction with main hall events.

Fountain Street, Middleton, Manchester, Greater Manchester M24 1AF
☎ 0161 643 2470
🕓 0161 643 2389
@ info@middletoncivic.com
🖰 www.middletoncivic.com
❂ Page 72-C4

Mint Lounge
Mint Lounge has every kind of music from the residents and live gigs from home-grown talent.

46–50 Oldham Street, Manchester, Greater Manchester M4 1LE
☎ 0161 228 1495
@ info@mintlounge.com
🖰 www.mintlounge.com
❂ Page 7-H3

Opus
Opus Manchester provides a variety of entertainment including club nights, stand-up comedy and live bands.

The Printworks, Units 21–23, Withy Grove, Manchester, Greater Manchester M4 2BS
☎ 0161 834 2414
@ robin@opusmanchester.com
🖰 www.opusmanchester.com
❂ Page 7-F2

Railway Inn
Situated in the West Riding of Yorkshire, The Railway is the gateway to Greenfield, literally steps away from the main Manchester-Wakefield train link and Oldham-Uppermill A road. Surrounded by scenic views, beautiful hills and pleasant valleys, it is a hidden gem of a watering hole and resting place, providing it's visitors with quality live entertainment and the warmest welcome.

11 Shaw Hall Bank Road, Greenfield, Saddleworth, Greater Manchester OL3 7JZ
☎ 01457 872307

@ info@railway-greenfield.
co.uk
www.railway-greenfield.
co.uk
Page 94-D1

White Hart

51 Stockport Road,
Lydgate, Oldham, Greater
Manchester OL4 4JJ
☎ 01457 872566
www.thewhitehart.co.uk
01457 875190
Page 93-H2

CLASSICAL MUSIC VENUES

Bamford Chapel

Jowkin Lane, Norden Road,
Bamford, Rochdale, Greater
Manchester OL11 5PQ
☎ 01706 648137
www.rochdale.gov.uk
Page 28-A5

The Bridgewater Hall

Lower Mosley Street,
Manchester, Greater
Manchester M2 3WS
☎ 0161 950 0000
☎ 0161 907 9000
@ admin@bridgewater-
hall.co.uk
www.bridgewater-hall.
co.uk
0161 950 0001
Page 6-D7

Chapel House

Stockport Road, Manchester,
Greater Manchester
M12 4JB
☎ 0161 432 6729
Page 129-F4

Chetham's School of Music

Long Millgate, Manchester,
Greater Manchester M31SB
☎ 0161 834 9644
@ chets@chethams.com
www.chethams.com
0161 839 3609
Page 6-E2

Manchester Cathedral

Manchester cathedral has
a stunning interior with
the best late medieval
woodwork in the north. The
cathedral helps children
and young people make a
stronger connection with
the Christian faith. Classical
concerts and performances
are also put on and the
cathedral welcomes visiting
choirs.

The Cathedral, Manchester,
Greater Manchester M3 1SX
☎ 0161 833 2220
@ office@manchester
cathedral.com
manchestercathedral.org
0161 839 6218
Page 6-E2

Manchester Opera House

Quay Street, Manchester,
Greater Manchester M3 3HP
☎ 0870 401 9000
www.manchester
operahouse.org.uk
Page 6-C5

The Maxwell Hall, Salford University

University of Salford,
Salford, Greater Manchester
M5 4WT
☎ 0161 295 5000
@ webmaster@salford.
ac.uk
www.salford.ac.uk
0161 295 5999
Page 113-H3

Royal Northern College of Music: Bruntwood Theatre

124 Oxford Road,
Manchester, Greater
Manchester M13 9RD
☎ 0161 907 5200
☎ 0161 907 5555
@ info@rncm.ac.uk
www.rncm.ac.uk
0161 273 7611
Page 128-B2

Royal Northern College of Music: Haden Freeman Concert Hall

124 Oxford Road,
Manchester, Greater
Manchester M13 9RD
☎ 0161 907 5200
☎ 0161 907 5555
@ info@rncm.ac.uk
www.rncm.ac.uk
0161 273 7611
Page 128-B2

Royal Northern College of Music: Lecture Theatre

124 Oxford Road,
Manchester, Greater
Manchester M13 9RD
☎ 0161 907 5200
☎ 0161 907 5555
@ info@rncm.ac.uk
www.rncm.ac.uk
0161 273 7611
Page 128-B2

Royal Northern College of Music: Lord Rhodes Room

124 Oxford Road,
Manchester, Greater
Manchester M13 9RD
☎ 0161 907 5200
@ info@rncm.ac.uk
www.rncm.ac.uk
0161 273 7611
Page 128-B2

Royal Northern College of Music: Studio Theatre

124 Oxford Road,
Manchester, Greater
Manchester M13 9RD
☎ 0161 907 5200
☎ 0161 907 5555
www.rncm.ac.uk
0161 273 7611
Page 128-B2

St Mary The Baum

St Mary's Gate, Rochdale,
Greater Manchester
OL16 1AP

☎ 01706 352604
@ canonfinney@
stmaryinthebaum.co.uk
www.stmaryinthebaum.
co.uk
Page 10-B5

St Ann's Church

St Ann's church is an
elegant, neo-classical
building dating from 1712,
and often ascribed to Sir
Christopher Wren or one
of his pupils. It is a Grade
I listed building of historic
and architectural merit.

St Ann Street, Manchester
Greater Manchester M2 7LF
☎ 0161 834 0239
www.stannsmanchester.
com
Page 6-E4

Studio 7, New Broadcasting House

Oxford Road, Manchester,
Greater Manchester
M60 1SJ
☎ 016 1244 4002
@ philharmonic@bbc.co.uk
www.bbc.co.uk/
philharmonic
Page 128-B1

CINEMAS

AMC Cinemas Great Northern 16

253 Deansgate, Manchester,
Greater Manchester M3 4EN
☎ 0870 755 5657
www.amctheatres.com/
theatres/international/uk
0161 817 3080
Page 6-D7

Apollo Cinema, Altrincham

Denmark Street, Altrincham,
Greater Manchester
WA14 2WG
☎ 0871 200 6000
www.apollocinemas.
co.uk
Page 165-G5

Cineworld Ashton-under-Lyne

Ashton Leisure Park, Fold Way, Ashton-under-Lyne, Greater Manchester OL7 0PG
☎ 08712 208000
🖰 www.cineworld.co.uk/
✆ Page 119-E5

Cineworld Bolton

The Valley, 15 Eagley Brook Way, Bolton, Greater Manchester BL1 8TS
☎ 0870 777 2775,
   0870 241 3445
🕽 08712 002000
🖰 www.cineworld.co.uk
✆ Page 34-B3

Cineworld Didsbury

Parrs Wood, East Didsbury, Manchester, Greater Manchester M20 5PG
☎ 0870 777 2775
🕽 08712 002000
🖰 www.cineworld.co.uk
✆ Page 158-A5

Cineworld Stockport

4 Grand Central Square, Wellington Road South, Stockport, Greater Manchester SK1 3TA
☎ 0870 777 2775
🕽 08712 002000
🖰 www.cineworld.co.uk
✆ Page 13-F5

New Curzon Cinema

Princess Road, Urmston, Manchester, Greater Manchester M41 5SQ
☎ 0161 748 2929
🕽 0161 755 0550
🖰 www.curzonmanchester. co.uk
✆ Page 124-A5

Odeon Manchester

Printworks Centre, 27 Withy Grove, Manchester, Greater Manchester M4 2BS
🕽 08712 244007
🖰 www.odeon.co.uk
✆ Page 7-F3

Odeon Rochdale

Sandbrook Park, Sandbrook Way, Rochdale, Greater Manchester OL11 1RY
☎ 08712 244007
🖰 www.odeon.co.uk
✆ Page 42-D2

Odeon Trafford Centre

201 The Dome, The Trafford Centre, Manchester, Greater Manchester M17 8DF
☎ 08712 244007
🖰 www.odeon.co.uk
✆ Page 124-C2

The Plaza Theatre

The Theatre hosts cinema, including classic British films, live stage shows, musicals, stand-up comedy and dance performances.

Mersey Square, Stockport, Greater Manchester SK1 1SP
☎ 0161 477 7779
🕽 0161 477 7779
@ boxoffice@ stockportplaza.co.uk
🖰 www.stockportplaza. co.uk
📄 0161 480 3818
✆ Page 13-F3

Regent, Marple

Stockport Road, Marple, Greater Manchester SK6 6BJ
☎ 0161 427 5951
@ marpleregent@cinemas-online.co.uk
🖰 www.regent-marple. co.uk
✆ Page 175-E3

Savoy Cinema

The Savoy is a privately owned independent cinema. The auditorium is stadium style with 460 comfortable seats, the films are presented in stereo surround sound and there is limited wheelchair access.

Heaton Moor Road, Heaton Moor, Stockport, Greater Manchester SK4 4HY
☎ 0161 432 2114
🖰 www.savoycinema.co.uk
✆ Page 158-D3

Showcase Cinema, Manchester

Hyde Road, Bell Vue, Manchester, Greater Manchester M12 5AL
☎ 08712 201000
🖰 www.showcasecinemas. co.uk
✆ Page 130-A3

Vue Bury

Park 66, Pilsworth Road, Bury, Greater Manchester BL9 8RS
☎ 08712 240240
@ customerservices@ vuemail.com
🖰 www.myvue.com
✆ Page 54-A3

Vue Manchester Lowry

The Lowry Designer Outlet, The Quays, Salford Quays, Salford, Greater Manchester M50 3AZ
☎ 08712 240240
@ customerservices@ vuemail.com
🖰 www.myvue.com
✆ Page 126-C1

THEATRES

Abraham Moss Centre Theatre

The Abraham Moss complex, home to a number of community groups, is used by national touring companies as well as by locally based theatre groups.

140 Crescent Road, Manchester, Greater Manchester M8 5UF
☎ 0161 908 8312
@ gdavis@notes. manchester.gov.uk
🖰 www.manchester.gov.uk
✆ Page 102-B2

Albert Halls

The Albert Halls has come a long way since re-opening for business back in 1985. The venue, which had been gutted by fire back in November 1981, spent three and half years undergoing a complete internal rebuild, converting what had for the previous 108 years been a single large concert hall, into two separate halls. The upper Albert Halls' capacity of 676 in its normal theatre setting is extremely versatile with the option to remove and reconfigure seats depending on the event.

Victoria Square, Bolton, Lancashire BL1 1YZ
☎ 01204 334400,
   01204 334433
@ info@alberthalls-boltn. co.uk
🖰 www.alberthalls-bolton. co.uk
✆ Page 2-E5

Altrincham Garrick Theatre

Barrington Road, Altrincham, Greater Manchester WA14 1HZ
☎ 0161 928 1677
🕽 0161 928 1677
@ info@garricktheatre. fsnet.co.uk
🖰 www.garricktheatre. co.uk
✆ Page 165-G3

The Blue Box Theatre

Nell Lane, Chorlton, Manchester, Greater Manchester M21 7SL
☎ 0161 882 1150
@ boxoffice@ blueboxtheatre.co.uk
🖰 www.blueboxtheatre. co.uk
📄 0161 861 8753
✆ Page 141-H5

Bolton Little Theatre

Hanover Street, Bolton,
Greater Manchester
BL1 4TG
☎ 01204 394223
✆ 01204 524469
@ info@blt.org.uk
✑ www.blt.org.uk
✆ Page 2-C5

Capitol Theatre

Cavendish Street,
Manchester, Greater
Manchester M15 6BH
☎ 0161 247 1305
✆ 0161 247 1306
✑ www.theatre.mmu.ac.uk
✆ Page 128-B2

Chapman Theatres

Chapman Building,
University of Salford,
Salford, Greater Manchester
M5 4WT
☎ 0161 295 5000,
0161 295 5223
✑ www.salford.ac.uk
✆ Page 113-H3

Contact Theatre

Located in the heart of the
University of Manchester's
student campus, the Contact
Theatre hosts a wide variety
of cutting-edge theatre
productions as well as
comedy evenings, artwork
exhibitions, gigs and student
nights. The theatre's Deluxe
bar serves Mediterranean
inspired lunches with music
from live DJs.

Oxford Road, Manchester,
Greater Manchester
M15 6JA
☎ 0161 274 0600
✆ 0161 274 0600
@ bookings@contact-
theatre.org
✑ www.contact-theatre.org
✆ Page 128-C3

Curtain Theatre

47 Milkstone Road,
Rochdale, Greater
Manchester OL11 1EB

☎ 01706 642008
@ enquiry@curtaintheatre
rochdale.org.uk
✑ www.curtaintheatre
rochdale.org.uk
✆ Page 30-A5

The Dancehouse Theatre

10 Oxford Road, Manchester,
Greater Manchester M1 5QA
☎ 0161 237 9753
@ admin@thedancehouse.
co.uk
✑ www.thedancehouse.
co.uk
🖹 0161 237 1408
✆ Page 128-B1

Didsbury Studio Theatre, MMU Campus

Manchester Metropolitan
University, 799 Wilmslow
Road, Didsbury, Greater
Manchester M20 2RR
☎ 0161 247 1565
@ venues@mmu.ac.uk
✑ www.mmu.ac.uk/
venues/locations/
suburbs/didsbury.php
🖹 0161 247 6887
✆ Page 157-G4

Farnworth Little Theatre

Cross Street, Farnworth,
Bolton, Greater Manchester
BL4 7AJ
☎ 01204 792599
✆ 01204 303808
@ tickets@farnworthlittle
theatre.co.uk
✑ www.farnworthlittle
theatre.co.uk
✆ Page 66-A4

The Forum Theatre

NK Theatre Arts is a
registered charity which
offers weekly workshops
in music, dance and drama
for anyone aged 5 years
to adult. The company
produces various theatrical
presentations throughout
the year and also offers a

versatile auditorium for hire,
be it for shows, corporate
functions, parties etc.

Compstall Road, Romiley,
Stockport, Greater
Manchester SK6 4EA
☎ 0870 777 8731
@ firstname@
nktheatrearts.org.uk
✑ www.nktheatrearts.
org.uk
🖹 0161 406 6782
✆ Page 162-C4

Gracie Fields Theatre

Hudson's Walk, Rochdale,
Greater Manchester
OL11 5EF
☎ 01706 716 682
@ sheila.ridgeway@
oulderhill.com
✆ Page 29-E4

Greenroom

Greenroom was established
in 1983 to develop and
present local, national and
international performance at
venues across Manchester.

54–56 Whitworth Street
West, Manchester, Greater
Manchester M1 5WW
☎ 0161 615 0515
✆ 0161 615 0500
@ info@greenroomarts.org
✑ www.greenroomarts.org
✆ Page 6-E7

Library Theatre

Central Library, St Peter's
Square, Manchester,
Greater Manchester M2 5PD
☎ 0161 236 7110
@ ltcmkt@libraries.
manchester.gov.uk
✑ www.librarytheatre.com
✆ Page 6-E6

Loading Deck Theatre Space

7 Constance Street, Knott
Mill, Greater Manchester
☎ 0161 237 9925
✆ Page 127-H1

Manchester Opera House

Quay Street, Manchester,
Greater Manchester M3 3HP
☎ 0870 401 9000
✑ www.manchester
operahouse.org.uk
✆ Page 6-C5

Martin Harris Centre for Music and Drama

The Martin Harris Centre
for Music and Drama is
situated at the heart of the
oldest part of the University
and is a refurbishment
of two existing buildings,
incorporating the John
Thaw Studio Theatre and the
newly built Cosmo Rodewald
Concert Hall.

The University of
Manchester, Bridgeford
Street, Manchester, Greater
Manchester M13 9PL
☎ 0161 275 8951
@ boxoffice@manchester.
ac.uk
✑ www.arts.manchester.
ac.uk/martinharriscentre
✆ Page 128-C2

Middleton Civic Hall

Middleton Civic Hall Offers
comedy, live theatre, music
and dance. In addition to
the main auditorium there
are three other meeting
rooms within the complex
which provide individual
facilities or can be used in
conjunction with main hall
events.

Fountain Street, Middleton,
Manchester, Greater
Manchester M24 1AF
☎ 0161 643 2470
✆ 0161 643 2389
@ info@middletoncivic.com
✑ www.middletoncivic.com
✆ Page 72-C4

The Octagon Theatre, Bolton

Established in 1967, the
Octagon Theatre, Bolton

hosts various events such as play, comedy, music and more.

Howell Croft South, Bolton, Greater Manchester BL1 1SB
☎ 01204 529407
✆ 01204 520661
@ info@octagonbolton. co.uk
🖱 www.octagonbolton.co.uk
🖨 01204 556502
❷ Page 2-E5

Odeon Rochdale

Sandbrook Park, Sandbrook Way, Rochdale, Greater Manchester OL11 1RY
☎ 08712 244007
🖱 www.odeon.co.uk
❷ Page 42-D2

Oldham Coliseum Theatre

Fairbottom Street, Oldham, Greater Manchester OL1 3SW
☎ 01616 241731
✆ 01616 242829
@ boxoffice@coliseum. org.uk
🖱 www.coliseum.org.uk
❷ Page 9-H3

Palace Theatre

First opened in 1891, The Palace Theatre has a long history of being one of Manchester's leading venues for touring theatre and musical productions ranging from *Nicholas Nickleby* to *Les Miserables*; Disney's *Beauty and the Beast* to *King Lear*. It also offers classical music concerts and comedy gigs.

Oxford Street, Manchester, Greater Manchester M1 6FT
☎ 0870 401 3000
🖱 www.livenationtheatres. co.uk
❷ Page 7-F7

Playhouse 2

The home of amateur theatre company Crompton Stage Society since 1966. A wide variety of entertainment, professional as well as amateur, is produced each year.

Newtown Street, Shaw, Oldham, Greater Manchester OL8 2NX
☎ 01706 847281
@ info@playhouse2.com
🖱 www.playhouse2.com
❷ Page 60-A3

The Plaza Theatre

The Theatre hosts cinema, including classic British films, live stage shows, musicals, stand-up comedy and dance performances.

Mersey Square, Stockport, Greater Manchester SK1 1SP
☎ 0161 477 7779
✆ 0161 477 7779
@ boxoffice@ stockportplaza.co.uk
🖱 www.stockportplaza. co.uk
🖨 0161 480 3818
❷ Page 13-F3

Robert Powell Theatre, Univeristy Of Salford, Allerton Building

Frederick Road Campus, Salford, Greater Manchester M6 6PU
☎ 0161 295 6108
@ artsunit-amss@salford. ac.uk
🖱 www.arts.salford.ac.uk
❷ Page 113-G2

Royal Exchange Theatre

The Royal Exchange Theatre was founded in 1976 in the old Cotton Exchange in Manchester by a group of artistic directors – Michael Elliott, Caspar Wrede, Richard Negri, James Maxwell and Braham Murray.

St Ann's Square, Manchester, Greater Manchester M2 7DH
☎ 0161 833 9833, 0161 833 0483
@ marketing@ royalexchange.co.uk
🖱 www.royalexchange. co.uk
❷ Page 6-E4

Stockport Garrick Theatre

Exchange Street, Wellington Road South, Stockport, Greater Manchester SK3 0EJ
☎ 0161 480 3287
✆ 0161 480 5866
@ garricktheatre@philm. co.uk
🖱 www.stockportgarrick. co.uk
❷ Page 13-F4

Stockport Town Hall

Stockport Town Hall, also referred to as 'The Wedding Cake', offers high quality services for the occasions such as wedding ceremonies, concerts, exhibitions and fairs and corporate events.

Edward Street, Stockport, Greater Manchester SK1 3XE
☎ 0845 833 0971
✆ 0845 833 0973
@ venue.management@ stockport.gov.uk
🖱 www.stockporttownhall. org.uk
❷ Page 13-G5

Studio Salford at The King's Arms

Studio Salford is an umbrella group representing and promoting several theatre companies, raising the profile of Salford as a viable artistic location and promoting artists from all over Salford and Manchester.

11 Bloom Street, Salford, Greater Manchester M3 6AN
☎ 0161 834 3896
@ mailinglist@ studiosalford.com
🖱 www.studiosalford.com
❷ Page 6-B3

BARS AND PUBS

The Abbey Inn

77 West Street, Oldham, Greater Manchester OL9 6EJ
☎ 0161 624 0888
❷ Page 8-C4

The Alma Inn

152–154 Bradshawgate, Bolton, Greater Manchester BL2 1BA
☎ 01204 364113
❷ Page 3-F6

Apollo Manchester

Opened in 1930 by the actress Margaret Lockwood, the Manchester Apollo was originally built as an ABC Cinema and variety hall. The venue has a tradition of bringing some of the biggest artists of the day to an intimate venue, as well as bringing through developing acts. Always diverse, the Apollo also caters for comedy shows, be they stand-up or larger scale touring productions.

Ardwick Green, Manchester, Greater Manchester M12 6AP
☎ 0161 273 6921
✆ 0870 401 8000
🖱 www.livenation.co.uk
❷ Page 128-D1

Atlas Bar

376 Deansgate, Manchester, Greater Manchester M3 4LY
☎ 0161 834 2124
❷ Page 6-C7

Axm Bar

Located in Manchester's Gay Village, Axm Bar won the Best Bar None award for Manchester and Best Bar in the Hot Village awards.

10 Canal Street, Manchester, Greater Manchester M1 3EZ
☎ 0161 236 6005
@ info@axm-bar.co.uk
⌐ www.axm-bar.co.uk/
▤ 0161 236 5118
◉ Page 7-G6

Baa Bar

27 Sackville Street, Manchester, Greater Manchester M1 3LZ
☎ 0161 247 7997
@ sackville@baabar.co.uk
⌐ www.baabar.co.uk/baa/index/htm
▤ 0161 247 7799
◉ Page 7-G6

Baa Deansgate

The bar was opened in a converted warehouse, and 13 years on, the original is formally established at the heart of the city centre nightlife.

Arch 11, Deansgate Locks, Manchester, Greater Manchester M1 5LH
☎ 0161 832 4446
@ deansgate@baabar.co.uk
⌐ www.baabar.co.uk/baa/index.htm
▤ 0161 839 5817
◉ Page 6-C7

Bar XS

This bar, in the heart of the student area, houses the XS Malarkey stand-up comedy night every Tuesday.

341–343 Wilmslow Road, Fallowfield, Manchester, Greater Manchester M14 6XS
☎ 0161 257 2403
◉ Page 143-E3

The Bay Horse

35–37 Thomas Street, Northern Quarter, Manchester, Greater Manchester M4 1NA
☎ 0161 661 1041
@ info@thebayhorsepub.co.uk
⌐ www.thebayhorsepub.co.uk
◉ Page 7-G3

Big Hands, Manchester

Conveniently located near the student union, the retro-bohemian decor of this bar provides a suitable atmosphere for a post-gig drink. Big Hands also offers DJ nights and live music.

296 Oxford Road, Manchester, Greater Manchester M13 9NS
☎ 0161 272 7779
◉ Page 128-C3

Billie Rox

106–108 Portland Street, Manchester, Greater Manchester M1 4RJ
☎ 01612 282036
⌐ www.billierox.com/manchester
▤ 0161 228 2079
◉ Page 7-F6

Bluu, Manchester

Smithfield Market, Thomas Street, Northern Quarter, Manchester, Greater Manchester M4 1BD
☎ 0161 839 7195
@ manchester@bluu.co.uk
⌐ www.bluu.co.uk/
▤ 0161 834 7364
◉ Page 7-G3

The Brook Tavern

260 Rochdale Road, Oldham, Greater Manchester OL1 2HF
☎ 0161 624 3789
◉ Page 75-F4

Cellar Vie

Lloyds House, 18–22 Lloyd Street, Manchester, Greater Manchester M2 5WA
☎ 0161 834 9696
◉ Page 6-D5

Chicago Rock Cafe, Bury

Chicago Rock Cafe offers a blend of eating, drinking and entertainment. The music played is the 'greatest classic hits of all time', catering for a wide variety of tastes and age groups, ranging from 1957–1995.

Haymarket Street, Bury Greater Manchester BL9 0AY
☎ 0161 763 6444
@ chicago-rock-cafe-bury@3d-entertainmentgroup.com
⌐ www.chicago-rock-cafe.co.uk
▤ 0161 763 5942
◉ Page 4-D5

Chicago Rock Cafe, Manchester

23 Peter Street, Manchester, Greater Manchester M2 5QR
☎ 0161 833 3000
@ chicago-rock-cafe-manchester@3d-entertainmentgroup.com
⌐ www.chicago-rock-cafe.co.uk
▤ 0161 839 4000
◉ Page 6-D6

Churchill's

Churchill's has developed a reputation as one of the most popular bars in Manchester's Gay Village with live entertainment every night of the week.

5 Canal Street, 37 Chorlton Street, Manchester, Greater Manchester M1 3HN
☎ 0161 236 5529
@ churchillsmanchester@hotmail.com
⌐ www.churchillsmanchester.com
▤ 0161 247 7789
◉ Page 7-G6

Company Cafe Bar

28, Richmond Street, Manchester, Greater Manchester M1 3NB
☎ 0161 237 9329
◉ Page 7-G6

Cord

The place to spend your weekend evenings, hosting some of the city's finest musical talent.

8 Dorsey Street, Tib Street, Manchester, Greater Manchester M4 1LU
☎ 0161 832 9494
@ info@cordbar.com
⌐ www.cordbar.com
◉ Page 7-H3

The Crown

37 Booth Street, Manchester, Greater Manchester M2 4AA
☎ 0161 237 0801 , 0161 237 0800
◉ Page 6-E5

Dry Bar

Since Dry Bar first opened its doors, it has been one of the most well-known and influential venues in the UK. Initially owned by Factory Records, Dry Bar opened on the 25th of July 1989 in the city's Northern Quarter. It is one of the places that gave birth to 'Madchester' in the early 90s and where many musicians still hang out today.

28–30 Oldham Street, Manchester, Greater Manchester M1 1JN
☎ 0161 236 9840
@ enquiries@drybar.co.uk
◉ Page 7-G4

Dunicans Bar
Sedgeborough Road, Moss Side, Manchester, Greater Manchester M16 7EZ
☎ 0161 226 2724
🌐 Page 127-H4

Equalz
174, Great Western Street, Manchester, Greater Manchester M14 4SN
☎ 0161 226 2061
🌐 Page 128-B4

The Farmers Arms
86–88 Chorley Street, Bolton, Greater Manchester BL1 4AL
☎ 01204 525834
🌐 Page 2-C3

The Fat Cat
Arch 8 Deansgate Locks, Manchester, Greater Manchester M1 5LH
☎ 0161 839 8243
@ manchester@ fatcatcafebars.co.uk
🌐 www.fatcatcafebars. co.uk/manchester
🌐 Page 6-C7

The Feathers
300 Barlow Moor Road, Chorlton, Manchester, Greater Manchester M21
☎ 0161 881 6612
🌐 Page 141-G5

Font Bar
7–9 New Wakefield Street, Manchester, Greater Manchester M1 5NP
☎ 0161 236 0944
@ fontbars@tiscali.co.uk
🌐 www.fontbar.com
🌐 Page 128-B1

Fuel, Manchester
448 Wilmslow Road, Withington, Manchester, Greater Manchester M20 3BW
☎ 01614 489702
@ fuelcafebar@hotmail. co.uk
🌐 Page 142-D4

The Garrett
127 Princess Street, Manchester, Greater Manchester M1 7AG
☎ 0161 228 6570
🌐 Page 7-F6

Glass Bar
258 Wilmslow Road, Fallowfield, Manchester, Greater Manchester M14 6JR
☎ 0161 257 0770
@ glass_bar@yahoo.co.uk
🌐 Page 143-F2

Gullivers
109 Oldham Street, Manchester, Greater Manchester M4 1LW
☎ 0161 832 5899
🌐 Page 7-G3

Hard Rock Cafe, Manchester
Located in the centre of the city, the UKs largest Hard Rock Cafe features a large collection of classic rock memorabilia from Manchester music greats such as The Smiths, Stone Roses, Happy Mondays and Herman's Hermits.

The Printworks, Corporation Street, Manchester, Greater Manchester M4 2BS
☎ 0161 831 6700
@ Iain_Duncan@hardrock. com
🌐 www.hardrock.com/ locations/cafes
🌐 Page 7-F2

The Hollywood
12 Bloom Street, Stockport, Greater Manchester SK3 9LA
☎ 0161 480 6525
🌐 Page 12-C6

Liquid Rock
Great George Street, Rochdale, Greater Manchester OL16 1PG
☎ 01706 750330
🌐 Page 10-D7

The Living Room
The Living Room on Deansgate in Manchester has now been open for over five years, and remains the restaurant and bar of choice for Manchester's discerning population. Situated directly above is The Dining Room, a standalone restaurant offering one of the chic-est dining experiences in Manchester. The Study above The Living Room and The Dining Room holds 50–100 people comfortably and is Manchester's premier private members' bar with an exceptional drinks list to match.

The Dining Room & The Study, 80 Deansgate, Manchester, Greater Manchester M3 2ER
☎ 0870 442 2537
@ manchester@ thelivingroom.co.uk
🌐 www.thelivingroom.co.uk
📄 0870 442 2538
🌐 Page 6-D4

M-Two
Peter Street, Manchester, Greater Manchester M2 3NQ
☎ 0161 839 1112
@ info@m-two.com
🌐 www.m-two.com
🌐 Page 6-D6

M19 Bar
847 Stockport Road, Levenshulme, Manchester, Greater Manchester M19 3PW
☎ 0161 224 8135
🌐 www.m19bar.com
🌐 Page 144-A2

Maloneys Bar
Provincial House, 6 Nelson Square, Bolton, Greater Manchester BL1 1LH
☎ 01204 366 111
📄 01204 366 111
🌐 Page 3-F5

Manchester Metropolitan University Students Union
99 Oxford Road, Manchester, Greater Manchester M1 7EL
☎ 01612 471162
@ mmunion@mmu.ac.uk
🌐 www.mmunion.co.uk
📄 01612 476314
🌐 Page 128-B1

Manchester Po Na Na
42 Charles Street, Oxford Road, Manchester, Greater Manchester M1 7DB
☎ 01612 726044
@ manchesterpnn@ ponana.com
🌐 www.ponana.com
📄 01612 726066
🌐 Page 7-G7

Napoleons
35 Bloom Street, Manchester, Greater Manchester M1 3LY
☎ 0161 236 8800
@ napoleonsmanchester@ yahoo.co.uk
🌐 www.napoleons.co.uk
🌐 Page 7-F7

O'Sheas Irish Bar
80 Princess Street, Manchester, Greater Manchester M1 6NF
🌐 Page 7-F6

The Old Market Tavern
Old Market Place, Altrincham, Greater Manchester WA14 4DN
☎ 0161 927 7062
🌐 Page 165-G4

The Old Pint Pot
Adelphi Street, Salford, Greater Manchester M3 6EN

☏ 0161 839 1514
Page 113-H3

One Central Street
One Central Street offers an extensive drinks menu in chic, contemporary surroundings.

1 Central Street, Manchester Greater Manchester M2 5WR
☏ 0161 211 9000
@ info@onecentralstreet.co.uk
🖰 www.onecentralstreet.co.uk
Page 6-E5

Othello's Cafe Bar
6 Brown Street, Stockport, Greater Manchester SK1 1RS
☏ 0161 477 0234
Page 13-F2

The Pack Horse
The Pack Horse has free events on all through the week from discos and karaoke, to live music and sport shown on large screens.

861 Stockport Road, Levenshulme, Manchester, Greater Manchester M19 3PW
☏ 0161 224 4355
🖰 www.levenshulme.com/packhorse
Page 144-A2

The Phoenix, Manchester
Precinct Centre, Oxford Road, Manchester, Greater Manchester M13 9RN
☏ 0161 272 5921
Page 128-B2

Pleasure Bar
489 Wilmslow Road, Withington, Manchester, Greater Manchester M20 4AN
☏ 0161 434 4300
Page 142-D4

Pure
21 Fletcher Street, Stockport, Greater Manchester SK1 1DY
☏ 0161 477 6655
Page 13-G3

Queen Anne
26 High Street, Bolton, Greater Manchester BL3 1NB
☏ 01204 572640
Page 67-E1

Red Bull Hotel
14 Middle Hillgate, Stockport, Greater Manchester SK1 3AY
☏ 01614 802087
Page 13-G4

Red On The Square
Nelson Square, Bolton, Greater Manchester BL1 1JT
☏ 01204 373805
Page 3-F5

The Retro Bar
Sackville Street, Manchester, Greater Manchester M1 3NJ
☏ 0161 274 4892
🖰 www.retrobarmanchester.com
Page 7-G7

Revolution Bar, Deansgate
Revolution Deansgate is the perfect place to have a party. Whether for chilling out in the lounge or dancing the night away in the Club Room.

Arch 7 Deansgate Lock, Whitworth Street, Deansgate, Manchester, Greater Manchester M1 5LH
☏ 0161 839 7558
@ deansgate-party@revolution-bars.co.uk
🖰 www.revolution-bars.co.uk/bars
📄 0161 839 7560
Page 6-C7

Revolution Bar, Fallowfield
Offering a wide variety of flavoured vodka drinks, food and music from resident DJs.

311–313 Wilmslow Road, Fallowfield, Manchester, Greater Manchester M14 6NW
☏ 0161 256 4754
🖰 www.revolution-bars.co.uk/bars
📄 0161 256 4754
Page 143-E3

Revolution Bar, Oxford Road
Offering a wide variety of flavoured vodka drinks, food and music from resident DJs.

90–94 Oxford Road, Manchester, Greater Manchester M1 5WH
☏ 0161 236 7470
@ manchester@revolution-bars.co.uk
🖰 www.revolution-bars.co.uk/bars
📄 0161 236 7470
Page 128-B1

Richmans
Moss Lane, Hale, Altrincham Greater Manchester WA15 8AP
☏ 0161 929 0111
Page 178-A1

Roscoes Bar
377 Chorley Road, Swinton, Greater Manchester M27 6AY
@ info@roscoesbar.co.uk
🖰 www.roscoesbar.co.uk
Page 98-D1

Royal Oak
440 Barlow Moor Road, Chorlton-cum-Hardy, Manchester, Greater Manchester M21 0BQ
☏ 0161 860 7438
@ 7953@greeneking.co.uk
Page 141-F3

Siberia Bar Club
107 The Rock, Bury, Greater Manchester BL9 0NB
☏ 0161 761 6568
@ info@siberiabury.com
🖰 www.siberiabury.com
Page 4-E4

The Slug And Lettuce
651 Wilmslow Road, Didsbury, Manchester Greater Manchester M20 6QZ
☏ 01614 341011
Page 157-G3

The Southern Hotel
Mauldeth Road West, Chorlton, Manchester, Greater Manchester M21 9AT
☏ 0161 881 7048
@ info@thesouthernhotel.co.uk
🖰 www.thesouthernhotel.co.uk
Page 142-A3

The Spread Eagle
526 Wilbraham Road, Chorlton, Manchester, Greater Manchester M21 9LD
☏ 0161 8610385
Page 141-E2

Star Inn
69 Church Street, Failsworth, Manchester, Greater Manchester M35 9JN
☏ 0161 681 2611
Page 105-E2

Studio 23
23 Peter Street, Manchester, Greater Manchester M2 5QR
Page 6-D6

TFI Mambos
19–21 Flixton Road, Urmston, Manchester, Greater Manchester M41 5AW
☏ 0161 749 4888
Page 138-C1

Taurus

Taurus hosts exhibitions, stand-up comics and performances by live bands.

1 Canal Street, Manchester, Greater Manchester M1 3HE
☎ 0161 236 4593
@ info@taurus-bar.co.uk
🖰 www.taurus-bar.co.uk
🖹 0161 236 5707
🗐 Page 7-G6

Teasers

Overlooking Peter Street, Teasers offers four bars spread between two different levels, each with its own dancefloor. The club's scantily-clad bar staff serve a capacity of 1,200 people.

Great Northern Warehouse, 231–233 Deansgate, Manchester, Greater Manchester M3 4EN
☎ 0161 833 3118
🖰 www.teaserscafe.co.uk
🖹 0161 833 3119
🗐 Page 6-C6

The Thirsty Scholar

50 New Wakefield Street, Manchester, Greater Manchester M1 5NP
☎ 0161 2366071
🗐 Page 128-A1

Tiger Tiger Manchester

With six bars, a grill and a lively club, Tiger Tiger hosts a variety of entertainment events, from after show parties to exhibitions and corporate dinners.

The Printworks, Withy Grove, Manchester, Greater Manchester M4 2BS
☎ 0161 385 8080
@ info@tigertiger-manch.co.uk
🖰 www.tigertiger-manch.co.uk
🖹 0161 385 8585
🗐 Page 7-F2

Tmesis

18–22 Lloyd Street, Manchester, Greater Manchester M2 5WA
☎ 0161 832 1111
🗐 Page 6-D5

Tokyo Project

57 Roscoe Street, Oldham, Greater Manchester OL1 1EA
☎ 01616 337000
🖰 www.tokyooldham.com
🗐 Page 9-H4

Trof

2a Landcross Road, Fallowfield, Manchester, Greater Manchester M14 6NA
☎ 0161 224 0467
🖰 www.trof.co.uk
🗐 Page 143-E2

Trof Northern Quarter

5–8 Thomas Street, Manchester, Greater Manchester M4 1EG
☎ 0161 833 3197
🗐 Page 7-G3

Waxy O'Connors

The Printworks, Manchester, Greater Manchester M4 2BS
☎ 0161 835 1210
@ manchester@waxyoconnors.co.uk
🖰 www.waxyoconnors.co.uk
🗐 Page 7-F2

White Hart

51 Stockport Road, Lydgate, Oldham, Greater Manchester OL4 4JJ
☎ 01457 872566
🖰 www.thewhitehart.co.uk
🖹 01457 875190
🗐 Page 93-H2

Zinc

Fully refurbished restaurant, bar and grill.

The Triangle, Hanging Ditch, Manchester, Greater Manchester M4 3ES

☎ 0161 827 4200
@ zinc.manchester@ircplc.co.uk
🖰 www.zincbar.co.uk
🗐 Page 6-E3

The Zumeroom

Oxford Road, Manchester, Greater Manchester M1 5QA
☎ 0161 236 8438
🖰 www.funkademia.net
🗐 Page 128-B1

NIGHTCLUBS

42nd Street Nightclub

2 Bootle Street, Manchester, Greater Manchester M2 5GU
☎ 0161 831 7108
@ info@42ndstreetnightclub.co.uk
🖰 www.42ndstreetnightclub.co.uk
🗐 Page 6-D5

5th Avenue

Sticking faithfully to it's Manchester style image, 5th Avenue presents wall-to-wall indie nights.

121 Princess Street, Manchester, Greater Manchester M1 7AG
☎ 0161 236 2754
🖰 www.5thavenuemanchester.com
🗐 Page 7-G7

Ampersand

A nightclub playing funky house music.

Longworth Street, St John Street, Deansgate, Manchester, Greater Manchester M3 4BQ
☎ 0161 832 3038
@ info@theampersand.co.uk
🖰 www.theampersand.co.uk
🗐 Page 6-C6

Area 51

Manchester's newest superclub which plays host to big name parties such as Cr2, Toolroom, Bitch, Sex

Toy, Filth and Kissdafunk, the successful Ibiza and Leeds house brand. With big line ups, new promotions and new decor attracting an 'up for it' party crowd.

2B Whitworth Street, Manchester, Greater Manchester M1 5WZ
☎ 07977 462522
🖰 www.area51club.co.uk
🗐 Page 6-D7

The Attic

An intimate dance music venue above the Thirsty Scholar pub with a range of cutting-edge club nights.

50 New Wakefield Street, Manchester, Greater Manchester M1 5NP
☎ 0161 236 6071
@ info@thirstyscholar.co.uk
🖰 www.thirstyscholar.co.uk
🗐 Page 128-A1

The Bay Horse

35–37 Thomas Street, Northern Quarter, Manchester, Greater Manchester M4 1NA
☎ 0161 661 1041
@ info@thebayhorsepub.co.uk
🖰 www.thebayhorsepub.co.uk
🗐 Page 7-G3

Billie Rox

106–108 Portland Street, Manchester, Greater Manchester M1 4RJ
☎ 01612 282036
🖰 www.billierox.com/manchester
🖹 0161 228 2079
🗐 Page 6-E6

Brannigans

Offering regular nights of 70s, 80s and 90s classics, plus fun and games events.

Albert Hall, Peter Street, Manchester, Greater Manchester M2 5QR

☎ 0161 835 9697
🖰 www.brannigansbars.com
📄 0161 835 9798
⊘ Page 6-D5

The Brickhouse
Specialising in indie, rock and pop classics from the 70s, 80s and 90s.

Arch 66, Whitworth Street West, Manchester, Greater Manchester M1 5WQ
☎ 0161 236 4418
@ info@brickhouse-nightclub.com
🖰 www.brickhouse-nightclub.com
⊘ Page 6-D7

Cafe Saki
A music venue and cafe with resident DJs and live bands.

2 Wilmslow Road, Rusholme, Greater Manchester M14 5TP
☎ 0161 257 0365
⊘ Page 128-C4

The Cinnamon Club
The Cinnamon Club is housed in a beautiful Edwardian building called The Bowdon Rooms which were built in 1903. With a fully sprung maple dance floor, and an arched ceiling towering above at over 40 feet, it makes a superb venue for concerts, cabarets, weddings and functions. Situated in leafy South Manchester/Cheshire, The Cinnamon Club is the premier live entertainment venue for music, private parties and corporate entertainment.

The Bowden Rooms, The Firs, Bowdon, Altrincham, Greater Manchester WA14 2TQ
☎ 0161 926 8992
@ information@thecinnamonclub.net
🖰 www.thecinnamonclub.net
⊘ Page 177-E2

The Club
Once home to legendary Mancunian record label, Factory Records and later gay club Paradise Factory, 112–116 Princess Street finally reopened its doors in 2008 under its new name, The Club.

112–116 Princess Street, Manchester, Greater Manchester M1 7EN
☎ 0161 272 7707
@ info@112-116princessstreet.co.uk
🖰 www.112-116princessstreet.co.uk
⊘ Page 7-G7

Club V
Venus is Manchester's longest running funky house night. Based at the famous V bar nightclub on Deansgate Manchester. Venus plays the best funky house music played by Manchester's and the UKs cream of the crop DJs.

111 Deansgate, Manchester, Greater Manchester M3 2BQ
☎ 07974 079961
@ les@2dope.co.uk
🖰 www.venusmanchester.co.uk
⊘ Page 6-D4

Copacabana
Copacabana is the best place for a Latin night out in Manchester. Whether you are an experienced salsero or you just enjoy a friendly, cosmopolitan atmosphere then Copacabana is the place for you. Specialising in parties, the range of options includes a latin-style celebration. Salsa classes run from Tuesday to Saturday and there are often bands, cultural events and student nights.

Sevendale House, Dale Street, Northern Quarter, Manchester, Greater Manchester M1 2HF
☎ 0161 237 3441
@ info@visitcopacabana.co.uk
🖰 www.visitcopacabana.co.uk
⊘ Page 7-G4

Cruz 101
Well-established gay venue on the Manchester strip. With a varied selection of in-house and hosted nights, the music policy ranges from disco to funky house, pop to trance and R'n'B to hard house.

101 Princess Street, Manchester, Greater Manchester M1 6DD
☎ 0161 2371554 , 0161 950 0101
🖰 www.cruz101.com
⊘ Page 7-F6

Fridays Nightclub
Fridays Nightclub has regular nights and special events featuring DJs playing party music, current chart, R'n'B, 80s and funky house.

Palatine Road, Didsbury, Manchester, Greater Manchester M20 8UF
☎ 0161 434 4986
🖰 www.fridaysnightclub.com
⊘ Page 157-E3

The Gateway
882 Wilmslow Road, East Didsbury, Manchester, Greater Manchester M20 5PG
☎ 0161 434 4122
@ thegatewaypub@yahoo.co.uk
🖰 www.thegatewaypub.co.uk
⊘ Page 157-H5

Hard Rock Cafe, Manchester
Located in the centre of the city, the UKs largest Hard Rock Cafe features a large collection of classic rock memorabilia from Manchester music greats such as The Smiths, Stone Roses, Happy Mondays and Herman's Hermits.

The Printworks, Corporation Street, Manchester, Greater Manchester M4 2BS
☎ 0161 831 6700
@ Iain_Duncan@hardrock.com
🖰 www.hardrock.com/locations/cafes
⊘ Page 7-F2

Hollywood Studio and Lounge
Hollywood Studio and Lounge opened with a host of entertainers and celebrities, playing 'old skool' classics, chart and pop music.

100 Bloom Street, Manchester, Greater Manchester M1 3LY
☎ 0161 228 1666
🖰 www.thehollywood.net
📄 0161 228 7474
⊘ Page 7-F6

Iguana Bar
A bar that hosts music for all tastes, with sounds such as the Country and Eastern Band's Turkish and Kurdish music, the Nile Band's Egyptian sounds, Jazz, Spanish and Irish music. It also hosts regular nights like Open Mic Night, Acoustic Gig Night, True Poets Society and World Music Night

115–117 Manchester Road, Chorlton, Manchester., Greater Manchester M21 9PG
☎ 0161 881 9338
@ Iguanabar@gmail.com
🖰 www.iguanabar.co.uk
⊘ Page 141-F1

Jabez Clegg
Jabez Clegg hosts events ranging from weekly quiz

and comedy nights to bands and club nights.

2 Portsmouth Street, Manchester, Greater Manchester M13 9GB
☎ 0161 272 8612
@ info@jabezclegg.co.uk
🖰 www.jabezclegg.co.uk
🖲 Page 128-C2

Jilly's Rockworld
Jilly's provides a variety of rock and alternative club nights, live music and one-off events.

65a Oxford Street, Manchester, Greater Manchester M1 6FQ
☎ 0161 236 9971
@ jillysrockworld@hotmail.co.uk
🖰 www.jillys.co.uk
📄 0161 236 9972
🖲 Page 7-F7

Joshua Brooks
Joshua Brooks is a great bar and nightclub situated on the corner of Charles Street and Princess Street next to the BBC. Home to some of the best club nights in Manchester, Joshua Brooks features indie, dance, live bands, and drum 'n' bass along with great DJs and a variety of different club night and live gigs.

106 Princess Street, Manchester, Greater Manchester M1 6NG
☎ 0161 273 7543
@ info@joshuabrooks.co.uk
🖰 www.joshuabrooks.co.uk
📄 0161 273 7336
🖲 Page 7-F7

Legends and The Outpost
4–6 Whitworth Street, Manchester, Greater Manchester M1 3QW
☎ 0161 236 5400
@ mail@legendsmanchester.com
🖰 www.legendsmanchester.com
🖲 Page 7-H6

Lime
Lime is situated between King Street and Albert Square, there are two-floors with 8,500 square feet of space. Downstairs is Sublime, with its large bar, dance floor and state of the art music system.

2 Booth Street, Manchester, Greater Manchester M2 4AT
☎ 0161 233 2929
@ kelvin@limeuk.com
🖰 www.limeuk.com/boothstreet
📄 0161 233 2925
🖲 Page 6-E5

Liquid Nightclub, Oldham
Two clubs in one, Liquid and Envy, hosting a wide range of music such as commercial dance, R'n'B, 'old skool', and club classics.

Retiro Street, Oldham, Greater Manchester OL1 1SA
☎ 0161 633 4585
@ liquid-oldham@luminar.co.uk
🖰 www.liquidclubs.com/oldham
📄 0161 627 5644
🖲 Page 9-G4

The Loft Nightclub
8–6 Old Street, Ashton-under-Lyne, Greater Manchester OL6 6LB
☎ 0161 343 1942
🖰 www.clubloft.co.uk
🖲 Page 119-G2

Manchester Metropolitan University Students Union
99 Oxford Road, Manchester, Greater Manchester M1 7EL
☎ 01612 471162
@ mmunion@mmu.ac.uk
🖰 www.mmunion.co.uk
📄 01612 476314
🖲 Page 128-B1

Manto
Manto opened in December 1990 when Manchester's Canal Street was a run-down back street and the Gay Village was in its infancy. After a 2-year break, the groundbreaking bar returned in October 2003 to its original location at 46 Canal Street. Manto is spread over three floors – the Main Arena, a two-floor open space with a dance floor, internet access and food, and the top-floor Lounge, the perfect antidote to Canal Street in every respect.

46 Canal Street, Manchester, Greater Manchester M1 3WD
☎ 0161 236 2667
@ enquires@mantobar.com
🖰 www.mantobar.com
📄 0161 236 3767
🖲 Page 7-G6

Mint Lounge
Mint Lounge has every kind of music from the residents and live gigs from home-grown talent.

46–50 Oldham Street, Manchester, Greater Manchester M4 1LE
☎ 0161 228 1495
@ info@mintlounge.com
🖰 www.mintlounge.com
🖲 Page 7-G4

Moho Live
MoHo Live is Manchester's newest independent live music, club and arts space.

Based in the heart of the City (just off Piccadilly) and in the exciting and bustling Northern Quarter, MoHo Live is set to be one of the best entertainment venues not only in the North West, but in the country.

Tibb Street, Northern Quarter, Manchester, Greater Manchester M4 1SH
☎ 0161 834 8188
@ info@moholive.co.uk
🖰 www.moholive.com
🖲 Page 7-G4

Music Box
Certified dance venue that hosts underground club nights, such as Electric Chair and Mr Scruff's Keep It Unreal at the weekend. Mid-week it presents up-and-coming live bands.

65 Oxford Street, Manchester, Greater Manchester M1 6QF
☎ 0161 236 9971
🖰 www.jillys.co.uk
🖲 Page 7-F7

Nicholsons
Nicholsons is a large stylish bar, nightclub and venue for private functions.There is a large, well-stocked bar area, at the front you'll find comfy leather sofas and other seating. The doors at the rear open up onto a separate bar area and dance floor.

102 School Road, Sale, Greater Manchester M33 7XB
☎ 0161 929 6116, 0161 962 3700
🖲 Page 154-B1

Night and Day Cafe
Night and Day Cafe is an intimate well-established live music venue offering local and international bands as well as breaking unsigned talent. Food and drink are served.

26 Oldham Street, Northern
Quarter, Manchester,
Greater Manchester M1 1JN
☎ 0161 236 1822
📞 0161 236 4597
@ jay@nightnday.org
🖰 www.nightnday.org
🖰 Page 7-G4

Opus

Opus Manchester provides
a variety of entertainment
including club nights, stand-
up comedy and live bands.

The Printworks, Units
21–23, Withy Grove,
Manchester, Greater
Manchester M4 2BS
☎ 0161 834 2414
@ robin@opusmanchester.
com
🖰 www.opusmanchester.
com
🖰 Page 7-F2

Paparazzi

Paparazzi has two floors
hosting regular nights with
DJs playing a wide range
of music including hip hop,
R'n'B, funk and vocal house.

The Printworks, Withy
Grove, Manchester, Greater
Manchester M4 2BS
☎ 0161 832 1234
@ info@thepaparazzi.co.uk
🖰 www.thepaparazzi.co.uk
📄 0161 832 1235
🖰 Page 7-F2

Pure

Pure has 80,000 square feet
of partying space, a 2,500
capacity, £300,000 Funktion-
One sound system split over
two cavernous rooms, and
Manchester's latest license.

The Printworks, Withy
Grove, Manchester, Greater
Manchester M4 2BS
☎ 0161 819 7770
@ pure@theprintworks.
com
🖰 www.puremanchester.
com
🖰 Page 7-F2

Pure Space

Pure Space is unique in its
use of three floors, each
with different feel and
function. Pure Space has
regular nights featuring DJs
playing a wide range music
from 80s and hip hop, to jazz
and soul.

11–13 New Wakefield
Street, Manchester, Greater
Manchester M1 5NP
☎ 0161 236 4899
@ info@purespacecafebar.
co.uk
🖰 www.purespacecafebar.
co.uk
📄 0161 923 4662
🖰 Page 128-B1

Rififi Nighclub &
Amber Lounge

Stylish nightclub with
regular big name DJs and
club nights.

26 Market Street,
Stalybridge, Greater
Manchester SK15 2AJ
☎ 0161 303 7111
🖰 www.rififi.co.uk/
📄 0161 303 7117
🖰 Page 120-D3

The Ritz

Whitworth Street West,
Manchester, Greater
Manchester M1 5NQ
☎ 0161 236 4355
@ info@ritznightclub.co.uk
🖰 www.ritznightclub.co.uk
📄 0161 236 7515
🖰 Page 6-E7

The Roadhouse

Live music venue featuring
a wide variety of acts
including punk, rock, indie
and retro music. Regular
club nights.

8 Newton Street, Piccadilly,
Manchester, Greater
Manchester M1 2AN
☎ 0161 832 1111,
0161 237 9789
@ info@theroadhouselive.
co.uk
🖰 www.theroadhouselive.
co.uk
📄 0161 236 9289
🖰 Page 7-H4

Sankeys Soap

Sankeys Soap offers a
variety of clubs nights
playing cutting edge dance
music, attracting renowned
international and national
DJs. The club is known for
its regular Tribal Sessions,
which attract a devoted
following.

Radium Street, Manchester,
Greater Manchester M4 6AY
☎ 0161 661 9668
🖰 www.sankeys.info
🖰 Page 7-K2

Sofa Lounge

236 Wilmslow Road,
Manchester, Greater
Manchester M14 6EL
☎ 0161 248 4820
🖰 Page 143-E1

Sol and Viva Night Club

Open four nights a week to
1,500 people, the club offers
top quality entertainment at
affordable prices. The club is
spread over three seperate
rooms playing everything
from 'old skool', big tunes,
R'n'B, pop, garage and soul.

Rochdale Road, Bury,
Greater Manchester BL9 0PL
☎ 0161 763 1951
@ sol-viva-bury@luminar.
co.uk
🖰 www.solandviva.com
📄 0161 763 1956
🖰 Page 4-E4

South

4a South King Street,
Manchester, Greater
Manchester M2 6DQ
☎ 0161 831 7756
@ info@southnightclub.
com
🖰 www.southnightclub.com
🖰 Page 6-D4

The Southern Venue

Mauldeth Road West,
Chorlton, Manchester,
Greater Manchester
M21 7SP
☎ 0161 881 7048
🖰 www.thesouthernhotel.
co.uk
🖰 Page 141-H4

The Swan

2–4 Churchgate, Bolton,
Greater Manchester
BL1 1HJ
☎ 01204 365174
🖰 Page 3-F4

Tiger Lounge

5 Cooper Street,
Manchester, Greater
Manchester M2 2FW
☎ 0161 236 6007
🖰 Page 6-E5

Tribeca and Bed

Tribeca Bar and Bed is
a chic and vibrant city
centre bar in the heart of
Manchester, with a distinct
and sophisticated New York
air. The bar offers a relaxed
atmosphere by day, and
a buzzy, vibrant scene by
night. A mix of raw tunes
and fresh cocktails.

50 Sackville Street,
Manchester, Greater
Manchester M1 3WF
☎ 0161 236 8300
@ ask@tribeca-bar.co.uk
🖰 www.tribeca-bar.co.uk
📄 0161 236 8244
🖰 Page 7-G6

Uppermill Conservative
Club

High Street, Uppermill,
Oldham, Greater
Manchester OL3 6AP
☎ 01457 873077
🖰 Page 79-E4

SPECIAL EVENTS' VENUES

BBC Screen, Manchester

Exchange Square, Hanging Ditch Lane, Manchester, Greater Manchester M4 3TR
🖰 Page 6-E3

City of Manchester Stadium

Rowsley Street, Manchester, Greater Manchester M11 3FF
☎ 0161 438 7745
@ tickets@mcfc.co.uk
🖰 www.mcfc.co.uk
🖰 Page 116-A3

Lancashire County Cricket Club

Lancashire's premier cricket ground also hosts special events and corporate functions.

County Ground, Old Trafford, Manchester, Greater Manchester M16 0PX
☎ 0870 062 5000
🖰 www.lccc.co.uk
📄 0161 873 8353
🖰 Page 126-D4

Manchester Central

Manchester Central, Petersfield, Manchester, Greater Manchester M2 3GX
☎ 0161 834 2700
@ info@manchester central.co.uk
🖰 www.manchester central.co.uk
📄 0161 833 3168
🖰 Page 6-D7

Manchester Evening News Arena (MEN Arena)

Opened in 1995, the Manchester Evening News Arena was originally conceived for Manchester's bid for the Olympics and was built despite the bid's failure. From U2 to Pavarotti, ice hockey to boxing, Disney shows and motorbike exhibitions through to blue-chip AGMs, this 21,000 capacity multi-purpose entertainment and sports arena caters for all.

21 Hunts Bank, Victoria Station, Manchester, Greater Manchester M3 1AR
☎ 0870 190 8000
@ enquiries@men-arena. com
🖰 www.men-arena.com
🖰 Page 6-E1

New Century Hall

Corporation Street, Manchester, Greater Manchester M60 4ES
☎ 0161 827 5198
🖰 www.newcenturyhouse. co.uk
📄 0161 827 5194
🖰 Page 7-K2

Old Trafford Football Stadium

Sir Matt Busby Way, Manchester Greater Manchester M16 0RA
☎ 08704 421994
🖰 www.manutd.com
📄 0161 868 8861
🖰 Page 126-C3

Piccadilly Gardens

Piccadilly Gardens hosts Manchester's winter festivals.

Piccadilly, Manchester, Greater Manchester M1 1RG
☎ 0161 234 5000 ,
0161 244 5765
🖰 www.onepiccadilly gardens.com/index.html
📄 0161 234 3760
🖰 Page 7-G5

Stalybridge Civic Hall

Trinity Street, Tameside, Stalybridge, Greater Manchester SK15 2BN
☎ 0161 303 8261
🖰 www.tameside.gov.uk/ stalybridge/civichall
📄 0161 303 8627
🖰 Page 120-D4

Trafford Centre

This large shopping centre also offers a range of entertainment events.

Barton Dock Road, Manchester, Greater Manchester M17 8AA
☎ 0161 749 1717,
0161 749 1718
🖰 www.traffordcentre.co.uk
🖰 Page 125-C2

Street by Street

MANCHESTER

BOLTON, BURY, OLDHAM, ROCHDALE, SALFORD, STOCKPORT

Altrincham, Ashton-under-Lyne, Bramhall, Hazel Grove, Hyde, Littleborough, Middleton, Prestwich, Ramsbottom, Sale, Stalybridge, Stretford, Wilmslow

Key to map pages	ii-iii
Key to map symbols	iv-1
Enlarged map pages	2-13
Main map pages	14-201
Index – towns & villages	202
Index – streets	203-261
Index – featured places	261-268
Acknowledgements	268

ii

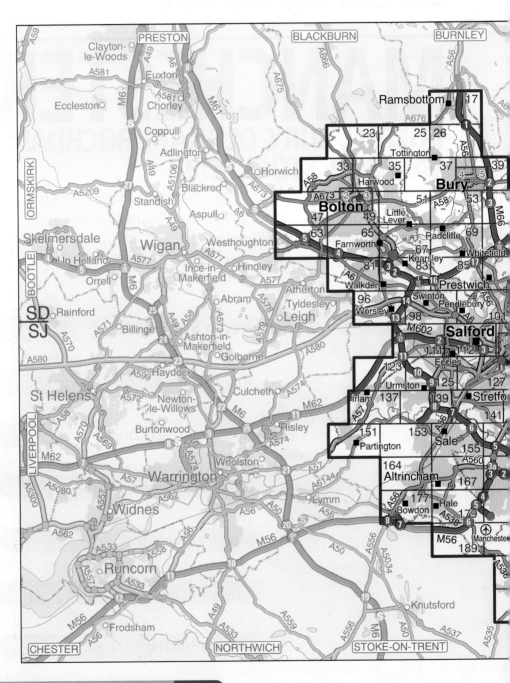

Scale of enlarged map pages 1:10,000   6.3 inches to 1 mile

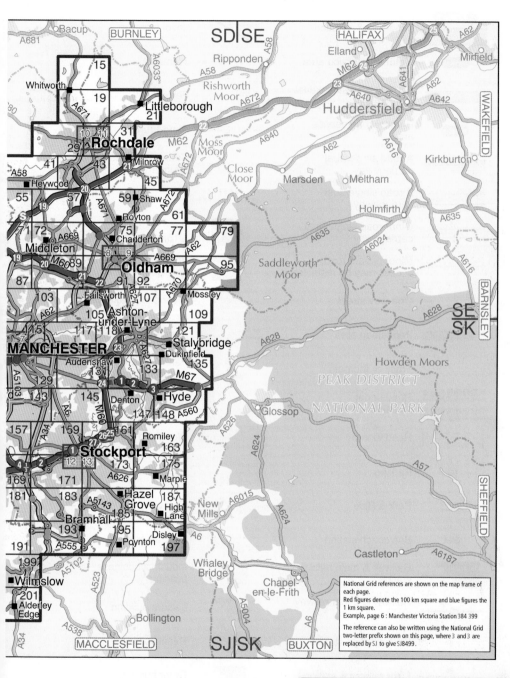

BURNLEY   HALIFAX

Bacup   Ripponden   Elland   Mirfield
A681   Rishworth   M62
Whitworth   Moor   Huddersfield   WAKEFIELD
15   A6033   A58   A672   A640   A641   A642
19   A671   Close   Marsden   Meltham   Kirkburton
Littleborough   Moss   Moor   Holmfirth   A635
21   Moor   A62   A6024   A616
10 11 31   M62   A672   A672   A635
Rochdale   A62   Saddleworth   Moor   BARNSLEY
29   41   43   Milnrow   A628
A58   45   A62   A628   SE
Heywood   20   59   Shaw   A670   SK
55   57   Royton   61   Howden Moors   PEAK DISTRICT
71 72   75   77   79   NATIONAL PARK   Glossop   A624
Middleton   Chadderton   A669   95   A626   A57
87   89   Oldham   92   A670   SHEFFIELD
103   Failsworth   107   Mossley   A624
A62   105   Ashton-   109   New   A6015   A57
115   117 118   under-Lyne   121   Mills   A6
MANCHESTER   23   Stalybridge   High   A6
129   131   133   Dukinfield   135   Lane   A6187
Audenshaw   24 1 2   M67   195   Disley   Castleton   A6187
143   145   3   Hyde   197   A6
157   Denton   147 148 A560   Whaley   Chapel-
159   25 26   161   Romiley   Bridge   en-le-Frith
169   27   163   A5004
Stockport   173   175   Bollington
1 2   12 13   Marple   A538
171   A626
181   183   Hazel   187
193   185   Grove   A5143
191   195   Bramhall   A555   Poynton   A6
199   A5102   A523   A5004
Wilmslow   A5   A6
201   Alderley   Edge   A34
A538   MACCLESFIELD   SJ|SK   BUXTON

National Grid references are shown on the map frame of each page.
Red figures denote the 100 km square and blue figures the 1 km square.
Example, page 6 : Manchester Victoria Station 384 399

The reference can also be written using the National Grid two-letter prefix shown on this page, where 3 and 3 are replaced by SJ to give SJ8499.

4.2 inches to 1 mile   **Scale of main map pages**   1:15,000

0   1/4   miles   1/2   3/4   1
0   1/4   1/2   kilometres 3/4   1   1 1/4   1 1/2

Junction 9	Motorway & junction	_LC_	Level crossing
Services	Motorway service area	•——•——•——•	Tramway
	Primary road single/dual carriageway	- - - - - - - - -	Ferry route
Services	Primary road service area	....	Airport runway
	A road single/dual carriageway	— · — · — · —	County, administrative boundary
	B road single/dual carriageway	▾▾▾▾▾▾▾▾▾▾	Mounds
	Other road single/dual carriageway	**17**	Page continuation 1:15,000
	Minor/private road, access may be restricted	**3**	Page continuation to enlarged scale 1:10,000
← ←	One-way street		River/canal, lake, pier
	Pedestrian area		Aqueduct, lock, weir
= = = = =	Track or footpath	465 ▲ Winter Hill	Peak (with height in metres)
▮▮▮▮▮▮▮▮	Road under construction		Beach
⊢ - - = = ⊣	Road tunnel		Woodland
P	Parking		Park
P+🚌	Park & Ride	✝✝✝✝✝	Cemetery
🚌	Bus/coach station		Built-up area
	Railway & main railway station		Industrial/business building
	Railway & minor railway station		Leisure building
⊖	Underground station		Retail building
⊖	Light railway & station		Other building
┼┼┼┼┼┼┼┼	Preserved private railway	**IKEA**	IKEA store

ᴪᴪᴪᴪ	City wall	♟	Castle
A&E	Hospital with 24-hour A&E department	🏛	Historic house or building
PO	Post Office	Wakehurst Place NT	National Trust property
📖	Public library	M	Museum or art gallery
i	Tourist Information Centre	🐎	Roman antiquity
i	Seasonal Tourist Information Centre	⚱	Ancient site, battlefield or monument
⛽⛽	Petrol station, 24 hour Major suppliers only	🏭	Industrial interest
†	Church/chapel	✳	Garden
🚻	Public toilets	◉	Garden Centre Garden Centre Association Member
♿	Toilet with disabled facilities	🌷	Garden Centre Wyevale Garden Centre
PH	Public house AA recommended	🌳	Arboretum
🍴	Restaurant AA inspected	🛒	Farm or animal centre
Madeira Hotel	Hotel AA inspected	🦌	Zoological or wildlife collection
🎭	Theatre or performing arts centre	🐦	Bird collection
🎥	Cinema	🦆	Nature reserve
⚑	Golf course	🐟	Aquarium
▲	Camping AA inspected	V	Visitor or heritage centre
🚐	Caravan site AA inspected	♀	Country park
▲🚐	Camping & caravan site AA inspected	⊙	Cave
🌴	Theme park	✘	Windmill
⛪	Abbey, cathedral or priory	🛢	Distillery, brewery or vineyard

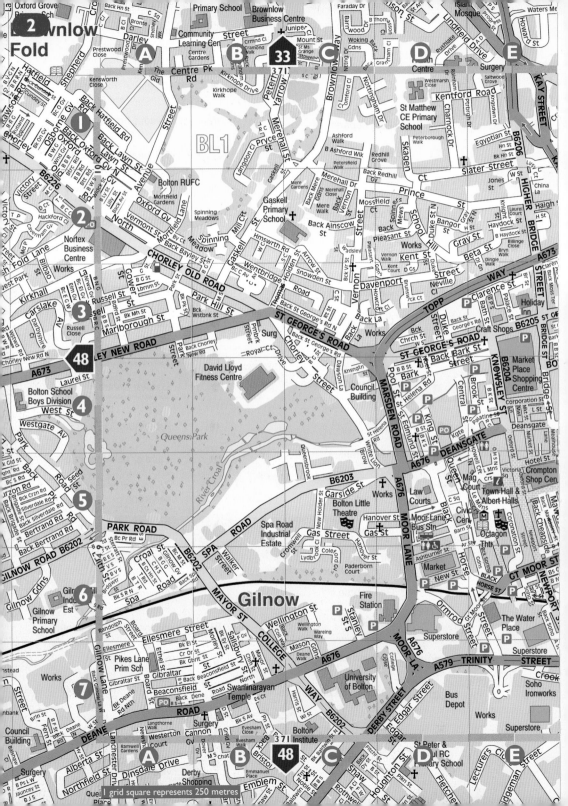

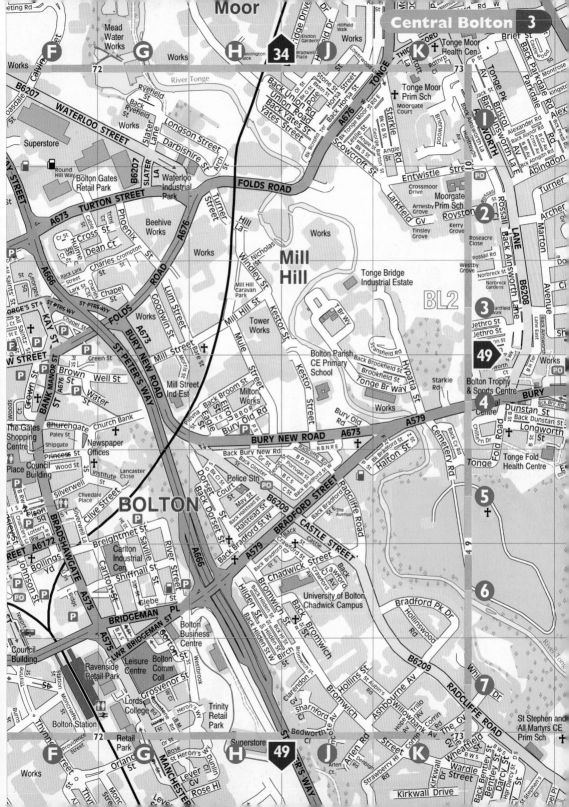

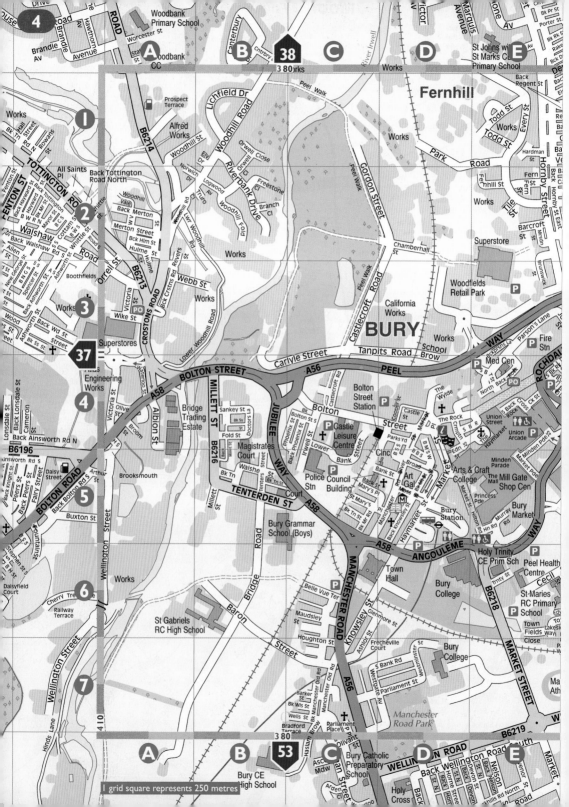

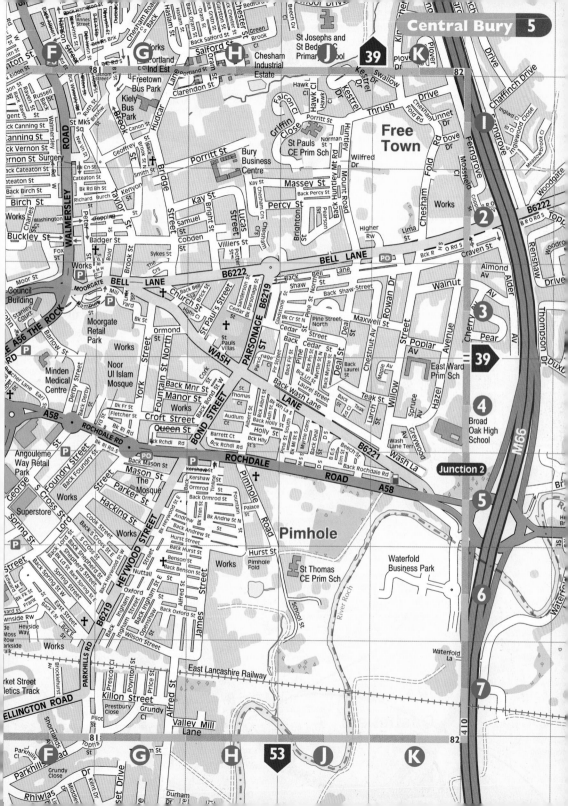

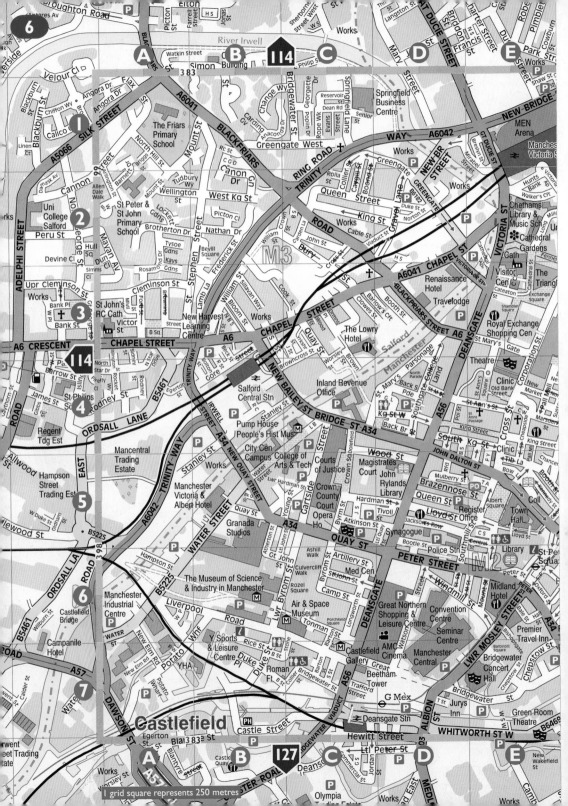

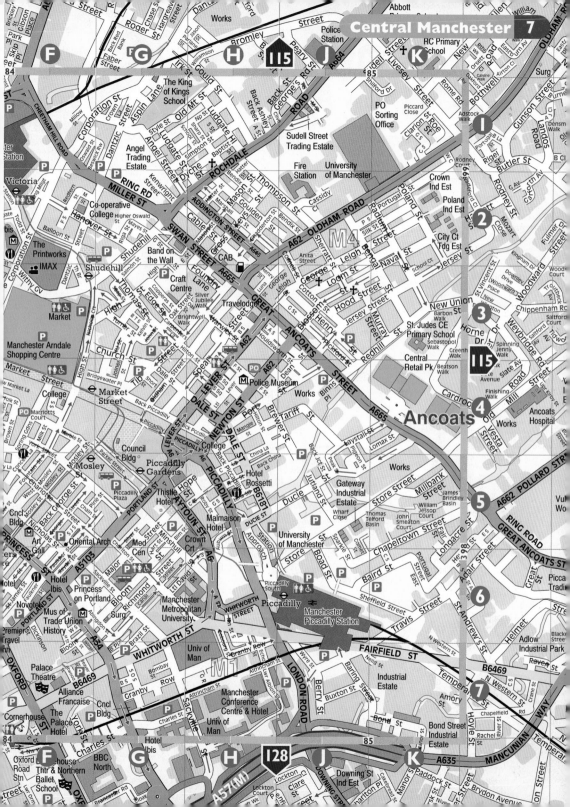

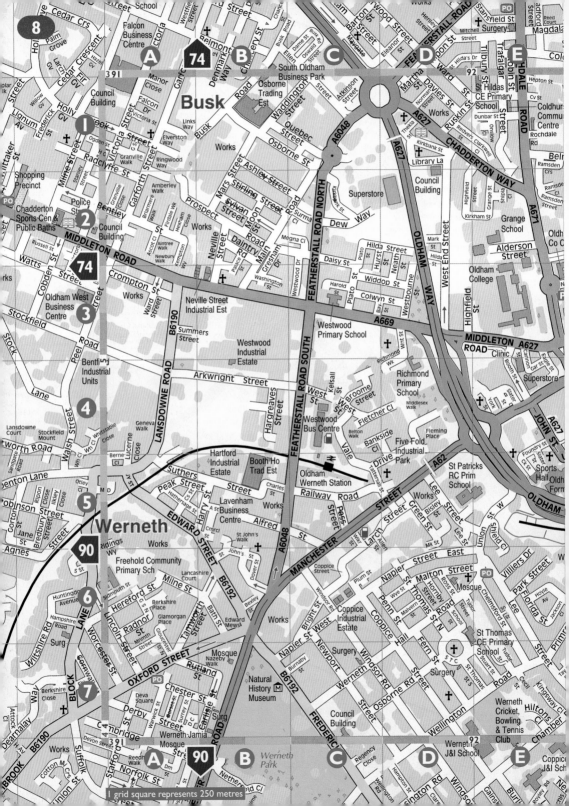

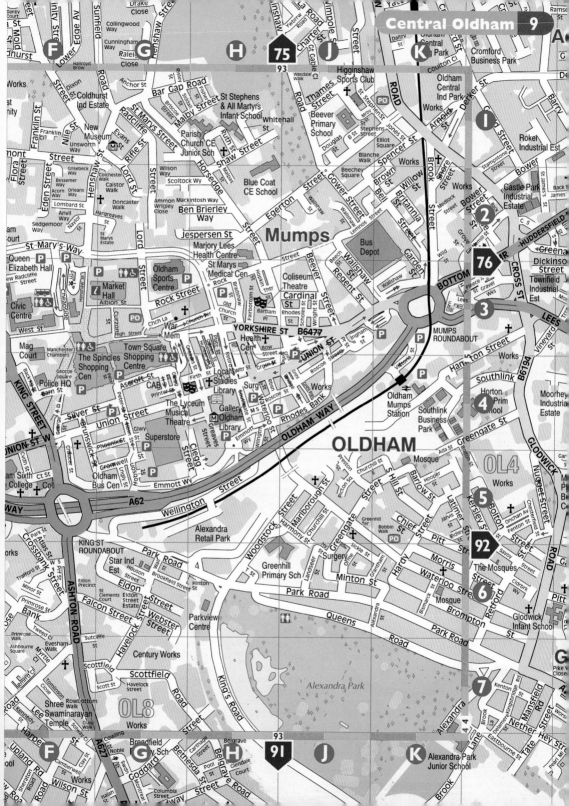

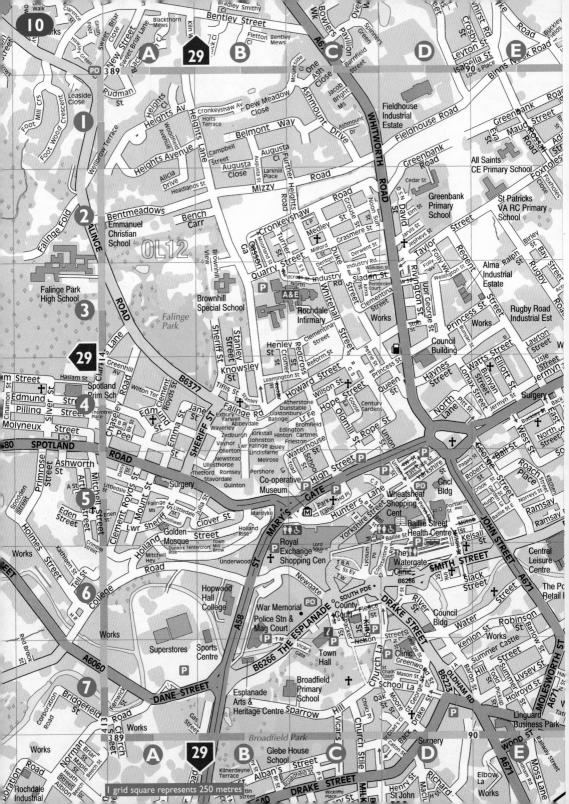

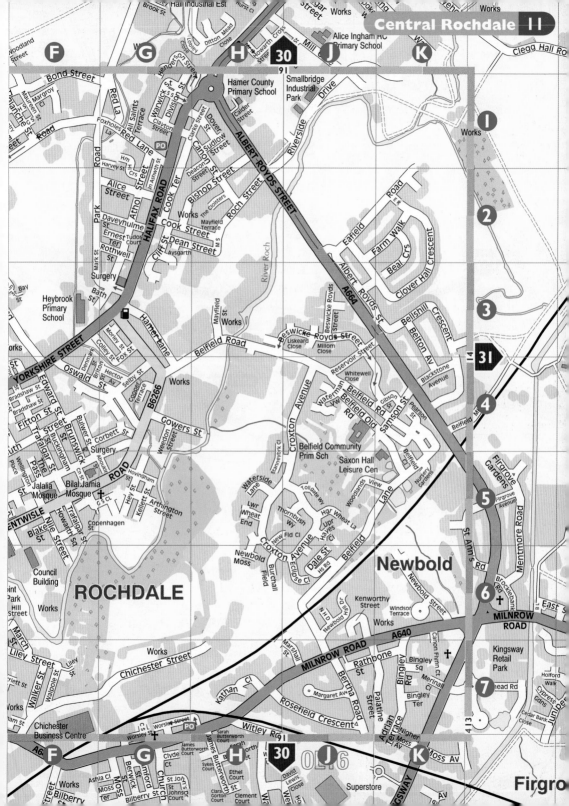

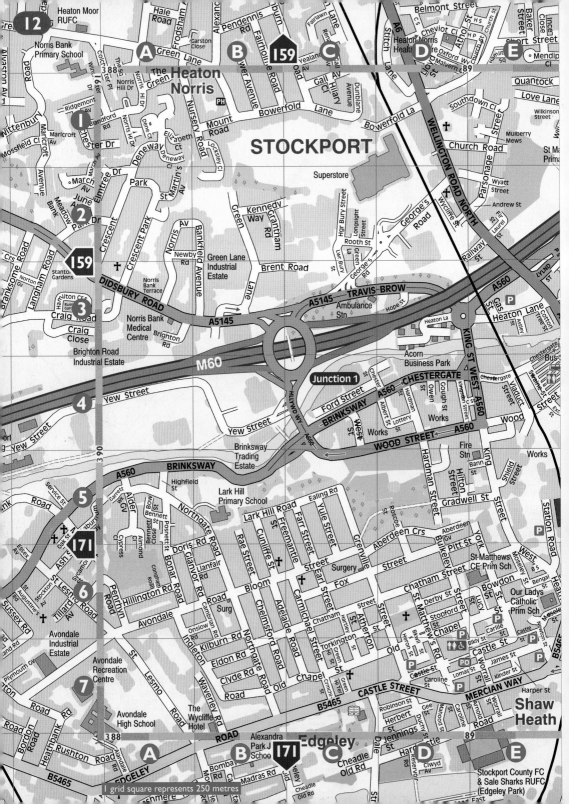

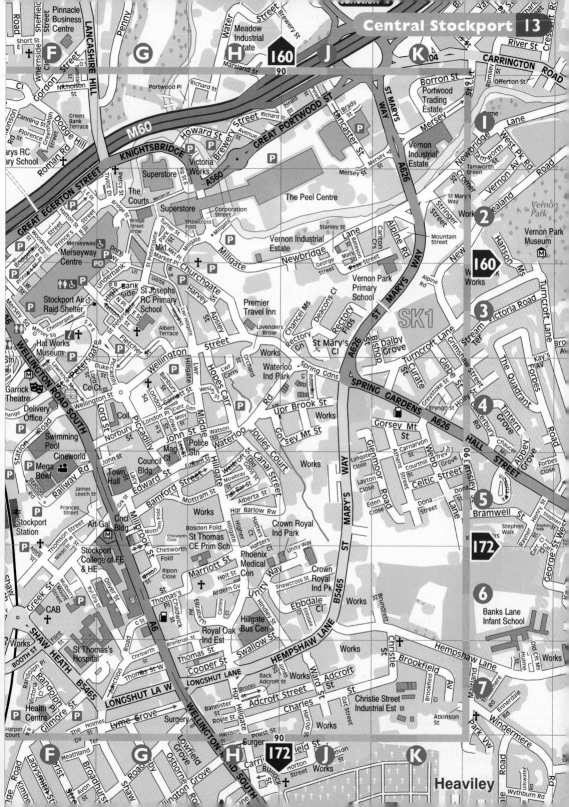

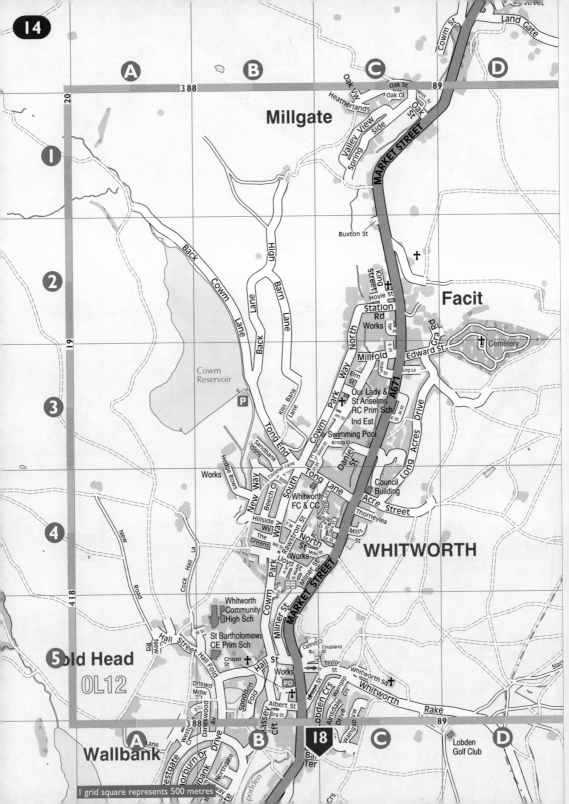

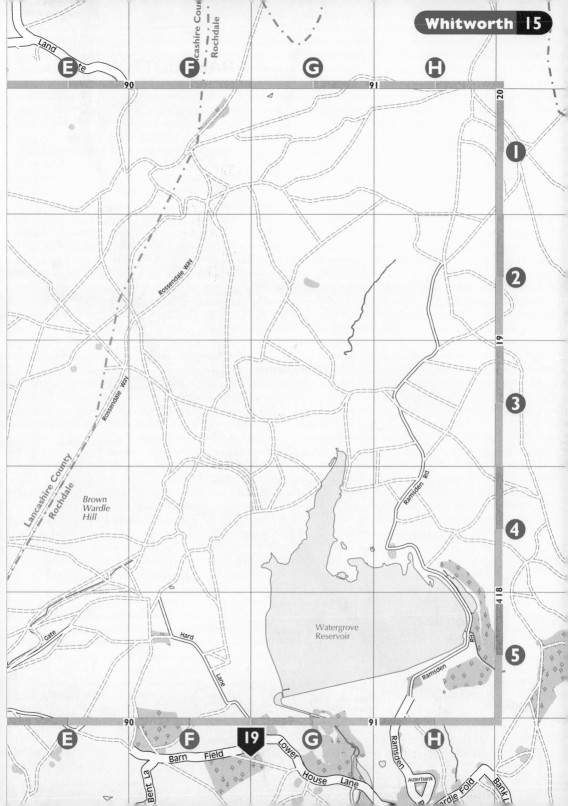

Land
Ete

E

F

Lancashire Cou
Rochdale

G

H

90

91

20

I

2

19

3

Rossendale Way

Rossendale Way

4

18

Lancashire County
Rochdale

Brown
Wardle
Hill

Ramsden Rd

Watergrove
Reservoir

Ramsden
Rd

5

Gate

Hard

Lane

Ramsden

E

90

F

19

Lower

G

91

H

Barn

Field

House

Lane

Bent La

Ramsden

Aiderbank

ardle Fold

Bank L

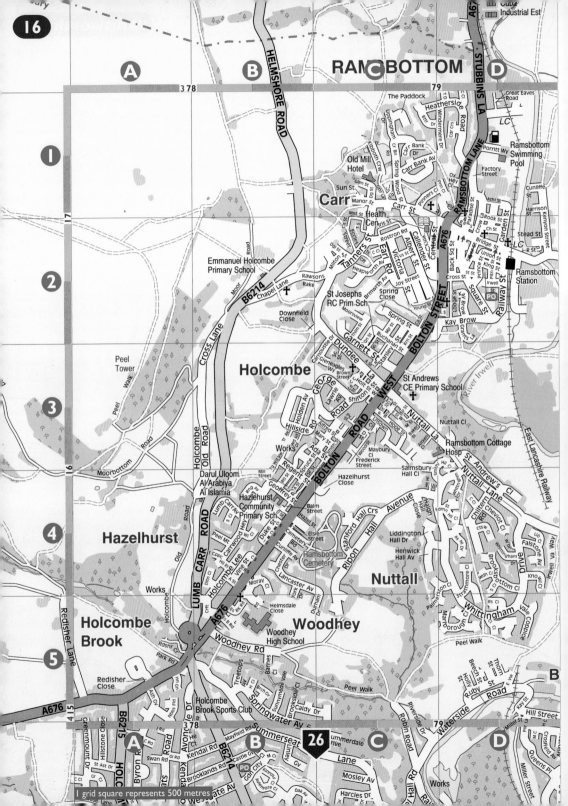

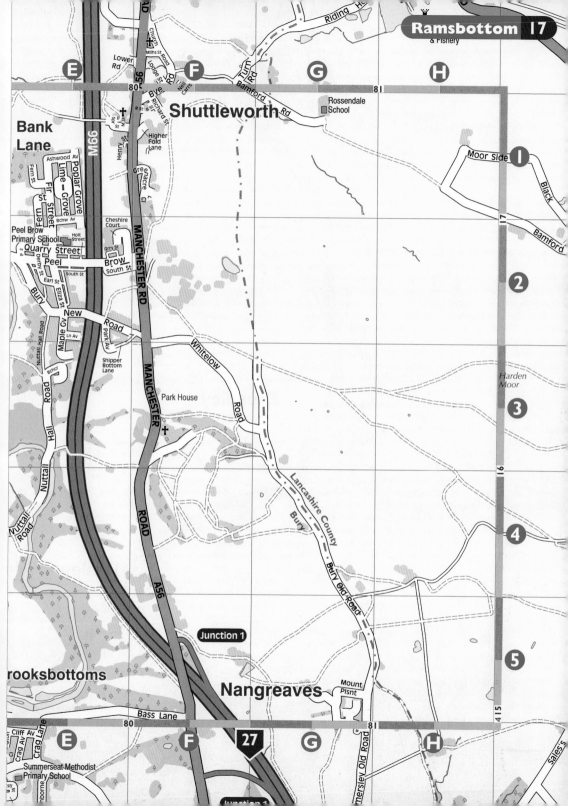

Riding Head
& Fishery

Church Road
Mills St
Lower Rd
Lodge St
E 80 95 Rd **F**
Turn Rd
Byer
Bamford Rd
G 81 **H**

Neil Carrs
Richard St
R St
Shuttleworth
Jas St
M St
Rossendale School

Henry St
Higher Fold Lane

Greenacre Cl

Moor Side **I**

Ashwood Av
Poplar Grove
Black

Bank Lane
Lime Grove
Fir Street
Fern St
Bchw Av

Bamford
17

Peel Brow Primary School
Holt Street
Cheshire Court
2

Quarry Street
Orry St
Derby St
South St
Brow South St
Earl St
Peel

Eliza St
Bury
Harden Moor
3

New Road
Maple Gv
Ln Av
Park Av
Whitelow Road
16

Nuttall Hall Road
Bchr
Shipper Bottom Lane

Park House

MANCHESTER RD

MANCHESTER
Road

4

Nuttall Hall Road
Lancashire County
Bury
Bury Old Road

A56

5

rooksbottoms

Junction 1

Mount Plsnt
Nangreaves

Bass Lane
80 **E**
81
F **27** **G**

Cliff Av
Crag Av
Crag Lane

Summerseat Methodist Primary School

mersley Old Road **H**
Sales
415

St

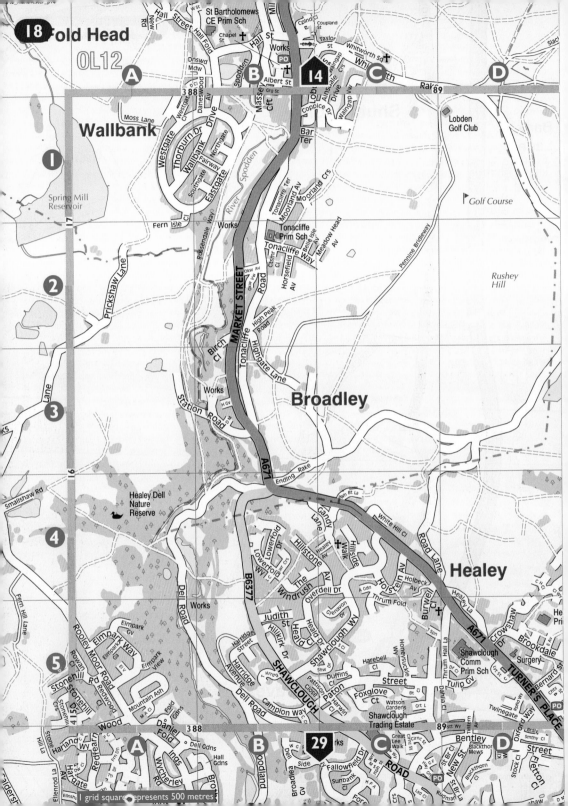

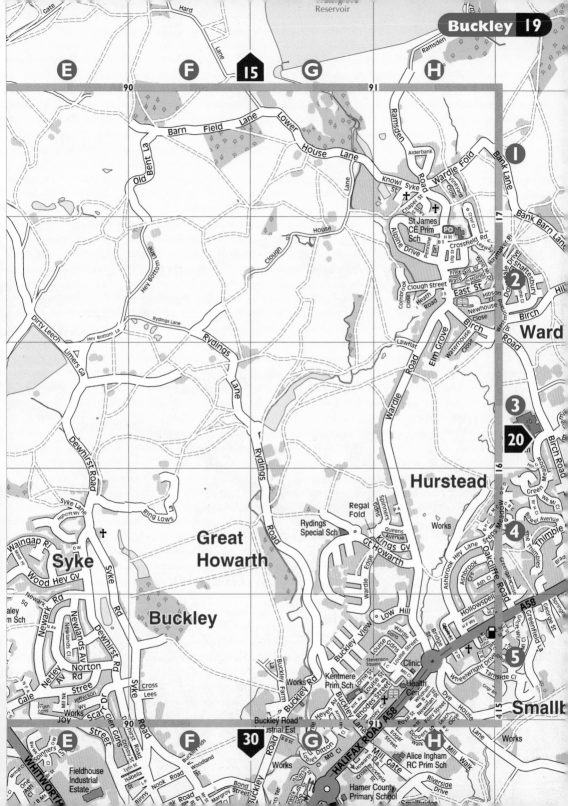

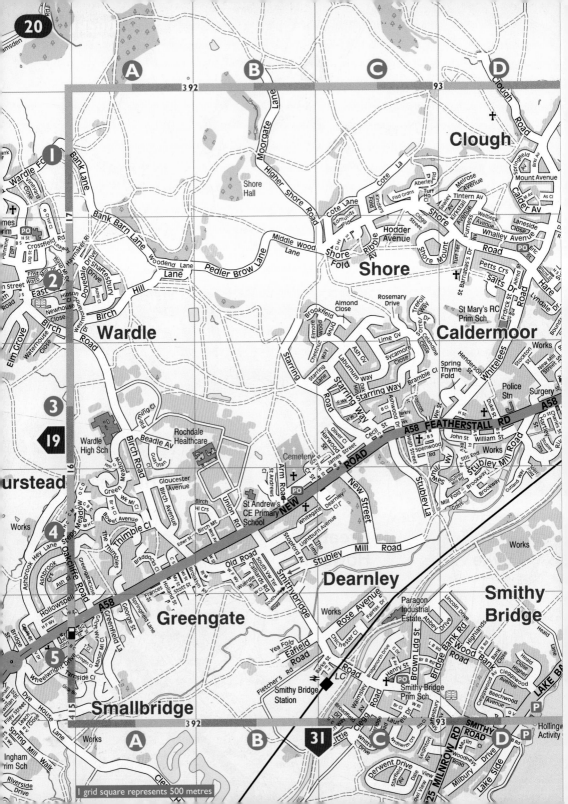

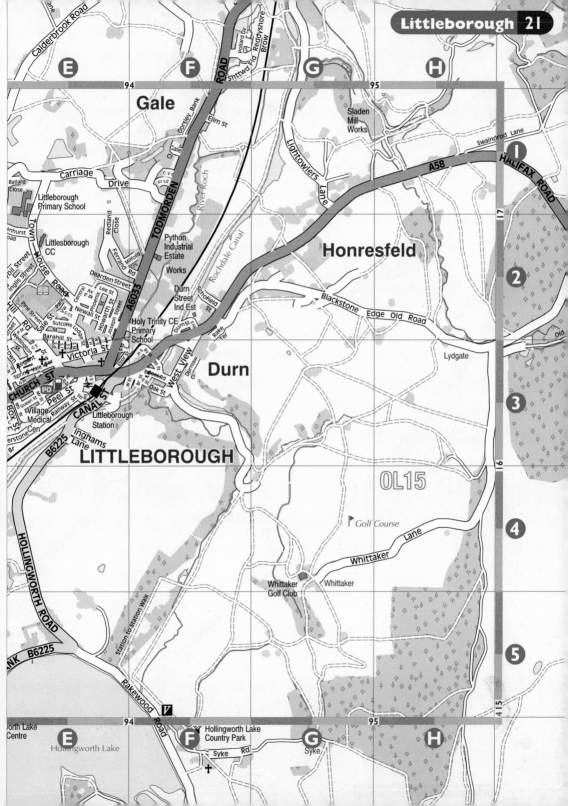

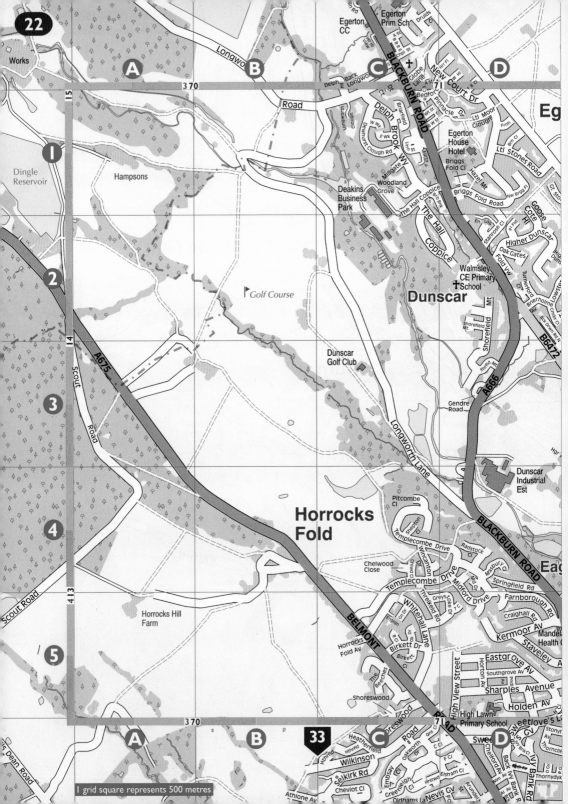

Works

Longwo

B

Road

C

BLACKBURN ROAD

Egerton Prim Sch
Egerton CC
Druids

New Court Dr

D

Eg

A 370

1

Dingle Reservoir

Hampsons

Delph

Back Longwo

Globe Lane

Bedfor
Pinnacle Dr

Lti Moor Clough

Egerton House Hotel

Briggs Fold Cl

Lti stones Road

Goose Cote Hl

Dewhurst Clough Rd

Delph Brook Wy

Millgate

Woodland Grove

The Hall Coppice

Briggs Fold Road

Nw Brga Fl

Hazel Mt

Higher Dunscar

Oak Gates

2

A675

Deakins Business Park

Golf Course

Walmsley CE Primary School

Dunscar

Stanrose Cl

Fold Vw

Turnerford Cl

Brierholme Cr

Scout

3

Dunscar Golf Club

Shorefield Mt

Longworth Lane

Gendre Road

Syfield Mt

A666

B6472

Road

4

Horrocks Fold

Pitcombe Cl

Templecombe Drive

Shelton

Wincanton

Raostock

BLACKBURN ROAD

Dunscar Industrial Est

Eag

414

413

5

Chelwood Close

Chelmsford

Midford Drive

Springfield Rd

Farnborough Rd

Horrocks Hill Farm

Templecombe Drive

Whitehall Lane

Greys

Coke Dr

Craighall Rd

Kermoor Av

Mandela
Health C

Staveley

The Beeches

Horrocks Fold Av

Birkett Dr

Birkett

English

Threlkeld Rd

High View Street

Horton La

Southgrove Av

Eastgrove Av

Sharples Avenue

Shoreswood

A 370

Belmont

Road

High Lawn Primary School

Holden Av

Sweetlove's L

A

Dean Road

B

33

C

Heatherfield

Oakworth

Wilkinson

Selkirk Rd

Cheviot Cl

Athlone Av

Road

Greenfield

Hirstwd

Oldhams La

Nevis Gv

D

Cherford

Sw

Back Ivy Bank Rd

Thornleigh

Stonyhu

Thorncliff

Arundel

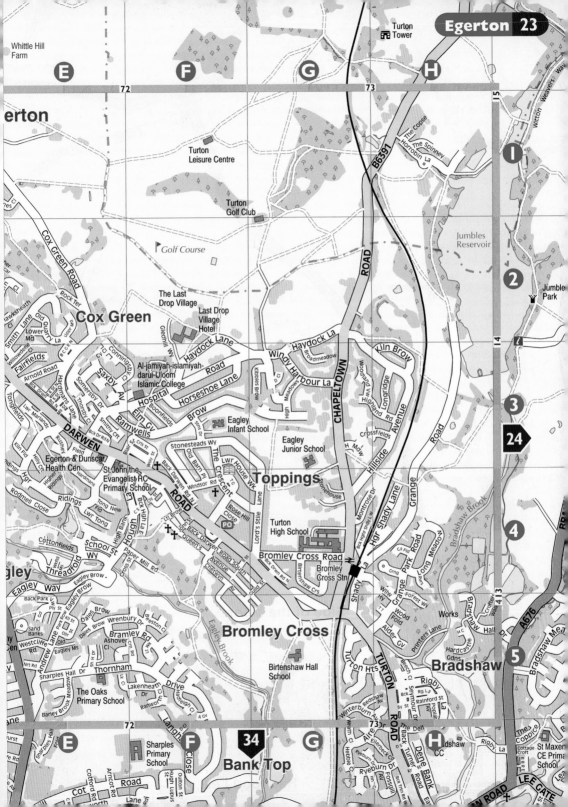

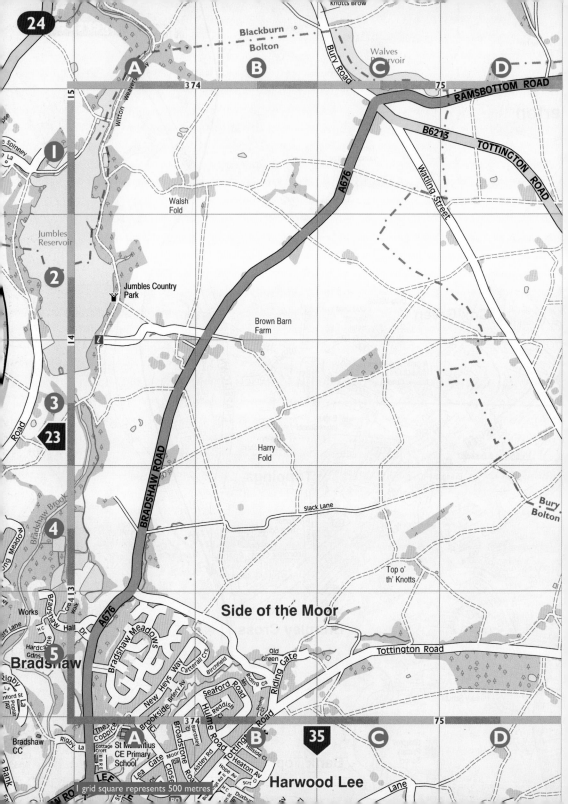

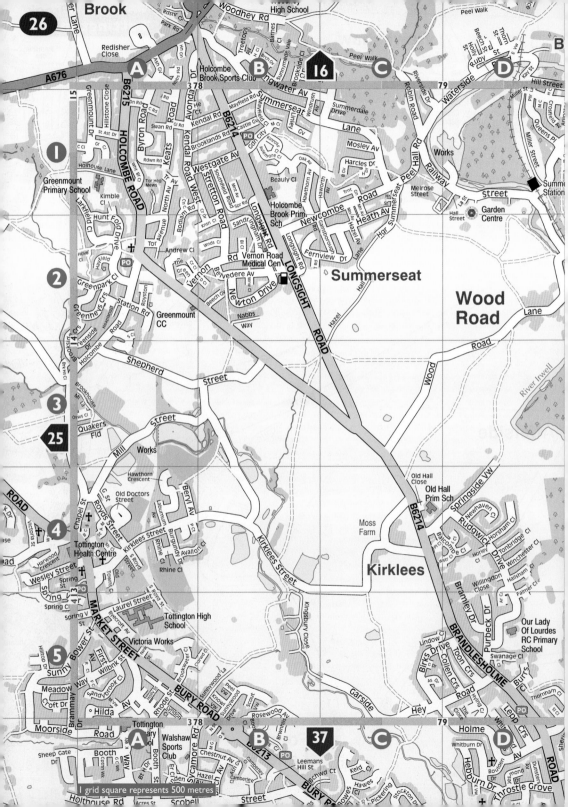

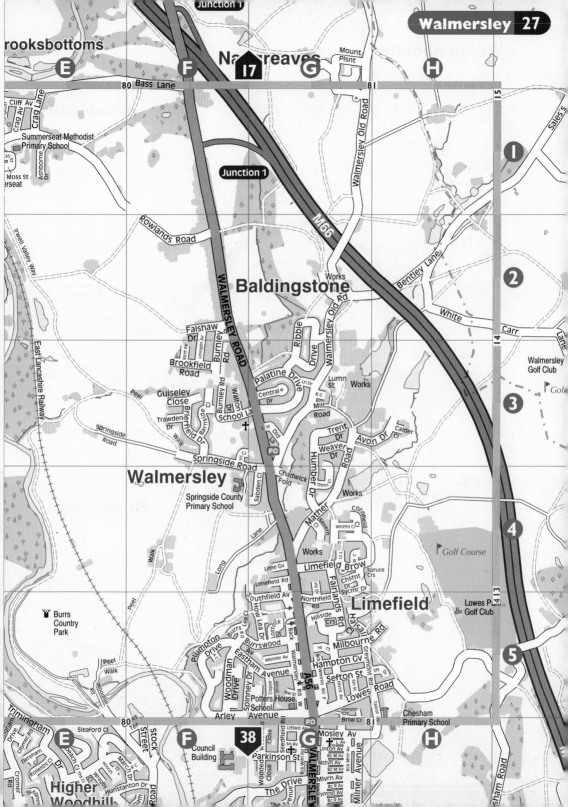

rooksbottoms

E **F** **G** **H**

17

80 Bass Lane 81

Mount Plsnt

Summerseat-Methodist Primary School

Crag Av
Cliff Av
Crag La
Ashborne Dr
Moss St
rseat

Irwell Valley Way

Rowlands Road

Junction 1

M66

Walmersley Old Road

Bentley Lane

White Carr Lane

Sales's Road

I

2

3

Walmersley Golf Club

Gol

Baldingstone

Works

Falshaw Dr
Burnley Rd
Ribble Drive
Walmersley Old Rd

Brookfield Road

Palatine Drive

Lumn St

Works

Guiseley Close

East Lancashire Railway

Trawdern Dr
Brierfield Dr
Barmsd Cl
Burnley Rd
Walton Dr
School La
Central Dr
Mill Road

Springside Road

Peel

springside Road

PO

Trent Dr
Weaver Dr
Avon Dr
Calder Cl

Chadwick Fold

Sabden Cl
Humber Dr

Walmersley

Springside Road

Springside County Primary School

Mather Cl
Severn Cl
Cornfield
Whtfld Cl

Works

4

Golf Course

Works

Lime Gv

Limefield Rd

Limefield Brow
Spruce Crs
Chstnt
Sycmr Dr

Burrs Country Park

Long Lane

Peel Walk

Southfield Av

Northfield Rd

Hillside Crs

Fairlands Rd
Halsall Rd
Greymont Rd

Limefield

Lowes Park Golf Club

5

Plumpton Drive

Burrswood Av

How Lea Dr

Eastham Avenue

Woodman Drive

Spinney Dr

Potters House School

Arley Avenue

Wstnhl Av

Back
Milbourne Gv
Hampton Gv
Sefton St
Lowes Road

Chesham Primary School

Peel Walk
Woodhll Rd

Trimingham Drive

80

E **F** **G** **H**

38

Council Building

Parkinson St

Higher Woodhill

Sleaford Cl

Cromer Dr
Derebam
Rollesby Cl
March Cl
Wendon
Hunstanton Dr

Stock Street

Wooded Close

Seedfield Rd
Lttlwd Cl

Mosley Av
Linton Av

A56 Walmersley Rd

PO

The Drive

Milner Avenue

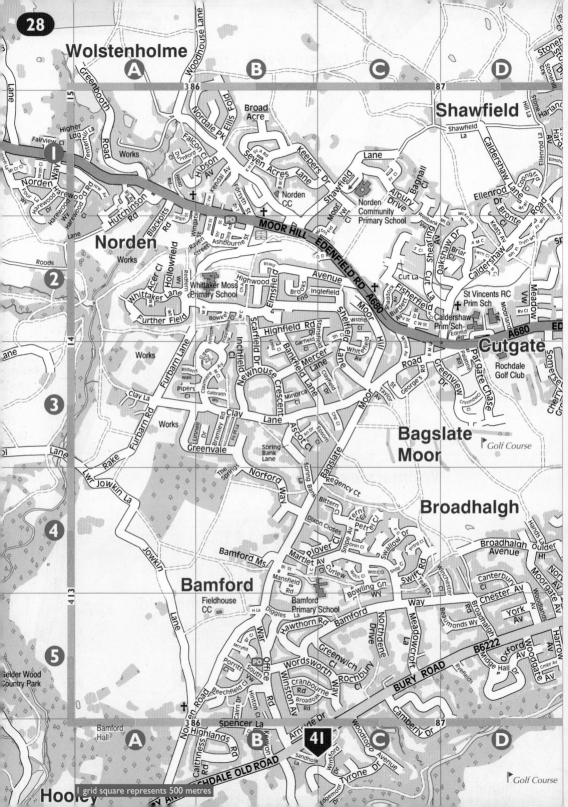

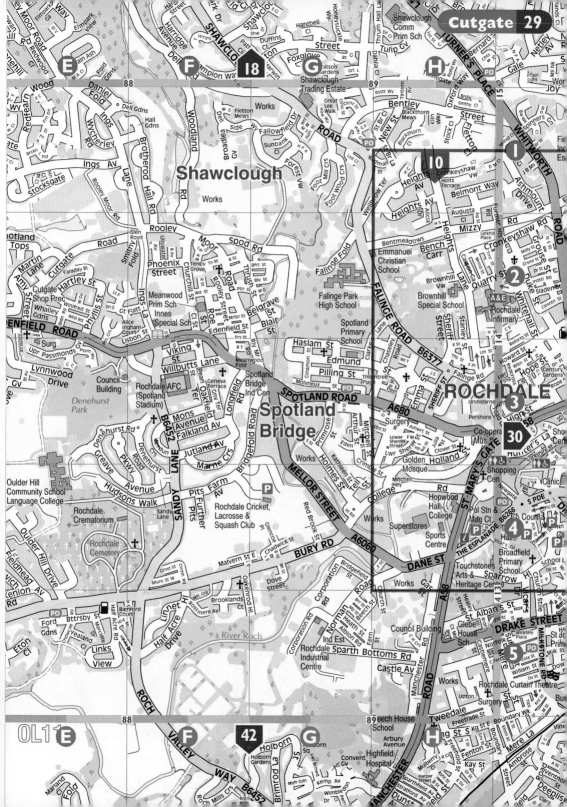

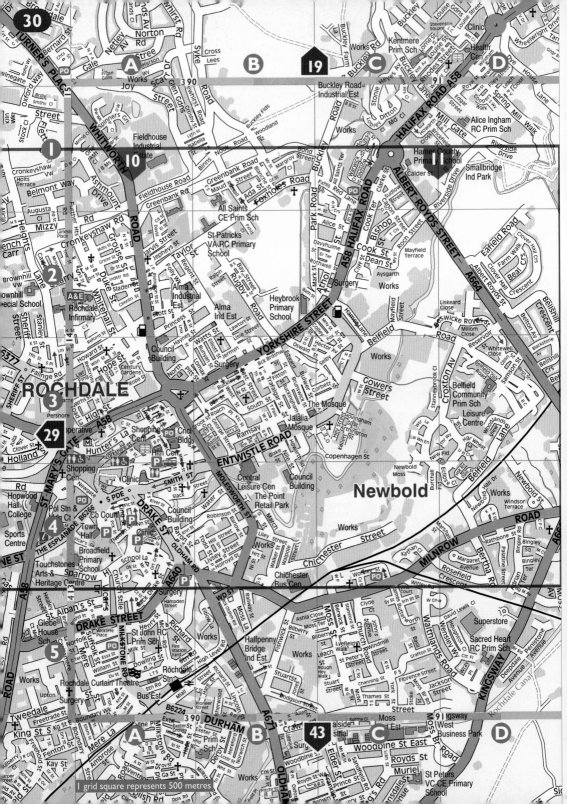

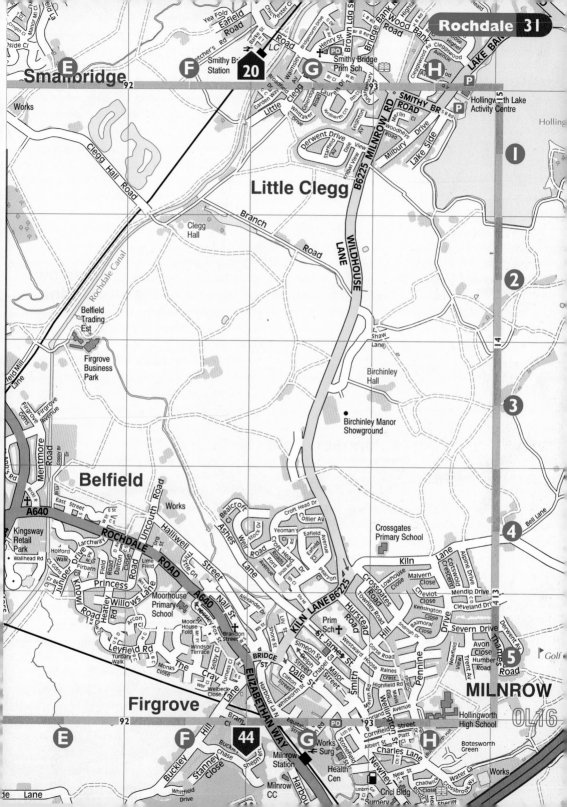

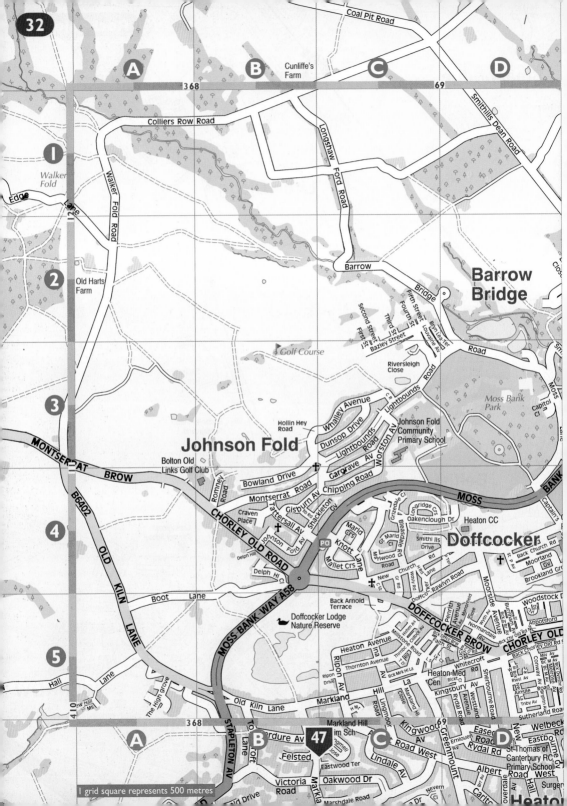

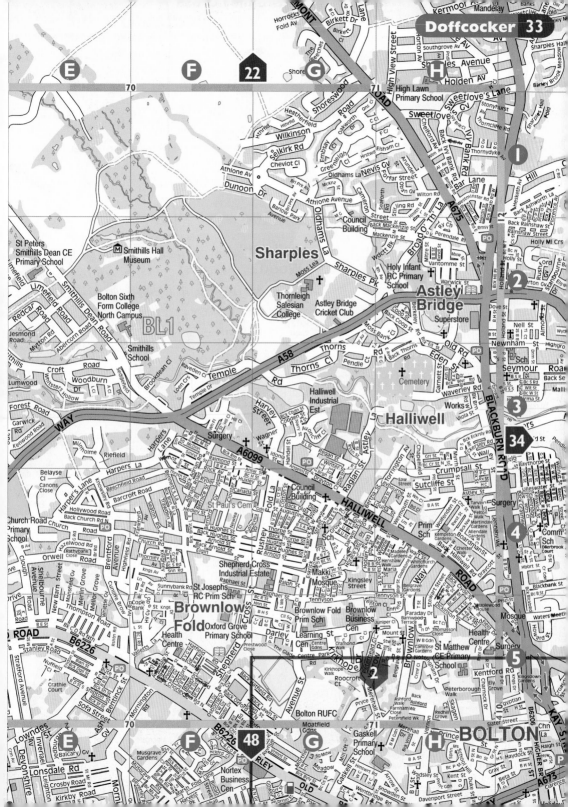

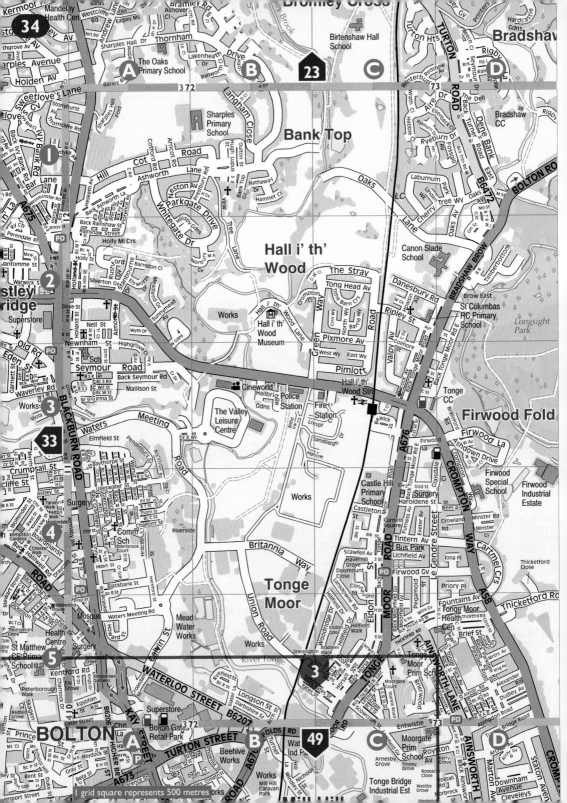

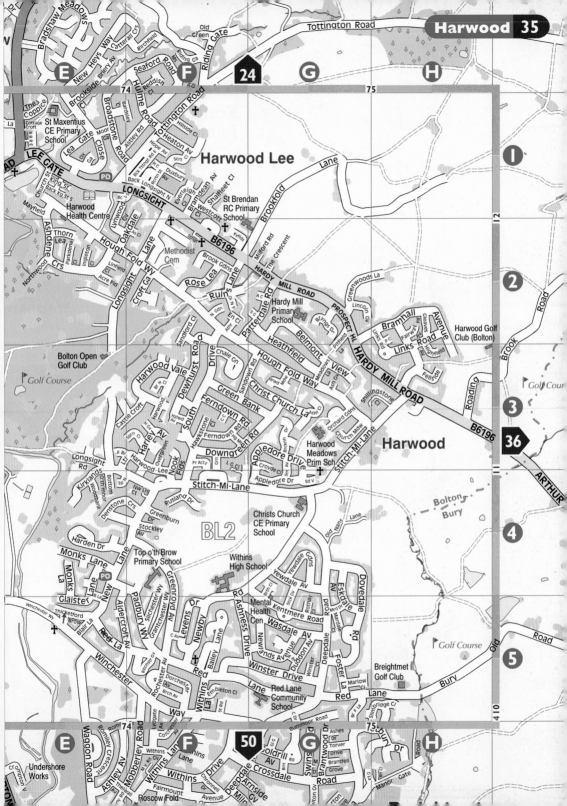

TOTTINGTON

36

A B 25 C D

Four Lane Ends

Bowstone Hill Road

Bowstone
Hill Road

1

Bradshaw Road

Harwood Road

Harwood Road

Bentley Hall Road

Walshaw

2

Brook Road

Harwood Golf
Club (Bolton)

Bentley Hall

Bentley Hall Road

Golf Course

3

Gisburn Dr

35

ARTHUR LANE

Bolton
Bury

4

Waddington
Close

Lowerc...
Primary
School

Ainsworth

Golf Course

5

Knowsley Road

COCKEY MOOR ROAD

B6196

Old Road

Bury

BURY OLD ROAD

Delph La

Greenside

Tommy
La

Well St

PO

CHURCH STREET

Church St

Thompson Av

Summer Av

B6292

Christchurch
Ainsworth CE
Prim Sch

Devon Dr

Newquay Av

Edgeworth Av

Moorside Av

Bankfield

Broomfield Close

Higher Pit La

A B 51 C D

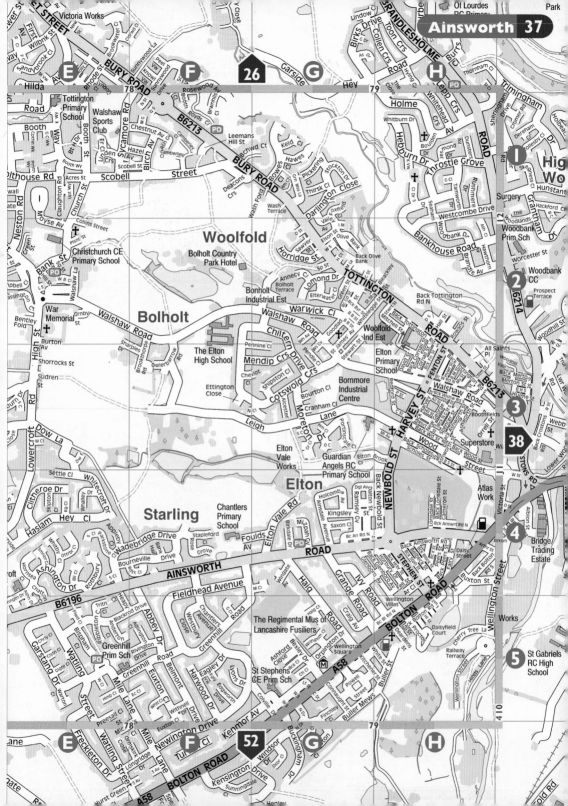

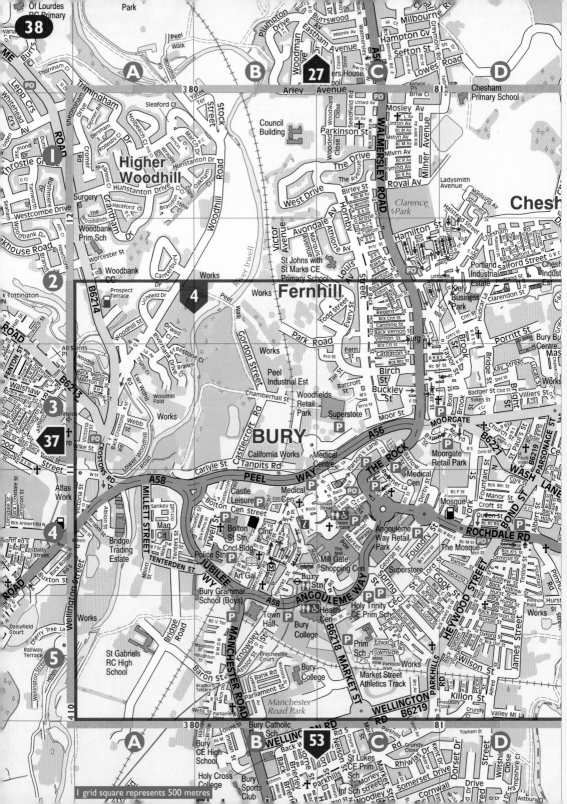

1 grid square represents 500 metres

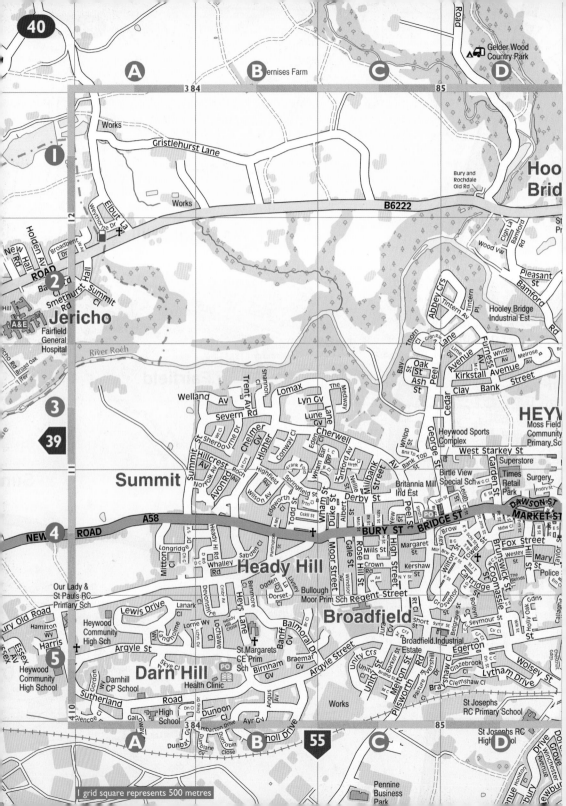

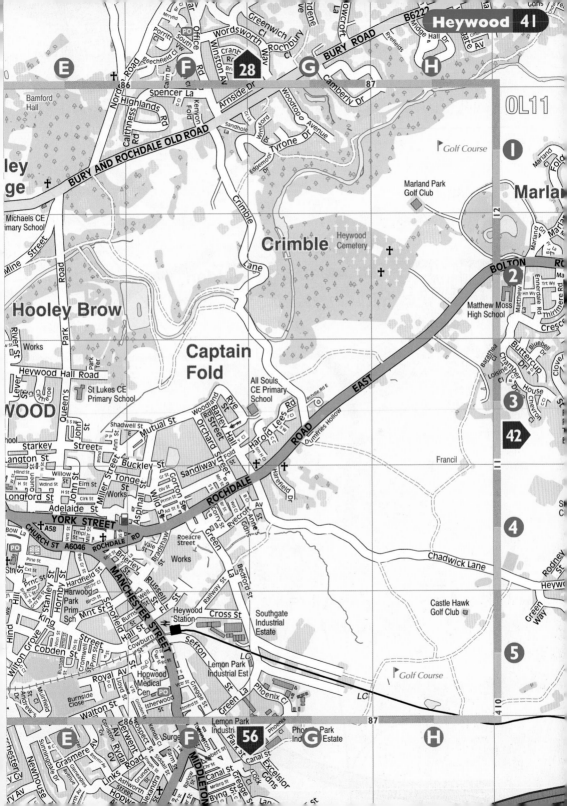

E   F   28   G   H

OL11

B6222

Midge Hall

Greenwich

Wordsworth

Rochbury Cl

BURY ROAD

Ryefields

Porritt Cl

South Vw

PO Office

Beechfield Rd

Winston Av

Cran

Camberly Dr

Spencer La

Nord Highlands Rd

Caithness Rd

Cairn Rd

Kenyon Fold

Arnside Dr

Windsor Dr

Woodtop Avenue

Sandhole La

Tyrone Dr

Edgemoor Dr

Golf Course

Bamford Hall

BURY AND ROCHDALE OLD ROAD

Crimble Lane

Crimble

Heywood Cemetery

Marland Park Golf Club

I

Marla

Marland Fold

ley ge

Michaels CE Primary School

Mine Street

River St

Works

Hooley Brow

Park Road

Heywood Hall Road

Lever

Queen's

Cliffe Vw

St Lukes CE Primary School

Captain Fold

All Souls CE Primary School

Rochdale Rd E

BOLTON

2

Matthew Moss High School

Ennerdale Rd

Thirlmere Rd

Cresc

Bargatea Cl

Loisine Cl

Chamber Dr

ButterCup Dr

Bluebell

House

Chevron

Clover

ROAD EAST

3

42

WOOD

Starkey

John Street

Langton St

Longford St

Adelaide St

YORK STREET

CHURCH ST

Shadwell St

Mutual St

Buckley St

Tonge St

Willow

Elm St

Clrk St

Woodland Rd

Barley Hall St

Orchard Street

Ann St

Rye St

Sandiway

Cotton St

Gr St E

Olv St E

Prmn St

Harold Lees Rd

Hartfield Dr

St Anne's

Dumfries Hollow

Francil

Castle Hawk Golf Club

Miller Street

Sandiway Fold

Corn St

ROCHDALE

A58

A6046

ROCHDALE RD

Brierley St

Vale St

Bradshaw

Ryecroft Gdns

Bedford St

Roeacre Street

Green

Works

Railway St

Chadwick Lane

Rodney St

Heywo

Green Way

4

5

Wilton Grove

Stanley St

Hornby St

Harwood Park Prim Sch

Hardfield St

Birch St

Schofield

MANCHESTER STREET

Russell St

Hall St

Fir St

Heywood Station

Cross St

Weil St

Burns St

Cowburn St

Southgate Industrial Estate

Golf Course

King Street

Cobden St

Cromwell St

Royal Av

Hopwood Medical Cen

Isherwood

Green La

Lemon Park Industrial Est

PO

LC

Phoenix Cl

LC

Burnside Close

Andrew's

Murfield

WALTON ST

Surge

Lemon Park Industri

Canal St

Phoenix

56

Phoenix Park Ind Estate

Excelsior Gdns

Grasmere Av

Rydal GV

Prospect

MIDDLETON

Ashworth

Alexandra

Byng St

E   F   56   G   H

87

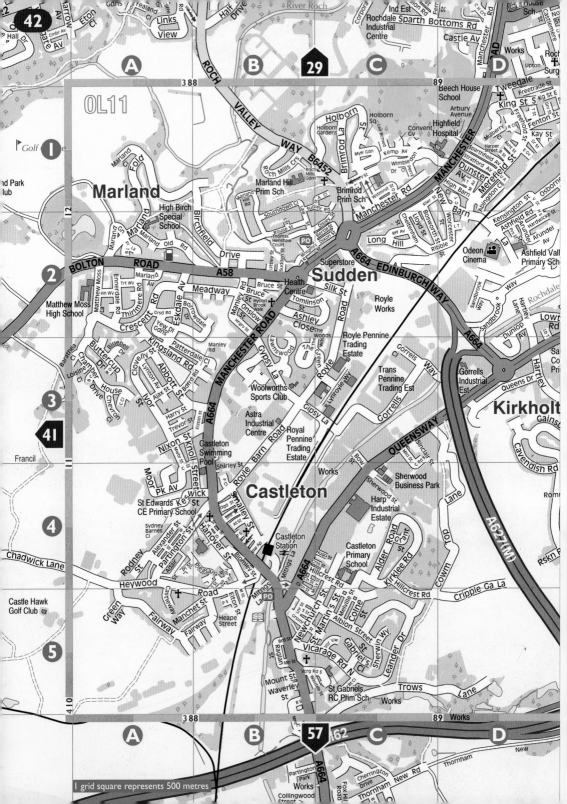

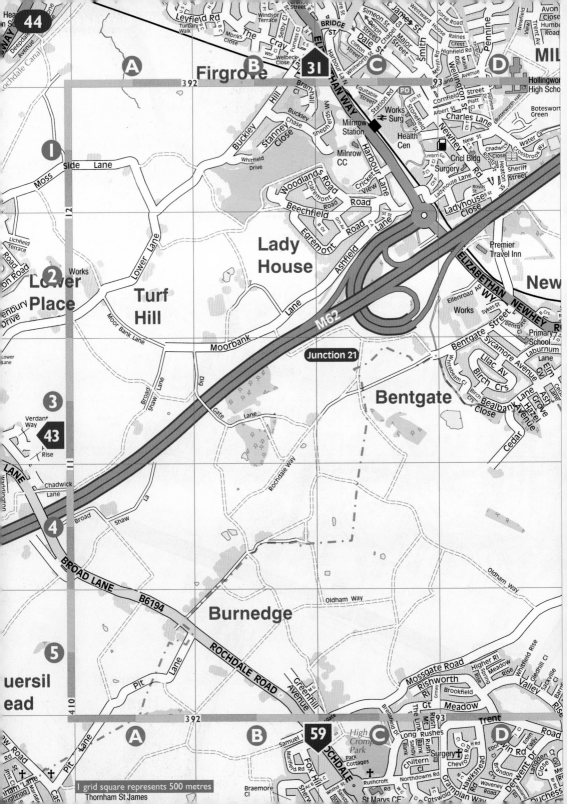

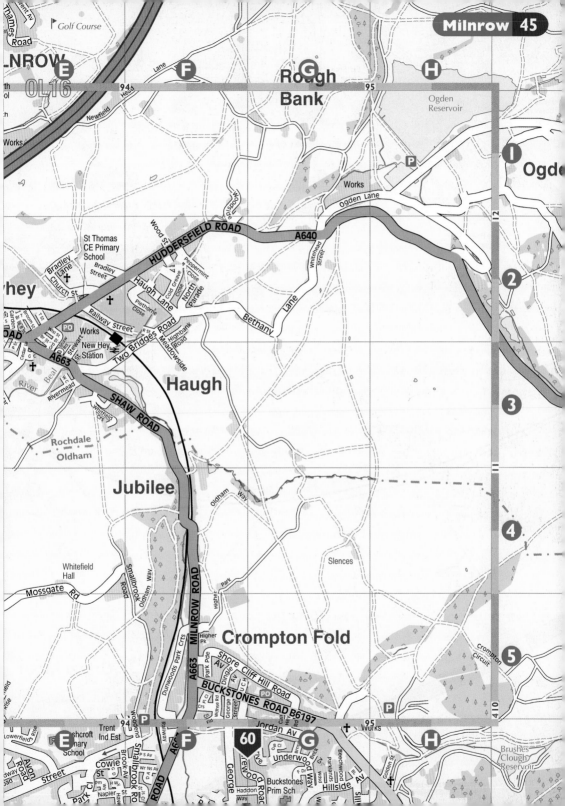

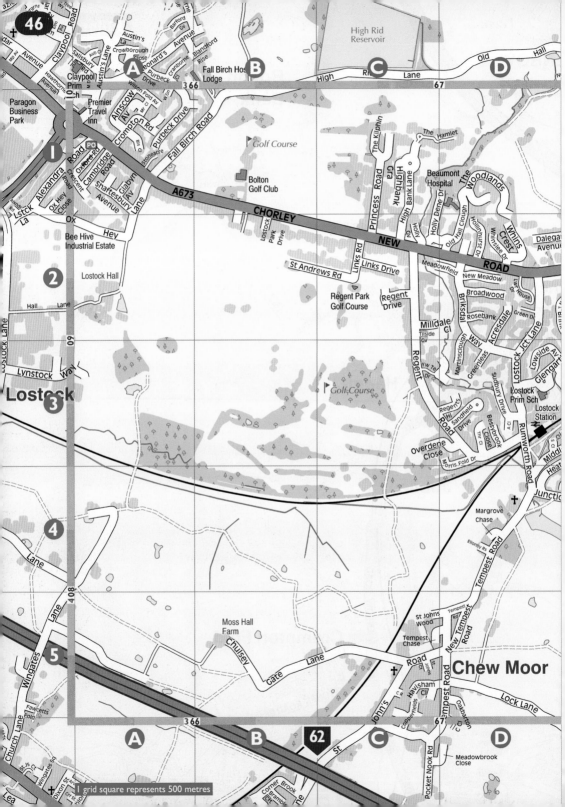

A   B   C   D

Paragon Business Park

Claypool Road
Claypool Prim Sch

Salisbury Rd
Austin's Lane
Austin's La
Crowborough Close
Leonard's Avenue
Barford Gv
Blandford Rise
Cranborne
Purbeck Drive

Fall Birch Hospital Lodge

High Rid Reservoir

Old Hall Road

High Rid Lane

67

Premier Travel Inn

Wilson Fold Av

Ainscow Av
Crompton Rd
Purbeck Drive

Fall Birch Road

Golf Course

The Kliphin
The Hamlet
Princess Road
Highbank
High Bank Lane

Beaumont Hospital

The Woodlands

Holly Dene Dr
Old Hall Clough

Whins Crest
Whinslee Dr
Dalegarth Avenue

1

Road
Oxford Rd
PO
Cambridge Road
Crescent
Glabvn Av
Shaftesbury Avenue
Lane

A673

CHORLEY
NEW
ROAD

Meadowfield
New Meadow
Lwr House
Broadwood
Rosebank
Green Dr

Alexandra
Ox Hey Close
Ox Hey La

Ox Hey

Bee Hive Industrial Estate

Lostock Park Drive

St Andrews Rd
Links Rd
Links Drive

Briksda
Acresdale
Lostock Jct Lane
Lowside Av
Glengarm

2

Lostock Hall

Hall Lane

Regent Park Golf Course

Regent Drive

Milldale Cl
Tilside Gv
Martinsclough
Greenleas
Sudbury Drive

Lostock Prim Sch

Lostock

3

Lynstock Way

Golf Course

Regent Road
Regent's Hill
Sandfield Drive
Bessybrook Close

YW Tel
YW Dr
Thr Cl

Lostock Station

Rumworth Road
Middle
Heath

Overdene Close
Orris Fold Dr

Junction

4

Lane

Margrove Chase

Ellonby Rs

Tempest Road

5

Wingates

Lane

Moss Hall Farm

Chulsey Gate Lane

St Johns Wood
Tempest Chase
Road
New Tempest Road
Tempest

Chew Moor

Lock Lane

Fawcetts Fold

Church Lane

3 66

Havisham Cl
John's St
Copperfields

Tempest Road

Oakbarton
Pocket Nook Rd

Meadowbrook Close

A   B   62   C   D

Dixon St
Wingates Sq

Corner Brook
Bramble

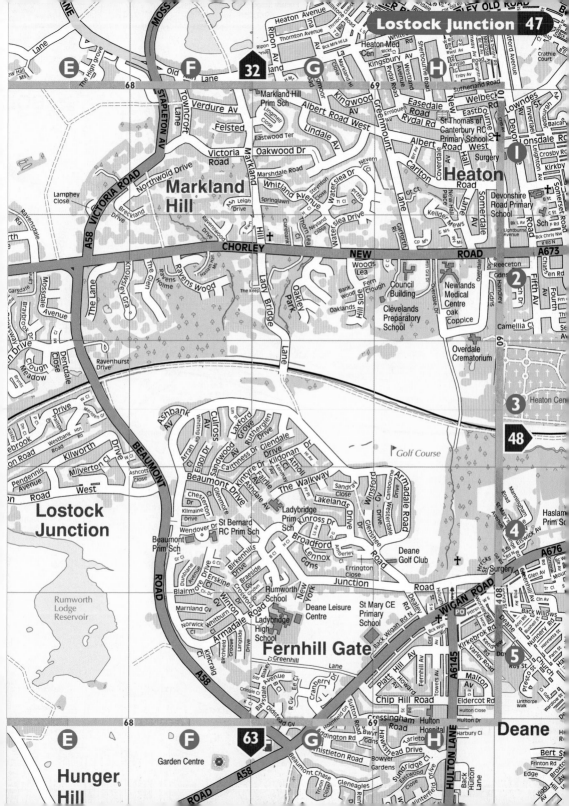

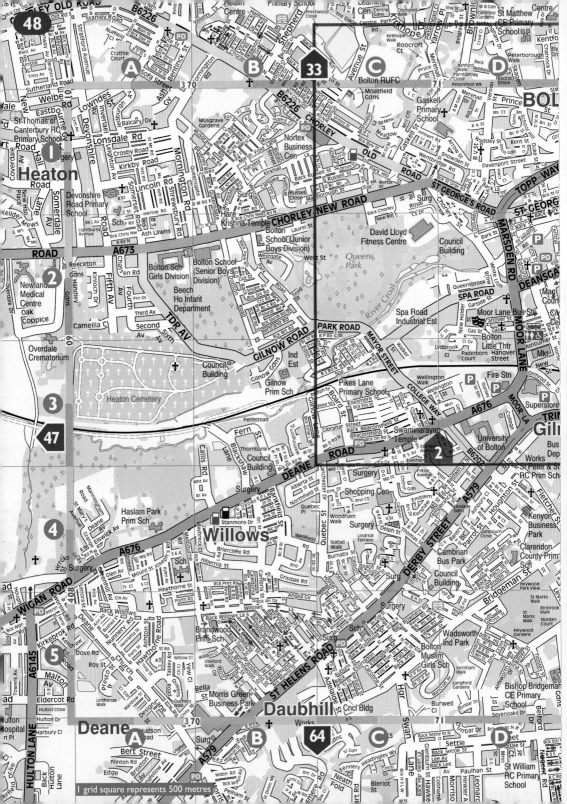

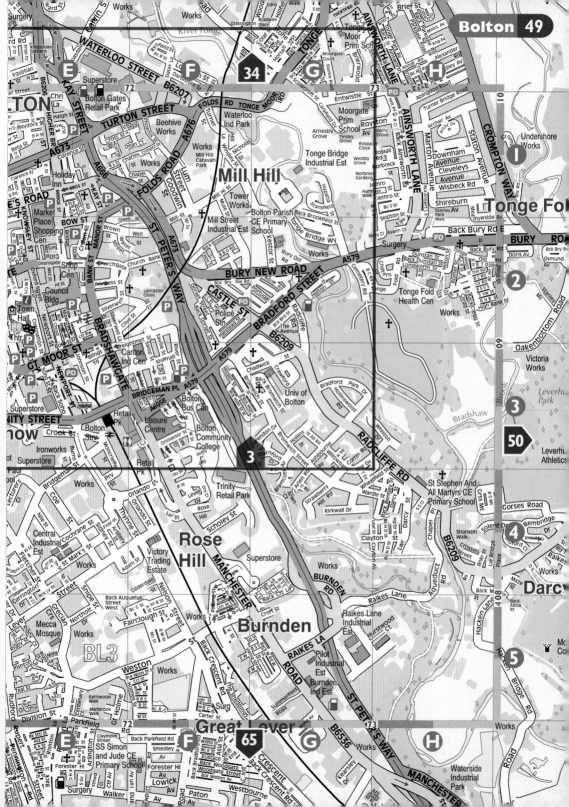

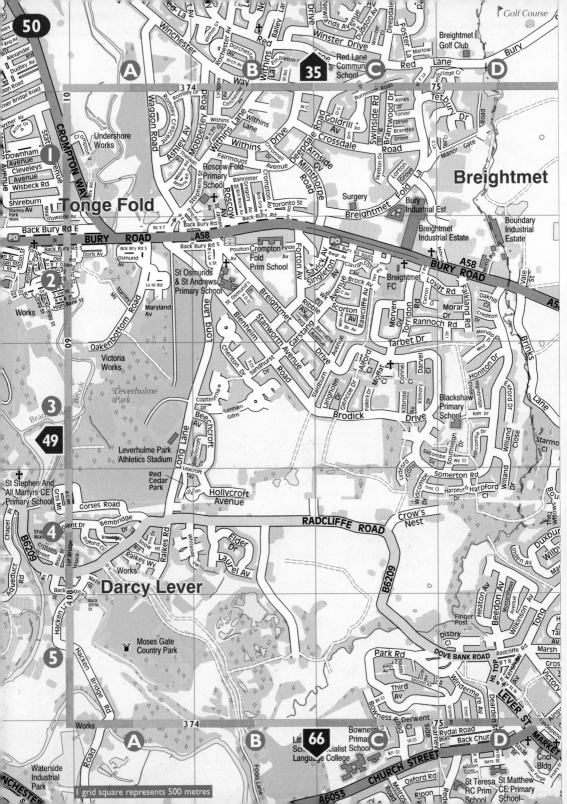

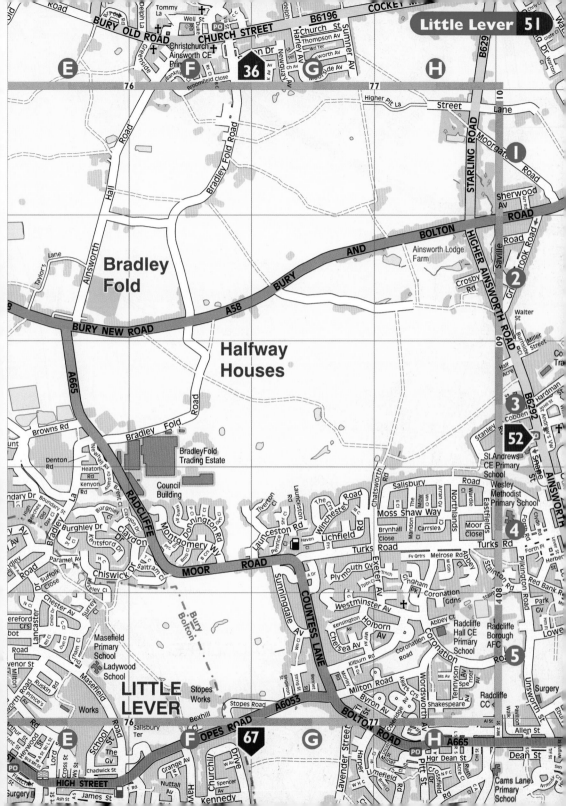

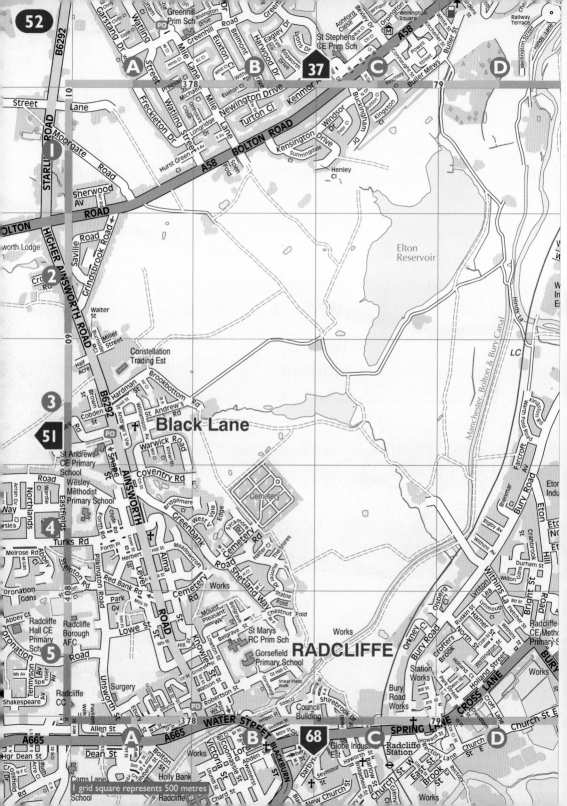

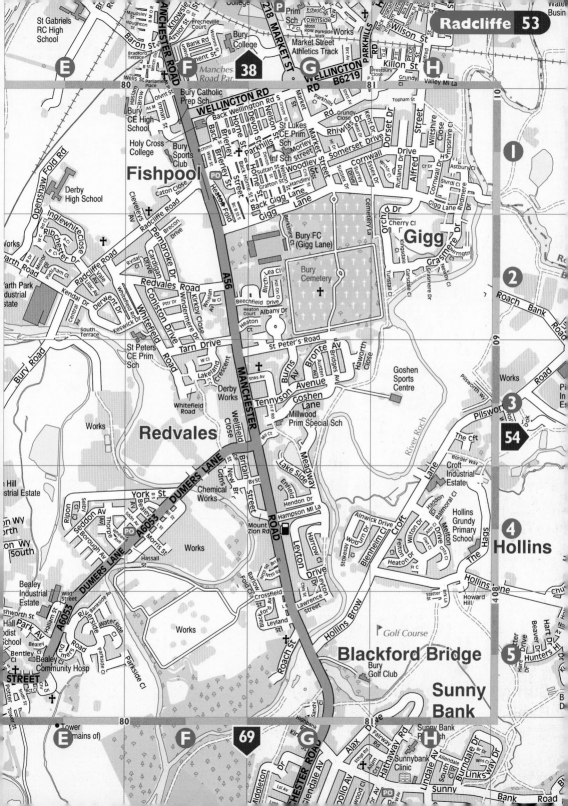

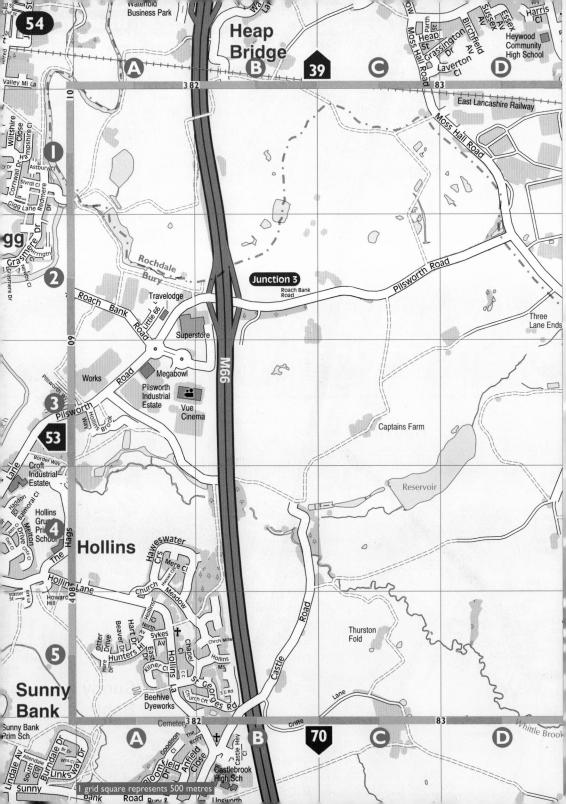

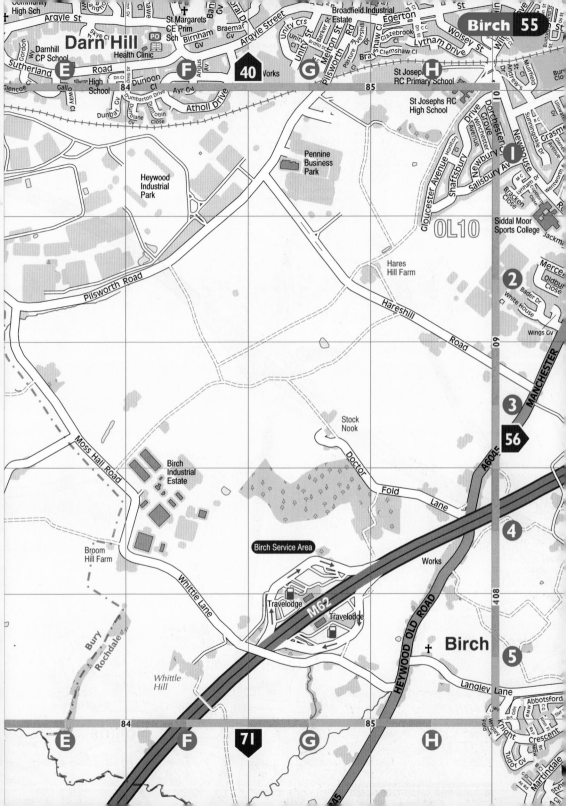

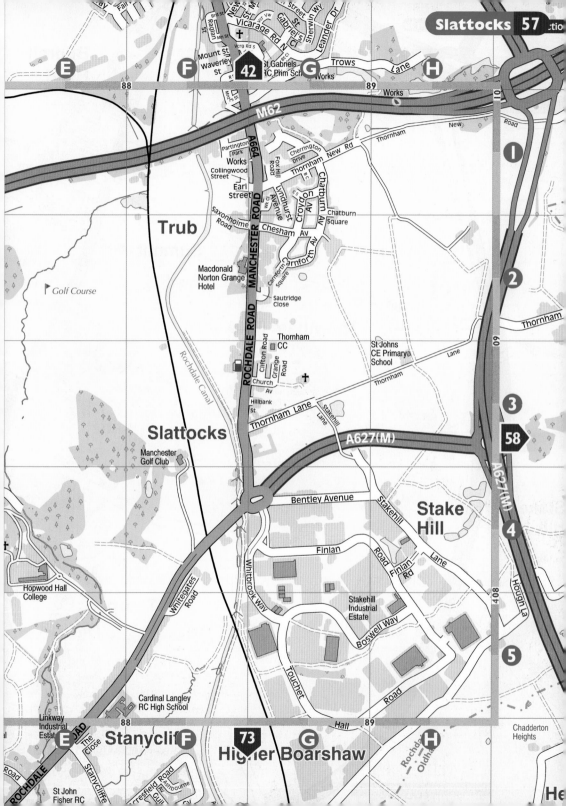

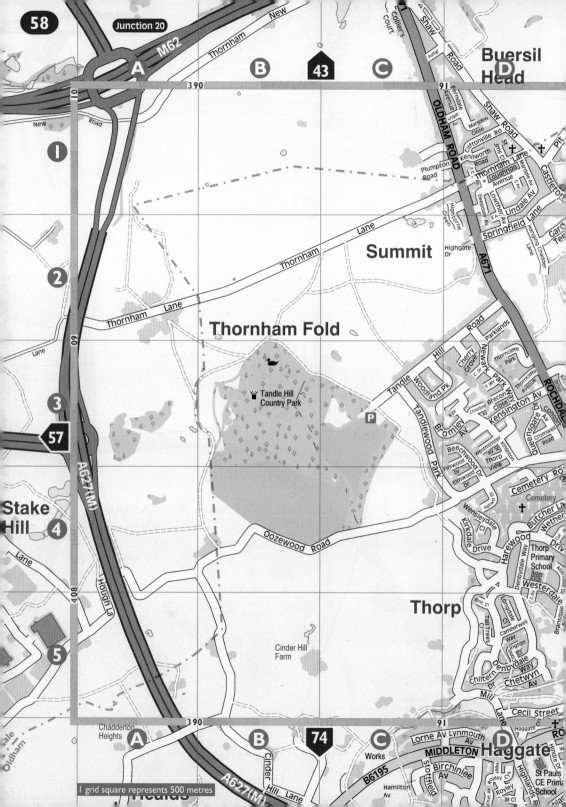

58

Junction 20

A M62

Thornham New

Collier's Court

Shaw Road

B

43

C

Buersil Head

D

New Road

OLDHAM ROAD

Ferndale Avenue

Adfar

Shaw Road

Marsden Close

Lingdl

Cliftonville Rd

Ken/worth Road

Jms Cl

Thornham Lane

Loughrigg Avenue

Marsdale Av

Castleton

Pit

Highcliffe Green

Plumpton Road

Lowther Av

Deepdale Av

Lindale Lane

Hanging Chadder

Gard
Ter

Springfield Lane

I

Thornham Lane

Summit

Highgate Dr

A671

2

Thornham Lane

Thornham Lane

Thornham Fold

Hill Road

Parklands

Tandle

Woodland Pk

Cherry Grove

Newark Park Way

Thorncliffe Park

ROCHDALE

Tandle Hill Country Park

Croydon Av

Brecon Close

Thorncliffe Avenue

S W Av

Kensington Av

Queensgate

Consort

Kirl

3

P

Bromley Av

Beechwood Dr

Firswood Dr

Elmwood Dr

Westminster

Kingston

Thorp View

Cemetery Rd

Cromwell Rd

Cemetery

57

A627(M)

Tandlewood Park

Stake Hill

4

Lane

Oozewood Road

Wensleydale Cl

Kirkdale Drive

Harewood Way

Denbydale Way

Butcher La

Wether

Dr

Thorp Primary School

Westerdale

Thorp

Brnt

Longdale Cl

Tall Trees Way

Camberwell Way

ngton

Bransled

C N

Hough La

5

A627(M)

A408

Cinder Hill Farm

Chiltern Dr

Chetwyn Av

Denbydale Way

Mill Lane

Cecil Street

Chadderton Heights

A

Cinder Hill Lane

B

74

C

Works

Lorne Av

Lynmouth Av

B6195

Stotfield

Birchinlee Av

Hamilton Av

MIDDLETON

Royley Cl

C N Av

Royley

M Cl

Highlands R

D

Haggate

St Pauls CE Prima School

RO

New Heads

Oldham

Lane

390

60

408

91

390

91

1 grid square represents 500 metres

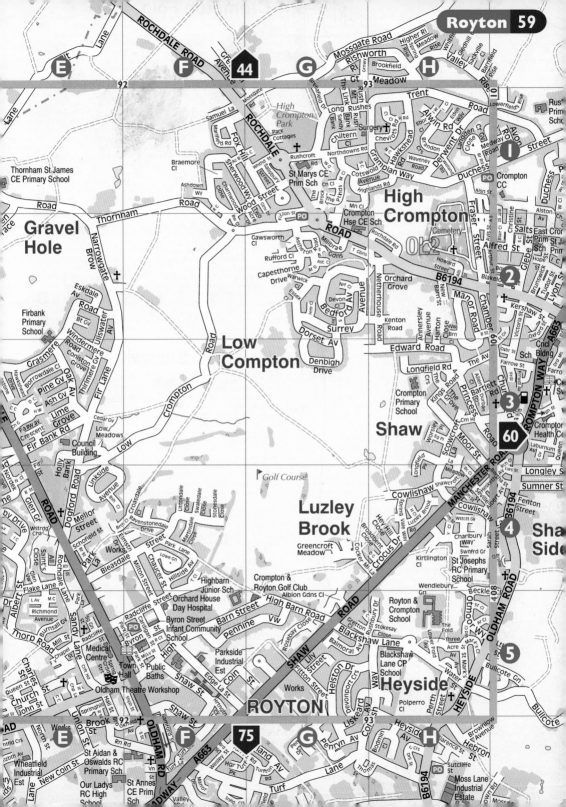

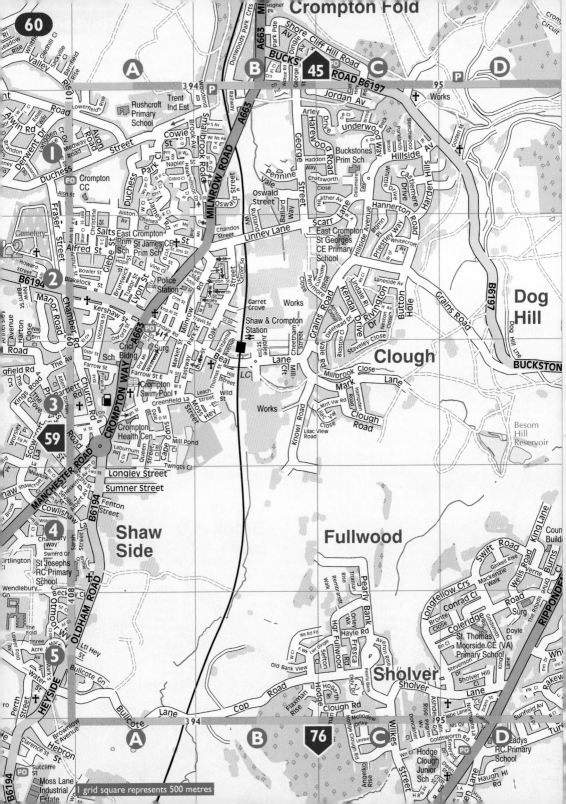

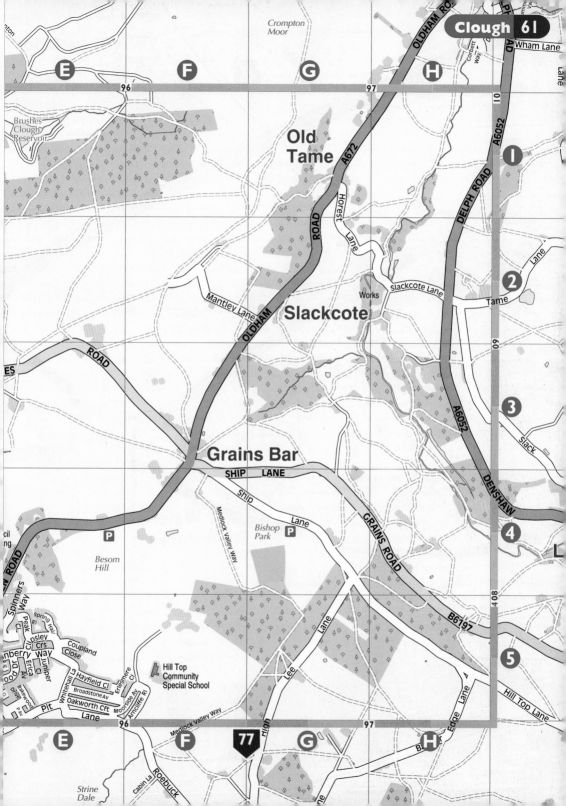

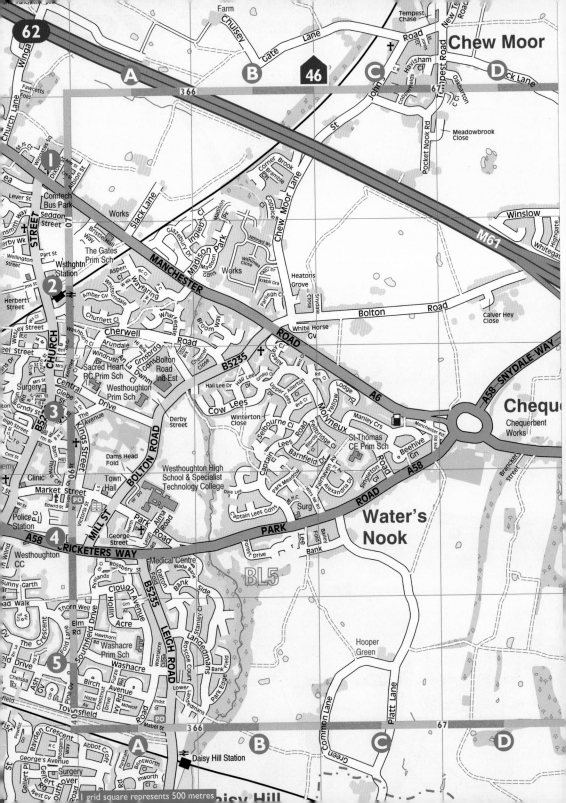

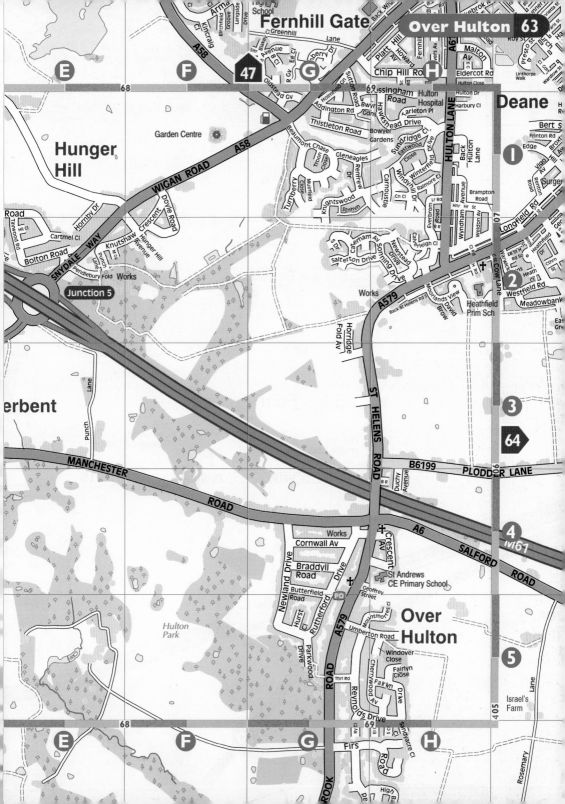

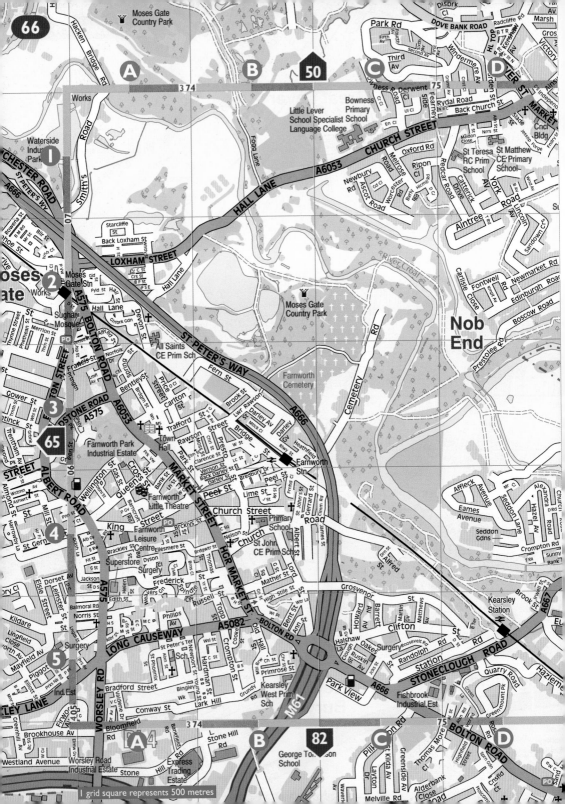

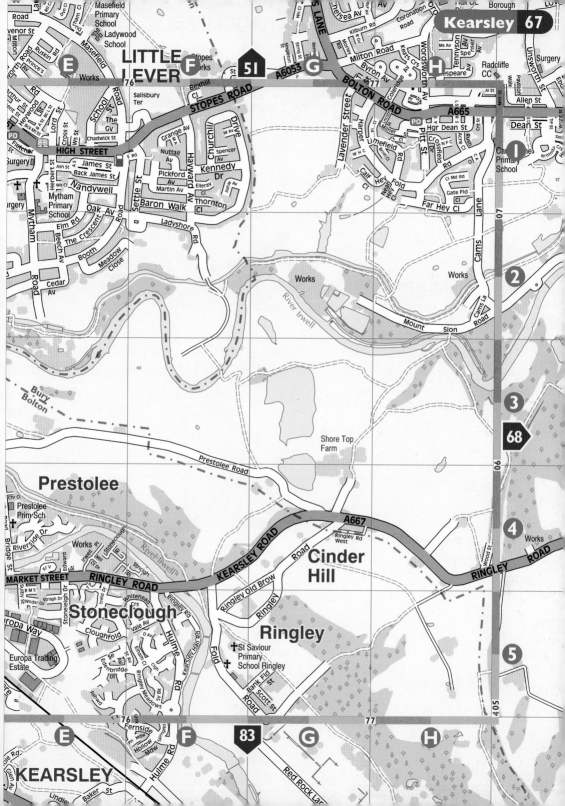

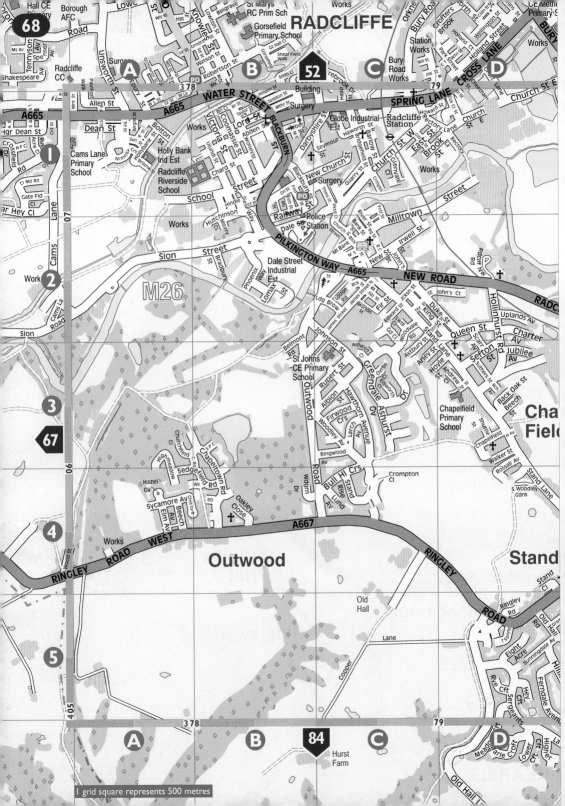

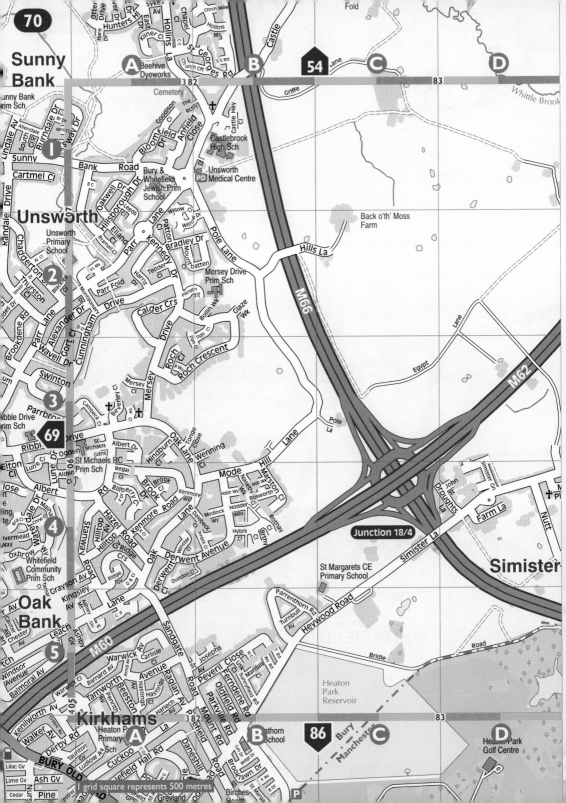

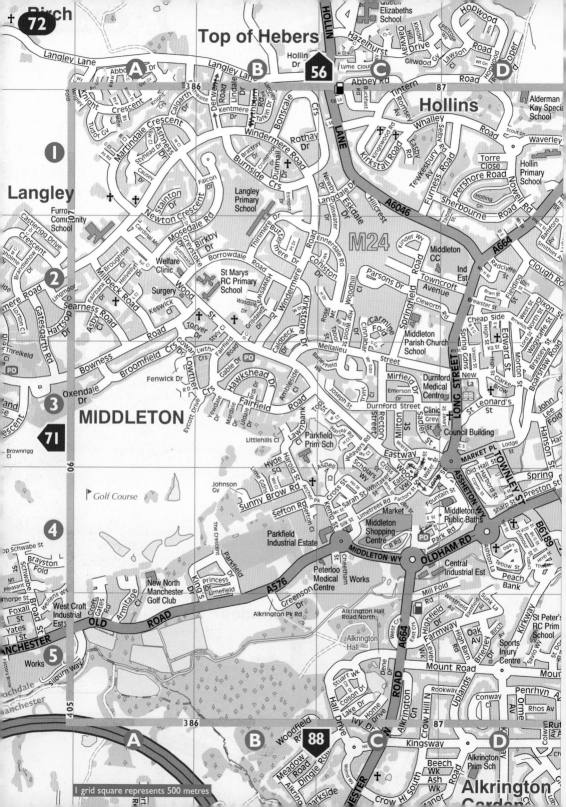

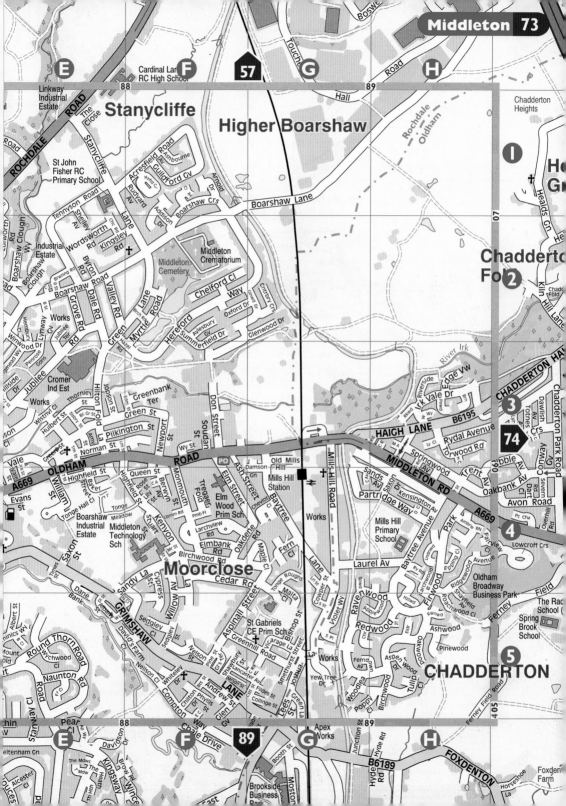

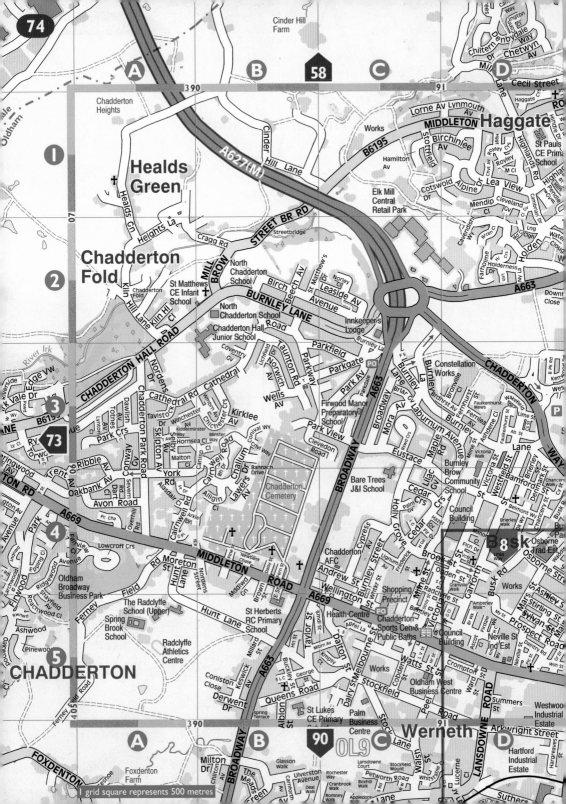

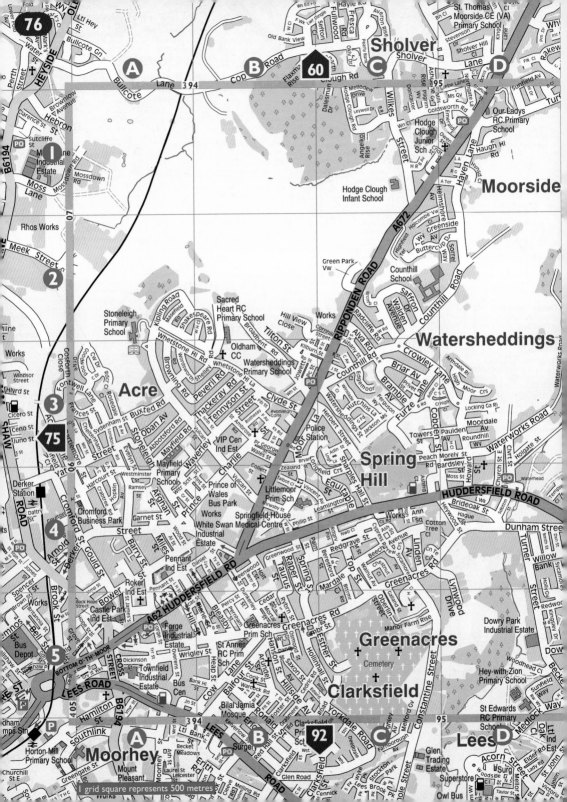

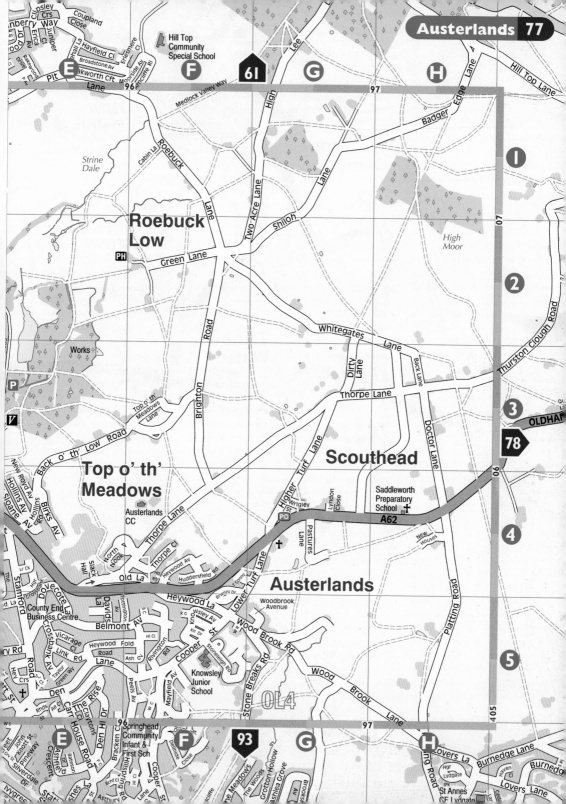

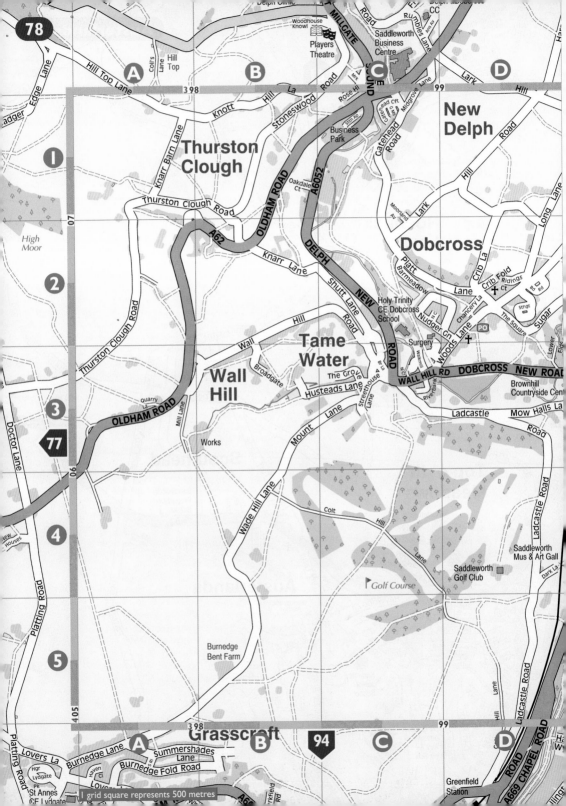

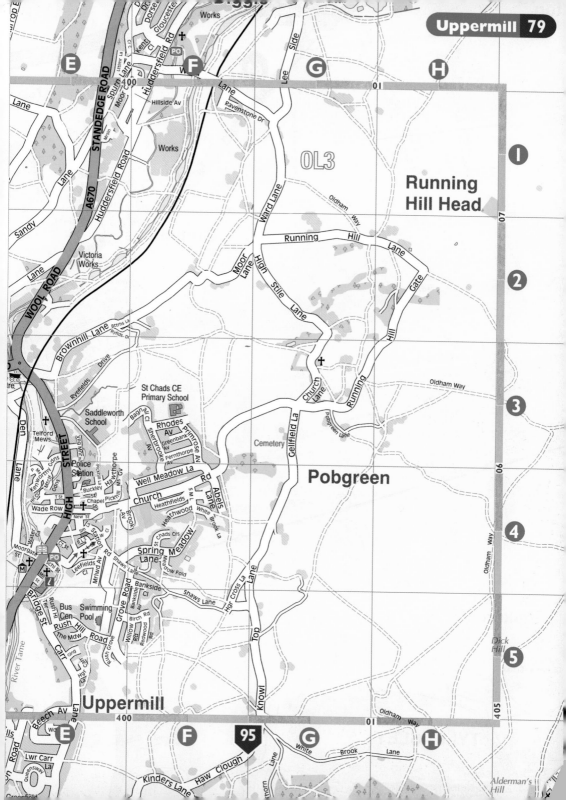

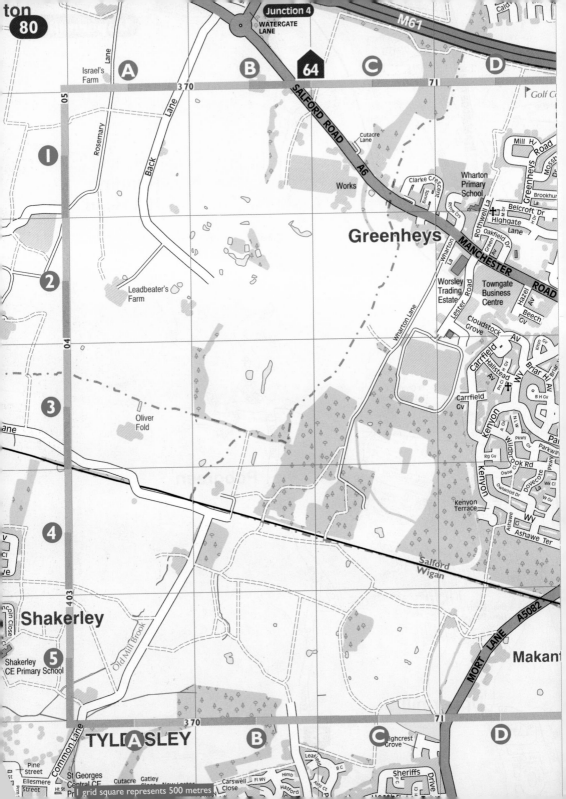

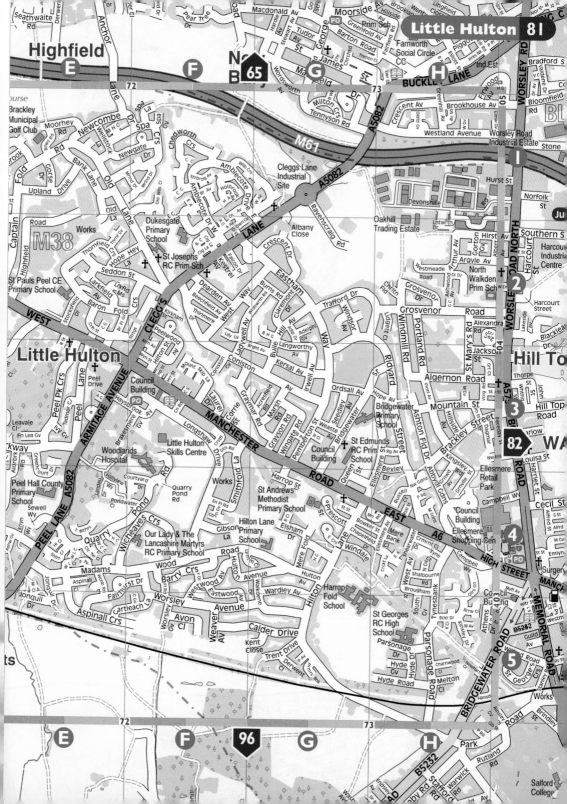

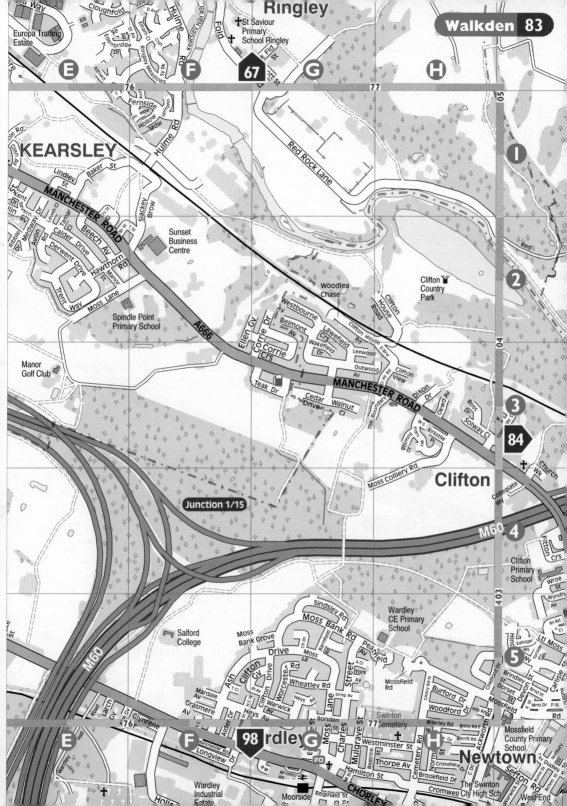

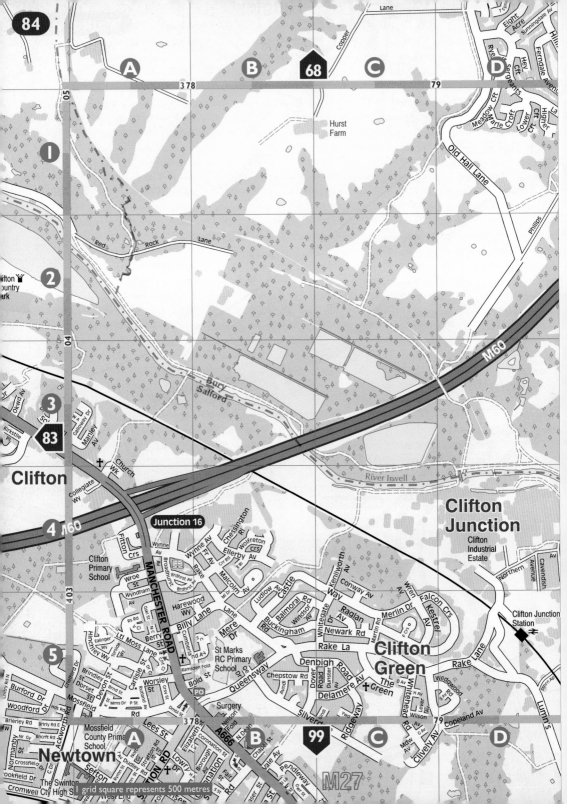

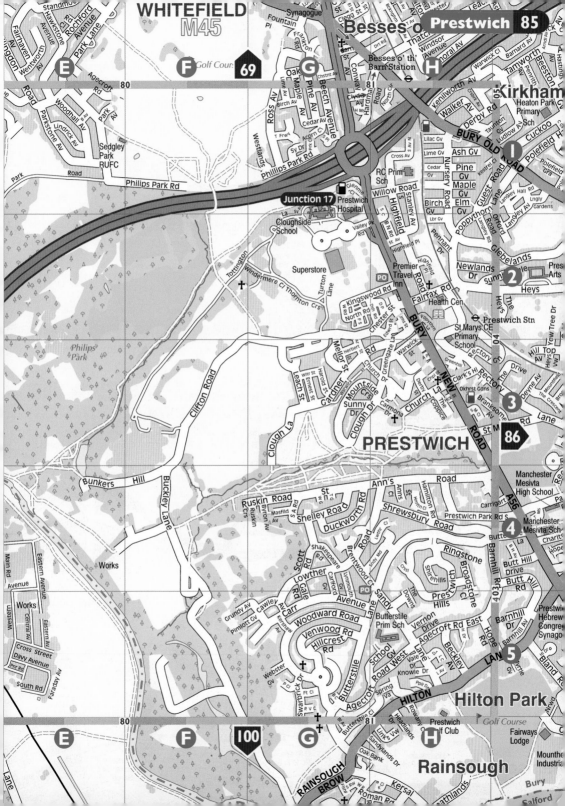

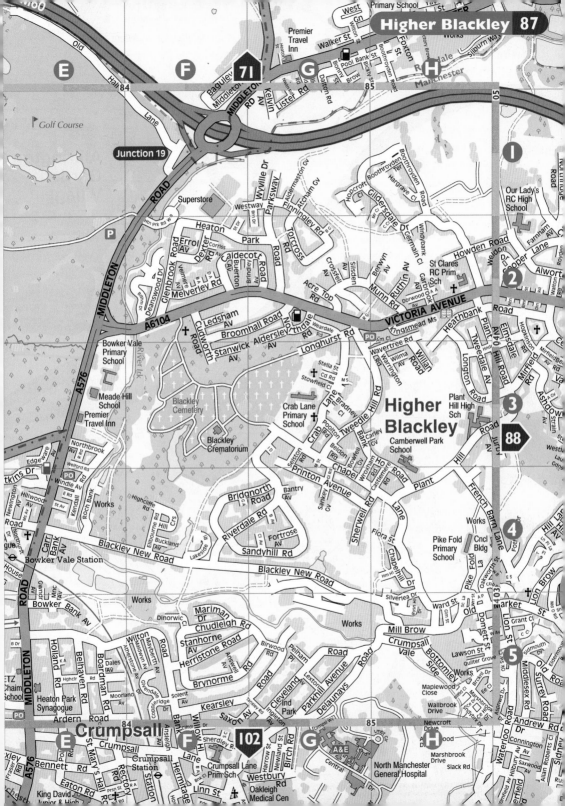

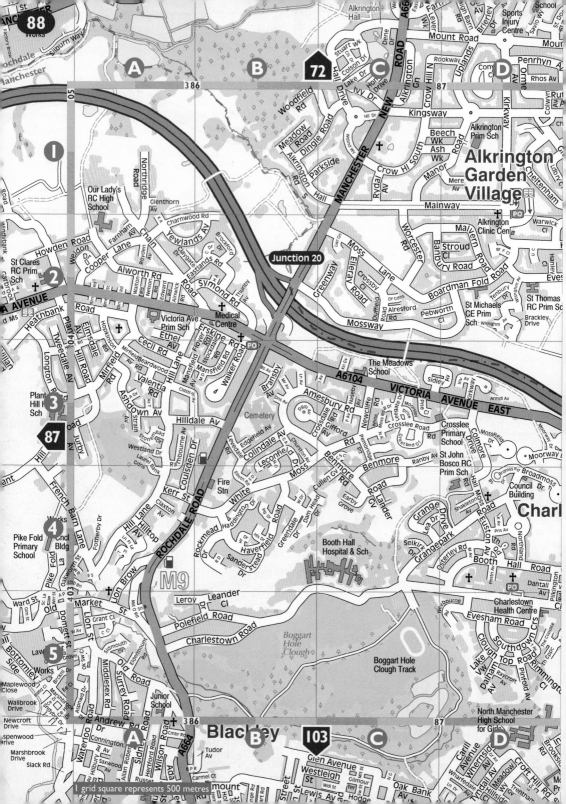

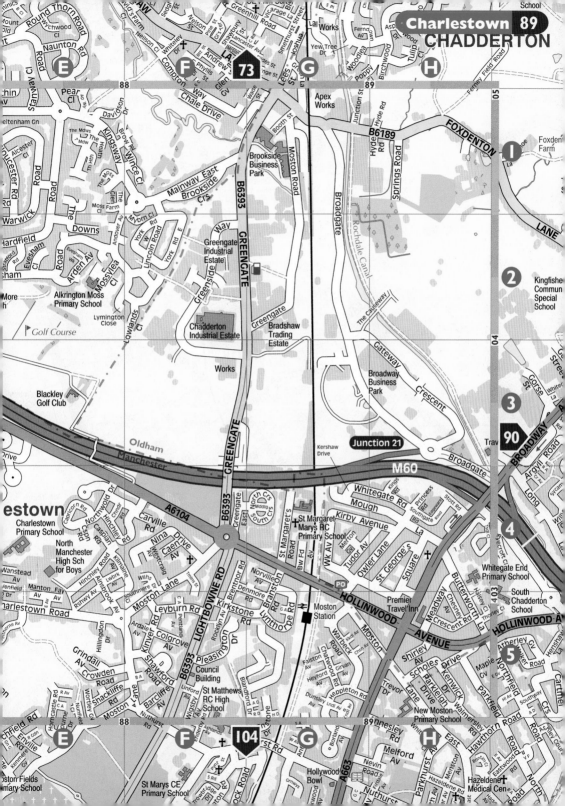

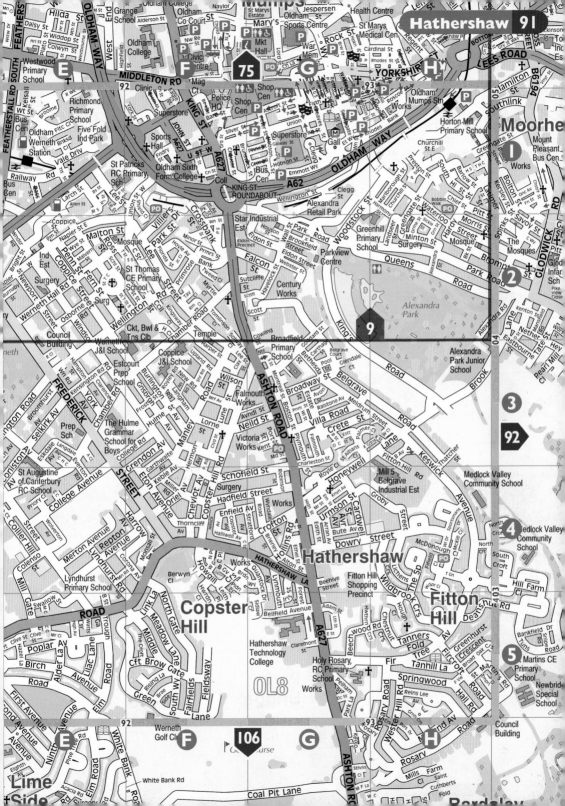

I grid square represents 500 metres

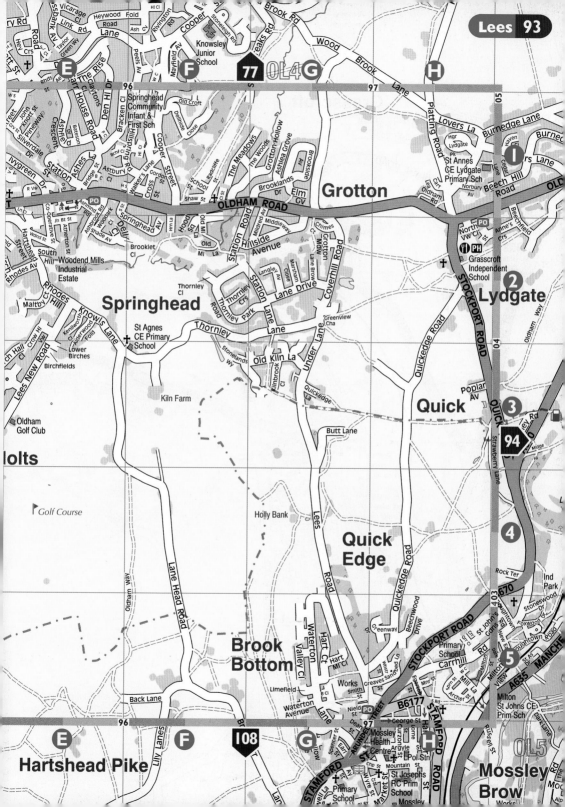

Map labels

Lees 93

E F 77 OL4 G H

Vicarage Rd · Heywood Fold · Rivington Rd · COOPER · Brook Rd · Wood Brook Lane
Link Rd · Ash C'
Taylor Green Wy · Peels Wy · Knowsley Junior School · Mayfield · reaks Rd
Heys Crs
Silverdale Dr · Ashfield · Pineway · Den Hi Dr · House Road · Bracken Cl · Springhillill · Old Croft · Dellhoe Close · Springhead Community Infant & First Sch · Lovers La · Burnedge Lane
Ivygreen Dr · Station · Ashes · Astbury Rd · Cooper Street · The Meadows · The Woods · Ashtea Grove · Brookside Av · Hgr Lydgate · St Annes CE Lydgate Primary Sch · Norbury Av · Beech Hill Road
Co-Operative St · Springhead Av · Hood Ln · Old Mill La · Shaw St · Radcliffe · Brooklands Dr · Elm GV · **Grotton** · Oldham Rd · North Vw Cl · Anne's Crs · Beechfield
OLDHAM ROAD
South Hill · Dell · Brooklet Cl · Hillside Avenue · Mildred · Middleway · Chimes · Grotton Mdw · Lane Brow · Grasscroft Independent School
Woodend Mills Industrial Estate · Rhodes Av · Maltby · Knowls Lane · Thornley Cl · Thornley Crs · Thornley Park · Station Road · Langley Av · Marsham Close · Lane Drive · Coverhill Road · Greenview Cha · **2 Lydgate**
Lees New Road · Birch Hall · Crow Hi · Aberwood Fold · Lower Birches · Birchfields · St Agnes CE Primary School · Thornley Lane · Stonelands Wy · Kilnbrook · Old Kiln La · Quickedge · **Quick** · Poplar Av · **3**
Oldham Golf Club · Kiln Farm · Kilnbrook Cl · Quickedge · Strawberry Lane · **94**
lolts · Butt Lane · Midge
Golf Course · Holly Bank · **Quick Edge** · **4**
Lane Way · Lees Road · Quickedge Road · Rock Ter · Ind Park · Stoneswood Dr · Foxwood
Lane Head Road · Greenway · Beechwood Drive · 670
Brook Bottom · Waterton Valley Cl · Hart Ct · Hart Mt Cl · St John's Gdns · Rd · Primary School Carrhill · **STOCKPORT ROAD** · Milton View · A635 · **MANCHE** · **5**
Back Lane · Limefield · Waterton Avenue · Works smith St · Greaves St · Sandbed La · Archer St · Mill La · Milton · St Johns CE Prim Sch
Nield St · Dean St · George St · **B6177** · Hart Road · Russell St
STAMFORD · **108** · **G** · Mossley Health Centre · Argyle · Pol Stn · **H** · Primary School · **OL5**
E · **F** · ARUNDEL STREET · Spencer St · Egmont St · Mountain St · St Josephs RC Prim School · Park La
Hartshead Pike · Lily Lanes · Primary School · Wyre St · Market St · Mossley · **Mossley Brow**

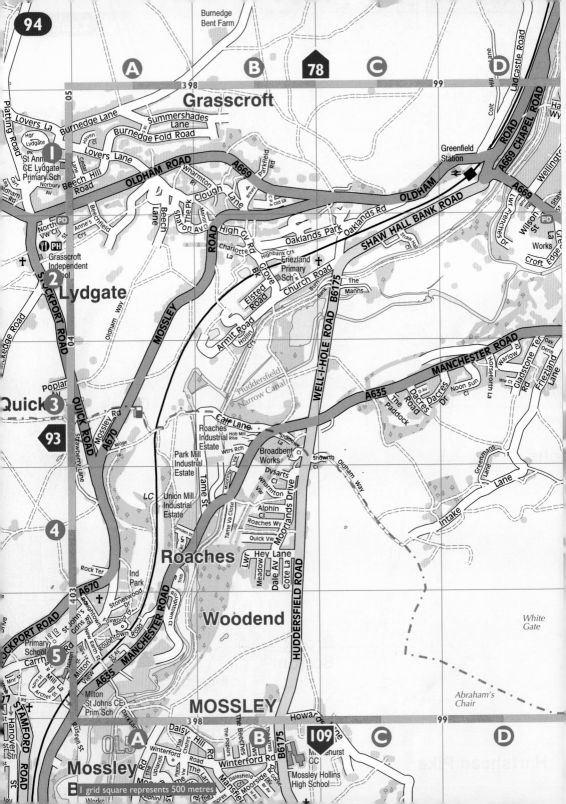

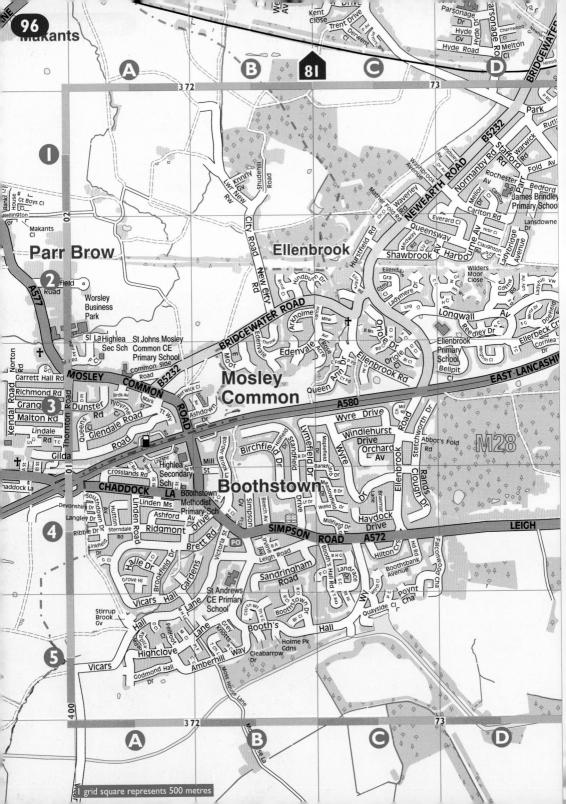

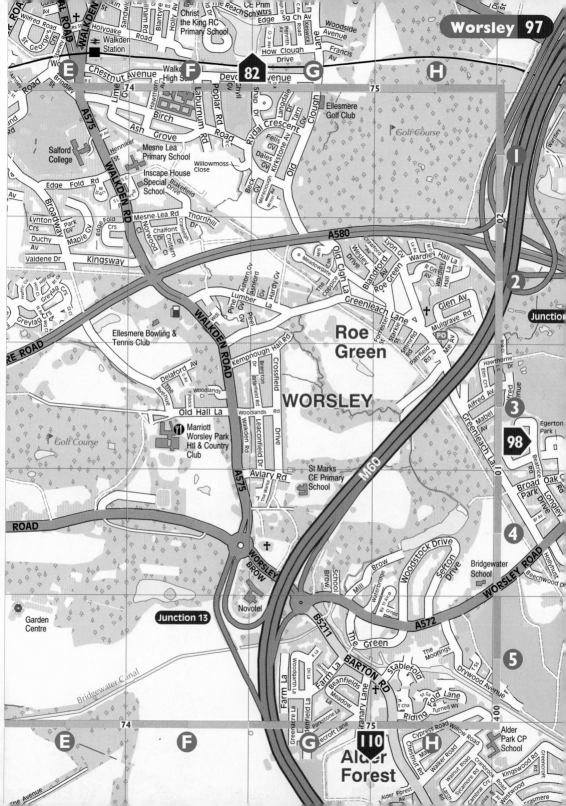

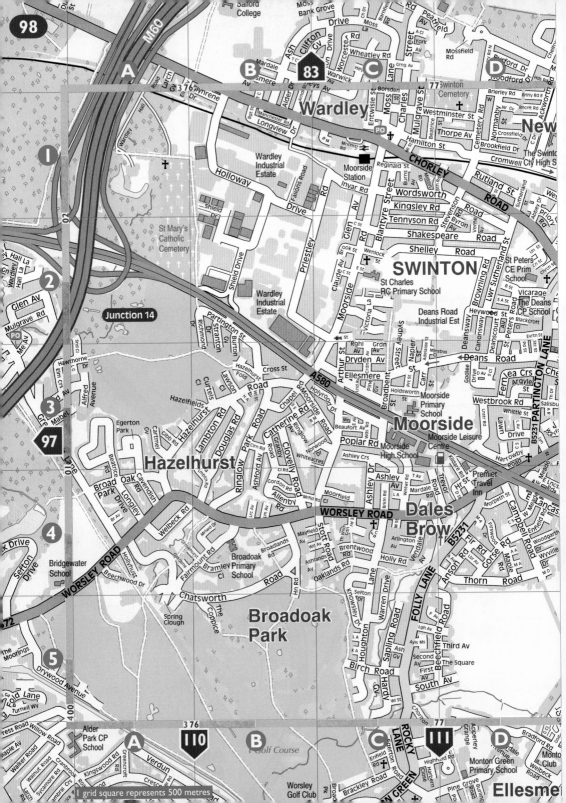

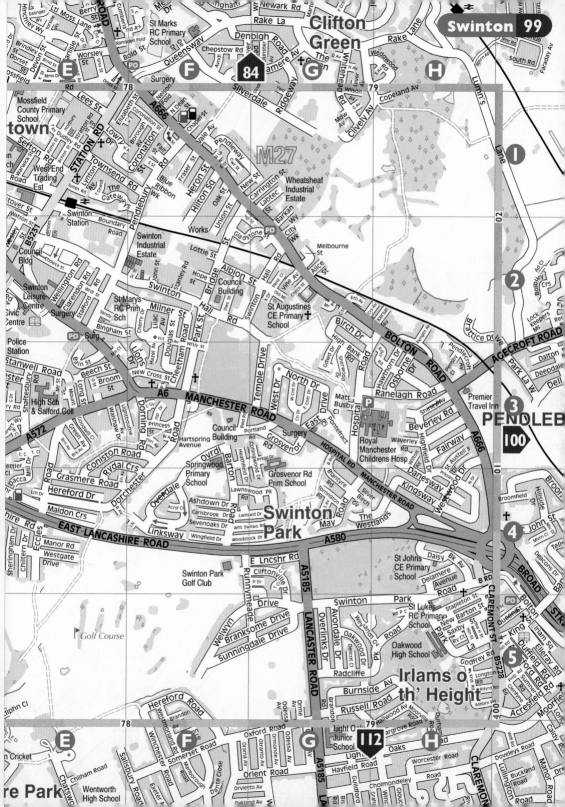

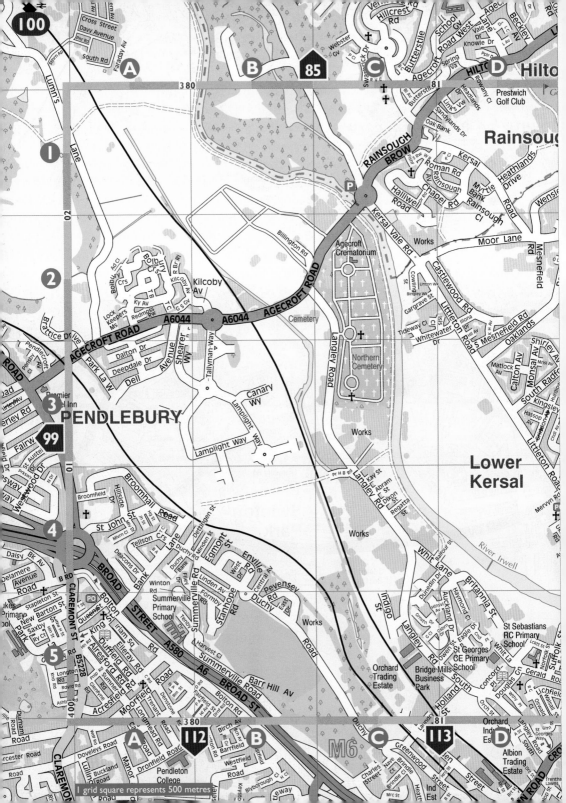

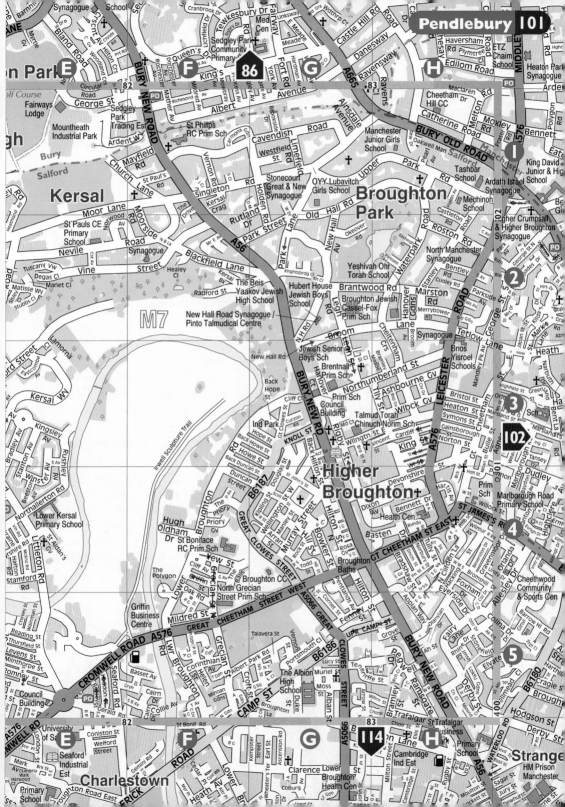

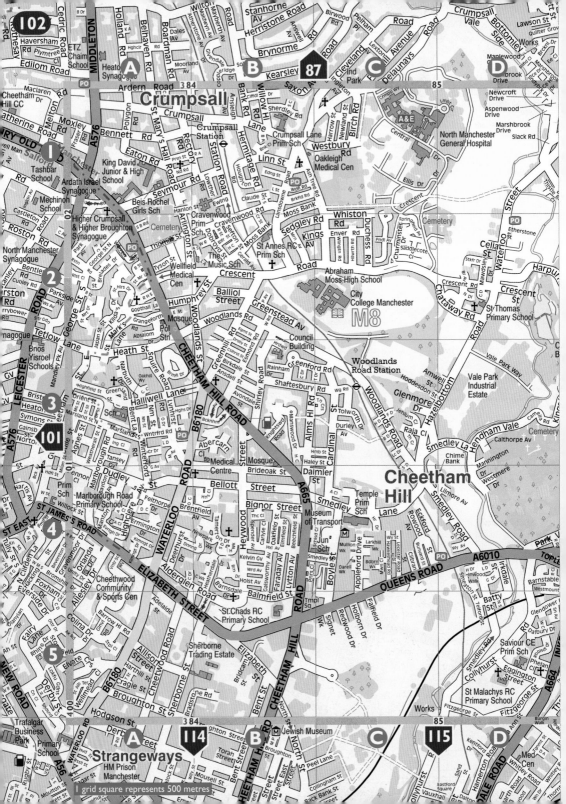

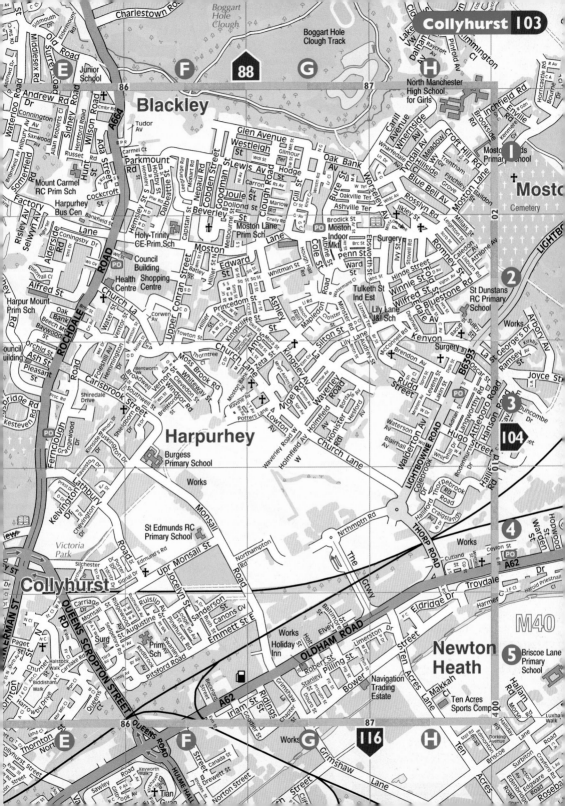

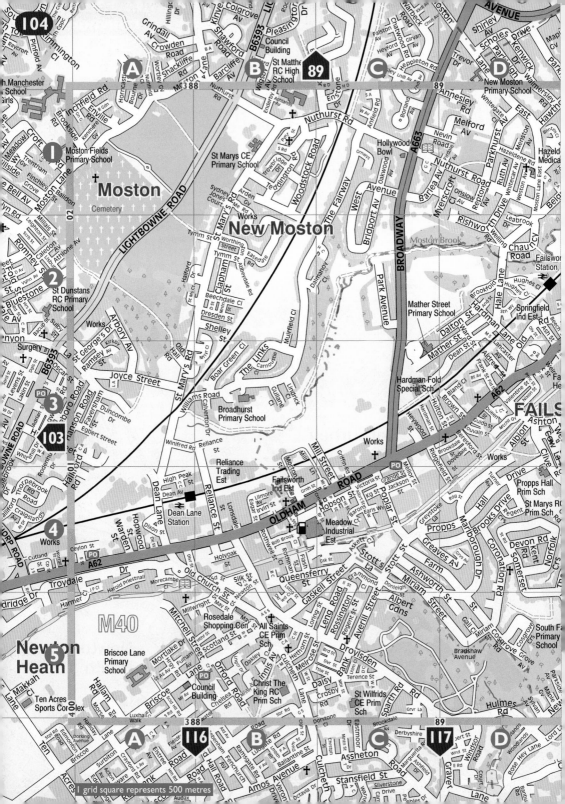

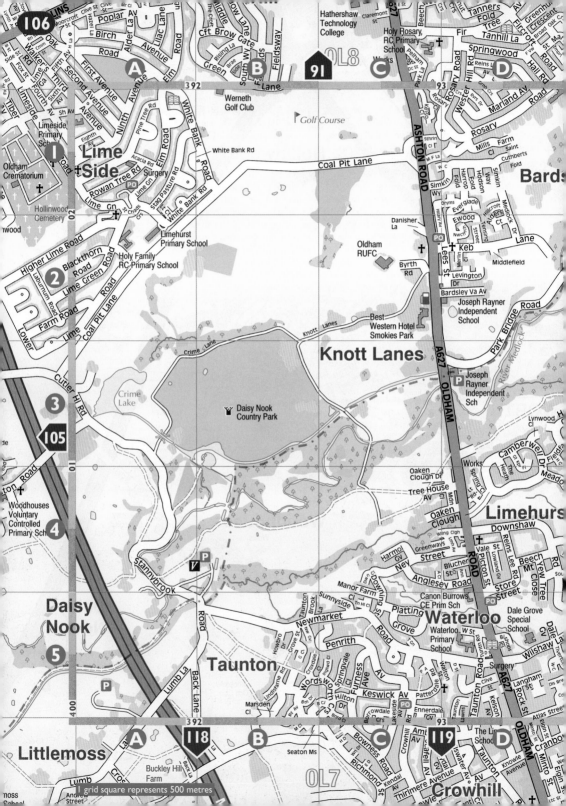

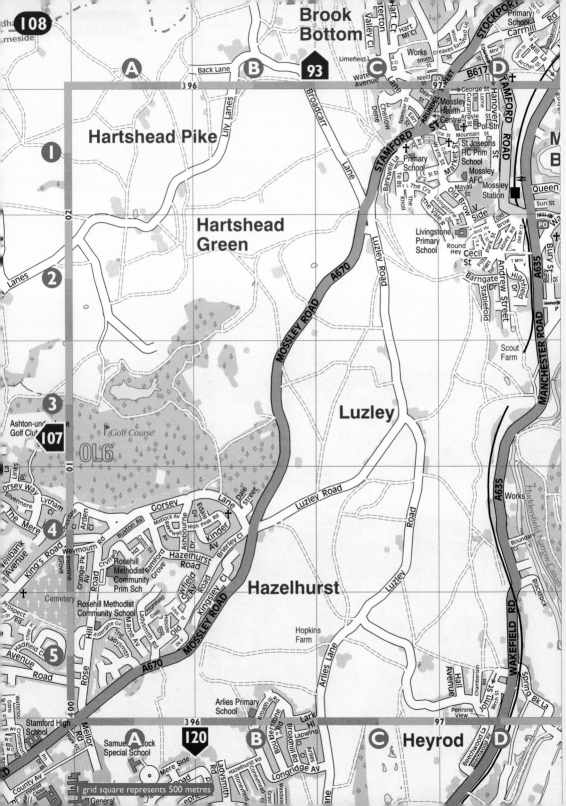

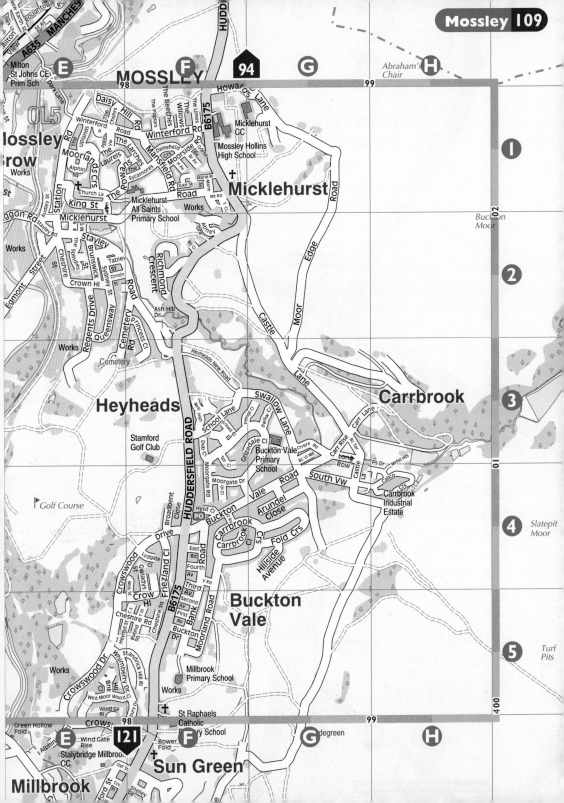

MOSSLEY

Milton View
Milton St Johns CE Prim Sch

A635 MANCHESTER

OL5

Mossley Brow
Works

E   **F**   94   **G**   **H**   Abraham's Chair

Daisy Hill Rd
Winterford Road
The Beeches
The Poplars
The Willows
The Limes
B6175
Howards Lane
Micklehurst CC
Mossley Hollins High School

Moorlands Crs
The Laurels
The Rowans
The Larches
The Sycamores
Mansfield Rd
Winterford Rd
Moorside Rd
Dalesfield
The Uplands
Alphin Sq
King St
Station Rd
Church La
Moorside Rd
Road
Works
Micklehurst

Micklehurst
Micklehurst All Saints Primary School

Mt Rd

Works

Eqmont Street
Waggon Rd
Staveley Rd
Stayley
Brunswick
Cheshire
The Spindles
Crown Hl
Sydney St
Tabley St
St Clrndn St
Richmond Crescent
Ash Hill Dr

2   Buckton Moor

Regents Drive
Queensway
Princess Cl
Cemetery Rd
Cemetery
Works

Heyheads New Road
Castle Lane
Moor Lane
Edge Road

3   **Carrbrook**

Heyheads

Golf Course

Stamford Golf Club

HUDDERSFIELD ROAD
School Lane
Swallow Lane
Grizedale Cl
Buckton Vale Primary School
Moorgate Rd
Moorgate Dr
Carr Lane
Carr Rise
Long Row
Castle
South Vw
Carrbrook Industrial Estate

Broadbent Close
Drive
Hysd Cl
PO
Buckton
Vale Road
Arundel Close
Carrbrook Cl
Carrbrook Crs
Fold Crs
Hillside Avenue

4   Slatepit Moor

Crowswood St
Lydgate Cl
Friezland Cl
Crow Hl
Cheshire Rd
Cheshire Sq
B6175
Bank
East Rd
Fourth Av
Third Avl
Second Av
First Av
Buckton Dr
Moorland Road

Buckton Vale

Crowswood Dr
Standrick Hill Rise
Whimberry Dr
Wild Moor Wood
Wind Ga Rl
Crows
Millbrook Primary School
Works

5   Turf Pits

Green Hollow Fold
Wind Gate Rise
E   121   Stalybridge Millbrook CC
F   St Raphaels Catholic Primary School
G   degreen
H

Bower Fold
Oxf St

Millbrook   **Sun Green**
Shelley Gv

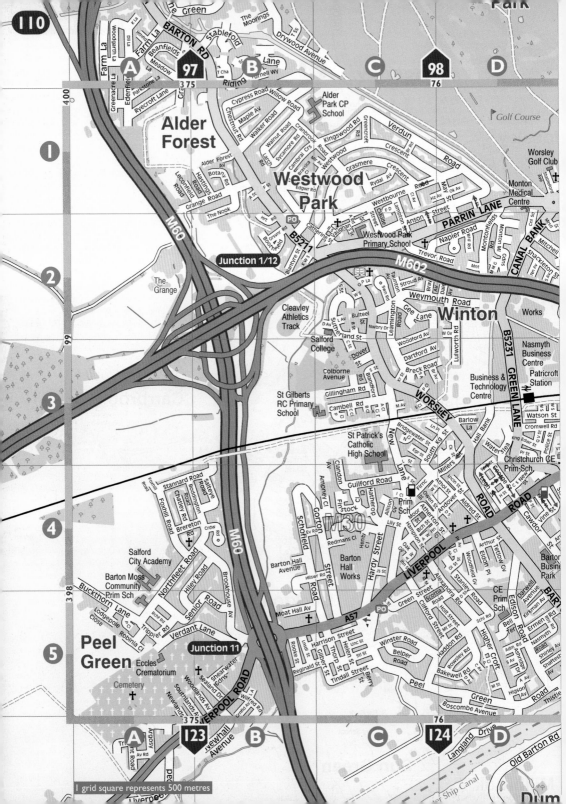

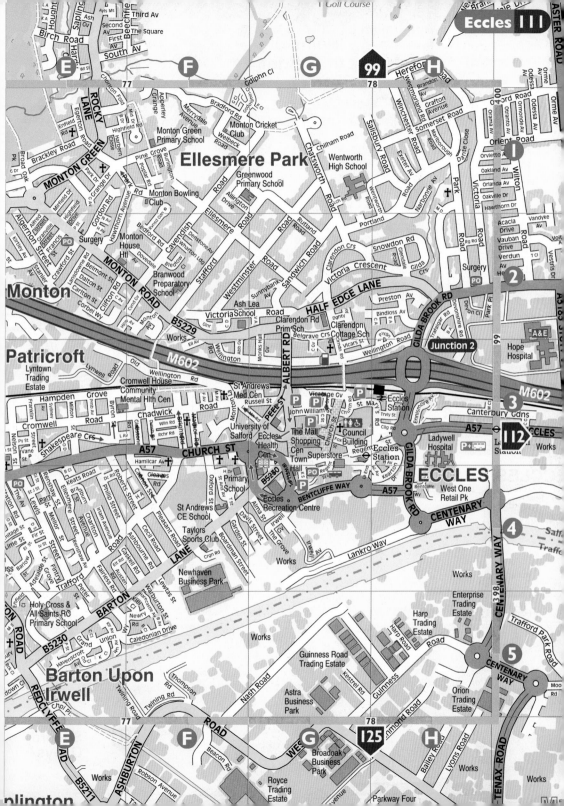

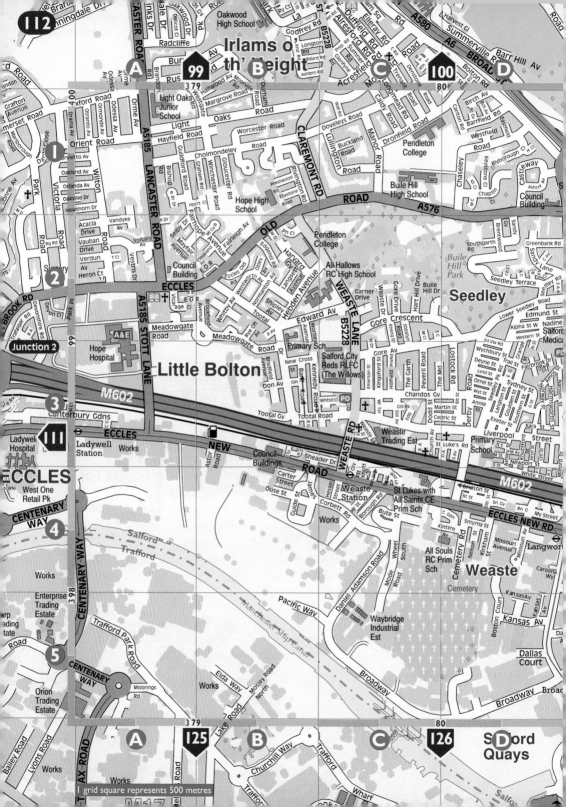

Strangeways

▪ 1 grid square represents 500 metres

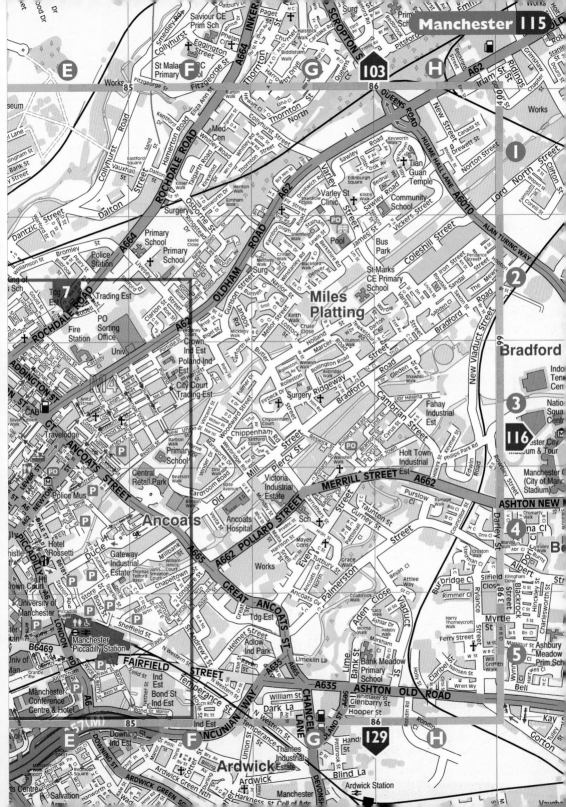

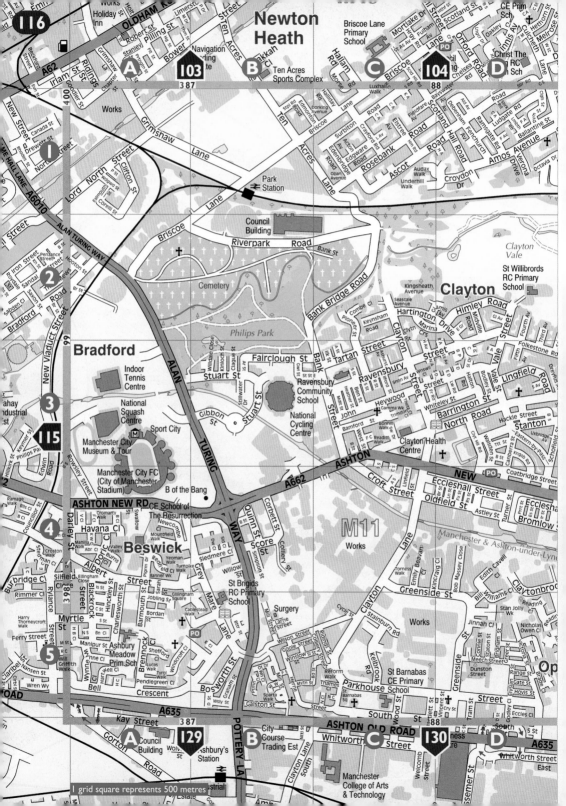

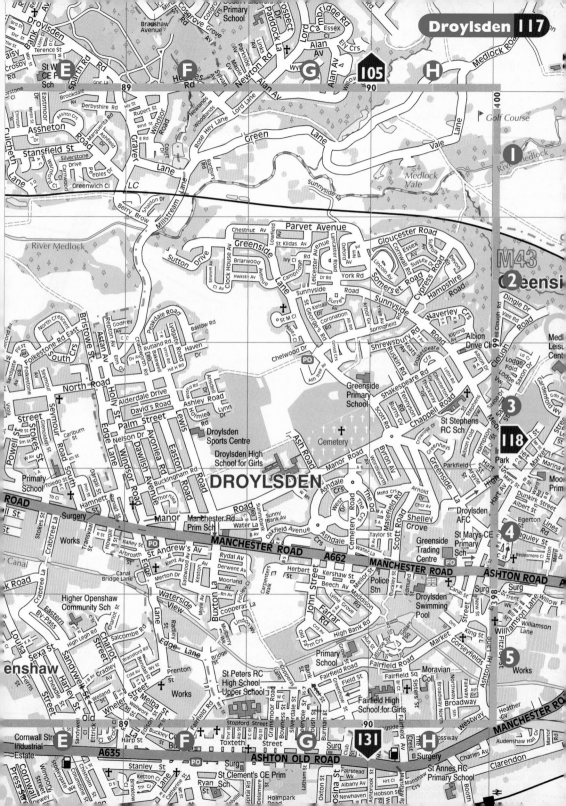

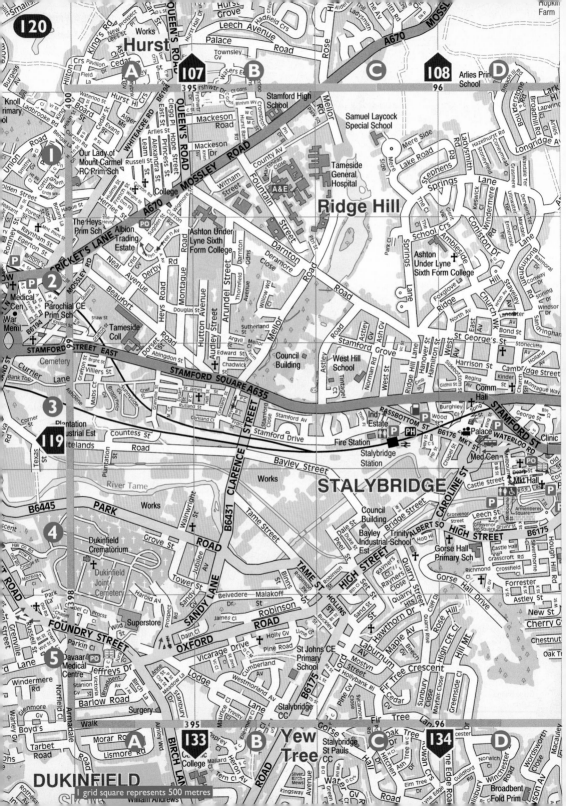

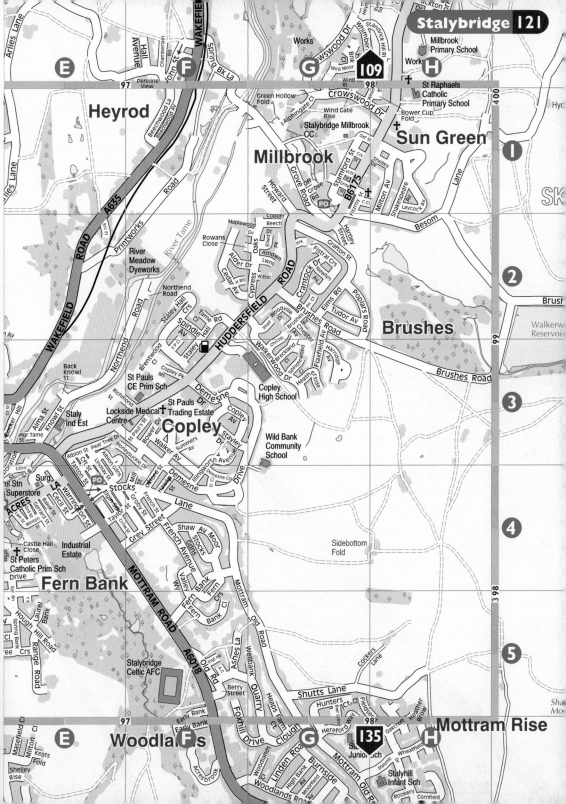

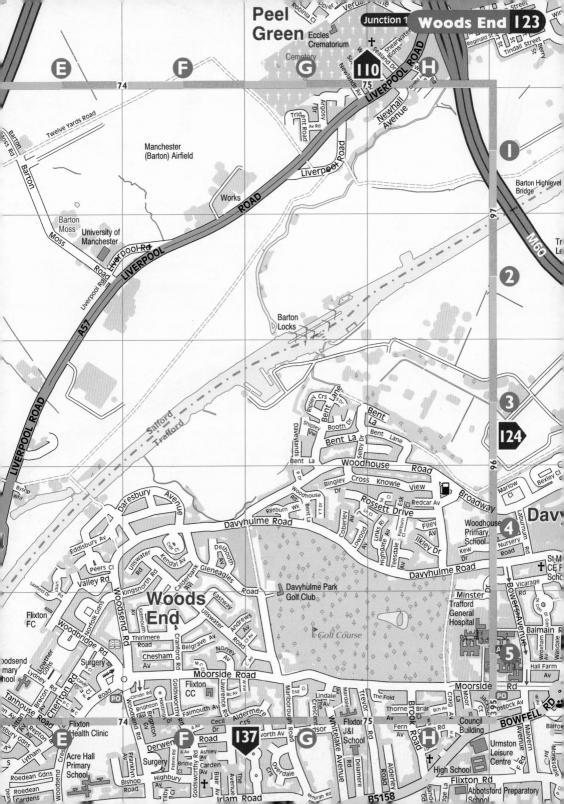

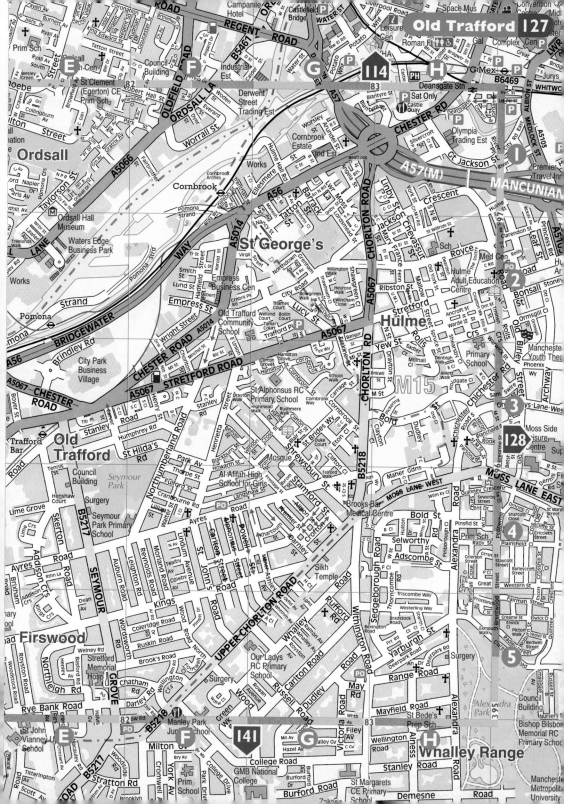

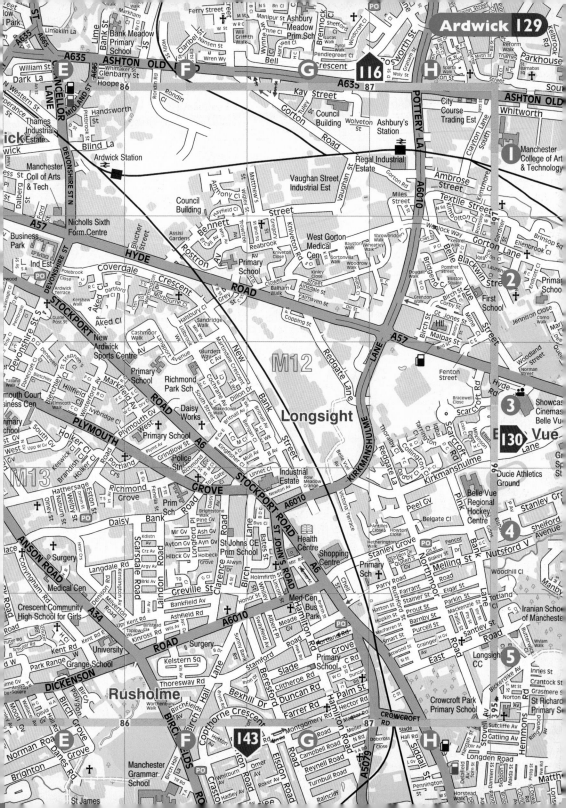

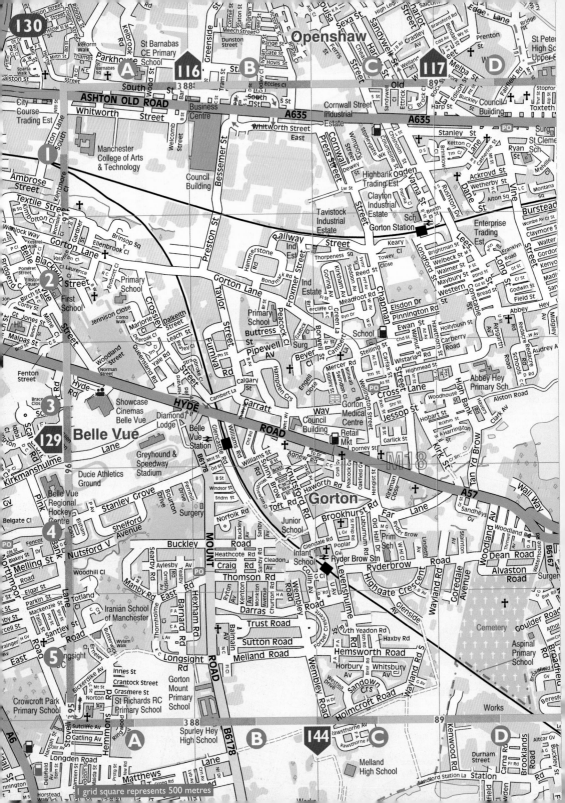

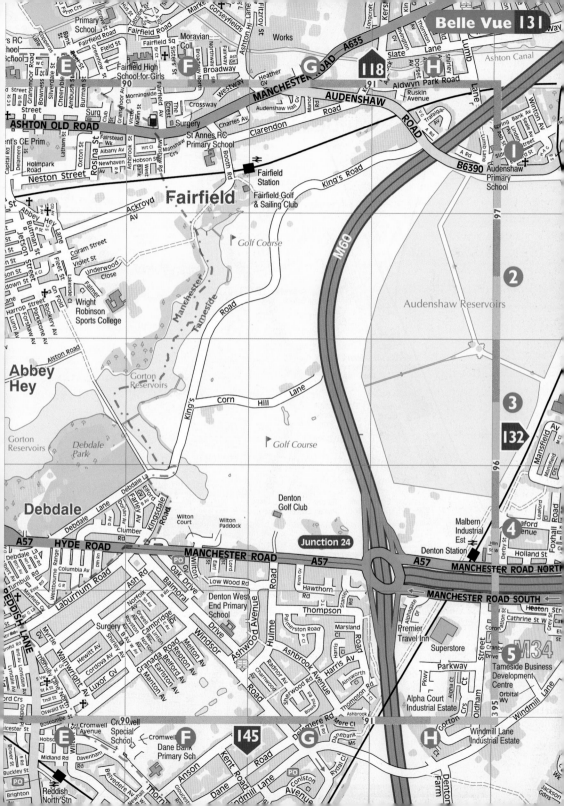

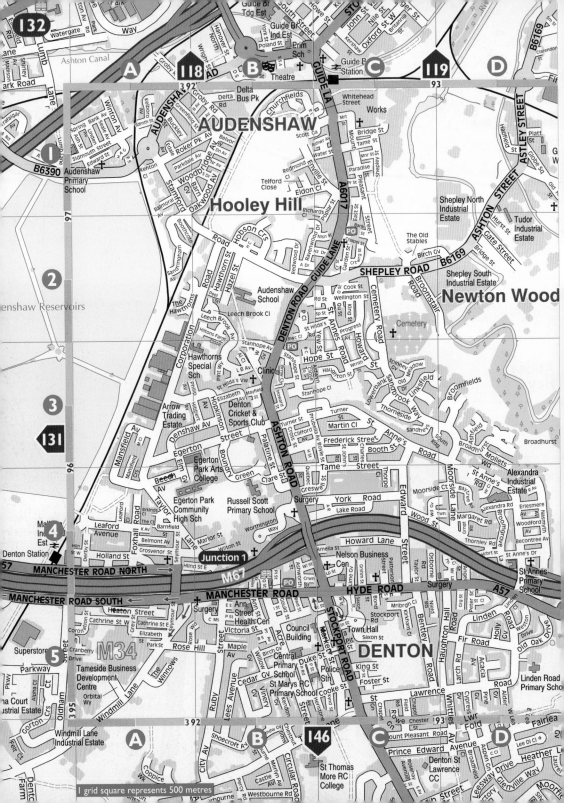

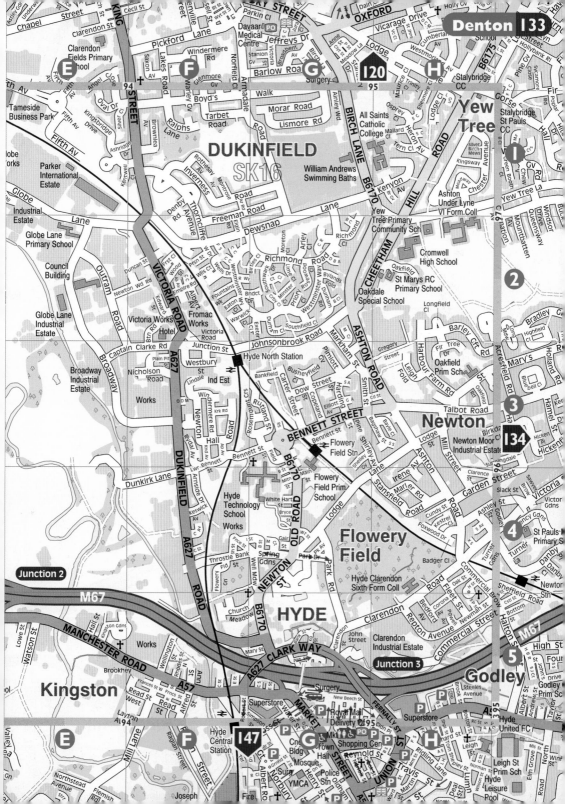

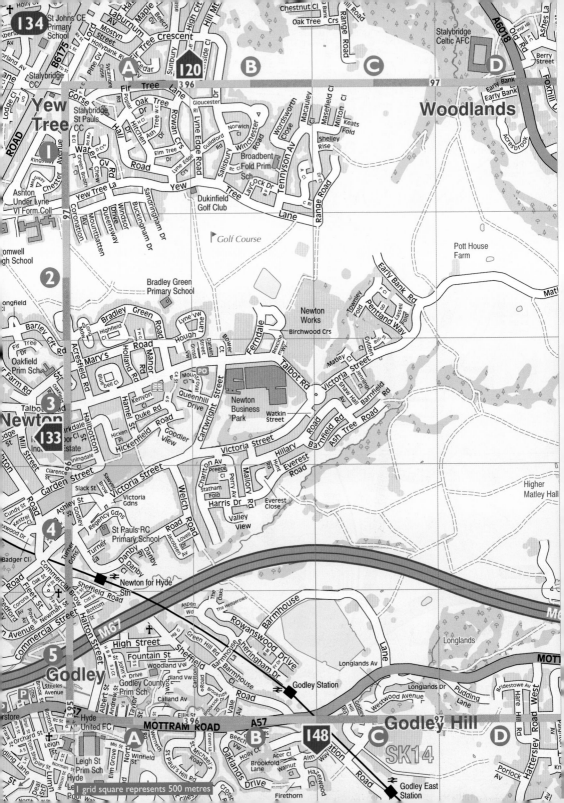

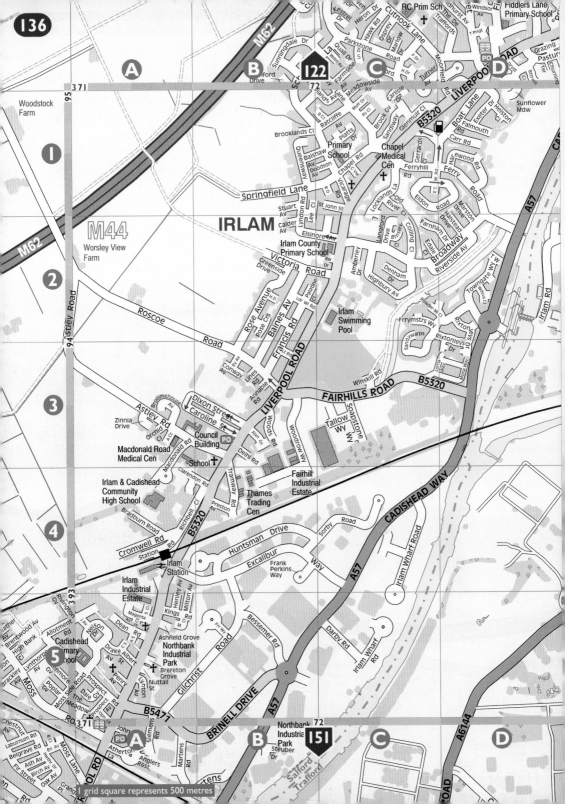

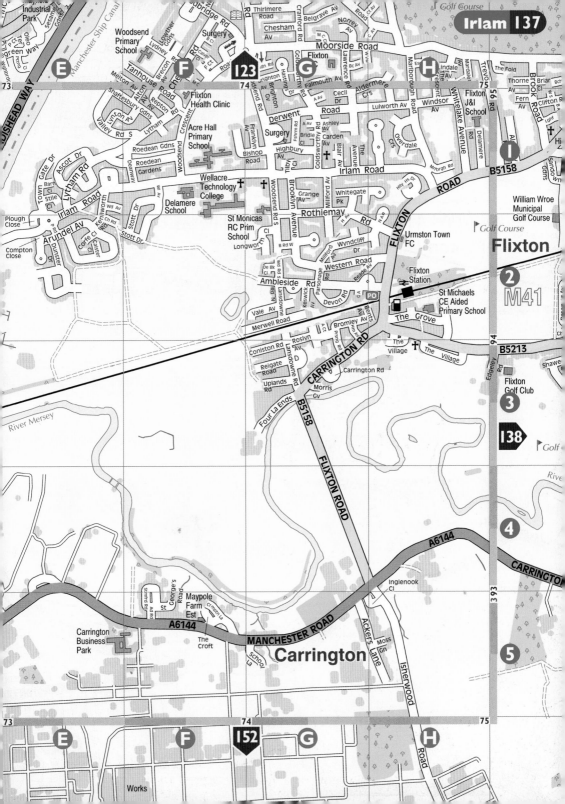

Golf Course

73

E

F

123

74

G

H

75

I

Industrial Park

Manchester Ship Canal

Woodsend Primary School

Surgery

Thirlmere Road

Chesham Av

Cranford Rd

Belgrave Av

Norley Av

Moorside Road

Flixton

Lawrence Rd

Falmouth Av

Aldermere Crs

Flixton J&I School

Windsor Av

Whitelake Avenue

Marlborough Road

Indale Av

Thorne Av

The Fold

Brook Rd

Briar Av

Clifton Av

Flixton Health Clinic

Derwent Road

Surgery

Cecil Av

Ashley Av

Carden Av

Lulworth Av

Overdale Crs

Delamere

I
B5158

Acre Hall Primary School

Roedean Gdns

Roedean Gardens

Franklyn Av

Bishop Road

Highbury Av

Blair Rd

Irlam Road

ROAD

Hilly Hs Gv

FLIXTON

William Wroe Municipal Golf Course

Wellacre Technology College

Delamere School

Brooklyn Av

Grange Av

Whitegate Pk

Rothiemay Rd

Golf Course

Flixton

St Monicas RC Prim School

Longworm

Milford Rd

Wyndcliff Dr

Urmston Town FC

Western Road

Reade Av

Parsonage

Flixton Station

St Michaels CE Aided Primary School

M41

Ambleside

Keswick Av

Lansdowne

Devon Rd

PO

2

Plough Close

Arundel Av

Compton Close

Irlam Road

Stott Dr

Corfe Cl

Merwell Road

Vale Av

Bromley Rd

The Grove

The Village

The Village

B5213

Flixton Golf Club

3

Coniston Rd

Roslyn Av

Reigate Road

Lansdowne Rd

Carrington Rd

Morris Gv

CARRINGTON RD

I 38

Golf

Four La Ends

Uplands Rd

B5158

FLIXTON ROAD

River Mersey

River

4

A6144

CARRINGTON

Inglenook Cl

5

Carrington Business Park

Maypole Farm Est

The Croft

A6144

MANCHESTER ROAD

Carrington

Ackers Lane

Isherwood Road

73

E

74

F

I52

G

75

H

Works

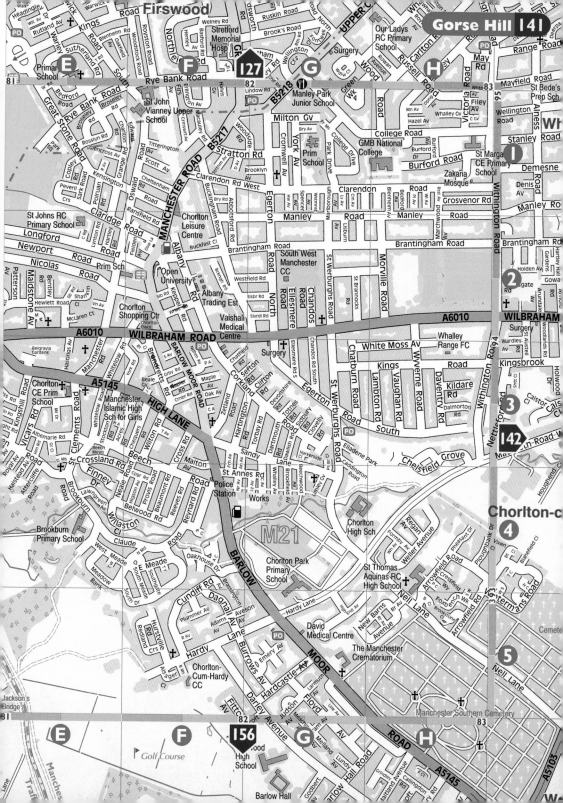

I grid square represents 500 metres

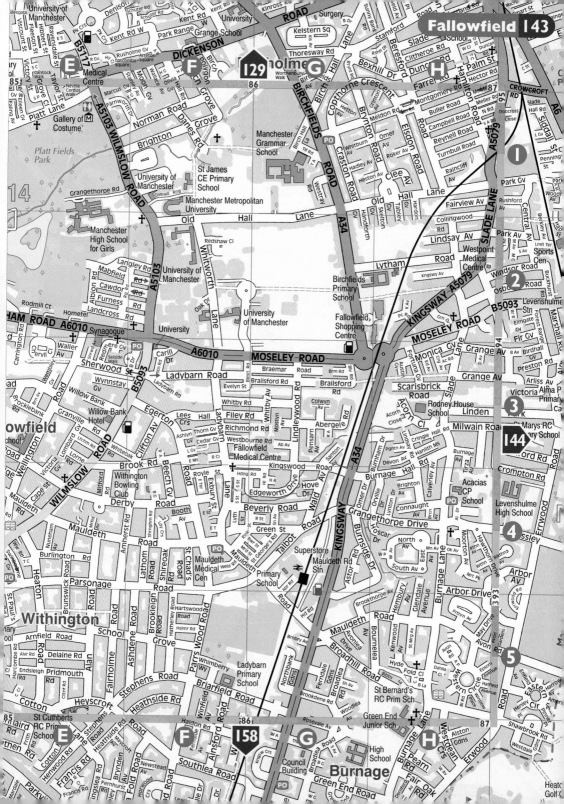

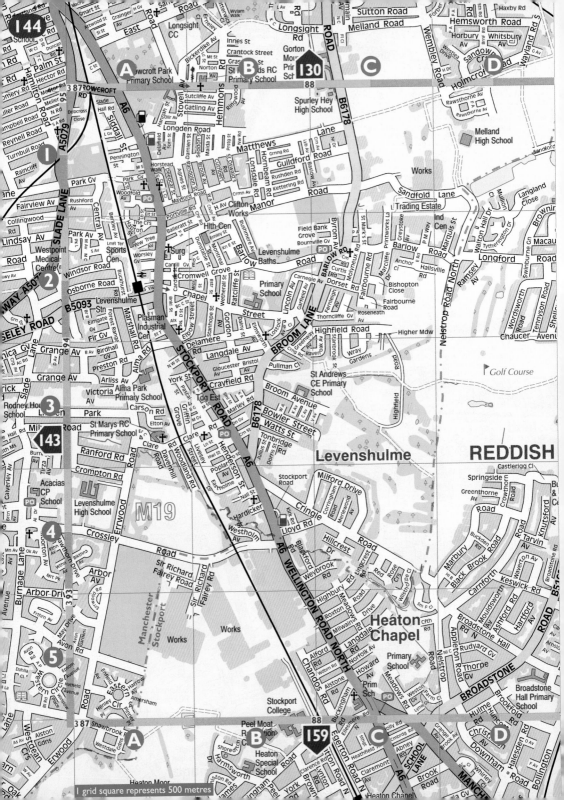

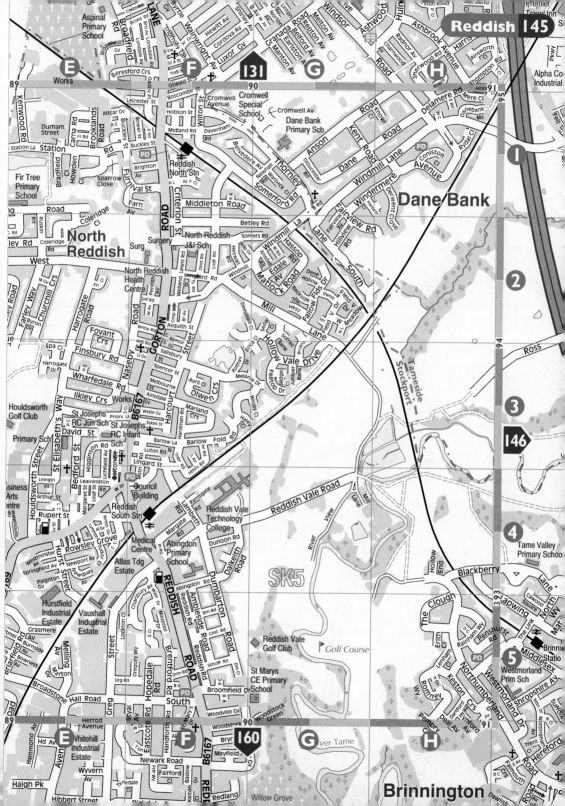

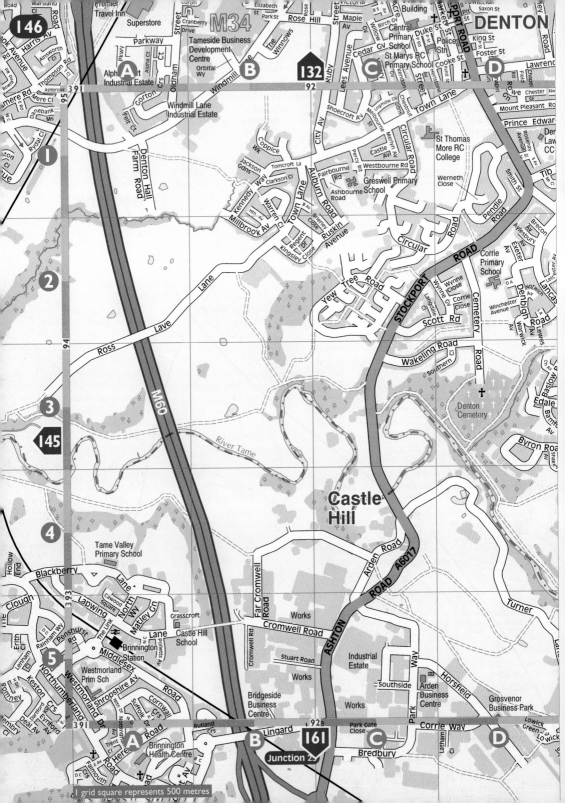

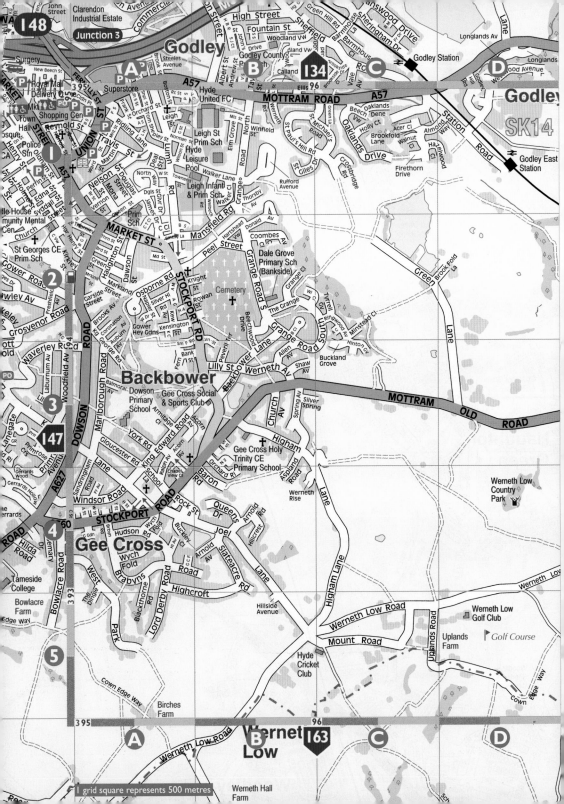

1 grid square represents 500 metres

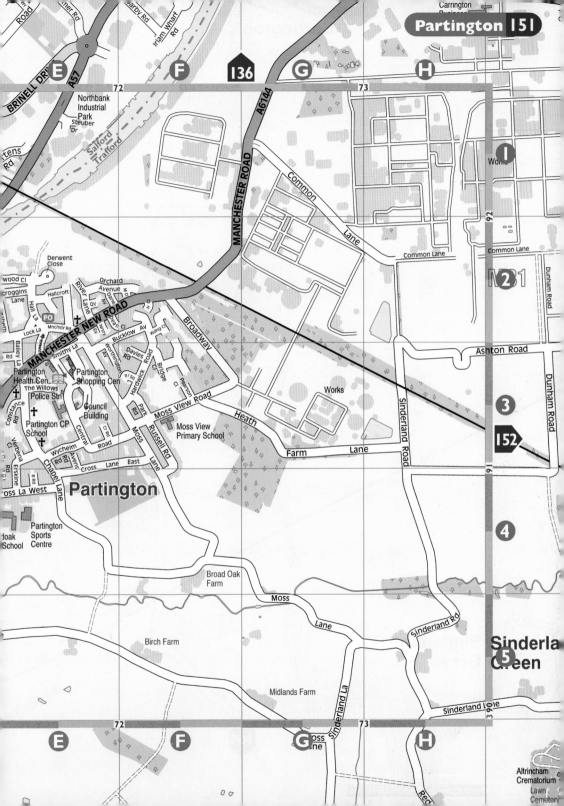

1 grid square represents 500 metres

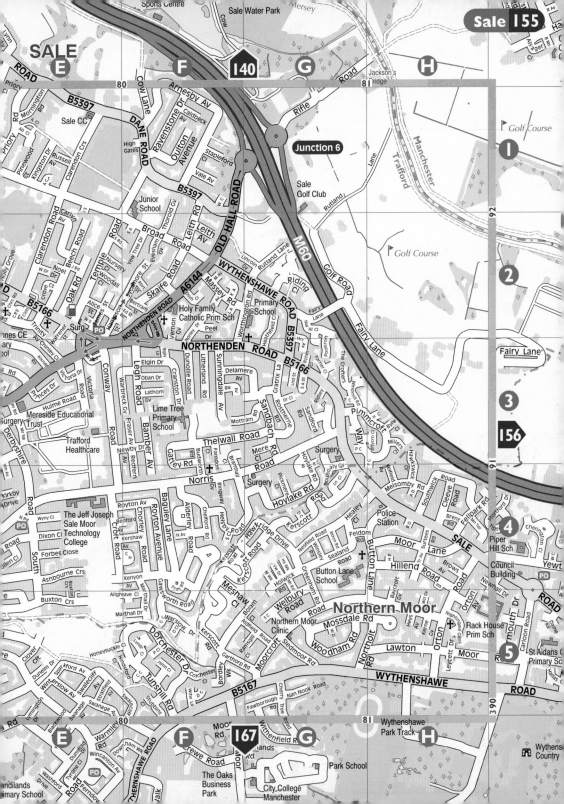

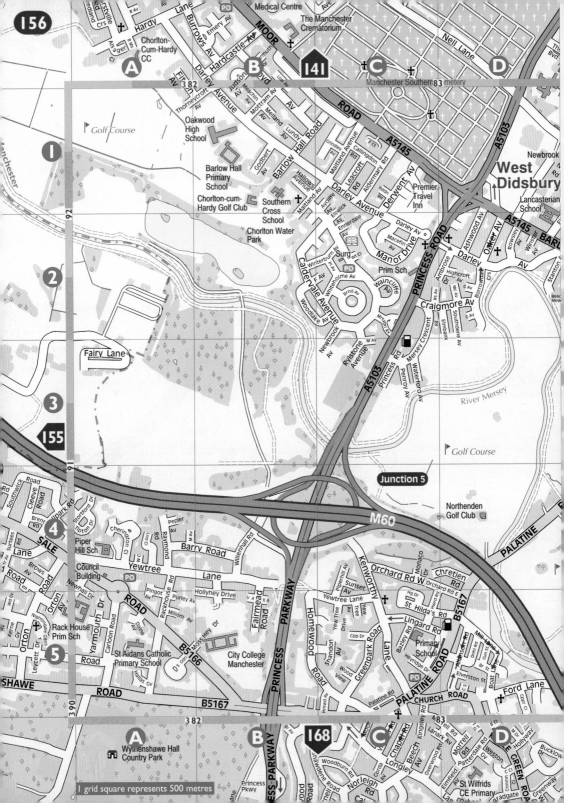

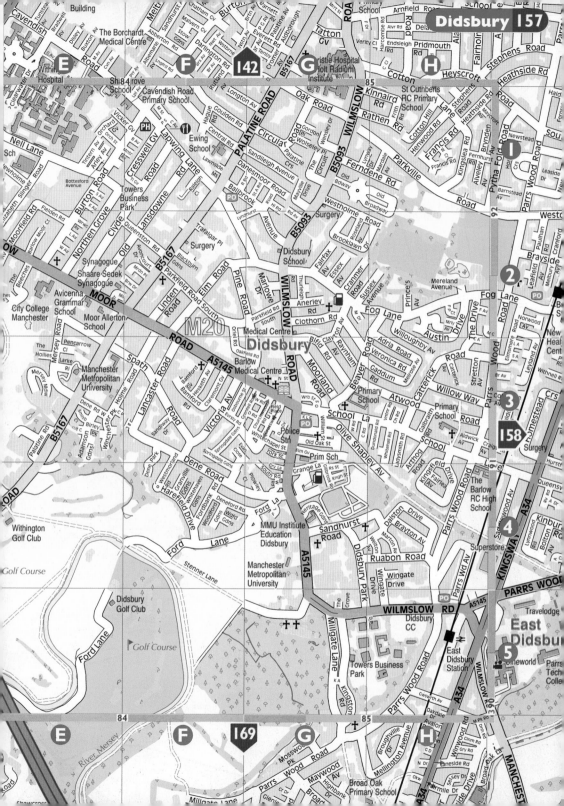

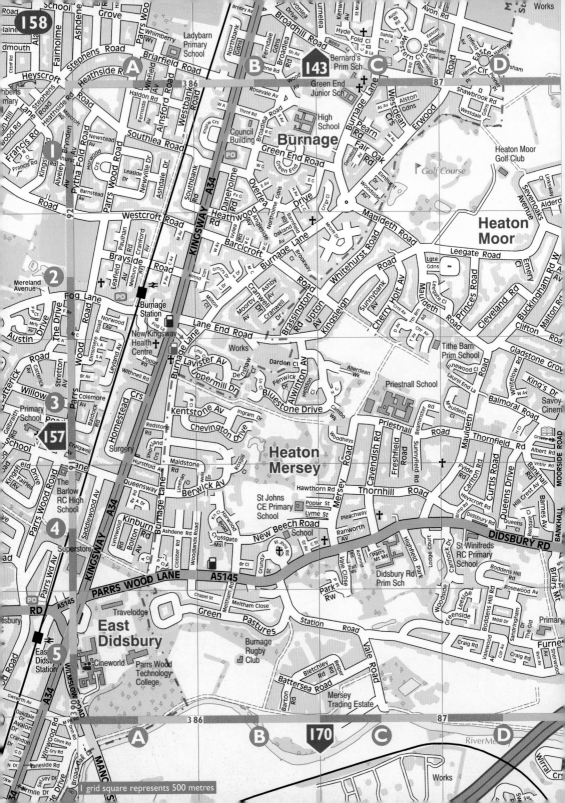

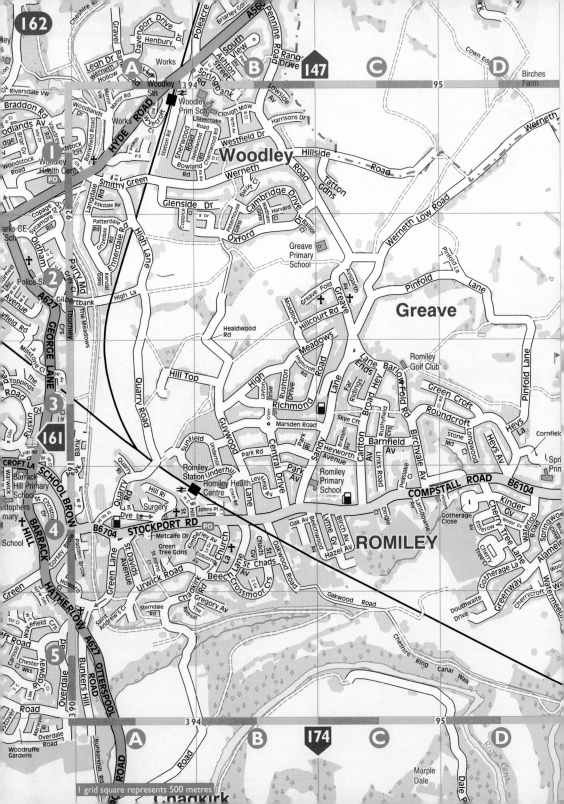

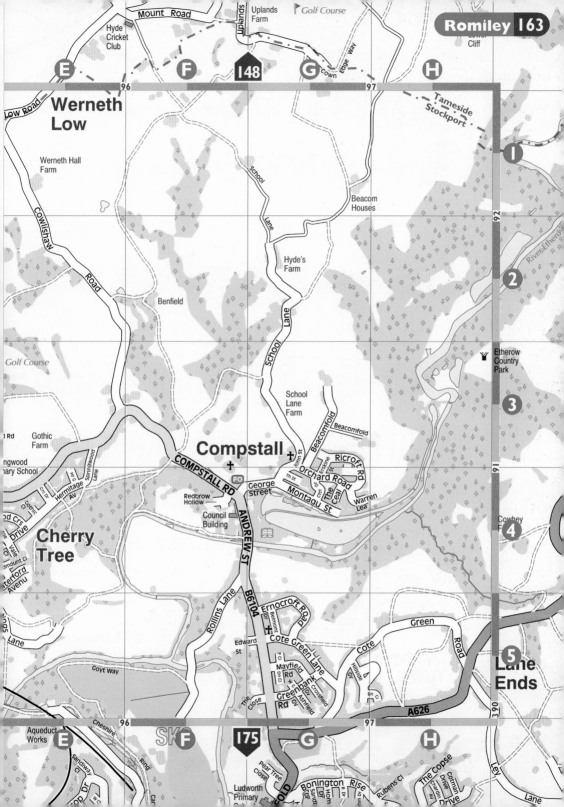

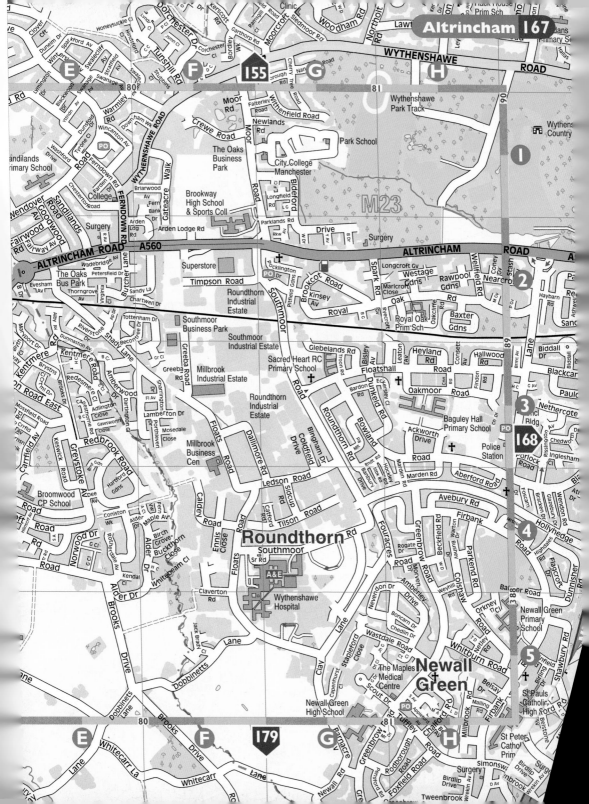

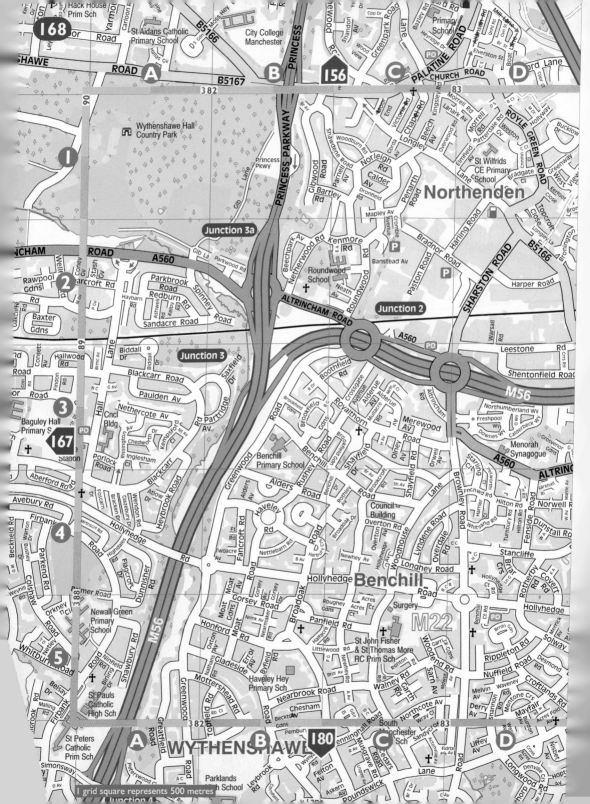

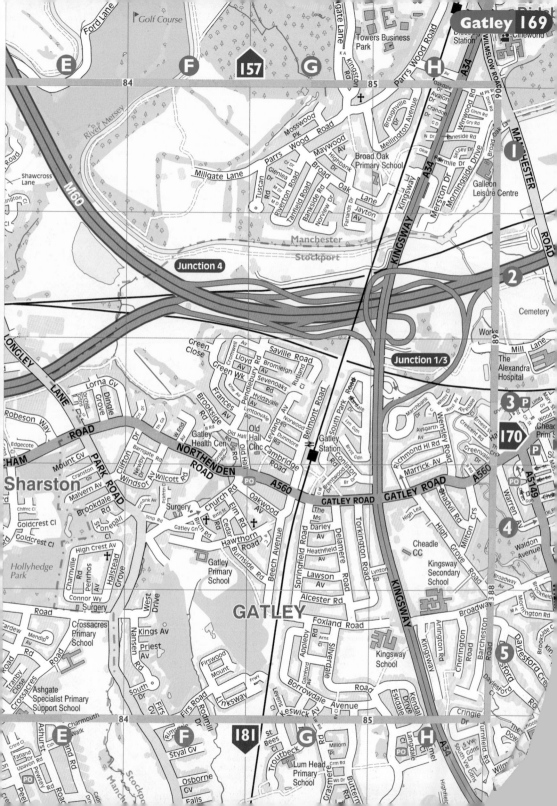

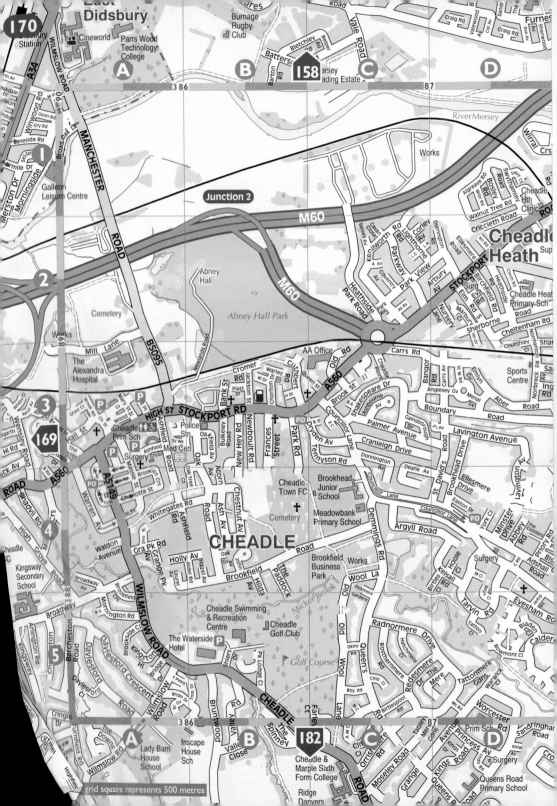

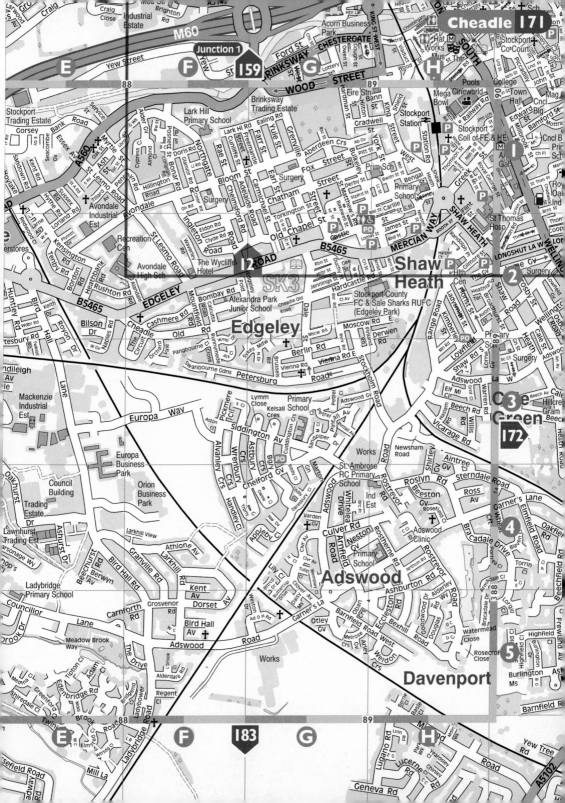

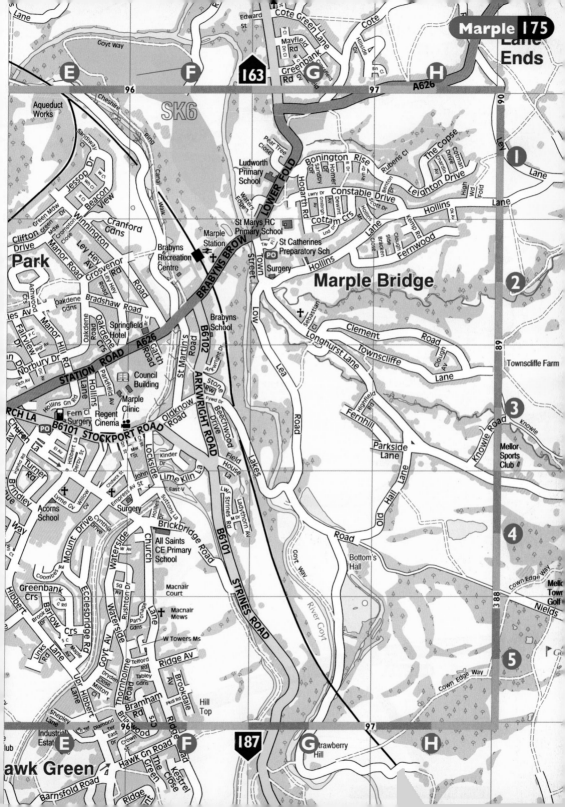

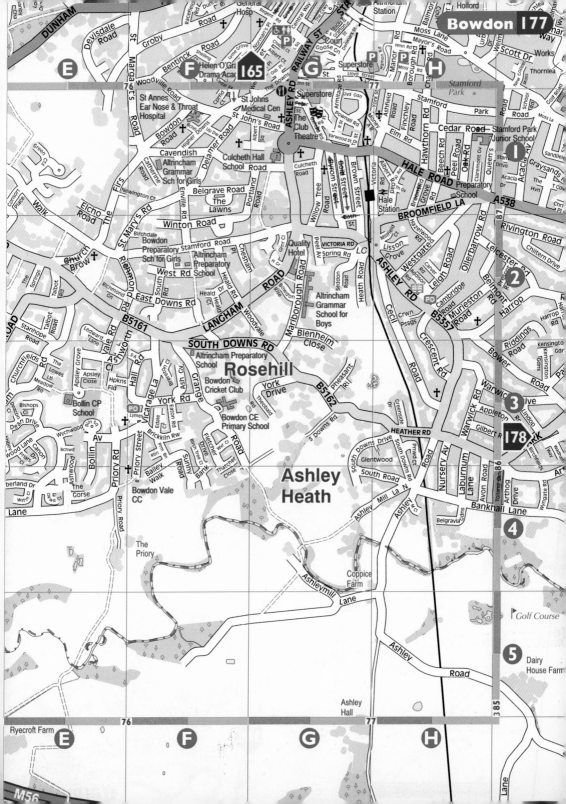

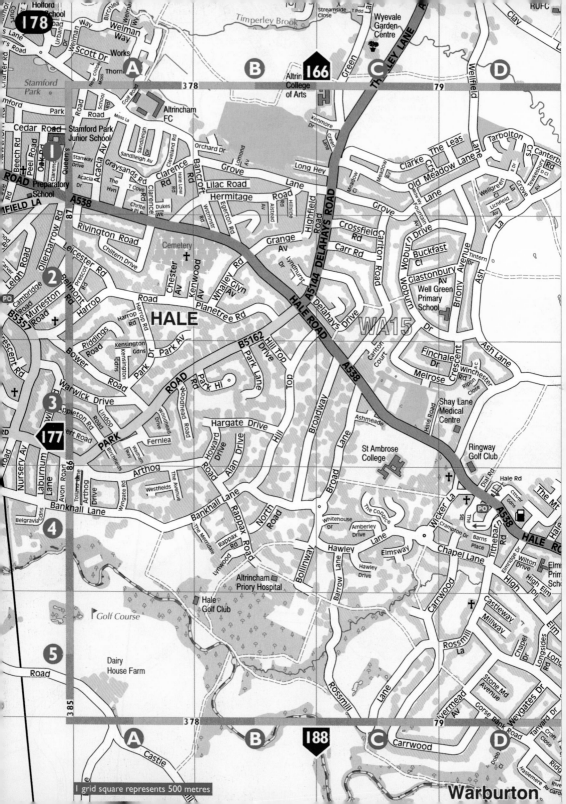

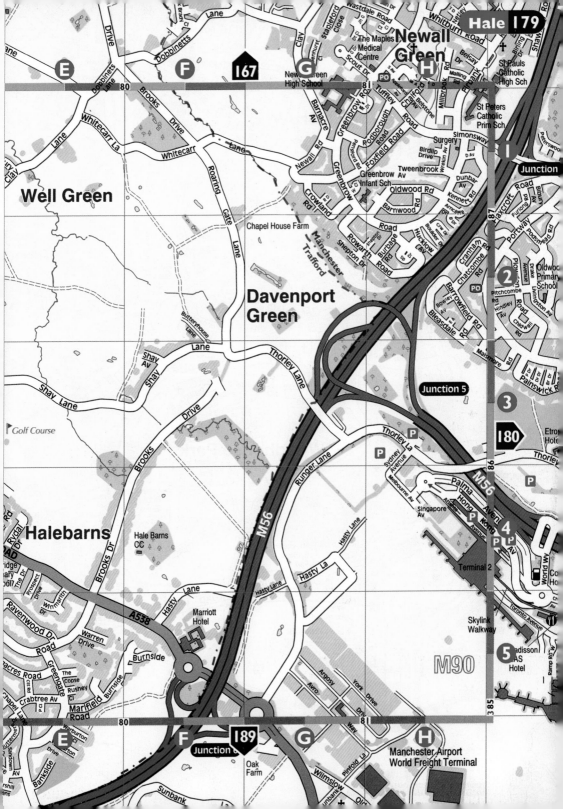

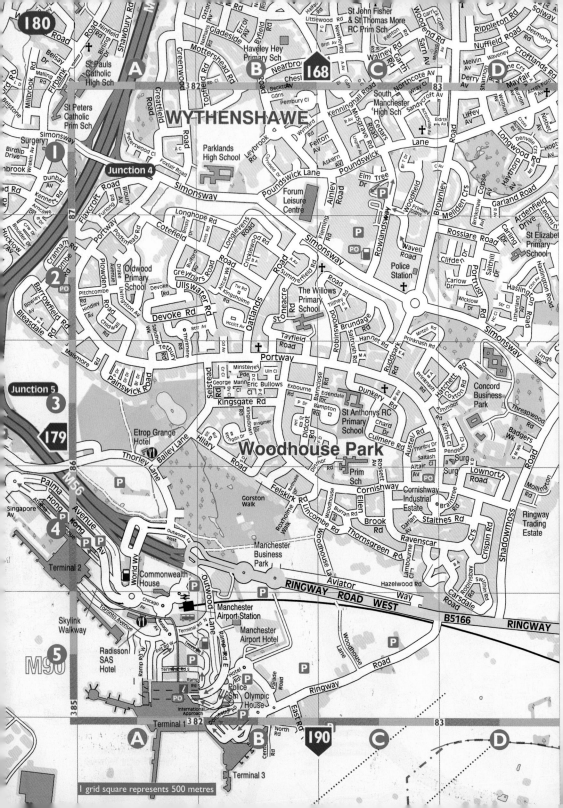

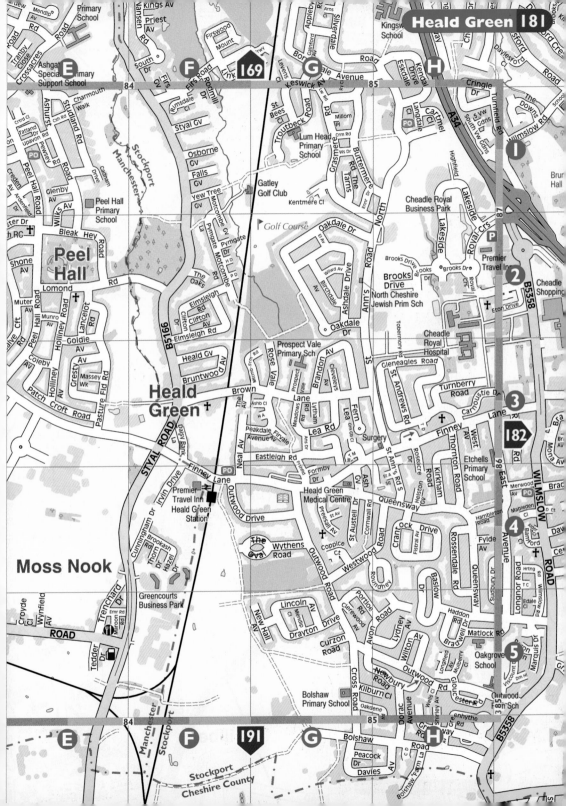

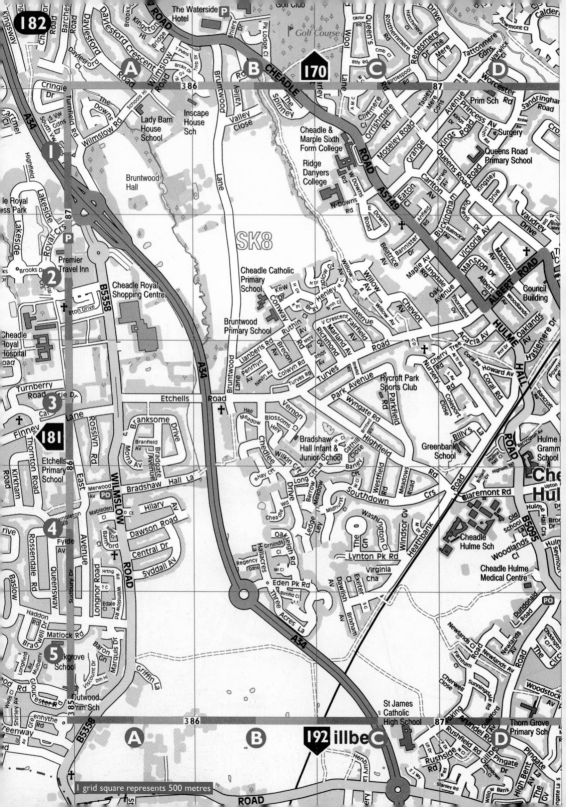

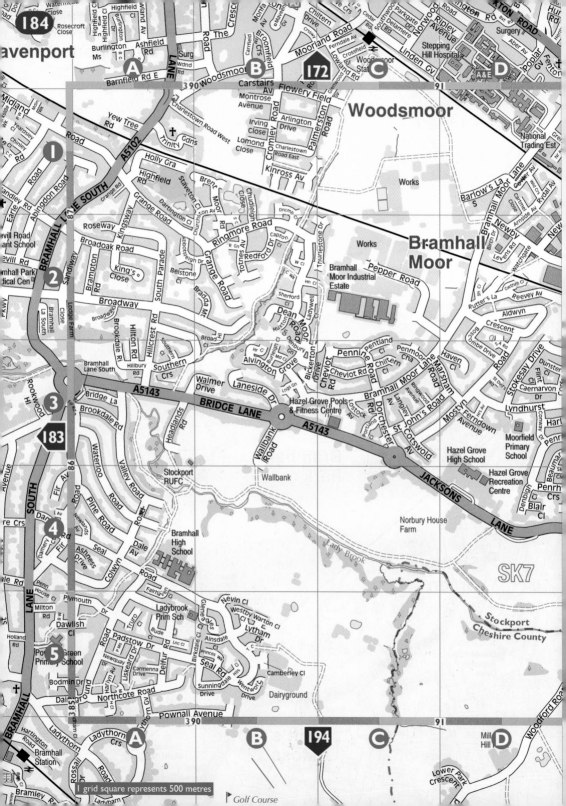

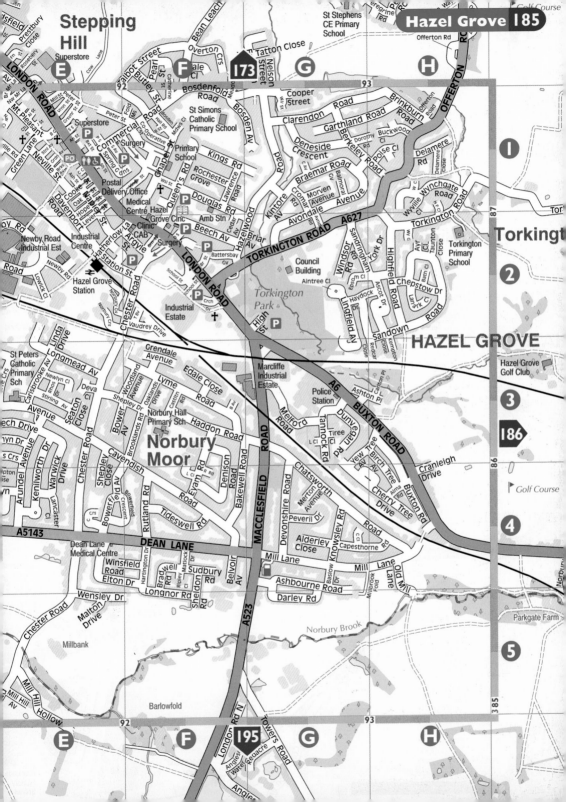

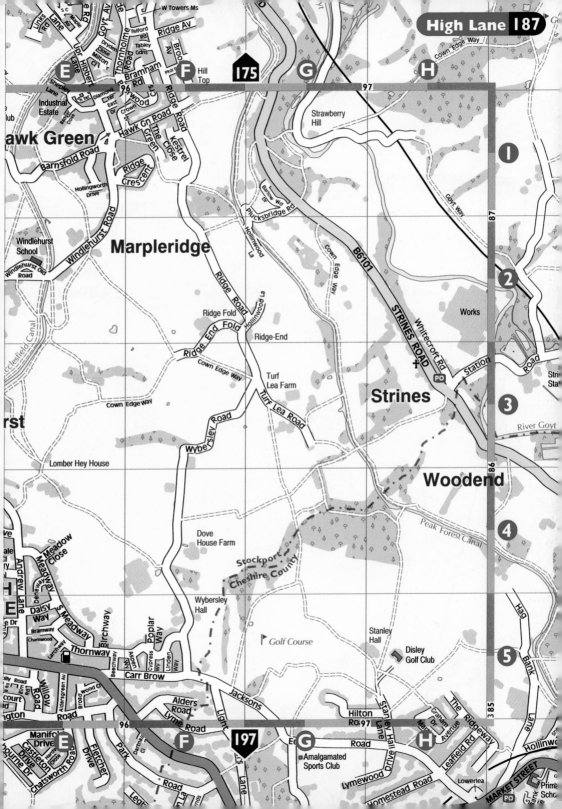

188

178

Road

Dairy
House Farm

A

B

C

D

3 78

85

1

Castle

Mill

Lane

M56

Warburton
Green

M56

Lane

Cow

Rossmill La

Rossmill

Roermead
Av

Corse Bank Road

79

Carrwood

Dobb Hedge

Haslemere Av

River Garden

Chapel
Dr

Longsides
Rd

Longs

Weygates Dr

Tanyard
Croft

stone
Aven

Tanyard Dr

Ridg

Close

Ashley
Station

Hough Green

Tanyard
Farm

Tanyard La

Castle Mill Lane

Thorns
Green

2

Back Lane

Back
Lane Farm

Back Lane

84

ough
Green
Farm

Castle Mill Lane

Brickhill Lane

Mead

3

Road

Lower House
Farm

Middle House

Mobberley

4

3 83

Lower House
Farm

Mobberley

5

Road

Breach

House

Blackshaw Heys
Farm

Stock-in-Hey
Farm

Kell House
Farm

84

Breach House
Farm

Lane

ley Brook

A

B

C

D

3 78

79

Pepp

M90

Hotel

E Marlfield
Road

F

179

G

H

Junction 6

Manchester Airport
World Freight Terminal

Oak
Farm

Sunbank Lane

WILMSLOW ROAD

Wilmslow Old Road

Pinfold La

†

I

Manc
Intern
Airpor

2

Aviation
Viewing
Park

Halebank
Farm

Sunbank Lane

Cloughbank
Farm

River Bollin

A538

Castle
Mill Farm

3

190

Mill Lane

Castle Mill Lane

owlands

4

Altrincham Road

Holiday
Inn

5

Bollin House
Farm

E

F

G

H

Wood Lane

Wood Farm

190
M90

Radisson SAS Hotel

Airport Hotel

P

Woodhouse Lane

P

A

Terminal Rd N

PO

Ramp Rd

Police Stn

B

Parade Road

East Rd

180

Road

C

D

85

Terminal 1

International A 3 82

North Rd

Central Rd

P

83

1

Manchester International Airport

iation ewing rk

2

84

Moss

Wilkins Lane

Lane

Holly

3

Manchester
Cheshire County

Moss
Lane

Norcliffe Hall

Styal Primary School

189

Oversley Farm

River Bollin

Styal Country Park NT

✝

4

Altrincham Road

83

Holiday Inn

ALTRINCHAM ROAD

Green Road

A538

M

5

Dooley's La

Nansmoss Lane

Quarr

382

83

A

B Morley

C

198

D

Wood Farm

Morley

1 grid square represents 500 metres

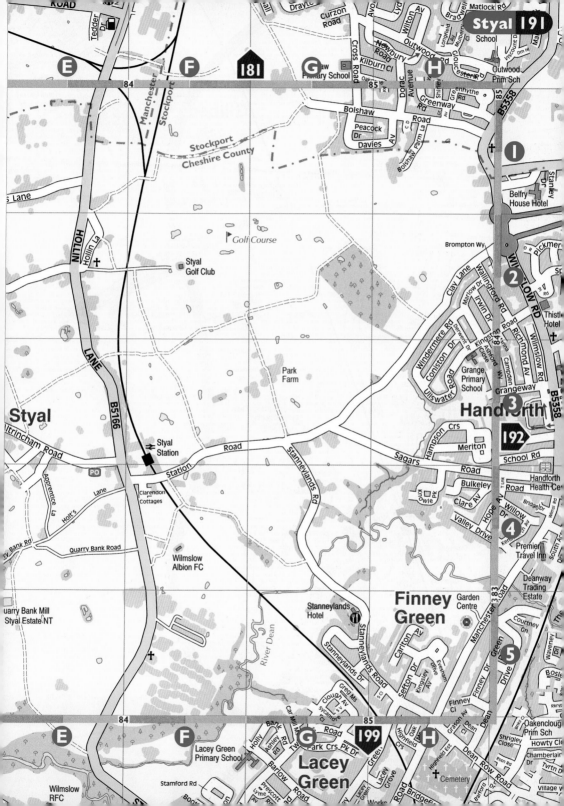

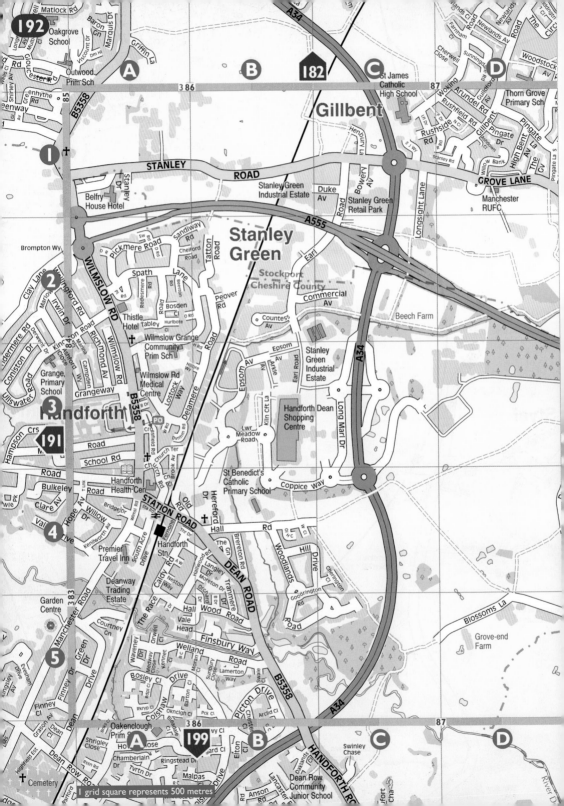

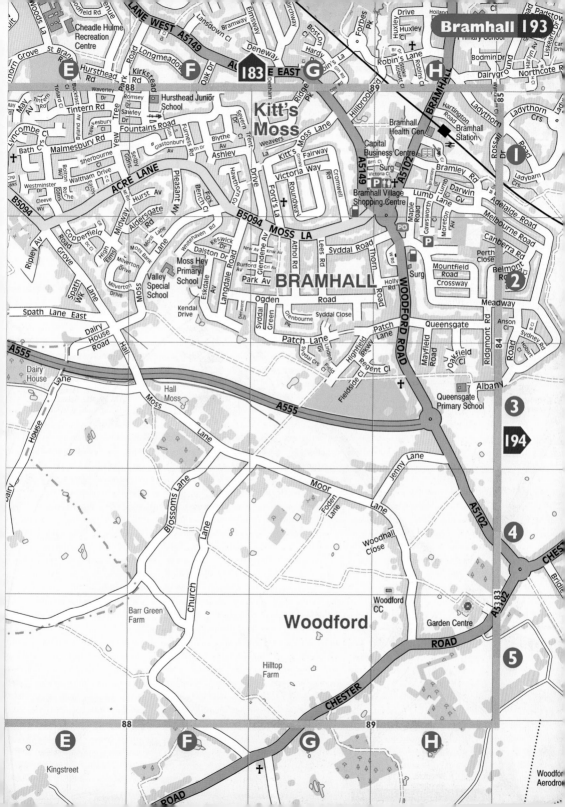

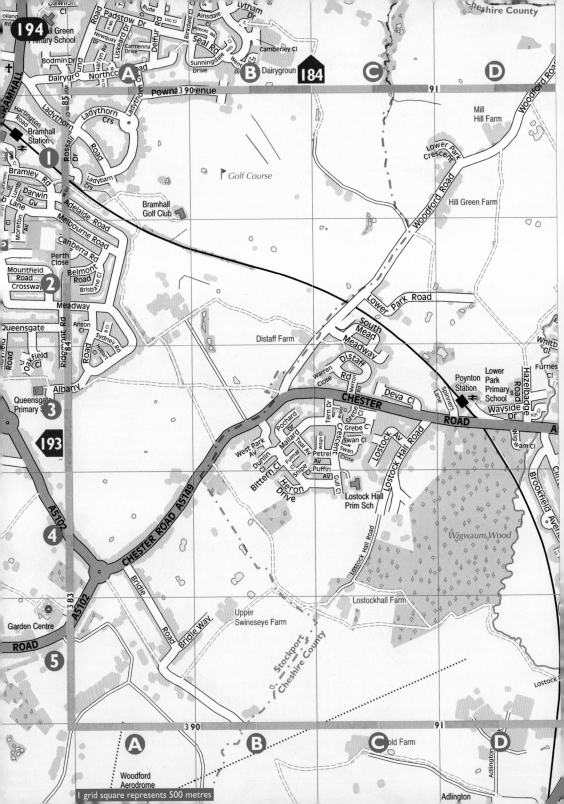

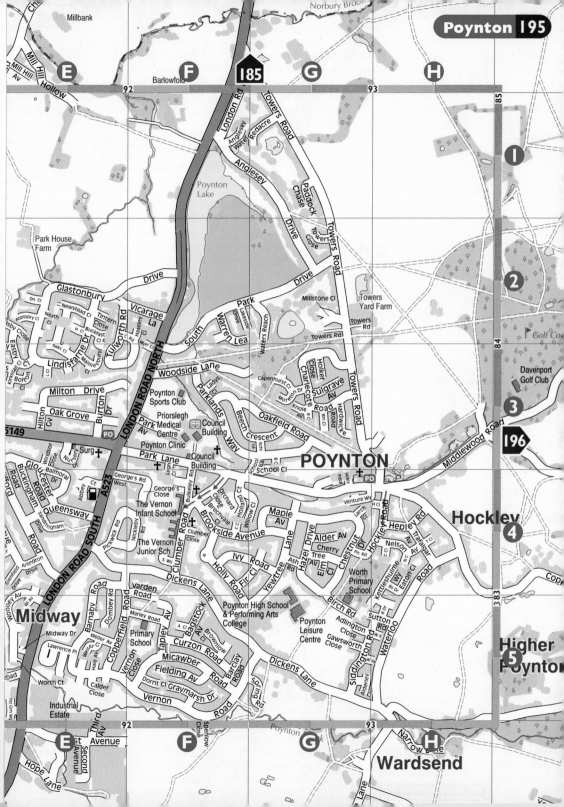

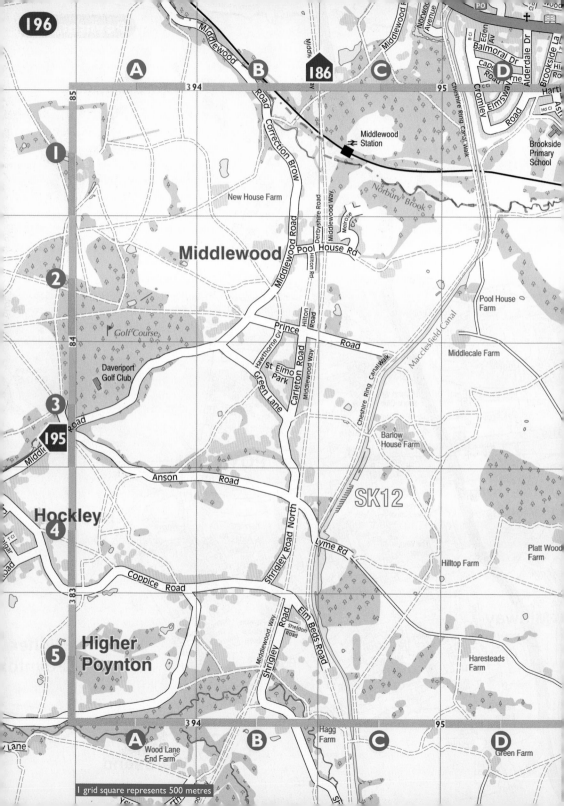

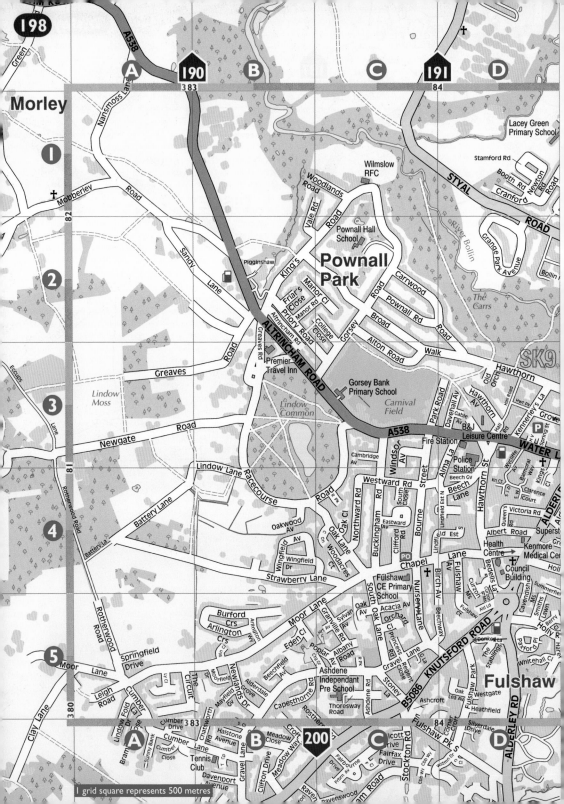

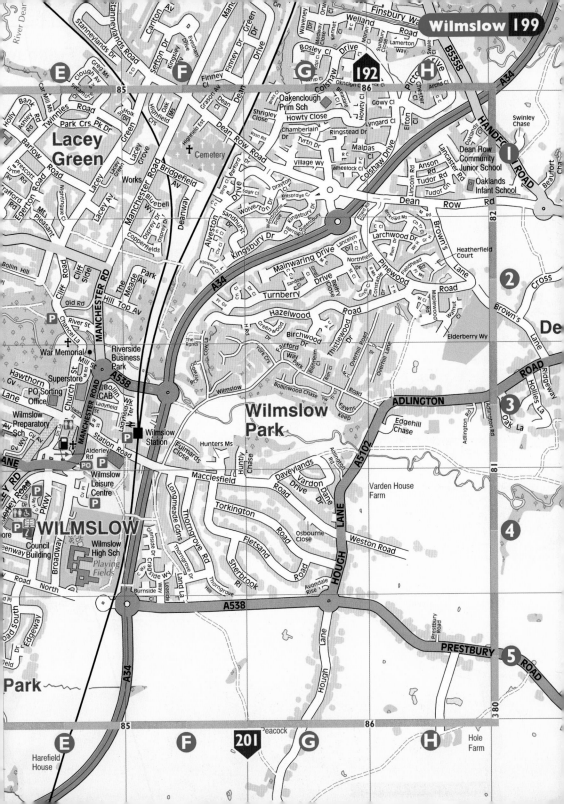

Park

E   **F**   199   **G**   **H**

I

2

3

4

5

85   86   80

79

378

Peacock

Hole Farm

Harefield House

Chonar Farm

Hough Green Farm

Harden Park

Heyes Lane

Brook Farm

Hough Lane

Lower Hou

Beech Close
Beech Road
The Circuit
Elm Crescent
Maple
Oakfield Close
Heywood Rd
Oakfield Rd
Annis Rd
Crescent Rd
Heywood Rd
Fairbourne Av
Elm Road

Davey Lane
Heyes Lane

Moss   Road

Moss Rose
Duke Street
Beaufort Close
Marlborough Avenue
Devonshire Drive
Moss Lane
Orchard Green
Alderley Edge CC

ALDERLEY EDGE

Hough

Mottram Road

Findlow Farm

Mottram Road
Squirrel's Jump
Swiss Hill
Woodbrook
Underwood Road
Tempest Road
Croston Cl

B5087
Alderley Edge Hotel
Oatlands

MACCLESFIELD ROAD

Alderley Edge

Clo
Far

Roan Way
Beechfield Road
Beechfield Road
Whitebarn Road

85   86

E   **F**   **G**   **H**

The Wizard

Edge House Farm

Artists Lane

Abbey Hey ... 131 E3
Acre ... 76 A3
Adswood ... 171 G4
Affetside ... 25 E3
Ainsworth ... 36 C5
Alder Forest ... 110 A1
Alderley Edge ... 201 F3
Alkrington Garden Village ... 88 D1
Alt ... 92 C4
Alt Hill ... 107 F2
Altrincham ... 166 A4
Ancoats ... 7 K4
Arden Park ... 181 E2
Ardwick ... 128 D1
Ashley Heath ... 177 G4
Ashton-under-Lyne ... 118 D2
Ashton Upon Mersey ... 139 F5
Astley Bridge ... 33 H2
Audenshaw ... 132 B1
Austerlands ... 78 A4
Backbower ... 148 A3
Bagslate Moor ... 28 C3
Balderstone ... 43 G3
Baldingstone ... 27 F2
Bamford ... 28 A4
Bank Lane ... 17 E1
Bank Top ... 34 B1
Bardsley ... 106 D1
Barrow Bridge ... 32 D2
Barton Upon Irwell ... 111 E5
Belfield ... 31 E4
Belle Vue ... 130 A3
Benchill ... 168 C4
Bentgate ... 44 C5
Besses o' th' Barn ... 69 G5
Beswick ... 116 A4
Birch ... 55 H5
Blackford Bridge ... 53 G3
Black Lane ... 52 A5
Blackley ... 103 F1
Bolholt ... 37 F2
Bolton ... 3 G5
Boothstown ... 96 B4
Bowdon ... 176 C3
Bowgreen ... 176 D3
Bowlee ... 71 F5
Bradford ... 116 A3
Bradley Fold ... 51 F2
Bradshaw ... 23 H5
Bramhall ... 193 G2
Bramhall Moor ... 184 C2
Bramhall Park ... 183 F3
Bredbury ... 161 F5
Bredbury Green ... 161 H4
Breightmet ... 50 D1
Brinnington ... 160 C1
Broadbottom ... 171 G4
Broadfield ... 40 C5
Broadhalgh ... 28 C4
Broadheath ... 165 F2
Broadley ... 18 B3
Broadoak Park ... 98 B5
Bromley Cross ... 23 H1
Brook Bottom ... 95 F5
Brooklands ... 154 C4
Brooksbottoms ... 16 D5
Broughton Park ... 101 G1
Brownlow Fold ... 33 F5
Brunswick ... 128 C2
Brushes ... 121 H2
Buckley ... 19 F5
Buckton Vale ... 109 F5
Buersil Head ... 43 H5
Burnage ... 158 B1
Burnden ... 49 F5
Burnedge ... 44 B5
Bury ... 4 C3
Busk ... 8 A1
Cadishead ... 150 B2
Caldermoor ... 20 C2
Cale Green ... 172 A3
Captain Fold ... 41 F3
Carr ... 16 C1
Carrbrook ... 109 H5
Carrington ... 137 C5
Carrington Moss ... 152 C5
Castlefield ... 6 A7
Castle Hill ... 146 C4
Castleton ... 42 B4
Chadderton ... 73 H5
Chadderton Fold ... 74 A2
Chadkirk ... 174 A1
Chapel Field ... 68 D3
Charlestown ... 88 D4
Charlestown ... 113 G1
Cheadle ... 170 B4
Cheadle Heath ... 170 D2
Cheadle Hulme ... 182 D4
Cheetham Hill ... 102 C4
Chequerbent ... 62 D5
Cherry Tree ... 163 E4
Chesham ... 38 D1
Chew Moor ... 46 D5
Choriton-cum-Hardy ... 141 H4
Cinder Hill ... 67 G4
Clarksfield ... 76 C5
Clayton ... 116 D2
Clifton ... 83 H4
Clifton Green ... 84 C5
Clifton Junction ... 84 D4
Clough ... 20 D1
Clough ... 60 C3
Collyhurst ... 103 E4
Compstall ... 163 F3
Copley ... 121 F5
Copster Hill ... 91 F5
Cox Green ... 23 E2
Crimble ... 41 G2
Crofts Bank ... 124 B4
Crompton Fold ... 45 F5
Crowhill ... 119 E1
Crumpsall ... 102 A1
Cutgate ... 28 D5
Daisy Nook ... 105 H5
Dales Brow ... 98 C4
Dane Bank ... 145 H1
Darcy Lever ... 50 A4
Darn Hill ... 40 A5
Daubhill ... 48 B5
Davenport ... 171 H5
Davenport Green ... 179 G2
Davenport Green ... 200 C2
Davyhulme ... 124 A4
Deane ... 64 A1
Dearnley ... 14 C5
Debdale ... 131 E4
Denton ... 132 C5
Didsbury ... 157 G3
Disley ... 197 G1
Dobcross ... 78 C2
Doffcocker ... 32 D4
Dog Hill ... 60 D2
Droylsden ... 117 F4
Dukinfield ... 133 F1
Dumplington ... 124 B1
Dunham Town ... 164 A5
Dunscar ... 22 C2
Durn ... 21 F3
Eagley ... 22 D4
East Didsbury ... 158 A5
Eccles ... 111 H4
Edge Fold ... 64 B3
Edgeley ... 171 F2
Egerton ... 22 D1
Ellenbrook ... 96 B2
Ellesmere Park ... 111 F1
Elton ... 37 G4
Facit ... 14 D2
Failsworth ... 104 D3
Fairfield ... 39 G3
Fairfield ... 131 F1
Fallowfield ... 142 D3
Farnworth ... 65 G4
Fern Bank ... 121 E4
Fernhill ... 4 D1
Fernhill Gate ... 47 G5
Finney Green ... 191 H5
Firgrove ... 31 F5
Firswood ... 127 E5
Firwood Fold ... 34 D3
Fishpool ... 51 H1
Fitton Hill ... 91 H4
Flixton ... 138 A2
Flowery Field ... 133 G4
Foggbrook ... 173 G2
Four Lane Ends ... 36 C1
Free Town ... 5 K1
Fullwood ... 60 C4
Fulshaw Park ... 198 D5
Gale ... 21 F1
Gatley ... 169 F5
Gee Cross ... 148 A4
Gigg ... 53 H2
Gillbent ... 192 C1
Gilnow ... 2 B6
Glodwick ... 92 A2
Godley ... 133 H5
Godley Hill ... 148 D1
Gorse Hill ... 126 B5
Gorton ... 130 B4
Grains Bar ... 61 F5
Grasscroft ... 78 A1
Gravel Hole ... 94 A1
Great Howarth ... 19 F4
Great Lever ... 65 F1
Great Moor ... 172 D3
Greave ... 162 C2
Greenacres ... 76 C5
Greenfield ... 95 E3
Greengate ... 20 A5
Greenheys ... 80 C2
Greenmount ... 25 H1
Greenside ... 118 A2
Grotton ... 93 G1
Guide Bridge ... 118 D4
Haggate ... 74 D1
Hale ... 178 A2
Halebarns ... 179 E4
Halfway House ... 51 F5
Hall i' th' Wood ... 34 B2
Halliwell ... 33 H3
Handforth ... 191 H5
Harden Park ... 201 E2
Harper Green ... 65 G3
Harpurhey ... 103 F3
Hartshead Green ... 108 B2
Hartshead Pike ... 108 A1
Harwood ... 35 H5
Harwood Lee ... 35 F1
Hathershaw ... 91 G4
Hattersley ... 149 F1
Haugh ... 45 F3
Haughton Green ... 147 E3
Hawk Green ... 186 D1
Hazel Grove ... 185 H5
Hazelhurst ... 16 A4
Hazelhurst ... 98 A4
Hazelhurst ... 108 B5
Heady Hill ... 40 B4
Heald Green ... 181 F3
Healds Green ... 74 A1
Healey ... 18 D4
Heap Bridge ... 39 F5
Heaton ... 47 H1
Heaton Chapel ... 144 C5
Heaton Mersey ... 158 B3
Heaton Moor ... 158 D2
Heaton Norris ... 12 A1
Heaviley ... 172 B2
Heyheads ... 109 E3
Heyrod ... 121 E1
Heyside ... 59 H5
Heywood ... 40 D5
Higginshaw ... 75 G2
High Crompton ... 59 H1
Higher Blackley ... 87 H5
Higher Boarshaw ... 73 E1
Higher Broughton ... 101 G4
Higher Poynton ... 196 A5
Higher Woodhill ... 38 A1
Highfield ... 65 E5
High Lane ... 186 D5
Hill Top ... 82 A3
Hilton Park ... 85 H5
Hockley ... 195 H4
Holcombe ... 16 B3
Holcombe Brook ... 16 A5
Holden End ... 75 E1
Hollins ... 54 A4
Hollins ... 64 C4
Hollins ... 72 C1
Hollinwood ... 105 F1
Holts ... 92 D3
Honresfeld ... 21 G2
Hooley Bridge ... 40 D1
Hooley Brow ... 41 E2
Hooley Hill ... 132 B1
Horrocks Fold ... 22 B4
Hough ... 201 G4
Hulme ... 127 H2
Hunger Hill ... 63 E1
Hurst ... 107 G5
Hurstead ... 19 H4
Hyde ... 133 G5
Irlam ... 136 B2
Irlams o' th' Height ... 99 H5
Jericho ... 39 H2
Johnson Fold ... 32 A3
Jubilee ... 45 E4
Kearsley ... 83 E1
Kersal ... 101 E1
Kingston ... 133 E5
Kirkhams ... 86 A1
Kirkholt ... 42 D5
Kirklees ... 26 C4
Kitt's Moss ... 193 G1
Knott Lanes ... 106 C3
Lacey Green ... 199 E1
Lady House ... 44 B2
Langley ... 71 H1
Lees ... 92 D1
Levenshulme ... 144 C3
Lever-Edge ... 64 C2
Ley Hey Park ... 174 D1
Limefield ... 27 G5
Limehurst ... 106 D4
Lime Side ... 106 A1
Linnyshaw ... 82 B4
Little Bolton ... 112 A3
Littleborough ... 21 E5
Little Clegg ... 31 F1
Little Hulton ... 81 E3
Little Lever ... 51 E5
Little Moor ... 173 E1
Littlemoss ... 118 B1
Long Sight ... 75 F2
Longsight ... 129 G3
Lostock Junction ... 47 E4
Low Compton ... 59 F3
Lower Bredbury ... 160 D4
Lower Broughton ... 113 H1
Lower Kersal ... 100 D4
Lower Place ... 43 H2
Luzley ... 108 C3
Luzley Brook ... 59 G6
Lydgate ... 93 H2
Makants ... 80 D5
Manchester ... 6 E3
Markland Hill ... 47 F1
Marland ... 42 A1
Marple ... 174 D5
Marple Bridge ... 175 G2
Marpleridge ... 187 F2
Matley ... 135 G2
Mickhurst ... 109 F1
Middleton ... 72 A3
Middlewood ... 196 A2
Midway ... 195 G5
Miles Platting ... 115 G2
Millbrook ... 121 G1
Millgate ... 14 B1
Mill Hill ... 3 H3
Milnrow ... 31 H5
Monton ... 111 E2
Moorclose ... 73 F4
Moorhey ... 92 A1
Mooriside ... 76 D1
Moorside ... 98 C3
Moses Gate ... 65 H2
Mosley Common ... 96 B3
Mossley ... 94 A5
Mossley Brow ... 108 D1
Moss Nook ... 181 E4
Moss Side ... 128 A4
Moston ... 104 A1
Mottram in Longdendale ... 135 G4
Mottram Rise ... 135 F1
Mumps ... 9 H2
Nangreaves ... 17 F5
Newall Green ... 167 H5
Newbold ... 11 K6
New Bury ... 65 F5
New Delph ... 78 D1
Newhey ... 44 D2
New Moston ... 104 B2
Newton ... 133 H5
Newton Heath ... 103 H5
Newton Wood ... 132 D2
Newtown ... 98 D1
Nob End ... 90 B5
Nob End ... 66 D2
Norbury Moor ... 185 F3
Norden ... 28 A2
Northenden ... 168 C1
Northern Moor ... 155 G5
North Reddish ... 145 E2
Nuttall ... 16 C4
Oak Bank ... 69 H5
Offerton ... 173 F2
Offerton Green ... 173 H5
Oldfield Brow ... 165 E4
Oldham ... 9 J5
Oldham Edge ... 75 G3
Old Tame ... 61 G1
Old Trafford ... 127 E5
Openshaw ... 116 D5
Ordsall ... 127 E1
Outwood ... 68 B4
Over Hulton ... 63 H5
Park Bridge ... 92 B5
Partington ... 151 E4
Patricroft ... 110 D3
Peel Green ... 110 A5
Peel Hall ... 181 E2
Pendlebury ... 99 H3
Pendleton ... 113 F2
Pinhole ... 5 J5
Pitses ... 92 C3
Pobgreen ... 79 G4
Portwood ... 160 B3
Pownall Park ... 198 C2
Poynton ... 195 G3
Prestolee ... 67 E4
Prestwich ... 85 G3
Quick ... 93 H3
Quick Edge ... 93 G4
Radcliffe ... 52 B5
Rainsough ... 100 D1
Ramsbottom ... 16 C1
Reddish ... 144 D3
Redvales ... 53 F3
Rhodes ... 71 G5
Ridge Hill ... 120 C1
Ringley ... 67 G5
Roaches ... 94 A4
Rochdale ... 11 F6
Roebuck Low ... 59 F2
Roe Cross ... 135 G3
Roe Green ... 97 G2
Romiley ... 162 C4
Rose Hill ... 49 F4
Rosehill ... 177 F3
Roundthorn ... 167 G3
Royton ... 59 G5
Running Hill Head ... 79 H1
Rusholme ... 129 G5
St George's ... 127 F2
Sale ... 140 B5
Salford ... 113 E4
Salford Quays ... 126 B1
Scouthead ... 77 G3
Sedgley Park ... 86 B5
Seedley ... 112 D2
Sharples ... 33 G2
Sharston ... 169 E4
Shaw ... 59 H3
Shawclough ... 29 F1
Shawfield ... 28 C1
Shaw Heath ... 12 E7
Shaw Side ... 60 A4
Shore ... 60 C5
Sholver ... 20 C2
Shuttleworth ... 17 F1
Side of the Moor ... 24 B5
Simister ... 70 D4
Sinderland Green ... 152 A5
Slackcote ... 61 G2
Slattocks ... 57 E3
Smallbridge ... 20 A5
Smallshaw ... 107 E4
Smithy Bridge ... 20 D5
Smithy Green ... 183 G4
South Reddish ... 159 H1
Spotland Bridge ... 29 G3
Springhead ... 93 E2
Spring Hill ... 76 C4
Stake Hill ... 57 H4
Stalybridge ... 120 C4
Stand ... 68 D4
Stanley Green ... 192 B2
Stancyliffe ... 73 E1
Stepping Hill ... 173 E5
Stockport ... 12 B1
Stoneclough ... 67 E5
Stoneyfield ... 43 E2
Strangeways ... 6 D1
Stretford ... 139 G2
Strines ... 187 H3
Styal ... 191 E5
Sudden ... 42 B2
Summerseat ... 26 C2
Summit ... 40 A4
Summit ... 58 C2
Sun Green ... 121 H1
Sunny Bank ... 53 H5
Swinton ... 98 C2
Swinton Park ... 99 G4
Syke ... 19 E4
Tame Water ... 78 B3
Taunton ... 106 B5
Thornham Fold ... 58 B2
Thornham Green ... 58 B1
Thorp ... 58 C5
Thurston Clough ... 78 A1
Timperley ... 166 B2
Tonge Fold ... 49 H1
Tonge Moor ... 34 B4
Top of Hebers ... 56 B5
Top o' th' Meadows ... 77 E4
Toppings ... 23 G4
Torkington ... 186 A2
Torrington ... 25 H5
Trafford Park ... 125 F3
Trub ... 57 F2
Tunstead ... 95 F2
Turf Hill ... 44 A2
Unsworth ... 69 H2
Uppermill ... 79 E5
Urmston ... 124 D4
Walkden ... 82 A3
Wallbank ... 18 A1
Wall Hill ... 78 B3
Walmersley ... 27 F4
Walshaw ... 36 D2
Warburton Green ... 188 D1
Wardle ... 20 A2
Wardley ... 98 B1
Waterloo ... 94 B1
Watersheddings ... 76 C3
Water's Nook ... 62 C4
Weaste ... 112 D4
Well Green ... 179 E1
Werneth ... 90 C1
Werneth Low ... 163 E4
West Didsbury ... 156 D1
Westwood Park ... 110 B1
Whalley Range ... 142 A1
Whitefield ... 69 F5
White Gate ... 91 G5
Whitworth ... 14 C4
Willows ... 48 B4
Wilmslow ... 199 E4
Wilmslow Park ... 199 F3
Windlehurst ... 186 D5
Winton ... 110 D2
Withington ... 143 E5
Woodend ... 94 B5
Woodend ... 187 H4
Woodford ... 193 G5
Woodgate Hill ... 39 G2
Woodhey ... 16 B5
Woodhouse Park ... 180 B3
Woodhouses ... 105 F4
Woodhouses ... 153 G4
Woodlands ... 134 C1
Woodley ... 162 B1
Wood Road ... 26 D2
Woods End ... 123 F5
Woodsmoor ... 184 C1
Woolfold ... 37 F2
Worsley ... 97 G3
Wythenshawe ... 180 A1
Yew Tree ... 133 H1

USING THE STREET INDEX

Street names are listed alphabetically. Each street name is followed by its postal town or area locality, the Postcode District, the page number, and the reference to the square in which the name is found.

Standard index entries are shown as follows:

Abberley Dr *NEWH/MOS* M40 ...... **89** G5

Street names and selected addresses not shown on the map due to scale restrictions are shown in the index with an asterisk:

Abbeyfield Sq *OP/CLY* M11 * ... **116** C5

GENERAL ABBREVIATIONS

ACC	ACCESS	CTYD	COURTYARD	HLS	HILLS	MWY	MOTORWAY	SE	SOUTH EAST

GENERAL ABBREVIATIONS

ACC ACCESS • ALY ALLEY • AP APPROACH • AR ARCADE • ASS ASSOCIATION • AV AVENUE • BCH BEACH • BLDS BUILDINGS • BND BEND • BNK BANK • BR BRIDGE • BRK BROOK • BTM BOTTOM • BUS BUSINESS • BVD BOULEVARD • BY BYPASS • CATH CATHEDRAL • CEM CEMETERY • CEN CENTRE • CFT CROFT • CH CHURCH • CHA CHASE • CHYD CHURCHYARD • CIR CIRCLE • CIRC CIRCUS • CL CLOSE • CLFS CLIFFS • CMP CAMP • CNR CORNER • CO COUNTY • COLL COLLEGE • COM COMMON • COMM COMMISSION • CON CONVENT • COT COTTAGE • COTS COTTAGES • CP CAPE • CPS COPSE • CR CREEK • CREM CREMATORIUM • CRS CRESCENT • CSWY CAUSEWAY • CT COURT • CTRL CENTRAL • CTS COURTS

CTYD COURTYARD • CUTT CUTTINGS • CV COVE • CYN CANYON • DEPT DEPARTMENT • DL DALE • DM DAM • DR DRIVE • DRO DROVE • DRY DRIVEWAY • DWGS DWELLINGS • E EAST • EMB EMBANKMENT • EMBY EMBASSY • ESP ESPLANADE • EST ESTATE • EX EXCHANGE • EXPY EXPRESSWAY • EXT EXTENSION • F/O FLYOVER • FC FOOTBALL CLUB • FK FORK • FLD FIELD • FLDS FIELDS • FLS FALLS • FM FARM • FTS FORT • FTS FLATS • FWY FREEWAY • FY FERRY • GA GATE • GAL GALLERY • GDN GARDEN • GDNS GARDENS • GLD GLADE • GLN GLEN • GN GREEN • GND GROUND • GRA GRANGE • GRG GARAGE • GT GREAT • GTWY GATEWAY • GV GROVE • HGR HIGHER • HL HILL

HLS HILLS • HO HOUSE • HOL HOLLOW • HOSP HOSPITAL • HRB HARBOUR • HTH HEATH • HTS HEIGHTS • HVN HAVEN • HWY HIGHWAY • IMP IMPERIAL • IN INLET • IND EST INDUSTRIAL ESTATE • INF INFIRMARY • INFO INFORMATION • INT INTERCHANGE • IS ISLAND • JCT JUNCTION • JTY JETTY • KG KING • KNL KNOLL • L LAKE • LA LANE • LDG LODGE • LGT LIGHT • LK LOCK • LKS LAKES • LNDG LANDING • LTL LITTLE • LWR LOWER • MAG MAGISTRATE • MAN MANSIONS • MD MEAD • MDW MEADOWS • MEM MEMORIAL • MI MILL • MKT MARKET • MKTS MARKETS • ML MALL • MNR MANOR • MS MEWS • MSN MISSION • MT MOUNT • MTN MOUNTAIN • MTS MOUNTAINS • MUS MUSEUM

MWY MOTORWAY • N NORTH • NE NORTH EAST • NW NORTH WEST • O/P OVERPASS • OFF OFFICE • ORCH ORCHARD • OV OVAL • PAL PALACE • PAS PASSAGE • PAV PAVILION • PDE PARADE • PH PUBLIC HOUSE • PK PARK • PKWY PARKWAY • PL PLACE • PLN PLAIN • PLNS PLAINS • PLZ PLAZA • POL POLICE STATION • PR PRINCE • PREC PRECINCT • PREP PREPARATORY • PRIM PRIMARY • PROM PROMENADE • PRS PRINCESS • PRT PORT • PT POINT • PTH PATH • PZ PIAZZA • QD QUADRANT • QU QUEEN • QY QUAY • R RIVER • RBT ROUNDABOUT • RD ROAD • RDG RIDGE • REP REPUBLIC • RES RESERVOIR • RFC RUGBY FOOTBALL CLUB • RI RISE • RP RAMP • RW ROW • S SOUTH • SCH SCHOOL

SE SOUTH EAST • SER SERVICE AREA • SH SHORE • SHOP SHOPPING • SKWY SKYWAY • SMT SUMMIT • SOC SOCIETY • SP SPUR • SPR SPRING • SQ SQUARE • ST STREET • STN STATION • STR STREAM • STRD STRAND • SW SOUTH WEST • TDG TRADING • TER TERRACE • THWY THROUGHWAY • TNL TUNNEL • TOLL TOLLWAY • TPK TURNPIKE • TR TRACK • TRL TRAIL • TWR TOWER • U/P UNDERPASS • UNI UNIVERSITY • UPR UPPER • V VALE • VA VALLEY • VIAD VIADUCT • VIL VILLA • VIS VISTA • VLG VILLAGE • VLS VILLAS • VW VIEW • W WEST • WD WOOD • WHF WHARF • WK WALK • WKS WALKS • WLS WELLS • WY WAY • YD YARD • YHA YOUTH HOSTEL

POSTCODE TOWNS AND AREA ABBREVIATIONS

ALT Altrincham • ANC Ancoats • AUL Ashton-under-Lyne • AULW Ashton-under-lyne west • ATH Atherton • BKLY Blackley • BOL Bolton • BOLE Bolton east • BOLS/LL Bolton south/Little Lever • BRAM/HZG Bramhall/Hazel Grove • BRO Broughton • BRUN/LGST Brunswick/Longsight • BNG/LEV Burnage/Levenshulme • BURY Bury • CMANE Central Manchester east • CMANW Central Manchester west • CSLFD Central Salford • CHAD Chadderton

CHD/CHDH Cheadle (Gtr. Man)/Cheadle Hulme • CHH Cheetham Hill • CCHDY Chorlton-cum-Hardy • DTN/ASHW Denton/Audenshaw • DID/WITH Didsbury/Withington • DROY Droylsden • DUK Dukinfield • ECC Eccles • EDGY/DAV Edgeley/Davenport • EDGW/EC Edgeworth/Egerton • FAIL Failsworth • FWTH Farnworth • GLSP Glossop • GOL/RIS/CUL Golborne/Risley/Culcheth • GTN Gorton • HALE/TIMP Hale/Timperley • HTNM Heaton Moor • HEY Heywood

HOR/BR Horwich/Blackrod • HULME Hulme • HYDE Hyde • IRL Irlam • KNUT Knutsford • LHULT Little Hulton • LIT Littleborough • LYMM Lymm • MCFLDN Macclesfield north • MANAIR Manchester Airport • MPL/ROM Marple/Romiley • MDTN Middleton (Gtr. Man) • MILN Milnrow • MOSL Mossley • NM/HAY New Mills/Hayfield • NEWH/MOS Newton Heath/Moston • NTHM/RTH Northern Moor/Roundthorn • OFTN Offerton • OLDTF/WHR Old Trafford/Whalley Range • OLD Oldham

OLDE Oldham east • OLDS Oldham south • OP/CLY Openshaw/Clayton • ORD Ordsall • PART Partington • POY/DIS Poynton/Disley • PWCH Prestwich • RAD Radcliffe • RAMS Ramsbottom • RDSH Reddish • ROCH Rochdale • ROY/SHW Royton/Shaw • RUSH/FAL Rusholme/Fallowfield • SALE Sale • SLFD Salford • SALQ Salford Quays • STLY Stalybridge • STKP Stockport • STRET Stretford • SWIN Swinton • TOT/BURYW Tottington/

BURY west • TRPK Trafford Park • TRPK Trafford Park • TYLD Tyldesley • UPML Uppermill • URM Urmston • WALK Walkden • WGTN/LGST West Gorton/Longsight • WHTN Westhoughton • WHTF Whitefield • WHIT Whitworth • WILM/AE Wilmslow/Alderley Edge • WYTH/NTH Wythenshawe/Northenden

Index - streets

Abb - Adr

A

Abberley Dr NEWH/MOS M40....89 G5
Abberton Rd DID/WITH M20...142 C1
Abbey Cl ALT WA14....176 D3
  BOLS/LL BL3....64 A2
  RAD M26....51 H4
  STRET M32....125 E5
Abbey Ct POY/DIS SK12....195 E4
  RAD M26....51 H5
Abbey Crs HEY OL10....40 C2
Abbeydale WHIT OL12....10 B4
Abbeydale Cl AUL OL6....107 H4
Abbeydale Gdns WALK M28....81 H5
Abbeydale Rd
  NEWH/MOS M40....104 B2
Abbey Dr LIT OL15....20 C5
  SWIN M27....98 D2
  TOT/BURYW BL8....37 F5
Abbeyfield Sq OP/CLY M11 *....116 C5
Abbey Gdns HYDE SK14....135 H5
Abbey Gv CHAD OL9....90 B3
  ECC M30....111 F3
  HYDE SK14....135 G5
  STKP SK1....172 C1
Abbey Hey La GTN M18....130 D2
Abbey Hills Rd OLDS OL8....92 A3
Abbey Lawn
  OLDTF/WHR M16....127 E5
Abbeylea Dr WHTN BL5....62 B2
Abbey Rd CHD/CHDH SK8....170 D4
  DROY M43....117 G2
  FAIL M35....105 G2
  MDTN M24....56 C5
  SALE M33....139 G5
Abbeyville Wk HULME M15 *....127 H3
Abbeywood Av GTN M18....130 D4
Abbotsbury Cl POY/DIS SK12....195 E2
Abbotts Cl SALE M33....154 D5
Abbotsfield Cl URM M41 *....123 E5
Abbot's Fold Rd WALK M28....96 C3
Abbotsford Dr MDTN M24....56 A5
Abbotsford Gv ALT WA14....165 H1

Abbotsford Rd BOL BL1....32 D5
  CCHDY M21....141 F2
  CHAD OL9 *....73 H4
  OLD OL1....76 A3
Abbotside Cl
  OLDTF/WHR M16....127 G5
Abbotsleigh Dr
  BRAM/HZG SK7....184 A2
Abbott St BOLS/LL BL3....48 D4
  ROCH OL11....42 A5
Abden St RAD M26....68 B1
Abels La UPML OL3....79 F4
Aber Av OFTN SK2....172 D5
Abercarn Cl CHH M8....102 B3
Abercorn Rd BOL BL1....33 E5
Abercorn St OLDE OL4 *....92 C1
Abercrombie Ct SALE M33....155 E1
Aberdaron Wk
  BRUN/LGST M13 *....128 C1
Aberdeen Crs EDGY/DAV SK3....12 C6
Aberdeen Gdns WHIT OL12....18 C4
Aberdeen Gv EDGY/DAV SK3....12 D5
Aberdeen St BRUN/LGST M13....128 C3
Aberford Rd NTHM/RTH M23....167 H4
Abergele Rd RUSH/FAL M14....143 G3
Abergele St OFTN SK2....172 A3
Aberley Fold LIT OL15....20 C1
Abernant Cl OP/CLY M11....116 A4
Aber Rd CHD/CHDH SK8....169 E2
Abersoch Av RUSH/FAL M14....143 G3
Abingdon Av WHTF M45....69 G2
Abingdon Cl CHAD OL9 *....90 C3
  ROCH OL11....42 D2
  WHTF M45....69 G2
Abingdon Rd BOLE BL2....49 H1
  BRAM/HZG SK7....183 H2
  RDSH SK5....145 F4
  URM M41....124 D5
Abingdon St AUL OL6....120 A3
  CMANE M1....7 F6
Abington Rd SALE M33....154 D5
Abney Gra MOSL OL5....109 F2
Abney Rd HTNM SK4....159 F1
  MOSL OL5....108 D2
Aboukir St MILN OL16....11 F5

Abram Cl RUSH/FAL M14....142 C2
Abram St SLFD M6....100 C4
Absalom Dr CHH M8....102 A3
Abson St OLD OL1....74 D5
Acacia Av CHD/CHDH SK8....182 D2
  DTN/ASHW M34....132 D5
  HALE/TIMP WA15....178 A1
  SWIN M27....98 D4
  WILM/AE SK9....198 C5
Acacia Dr HALE/TIMP WA15....178 A1
  SLFD M6....112 A2
Acacia Gv RDSH SK5....160 A2
Acacia Rd OLDS OL8....106 A1
The Acacias URM M41 *....139 E1
Academy Wk HULME M15 *....127 H3
Ace Mi CHAD OL9 *....90 A3
Acer Cl HYDE SK14....148 C1
  ROCH OL11....28 A2
Acer Gv BRO M7....100 C1
Acheson St GTN M18....130 C3
Ackers La PART M31....137 G5
Ackers St BRUN/LGST M13....128 C3
Acker St MILN OL16 *....10 D5
Ackroyd Av GTN M18....131 F2
Ackroyd St OP/CLY M11....130 D1
Ackworth Dr NTHM/RTH M23....167 H3
Ackworth Rd SWIN M27....98 D1
Acme Dr SWIN M27....99 G2
Acomb St HULME M15....128 C3
  RUSH/FAL M14....128 C5
Acorn Av CHD/CHDH SK8....170 B4
  HYDE SK14....148 A3
Acorn Cl BNG/LEV M19....143 H5
  WHTF M45....85 G1
Acorn St OLDE OL4....92 D1
Acorn Wy OLD OL1....9 F2
Acre Barn ROY/SHW OL2....59 F1
Acre Fld BOLE BL2....35 E2
Acrefield SALE M33....154 B3
Acrefield Av HTNM SK4....158 D2
  URM M41....139 F2
Acre La CHD/CHDH SK8....193 E1
  OLD OL1....75 H3

Acresbrook STLY SK15....134 D1
Acres Ct WYTH/NTH M22....168 C5
Acresdale HOR/BR BL6....46 D3
Acresfield Rd
  DTN/ASHW M34....118 A4
Acresfield Cl SWIN M27....99 F4
Acresfield Rd
  HALE/TIMP WA15....166 B1
  HYDE SK14....134 A3
  LHULT M38....81 G3
  MDTN M24....73 F1
  SLFD M6....100 A5
Acres Fold Av
  WYTH/NTH M22....180 C1
Acres La STLY SK15....121 E4
Acres Rd CCHDY M21....141 E3
  CHD/CHDH SK8 *....169 F4
Acres St TOT/BURYW BL8....37 E1
Acre Top Rd BKLY M9....87 G2
Acton Av NEWH/MOS M40....116 C1
Acton St OLD OL1....75 H4
  WHIT OL12....10 E3
Actonville Av
  WYTH/NTH M22....180 C1
Adair St CMANE M1....7 F5
  ROCH OL11....42 A4
Adam Cl CHD/CHDH SK8....171 E5
Adams Av CCHDY M21....141 F5
Adams Cl POY/DIS SK12....195 F5
Adamson Gdns
  DID/WITH M20....157 E3
Adamson Rd ECC M30....110 D5
Adamson Wk
  RUSH/FAL M14 *....128 C5
Adam St AUL OL6....119 H2
  BOLS/LL BL3....48 C4
  OLDS OL8....91 G5
Ada St BKLY M9....103 E1
  OLDE OL4....9 K5
  RAMS BL0....16 B3
  WHIT OL12....10 E1

Adbaston Rd STRET M32....125 F3
Adcroft St STKP SK1....13 J7
Addenbrook Rd CHH M8....101 H5
Addingham Cl BKLY M9....87 H3
Addington Rd BOLS/LL BL3....63 G1
Addison Av AUL OL6....120 A2
Addison Cl BRUN/LGST M13....128 D2
Addison Crs OLDTF/WHR M16....127 E5
Addison Dr MDTN M24....73 F2
Addison Rd HALE/TIMP WA15....177 H2
  IRL M44....122 D4
  PART M31....137 F5
  URM M41....138 D2
Adelaide Rd BRAM/HZG SK7....193 H1
  EDGY/DAV SK3....12 B6
Adelaide St BOLS/LL BL3....48 C5
  CHH M8....102 A5
  ECC M30....111 E4
  HEY OL10....41 E4
  MDTN M24....72 D4
  RAMS BL0....16 B4
  SWIN M27....98 C5
Adelaide St East HEY OL10....41 F4
Adelphi Dr LHULT M38....81 G2
Adelphi Gv LHULT M38....81 G2
Adelphi St CSLFD M3....114 A3
  RAD M26....52 A4
Aden Cl WGTN/LGST M12....115 G5
Aden St OLDE OL4....92 C2
  WHIT OL12 *....10 E2
Adisham Dr BOL BL1....34 A5
Adlington Cl
  HALE/TIMP WA15....167 E3
  POY/DIS SK12....195 G5
  TOT/BURYW BL8....37 F5
Adlington Dr STRET M32....126 C4
Adlington Rd WILM/AE SK9....199 G1
Adlington St BOLS/LL BL3....64 C1
  OLDE OL4....76 C3
  WGTN/LGST M12....115 G5
Adrian Rd BOL BL1....33 F4
Adrian St NEWH/MOS M40....103 H3
Adrian Ter MILN OL16....30 D5

Adria Rd DID/WITH M20 157 H3
Adscombe St
OLDTF/WHR M16 127 H4
Adshall Rd CHD/CHDH SK8 170 D4
Adshead Cl WYTH/NTH M22 180 A1
Adstock Wk NEWH/MOS M40 7 K1
Adstone Cl ANC M4 115 G4
Adswood Cl OLDE OL4 76 C3
Adswood Gv EDGY/DAV SK3 171 G3
Adswood La East OFTN SK2 172 A3
Adswood La West
EDGY/DAV SK3 171 H3
Adswood Old Hall Rd
CHD/CHDH SK8 171 G5
Adswood Rd CHD/CHDH SK8 171 F5
Adswood St NEWH/MOS M40 115 H3
Adswood Ter EDGY/DAV SK3 171 H3
Aegean Cl BRO M7 101 F5
Aegean Rd ALT WA14 164 D3
Affetside Dr TOT/BURYW BL8 36 D4
Affleck Av RAD M26 66 D4
Afghan St OLD OL1 76 A4
Age Cft OLDS OL8 92 B4
Agecroft Enterprise Pk
SWIN M27 100 B3
Agecroft Rd MPL/ROM SK6 161 H5
SWIN M27 100 B2
WHTF M45 85 E1
Agecroft Rd East PWCH M25 85 H5
Agecroft Rd West PWCH M25 85 H5
Agincourt St HEY OL10 * 40 C4
Agnes Cl CHAD OL9 90 D3
Agnes St BNG/LEV M19 144 A1
BRO M7 102 A3
CHAD OL9 90 C2
Agnew Pl SLFD M6 113 F1
Agnew Rd GTN M18 130 B3
Aigburth Gv RDSH SK5 145 E1
Ailsa Cl NEWH/MOS M40 103 E5
Aimson Rd East
HALE/TIMP WA15 166 D3
Aimson Rd West
HALE/TIMP WA15 166 D3
Ainley Rd WYTH/NTH M22 180 C1
Ainley Wd DUK SK16 133 G1
Ainsbrook Av BKLY M9 89 E4
Ainscow Av HOR/BR BL6 46 A1
Ainsdale Av BRO M7 101 G1
TOT/BURYW BL8 37 G4
Ainsdale Cl BRAM/HZG SK7 184 B5
OLDS OL8 91 E3
Ainsdale Crs ROY/SHW OL2 75 F2
Ainsdale Dr CHD/CHDH SK8 181 G3
SALE M33 153 H4
WHIT OL12 18 C1
Ainsdale Gv RDSH SK5 145 F3
Ainsdale Rd BOLS/LL BL3 64 D2
Ainsdale St WGTN/LGST M12 129 G2
Ainsford Rd DID/WITH M20 158 A1
Ainsley Gv WALK M28 82 A5
Ainslie Rd BOL BL1 32 D5
Ainsty Rd RUSH/FAL M14 128 B4
Ainsworth Cl DTN/ASHW M34 131 G5
Ainsworth Ct BOLE BL2 49 H2
Ainsworth Hall Rd BOLE BL2 51 E2
Ainsworth La BOLE BL2 49 H1
Ainsworth Rd BOLS/LL BL3 66 D1
RAD M26 52 A4
TOT/BURYW BL8 37 F4
Ainsworth St BOL BL1 33 F4
MILN OL16 30 B5
Aintree Av SALE M33 153 F3
Aintree Cl BRAM/HZG SK7 185 G2
Aintree Dr ROCH OL11 28 B3
Aintree Gv EDGY/DAV SK3 171 H4
Aintree Rd BOLS/LL BL3 66 D2
Aintree St OP/CLY M11 116 C4
Aintree Wk CHAD OL9 8 A2
Airedale Cl CHD/CHDH SK8 169 H3
Airedale Ct ALT WA14 * 165 H4
Aire Dr BOLE BL2 34 C1
Air Hill Ter WHIT OL12 * 29 F2
Airton Cl NEWH/MOS M40 115 F2
Aitken Cl RAMS BL0 16 C3
Aitken St BNG/LEV M19 * 144 C2
Ajax Dr BURY BL9 69 G1
Ajax St RAMS BL0 16 C3
ROCH OL11 42 A3
Aked Cl WGTN/LGST M12 129 E2
Akesmoor Dr OFTN SK2 172 C3
Alamein Dr MPL/ROM SK6 162 D4
Alan Av FAIL M35 105 E5
Alanbrooke Wk HULME M15 * 127 H3
Alandale Av DTN/ASHW M34 132 B1
Alandale Rd EDGY/DAV SK3 171 F2
Alan Dr HALE/TIMP WA15 178 B4
MPL/ROM SK6 174 D3
Alan Rd DID/WITH M20 143 E5
HTNM SK4 159 E3
Alan St BOL BL1 33 G3
Alan Turing Wy
NEWH/MOS M40 115 H2
Alasdair Cl CHAD OL9 74 A4
Alba Cl ECC M30 111 E4
Alban St BRO M7 101 G5
Albany Av OP/CLY M11 131 E1
Albany Cl LHULT M38 81 G2
Albany Ct URM M41 124 A5
Albany Dr BURY BL9 53 G2
Albany Rd BRAM/HZG SK7 193 H3
CCHDY M21 141 F2
ECC M30 110 C2
WILM/AE SK9 198 C5
Albany St MDTN M24 73 E5
OLDE OL4 76 C3
ROCH OL11 43 F1
Albany Wy SLFD M6 113 F2
Alba Wy STRET M32 125 F3
Albemarle Av DID/WITH M20 142 C5
Albemarle Rd CCHDY M21 141 E3
Albemarle St AUL OL6 119 H2
RUSH/FAL M14 128 B4
Albemarle Ter AUL OL6 * 119 H2
Alberbury Av
HALE/TIMP WA15 167 E2
Albermarle Rd SWIN M27 98 D3
Alberta St BOLS/LL BL3 48 B4
STKP SK1 13 H5
Albert Av DUK SK16 133 F2
GTN M18 130 D4
PWCH M25 101 F1
ROY/SHW OL2 59 H4
URM M41 139 E1
WALK M28 82 A2
Albert Cl CHD/CHDH SK8 182 D2
WHTF M45 69 H4
Albert Ct ALT WA14 165 G5
Albert Dr WHTF M45 70 A3
Albert Gdns NEWH/MOS M40 104 C5
Albert Gv FWTH BL4 66 A4
WGTN/LGST M12 129 H4
Albert Hill St DID/WITH M20 * 157 G3
Albert Park Rd BRO M7 101 F5
Albert Pl ALT WA14 165 G4
BRUN/LGST M13 129 G5
Albert Rd CHD/CHDH SK8 182 D2
ECC M30 111 G3
FWTH BL4 66 A4
HALE/TIMP WA15 177 H1
HTNM SK4 158 D3
HYDE SK14 147 H1
SALE M33 154 D2
WHTF M45 69 H4
WILM/AE SK9 198 D4
Albert Rd East
HALE/TIMP WA15 177 H1
Albert Rd West BOL BL1 47 H1
Albert Royds St MILN OL16 11 H1
Albert Sq ALT WA14 177 G1
CMANW M2 6 E5
STLY SK15 120 C4
Albert St BOLS/LL BL3 * 67 E1
BRAM/HZG SK7 185 E1
BURY BL9 5 H4
CHAD OL9 90 C4
DROY M43 118 A4
DTN/ASHW M34 * 132 C5
EDGY/DAV SK3 12 D4
FWTH BL4 66 B4
HEY OL10 40 C4
HYDE SK14 134 A5
IRL M44 136 A5
LIT OL15 20 D3
MDTN M24 73 E5
MILN OL16 44 C1
OLDE OL4 92 D2
OLDS OL8 105 G1
OLDTF/WHR M16 127 F2
OP/CLY M11 116 A4
PWCH M25 * 86 B2
RAMS BL0 16 C2
ROY/SHW OL2 59 E5
ROY/SHW OL2 59 H2
WHIT OL12 14 B5
Albert St West FAIL M35 104 C4
Albert Ter STKP SK1 13 G3
Albine St NEWH/MOS M40 103 G2
Albion Cl HTNM SK4 159 H3
Albion Dr DROY M43 117 H3
Albion Fold DROY M43 117 H3
Albion Gdns STLY SK15 121 E3
Albion Gardens Cl
ROY/SHW OL2 59 G5
Albion Gv SALE M33 154 B2
Albion Pl BRAM/HZG SK7 * 185 E1
BRO M7 * 101 F5
ORD M5 113 H3
PWCH M25 85 H3
Albion Rd ROCH OL11 29 G5
RUSH/FAL M14 143 E2
Albion St AUL OL6 119 H2
BOLS/LL BL3 49 E4
CHAD OL9 90 B1
CMANE M1 6 D7
FAIL M35 104 D3
FWTH BL4 82 D1
HULME M15 128 A1
LIT OL15 20 D3
OLD OL1 9 G3
OLDTF/WHR M16 127 G4
RAD M26 68 C3
ROCH OL11 42 C5
SALE M33 154 C2
STLY SK15 121 E3
SWIN M27 99 F2
TOT/BURYW BL8 4 A4
Albion Wy ORD M5 113 G4
Albury Dr BNG/LEV M19 158 A4
WHIT OL12 28 C1
Albyns Av CHH M8 102 B3
Alcester Av EDGY/DAV SK3 170 C2
Alcester Cl MDTN M24 89 E1
TOT/BURYW BL8 37 G3
Alcester Rd CHD/CHDH SK8 169 G5
SALE M33 154 C4
Alcester St CHAD OL9 90 B4
Aldborough Cl DID/WITH M20 142 D5
Aldbourne Cl
NEWH/MOS M40 103 E5
Aldbury Ter BOL BL1 * 33 G5
Aldcroft St GTN M18 * 131 E2
Alden Cl WHTF M45 69 H4
Alder Av BURY BL9 39 F3
POY/DIS SK12 195 G4
Alderbank WHIT OL12 19 H1
Alderbank Cl FWTH BL4 82 C1
Alderbrook Rd LHULT M38 81 E4
Alder Cl AUL OL6 107 E3
CHD/CHDH SK8 182 A4
TOT/BURYW BL8 37 H4
Alder Ct CHH M8 * 102 A1
Aldercroft Av BOLE BL2 35 E5
WYTH/NTH M22 180 B2
Alderdale Dr DROY M43 117 E3
HTNM SK4 158 D1
MPL/ROM SK6 186 D5
Alderdale Gv WILM/AE SK9 198 B5
Alderdale Rd CHD/CHDH SK8 171 F5
Alder Dr HALE/TIMP WA15 167 F4
STLY SK15 121 F2
SWIN M27 98 B1
Alderfield Rd STRET M32 140 D2
Alder Forest Av ECC M30 110 B1
Aldergate Gv AUL OL6 108 A5
Alderglen Rd CHH M8 102 A4
Alder Gv DTN/ASHW M34 132 D5
EDGW/EG BL7 23 H5
EDGY/DAV SK3 12 A5
STRET M32 140 C1
Alder La OLDS OL8 91 E5
Alderley Av BOL BL1 33 H1
Alderley Cl BRAM/HZG SK7 185 G4
POY/DIS SK12 195 G5
Alderley Dr MPL/ROM SK6 161 F2
Alderley Ldg WILM/AE SK9 198 D5
Alderley Rd RDSH SK5 160 A1
SALE M33 155 F4
URM M41 138 A1
WILM/AE SK9 198 D4
Alderley St AUL OL6 107 G5
Alderley Wy EDGY/DAV SK3 171 H5
Alderman Foley Dr WHIT OL12 28 D1
Alderman Sq
WGTN/LGST M12 115 H5
Aldermary Rd CCHDY M21 156 C1
Aldermaston Gv BKLY M9 87 G1
Alder Meadow Cl WHIT OL12 28 D2
Aldermere Crs URM M41 137 G1
Alderminster Av LHULT M38 81 F2
Aldermoor Cl OP/CLY M11 116 D5
Alder Rd CHD/CHDH SK8 170 A4
FAIL M35 105 F4
MDTN M24 * 73 F2
ROCH OL11 42 C4
Alders Av WYTH/NTH M22 168 B4
Alders Ct OLDS OL8 106 D2
Aldersgate Rd
CHD/CHDH SK8 193 F2
OFTN SK2 172 C3
Aldersgreen Av
MPL/ROM SK6 187 E5
Alderside Rd BKLY M9 103 E2
Aldersley Av BKLY M9 87 G3
Alderson St CHAD OL9 8 E2
SLFD M6 113 F1
Alders Rd POY/DIS SK12 187 F5
WYTH/NTH M22 168 B4
Alder St BOLS/LL BL3 65 E1
ECC M30 110 B1
SLFD M6 113 E5
Aldersyde St BOLS/LL BL3 64 C1
Alderue Av WYTH/NTH M22 168 C3
Alderwood Fold OLDE OL4 93 E3
Aldfield Rd NTHM/RTH M23 155 G5
Aldford Cl DID/WITH M20 * 157 H3
Aldford Gv BOLE BL2 51 E4
Aldford Pl WILM/AE SK9 200 C3
Aldham Av NEWH/MOS M40 116 D1
Aldon St AUL OL6 119 H1
Aldred Cl CHH M8 102 C4
Aldred St BOLS/LL BL3 64 A1
ECC M30 110 D4
FAIL M35 104 D3
ORD M5 113 G3
Aldsworth Dr BOLS/LL BL3 48 D5
NEWH/MOS M40 103 F5
Aldwick Av DID/WITH M20 157 H3
Aldwinians Cl DTN/ASHW M34 132 B3
Aldworth Gv SALE M33 153 G2
Aldwych ROCH OL11 43 E3
Aldwych Av RUSH/FAL M14 128 C5
Aldwyn Cl DTN/ASHW M34 132 B3
RAD M26 68 C3
Aldwyn Crs BRAM/HZG SK7 184 D2
Aldwyn Park Rd
DTN/ASHW M34 131 H1
Alexander Av FAIL M35 105 F2
Alexander Briant Ct
FWTH BL4 * 65 H5
Alexander Dr BURY BL9 69 H3
HALE/TIMP WA15 166 B3
MILN OL16 31 G5
Alexander Gdns BRO M7 114 A1
Alexander Rd BOLE BL2 34 D5
Alexander St ROCH OL11 42 A4
SLFD M6 * 112 D3
Alexandra Av HYDE SK14 147 G1
RUSH/FAL M14 142 B1
WHTF M45 69 H4
Alexandra Cl EDGY/DAV SK3 171 F3
Alexandra Ct URM M41 137 G2
Alexandra Crs OLD OL1 76 A4
Alexandra Dr BNG/LEV M19 143 H4
Alexandra Gv IRL M44 136 B3
Alexandra Ms OLDS OL8 * 9 K7
Alexandra Rd AUL OL6 119 H1
DTN/ASHW M34 132 D4
ECC M30 110 C4
FWTH BL4 82 D1
HTNM SK4 159 F3
OLDTF/WHR M16 127 H4
RAD M26 66 D4
SALE M33 155 E3
WALK M28 81 H2
Alexandra Rd South
OLDTF/WHR M16 127 H5
Alexandra St AUL OL6 120 A1
BOLS/LL BL3 * 48 C5
BRO M7 * 114 A2
FWTH BL4 66 A5
HEY OL10 56 B1
HYDE SK14 147 G2
OLDS OL8 9 K6
Alexandra Ter BNG/LEV M19 144 A2
OLDE OL4 76 D1
Alexandria Dr AULW OL7 118 D4
AULW OL7 119 F4
WHTN BL5 62 C4
Alford Av DID/WITH M20 142 C3
Alford Cl BOLE BL2 50 B3
Alford Rd HTNM SK4 144 B5
Alford St CHAD OL9 90 C5
Alfred Av WALK M28 98 A3
Alfred James Cl
NEWH/MOS M40 115 G2
Alfred St AUL OL6 * 120 A1
BKLY M9 103 E2
BOLS/LL BL3 49 G4
BURY BL9 53 H1
CHAD OL9 8 B5
ECC M30 111 E2
FWTH BL4 66 A2
FWTH BL4 66 C4
HYDE SK14 133 F5
IRL M44 136 A5
LIT OL15 20 D2
RAMS BL0 16 C3
ROY/SHW OL2 59 H2
WALK M28 82 A4
WHIT OL12 14 C3
Alfreton Av DTN/ASHW M34 147 E3
Alfreton Rd OFTN SK2 173 E3
Alfriston Dr NTHM/RTH M23 155 H4
Alger Ms AUL OL6 120 A1
Algernon Rd WALK M28 81 H3
Algernon St ECC M30 111 E2
SWIN M27 98 C2
Alger St AUL OL6 120 A1
Algreave Rd EDGY/DAV SK3 170 D1
Alice Ingham Ct ROCH OL11 29 E2
Alice St BOLS/LL BL3 48 B4
HYDE SK14 148 A4
SALE M33 155 E2
SWIN M27 99 G2
WHIT OL12 11 G2
Alicia Dr WHIT OL12 10 A2
Alison Kelly Cl BKLY M9 103 G2
Alison St ROY/SHW OL2 59 H1
RUSH/FAL M14 128 A5
Alker Rd NEWH/MOS M40 * 115 G2
Alkrington Cl BURY BL9 69 H2
Alkrington Gn MDTN M24 88 C1
Alkrington Hall Rd North
MDTN M24 72 C5
Alkrington Hall Rd South
MDTN M24 88 B1
Alkrington Park Rd MDTN M24 72 B5
Allama Iqbal Rd OLDE OL4 92 B2
Allandale ALT WA14 165 E5
Allandale Dr ROY/SHW OL2 58 D4
Allandale Rd BNG/LEV M19 * 143 H2
Allan Roberts Cl BKLY M9 103 E1
Allanson Rd WYTH/NTH M22 156 D5
Alldis Cl WGTN/LGST M12 129 F3
Alldis St OFTN SK2 172 C4
Allen Av HYDE SK14 148 B3
Allenby Rd IRL M44 150 C2
SWIN M27 98 B4
Allenby St ROY/SHW OL2 60 A2
Allen Cl ROY/SHW OL2 59 H3
Allendale Dr BURY BL9 69 H1
Allendale Gdns BOL BL1 33 H4
Allen Dale Wk CSLFD M3 114 A3
Allen Rd URM M41 139 F2
Allen St BOLS/LL BL3 66 D1
MILN OL16 43 F1
OLDS OL8 8 C5
RAD M26 68 A1
TOT/BURYW BL8 37 H3
Allerdean Wk HTNM SK4 158 C3
Allerford St OLDTF/WHR M16 127 H4
Allerton Cl WHTN BL5 62 B3
Allerton Wk
BRUN/LGST M13 * 128 C2
Allesley Cl WHTN BL5 62 B3
Allesley Dr BRO M7 102 A5
Allgreave Cl SALE M33 155 F5
Alligin Cl CHAD OL9 74 B4
Allingham St BRUN/LGST M13 129 F4
Allington ROCH OL11 * 29 H5
Allington Dr ECC M30 111 F1
Alliott Wk HULME M15 127 H3
Allison Gv ECC M30 110 C4
Allison St CHH M8 102 A5
All Saint's Cl ROY/SHW OL2 59 E4
All Saints Ct STRET M32 * 139 H1
All Saints Pl TOT/BURYW BL8 37 H3
All Saints' Rd HTNM SK4 159 G3
All Saints' St BOL BL1 2 E3
NEWH/MOS M40 104 B5
All Saints Ter WHIT OL12 11 G1
Allsopp St BOLS/LL BL3 2 E7
Alma La WILM/AE SK9 198 D4
Alma Rd BNG/LEV M19 144 A3
BRAM/HZG SK7 185 H4
HTNM SK4 159 E1
SALE M33 153 H4
WHTN BL5 62 A4
Alma St BOLS/LL BL3 48 B5
BOLS/LL BL3 67 E1
ECC M30 111 G4
FWTH BL4 * 83 E2
RAD M26 52 A4
STLY SK15 121 E3
WHIT OL12 10 C3
Alminstone Cl
NEWH/MOS M40 117 E1
Almond Av BURY BL9 39 F3
Almond Cl EDGY/DAV SK3 12 A5
FAIL M35 105 E4
LIT OL15 20 C2
SLFD M6 113 F3
Almond Dr SALE M33 139 F5
Almond Gv BOL BL1 * 34 A3
Almond Rd OLDE OL4 76 C3
Almond St BOL BL1 34 A2
FWTH BL4 65 H4
NEWH/MOS M40 * 115 E1
Almond Tree Rd
CHD/CHDH SK8 182 D3
Almond Wy HYDE SK14 148 D1
Alms Hill Rd CHH M8 102 B3
Alness Rd OLDTF/WHR M16 142 A1
Alnwick Dr BURY BL9 53 H4
Alnwick Rd BKLY M9 88 A2
Alpha Ct DTN/ASHW M34 131 H5
Alphagate Dr DTN/ASHW M34 131 H5
Alpha Pl HULME M15 127 H1
Alpha Rd STRET M32 140 A1
Alpha St OP/CLY M11 130 D1
SLFD M6 113 E2
Alpha St West SLFD M6 112 D2
Alphin Cl MOSL OL5 94 B4
UPML OL3 95 E2
Alphingate Cl STLY SK15 121 G1
Alphin Sq MOSL OL5 109 E1
Alphonsus St
OLDTF/WHR M16 127 F4
Alpine Dr MILN OL16 31 H4
ROY/SHW OL2 74 D1
WHIT OL12 19 H2
Alpine Rd STKP SK1 13 K3
Alpine St OP/CLY M11 116 C3
Alport Av OLDTF/WHR M16 * 141 G1
Alresford Rd MDTN M24 88 C2
SLFD M6 100 A5
Alsager Cl CCHDY M21 141 F5
Alsop Av BRO M7 * 101 E3
Alstead Av HALE/TIMP WA15 178 B1
Alston Av ROY/SHW OL2 60 A2
SALE M33 154 A3
STRET M32 125 G5
Alston Cl BRAM/HZG SK7 * 184 B3
Alstone Dr ALT WA14 164 D3
Alstone Rd HTNM SK4 144 C5
Alston Gdns BNG/LEV M19 158 C1
Alston Rd GTN M18 130 D3
Alston St BOLS/LL BL3 * 64 D1
TOT/BURYW BL8 * 37 H2
Altair Av WYTH/NTH M22 180 C4
Altair Pl BRO M7 113 H1
Altcar Gv RDSH SK5 145 E1
Altcar Wk WYTH/NTH M22 180 B2
Alt Fold Dr OLDS OL8 92 B4
Alt Gv AUL OL6 107 E4
Altham Cl BURY BL9 53 E2
Alt Hill La AUL OL6 107 F2
Alt La OLDS OL8 92 C4
Alton Av URM M41 137 F1
Alton Cl AUL OL6 107 F3
BURY BL9 53 H4
Alton Rd WILM/AE SK9 198 C2
Alton Sq OP/CLY M11 130 D1
Alton St OLDS OL8 91 G4
Altrincham Rd
NTHM/RTH M23 167 E2
WILM/AE SK9 189 H4
WYTH/NTH M22 168 C2
Altrincham St CMANE M1 7 H7
Alum Crs BURY BL9 69 H1
Alvanley Cl SALE M33 154 C5
Alvanley Crs EDGY/DAV SK3 171 F3
Alvan Sq OP/CLY M11 * 130 D1
Alva Rd OLDE OL4 76 C2
Alvaston Av HTNM SK4 159 E3
Alvaston Rd GTN M18 130 D4
Alveley Av DID/WITH M20 157 H1
Alverstone Rd DID/WITH M20 143 E5
Alveston Dr WILM/AE SK9 199 F2
Alvington Gv BRAM/HZG SK7 184 B3
Alwin Rd ROY/SHW OL2 59 H1
Alwinton Av HTNM SK4 158 B3
Alworth Rd BKLY M9 88 A2
Alwyn Dr BRUN/LGST M13 129 F4
Ambassador Pl
HALE/TIMP WA15 * 165 H4
Amber Gdns DUK SK16 * 119 G5
Amber Gv WHTN BL5 62 A2
Amberhill Wy WALK M28 96 B5
Amberley Cl BOLS/LL BL3 47 G4
Amberley Dr
HALE/TIMP WA15 178 C4
IRL M44 136 C2
NTHM/RTH M23 167 H5
Amberley Rd SALE M33 153 H1
Amberley Wk CHAD OL9 8 A2
Amberwood CHAD OL9 73 H4
Amberwood Dr
NTHM/RTH M23 167 E3
Amblecote Dr East LHULT M38 81 F1
Amblecote Dr West
LHULT M38 81 F1
Ambleside STLY SK15 120 D2
Ambleside Av AULW OL7 119 E1
HALE/TIMP WA15 166 D4
Ambleside Cl BOLE BL2 35 G2
MDTN M24 72 B3
Ambleside Rd RDSH SK5 145 F5
URM M41 137 G2
Ambrose Ct WYTH/NTH M22 * 156 C5
Ambrose Dr DID/WITH M20 156 D2
Ambrose St ROCH OL11 43 E1
WGTN/LGST M12 129 H1
Ambush St OP/CLY M11 131 E1
Amelia St DTN/ASHW M34 132 C4
HYDE SK14 148 A1
Amersham Cl URM M41 124 A3
Amersham Pl BNG/LEV M19 144 A5
Amersham St ORD M5 113 E4
Amesbury Gv RDSH SK5 160 A1
Amesbury Rd BKLY M9 88 B3
Amherst Rd DID/WITH M20 143 E4
Amlwch Av OFTN SK2 173 E3
Ammon Wrigley Cl OLD OL1 9 G2
Amory St WGTN/LGST M12 7 K7
Amos Av NEWH/MOS M40 116 D1
Amos St BKLY M9 103 G3
SLFD M6 112 D3
Ampney Cl ECC M30 110 C4
Amwell St CHH M8 102 C3
Amy St MDTN M24 73 E3
WHIT OL12 29 E2
Anaconda Dr CSLFD M3 6 B1
Anchorage Quay SALQ M50 113 F5
Anchorage Rd URM M41 139 G2
Anchor Cl BNG/LEV M19 144 C2
Anchor Ct CHH M8 * 102 A1
Anchor La FWTH BL4 65 E5
Anchorside Cl CCHDY M21 141 F4
Anchor St OLD OL1 9 G1
Ancoats Gv ANC M4 115 G4
Ancoats Gv North ANC M4 115 G4
Ancoats St OLDE OL4 92 D1
Ancroft St HULME M15 127 H2
Anderton Cl TOT/BURYW BL8 37 E5
Anderton Gv AUL OL6 107 H5
Anderton Wy WILM/AE SK9 192 A4
Andoc Av ECC M30 111 G4
Andover Av MDTN M24 89 E2
Andover St ECC M30 110 D4
Andre St OP/CLY M11 * 116 D3
Andrew Cl RAD M26 68 D3
TOT/BURYW BL8 26 A2
Andrew La BOL BL1 23 E5
MPL/ROM SK6 186 D3
Andrew Rd BKLY M9 103 E1
Andrews Av URM M41 123 F5
Andrew St AUL OL6 * 107 G5
BURY BL9 5 G5
CHAD OL9 74 B4
DROY M43 118 B1
FAIL M35 104 D2
HTNM SK4 12 E2
HYDE SK14 134 A5
MDTN M24 73 F5
MOSL OL5 108 D2
MPL/ROM SK6 163 F4
Anerley Rd DID/WITH M20 157 G2
Anfield Cl BURY BL9 70 A1
Anfield Rd BOLS/LL BL3 64 D2

CHD/CHDH SK8 182 C2
NEWH/MOS M40 104 C1
SALE M33 154 D1
Angela Av ROY/SHW OL2 75 F2
Angela St HULME M15 127 G1
Angel Cl DUK SK16 133 E1
Angelko Ri OLD OL1 76 C1
Angelo St BOL BL1 33 G3
Angel St ANC M4 7 G1
BRAM/HZG SK7 185 E1
DTN/ASHW M34 132 D4
Anglers Rest IRL M44 150 D1
Anglesea Av OFTN SK2 172 A3
Anglesey Cl AULW OL7 106 C4
Anglesey Dr POY/DIS SK12 195 F1
Anglesey Gv CHD/CHDH SK8 170 C3
Anglesey Rd AULW OL7 106 C4
Anglesey Water
POY/DIS SK12 195 F1
Angleside Av BNG/LEV M19 158 B2
Angle St BOLE BL2 3 K1
Anglia Gv BOLS/LL BL3 48 B5
Angora Dr CSLFD M3 114 A2
Angouleme Wy BURY BL9 4 D6
Angus Av HEY OL10 40 B5
Anita St ANC M4 7 J2
Annable Rd DROY M43 118 A4
GTN M18 130 D2
IRL M44 136 B3
MPL/ROM SK6 161 E3
Annald Sq DROY M43 117 H5
Annan St DTN/ASHW M34 * 132 C4
Anne Cl AULW OL7 106 D4
Annecy Cl TOT/BURYW BL8 37 G2
Anne Nuttall Rd HULME M15 127 G1
Annersley Av ROY/SHW OL2 59 H3
Annesley Rd NEWH/MOS M40 104 D1
Anne St DUK SK16 120 A5
Annie St ORD M5 112 D3
RAMS BL0 16 B4
Annis Cl WILM/AE SK9 201 E3
Annisdale Cl ECC M30 110 C3
Annisfield Av UPML OL3 95 F2
Annis Rd BOLS/LL BL3 48 A5
WILM/AE SK9 201 E3
Annis St BKLY M9 103 F3
Ann Sq OLDE OL4 76 C4
Ann St AULW OL7 119 E5
DTN/ASHW M34 132 B5
FWTH BL4 66 B5
HEY OL10 41 E3
HYDE SK14 133 F5
RDSH SK5 159 H2
ROCH OL11 * 30 A5
Anscombe Cl
NEWH/MOS M40 115 G2
Ansdell Av CCHDY M21 141 F4
Ansdell Dr DROY M43 117 F3
Ansdell Rd MILN OL16 43 G2
RDSH SK5 145 G2
Ansdell St CHH M8 102 B3
Ansell Cl GTN M18 130 C2
Anselms Ct OLDS OL8 90 D3
Ansleigh Av CHH M8 102 B1
Ansley Gv HTNM SK4 159 E3
Anslow Cl NEWH/MOS M40 103 E5
Anson Av SWIN M27 98 D4
Anson Cl BRAM/HZG SK7 194 A2
Anson Rd DTN/ASHW M34 145 G1
POY/DIS SK12 196 A4
RUSH/FAL M14 129 E4
SWIN M27 98 D4
WILM/AE SK9 199 H1
Anson St BOL BL1 34 A3
ECC M30 110 C2
Answell Av CHH M8 87 F5
Antares Av BRO M7 114 A2
Anthony Cl WGTN/LGST M12 129 F1
Anthony St MOSL OL5 108 C1
Antilles Cl WGTN/LGST M12 129 H4
Antrim Cl BNG/LEV M19 158 A4
Anvil Wy OLD OL1 9 F2
Apethorn La HYDE SK14 147 G3
Apfel La CHAD OL9 74 C5
Apollo Av BURY BL9 69 G1
Apperley Gra ECC M30 111 F1
Appian Wy BRO M7 101 H5
Appleby Av HALE/TIMP WA15 166 D4
HYDE SK14 133 F3
Appleby Cl EDGY/DAV SK3 171 G4
TOT/BURYW BL8 37 E4
Appleby Gdns BOLE BL2 * 3 H1
Appleby Rd CHD/CHDH SK8 169 G5
Apple Cl OLDS OL8 92 B4
Appledore Dr BOLE BL2 35 G4
NTHM/RTH M23 167 E2
Appledore Wk CHAD OL9 90 C1
Appleford Av NTHM/RTH M23 167 H5
Appleford Dr CHH M8 102 C4
Apple St HYDE SK14 149 E4
Appleton Gv SALE M33 153 H4
Appleton La WHTN BL5 62 A3
Appleton Rd
HALE/TIMP WA15 177 H3
HTNM SK4 144 D5
Apple Tree Ct ORD M5 113 F3
Apple Wy MDTN M24 89 E1
Applewood CHAD OL9 73 G5
Appleyard Cl SWIN M27 100 A2
Apprentice La WILM/AE SK9 191 E4
April Cl OLDS OL8 92 B3
Apsley Cl ALT WA14 177 E3
Apsley Gv ALT WA14 177 E3
WGTN/LGST M12 128 D2
Apsley Rd DTN/ASHW M34 132 C4
Apsley St STKP SK1 13 H3
Aquarius La SLFD M6 * 113 H1
Aquarius St HULME M15 128 B3
Aqueduct Rd BOLS/LL BL3 49 H5
Aragon Dr HEY OL10 40 D4
Aragon Wy MPL/ROM SK6 174 D3
Arbor Av BNG/LEV M19 144 A4
Arbor Dr BNG/LEV M19 143 H4
Arbor Gv DROY M43 117 G2
LHULT M38 80 D3
Arbory Av NEWH/MOS M40 104 A2
Arbour Cl BURY BL9 27 F5
SLFD M6 113 E2
Arbour Rd OLDE OL4 92 D3
Arbroath St DROY M43 117 F4
Arbury Av EDGY/DAV SK3 170 C2
ROCH OL11 42 D1
The Arcades AUL OL6 * 119 G2
Arcadia Av SALE M33 154 B5
Archer Av BOLE BL2 49 H1
Archer Gv BOLE BL2 49 H1
Archer Pk MDTN M24 72 B4
Archer Pl STRET M32 139 F1
Archer St MOSL OL5 93 H5
OFTN SK2 172 D4
OP/CLY M11 116 B3
Archie St ORD M5 126 D1
Arch St BOL BL1 3 H2
Archway HULME M15 128 A3
Arclid Cl WILM/AE SK9 192 B5
Arcon Cl MILN OL16 31 F5
Arcon Dr OLDTF/WHR M16 127 H5
Arcon Pl ALT WA14 164 D3
Ardale Av NEWH/MOS M40 89 F5
Ardcombe Av BKLY M9 87 H2
Ardeen Wk BRUN/LGST M13 * 128 D2
Arden Av MDTN M24 89 E2
Arden Cl AUL OL6 108 A4
BURY BL9 * 53 F1
Arden Ct BRAM/HZG SK7 183 G3
Ardenfield DTN/ASHW M34 147 E4
Ardenfield Dr
WYTH/NTH M22 180 D2
Arden Gv NEWH/MOS M40 104 B1
Arden Lodge Rd
NTHM/RTH M23 167 F2
Arden Rd MPL/ROM SK6 146 C4
Ardens Cl SWIN M27 83 G5
Arden St CHAD OL9 90 B4
Ardent Wy PWCH M25 101 E1
Arderne Pl WILM/AE SK9 200 D4
Arderne Rd HALE/TIMP WA15 166 B1
Ardern Gv STKP SK1 13 H6
Ardern Rd CHH M8 102 A1
Ardwick Gn North
WGTN/LGST M12 128 D1
Ardwick Gn South
BRUN/LGST M13 128 C1
Ardwick Ter WGTN/LGST M12 129 E2
Argo St BOLS/LL BL3 48 C5
Argosy Dr ECC M30 123 G1
MANAIR M90 179 G5
Argus St OLDS OL8 90 D5
Argyle Av RUSH/FAL M14 129 F4
WALK M28 81 H2
WHTF M45 69 H4
Argyle Crs HEY OL10 40 C5
Argyle St BRAM/HZG SK7 185 F2
BURY BL9 38 C2
DROY M43 117 H4
GTN M18 130 C3
HEY OL10 40 A5
MILN OL16 43 F2
MOSL OL5 108 D1
OLD OL1 76 A4
SWIN M27 98 D3
Argyll Av STRET M32 139 H1
Argyll Cl FAIL M35 105 G3
Argyll Park Rd FAIL M35 105 G3
Argyll Rd CHAD OL9 90 A4
CHD/CHDH SK8 170 C4
Argyll St AUL OL6 120 B2
Arkendale Cl FAIL M35 * 105 H3
Arkholme WALK M28 96 B2
Arkle Av WILM/AE SK9 192 B3
Arkle Dr CHAD OL9 74 A4
Arkley Wk BRUN/LGST M13 128 C2
Ark St BNG/LEV M19 144 A1
Arkwright Cl BOL BL1 33 F5
Arkwright Dr MPL/ROM SK6 175 F3
Arkwright Rd MPL/ROM SK6 175 F3
Arkwright St CHAD OL9 8 A4
Arlen Ct BOLE BL2 49 G4
Arlen Rd BOLE BL2 49 G4
Arlen Wy HEY OL10 * 40 C4
Arley Av BURY BL9 38 B1
DID/WITH M20 157 E1
Arley Cl ALT WA14 165 G1
DUK SK16 133 G2
Arley Dr ROY/SHW OL2 60 B1
SALE M33 154 B4
Arley Gv EDGY/DAV SK3 171 G5
Arley Mere Cl CHD/CHDH SK8 182 C1
Arley Moss Wk
BRUN/LGST M13 * 128 C1
Arley St RAD M26 68 C3
Arlies Cl STLY SK15 120 D1
Arlies La STLY SK15 120 D1
Arlies St AUL OL6 120 A1
Arlington Av DTN/ASHW M34 147 E1
PWCH M25 86 A5
SWIN M27 98 C4
Arlington Cl BURY BL9 26 D1
ROY/SHW OL2 75 F2
Arlington Crs WILM/AE SK9 198 B5
Arlington Dr OFTN SK2 184 B1
POY/DIS SK12 195 E4
Arlington Rd CHD/CHDH SK8 169 H5
STRET M32 139 H2
Arlington St AUL OL6 119 H2
BOLS/LL BL3 65 E1
CHH M8 102 A1
CSLFD M3 6 A1
Arlington Wy WILM/AE SK9 198 B5
Arliss Av BNG/LEV M19 144 A3
Armadale Av BKLY M9 88 D3
Armadale Cl EDGY/DAV SK3 171 H5
Armadale Rd BOLS/LL BL3 47 F5
DUK SK16 119 H5
Armdale Ri OLDE OL4 76 D3
Armentieres STLY SK15 120 D4
Armitage Av LHULT M38 81 E3
Armitage Cl HYDE SK14 148 A3
MDTN M24 72 A5
OLDS OL8 90 D4
Armitage Gv LHULT M38 81 E3
Armitage Rd ALT WA14 177 G1
Armitage St ECC M30 110 D4
Armit Rd UPML OL3 94 B3
Armour Pl BKLY M9 87 H5
Armoury St EDGY/DAV SK3 13 F6
Arm Rd LIT OL15 20 B3
Armstrong Hurst Cl
WHIT OL12 30 C1
Arncliffe Dr NTHM/RTH M23 179 H1
Arncliffe Ri OLDE OL4 61 F5
Arncot Rd BOL BL1 34 A1
Arncott Cl ROY/SHW OL2 59 H5
Arne Cl OFTN SK2 173 H4
Arnesby Av SALE M33 140 C5
Arnesby Gv BOLE BL2 3 K2
Arne St CHAD OL9 * 90 B2
Arnfield Dr WALK M28 96 C4
Arnfield Rd DID/WITH M20 143 E5
EDGY/DAV SK3 171 G4
Arnold Av HEY OL10 56 B2
HYDE SK14 148 B4
Arnold Cl DUK SK16 134 B1
Arnold Dr DROY M43 117 H4
MDTN M24 73 F1
Arnold Rd EDGW/EG BL7 23 E3
HYDE SK14 148 B4
OLDTF/WHR M16 142 A2
Arnold St BOL BL1 33 G4
EDGY/DAV SK3 12 E7
OLD OL1 9 K1
Arnott Crs HULME M15 128 A3
Arnside Av BRAM/HZG SK7 184 D2
CHAD OL9 90 B2
HTNM SK4 144 D5
Arnside Cl CHD/CHDH SK8 169 G5
MPL/ROM SK6 186 D4
ROY/SHW OL2 60 C2
Arnside Dr HYDE SK14 133 F4
ROCH OL11 41 F1
SLFD M6 112 A2
Arnside Gv BOLE BL2 50 B1
SALE M33 154 C1
Arnside St RUSH/FAL M14 142 D1
Arran Av OLDS OL8 91 G4
SALE M33 154 D3
STRET M32 139 G1
Arran Cl BOLS/LL BL3 47 F4
Arrandale Ct URM M41 * 124 C5
Arran Gdns URM M41 124 C3
Arran Gv RAD M26 51 H4
Arran Rd DUK SK16 133 F1
Arran St BRO M7 101 G4
NEWH/MOS M40 103 G2
Arras Gv RDSH SK5 131 E5
Arreton Sq RUSH/FAL M14 129 E5
Arrowfield Rd CCHDY M21 141 H5
Arrowhill Rd RAD M26 52 A1
Arrow St BOL BL1 2 C2
BRO M7 101 G5
Arthington St MILN OL16 11 G5
Arthog Dr HALE/TIMP WA15 178 A4
Arthog Rd DID/WITH M20 157 H4
HALE/TIMP WA15 178 A4
Arthur Av WALK M28 81 H2
Arthur La BOLE BL2 36 A4
Arthur Rd OLDTF/WHR M16 127 F5
Arthurs La UPML OL3 95 E2
Arthur St BOLS/LL BL3 66 D1
ECC M30 110 D4
FWTH BL4 66 A4
HEY OL10 * 41 E4
HYDE SK14 147 G2
PWCH M25 85 G3
RDSH SK5 145 E4
ROY/SHW OL2 59 H2
SWIN M27 98 C3
TOT/BURYW BL8 37 H4
WALK M28 82 C5
WALK M28 97 E1
WHIT OL12 29 G3
Artillery Pl WYTH/NTH M22 * 169 E5
Artillery St BOLS/LL BL3 49 E4
CSLFD M3 6 C6
Arundale WHTN BL5 62 A2
Arundale Av OLDTF/WHR M16 142 A2
Arundale Cl HYDE SK14 135 G5
Arundale Gv HYDE SK14 135 G5
Arundel Av BRAM/HZG SK7 185 E4
ROCH OL11 42 D2
URM M41 137 E2
WHTF M45 70 A5
Arundel Cl HALE/TIMP WA15 178 D3
STLY SK15 109 G4
TOT/BURYW BL8 26 D5
Arundel Gv OFTN SK2 172 C5
Arundel Rd CHD/CHDH SK8 192 D1
Arundel St AUL OL6 120 B2
BOL BL1 33 H1
HULME M15 127 G1
MOSL OL5 108 D1
OLDE OL4 76 B5
ROCH OL11 42 D2
SWIN M27 98 B1
Asby Cl MDTN M24 72 A2
Ascension Rd BRO M7 114 A1
Ascot Av SALE M33 153 F3
STRET M32 126 C5
Ascot Cl CHAD OL9 8 A2
ROCH OL11 28 B3
Ascot Dr BRAM/HZG SK7 185 H2
URM M41 137 E1
Ascot Mdw BURY BL9 53 F1
Ascot Pde BNG/LEV M19 143 H5
Ascot Rd BOLS/LL BL3 66 C1
NEWH/MOS M40 116 C1
Ascroft St OLD OL1 9 G4
Asgard Dr ORD M5 113 H5
Asgard Gv ORD M5 113 H5
Ash Av ALT WA14 164 D4
CHD/CHDH SK8 170 B4
IRL M44 150 C1
Ashawe Cl LHULT M38 80 D4
Ashawe Gv LHULT M38 81 E4
Ashawe Ter LHULT M38 80 D4
Ashbank Av BOLS/LL BL3 47 F3
Ashbee St BOL BL1 33 H3
Ashberry Cl WILM/AE SK9 199 G2
Ashborne Dr BURY BL9 27 E1
Ashbourne Av BOLE BL2 3 K7
CHD/CHDH SK8 170 C3
MDTN M24 73 F1
URM M41 137 G1
Ashbourne Cl WHIT OL12 20 A2
Ashbourne Crs SALE M33 155 E4
Ashbourne Dr AUL OL6 108 B4
MPL/ROM SK6 196 D1
Ashbourne Gv BRO M7 101 H3
WALK M28 97 F2
WHTF M45 69 F4
Ashbourne Rd
BRAM/HZG SK7 185 G4
DTN/ASHW M34 146 C1
ECC M30 111 F4
SLFD M6 99 H5
STRET M32 125 F4
Ashbourne Sq OLDS OL8 9 F7
Ashbourne St ROCH OL11 28 B2
Ashbridge TRPK M17 125 G2
Ashbridge Rd FAIL M35 105 G4
Ashbrook Av DTN/ASHW M34 131 G5
Ashbrook Cl CHD/CHDH SK8 181 G3
DTN/ASHW M34 131 G5
Ashbrook Crs WHIT OL12 19 H4
Ashbrook Farm Cl RDSH SK5 145 F1
Ashbrook Hey La WHIT OL12 19 H4
Ashbrook La RDSH SK5 145 F1
Ashbrook Rd OLDE OL4 93 E2
Ashbrook St OP/CLY M11 131 F1
Ashburn Av BNG/LEV M19 158 C1
Ashburner St BOL BL1 2 D6
Ashburn Gv HTNM SK4 159 F3
Ashburn Rd HTNM SK4 159 F3
Ashburton Cl HYDE SK14 149 G1
Ashburton Rd EDGY/DAV SK3 171 H5
Ashburton Rd West
TRPK M17 124 D1
Ashbury Cl BOLS/LL BL3 48 D4
Ashbury Pl NEWH/MOS M40 * 115 H1
Ashby Av BNG/LEV M19 158 B2
Ashby Cl FWTH BL4 65 G1
Ashby Gv WHTF M45 69 H5
Ash Cl AUL OL6 107 G5
HYDE SK14 135 H4
OFTN SK2 172 D4
WHIT OL12 19 H4
Ashcombe Dr BOLE BL2 50 D3
RAD M26 51 G4
Ashcott Av WYTH/NTH M22 168 C5
Ashcott Cl HOR/BR BL6 47 E4
Ashcroft WILM/AE SK9 198 C5
Ashcroft Av SLFD M6 112 D1
Ashcroft St CHAD OL9 90 B2
Ashdale Av BOLS/LL BL3 47 F4
Ashdale Cl RDSH SK5 160 A1
Ashdale Crs DROY M43 117 G4
Ashdale Dr CHD/CHDH SK8 181 G2
DID/WITH M20 158 A1
Ashdene AUL OL6 119 H3
Ashdene Cl CHAD OL9 74 D3
OLDE OL4 77 E5
Ashdene Crs BOLE BL2 35 E2
Ashdene Ri OLD OL1 60 C5
Ashdene Rd BNG/LEV M19 158 A4
DID/WITH M20 143 F5
WILM/AE SK9 198 C5
Ashdown Av BKLY M9 88 A3
MPL/ROM SK6 162 B1
Ashdown Cl CHD/CHDH SK8 192 D1
Ashdown Dr BOLE BL2 34 D3
SWIN M27 99 F4
WALK M28 96 A3
Ashdowne Lawns STLY SK15 121 G2
Ashdown Gv BKLY M9 88 A3
Ashdown Rd HTNM SK4 159 F3
Ashdown Ter BKLY M9 88 A3
Ashdown Wy ROY/SHW OL2 59 F1
Ash Dr SWIN M27 83 F5
Asher St BOLS/LL BL3 64 B1
Ashes Cl STLY SK15 121 F5
Ashes Dr BOLE BL2 50 C1
Ashes La MILN OL16 31 F4
OLDE OL4 93 E1
STLY SK15 121 F5
Ashfield DTN/ASHW M34 132 D3
Ashfield Av ROCH OL11 43 E1
Ashfield Cl SLFD M6 112 D2
Ashfield Crs CHD/CHDH SK8 170 A3
OLDE OL4 93 E1
Ashfield Dr NEWH/MOS M40 117 E1
Ashfield Gv BOL BL1 23 F5
EDGY/DAV SK3 * 172 A5
GTN M18 * 131 E4
IRL M44 136 A5
MPL/ROM SK6 163 G5
Ashfield La MILN OL16 44 C2
Ashfield Rd BRUN/LGST M13 129 F5
CHD/CHDH SK8 170 A4
EDGY/DAV SK3 172 A5
HALE/TIMP WA15 177 H1
ROCH OL11 42 D2
SALE M33 154 C1
URM M41 138 D1
Ashfield Sq DROY M43 117 G4
Ashford SALE M33 153 F2
Ashford Av ECC M30 110 D5
RDSH SK5 * 145 F1
SWIN M27 98 B4
WALK M28 96 A4
Ashford Cl BOLE BL2 35 F2
TOT/BURYW BL8 37 G5
WILM/AE SK9 191 H3
Ashford Ct OLDE OL4 76 C4
Ashford Gv WALK M28 97 G2
Ashford Rd DID/WITH M20 142 C4
HTNM SK4 144 D5
WILM/AE SK9 200 D1
Ashford St HEY OL10 40 A4
Ashford Wk BOL BL1 2 C1
CHAD OL9 * 90 B1
Ashgate Av WYTH/NTH M22 168 D5
Ash Gv ALT WA14 177 F3
BOL BL1 48 A1
BOLE BL2 35 G3
CHD/CHDH SK8 181 G4
DROY M43 117 H5
HALE/TIMP WA15 166 A2
HTNM SK4 159 G1
LIT OL15 20 C3
MILN OL16 44 D3
MPL/ROM SK6 174 D4
OLDE OL4 77 F5
PWCH M25 85 H1
RAMS BL0 16 A5
ROY/SHW OL2 59 E3
RUSH/FAL M14 129 F4
STLY SK15 120 C3
STRET M32 140 A3
SWIN M27 98 C5
TOT/BURYW BL8 37 F1
WALK M28 97 F1
Ashgrove MILN OL16 43 G5
Ash Hill Dr MOSL OL5 109 F2
Ashia Cl MILN OL16 30 B5
Ashill Wk CSLFD M3 6 C6
Ashington Cl BOL BL1 33 E3
Ashington Dr TOT/BURYW BL8 36 D5
Ashkirk St GTN M18 130 C3
Ashlands SALE M33 154 B1
Ashlands Av NEWH/MOS M40 104 B1
WALK M28 96 B3
WALK M28 98 B4
Ashlands Dr DTN/ASHW M34 132 B2
Ashlands Rd
HALE/TIMP WA15 154 A5
Ash La HALE/TIMP WA15 178 D3
Ashlar Dr WGTN/LGST M12 115 G5
Ash Lawns BOL BL1 48 A2
Ashlea Gv OLDE OL4 93 G1
Ashleigh Cl ROY/SHW OL2 75 F2
Ash Leigh Dr BOL BL1 47 F1
Ashleigh Rd HALE/TIMP WA15 166 C1
Ashley Av BOLE BL2 50 A1
OLDTF/WHR M16 127 G4
SWIN M27 98 C4
URM M41 137 G1
Ashley Cl ROCH OL11 42 B2
Ashley Court Dr
NEWH/MOS M40 105 E1
Ashley Crs SWIN M27 98 C3
Ashley Dr BRAM/HZG SK7 193 F1
SALE M33 153 H4
SWIN M27 98 C4
Ashley Gdns HYDE SK14 148 A2
MPL/ROM SK6 186 C4
Ashley La BKLY M9 103 G2
Ashley Ms HYDE SK14 148 A2
WHTF M45 70 A5
Ashleymill La ALT WA14 177 G4
Ashley Mill La North
ALT WA14 177 H4
Ashley Rd ALT WA14 177 G1
DROY M43 117 F3
OFTN SK2 172 D1
WILM/AE SK9 199 E1
Ashley St ANC M4 7 H1
CHAD OL9 8 B1
HYDE SK14 133 H4
SLFD M6 112 D3
Ashlor St BURY BL9 4 C7
Ashlyn Gv RUSH/FAL M14 143 F3
Ashlynne AUL OL6 119 H2
Ashmeade HALE/TIMP WA15 178 C3
Ashmond Rd OLDE OL4 93 E1
Ashmoor Rd
WYTH/NTH M22 180 C3
Ashmore Av EDGY/DAV SK3 170 C2
Ashmount Dr WHIT OL12 10 C1
Ashness Dr BOLE BL2 35 F5
BRAM/HZG SK7 183 H4
MDTN M24 72 A1
Ashover Av
WGTN/LGST M12 * 129 G2
Ashover Cl BOL BL1 23 E5
Ashover St STRET M32 126 B5
Ashridge Cl HOR/BR BL6 46 D3
Ashridge Dr DUK SK16 133 E1
ECC M30 110 D5
Ash Rd DROY M43 117 G3
DTN/ASHW M34 131 F4
FWTH BL4 82 C2
PART M31 150 C3
POY/DIS SK12 195 G4
Ash Sq OLDE OL4 76 C4
Ashstead Rd SALE M33 154 D5
Ash St BKLY M9 103 E3
BOLE BL2 3 G6
BRAM/HZG SK7 185 E1
BURY BL9 5 H4
DTN/ASHW M34 132 A1
EDGY/DAV SK3 171 E1
FAIL M35 104 D2
HEY OL10 40 C3
MDTN M24 73 F3
OLDE OL4 92 A1
ROCH OL11 42 B4
SLFD M6 113 E3
Ashton Av ALT WA14 165 H3
Ashton Crs CHAD OL9 90 B4
Ashton Field Dr WALK M28 81 H3
Ashton Hill La DROY M43 117 H5
Ashton La MDTN M24 72 D4
SALE M33 154 A1
Ashton New Rd OP/CLY M11 116 A4
Ashton Old Rd OP/CLY M11 115 H5
Ashton Pl BRAM/HZG SK7 185 H3
Ashton Rd BKLY M9 88 A2
DROY M43 117 H4
DTN/ASHW M34 132 B3
FAIL M35 105 H4
HYDE SK14 133 H3
MPL/ROM SK6 146 C5
OLDS OL8 9 F6
PART M31 151 H3
SALE M33 153 F2
Ashton Rd East FAIL M35 105 F3
Ashton Rd West FAIL M35 104 D3
Ashton St BOLS/LL BL3 48 A5
BOLS/LL BL3 67 E1
CHAD OL9 90 A4
DUK SK16 132 D2
HEY OL10 40 D4
MPL/ROM SK6 147 G5
ROCH OL11 42 D1
Ash Tree Av DROY M43 117 G3
Ash Tree Dr DUK SK16 134 A1
Ash Tree Rd CHH M8 102 B1
HYDE SK14 134 C3
Ashurst Av OP/CLY M11 116 C3
Ashurst Cl BOLE BL2 35 G3
HYDE SK14 148 C2
Ashurst Dr EDGY/DAV SK3 171 E4
Ashurst Gv RAD M26 68 C3
Ashurst Rd WYTH/NTH M22 181 E1
Ashville Ter NEWH/MOS M40 103 G1
Ash Wk CHAD OL9 * 74 C4
MDTN M24 88 C1
Ashway AUL OL6 * 119 F2
Ashway Clough North
OFTN SK2 * 173 E4

Ashway Clough South
OFTN SK2 * 173 E4
Ashwell Rd NTHM/RTH M23 168 A2
Ashwell St BOLE BL2 * 34 C3
Ashwood ALT WA14 177 E4
CHAD OL9 73 H5
RAD M26 67 E5
Ashwood Av DID/WITH M20 156 D2
DTN/ASHW M34 131 F5
RAMS BL0 17 E1
SALE M33 153 H3
WALK M28 81 H2
Ashwood Crs MPL/ROM SK6 175 E2
Ashwood Dr LIT OL15 20 C3
ROY/SHW OL2 58 D4
TOT/BURYW BL8 26 C5
Ashworth Av BOLS/LL BL3 67 F1
DTN/ASHW M34 132 B1
URM M41 137 G1
Ashworth Cl ALT WA14 177 E3
CHAD OL9 90 C3
LIT OL15 20 D1
Ashworth Gdns UPML OL3 95 E2
Ashworth La BOL BL1 34 A1
HYDE SK14 135 G5
Ashworth Ms HEY OL10 40 B4
Ashworth St CHH M8 101 H5
DTN/ASHW M34 132 B4
FAIL M35 104 C4
FWTH BL4 65 H4
HEY OL10 56 A1
RAD M26 52 D5
TOT/BURYW BL8 37 H3
Asia St BOLS/LL BL3 65 F1
Askern Av WYTH/NTH M22 180 C1
Askett Cl NEWH/MOS M40 104 C4
Aspell Cl MDTN M24 72 C4
Aspen Cl HALE/TIMP WA15 167 F4
WHTN BL5 62 A2
Aspen Gdns WHIT OL12 * 28 D2
Aspen Gn DTN/ASHW M34 147 E1
The Aspens CHD/CHDH SK8 * 169 F3
Aspen Wy MPL/ROM SK6 187 F5
Aspen Wd HYDE SK14 134 A5
Aspenwood Cl MPL/ROM SK6 174 D2
Aspenwood Dr BKLY M9 102 D1
Aspen Wood Dr CHAD OL9 73 H5
Aspenwood Dr SALE M33 153 F2
Aspinall Cl WALK M28 81 E4
Aspinall Crs WALK M28 81 E5
Aspinall St HEY OL10 41 F4
MDTN M24 73 F5
RUSH/FAL M14 128 D5
Aspin La ANC M4 7 G1
Aspland Rd HYDE SK14 148 B4
Aspull St OLDE OL4 92 B2
Asquith Av DUK SK16 133 F2
Asquith St RDSH SK5 145 F2
Assheton Av DTN/ASHW M34 118 C5
Assheton Cl AUL OL6 119 G2
Assheton Crs
NEWH/MOS M40 117 E1
Assheton Rd NEWH/MOS M40 117 E1
ROY/SHW OL2 59 G2
Assheton St MDTN M24 72 D2
Assheton Wy MDTN M24 72 D4
Assisi Gdns WGTN/LGST M12 129 F2
Assumpton Rd MDTN M24 72 A1
Astan Av DROY M43 117 E2
Astbury Av DTN/ASHW M34 118 C4
Astbury Cl BURY BL9 53 H1
HALE/TIMP WA15 * 165 H3
OLDE OL4 93 E1
Astbury Crs EDGY/DAV SK3 171 G3
Astbury St RAD M26 68 C3
Aster Av FWTH BL4 65 F3
Aster St OLD OL1 75 F3
Astley Cl ROY/SHW OL2 59 G2
Astley Ct IRL M44 136 A3
Astley Gdns DUK SK16 119 G5
Astley Gv STLY SK15 120 C2
Astley Hall Dr RAMS BL0 16 D4
Astley La BOL BL1 33 G3
Astley Rd BOLE BL2 35 F1
STLY SK15 120 C3
Astley St BOL BL1 33 H4
DUK SK16 119 G5
HTNM SK4 12 E3
OP/CLY M11 116 D4
STLY SK15 120 D5
Aston Av RUSH/FAL M14 142 C2
Aston Cl EDGY/DAV SK3 171 F3
Astor Rd BNG/LEV M19 143 G4
SALQ M50 112 B4
Atcham Gv BKLY M9 87 G1
Athenian Gdns BRO M7 101 F5
Athens Dr WALK M28 81 H5
Athens St STKP SK1 13 K4
Athens Wy OLDE OL4 92 D1
Atherfield BOLE BL2 35 F2
Atherley Gv NEWH/MOS M40 90 A5
Atherstone WHIT OL12 10 B4
Atherstone Av CHH M8 87 F5
Atherstone Cl
TOT/BURYW BL8 37 H2
Atherton Av HYDE SK14 135 H5
Atherton Cl FAIL M35 105 G5
Atherton Gv HYDE SK14 135 H4
Atherton La IRL M44 150 D1
Atherton St CSLFD M3 6 B6
ECC M30 110 D4
EDGY/DAV SK3 12 C6
OLDE OL4 92 D2
Atherton Wy ECC M30 110 D4
Athlone Av BOL BL1 33 G1
BURY BL9 38 C2
CHD/CHDH SK8 171 F4
NEWH/MOS M40 103 H2
Athole St ORD M5 113 E4
Atholl Av STRET M32 139 G1
Atholl Cl BOLS/LL BL3 47 G3
Atholl Dr HEY OL10 55 F1
Athol Rd BRAM/HZG SK7 193 G2
OLDTF/WHR M16 142 A2
Athol St AUL OL6 119 H2
ECC M30 110 D4
GTN M18 130 D5
HTNM SK4 159 G3
RAMS BL0 16 D1
WHIT OL12 11 G2
Atkinson Av BOLS/LL BL3 65 G1
Atkinson Rd SALE M33 139 G5
URM M41 138 D1
Atkinson St CHAD OL9 8 C1
CSLFD M3 6 C5
ROCH OL11 42 B4
STKP SK1 13 K7
Atkin St WALK M28 82 A5
Atlanta Av MANAIR M90 179 H4
Atlantic St ALT WA14 164 D3
Atlas Pk WYTH/NTH M22 * 181 E3
Atlas St AULW OL7 119 F1
DUK SK16 * 120 A5
OLDS OL8 9 F5
Atlow Dr NTHM/RTH M23 168 A4
Attenbury's La ALT WA14 165 H1
Attenburys Park Est
ALT WA14 * 165 H1
Attercliffe Rd CCHDY M21 141 E4
Attewell St OP/CLY M11 * 116 B5
Attleboro Rd
NEWH/MOS M40 103 H3
Attlee Wy WGTN/LGST M12 115 H4
Attock Cl CHAD OL9 90 C2
Attwood Rd HALE/TIMP WA15 166 C4
Attwood St WGTN/LGST M12 129 H5
Atwood Rd DID/WITH M20 157 H3
Atwood St CMANE M1 7 F7
Auberson Rd BOLS/LL BL3 64 C1
Aubrey Rd RUSH/FAL M14 143 G5
Aubrey St ROCH OL11 43 E1
SALQ M50 126 D1
Auburn Av HYDE SK14 148 A3
MPL/ROM SK6 161 G2
Auburn Dr URM M41 139 E2
Auburn Rd DTN/ASHW M34 146 B1
OLDTF/WHR M16 127 E4
Auburn St BOLS/LL BL3 48 C5
CMANE M1 7 H6
Auckland Dr SLFD M6 100 D5
Auckland Rd BNG/LEV M19 143 H3
Audax Wk NEWH/MOS M40 116 C1
Auden Cl OP/CLY M11 117 E4
Audenshaw Hall Gv
DTN/ASHW M34 131 G1
Audenshaw Rd
DTN/ASHW M34 131 H1
Audlem Cl NEWH/MOS M40 115 G3
Audley Av STRET M32 125 E4
Audley Rd BNG/LEV M19 * 144 B1
Audley St AUL OL6 120 B3
MOSL OL5 109 E2
Audlum Ct BURY BL9 5 H4
Audrey Av GTN M18 130 D3
Audrey St BKLY M9 103 G2
Augusta Cl WHIT OL12 10 B2
Augusta St WHIT OL12 10 B1
Augustine Webster Cl
BKLY M9 103 F2
Augustus St ANC M4 114 D1
BOLS/LL BL3 49 F5
Augustus Wy HULME M15 127 G4
Auriga Wk BRO M7 113 H2
Austell Rd WYTH/NTH M22 180 C3
Austen Av BURY BL9 53 G3
Austen Rd ECC M30 111 E4
Austin Dr DID/WITH M20 157 H2
Austin Gv BNG/LEV M19 143 H3
Autumn St BRUN/LGST M13 128 D4
Avallon Cl TOT/BURYW BL8 26 B4
Avalon Dr DID/WITH M20 169 H1
Avebury Cl BRO M7 102 A4
Avebury Rd NTHM/RTH M23 167 H4
Avens Rd PART M31 151 E3
Avenue St BOL BL1 2 A2
STKP SK1 13 H1
The Avenue BOLE BL2 3 J5
BRO M7 101 F5
BURY BL9 38 C1
CHD/CHDH SK8 181 F3
ECC M30 111 E4
HALE/TIMP WA15 178 A4
MPL/ROM SK6 161 E3
ROY/SHW OL2 59 H3
SALE M33 153 G3
URM M41 137 G1
WALK M28 97 F3
WHTN BL5 62 A3
WILM/AE SK9 200 D4
Averhill WALK M28 96 C2
Averill St NEWH/MOS M40 104 C5
Averon Ri OLD OL1 60 C5
Aveson Av CCHDY M21 141 F5
Avian Dr RUSH/FAL M14 142 D3
Aviary Rd WALK M28 97 F4
Aviator Wy WYTH/NTH M22 180 C4
Aviemore Cl RAMS BL0 26 B1
Avis St ROY/SHW OL2 59 H2
Avocet Dr ALT WA14 165 E1
IRL M44 122 B5
Avonbrook Dr
NEWH/MOS M40 90 A5
Avoncliff Cl BOL BL1 33 G3
Avon Cl MILN OL16 31 H5
MPL/ROM SK6 174 D4
WALK M28 81 F5
Avoncourt Dr DID/WITH M20 157 F2
Avondale SWIN M27 84 B5
Avondale Av BRAM/HZG SK7 185 G2
BURY BL9 38 B2
Avondale Crs URM M41 124 B5
Avondale Dr RAMS BL0 26 A1
SLFD M6 99 G5
Avondale Ri WILM/AE SK9 199 G4
Avondale Rd BRAM/HZG SK7 185 G2
EDGY/DAV SK3 12 A6
FWTH BL4 65 E4
STRET M32 126 B4
WHTF M45 69 F3
Avondale St BOL BL1 33 F5
CHH M8 102 B3
OLDS OL8 91 F3
Avon Dr BURY BL9 27 G3
Avon Gdns BNG/LEV M19 144 A5
Avonlea Dr BNG/LEV M19 143 G5
Avonlea Rd DROY M43 117 F3
SALE M33 153 G5
Avonleigh Gdns OLD OL1 76 B3
Avon Rd BNG/LEV M19 143 H5
CHAD OL9 74 A4
CHD/CHDH SK8 181 G5
FWTH BL4 83 E2
HALE/TIMP WA15 177 H4
HEY OL10 40 B4
ROY/SHW OL2 60 A1
Avon St BOL BL1 33 E5
EDGY/DAV SK3 171 H2
OLDS OL8 91 G3
Avril Cl RDSH SK5 145 F3
Avro Cl RUSH/FAL M14 142 D2
Avroe Rd ECC M30 123 G1
Avro Wy MANAIR M90 179 G5
Awburn Rd HYDE SK14 149 G2
Axbridge Wk
NEWH/MOS M40 115 G3
Axford Cl BRO M7 102 A4
Axon Sq OLDTF/WHR M16 128 A4
Aycliffe Av CCHDY M21 156 C1
Aycliffe Gv BRUN/LGST M13 129 F5
Aylesbury Av DTN/ASHW M34 146 D2
URM M41 124 D4
Aylesbury Cl ORD M5 113 F4
Aylesbury Gv MDTN M24 73 F2
Aylesby Av GTN M18 130 A4
Aylesford Rd RUSH/FAL M14 129 E5
Aylesford Wk BOL BL1 * 2 D1
Aylsham Cl MPL/ROM SK6 161 G1
Aylsham Ms SWIN M27 98 C5
Aylwin Dr SALE M33 154 C3
Ayr Av OLDS OL8 91 G4
Ayr Cl BRAM/HZG SK7 185 H2
Ayres Rd OLDTF/WHR M16 127 F4
Ayr Gv HEY OL10 55 F1
Ayrshire Rd BRO M7 100 D4
Ayr St BOLE BL2 34 C2
Ayrton Gv LHULT M38 81 F2
Aysgarth MILN OL16 11 G2
Aysgarth Av CHD/CHDH SK8 169 H3
GTN M18 130 D2
MPL/ROM SK6 162 C2
Aysgarth Cl SALE M33 153 G3
Ayshford Cl ALT WA14 165 E3
Ayton Gv RUSH/FAL M14 129 F4
Aytoun St CMANE M1 7 H5
Azalea Av GTN M18 130 C2

B

Babbacombe Gv BKLY M9 87 G2
Babbacombe Rd OFTN SK2 172 D3
Back Abingdon Rd BOLE BL2 34 D5
Back Acton St CMANE M1 * 7 H6
Back Adcroft St STKP SK1 13 H7
Back Adrian Rd BOL BL1 33 F4
Back Adrian Rd East BOL BL1 * 33 F4
Back Ainscow St BOL BL1 2 C2
Back Ainsworth La BOLE BL2 3 K1
Back Ainsworth La East
BOLE BL2 49 H1
Back Ainsworth Rd North
TOT/BURYW BL8 37 H4
Back Ainsworth Rd South
TOT/BURYW BL8 37 H4
Back Ainsworth St BOL BL1 33 G4
Back Albert St BURY BL9 5 H4
Back Albion Pl BURY BL9 38 C2
Back Alder St BOLS/LL BL3 65 E1
Back Alexander Rd BOLE BL2 34 D5
Back Alexandra St
BOLS/LL BL3 48 B5
Back Alfred St BOLS/LL BL3 * 49 G5
Back Alice St BOLS/LL BL3 * 48 B4
BOLS/LL BL3 67 E1
Back Alicia St BOLS/LL BL3 50 A5
Back All Saints' St BOL BL1 3 F3
Back Alston St BOLS/LL BL3 64 D1
Back Andrew St BURY BL9 5 G5
Back Andrew St North
BURY BL9 5 H5
Back Anglia Gv BOLS/LL BL3 48 B5
Back Annis Rd BOLS/LL BL3 * 48 A5
Back Anson St BOL BL1 * 34 A3
Back Apple Ter BOL BL1 * 33 G4
Back Argo St BOLS/LL BL3 48 C5
Back Argyle St BURY BL9 38 C1
Back Arlington St BOLS/LL BL3 65 E1
Back Arnold St BOL BL1 33 F4
Back Arnold Ter BOL BL1 32 C5
Back Ashbee St BOL BL1 33 H3
Back Ashford Wk BOL BL1 2 C1
Back Ashley St ANC M4 7 H1
Back Ash St BOLE BL2 3 G6
BURY BL9 * 5 H4
Back Ashton St BOLS/LL BL3 * 48 A5
Back Ashworth La BOL BL1 34 A1
Back Ashworth St
TOT/BURYW BL8 37 H3
Back Astley St BOL BL1 33 H4
Back Augustus St
BOLS/LL BL3 * 49 F5
Back Augustus St West
BOLS/LL BL3 49 E5
Back Avenue St BOL BL1 2 A2
Back Avondale St BOL BL1 * 33 F5
Back Baldwin St BOLS/LL BL3 * 48 D4
Back Baldwin St North
BOLS/LL BL3 48 D4
Back Balloon St ANC M4 * 7 F2
Back Banbury St BOLE BL2 34 D5
Back Bankfield St BOLS/LL BL3 48 B4
Back Bank St CHH M8 114 D1
Back Bantry St BOLS/LL BL3 * 48 D4
Back Barbara St BOLS/LL BL3 48 C5
Back Bark St BOL BL1 2 D4
Back Bashall St BOL BL1 48 B1
Back Battenberg Rd BOL BL1 48 B1
Back Baxendale St BOL BL1 33 H2
Back Bayley St BOL BL1 2 A2
Back Baythorpe St BOL BL1 * 34 A4
Back Baytorpe St North
BOL BL1 * 34 A3
Back Beaconsfield St
BOLS/LL BL3 2 A7
Back Beaconsfield Ter
BOLE BL2 3 J1
Back Bedford St BOL BL1 2 A3
Back Beech St BOL BL1 34 A4
Back Beechwood St
BOLS/LL BL3 65 E1
Back Belbeck St
TOT/BURYW BL8 37 H4
Back Bell La BURY BL9 5 G3
Back Belmont Rd BOL BL1 33 H1
Back Belmont Rd East
BOL BL1 33 H1
Back Bennett's La BOL BL1 33 F4
Back Bennett's La East
BOL BL1 33 F4
Back Benson St BURY BL9 5 G6
Back Bentinck St BOL BL1 33 E5
Back Bentley St BOLE BL2 49 H4
Back Bertrand Rd BOL BL1 48 B3
Back Beverley Rd BOL BL1 48 B1
Back Birch St BURY BL9 5 F2
Back Blackbank St BOL BL1 34 A5
Back Blackburn Rd BOL BL1 34 A4
Back Blackburn Rd West
BOL BL1 33 H3
EDGW/EG BL7 * 22 D3
Back Blackburn St BOL BL1 34 A3
Back Blackwood St
BOLS/LL BL3 49 F5
Back Bolton Rd North
TOT/BURYW BL8 37 H5
Back Bolton Rd South
TOT/BURYW BL8 37 H5
Back Bolton St BOL BL1 34 A4
Back Bolton St South BURY BL9 4 C4
Back Bond St West BURY BL9 5 H4
Back Boundary St BOL BL1 33 G4
Back Bowen St BOL BL1 * 33 E5
Backbower La HYDE SK14 148 B3
Back Bowness Rd
BOLS/LL BL3 48 C5
Back Bradford Rd
BOLS/LL BL3 65 F1
Back Bradford Rd West
BOLS/LL BL3 65 F1
Back Bradford St BOLE BL2 3 K5
Back Bradford St East
BOLE BL2 3 J5
Back Bradford St South
BOLE BL2 3 H6
Back Bradford St West
BOLE BL2 3 J5
Back Bradshaw BOLE BL2 34 D2
Back Bradshaw Brow West
BOLE BL2 * 34 D2
Back Bradshawgate BOL BL1 3 F5
Back Bradshaw Rd East
BOLE BL2 35 E1
Back Bradshaw St MILN OL16 10 E4
Back Brandon St BOLS/LL BL3 48 C5
Back Brandon St North
BOLS/LL BL3 48 C5
Back Brandwood St
BOLS/LL BL3 48 B5
Back Bridgeman St
BOLS/LL BL3 48 D5
Back Bridge St BOL BL1 2 E3
CSLFD M3 6 D4
RAMS BL0 16 D2
Back Brierley St BURY BL9 53 F1
Back Brierley St South
BURY BL9 53 F1
Back Brigade St BOL BL1 48 B2
Back Brindley St BOL BL1 34 A2
Back Brink's Pl BOL BL1 * 2 C4
Back Bristol Av BOLE BL2 34 D5
Back Bristol St BOLS/LL BL3 48 C4
Back Broach St BOLS/LL BL3 48 D5
Back Broad o' th' La BOL BL1 * 33 H2
Back Broad St BURY BL9 4 D5
Back Bromwich St BOLE BL2 3 J6
Back Brookfield St BOLE BL2 3 J4
Back Brook St North BURY BL9 5 G1
Back Broom St BOLE BL2 3 H4
MILN OL16 45 E2
Back Burnaby St BOLS/LL BL3 48 C4
Back Burnham Av BOL BL1 32 D5
Back Bury New Rd BOLE BL2 3 H5
Back Bury New Rd East
BOLE BL2 3 J5
Back Bury Old Rd BOLE BL2 3 H4
Back Bury Rd BOLE BL2 50 A2
Back Bury Rd East BOLE BL2 49 H2
Back Bury Rd South BOLE BL2 50 A2
Back Bushell St BOLS/LL BL3 * 48 A5
Back Byrom St
TOT/BURYW BL8 37 G2
Back Byrom St South
TOT/BURYW BL8 37 G2
Back Calder Rd BOLS/LL BL3 64 D1
Back Caledonia St BOLS/LL BL3 48 B4
Back Calvert Rd BOLS/LL BL3 65 E1
Back Cambridge St AULW OL7 119 E4
Back Camp St BRO M7 * 101 G5
Back Canada St BOL BL1 33 G4
Back Canning St BURY BL9 4 E1
Back Carl St BOL BL1 33 G4
Back Carter St BOLS/LL BL3 49 F5
Back Castle St BOLE BL2 3 J5
Back Cateaton St BURY BL9 4 E2
Back Cecilia St BOLS/LL BL3 49 F5
Back Cecil St BOLE BL2 3 J5
MOSL OL5 * 108 D2
Back Cedar St BURY BL9 5 J3
Back Cedar St North BURY BL9 5 J3
Back Cemetery Rd East
BOLE BL2 3 K4
Back Cestrian St BOLS/LL BL3 * 65 E1
Back Chalfont St BOL BL1 34 A4
Back Chapel St BNG/LEV M19 144 A2
BRAM/HZG SK7 * 185 F1
TOT/BURYW BL8 26 A4
WHIT OL12 * 19 H1
Back Chapman St BOL BL1 33 E5
Back Charles Holden St
BOL BL1 2 A6
Back Chaucer St BOL BL1 33 G5
Back Cheapside BOL BL1 2 E5
Back Chesham Rd North
BURY BL9 38 D2
Back Chesham Rd South
BURY BL9 38 D2
Back Chester St BURY BL9 38 D2
Back China La CMANE M1 7 H5
Back Chorley New Rd BOL BL1 2 A3
Back Chorley New Rd North
BOL BL1 48 A2
Back Chorley Old Rd BOL BL1 32 D5
Back Chorley Old Rd North
BOL BL1 33 E5
Back Chorley Old Rd South
BOL BL1 32 D5
Back Chorley St BOL BL1 2 C4
Back Chorley St East BOL BL1 * 2 C3
Back Church Av BOLS/LL BL3 48 B5
Back Church Rd BOL BL1 32 D4
BOL BL1 33 F4
Back Church Rd North BOL BL1 33 F4
Back Church St BOL BL1 2 D3
BOLS/LL BL3 66 D1
Back Clarendon Rd BOLE BL2 49 H2
Back Clarke St BOL BL1 * 48 B1
Back Clay St East
EDGW/EG BL7 * 23 F4
Back Clay St West
EDGW/EG BL7 * 23 F4
Back Clegg's Buildings
BOL BL1 * 2 C3
Back Clegg St BOLE BL2 49 H2
Back Clifton St BURY BL9 38 C2
Back Cloister St BOL BL1 * 33 F4
Back Clyde St BOL BL1 33 H4
Back Cobden St BOL BL1 33 G3
Back Colenso Rd BOLE BL2 * 50 A2
Back College Land CSLFD M3 * 6 D4
Back College Wy BOLS/LL BL3 2 B6
Back Columbia Rd BOL BL1 * 48 B1
Back Coniston St BOL BL1 * 34 A3
Back Coop St BOL BL1 33 H2
Back Cornall St
TOT/BURYW BL8 37 H3
Back Corson St BOLS/LL BL3 66 A2
Back Cottam St
TOT/BURYW BL8 * 37 H3
Back Cotton St BOL BL1 33 G4
Back Cowm La WHIT OL12 14 B2
Back Cox Green Rd North
EDGW/EG BL7 23 E3
Back Crawford Av BOLE BL2 3 J6
Back Crawford St BOLE BL2 * 3 J6
Back Crescent Av BOL BL1 2 B3
Back Crescent Rd BOLS/LL BL3 49 F5
Back Crescent Rd West
BOLS/LL BL3 65 F1
Back Croft La BOLS/LL BL3 49 G5
Back Cromer Av BOLE BL2 34 D5
Back Crostons Rd
TOT/BURYW BL8 4 A3
Back Croston St BOLS/LL BL3 48 B5
Back Crumpsall St North
BOL BL1 33 H3
Back Cundey St BOL BL1 * 33 F5
Back Curzon Rd BOL BL1 48 B2
Back Cyril St BOLS/LL BL3 * 49 F4
Back Daisy St BOLS/LL BL3 48 B5
Back Darley St FWTH BL4 66 B4
Back Darwen Rd North
EDGW/EG BL7 23 E3
Back Darwen Rd South
EDGW/EG BL7 23 F4
Back Darwin St BOL BL1 * 33 G4
Back Deal St BOLS/LL BL3 * 65 E1
BURY BL9 5 J5
Back Deane Church La
BOLS/LL BL3 * 48 A5
Back Deane Church La West
BOLS/LL BL3 * 48 A5
Back Deane Rd BOLS/LL BL3 48 B4
Back Deane Rd North
BOLS/LL BL3 2 B7
Back Delamere St South
BURY BL9 * 38 D1
Back Denton St BURY BL9 38 C2
Back Derby St BOLS/LL BL3 48 D4
BURY BL9 5 F4
Back Design St BOLS/LL BL3 * 48 A5
Back Devonshire Rd BOL BL1 32 D5
Back Devon St North
BURY BL9 * 53 F1
Back Devon St South
BURY BL9 * 53 G1
Back Dijon St BOLS/LL BL3 48 B5
Back Dijon St North
BOLS/LL BL3 48 B5
Back Dobie St BOLS/LL BL3 * 49 F5
Back Doffcocker Brow
BOL BL1 32 C5
Back Dorset St BOLE BL2 3 H5
Back Dougill St BOL BL1 33 E5
Back Dougill St South BOL BL1 33 E5
Back Drake St MILN OL16 10 D7
Back Drummond St BOL BL1 * 33 H2
Back Ducie Av BOL BL1 48 B2
Back Duckworth St BURY BL9 38 D2
Back Duncan St BRO M7 101 F3
Back Dunstan St BOLE BL2 49 H2
Back Durham St ROCH OL11 43 F1
Back Duxbury St BOL BL1 * 33 G4
Back Earnshaw St
BOLS/LL BL3 * 64 B1
Back Eastbank St BOL BL1 34 A3
Back East St BURY BL9 5 F6
Back Eckersley Rd BOL BL1 33 H3
Back Edditch Gv BOLE BL2 49 H2
Back Eden St BOL BL1 33 H3
Back Edgmont Av
BOLS/LL BL3 * 48 C5
Back Eldon St BURY BL9 4 E1
Back Ellesmere Rd BOLS/LL BL3 64 B1
Back Ellesmere St BOLS/LL BL3 2 A7
Back Elm St BURY BL9 5 J5
Back Elmwood Gv BOL BL1 * 48 B1
Back Elmwood Gv West
BOL BL1 * 48 B1
Back Elsworth St CSLFD M3 114 D2
Back Empire Rd BOLE BL2 50 A1
Back Empress St BOL BL1 33 E5
Back Ena St BOLS/LL BL3 * 65 F1
Back Ernest St BOL BL1 2 A6
Back Eskrick St BOL BL1 * 33 G4
Back Eskrick St East BOL BL1 * 33 G4
Back Eskrick St South BOL BL1 33 G4
Back Eskrick St West BOL BL1 33 G4
Back Essingdon St BOLS/LL BL3 48 C5

Back Essingdon St South
BOLS/LL BL3 48 C5
Back Eustace St BOLS/LL BL3 65 F1
Back Euxton St BOLS/LL BL3 48 C5
Back Everton St North
BOL BL1 * 34 A4
Back Ewart St BOL BL1 * 33 H4
Back Fairhaven Rd BOL BL1 34 A3
Back Fair St BOLS/LL BL3 64 B2
Back Fenton St
TOT/BURYW BL8 37 H3
Back Fern St East BOLS/LL BL3 48 B3
Back Fir St BURY BL9 5 J4
Back Fletcher St BURY BL9 5 G4
RAD M26 * 67 E5
Back Flora St BOLS/LL BL3 * 48 D5
Back Florence Av BOL BL1 34 A2
Back Fortune St BOLS/LL BL3 49 G4
Back Foundry St BURY BL9 5 F5
Back Frances St BOL BL1 33 G4
Back Frank St BOL BL1 * 33 G5
BURY BL9 5 F6
Back Fylde St BOLS/LL BL3 66 A2
Back Gainsborough Av
BOLS/LL BL3 64 B1
Back Garside Gv BOL BL1 * 33 F4
Back Garston St BURY BL9 38 D2
Back Gaskell St BOL BL1 2 B3
Back Gaskell St East BOL BL1 * 2 B3
Back Gaythorne St BOL BL1 * 34 A3
Back George Barton St
BOLE BL2 3 K1
Back George St BOLS/LL BL3 49 F5
CMANE M1 7 F5
Back Gibraltar St BOLS/LL BL3 2 B7
Back Gibraltar St South
BOLS/LL BL3 * 2 A7
Back Gigg La BURY BL9 53 G1
Back Gilmour St MDTN M24 72 D4
Back Gilnow Gv BOL BL1 2 A6
Back Gilnow La West
BOLS/LL BL3 48 B3
Back Gilnow Rd BOL BL1 48 B3
Back Glen Av BOLS/LL BL3 * 48 A4
Back Glenboro Av
TOT/BURYW BL8 37 G4
Back Glen Bott St BOL BL1 * 33 G4
Back Gloster St BOLE BL2 3 H5
Back Goldsmith St
BOLS/LL BL3 48 C5
Back Goodlad St
TOT/BURYW BL8 37 G2
Back Gordon Av BOLS/LL BL3 48 B4
Back Gorses Mt BOLE BL2 49 H4
Back Grafton St ALT WA14 165 G5
BOL BL1 2 A3
Back Grantham Cl BOL BL1 * 33 H5
Back Grasmere St BOL BL1 34 A4
Back Greaves St OLD OL1 * 9 H4
Back Greenhalgh St
BOLS/LL BL3 * 66 D1
Back Greenland Rd
BOLS/LL BL3 65 E1
Back Green La BOLS/LL BL3 65 G2
Back Green La South
BOLS/LL BL3 65 E1
Back Green St MDTN M24 73 E3
Back Gregory Av BOLE BL2 50 B1
Back Grendon St BOLS/LL BL3 64 B1
Back Gresham St BOL BL1 * 34 A3
Back Grosvenor St STLY SK15 120 D4
Back Grove St BOL BL1 33 G4
Back Hadwin St BOL BL1 2 E1
Back Halliwell La CHH M8 * 102 A3
Back Halliwell Rd BOL BL1 33 H4
Back Halliwell Rd South
BOL BL1 33 G4
Back Halstead St BOLE BL2 3 H5
BURY BL9 38 D2
Back Hamilton St BRO M7 * 101 G4
BURY BL9 38 C2
Back Hampson St
NEWH/MOS M40 115 G1
Back Hanson St BURY BL9 38 C2
Back Hargreaves St BOL BL1 33 H4
Back Harper's La South
BOL BL1 * 33 E4
Back Hartington Rd BOL BL1 * 48 B1
Back Harvey St
TOT/BURYW BL8 37 H3
Back Haslam St BURY BL9 * 38 D2
Back Hatfield Rd BOL BL1 33 F5
Back Hawthorne Rd
BOLS/LL BL3 * 48 A5
Back Hawthorne Rd East
BOLS/LL BL3 * 48 A4
Back Hawthorn Rd West
BOLS/LL BL3 * 48 A4
Back Haydn St BOL BL1 33 G4
Back Haydock St BOL BL1 2 E2
Back Hayward St
TOT/BURYW BL8 * 37 H3
Back Hengist St BOLE BL2 49 H2
Back Hennon St BOL BL1 33 G5
Back Henrietta St
BOLS/LL BL3 * 48 A5
Back Henry Lee St
BOLS/LL BL3 64 B1
Back Heywood St East
BURY BL9 5 G5
Back Heywood St West
BURY BL9 5 G6
Back High Bank St BOLE BL2 49 H2
Back Higher Darcy St
BOLE BL2 49 H4
Back Higher Shady La West
EDGW/EG BL7 23 G4
Back Higher Swan La
BOLS/LL BL3 64 C1
Back Higher Swan La West
BOLS/LL BL3 64 C1
Back High St BOLS/LL BL3 48 D5
Back High St South
BOLS/LL BL3 48 D5
Back High St West
BOLS/LL BL3 * 48 D5
Back Hilden St BOLE BL2 3 H6
Back Hilden St West BOLE BL2 3 H6
Back Hilton St BRO M7 101 G3
BURY BL9 5 F1
Back Hind St BOLE BL2 49 H2
Back Holland St BOL BL1 34 A2
Back Holland St East
BOL BL1 * 34 A2
Back Holly Pl BOL BL1 33 H2
Back Holly St BOL BL1 34 A2
BURY BL9 5 H4
Back Holly St South BURY BL9 5 H4
Back Hopefield St BOLS/LL BL3 48 C5
Back Hope St BRO M7 101 G3
OLD OL1 76 A5
Back Horbury St
TOT/BURYW BL8 37 H4
Back Horeb St East
BOLS/LL BL3 * 48 C4
Back Hornby St BURY BL9 38 C1
Back Hornby St East BURY BL9 4 E2
Back Hornby St West
BURY BL9 * 4 E2
Back Horne St North
BURY BL9 * 53 F1
Back Horne St South
BURY BL9 53 F1
Back Horsa St BOLE BL2 3 J1
Back Horsa St North BOLE BL2 * 3 J1
Back Hotel St BOL BL1 * 2 E4
Back Hough La East
EDGW/EG BL7 23 F4
Back Howarden St BOL BL1 * 33 H1
Back Howcroft St
BOLS/LL BL3 * 48 C5
Back Howe St BRO M7 101 F3
Back Hughes St BOL BL1 33 G4
Back Hulbert St
TOT/BURYW BL8 * 37 H5
Back Hulme St ORD M5 113 H4
TOT/BURYW BL8 4 A2
Back Hulton La BOLS/LL BL3 63 H2
Back Hulton La South
BOLS/LL BL3 * 63 H2
Back Hulton La West
BOLS/LL BL3 * 47 H5
Back Huntley Mount Rd
BURY BL9 5 J2
Back Hurst St BOLS/LL BL3 64 B1
BURY BL9 5 G6
Back Huxley St BOL BL1 33 F4
Back Ingham St BURY BL9 5 G6
Back Ingham St East BURY BL9 5 G6
Back Irlam St BOL BL1 33 H3
Back Irlam St North BOL BL1 * 33 H3
Back Ivy Bank Rd BOL BL1 33 H1
Back Ivy Rd BOL BL1 33 F5
Back Ivy Rd West BOL BL1 * 33 F4
Back James St BOLS/LL BL3 67 E1
Back Jauncey St BOLS/LL BL3 48 B4
Back John Brown St BOL BL1 * 2 B3
Back John Cross St
BOLS/LL BL3 * 48 D5
Back Johnson St BOL BL1 * 3 F6
Back Junction St CMANE M1 7 J4
Back Keighley St BOL BL1 33 F4
Back Kendal Rd BOL BL1 48 B1
Back Kershaw St BURY BL9 5 H5
Back Kingholm Gdns BOL BL1 * 33 G5
Back Kingsley St BOL BL1 33 G4
Back King St BOL BL1 2 D4
OLDS OL8 9 F4
Back King St North
EDGW/EG BL7 23 E3
Back King St South BOLE BL2 35 E1
Back Knight St
TOT/BURYW BL8 37 H4
Back Knowl St STLY SK15 121 E3
Back Knowsley Rd BOL BL1 * 33 E4
Back Knowsley St BOL BL1 2 E4
BURY BL9 4 D5
Back Kylemore Av
BOLS/LL BL3 * 48 A4
Back La AULW OL7 118 D1
BOL BL1 2 C3
DROY M43 106 A5
HALE/TIMP WA15 188 A2
HYDE SK14 135 H5
MOSL OL5 93 F5
OLDE OL4 77 H3
WHIT OL12 14 B3
WHTN BL5 80 A1
Back Lark St BOL BL1 3 F3
Back Latham St BOL BL1 34 A4
Back Lathom St BURY BL9 38 D2
Back Laurel St BURY BL9 5 J4
Back Lawn St BOL BL1 33 F5
Back Leachfield St BOL BL1 33 G3
Back Leach St BOLS/LL BL3 48 D4
Back Lee Av BOLS/LL BL3 64 D1
Back Lee St UPML OL3 79 E4
Back Lena St BOL BL1 34 A4
Back Lenora St BOLS/LL BL3 * 48 A4
Back Lever Edge La
BOLS/LL BL3 64 B2
BOLS/LL BL3 65 E1
Back Lever Edge La South
BOLS/LL BL3 64 D1
Back Lever St BOLS/LL BL3 49 E5
Back Lever St North
BOLS/LL BL3 50 D5
Back Lever St South
BOLS/LL BL3 * 48 D5
Back Lightburne Av BOL BL1 48 A2
Back Lilly St BOL BL1 2 A2
Back Lincoln Rd BOL BL1 * 48 B1
Back Lindley St BOLS/LL BL3 * 67 E1
Back Linton Av BURY BL9 38 C1
Back Longden St BOL BL1 48 B1
Back Longfield Rd
BOLS/LL BL3 * 64 A1
Back Long La BOLE BL2 50 B2
Back Longsight North
BOLE BL2 35 F1
Back Longsight South
BOLE BL2 35 E1
Back Lonsdale St
TOT/BURYW BL8 37 H4
Back Lord St BOLS/LL BL3 67 E1
BURY BL9 5 F6
Back Loxham St BOLS/LL BL3 66 A2
Back Lumsden St BOLS/LL BL3 48 D4
Back Luton St BOLS/LL BL3 49 F5
Back Lytton St BOL BL1 33 G5
Back Mackenzie St BOL BL1 33 G2
Back Malvern Av BOL BL1 32 D5
BURY BL9 38 C1
Back Manchester Old Rd
BURY BL9 4 C7
Back Manchester Rd
BOLE BL2 3 G7
BOLS/LL BL3 65 H2
BURY BL9 4 C5
Back Manchester Rd South
BOLS/LL BL3 49 F5
Back Manchester Rd West
BOLS/LL BL3 49 G5
Back Manchester St
HEY OL10 * 41 F5
Back Manor St BURY BL9 5 G4
Back Maple St BOLS/LL BL3 * 48 C4
Back Marion St South
BOLS/LL BL3 * 65 H2
Back Market St BOLS/LL BL3 67 E1
BURY BL9 4 D5
RAD M26 67 E5
Back Market St West BURY BL9 4 D4
Back Markland Hill La BOL BL1 32 C5
Back Markland Hill La East
BOL BL1 * 32 C5
Back Markland Hill La West
BOL BL1 * 32 C5
Back Marlborough St BOL BL1 2 A3
Back Marsh Fold La BOL BL1 * 48 B1
Back Mary St BOLS/LL BL3 * 48 C4
Back Mason St BURY BL9 5 G5
Back Massie St
CHD/CHDH SK8 * 170 A3
Back Mawdsley St BOL BL1 2 E5
Back Maxwell St BOL BL1 * 33 H2
Back Maybank St BOLS/LL BL3 48 C4
Back Mayfield Av BOLS/LL BL3 65 G1
Back Mayor St BOL BL1 2 A6
TOT/BURYW BL8 37 H3
Back Maze St BOLS/LL BL3 49 H4
Back McDonna St BOL BL1 33 F3
Back McKean St BOLS/LL BL3 49 F5
Back McKean St North
BOLS/LL BL3 * 49 F5
Back Melbourne Rd
BOLS/LL BL3 48 B4
Back Melbourne St STLY SK15 120 D3
Back Mellor Gv BOL BL1 * 33 E5
Back Mellor Gv West BOL BL1 * 33 E5
Back Melrose Av BOL BL1 32 D5
Back Melville St BOLS/LL BL3 65 F1
Back Mercia St BOLS/LL BL3 48 B4
Back Meredith St BOLS/LL BL3 65 E1
Back Mere Gdns BOL BL1 2 C2
Back Merlin Gv BOL BL1 * 33 E5
Back Merton St
TOT/BURYW BL8 4 A2
Back Methwold St
BOLS/LL BL3 * 48 B5
Back Milford Rd BOLS/LL BL3 64 D1
Back Miller St BOL BL1 * 33 H2
Back Millet St BURY BL9 4 B5
Back Mill St North
EDGW/EG BL7 * 23 E3
Back Mill St South
EDGW/EG BL7 * 23 E3
Back Milner Av BURY BL9 38 C1
Back Minorca St BOLS/LL BL3 * 48 D5
Back Monmouth Av BURY BL9 38 C1
Back Moor HYDE SK14 135 H4
Back Moorfield Gv BOLE BL2 34 C5
Back Moorgate West BURY BL9 5 G3
Back Mornington Rd East
BOL BL1 48 B1
Back Morris Green La
BOLS/LL BL3 64 B2
Back Morris Green La East
BOLS/LL BL3 64 B2
Back Moss Ter BOL BL1 2 E3
Back Mostyn Av BURY BL9 38 C1
Back Mowbray St BOL BL1 * 33 E5
Back Murton Ter BOL BL1 34 A2
Back Musgrave Rd BOL BL1 48 B1
Back Musgrave Rd North
BOL BL1 48 B1
Back Myrtle St BURY BL9 5 J4
Back Myrtle St South BURY BL9 5 J5
Back Nebo St BOLS/LL BL3 48 C5
Back Nelson St South
BURY BL9 * 53 G1
Back Nevada St BOL BL1 33 H5
Back Newbold St
TOT/BURYW BL8 37 H4
Back New George St
TOT/BURYW BL8 37 H3
Back Newhall La BOL BL1 32 D5
Back Newport Rd
BOLS/LL BL3 * 49 F5
Back Newport St BOL BL1 2 E6
Back Newton St BOL BL1 33 H4
Back Nixon Rd BOLS/LL BL3 64 B1
Back Normanby St
BOLS/LL BL3 64 B2
Back Norris St BOLS/LL BL3 * 66 D1
Back Northern Gv BOL BL1 33 F5
Back Nunnery Rd
BOLS/LL BL3 * 48 A5
Back Nut St BOL BL1 33 G4
Back Oak St RAD M26 68 D3
Back Olaf St BOLE BL2 3 J1
Back Oldham Rd MILN OL16 30 B5
Back Olga St BOL BL1 33 G4
Back Olga St North BOL BL1 * 33 G4
Back Olive Bank
TOT/BURYW BL8 37 G2
Back Oram St BURY BL9 38 D2
Back Oriel St BOLS/LL BL3 48 B4
Back Ormrod St BURY BL9 5 H5
Back Osborne Gv BOL BL1 33 F5
Back o' th' Low Rd OLDE OL4 77 E4
Back Oxford Gv North
BOL BL1 33 F5
Back Oxford St BURY BL9 5 G6
Back Packer St BOL BL1 33 F4
Back Palace St BOL BL1 2 E3
Back Palm St BOL BL1 34 A3
Back Parkdale Rd BOLE BL2 34 D5
Back Parkfield Rd
BOLS/LL BL3 65 F1
Back Parkhills Rd North
BURY BL9 * 53 F1
Back Parkinson St
BOLS/LL BL3 * 48 B4
Back Park Rd BOL BL1 2 A5
Back Park St BOL BL1 2 A3
Back Park Vw BOL BL1 23 E5
Back Park View Rd
BOLS/LL BL3 * 48 B5
Back Parsonage St BURY BL9 5 H3
Backparsons La BURY BL9 4 E4
Back Partington St
BOLS/LL BL3 64 B2
Back Patience St WHIT OL12 * 29 F2
Back Patterson St
BOLS/LL BL3 * 47 H5
Back Peabody St
BOLS/LL BL3 * 48 D5
Back Peace St BOLS/LL BL3 48 C4
Back Pedder St BOL BL1 33 F5
Back Peers St TOT/BURYW BL8 37 H4
Back Penarth Rd
BOLS/LL BL3 * 48 A5
Back Pennington Rd
BOLS/LL BL3 65 E1
Back Percy St BURY BL9 5 J2
Back Peter St BURY BL9 5 G3
Back Peveril St BOLS/LL BL3 64 A1
Back Phoenix St BURY BL9 4 C5
Back Piccadilly CMANE M1 7 H5
Back Pikes La West
BOLS/LL BL3 48 B4
Back Pine St BOL BL1 34 A4
BURY BL9 5 J4
Back Pleasant St BOL BL1 2 D2
Back Pool Fold CMANW M2 * 6 E4
Back Poplar Av BOL BL1 34 A2
Back Porter St BURY BL9 38 C2
Back Portland St AUL OL6 119 F3
Back Portugal St BOLE BL2 3 J5
Back Primrose St BOL BL1 * 34 A2
Back Primula St BOL BL1 34 A2
Back Proctor St
TOT/BURYW BL8 * 37 H5
Back Progress St BOL BL1 * 34 A5
Back Quay St CSLFD M3 6 B5
Back Quebec St BOLS/LL BL3 48 B4
Back Queensgate BOL BL1 48 B1
Back Queen St BOL BL1 * 2 D5
Back Radcliffe Rd East
BOLE BL2 * 3 J4
Back Raimond St BOL BL1 33 F3
Back Rainshaw St BOL BL1 34 A2
Back Rake St BURY BL9 38 C2
Back Randal St BOLS/LL BL3 * 48 B5
Back Range St BOLS/LL BL3 * 48 C5
Back Raphael St BOL BL1 33 G5
Back Raven St BURY BL9 5 F1
Back Rawson Rd BOL BL1 33 F5
Back Rawson Rd North
BOL BL1 33 F5
Back Raymond Av BURY BL9 38 C1
Back Red Bank ANC M4 114 D2
Back Redhill Gv BOL BL1 2 C2
Back Regent St BURY BL9 4 E1
Back Ribblesdale Rd
BOLS/LL BL3 48 C5
Back Richard Burch St
BURY BL9 5 F2
Back Richelieu St BOLS/LL BL3 49 F5
Back Rigby La North
BOLE BL2 * 23 H5
Back Rigby La South BOLE BL2 23 H5
Back Rishton La BOLS/LL BL3 65 E1
Back Rishton La East
BOLS/LL BL3 65 E1
Back Rochdale Old Rd North
BURY BL9 39 F3
Back Rochdale Old Rd South
BURY BL9 5 K2
Back Rochdale Rd BURY BL9 5 G4
Back Rochdale Rd South
BURY BL9 5 G5
Back Rock Av BOL BL1 33 F3
Back Roland Rd BOLS/LL BL3 48 B4
Back Romer St BOLE BL2 49 H2
Back Rosamond St
BOLS/LL BL3 48 B5
Back Roscow Av BOLE BL2 50 B1
Back Rose Bank BURY BL9 * 38 C2
Back Roseberry St
BOLS/LL BL3 48 B5
Back Rossini St BOL BL1 * 33 G3
Back Rw WHIT OL12 * 18 A2
Back Rowena St BOLS/LL BL3 * 65 H2
Back Rowland St
BOLS/LL BL3 * 64 A1
Back Roxalina St BOLS/LL BL3 48 D5
Back Royal Av BURY BL9 38 C1
Back Royds St MILN OL16 43 F1
Back Rudolph St BOLS/LL BL3 65 E1
Back Rumworth St
BOLS/LL BL3 48 C5
Back Rushton Rd BOL BL1 * 33 E5
Back Russell Cl BOL BL1 * 48 B1
Back Russell St BOL BL1 48 B1
Back Rutland Gv BOL BL1 33 F5
Back Ryefield St BOL BL1 3 G1
Back St Anne's St BURY BL9 38 C2
Back St Ann St BOL BL1 33 H5
Back St Augustine St
BOL BL1 33 G4
Back St George's Rd ANC M4 7 H1
BOL BL1 2 D3
Back St George's Rd North
BOL BL1 2 B3
Back St Helens Rd
BOLS/LL BL3 * 48 C5
Back St Helens Rd South
BOLS/LL BL3 64 A2
Back St James's St OLD OL1 * 76 A5
Back St Mark's La CHH M8 * 102 A2
Back St Mary's Pl BURY BL9 4 C5
Back St Philip's Av
BOLS/LL BL3 48 C5
Back St Thomas St East
BOL BL1 * 33 G4
Back Salford St BURY BL9 38 D2
Back Salisbury St BOLS/LL BL3 2 B6
Back Salisbury Ter BOLE BL2 50 A2
Back Sandon St West
BOLS/LL BL3 * 48 C5
Back Sankey St BURY BL9 4 B4
Back Sapling Rd BOLS/LL BL3 * 64 A2
Back Sapling Rd South
BOLS/LL BL3 * 64 A2
Back Scholes St
TOT/BURYW BL8 37 H3
Back Scott St OLDS OL8 * 9 F7
Back Scowcroft St BOLE BL2 3 J1
Back Settle St BOLS/LL BL3 64 C1
Back Settle St North
BOLS/LL BL3 64 D1
Back Seymour Rd BOL BL1 34 A3
Back Sharman St BOLS/LL BL3 49 G4
Back Shaw-Street BURY BL9 5 J3
Back Shepherd St BURY BL9 5 F5
Back Sherwood St BOL BL1 34 A3
Back Shipton St BOL BL1 33 E5
Back Silverdale Rd BOL BL1 48 B2
Back Silver St BURY BL9 4 D5
Back Skipton St BOLE BL2 49 H1
Back Smethurst La
BOLS/LL BL3 64 A2
Back Smethurst La West
BOLS/LL BL3 * 64 A2
Back Sofa St BOL BL1 33 E5
Back Soho St BOL BL1 2 E6
Back Somerset Rd BOL BL1 48 A2
Back Somerville St BOL BL1 * 33 F3
Back South Cross St East
BURY BL9 5 F5
Back South Pde CSLFD M3 6 D4
Back South St BOLS/LL BL3 64 D1
Back South View St BOLE BL2 49 H2
Back Spa Rd BOL BL1 2 A6
Back Spa Rd North BOL BL1 2 A6
Back Spa Rd West BOL BL1 * 2 A6
Back Spear St ANC M4 * 7 H3
Back Springfield St
BOLS/LL BL3 49 G5
Back Spring Gdns BOL BL1 2 E6
MDTN M24 72 D2
Back Spring St East BURY BL9 5 F6
Back Spring St West BURY BL9 5 F6
Back Square St RAMS BL0 16 D2
Back Stainsbury St
BOLS/LL BL3 48 B5
Back Stanley St RAMS BL0 * 16 C3
Back Stephen St
TOT/BURYW BL8 37 H4
Back Stewart St BOL BL1 33 H5
Backstone St BOLE BL2 3 J1
Back Sunlight Rd BOL BL1 48 B2
Back Sunning Hill St
BOLS/LL BL3 * 48 C5
Back Sunnyside Rd BOL BL1 33 F4
Back Swan La BOLS/LL BL3 * 48 C5
Back Tavistock Rd BOL BL1 2 A6
Back Teak St BURY BL9 5 J4
Back Tenterden St BURY BL9 4 C5
Back Thicketford Rd
BOLE BL2 * 34 D5
Back Thicketford Rd West
BOLE BL2 34 C5
Back Thomasson Cl BOL BL1 33 H5
Back Thomas St ANC M4 * 7 G3
Back Thorns Rd BOL BL1 33 H3
Back Thorn St BOL BL1 34 A4
Back Thorpe St BOL BL1 33 G4
Back Thurnham St
BOLS/LL BL3 * 64 B1
Back Tinline St BURY BL9 5 H5
Back Tonge Moor Rd
BOLE BL2 34 C4
Back Tonge Moor Rd East
BOLE BL2 3 J1
BOLE BL2 34 D3
Back Tonge Old Rd BOLE BL2 49 H2
Back Tong Rd BOLS/LL BL3 50 D5
Back Tottington Rd
TOT/BURYW BL8 * 37 G2
Back Tottington Rd East
BOLE BL2 35 F1
Back Tottington Rd North
TOT/BURYW BL8 37 H3
Back Tottington Rd South
TOT/BURYW BL8 37 H3
Back Tudor St BOLS/LL BL3 * 48 B5
Back Turner St ANC M4 7 G3
Back Turton Rd East BOLE BL2 34 D1
Back Turton Rd West
BOLE BL2 34 D2
Back Uganda St BOLS/LL BL3 64 B1
Back Ulleswater St BOL BL1 34 A4
Back Union Rd BOLE BL2 3 H1
Back Unsworth St South
BOLS/LL BL3 48 C4
Back Uttley St BOL BL1 33 G4
Back Venice St BOLS/LL BL3 48 B5
Back Vernon St BOL BL1 2 C3
BURY BL9 4 E1
Back Vernon St South
BOL BL1 * 2 C3
Back Vickerman St BOL BL1 33 G4
Back Victoria Gv BOL BL1 33 F5
Back Victoria Gv North
BOL BL1 33 F5
Back Victory St East BOL BL1 48 B1
Back View St BOLS/LL BL3 48 C4
Back Vincent St BOL BL1 2 A6
Back Vine St BOLS/LL BL3 * 48 B3
Back Viola St BOL BL1 33 H3
Back Waldeck St BOL BL1 48 B1
Back Walmersley Rd East
BURY BL9 5 F2
Back Walmersley Rd West
BURY BL9 5 F1
Back Walnut St BOL BL1 34 A3
Back Walshaw Rd North
TOT/BURYW BL8 37 H3
Back Walshaw Rd South
TOT/BURYW BL8 37 H3
Back Wapping St BOL BL1 * 33 G4
Back Wardle St BOLE BL2 * 49 G4
Back Wash La BURY BL9 5 H4
Back Wash La South BURY BL9 5 H4
Back Water St EDGW/EG BL7 22 C1
STKP SK1 * 13 H1
Back Waverley Rd BOL BL1 33 H3

Back Webster St
BOLS/LL BL3 * 49 G5
Back Wellington Rd South
BURY BL9 53 F1
Back Wells St *BURY* BL9 4 C7
Back Westbank St *BOL* BL1 2 B3
Back Westbourne Av
BOLS/LL BL3 65 F1
Back Weston St North
BOLS/LL BL3 49 F5
Back Weston St South
BOLS/LL BL3 49 E5
Back Westwood Rd *BOL* BL1 * 48 B1
Back Whittle Gv *BOL* BL1 * 33 E5
Back Whittle St
TOT/BURYW BL8 * 37 H3
Back Wigan Rd *BOLS/LL* BL3 47 H5
Back Wigan Rd North
BOLS/LL BL3 47 H5
Back Wigan Rd South
BOLS/LL BL3 * 48 A4
Back Willows *BOLS/LL* BL3 48 A5
Back Willows La *BOLS/LL* BL3 48 C5
Back Willows La North
BOLS/LL BL3 48 A5
Back Willows La South
BOLS/LL BL3 48 B5
Back Wilmot St *BOL* BL1 * 33 F3
Back Wilton St *BOL* BL1 34 A3
Back Windermere St *BOL* BL1 34 A3
Back Windsor Gv *BOL* BL1 33 F5
Back Wolfenden St *BOL* BL1 * 33 H4
Back Woodbine Rd
BOLS/LL BL3 64 B1
Back Woodfield St
BOLS/LL BL3 * 65 F1
Back Woodgate St
BOLS/LL BL3 65 F1
Back Wood St *TOT/BURYW* BL8 37 H3
Back Worcester St *BOL* BL1 33 H5
Back Wordsworth St *BOL* BL1 33 G4
Back Worsel St *BOLS/LL* BL3 48 B5
Back Worsel St North
BOLS/LL BL3 * 48 B5
Back Wynne St *BOL* BL1 33 H4
Back Yates St *BOLE* BL2 3 H1
Bacon Av *DTN/ASHW* M34 147 E4
Bacup St *NEWH/MOS* M40 103 H2
Badby Cl *ANC* M4 115 G4
Baddeley Cl *EDGY/DAV* SK3 171 G4
Badder St *BOL* BL1 2 E3
Bader Dr *HEY* OL10 56 A2
Badger Cl *HYDE* SK14 133 H4
MILN OL16 43 H3
MPL/ROM SK6 187 E1
Badger Edge La *OLDE* OL4 77 H1
UPML OL3 61 H5
Badger La *MILN* OL16 43 H3
Badger Rd *ALT* WA14 165 F1
Badger St *BURY* BL9 5 F2
Badgers Wk *WYTH/NTH* M22 180 D3
Bagnall Cl *UPML* OL3 79 F3
WHIT OL12 28 C1
Bagot St *OP/CLY* M11 116 D3
SWIN M27 98 B1
Bagshaw St *HYDE* SK14 133 G3
Bagslate Moor La *ROCH* OL11 28 C3
Bagslate Moor Rd *ROCH* OL11 28 C4
Bagstock Av *POY/DIS* SK12 195 F5
Baguley Crs *EDGY/DAV* SK3 171 G3
MDTN M24 87 F1
Baguley Dr *BURY* BL9 69 H2
Baguley La *SALE* M33 155 F4
Baguley Rd *SALE* M33 155 F2
Baguley St *DROY* M43 118 A4
Baildon Rd *ROCH* OL11 29 E2
Baildon St
NEWH/MOS M40 103 H1
Bailey Fold *WHTN* BL5 62 C4
Bailey La *BOLE* BL2 35 F5
MANAIR M90 180 A3
PART M31 151 E2
Bailey Rd *TRPK* M17 125 F1
Bailey St *OLD* OL1 * 9 J3
OP/CLY M11 117 E4
PWCH M25 86 B2
Bailey Wk *ALT* WA14 177 F4
Baillie St *MILN* OL16 10 D5
RAD M26 53 F4
Baillie St East *MILN* OL16 10 E5
The Bails *BRO* M7 101 F4
Bainbridge Cl
WGTN/LGST M12 * 129 E2
Bainbridge Rd *OLDE* OL4 76 C3
Bainburgh Clough *OLDS* OL8 92 B3
Baines Av *IRL* M44 136 B2
Baines St *BOL* BL1 48 A1
Bain St *SWIN* M27 99 E3
Baird St *CMANE* M1 7 J6
Baker St *FWTH* BL4 83 E1
HEY OL10 56 B1
HTNM SK4 159 H3
MDTN M24 73 E4
RAMS BL0 16 C3
STLY SK15 121 E4
Bakewell Av *AUL* OL6 108 A4
DTN/ASHW M34 147 E3
Bakewell Rd
BRAM/HZG SK7 185 F4
DROY M43 117 F3
ECC M30 110 C5
STRET M32 125 F5
Bakewell St *EDGY/DAV* SK3 12 D6
GTN M18 130 B4
Bala Cl *ORD* M5 113 F3
Balcary Gv *BOL* BL1 48 A1
Balcombe Cl
TOT/BURYW BL8 26 C4
Balderstone Rd *ROCH* OL11 43 F4
Baldock Rd *DID/WITH* M20 158 A3
Baldwin Rd *BNG/LEV* M19 143 H5
Bale St *CMANW* M2 6 E6
Balfour Gv *RDSH* SK5 145 F3
Balfour Rd *ALT* WA14 165 G2
URM M41 138 B1
WHIT OL12 29 F2
Balfour St *BOLS/LL* BL3 2 A7
CHH M8 102 B2
OLDE OL4 76 B5
ROY/SHW OL2 60 A1
SLFD M6 100 C4
Balham Wk
WGTN/LGST M12 129 G2
Balinge *WHIT* OL12 10 B4
Ballantine St
NEWH/MOS M40 116 D1
Ballard Cl *LIT* OL15 21 E1
Ballard Wy *ROY/SHW* OL2 60 B2
Ballater Av *URM* M41 138 A2
Ballbrook Av *DID/WITH* M20 157 F1
Balleratt St *BNG/LEV* M19 144 A2
Ball Gn *STRET* M32 125 G3
Balliol Cl *MPL/ROM* SK6 162 B2
Balliol St *CHH* M8 102 B2
SWIN M27 98 D2
Balloon St *ANC* M4 7 F2
Ball St *MILN* OL16 10 E5
Ball Wk *HYDE* SK14 149 H2
Balmain Av *GTN* M18 130 B5
Balmain Rd *URM* M41 124 A5
Balmer Rd *NTHM/RTH* M23 167 H4
Balmfield St *CHH* M8 102 B5
Balmforth St *HULME* M15 127 G1
Balmoral Av *BOLS/LL* BL3 66 D1
CHD/CHDH SK8 182 D2
DTN/ASHW M34 132 A1
HYDE SK14 148 A3
ROCH OL11 29 E3
ROY/SHW OL2 59 G5
STRET M32 126 A5
URM M41 138 B2
WHTF M45 69 H5
Balmoral Cl *BURY* BL9 53 H4
MILN OL16 31 H5
TOT/BURYW BL8 26 B2
Balmoral Dr *ALT* WA14 166 A1
DTN/ASHW M34 131 F4
HEY OL10 40 B5
MPL/ROM SK6 186 D5
POY/DIS SK12 195 E4
STLY SK15 120 D2
Balmoral Gra *PWCH* M25 86 D4
Balmoral Gv *BRAM/HZG* SK7 185 G1
Balmoral Rd *FWTH* BL4 65 H5
HALE/TIMP WA15 165 H5
HTNM SK4 158 D3
RUSH/FAL M14 143 F3
SWIN M27 84 B5
URM M41 138 A2
Balmoral St *GTN* M18 130 B4
Balmoral Wy *WILM/AE* SK9 198 D4
Balmore Cl *BOLS/LL* BL3 63 H1
Balm St *RAMS* BL0 16 B4
Balsam Cl *BRUN/LGST* M13 128 D1
Balshaw Av *IRL* M44 136 B1
Balshaw Cl *BOLS/LL* BL3 48 B4
Balshaw Ct *IRL* M44 136 C1
Baltic Rd *ALT* WA14 164 D3
Baltic St *ORD* M5 112 D3
Baltimore St *NEWH/MOS* M40 103 G5
Bamber Av *SALE* M33 155 F5
Bamber St *BKLY* M9 88 A2
Bamber Wk *BOLS/LL* BL3 * 48 C4
Bamburgh Cl *RAD* M26 51 F4
Bamburgh Dr *AULW* OL7 106 B5
Bambury St *BURY* BL9 5 F3
Bamford Av *DTN/ASHW* M34 146 D3
MDTN M24 72 D2
Bamford Cl *BURY* BL9 39 H2
CHD/CHDH SK8 182 A4
Bamford Ct *ROCH* OL11 29 E5
Bamford Gdns
HALE/TIMP WA15 167 E4
Bamford Gv *AUL* OL6 108 A4
DID/WITH M20 157 F3
Bamford Ms *ROCH* OL11 28 B4
Bamford Prec *ROCH* OL11 * 28 B4
Bamford Rd *DID/WITH* M20 157 F3
HEY OL10 40 D2
Bamford St *CHAD* OL9 74 D4
LIT OL15 20 C3
OP/CLY M11 116 C3
ROY/SHW OL2 59 F5
STKP SK1 13 G5
Bamford Wy *ROCH* OL11 28 C5
Bampton Cl *OFTN* SK2 172 C2
Bampton Rd *WYTH/NTH* M22 180 B3
Banbury Dr *ALT* WA14 165 H1
Banbury Ms *SWIN* M27 98 C1
Banbury Rd *FAIL* M35 117 F1
MDTN M24 88 C2
NTHM/RTH M23 167 G4
Banbury St *BOLE* BL2 34 D5
STKP SK1 13 G4
Bancroft Av *CHD/CHDH* SK8 182 D3
Bancroft Cl *MPL/ROM* SK6 161 F3
Bancroft Fold *HYDE* SK14 134 C3
Bancroft Rd
HALE/TIMP WA15 178 B1
SWIN M27 98 D1
Banff Gv *HEY* OL10 40 B5
Banff Rd *RUSH/FAL* M14 128 D4
Bangor Rd *CHD/CHDH* SK8 170 D3
Bangor St *AUL* OL6 120 B3
BOL BL1 2 D2
HULME M15 127 G3
MILN OL16 * 30 C5
RDSH SK5 160 A2
Bank Barn La *WHIT* OL12 20 A2
Bank Bridge Rd *OP/CLY* M11 116 B2
Bank Cl *LIT* OL15 20 D5
Banker St *BOLS/LL* BL3 49 H4
Bankfield *HYDE* SK14 133 G3
Bank Fld *WHTN* BL5 62 B5
Bankfield Av *BRUN/LGST* M13 129 F5
DROY M43 117 H3
HTNM SK4 12 B2
IRL M44 150 C1
Bankfield Cl *BOLE* BL2 36 B5
Bankfield Dr *OLDS* OL8 92 A5
WALK M28 96 B4
Bankfield La *ROCH* OL11 28 B3
Bankfield Rd *CHD/CHDH* SK8 182 C3
FWTH BL4 82 A1
MPL/ROM SK6 162 A1
SALE M33 139 E5
Bankfield St *BKLY* M9 103 E1
BOLS/LL BL3 48 B5
HTNM SK4 159 H3
Bank Field St *RAD* M26 67 G5
Bank Hall *TOT/BURYW* BL8 37 F4
Bankhall La *HALE/TIMP* WA15 177 H4
Bankhall Rd *HTNM* SK4 158 D4
Bank Hey *WHTN* BL5 * 62 A4
Bank Hill St *OLDE* OL4 76 A5
Bankhirst Cl *CHH* M8 102 B1
Bank House Rd *BKLY* M9 87 H4
Bankhouse Rd
TOT/BURYW BL8 37 H2
Banklands Cl *IRL* M44 150 C1
Bank La *LHULT* M38 81 E1
SLFD M6 100 A4
UPML OL3 95 G3
WHIT OL12 19 H1
Bankley St *BNG/LEV* M19 144 A2
Bankmill Cl *BRUN/LGST* M13 128 C1
Bank Pl *CSLFD* M3 114 A3
Bank Rd *CHH* M8 87 F5
MPL/ROM SK6 161 H3
STLY SK15 109 F5
Banks Cft *HEY* OL10 56 A2
Bankside *HALE/TIMP* WA15 189 E1
HYDE SK14 149 F2
Bank Side *WHTN* BL5 62 A4
Bankside Av *RAD* M26 53 E5
UPML OL3 79 F5
Bankside Cl *CHAD* OL9 8 C4
MPL/ROM SK6 163 G5
UPML OL3 79 F4
WILM/AE SK9 199 G1
Bankside Ct *HTNM* SK4 * 158 D4
Bankside Rd *DID/WITH* M20 169 G2
Banks La *STKP* SK1 172 C1
Bank Stanway Av *BOLS/LL* BL3 2 B7
Bank St *AUL* OL6 119 G3
BOL BL1 3 F4
BRO M7 102 A2
BURY BL9 4 C5
CHD/CHDH SK8 170 B3
CSLFD M3 114 A3
DROY M43 117 G5
DTN/ASHW M34 132 C2
DTN/ASHW M34 147 F3
FWTH BL4 66 A4
HEY OL10 40 C4
HYDE SK14 133 G5
MPL/ROM SK6 162 A1
OLDE OL4 92 C1
OP/CLY M11 116 B3
RAD M26 68 C2
RAMS BL0 17 F1
ROCH OL11 43 F2
ROY/SHW OL2 59 H2
SALE M33 154 D1
TOT/BURYW BL8 37 E2
WHTF M45 69 F3
Bank Top *AUL* OL6 119 H3
HEY OL10 40 C3
Bank Top Gv *BOL* BL1 34 B1
Bank Top Pk *OLDE* OL4 92 C1
Bank Top St *HEY* OL10 40 C3
Bankwell St *HULME* M15 127 H3
Bank Wd *BOL* BL1 47 G2
Banky La *SALE* M33 138 C5
Bannach Dr *CHAD* OL9 74 B4
Bannatyne Cl
NEWH/MOS M40 104 D1
Banner Dale Cl
BRUN/LGST M13 129 G4
Bannerman Av *PWCH* M25 86 A4
Bannerman Rd *DROY* M43 118 A4
Banner Wk *OP/CLY* M11 116 A4
Bannister Dr *CHD/CHDH* SK8 182 C2
Bannister St *BOLE* BL2 50 B1
OFTN SK2 13 H7
Bann St *EDGY/DAV* SK3 12 E5
Banstead Av *WYTH/NTH* M22 168 C2
Bantry Av *BKLY* M9 87 G4
Bantry St *BOLS/LL* BL3 48 D4
WHIT OL12 10 E1
Baptist St *ANC* M4 7 H1
Barathea Cl *ROCH* OL11 41 H3
Barbara Rd *BOLS/LL* BL3 63 H2
Barbara St *BOLS/LL* BL3 48 C5
Barbeck Cl *NEWH/MOS* M40 115 H2
Barberry Bank *EDGW/EG* BL7 22 C3
Barberry Cl *ALT* WA14 165 E2
Barber St *OP/CLY* M11 * 130 D1
Barbican St *DID/WITH* M20 142 D4
Barbirolli Sq *CMANW* M2 6 E7
Barbon Wk *ANC* M4 7 K3
Barchester Av *BOLE* BL2 35 F5
Barcheston Rd
CHD/CHDH SK8 169 H5
Barcicroft Rd *BNG/LEV* M19 158 B2
Barclay Rd *POY/DIS* SK12 195 F5
Barclays Av *SLFD* M6 100 A4
Barcliffe Av *NEWH/MOS* M40 89 F5
Barclyde St *ROCH* OL11 42 D1
Barcombe Cl *OLDE* OL4 76 C2
STRET M32 125 E5
Barcroft Rd *BOL* BL1 33 E4
Barcroft St *BURY* BL9 4 E2
Bardell Cl *POY/DIS* SK12 * 195 E5
Bardon Cl *BOL* BL1 * 33 G5
Bardon Rd *NTHM/RTH* M23 167 G3
Bardsea Av *WYTH/NTH* M22 180 C3
Bardsley Av *FAIL* M35 105 E3
Bardsley Cl *BOLE* BL2 35 E1
HYDE SK14 149 G1
Bardsley Gate Av *STLY* SK15 135 F2
Bardsley St *CHAD* OL9 90 A4
HTNM SK4 159 G3
MDTN M24 * 72 D3
NEWH/MOS M40 104 C5
OLDE OL4 * 92 D2
Bardsley Vale Av *OLDS* OL8 106 C2
Barehill St *LIT* OL15 21 E2
Bare St *BOL* BL1 3 H3
Barff Rd *ORD* M5 112 B3
Barfold Cl *OFTN* SK2 173 H4
Barfoot Aqueduct
STRET M32 140 A4
Barford Dr *WILM/AE* SK9 199 F1
Bar Gap Rd *OLD* OL1 9 G1
Baring St *CMANE* M1 7 J7
Barkan Wy *SWIN* M27 99 G2
Barker Rd *MPL/ROM* SK6 161 G3
Barker's La *SALE* M33 154 A1
Barker St *BURY* BL9 4 C7
CSLFD M3 114 C1
HEY OL10 40 C5
Barke St *LIT* OL15 20 C5
Barking St *NEWH/MOS* M40 115 H2
Bark St *BOL* BL1 2 D4
FWTH BL4 83 E2
Bark St East *BOL* BL1 2 E3
Bark Wk *HULME* M15 128 A2
Barkway Rd *STRET* M32 139 G2
Barkwell La *MOSL* OL5 108 C1
Bar La *BOL* BL1 33 H1
Barlea Av *NEWH/MOS* M40 104 C1
Barley Brook Meadow
BOL BL1 23 E5
Barleycorn Cl *SALE* M33 155 H3
Barley Cft *CHD/CHDH* SK8 182 C4
Barley Croft Rd *HYDE* SK14 133 H3
Barleycroft St
OLDTF/WHR M16 128 A4
Barley Dr *BRAM/HZG* SK7 183 H5
Barleyfield Wk *MDTN* M24 72 B3
Barley Hall St *HEY* OL10 41 F3
Barlow Cl *BURY* BL9 38 C1
Barlow Ct *WALK* M28 * 82 B4
Barlow Crs *MPL/ROM* SK6 175 E5
Barlow Fold *BURY* BL9 53 G4
Barlow Fold Cl *BURY* BL9 53 F4
Barlow Fold Rd
MPL/ROM SK6 162 C3
RDSH SK5 145 F3
Barlow Hall Rd *CCHDY* M21 156 B1
Barlow La *ECC* M30 110 D3
Barlow La North *RDSH* SK5 145 F3
Barlow Moor Cl *WHIT* OL12 28 B1
Barlow Moor Ct
DID/WITH M20 157 E2
Barlow Moor Rd *CCHDY* M21 141 F4
DID/WITH M20 156 D2
Barlow Park Av *BOL* BL1 33 G1
Barlow Pl *BRUN/LGST* M13 128 D1
Barlow Rd *ALT* WA14 165 E1
BNG/LEV M19 144 C2
DUK SK16 120 A5
ORD M5 113 H4
STRET M32 126 C4
WILM/AE SK9 199 E1
Barlow's Cft *CSLFD* M3 6 C3
Barlow's La South
BRAM/HZG SK7 184 D1
Barlow St *BURY* BL9 5 F3
ECC M30 111 E4
HEY OL10 56 B1
MILN OL16 10 E6
OLDE OL4 9 K5
RAD M26 68 C1
WALK M28 82 A3
Barlow Wood Dr
PL/ROM SK6 187 G1
Barmeadow *UPML* OL3 78 C2
Barmhouse Cl *HYDE* SK14 134 B5
Barmhouse La *HYDE* SK14 134 C5
Barmhouse Ms *HYDE* SK14 134 B5
Barmouth St *OP/CLY* M11 116 A5
Barmouth Wk *OLDS* OL8 90 C5
Barnaby Rd *POY/DIS* SK12 195 E5
Barnacre Av *BOLE* BL2 50 C2
NTHM/RTH M23 179 G1
Barnard Av *HTNM* SK4 159 E4
WHTF M45 70 A5
Barnard Cl *AULW* OL7 106 C5
Barnard Rd *GTN* M18 130 A5
Barnbrook St *BURY* BL9 5 G3
Barnby St *WGTN/LGST* M12 129 H5
Barn Cl *URM* M41 137 E1
Barnclose Rd *WYTH/NTH* M22 180 C3
Barn Ct *BOLE* BL2 * 34 D4
Barncroft Gdns
WYTH/NTH M22 * 168 B4
Barncroft Rd *FWTH* BL4 66 A4
Barnes Av *HTNM* SK4 158 D4
Barnes Cl *FWTH* BL4 66 A4
RAMS BL0 16 B5
Barnes Dr *FWTH* BL4 65 E3
Barnes St *FWTH* BL4 65 G3
Barnes Ter *FWTH* BL4 66 D5
Barneswell St
NEWH/MOS M40 104 B5
Barnet Rd *BOL* BL1 33 E4
Barnett Av *DID/WITH* M20 142 D5
Barnett Dr *CSLFD* M3 6 A2
Barnfield *URM* M41 138 B3
Barnfield Av *MPL/ROM* SK6 162 C3
Barnfield Cl *EDGW/EG* BL7 22 D1
ORD M5 113 E4
RAD M26 67 H1
Barnfield Crs *SALE* M33 154 A1
Barnfield Dr *WALK* M28 96 C4
WHTN BL5 62 B3
Barn Field La *WHIT* OL12 19 F1
Barnfield Ri *ROY/SHW* OL2 44 D5
Barnfield Rd *BNG/LEV* M19 158 B2
HYDE SK14 134 C3
SWIN M27 83 G5
Barnfield Rd East
EDGY/DAV SK3 172 A5
Barnfield Rd West
EDGY/DAV SK3 171 G5
Barnfield St *DTN/ASHW* M34 132 A4
HEY OL10 41 F4
WHIT OL12 30 A1
Barn Fold *OLDE* OL4 92 D2
Barngate Dr *MOSL* OL5 108 D2
Barngate Rd *CHD/CHDH* SK8 169 F3
Barn Gv *DTN/ASHW* M34 132 A1
Barnhill Av *PWCH* M25 86 A5
Barnhill Dr *PWCH* M25 86 A5
Barnhill Rd *PWCH* M25 85 H4
Barnhill St *RUSH/FAL* M14 128 A4
Barnley Cl *IRL* M44 122 C5
Barnsdale Cl *BOLE* BL2 36 B5
Barnsdale Dr *CHH* M8 102 B5
Barnsfold Av *RUSH/FAL* M14 143 E3
Barnsfold Rd *MPL/ROM* SK6 187 E1
Barnside Av *WALK* M28 82 B5
Barnside Cl *BURY* BL9 27 F3
Barnside Wy *FAIL* M35 105 H3
Barnsley St *STKP* SK1 13 K5
Barns Pl *HALE/TIMP* WA15 178 D4
Barnstable Dr
NEWH/MOS M40 102 D4
Barnstead Av *DID/WITH* M20 158 A1
Barnston Av *RUSH/FAL* M14 142 D1
Barnston Cl *BOL* BL1 34 A2
Barn St *BOL* BL1 2 D5
OLDS OL8 9 F4
WHTF M45 69 G5
Barnview Dr *IRL* M44 136 C2
Barnwell Cl *DTN/ASHW* M34 132 B3
Barnwood Cl *BOL* BL1 * 33 H5
Barnwood Dr *BOL* BL1 33 H5
Barnwood Rd
NTHM/RTH M23 179 H1
Barnwood Ter *BOL* BL1 33 H5
Baroness Gv *BRO* M7 113 H1
Baron Fold Crs *LHULT* M38 81 E2
Baron Fold Gv *LHULT* M38 81 E2
Baron Fold Rd *LHULT* M38 * 81 E2
Baron Gn *CHD/CHDH* SK8 182 A5
Baron Rd *HYDE* SK14 148 B4
Barons Ct *FAIL* M35 104 C4
Baron St *BURY* BL9 4 B6
MILN OL16 10 D7
Baron Wk *BOLS/LL* BL3 67 F1
Barrack Hl *MPL/ROM* SK6 161 H4
Barrack Hill Cl *MPL/ROM* SK6 161 H3
Barrack St *HULME* M15 127 G1
Barra Dr *URM* M41 124 C3
Barrass St *OP/CLY* M11 130 C1
Barratt Gdns *MDTN* M24 72 A1
Barrett Av *FWTH* BL4 66 C5
Barrett Ct *BURY* BL9 5 H4
Barrfield Rd *SLFD* M6 112 D1
Barr Hill Av *SLFD* M6 100 B5
Barrhill Cl *HULME* M15 127 G2
Barrie Wy *BOL* BL1 34 C2
Barrington Av *CHD/CHDH* SK8 182 D3
DROY M43 117 G4
Barrington Cl *ALT* WA14 165 G3
Barrington Rd *ALT* WA14 165 G3
Barrington St *OP/CLY* M11 116 D3
Barrisdale Cl *BOLS/LL* BL3 47 G4
Barrow Bridge Rd *BOL* BL1 32 D3
Barrowfield Rd
WYTH/NTH M22 179 H2
Barrowfields *MDTN* M24 72 D2
Barrow Hill Rd *CHH* M8 102 A5
Barrow La *HALE/TIMP* WA15 178 C5
Barrow Meadow
CHD/CHDH SK8 182 C4
Barrows Ct *BOL* BL1 2 E6
Barrowshaw Cl *WALK* M28 81 H5
Barrow St *CSLFD* M3 114 A4
Barrule Av *BRAM/HZG* SK7 185 F3
Barry Crs *WALK* M28 81 F4
Barry Lawson Cl *CHH* M8 * 102 A3
Barry Ri *ALT* WA14 176 D2
Barry Rd *NTHM/RTH* M23 156 A4
RDSH SK5 160 A1
Barry St *OLD* OL1 76 A4
Barsham Dr *BOLS/LL* BL3 48 C4
Bar Ter *WHIT* OL12 18 B1
Bartlam Pl *OLD* OL1 9 H3
Bartlemore St *OLD* OL1 75 H3
Bartlett Rd *ROY/SHW* OL2 59 H3
Bartlett St *OP/CLY* M11 130 A1
Bartley Rd *WYTH/NTH* M22 168 B1
Barton Av *URM* M41 138 B1
Barton Cl *WILM/AE* SK9 192 A5
Barton Dock Rd *STRET* M32 125 F4
URM M41 124 D2
Barton Fold *HYDE* SK14 147 H2
Barton Hall Av *ECC* M30 110 B4
Barton Highlevel Br
TRPK M17 124 A1
Barton La *ECC* M30 111 E5
Barton Moss Rd *ECC* M30 122 D1
Barton Rd *ECC* M30 110 D5
FWTH BL4 65 G5
HTNM SK4 158 B5
HYDE SK14 133 F3
MDTN M24 72 C4
STRET M32 125 F5
SWIN M27 99 F3
URM M41 124 B4
WALK M28 97 G5
Barton St *CHAD* OL9 75 E4
CSLFD M3 6 C7
FWTH BL4 66 B5
Barway Rd *CCHDY* M21 140 D2
Barwell Rd *SALE* M33 153 H1
Barwell Sq *FWTH* BL4 65 G2
Barwick Pl *SALE* M33 154 B2
Basechurch Wk
WGTN/LGST M12 * 129 G2
Basford Rd *OLDTF/WHR* M16 127 E5
Bashall St *BOL* BL1 48 B1
Basil Ct *MILN* OL16 * 30 C5
Basildon Cl *BRUN/LGST* M13 129 E3
Basil St *BOLS/LL* BL3 48 D4
HTNM SK4 159 G3
MILN OL16 30 C5
RUSH/FAL M14 * 128 D5
Basle Cl *BRAM/HZG* SK7 183 H1
Baslow Av *BNG/LEV* M19 144 B1
Baslow Dr *BRAM/HZG* SK7 185 G4
CHD/CHDH SK8 181 H4
Baslow Gv *RDSH* SK5 160 A1
Baslow Rd *DROY* M43 117 F2
DTN/ASHW M34 146 D3
STRET M32 125 F5
Baslow St *OP/CLY* M11 115 H4
Bassenthwaite Cl
MDTN M24 72 A1
Basset Av *SLFD* M6 101 F5
Bassett Wy *WHIT* OL12 29 H1
Bass La *BURY* BL9 17 F5
Bass St *DUK* SK16 119 G5
Basten Dr *BRO* M7 101 G4
Batchelor Cl *CCHDY* M21 142 A4
Bates Cl *ROCH* OL11 42 C5
Bateson Dr *OLDE* OL4 93 E1
Bateson St *STKP* SK1 13 J2
Bateson Wy *OLDS* OL8 * 9 G6
Bates St *BRUN/LGST* M13 129 G4
DUK SK16 119 H5
Bath Cl *BRAM/HZG* SK7 185 H2
Bath Crs *CHD/CHDH* SK8 193 E1
OLDTF/WHR M16 127 F3
Bath St *ALT* WA14 177 G2
BOL BL1 2 E3

CHAD OL9 8 B6
WHIT OL12 11 F3
Batley St BKLY M9 103 F2
MOSL OL5 108 C1
Batsmans Dr SWIN M27 83 H3
Battenberg Rd BOL BL1 48 B1
Battersbay Gv
BRAM/HZG SK7 185 F2
Battersby Ct OFTN SK2 * 173 F3
Battersby St BURY BL9 39 G3
OP/CLY M11 * 130 D1
ROCH OL11 29 E5
Battersea Rd HTNM SK4 158 B5
Battery La WILM/AE SK9 198 A4
Batty St CHH M8 102 D5
The Baum MILN OL16 10 C5
Baxendale St BOL BL1 33 H2
Baxter Gdns NTHM/RTH M23 167 H2
Baxter Rd SALE M33 154 C2
Baxter St OLDS OL8 90 C5
Baybutt St RAD M26 * 68 D1
Baycroft Gv NTHM/RTH M23 155 H5
Baydon Av BRO M7 102 A4
Bayfield Gv
NEWH/MOS M40 * 103 H1
Bayle Cl HYDE SK14 133 H3
Bayley Ct BOL BL1 2 A2
Bayley St STLY SK15 120 B3
Baysdale Av BOLS/LL BL3 47 G5
Bayston Wk WGTN/LGST M12 129 G2
Bay St CHAD OL9 8 C3
HEY OL10 40 C3
WHIT OL12 10 E2
Bayswater Av
NEWH/MOS M40 116 D1
Bayswater St BOLS/LL BL3 64 B2
Baythorpe St BOL BL1 34 A3
Baytree Av CHAD OL9 73 H4
DTN/ASHW M34 132 D4
Bay Tree Av WALK M28 97 H5
Baytree Dr MPL/ROM SK6 161 G2
Baytree Gv RAMS BL0 26 C1
Baytree La MDTN M24 73 G4
Baytree Wk WHIT OL12 14 B4
Baywood St BKLY M9 103 E2
Bazaar St SLFD M6 113 F1
Bazley Rd WYTH/NTH M22 156 C5
Bazley St BOL BL1 32 C3
Beacomfold MPL/ROM SK6 163 G3
Beacon Dr NTHM/RTH M23 179 H2
Beacon Gv OLDS OL8 92 B3
Beacon Rd MPL/ROM SK6 161 H5
TRPK M17 124 D1
Beaconsfield
RUSH/FAL M14 * 143 E4
Beaconsfield Rd ALT WA14 165 G2
Beaconsfield St BOLS/LL BL3 2 A7
Beaconsfield Ter STLY SK15 109 G3
Beacon Vw MPL/ROM SK6 175 E1
Beadham Dr BKLY M9 87 F2
Beadle Av WHIT OL12 20 A3
Bealbank Cl MILN OL16 44 D3
Beal Cl HTNM SK4 158 A3
Beal Crs MILN OL16 11 K3
Bealcroft Cl MILN OL16 31 F4
Beale Gv CCHDY M21 141 F3
Bealey Av RAD M26 53 F4
Bealey Cl GTN M18 130 A2
RAD M26 53 E5
Bealey Dr BURY BL9 53 E2
Beal La ROY/SHW OL2 60 B3
Beaminster Rd HTNM SK4 158 C3
Beaminster Wk
BRUN/LGST M13 * 128 D3
Beamish Cl BRUN/LGST M13 128 D2
Beamsley Dr WYTH/NTH M22 180 A2
Beanfields WALK M28 97 G5
Bean Leach Av OFTN SK2 173 G3
Bean Leach Dr OFTN SK2 173 G3
Bean Leach Rd
BRAM/HZG SK7 173 F5
Beard Rd GTN M18 * 130 B4
Beard St DROY M43 117 G4
ROY/SHW OL2 75 F1
Beardwood Rd BKLY M9 88 A3
Bearswood Cl HYDE SK14 148 B2
Beathwaite Dr
BRAM/HZG SK7 183 F3
Beatrice Av CHD/CHDH SK8 182 C2
GTN M18 131 E4
Beatrice Rd BOL BL1 48 B1
WALK M28 98 A3
Beatrice St DTN/ASHW M34 132 B5
FWTH BL4 65 G4
ROCH OL11 29 G4
SWIN M27 98 D1
Beatrice Wignall St
DROY M43 * 117 H5
Beatson Wk ANC M4 7 K4
Beattock Cl HULME M15 127 G1
Beattock St HULME M15 127 G1
Beauchamp St AUL OL6 119 H2
Beaufont Dr OLDE OL4 92 B2
Beaufort Av DID/WITH M20 157 F1
SALE M33 154 D4
SWIN M27 98 C3
Beaufort Cl HYDE SK14 149 G2
WILM/AE SK9 201 E3
Beaufort Rd AUL OL6 120 A2
HYDE SK14 149 G1
OFTN SK2 173 E5
SALE M33 154 D3
Beaufort St CSLFD M3 6 B7
ECC M30 110 C2
PWCH M25 86 B3
WHIT OL12 29 G2
Beauly Cl RAMS BL0 26 B1
Beaumaris Crs
BRAM/HZG SK7 184 D4
Beaumonds Wy ROCH OL11 28 C5
Beaumont Cha BOLS/LL BL3 63 G1
Beaumont Cl LIT OL15 20 C3
Beaumont Dr BOLS/LL BL3 47 F4
Beaumont Rd CCHDY M21 141 F4
HOR/BR BL6 47 F3
Beaumont St AUL OL6 119 H2
Beauvale Av OFTN SK2 172 D2
Beaver Dr BURY BL9 54 A5
Beaver Rd DID/WITH M20 157 G3
Beaver St CMANE M1 7 F7
Bebbington Cl SALE M33 155 G4
Bebbington St OP/CLY M11 * 116 D4
Beccles Rd SALE M33 154 C5
Beckenham Cl
TOT/BURYW BL8 37 G5
Beckenham Rd CHH M8 102 B3
Becket Av BRO M7 101 H4
Becket Mdw OLDE OL4 92 A1
Beckett St GTN M18 130 B4
OLDE OL4 76 D5
Beckfield Rd NTHM/RTH M23 167 H4
Beckfoot Dr BRUN/LGST M13 129 F5
Beckford St NEWH/MOS M40 103 F5
Beck Gv ROY/SHW OL2 60 C1
WALK M28 97 G1
Beckhampton Cl
BRUN/LGST M13 128 D3
Beckley Av PWCH M25 85 H5
Beckley Cl ROY/SHW OL2 59 H5
Beckside RDSH SK5 145 G2
Beck St CSLFD M3 6 B3
OP/CLY M11 * 130 D1
Beckton Gdns
WYTH/NTH M22 180 B1
Becontree Av
DTN/ASHW M34 132 D4
Becontree Dr
NTHM/RTH M23 167 E3
Bedells La WILM/AE SK9 198 D4
Bede St BOL BL1 33 F4
Bedford Av HYDE SK14 133 H5
OLDTF/WHR M16 141 H1
ROY/SHW OL2 59 G2
SALE M33 155 E4
SWIN M27 * 98 D3
WALK M28 96 D1
Bedford Dr HALE/TIMP WA15 166 D3
Bedford Rd ECC M30 111 F2
OLDTF/WHR M16 141 E1
URM M41 124 B4
Bedfordshire Cl CHAD OL9 90 C2
Bedford St BOL BL1 2 A3
BURY BL9 38 D2
EDGW/EG BL7 22 C1
HEY OL10 41 F4
PWCH M25 86 B2
RDSH SK5 145 E4
Bedlam Gn BURY BL9 4 E4
Bednal Av NEWH/MOS M40 115 H1
Bedwell St OLDTF/WHR M16 128 A5
Bedworth Cl BOLE BL2 49 G4
Beechacre RAMS BL0 17 E3
Beech Av BOLS/LL BL3 67 E2
BRAM/HZG SK7 185 F2
CHD/CHDH SK8 169 G4
DROY M43 117 G4
DTN/ASHW M34 132 A4
EDGY/DAV SK3 172 A3
FWTH BL4 65 F4
FWTH BL4 83 E2
IRL M44 122 D5
MPL/ROM SK6 174 C3
OLD OL1 74 B2
OLDE OL4 76 C4
RAD M26 68 A4
SLFD M6 112 D1
UPML OL3 95 E1
URM M41 138 C2
WALK M28 96 B4
WHTF M45 69 G5
WYTH/NTH M22 168 C1
Beech Cl BOLE BL2 23 H5
PWCH M25 86 B4
WHIT OL12 14 B4
WILM/AE SK9 201 E2
Beech Cottages WILM/AE SK9 200 D5
Beech Ct WILM/AE SK9 * 199 G4
Beech Crs POY/DIS SK12 195 F3
Beechcroft PWCH M25 86 B5
Beechcroft Av BOLE BL2 50 A3
Beechcroft Cl
NEWH/MOS M40 115 F2
Beechcroft Gv BOLE BL2 50 B3
Beechdale Cl
NEWH/MOS M40 104 B2
Beeches Ms DID/WITH M20 156 D2
The Beeches BOL BL1 22 C5
DID/WITH M20 157 E2
MOSL OL5 94 B5
Beechey Sq OLD OL1 9 J2
Beechfield ALT WA14 177 F1
OLDE OL4 94 A1
SALE M33 154 A4
Beechfield Av LHULT M38 81 F2
RAD M26 68 D3
URM M41 123 H5
WILM/AE SK9 198 B5
Beechfield Cl OLDE OL4 93 E1
ROCH OL11 28 B5
Beechfield Dr BURY BL9 53 G2
Beechfield Ms HYDE SK14 * 134 B5
Beechfield Rd BOL BL1 33 E4
CHD/CHDH SK8 183 E4
EDGY/DAV SK3 172 A5
MILN OL16 44 B1
SWIN M27 98 D5
WILM/AE SK9 200 D5
Beechfield St CHH M8 102 B4
Beech Gv AULW OL7 119 E4
LHULT M38 80 D2
RUSH/FAL M14 143 F3
SALE M33 154 A2
SLFD M6 112 D1
STLY SK15 120 C5
TOT/BURYW BL8 26 B2
WILM/AE SK9 198 D4
Beech Grove Cl BURY BL9 39 E2
Beech Hill Rd OLDE OL4 93 H1
Beech Holme Gv STKP SK1 172 D1
Beech Hurst Cl
OLDTF/WHR M16 * 141 H1
Beech La MPL/ROM SK6 162 B4
OLDE OL4 94 A1
WILM/AE SK9 198 D4
Beech Ms CCHDY M21 141 E3
OFTN SK2 172 B4
Beech Mt AULW OL7 106 D4
BKLY M9 103 E2
Beechpark Av
WYTH/NTH M22 168 B2
Beech Rd CCHDY M21 141 F3
CHD/CHDH SK8 183 E3
EDGY/DAV SK3 171 H3
HALE/TIMP WA15 177 H1
MPL/ROM SK6 187 E5
SALE M33 155 E2
WILM/AE SK9 201 E2
Beech St BOL BL1 34 A4
BURY BL9 5 J4
BURY BL9 16 D5
ECC M30 110 C4
FAIL M35 104 D2
MDTN M24 * 72 C4
MILN OL16 44 D2
OLD OL1 9 J3
RAD M26 68 D3
ROCH OL11 29 G5
SWIN M27 99 E3
Beechurst Rd CHD/CHDH SK8 171 E4
Beech Vw HYDE SK14 148 C1
Beech Wk MDTN M24 88 C1
STRET M32 140 A3
Beechway MPL/ROM SK6 187 E5
WILM/AE SK9 198 C5
Beechwood ALT WA14 177 E3
ROY/SHW OL2 60 C1
Beechwood Av CCHDY M21 141 G4
LIT OL15 20 D5
MPL/ROM SK6 162 B4
RAMS BL0 17 E2
STLY SK15 121 F1
URM M41 123 F5
Beechwood Ct
TOT/BURYW BL8 37 G1
Beechwood Dr HYDE SK14 148 B2
MOSL OL5 93 H5
MPL/ROM SK6 175 F3
ROY/SHW OL2 58 D3
SALE M33 153 F2
WALK M28 98 A4
WILM/AE SK9 * 199 H2
Beechwood Gv
CHD/CHDH SK8 182 D4
Beechwood La STLY SK15 121 F1
Beechwood Rd OLDS OL8 91 G5
PWCH M25 86 C4
Beechwood St BOLS/LL BL3 65 E1
Beede St OP/CLY M11 116 C5
Beedon Av BOLS/LL BL3 50 D5
Beehive Gn WHTN BL5 62 C3
Beehive St OLDS OL8 91 G4
Beeley St HYDE SK14 148 A1
SLFD M6 101 E5
Beenham Cl SALE M33 153 F3
Beeston Av BRO M7 101 E4
HALE/TIMP WA15 166 A3
Beeston Cl BOL BL1 23 F5
Beeston Gv EDGY/DAV SK3 171 H4
WHTF M45 70 A5
Beeston Rd SALE M33 153 H2
WILM/AE SK9 192 A2
Beeston St BKLY M9 103 F3
Beeth St OP/CLY M11 130 D2
Beeton Gv BRUN/LGST M13 129 F4
Beever St OLD OL1 9 J2
OLDTF/WHR M16 127 F3
Begley Cl MPL/ROM SK6 161 G5
Begonia Av FWTH BL4 65 F3
Belayse Cl BOL BL1 33 E4
Belbeck St TOT/BURYW BL8 37 H4
Belbeck St South
TOT/BURYW BL8 * 37 H4
Belcroft Cl WYTH/NTH M22 168 D1
Belcroft Dr LHULT M38 80 D1
Belcroft Gv LHULT M38 * 80 D2
Belding Av NEWH/MOS M40 105 E1
Beldon Rd BKLY M9 87 G3
Belfairs Cl AULW OL7 107 E4
Belfield Cl MILN OL16 11 K4
Belfield La MILN OL16 11 J6
Belfield Mill La MILN OL16 11 K4
Belfield Old Rd MILN OL16 11 J4
Belfield Rd DID/WITH M20 157 G3
MILN OL16 11 H4
PWCH M25 86 D4
Belford Av DTN/ASHW M34 131 F5
Belford Dr BOLS/LL BL3 64 D1
Belford Rd STRET M32 126 A5
Belfort Dr ORD M5 113 G5
Belfry Cl WILM/AE SK9 199 G2
Belgate Cl WGTN/LGST M12 129 H4
Belgium St ROCH OL11 28 B4
Belgrave Av FAIL M35 105 G2
MPL/ROM SK6 175 E3
OLDS OL8 91 H3
URM M41 123 F5
Belgrave Ct OLDS OL8 91 G3
Belgrave Crs ECC M30 111 G2
OFTN SK2 172 C5
Belgrave Dr RAD M26 52 B5
Belgrave Gdns BOL BL1 33 H4
Belgrave Rd ALT WA14 177 F1
IRL M44 150 C1
NEWH/MOS M40 104 D1
OLDS OL8 91 G3
SALE M33 154 B2
Belgrave St BOL BL1 33 H4
HEY OL10 40 D5
RAD M26 52 B5
WHIT OL12 29 G2
Belgrave St South BOL BL1 2 C1
Belgravia Gdns CCHDY M21 141 E3
HALE/TIMP WA15 177 H4
Belgravia Ms ROY/SHW OL2 60 B2
Belhaven Rd CHH M8 87 E5
Bellairs St BOLS/LL BL3 64 B1
Bella St BOLS/LL BL3 48 B5
Bell Clough Rd DROY M43 118 A2
Bell Crs OP/CLY M11 116 A5
Belldale Cl HTNM SK4 158 D4
Belle Isle Av WHIT OL12 18 C2
Bellerby Cl WHTF M45 69 F4
Belleville Av WYTH/NTH M22 180 D4
Belle Vue Av WGTN/LGST M12 129 G3
Belle Vue St WGTN/LGST M12 129 H2
Belle Vue Ter BURY BL9 4 C6
Bellfield Av CHD/CHDH SK8 183 E3
OLDS OL8 91 G5
Bellfield Cl BKLY M9 87 H5
Bellfield Vw BOL BL1 34 B3
Bellhill Gdns SLFD M6 113 E2
Bellingham Cl ROY/SHW OL2 60 A1
TOT/BURYW BL8 37 E4
Bellis Cl WGTN/LGST M12 115 H4
Bell La BURY BL9 5 G3
Bellott St CHH M8 102 B4
Bellott Wk OLD OL1 * 75 F4
Bellpit Cl WALK M28 96 D3
Bells Croft Av
NEWH/MOS M40 * 104 A3
Bellshill Crs MILN OL16 11 K3
Bell St DROY M43 118 A3
MILN OL16 10 C5
OLD OL1 9 K2
Bell Ter ECC M30 110 D5
Belmont Av DTN/ASHW M34 132 A4
OLDE OL4 77 F5
SLFD M6 111 H2
SWIN M27 83 G2
Belmont Cl HTNM SK4 159 H3
Belmont Dr MPL/ROM SK6 163 G5
TOT/BURYW BL8 37 F5
Belmont Rd BOL BL1 22 C5
BRAM/HZG SK7 194 A2
CHD/CHDH SK8 169 G3
HALE/TIMP WA15 177 H2
RAD M26 68 B3
SALE M33 139 G5
Belmont St ECC M30 111 E2
HTNM SK4 159 H3
OLD OL1 8 E1
OLDE OL4 92 D2
SALQ M50 112 C4
Belmont Ter PART M31 * 137 F5
Belmont Vw BOLE BL2 35 G2
Belmont Wk
BRUN/LGST M13 * 128 D2
Belmont Wy CHAD OL9 74 D4
HTNM SK4 159 H3
WHIT OL12 10 B1
Belmore Rd SALE M33 154 C5
Belper Rd ECC M30 110 C5
HTNM SK4 158 C5
Belroy Ct PWCH M25 * 86 A4
Belsay Cl AULW OL7 106 B5
Belsay Dr NTHM/RTH M23 167 H5
Belsfield Ter AUL OL6 * 107 F2
Belstone Av
NTHM/RTH M23 179 H1
Belstone Cl BRAM/HZG SK7 184 A2
Belthorne Av BKLY M9 88 D5
Belton Av MILN OL16 11 K3
Beltone Cl STRET M32 139 H2
Belton Wk CHAD OL9 8 C4
Belvedere Av RDSH SK5 145 F1
TOT/BURYW BL8 26 B2
Belvedere Ct PWCH M25 * 85 H4
Belvedere Dr DUK SK16 120 B5
MPL/ROM SK6 160 D3
Belvedere Ri OLD OL1 76 C1
Belvedere Rd RUSH/FAL M14 143 G3
SLFD M6 113 F2
Belvedere St SLFD M6 * 113 G2
Belvoir Av BNG/LEV M19 * 144 A1
BRAM/HZG SK7 185 F4
Belvoir Mdw MILN OL16 20 B4
Belvoir St BOLE BL2 49 H2
WHIT OL12 29 G2
Belvor Av DTN/ASHW M34 132 B1
Belwood Rd CCHDY M21 141 E4
Bembridge Cl RUSH/FAL M14 128 D5
Bembridge Dr BOLS/LL BL3 50 A4
Bembridge Rd
DTN/ASHW M34 147 F3
Bempton Cl OFTN SK2 173 H4
Bemrose Av ALT WA14 165 F3
Bemsley Pl ORD M5 * 113 F5
Benbecula Wy URM M41 124 C3
Benbow Av WGTN/LGST M12 129 G3
Benbow St SALE M33 154 C1
Ben Brierley Wy OLD OL1 9 H2
Bench Carr WHIT OL12 10 A2
Benchill Court Rd
WYTH/NTH M22 168 D5
Benchill Dr WYTH/NTH M22 168 C4
Benchill Rd WYTH/NTH M22 168 B3
Bendall St OP/CLY M11 117 F5
Ben Davies Ct
MPL/ROM SK6 * 162 B4
Bendemeer URM M41 124 B5
Bendix St ANC M4 7 H2
Benedict Cl BRO M7 101 F5
Benedict Dr DUK SK16 133 F2
Benfield Av NEWH/MOS M40 89 F5
Benfield St HEY OL10 41 E4
Benfleet Cl WGTN/LGST M12 * 129 H2
Bengal La AUL OL6 119 H1
Bengal St ANC M4 7 J2
EDGY/DAV SK3 12 E6
Benjamin St AULW OL7 119 F4
Benmore Cl HEY OL10 40 B4
Benmore Rd BKLY M9 88 C4
Bennet St RAD M26 51 G5
Bennett Cl EDGY/DAV SK3 12 A5
Bennett Dr BRO M7 101 H4
Bennett Rd CHH M8 102 A1
Bennett's La BOL BL1 33 F4
Bennett St AULW OL7 119 E4
EDGY/DAV SK3 12 A5
HYDE SK14 133 G3
STLY SK15 * 120 D4
STRET M32 * 140 A2
WGTN/LGST M12 129 F2
Benny La DROY M43 118 C2
Benson Cl BRO M7 101 H5
Benson St BURY BL9 5 G6
Ben St OP/CLY M11 116 C3
Bentcliffe Wy ECC M30 111 H4
Bentfield Crs MILN OL16 44 D2
Bent Fold Dr BURY BL9 * 69 H3
Bentgate Cl MILN OL16 44 D2
Bentgate St MILN OL16 44 D3
Bentham Cl TOT/BURYW BL8 36 D3
Bent Hill St BOLS/LL BL3 * 47 H5
Bentinck Cl ALT WA14 * 165 F5
Bentinck Rd ALT WA14 165 F5
Bentinck St AUL OL6 119 F3
BOL BL1 33 E5
FWTH BL4 65 H3
HULME M15 127 G1
WHIT OL12 29 F2
Bent La CHH M8 102 A3
PWCH M25 86 B3
Bent Lanes URM M41 123 H3
Bentley Av MDTN M24 57 G4
Bentley Cl RAD M26 53 E5
Bentley Ct FWTH BL4 66 A3
Bentley Fold TOT/BURYW BL8 37 E2
Bentley Fold Cottages
TOT/BURYW BL8 * 37 E2
Bentley Hall Rd
TOT/BURYW BL8 36 B2
Bentley La BURY BL9 27 H2
Bentley Ms WHIT OL12 * 29 H1
Bentley Rd BRO M7 101 H2
CCHDY M21 141 E2
DTN/ASHW M34 132 C5
Bentley St CHAD OL9 74 C5
FWTH BL4 66 A3
OLD OL1 76 A4
WHIT OL12 29 H1
Bentmeadows WHIT OL12 10 A2
Benton Dr MPL/ROM SK6 175 H1
Benton St BKLY M9 103 G3
Bents Av MPL/ROM SK6 161 H3
URM M41 137 G2
Bents Farm Cl LIT OL15 * 20 C3
Bent Spur Rd FWTH BL4 82 D2
Bent St CHH M8 102 B5
FWTH BL4 66 B5
Bentworth Wk BKLY M9 103 F3
Beresford Av BOLS/LL BL3 48 B4
Beresford Crs OLDE OL4 76 C4
RDSH SK5 130 D5
Beresford Rd
BRUN/LGST M13 129 G5
STRET M32 126 B4
Beresford St FAIL M35 104 D3
MILN OL16 45 E2
OLDE OL4 76 C4
RUSH/FAL M14 128 A5
Berigan Cl WGTN/LGST M12 129 F3
Berisford Cl HALE/TIMP WA15 165 H2
Berkeley Av CHAD OL9 90 A4
RUSH/FAL M14 129 F4
STRET M32 125 F4
Berkeley Cl HYDE SK14 147 H2
OFTN SK2 172 D1
Berkeley Crs HYDE SK14 147 H2
RAD M26 51 F4
Berkeley Dr MILN OL16 43 G2
Berkeley Rd BOL BL1 33 H2
BRAM/HZG SK7 185 G1
Berkeley St AUL OL6 119 F2
Berkley Av BNG/LEV M19 144 A1
Berkley Dr ROY/SHW OL2 75 E2
Berkley St ROY/SHW OL2 59 E4
Berkley Wk LIT OL15 20 C3
Berkshire Cl CHAD OL9 90 C2
Berkshire Ct BURY BL9 53 G2
Berkshire Pl CHAD OL9 8 A6
Berkshire Rd
NEWH/MOS M40 115 G2
Berlin Rd EDGY/DAV SK3 171 G3
Berlin St BOLS/LL BL3 48 B3
Bermondsay St ORD M5 113 G5
Bernard Gv BOL BL1 33 F4
Bernard St BKLY M9 103 E2
WHIT OL12 18 D5
Berne Cl BRAM/HZG SK7 171 H5
CHAD OL9 8 A5
Bernice Av CHAD OL9 90 C1
Bernice St BOL BL1 33 F4
Berriedale Cl
OLDTF/WHR M16 * 141 H1
Berrie Gv BNG/LEV M19 144 A3
Berry Brow NEWH/MOS M40 117 F1
UPML OL3 95 E2
Berry Cl WILM/AE SK9 198 D5
Berrycroft La MPL/ROM SK6 161 H3
Berry St CMANE M1 7 J7
ECC M30 110 C5
STLY SK15 121 F5
SWIN M27 84 A5
UPML OL3 95 E2
Bertha Rd MILN OL16 11 J7
Bertha St BOL BL1 33 G4
OP/CLY M11 130 A1
ROY/SHW OL2 60 A4
Bertie St ROCH OL11 42 C2
Bertram St SALE M33 155 F2
WGTN/LGST M12 * 129 H2
Bertrand Rd BOL BL1 48 B2
Bert St BOLS/LL BL3 64 A1
Berwick Av HTNM SK4 158 A4
URM M41 139 G1
WHTF M45 69 H5
Berwick Cl HEY OL10 40 B5
WALK M28 96 A3
Berwick St MILN OL16 30 C5
Berwyn Av BKLY M9 87 H2
CHD/CHDH SK8 171 E4
MDTN M24 73 F4
Berwyn Cl OLDS OL8 91 F4
Beryl Av TOT/BURYW BL8 26 A4
Beryl St BOL BL1 34 A3
Besom La STLY SK15 121 H2
Bessemer Rd IRL M44 136 B5
Bessemer St OP/CLY M11 130 B1
Bessemer Wy OLD OL1 9 F2
Bessybrook Cl HOR/BR BL6 46 D3
Beswick Dr FAIL M35 105 F4
Beswicke Royds St MILN OL16 11 J3
Beswicke St LIT OL15 21 F3
WHIT OL12 10 A4
Beswick Rw ANC M4 7 F2
Beswick St ANC M4 115 G3
DROY M43 118 A4
Beta Av STRET M32 140 A2
Beta St BOL BL1 2 D2
Bethany La MILN OL16 45 F2
Bethel Av FAIL M35 104 D3
Bethel St HEY OL10 40 D4
Bethesda St OLDS OL8 91 G3
Bethnall Dr RUSH/FAL M14 142 C3
Betjeman Pl ROY/SHW OL2 60 C2
Betleymere Rd
CHD/CHDH SK8 170 C5
Betley Rd RDSH SK5 145 F2
Betley St CMANE M1 7 K6

HEY OL10 * 40 D5
RAD M26 52 D5
Betnor Av STKP SK1 160 C5
Betony Cl WHIT OL12 18 C5
Betsham St HULME M15 128 A3
Bettwood Dr CHH M8 87 E5
Betula Gv BRO M7 101 G3
Betula Ms ROCH OL11 28 A2
Bevan Cl WGTN/LGST M12 115 H4
Bevendon Sq BRO M7 101 H4
Beveridge St RUSH/FAL M14 128 B5
Beverley Av DTN/ASHW M34 147 E1
URM M41 124 D4
Beverley Cl WHTF M45 70 A3
Beverley Pl MILN OL16 * 10 E5
Beverley Rd BOL BL1 48 B1
BOLS/LL BL3 66 C1
OFTN SK2 172 D1
SWIN M27 99 H3
Beverley St BKLY M9 103 F1
Beverley Wk OLDS OL8 * 9 F7
Beverly Cl AUL OL6 107 E4
Beverly Rd RUSH/FAL M14 143 F4
Beverston ROCH OL11 * 29 H5
Beverston Dr BRO M7 101 H4
Bevill Sq CSLFD M3 6 B2
Bevis Gn BURY BL9 27 G3
Bewick St BOLE BL2 34 C3
Bewley St OLDS OL8 91 E5
Bexhill Av HALE/TIMP WA15 166 A3
Bexhill Cl BOLS/LL BL3 67 F1
Bexhill Dr BRUN/LGST M13 129 F5
Bexhill Rd EDGY/DAV SK3 171 H5
Bexhill Wk CHAD OL9 90 C1
Bexington Rd
OLDTF/WHR M16 127 G5
Bexley Cl URM M41 124 A4
Bexley Dr LHULT M38 81 H4
TOT/BURYW BL8 37 G5
Bexley Sq CSLFD M3 6 A3
Bexley St CHAD OL9 8 B6
Beyer Cl GTN M18 130 B3
Bibby La BNG/LEV M19 143 H5
Bibby St BURY BL9 53 G4
HYDE SK14 * 133 G3
Bibury Av WYTH/NTH M22 180 A1
Bickerdike Av
WGTN/LGST M12 130 A5
Bickershaw Dr WALK M28 81 H5
Bickerstaffe Cl ROY/SHW OL2 59 H4
Bickerton Dr BRAM/HZG SK7 184 C3
Bickerton Rd ALT WA14 165 E4
Biddall Dr NTHM/RTH M23 168 A3
Biddisham Wk
NEWH/MOS M40 * 115 G1
Biddulph Av OFTN SK2 172 D4
Bideford Dr BOLE BL2 50 D3
NTHM/RTH M23 167 G2
Bideford Rd OFTN SK2 160 D5
ROCH OL11 42 A3
Bidston Av RUSH/FAL M14 142 D1
Bidston Cl ROY/SHW OL2 60 C3
TOT/BURYW BL8 37 E4
Bidston Dr WILM/AE SK9 192 B5
Biggin Gdns HEY OL10 56 B2
Bignor St CHH M8 102 B4
Bilbao St BOL BL1 48 B1
Bilberry St MILN OL16 30 C5
Bilbrook St ANC M4 115 E2
Billberry Cl WHTF M45 70 A4
Billing Av WGTN/LGST M12 128 D1
Billinge Cl BOL BL1 2 E2
Billington Rd SWIN M27 100 B2
Bill Williams Cl OP/CLY M11 116 D5
Billy La SWIN M27 84 A5
Billy's La CHD/CHDH SK8 182 D3
Bilson Dr EDGY/DAV SK3 171 E2
Binbrook Wk BOLS/LL BL3 48 D5
Bindloss Av ECC M30 111 H2
Bingham Dr NTHM/RTH M23 167 G3
Bingham St SWIN M27 99 E2
Bingley Cl OP/CLY M11 116 A5
Bingley Dr URM M41 123 G4
Bingley Rd MILN OL16 11 K7
Bingley Sq MILN OL16 11 K7
Bingley Ter MILN OL16 11 K7
Bingley Wk BRO M7 100 C2
FWTH BL4 66 A5
Binns Nook Rd WHIT OL12 10 E1
Binns Pl ANC M4 7 J4
Binns St STLY SK15 120 B4
Binsley Cl IRL M44 136 C2
Binstead Cl RUSH/FAL M14 129 F5
Birbeck St MOSL OL5 * 93 H5
Birchacre Gv RUSH/FAL M14 145 F4
Birchall Cl DUK SK16 133 G2
Birchall Gn MPL/ROM SK6 161 H1
Birchall Wy HULME M15 128 A2
Birch Av FAIL M35 105 E5
HTNM SK4 159 E2
IRL M44 150 C1
MDTN M24 72 D5
MPL/ROM SK6 162 C4
OLD OL1 74 B2
OLDS OL8 91 E5
OLDTF/WHR M16 126 D4
SALE M33 154 C3
SLFD M6 112 D1
TOT/BURYW BL8 37 F1
WHIT OL12 20 A4
WHTF M45 85 G1
WHTN BL5 62 A5
WILM/AE SK9 198 C4
Birch Cl WHIT OL12 18 B3
Birch Crs MILN OL16 44 D3
Birchdale ALT WA14 177 F2
Birchdale Av CHD/CHDH SK8 181 G2
Birch Dr BRAM/HZG SK7 184 D2
OLDE OL4 92 D2
SWIN M27 99 G2
Birchenall St NEWH/MOS M40 103 G2
Birchenlea St CHAD OL9 90 B4
The Birches MOSL OL5 108 C1
SALE M33 153 H1
Birchfield BOLE BL2 24 B5
Birchfield Av BURY BL9 39 H5
Birchfield Dr ROCH OL11 42 B1
WALK M28 96 B3
Birchfield Gv BOLS/LL BL3 47 F5
Birchfield Ms HYDE SK14 * 147 H1
Birchfield Rd EDGY/DAV SK3 170 D2
Birchfields HALE/TIMP WA15 178 A3
OLDE OL4 93 E3
Birchfields Av
BRUN/LGST M13 143 G1
Birchfields Rd
BRUN/LGST M13 129 F5
Birchfold Cl LHULT M38 81 G3
Birchgate Wk BOLS/LL BL3 48 D4
Birch Gv DTN/ASHW M34 132 B5
DTN/ASHW M34 132 C2
HALE/TIMP WA15 167 F4
PWCH M25 85 H1
RAMS BL0 16 B5
RUSH/FAL M14 129 E5
Birch Hall Cl OLDE OL4 92 D3
Birch Hall La BRUN/LGST M13 143 G1
Birch Hey Cl WHIT OL12 19 H4
Birch Hill Crs WHIT OL12 20 B4
Birch Hill La WHIT OL12 20 A2
Birchington Rd
DID/WITH M20 142 C3
Birchinlee Av ROY/SHW OL2 74 C1
Birchin Pl ANC M4 * 7 G4
Birch La BRUN/LGST M13 129 F4
DUK SK16 120 A5
Birchlea HALE/TIMP WA15 166 A5
Birch-lea Cl BURY BL9 53 G2
Birchleaf Gv ORD M5 112 B3
Birch Mt WHIT OL12 20 B4
Birch Polygon RUSH/FAL M14 129 E5
Birch Rd CHD/CHDH SK8 169 F4
CHH M8 102 C1
FWTH BL4 82 C1
GOL/RIS/CUL WA3 150 A4
MDTN M24 73 F2
PART M31 152 C3
POY/DIS SK12 195 G5
SWIN M27 98 C5
UPML OL3 79 F5
WALK M28 97 F1
WHIT OL12 19 H2
Birch St AULW OL7 118 D4
BOLE BL2 3 J7
BURY BL9 5 F2
DROY M43 * 118 A5
HEY OL10 41 E5
RAD M26 53 F4
STLY SK15 108 D5
WGTN/LGST M12 129 H2
WHIT OL12 19 H2
Birch Ter HYDE SK14 * 147 G1
Birch Tree Av BRAM/HZG SK7 185 H3
Birch Tree Cl ALT WA14 177 F3
Birch Tree Dr WYTH/NTH M22 180 C1
Birchvale Av MPL/ROM SK6 162 C3
Birchway BRAM/HZG SK7 183 G5
MPL/ROM SK6 187 E5
Birchwood CHAD OL9 73 H5
DROY M43 118 A2
Birchwood Crs HYDE SK14 134 B2
Birchwood Dr
NEWH/MOS M40 103 E4
WILM/AE SK9 199 G3
Birchwood Rd MDTN M24 73 F4
Birchwood Wy DUK SK16 * 133 G2
Bird Hall Av CHD/CHDH SK8 171 F5
Birdhall Gv BNG/LEV M19 144 A3
Bird Hall La EDGY/DAV SK3 171 E2
Bird Hall Rd CHD/CHDH SK8 171 E4
Birdlip Dr NTHM/RTH M23 179 H1
Birkby Dr MDTN M24 72 B2
Birkdale Av ROY/SHW OL2 75 F2
WHTF M45 85 E1
Birkdale Cl BRAM/HZG SK7 184 A5
HEY OL10 56 A1
HYDE SK14 133 H3
Birkdale Dr SALE M33 153 H4
TOT/BURYW BL8 37 G4
Birkdale Gdns BOLS/LL BL3 48 C4
Birkdale Gv ECC M30 111 G3
RDSH SK5 160 A1
Birkdale Pl SALE M33 * 139 F5
Birkdale Rd MILN OL16 43 H2
RDSH SK5 160 A1
Birkdale St CHH M8 102 B3
Birkenhills Dr BOLS/LL BL3 47 F4
Birkett Cl BOL BL1 22 C5
Birkett Dr BOL BL1 22 C5
Birkinbrook Cl WHTF M45 69 H3
Birks Av OLDE OL4 77 E4
Birks Dr TOT/BURYW BL8 26 C5
Birkworth Ct OFTN SK2 173 E3
Birley Cl HALE/TIMP WA15 166 A2
Birley Pk DID/WITH M20 157 E3
Birley St BOL BL1 33 H2
BURY BL9 38 C1
WHIT OL12 10 E2
Birling Dr NTHM/RTH M23 168 A5
Birnham Gv HEY OL10 40 B5
Birshaw Cl ROY/SHW OL2 60 A4
Birtenshaw Crs EDGW/EG BL7 23 G4
Birtles Av RDSH SK5 131 E5
Birtles Cl CHD/CHDH SK8 170 D5
DUK SK16 133 G2
Birtlespool Rd
CHD/CHDH SK8 170 C5
Birtley Wk NEWH/MOS M40 * 115 F2
Birt St NEWH/MOS M40 115 G1
Birwood Rd CHH M8 87 G5
Biscay Cl OP/CLY M11 116 A4
Bishopbridge Cl BOLS/LL BL3 49 E5
Bishop Cl OLDTF/WHR M16 127 H4
Bishopdale Cl ROY/SHW OL2 59 E4
Bishopgate St CHAD OL9 90 B2
Bishop Marshall Cl
NEWH/MOS M40 * 103 E5
Bishop Marshall Wy
MDTN M24 56 A5
Bishop Rd SLFD M6 112 A1
URM M41 137 G1
Bishops Cl ALT WA14 177 E3
AULW OL7 106 D5
BOLS/LL BL3 65 F2
CHD/CHDH SK8 170 D4
Bishopsgate CMANW M2 6 E6
Bishopsgate Wk MILN OL16 43 H2
Bishops Meadow MDTN M24 72 A1
Bishops Ms SALE M33 139 E5
Bishop's Rd BOLS/LL BL3 65 F2
PWCH M25 86 B4
Bishop St MDTN M24 73 G5
MILN OL16 11 G2
STKP SK1 13 J3
Bishopton Cl BNG/LEV M19 144 C2
Bisley Av NTHM/RTH M23 167 G3
Bisley St OLDS OL8 8 D5
Bismarck St OLDE OL4 9 K6
Bispham Av BOLE BL2 50 C2
Bispham Cl TOT/BURYW BL8 37 E5
Bispham Gv BRO M7 101 H3
Bispham St BOLE BL2 * 49 H1
Bittern Cl POY/DIS SK12 194 B4
ROCH OL11 28 C4
Bittern Dr DROY M43 118 B2
Blackbank St BOL BL1 34 A4
Blackberry Cl ALT WA14 165 E1
Blackberry La RDSH SK5 145 H4
Black Brook Rd HTNM SK4 144 D4
Blackburn Gdns
DID/WITH M20 157 F2
Blackburn Pl ORD M5 113 H4
Blackburn St CSLFD M3 114 A2
OLDTF/WHR M16 127 F3
PWCH M25 86 B3
RAD M26 68 C2
Blackcap Cl WALK M28 96 C3
Blackcarr Rd NTHM/RTH M23 168 A4
Blackchapel Dr MILN OL16 43 G3
Blackcroft Cl SWIN M27 98 D2
Blackdown Gv OLDS OL8 91 F4
Blackett St WGTN/LGST M12 * 115 F5
Blackfield La BRO M7 101 F2
Blackfields BRO M7 * 101 G2
Blackford Av BURY BL9 53 G5
Blackford Rd BNG/LEV M19 144 B4
Blackford Wk
NEWH/MOS M40 115 G2
Blackfriars Rd CSLFD M3 6 B1
Blackfriars St CSLFD M3 6 D3
Blackhill Cl BRUN/LGST M13 128 C1
Black Horse St BOL BL1 2 E6
FWTH BL4 66 B5
Blackleach Dr WALK M28 82 A3
Blackledge St BOLS/LL BL3 48 B5
Blackley Cl BURY BL9 69 H2
Blackley New Rd BKLY M9 87 E4
Blackley Park Rd BKLY M9 103 E1
Blackley St MDTN M24 71 G5
OLDTF/WHR M16 127 F3
Blacklock St CSLFD M3 114 C1
Blackmore Rd STRET M32 125 G3
Black Moss Cl RAD M26 * 67 G1
Black Moss Rd ALT WA14 164 B2
Blackpits Rd ROCH OL11 28 A2
Blackpool St OP/CLY M11 116 D3
Blackrock MOSL OL5 108 D4
Blackrock St OP/CLY M11 116 A4
Blackrod Dr TOT/BURYW BL8 37 F5
Black Sail Wk OLD OL1 75 G3
Blackshaw La BOLS/LL BL3 48 B3
ROY/SHW OL2 59 G5
WILM/AE SK9 200 C4
Blackshaw St EDGY/DAV SK3 13 F5
Blacksmith La ROCH OL11 42 A2
Blackstock St
BRUN/LGST M13 128 D4
Blackstone Av MILN OL16 11 K4
Blackstone Edge Old Rd
LIT OL15 21 H2
Blackstone Rd OFTN SK2 173 E4
Blackthorn Av BNG/LEV M19 144 A4
Blackthorn Cl WHIT OL12 29 H1
Blackthorne Cl BOL BL1 32 D5
Blackthorne Dr SALE M33 153 G4
Blackthorne Rd HYDE SK14 148 A5
Blackthorn Ms WHIT OL12 29 H1
Blackthorn Rd OLDS OL8 105 H2
Blackwin St WGTN/LGST M12 129 H2
Blackwood Dr
NTHM/RTH M23 167 E1
Blackwood St BOLS/LL BL3 49 F5
Bladen Cl CHD/CHDH SK8 170 D5
Bladon St CMANE M1 * 7 H6
Blair Av LHULT M38 81 G3
URM M41 137 G1
Blair Cl BRAM/HZG SK7 184 D4
ROY/SHW OL2 60 A2
SALE M33 153 F5
Blairhall Av NEWH/MOS M40 103 H3
Blair La BOLE BL2 35 E5
Blairmore Dr BOLS/LL BL3 47 F5
Blair Rd OLDTF/WHR M16 142 A2
Blair St EDGW/EG BL7 23 E3
FWTH BL4 82 D1
OLDTF/WHR M16 127 G3
WHIT OL12 29 G2
Blakedown Wk
WGTN/LGST M12 129 F3
Blake Dr OFTN SK2 173 F2
Blakefield Dr WALK M28 97 F1
Blake Gdns BOL BL1 33 G4
Blakelock St ROY/SHW OL2 59 H2
Blakemere Av SALE M33 155 F3
Blakemore Wk
WGTN/LGST M12 * 115 H4
Blake St BOL BL1 33 G4
EDGW/EG BL7 23 F4
MILN OL16 11 F5
Blakeswell Cl URM M41 123 E5
Blakey Cl BOLS/LL BL3 47 G5
Blakey St WGTN/LGST M12 129 H4
Blanchard St HULME M15 127 H3
Blanche St WHIT OL12 10 E1
Blanche Wk OLD OL1 9 J1
Bland Cl FAIL M35 104 D3
Blandford Av WALK M28 97 H2
Blandford Cl TOT/BURYW BL8 38 A1
Blandford Ct STLY SK15 120 D3
Blandford Dr NEWH/MOS M40 89 F5
Blandford Rd ECC M30 110 C3
HTNM SK4 12 A1
SLFD M6 101 E5
Blandford St AUL OL6 119 F2
STLY SK15 * 120 D3
Bland Rd PWCH M25 86 A5
Bland St OLDTF/WHR M16 * 127 H4
Blanefield Cl CCHDY M21 142 A4
Blantyre Av WALK M28 82 B5
Blantyre Rd SWIN M27 99 G4
Blantyre St ECC M30 110 B2
HULME M15 127 G1
SWIN M27 98 C2
Blanwood Dr CHH M8 102 C3
Blaven Cl EDGY/DAV SK3 172 A4
Blazemoss Bank OFTN SK2 173 E4
Bleackley St TOT/BURYW BL8 37 H2
Bleadale Cl WILM/AE SK9 199 G1
Bleak Hey Rd WYTH/NTH M22 181 E2
Bleakley St WHTF M45 69 F3
Bleak St BOLE BL2 34 C4
Bleasby St OLDE OL4 76 B5
Bleasdale Cl HOR/BR BL6 46 A1
Bleasdale Rd BOL BL1 32 C4
WYTH/NTH M22 179 H2
Bleasdale St ROY/SHW OL2 59 E4
Bleasefell Cha WALK M28 96 B5
Bleatarn Rd STKP SK1 172 C2
Bledlow Cl ECC M30 111 F2
Blenheim Av
OLDTF/WHR M16 141 H1
Blenheim Cl ALT WA14 177 G3
BURY BL9 53 G4
HEY OL10 41 F4
POY/DIS SK12 195 G3
WILM/AE SK9 199 G3
Blenheim Rd BOLE BL2 50 B2
CHD/CHDH SK8 183 E2
OLDTF/WHR M16 126 D5
Blenheim St OLDE OL4 76 C3
WHIT OL12 * 29 F2
Blenheim Wy AUL OL6 120 B1
Blenhiem Av OLD OL1 76 C1
Blenmar Cl RAD M26 52 D4
Bleriot St BOLS/LL BL3 64 C1
Bletchley Cl BRUN/LGST M13 129 E3
Bletchley Rd HTNM SK4 158 B5
Blethyn St BOLS/LL BL3 64 A2
Blinco Rd URM M41 139 F2
Blind La WGTN/LGST M12 129 E1
Blindsill Rd FWTH BL4 65 G5
Blisworth Av ECC M30 111 F5
Blisworth Cl ANC M4 115 G4
Block La CHAD OL9 90 C2
Blodwell St SLFD M6 113 E3
Blomley St ROCH OL11 42 B4
Bloomfield Cl CHD/CHDH SK8 182 B5
Bloomfield Dr BURY BL9 70 A1
WALK M28 96 B3
Bloomfield Rd FWTH BL4 82 A1
Bloomfield St BOL BL1 33 H3
Bloomsbury Gv
HALE/TIMP WA15 166 B3
Bloomsbury La
HALE/TIMP WA15 166 B3
Bloom St CMANE M1 7 G6
CSLFD M3 6 B3
EDGY/DAV SK3 12 B6
RAMS BL0 16 B4
Blossom Pl MILN OL16 * 10 C5
Blossom Rd PART M31 150 D4
Blossoms Hey CHD/CHDH SK8 182 B3
Blossoms La BRAM/HZG SK7 192 D5
Blossoms St OFTN SK2 172 A2
Blossom St ANC M4 7 J3
CSLFD M3 6 C2
Blucher St AULW OL7 106 D4
ORD M5 113 H4
WGTN/LGST M12 129 F2
Blueball La PWCH M25 71 F3
Blue Bell Av NEWH/MOS M40 103 H1
Bluebell Cl HYDE SK14 134 A3
Bluebell Dr ROCH OL11 42 A3
Bluebell Gv CHD/CHDH SK8 170 A5
Bluebell Wy WILM/AE SK9 199 F1
Blueberry Dr ROY/SHW OL2 60 C2
Blueberry Rd ALT WA14 176 D2
Bluefields ROY/SHW OL2 60 C1
Blue Ribbon Wk SWIN M27 99 F1
Bluestone Dr HTNM SK4 158 B3
Bluestone Rd
NEWH/MOS M40 103 H2
RDSH SK5 145 G1
Blundell Cl BURY BL9 70 A1
Blundell St BOL BL1 2 D4
Blundering La STLY SK15 135 E2
Blunn St OLDS OL8 91 G3
Blyborough Cl SLFD M6 112 D1
Blyth Av LIT OL15 * 20 C5
Blyth Cl HALE/TIMP WA15 167 E3
Blythe Av BRAM/HZG SK7 193 F1
Blyton St HULME M15 128 C3
Boad St CMANE M1 7 J6
Boardale Dr MDTN M24 72 B3
Boardman Cl BOL BL1 33 H4
RDSH SK5 159 H2
Boardman Fold Cl MDTN M24 88 D2
Boardman Fold Rd MDTN M24 88 D2
Boardman La MDTN M24 71 G4
Boardman Rd CHH M8 87 E5
Boardman St BOL BL1 33 H4
ECC M30 111 F4
HYDE SK14 147 H1
Board St AUL OL6 120 A1
BOL BL1 2 A6
Boar Green Cl
NEWH/MOS M40 104 B3
Boarshaw Clough MDTN M24 73 E2
Boarshaw Clough Wy
MDTN M24 73 E2
Boarshaw Crs MDTN M24 73 F2
Boarshaw La MDTN M24 73 G1
Boarshaw Rd MDTN M24 72 D3
Boarshurst La UPML OL3 95 F2
Boat La IRL M44 136 D1
WYTH/NTH M22 156 D5
Bobbin Wk ANC M4 * 7 K4
OLDE OL4 9 K5
Bob Brook Cl
NEWH/MOS M40 104 B4
Bob Massey Cl OP/CLY M11 116 D5
Bob's La IRL M44 150 C2
Boddens Hill Rd HTNM SK4 158 D5
Boddington Rd ECC M30 110 A4
Bodiam Rd TOT/BURYW BL8 26 A2
Bodley St OP/CLY M11 116 D3
Bodmin Cl ROY/SHW OL2 75 H1
Bodmin Crs RDSH SK5 160 C1
Bodmin Dr BRAM/HZG SK7 185 A5
Bodmin Rd SALE M33 153 G1
Bolam Cl NTHM/RTH M23 155 G5
Boland Dr RUSH/FAL M14 143 F3
Bolbury Crs SWIN M27 100 A2
Bolderod Pl OLD OL1 * 9 J1
Bolderstone Pl OFTN SK2 173 F5
Bold St ALT WA14 177 G1
BOL BL1 2 E6
BURY BL9 5 G2
HULME M15 127 H3
SWIN M27 84 B5
Bolesworth Cl CCHDY M21 140 D3
Boleyn Ct HEY OL10 40 D5
Bolholt Ter TOT/BURYW BL8 37 G2
Bolivia St ORD M5 112 B3
Bollin Av ALT WA14 177 E4
Bollin Cl FWTH BL4 82 D1
Bollin Ct HULME M15 127 G2
Bollin Dr ALT WA14 165 H1
SALE M33 154 C4
Bollings Yd BOL BL1 3 F6
Bollington Rd HTNM SK4 159 G1
NEWH/MOS M40 115 G3
Bollington St AULW OL7 119 F4
Bollin Hl WILM/AE SK9 198 D2
Bollin Sq ALT WA14 177 E3
Bollin Wk WHTF M45 70 B2
WILM/AE SK9 199 E3
Bollinway HALE/TIMP WA15 178 B4
Bollinwood Cha WILM/AE SK9 199 G3
Bolshaw Farm La
CHD/CHDH SK8 191 H1
Bolshaw Rd CHD/CHDH SK8 191 G1
Bolton Av BNG/LEV M19 158 A4
CHD/CHDH SK8 193 E1
Bolton Cl POY/DIS SK12 195 E3
PWCH M25 85 G5
Bolton Rd BOLE BL2 34 D1
FWTH BL4 66 A2
FWTH BL4 66 B5
RAD M26 51 G5
ROCH OL11 41 H2
SLFD M6 99 H4
SWIN M27 99 H2
TOT/BURYW BL8 25 F1
TOT/BURYW BL8 52 B1
WALK M28 82 A3
WHTN BL5 62 A4
Bolton Rd West RAMS BL0 16 C4
Bolton St CSLFD M3 6 B4
OLDE OL4 9 K4
RAD M26 68 A1
RAMS BL0 16 C3
RDSH SK5 145 E4
TOT/BURYW BL8 4 A4
Bombay Rd EDGY/DAV SK3 171 F2
Bombay St AUL OL6 120 A1
CMANE M1 7 G7
Bonar Cl EDGY/DAV SK3 * 12 A5
Bonar Rd EDGY/DAV SK3 12 A6
Boncarn Dr NTHM/RTH M23 167 H5
Bonchurch Wk
WGTN/LGST M12 130 A2
Bondmark Rd GTN M18 130 B2
Bond Sq BRO M7 * 101 H4
Bond St BURY BL9 5 H4
DTN/ASHW M34 132 C5
STLY SK15 120 D2
WGTN/LGST M12 7 K7
WHIT OL12 11 F1
Bongs Rd OFTN SK2 173 G3
Bonhill Wk OP/CLY M11 116 C3
Bonington Ri MPL/ROM SK6 175 G1
Bonis Crs OFTN SK2 172 D5
Bonny Brow St MDTN M24 71 G5
Bonsall St HULME M15 128 B2
Bonscale Crs MDTN M24 72 B1
Bonville Cha ALT WA14 164 D5
Bonville Rd ALT WA14 164 D4
Boodle St AUL OL6 119 G2
Boond St ANC M4 115 G4
CSLFD M3 6 C2
Boonfields EDGW/EG BL7 23 F3
Booth Av RUSH/FAL M14 143 F4
Booth Bridge Cl MDTN M24 * 71 H5
Boothby Rd SWIN M27 98 D1
Boothby St OFTN SK2 172 D5
Booth Cl STLY SK15 120 C4
TOT/BURYW BL8 37 F1
Boothcote DTN/ASHW M34 132 A2
Booth Dr URM M41 123 G3
Boothfield ECC M30 110 B2
Boothfield Rd
WYTH/NTH M22 168 C3
Boothfields TOT/BURYW BL8 37 H3
Booth Hall Dr TOT/BURYW BL8 37 E1
Booth Hall Rd BKLY M9 88 D4
Booth Hill La OLD OL1 75 F3
Booth Rd ALT WA14 165 F5
BOLS/LL BL3 67 E2
DTN/ASHW M34 131 F1
OLDTF/WHR M16 127 F5
SALE M33 139 H5
WILM/AE SK9 198 D1
Boothroyden Rd BKLY M9 87 H1
Boothroyden Ter BKLY M9 87 H1
Boothsbank Av WALK M28 96 C4
Booth's Hall WALK M28 96 C4
Booth's Hall Gv WALK M28 96 C4
Booth's Hall Rd WALK M28 96 C4
Booth's Hall Wy WALK M28 96 C5
Boothstown Dr WALK M28 96 B5
Booth St AUL OL6 * 119 G3
BOL BL1 33 F3
CHAD OL9 8 E4
CMANW M2 6 E5
CSLFD M3 6 D3
DTN/ASHW M34 132 C3
EDGY/DAV SK3 13 F7
HYDE SK14 148 A2
MDTN M24 89 G1
OLDE OL4 92 D1
STLY SK15 120 C5
TOT/BURYW BL8 37 E1
Booth St East
BRUN/LGST M13 128 C2
Booth St West HULME M15 128 B2
Booth Wy TOT/BURYW BL8 37 E1
Boot La BOL BL1 32 A5
Bootle St CMANW M2 6 D5
Bordale Av BKLY M9 103 G3

Bordan St OP/CLY M11 116 A5
Border Brook La WALK M28 96 B3
Border Wy BURY BL9 53 H3
Bordley Wk NTHM/RTH M23 155 F5
Bordon Rd EDGY/DAV SK3 171 E2
Boringdon Cl
NEWH/MOS M40 * 104 A4
Borland Av NEWH/MOS M40 104 C1
Borough Av RAD M26 53 E4
SWIN M27 99 F1
Borough Rd HALE/TIMP WA15 165 H5
SALQ M50 112 C4
Borough St STLY SK15 120 D4
The Borrans WALK M28 * 96 A5
Borron St STKP SK1 13 K1
Borrowdale Av BOL BL1 47 H1
CHD/CHDH SK8 169 G5
Borrowdale Cl ROY/SHW OL2 59 E3
Borrowdale Crs AULW OL7 119 E1
DID/WITH M20 156 D2
Borrowdale Dr BURY BL9 69 H1
ROCH OL11 42 A2
Borrowdale Rd MDTN M24 72 B2
OFTN SK2 172 C3
Borsden St SWIN M27 98 C1
Borth Av OFTN SK2 172 D2
Borwell St GTN M18 130 C3
Boscobel Rd BOLS/LL BL3 65 G2
Boscombe Av ECC M30 110 D5
Boscombe Dr BRAM/HZG SK7 184 D2
Boscombe St RDSH SK5 145 F1
RUSH/FAL M14 142 D1
Boscow Rd BOLS/LL BL3 66 D2
Bosden Av BRAM/HZG SK7 185 F1
Bosden Cl WILM/AE SK9 192 A2
Bosden Fold STKP SK1 13 H5
Bosdenfold Rd
BRAM/HZG SK7 185 F1
Bosden Hall Rd
BRAM/HZG SK7 185 F1
Bosdin Rd East URM M41 * 137 G2
Bosdin Rd West URM M41 137 G2
Bosley Av DID/WITH M20 142 C3
Bosley Cl WILM/AE SK9 192 A5
Bosley Dr POY/DIS SK12 195 H4
Bosley Rd EDGY/DAV SK3 170 D1
Bossall Av BKLY M9 88 B3
Bossington Cl OFTN SK2 172 D1
Bostock Wk
BRUN/LGST M13 * 128 C1
Boston Cl BRAM/HZG SK7 183 G5
FAIL M35 105 E2
Boston Ct SALQ M50 112 D5
Boston St BOL BL1 * 33 H4
HULME M15 128 A3
HYDE SK14 133 H5
OLDS OL8 91 G3
Boswell Av DTN/ASHW M34 118 C4
Boswell Wy MDTN M24 57 G5
Bosworth Cl WHTF M45 70 B4
Bosworth Sq ROCH OL11 * 42 C2
Bosworth St OP/CLY M11 116 B5
ROCH OL11 42 C1
Botanical Av
OLDTF/WHR M16 126 D3
Botany Cl HEY OL10 40 C3
Botany La AUL OL6 119 H1
Botany Rd ECC M30 110 B1
MPL/ROM SK6 147 E5
Botesworth Gn MILN OL16 44 D1
Botham Cl HULME M15 128 B3
Bothwell Rd
NEWH/MOS M40 * 115 F2
Bottesford Av DID/WITH M20 157 E1
Bottomfield Cl OLD OL1 75 H3
Bottomley Side BKLY M9 87 H5
Bottom o' th' Moor BOLE BL2 35 E4
OLD OL1 9 K3
Bottom St HYDE SK14 134 A5
Boulden Dr TOT/BURYW BL8 37 H1
Boulder Dr NTHM/RTH M23 179 H2
Boulderstone Rd STLY SK15 120 D1
The Boulevard
BRAM/HZG SK7 185 F2
DID/WITH M20 142 A5
Boundary Cl MOSL OL5 108 D4
MPL/ROM SK6 162 B1
Boundary Dr BOLE BL2 50 D4
Boundary Gdns BOL BL1 * 33 G4
OLD OL1 75 F4
Boundary Gv NTHM/RTH M23 155 G4
Boundary La HULME M15 128 B2
Boundary Park Rd OLD OL1 74 D3
Boundary Rd CHD/CHDH SK8 170 C3
IRL M44 122 D5
SWIN M27 99 E2
Boundary St BOL BL1 33 G4
BOLE BL2 51 E4
LIT OL15 20 D2
ROCH OL11 42 D1
WGTN/LGST M12 129 H3
Boundary St West
HULME M15 128 B2
Boundary Ter
WYTH/NTH M22 * 191 E1
The Boundary SWIN M27 83 G3
Boundary Wk ROCH OL11 43 E1
Boundry Gn DTN/ASHW M34 132 B3
Bourdon St NEWH/MOS M40 115 G2
Bourget St BRO M7 102 A2
Bournbrook Av LHULT M38 81 F1
Bourne Av SWIN M27 99 E3
Bourne Dr NEWH/MOS M40 104 A1
Bournelea Av BNG/LEV M19 143 G5
Bourne Rd ROY/SHW OL2 59 H1
Bourne St CHAD OL9 90 C5
HTNM SK4 159 H2
WILM/AE SK9 198 C4
Bourneville Dr
TOT/BURYW BL8 37 F4
Bournville Av HTNM SK4 159 H2
Bournville Gv BNG/LEV M19 144 B2
Bourton Cl TOT/BURYW BL8 37 G3
Bourton Dr GTN M18 130 A4
Bowden Cl HYDE SK14 149 G2
ROCH OL11 57 G1
Bowden La MPL/ROM SK6 174 D2
Bowden Rd SWIN M27 99 F3
Bowden St BRAM/HZG SK7 185 F1
DTN/ASHW M34 132 B5
Bowdon Av RUSH/FAL M14 142 B2
Bowdon Ri ALT WA14 177 G2
Bowdon Rd ALT WA14 177 F1
Bowdon St EDGY/DAV SK3 12 E6
Bowen Cl BRAM/HZG SK7 194 A2
Bowen St BOL BL1 33 E5
Bower Av BRAM/HZG SK7 185 E3
HTNM SK4 159 F3
WHIT OL12 20 A4
Bower Ct HYDE SK14 134 B3
Bower Cup Fold STLY SK15 121 H1
Bowerfield Av BRAM/HZG SK7 185 E4
Bowerfield Crs
BRAM/HZG SK7 185 F4
Bowerfold La HTNM SK4 12 C1
Bower Gdns STLY SK15 121 G5
Bower Gv STLY SK15 121 F3
Bower Rd HALE/TIMP WA15 177 H3
Bowers Av URM M41 124 A4
Bowers St RUSH/FAL M14 143 F4
Bower St BRO M7 * 101 H3
NEWH/MOS M40 103 G5
OLD OL1 9 K2
RDSH SK5 145 F1
Bower Ter DROY M43 118 B2
Bowery Av CHD/CHDH SK8 192 C1
Bowes Cl TOT/BURYW BL8 37 G1
Bowes St RUSH/FAL M14 128 A5
Bowfell Dr MPL/ROM SK6 186 D4
Bowfell Gv BKLY M9 87 G4
Bowfell Rd URM M41 138 B1
Bowgreave Av BOLE BL2 50 C2
Bow Green Rd ALT WA14 176 D3
Bowgreen Wk HULME M15 127 G2
Bowker Av DTN/ASHW M34 147 F3
Bowker Bank Av CHH M8 87 E5
Bowker Cl ROCH OL11 28 B2
Bowkers Rw BOL BL1 3 F5
Bowker St BRO M7 101 G4
HYDE SK14 133 H5
RAD M26 68 B1
WALK M28 81 G4
Bowlacre Rd HYDE SK14 147 H5
Bowland Av GTN M18 131 F4
Bowland Cl AUL OL6 107 F3
OFTN SK2 173 F4
ROY/SHW OL2 59 F2
TOT/BURYW BL8 36 D3
Bowland Dr BOL BL1 32 B4
Bowland Gv MILN OL16 44 C2
Bowland Rd DTN/ASHW M34 131 E5
MPL/ROM SK6 162 A1
NTHM/RTH M23 167 G3
Bow La ALT WA14 176 D4
CMANW M2 6 E5
HEY OL10 40 D4
Bowlee Cl WHTF M45 69 H3
Bowler St BNG/LEV M19 144 B3
ROY/SHW OL2 60 A2
Bowlers Wk WHIT OL12 30 A1
Bowley Av WYTH/NTH M22 179 H2
Bowling Green Cl CHAD OL9 90 B3
Bowling Green St HEY OL10 41 E4
HYDE SK14 147 G1
Bowling Green Wy ROCH OL11 28 C5
Bowling Rd GTN M18 130 D5
Bowling St CHAD OL9 90 C5
Bowman Crs AUL OL6 120 A2
Bow Meadow Gra
WGTN/LGST M12 129 G4
Bowmont Cl CHD/CHDH SK8 170 D5
Bowness Av CHD/CHDH SK8 183 E3
HTNM SK4 145 E5
IRL M44 150 C2
WHIT OL12 29 F2
Bowness Dr SALE M33 154 A1
Bowness Rd AULW OL7 119 E1
BOLS/LL BL3 48 C5
BOLS/LL BL3 50 C5
MDTN M24 72 A3
Bowness St OP/CLY M11 131 E1
STRET M32 126 A5
Bowring St BRO M7 * 101 F5
Bowscale Cl BRUN/LGST M13 129 G4
Bowstone Hill Rd BOLE BL2 36 A1
Bow St BOL BL1 2 E4
CMANW M2 6 D5
DUK SK16 119 H3
EDGY/DAV SK3 12 A5
OLD OL1 9 H3
ROCH OL11 42 C3
Bowyer Gdns BOLS/LL BL3 63 G1
Boxgrove Rd SALE M33 153 H1
Boxhill Dr NTHM/RTH M23 * 155 H5
Box St LIT OL15 20 D3
RAMS BL0 * 17 E2
Boxtree Av GTN M18 130 C5
Boyd St WGTN/LGST M12 129 H1
Boyd's Wk DUK SK16 133 F1
Boyer St OLDTF/WHR M16 127 E3
Boyle St BOL BL1 32 D5
CHH M8 102 C4
Boysnope Whf ECC M30 123 E4
Brabant Rd CHD/CHDH SK8 183 E2
Brabham Cl CCHDY M21 141 F3
Brabham Ms SWIN M27 98 B3
Brabyns Av MPL/ROM SK6 162 C3
Brabyns Brow MPL/ROM SK6 175 F2
Brabyns Rd HYDE SK14 148 A4
Bracadale Dr EDGY/DAV SK3 171 H5
Bracewell Cl WGTN/LGST M12 129 H3
Bracken Av WALK M28 82 B4
Bracken Cl BOL BL1 22 C5
DROY M43 118 B3
HEY OL10 56 A1
MPL/ROM SK6 175 H2
OLDE OL4 93 E1
SALE M33 153 F1
Bracken Dr NTHM/RTH M23 168 A4
Brackenhurst Av MOSL OL5 109 F1
Brackenlea Dr BKLY M9 87 H5
Bracken Lea Fold WHIT OL12 29 E1
Brackenlea Pl EDGY/DAV SK3 171 G4
Brackenside RDSH SK5 145 G3
Brackenwood Cl
ROY/SHW OL2 74 D2
Brackenwood Dr
CHD/CHDH SK8 170 A5
Brackenwood Ms
WILM/AE SK9 199 H1
Brackley Av HULME M15 127 G1
Brackley Dr MDTN M24 88 D2
Brackley Ldg ECC M30 * 111 G2
Brackley Rd ECC M30 111 E1
HTNM SK4 159 G1
WHTN BL5 63 H4
Brackley Sq OLD OL1 * 9 K1
Brackleys St FWTH BL4 66 A4
Brackley St FWTH BL4 66 A4
OLD OL1 * 9 J1
WALK M28 81 H3
Bracondale Av BOL BL1 33 E4
Bradbourne Cl BOLS/LL BL3 48 D4
Bradburn Cl ECC M30 111 E4
Bradburn Rd IRL M44 136 A4
Bradburn St ECC M30 111 E4
Bradburn Wk CHH M8 102 C4
Bradbury Av ALT WA14 164 D4
Bradbury's La UPML OL3 95 G4
Bradbury St AULW OL7 * 119 F1
HYDE SK14 148 A2
RAD M26 68 B2
Bradda Mt BRAM/HZG SK7 184 A2
Braddan Av SALE M33 154 D3
Bradden Cl ORD M5 113 F4
Braddocks Cl WHIT OL12 20 A4
Braddon Av URM M41 124 C5
Braddon Rd MPL/ROM SK6 161 H1
Braddon St OP/CLY M11 116 D4
Braddyll Rd WHTN BL5 63 G4
Brade Cl OP/CLY M11 116 D5
Bradfield Av SLFD M6 112 B3
Bradfield Cl RDSH SK5 145 E1
Bradfield Rd URM M41 139 F1
Bradford Av BOLS/LL BL3 65 G1
Bradford Crs BOLS/LL BL3 * 49 F5
Bradford Park Dr BOLE BL2 3 K6
Bradford Rd BOLS/LL BL3 65 F2
ECC M30 111 F1
NEWH/MOS M40 115 H2
Bradford St BOLE BL2 3 H5
FWTH BL4 66 A5
OLD OL1 75 F4
Bradford Ter BURY BL9 4 B7
Bradgate Av CHD/CHDH SK8 182 A3
Bradgate Cl WYTH/NTH M22 168 D1
Bradgate Rd ALT WA14 164 D4
SALE M33 154 C4
Bradgate St AULW OL7 119 F4
Bradgreen Rd ECC M30 110 D2
Bradley Av BRO M7 101 E3
Bradley Cl HALE/TIMP WA15 165 H2
Bradley Dr BURY BL9 70 A2
Bradley Fold Rd BOLE BL2 51 E3
Bradley Green Rd HYDE SK14 134 A2
Bradley La MILN OL16 45 E2
RAD M26 51 E4
STRET M32 139 G4
Bradleys Count CMANE M1 * 7 H4
Bradley Smithy Cl WHIT OL12 29 H1
Bradley St CMANE M1 7 H3
MILN OL16 45 E2
Bradney Cl BKLY M9 87 G3
Bradnor Rd WYTH/NTH M22 168 C2
Bradshaw Av DID/WITH M20 142 D4
FAIL M35 104 D5
WHTF M45 69 F2
Bradshaw Brow BOLE BL2 34 D2
Bradshaw Crs MPL/ROM SK6 175 F2
Bradshaw Fold Av NEWH/MOS M40 89 G4
Bradshawgate BOL BL1 3 F5
Bradshaw Hall Dr BOLE BL2 23 H5
Bradshaw Hall Fold BOLE BL2 * 24 A5
Bradshaw Hall La CHD/CHDH SK8 182 A4
Bradshaw La STRET M32 140 B3
Bradshaw Mdw BOLE BL2 24 A5
Bradshaw Rd BOLE BL2 24 A4
MPL/ROM SK6 175 E2
TOT/BURYW BL8 25 F5
Bradshaw St ANC M4 * 7 F2
BRO M7 101 H4
FWTH BL4 66 A5
HEY OL10 41 F4
OLD OL1 9 H3
RAD M26 68 A1
Bradshaw St North BRO M7 101 G3
Bradstock Rd OLDTF/WHR M16 127 H5
Bradstone Rd CHH M8 102 A5
Bradwell Av DID/WITH M20 142 B5
STRET M32 125 F5
Bradwell Dr CHD/CHDH SK8 181 H5
Bradwell Pl BOLE BL2 34 C5
Bradwell Rd BRAM/HZG SK7 185 F4
Bradwen Av CHH M8 102 B1
Bradwen Cl DTN/ASHW M34 147 E2
Brady St STKP SK1 13 J1
Braemar Av STRET M32 139 G1
URM M41 138 A2
Braemar Dr BURY BL9 39 G4
Braemar Gv HEY OL10 40 B5
Braemar La WALK M28 96 C4
Braemar Rd BRAM/HZG SK7 185 G1
RUSH/FAL M14 143 G3
SALE M33 153 F4
Braemore Cl ROY/SHW OL2 59 F1
Braemore Dr HYDE SK14 149 H2
Brae Side OLDS OL8 91 F5
Braeside STRET M32 * 139 G2
Braeside Cl OFTN SK2 173 G4
Braeside Gv BOLS/LL BL3 47 F4
Braewood Cl BURY BL9 39 F3
Bragenham St GTN M18 130 B3
Brailsford Rd BOLE BL2 34 D3
RUSH/FAL M14 143 G3
Braintree Rd WYTH/NTH M22 180 D4
Braithwaite Rd MDTN M24 56 A5
Brakehouse Cl MILN OL16 31 F5
Brakenhurst Dr BRO M7 * 102 A4
Brakesmere Gv WALK M28 81 E3
Braley St CMANE M1 * 128 C1
Bramall Cl BURY BL9 70 A2
Bramall St HYDE SK14 133 G4
Bramble Av OLDE OL4 76 C3
ORD M5 127 F1
Bramble Cl LIT OL15 20 C3
Bramble Cft HOR/BR BL6 62 B1
Brambling Cl DTN/ASHW M34 118 B3
OFTN SK2 173 H5
Bramcote Av BOLE BL2 49 G4
NTHM/RTH M23 168 A3
Bramdean Av BOLE BL2 35 F1
Bramfield Wk HULME M15 * 127 G1
Bramhall Av BOLE BL2 35 H2
Bramhall Cl DUK SK16 133 G2
HALE/TIMP WA15 167 E3
MILN OL16 31 F5
SALE M33 155 F3
Bramhall La EDGY/DAV SK3 172 A5
Bramhall La South
BRAM/HZG SK7 193 H1
Bramhall Moor La
BRAM/HZG SK7 184 D2
Bramhall Park Rd
BRAM/HZG SK7 183 F3
Bramhall St BOLS/LL BL3 65 G1
GTN M18 * 130 D3
Branham Rd MPL/ROM SK6 175 F5
Bramley Av BNG/LEV M19 144 A3
STRET M32 139 H1
Bramley Cl BRAM/HZG SK7 193 H1
SWIN M27 98 B4
WILM/AE SK9 200 A1
Bramley Crs HTNM SK4 159 E5
Bramley Dr BRAM/HZG SK7 193 H1
TOT/BURYW BL8 26 D4
Bramley Meade BRO M7 101 H3
Bramley Rd BOL BL1 23 E5
BRAM/HZG SK7 193 H1
ROCH OL11 28 B3
Bramley St BRO M7 101 H5
Brammay Dr TOT/BURYW BL8 36 D1
Brampton Rd BOLS/LL BL3 63 H1
BRAM/HZG SK7 184 A2
Bramway BRAM/HZG SK7 183 F5
MPL/ROM SK6 187 E5
Bramwell Dr BRUN/LGST M13 128 D2
Bramwell St STKP SK1 172 C1
Bramworth Av RAMS BL0 16 C2
Brancaster Rd CMANE M1 128 B1
Branch Cl TOT/BURYW BL8 4 B2
Branch Rd LIT OL15 31 F2
Brancker St WHTN BL5 62 D4
Brandish Cl BRUN/LGST M13 129 E4
Brandle Av TOT/BURYW BL8 37 H2
Brandlehow Dr MDTN M24 71 H2
Brandlesholme Rd
TOT/BURYW BL8 26 D5
Brandon Av CHD/CHDH SK8 181 G3
DTN/ASHW M34 131 E5
ECC M30 111 H1
WYTH/NTH M22 168 B1
Brandon Brow OLD OL1 * 75 F4
Brandon Cl TOT/BURYW BL8 38 A1
WILM/AE SK9 192 A5
Brandon Crs ROY/SHW OL2 59 H1
Brandon Rd SLFD M6 99 G5
Brandon St BOLS/LL BL3 48 C5
MILN OL16 31 F5
Brandram Rd PWCH M25 * 86 A3
Brandsby Gdns ORD M5 * 113 F5
Brandwood OLD OL1 73 H3
Brandwood Av CCHDY M21 156 C2
Brandwood Cl WALK M28 96 B2
Brandwood St BOLS/LL BL3 48 B5
Branfield Av CHD/CHDH SK8 182 A3
Branksome Av PWCH M25 85 H3
Branksome Dr BKLY M9 87 G1
CHD/CHDH SK8 182 A3
SLFD M6 99 F5
Branksome Rd HTNM SK4 159 E5
Brannach Dr CHAD OL9 74 B4
Bransby Av BKLY M9 88 B3
Branscombe Dr SALE M33 153 F1
Branscombe Gdns
BOLS/LL BL3 * 50 A4
Bransdale Av ROY/SHW OL2 58 D5
Bransdale Cl BOLS/LL BL3 47 G5
Bransford Rd OP/CLY M11 117 E5
URM M41 124 B5
Branson St ANC M4 115 G3
Branson Wk
HALE/TIMP WA15 166 D3
Branston Rd NEWH/MOS M40 89 G5
Brantfell Gv BOLE BL2 50 C1
Brantingham Rd CCHDY M21 141 F2
Brantwood Cl ROY/SHW OL2 58 D5
Brantwood Dr BOLE BL2 50 C1
Brantwood Rd BRO M7 101 G2
CHD/CHDH SK8 182 C3
HTNM SK4 159 F2
Brantwood Ter BKLY M9 * 103 G3
Brassey St AUL OL6 119 G1
MDTN M24 72 D3
Brassica Cl ECC M30 110 B1
Brassington Av CCHDY M21 141 F4
ORD M5 113 G5
Brassington Rd HTNM SK4 158 B2
Brathay Cl BOLE BL2 35 G5
WHTF M45 70 B4
Brattice Dr SWIN M27 99 H2
Bratton Wk
BRUN/LGST M13 * 129 E2
Brattray Dr MDTN M24 72 B1
Braunston Cl ECC M30 111 F5
Bray Av ECC M30 110 C2
Braybrook Dr BOL BL1 47 E2
Bray Cl CHD/CHDH SK8 182 B2
Brayford Rd WYTH/NTH M22 180 C3
Brayshaw Cl HEY OL10 40 C5
Brayside Rd DID/WITH M20 158 A2
Braystan Gdns
CHD/CHDH SK8 169 G3
Braystones Cl
HALE/TIMP WA15 167 E3
Brayston Fold MDTN M24 71 H4
Brayton Av DID/WITH M20 157 H4
SALE M33 153 G1
Brazennose St CMANW M2 6 D5
Brazil Pl CMANE M1 7 G7
Brazil St CMANE M1 7 G7
Brazley Av BOLS/LL BL3 65 F1
Breach House La KNUT WA16 188 B5
Bread St GTN M18 130 D2
Brechvale Cl POY/DIS SK12 195 F4
Breckland Cl STLY SK15 121 G3
Breckland Dr BOL BL1 47 E2
Breckles Pl BOLS/LL BL3 * 48 C4
Breck Rd ECC M30 110 C3
Brecon Av BNG/LEV M19 143 H4
CHD/CHDH SK8 182 B3
DTN/ASHW M34 146 D2
URM M41 123 E5
Brecon Cl POY/DIS SK12 195 G3
ROY/SHW OL2 58 D3
Brecon Crs AUL OL6 107 E4
Brecon Dr BURY BL9 53 F2
Brecon Wk OLDS OL8 * 90 C5
Bredbury Dr FWTH BL4 66 B4
Bredbury Gn MPL/ROM SK6 161 H5
Bredbury Park Wy
MPL/ROM SK6 146 C5
Bredbury Rd RUSH/FAL M14 142 D1
Bredbury St CHAD OL9 90 C1
HYDE SK14 * 133 G3
Bredon Wy OLDS OL8 91 F4
Breeze Hill Rd OLDE OL4 92 C2
Breeze Mt PWCH M25 86 A5
Breightmet Dr BOLE BL2 50 B2
Breightmet Fold La BOLE BL2 50 C2
Breightmet St BOLE BL2 3 F6
Brellafield Dr ROY/SHW OL2 44 C5
Brenbar Crs WHIT OL12 14 C4
Brenchley Dr NTHM/RTH M23 155 H4
Brencon Av NTHM/RTH M23 154 D5
Brendall Cl OFTN SK2 173 H4
Brendon Av NEWH/MOS M40 103 H3
RDSH SK5 145 F5
Brendon Dr DTN/ASHW M34 118 C4
Brendon Hills ROY/SHW OL2 74 D1
Brennan Cl HULME M15 128 B3
Brennan Ct OLDS OL8 90 D5
Brennock Cl OP/CLY M11 116 A5
Brentbridge Rd
DID/WITH M20 142 D4
Brent Cl BOLE BL2 51 E4
POY/DIS SK12 194 C3
Brentfield Av CHH M8 102 A4
Brentford Av BOL BL1 33 E4
Brentford Rd RDSH SK5 145 F5
Brentford St BKLY M9 103 F3
Brent Moor Rd
BRAM/HZG SK7 184 B2
Brentnall St STKP SK1 13 G7
Brentnor Rd NEWH/MOS M40 89 F5
Brenton Av SALE M33 154 B2
Brent Rd HTNM SK4 12 B3
NTHM/RTH M23 155 H4
Brentwood SALE M33 154 B2
SLFD M6 112 D2
Brentwood Av ALT WA14 165 H2
URM M41 138 D1
WALK M28 98 A4
Brentwood Cl LIT OL15 20 C5
OLDTF/WHR M16 128 A5
RDSH SK5 161 E1
STLY SK15 121 F3
Brentwood Ct PWCH M25 85 G4
Brentwood Crs ALT WA14 165 H3
Brentwood Dr
CHD/CHDH SK8 169 G4
ECC M30 111 E1
FWTH BL4 65 G2
Brentwood Rd SWIN M27 98 C4
Brereton Cl ALT WA14 177 F3
Brereton Dr WALK M28 97 G3
Brereton Gv IRL M44 136 A5
Brereton Rd ECC M30 110 A4
WILM/AE SK9 192 B4
Breslyn St CSLFD M3 6 E1
Brethren's Cl DROY M43 117 H5
Bretland Gdns HYDE SK14 149 G2
Brettargh St SLFD M6 113 F1
Brett Rd WALK M28 96 A4
Brett St WYTH/NTH M22 156 D5
Brewer's Gn BRAM/HZG SK7 185 E1
Brewer St CMANE M1 7 H4
Brewerton Rd OLDE OL4 92 B2
Brewery St ALT WA14 165 G5
STKP SK1 13 H1
Brewster St BKLY M9 * 103 E2
MDTN M24 72 D2
Brian Av DROY M43 * 118 B2
Brian Redhead Ct
HULME M15 127 H1
Brian Rd FWTH BL4 65 F2
Brian St ROCH OL11 42 A4
Briaracre Ter AUL OL6 * 107 F2
Briar Av BRAM/HZG SK7 185 G2
GOL/RIS/CUL WA3 150 A4
OLDE OL4 76 C3
Briar Cl SALE M33 153 F2
URM M41 123 H5
WHIT OL12 28 D2
Briar Crs WYTH/NTH M22 168 D4
Briardene DTN/ASHW M34 * 132 D4
Briardene Gdns
WYTH/NTH M22 168 D5
Briarfield EDGW/EG BL7 22 C1
Briarfield Rd CHD/CHDH SK8 183 E1
DID/WITH M20 143 F5
FWTH BL4 65 F3
HALE/TIMP WA15 166 D3
HTNM SK4 145 E5
UPML OL3 78 D2
WALK M28 97 G3
Briar Gv CHAD OL9 74 C3
MPL/ROM SK6 161 H1
Briar Hill Av LHULT M38 80 D3
Briar Hill Cl LHULT M38 80 D3
Briar Hill Gv LHULT M38 80 D3
Briar Hill Wy SLFD M6 * 113 F2
Briar Hollow HTNM SK4 159 E5
Briarlands Av SALE M33 154 A4
Briarlands Cl BRAM/HZG SK7 193 G1
Briarlea Gdns BNG/LEV M19 158 B1
Briarley Gdns MPL/ROM SK6 147 G5
Briarmere Wk CHAD OL9 8 A2
Briars Mt HTNM SK4 158 D4
Briars Pk BRAM/HZG SK7 183 F3
Briarstead Cl
BRAM/HZG SK7 183 G5
Briar St BOLE BL2 * 50 A2
ROCH OL11 29 G5
Briarwood WILM/AE SK9 199 F3
Briarwood Av DROY M43 117 F2
NTHM/RTH M23 167 E1
Briarwood Cha
CHD/CHDH SK8 183 E3

Briarwood Crs MPL/ROM SK6 175 E5
Brice St DUK SK16 119 G5
Brickbridge Rd
MPL/ROM SK6 175 F4
Brickfield St MILN OL16 30 C1
Brickhill La HALE/TIMP WA15 188 C3
Brickkiln Rw ALT WA14 177 F3
Brickley St CSLFD M3 114 D2
Brick St ANC M4 * 7 G3
BURY BL9 5 H3
Bridcam St CHH M8 102 B5
Briddon St CSLFD M3 114 C2
Brideoak St CHH M8 102 B4
OLDE OL4 76 D4
Bridestowe Av HYDE SK14 134 D5
Bride St BOL BL1 33 H4
Bridge Av MPL/ROM SK6 161 H1
Bridge Bank Rd LIT OL15 20 D5
Bridge Cl PART M31 151 F3
RAD M26 68 C2
Bridgecrest Ct
CHD/CHDH SK8 * 182 D2
Bridge Dr CHD/CHDH SK8 170 A5
WILM/AE SK9 192 A4
Bridgefield Av WILM/AE SK9 199 F1
Bridgefield Crs OLDE OL4 93 E1
Bridgefield Dr BURY BL9 39 G4
Bridgefield St RAD M26 68 C1
ROCH OL11 29 G4
STKP SK1 13 F3
Bridgefold Rd ROCH OL11 29 F4
Bridgefoot Cl WALK M28 96 B5
Bridge Gv HALE/TIMP WA15 166 A2
Bridge Hall Dr BURY BL9 39 F4
Bridge Hall Fold BURY BL9 39 F4
Bridge Hall La BURY BL9 39 G4
Bridge La BRAM/HZG SK7 184 B3
Bridgelea Ms DID/WITH M20 142 D5
Bridgelea Rd DID/WITH M20 142 D5
Bridgeman Pl BOLE BL2 3 G6
Bridgeman St BOLS/LL BL3 48 D5
FWTH BL4 66 A3
Bridgemere Cl RAD M26 52 A4
Bridgend Cl CHD/CHDH SK8 171 F5
WGTN/LGST M12 129 H2
Bridgenorth Av URM M41 139 F1
Bridgenorth Dr LIT OL15 20 C5
Bridge Rd BURY BL9 4 B6
HALE/TIMP WA15 166 D2
Bridges Av BURY BL9 53 G3
Bridges Ct BOL BL1 * 2 E6
Bridge St BOL BL1 2 E4
BURY BL9 5 G1
CSLFD M3 6 C4
DROY M43 117 F5
DTN/ASHW M34 132 C1
FWTH BL4 66 B3
HEY OL10 40 C4
MDTN M24 * 72 D4
MILN OL16 31 G5
OLD OL1 9 J4
OLDE OL4 93 E1
RAD M26 67 E4
RAMS BL0 16 D2
ROCH OL11 42 B5
ROY/SHW OL2 * 60 B1
STKP SK1 13 G2
STLY SK15 120 C4
SWIN M27 99 F2
UPML OL3 79 E5
WHIT OL12 * 14 B4
WHIT OL12 19 H5
Bridge St Brow STKP SK1 13 G2
Bridgewater Cir TRPK M17 124 B2
Bridgewater Pl CMANE M1 7 F4
Bridgewater Rd ALT WA14 165 G2
SWIN M27 99 G3
WALK M28 96 B3
Bridgewater St BOL BL1 2 A6
CSLFD M3 6 B7
ECC M30 110 C3
FWTH BL4 66 A4
LHULT M38 81 G3
OLD OL1 9 J1
SALE M33 154 C1
STRET M32 * 140 C1
Bridgewater Viad CSLFD M3 * 127 H1
Bridgewater Wy
OLDTF/WHR M16 127 F2
Bridgfield Cl MPL/ROM SK6 186 D5
Bridgnorth Rd BKLY M9 87 F4
Bridle Cl DROY M43 118 B2
URM M41 137 G1
Bridle Fold RAD M26 52 B5
Bridle Rd BRAM/HZG SK7 194 A4
PWCH M25 70 D5
Bridle Wy BRAM/HZG SK7 194 A5
Bridlington Av SLFD M6 * 112 B2
Bridlington Cl
NEWH/MOS M40 104 B4
Bridport Av NEWH/MOS M40 104 C2
Bridson La BOLE BL2 35 E5
Bridson St OLDE OL4 76 B5
ORD M5 112 D4
Brief St BOLE BL2 34 D5
Brien Av ALT WA14 165 G3
Briercliffe Cl GTN M18 130 B2
Briercliffe Rd BOLS/LL BL3 48 B4
Brierfield Dr BURY BL9 27 F3
Brierholme Av EDGW/EG BL7 22 D2
Brierley Av FAIL M35 105 F3
WHTF M45 69 F2
Brierley Cl AUL OL6 108 B4
DTN/ASHW M34 146 C1
Brierley Dr MDTN M24 72 D5
Brierley Rd East SWIN M27 98 D1
Brierley Rd West SWIN M27 98 D1
Brierley St BURY BL9 53 F1
CHAD OL9 74 D4
DUK SK16 * 120 A4
HEY OL10 41 E4
OLDS OL8 91 G4
Brierley Wk CHAD OL9 74 D4
Brierton Dr WYTH/NTH M22 180 A3
Brierwood BOLE BL2 3 K1
Brierwood Cl ROY/SHW OL2 75 F3
Briery Av BOLE BL2 24 A5
Brigade Dr STRET M32 125 H5
Brigade St BOL BL1 48 B2
Brigadier Cl DID/WITH M20 142 D5
Brigantine Cl ORD M5 113 F5
Briggs Cl SALE M33 153 F5
Briggs Fold Cl EDGW/EG BL7 22 D1
Briggs Fold Rd EDGW/EG BL7 22 D1
Briggs Rd STRET M32 * 126 C4
Briggs St CSLFD M3 6 A1
Brigham St OP/CLY M11 116 D5
Bright Cir URM M41 124 D2
Brightgate Wy STRET M32 125 F3
Brightman St GTN M18 130 C2
Brighton Av BNG/LEV M19 143 H4
BOL BL1 32 D5
BRO M7 101 H4
RDSH SK5 145 F1
URM M41 123 F5
Brighton Gv HYDE SK14 148 A2
RUSH/FAL M14 143 F1
SALE M33 154 B1
URM M41 123 F5
Brighton Pl BRUN/LGST M13 128 C2
Brighton Range GTN M18 * 131 E4
Brighton Rd HTNM SK4 12 A3
OLDE OL4 77 F3
Brighton St ANC M4 114 D2
BURY BL9 5 J2
Bright Rd ECC M30 111 F3
Brightstone Wk
RUSH/FAL M14 129 F4
Bright St AUL OL6 120 A3
BURY BL9 5 H2
CHAD OL9 90 B4
DROY M43 118 A4
MILN OL16 43 F1
OLDS OL8 8 C6
RAD M26 52 D5
Brightwater Cl WHTF M45 69 H4
Brightwell Wk ANC M4 7 G3
Brigstock Av GTN M18 130 B3
Briksdal Wy HOR/BR BL6 46 D2
Brimelow St MPL/ROM SK6 160 D3
Brimrod La ROCH OL11 42 C1
Brimscombe Av
WYTH/NTH M22 180 B2
Brindale Rd RDSH SK5 160 D2
Brindle Cl SLFD M6 113 E1
Brindle Heath Rd SLFD M6 113 E1
Brindley Av BKLY M9 87 G2
MPL/ROM SK6 174 D4
SALE M33 140 A5
WALK M28 96 B4
Brindley Cl FWTH BL4 65 G4
Brindley Rd OLDTF/WHR M16 127 E3
Brindley St ECC M30 110 C2
SWIN M27 84 A5
WALK M28 82 A5
WALK M28 96 A4
Brinell Dr IRL M44 151 E1
Brinkburn Rd BRAM/HZG SK7 185 H1
Brinklow Cl OP/CLY M11 130 D1
Brinkshaw Av
WYTH/NTH M22 180 D2
Brinks La BOLE BL2 50 D2
Brinksway BOL BL1 46 D2
EDGY/DAV SK3 12 A5
Brinksworth Cl BOLE BL2 50 D1
Brinnington Crs RDSH SK5 160 C2
Brinnington Rd RDSH SK5 160 D2
STKP SK1 160 B3
Brinsop Sq WGTN/LGST M12 130 A2
Brinsworth Dr CHH M8 102 B4
Briony Av HALE/TIMP WA15 178 D2
Briony Cl ROY/SHW OL2 75 F2
Brisbane Cl BRAM/HZG SK7 194 A2
Brisbane St BRUN/LGST M13 128 C3
Briscoe La NEWH/MOS M40 116 B1
Briscoe Ms BOLS/LL BL3 49 F5
Briscoe St OLD OL1 9 G1
Bristle Hall Wy WHTN BL5 62 A2
Bristle St HULME M15 128 B2
Bristol Av AUL OL6 107 E3
BNG/LEV M19 144 B3
BOLE BL2 34 D5
Bristol St BRO M7 101 H3
Bristowe St OP/CLY M11 117 E2
Britain St BURY BL9 53 F3
Britannia Av ROY/SHW OL2 60 B3
Britannia Cl RAD M26 68 B1
Britannia Rd SALE M33 154 C1
Britannia St AULW OL7 119 E5
HEY OL10 40 C4
OLD OL1 9 K2
SLFD M6 100 D4
Britannia Wy BOLE BL2 34 B4
Britnall Av WGTN/LGST M12 129 F3
Briton St MILN OL16 11 G4
ROY/SHW OL2 75 F2
Brixham Av CHD/CHDH SK8 182 C5
Brixham Dr SALE M33 138 D5
Brixham Rd OLDTF/WHR M16 127 E4
Brixham Wk BRAM/HZG SK7 183 H5
BRUN/LGST M13 128 D3
Brixton Av DID/WITH M20 142 C5
Broach St BOLS/LL BL3 48 D5
Broadacre STLY SK15 135 F2
Broad Acre WHIT OL12 28 B1
Broadacre Pl WILM/AE SK9 200 A2
Broadbent Av AUL OL6 107 F4
DUK SK16 120 A5
Broadbent Cl ROY/SHW OL2 59 G4
STLY SK15 109 F4
Broadbent Dr BURY BL9 39 H2
Broadbent Gv HYDE SK14 149 G2
Broadbent Rd OLD OL1 76 B2
Broadbent St HYDE SK14 133 G4
SWIN M27 98 C3
Broadbottom Rd HYDE SK14 149 H1
Broadcarr La MOSL OL5 108 B1
Broadfield Cl
DTN/ASHW M34 147 E1
Broadfield Dr LIT OL15 20 C5
Broadfield Gv RDSH SK5 130 D5
Broadfield Rd RDSH SK5 130 D5
RUSH/FAL M14 128 B5
Broadfield Stile MILN OL16 29 H5
Broadfield St HEY OL10 40 C5
MILN OL16 29 H5
Broadford Rd BOLS/LL BL3 47 G4
Broadgate CHAD OL9 89 H3
MDTN M24 89 G1
UPML OL3 78 B3
Broadgate Meadow
SWIN M27 * 99 E3
Broadgreen Gdns FWTH BL4 * 66 A2
Broadhalgh Av ROCH OL11 28 D4
Broadhalgh Rd ROCH OL11 28 D5
Broadheath Cl WHTN BL5 62 B3
Broad Hey MPL/ROM SK6 162 C3
Broad Hill Cl BRAM/HZG SK7 184 B3
Broadhill Rd BNG/LEV M19 143 G5
STLY SK15 120 D1
Broadhurst DTN/ASHW M34 132 D3
Broadhurst Av OLD OL1 74 D3
SWIN M27 84 A4
Broadhurst Ct BOLS/LL BL3 48 C5
Broadhurst Gv AUL OL6 107 F4
Broadhurst St BOLS/LL BL3 * 48 C5
EDGY/DAV SK3 171 H2
Broad Ing ROCH OL11 * 29 E2
Broadlands Rd WALK M28 98 B4
Broad La HALE/TIMP WA15 178 C4
MILN OL16 43 H3
Broad Lea URM M41 124 B5
Broadlea Gv WHIT OL12 29 F1
Broadlea Rd BNG/LEV M19 158 B1
Broadley Av WYTH/NTH M22 168 C5
Broadmeadow EDGW/EG BL7 23 G3
Broadmeadow Av
OLDTF/WHR M16 142 B2
Broadmoss Dr BKLY M9 88 D4
Broadmoss Rd BKLY M9 88 D4
Broadmount Ter CHAD OL9 * 90 C3
Broadoak Av WALK M28 96 A3
WYTH/NTH M22 168 B4
Broadoak Crs AUL OL6 107 E5
Broad Oak Crs OLDS OL8 91 H5
Broadoak Dr WYTH/NTH M22 168 C4
Broad Oak La BURY BL9 39 G3
DID/WITH M20 169 H1
Broad Oak Pk ECC M30 111 E1
WALK M28 98 A4
Broad Oak Rd BOLS/LL BL3 65 F2
Broadoak Rd AUL OL6 107 F4
BRAM/HZG SK7 184 A2
ROCH OL11 28 B5
WYTH/NTH M22 168 B5
Broadoaks BURY BL9 39 G3
Broadoaks Rd SALE M33 154 B2
URM M41 138 B2
Broad Oak Ter BURY BL9 39 H3
Broad o' th' La BOL BL1 33 H2
Broad Rd SALE M33 154 D1
Broad Shaw La MILN OL16 44 A4
Broadstone Av OLDE OL4 61 E5
Broadstone Cl PWCH M25 85 H5
WHIT OL12 28 D2
Broadstone Hall Rd North
HTNM SK4 144 D5
Broadstone Hall Rd South
HTNM SK4 145 E5
Broadstone Rd BOLE BL2 35 E1
HTNM SK4 144 D5
Broad St BURY BL9 4 D5
MDTN M24 71 H5
SLFD M6 100 B5
Broad Wk WILM/AE SK9 198 C2
Broadway BRAM/HZG SK7 184 A2
CHAD OL9 74 C3
CHAD OL9 90 A4
CHD/CHDH SK8 169 H5
DROY M43 117 H5
FAIL M35 104 C2
FWTH BL4 65 F2
HALE/TIMP WA15 178 B3
HYDE SK14 133 E3
IRL M44 136 C2
OFTN SK2 172 D2
PART M31 151 F2
ROY/SHW OL2 75 F1
SALE M33 154 B1
SALQ M50 112 D5
URM M41 123 H4
WALK M28 97 E1
WILM/AE SK9 199 E4
Broadway Av CHD/CHDH SK8 170 A4
Broadway Cl URM M41 124 B4
Broadway North DROY M43 117 H5
Broadway St OLDS OL8 91 G3
The Broadway MPL/ROM SK6 161 F2
Broadwell Dr BKLY M9 103 F3
Broadwood HOR/BR BL6 46 D2
Broadwood Cl POY/DIS SK12 187 E5
Brocade Cl CSLFD M3 114 A2
Broche Cl ROCH OL11 42 A3
Brock Av BOLE BL2 50 C2
Brock Cl OP/CLY M11 130 C1
Brock Dr CHD/CHDH SK8 182 D4
Brockenhurst Dr BOLE BL2 35 G3
Brockford Dr BKLY M9 88 B2
Brocklebank Rd MILN OL16 31 E4
RUSH/FAL M14 143 E3
Brocklehurst Av BURY BL9 5 F7
Brocklehurst St BKLY M9 103 H2
Brockley Av RUSH/FAL M14 142 D1
Brock St CMANE M1 * 7 J4
The Brock ROY/SHW OL2 59 G1
Brockway MILN OL16 43 H3
Brodick Dr BOLE BL2 50 C3
Brodick St NEWH/MOS M40 103 G2
Brodie Cl ECC M30 110 C3
Brogan St GTN M18 130 C3
Brogden Dr CHD/CHDH SK8 169 G4
Brogden Gv SALE M33 154 B3
Brogden Ter SALE M33 154 B2
Bromborough Av
DID/WITH M20 142 C3
Bromfield WHIT OL12 10 C4
Bromfield Av BKLY M9 103 E1
Bromleigh Av CHD/CHDH SK8 169 G3
Bromley Av ROY/SHW OL2 58 D3
URM M41 137 G2
Bromley Crs AUL OL6 107 E4
Bromley Cross Rd
EDGW/EG BL7 23 G4
Bromley Rd SALE M33 154 D4
Bromley St ANC M4 115 E2
CHAD OL9 90 B5
DTN/ASHW M34 * 132 C5
Bromlow St OP/CLY M11 116 D4
Brompton Av FAIL M35 105 G2
Brompton Rd HTNM SK4 158 D4
RUSH/FAL M14 142 D1
STRET M32 125 E5
Brompton St OLDE OL4 9 K6
Brompton Wy WILM/AE SK9 191 H2
Bromsgrove Av ECC M30 110 C3
Bromshill Dr BRO M7 101 H4
Bromwich St BOLE BL2 3 J7
Bronington Cl
WYTH/NTH M22 168 D2
Bronte Av BURY BL9 53 G3
Bronte Cl BOL BL1 33 G5
OLD OL1 60 C5
WHIT OL12 28 D2
Bronte St HULME M15 128 B3
Bronville Cl OLD OL1 74 D3
Brookash Rd WYTH/NTH M22 181 F4
Brook Av BNG/LEV M19 144 B1
DROY M43 * 117 F4
HALE/TIMP WA15 165 H3
HTNM SK4 159 G1
ROY/SHW OL2 60 A1
SWIN M27 99 E3
UPML OL3 79 E4
WILM/AE SK9 192 A4
Brook Bank BOLE BL2 * 35 E3
Brookbank Cl MDTN M24 73 E5
Brookbottom Rd RAD M26 52 A3
Brookburn Rd CCHDY M21 141 E4
Brook Cl HALE/TIMP WA15 165 H3
WHTF M45 70 A4
Brookcot Rd NTHM/RTH M23 167 G2
Brookcroft Av
WYTH/NTH M22 168 C4
Brookcroft Rd
WYTH/NTH M22 168 C4
Brookdale WHIT OL12 18 D5
Brookdale Av DTN/ASHW M34 132 B1
MPL/ROM SK6 175 F5
NEWH/MOS M40 117 E1
Brookdale Cl BOL BL1 34 A4
MPL/ROM SK6 161 G3
Brookdale Pk LHULT M38 * 81 G1
Brookdale Ri BRAM/HZG SK7 184 A2
Brookdale Rd BRAM/HZG SK7 184 A3
CHD/CHDH SK8 169 E4
Brookdale St FAIL M35 104 D3
Brookdean Cl BOL BL1 33 F3
Brookdene Rd BNG/LEV M19 143 G5
Brook Dr MPL/ROM SK6 175 E5
WHTF M45 70 A4
Brooke Dr WILM/AE SK9 192 A3
Brookes St MDTN M24 73 E2
Brooke Wy WILM/AE SK9 * 192 A3
Brook Farm Cl PART M31 150 D5
Brookfield PWCH M25 86 A3
ROY/SHW OL2 44 D5
Brookfield Av BOLE BL2 36 B5
CCHDY M21 141 G4
HALE/TIMP WA15 166 A1
MPL/ROM SK6 161 H2
POY/DIS SK12 194 D4
ROY/SHW OL2 75 F1
SLFD M6 112 B2
STKP SK1 13 K7
URM M41 138 A1
Brookfield Cl STKP SK1 13 K7
Brookfield Crs
CHD/CHDH SK8 170 A5
Brookfield Dr
HALE/TIMP WA15 166 B2
LIT OL15 20 C2
SWIN M27 98 D1
WALK M28 96 A4
Brookfield Gdns
WYTH/NTH M22 168 C3
Brookfield Gv AUL OL6 120 A3
Brookfield Rd BURY BL9 27 F3
CHD/CHDH SK8 170 B4
CHH M8 102 B1
ECC M30 110 C1
Brookfield St BOLE BL2 3 J4
OLDS OL8 9 G6
Brookfold FAIL M35 104 D2
Brookfold La BOLE BL2 35 G2
HYDE SK14 148 C1
Brook Fold La HYDE SK14 148 D2
Brookfold Rd HTNM SK4 159 G1
Brook Gdns BOLE BL2 35 F2
HEY OL10 40 D4
Brook Green La GTN M18 131 E5
Brook Gv IRL M44 136 C1
Brookhead Av
DID/WITH M20 * 142 B4
Brookhead Dr
CHD/CHDH SK8 170 D4
Brookhey HYDE SK14 133 E5
Brookhey Av BOLS/LL BL3 65 E1
Brook Hey Cl WHIT OL12 20 A4
Brookheys Rd PART M31 152 B2
Brookhill St
NEWH/MOS M40 115 H2
Brookhouse Av ECC M30 110 B4
FWTH BL4 81 H1
Brook House Cl BOLE BL2 35 F3
TOT/BURYW BL8 25 H3
Brookhouse Mill La
TOT/BURYW BL8 26 A3
Brookhurst La LHULT M38 80 D1
Brookhurst Rd GTN M18 130 C4
Brookland Av
DTN/ASHW M34 146 B1
FWTH BL4 65 H5
Brookland Gv BOL BL1 32 D4
Brooklands Av CHAD OL9 90 C2
DID/WITH M20 142 C5
Brooklands Cl
DTN/ASHW M34 132 A4
HTNM SK4 159 G1
IRL M44 136 B1
MOSL OL5 93 G5
Brooklands Ct ROCH OL11 29 F5
Brooklands Crs SALE M33 154 C3
Brooklands Dr DROY M43 118 B2
OLDE OL4 93 G1
Brooklands Pde
OLDE OL4 * 93 G1
Brooklands Rd
BRAM/HZG SK7 185 F3
NTHM/RTH M23 166 D1
PWCH M25 86 D5
RAMS BL0 26 A1
RDSH SK5 145 E1
SALE M33 154 C3
SWIN M27 98 C4
Brooklands Station Ap
SALE M33 154 B3
Brooklands St ROY/SHW OL2 59 E4
The Brooklands HEY OL10 40 D4
Brookland St MILN OL16 * 43 G3
Brook La BURY BL9 53 H4
HALE/TIMP WA15 165 H3
MILN OL16 43 G3
OLDE OL4 92 D1
OLDS OL8 91 H3
UPML OL3 78 C3
WILM/AE SK9 200 C2
Brooklawn Dr DID/WITH M20 157 G2
PWCH M25 86 B1
Brookleigh Rd DID/WITH M20 143 F5
Brooklet Cl OLDE OL4 93 F2
Brooklyn Av LIT OL15 20 D1
MILN OL16 20 B4
OLDTF/WHR M16 141 F1
URM M41 137 G1
Brooklyn Crs CHD/CHDH SK8 170 A4
Brooklyn Rd CHD/CHDH SK8 170 A4
OFTN SK2 172 D3
Brooklyn St BOL BL1 33 H5
OLD OL1 * 76 B3
Brook Meadow WHTN BL5 * 62 B4
Brook Rd CHD/CHDH SK8 170 A3
HTNM SK4 159 F1
RUSH/FAL M14 143 E4
URM M41 123 H5
Brooks Av BRAM/HZG SK7 185 E1
HYDE SK14 148 A2
RAD M26 52 A3
Brooksbottom Cl RAMS BL0 16 D4
Brooks Dr CHD/CHDH SK8 181 H2
FAIL M35 104 D4
HALE/TIMP WA15 167 E3
HALE/TIMP WA15 179 F4
Brooks End ROCH OL11 28 B2
Brookshaw St BURY BL9 5 G1
OP/CLY M11 116 B4
Brookside OLDE OL4 92 C1
Brookside Av DROY M43 118 B2
FWTH BL4 65 H5
OFTN SK2 173 F3
OLDE OL4 93 G1
POY/DIS SK12 195 F4
Brookside Cl BOLE BL2 35 E1
CHD/CHDH SK8 170 A5
HYDE SK14 134 B5
RAMS BL0 16 B5
Brookside Crs MDTN M24 89 F1
TOT/BURYW BL8 26 A3
WALK M28 82 B4
Brookside Dr HYDE SK14 134 B5
PWCH M25 101 G1
Brookside La MPL/ROM SK6 186 D5
Brookside Rd BOLE BL2 50 A1
CHD/CHDH SK8 169 F3
NEWH/MOS M40 103 H1
SALE M33 154 B4
Brooksmouth TOT/BURYW BL8 4 A5
Brook's Pl WHIT OL12 10 A4
Brook's Rd OLDTF/WHR M16 127 F5
Brooks St STKP SK1 13 H7
Brookstone Cl CCHDY M21 141 H5
Brook St BOL BL1 2 E4
BRAM/HZG SK7 185 F2
BURY BL9 5 G1
CHAD OL9 74 C4
CHD/CHDH SK8 170 C3
FAIL M35 104 C4
FWTH BL4 66 B3
HYDE SK14 133 H5
LIT OL15 21 F3
OLD OL1 9 K1
RAD M26 66 D5
RAD M26 68 D1
ROY/SHW OL2 75 E1
SALE M33 154 D1
SLFD M6 113 G1
SWIN M27 98 C2
WHIT OL12 19 H2
WHTN BL5 * 62 A3
Brook St East AUL OL6 119 F3
Brook St West AUL OL6 119 F3
Brookthorn Cl OFTN SK2 173 G4
Brookthorpe Av
BNG/LEV M19 143 G5
Brookthorpe Rd
TOT/BURYW BL8 37 F3
Brookwater Cl
TOT/BURYW BL8 26 A5
Brookway
HALE/TIMP WA15 166 A3
LIT OL15 20 D4
OLDE OL4 92 D2
OLDE OL4 94 B1
Brookway Cl BNG/LEV M19 158 B2
Brookwood Av CHH M8 102 D2
SALE M33 153 H3
Brookwood Cl
DTN/ASHW M34 147 E4
Broom Av BNG/LEV M19 144 B3
BRO M7 101 H2
RDSH SK5 145 F5
Broome Gv FAIL M35 105 E4
Broomehouse Av IRL M44 136 A3
Broome St CHAD OL9 8 C4
Broomfield SWIN M27 100 A4
Broomfield Cl BOLE BL2 51 F1
RDSH SK5 145 F5
WILM/AE SK9 * 199 H2
Broomfield Crs MDTN M24 72 A3
OFTN SK2 172 B5
Broomfield Dr CHH M8 102 A3
RDSH SK5 145 F5
Broomfield La
HALE/TIMP WA15 177 H2
Broomfield Rd BOLS/LL BL3 48 B4
HTNM SK4 159 F2
Broomfields
DTN/ASHW M34 132 D3
Broomfield Sq ROCH OL11 * 43 E1
Broomfield Ter MILN OL16 45 E2

Broomgrove La
DTN/ASHW M34 132 D4
Broomhall Rd BKLY M9 87 F2
SWIN M27 100 A4
Broomhill Dr BRAM/HZG SK7 183 G3
Broomhurst Av OLDS OL8 91 E3
Broom La BNG/LEV M19 144 B3
BRO M7 101 G2
Broom Rd HALE/TIMP WA15 177 H1
PART M31 151 E4
Broomstair Rd
DTN/ASHW M34 132 C2
Broom St MILN OL16 45 E2
SWIN M27 99 E3
TOT/BURYW BL8 4 A4
Broomville Av SALE M33 154 C2
Broom Wy WHTN BL5 62 B2
Broomwood Rd
HALE/TIMP WA15 166 D4
Broomwood Wk
HULME M15 * 128 A2
Broseley Av DID/WITH M20 158 A3
Broseley Rd OLDTF/WHR M16 141 E1
Brotherdale Cl ROY/SHW OL2 59 E4
Brotherod Hall Rd WHIT OL12 29 F1
Brotherton Cl HULME M15 127 G1
Brotherton Dr CSLFD M3 6 A2
Brougham St WALK M28 81 H5
Broughton Av LHULT M38 81 F3
Broughton Cl MDTN M24 72 A2
Broughton La BRO M7 101 G5
Broughton Rd RDSH SK5 160 A2
SLFD M6 113 F2
Broughton Rd East SLFD M6 113 G1
Broughton St BOL BL1 33 G4
CHH M8 102 A5
Broughville Dr DID/WITH M20 169 H1
Brow Av MDTN M24 89 E1
Brow East BOLE BL2 34 D2
Browfield Av ORD M5 127 E1
Browfield Wy OLD OL1 75 F3
Browmere Dr DID/WITH M20 157 E2
Brownacre St DID/WITH M20 142 D5
Brown Bank Rd LIT OL15 20 C5
Browncross St CSLFD M3 6 B4
Brown Edge Rd OLDE OL4 92 D3
Brownhill Dr OLDE OL4 77 F5
Brownhill La UPML OL3 79 E3
Brownhills Cl TOT/BURYW BL8 37 F1
Brownhills Ct CCHDY M21 * 141 F3
Brownhill St OP/CLY M11 * 116 B5
Brownhill Vw WHIT OL12 10 B2
Browning Av DROY M43 117 H4
Browning Cl BOL BL1 33 G5
Browning Rd MDTN M24 73 E2
OLD OL1 76 A3
RDSH SK5 144 D2
SWIN M27 98 D2
Browning St CSLFD M3 6 A3
HULME M15 127 G2
Brown La CHD/CHDH SK8 181 F3
Brownlea Av DUK SK16 133 F1
Brownley Court Rd
WYTH/NTH M22 168 D4
Brownley Rd WYTH/NTH M22 168 D4
Brown Lodge St LIT OL15 20 C5
Brownlow Av ROY/SHW OL2 75 H1
Brownlow Cl POY/DIS SK12 195 F5
Brownlow Wy BOL BL1 2 C1
Brownrigg Cl MDTN M24 71 H3
Brownside Cl MILN OL16 19 H5
Brown's La WILM/AE SK9 199 H2
Brownslow Wk
BRUN/LGST M13 * 128 C1
Browns Rd BOLE BL2 51 E3
Brown St ALT WA14 177 G1
BOL BL1 3 F4
CHAD OL9 74 B5
CSLFD M3 6 C4
FAIL M35 104 D3
HEY OL10 40 D3
LIT OL15 20 D3
MDTN M24 72 D2
OLD OL1 9 K2
RAD M26 52 A3
RAMS BL0 16 C3
SLFD M6 113 E4
STKP SK1 13 F2
WILM/AE SK9 200 D4
Brownsville Rd HTNM SK4 159 E1
Brownville Gv DUK SK16 133 H1
Brownwood Av STKP SK1 160 C5
Brownwood Cl SALE M33 154 D5
Brows Av NTHM/RTH M23 155 H4
Brow St ROCH OL11 43 F2
Broxton Av BOLS/LL BL3 64 A1
Broxton St NEWH/MOS M40 116 A2
Broxwood Cl GTN M18 * 130 C3
Bruce St ROCH OL11 42 B2
Brundage Rd WYTH/NTH M22 180 C2
Brundretts Rd CCHDY M21 141 F3
Brundrett St STKP SK1 13 K6
Brunel Av ORD M5 113 G4
Brunel Cl STRET M32 140 C1
Brunel St BOL BL1 33 G3
Brunet Wk WGTN/LGST M12 * 129 G2
Brunstead Cl NTHM/RTH M23 167 E3
Brunswick Ct BOL BL1 2 D3
Brunswick Rd ALT WA14 165 G2
DID/WITH M20 143 E5
Brunswick Sq OLD OL1 * 9 G4
Brunswick St
BRUN/LGST M13 128 D2
BURY BL9 4 E3
DUK SK16 119 H5
HEY OL10 40 D4
MILN OL16 11 F4
MOSL OL5 109 E2
OLD OL1 9 F4
ROY/SHW OL2 60 A2
STRET M32 140 A3
Brunton Rd RDSH SK5 145 F5
Brunt St RUSH/FAL M14 128 C5
Bruntwood Av
CHD/CHDH SK8 181 F3
Bruntwood La
CHD/CHDH SK8 170 B5
Brushes Av STLY SK15 121 G2
Brushes Rd STLY SK15 121 G2
Brussels Rd EDGY/DAV SK3 171 G3
Bruton Av STRET M32 139 H2
Bryan Rd CCHDY M21 141 F1
Bryan St OLDE OL4 76 B3
Bryant Cl BRUN/LGST M13 128 D3
Bryantsfield BOL BL1 47 E3
Bryce St HYDE SK14 133 G4
Brydges Rd MPL/ROM SK6 174 D4
Brydon Av WGTN/LGST M12 128 D1
Brydon Cl SLFD M6 113 F3
Bryndale Gv SALE M33 154 A5
Brynden Av DID/WITH M20 157 H1
Bryn Dr RDSH SK5 160 A1
Brynford Av BKLY M9 87 F2
Bryngs Dr BOLE BL2 35 G2
Brynhelys Cl RAD M26 51 H4
Brynheys Cl LHULT M38 81 F2
Bryn Lea Ter BOL BL1 32 C2
Brynorme Rd CHH M8 87 F5
Brynton Rd BRUN/LGST M13 143 G1
Bryn Wk BOL BL1 2 E2
Bryone Dr OFTN SK2 172 C4
Bryony Cl WYTH/NTH M22 180 B3
Buchanan St RAMS BL0 16 C2
SWIN M27 99 E1
Buchan St OP/CLY M11 116 C3
Buckden Rd HTNM SK4 144 D4
Buckfast Av OLDS OL8 92 B4
Buckfast Cl CCHDY M21 141 F2
CHD/CHDH SK8 183 E5
HALE/TIMP WA15 178 C2
POY/DIS SK12 195 E2
Buckfast Rd MDTN M24 56 C5
SALE M33 138 D5
Buckfield Av ORD M5 127 E1
Buckhurst Rd BNG/LEV M19 144 A2
Buckingham Av SLFD M6 112 C3
WHTF M45 69 H5
Buckingham Dr DUK SK16 134 A2
TOT/BURYW BL8 52 C1
Buckingham Park Cl
ROY/SHW OL2 60 A1
Buckingham Rd ALT WA14 154 A5
CCHDY M21 141 F2
CHD/CHDH SK8 182 C2
DROY M43 117 F4
HTNM SK4 159 F1
IRL M44 150 B1
POY/DIS SK12 195 E4
PWCH M25 * 86 A5
STLY SK15 120 D2
STRET M32 126 C3
SWIN M27 84 B5
WILM/AE SK9 198 C4
Buckingham Rd West
HTNM SK4 158 D2
Buckingham St MILN OL16 11 F4
OFTN SK2 * 172 B3
ORD M5 113 E4
Buckingham Wy
HALE/TIMP WA15 166 B3
Buckland Av BKLY M9 87 F4
Buckland Gv HYDE SK14 148 C3
Buckland Rd SLFD M6 112 C1
Buck La SALE M33 139 E5
Buckley Av GTN M18 130 B4
Buckley Brook St WHIT OL12 30 C1
Buckley Cha MILN OL16 44 B1
Buckley Cl HYDE SK14 148 A4
Buckley Dr MPL/ROM SK6 161 H5
Buckley Farm La WHIT OL12 19 G5
Buckley Flds WHIT OL12 30 B1
Buckley Hill La MILN OL16 44 B1
Buckley La FWTH BL4 65 H5
WHIT OL12 19 G5
WHTF M45 85 F4
Buckley Rd GTN M18 130 A4
WHIT OL12 19 G5
Buckley Sq FWTH BL4 81 H1
Buckley St BURY BL9 5 F2
CHAD OL9 74 B5
DROY M43 117 H5
DTN/ASHW M34 132 A1
HEY OL10 41 E3
MILN OL16 11 G3
OLDE OL4 92 D2
OP/CLY M11 130 D1
RDSH SK5 145 E1
ROY/SHW OL2 60 B2
STLY SK15 120 C5
UPML OL3 79 E4
Buckley Vw WHIT OL12 19 G5
Bucklow Av PART M31 151 F2
RUSH/FAL M14 142 D2
Bucklow Cl HYDE SK14 149 H2
OLDE OL4 76 D1
Bucklow Dr WYTH/NTH M22 168 D1
Bucklow Vw ALT WA14 176 D1
Buckstones Rd OLD OL1 60 D3
ROY/SHW OL2 45 F5
Buckthorn Cl CCHDY M21 141 H5
HALE/TIMP WA15 167 F4
WHTN BL5 62 A2
Buckthorn La ECC M30 110 A4
Buckton Dr STLY SK15 109 F5
Buckton Vale Ms STLY SK15 109 G3
Buckton Vale Rd STLY SK15 109 F4
Buckwood Cl BRAM/HZG SK7 185 H1
Buddleia Gv BRO M7 * 101 G4
Bude Av RDSH SK5 160 C1
URM M41 138 B3
Bude Cl BRAM/HZG SK7 184 A5
Budsworth Av DID/WITH M20 142 D4
Budworth Rd SALE M33 155 F3
Buersil Av MILN OL16 43 G2
Buersil St MILN OL16 43 G3
Buerton Av BKLY M9 87 F2
Bugle St CMANE M1 * 6 C7
Buile Dr BKLY M9 88 C3
Buile Hill Av LHULT M38 81 G3
Buile Hill Dr ORD M5 112 C2
Buile Hill Gv LHULT M38 81 G2
Buile St BRO M7 101 H3
Bulford Av WYTH/NTH M22 180 A2
Bulkeley Rd CHD/CHDH SK8 170 B3
POY/DIS SK12 195 F4
WILM/AE SK9 191 H4
Bulkeley St EDGY/DAV SK3 12 D5
Bullcote Gn ROY/SHW OL2 59 H5
Bullcote La ROY/SHW OL2 60 A5
Buller Ms TOT/BURYW BL8 37 G5
Buller Rd BRUN/LGST M13 143 H1
Buller St BOLS/LL BL3 65 H2
DROY M43 118 A5
TOT/BURYW BL8 37 H5
Bullfinch Dr BURY BL9 39 E1
Bull Hill Crs RAD M26 68 C4
Bullock St STKP SK1 172 A2
Bullows Rd LHULT M38 81 E1
Bulteel St BOLS/LL BL3 64 B2
ECC M30 110 C2
Bulwer St MILN OL16 11 F4
The Bungalows
BRAM/HZG SK7 * 173 G5
Bunkers Hl MPL/ROM SK6 162 A5
WHTF M45 85 F4
Bunkers Hill Rd HYDE SK14 149 G2
Bunkershill Rd MPL/ROM SK6 174 A1
Bunsen St CMANE M1 * 7 H4
Bunting Ms WALK M28 96 C2
Bunyan Cl OLD OL1 60 C5
Bunyan St WHIT OL12 10 E4
Bunyard St CHH M8 102 C4
Burbage Rd NTHM/RTH M23 179 H2
Burbridge Cl OP/CLY M11 115 H5
Burchall Fld MILN OL16 11 H6
Burdale Dr SLFD M6 112 A1
Burdett Av OLDS OL8 90 D5
Burdett Av WHIT OL12 28 C2
Burdett Wy WGTN/LGST M12 129 F3
Burdith Av RUSH/FAL M14 142 C1
Burdon Av WYTH/NTH M22 168 D5
Burford Av BRAM/HZG SK7 193 F2
OLDTF/WHR M16 141 H1
URM M41 124 D5
Burford Crs WILM/AE SK9 198 B5
Burford Dr BOLS/LL BL3 48 D4
OLDTF/WHR M16 141 H1
SWIN M27 83 H5
Burford Gv SALE M33 153 H5
Burford Rd OLDTF/WHR M16 141 H1
Burgess Av AUL OL6 107 F5
Burgess Dr FAIL M35 105 E3
Burghley Av OLDE OL4 92 C1
Burghley Cl RAD M26 51 E4
STLY SK15 120 D3
Burghley Dr RAD M26 51 E4
Burgin Wk NEWH/MOS M40 115 F1
Burgundy Dr TOT/BURYW BL8 26 A4
Burke St BOL BL1 33 G4
Burkitt St HYDE SK14 148 A1
Burland Cl BRO M7 101 G5
Burleigh Cl BRAM/HZG SK7 184 B3
Burleigh Ms CCHDY M21 141 F5
Burleigh Rd STRET M32 126 B4
Burleigh St HULME M15 128 C3
Burlescombe Cl ALT WA14 165 E3
Burley Ct HTNM SK4 * 12 A1
Burlington Av OLDS OL8 91 F3
Burlington Cl HTNM SK4 158 B4
Burlington Dr EDGY/DAV SK3 172 A5
Burlington Gdns
EDGY/DAV SK3 172 A5
Burlington Ms EDGY/DAV SK3 172 A5
Burlington Rd ALT WA14 165 G4
DID/WITH M20 143 E4
ECC M30 111 F1
Burlington St AULW OL7 119 E3
BRUN/LGST M13 128 C3
ROCH OL11 43 F2
Burman St OP/CLY M11 131 E1
Burnaby St BOLS/LL BL3 48 C4
OLDS OL8 8 B7
Burnage Av BNG/LEV M19 143 H3
Burnage Hall Rd
BNG/LEV M19 143 G4
Burnage La BNG/LEV M19 158 A4
Burnage Range
BNG/LEV M19 144 A2
Burn Bank UPML OL3 94 B2
Burnbray Av BNG/LEV M19 143 G5
Burndale Dr BURY BL9 69 H1
Burnden Rd BOLS/LL BL3 49 G4
Burnedge Cl WHIT OL12 14 C3
Burnedge Fold Rd OLDE OL4 94 A1
Burnedge La OLDE OL4 93 H1
Burnell Cl NEWH/MOS M40 115 F2
Burnet Cl MILN OL16 43 H2
Burnett Av ORD M5 113 G5
Burnett Cl NEWH/MOS M40 103 E5
Burnfield Rd GTN M18 130 C5
Burnham Av BOL BL1 32 D5
RDSH SK5 145 F2
Burnham Cl CHD/CHDH SK8 182 C2
Burnham Dr BNG/LEV M19 143 H4
URM M41 124 B5
Burnham Rd
DTN/ASHW M34 131 F5
Burnley La CHAD OL9 74 B2
Burnley Rd BURY BL9 27 F3
Burnley St CHAD OL9 74 C5
FAIL M35 105 F3
Burnmoor Rd BOLE BL2 50 C1
Burnsall Av WHTF M45 69 E4
Burnsall Gv ROY/SHW OL2 59 E5
Burns Av BURY BL9 53 E2
CHD/CHDH SK8 170 C3
SWIN M27 98 C1
Burns Cl OLD OL1 60 D4
OP/CLY M11 116 A4
Burns Crs OFTN SK2 173 F2
Burns Fold DUK SK16 134 B1
Burns Gdns PWCH M25 * 85 G4
Burns Gv DROY M43 117 H3
Burnside HALE/TIMP WA15 179 F5
ROY/SHW OL2 60 C1
STLY SK15 135 E1
Burnside Av HTNM SK4 145 E5
SLFD M6 99 G5
Burnside Cl HEY OL10 41 E5
MPL/ROM SK6 161 G3
RAD M26 52 A3
STLY SK15 135 E1
WILM/AE SK9 199 F5
Burnside Crs MDTN M24 72 B1
Burnside Dr BNG/LEV M19 143 G4
Burnside Rd BOL BL1 33 E4
CHD/CHDH SK8 169 F4
MILN OL16 30 D5
Burns Rd DTN/ASHW M34 147 E4
LHULT M38 81 G2
Burns St BOLS/LL BL3 2 E7
HEY OL10 41 E5
Burnthorp Av BKLY M9 87 G4
Burnthorpe Cl ROCH OL11 28 B5
Burran Rd WYTH/NTH M22 180 C4
Burrows Av CCHDY M21 141 F5
Burrs Cl TOT/BURYW BL8 26 D5
Burrs Lea Cl BURY BL9 27 F5
Burrswood Av BURY BL9 27 F5
Burrswood Dr BURY BL9 27 F5
Burslem Av DID/WITH M20 142 C3
Burstead St GTN M18 130 D2
Burstock St ANC M4 115 E2
Burston St GTN M18 130 B2
Burton Av DID/WITH M20 142 D5
HALE/TIMP WA15 154 B5
TOT/BURYW BL8 37 E2
Burton Dr POY/DIS SK12 195 E3
Burton Gv WALK M28 98 B2
Burton Rd DID/WITH M20 157 E2
Burton St HTNM SK4 159 H3
MDTN M24 72 C4
OLDE OL4 92 D1
Burton Wk CSLFD M3 6 A2
HTNM SK4 159 H2
Burtonwood Ct MDTN M24 72 C3
Burtree St WGTN/LGST M12 * 129 H2
Burwell Cl BOLS/LL BL3 48 C5
WHIT OL12 18 C5
Burwell Gv NTHM/RTH M23 167 G2
Bury & Bolton Rd RAD M26 51 G2
Bury & Rochdale Old Rd
HEY OL10 40 D1
Bury Av OLDTF/WHR M16 141 G1
Bury New Rd BOL BL1 3 G3
BOLE BL2 51 E2
BRO M7 101 G3
BURY BL9 39 G4
PWCH M25 85 H2
RAMS BL0 17 E2
WHTF M45 69 G3
Bury Old Rd BOLE BL2 3 J4
BOLE BL2 36 A5
BRO M7 101 H1
BURY BL9 17 G4
BURY BL9 39 H5
WHTF M45 85 H1
Bury Pl OP/CLY M11 116 D3
Bury Rd BOLE BL2 50 A2
RAD M26 52 C5
ROCH OL11 28 C5
TOT/BURYW BL8 26 A5
Bury St CSLFD M3 6 C2
HEY OL10 40 C4
MOSL OL5 108 D2
RAD M26 52 D5
RDSH SK5 160 A3
Bushell St BOLS/LL BL3 48 A5
Bushey Dr NTHM/RTH M23 167 H4
Busheyfield Cl HYDE SK14 133 G3
Bush St NEWH/MOS M40 103 F5
Busk Rd CHAD OL9 8 B1
Busk Wk CHAD OL9 * 74 D4
Butcher La BURY BL9 4 E4
NTHM/RTH M23 167 E2
ROY/SHW OL2 58 D4
Bute Av OLDS OL8 91 G4
Bute St BOL BL1 33 E5
NEWH/MOS M40 103 G1
SALQ M50 112 C4
Butler Gn CHAD OL9 90 B3
Butler La NEWH/MOS M40 115 F2
Butler St ANC M4 115 G3
RAMS BL0 16 B4
Butley St BRAM/HZG SK7 173 F5
Butman St GTN M18 131 E2
Buttercup Av WALK M28 * 81 E4
Buttercup Dr EDGY/DAV SK3 171 G5
OLDE OL4 76 C2
ROCH OL11 42 A3
Butterfield Cl CHD/CHDH SK8 183 E3
Butterfield Rd WHTN BL5 63 G4
Butterhouse La UPML OL3 79 E2
Butter La CSLFD M3 * 6 D4
Butterley Cl DUK SK16 134 A1
Buttermere Av HEY OL10 56 A1
SWIN M27 99 E4
WYTH/NTH M22 180 A2
Buttermere Cl BOLS/LL BL3 50 C5
STRET M32 125 H5
Buttermere Dr
HALE/TIMP WA15 188 D1
MDTN M24 72 B2
RAMS BL0 16 C1
Buttermere Gv
ROY/SHW OL2 59 E2
Buttermere Rd AULW OL7 119 E1
CHD/CHDH SK8 181 G1
FWTH BL4 64 D4
OLDE OL4 76 C4
PART M31 150 D3
Buttermill Cl IRL M44 122 C5
Butterstile Av PWCH M25 100 C1
Butterstile Cl PWCH M25 100 C1
Butterstile La PWCH M25 85 H4
Butterwick Cl
WGTN/LGST M12 130 A5
Butterworth Hall MILN OL16 44 D1
Butterworth La CHAD OL9 89 H4
Butterworth St CHAD OL9 * 74 C5
LIT OL15 20 D3
MDTN M24 73 F5
OLDE OL4 76 B5
OP/CLY M11 116 B5
Butterworth Wy UPML OL3 95 E2
Butteryhouse La
HALE/TIMP WA15 179 F2
Butt Hill Av PWCH M25 86 A4
Butt Hill Dr PWCH M25 86 A4
Butt Hill Rd PWCH M25 86 A5
Butt La OLDE OL4 93 G3
Button Hole ROY/SHW OL2 60 C2
Button La NTHM/RTH M23 155 G4
Buttress St GTN M18 130 B2
The Butts Av MILN OL16 10 C6
Buxted Rd OLD OL1 76 A3
Buxton Av AUL OL6 108 A4
DID/WITH M20 142 B5
Buxton Crs MILN OL16 43 G2
SALE M33 155 E5
Buxton La DROY M43 117 F5
MPL/ROM SK6 174 D4
Buxton Pl OLDS OL8 * 9 F7
Buxton Rd BRAM/HZG SK7 185 H4
OFTN SK2 172 D5
STRET M32 125 F5
Buxton St BRAM/HZG SK7 185 E1
CHD/CHDH SK8 169 F4
CMANE M1 7 J7
HEY OL10 41 E5
TOT/BURYW BL8 37 H4
WHIT OL12 14 C2
Bye Rd RAMS BL0 17 F1
Byfield Rd WYTH/NTH M22 168 B5
Byland Av CHD/CHDH SK8 193 E1
OLDE OL4 92 C3
Byland Cl BOL BL1 33 H4
Bylands Cl POY/DIS SK12 * 195 E3
Bylands Fold DUK SK16 133 G2
Byng Av IRL M44 150 B2
Byng St FWTH BL4 66 A4
HEY OL10 56 B1
Byrcland Cl WGTN/LGST M12 115 H5
Byre Cl SALE M33 155 H3
Byrom Av BNG/LEV M19 144 C2
Byrom St ALT WA14 177 G1
CSLFD M3 6 C6
OLDTF/WHR M16 127 G4
ORD M5 113 F5
Byron Av DROY M43 117 H3
PWCH M25 85 G4
RAD M26 51 G5
SWIN M27 98 D2
Byron Dr CHD/CHDH SK8 170 C3
Byron Gv RDSH SK5 145 E2
Byron Rd DTN/ASHW M34 146 D3
MDTN M24 73 E2
STRET M32 126 B5
TOT/BURYW BL8 26 A1
Byron's Dr HALE/TIMP WA15 166 B3
Byron St ECC M30 111 E3
OLDS OL8 90 C5
ROY/SHW OL2 59 F5
Byron Wk FWTH BL4 81 G1
Byrth Rd OLDS OL8 106 C2

C

Cabin La OLDE OL4 77 F1
Cablestead Wk OP/CLY M11 116 A5
Cable St ANC M4 7 G2
BOL BL1 3 F2
CSLFD M3 6 C2
Cabot Pl RDSH SK5 160 A2
Cabot St BRUN/LGST M13 * 128 C2
Caddington Rd CCHDY M21 141 G3
Cadishead Wy IRL M44 136 C4
Cadnam Dr WYTH/NTH M22 181 E1
Cadogan Pl BRO M7 * 101 H1
Cadogan St RUSH/FAL M14 128 B4
Cadum Wk BRUN/LGST M13 128 D2
Caen Av NEWH/MOS M40 89 F4
Caernarvon Cl
TOT/BURYW BL8 26 A2
Caernarvon Dr
BRAM/HZG SK7 184 D3
Caesar St ROCH OL11 43 F4
Cairn Dr ROCH OL11 41 F1
SLFD M6 113 H1
Cairngorm Dr BOLS/LL BL3 47 F4
Cairns Pl AUL OL6 107 G5
Cairn Wk OP/CLY M11 * 116 A4
Cairnwell Rd CHAD OL9 74 B4
Caister Av WHTF M45 69 H5
Caister Cl URM M41 137 E2
Caistor Cl OLDTF/WHR M16 142 A3
Caistor St STKP SK1 160 C3
Caistor Wk OLD OL1 9 G2
Caithness Cl NTHM/RTH M23 167 H5
Caithness Dr BOLS/LL BL3 47 F4
Caithness Rd HEY OL10 41 F1
Cakebread St
WGTN/LGST M12 128 D1
Calbourne Crs
WGTN/LGST M12 130 A5
Calcutta Rd EDGY/DAV SK3 171 F2
Caldbeck Av BOL BL1 32 C5
SALE M33 155 F1
Caldbeck Dr FWTH BL4 64 D5
MDTN M24 72 B3
Caldecott Rd BKLY M9 87 F2
Calder Av IRL M44 136 B2
LIT OL15 20 D1
WYTH/NTH M22 168 C1
Calderbank Av URM M41 123 F5
Calderbeck Wy
WYTH/NTH M22 168 D3
Calderbrook Dr
CHD/CHDH SK8 170 D5
Calderbrook Wy OLDE OL4 92 A2
Calder Cl BURY BL9 27 H3
POY/DIS SK12 195 E5
RDSH SK5 160 B1
Calder Ct URM M41 123 F4
Calder Crs WHTF M45 70 A2
Calder Dr FWTH BL4 83 E2
SWIN M27 98 D1
WALK M28 81 F5
Calder Gv ROY/SHW OL2 59 H1
Calder Rd BOLS/LL BL3 64 D1
Caldershaw La WHIT OL12 28 D1
Caldershaw Rd WHIT OL12 28 D2
Calder St MILN OL16 11 H1
ORD M5 113 H5
Caldervale Av CCHDY M21 156 B2
Calderwood Cl
TOT/BURYW BL8 26 A5
Caldey Rd NTHM/RTH M23 167 F4
Caldon Cl ECC M30 111 E5
Caldwell St RDSH SK5 145 F2
Caldy Dr RAMS BL0 16 B5
Caldy Rd SLFD M6 112 C1
WILM/AE SK9 192 A4
Caledon Av NEWH/MOS M40 103 H2
Caledonian Dr ECC M30 111 F5
Caledonia St BOLS/LL BL3 48 B4
RAD M26 52 D5

Caledonia Wy STRET M32 125 F3
Cale Gn OFTN SK2 172 A3
Cale St OFTN SK2 172 A2
Caley St BOL BL1 32 C4
CMANE M1 * 128 B1
Calf Hey LIT OL15 20 C2
Calf Hey Cl RAD M26 67 H1
Calf Hey North ROCH OL11 43 F2
Calf Hey Rd ROY/SHW OL2 60 C1
Calf Hey South ROCH OL11 43 F2
Calf La MOSL OL5 94 B3
Calgarth Dr MDTN M24 72 A1
Calgary St GTN M18 130 B3
Calico Cl CSLFD M3 114 A2
Calico Crs STLY SK15 109 H4
Callaghan Wk HEY OL10 40 D5
Calland Av HYDE SK14 134 A5
Callender St RAMS BL0 16 C2
Calliards Rd MILN OL16 20 B4
Callingdon Rd CCHDY M21 156 C1
Callington Cl HYDE SK14 149 G1
Callington Dr HYDE SK14 149 G1
Callis Rd BOLS/LL BL3 48 B3
Callum Wk BRUN/LGST M13 * 128 D2
Calluna Ms DID/WITH M20 * 157 F2
Caltha St RAMS BL0 16 C2
Calthorpe Av BKLY M9 102 D3
Calton Av BRO M7 100 D3
Calve Croft Rd
WYTH/NTH M22 180 D3
Calver Av ECC M30 110 D5
Calver Cl URM M41 123 E5
Calver Hey Cl WHTN BL5 62 D2
Calverleigh Cl BOLS/LL BL3 63 H2
Calverley Av BNG/LEV M19 143 H4
Calverley Cl WILM/AE SK9 199 F2
Calverley Wy WHIT OL12 18 D4
Calverly Rd CHD/CHDH SK8 170 D4
Calverton Dr
NEWH/MOS M40 104 B3
Calvert Rd BOLS/LL BL3 65 E1
Calvert St ORD M5 112 C3
Calver Wk NEWH/MOS M40 * 115 F2
Calvine Wk NEWH/MOS M40 * 115 F2
Calvin St BOL BL1 3 F1
Cambeck Cl WHTF M45 70 A3
Cambell Rd ECC M30 110 C3
Camberley Cl BRAM/HZG SK7 184 B5
TOT/BURYW BL8 37 F1
Camberly Dr ROCH OL11 28 C5
Cambert La GTN M18 130 B3
Camberwell Dr AULW OL7 106 D3
Camberwell St CHH M8 * 114 D1
OLDS OL8 * 91 F3
Camberwell Wy ROY/SHW OL2 58 D5
Camborne Rd HYDE SK14 135 F5
Camborne St RUSH/FAL M14 142 D1
Cambourne Dr BOLS/LL BL3 47 H4
Cambo Wk HTNM SK4 158 C3
Cambrai Crs ECC M30 110 B1
Cambrian Dr MILN OL16 31 H5
ROY/SHW OL2 74 D2
Cambrian Rd EDGY/DAV SK3 12 B6
Cambrian St NEWH/MOS M40 115 H3
Cambria Sq BOLS/LL BL3 * 48 B4
Cambria St BOLS/LL BL3 48 B4
OLDE OL4 76 B5
Cambridge Av
OLDTF/WHR M16 141 G1
ROCH OL11 28 D5
WILM/AE SK9 198 C3
Cambridge Cl FWTH BL4 65 E3
SALE M33 153 G3
Cambridge Dr BOLS/LL BL3 51 E5
DTN/ASHW M34 131 F5
MPL/ROM SK6 162 B1
Cambridge Gv ECC M30 111 G3
WHTF M45 69 H4
Cambridge Rd BKLY M9 103 E1
CHD/CHDH SK8 169 G3
DROY M43 117 G2
FAIL M35 105 E5
HALE/TIMP WA15 177 H2
HOR/BR BL6 46 A1
HTNM SK4 159 F1
URM M41 138 B2
Cambridge St AULW OL7 119 E4
BRO M7 114 B1
CHAD OL9 90 D3
CMANE M1 128 A1
DUK SK16 119 H4
OFTN SK2 172 B3
STLY SK15 120 D3
Camden Av NEWH/MOS M40 116 D1
Camden Cl BOLE BL2 36 B5
Camden St MOSL OL5 94 A4
Camelford Cl HULME M15 * 128 B2
Camelia Rd BKLY M9 102 D3
Camellia Cl BOL BL1 48 A2
Cameron Ct ROY/SHW OL2 59 E3
Cameron St BOL BL1 33 G1
CMANE M1 * 6 D7
TOT/BURYW BL8 37 H4
Campania St ROY/SHW OL2 75 F2
Campbell Cl TOT/BURYW BL8 36 D2
Campbell Ct FWTH BL4 65 H2
Campbell Rd BOLS/LL BL3 63 H2
BRUN/LGST M13 143 H1
SALE M33 154 B3
SWIN M27 98 D4
Campbell St FWTH BL4 65 G3
RDSH SK5 145 F2
WHIT OL12 10 B1
Campbell Wy WALK M28 81 H4
Campden Wy WILM/AE SK9 192 A3
Campion Wy WHIT OL12 18 B5
Camp St AUL OL6 119 G2
BRO M7 113 H1
CSLFD M3 6 C6
TOT/BURYW BL8 37 H3
Camrose Gdns BOL BL1 33 H5
Camrose Wk
BRUN/LGST M13 * 129 E3
Cams Acre Cl RAD M26 67 H1
Cams La RAD M26 67 H2
Canada St BOL BL1 33 F4
NEWH/MOS M40 115 H1
OFTN SK2 172 B3
Canal Bank ECC M30 110 D2
Canal Bridge La DROY M43 117 E4
Canal Cottages Yd ANC M4 * 115 F4
Canal Rd ALT WA14 165 H2
Canal Side ECC M30 110 D2
Canal St CHAD OL9 90 C4
CMANE M1 7 G6
DROY M43 117 H5
HEY OL10 56 B1
HYDE SK14 133 F5
LIT OL15 21 E3
MPL/ROM SK6 175 F3
ORD M5 * 113 H4
ROCH OL11 43 F1
STKP SK1 13 H5
STLY SK15 * 120 D4
Canary Wy SWIN M27 100 B3
Canberra Rd BRAM/HZG SK7 194 A2
Canberra St OP/CLY M11 116 D3
Canberra Wy ROCH OL11 43 F3
Candahar St BOLS/LL BL3 65 F1
Candleford Pl OFTN SK2 173 F5
Candleford Rd
DID/WITH M20 * 142 D5
Candlestick Ct BURY BL9 39 G2
Canisp Cl CHAD OL9 74 B4
Canley Cl STKP SK1 13 H6
Canmore Cl BOLS/LL BL3 63 H1
Cannel Fold WALK M28 96 C3
Canning Dr BOL BL1 33 H4
Canning St BOL BL1 * 33 H4
BURY BL9 4 E1
HTNM SK4 13 F1
Cannock Dr HTNM SK4 158 D4
Cannon Cl CSLFD M3 6 E3
Cannon St BOLS/LL BL3 48 C4
CHAD OL9 8 E3
CSLFD M3 114 A3
ECC M30 111 F4
RAD M26 52 A4
RAMS BL0 16 B4
Cannon St North BOLS/LL BL3 * 2 B7
Cann St TOT/BURYW BL8 25 G4
Canon Dr ALT WA14 177 E3
Canon Flynn Ct MILN OL16 11 K6
Canon Green Dr CSLFD M3 6 B2
Canons Cl BOL BL1 33 E4
Canons Gv NEWH/MOS M40 103 F5
Canonsleigh Cl CHH M8 101 H5
Canon St BURY BL9 5 G1
MILN OL16 11 G1
Canonsway SWIN M27 98 D3
Canon Tighe Ct CHAD OL9 * 74 B5
Cansfield Ct FWTH BL4 82 D1
Canterbury Cl DUK SK16 133 G2
ROCH OL11 28 D4
Canterbury Crs MDTN M24 73 G2
Canterbury Dr PWCH M25 86 B5
TOT/BURYW BL8 38 A2
Canterbury Gdns ORD M5 111 H3
Canterbury Gv BOLS/LL BL3 64 C1
Canterbury Pk DID/WITH M20 157 E3
Canterbury Rd
HALE/TIMP WA15 178 D1
STKP SK1 160 C5
URM M41 124 A5
Canterbury St AUL OL6 119 H1
Canterfield Cl DROY M43 118 C3
Cantrell St OP/CLY M11 116 C4
Canute Rd STRET M32 126 B5
Canute St BOLE BL2 34 D5
ORD M5 * 113 G3
RAD M26 67 H1
Cape Gdns ROY/SHW OL2 60 A3
Capella Wk BRO M7 113 H1
Capenhurst Cl
NTHM/RTH M23 167 G5
POY/DIS SK12 195 G3
Capesthorne Cl
BRAM/HZG SK7 185 G4
Capesthorne Dr
ROY/SHW OL2 59 G2
Capesthorne Rd
BRAM/HZG SK7 185 G4
DUK SK16 133 G2
HALE/TIMP WA15 167 E3
MPL/ROM SK6 186 D5
WILM/AE SK9 198 B5
Cape St DID/WITH M20 143 E4
Capital Rd OP/CLY M11 131 E1
Capitol Cl BOL BL1 32 D3
Capricorn Rd BKLY M9 89 E4
Capricorn Wy SLFD M6 * 113 H1
Capstan St BKLY M9 103 F2
Captain Clarke Rd HYDE SK14 133 E3
Captain Fold HEY OL10 * 41 F4
Captain Fold Rd LHULT M38 81 E2
Captain Lees Gdns WHTN BL5 62 B4
Captain Lees Rd WHTN BL5 62 B4
Captain's Clough Rd BOL BL1 33 E4
Capton Cl BRAM/HZG SK7 184 B2
Carberry Rd GTN M18 130 D3
Carden Av SWIN M27 98 C3
URM M41 137 G1
Carder Cl SWIN M27 99 E3
Cardew Av WYTH/NTH M22 168 D5
Cardiff Cl OLDS OL8 105 G1
Cardiff St BRO M7 101 H3
Cardigan Dr BURY BL9 53 F2
Cardigan Rd OLDS OL8 90 C5
Cardigan St ROY/SHW OL2 59 F5
SLFD M6 * 112 D4
WHIT OL12 18 D5
Cardinal Ms MDTN M24 72 A2
Cardinal St CHH M8 102 C4
OLD OL1 9 J3
Carding Gv CSLFD M3 6 B1
Cardroom Rd ANC M4 7 K4
Cardus St BNG/LEV M19 144 A2
Cardwell Gdns BOL BL1 * 33 H4
Cardwell Rd ECC M30 110 B4
Cardwell St OLDS OL8 91 G4
Caremine Av BNG/LEV M19 144 B1
Carey Cl BRO M7 * 114 A1
Carey Wk HULME M15 128 A3
Carfax Fold WHIT OL12 29 E1
Carfax St GTN M18 130 C3
Carill Av NEWH/MOS M40 103 H1
Carill Dr RUSH/FAL M14 143 F3
Carina Pl BRO M7 113 H1
Carisbrook Av URM M41 138 C2
WHTF M45 85 H1
Carisbrook Dr SWIN M27 99 F4
Carisbrooke Av
BRAM/HZG SK7 185 E3
Carisbrooke Dr BOL BL1 34 A3
Carisbrooke St BKLY M9 103 E3
Carlburn St OP/CLY M11 117 E3
Carleton Rd POY/DIS SK12 196 B3
Carley Gv BKLY M9 87 H3
Carlford Gv PWCH M25 85 G4
Carlile St EDGY/DAV SK3 12 E6
Carlin Ga HALE/TIMP WA15 166 B3
Carling Dr WYTH/NTH M22 180 D2
Carlingford Cl
EDGY/DAV SK3 171 H4
Carlisle Cl BOLS/LL BL3 66 D2
MPL/ROM SK6 161 H5
WHTF M45 70 A5
Carlisle Crs AUL OL6 107 F3
Carlisle Dr ALT WA14 165 H1
IRL M44 136 C1
Carlisle St CHAD OL9 90 D3
EDGW/EG BL7 23 F3
SWIN M27 84 A5
WHIT OL12 18 D5
WILM/AE SK9 200 D5
Carloon Rd NTHM/RTH M23 156 A5
Carlow Dr WYTH/NTH M22 180 D2
Carl St BOL BL1 * 33 G4
Carlton Av BOLS/LL BL3 47 H5
BRAM/HZG SK7 193 G2
CHD/CHDH SK8 182 C1
MPL/ROM SK6 162 C3
OLDE OL4 76 C3
PWCH M25 86 D5
WHTF M45 69 E3
WILM/AE SK9 191 H5
Carlton Cl BOLE BL2 35 F3
WALK M28 96 D1
Carlton Ct HALE/TIMP WA15 178 C3
Carlton Crs STKP SK1 13 K2
URM M41 138 D2
Carlton Dr CHD/CHDH SK8 169 F3
PWCH M25 86 D5
Carlton Pl BRAM/HZG SK7 185 H3
FWTH BL4 * 66 A3
Carlton Range GTN M18 * 131 E4
Carlton Rd AUL OL6 107 F5
BOL BL1 47 H1
HALE/TIMP WA15 178 C2
HTNM SK4 158 D4
HYDE SK14 134 B5
OLDTF/WHR M16 127 G5
SALE M33 139 G5
SLFD M6 112 D1
URM M41 138 C2
WALK M28 96 D1
Carlton St BOLE BL2 3 G6
BURY BL9 53 G1
ECC M30 111 E2
FWTH BL4 66 A3
OLDTF/WHR M16 127 F4
Carlton Wy
GOL/RIS/CUL WA3 150 B1
ROY/SHW OL2 75 E2
Carlyle Cl CHH M8 102 B4
Carlyle St BURY BL9 4 B4
Carlyn Av SALE M33 155 E2
Carmel Av ORD M5 127 F1
Carmel Cl ORD M5 113 H5
Carmel Ct BKLY M9 103 E1
Carmenna Dr BRAM/HZG SK7 184 A5
Carmichael Cl PART M31 150 D3
Carmichael St EDGY/DAV SK3 12 C7
Car Mill Ms WILM/AE SK9 191 G5
Carmine Fold MDTN M24 72 C2
Carmona Dr PWCH M25 85 H3
Carmona Gdns BRO M7 101 F1
Carmoor Rd BRUN/LGST M13 128 D3
Carnaby St BKLY M9 103 G1
Carna Rd RDSH SK5 145 E1
Carnarvon St BRO M7 * 101 H3
CSLFD M3 114 C2
OLDS OL8 90 C5
STKP SK1 13 K5
Carnation Rd FWTH BL4 65 F3
OLDE OL4 92 D3
Carnegie Av BNG/LEV M19 144 A2
Carnegie Cl SALE M33 153 G3
Carnforth Av CHAD OL9 90 B1
ROCH OL11 57 G2
Carnforth Dr SALE M33 154 B3
TOT/BURYW BL8 26 B1
Carnforth Rd CHD/CHDH SK8 171 F5
HTNM SK4 144 C5
Carnforth Sq MDTN M24 57 G2
Carnforth St RUSH/FAL M14 128 C5
Carnoustie BOLS/LL BL3 63 H1
Carnoustie Cl
NEWH/MOS M40 104 B3
WILM/AE SK9 199 G2
Carnoustie Dr CHD/CHDH SK8 181 H3
RAMS BL0 16 C2
Carnwood Cl
NEWH/MOS M40 117 E1
Carolina Wy SALQ M50 112 D4
Caroline St AUL OL6 119 H2
BOLS/LL BL3 48 C5
BRO M7 114 B1
EDGY/DAV SK3 12 D7
IRL M44 136 A3
STLY SK15 120 D4
Carpenters La ANC M4 7 G3
Carpenters Wk DROY M43 117 G4
Carpenters Wy MILN OL16 43 G2
Carradale Dr SALE M33 153 F1
Carr Av PWCH M25 85 G5
Carr Bank Av BKLY M9 87 E4
RAMS BL0 16 C1
Carr Bank Dr RAMS BL0 16 C1
Carr Bank Rd RAMS BL0 16 C1
Carrbrook Cl STLY SK15 109 G4
Carrbrook Crs STLY SK15 109 G4
Carrbrook Dr ROY/SHW OL2 75 F3
Carrbrook Rd STLY SK15 109 G3
Carrbrook Ter RAD M26 52 D5
Carr Brow MPL/ROM SK6 187 F5
Carr Cl STKP SK1 172 C1
Carr Dr FWTH BL4 65 E3
Carrfield Av EDGY/DAV SK3 172 B5
HALE/TIMP WA15 167 E4
LHULT M38 80 D3
Carrfield Gv LHULT M38 80 D3
Carr Fold RAMS BL0 16 C1
Carrgate Rd DTN/ASHW M34 147 F2
Carrgreen Cl BNG/LEV M19 158 C1
Carrhill Quarry Cl MOSL OL5 93 H5
Carrhill Rd MOSL OL5 93 H5
Carrhill Ter MOSL OL5 * 93 H5
Carr House Rd OLDE OL4 77 E5
Carriage Dr LIT OL15 21 E1
NEWH/MOS M40 103 E5
The Carriages ALT WA14 * 165 F5
Carriage St OLDTF/WHR M16 127 G3
Carrick Gdns MDTN M24 56 C5
Carrie St BOL BL1 48 A1
Carrigart PWCH M25 85 H4
Carrill Gv East BNG/LEV M19 144 A2
Carrington Cl MILN OL16 20 A5
Carrington Dr BOLS/LL BL3 49 E5
Carrington Field St OFTN SK2 172 A2
Carrington La SALE M33 138 D5
Carrington Rd RUSH/FAL M14 143 E3
STKP SK1 160 C4
URM M41 137 G3
Carrington St CHAD OL9 90 C4
SWIN M27 99 G1
Carrington Ter SWIN M27 * 99 F1
Carr La STLY SK15 109 G3
UPML OL3 79 E5
WILM/AE SK9 200 A3
Carr Lea OLDE OL4 93 H1
Carr Mill Ms WILM/AE SK9 * 199 E1
Carron Av BKLY M9 103 F1
Carron Gv BOLE BL2 50 C2
Carr Ri STLY SK15 109 G3
Carr Rd HALE/TIMP WA15 178 C2
IRL M44 136 D1
Carrs Av CHD/CHDH SK8 170 D3
Carrsdale Dr BKLY M9 87 H5
Carrsfield Rd WYTH/NTH M22 168 D3
Carrslea Cl RAD M26 51 H4
Carrs Rd CHD/CHDH SK8 170 C3
Carr St AUL OL6 107 G5
RAMS BL0 16 C1
SWIN M27 98 C3
Carrsvale Av URM M41 124 A5
Carrswood Rd
NTHM/RTH M23 166 D1
Carruthers Cl HEY OL10 41 G3
Carruthers St ANC M4 115 G4
Carrwood HALE/TIMP WA15 178 C5
Carrwood Av BRAM/HZG SK7 183 H4
Carrwood Hey RAMS BL0 16 B4
Carrwood Rd BRAM/HZG SK7 183 G3
WILM/AE SK9 198 C2
Carsdale Rd WYTH/NTH M22 180 D5
Carslake Av BOL BL1 48 B1
Carslake Rd NEWH/MOS M40 103 E5
Carson Rd BNG/LEV M19 144 A3
Carstairs Av OFTN SK2 172 B5
Carstairs Cl CHH M8 102 A3
Carter Cl DTN/ASHW M34 * 146 D1
Carter Pl HYDE SK14 * 133 G3
Carter St BOLS/LL BL3 49 F5
BRO M7 * 101 G5
FWTH BL4 * 66 B5
HYDE SK14 133 G3
MOSL OL5 108 D2
SALQ M50 112 B4
STLY SK15 121 E3
Carthage St OLDS OL8 91 G3
Cartleach Gv WALK M28 81 F5
Cartleach La WALK M28 81 E5
Cartmel WHIT OL12 10 C4
Cartmel Av HTNM SK4 144 D5
MILN OL16 44 C2
Cartmel Cl BOLS/LL BL3 63 E2
BRAM/HZG SK7 184 D1
BURY BL9 69 H1
CHD/CHDH SK8 181 H1
OLDS OL8 91 E4
Cartmel Crs BOLE BL2 34 D4
CHAD OL9 90 A5
Cartmel Dr HALE/TIMP WA15 167 E3
Cartmel Gv WALK M28 98 A3
Cartridge Cl WYTH/NTH M22 181 E1
Cartridge St HEY OL10 40 D4
Cartwright Rd CCHDY M21 141 E3
Cartwright St
DTN/ASHW M34 132 C2
HYDE SK14 134 B3
Carver Av PWCH M25 86 B2
Carver Cl OLDTF/WHR M16 127 E3
Carver Dr MPL/ROM SK6 174 D4
Carver Rd HALE/TIMP WA15 177 H2
MPL/ROM SK6 174 D4
Carver St OLDTF/WHR M16 127 E3
Carver Wk HULME M15 * 128 A3
Carville Rd BKLY M9 89 F4
Cascade Dr BRO M7 101 H5
Cashgate Ct OLDS OL8 90 D4
Cashmere Rd EDGY/DAV SK3 171 F2
Cashmoor Wk
WGTN/LGST M12 129 F2
Caspian Rd ALT WA14 164 D3
BKLY M9 89 E4
Cass Av ORD M5 113 F5
Cassidy Cl ANC M4 7 J2
Cassidy Gdns MDTN M24 56 A5
Casson Ga WHIT OL12 10 B2
Casson St FAIL M35 105 E3
Casterton Wy WALK M28 96 B5
Castle Av DTN/ASHW M34 146 C1
ROCH OL11 29 H5
Castlebrook Cl BURY BL9 54 A5
Castle Cl DROY M43 118 A3
Castle Ct AUL OL6 107 E3
Castle Cft BOLE BL2 35 E3
Castlecroft Rd BURY BL9 4 C4
Castledene Av SLFD M6 112 D2
Castle Farm Dr OFTN SK2 172 C3
Castle Farm La OFTN SK2 * 172 D4
Castlefield Av BRO M7 101 H2
Castlefield Br ORD M5 114 A5
Castleford Cl BOL BL1 * 2 B2
Castleford St OLD OL1 74 D3
Castle Gv RAMS BL0 26 B1
Castle Hall Cl STLY SK15 121 E4
Castle Hall Ct STLY SK15 * 120 D4
Castle Hall Vw STLY SK15 120 D4
Castle Hey Cl BURY BL9 70 B1
Castle Hill Crs ROCH OL11 29 H5
Castle Hill Dr BKLY M9 102 D1
Castle Hill Pk MPL/ROM SK6 * 146 D5
Castle Hill Rd BURY BL9 39 G2
PWCH M25 86 C5
Castle Hill St BOLE BL2 34 C4
Castle La STLY SK15 109 G2
Castlemere Dr ROY/SHW OL2 60 C1
Castlemere Rd BKLY M9 87 H4
Castlemere St ROCH OL11 29 H5
Castlemere Ter ROCH OL11 29 H5
Castle Mill La
HALE/TIMP WA15 188 B2
Castlemoor Av BRO M7 101 E2
Castle Quay HULME M15 127 H1
Castlerea Cl ECC M30 111 E5
Castlerigg Cl HTNM SK4 144 D4
Castlerigg Dr MDTN M24 71 H2
ROY/SHW OL2 58 D3
Castle Rd BURY BL9 54 B5
Castle Shaw Rd OFTN SK2 173 F4
Castle St BOLE BL2 3 J6
BURY BL9 4 D4
BURY BL9 26 D1
CSLFD M3 6 B7
ECC M30 111 G3
EDGY/DAV SK3 12 C7
FWTH BL4 * 66 A5
HYDE SK14 134 A5
MDTN M24 73 G5
STLY SK15 120 D4
Castleton Av STRET M32 125 G5
Castleton Dr MPL/ROM SK6 197 E1
Castleton Gv AUL OL6 108 A4
Castleton Rd BRAM/HZG SK7 185 F3
BRO M7 101 H2
ROY/SHW OL2 58 D1
STRET M32 125 F4
Castleton Rd South
ROCH OL11 42 C4
Castleton St ALT WA14 165 F2
BOLE BL2 34 C4
CHAD OL9 8 A5
Castleton Wk OP/CLY M11 * 116 A4
Castleway HALE/TIMP WA15 178 D5
ROCH OL11 42 A4
SLFD M6 112 D1
Castle Wy SWIN M27 84 B5
Castlewood Gdns OFTN SK2 172 D4
Castlewood Rd BRO M7 100 C2
Castlewood Sq BOLE BL2 34 D5
Catchdale Cl BKLY M9 87 H2
Catches Cl ROCH OL11 29 E3
Catches La ROCH OL11 29 E2
Cateaton St BURY BL9 4 E2
CSLFD M3 6 E3
Caterham Av BOLS/LL BL3 63 G2
Caterham St ANC M4 115 G4
Catfield Wk HULME M15 * 127 G1
Catford Rd NTHM/RTH M23 167 G4
Cathedral Ap CSLFD M3 6 E2
Cathedral Cl DUK SK16 133 G2
Cathedral Gdns ANC M4 * 6 E2
Cathedral Gates CSLFD M3 * 6 E3
Cathedral Rd CHAD OL9 74 B3
Cathedral St CSLFD M3 6 E3
Catherine Houses
HTNM SK4 * 158 C4
Catherine Rd ALT WA14 177 F1
CHH M8 101 H1
MPL/ROM SK6 161 G5
SWIN M27 98 B3
Catherine St BOLS/LL BL3 64 A2
BRAM/HZG SK7 173 F5
BURY BL9 53 F3
ECC M30 110 B2
HYDE SK14 133 G5
OLDE OL4 92 D1
OP/CLY M11 130 D1
Catherston Cl
OLDTF/WHR M16 127 H5
Cathrine St East
DTN/ASHW M34 132 A5
Cathrine St West
DTN/ASHW M34 132 A5
Catlow La ANC M4 * 7 G3
Catlow St BRO M7 114 B1
Caton Cl BURY BL9 53 F1
Caton St MILN OL16 30 A5
Cato St RAMS BL0 16 B4
Catterall Crs BOLE BL2 24 A5
Catterick Av DID/WITH M20 157 H3
SALE M33 153 F4
Catterick Dr BOLS/LL BL3 66 D1
Catterick Rd DID/WITH M20 157 H3
Catterwood Dr
MPL/ROM SK6 163 G4
Cattlin Wy OLDS OL8 90 D5
The Causeway ALT WA14 165 G5
CHAD OL9 89 G2
Causewood Cl OLDE OL4 60 D5
Causey Dr MDTN M24 72 A1
Cavanagh Cl BRUN/LGST M13 129 E2
Cavan Cl EDGY/DAV SK3 170 C2
Cavell St CMANE M1 * 7 H4
Cavell Wy ORD M5 113 F4
Cavendish Av DID/WITH M20 142 B5
SWIN M27 84 D4
Cavendish Gdns BOLS/LL BL3 64 B1
Cavendish Gv ECC M30 111 F2
Cavendish Ms WILM/AE SK9 198 D5
Cavendish Pl AUL OL6 * 119 F2
Cavendish Rd ALT WA14 177 F1
BRAM/HZG SK7 185 E3
BRO M7 101 G1
DID/WITH M20 142 B5
ECC M30 111 F2
HTNM SK4 158 C4
ROCH OL11 42 D3
STRET M32 126 B4
URM M41 139 E1
WALK M28 98 A4
Cavendish St AUL OL6 119 G3
HULME M15 128 B2
OLDS OL8 9 F5
Cavendish Wy ROY/SHW OL2 74 D2
Cavenham Gv BOL BL1 48 B1
Caversham Dr BKLY M9 103 F2
Cawdor Ct FWTH BL4 65 H2

Cawdor Pl HALE/TIMP WA15 166 D3
Cawdor Rd RUSH/FAL M14 143 E2
Cawdor St ECC M30 110 D4
FWTH BL4 65 G2
HULME M15 127 G1
SWIN M27 98 C2
WALK M28 82 B5
Cawley Av PWCH M25 85 G5
Cawley Ter BKLY M9 * 87 F2
Cawood Sq RDSH SK5 146 A5
Cawston Wk CHH M8 102 B4
Caxton Rd RUSH/FAL M14 142 D2
Caxton St CSLFD M3 * 6 C3
HEY OL10 41 E4
ROCH OL11 42 B4
Caxton Wy ORD M5 113 G4
Caygill St CSLFD M3 6 C2
Cayley St MILN OL16 11 G7
Caythorpe St RUSH/FAL M14 128 B5
Cayton St WGTN/LGST M12 129 H5
The Ceal MPL/ROM SK6 163 G4
Cecil Av SALE M33 153 H3
Cecil Dr URM M41 137 G1
Cecil Gv GTN M18 130 C4
Cecilia St BOLS/LL BL3 49 F5
Cecil Rd BKLY M9 88 A3
ECC M30 111 F4
HALE/TIMP WA15 177 H2
STRET M32 140 A2
Cecil St BOLE BL2 3 J5
BURY BL9 4 E6
DUK SK16 119 G5
EDGY/DAV SK3 * 12 E7
HULME M15 128 C3
LIT OL15 20 C3
MOSL OL5 108 D2
OLDS OL8 8 E7
ROCH OL11 43 E1
ROY/SHW OL2 58 D5
STLY SK15 121 E4
WALK M28 82 A4
Cedar Av ALT WA14 165 F5
AUL OL6 107 G5
BOLS/LL BL3 67 E2
BRAM/HZG SK7 185 F2
HEY OL10 40 D3
STLY SK15 121 F2
WHTF M45 85 G1
Cedar Bank Cl MILN OL16 31 E4
Cedar Cl POY/DIS SK12 195 F4
Cedar Ct HALE/TIMP WA15 * 166 C4
Cedar Crs CHAD OL9 74 C4
RAMS BL0 16 D1
Cedar Dr DROY M43 118 A3
SWIN M27 83 G3
URM M41 138 C2
Cedar Gv DTN/ASHW M34 132 B5
DUK SK16 120 C5
FWTH BL4 65 G4
HTNM SK4 159 F1
PWCH M25 85 H1
ROY/SHW OL2 59 E3
ROY/SHW OL2 60 A3
RUSH/FAL M14 143 F3
Cedar La MILN OL16 44 D3
OLDE OL4 94 A1
Cedar Lawn
CHD/CHDH SK8 * 182 D2
Cedar Ms AULW OL7 106 D5
Cedar Pl BRO M7 113 H1
Cedar Rd CHD/CHDH SK8 169 F4
FAIL M35 105 E4
HALE/TIMP WA15 177 H1
MDTN M24 73 F4
MPL/ROM SK6 174 D5
OFTN SK2 172 C5
PART M31 150 D3
SALE M33 138 D5
Cedars Rd WYTH/NTH M22 180 C1
Cedar St AUL OL6 120 A1
BURY BL9 5 H3
HYDE SK14 133 G3
OLDE OL4 76 B5
WHIT OL12 10 D2
Cedar Vw AUL OL6 * 107 H5
Cedarwood Av HTNM SK4 158 D5
Cedarwood Cl
WYTH/NTH M22 168 D1
Cedar Wood Ct BOL BL1 * 47 G1
Cedric Rd CHH M8 86 D5
OLDE OL4 76 B5
Cedric St ORD M5 112 C3
Celandine Cl LIT OL15 20 C3
Celia St CHH M8 102 D2
Cellini Sq BOL BL1 33 G5
Celtic St STKP SK1 13 K5
Cemetery La BURY BL9 53 G1
Cemetery Rd BOLE BL2 3 K4
DROY M43 117 G4
DTN/ASHW M34 132 C2
DTN/ASHW M34 146 D2
FAIL M35 105 E4
FWTH BL4 66 C3
MOSL OL5 109 E3
ORD M5 112 D4
RAD M26 52 B4
RAMS BL0 16 B4
ROY/SHW OL2 58 D4
SWIN M27 98 D1
Cemetery Rd North
SWIN M27 83 H5
Cemetery St MDTN M24 72 D3
Cennick Cl OLDE OL4 92 C1
Ceno St OLD OL1 75 H3
Centaur Cl SWIN M27 84 A5
Centenary Ct BOLS/LL BL3 49 E5
Centenary Wy SALQ M50 111 H4
TRPK M17 112 A5
Central Av BNG/LEV M19 144 A1
BURY BL9 53 E2
FWTH BL4 65 F4
LIT OL15 21 E2
SALE M33 153 G5
SLFD M6 100 B5
SWIN M27 85 E5
UPML OL3 95 F2
URM M41 124 D2
WALK M28 81 H2
Central Dr BRAM/HZG SK7 183 G2
BURY BL9 27 G3
CHD/CHDH SK8 182 A4
CHH M8 102 C1
MPL/ROM SK6 162 B3
RDSH SK5 160 B1
SWIN M27 99 G3
URM M41 138 D1
Central Park Est TRPK M17 * 125 H2
Central Rd DID/WITH M20 157 F1
MANAIR M90 190 B1
PART M31 151 E3
Central St BOL BL1 2 D4
CMANW M2 6 E6
RAMS BL0 16 C2
Central Wy ALT WA14 165 G5
Centre Gdns BOL BL1 33 G5
Centre Park Rd BOL BL1 2 A1
Centre Vale Cl LIT OL15 21 F1
Centurion Gv BRO M7 101 H5
Century Gdns WHIT OL12 10 C4
Century Ldg FWTH BL4 65 H4
Cestrian St BOLS/LL BL3 65 E1
Ceylon St NEWH/MOS M40 103 H4
OLDE OL4 92 C2
Chadbury Cl HOR/BR BL6 62 D1
Chadderton Dr BURY BL9 69 H2
Chadderton Fold OLD OL1 74 A2
Chadderton Hall Rd CHAD OL9 74 A3
Chadderton Park Rd CHAD OL9 74 A3
Chadderton Prec CHAD OL9 * 74 C5
Chadderton St ANC M4 7 H2
Chadderton Wy CHAD OL9 8 D1
OLD OL1 74 D3
Chaddesley Wk OP/CLY M11 * 116 B5
The Chaddock Level WALK M28 96 B5
Chadkirk Rd MPL/ROM SK6 162 B5
Chadvil Rd CHD/CHDH SK8 169 H4
Chadwell Rd OFTN SK2 173 F2
Chadwick Cl MILN OL16 44 D1
RUSH/FAL M14 * 128 C5
WILM/AE SK9 199 F1
Chadwick Fold BURY BL9 27 G4
Chadwick Hall Rd ROCH OL11 29 E5
Chadwick La MILN OL16 43 H4
ROCH OL11 41 H4
Chadwick Rd ECC M30 111 F3
URM M41 139 F1
Chadwick St AUL OL6 120 B3
BOLE BL2 3 H6
BOLS/LL BL3 67 E1
BURY BL9 39 H2
MILN OL16 31 F4
MPL/ROM SK6 175 E4
ROCH OL11 29 G4
STKP SK1 13 G6
SWIN M27 99 E2
Chaffinch Cl DROY M43 118 B2
OLDE OL4 92 D3
WYTH/NTH M22 169 E4
Chaffinch Dr BURY BL9 39 F2
Chaffinch Gv STLY SK15 * 109 F3
Chain Bar La HYDE SK14 149 H1
Chain Rd BKLY M9 88 A2
Chain St CMANE M1 7 F5
Chalcombe Gra
WGTN/LGST M12 * 129 G4
Chale Cl NEWH/MOS M40 115 G2
Chale Dr MDTN M24 89 F1
Chale Gn BOLE BL2 35 F3
Chalfont Av URM M41 * 139 E1
Chalfont Cl OLDS OL8 * 92 A3
Chalfont Dr CHH M8 102 B3
WALK M28 97 F2
Chalfont St BOL BL1 34 A4
Chalford Rd NTHM/RTH M23 179 H1
Challenor Sq
WGTN/LGST M12 * 129 H2
Challum Dr CHAD OL9 74 B4
Chamber Hall Cl OLDS OL8 91 E3
Chamberhall St BURY BL9 4 D2
Chamber House Dr ROCH OL11 42 A3
Chamberlain Dr WILM/AE SK9 199 G1
Chamberlain Rd STLY SK15 108 D5
Chamberlain St BOLS/LL BL3 2 B7
Chamber Rd OLDS OL8 90 D4
ROY/SHW OL2 59 H2
Chambers Ct HYDE SK14 135 H5
Chambers Field Ct ORD M5 113 F4
Champness Hall MILN OL16 * 10 D7
Chancel Av ORD M5 113 H5
Chancel Cl DUK SK16 133 F2
Chancel La WILM/AE SK9 199 E2
Chancellor La
WGTN/LGST M12 115 G5
Chancel Ms STKP SK1 13 J3
Chancel Pl CMANE M1 * 7 K5
MILN OL16 10 C7
Chancery La BOL BL1 3 F5
CMANW M2 6 E5
ROY/SHW OL2 * 60 B2
UPML OL3 78 D2
Chancery St OLDE OL4 92 B1
Chancery Wk CHAD OL9 74 D4
Chandley St CHD/CHDH SK8 * 170 A3
Chandos Gv ORD M5 112 C3
Chandos Rd CCHDY M21 141 G2
HTNM SK4 144 B5
PWCH M25 86 A5
Chandos Rd South
CCHDY M21 141 G2
Chandos St ROY/SHW OL2 60 B2
Change Wy CSLFD M3 6 B1
Channing Ct MILN OL16 * 30 C5
Channing Sq MILN OL16 30 C5
Channing St MILN OL16 30 C5
The Chanters WALK M28 96 D3
Chantlers Av
TOT/BURYW BL8 37 F5
Chantry Cl RDSH SK5 145 E4
Chapel Aly BOL BL1 * 2 E4
Chapel Cl BURY BL9 54 A5
DUK SK16 119 H5
Chapel Ct ALT WA14 165 G5
Chapel Cft ROY/SHW OL2 59 E5
Chapel Dr AUL OL6 107 H5
HALE/TIMP WA15 178 D5
Chapelfield RAD M26 68 D3
Chapelfield Cl STLY SK15 121 G1
Chapelfield Dr WALK M28 81 G4
Chapel Field Rd
DTN/ASHW M34 132 C5
Chapelfield Rd
WGTN/LGST M12 115 F5
Chapelfield St BOL BL1 33 H3
Chapel Gdns TOT/BURYW BL8 25 H2
Chapel Ga MILN OL16 31 G5
Chapel Gn DTN/ASHW M34 132 C5
Chapel Gv URM M41 139 E1
Chapel Hl LIT OL15 21 E2
Chapelhill Dr BKLY M9 87 H4
Chapel La BKLY M9 87 G4
HALE/TIMP WA15 178 D5
PART M31 151 E3
ROY/SHW OL2 59 E5
SALE M33 139 E5
TOT/BURYW BL8 16 B2
WILM/AE SK9 198 C4
Chapel Meadow WALK M28 96 C3
Chapel Pl BOLS/LL BL3 49 H4
URM M41 111 E5
Chapel Rd IRL M44 136 C1
OLDS OL8 90 D4
PWCH M25 100 C1
SALE M33 154 C1
SWIN M27 98 B3
UPML OL3 94 D1
WILM/AE SK9 200 D4
WYTH/NTH M22 168 C1
Chapel St AUL OL6 119 H2
BNG/LEV M19 144 A2
BOL BL1 3 G3
BOLS/LL BL3 * 66 D1
BRAM/HZG SK7 185 F1
BURY BL9 4 E4
CHD/CHDH SK8 170 A4
CSLFD M3 6 B3
DROY M43 118 A4
DTN/ASHW M34 132 C2
DUK SK16 119 H5
ECC M30 110 D4
FWTH BL4 * 66 B4
HEY OL10 * 41 E4
HTNM SK4 158 A5
HYDE SK14 147 H2
MDTN M24 * 71 H5
MDTN M24 72 C4
MOSL OL5 108 C1
MPL/ROM SK6 162 A1
OLDE OL4 92 D1
PWCH M25 85 H3
ROCH OL11 43 F2
ROY/SHW OL2 59 E5
ROY/SHW OL2 * 60 A2
STLY SK15 120 D3
SWIN M27 99 F1
TOT/BURYW BL8 26 A4
UPML OL3 79 E4
WALK M28 96 A4
WHIT OL12 14 B5
WHIT OL12 19 H1
WILM/AE SK9 200 D4
Chapeltown Rd EDGW/EG BL7 23 G3
RAD M26 68 B3
Chapeltown St CMANE M1 7 K6
Chapel Vw DUK SK16 119 H5
Chapel View Cl HYDE SK14 148 A4
Chapel Wk OLD OL1 75 E3
Chapel Wks CHD/CHDH SK8 193 E1
CMANW M2 6 E4
Chapelway Gdns
ROY/SHW OL2 59 E3
Chaplin Cl SLFD M6 112 D1
Chapman Ms GTN M18 * 130 C3
Chapman Rd HYDE SK14 149 G2
Chapman St BOL BL1 33 E5
GTN M18 130 C2
Chappell Rd DROY M43 117 H3
Chappeltown Rd RAD M26 68 A3
Chapter St NEWH/MOS M40 116 A1
Charcoal Rd ALT WA14 176 C1
Charcoal Woods ALT WA14 176 D1
Chard Dr WYTH/NTH M22 180 C3
Chardin Av MPL/ROM SK6 175 H1
Chard St RAD M26 68 B1
Charges St AULW OL7 119 E4
Chariot St OP/CLY M11 117 E5
Charlbury Av PWCH M25 86 C4
RDSH SK5 145 F5
Charlbury Wy ROY/SHW OL2 59 H4
Charlecote Rd POY/DIS SK12 195 G3
Charles Av DTN/ASHW M34 131 F1
MPL/ROM SK6 174 B3
Charles Ct BOL BL1 * 3 F3
Charles Halle Rd
RUSH/FAL M14 128 B3
Charles Holden St BOL BL1 2 A6
Charles La MILN OL16 44 D1
Charles Ms MILN OL16 * 44 D1
Charles Morris Cl FAIL M35 105 G2
Charles Shaw Cl OLDE OL4 76 D3
Charles St AULW OL7 119 G3
BOL BL1 3 G3
BRAM/HZG SK7 185 E1
BURY BL9 5 F2
CHAD OL9 8 B5
CMANE M1 7 G7
DROY M43 * 117 F4
DTN/ASHW M34 132 C3
EDGW/EG BL7 22 C1
FWTH BL4 66 B3
HEY OL10 56 B1
IRL M44 136 A5
LIT OL15 20 D3
ROY/SHW OL2 59 E5
SLFD M6 113 E1
STKP SK1 13 J7
SWIN M27 98 C1
WHTF M45 69 G5
Charleston Cl SALE M33 153 G4
Charleston Sq URM M41 124 A5
Charleston St OLDS OL8 91 G3
Charlestown Rd BKLY M9 88 A5
Charlestown Rd East
OFTN SK2 184 B1
Charlestown Rd West
EDGY/DAV SK3 184 A1
Charlestown Wy AUL OL6 119 F2
Charles Whittaker St
WHIT OL12 28 C2
Charlesworth Av BOLS/LL BL3 65 G2
DTN/ASHW M34 146 D3
Charlesworth St OP/CLY M11 116 A5
STKP SK1 13 G7
Charlock Sq ALT WA14 165 E1
Charlotte La OLDE OL4 94 B2
Charlotte Pl HALE/TIMP WA15 178 A1
Charlotte St BOL BL1 33 H4
CHD/CHDH SK8 170 A4
CMANW M2 7 F5
MILN OL16 43 G3
RAMS BL0 16 C3
STKP SK1 160 C3
Charlton Av ECC M30 111 E4
HYDE SK14 134 B4
PWCH M25 86 A4
Charlton Dr SALE M33 154 D2
SWIN M27 83 G5
Charlton Fold WALK M28 81 H2
Charlton Pl CMANE M1 128 C1
Charlton Rd BNG/LEV M19 144 B1
Charminster Dr CHH M8 102 C2
Charmouth Wk
WYTH/NTH M22 181 E1
Charnley Cl NEWH/MOS M40 115 H2
Charnley St WHTF M45 69 G4
Charnock Dr BOL BL1 2 D1
Charnville Rd CHD/CHDH SK8 169 E5
Charnwood MPL/ROM SK6 187 E5
Charnwood Av
DTN/ASHW M34 131 G5
Charnwood Cl AUL OL6 107 F3
ROY/SHW OL2 59 F1
WALK M28 81 H5
Charnwood Crs
BRAM/HZG SK7 185 E4
Charnwood Rd BKLY M9 88 A2
MPL/ROM SK6 162 B1
Charter Av RAD M26 68 D3
Charter Cl SALE M33 153 G3
Charter Rd HALE/TIMP WA15 165 H5
Charter St CSLFD M3 114 C2
MILN OL16 43 F2
OLD OL1 75 H4
Chartwell Cl SLFD M6 113 E3
Chartwell Dr NTHM/RTH M23 167 E2
Chase Briar Wd
CHD/CHDH SK8 * 183 E3
Chasefield ALT WA14 176 D2
Chaseley Rd SLFD M6 112 D1
WHIT OL12 10 A4
The Chase WALK M28 97 H5
Chasewood BNG/LEV M19 * 144 A2
Chassen Av URM M41 * 138 A1
Chassen Ct URM M41 * 138 B2
Chassen Rd BOL BL1 48 A2
URM M41 138 B2
Chataway Rd CHH M8 102 C2
Chatburn Av ROCH OL11 57 G2
Chatburn Gdns HEY OL10 40 A4
Chatburn Rd BOL BL1 32 C3
CCHDY M21 141 G3
Chatburn Sq ROCH OL11 57 G1
Chatcombe Rd
WYTH/NTH M22 179 H2
Chatfield Rd CCHDY M21 141 F3
Chatford Cl BRO M7 114 B1
Chatham Ct DID/WITH M20 * 142 C5
Chatham Gdns BOLS/LL BL3 48 C4
Chatham Gv DID/WITH M20 142 C5
Chatham Pl BOLS/LL BL3 * 48 C4
Chatham Rd GTN M18 * 130 D5
OLDTF/WHR M16 127 F5
Chatham St CMANE M1 7 H5
EDGY/DAV SK3 12 C6
HYDE SK14 147 H4
Chatley Rd ECC M30 110 A4
Chatley St CSLFD M3 114 C1
Chatswood Av OFTN SK2 172 A3
Chatsworth Av PWCH M25 86 A3
Chatsworth Cl BURY BL9 53 H4
DROY M43 117 E2
HALE/TIMP WA15 166 D4
ROY/SHW OL2 60 C1
URM M41 139 E1
Chatsworth Gv
OLDTF/WHR M16 141 H1
Chatsworth Ms
BRAM/HZG SK7 183 G2
Chatsworth Rd
BRAM/HZG SK7 185 G3
DROY M43 117 F3
ECC M30 111 G1
GTN M18 130 B3
MPL/ROM SK6 197 E1
RAD M26 51 H4
STRET M32 125 E5
WALK M28 98 A5
WILM/AE SK9 200 B1
Chatsworth St OLDE OL4 92 B2
WHIT OL12 18 D5
Chatterton Cl DID/WITH M20 143 E5
Chattock St OLDTF/WHR M16 127 H5
Chatton Cl TOT/BURYW BL8 37 E5
Chatwood Rd
NEWH/MOS M40 89 G5
Chaucer Av DROY M43 117 H4
DTN/ASHW M34 147 E4
RDSH SK5 144 D3
Chaucer Ms STKP SK1 160 C5
Chaucer Ri DUK SK16 134 B1
Chaucer Rd MDTN M24 73 E2
Chaucer St BOL BL1 33 G5
OLDS OL8 9 F4
ROCH OL11 42 B4
ROY/SHW OL2 59 F4
Chaucer Wk BRUN/LGST M13 128 D2
Chauncy Rd NEWH/MOS M40 104 D2
Chaytor Av NEWH/MOS M40 104 A3
Cheadle Av BRO M7 100 D3
Cheadle Old Rd
EDGY/DAV SK3 171 G2
Cheadle Pl CHD/CHDH SK8 * 171 E4
Cheadle Point CHD/CHDH SK8 170 C3
Cheadle Rd CHD/CHDH SK8 170 B5
Cheadle Sq BOL BL1 2 D5
Cheadle St OP/CLY M11 117 E5
Cheadle Wd CHD/CHDH SK8 182 B4
Cheam Rd HALE/TIMP WA15 166 A1
Cheap Side MDTN M24 72 D2
Cheapside CMANW M2 6 E4
HYDE SK14 133 H5
OLD OL1 9 F3
Cheapside Sq BOL BL1 * 2 E5
Cheddar St GTN M18 130 C3
Cheddington Cl
CHD/CHDH SK8 182 D5
Chedlee Dr CHD/CHDH SK8 182 B3
Chedlin Dr NTHM/RTH M23 167 H5
Chedworth Crs LHULT M38 81 F1
Chedworth Dr
NTHM/RTH M23 168 A3
Chedworth Gv BOLS/LL BL3 * 48 D4
Cheeryble St DROY M43 117 G5
Cheetham Fold Rd
HYDE SK14 147 H3
Cheetham Hl ROY/SHW OL2 59 H3
Cheetham Hill Rd ANC M4 7 F1
CHH M8 102 B3
DUK SK16 133 G2
Cheetham Pl MPL/ROM SK6 161 G2
Cheetham Rd SWIN M27 99 F3
Cheetham St FAIL M35 105 F2
MDTN M24 72 C4
MILN OL16 10 C5
NEWH/MOS M40 * 103 F5
OLD OL1 * 76 A5
RAD M26 52 D5
ROY/SHW OL2 60 B3
Cheetwood Rd CHH M8 102 A5
Cheetwood St BRO M7 114 B1
Chelbourne Dr OLDS OL8 * 90 C5
Chelburn Cl OFTN SK2 173 E4
Chelford Av BOL BL1 33 H1
Chelford Cl HALE/TIMP WA15 165 H3
MDTN M24 73 F2
Chelford Dr SWIN M27 83 H5
Chelford Gv EDGY/DAV SK3 171 F4
Chelford Rd OLDTF/WHR M16 127 F5
SALE M33 155 F4
WILM/AE SK9 192 A2
Chellow Dene MOSL OL5 108 C1
Chell St BRUN/LGST M13 129 G4
Chelmer Cl WHTN BL5 62 A3
Chelmer Gv HEY OL10 40 B3
Chelmsford Av
NEWH/MOS M40 116 C1
Chelmsford Rd EDGY/DAV SK3 12 B6
Chelmsford St OLDS OL8 8 E6
Chelsea Av RAD M26 51 G5
Chelsea Cl ROY/SHW OL2 60 A2
Chelsea Rd BOLS/LL BL3 64 B1
NEWH/MOS M40 104 B5
URM M41 137 E2
Chelsea St BURY BL9 53 G4
ROCH OL11 * 42 C1
Chelsfield Gv CCHDY M21 141 H3
Chelston Av NEWH/MOS M40 89 G5
Chelston Dr CHD/CHDH SK8 191 H1
Cheltenham Crs BRO M7 101 H3
Cheltenham Dr SALE M33 154 D2
Cheltenham Gn MDTN M24 88 D1
Cheltenham Rd CCHDY M21 141 F1
EDGY/DAV SK3 170 D2
MDTN M24 88 D1
Cheltenham St OLD OL1 76 A3
ROCH OL11 42 C2
SLFD M6 113 F1
Chelwood Cl BOL BL1 22 C4
Chelwood Dr DROY M43 117 G3
Chelwood Ms HOR/BR BL6 * 46 C2
Chendre Rd BKLY M9 89 E4
Cheney Cl OP/CLY M11 * 130 C1
Chepstow Av SALE M33 153 F3
Chepstow Cl ROCH OL11 28 C3
Chepstow Dr BRAM/HZG SK7 185 H2
OLD OL1 76 A3
Chepstow Rd CCHDY M21 141 E2
SWIN M27 84 B5
Chepstow St CMANE M1 6 E7
Chepstow St South
CMANE M1 * 6 E7
Chequers Rd CCHDY M21 141 F3
Cherington Cl
NTHM/RTH M23 156 A4
WILM/AE SK9 192 C4
Cherington Rd
CHD/CHDH SK8 169 H5
Cheriton Av SALE M33 154 D1
Cheriton Cl HYDE SK14 149 F1
Cheriton Dr BOLE BL2 50 B3
Cheriton Ri OFTN SK2 173 H3
Cheriton Rd URM M41 137 F1
Cherrington Dr ROCH OL11 57 G1
Cherry Av AUL OL6 107 E4
BURY BL9 39 F3
OLDS OL8 92 B4
Cherry Cl BURY BL9 53 H2
OFTN SK2 173 F2
Cherrycroft MPL/ROM SK6 162 D5
Cherry Dr SWIN M27 99 F2
Cherry Gv ROCH OL11 28 D3
ROY/SHW OL2 58 D3
STLY SK15 120 D5
Cherry Hall Dr ROY/SHW OL2 * 59 F2
Cherry Hinton OLD OL1 * 75 E4
Cherry Holt Av HTNM SK4 158 C2
Cherry La SALE M33 153 F4
Cherry Orchard Cl
BRAM/HZG SK7 183 G3
Cherry St PWCH M25 * 86 B2
Cherryton Wk
BRUN/LGST M13 128 D2
Cherry Tree Av FWTH BL4 65 E4
POY/DIS SK12 195 G4
Cherry Tree Cl
HALE/TIMP WA15 166 C4
MPL/ROM SK6 162 D4
WILM/AE SK9 199 H2
Cherry Tree Ct OFTN SK2 172 D5
Cherry Tree Dr
BRAM/HZG SK7 185 H4
Cherry Tree La MPL/ROM SK6 162 D4
OFTN SK2 172 D4
TOT/BURYW BL8 37 H5
Cherry Tree Rd
CHD/CHDH SK8 182 C3
NTHM/RTH M23 155 G5
Cherry Tree Wk STRET M32 139 H2
Cherry Tree Wy BOLE BL2 34 D1
Cherry Wk CHD/CHDH SK8 183 F4
Cherrywood CHAD OL9 73 G5

Cherrywood Av WHTN BL5 63 H5
Cherrywood Cl WALK M28 96 C2
Chertsey Cl GTN M18 130 D3
ROY/SHW OL2 60 A1
Chervil Cl RUSH/FAL M14 142 D2
Chervil Cl RUSH/FAL M14 143 E3
Cherwell Av HEY OL10 40 B3
Cherwell Cl CHD/CHDH SK8 182 D5
OLDS OL8 105 H1
WHTF M45 69 H4
Cherwell Rd WHTN BL5 62 A2
Chesham Av BOL BL1 33 H4
ROCH OL11 57 G2
URM M41 123 F5
WYTH/NTH M22 168 B5
Chesham Cl WILM/AE SK9 200 C1
Chesham Crs BURY BL9 5 H2
Chesham Fold Rd BURY BL9 5 K2
Chesham Pl ALT WA14 177 F2
Chesham Rd BURY BL9 39 E1
ECC M30 * 110 D5
OLDE OL4 92 B1
WILM/AE SK9 200 C1
Cheshire Cl STRET M32 139 H2
Cheshire Ct RAMS BL0 17 E2
Cheshire Ring Canal Wk
ALT WA14 164 B4
MPL/ROM SK6 147 F5
MPL/ROM SK6 162 D5
POY/DIS SK12 196 C3
Cheshire Rd PART M31 150 C4
STLY SK15 109 E5
Cheshire Sq STLY SK15 109 F5
The Cheshires MOSL OL5 109 E1
Cheshire St MOSL OL5 109 E2
Chesney Av CHAD OL9 89 H5
Chesshyre Av ANC M4 * 115 G4
Chessington Ri SWIN M27 84 B4
Chester Av BOLS/LL BL3 51 E5
DUK SK16 133 H1
HALE/TIMP WA15 178 A2
ROCH OL11 28 D5
SALE M33 153 E5
STLY SK15 121 G2
URM M41 124 D5
WHTF M45 69 H5
Chester Cl BOLS/LL BL3 51 E5
IRL M44 150 C1
WILM/AE SK9 199 H1
Chester Dr RAMS BL0 16 B4
Chesterfield Gv AUL OL6 120 A2
Chesterfield St OLDE OL4 92 A1
Chestergate EDGY/DAV SK3 12 E4
STKP SK1 13 F3
Chester Rd BRAM/HZG SK7 193 G5
HULME M15 127 H1
OLDTF/WHR M16 127 F3
POY/DIS SK12 185 E5
POY/DIS SK12 194 C3
STRET M32 140 A3
Chester St BURY BL9 38 D2
CHAD OL9 8 A7
DTN/ASHW M34 146 D1
EDGY/DAV SK3 12 C4
HULME M15 128 A1
PWCH M25 85 H2
SWIN M27 98 D3
Chesterton Dr BOLS/LL BL3 47 F4
Chesterton Gv DROY M43 117 H3
Chesterton Rd
NTHM/RTH M23 167 E1
Chester Wk BOL BL1 33 H4
Chester Wks MPL/ROM SK6 161 H5
Chestnut Av BURY BL9 5 J4
CCHDY M21 141 F3
CHD/CHDH SK8 170 B4
DROY M43 117 F2
IRL M44 150 C1
TOT/BURYW BL8 37 F1
WALK M28 82 A5
WHTF M45 69 G5
Chestnut Cl BOLS/LL BL3 48 A5
OLDE OL4 76 C4
STLY SK15 120 D5
WILM/AE SK9 199 H2
Chestnut Crs OLDS OL8 91 H5
Chestnut Dr BURY BL9 27 G4
POY/DIS SK12 195 G4
SALE M33 153 G5
WHTN BL5 62 A5
Chestnut Fold RAD M26 52 B5
Chestnut Gdns
DTN/ASHW M34 146 C1
HEY OL10 40 D5
Chestnut Gv FAIL M35 105 E4
RAD M26 68 A4
Chestnut Rd ECC M30 110 B1
Chestnut St CHAD OL9 90 B4
Chestnut Wy LIT OL15 20 C3
Chesworth Cl STKP SK1 13 G5
Chesworth Fold STKP SK1 13 G6
Chetham Cl ORD M5 * 127 E1
Chetwyn Av EDGW/EG BL7 23 F4
ROY/SHW OL2 58 D5
Chetwynd Av URM M41 138 C2
Chetwynd Cl SALE M33 139 E5
Chevassut St HULME M15 127 H2
Chevington Dr BKLY M9 103 E4
HTNM SK4 158 A3
Cheviot Av CHD/CHDH SK8 182 C2
OLDS OL8 91 F4
ROY/SHW OL2 74 D1
Cheviot Cl BOL BL1 33 G1
CHAD OL9 90 B2
HTNM SK4 159 G3
MDTN M24 73 G4
MILN OL16 31 H5
RAMS BL0 16 D4
SLFD M6 112 D2
TOT/BURYW BL8 37 F3
Cheviot Rd BRAM/HZG SK7 184 C3
Cheviots Rd ROY/SHW OL2 59 H1
Cheviot St CSLFD M3 114 C2
Chevithorne Cl ALT WA14 165 E4
Chevril Cl HULME M15 128 B2
Chevron Cl ROCH OL11 42 A3
SLFD M6 113 G3
Chevron Pl ALT WA14 165 G2
Chew Brook Dr UPML OL3 95 E2
Chew Moor La WHTN BL5 62 B2
Chew V DUK SK16 134 A1
UPML OL3 95 E2
Chew Valley Rd UPML OL3 95 E2
Chicago Av MANAIR M90 180 A5
Chichester Cl LIT OL15 20 C5
SALE M33 153 G3
Chichester Crs CHAD OL9 74 B3
Chichester Rd HULME M15 127 H3
MPL/ROM SK6 162 B4
Chichester Rd South
HULME M15 * 127 H3
Chichester St MILN OL16 11 G7
Chidlow Av DID/WITH M20 142 C4
Chidwall Rd WYTH/NTH M22 180 A2
Chief St OLDE OL4 9 K5
Chiffon Wy CSLFD M3 114 A2
Chigwell Cl WYTH/NTH M22 168 D4
Chilcote Av SALE M33 153 H2
Childwall Cl BOLS/LL BL3 64 D2
Chilham Rd ECC M30 111 G1
WALK M28 82 B5
Chilham St BOLS/LL BL3 64 A2
SWIN M27 98 D4
Chilmark Dr NTHM/RTH M23 167 H3
Chiltern Av URM M41 123 G5
Chiltern Cl BRAM/HZG SK7 184 C3
RAMS BL0 16 D4
ROY/SHW OL2 59 G1
WALK M28 97 F2
Chiltern Dr BOLE BL2 49 H2
HALE/TIMP WA15 178 A2
OFTN SK2 172 B5
ROY/SHW OL2 58 D5
SWIN M27 99 E4
TOT/BURYW BL8 37 G2
Chiltern Gdns SALE M33 166 D1
Chiltern Rd RAMS BL0 16 D4
Chilton Av CHAD OL9 90 B1
Chilton Dr MDTN M24 73 F5
Chilworth St RUSH/FAL M14 142 D1
Chime Bank CHH M8 102 D3
Chimes Ct OLDE OL4 93 G2
China La BOL BL1 2 E2
CMANE M1 7 H5
Chingford Wk
BRUN/LGST M13 * 129 G4
Chinley Av NEWH/MOS M40 103 H2
STRET M32 125 F4
Chinley Cl BRAM/HZG SK7 183 H1
HTNM SK4 159 E3
SALE M33 155 E3
Chinley St SLFD M6 101 E5
Chinwell Vw BNG/LEV M19 * 144 A2
Chip Hill Rd BOLS/LL BL3 47 H5
Chippendale Pl AUL OL6 107 H5
Chippenham Av OFTN SK2 172 D2
Chippenham Ct ANC M4 115 G3
Chippenham Rd ANC M4 115 F3
Chipping Fold MILN OL16 44 C1
Chipping Rd BOL BL1 32 C4
Chipstead Av
WGTN/LGST M12 129 F3
Chirmside St TOT/BURYW BL8 37 G5
Chiseldon Av WYTH/NTH M22 180 D2
Chiselhurst St CHH M8 102 B3
Chisholme Cl TOT/BURYW BL8 26 A1
Chisholm St OP/CLY M11 130 C1
Chisledon Av BRO M7 * 102 A4
Chislehurst Av URM M41 124 C5
Chislehurst Cl TOT/BURYW BL8 37 G5
Chiswick Dr RAD M26 51 E4
Chiswick Rd DID/WITH M20 157 H3
Chisworth Cl BRAM/HZG SK7 183 H1
Chisworth St BOLE BL2 34 C3
Choir St BRO M7 114 B1
Chokeberry Cl ALT WA14 165 E1
Cholmondeley Av ALT WA14 * 165 H1
Cholmondeley Rd SLFD M6 112 A1
Chomlea Mnr SLFD M6 * 112 B1
Choral Gv BRO M7 101 G5
Chorley Cl TOT/BURYW BL8 37 E5
Chorley Hall Cl WILM/AE SK9 200 C4
Chorley Hall La
WILM/AE SK9 200 D4
Chorley New Rd BOL BL1 47 F2
HOR/BR BL6 46 B1
Chorley Old Rd BOL BL1 2 A2
BOL BL1 32 B4
Chorley Rd SALE M33 155 F4
SWIN M27 98 C1
Chorley St BOL BL1 2 C3
STRET M32 126 C3
Chorley Wood Av
BNG/LEV M19 * 143 H5
Chorlton Dr CHD/CHDH SK8 170 B3
Chorlton Fold ECC M30 98 C5
Chorlton Gv STKP SK1 172 C2
Chorlton Pl CCHDY M21 141 F2
Chorlton Rd HULME M15 127 H2
Chorlton St CMANE M1 7 G5
OLDTF/WHR M16 127 F3
Chorlton Ter
BRUN/LGST M13 * 128 C2
Chretien Rd WYTH/NTH M22 156 D4
Christchurch Av ORD M5 113 G3
Christ Church Cl BOLE BL2 * 35 G4
Christ Church La BOLE BL2 35 G3
Christchurch Rd SALE M33 153 F1
Christie Rd STRET M32 140 C1
Christie St STKP SK1 13 K7
Christine St ROY/SHW OL2 60 A2
Christleton Av HTNM SK4 159 G1
Christopher Acre ROCH OL11 28 B2
Christopher St
NEWH/MOS M40 117 E1
ORD M5 113 F4
Chronnell Dr BOLE BL2 50 B1
Chudleigh Cl ALT WA14 165 E3
BRAM/HZG SK7 184 B1
Chudleigh Rd CHH M8 87 F5
Chulsey Gate La HOR/BR BL6 46 B5
Chulsey St BOLS/LL BL3 64 A1
Church Av BOLS/LL BL3 48 B5
DTN/ASHW M34 147 E3
HYDE SK14 148 B3
MDTN M24 57 G3
NEWH/MOS M40 104 B5
SLFD M6 112 C3
Church Bank BOL BL1 3 F4
Churchbank STLY SK15 121 G3
Church Brow ALT WA14 177 E2
HYDE SK14 135 H5
HYDE SK14 147 H2
Church Cl RAD M26 67 E4
RAMS BL0 16 C3
WILM/AE SK9 192 A4
Church Ct BURY BL9 * 5 G3
DUK SK16 119 G4
Church Cft BURY BL9 54 A5
Churchdale Rd BKLY M9 87 G3
Church Dr PWCH M25 85 G3
Churchfield Cl RAD M26 68 A3
Churchfield Rd SLFD M6 100 A5
Churchfields ALT WA14 177 E3
DTN/ASHW M34 132 B1
SALE M33 138 D5
Churchfield Wk
OP/CLY M11 * 116 B5
Churchgate BOL BL1 3 F4
STKP SK1 13 G3
URM M41 139 E2
Churchgate Buildings
CMANE M1 * 7 K6
Church Gn RAD M26 53 E5
SLFD M6 * 113 E2
Church Gv BRAM/HZG SK7 185 F2
Churchill Av BOLE BL2 36 C5
Churchill Cl HEY OL10 56 B1
Churchill Crs MPL/ROM SK6 174 C2
RDSH SK5 145 E2
Churchill Dr BOLS/LL BL3 67 F1
FWTH BL4 65 E2
Churchill Rd ALT WA14 165 G2
Churchill St BOLE BL2 49 H2
HTNM SK4 159 G3
OLDE OL4 9 J5
WHIT OL12 29 F2
Churchill St East OLDE OL4 9 K5
Churchill Wy SLFD M6 113 F3
TRPK M17 125 H1
Church La BKLY M9 103 F3
BNG/LEV M19 143 H5
BRAM/HZG SK7 193 F5
BRO M7 101 E1
MILN OL16 10 C7
MOSL OL5 109 E1
MPL/ROM SK6 162 B4
MPL/ROM SK6 174 D3
MPL/ROM SK6 175 F4
OLD OL1 9 G3
PWCH M25 85 H3
SALE M33 139 E5
UPML OL3 79 G3
WHTF M45 69 F4
WILM/AE SK9 200 D3
Churchley Cl EDGY/DAV SK3 170 D3
Churchley Rd EDGY/DAV SK3 170 D2
Church Meadow BURY BL9 54 B5
HYDE SK14 133 F5
UPML OL3 94 B2
Church Mdw BOLE BL2 35 G3
Church Ms
DTN/ASHW M34 132 B5
Church Rd BOL BL1 33 E4
CHD/CHDH SK8 169 F4
CHD/CHDH SK8 183 E5
ECC M30 111 G3
FWTH BL4 66 B4
HTNM SK4 12 D1
MDTN M24 73 G5
MILN OL16 30 C5
RAD M26 66 D4
ROY/SHW OL2 60 A3
SALE M33 155 E2
UPML OL3 79 F4
UPML OL3 94 B2
URM M41 138 A3
URM M41 138 D2
WALK M28 82 A4
WILM/AE SK9 192 A4
WILM/AE SK9 200 B1
WYTH/NTH M22 156 D5
Church Rd East SALE M33 155 E2
Church Rd West
SALE M33 154 D2
Churchside FWTH BL4 65 G5
Churchside Cl BKLY M9 88 A5
Church Stile MILN OL16 10 C7
Churchston Av
BRAM/HZG SK7 184 B2
Church St ALT WA14 165 G4
ANC M4 7 G3
AUL OL6 119 H3
BOLE BL2 35 E1
BOLE BL2 36 C5
BOLS/LL BL3 66 C1
BURY BL9 5 G3
CHD/CHDH SK8 170 A3
DROY M43 118 A4
DTN/ASHW M34 * 132 C1
DUK SK16 119 G5
ECC M30 111 F3
FAIL M35 105 E2
FWTH BL4 66 B5
HEY OL10 41 E4
HTNM SK4 159 H3
HYDE SK14 147 H2
LIT OL15 21 E3
MDTN M24 * 72 D2
MILN OL16 20 A5
MILN OL16 45 E2
MPL/ROM SK6 161 H1
MPL/ROM SK6 175 E4
OLDE OL4 92 D2
RAD M26 68 C2
RAMS BL0 16 D2
ROY/SHW OL2 59 E5
STLY SK15 120 D3
STRET M32 140 A2
SWIN M27 98 D2
SWIN M27 99 G2
TOT/BURYW BL8 37 E1
WHIT OL12 10 A7
WHIT OL12 14 B5
WILM/AE SK9 199 E3
Church St East OLDE OL4 76 D4
RAD M26 52 D5
Church St West RAD M26 68 C1
Church Ter MILN OL16 44 D1
OLD OL1 9 G3
SALE M33 * 139 G5
WILM/AE SK9 192 A3
Churchtown Av BOLE BL2 50 C2
Church Vw HYDE SK14 135 H5
IRL M44 136 C1
WHIT OL12 28 B1
Church Wk ALT WA14 165 G4
FWTH BL4 * 65 H4
STLY SK15 120 D2
SWIN M27 84 A3
TOT/BURYW BL8 * 25 G2
Churchwood Rd
DID/WITH M20 157 G3
Churnet St NEWH/MOS M40 103 E5
Churnett Cl WHTN BL5 62 A2
Churning Ter IRL M44 122 C5
Churston Av BKLY M9 88 B3
Churton Av SALE M33 153 H3
Churton Rd GTN M18 130 B5
Churwell Av HTNM SK4 158 C2
Cicero St BKLY M9 103 F2
OLD OL1 75 H3
Cinamon St WHIT OL12 29 G3
Cinder Hill La OLD OL1 74 B1
Cinder St ANC M4 * 7 K2
Cinnabar Dr MDTN M24 72 C2
Cinnamon Cl WYTH/NTH M22 168 D1
Cipher St ANC M4 7 K1
Circle South TRPK M17 126 B2
The Circuit CHD/CHDH SK8 182 D5
DID/WITH M20 157 G1
EDGY/DAV SK3 171 F3
WILM/AE SK9 198 A5
WILM/AE SK9 201 E2
Circular Rd DID/WITH M20 157 G1
DTN/ASHW M34 146 C2
PWCH M25 101 E1
Circus St CMANE M1 * 7 H5
Cirencester Cl LHULT M38 81 F1
Ciss La URM M41 139 E1
Citrus Wy SLFD M6 113 F3
City Av DTN/ASHW M34 146 C1
City Gdns DTN/ASHW M34 * 146 C1
City Rd HULME M15 127 G2
WALK M28 96 B2
City Rd East HULME M15 128 A1
City Wk SWIN M27 99 G2
Clacton Wk BRUN/LGST M13 * 128 D2
Clague St OP/CLY M11 116 B3
Claife Av NEWH/MOS M40 89 E5
Clammerclough Rd FWTH BL4 66 C4
Clandon Av ECC M30 110 C3
Clapgate MPL/ROM SK6 161 H5
Clapgate Rd ROCH OL11 28 B2
Clapham St NEWH/MOS M40 104 B2
Clara Gorton Ct MILN OL16 * 30 C5
Clara St CHAD OL9 90 D3
ROCH OL11 43 E1
WHIT OL12 14 C4
Clare Av WILM/AE SK9 191 H4
Clarebank BOL BL1 47 G2
Clare Cl TOT/BURYW BL8 38 A1
Claremont Av ALT WA14 165 G1
DID/WITH M20 157 F1
HTNM SK4 159 F1
MPL/ROM SK6 174 B3
Claremont Ct BOL BL1 * 33 H5
Claremont Dr ALT WA14 165 H1
LHULT M38 81 G2
Claremont Gdns AUL OL6 120 B1
Claremont Gv
DID/WITH M20 157 F3
HALE/TIMP WA15 177 H1
Claremont Range GTN M18 * 131 E4
Claremont Rd
CHD/CHDH SK8 182 D4
MILN OL16 44 C1
OFTN SK2 172 C5
OLDTF/WHR M16 128 A5
ROCH OL11 29 F4
SALE M33 154 C1
SLFD M6 112 B1
Claremont St AUL OL6 120 A1
CHAD OL9 * 74 D3
FAIL M35 105 E2
OLDS OL8 91 G5
SLFD M6 99 H4
Clarence Ar AUL OL6 * 119 G3
Clarence Av OLDS OL8 91 E3
TRPK M17 125 E2
WHTF M45 69 H5
Clarence Ct BOL BL1 * 2 C3
WILM/AE SK9 198 D4
Clarence Rd AUL OL6 119 H1
BRUN/LGST M13 129 F5
HALE/TIMP WA15 178 A1
HTNM SK4 159 E1
SWIN M27 98 B3
Clarence St BOL BL1 2 E3
BRO M7 114 A1
CMANW M2 * 6 E5
FWTH BL4 66 B3
HYDE SK14 133 H4
ROY/SHW OL2 75 H1
STLY SK15 120 B4
WHIT OL12 29 G1
Clarendon Av
HALE/TIMP WA15 165 H4
HTNM SK4 159 E3
Clarendon Cottages
WILM/AE SK9 191 F4
Clarendon Crs ECC M30 111 G2
SALE M33 155 E1
Clarendon Gv BOLE BL2 3 J7
Clarendon Pl HYDE SK14 148 A1
Clarendon Rd BOLE BL2 49 H2
BRAM/HZG SK7 185 G1
DTN/ASHW M34 131 G1
DTN/ASHW M34 147 F1
ECC M30 111 G2
HYDE SK14 133 G5
IRL M44 136 A4
OLDTF/WHR M16 141 G1
SALE M33 155 E2
SWIN M27 99 E2
URM M41 123 F5
Clarendon Rd West
CCHDY M21 141 F1
Clarendon St BOLS/LL BL3 48 D5
BURY BL9 5 G1
DUK SK16 119 G5
HULME M15 128 A2
HYDE SK14 133 G5
MILN OL16 43 G2
MOSL OL5 109 E2
RDSH SK5 * 160 A3
WHTF M45 69 G4
Clare Rd BNG/LEV M19 144 A3
RDSH SK5 * 160 A2
Clare St CMANE M1 128 C1
DTN/ASHW M34 132 B4
ORD M5 * 113 H4
Claribel St OP/CLY M11 115 H5
Claridge Rd CCHDY M21 141 E2
Clarion St ANC M4 7 K1
Clark Av GTN M18 130 D3
Clarke Av ORD M5 127 E1
Clarke Brow MDTN M24 72 D3
Clarke Crs HALE/TIMP WA15 178 C1
LHULT M38 80 C1
Clarkes Cft BURY BL9 39 F3
Clarke's La WHIT OL12 29 G3
Clarke St AULW OL7 * 119 E5
BOL BL1 48 B1
HEY OL10 41 E4
MILN OL16 11 G1
Clarksfield Rd OLDE OL4 92 B1
Clarksfield St OLDE OL4 92 C1
Clark's Hl PWCH M25 85 H3
Clarkson Cl DTN/ASHW M34 146 B1
Clark Wy HYDE SK14 133 G5
Clarkwell Cl OLD OL1 8 E1
Claude Av SWIN M27 98 C2
Claude Rd CCHDY M21 141 E4
Claude St CHH M8 102 B1
ECC M30 110 C1
SWIN M27 98 C2
Claudia Sq STLY SK15 109 F5
Claughton Av BOLE BL2 50 C2
WALK M28 96 D2
Claughton Rd TOT/BURYW BL8 37 E1
Claverton Rd NTHM/RTH M23 167 F5
Claxton Av BKLY M9 88 A4
Clay Bank DROY M43 117 F4
Claybank Dr TOT/BURYW BL8 25 H4
Clay Bank St HEY OL10 40 D3
Claybar Dr ECC M30 111 F2
Claybrook Wk OP/CLY M11 * 116 B4
Clayburn Rd HULME M15 127 H2
Claycourt Av ECC M30 110 C1
Claydon Dr RAD M26 51 E4
Clayfield Dr ROCH OL11 28 C3
Claygate Dr BKLY M9 88 A2
Clay La HALE/TIMP WA15 166 D5
NTHM/RTH M23 167 G5
ROCH OL11 28 B3
WILM/AE SK9 191 H2
Claymere Av ROCH OL11 28 B3
Claymore St BOLS/LL BL3 65 E1
GTN M18 130 D2
Clay St EDGW/EG BL7 23 F4
LIT OL15 20 C3
OLDS OL8 91 F3
Claythorpe Wk PWCH M25 86 D5
Clayton Av BOLE BL2 49 G4
DID/WITH M20 157 G3
Claytonbrook Rd
OP/CLY M11 116 D4
Clayton Cl HULME M15 127 H3
TOT/BURYW BL8 37 E5
Clayton Hall Rd OP/CLY M11 116 D3
Clayton La OP/CLY M11 116 C5
Clayton La South
WGTN/LGST M12 129 H1
Claytons Cl OLDE OL4 77 E5
Clayton St BOLE BL2 49 H4
CHAD OL9 90 B4
DTN/ASHW M34 146 D1
DUK SK16 120 A5
FAIL M35 * 104 D3
OP/CLY M11 116 C2
WHIT OL12 11 G1
Cleabarrow Dr WALK M28 96 B5
Cleadon Av GTN M18 130 B4
Cleadon Dr South
TOT/BURYW BL8 37 H1
Clearwater Dr DID/WITH M20 157 E1
Cleavley St ECC M30 110 C3
Clee Av BRUN/LGST M13 143 H1
Cleethorpes Av BKLY M9 87 G4
Cleeve Rd NTHM/RTH M23 155 H4
OLDE OL4 92 B1
Cleeve Wy CHD/CHDH SK8 193 E1
Clegg Hall Rd MILN OL16 31 E1
Clegg Pl AUL OL6 120 A1
Clegg's Buildings BOL BL1 * 2 C3
Clegg's La LHULT M38 81 F2
Clegg St BOLE BL2 49 H2
DROY M43 * 117 G4
LIT OL15 20 C1
MILN OL16 44 D1
MPL/ROM SK6 161 G3
OLD OL1 9 H4
OLDE OL4 93 F1
WHIT OL12 14 B3
WHTF M45 69 G5
Cleggswood Av LIT OL15 20 D5
Clelland St FWTH BL4 66 B5
Clement Ct MILN OL16 * 30 C5
Clementina St WHIT OL12 10 C3
Clementine Cl SLFD M6 113 G3
Clement Rd MPL/ROM SK6 175 G2
Clement Royds St WHIT OL12 10 A5
Clement Stott Cl BKLY M9 88 C3
Clement St HTNM SK4 159 H3
Cleminson St CSLFD M3 6 A3
Clemshaw Cl HEY OL10 40 D5
Clerewood Av CHD/CHDH SK8 181 G5
Clerke St BURY BL9 4 E4
Clevedon Av URM M41 139 G1
Clevedon Rd CHAD OL9 74 B3
Clevedon St BKLY M9 103 F3
Cleveland Av BNG/LEV M19 144 B1
HYDE SK14 * 147 G1
SLFD M6 112 B2
Cleveland Cl RAMS BL0 16 D5
Cleveland Dr MILN OL16 31 H5
Cleveland Gdns BOLS/LL BL3 48 A5
Cleveland Gv ROY/SHW OL2 74 D2
Cleveland Rd CHH M8 87 G5

HALE/TIMP WA15 178 A1
HTNM SK4 158 D2
Cleveland St BOLS/LL BL3 * 48 A5
Cleveleys Av BOLE BL2 49 H1
BURY BL9 53 F2
CCHDY M21 141 G4
CHD/CHDH SK8 181 G3
MILN OL16 43 G3
Cleveleys Gv BRO M7 101 H3
Cleves Ct HEY OL10 40 D5
Clevlands Cl ROY/SHW OL2 59 H1
Cleworth Rd MDTN M24 72 C2
Cleworth St HULME M15 127 G1
Cleworth Wk HULME M15 * 127 G1
Clibran St CHH M8 102 C4
Clifden Dr WYTH/NTH M22 180 D2
Cliff Av BRO M7 101 F4
BURY BL9 27 E1
TOT/BURYW BL8 25 H4
Cliff Crs BRO M7 101 G3
Cliff Dl STLY SK15 120 C5
Cliffdale Dr CHH M8 102 B1
Cliff Gv HTNM SK4 159 E2
Cliff Hill Rd ROY/SHW OL2 45 G5
Cliffmere Cl CHD/CHDH SK8 182 C1
Clifford Av DTN/ASHW M34 132 B3
HALE/TIMP WA15 166 B3
Clifford Rd BOLS/LL BL3 * 63 H2
POY/DIS SK12 194 D3
WILM/AE SK9 198 C4
Clifford St ECC M30 110 C5
ROCH OL11 43 E1
SWIN M27 99 G2
Cliff Rd WILM/AE SK9 199 E2
Cliff Side WILM/AE SK9 199 E2
Cliff St MILN OL16 11 G2
Clifton Av CHD/CHDH SK8 181 F2
ECC M30 111 E2
HALE/TIMP WA15 165 H4
OLDE OL4 * 92 A2
RUSH/FAL M14 143 F3
Clifton Cl HEY OL10 40 D5
OLDE OL4 92 A2
OLDTF/WHR M16 127 G3
Clifton Ct FWTH BL4 65 G2
Clifton Crs ROY/SHW OL2 75 H1
Clifton Dr CHD/CHDH SK8 169 E4
CHD/CHDH SK8 181 F2
MPL/ROM SK6 175 E2
SWIN M27 83 G5
WILM/AE SK9 200 B1
Clifton Gv OLDTF/WHR M16 127 G3
SWIN M27 83 G5
Clifton House Rd SWIN M27 83 H3
Clifton Park Rd OFTN SK2 172 B4
Clifton Pl PWCH M25 * 85 H2
Clifton Rd CCHDY M21 141 G3
ECC M30 111 E2
HTNM SK4 158 D2
MDTN M24 57 G3
PWCH M25 85 F3
SALE M33 154 C3
URM M41 138 A1
Clifton St AUL OL6 119 F2
BOL BL1 2 C3
BURY BL9 38 C2
FAIL M35 105 F1
FWTH BL4 65 G2
FWTH BL4 66 C5
MILN OL16 31 G5
NEWH/MOS M40 116 A1
OLDTF/WHR M16 127 G3
ROCH OL11 * 43 F1
UPML OL3 95 E2
WILM/AE SK9 200 D4
Clifton Vw SWIN M27 83 H3
Cliftonville Dr SWIN M27 99 G4
Cliftonville Rd MILN OL16 58 D1
Clinton Av RUSH/FAL M14 142 C1
Clinton Gdns RUSH/FAL M14 142 C1
Clinton St AUL OL6 * 120 A1
Clinton Wk OLDE OL4 * 9 J5
Clippers Quay SALQ M50 126 D2
Clipsley Crs OLDE OL4 61 E5
Cliston Wk BRAM/HZG SK7 184 B2
Clitheroe Cl HEY OL10 41 E3
Clitheroe Dr TOT/BURYW BL8 37 E4
Clitheroe Rd BRUN/LGST M13 129 G5
Clito St BKLY M9 103 G2
Clive Av WHTF M45 69 F3
Clivedale Pl BOL BL1 3 F5
Clively Av SWIN M27 99 G1
Clive Rd FAIL M35 104 D3
Clive St ANC M4 7 H1
AULW OL7 106 D5
BOL BL1 3 F5
OLDS OL8 91 E5
Clivia Gv BRO M7 * 101 G4
Clock House Av DROY M43 117 F2
Clockhouse Ms DROY M43 * 117 F2
Clock St CHAD OL9 90 C5
Clock Tower Cl HYDE SK14 148 A2
WALK M28 81 E4
Cloister Cl DUK SK16 133 F2
Cloister Rd HTNM SK4 158 A4
The Cloisters CHD/CHDH SK8 170 D4
MILN OL16 11 H2
SALE M33 155 E2
Cloister St BKLY M9 103 G2
BOL BL1 33 F4
Clopton Wk HULME M15 127 H2
Closes Farm BOLS/LL BL3 64 A2
The Close ALT WA14 165 F4
BOLE BL2 34 C3
DTN/ASHW M34 132 A4
MDTN M24 73 E1
MPL/ROM SK6 163 G5
STLY SK15 120 C2
TOT/BURYW BL8 26 D5
Clothorn Rd DID/WITH M20 157 G2
Cloudstock Gv LHULT M38 80 D2
Clough Av MPL/ROM SK6 175 H3
SALE M33 153 G5
WHTN BL5 62 A4
WILM/AE SK9 191 G5
Clough Bank BKLY M9 * 88 A5
Cloughbank RAD M26 67 F5
Clough Dr PWCH M25 85 G3
Clough End Rd HYDE SK14 149 H2
Cloughfield Av ORD M5 113 G5
Cloughfold RAD M26 67 E5
Clough Fold Rd HYDE SK14 147 H2
Clough Ga HYDE SK14 * 148 B3
OLDS OL8 91 E5
Clough Gv WHTF M45 69 E2
Clough House La WHIT OL12 19 G2
Clough La HEY OL10 40 D2
OLDE OL4 94 B1
PWCH M25 85 G3
Clough Meadow BOL BL1 47 E3
MPL/ROM SK6 162 B1
Clough Meadow Rd RAD M26 67 H1
Clough Park Av OLDE OL4 94 B1
Clough Rd BKLY M9 103 G2
DROY M43 118 A3
FAIL M35 105 F3
MDTN M24 72 D2
ROY/SHW OL2 60 C3
Cloughs Av CHAD OL9 73 G4
Clough Side MPL/ROM SK6 175 H2
Clough St FWTH BL4 66 C5
MDTN M24 73 E2
NEWH/MOS M40 116 D1
RAD M26 68 D3
WHIT OL12 19 H2
Clough Ter LIT OL15 * 20 D1
The Clough AULW OL7 106 D4
BOL BL1 * 47 F1
RDSH SK5 145 H5
Clough Top Rd BKLY M9 88 D5
Clovelly Av OLDS OL8 90 D5
Clovelly Rd CCHDY M21 141 G3
OFTN SK2 172 D1
SWIN M27 98 B3
Clovelly St NEWH/MOS M40 * 104 C5
ROCH OL11 42 A3
Clover Av EDGY/DAV SK3 171 G5
Cloverbank Av BNG/LEV M19 158 A2
Clover Crs OLDS OL8 92 B4
Clover Cft SALE M33 155 E5
Cloverdale Sq BOL BL1 32 D5
Clover Hall Crs MILN OL16 11 K3
Cloverley Dr
HALE/TIMP WA15 166 B5
Clover Rd HALE/TIMP WA15 166 B4
MPL/ROM SK6 162 D3
Clover St WHIT OL12 10 B5
Clover Vw MILN OL16 * 11 H5
Clowes St CHAD OL9 90 B5
CSLFD M3 6 C3
WGTN/LGST M12 129 H2
Club St OP/CLY M11 131 E1
Clumber Cl POY/DIS SK12 195 F4
Clumber Rd GTN M18 131 E4
POY/DIS SK12 195 F4
Clunton Av BOLS/LL BL3 48 A5
Clutha Rd EDGY/DAV SK3 172 A5
Clwyd Av EDGY/DAV SK3 171 G2
Clyde Av WHTF M45 85 G1
Clyde Ct MILN OL16 30 C5
Clyde Rd DID/WITH M20 157 E2
EDGY/DAV SK3 12 B7
RAD M26 52 A4
Clydesdale St OLDS OL8 91 F3
Clyde St AULW OL7 119 E4
BOL BL1 * 33 H4
OLD OL1 76 B3
Clyde Ter RAD M26 * 52 A4
Clyne St STRET M32 126 C3
Coach La ROCH OL11 41 F1
Coalbrook Wk
WGTN/LGST M12 115 G5
Coalburn St WGTN/LGST M12 129 H3
Coal Pit La OLDS OL8 106 A3
Coalshaw Green Rd CHAD OL9 90 B4
Coatbridge St OP/CLY M11 116 D4
Cobalt Av URM M41 125 E2
Cobb Cl CHH M8 86 D4
Cobbett's Wy WILM/AE SK9 200 C1
Cobble Bank BKLY M9 87 H4
Cobden St AUL OL6 * 120 A3
BKLY M9 103 F1
BOL BL1 33 G3
BURY BL9 5 G2
CHAD OL9 74 C5
EDGW/EG BL7 * 22 C1
HEY OL10 41 E5
OLDE OL4 76 C3
RAD M26 52 A3
SLFD M6 113 E1
Coberley Av URM M41 123 G4
Cob Hall Rd STRET M32 140 A2
Cobham Av BOLS/LL BL3 64 C1
NEWH/MOS M40 89 F5
Cobourg St CMANE M1 7 H6
Coburg Av BRO M7 114 A1
Cochrane Av WGTN/LGST M12 129 F3
Cochrane St BOLS/LL BL3 49 E4
Cock Brow HYDE SK14 149 E4
Cock Clod St RAD M26 68 D1
Cockcroft Rd ORD M5 113 H3
Cockcroft St BKLY M9 103 E1
Cockerell Springs BOLE BL2 * 3 G6
Cocker Hl STLY SK15 121 E3
Cocker Mill La ROY/SHW OL2 59 G4
Cockers La STLY SK15 121 H5
Cocker St LHULT M38 81 F3
Cockey Moor Rd BOLE BL2 36 C5
Cock Hall La WHIT OL12 14 A4
Cockhall La WHIT OL12 14 B4
Coconut Gv SLFD M6 113 F3
Codale Dr BOLE BL2 50 C1
Coddington Av OP/CLY M11 117 F5
Coe St BOLS/LL BL3 49 E4
Coghlan Cl OP/CLY M11 * 116 C3
Coin St ROY/SHW OL2 59 F5
Colborne Av ECC M30 110 C3
MPL/ROM SK6 162 A4
RDSH SK5 * 131 E5
Colbourne Av CHH M8 102 A1
Colbourne Gv HYDE SK14 135 F5
Colchester Av BOLE BL2 50 B1
Colchester Cl NTHM/RTH M23 155 F5
Colchester Dr FWTH BL4 65 E3
Colchester Pl HTNM SK4 159 E3
Colchester Wk OLD OL1 9 G2
Colclough Cl NEWH/MOS M40 104 A4
Coldfield Dr NTHM/RTH M23 167 G3
Cold Greave Cl MILN OL16 45 F2
Coldhurst St OLD OL1 75 F4
Coldstream Av BKLY M9 88 A3
Colebrook Dr
NEWH/MOS M40 103 H4
Colebrook Rd
HALE/TIMP WA15 166 B3
Coleby Av OLDTF/WHR M16 127 F4
WYTH/NTH M22 181 E3
Coledale Dr MDTN M24 71 H2
Coleford Gv BOL BL1 2 C6
Colemore Av DID/WITH M20 158 A3
Colenso Ct BOLE BL2 * 49 H2
Colenso Gv HTNM SK4 159 E3
Colenso St OLDS OL8 91 E4
Coleport Cl CHD/CHDH SK8 182 D3
Coleridge Av MDTN M24 73 F1
RAD M26 67 H1
Coleridge Cl RDSH SK5 145 E2
Coleridge Rd LIT OL15 31 G1
OLD OL1 60 D5
OLDTF/WHR M16 127 F5
RDSH SK5 145 E2
TOT/BURYW BL8 26 A1
Colesbourne Cl LHULT M38 81 F1
Coleshill St NEWH/MOS M40 115 H2
Cole St NEWH/MOS M40 103 G2
Colgate Crs RUSH/FAL M14 142 D3
Colgate La ORD M5 126 D2
Colgrove Av NEWH/MOS M40 89 F5
Colina Dr BRO M7 101 H5
Colindale Av BKLY M9 88 B3
Colindale Cl BOLS/LL BL3 * 48 B4
Colin Murphy Rd HULME M15 127 H1
Colin Rd HTNM SK4 159 H2
Colinton Cl BOL BL1 33 G5
Colinwood Cl BURY BL9 69 G1
Coll Dr URM M41 124 C3
College Av OLDS OL8 91 E4
College Cl BOLS/LL BL3 2 D7
OFTN SK2 172 C3
WILM/AE SK9 198 B2
College Dr OLDTF/WHR M16 141 G1
College Rd ECC M30 111 H3
OLDS OL8 91 E3
OLDTF/WHR M16 141 H1
WHIT OL12 29 G4
College Wy BOLS/LL BL3 2 C7
Collegiate Wy SWIN M27 84 A4
Collen Crs TOT/BURYW BL8 26 C5
Collett St OLD OL1 76 B4
Colley St MILN OL16 11 F3
STRET M32 126 C3
Collie Av SLFD M6 101 F5
Collier Av MILN OL16 31 G4
Collier Cl HYDE SK14 149 G2
Collier Hl OLDS OL8 91 E4
Collier Hill Av OLDS OL8 90 D4
Collier's Ct ROCH OL11 43 G5
Colliers Row Rd BOL BL1 32 A1
Collier St CSLFD M3 6 C2
CSLFD M3 6 C7
SWIN M27 98 D3
Colliery St OP/CLY M11 116 B4
Collin Av GTN M18 130 B4
Collingburn Av ORD M5 127 E1
Colling Cl IRL M44 136 C2
Collinge Av MDTN M24 73 F4
Collinge St HEY OL10 40 D4
MDTN M24 73 G5
ROY/SHW OL2 * 60 A2
TOT/BURYW BL8 37 G2
Collingham St CHH M8 114 D1
Colling St RAMS BL0 * 16 C3
Collington Cl WGTN/LGST M12 129 H3
Collingwood Av DROY M43 117 F2
Collingwood Cl POY/DIS SK12 195 H4
Collingwood Dr SWIN M27 99 F3
Collingwood Rd
BNG/LEV M19 143 H2
Collingwood St ROCH OL11 57 F1
Collingwood Wy OLD OL1 * 75 G4
Collins St TOT/BURYW BL8 37 E2
Collins Wy CHAD OL9 90 D4
Collop Dr HEY OL10 56 B2
Collyhurst Av WALK M28 82 B5
Collyhurst Rd
NEWH/MOS M40 115 E1
Collyhurst St
NEWH/MOS M40 115 F1
Colman Gdns ORD M5 127 E1
Colmore Dr BKLY M9 88 D3
Colmore Gv BOLE BL2 34 C2
Colmore St BOLE BL2 34 C3
Colne St ROCH OL11 42 C5
Colonial Rd OFTN SK2 172 B3
Colshaw Dr WILM/AE SK9 199 G1
Colshaw Rd NTHM/RTH M23 167 H4
Colson Dr MDTN M24 72 C5
Colt Hill La UPML OL3 78 D5
Coltsfoot Dr ALT WA14 165 E1
Columbia Av GTN M18 131 E4
Columbia Rd BOL BL1 48 B1
Columbia St OLDS OL8 * 91 G3
Columbine Cl WHIT OL12 18 B5
Columbine St OP/CLY M11 130 C1
Colville Dr TOT/BURYW BL8 37 G5
Colville Gv HALE/TIMP WA15 166 B3
SALE M33 153 H5
Colville Rd OLD OL1 75 E3
Colwell Av STRET M32 139 H2
Colwick Av ALT WA14 165 H3
Colwith Av BOLE BL2 35 F5
Colwyn Av MDTN M24 88 D1
RUSH/FAL M14 143 G3
Colwyn Crs RDSH SK5 160 A1
Colwyn Rd BRAM/HZG SK7 184 A4
CHD/CHDH SK8 182 B3
SWIN M27 98 B4
Colwyn St CHAD OL9 8 C3
ROCH OL11 42 A4
SLFD M6 113 E2
Combe Cl OP/CLY M11 116 C2
Combermere Av
DID/WITH M20 142 C4
Combermere Cl
CHD/CHDH SK8 170 C5
Combermere St DUK SK16 119 H4
Comer Ter SALE M33 154 B2
Comet St CMANE M1 7 J5
Commercial Av
CHD/CHDH SK8 192 B2
Commercial Brow HYDE SK14 133 H4
Commercial Rd
BRAM/HZG SK7 185 E1
Commercial St CHAD OL9 8 B5
HULME M15 127 H1
HYDE SK14 133 H5
Common La PART M31 151 H2
Common Side Rd WALK M28 96 A3
Community St AULW OL7 119 E4
Como St BOLS/LL BL3 * 48 B5
Como Wk GTN M18 130 A2
Compass St OP/CLY M11 130 B1
Compstall Av RUSH/FAL M14 142 D2
Compstall Gv GTN M18 * 130 D2
Compstall Mills Est
MPL/ROM SK6 * 163 G4
Compstall Rd MPL/ROM SK6 162 C4
Compton Cl URM M41 137 E2
Compton Dr
NTHM/RTH M23 * 179 H2
Compton Fold ROY/SHW OL2 45 F5
Compton Wy MDTN M24 73 F5
Comus St ORD M5 113 H5
Concert La CMANW M2 7 F5
Concord Pl SLFD M6 100 D5
Condor Cl DROY M43 * 118 B2
Condor Pl SLFD M6 100 D5
Condor Wk BRUN/LGST M13 * 128 C2
Conduit St AUL OL6 119 H3
OLD OL1 76 C1
Conewood Wk
BRUN/LGST M13 128 D2
Coney Gv NTHM/RTH M23 167 H2
Coneymead STLY SK15 120 D1
Congham Rd EDGY/DAV SK3 12 A6
Congleton Av RUSH/FAL M14 142 C1
Congleton Cl WILM/AE SK9 200 D5
Congou St CMANE M1 7 K6
Congreave St OLD OL1 8 E1
Coningsby Dr BKLY M9 103 E2
Conisber Cl EDGW/EG BL7 22 D2
Conisborough ROCH OL11 * 29 H5
Conisborough Pl WHTF M45 70 A5
Coniston BOL BL1 * 34 A3
Coniston Av BKLY M9 103 E2
FWTH BL4 64 D5
HYDE SK14 133 F4
LHULT M38 81 F3
OLDS OL8 91 E4
SALE M33 154 D4
WHTF M45 69 G4
Coniston Cl BOLS/LL BL3 50 D5
CHAD OL9 74 B5
DTN/ASHW M34 145 H1
RAMS BL0 16 D1
Coniston Dr BURY BL9 53 F2
MDTN M24 72 B2
STLY SK15 120 D2
WILM/AE SK9 191 H3
Coniston Gv AULW OL7 119 F1
HEY OL10 56 A1
LHULT M38 81 F3
ROY/SHW OL2 59 E3
Coniston Rd CHD/CHDH SK8 169 G3
MPL/ROM SK6 186 D4
PART M31 150 D2
RDSH SK5 145 F5
STRET M32 125 H5
SWIN M27 99 E4
URM M41 137 G3
Coniston St NEWH/MOS M40 104 B5
SLFD M6 113 G1
Coniston Wk
HALE/TIMP WA15 167 E4
Conival Wy CHAD OL9 74 B3
Conmere Sq HULME M15 128 A1
Connaught Av BNG/LEV M19 143 H4
MILN OL16 43 G3
WHTF M45 69 H5
Connaught Cl WILM/AE SK9 199 F2
Connaught Sq BOLE BL2 34 C5
Connaught St OLDS OL8 9 F5
TOT/BURYW BL8 37 G5
Connel Cl BOLE BL2 50 C3
Connell Rd NTHM/RTH M23 167 H3
Connell Wy HEY OL10 * 41 G3
Connery Crs AUL OL6 107 G4
Connie St OP/CLY M11 116 D5
Conningsby Cl EDGW/EG BL7 23 E3
Connington Av BKLY M9 103 E1
Connington Cl ROY/SHW OL2 58 D5
Connor Wy CHD/CHDH SK8 169 E5
Conrad Cl OLD OL1 60 D5
Conran St BKLY M9 103 E3
Consett Av NTHM/RTH M23 167 H3
Consort Av ROY/SHW OL2 58 D3
Consort Cl DUK SK16 133 F2
Consort Pl ALT WA14 177 E1
Constable Cl BOL BL1 33 G5
Constable Dr MPL/ROM SK6 175 G1
WILM/AE SK9 199 H2
Constable St GTN M18 130 D2
Constance Gdns ORD M5 113 E4
Constance Rd BOLS/LL BL3 48 B4
PART M31 151 E3
Constance St
HULME M15 * 127 H1
Constantine Rd MILN OL16 10 D6
Constantine St OLDE OL4 92 C1
Consul St WYTH/NTH M22 156 D5
Convamore Rd
BRAM/HZG SK7 193 G1
Convent Gv ROCH OL11 42 C1
Convent St OLDE OL4 92 B3
Conway Av BOL BL1 32 D5
IRL M44 136 B3
SWIN M27 84 C5
WHTF M45 69 G5
Conway Cl HEY OL10 40 B3
MDTN M24 72 D5
OLDTF/WHR M16 * 126 D5
RAMS BL0 16 C2
Conway Crs TOT/BURYW BL8 26 A1
Conway Dr BRAM/HZG SK7 184 D3
BURY BL9 39 G4
HALE/TIMP WA15 166 D3
STLY SK15 120 D2
Conway Gv CHAD OL9 74 A4
Conway Rd CHD/CHDH SK8 182 B2
SALE M33 155 E3
URM M41 124 C4
Conway St FWTH BL4 66 A5
RDSH SK5 159 H2
Conyngham Rd
RUSH/FAL M14 129 E4
Cooke St BRAM/HZG SK7 185 E1
DTN/ASHW M34 132 C5
FAIL M35 105 E2
FWTH BL4 66 B5
HYDE SK14 134 A3
Cook St BURY BL9 5 F5
CSLFD M3 6 B3
DTN/ASHW M34 132 C2
ECC M30 110 D3
EDGY/DAV SK3 12 E4
MILN OL16 11 G2
OLDE OL4 76 B5
Cook Ter MILN OL16 11 G2
Coomassie St HEY OL10 40 D4
RAD M26 68 B1
SLFD M6 * 113 E2
Coombes Av HYDE SK14 148 B2
MPL/ROM SK6 175 E4
Coombes St OFTN SK2 172 C4
Coombes Vw HYDE SK14 149 H3
Co-operation St FAIL M35 105 E1
Co-operative St
BRAM/HZG SK7 185 F1
LHULT M38 * 80 D2
OLDE OL4 93 E1
ROY/SHW OL2 * 60 A2
SLFD M6 113 E3
UPML OL3 * 79 E4
Cooper Fold MDTN M24 56 D5
Cooper La BKLY M9 88 A2
MDTN M24 72 C1
Cooper St BRAM/HZG SK7 185 G1
BURY BL9 4 D4
CMANW M2 6 E5
DROY M43 * 117 F4
DUK SK16 119 G4
OFTN SK2 13 H7
OLDE OL4 77 F5
STRET M32 140 B2
WHIT OL12 20 A4
Coopers Wk MILN OL16 30 D1
Cooper Ter MILN OL16 11 G4
Coop St ANC M4 * 7 H2
BOL BL1 33 H2
Copage Dr MPL/ROM SK6 161 H2
Cope Bank BOL BL1 33 F5
Cope Bank West BOL BL1 * 33 E4
Cope Cl OP/CLY M11 * 130 D1
Copeland Av SWIN M27 99 H1
Copeland Cl MDTN M24 71 H3
Copeland Ms BOL BL1 47 H2
Copeland St HYDE SK14 133 G3
Copeman Cl BRUN/LGST M13 128 D2
Copenhagen Sq MILN OL16 * 11 F5
Copenhagen St MILN OL16 11 F5
NEWH/MOS M40 103 H4
Cope St BOL BL1 33 F5
Copgrove Rd CCHDY M21 141 F4
Copley Av STLY SK15 121 F3
Copley Park Ms STLY SK15 121 F3
Copley Rd CCHDY M21 141 E1
Copley St ROY/SHW OL2 * 60 A1
Copperas La DROY M43 117 F5
Copperas St ANC M4 7 G3
Copperbeech Cl
WYTH/NTH M22 156 D5
Copper Beech Dr STLY SK15 121 G2
Copperfield Ct ALT WA14 177 F1
Copperfield Rd
CHD/CHDH SK8 193 E2
POY/DIS SK12 195 E5
Copperfields HOR/BR BL6 62 C1
WILM/AE SK9 199 F2
Copper La WHTF M45 68 C5
Coppice Av POY/DIS SK12 197 F1
SALE M33 153 G4
Coppice Cl HOR/BR BL6 62 B1
MPL/ROM SK6 162 A2
Coppice Ct CHD/CHDH SK8 181 G4
Coppice Dr WHIT OL12 18 B1
WYTH/NTH M22 156 C5
Coppice La POY/DIS SK12 197 F1
Coppice Rd POY/DIS SK12 196 A4
Coppice St OLDS OL8 8 C6
The Coppice BKLY M9 88 D5
BOLE BL2 35 E1
HALE/TIMP WA15 178 C4
PWCH M25 85 H3
RAMS BL0 16 B4
WALK M28 97 G2
WALK M28 98 B5
Coppice Wk DTN/ASHW M34 146 B1
Coppice Wy WILM/AE SK9 192 B4
Coppingford Cl WHIT OL12 28 D1
Copping St WGTN/LGST M12 129 G2
The Coppins WILM/AE SK9 200 B1
Coppleridge Dr CHH M8 87 F5
Copplestone Dr SALE M33 153 F1
Coppy Bridge Dr MILN OL16 31 E3
Cop Rd OLD OL1 60 B5
Copse Av WYTH/NTH M22 180 D1
Copse Dr BURY BL9 27 G5
The Copse EDGW/EG BL7 23 H1
HALE/TIMP WA15 179 E5
MPL/ROM SK6 175 H1
Copson St DID/WITH M20 142 D4
Copster Av OLDS OL8 91 F4
Copster Hill Rd OLDS OL8 91 F4
Copster Pl OLDS OL8 91 F4
Copthall La CHH M8 102 A2
Copthorne Cl HEY OL10 56 A1
Copthorne Crs
BRUN/LGST M13 143 G1
Copthorne Dr BOLE BL2 50 B3
Copthorn Wk
TOT/BURYW BL8 37 E1
Coptrod Head Cl WHIT OL12 18 D4
Coral Av CHD/CHDH SK8 182 D3
Coral Rd CHD/CHDH SK8 182 D3
Coral St BRUN/LGST M13 128 D1
Coram St GTN M18 131 E2
Corbar Rd OFTN SK2 172 C4
Corbel Wy ECC M30 111 E2
Corbett St MILN OL16 11 F4
OP/CLY M11 116 B4

Corbrook Rd CHAD OL9 73 H3
Corby St WGTN/LGST M12 129 H2
Corcoran Dr MPL/ROM SK6 163 E4
Corda Av WYTH/NTH M22 168 C1
Cordingley Av DROY M43 117 G5
Cordova Av DTN/ASHW M34 131 E5
Corelli St NEWH/MOS M40 116 A1
Corfe Cl URM M41 137 E2
Corfe Crs BRAM/HZG SK7 185 E3
Corinthian Av BRO M7 101 F5
Corkland Cl AUL OL6 120 A3
Corkland Rd CCHDY M21 141 F3
Corkland St AUL OL6 120 B3
Cork St BURY BL9 5 H4
WGTN/LGST M12 115 G5
Corley Av EDGY/DAV SK3 170 C2
Corley Wk OP/CLY M11 * 116 A4
Cormallen Gv FAIL M35 105 F3
Cormorant Cl LHULT M38 81 H4
Cornall St TOT/BURYW BL8 37 H3
Cornbrook Arches
HULME M15 127 F1
Cornbrook Cl WHIT OL12 19 H2
Cornbrook Gv
OLDTF/WHR M16 127 G3
Cornbrook Park Rd
HULME M15 127 F2
Cornbrook St
OLDTF/WHR M16 127 G3
Cornbrook Wy
OLDTF/WHR M16 127 G3
Corn Cl BRUN/LGST M13 128 D3
Cornell St ANC M4 7 J2
Corner Brook HOR/BR BL6 62 B1
Corner Cft WILM/AE SK9 200 D1
Corner St AUL OL6 119 H3
Cornet St BRO M7 101 G5
Cornfield STLY SK15 135 F1
Cornfield Cl BURY BL9 27 G4
SALE M33 * 155 G3
Cornfield Dr
WYTH/NTH M22 180 B1
Cornfield Rd MPL/ROM SK6 162 D3
Cornfield St MILN OL16 44 D1
Cornford Av GTN M18 130 A5
Corn Hey Rd SALE M33 153 F4
Cornhill Av URM M41 124 A5
Corn Hill La DTN/ASHW M34 131 F3
Cornhill Rd URM M41 124 A5
Cornhill St OLD OL1 76 B2
Cornish Wy ROY/SHW OL2 75 G1
Cornishway WYTH/NTH M22 180 C4
Cornlea Dr WALK M28 96 D3
Corn Mill Cl WHIT OL12 19 H4
Corn Mill La STLY SK15 121 E4
Corn St FAIL M35 104 B4
OLDE OL4 9 K3
Cornwall Av BNG/LEV M19 144 B3
WHTN BL5 63 G4
Cornwall Cl MPL/ROM SK6 186 D5
Cornwall Crs RDSH SK5 146 A5
Cornwall Dr BURY BL9 53 H1
Cornwall Rd CHD/CHDH SK8 181 G4
DROY M43 117 H2
IRL M44 150 C1
Cornwall St CHAD OL9 90 C2
ECC M30 110 D4
OP/CLY M11 130 C1
Cornwell Cl WILM/AE SK9 199 G2
Corona Av HYDE SK14 133 H5
OLDS OL8 91 E4
Coronation Av DUK SK16 133 H1
HEY OL10 56 B1
HYDE SK14 148 A2
Coronation Gdns RAD M26 51 H5
Coronation Rd AUL OL6 107 F4
DROY M43 117 G2
FAIL M35 104 D4
RAD M26 51 H5
Coronation Sq
WGTN/LGST M12 115 F5
Coronation St BOL BL1 2 E5
DTN/ASHW M34 131 H5
OP/CLY M11 * 116 D5
ORD M5 113 G5
RDSH SK5 159 H2
SWIN M27 99 F1
Corporation Rd
DTN/ASHW M34 132 A3
ROCH OL11 29 G5
Corporation St BOL BL1 2 E4
CMANW M2 6 E4
HYDE SK14 * 147 H1
MDTN M24 72 D4
STKP SK1 13 H2
STLY SK15 120 D4
Corran Cl ECC M30 110 C3
Correction Brow
POY/DIS SK12 196 B1
Corrie Cl DTN/ASHW M34 146 D2
Corrie Crs FWTH BL4 83 G3
Corrie Dr FWTH BL4 83 G3
Corrie Rd SWIN M27 84 B4
Corrie St LHULT M38 81 F3
Corrie Wy MPL/ROM SK6 161 F1
Corrigan St GTN M18 130 D2
Corringham Rd BNG/LEV M19 144 C4
Corring Wy BOL BL1 34 C2
Corriss Av BKLY M9 87 F2
Corry St HEY OL10 41 F4
Corson St BOLS/LL BL3 66 A2
Corwen Av BKLY M9 103 F2
Corwen Cl OLDS OL8 90 C5
Cosgrove Crs FAIL M35 104 D5
Cosgrove Rd FAIL M35 104 D5
Cosham Rd WYTH/NTH M22 181 E1
Costobadie Cl HYDE SK14 135 G5
Cotaline Cl ROCH OL11 42 A3
Cotefield Av BOLS/LL BL3 65 E1
Cotefield Cl MPL/ROM SK6 * 175 E4
Cotefield Rd WYTH/NTH M22 180 A2
Cote Green La MPL/ROM SK6 163 G5
Cote Green Rd MPL/ROM SK6 163 H5
Cote La LIT OL15 20 C2
MOSL OL5 94 B4
Cotford Rd BOL BL1 34 A1
Cotham St CSLFD M3 114 C2
Cotman Dr MPL/ROM SK6 175 H1
Cotswold Av BRAM/HZG SK7 184 C3
CHAD OL9 90 B2
ROY/SHW OL2 59 G1
URM M41 123 G5
Cotswold Cl PWCH M25 86 B2
RAMS BL0 16 D4
Cotswold Crs MILN OL16 31 H4
TOT/BURYW BL8 37 G3
Cotswold Dr ROY/SHW OL2 74 C1
SLFD M6 113 E2
Cotswold Rd HTNM SK4 159 G3
Cottage Cft BOLE BL2 35 E1
Cottage Gdns MPL/ROM SK6 161 E3
Cottage Gv WILM/AE SK9 198 B5
The Cottages OLDE OL4 * 77 E5
Cottam Crs MPL/ROM SK6 175 G2
Cottam Gv SWIN M27 99 F3
Cottam St OLD OL1 75 E4
TOT/BURYW BL8 37 H3
Cottenham La BRO M7 114 B1
Cottenham St
BRUN/LGST M13 128 C2
Cotterdale Cl
OLDTF/WHR M16 141 H1
Cotterill Cl SALE M33 154 D5
Cotterill St SLFD M6 113 F3
Cotter St WGTN/LGST M12 128 D1
Cottesmore Cl WHIT OL12 18 B2
Cottesmore Dr CHH M8 102 D2
Cottesmore Gdns
HALE/TIMP WA15 178 D4
Cottingham Dr AUL OL6 119 H1
Cottingham Rd
WGTN/LGST M12 129 F2
Cottingley Cl BOL BL1 33 G1
Cotton Cl HYDE SK14 148 A2
Cottonfield Rd DID/WITH M20 143 E5
Cottonfields EDGW/EG BL7 23 E4
Cotton Fold MILN OL16 30 D5
Cotton Hl DID/WITH M20 157 H1
Cotton La DID/WITH M20 143 E5
Cotton Mill Crs CHAD OL9 90 C3
Cotton St ANC M4 7 J3
BOL BL1 33 G4
Cotton St East AUL OL6 119 G2
Cotton St West AUL OL6 119 F3
Cotton Tree Cl OLDE OL4 76 C4
Cotton Tree St HTNM SK4 12 E3
Cottonwood Dr SALE M33 153 F1
Cottrell Rd HALE/TIMP WA15 179 E5
Coucill Sq FWTH BL4 66 B4
Coulsden Dr BKLY M9 88 A4
Coulthart St AUL OL6 119 G2
Coulthurst St RAMS BL0 16 C2
Coulton Cl OLD OL1 9 K1
OLD OL1 75 H4
Councillor La CHD/CHDH SK8 170 C4
Councillor St
WGTN/LGST M12 115 H4
Countess Av CHD/CHDH SK8 192 B2
Countess Gv BRO M7 101 G5
Countess La RAD M26 51 G4
Countess Pl PWCH M25 86 B3
Countess Rd DID/WITH M20 157 G3
Countess St AUL OL6 120 A3
OFTN SK2 172 B4
Counthill Dr CHH M8 86 D5
Counthill Rd OLDE OL4 76 C3
Count St MILN OL16 43 F2
County Av AUL OL6 120 B1
County Rd LHULT M38 81 F3
County St CMANW M2 6 E5
OLDS OL8 90 D5
Coupland Cl OLDE OL4 61 E5
WHIT OL12 14 B5
Coupland St HULME M15 128 B3
WHIT OL12 14 C5
Courier St GTN M18 130 D2
Course Vw OLDE OL4 92 D4
Court Dr NEWH/MOS M40 117 F1
Courtfield Av BKLY M9 * 88 A3
Courthill St STKP SK1 13 K5
Courtney Gn WILM/AE SK9 192 A5
Courtney Pl ALT WA14 176 D3
Court St BOLE BL2 3 H5
UPML OL3 79 E4
Courts Vw SALE M33 154 D1
Courtyard Dr WALK M28 81 E4
The Courtyard BOL BL1 * 34 A5
HEY OL10 * 41 G5
Cousin Flds EDGW/EG BL7 23 H4
Covell Rd POY/DIS SK12 195 E2
Covent Gdn STKP SK1 13 G4
Coventry Av EDGY/DAV SK3 170 C2
Coventry Gv CHAD OL9 74 B3
Coventry Rd RAD M26 52 A4
Coventry St ROCH OL11 30 A5
Coverdale Av BOL BL1 47 H1
ROY/SHW OL2 58 D4
Coverdale Cl HEY OL10 40 D5
Coverdale Crs
WGTN/LGST M12 129 E2
Coverham Av OLDE OL4 92 C3
Coverhill Rd OLDE OL4 93 G2
Covert Rd OLDE OL4 92 D4
WYTH/NTH M22 168 D4
The Cove HALE/TIMP WA15 178 A1
Covington Pl WILM/AE SK9 199 E4
Cowan St NEWH/MOS M40 115 G3
Cowburn St CSLFD M3 114 D2
HEY OL10 41 F5
Cowdals Rd HOR/BR BL6 46 C5
Cowesby St RUSH/FAL M14 128 B5
Cowhill La AUL OL6 119 H2
Cowie St ROY/SHW OL2 60 A1
Cow La BOLS/LL BL3 64 A2
BRAM/HZG SK7 173 E5
FAIL M35 104 D3
HALE/TIMP WA15 188 A2
OLDE OL4 76 B5
ORD M5 113 H4
SALE M33 140 C5
WILM/AE SK9 199 F3
Cow Lees WHTN BL5 62 B3
Cowley Rd BOL BL1 34 A1
Cowley St NEWH/MOS M40 104 B4
Cowling St BRO M7 100 C2
Cowlishaw ROY/SHW OL2 59 H4
Cowlishaw La ROY/SHW OL2 59 H4
Cowlishaw Rd HYDE SK14 163 E1
Cowm Park Wy North
WHIT OL12 14 B3
Cowm Park Wy South
WHIT OL12 14 B5
Cowm Top La ROCH OL11 42 D4
Cown Edge Wy GLSP SK13 149 H5
HYDE SK14 147 H5
MPL/ROM SK6 175 H5
MPL/ROM SK6 187 F3
OFTN SK2 173 H5
Cowper St AUL OL6 119 H2
MDTN M24 73 G5
Coxton Rd WYTH/NTH M22 180 D3
Crabbe St ANC M4 114 D2
Crab La BKLY M9 87 G3
Crabtree Av
HALE/TIMP WA15 179 E5
Crabtree La OP/CLY M11 117 E5
Crabtree Rd OLD OL1 76 A4
Craddock Rd SALE M33 154 D4
Craddock St MOSL OL5 108 D1
Cradley Av OP/CLY M11 117 E5
Crag Av BURY BL9 27 E1
Cragg Fold BURY BL9 * 27 E1
Cragg Rd OLD OL1 74 B2
Cragie St CHH M8 102 A5
Crag La BURY BL9 27 E1
Cragside Wy WILM/AE SK9 199 F4
Craig Av TOT/BURYW BL8 37 G5
URM M41 123 H5
Craig Cl HTNM SK4 159 E5
Craighall Av BNG/LEV M19 143 H3
Craighall Rd BOL BL1 22 D5
Craiglands MILN OL16 43 G4
Craigmore Av DID/WITH M20 156 C2
Craignair Ct SWIN M27 * 99 H2
Craig Rd GTN M18 130 B4
HTNM SK4 158 D5
Craigslands Av
NEWH/MOS M40 103 H4
Craig Wk OLDS OL8 9 F7
Craigweil Av DID/WITH M20 157 H3
Craigwell Rd PWCH M25 86 C5
Cramer St NEWH/MOS M40 * 103 G5
Crammond Cl
NEWH/MOS M40 104 C4
Cramond Cl BOL BL1 33 G5
Cramond Wk BOL BL1 33 G5
Crampton Dr
HALE/TIMP WA15 178 D4
Crampton La PART M31 137 F5
Cranage Rd BNG/LEV M19 144 B3
Cranark Cl BOL BL1 47 H2
Cranberry Cl ALT WA14 165 E1
Cranberry Dr BOLS/LL BL3 47 G5
DTN/ASHW M34 131 H5
Cranberry Rd PART M31 151 E3
Cranberry St OLDE OL4 92 A2
Cranbourne Av
CHD/CHDH SK8 183 E2
Cranbourne Cl
HALE/TIMP WA15 166 B3
Cranbourne Rd AULW OL7 107 E5
CCHDY M21 141 F3
HTNM SK4 159 E2
OLDTF/WHR M16 127 F4
ROCH OL11 28 B5
Cranbourne St ORD M5 113 H4
Cranbourne Ter AUL OL6 107 E5
Cranbrook Dr PWCH M25 86 B5
Cranbrook Gdns AULW OL7 * 119 G1
Cranbrook Rd ECC M30 110 B1
GTN M18 130 D5
Cranbrook St AULW OL7 119 G1
OLDE OL4 92 B1
RAD M26 52 D4
Cranbrook Wk CHAD OL9 * 90 B1
Crandon Dr DID/WITH M20 169 H1
Cranesbill Cl WYTH/NTH M22 180 B3
Crane St BOLS/LL BL3 * 64 A1
WGTN/LGST M12 115 F5
Cranfield Cl NEWH/MOS M40 115 G3
Cranford Av DID/WITH M20 158 A2
SALE M33 140 A5
STRET M32 126 C5
WHTF M45 69 F2
Cranford Cl SWIN M27 99 G4
WHTF M45 69 F2
Cranford Dr IRL M44 122 A5
Cranford Gdns MPL/ROM SK6 175 E2
URM M41 * 123 F5
Cranford Rd URM M41 123 F5
WILM/AE SK9 198 D1
Cranford St BOLS/LL BL3 64 B2
Cranham Cl TOT/BURYW BL8 37 G3
Cranham Close Crs
LHULT M38 * 81 F1
Cranham Rd WYTH/NTH M22 179 H2
Cranleigh Av HTNM SK4 158 C2
Cranleigh Cl OLDE OL4 76 D3
Cranleigh Dr BRAM/HZG SK7 185 H4
CHD/CHDH SK8 170 C3
SALE M33 154 B1
SALE M33 154 D5
WALK M28 97 F2
Cranlington Dr CHH M8 102 A4
Cranmer Ct HEY OL10 40 D5
Cranmere Av BNG/LEV M19 144 C1
Cranmere Dr SALE M33 153 G4
Cranmer Rd DID/WITH M20 157 G2
Cranston Dr DID/WITH M20 169 G1
SALE M33 155 F3
Cranston Gv CHD/CHDH SK8 169 E4
Cranswick St RUSH/FAL M14 128 B5
Crantock Dr CHD/CHDH SK8 181 H4
STLY SK15 121 G2
Crantock St WGTN/LGST M12 130 A5
Cranwell Dr BNG/LEV M19 158 B2
Cranworth St STLY SK15 121 E4
Craston Rd BRUN/LGST M13 143 G1
Crathie Ct BOL BL1 33 E5
Craven Av ORD M5 113 G5
Craven Ct ALT WA14 * 165 F2
Craven Dr ALT WA14 165 F1
ORD M5 126 D2
Craven Gdns ROCH OL11 * 42 D1
Cravenhurst Av
NEWH/MOS M40 116 C1
Craven Pl BOL BL1 32 B4
OP/CLY M11 116 D3
Craven Rd ALT WA14 165 F2
RDSH SK5 * 145 F5
Craven St AUL OL6 * 107 G5
BURY BL9 5 K2
OLD OL1 75 F3
ORD M5 113 H4
Craven Ter SALE M33 154 D2
Cravenwood AUL OL6 108 A4
Cravenwood Rd CHH M8 102 B2
Crawford Av BOLE BL2 3 J6
WALK M28 97 G2
Crawford St AUL OL6 120 A3
BOLE BL2 3 H5
ECC M30 111 E1
MILN OL16 43 F1
NEWH/MOS M40 * 104 B5
Crawley Av ECC M30 111 H2
WYTH/NTH M22 180 C1
Crawley Gv OFTN SK2 172 C3
Craydon St OP/CLY M11 116 D5
Crayfield Rd BNG/LEV M19 144 B3
Crayford Rd NEWH/MOS M40 116 C1
The Cray MILN OL16 31 F5
Cray Wk BRUN/LGST M13 * 128 C1
Creaton Wy MDTN M24 56 A5
Creden Av WYTH/NTH M22 180 D1
Crediton Cl ALT WA14 165 E3
HULME M15 128 A3
Crediton Dr BOLE BL2 50 D2
Cresbury St
WGTN/LGST M12 * 129 E1
Crescent ORD M5 113 H3
Crescent Av BOL BL1 2 B3
CHH M8 * 102 B2
FWTH BL4 81 H1
PWCH M25 86 A5
SWIN M27 99 G2
WHTN BL5 63 H4
Crescent Cl DUK SK16 119 H4
EDGY/DAV SK3 172 B4
Crescent Dr CHH M8 102 C1
LHULT M38 81 G2
Crescent Fold HYDE SK14 * 149 H3
Crescent Gv BNG/LEV M19 * 144 A2
PWCH M25 86 A5
Crescent Pk HTNM SK4 12 A3
Crescent Range
RUSH/FAL M14 128 D5
Crescent Rd ALT WA14 164 D3
BOLS/LL BL3 65 G1
CHAD OL9 89 H5
CHD/CHDH SK8 169 H3
CHH M8 102 B2
DUK SK16 119 H4
FWTH BL4 82 C1
HALE/TIMP WA15 177 H2
ROCH OL11 42 A2
STKP SK1 160 C3
WILM/AE SK9 201 E3
Crescent St CHH M8 102 D2
The Crescent ALT WA14 164 D4
BNG/LEV M19 144 A2
BOLE BL2 35 G2
BOLS/LL BL3 67 E2
BURY BL9 5 G3
CHD/CHDH SK8 169 H3
DROY M43 117 G4
EDGW/EG BL7 23 F3
EDGY/DAV SK3 172 B5
HALE/TIMP WA15 166 A2
IRL M44 122 C5
MDTN M24 72 B4
MOSL OL5 108 C1
MPL/ROM SK6 161 E2
PWCH M25 86 A3
RAD M26 51 G4
ROY/SHW OL2 59 H3
STLY SK15 135 E2
URM M41 123 G5
WHIT OL12 * 14 B5
Crescent Wy EDGY/DAV SK3 172 B4
Cressfield Wy CCHDY M21 141 H4
Cressingham Rd BOLS/LL BL3 63 H1
STRET M32 139 H2
Cressington Cl ORD M5 * 112 D3
Cresswell Gv DID/WITH M20 157 F1
Crestfold LHULT M38 81 F3
Crest St CSLFD M3 6 E1
The Crest DROY M43 131 F1
Crete St OLDS OL8 91 G3
Crewe Rd NTHM/RTH M23 167 F1
Crib Fold UPML OL3 78 D2
Crib La UPML OL3 78 D2
Criccieth Rd EDGY/DAV SK3 170 D2
Criccieth St OLDTF/WHR M16 128 A4
Cricketfield La WALK M28 81 H4
Cricket's La AUL OL6 119 H2
Cricket's La North AUL OL6 119 H2
Cricket St BOLS/LL BL3 48 D4
DTN/ASHW M34 * 132 D4
Cricket Vw MILN OL16 44 C1
Cricklewood Rd
WYTH/NTH M22 180 B2
Crimble La ROCH OL11 41 F1
Crimble St WHIT OL12 29 G3
Crime La OLDS OL8 106 A3
Crimsworth Av
OLDTF/WHR M16 141 F1
Crinan Wk NEWH/MOS M40 115 G2
Cringlebarrow Cl WALK M28 96 A5
Cringle Cl BOLS/LL BL3 47 F5
Cringle Dr CHD/CHDH SK8 169 H5
Cringleford Wk
WGTN/LGST M12 129 G3
Cringle Hall Rd BNG/LEV M19 143 H3
Cringle Rd BNG/LEV M19 144 B4
Cripple Gate La ROCH OL11 42 D5
Crispin Rd WYTH/NTH M22 180 D4
Critchley Cl HYDE SK14 148 B2
Criterion St RDSH SK5 145 F1
Croal St BOL BL1 2 A6
Croasdale Av RUSH/FAL M14 142 D2
Croasdale Cl ROY/SHW OL2 59 F4
Croasdale St BOL BL1 2 E1
Crocus Dr ROY/SHW OL2 59 H4
Crocus St BOL BL1 34 A2
Croft Av PWCH M25 71 E4
Croft Bank BRO M7 * 101 F5
GTN M18 130 D3
Croft Brow OLDS OL8 91 F5
Croft Cl HALE/TIMP WA15 188 D1
Croft Dr TOT/BURYW BL8 25 H5
Croft Edge UPML OL3 94 D2
Crofters Brook RAD M26 52 D5
Crofters Gn WILM/AE SK9 198 C4
The Crofters SALE M33 155 G3
Crofters Wk BOLE BL2 23 H5
Croft Ga BOLE BL2 35 F2
Croft Gates Rd MDTN M24 72 A5
Croft Gv LHULT M38 81 E2
Croft Head ROY/SHW OL2 59 E5
Croft Head Dr MILN OL16 31 G4
Croft Hill Rd NEWH/MOS M40 103 H1
Croftlands RAMS BL0 16 B5
Croftlands Rd WYTH/NTH M22 168 D5
Croft La BOLS/LL BL3 49 G4
BURY BL9 53 H4
RAD M26 52 D5
Croftleigh Cl WHTF M45 69 F2
Crofton Av HALE/TIMP WA15 166 B1
Crofton St OLDS OL8 91 F4
OLDTF/WHR M16 127 G4
RUSH/FAL M14 128 C5
Croft Rd CHD/CHDH SK8 183 E1
SALE M33 155 F4
WILM/AE SK9 200 B1
Crofts Bank Rd URM M41 124 B4
Croftside Av WALK M28 82 B4
Croftside Cl WALK M28 82 B4
Croftside Gv WALK M28 82 B4
Croftside Wy WILM/AE SK9 199 F4
Croft St BOLS/LL BL3 49 G5
BRO M7 101 F5
BURY BL9 5 G4
FAIL M35 105 F1
HYDE SK14 147 H1
LHULT M38 81 E2
OP/CLY M11 116 C4
STLY SK15 121 E3
WHIT OL12 19 H5
The Croft BURY BL9 53 H3
HYDE SK14 135 H4
OLDS OL8 91 F5
PART M31 137 F5
Croichbank TOT/BURYW BL8 25 E1
Cromar Rd BRAM/HZG SK7 185 G1
Cromarty Av CHAD OL9 90 A4
Cromarty Wk OP/CLY M11 116 A4
Crombie Av WYTH/NTH M22 168 C1
Crombouke Fold WALK M28 96 C3
Cromdale Av BOL BL1 48 A1
BRAM/HZG SK7 185 G1
Cromer Av BOLE BL2 34 D5
DID/WITH M20 142 D5
DTN/ASHW M34 131 F5
Cromer Rd CHD/CHDH SK8 170 B3
SALE M33 154 D3
TOT/BURYW BL8 38 A1
Cromer St MDTN M24 72 D3
OP/CLY M11 * 117 E4
ROY/SHW OL2 * 60 A2
STKP SK1 13 K2
WHIT OL12 10 B3
Cromford Av STRET M32 125 G5
Cromford Cl BOL BL1 2 C1
Cromford Gdns BOL BL1 34 A4
Cromford St OLD OL1 75 H4
Cromhurst St CHH M8 102 B2
Cromley Rd MPL/ROM SK6 186 D5
OFTN SK2 184 B1
Crompton Av BOLE BL2 50 B1
MILN OL16 43 G3
Crompton Circuit
ROY/SHW OL2 45 H5
Crompton Cl BOL BL1 34 B2
MPL/ROM SK6 175 E2
RAD M26 68 C4
Crompton Pl BOL BL1 * 3 F5
RAD M26 68 C1
Crompton Rd BNG/LEV M19 144 A4
HOR/BR BL6 46 A1
RAD M26 66 D4
Crompton St AUL OL6 120 B1
BOL BL1 3 G3
BURY BL9 4 D4
CHAD OL9 8 A3
FWTH BL4 66 B5
OLD OL1 75 F4
ROY/SHW OL2 60 A2
ROY/SHW OL2 * 75 F1
SWIN M27 98 D2
WALK M28 82 C5
Crompton V BOLE BL2 50 A1
Crompton Wy BOLE BL2 34 D3
ROY/SHW OL2 60 A3
Cromwell Av CHD/CHDH SK8 169 F3
MPL/ROM SK6 174 C3
OLDTF/WHR M16 141 G1
RDSH SK5 145 G1
Cromwell Gv BNG/LEV M19 144 A2
BRO M7 101 F5
Cromwell Range
RUSH/FAL M14 143 F1
Cromwell Rd
BRAM/HZG SK7 193 G1
ECC M30 110 D3
IRL M44 136 A4
MPL/ROM SK6 146 B5
PWCH M25 86 B3
ROY/SHW OL2 58 D3
SLFD M6 113 F1
STRET M32 140 C2
SWIN M27 98 D1
WHTF M45 69 E2
Cromwell St BOL BL1 2 C6
HEY OL10 41 E5
HTNM SK4 159 G3
OLD OL1 9 G5
Crondall St RUSH/FAL M14 128 B5
Cronkeyshaw Av WHIT OL12 10 B1
Cronkeyshaw Rd WHIT OL12 10 B2
Cronshaw St BNG/LEV M19 144 B3
Crookhill Dr CHH M8 102 A3
Crookilley Wy
MPL/ROM SK6 161 E1
STKP SK1 160 C3
Crook St BOLS/LL BL3 2 E7
HYDE SK14 147 H1
MILN OL16 10 E5
Crosby Av WALK M28 82 C5
Crosby Rd BOL BL1 48 A1
NEWH/MOS M40 104 C5

RAD M26 51 H2
SLFD M6 * 100 A5
Crosby St OFTN SK2 172 A2
WHIT OL12 30 A1
Crosfield Av BURY BL9 26 D1
Crosfield Gv GTN M18 130 C4
Crossacres Rd
WYTH/NTH M22 169 E5
Cross Acres Rd
WYTH/NTH M22 180 D1
Cross Av PWCH M25 85 H1
Crossbank Av OLDE OL4 77 E5
Crossbank Cl BRUN/LGST M13 129 E3
Crossbank St OLDS OL8 8 E5
Crossbridge Rd HYDE SK14 148 C1
Crossbrook Wy MILN OL16 44 D1
Crossby Cl MDTN M24 88 C2
Crosscliffe St
OLDTF/WHR M16 128 A4
Crossdale Rd BKLY M9 88 B3
BOLE BL2 50 C1
Crossefield Rd CHD/CHDH SK8 182 D1
Crossen St BOLS/LL BL3 49 H4
Crossfell Av BKLY M9 87 G2
Cross Field Cl ROY/SHW OL2 45 F5
Crossfield Cl DTN/ASHW M34 147 E1
STLY SK15 120 D4
WHIT OL12 19 H1
Crossfield Dr RAD M26 67 H1
SWIN M27 98 D1
WALK M28 97 G3
Crossfield Gv MPL/ROM SK6 163 G5
OFTN SK2 172 C5
Crossfield Pl ROCH OL11 43 F1
Crossfield Rd ECC M30 122 D4
HALE/TIMP WA15 178 C2
WHIT OL12 19 H2
WILM/AE SK9 192 A3
Crossfields EDGW/EG BL7 23 G3
Crossfield St BURY BL9 53 G5
Crossford Br SALE M33 140 A4
Crossford Cl SALE M33 * 139 H5
Crossford Dr BOLS/LL BL3 47 F4
Crossford St STRET M32 140 B2
Crossgate Av WYTH/NTH M22 168 C3
Crossgate Ms HTNM SK4 158 B4
Crossgates Rd MILN OL16 31 G4
Cross Glebe St AUL OL6 * 119 H2
Cross Gv HALE/TIMP WA15 166 A1
Crosshill St OLDTF/WHR M16 128 A4
Cross Keys St ANC M4 7 H2
Cross Knowle Vw URM M41 123 H4
Crossland Rd CCHDY M21 141 E3
DROY M43 117 H3
Crosslands PWCH M25 85 H4
Crosslands Rd WALK M28 96 A4
Cross La DROY M43 118 C1
GTN M18 130 C3
MPL/ROM SK6 174 D4
ORD M5 113 F4
RAD M26 52 D5
TOT/BURYW BL8 16 B3
Cross La East PART M31 151 F3
Cross La West PART M31 150 D4
Crosslee Rd BKLY M9 88 C3
Cross Lees WHIT OL12 19 F5
Crossley Ct ANC M4 115 G4
Crossley Crs AUL OL6 107 H4
Crossley Rd BNG/LEV M19 144 A4
SALE M33 139 G5
Crossley St BOLS/LL BL3 50 D5
GTN M18 130 A2
MILN OL16 31 F5
ROY/SHW OL2 60 B2
ROY/SHW OL2 75 F2
STLY SK15 120 C3
Crossmead Dr BKLY M9 88 B2
Crossmeadow Cl ROCH OL11 28 D3
Crossmoor Crs MPL/ROM SK6 162 B4
Crossmoor Dr BOLE BL2 3 K2
Crossmoor Gv MPL/ROM SK6 162 B4
Cross Ormrod St BOLS/LL BL3 2 B7
Cross Rd CCHDY M21 141 F4
CHD/CHDH SK8 181 G5
Cross St ALT WA14 165 G5
AUL OL6 107 G5
AUL OL6 119 F3
BOL BL1 3 F2
BOLS/LL BL3 67 E1
BURY BL9 4 E4
CMANW M2 6 E4
CSLFD M3 6 C3
DTN/ASHW M34 132 B3
EDGW/EG BL7 23 E4
FWTH BL4 66 A3
FWTH BL4 83 E2
HEY OL10 41 F5
HYDE SK14 147 H1
MDTN M24 72 C4
MILN OL16 31 E4
MOSL OL5 * 93 H5
OLDE OL4 76 A5
OLDE OL4 93 F1
OLDTF/WHR M16 127 G3
RAMS BL0 16 D2
ROCH OL11 42 B4
SALE M33 154 C1
STLY SK15 121 G1
STRET M32 140 B1
SWIN M27 85 E5
URM M41 138 C2
WALK M28 98 B3
WHTF M45 69 F3
The Cross TOT/BURYW BL8 * 26 A5
Crosswaite Rd OFTN SK2 173 E3
Crossway BRAM/HZG SK7 193 H2
DID/WITH M20 157 G3
DROY M43 131 F1
OFTN SK2 172 B5
Crossways OLDS OL8 106 D1
Croston Cl WILM/AE SK9 201 F4
Crostons Rd TOT/BURYW BL8 4 A3
Croston St BOLS/LL BL3 48 B5
Croston Wk OP/CLY M11 115 H4
Croton St HTNM SK4 158 B4
Croughton Cl OP/CLY M11 * 130 C1
Crowborough Wk
HULME M15 128 A3
Crowcroft Rd
BRUN/LGST M13 144 A1
Crowden Rd NEWH/MOS M40 89 E5
Crow Hl STLY SK15 109 F5
Crow Hl North MDTN M24 88 C1
Crowhill Rd AULW OL7 119 E1
Crow Hl South MDTN M24 88 C1
Crow Hill Vw OLDE OL4 93 E3
Crowland Gdns
CHD/CHDH SK8 193 E1
Crowland Rd BOLE BL2 34 D4
NTHM/RTH M23 179 G1
Crow La RAMS BL0 16 D2
Crowley La OLDE OL4 76 C3
Crowley Rd BKLY M9 103 G2
HALE/TIMP WA15 166 C3
Crown Ct BRAM/HZG SK7 185 E1
Crowneast St ROCH OL11 29 F4
Crown Gdns MILN OL16 43 F1
Crowngreen Rd ECC M30 111 F4
Crown Hl MOSL OL5 109 E2
Crownhill Dr DROY M43 117 H3
Crown La ANC M4 7 G1
Crown Passages
HALE/TIMP WA15 177 H2
Crown Point Av
NEWH/MOS M40 * 104 B5
Crown Rd HEY OL10 40 C4
Crown Sq CSLFD M3 6 C5
Crown St AUL OL6 119 G3
BOL BL1 3 F4
CSLFD M3 6 C2
DTN/ASHW M34 132 B4
FAIL M35 105 E2
HULME M15 127 H1
MILN OL16 43 G1
MPL/ROM SK6 * 161 G2
MPL/ROM SK6 187 E1
NEWH/MOS M40 104 B5
ROY/SHW OL2 * 60 A2
Crowsdale Pl OFTN SK2 173 F5
Crowshaw Dr WHIT OL12 18 D5
Crow's Nest BOLS/LL BL3 50 C4
Crowswood Dr STLY SK15 109 E5
Crowther Av ORD M5 113 F5
Crowther St GTN M18 130 C3
LIT OL15 20 B4
MILN OL16 43 G2
Crowthorn Dr
NTHM/RTH M23 179 H2
Crowthorn Rd AULW OL7 119 E4
HTNM SK4 144 D4
Crowton Av SALE M33 153 G4
Croxdale Cl AULW OL7 106 C5
Croxton Av MILN OL16 11 J5
Croxton Cl MPL/ROM SK6 174 D4
SALE M33 153 G4
Croyde Cl BOLE BL2 35 G4
WYTH/NTH M22 181 E5
Croydon Av ROCH OL11 57 G2
ROY/SHW OL2 58 D3
Croydon Dr NEWH/MOS M40 116 D1
Croydon Sq ROCH OL11 57 G1
Crummock Cl BOLS/LL BL3 66 C1
Crummock Dr MDTN M24 72 B1
Crummock Rd
CHD/CHDH SK8 181 G1
FWTH BL4 64 D5
Crumpsall La CHH M8 102 A1
Crumpsall St BOL BL1 33 H4
Crumpsall V CHH M8 87 H5
Crumpsall Wy CHH M8 102 C1
Crundale Rd BOL BL1 23 E5
Cruttenden Rd OFTN SK2 172 D5
Cryer St DROY M43 118 B1
Cubley Rd BRO M7 101 H2
Cuckoo Gv PWCH M25 86 A1
Cuckoo La BURY BL9 39 F4
PWCH M25 86 A1
Cuddington Av
DID/WITH M20 142 C3
Cuddington Crs
EDGY/DAV SK3 171 G3
Cudworth Rd BKLY M9 87 F2
Culand St WGTN/LGST M12 129 F2
Culbert Av DID/WITH M20 157 H3
Culchetch Av MPL/ROM SK6 175 E3
Culcheth La NEWH/MOS M40 116 D1
Culcheth Rd ALT WA14 177 G1
Culford Cl WGTN/LGST M12 129 F3
Culham Cl BOL BL1 * 33 G4
Cullen Gv BKLY M9 88 B4
Cullercoats Wk
WGTN/LGST M12 * 130 A5
Culmere Rd WYTH/NTH M22 180 C3
Culross Av BOLS/LL BL3 47 F3
NEWH/MOS M40 104 D1
Culvercliff Wk CSLFD M3 6 C6
Culver Rd EDGY/DAV SK3 171 G4
Culvert St MILN OL16 43 G4
OLDE OL4 76 D3
Culverwell Dr ORD M5 113 G3
Cumber Cl WILM/AE SK9 200 A1
Cumber Dr WILM/AE SK9 200 A1
Cumberland Av DUK SK16 120 B5
HEY OL10 40 B4
IRL M44 150 B1
RDSH SK5 160 D2
SWIN M27 84 A5
Cumberland Cl BURY BL9 53 F3
Cumberland Dr ALT WA14 176 D4
OLD OL1 75 E3
Cumberland Gv AULW OL7 119 G1
Cumberland Rd BKLY M9 * 103 E1
PART M31 150 C4
ROCH OL11 43 E4
SALE M33 154 D4
URM M41 138 C2
Cumberland St BRO M7 114 A1
STLY SK15 120 C3
Cumber La WILM/AE SK9 200 A1
Cumbrae Gdns ORD M5 112 D4
Cumbrae Rd BNG/LEV M19 144 C2
Cumbrian Cl
BRUN/LGST M13 * 128 D2
ROY/SHW OL2 59 G1
Cumbria Wk SLFD M6 113 G1
Cummings St OLDS OL8 90 D5
Cunard Cl BRUN/LGST M13 128 D2
Cuncliffe Dr ROY/SHW OL2 60 C2
Cundey St BOL BL1 * 33 F5
Cundiff Rd CCHDY M21 141 F5
Cundy St HYDE SK14 133 H4
Cunliffe Av RAMS BL0 16 B4
Cunliffe Brow BOL BL1 33 E5
Cunliffe Dr SALE M33 154 D3
Cunliffe St EDGY/DAV SK3 12 B5
HYDE SK14 133 F4
RAMS BL0 16 D1
Cunningham Dr BURY BL9 70 A3
WYTH/NTH M22 181 F4
Cunningham Wy OLD OL1 * 75 F4
Curate St STKP SK1 13 K4
Curlew Cl ROCH OL11 28 C4
Curlew Dr IRL M44 122 B4
Curlew Rd OLDE OL4 92 D3
Currier La AUL OL6 119 H3
Curtels Cl WALK M28 98 B3
Curtis Rd BNG/LEV M19 144 C2
HTNM SK4 158 D4
Curtis St BOLS/LL BL3 64 B2
Curzon Av RUSH/FAL M14 129 F4
Curzon Cl ROCH OL11 43 E4
Curzon Dr HALE/TIMP WA15 166 C3
Curzon Gn OFTN SK2 173 E1
Curzon Ms WILM/AE SK9 198 D4
Curzon Rd AUL OL6 119 H1
BOL BL1 48 B2
BRO M7 101 G3
CHD/CHDH SK8 181 G5
OFTN SK2 173 E2
POY/DIS SK12 195 F5
ROCH OL11 43 E4
SALE M33 154 C1
STRET M32 125 F5
Curzon St MOSL OL5 108 D1
OLD OL1 9 G3
Cutacre La WHTN BL5 80 C1
Cutgate Cl NTHM/RTH M23 155 F5
Cutgate Rd WHIT OL12 29 E2
Cuthbert Av BNG/LEV M19 144 B1
Cuthbert Mayne Ct MILN OL16 29 H5
Cuthbert Rd CHD/CHDH SK8 170 B3
Cuthbert St BOLS/LL BL3 63 H2
Cutland St NEWH/MOS M40 103 H4
Cutland Wy LIT OL15 20 D4
Cut La WHIT OL12 28 C2
Cutler Hill Rd FAIL M35 105 H3
Cutnook La IRL M44 122 A3
Cutter Cl ORD M5 113 F5
Cycle St OP/CLY M11 116 C5
Cyclone St OP/CLY M11 116 A5
Cygnus Av BRO M7 113 H2
Cymbal Ct RDSH SK5 159 H3
Cynthia Dr MPL/ROM SK6 175 E4
Cypress Av CHAD OL9 74 C4
Cypress Cl EDGY/DAV SK3 12 A5
Cypress Gdns MILN OL16 31 E4
Cypress Gv DTN/ASHW M34 132 D5
FWTH BL4 * 66 C5
Cypress Oaks STLY SK15 121 G2
Cypress Rd DROY M43 117 H2
ECC M30 110 B1
OLDE OL4 76 C4
Cypress St MDTN M24 73 F4
Cypress Wy MPL/ROM SK6 187 F5
Cyprus Cl OLDE OL4 92 C2
ORD M5 113 E4
Cyprus St STRET M32 140 B1
Cyril St BOLS/LL BL3 49 F4
ROY/SHW OL2 60 B2
RUSH/FAL M14 128 C5
Cyrus St NEWH/MOS M40 115 H3

D

Daccamill Dr SWIN M27 99 E4
Dacre Av OLDTF/WHR M16 141 F1
Dacre Cl MDTN M24 71 G3
Dacre Rd ROCH OL11 43 E2
Dacres Av UPML OL3 94 C3
Dacres Dr UPML OL3 94 D3
Dacres Rd UPML OL3 94 C3
Daffodil Cl WHIT OL12 18 D5
Daffodil Rd FWTH BL4 65 F3
Daffodil St BOL BL1 34 A1
Dagenham Rd
RUSH/FAL M14 * 128 D5
Dagmar St WALK M28 81 H3
Dagnall Av CCHDY M21 141 F5
Dahlia Cl BNG/LEV M19 143 H5
WHIT OL12 18 C5
Daimler St CHH M8 102 B4
Dain Cl DUK SK16 120 A5
Daine Av NTHM/RTH M23 156 A5
Dainton St WGTN/LGST M12 129 E1
Daintry Cl HULME M15 128 A2
Daintry Rd CHAD OL9 8 B2
Dairydale Cl IRL M44 122 C5
Dairyground Rd
BRAM/HZG SK7 183 H5
Dairyhouse La ALT WA14 165 E2
Dairy House La
BRAM/HZG SK7 193 E4
Dairy House Rd
BRAM/HZG SK7 193 E2
Dairy St CHAD OL9 74 C5
Daisy Av BRUN/LGST M13 129 F4
FWTH BL4 65 F3
Daisy Bank NEWH/MOS M40 104 B5
Daisy Bank Av SWIN M27 99 H4
Daisy Bank La CHD/CHDH SK8 181 F3
Daisy Bank Rd RUSH/FAL M14 129 F4
Daisyfield Cl WYTH/NTH M22 180 B3
Daisyfield Ct TOT/BURYW BL8 37 H5
Daisyhill Cl SALE M33 155 F2
Daisy Hill Rd MOSL OL5 109 E1
Daisy Ms EDGY/DAV SK3 171 G5
Daisy St BOLS/LL BL3 48 B5
CHAD OL9 8 C2
CHAD OL9 74 B4
OFTN SK2 172 A2
TOT/BURYW BL8 37 H4
WHIT OL12 10 A5
Daisy Wy MPL/ROM SK6 187 E5
Dakerwood Cl
NEWH/MOS M40 104 B5
Dakley St OP/CLY M11 130 B1
Dakota Av SALQ M50 112 D5
Dakota South SALQ M50 113 E5
Dalbeattie St BKLY M9 103 F2
Dalberg St WGTN/LGST M12 129 E1
Dalbury Dr NEWH/MOS M40 102 D5
Dalby Av SWIN M27 98 D3
Dalby Gv STKP SK1 13 K3
Dale Av BRAM/HZG SK7 184 A4
ECC M30 110 D2
MOSL OL5 94 B4
Dalebank Ms SWIN M27 * 83 G2
Dalebeck Cl WHTF M45 70 A4
Dale Brook Av DUK SK16 133 G2
Dalebrook Ct HTNM SK4 * 12 B3
Dalebrook Rd SALE M33 154 D5
Daleford Sq
BRUN/LGST M13 * 128 C1
Dalegarth Av BOL BL1 46 D2
Dale Gv AULW OL7 106 D5
HALE/TIMP WA15 166 A2
IRL M44 136 A5
Dalehead Dr ROY/SHW OL2 60 C2
Dale Lee WHTN BL5 62 B4
Dale Rd MDTN M24 73 E2
MPL/ROM SK6 174 D2
Dales Av CHH M8 87 E5
WHTF M45 69 E3
Dalesbrook Cl BOLS/LL BL3 50 D5
Dales Brow BOL BL1 23 E5
SWIN M27 * 98 C4
Dales Brow Av AULW OL7 106 D5
Dalesfield Crs MOSL OL5 109 F1
Dales Gv WALK M28 97 G1
Dales La WHTF M45 69 F3
Dalesman Cl BKLY M9 103 G2
Dalesman Dr OLD OL1 76 C1
Dalesman Wk HULME M15 * 128 A2
Dales Park Dr SWIN M27 * 98 C4
Dale St AUL OL6 108 B4
CMANE M1 7 H4
EDGY/DAV SK3 171 G2
FWTH BL4 * 66 B3
MDTN M24 73 E5
MILN OL16 11 J6
MILN OL16 31 G5
RAD M26 68 B2
ROY/SHW OL2 60 A3
STLY SK15 120 C4
SWIN M27 98 D4
TOT/BURYW BL8 37 H2
WHTF M45 69 F3
Dale St East AUL OL6 119 F3
Dale St West AUL OL6 119 F3
Daleswood Av WHTF M45 69 E3
Dale Vw DTN/ASHW M34 147 E4
HYDE SK14 147 H3
LIT OL15 31 G1
Dalham Av BKLY M9 88 D5
Dalkeith Gv BOLS/LL BL3 47 G4
Dalkeith Rd RDSH SK5 145 F4
Dalkeith St GTN M18 130 A2
Dallas Ct SALQ M50 112 D5
Dalley Av BRO M7 114 A1
Dallimore Rd NTHM/RTH M23 167 F3
Dalmahoy Cl NEWH/MOS M40 104 B2
Dalmain Cl CHH M8 102 A4
Dalmeny Ter ROCH OL11 43 E2
Dalmorton Rd CCHDY M21 141 H3
Dalny St BNG/LEV M19 144 B2
Dalston Av FAIL M35 105 G2
Dalston Dr BRAM/HZG SK7 193 F2
DID/WITH M20 157 H4
Dalton Av MILN OL16 31 E4
RUSH/FAL M14 142 C1
STRET M32 125 E4
WHTF M45 69 H5
Dalton Cl MILN OL16 31 F4
RAMS BL0 16 B4
Dalton Dr SWIN M27 100 A3
Dalton Fold WHTN BL5 62 A4
Dalton Gdns URM M41 124 A5
Dalton Gv HTNM SK4 159 F2
Dalton Rd BKLY M9 88 A2
MDTN M24 71 G5
Dalton St ANC M4 115 E2
CHAD OL9 74 C5
ECC M30 111 E2
FAIL M35 104 D2
OLD OL1 * 76 A5
SALE M33 140 A5
TOT/BURYW BL8 37 G4
Daltry St OLD OL1 75 H4
Dalveen Av URM M41 124 B4
Dalveen Dr HALE/TIMP WA15 166 A2
Dalymount Cl BOLE BL2 34 C4
Damask Av CSLFD M3 114 A3
Dame Hollow CHD/CHDH SK8 182 A5
Dameral Cl CHH M8 * 102 B4
Damery Ct BRAM/HZG SK7 183 H4
Damery Rd BRAM/HZG SK7 183 H4
Dame St CHAD OL9 75 E4
Dam Head Dr BKLY M9 88 B4
Damien St BNG/LEV M19 144 B1
Dams Head Fold WHTN BL5 62 A3
Damson Gn MDTN M24 73 F4
Dan Bank MPL/ROM SK6 174 B3
Danby Cl HYDE SK14 134 A4
Danby Ct OLD OL1 * 75 F4
Danby Pl HYDE SK14 134 A4
Danby Rd BOLS/LL BL3 64 D1
HYDE SK14 134 A4
Dane Av EDGY/DAV SK3 * 170 D1
PART M31 151 E2
Dane Bank MDTN M24 73 E5
Danebank Ms
DTN/ASHW M34 145 H1
Danebank Wk
BRUN/LGST M13 128 C1
Danebridge Cl FWTH BL4 * 66 B4
Dane Cl BRAM/HZG SK7 183 G2
Danecroft Cl BRUN/LGST M13 129 E3
Dane Dr WILM/AE SK9 199 G4
Danefield Ct CHD/CHDH SK8 182 A4
Danefield Rd SALE M33 140 A5
Daneholme Rd BNG/LEV M19 158 B1
Dane Ms SALE M33 * 139 H5
Dane Rd DTN/ASHW M34 145 G1
SALE M33 140 A5
Danesbury Ri CHD/CHDH SK8 170 A4
Danesbury Rd BOLE BL2 34 C2
Daneshill PWCH M25 86 A1
Danesmoor Dr BURY BL9 38 D2
Danesmoor Rd
DID/WITH M20 157 F1
Danes Rd RUSH/FAL M14 143 F1
Dane St BOLS/LL BL3 * 48 B5
OLDE OL4 76 B5
OP/CLY M11 130 D1
WHIT OL12 10 A7
Danesway PWCH M25 86 C5
SWIN M27 99 H4
Danesway Ct BOL BL1 33 G4
Daneswood Av BKLY M9 * 88 C3
WHIT OL12 18 B1
Daneswood Cl WHIT OL12 14 A5
Daneswood Meadow
WHIT OL12 14 A5
Danett Cl WGTN/LGST M12 129 H2
Danforth Gv BNG/LEV M19 144 B3
Daniel Adamson Av
PART M31 150 C3
Daniel Adamson Rd
SALQ M50 112 C5
Daniel Fold WHIT OL12 29 E1
Daniel's La STKP SK1 * 13 G2
Daniel St BRAM/HZG SK7 185 F2
HEY OL10 * 40 C4
OLD OL1 76 B4
ROY/SHW OL2 75 H1
WHIT OL12 14 C4
Danisher La OLDS OL8 106 C2
Dannywood Cl HYDE SK14 147 G3
Danson St NEWH/MOS M40 115 H2
Dantall Av BKLY M9 88 D5
Dante Cl ECC M30 111 H1
Danty St DUK SK16 * 119 G4
Dantzic St ANC M4 7 F3
Danwood Cl DTN/ASHW M34 147 F2
Darbishire St BOL BL1 3 G1
Darby Rd IRL M44 136 C5
Darbyshire Cl BOL BL1 48 B1
Darbyshire St RAD M26 68 B1
Darcy St BOLE BL2 49 H4
Darden Cl HTNM SK4 158 B3
Darell Wk CHH M8 102 C4
Daresbury Av URM M41 123 E4
Daresbury Cl EDGY/DAV SK3 171 G4
SALE M33 155 G3
Daresbury Rd CCHDY M21 140 D2
Daresbury St CHH M8 102 B3
Dargai St OP/CLY M11 117 E4
Dargle Rd SALE M33 139 H5
Darian Av WYTH/NTH M22 180 C4
Dark La MOSL OL5 94 A5
MPL/ROM SK6 161 E3
UPML OL3 78 D4
WGTN/LGST M12 115 G5
Darley Av CCHDY M21 141 G5
CHD/CHDH SK8 169 G4
DID/WITH M20 156 D2
ECC M30 110 D5
FWTH BL4 66 B3
Darley Gv FWTH BL4 66 B3
Darley Rd BRAM/HZG SK7 185 G5
OLDTF/WHR M16 127 F5
ROCH OL11 43 E2
Darley St BOL BL1 33 G5
FWTH BL4 66 B4
OP/CLY M11 115 H4
SALE M33 154 C2
STRET M32 126 B4
Darley Ter BOL BL1 * 33 G5
Darlington Cl TOT/BURYW BL8 37 G2
Darlington Rd DID/WITH M20 142 C5
ROCH OL11 43 E3
Darliston Av BKLY M9 87 F2
Darnall Av DID/WITH M20 142 C3
Darnbrook Dr WYTH/NTH M22 180 A3
Darncombe Cl
OLDTF/WHR M16 128 A4
Darnley Av WALK M28 96 D1
Darnley St OLDTF/WHR M16 127 G4
Darnton Gdns AUL OL6 120 B2
Darnton Rd AUL OL6 120 B2
Darras Rd GTN M18 130 B5
Dart Cl CHAD OL9 74 A4
Dartford Av ECC M30 110 C3
RDSH SK5 145 H5
Dartford Cl WGTN/LGST M12 129 E2
Dartford Rd URM M41 138 C2
Dartington Cl BRAM/HZG SK7 184 A1
NTHM/RTH M23 167 E3
Dartmouth Cl OLDS OL8 91 G3
Dartmouth Crs RDSH SK5 160 D1
Dartmouth Rd CCHDY M21 141 G3
WHTF M45 69 H5
Dartnall Cl POY/DIS SK12 197 F1
Darton Av NEWH/MOS M40 115 H2
Darvel Cl BOLE BL2 50 C3
Darwell Av ECC M30 110 D5
Darwen Rd EDGW/EG BL7 23 E3
Darwen St OLDTF/WHR M16 127 F3
Darwin Gv BRAM/HZG SK7 193 H1
Darwin St AULW OL7 119 F3
BOL BL1 33 G4
HYDE SK14 134 B2
OLDE OL4 92 B2
Dashwood Rd PWCH M25 85 G2
Datchett Ter ROCH OL11 43 E2
Dauntesy Av SWIN M27 * 100 A3
Davehall Av WILM/AE SK9 198 D3
Davenfield Gv DID/WITH M20 157 G3
Davenfield Rd DID/WITH M20 157 G3
Davenham Rd RDSH SK5 145 F1
SALE M33 139 E5
WILM/AE SK9 192 A3
Davenhill Rd BNG/LEV M19 144 A3
Davenport Av DID/WITH M20 142 D4
WILM/AE SK9 200 B1
Davenport Dr MPL/ROM SK6 147 F5
Davenport Fold Rd BOLE BL2 * 35 H2
Davenport Gdns BOL BL1 2 D3
Davenport Park Rd OFTN SK2 172 B4
Davenport Rd BRAM/HZG SK7 185 E1
Davenport St BOL BL1 2 C3
DROY M43 * 117 F4
DTN/ASHW M34 118 D5
Daventry Rd CCHDY M21 141 H3
ROCH OL11 43 E3
Daveyhulme St WHIT OL12 11 G2
Daveylands URM M41 123 G3

WILM/AE SK9 199 G4
Davey La WILM/AE SK9 200 D3
David Brow BOLS/LL BL3 63 H2
David Cl DTN/ASHW M34 * 147 E2
David Lewis Cl MILN OL16 30 D5
David's Farm Cl MDTN M24 73 F5
Davids La OLDE OL4 77 E5
Davidson Dr MDTN M24 89 F1
David's Rd DROY M43 117 F3
David St DTN/ASHW M34 147 E2
RDSH SK5 145 E3
TOT/BURYW BL8 37 H3
WHIT OL12 10 D2
David St North WHIT OL12 10 D2
Davies Av CHD/CHDH SK8 191 G1
Davies Rd MPL/ROM SK6 161 E3
PART M31 151 F3
Davies Sq RUSH/FAL M14 128 B4
Davies St AULW OL7 119 E4
FWTH BL4 66 D5
OLD OL1 8 D1
Davis St ECC M30 111 F4
Davy Av SWIN M27 85 E5
Davyhulme Rd STRET M32 125 H5
URM M41 123 F4
Davyhulme Rd East
STRET M32 126 A5
Davy St NEWH/MOS M40 * 115 E1
Dawlish Av CHAD OL9 74 A3
CHD/CHDH SK8 182 C4
DROY M43 117 F3
RDSH SK5 160 D1
Dawlish Cl BRAM/HZG SK7 183 H5
GOL/RIS/CUL WA3 150 A3
HYDE SK14 135 F5
Dawlish Rd CCHDY M21 141 G3
SALE M33 153 H1
Dawnay St OP/CLY M11 * 130 A1
Dawn St ROY/SHW OL2 * 60 A3
Dawson La BOL BL1 2 C4
Dawson Rd ALT WA14 165 G2
CHD/CHDH SK8 182 A4
Dawson St BURY BL9 38 D2
CSLFD M3 6 A7
CSLFD M3 * 6 D2
HEY OL10 40 D4
HYDE SK14 148 A2
OLDE OL4 92 D2
STKP SK1 160 C3
SWIN M27 99 F2
Day Dr FAIL M35 105 E4
Day Gv HYDE SK14 135 H5
Daylesford Cl CHD/CHDH SK8 169 H5
Daylesford Crs
CHD/CHDH SK8 170 A5
Daylesford Rd
CHD/CHDH SK8 170 A5
Deacon Cl ALT WA14 177 E3
Deacons Cl STKP SK1 13 J3
Deacons Crs TOT/BURYW BL8 37 H5
Deacons Dr SLFD M6 100 A4
Deacon St MILN OL16 11 G2
Deal Av RDSH SK5 145 H5
Deal Cl NEWH/MOS M40 104 C5
Dealey Rd BOLS/LL BL3 47 H5
Deal St BOLS/LL BL3 65 E1
BURY BL9 5 J3
CSLFD M3 * 6 C3
HYDE SK14 148 A1
Deal Wk CHAD OL9 90 B1
Dean Av NEWH/MOS M40 104 A4
OLDTF/WHR M16 127 E5
Deanbank Av BNG/LEV M19 143 H3
Dean Bank Dr MILN OL16 43 G5
Dean Brook Cl
NEWH/MOS M40 104 B3
Dean Cl FWTH BL4 65 E4
PART M31 151 E2
WHTF M45 69 E5
WILM/AE SK9 199 F1
Dean Ct BOL BL1 3 F2
HULME M15 * 127 G2
Deancourt ROCH OL11 42 D2
Dean Dr ALT WA14 177 E3
WILM/AE SK9 199 F1
Deane Av BOLS/LL BL3 48 A4
CHD/CHDH SK8 170 C4
HALE/TIMP WA15 166 B4
Deane Church La BOLS/LL BL3 48 A5
Deane Rd BOLS/LL BL3 48 B4
Deanery Wy STKP SK1 13 G2
Deane Wk BOLS/LL BL3 2 C7
Dean La BRAM/HZG SK7 185 F4
NEWH/MOS M40 104 A4
Dean Moor Rd BRAM/HZG SK7 184 B2
Dean Rd CSLFD M3 6 C1
GTN M18 130 D4
IRL M44 136 A5
WILM/AE SK9 192 B4
Dean Row Rd WILM/AE SK9 199 F1
Deanscourt Av SWIN M27 98 D3
Deansgate BOL BL1 2 E4
HULME M15 127 H1
Deansgate La
HALE/TIMP WA15 165 H2
Deanshut Rd OLDS OL8 91 H5
Deans Rd SWIN M27 98 D3
Dean St AUL OL6 119 F2
CMANE M1 7 J4
FAIL M35 104 D3
MILN OL16 11 G2
MOSL OL5 108 C1
RAD M26 68 A1
STLY SK15 120 D4
Deansway SWIN M27 98 D3
Deanswood Dr BKLY M9 87 F2
Dean Ter AUL OL6 107 E1
Deanwater Cl
BRUN/LGST M13 128 C1
Deanwater Ct
CHD/CHDH SK8 * 182 A5
STRET M32 * 140 A3
Deanway NEWH/MOS M40 103 H2
URM M41 137 F1
WILM/AE SK9 199 F2
Dearden Av LHULT M38 81 F2
Dearden Fold
TOT/BURYW BL8 * 37 H5
Deardens St TOT/BURYW BL8 37 H5
Dearden St BOLS/LL BL3 50 D5
HULME M15 127 H2
LIT OL15 21 E2
STLY SK15 * 120 D3
Dearmans Pl CSLFD M3 6 C3
Dearnalay Wy CHAD OL9 90 C2
Dearne Dr STRET M32 140 C1
Dearnley Cl LIT OL15 20 C4
Debdale Av GTN M18 131 E4
Debdale La GTN M18 131 E4
Debenham Av
NEWH/MOS M40 116 D1
Debenham Ct FWTH BL4 * 66 A5
Debenham Rd STRET M32 139 G2
De Brook Cl URM M41 137 G2
Dee Av HALE/TIMP WA15 167 E4
Dee Dr FWTH BL4 82 D2
Deepcar St BNG/LEV M19 144 A1
Deepdale OLDE OL4 92 C1
Deepdale Av DID/WITH M20 142 C3
MILN OL16 30 D5
ROY/SHW OL2 58 D1
Deepdale Cl RDSH SK5 145 F2
Deepdale Dr SWIN M27 100 A3
Deepdale Rd BOLE BL2 35 G5
Deeping Av OLDTF/WHR M16 141 H1
Deeplish Rd ROCH OL11 43 E1
Deeplish St ROCH OL11 43 E1
Deeracre Av OFTN SK2 172 D3
Deerfold Cl GTN M18 * 130 C3
Deerhurst Dr CHH M8 102 A4
Deeroak Cl GTN M18 130 A2
Deerpark Rd
OLDTF/WHR M16 127 H5
Deerwood V HYDE SK14 149 G2
Defence St BOLS/LL BL3 2 B7
Deganwy Gv RDSH SK5 160 A1
Degas Cl BRO M7 101 E2
Delacourt Rd RUSH/FAL M14 142 C3
Delafield Av WGTN/LGST M12 144 A1
Delaford Av WALK M28 97 F3
Delaford Cl EDGY/DAV SK3 171 H5
Delahays Dr HALE/TIMP WA15 178 B2
Delahays Range GTN M18 131 E4
Delahays Rd HALE/TIMP WA15 178 C2
Delaine Rd DID/WITH M20 143 E5
Delamere Av ROY/SHW OL2 60 C1
SALE M33 155 F3
SLFD M6 99 H4
STRET M32 140 B1
SWIN M27 84 C5
WHTF M45 69 F4
Delamere Cl BRAM/HZG SK7 185 H1
MPL/ROM SK6 162 B1
STLY SK15 109 F4
Delamere Rd BNG/LEV M19 144 A3
BRAM/HZG SK7 185 H1
CHD/CHDH SK8 169 G4
DTN/ASHW M34 145 H1
MILN OL16 43 H2
OFTN SK2 172 C5
URM M41 137 H1
WILM/AE SK9 192 A3
Delamere St AUL OL6 119 G3
BURY BL9 38 D1
OLDS OL8 92 A3
OP/CLY M11 131 E1
Delamer Rd ALT WA14 177 F1
Delaunays Rd CHH M8 87 G5
SALE M33 154 A2
Delbooth Av URM M41 123 F4
Delfur Rd BRAM/HZG SK7 184 A5
Delhi Rd IRL M44 136 B3
Dellar St WHIT OL12 29 F2
Dell Av SWIN M27 100 A3
Dell Cl OLDE OL4 93 E2
Dellcot Cl PWCH M25 86 C5
SLFD M6 99 G5
Dellcot La WALK M28 97 G5
Dell Gdns WHIT OL12 29 E1
Dellhide Cl OLDE OL4 93 F1
Dell Meadow WHIT OL12 18 B3
Dell Rd WHIT OL12 18 A4
Dell Side MPL/ROM SK6 161 F3
Dellside Gv WALK M28 82 B4
Dell Side Wy WHIT OL12 29 F1
The Dell BOLE BL2 34 D1
Delph Brook Wy EDGW/EG BL7 22 C1
Delph Hl BOL BL1 32 B4
Delph Hill Cl BOL BL1 32 B4
Delphi Av WALK M28 82 A5
Delph La BOLE BL2 36 B5
Delph New Rd UPML OL3 78 C2
Delph Rd UPML OL3 61 H2
Delph St BOLS/LL BL3 48 C4
MILN OL16 31 G5
The Delph WALK M28 * 97 G4
Delside Av NEWH/MOS M40 103 H2
Delta Cl ROY/SHW OL2 75 E2
Delta Rd DTN/ASHW M34 132 B1
Delves Rd ALT WA14 165 G1
Delvino Wk RUSH/FAL M14 128 B4
Delwood Gdns
WYTH/NTH M22 168 C5
De-massey Cl
MPL/ROM SK6 * 147 F5
Demesne Cl STLY SK15 121 F4
Demesne Crs STLY SK15 121 F4
Demesne Dr STLY SK15 121 F4
Demesne Rd OLDTF/WHR M16 142 A1
Demmings Rd CHD/CHDH SK8 170 C4
Dempsey Dr BURY BL9 70 A2
Denbigh Cl BRAM/HZG SK7 184 D4
Denbigh Dr ROY/SHW OL2 59 G3
Denbigh Pl ORD M5 113 F4
Denbigh Rd BOLE BL2 49 G4
DTN/ASHW M34 146 D2
SWIN M27 84 B5
Denbigh St HTNM SK4 159 G3
OLDS OL8 * 91 G4
Denbigh Wk HULME M15 127 H3
Denbury Dr ALT WA14 165 E4
Denbury Gn BRAM/HZG SK7 184 B3
Denbydale Wy ROY/SHW OL2 58 D5
Denby La HTNM SK4 159 G2
Denby Rd DUK SK16 133 F1
Dencombe St
BRUN/LGST M13 129 G4
Dene Bank BOLE BL2 34 D1
Dene Brow DTN/ASHW M34 147 F3
Dene Ct HTNM SK4 12 A1
Dene Dr MDTN M24 72 C5
Denefield Cl MPL/ROM SK6 163 G5
Deneford Rd DID/WITH M20 157 F4
Dene Hollow RDSH SK5 145 G2
Denehurst Rd ROCH OL11 29 F3
Denehurst St
WGTN/LGST M12 * 129 G2
Dene Pk DID/WITH M20 157 F4
Dene Rd DID/WITH M20 157 F3
Dene Rd West DID/WITH M20 157 E3
Deneside Crs BRAM/HZG SK7 185 G1
Dene St BOLE BL2 34 D1
Denesway SALE M33 153 H3
Deneway BRAM/HZG SK7 183 F5
HTNM SK4 12 A1
MPL/ROM SK6 187 E5
Deneway Cl HTNM SK4 12 A2
Deneway Ms HTNM SK4 * 12 A1
Denewell Cl BRUN/LGST M13 129 E3
Denham Cl BOL BL1 34 B1
Denham Dr BRAM/HZG SK7 183 G5
IRL M44 136 C2
Denham St BRUN/LGST M13 129 E4
Den Hill Dr OLDE OL4 93 E1
Denhill Rd HULME M15 128 A4
Denholme Rd ROCH OL11 43 E2
Denholm Rd DID/WITH M20 169 H1
Denhurst Rd LIT OL15 20 D2
Denis Av OLDTF/WHR M16 142 A1
Denison Rd BRAM/HZG SK7 185 F4
RUSH/FAL M14 129 E5
Denison St RUSH/FAL M14 128 D5
Deniston Rd HTNM SK4 159 E1
Den La OLDE OL4 77 E5
UPML OL3 79 E4
Denmark Rd HULME M15 128 B4
SALE M33 139 H5
Denmark St ALT WA14 165 G5
CHAD OL9 74 D4
MILN OL16 11 F4
OLDE OL4 * 76 A5
Denmark Wy CHAD OL9 8 B1
Denmore Rd
NEWH/MOS M40 89 F5
Dennington Dr URM M41 124 B4
Dennison Av DID/WITH M20 142 D4
Dennison Rd CHD/CHDH SK8 182 D4
Denshaw Av DTN/ASHW M34 132 A3
Denshaw Cl BNG/LEV M19 158 B3
Denshaw Rd UPML OL3 61 H4
Densmead Wk
NEWH/MOS M40 * 115 F2
Densmore St FAIL M35 * 104 D3
Denson Rd HALE/TIMP WA15 166 C1
Denstone Av ECC M30 111 F2
SALE M33 153 H3
URM M41 124 B5
Denstone Crs BOLE BL2 35 E4
Denstone Rd RDSH SK5 145 F2
SLFD M6 100 A5
URM M41 124 B5
Dentdale Cl BOL BL1 47 E3
Denton Hall Farm Rd
DTN/ASHW M34 146 A1
Denton La CHAD OL9 90 B2
Denton Rd BOLE BL2 51 E3
DTN/ASHW M34 132 B3
Denton St BURY BL9 4 E1
HEY OL10 40 D5
WHIT OL12 10 C3
Denver Av NEWH/MOS M40 115 G2
Denver Dr HALE/TIMP WA15 166 B3
Denver Rd ROCH OL11 43 E2
Denville Crs WYTH/NTH M22 180 D1
Denzell Gdns ALT WA14 * 176 D1
Depleach Rd CHD/CHDH SK8 170 A4
Deptford Av NTHM/RTH M23 179 H1
De Quincey Rd ALT WA14 153 G5
Deramore Cl AUL OL6 120 B2
Deramore St RUSH/FAL M14 128 C5
Derby Av SLFD M6 112 D3
Derby Cl IRL M44 150 B1
Derby Ct CHAD OL9 8 A7
SALE M33 154 D3
Derby Gv BNG/LEV M19 144 B2
Derby Range HTNM SK4 159 E2
Derby Rd AUL OL6 120 A2
HTNM SK4 159 F2
ORD M5 112 D3
RAD M26 66 D4
RUSH/FAL M14 143 E4
SALE M33 139 E5
URM M41 124 C5
WHTF M45 85 H1
Derbyshire Av STRET M32 125 G5
Derbyshire Crs STRET M32 125 G5
Derbyshire Gv STRET M32 125 F5
Derbyshire La STRET M32 140 A1
Derbyshire La West
STRET M32 125 F5
Derbyshire Rd
NEWH/MOS M40 117 E1
PART M31 150 C4
POY/DIS SK12 196 C2
SALE M33 154 D3
Derbyshire Rd South
SALE M33 155 E4
Derbyshire Rw BOL BL1 * 33 H3
Derbyshire St OP/CLY M11 130 B1
Derby St ALT WA14 165 H4
AULW OL7 106 D5
BOLS/LL BL3 48 C4
BURY BL9 5 F4
CHAD OL9 8 A7
CHH M8 101 H5
DTN/ASHW M34 132 A4
EDGY/DAV SK3 12 D6
FAIL M35 105 F1
HEY OL10 40 C4
MOSL OL5 * 109 E2
MPL/ROM SK6 175 E4
PWCH M25 85 H3
RAMS BL0 17 E2
ROCH OL11 43 F1
WHTN BL5 62 A3
Dereham Cl TOT/BURYW BL8 38 A1
Derg St SLFD M6 113 E3
Derker St OLD OL1 9 K1
Dermot Murphy Cl
DID/WITH M20 142 B5
Dernford Av BNG/LEV M19 158 C1
Derry Av WYTH/NTH M22 168 D5
Derwen Rd EDGY/DAV SK3 171 H3
Derwent Av AULW OL7 119 F1
CCHDY M21 156 C1
DROY M43 117 F4
HALE/TIMP WA15 * 167 E4
HEY OL10 56 A1
WHTF M45 70 A4
Derwent Cl BOLS/LL BL3 66 C1
DTN/ASHW M34 145 H1
PART M31 151 E2
WALK M28 81 G5
WHTF M45 70 A5
Derwent Dr BRAM/HZG SK7 193 F2
BURY BL9 53 E2
CHAD OL9 74 B5
FWTH BL4 83 E2
LIT OL15 31 G1
ROY/SHW OL2 59 H1
SALE M33 154 B4
WILM/AE SK9 191 H2
Derwent Rd FWTH BL4 65 E5
MDTN M24 72 B1
MPL/ROM SK6 186 D4
STRET M32 126 A5
URM M41 137 G1
Derwent St CHH M8 102 D4
DROY M43 * 117 E4
ORD M5 113 H5
WHIT OL12 10 C2
Derwent Ter STLY SK15 120 D1
Design St BOLS/LL BL3 64 A1
Desmond Rd WYTH/NTH M22 168 D5
The De Traffords IRL M44 122 C5
Dettingen St SLFD M6 100 B4
Deva Cl BRAM/HZG SK7 185 E3
POY/DIS SK12 194 C3
Deva Sq CHAD OL9 8 A7
Devas St HULME M15 128 C3
Deverill Av GTN M18 131 E4
Devine Cl CSLFD M3 114 A3
ROY/SHW OL2 59 E3
Devisdale Gra ALT WA14 * 177 E1
Devisdale Rd ALT WA14 165 E5
Devoke Av WALK M28 82 B5
Devoke Gv FWTH BL4 64 D4
Devoke Rd WYTH/NTH M22 180 A2
Devon Av BNG/LEV M19 143 H3
WHTF M45 69 F3
Devon Cl BOLS/LL BL3 51 E5
RDSH SK5 160 D2
ROY/SHW OL2 59 G2
SLFD M6 111 H2
Devon Dr BOLE BL2 36 B5
Devonport Crs ROY/SHW OL2 59 G5
Devon Rd DROY M43 117 H2
FAIL M35 104 D4
IRL M44 150 C1
PART M31 150 D4
URM M41 137 G2
Devonshire Cl HEY OL10 40 B5
URM M41 139 E1
Devonshire Dr WILM/AE SK9 201 E3
Devonshire Park Rd
OFTN SK2 172 B4
Devonshire Pl PWCH M25 85 H2
Devonshire Rd ALT WA14 165 G3
BOL BL1 48 A1
BRAM/HZG SK7 185 G4
CCHDY M21 141 G3
ECC M30 111 F3
HTNM SK4 159 E4
ROCH OL11 43 E4
SLFD M6 111 H2
WALK M28 81 H1
Devonshire St BRO M7 101 H4
BRUN/LGST M13 129 E2
Devonshire St East
FAIL M35 * 104 C5
Devonshire St North
WGTN/LGST M12 129 E1
Devonshire St South
BRUN/LGST M13 129 E3
Devon St BOLE BL2 3 H5
BURY BL9 53 G1
CHAD OL9 90 C3
FWTH BL4 66 A2
ROCH OL11 30 A5
SWIN M27 84 A5
Devon Wy OLDS OL8 90 D5
Dewar Cl OP/CLY M11 116 B4
Dewes Av SWIN M27 84 C5
Dewey St OP/CLY M11 130 C1
Dewham Cl WHTN BL5 62 A3
Dewhirst Rd WHIT OL12 19 E3
Dewhirst Wy WHIT OL12 19 E4
Dewhurst Clough Rd
EDGW/EG BL7 22 C1
Dewhurst Rd BOLE BL2 35 F3
Dewhurst St CHH M8 114 C1
HEY OL10 * 41 F4
Dewint Av MPL/ROM SK6 175 G1
Dew Meadow Cl WHIT OL12 10 B1
Dewsnap Cl DUK SK16 * 133 F2
Dewsnap La DUK SK16 133 F2
HYDE SK14 135 H2
Dew Wy CHAD OL9 88 D5
Dexter Rd BKLY M9 87 F2
Deyne Av PWCH M25 86 A3
RUSH/FAL M14 128 D4
Deyne St ORD M5 112 D3
Dial Ct FWTH BL4 * 66 A4
Dial Park Rd OFTN SK2 173 E5
Dial Rd HALE/TIMP WA15 178 D4
OFTN SK2 172 D4
Dialstone La OFTN SK2 172 D2
Diamond St OFTN SK2 172 B3
Diamond Ter MPL/ROM SK6 187 E1
Dicken Gn ROCH OL11 43 E2
Dicken Green La ROCH OL11 43 E2
Dickens Cl CHD/CHDH SK8 193 E2
Dickens La POY/DIS SK12 195 F4
Dickenson Rd RUSH/FAL M14 129 E5
Dickens Rd ECC M30 111 E4
Dickens St HEY OL10 * 40 C4
OLD OL1 60 D5
Dickinson Cl BOL BL1 * 33 H5
Dickinson St BOL BL1 33 H5
CMANE M1 7 F6
OLDE OL4 76 A5
Didcot Rd WYTH/NTH M22 180 B3
Didley Sq WGTN/LGST M12 * 129 H2
Didsbury Pk DID/WITH M20 157 H5
Didsbury Rd HTNM SK4 158 D4
Digby Rd ROCH OL11 43 E2
Dig Gate La MILN OL16 44 B3
Diggles La ROCH OL11 28 B5
Diggle St ROY/SHW OL2 60 A3
Dijon St BOLS/LL BL3 48 B5
Dilham Ct BOL BL1 48 B1
Dillmoss Wk HULME M15 * 127 G2
Dillon Dr WGTN/LGST M12 129 F3
Dilworth Cl HEY OL10 40 A4
Dilworth Ct OFTN SK2 173 F4
Dilworth St HULME M15 128 C3
Dingle Av ROY/SHW OL2 45 F5
WILM/AE SK9 200 A2
Dingle Bank Rd
BRAM/HZG SK7 183 G3
Dingle Cl MPL/ROM SK6 162 C4
Dingle Dr DROY M43 118 A2
Dingle Gv CHD/CHDH SK8 169 E3
Dingle Rd MDTN M24 88 B1
Dingle Ter AUL OL6 92 A5
The Dingle BRAM/HZG SK7 183 F3
HYDE SK14 148 A5
Dingle Wk BOL BL1 2 E2
Dinmor Rd WYTH/NTH M22 180 C4
Dinnington Dr CHH M8 102 A4
Dinorwic Cl CHH M8 87 F5
Dinsdale Dr BOLS/LL BL3 48 C4
Dinting Av DID/WITH M20 142 C4
Dinton St HULME M15 127 F1
Dirty La OLDE OL4 77 G3
Dirty Leech WHIT OL12 19 E2
Discovery Pk HTNM SK4 * 159 F1
Disley Av DID/WITH M20 142 B5
Disley St ROCH OL11 42 C2
Distaff Rd POY/DIS SK12 194 C3
Ditton Brook WHTN BL5 62 A3
Ditton Mead Cl WHIT OL12 30 C1
Division St BOLS/LL BL3 65 E1
WHIT OL12 11 G1
Dixon Av BRO M7 101 G4
Dixon Cl SALE M33 155 E4
Dixon Closes ROCH OL11 28 B4
Dixon Dr SWIN M27 83 H3
Dixon Green Dr FWTH BL4 65 H4
Dixon Rd DTN/ASHW M34 147 F2
Dixon St AUL OL6 120 A1
IRL M44 136 A3
MDTN M24 72 D2
NEWH/MOS M40 104 A4
OLD OL1 9 F1
OLDE OL4 76 D4
ROCH OL11 42 C2
SLFD M6 100 C4
Dobb Hedge Cl
HALE/TIMP WA15 188 D1
Dobbin Dr ROCH OL11 43 E3
Dobbinets La
HALE/TIMP WA15 179 E1
Dobbinetts La
HALE/TIMP WA15 167 F5
Dobcross Cl BRUN/LGST M13 144 A1
Dobcross New Rd UPML OL3 78 D3
Dobhill St FWTH BL4 66 A4
Dobroyd St CHH M8 102 B2
Dobson Cl BRUN/LGST M13 129 E2
Dobson Rd BOL BL1 48 B2
Dobson St BOL BL1 33 G4
Doctor Fold La HEY OL10 55 H4
Doctor La OLDE OL4 77 H3
Doctors La BURY BL9 4 B4
Dodd Cft MILN OL16 43 G4
Doddington La ORD M5 113 F5
Doddington Wk
DTN/ASHW M34 * 146 C2
Dodd St ORD M5 112 C3
Dodge Fold OFTN SK2 173 F3
Dodge Hl HTNM SK4 13 F1
Dodgson St MILN OL16 30 B5
Dodworth Cl HULME M15 128 A2
Doe Brow SWIN M27 83 H3
Doefield Av WALK M28 97 E2
Doe Hey Gv FWTH BL4 65 G2
Doe Hey Rd BOLS/LL BL3 65 G2
Doffcocker Brow BOL BL1 32 C5
Doffcocker La BOL BL1 32 C5
Dogford Rd ROY/SHW OL2 59 E4
Dog Hill Lne ROY/SHW OL2 60 D2
Dolbey St ORD M5 112 D4
Dolefield CSLFD M3 6 C5
D'Olivera Ct MDTN M24 72 B2
Dollond St BKLY M9 103 F1
Dolphin Pl WGTN/LGST M12 128 D1
Dolphin St WGTN/LGST M12 128 D1
Doman St BOLS/LL BL3 49 E4
Dombey Rd POY/DIS SK12 195 E5
Domestic Ap MANAIR M90 180 B5
The Dome ALT WA14 * 165 G5
Domett St BKLY M9 87 H5
Dominic Cl NTHM/RTH M23 155 F5
Donald Av HYDE SK14 148 B2
Donald St CMANE M1 * 7 G7
Dona St STKP SK1 13 K5
Don Av SLFD M6 112 B3
Doncaster Av DID/WITH M20 142 C4
Doncaster Cl BOLS/LL BL3 66 C1
OLD OL1 60 C5
Doncaster Wk OLD OL1 9 G2
Donhead Wk
BRUN/LGST M13 * 128 D2
Donkey La WILM/AE SK9 198 D5
Donleigh St NEWH/MOS M40 104 C5
Donnington ROCH OL11 * 29 H5
Donnington Av
CHD/CHDH SK8 170 C4
Donnington Gdns WALK M28 * 82 A4
Donnington Rd GTN M18 130 D3
RAD M26 51 F4
Donnison St WGTN/LGST M12 129 G2
Donovan Av NEWH/MOS M40 115 F1
Don St BOLS/LL BL3 64 C1
MDTN M24 73 F3
Doodson Av IRL M44 136 B1
Doodson Sq FWTH BL4 66 A4
Dooley La MPL/ROM SK6 174 A2
Dooley's La WILM/AE SK9 190 A5

Dorac Av CHD/CHDH SK8 191 H1
Dora St RAMS BL0 16 B4
Dorchester Av BOLE BL2 35 F5
DTN/ASHW M34 146 D2
PWCH M25 86 B5
URM M41 125 E5
Dorchester Cl
HALE/TIMP WA15 178 D1
WILM/AE SK9 199 G2
Dorchester Ct
CHD/CHDH SK8 183 E3
SALE M33 154 C4
Dorchester Dr
NTHM/RTH M23 155 F5
ROY/SHW OL2 75 E2
Dorchester Gv HEY OL10 55 H1
Dorchester Rd
BRAM/HZG SK7 184 C3
SWIN M27 99 E4
Dorclyn Av URM M41 138 D1
Dorfield Cl MPL/ROM SK6 161 F3
Doric Av MPL/ROM SK6 161 E4
Doric Cl OP/CLY M11 116 A4
Doris Av BOLE BL2 50 A2
Doris Rd EDGY/DAV SK3 12 A6
Doris St MDTN M24 72 D2
Dorking Av NEWH/MOS M40 116 B1
Dorking Cl BOL BL1 34 A4
STKP SK1 172 C2
Dorlan Av GTN M18 131 E4
Dorland Gv OFTN SK2 172 C2
Dorman St OP/CLY M11 130 C1
Dormer St BOL BL1 34 A3
Dorney St GTN M18 130 C3
Dorning Rd SWIN M27 99 F3
Dorning St ECC M30 111 E4
FWTH BL4 66 C4
TOT/BURYW BL8 37 G2
Dorothy Rd BRAM/HZG SK7 185 G1
Dorothy St BRO M7 102 A3
RAMS BL0 16 C3
Dorrington Rd EDGY/DAV SK3 170 D2
SALE M33 153 G2
Dorris St BNG/LEV M19 144 B3
BOLS/LL BL3 * 64 B1
Dorrit Cl POY/DIS SK12 195 F5
Dorset Av BRAM/HZG SK7 183 G3
CHD/CHDH SK8 171 F5
DTN/ASHW M34 118 B5
FWTH BL4 65 H4
RDSH SK5 160 D1
ROY/SHW OL2 59 G2
RUSH/FAL M14 142 C1
Dorset Cl FWTH BL4 65 H4
HEY OL10 40 B5
Dorset Dr BURY BL9 53 H1
Dorset Rd ALT WA14 165 E5
BNG/LEV M19 144 C2
DROY M43 117 G2
FAIL M35 105 E5
IRL M44 150 C1
Dorset St AUL OL6 120 A3
BOLE BL2 3 H5
CHAD OL9 8 A7
ROCH OL11 30 A5
STRET M32 140 B2
SWIN M27 84 A5
Dorsey St ANC M4 * 7 H3
Dorstone Cl NEWH/MOS M40 116 D1
Dorwood Av BKLY M9 87 H2
Dougall Wk WGTN/LGST M12 129 H2
Doughty Av ECC M30 111 G2
Douglas Av STRET M32 126 A5
TOT/BURYW BL8 37 G4
Douglas Cl WHTF M45 70 B3
Douglas Gn SLFD M6 100 D5
Douglas Rd BRAM/HZG SK7 185 F1
EDGY/DAV SK3 171 H5
WALK M28 98 B3
Douglas St AUL OL6 120 A2
BOL BL1 * 33 H1
BRO M7 101 G4
FAIL M35 105 F3
HYDE SK14 148 A1
NEWH/MOS M40 103 H3
OLD OL1 9 J1
RAMS BL0 16 C2
SWIN M27 99 F3
Doulton St NEWH/MOS M40 104 B2
Dounby Av ECC M30 110 C2
Douro St NEWH/MOS M40 103 G5
Douthwaite Dr MPL/ROM SK6 162 D5
Dove Bank Rd BOLS/LL BL3 50 C5
Dovebrook Cl STLY SK15 109 F3
Dovecote DROY M43 118 C2
Dovecote Cl EDGW/EG BL7 23 G3
Dovecote La LHULT M38 80 D4
OLDE OL4 77 E5
Dovecote Ms CCHDY M21 141 E4
Dovedale Av DID/WITH M20 142 D4
DROY M43 117 F3
ECC M30 111 F2
PWCH M25 86 C4
URM M41 138 D1
Dovedale Cl MPL/ROM SK6 186 D5
Dovedale Dr WHIT OL12 20 A2
Dovedale Rd BOLE BL2 35 G5
OFTN SK2 173 E2
Dovedale St FAIL M35 104 D3
Dove Dr BURY BL9 5 K1
IRL M44 122 B5
Dovehouse Cl WHTF M45 69 E4
Doveleys Rd SLFD M6 112 C1
Dover Cl TOT/BURYW BL8 26 B2
Dovercort Av HTNM SK4 158 C2
Dovercourt Av HTNM SK4 * 158 C3
Dover Gv BOLS/LL BL3 48 C4
Doveridge Gdns SLFD M6 113 E2
Dove Rd BOLS/LL BL3 48 A5
Dover Pk URM M41 124 C4
Dover Rd SWIN M27 84 B5
Dover St BRUN/LGST M13 128 C2
CHAD OL9 8 B6
ECC M30 110 C3
FWTH BL4 65 H2
MILN OL16 11 H1
RDSH SK5 * 145 E4
Dovestone Crs DUK SK16 134 A1
Dovestone Wk
NEWH/MOS M40 * 104 D1
Doveston Rd SALE M33 139 H5
Dove St BOL BL1 33 H2
OLDE OL4 92 C2
ROCH OL11 29 G4
Dow Fold TOT/BURYW BL8 37 E3
Dowland Cl NTHM/RTH M23 * 155 G4
Dow La TOT/BURYW BL8 37 E3
Dowling St ROCH OL11 30 A5
Downesway WILM/AE SK9 200 C4
Downes Wy WYTH/NTH M22 168 D3
Downfield Cl RAMS BL0 16 B2
Downfields RDSH SK5 145 G2
Downgreen Rd BOLE BL2 35 F3
Downhall Gn BOL BL1 2 E2
Downham Av BOLE BL2 49 H1
Downham Cha
HALE/TIMP WA15 166 C3
Downham Cl ROY/SHW OL2 74 D2
Downham Crs PWCH M25 86 D4
Downham Gdns PWCH M25 86 D4
Downham Rd HEY OL10 40 B4
HTNM SK4 159 G1
Downham Wk
NTHM/RTH M23 167 E1
Downhill Cl OLD OL1 75 F3
Downing Cl AULW OL7 106 C4
Downing St AULW OL7 106 C4
CMANE M1 128 C1
Downley Cl WHIT OL12 28 D1
Downley Dr ANC M4 115 F3
Downs Dr ALT WA14 165 H1
Downshaw Rd AULW OL7 106 D4
The Downs ALT WA14 177 G1
CHD/CHDH SK8 182 A1
MDTN M24 89 E1
PWCH M25 85 H4
Dowry Rd OLDE OL4 76 D5
Dowry St OLDS OL8 91 G4
Dowson Rd HYDE SK14 148 A3
Dowson St BOLE BL2 3 H5
Dow St HYDE SK14 133 G3
Doyle Av MPL/ROM SK6 161 E3
Doyle Cl OLD OL1 60 D5
Doyle Rd BOLS/LL BL3 63 F1
Drake Av FWTH BL4 82 A1
IRL M44 136 A5
WYTH/NTH M22 180 A2
Drake Cl OLD OL1 75 G4
Drake Ct RDSH SK5 159 H2
Drake Rd ALT WA14 165 E1
Drake St MILN OL16 10 C6
ROCH OL11 30 A5
Draycott St BOL BL1 34 A4
Draycott St East BOL BL1 34 A4
Drayfields DROY M43 118 C3
Drayford Cl NTHM/RTH M23 155 G4
Drayton Cl BOL BL1 33 G4
SALE M33 153 G4
WILM/AE SK9 199 G1
Drayton Dr CHD/CHDH SK8 181 G5
Drayton Gv HALE/TIMP WA15 166 B5
Drayton St HULME M15 127 H3
Drayton Wk OLDTF/WHR M16 127 G2
Dresden St NEWH/MOS M40 104 B2
Drewett St NEWH/MOS M40 115 H1
Dreyfus Av OP/CLY M11 116 D3
Driffield St ECC M30 110 D5
RUSH/FAL M14 128 B5
Drill Wk ANC M4 115 F4
Drinkwater Rd PWCH M25 100 C1
Driscoll St BRUN/LGST M13 129 G5
The Drive BRO M7 101 F2
BURY BL9 38 C1
CHD/CHDH SK8 171 F5
DID/WITH M20 157 H3
HALE/TIMP WA15 179 E4
MPL/ROM SK6 161 E3
MPL/ROM SK6 174 D3
PWCH M25 86 A3
RDSH SK5 160 D2
SALE M33 153 H5
Droitwich Rd NEWH/MOS M40 115 G1
Dronfield Rd SLFD M6 112 C1
WYTH/NTH M22 168 C1
Droughts La PWCH M25 70 C4
Droylsden Rd DTN/ASHW M34 118 A4
NEWH/MOS M40 104 C5
Drummond St BOL BL1 * 33 H2
Drury La CHAD OL9 90 B4
Drury St BNG/LEV M19 144 A2
Dryad Cl SWIN M27 84 A5
Drybrook Cl BRUN/LGST M13 129 F3
Dryburgh Av BOL BL1 33 G3
Dryden Av CHD/CHDH SK8 170 B3
SWIN M27 98 C3
Dryden Cl DUK SK16 134 C1
MPL/ROM SK6 175 E5
Dryden Rd OLDTF/WHR M16 127 F5
Dryden St BRUN/LGST M13 128 D2
Dryhurst Wk HULME M15 128 B2
Drymoss OLDS OL8 106 C1
Drysdale Vw BOL BL1 33 H2
Drywood Av WALK M28 97 H5
Ducal St ANC M4 115 E1
Duchess Park Cl ROY/SHW OL2 60 A1
Duchess Rd CHH M8 102 C2
Duchess St ROY/SHW OL2 59 H1
Duchess Wk BOLS/LL BL3 48 A5
Duchy Av WALK M28 97 E2
WHTN BL5 63 H4
Duchy Bank SLFD M6 100 A4
Duchy Rd SLFD M6 100 B5
Duchy St EDGY/DAV SK3 12 D7
SLFD M6 113 E3
Ducie Av BOL BL1 48 B2
Ducie St CMANE M1 7 H5
OLDS OL8 91 G5
RAD M26 52 A4
WHTF M45 69 G4
Duckshaw La FWTH BL4 65 H4
Duckworth Rd PWCH M25 85 G4
Duckworth St BURY BL9 38 D2
ROY/SHW OL2 60 B2
Duddon Av BOLE BL2 35 G5
Duddon Cl WHTF M45 70 A4
Dudley Av BOLE BL2 34 D5
WHTF M45 69 G4
Dudley Cl HULME M15 127 H3
Dudley Rd HALE/TIMP WA15 166 C2
IRL M44 150 C2
OLDTF/WHR M16 127 G5
SALE M33 140 A5
SWIN M27 99 E1
Dudley St BRO M7 102 A4
ECC M30 110 D4
OLDE OL4 92 C1
Dudlow Wk HULME M15 * 127 G2
Dudwell Cl BOL BL1 33 F5
Duerden St BOLS/LL BL3 * 63 H2
Duffield Ct MDTN M24 * 88 C2
Duffield Gdns MDTN M24 88 C2
Duffield Rd MDTN M24 88 C2
SLFD M6 100 A5
Duffins Cl WHIT OL12 18 C5
Dugdale Av BKLY M9 88 B3
Dugie St RAMS BL0 16 C1
Duke Av CHD/CHDH SK8 192 C1
Duke Ct OLDTF/WHR M16 127 G3
Dukefield St WYTH/NTH M22 168 D1
Duke Pl CSLFD M3 6 B7
Duke Rd BOLE BL2 36 B5
HYDE SK14 134 A3
Dukes Platting AUL OL6 108 A5
Duke St AUL OL6 * 119 G3
BOL BL1 2 D3
BRO M7 101 G5
CSLFD M3 6 B7
CSLFD M3 6 D2
DTN/ASHW M34 132 B5
ECC M30 110 D1
FAIL M35 105 F2
HEY OL10 40 C4
LHULT M38 81 F2
LIT OL15 20 D3
MOSL OL5 109 F1
RAD M26 68 C2
RAMS BL0 16 B4
ROY/SHW OL2 60 B3
STKP SK1 13 G4
STLY SK15 120 C4
WALK M28 83 E5
WHIT OL12 10 C2
WILM/AE SK9 201 E3
Duke St North BOL BL1 2 D2
Dukes Wk HALE/TIMP WA15 178 A1
Dukinfield Rd HYDE SK14 133 F3
Dulford Wk BRUN/LGST M13 * 128 D3
Dulgar St OP/CLY M11 * 116 C5
Dulverton Gdns BOLS/LL BL3 * 67 E2
Dulverton St NEWH/MOS M40 104 A4
Dulwich Cl SALE M33 153 G3
Dulwich St ANC M4 115 E2
Dumbarton Cl RDSH SK5 145 F5
Dumbarton Dr HEY OL10 40 B5
Dumbarton Rd RDSH SK5 145 F4
Dumbell St SWIN M27 84 A5
Dumber La SALE M33 139 F5
Dumers Cl RAD M26 53 E5
Dumers La RAD M26 53 F4
Dumfries Hollow HEY OL10 41 G3
Dunbar Av NTHM/RTH M23 179 H1
Dunbar Dr BOLS/LL BL3 64 D1
Dunbar Gv HEY OL10 55 E1
Dunbar St OLD OL1 8 E1
Dunblane Av BOLS/LL BL3 47 F4
HTNM SK4 12 C1
Dunblane Gv HEY OL10 55 F1
Duncan Rd BRUN/LGST M13 129 G5
Duncan St BRO M7 101 F4
DUK SK16 133 E2
ORD M5 113 H5
Dunchurch Cl HOR/BR BL6 47 E3
Dunchurch Rd SALE M33 153 H2
Dun Cl CSLFD M3 6 A3
Duncombe Cl BRAM/HZG SK7 184 B1
Duncombe Dr
NEWH/MOS M40 104 A3
Duncombe Rd BOLS/LL BL3 64 D2
Duncombe St BRO M7 101 H4
Duncote Gv ROY/SHW OL2 59 G4
Dundee Cl HEY OL10 40 A5
Dundee La RAMS BL0 16 C2
Dundonald Rd
CHD/CHDH SK8 182 D5
DID/WITH M20 157 H3
Dundonald St OFTN SK2 172 A3
Dundraw Cl MDTN M24 71 G3
Dundrennan Cl POY/DIS SK12 195 E2
Dunecroft DTN/ASHW M34 * 132 D4
Dunedin Dr SLFD M6 100 C5
Dunedin Rd TOT/BURYW BL8 26 A1
Dunelm Dr SALE M33 155 E5
Dunham Lawn ALT WA14 165 E5
Dunham Ms ALT WA14 * 176 C3
Dunham Ri ALT WA14 165 F5
Dunham Rd ALT WA14 176 C2
DUK SK16 133 G2
PART M31 152 A3
WILM/AE SK9 192 A2
Dunham St HULME M15 127 H2
OLDE OL4 76 D4
Dunkeld Rd NTHM/RTH M23 167 G3
Dunkerley Av FAIL M35 105 E3
Dunkerley St AULW OL7 106 D5
OLDE OL4 76 B5
ROY/SHW OL2 * 59 E5
Dunkery Rd WYTH/NTH M22 180 C3
Dunkirk La HYDE SK14 133 E4
Dunkirk Ri WHIT OL12 10 A6
Dunkirk Rd WHTF M45 69 G3
Dunkirk St DROY M43 118 A4
Dunley Cl WGTN/LGST M12 129 H3
Dunlin Cl BOLE BL2 49 F4
OFTN SK2 173 H4
POY/DIS SK12 194 B4
ROCH OL11 28 C4
Dunlin Dr IRL M44 122 B5
Dunlop Av ROCH OL11 42 D3
Dunlop St CSLFD M3 * 6 D4
Dunmail Dr MDTN M24 72 B1
Dunmaston Av
HALE/TIMP WA15 167 E2
Dunmore Rd CHD/CHDH SK8 169 G3
Dunmow Ct OFTN SK2 173 F4
Dunnisher Rd
NTHM/RTH M23 168 A5
Dunnock Cl OFTN SK2 173 G4
Dunollie Rd SALE M33 155 F3
Dunoon Cl HEY OL10 40 B5
Dunoon Dr BOL BL1 33 G1
Dunoon Rd RDSH SK5 145 F4
Dunrobin Cl HEY OL10 55 F1
Dunscar Cl WHTF M45 69 E5
Dunsfold Dr NTHM/RTH M23 167 E1
Dunsley Av NEWH/MOS M40 89 G5
Dunsmore Cl
OLDTF/WHR M16 127 G4
Dunsop Dr BOL BL1 32 C3
Dunstable WHIT OL12 10 B4
Dunstable St BNG/LEV M19 144 B2
Dunstall Rd WYTH/NTH M22 168 D4
Dunstan St BOLE BL2 49 H2
Dunstar Av DTN/ASHW M34 132 B1
Dunster Av BKLY M9 88 B3
RDSH SK5 160 D1
ROCH OL11 42 D1
SWIN M27 84 C5
Dunster Cl BRAM/HZG SK7 184 D3
Dunster Dr URM M41 137 E2
Dunster Pl WALK M28 96 A3
Dunster Rd WALK M28 96 A3
Dunsters Av TOT/BURYW BL8 37 H1
Dunston St OP/CLY M11 116 D5
Dunton Gn RDSH SK5 145 H5
Dunvegan Rd BRAM/HZG SK7 185 G3
Dunwood Av ROY/SHW OL2 60 B1
Dunwoods Park Cts
ROY/SHW OL2 45 F5
Dunworth St RUSH/FAL M14 128 C5
Durant St ANC M4 * 7 H1
Durban Cl ROY/SHW OL2 59 H3
Durban Rd BOL BL1 33 H1
Durban St AULW OL7 118 D4
OLDS OL8 90 D4
ROCH OL11 42 B4
Durden Ms ROY/SHW OL2 60 A3
Durham Av URM M41 124 D5
Durham Cl BOLS/LL BL3 51 E5
DUK SK16 133 G2
MPL/ROM SK6 161 H5
Durham Crs FAIL M35 105 F4
Durham Dr AUL OL6 107 G2
BURY BL9 * 53 H1
RAMS BL0 16 B5
Durham Rd SLFD M6 112 B1
Durham St BKLY M9 * 103 F3
BOL BL1 34 A4
CHAD OL9 90 D3
DROY M43 117 H5
RAD M26 52 D4
RDSH SK5 145 E1
ROCH OL11 43 F1
Durley Av CHH M8 102 C3
HALE/TIMP WA15 166 C2
Durling St WGTN/LGST M12 128 D1
Durnford Av URM M41 139 G1
Durnford Cl WHIT OL12 28 A1
Durnford St MDTN M24 72 C3
Durnlaw Cl LIT OL15 21 F3
Durn St LIT OL15 21 F2
Dutton St CSLFD M3 114 C2
Duty St BOL BL1 33 H3
Duxbury Av BOLE BL2 35 F1
BOLS/LL BL3 50 D4
Duxbury Dr BURY BL9 39 F4
Duxbury St BOL BL1 33 G4
Dyche St ANC M4 7 H2
Dye House La MILN OL16 19 H5
Dye La MPL/ROM SK6 162 A4
Dyers Ct LIT OL15 * 20 D2
Dyer St OP/CLY M11 116 B5
ORD M5 127 F1
Dymchurch Av RAD M26 67 F5
Dymchurch St
NEWH/MOS M40 116 D1
Dysarts Cl MOSL OL5 94 B4
Dysart St AUL OL6 120 A3
OFTN SK2 172 C4
Dyserth Gv RDSH SK5 160 A1
Dyson Cl FWTH BL4 66 A4
Dyson Gv OLDE OL4 * 77 E4
Dyson St FWTH BL4 * 66 A5
MOSL OL5 * 93 G5

E

Eades St SLFD M6 113 F2
Eadington St CHH M8 102 B1
Eafield Av MILN OL16 31 G4
Eafield Cl MILN OL16 31 G4
Eafield Rd LIT OL15 20 B5
MILN OL16 11 K2
Eagar St NEWH/MOS M40 104 B4
Eagle Dr SLFD M6 100 D5
Eagle St ANC M4 7 G2
BOLE BL2 3 H4
CHAD OL9 8 E3
ROCH OL11 * 10 E7
Eagley Brook Wy BOL BL1 34 A3
Eagley Brow BOL BL1 23 E4
Eagley Dr TOT/BURYW BL8 37 F5
Eagley Vw TOT/BURYW BL8 37 F5
Eagley Wy BOL BL1 23 E5
Ealees Rd LIT OL15 21 F3
Ealing Av RUSH/FAL M14 142 D1
Ealinger Wy SWIN M27 84 A5
Ealing Pl BNG/LEV M19 * 144 A5
Ealing Rd EDGY/DAV SK3 12 C5
Eames Av RAD M26 66 D4
Earby Gv BKLY M9 88 C4
Earle Rd BRAM/HZG SK7 183 H2
Earlesdon Crs LHULT M38 81 F2
Earlesfield Cl SALE M33 153 G4
Earle St AULW OL7 119 E4
Earl Rd CHD/CHDH SK8 192 B2
HTNM SK4 159 F2
RAMS BL0 16 C2
Earlston Av DTN/ASHW M34 131 F5
Earl St BRO M7 114 A1
BURY BL9 5 F4
DTN/ASHW M34 131 F4
EDGY/DAV SK3 12 C6
HEY OL10 40 D4
MOSL OL5 108 C1
PWCH M25 86 B3
RAMS BL0 17 E2
ROCH OL11 57 F1
SALE M33 * 154 D1
Earls Wy FAIL M35 104 C4
Earlswood Wk BOLS/LL BL3 49 E5
Earl Wk WGTN/LGST M12 * 129 G4
Early Bank STLY SK15 121 F5
Early Bank Rd HYDE SK14 134 C2
Earnshaw Av STKP SK1 160 C5
WHIT OL12 18 D5
Earnshaw Cl AULW OL7 * 106 C5
Earnshaw St BOLS/LL BL3 * 64 B1
Easby Cl CHD/CHDH SK8 193 E1
POY/DIS SK12 195 E2
Easby Rd MDTN M24 72 C1
Easedale Cl URM M41 123 G5
Easedale Rd BOL BL1 47 H1
NEWH/MOS M40 104 B2
East Aisle Rd TRPK M17 125 H4
East Av BNG/LEV M19 143 H4
CHD/CHDH SK8 182 A4
STLY SK15 120 D2
WHTF M45 69 F2
Eastbank St BOL BL1 34 A4
Eastbourne Gv BOL BL1 47 H1
Eastbourne St OLDS OL8 92 A3
ROCH OL11 43 E1
Eastbrook Av RAD M26 * 52 D5
Eastburn Av NEWH/MOS M40 115 F2
East Central Dr SWIN M27 99 G3
Eastchurch Cl FWTH BL4 66 A5
Eastcombe Av BRO M7 101 E3
Eastcote Rd RDSH SK5 160 A1
East Crs MDTN M24 72 C5
Eastdale Pl ALT WA14 * 165 G2
East Downs Rd ALT WA14 177 F2
CHD/CHDH SK8 182 C2
East Dr BURY BL9 54 A5
MPL/ROM SK6 187 E1
SLFD M6 100 B5
SWIN M27 99 G3
Easterdale OLDE OL4 92 B1
Eastern Av SWIN M27 85 E5
Eastern By-Pass OP/CLY M11 116 D3
OP/CLY M11 117 E5
Eastern Cir BNG/LEV M19 144 A5
Eastfield SLFD M6 112 D1
Eastfield Av MDTN M24 72 D5
NEWH/MOS M40 115 H2
Eastfields RAD M26 51 H4
Eastford Sq NEWH/MOS M40 115 E1
Eastgate WHIT OL12 18 B1
Eastgate St AULW OL7 119 F4
East Gate St MILN OL16 10 D5
East Gra OP/CLY M11 116 D2
East Gv BRUN/LGST M13 128 D3
Eastgrove Av BOL BL1 22 D5
Eastham Av BURY BL9 27 F5
RUSH/FAL M14 142 D2
Eastham Wy LHULT M38 81 G2
Easthaven Av OP/CLY M11 116 D3
East Hill St OLDE OL4 * 9 K5
Eastholme Dr BNG/LEV M19 144 B4
Easthope Cl DID/WITH M20 142 D4
East Lancashire Rd SWIN M27 99 G4
WALK M28 96 A3
Eastlands Rd BKLY M9 88 A2
East Lea DTN/ASHW M34 132 D5
Eastleigh Av BRO M7 101 H2
Eastleigh Dr NEWH/MOS M40 115 G2
Eastleigh Rd CHD/CHDH SK8 181 G3
PWCH M25 86 D4
East Lynn Dr WALK M28 82 D5
East Meade BOLS/LL BL3 64 D2
CCHDY M21 141 F4
PWCH M25 86 C5
SWIN M27 98 D4
East Moor WALK M28 96 B3
Eastmoor Dr NEWH/MOS M40 117 E1
Eastmoor Gv BOLS/LL BL3 64 A2
East Newton St ANC M4 115 F2
Easton Cl MDTN M24 73 F5
Easton Dr CHD/CHDH SK8 170 D4
Easton Rd DROY M43 117 F3
East Ordsall La CSLFD M3 6 A4
Eastover MPL/ROM SK6 173 H1
East Park Cl BRUN/LGST M13 128 D2
Eastpark Cl BRUN/LGST M13 128 D2
East Philip St CSLFD M3 114 B2
East Rd BOL BL1 33 H2
GTN M18 130 A5
MANAIR M90 180 B5
STLY SK15 109 F4
STRET M32 125 G4
URM M41 125 E3
WGTN/LGST M12 129 H5
Eastry Av RDSH SK5 160 C1
East St AUL OL6 120 A1
BURY BL9 5 F6
DTN/ASHW M34 132 C2
LIT OL15 21 F3
MILN OL16 10 E4
RAD M26 68 C1
WHIT OL12 19 H2
East Union St
OLDTF/WHR M16 127 F2
East V MPL/ROM SK6 175 F4
East Vw BURY BL9 16 D5
MDTN M24 72 C4
Eastville Gdns BNG/LEV M19 158 B1
East Wk EDGW/EG BL7 22 C1
Eastward Av WILM/AE SK9 198 C4
East Wy BOL BL1 34 C3
OLD OL1 75 F3
Eastway MDTN M24 72 C3
ROY/SHW OL2 60 A3
SALE M33 154 A5
URM M41 123 F5
Eastwood Av DROY M43 117 F4
NEWH/MOS M40 105 E1
URM M41 138 D1
WALK M28 81 F4
Eastwood Cl BOLS/LL BL3 63 H1
BURY BL9 5 J4
Eastwood Rd
NEWH/MOS M40 105 E1
Eastwood St
DTN/ASHW M34 132 A1
LIT OL15 21 E3
Eastwood Ter BOL BL1 47 G1
Eaton Cl CHD/CHDH SK8 182 C1
DUK SK16 133 F2

POY/DIS SK12 195 H4
Eaton Dr AULW OL7 119 E1
HALE/TIMP WA15 166 B1
WILM/AE SK9 200 C3
Eaton Rd ALT WA14 177 F3
CHH M8 102 A1
SALE M33 154 B2
Eaves La CHAD OL9 90 B2
Ebbdale Cl STKP SK1 13 J6
Ebberstone St RUSH/FAL M14 142 C1
Ebden St CMANE M1 * 7 H7
Ebor Cl ROY/SHW OL2 59 H1
Ebor Rd WYTH/NTH M22 * 168 D5
Ebor St LIT OL15 21 E3
Ebsworth St NEWH/MOS M40 103 G2
Ebury St RAD M26 68 A1
Ecclesbridge Rd
MPL/ROM SK6 175 E4
Eccles Cl OP/CLY M11 116 D5
Eccleshall St OP/CLY M11 116 D4
Eccles New Rd SALQ M50 112 A3
Eccles Old Rd SLFD M6 112 B2
Eccles Rd SWIN M27 99 E4
Eccles St RAMS BL0 16 C2
Eccleston Av BOLE BL2 34 C5
RUSH/FAL M14 142 C2
SWIN M27 98 C3
Eccleston Cl TOT/BURYW BL8 37 F5
Eccleston Pl BRO M7 * 101 G2
Eccleston Rd EDGY/DAV SK3 171 H5
Eccleston St FAIL M35 * 105 F2
Echo St CMANE M1 7 H7
Eckersley Cl NTHM/RTH M23 167 G3
Eckersley Rd BOL BL1 33 H3
Eckersley St BOLS/LL BL3 48 B5
Eckford St CHH M8 102 C4
Eclipse Cl MILN OL16 11 J6
Edale Av DTN/ASHW M34 132 A1
DTN/ASHW M34 146 D3
NEWH/MOS M40 103 H2
RDSH SK5 145 G2
URM M41 138 B2
Edale Cl ALT WA14 177 F3
BRAM/HZG SK7 185 F3
CHD/CHDH SK8 182 A5
IRL M44 136 C2
Edale Gv AUL OL6 108 B4
SALE M33 153 H4
Edale Rd BOLS/LL BL3 * 47 H5
FWTH BL4 65 H5
STRET M32 125 G5
Edale St SLFD M6 101 E5
Edbrook Wk
BRUN/LGST M13 * 129 E3
Eddie Colman Cl
NEWH/MOS M40 * 104 A5
Eddisbury Av DID/WITH M20 142 B3
URM M41 123 E4
Edditch Gv BOLE BL2 49 H2
Eddystone Cl ORD M5 113 F4
Eden Av BOL BL1 33 H3
MPL/ROM SK6 186 D5
Edenbridge Dr RAD M26 67 E5
Edenbridge Rd
CHD/CHDH SK8 171 E5
NEWH/MOS M40 116 C1
Eden Cl HEY OL10 40 B3
HULME M15 128 B3
STKP SK1 13 J5
WILM/AE SK9 198 B5
Edendale Dr WYTH/NTH M22 180 C3
Edenfield La WALK M28 110 A1
Edenfield Rd PWCH M25 86 D4
ROCH OL11 * 28 A1
ROCH OL11 28 D2
Edenfield St ROCH OL11 29 F2
Eden Gv BOL BL1 33 H3
Edenhall Av BNG/LEV M19 143 H3
Edenhurst Dr
HALE/TIMP WA15 166 C4
Edenhurst Rd OFTN SK2 172 C5
Eden Park Rd CHD/CHDH SK8 182 B4
Eden Pl CHD/CHDH SK8 170 A3
Edensor Dr HALE/TIMP WA15 178 D1
Eden St BOL BL1 33 H3
OLD OL1 9 F2
WHIT OL12 29 G3
Edenvale WALK M28 96 B3
Eden Wy ROY/SHW OL2 59 H1
Edgar St BOLS/LL BL3 48 D4
MILN OL16 30 D1
RAMS BL0 16 C3
Edgar St West RAMS BL0 16 C3
Edgbaston Dr
OLDTF/WHR M16 126 D5
Edgecote Cl WYTH/NTH M22 169 E3
Edgedale Av BNG/LEV M19 158 B1
Edgefield Av BKLY M9 88 B3
Edge Fold FWTH BL4 * 64 B3
Edge Fold Crs WALK M28 97 E2
Edge Fold Rd WALK M28 97 E1
Edge Gn WALK M28 * 96 D2
Edge Hill Av ROY/SHW OL2 75 F2
Edgehill Cha WILM/AE SK9 199 H3
Edgehill Cl ORD M5 113 E3
Edge Hill Rd BOLS/LL BL3 64 A1
ROY/SHW OL2 75 F1
Edgehill Rd SLFD M6 112 B2
Edgehill St ANC M4 * 7 G3
Edge La DROY M43 117 F4
HYDE SK14 135 F5
STRET M32 140 C2
Edge Lane Rd OLD OL1 75 H4
Edge Lane St ROY/SHW OL2 59 F5
Edgeley Fold EDGY/DAV SK3 171 F2
Edgeley Rd EDGY/DAV SK3 171 F2
URM M41 138 A3
Edgemoor ALT WA14 176 D2
Edgemoor Cl OLDE OL4 76 C3
RAD M26 51 H4
Edgemoor Dr ROCH OL11 41 G1
Edge St ANC M4 7 G3
Edge Vw OLD OL1 73 H3
Edgeware Av PWCH M25 87 E3
Edgeware Rd CHAD OL9 89 H4
ECC M30 110 B1
Edgewater ORD M5 112 C3
Edgeway WILM/AE SK9 199 E5
Edgeworth Av BOLE BL2 36 C5
Edgeworth Dr RUSH/FAL M14 143 G4
Edgmont Av BOLS/LL BL3 48 C5
Edgware Rd NEWH/MOS M40 116 C1
Edgworth Cl HEY OL10 40 B4
Edgworth Dr TOT/BURYW BL8 37 F5
Edilom Rd CHH M8 86 D5
Edinburgh Cl CHD/CHDH SK8 170 C3
Edinburgh Dr MPL/ROM SK6 162 B2
Edinburgh Rd BOLS/LL BL3 66 D2
Edinburgh Sq
NEWH/MOS M40 115 G1
Edinburgh Wy ROCH OL11 42 C2
Edington WHIT OL12 10 B4
Edison Rd ECC M30 110 D5
Edison St OP/CLY M11 130 D1
Edith Av RUSH/FAL M14 142 C1
Edith Cavell Cl OP/CLY M11 116 D4
Edith St BOL BL1 48 B3
FWTH BL4 66 A5
OLDS OL8 91 G4
Edlin Cl WGTN/LGST M12 129 F3
Edlingham ROCH OL11 * 29 H5
Edlinburgh Cl SALE M33 153 G3
Edmonds St MDTN M24 73 E3
Edmonton Rd EDGY/DAV SK3 172 B5
NEWH/MOS M40 116 B1
Edmund Cl HTNM SK4 159 H3
Edmunds Ct BOLS/LL BL3 2 B7
Edmunds Fold LIT OL15 20 C2
Edmund St CSLFD M3 * 6 B3
DROY M43 117 H5
FAIL M35 * 105 E2
RAD M26 * 52 D5
ROY/SHW OL2 60 B2
SLFD M6 112 D2
WHIT OL12 10 A4
Edna St HYDE SK14 147 H1
Edson Rd CHH M8 87 E4
Edstone Cl BOLS/LL BL3 47 G5
Edward Av CCHDY M21 140 D4
LIT OL15 20 C5
MPL/ROM SK6 161 F3
SLFD M6 112 B2
Edward Charlton Rd
OLDTF/WHR M16 141 E1
Edward Ct ALT WA14 165 E2
Edward Ms CHAD OL9 8 B6
Edward Rd BKLY M9 88 A2
ROY/SHW OL2 59 H3
Edwards Cl MPL/ROM SK6 174 D4
Edwards Dr WHTF M45 70 A4
Edward St AUL OL6 120 B3
BKLY M9 103 F2
BOLS/LL BL3 48 C4
BRO M7 114 B1
BURY BL9 4 E6
CHAD OL9 8 A5
DROY M43 * 117 H5
DTN/ASHW M34 132 A1
DUK SK16 133 F2
FWTH BL4 65 G2
HYDE SK14 133 F5
MDTN M24 72 D2
MILN OL16 11 F4
MPL/ROM SK6 163 F5
PWCH M25 85 H2
RAD M26 67 E4
RAD M26 68 C2
SALE M33 155 F2
STKP SK1 13 G5
WHIT OL12 14 C3
WHIT OL12 20 A4
Edwards Wy MPL/ROM SK6 174 D4
Edwin Rd OP/CLY M11 115 H4
Edwin St BURY BL9 4 D5
STKP SK1 172 C1
Eeasbrook URM M41 138 D2
Egbert St NEWH/MOS M40 104 A3
Egerton Ct WALK M28 * 97 H2
Egerton Crs DID/WITH M20 * 142 D4
Egerton Dr SALE M33 * 154 C1
Egerton Gv WALK M28 82 A4
Egerton Ldg EDGW/EG BL7 22 D2
Egerton Ms DROY M43 * 117 H5
RUSH/FAL M14 143 F3
Egerton Pk WALK M28 98 A3
Egerton Pl ROY/SHW OL2 59 H3
Egerton Rd ECC M30 111 E1
EDGY/DAV SK3 172 B5
HALE/TIMP WA15 178 B2
RUSH/FAL M14 143 F3
WALK M28 82 A4
WHTF M45 69 G5
WILM/AE SK9 199 E2
Egerton Rd North
CCHDY M21 141 G2
HTNM SK4 159 F1
Egerton Rd South
CCHDY M21 141 G3
HTNM SK4 159 F2
Egerton St AUL OL6 119 H2
CSLFD M3 6 A4
DROY M43 118 A4
DTN/ASHW M34 132 A3
ECC M30 110 C3
FWTH BL4 65 H3
HEY OL10 40 D5
MDTN M24 * 71 H5
MOSL OL5 93 H5
OLD OL1 9 H2
PWCH M25 86 B3
Egerton Ter RUSH/FAL M14 143 F4
Egerton V EDGW/EG BL7 22 C1
Eggington St
NEWH/MOS M40 102 D5
Egham Ct BOLE BL2 * 3 J1
Egmont St CHH M8 102 B2
MOSL OL5 109 E2
SLFD M6 100 B4
Egremont Av DID/WITH M20 142 C4
Egremont Cl WHTF M45 69 H3
Egremont Ct BRO M7 * 101 F2
Egremont Gv EDGY/DAV SK3 171 E1
Egremont Rd MILN OL16 44 B2
Egret Dr IRL M44 * 122 B5
Egyptian St BOL BL1 2 E1
Egypt La PWCH M25 70 D2
Eida Wy TRPK M17 112 B5
Eight Acre WHTF M45 68 D5
Eighth Av OLDS OL8 106 A1
Eighth St TRPK M17 125 H2
Eileen Gv RUSH/FAL M14 143 E1
Eileen Gv West
RUSH/FAL M14 142 D1
Elaine Av BKLY M9 89 E5
Elbe St WGTN/LGST M12 115 F5
Elbow La ROCH OL11 30 B5
Elbow St BNG/LEV M19 144 A2
Elbut La BURY BL9 40 A1
Elcho Ct ALT WA14 * 177 E2
Elcho Rd ALT WA14 177 E1
Elcot Cl NEWH/MOS M40 * 102 D5
Elderberry Wy WILM/AE SK9 199 H2
Elder Cl OFTN SK2 173 E1
TOT/BURYW BL8 37 E1
Eldercot Gv BOLS/LL BL3 47 H5
Eldercot Rd BOLS/LL BL3 47 H5
Eldercroft Rd
HALE/TIMP WA15 166 D4
Elder Dr BOLS/LL BL3 50 B4
Elderfield Dr MPL/ROM SK6 161 G2
Elder Gv NEWH/MOS M40 90 A5
Eldermount Rd BKLY M9 88 A5
Elder Rd OLDE OL4 92 D1
Elder St MILN OL16 43 G1
Elderwood CHAD OL9 73 H5
Eldon Cl DTN/ASHW M34 132 B1
Eldon Pl ECC M30 110 D4
Eldon Prec OLDS OL8 9 F6
Eldon Rd EDGY/DAV SK3 12 B7
IRL M44 136 C1
Eldon St BOLE BL2 34 C5
BURY BL9 4 E1
OLDS OL8 9 G6
Eldon Street Est OLDS OL8 9 G6
Eldridge Dr NEWH/MOS M40 103 H5
Eldroth Av WYTH/NTH M22 180 C1
Eleanor Rd CCHDY M21 140 D3
ROY/SHW OL2 75 F2
Eleanor St BOL BL1 34 B1
OLD OL1 75 E4
Electo St OP/CLY M11 130 D1
Elevator Rd TRPK M17 126 B2
Eleventh St TRPK M17 126 A2
Elf Mill Cl EDGY/DAV SK3 171 H3
Elford Gv GTN M18 131 F4
Elgar St WGTN/LGST M12 129 H5
Elgin Av DID/WITH M20 * 158 A3
Elgin Dr SALE M33 155 F3
Elgin Rd DUK SK16 133 F2
OLDE OL4 92 A1
Elgin St AULW OL7 119 F1
BOL BL1 33 F4
STLY SK15 121 E4
Elgol Cl EDGY/DAV SK3 172 A4
Elgol Dr BOLS/LL BL3 47 F4
Elham Cl RAD M26 67 F5
Elim St LIT OL15 21 F1
Eliot Rd ECC M30 111 E4
Eli St CHAD OL9 90 B4
Eliza Ann St ECC M30 110 D4
NEWH/MOS M40 115 F1
Elizabethan Wy MILN OL16 31 F5
Elizabeth Av CHAD OL9 90 B4
DTN/ASHW M34 132 B3
ROY/SHW OL2 74 D1
STKP SK1 13 H6
Elizabeth Cl STRET M32 140 B1
Elizabeth Ct HTNM SK4 12 A1
Elizabeth Gv ROY/SHW OL2 60 A3
Elizabeth Rd PART M31 150 D2
Elizabeth Slinger Rd
DID/WITH M20 156 D2
Elizabeth St AUL OL6 119 G1
CHH M8 102 B5
DTN/ASHW M34 132 B5
HEY OL10 40 D4
HYDE SK14 133 G5
RAD M26 68 B1
ROCH OL11 42 B3
SWIN M27 99 F1
WHTF M45 69 G5
Eliza St HULME M15 127 H2
RAMS BL0 17 E2
Elkanagh Gdns SLFD M6 113 E2
Elkstone Av LHULT M38 81 F1
Elladene Pk CCHDY M21 141 G3
Ellanby Cl RUSH/FAL M14 128 C5
Elland Cl BURY BL9 70 A2
Ellaston Dr URM M41 * 138 D1
Ellastone Rd SLFD M6 112 B1
Ellbourne Rd BKLY M9 87 F4
Ellenbrook Cl
WGTN/LGST M12 130 A2
Ellenbrook Rd WALK M28 96 C2
Ellen Brook Rd
WYTH/NTH M22 180 C4
Ellendale Gra WALK M28 96 C2
Ellen Gv FWTH BL4 83 G2
Ellenhall Cl BKLY M9 103 E2
Ellenroad Ap MILN OL16 44 D2
Ellenrod Dr WHIT OL12 28 D1
Ellenrod La WHIT OL12 28 D1
Ellenshaw Cl WHIT OL12 28 D1
Ellen St BOL BL1 33 F3
CHAD OL9 8 C1
DROY M43 118 A5
HTNM SK4 159 G3
Ellen Wilkinson Crs
WGTN/LGST M12 129 H3
Elleray Cl BOLS/LL BL3 67 F1
Elleray Rd MDTN M24 88 C2
SLFD M6 100 A5
Ellerbeck Cl BOLE BL2 34 D1
Ellerbeck Crs WALK M28 96 D3
Ellerby Av SWIN M27 84 B4
Ellesmere Av AUL OL6 107 F3
ECC M30 111 F3
MPL/ROM SK6 175 E3
WALK M28 81 H4
Ellesmere Cir URM M41 124 C1
Ellesmere Cl DUK SK16 133 H1
Ellesmere Dr CHD/CHDH SK8 170 D4
Ellesmere Gdns BOLS/LL BL3 64 C1
Ellesmere Rd ALT WA14 165 G3
BOLS/LL BL3 64 B1
CCHDY M21 141 G2
ECC M30 111 F1
EDGY/DAV SK3 170 D2
Ellesmere Rd North
HTNM SK4 159 F1
Ellesmere Rd South
CCHDY M21 141 G3
Ellesmere St BOLS/LL BL3 2 A7
ECC M30 111 E4
FAIL M35 105 E2
FWTH BL4 66 A4
HULME M15 127 G1
LHULT M38 81 H4
ROCH OL11 43 E1
SWIN M27 98 C3
SWIN M27 99 F1
Ellesmere Ter RUSH/FAL M14 143 F4
Ellingham Cl OP/CLY M11 116 A4
Elliot Sq OLD OL1 9 K1
Elliot St BOL BL1 33 F3
OLDE OL4 92 D1
Elliott Av HYDE SK14 133 G3
Elliott Dr SALE M33 153 H2
Elliott St FWTH BL4 65 H5
WHIT OL12 10 E4
Ellis Crs WALK M28 81 G4
Ellis Dr CHH M8 102 C1
Ellis Fold WHIT OL12 28 B1
Ellis La MDTN M24 71 G4
Ellis St BOLS/LL BL3 48 C4
CHH M8 114 B1
HULME M15 127 H2
HYDE SK14 148 B1
TOT/BURYW BL8 * 37 G4
Elliston Sq WGTN/LGST M12 129 H2
Ellonby Ri HOR/BR BL6 46 D4
Ellor St SLFD M6 113 E2
Ellwood Rd STKP SK1 160 C5
Elly Clough ROY/SHW OL2 * 74 D1
Elm Av RAD M26 68 A4
Elmbank Av DID/WITH M20 156 D2
Elmbank Rd MDTN M24 73 F4
Elm Beds Rd POY/DIS SK12 196 B5
Elmbridge Wk BOLS/LL BL3 48 C4
Elm Cl HYDE SK14 135 H4
POY/DIS SK12 195 G4
Elm Crs WALK M28 97 H3
WILM/AE SK9 201 E3
Elmdale Av CHD/CHDH SK8 181 G2
Elmdale Wk HULME M15 * 128 B2
Elm Dr STRET M32 139 H2
STRET M32 140 A3
Elmfield Av WYTH/NTH M22 168 D1
Elmfield Dr MPL/ROM SK6 174 D3
Elmfield Rd DTN/ASHW M34 118 B5
EDGY/DAV SK3 172 A4
WILM/AE SK9 201 E3
Elmfield St BOL BL1 34 A4
CHH M8 102 B4
Elmgate Gv BNG/LEV M19 144 A2
Elm Gv AUL OL6 107 F5
DID/WITH M20 157 G3
DROY M43 117 E3
DTN/ASHW M34 132 A4
EDGW/EG BL7 23 F3
FWTH BL4 65 G4
HYDE SK14 148 B1
MILN OL16 44 D3
OLDE OL4 93 G1
PWCH M25 85 H1
ROCH OL11 42 D1
SALE M33 139 H5
SWIN M27 98 A1
URM M41 139 E1
WHIT OL12 19 H3
WILM/AE SK9 200 D3
Elmham Wk NEWH/MOS M40 115 F1
Elmhurst Dr BNG/LEV M19 158 C1
Elmira Wy ORD M5 126 D2
Elmley Cl OFTN SK2 173 H4
Elmore Wd LIT OL15 20 C2
Elmpark Ga WHIT OL12 18 A5
Elmpark Gv WHIT OL12 18 A5
Elmpark V WHIT OL12 18 A5
Elmpark Vw WHIT OL12 18 A5
Elmpark Wy WHIT OL12 18 A5
Elmridge Dr HALE/TIMP WA15 178 D4
Elm Rd BOLS/LL BL3 67 E2
CHD/CHDH SK8 169 F4
DID/WITH M20 157 F2
FWTH BL4 82 C2
HALE/TIMP WA15 177 H1
MPL/ROM SK6 165 G2
OLDS OL8 106 A1
Elm Rd South EDGY/DAV SK3 170 D2
Elms Cl WHTF M45 69 G2
Elmscott Wk BRUN/LGST M13 129 E3
Elmsdale Av BKLY M9 87 H2
Elmsfield Av ROCH OL11 28 B2
Elmsleigh Rd CHD/CHDH SK8 181 F3
Elmsmere Rd DID/WITH M20 158 A3
Elms Rd HTNM SK4 159 E1
STLY SK15 121 G2
WHTF M45 69 G3
Elms St WHTF M45 69 G3
Elmstead Av DID/WITH M20 142 C5
Elmsted Cl CHD/CHDH SK8 183 E1
The Elms LIT OL15 20 B4
MOSL OL5 * 108 C1
Elmstone Cl BKLY M9 87 H5
Elmstone Dr ROY/SHW OL2 59 E4
Elmstone Gv BOL BL1 * 2 E1
Elm St BURY BL9 5 J5
ECC M30 111 E4
FAIL M35 105 E2
FWTH BL4 66 A3
HEY OL10 41 E4
MDTN M24 73 F4
MPL/ROM SK6 161 G2
RAMS BL0 * 17 E2
SWIN M27 98 D1
WHIT OL12 10 D2
WHIT OL12 14 C3
Elmsway BRAM/HZG SK7 183 F5
HALE/TIMP WA15 178 C4
MPL/ROM SK6 196 D1
Elmswood Av RUSH/FAL M14 142 B1
Elmswood Dr HYDE SK14 * 134 B5
Elmsworth Av BNG/LEV M19 144 B2
Elmton Rd BKLY M9 88 B4
Elm Tree Cl FAIL M35 105 G3
Elm Tree Dr DUK SK16 134 A1
WYTH/NTH M22 180 C1
Elmtree Dr HTNM SK4 159 E4
Elm Tree Rd MPL/ROM SK6 160 D3
Elmwood SALE M33 153 F2
Elmwood Dr ROY/SHW OL2 58 D4
Elmwood Gv BKLY M9 103 G3
BOL BL1 * 48 B1
FWTH BL4 81 H1
Elmwood Pk STLY SK15 121 G2
Elsa Rd BNG/LEV M19 144 C2
Elsdon Dr GTN M18 130 C2
Elsdon Gdns BOLE BL2 34 C5
Elsdon Rd BRUN/LGST M13 143 H1
Elsfield Cl BOL BL1 * 33 G4
Elsham Cl BOL BL1 33 H1
Elsham Dr WALK M28 81 G4
Elsham Gdns GTN M18 129 H4
Elsie St BKLY M9 103 F2
FWTH BL4 65 H5
RAMS BL0 16 B4
Elsinore Av IRL M44 136 C2
Elsinore Cl FAIL M35 105 G3
Elsinore Rd OLDTF/WHR M16 126 D4
Elsinore St BOLE BL2 34 C3
Elsma Rd NEWH/MOS M40 117 F1
Elsmore Rd RUSH/FAL M14 142 C2
Elson St TOT/BURYW BL8 37 G2
Elsted Rd UPML OL3 94 B2
Elstree Av NEWH/MOS M40 116 C1
Elswick Av BOLS/LL BL3 48 A4
BRAM/HZG SK7 183 H5
CCHDY M21 156 C2
Elsworth Cl RAD M26 68 C3
Elsworth Dr BOL BL1 34 A2
Elsworth St CSLFD M3 114 D2
Elterwater Cl TOT/BURYW BL8 37 G2
Elterwater Rd FWTH BL4 64 D5
Eltham Av OFTN SK2 * 172 D4
Eltham Dr URM M41 124 B4
Eltham St BNG/LEV M19 144 A1
Elton Av BNG/LEV M19 144 A3
FWTH BL4 65 E4
Elton Brook Cl
TOT/BURYW BL8 37 G3
Elton Cl WHTF M45 69 H4
WILM/AE SK9 199 H1
Elton Dr BRAM/HZG SK7 185 E4
Elton Rd SALE M33 153 G4
Elton St BOLE BL2 3 H4
BRO M7 114 A2
ROCH OL11 42 B5
STRET M32 126 C3
Elton's Yd BRO M7 114 A2
Elton Vale Rd TOT/BURYW BL8 37 G4
Elvate Crs CHH M8 101 H5
Elverdon Cl HULME M15 127 H3
Elverston St WYTH/NTH M22 156 D5
Elverston Wy CHAD OL9 8 A1
Elvey St NEWH/MOS M40 103 G5
Elvington Crs WALK M28 96 D2
Elwick Cl OLDTF/WHR M16 128 A5
Elwyn Av WYTH/NTH M22 168 C2
Ely Av STRET M32 125 E5
Ely Cl WALK M28 96 C2
Ely Crs FAIL M35 105 E5
Ely Dr TOT/BURYW BL8 4 B1
Ely Gv BOL BL1 * 2 D1
Elysian St OP/CLY M11 116 D5
Ely St CHAD OL9 90 C2
Emaline Gra SLFD M6 112 D3
Ember St OP/CLY M11 * 117 E3
Embla Wk BOLS/LL BL3 49 F5
Emblem St BOLS/LL BL3 48 C4
Embleton Cl BOLE BL2 35 F2
BOLE BL2 35 F5
Embsay Cl BOL BL1 33 G1
Emerald Dr OLD OL1 76 D1
Emerald Rd WYTH/NTH M22 181 E5
Emerald St BOL BL1 34 A3
DTN/ASHW M34 132 B5
Emerson Av ECC M30 111 H2
Emerson Dr MDTN M24 72 C3
Emerson St ORD M5 112 C3
Emery Av CCHDY M21 141 G5
Emery Cl ALT WA14 165 G2
HTNM SK4 158 D2
Emily Beavan Cl OP/CLY M11 116 C4
Emily Cl FAIL M35 105 F1
Emily Pl DROY M43 117 G4
Emley St BNG/LEV M19 144 B2
Emlyn Gv CHD/CHDH SK8 170 D3
Emlyn St FWTH BL4 65 H3
SWIN M27 98 C2
WALK M28 82 A4
Emmanuel Cl BOLS/LL BL3 * 48 C4
Emmanuel Pl BOLS/LL BL3 * 48 C4
Emma St OLDS OL8 91 G4
WHIT OL12 10 A4
Emmerson St SWIN M27 99 E1
Emmett St East
NEWH/MOS M40 103 F5
Emmott Cl HEY OL10 40 D4
Emmott Wy OLD OL1 9 H4
Empire Rd BOLE BL2 50 A1
DUK SK16 133 F2
Empire St CHH M8 114 C1
Empress Av MPL/ROM SK6 175 E4
Empress Dr HTNM SK4 159 G2
Empress St BOL BL1 * 33 E5
CHH M8 102 A2
OLDTF/WHR M16 127 F2
Emsworth Dr SALE M33 154 D5
Ena St BOLS/LL BL3 65 F1
OLD OL1 76 B3
Enbridge St ORD M5 * 113 F5
Encombe Pl CSLFD M3 * 114 A3
Endcott Cl GTN M18 130 A2
Enderby Rd NEWH/MOS M40 104 B1
Ending Rake WHIT OL12 18 B4
Endon Dr CCHDY M21 142 B3
Endon St BOL BL1 33 E5
Endsleigh Rd DID/WITH M20 143 E5
Endsley Av WALK M28 96 D1
Energy St NEWH/MOS M40 * 115 H2
Enfield Av BNG/LEV M19 144 A5
OLDS OL8 91 F4
Enfield Cl BOL BL1 33 H5
BURY BL9 53 G4
ECC M30 111 E5
ROCH OL11 28 B2
Enfield Dr OP/CLY M11 116 D3
Enfield Rd ECC M30 111 E1
SWIN M27 98 D4

Enfield St HYDE SK14 * 148 A4
WALK M28 82 A2
Enford Av WYTH/NTH M22 179 H2
Engell Cl GTN M18 130 B3
Engine Fold Rd WALK M28 81 F4
Engine St CHAD OL9 90 C3
Engledene BOL BL1 22 C5
Enid Cl BRO M7 101 H5
Ennerdale Av BOLE BL2 35 G5
CCHDY M21 156 C2
ROY/SHW OL2 58 D2
SWIN M27 99 E4
Ennerdale Cl BOLS/LL BL3 66 C1
Ennerdale Dr BURY BL9 69 H2
CHD/CHDH SK8 181 G1
HALE/TIMP WA15 166 B2
SALE M33 153 H1
Ennerdale Gv AULW OL7 106 C5
FWTH BL4 64 D4
Ennerdale Rd MDTN M24 72 B2
MPL/ROM SK6 162 A2
PART M31 150 D3
ROCH OL11 42 A2
STKP SK1 172 C2
STRET M32 * 125 H5
Ennerdale Ter STLY SK15 120 D2
Ennis Cl NTHM/RTH M23 167 F4
Ennismore Av ECC M30 111 H3
Enstone Dr
NEWH/MOS M40 104 C1
Enticott Rd IRL M44 150 B1
Entwisle Av URM M41 124 A5
Entwisle Rd MILN OL16 10 E5
Entwisle Rw FWTH BL4 66 A4
Entwisle St FWTH BL4 * 66 A3
MILN OL16 31 F5
SWIN M27 98 C1
Entwistle St BOLE BL2 3 K2
Enver Rd CHH M8 102 C2
Enville Rd ALT WA14 177 F1
NEWH/MOS M40 104 A1
SLFD M6 100 B4
Enville St AUL OL6 119 H2
BKLY M9 88 A4
DTN/ASHW M34 132 B1
Epping Cl AUL OL6 107 F3
CHAD OL9 73 H4
Epping Dr SALE M33 153 F1
Epping Rd
DTN/ASHW M34 145 H1
Epping St HULME M15 128 A2
Eppleworth Ri SWIN M27 84 B4
Epsom Av BNG/LEV M19 143 H5
SALE M33 153 F4
WILM/AE SK9 192 B3
Epsom Cl
BRAM/HZG SK7 185 G2
ROCH OL11 28 B3
Epworth St ANC M4 115 F4
Equitable St MILN OL16 44 C1
OLDE OL4 76 C4
Era St BOLE BL2 50 A2
SALE M33 154 C2
Ercall Av WGTN/LGST M12 129 F2
Erica Av OLDE OL4 61 E5
Erica Cl RDSH SK5 145 F3
Erica Dr BNG/LEV M19 158 B2
Eric Brook Cl RUSH/FAL M14 128 B5
Eric Bullows Cl
WYTH/NTH M22 180 B3
Eric St LIT OL15 20 D2
OLDE OL4 92 B1
Erin Cl CHAD OL9 90 C2
Erin St OP/CLY M11 * 130 D1
Erith Cl RDSH SK5 145 H5
Erith Rd OLDE OL4 92 A1
Erlesmere Av DTN/ASHW M34 132 D4
Erlesmere Cl OLDE OL4 61 F5
Erlington Av
OLDTF/WHR M16 127 E5
Ermen Rd ECC M30 110 D5
Ermington Dr CHH M8 102 A4
Erneley Cl WGTN/LGST M12 130 A5
Ernest St BOL BL1 2 A5
CHD/CHDH SK8 169 H3
OFTN SK2 172 B3
PWCH M25 85 G3
Ernest Ter WHIT OL12 11 G2
Ernlouen Av BOL BL1 47 H1
Ernocroft Gv GTN M18 * 130 D2
Ernocroft Rd MPL/ROM SK6 163 G5
Erringdon Cl OFTN SK2 173 F3
Errington Cl BOLS/LL BL3 47 G4
Errington Dr BRO M7 114 A1
Errol Av BKLY M9 87 F2
WYTH/NTH M22 168 B5
Errwood Crs BNG/LEV M19 144 A3
Errwood Rd BNG/LEV M19 144 A5
Erskine Cl BOLS/LL BL3 47 F4
Erskine Rd BKLY M9 88 B2
PART M31 151 E3
Erskine St HULME M15 127 G2
MPL/ROM SK6 163 G4
Erwin St NEWH/MOS M40 104 A4
Erwood Rd BNG/LEV M19 144 A5
Eryngo St STKP SK1 13 K4
Escott St OLDTF/WHR M16 128 A5
Esher Dr SALE M33 166 C1
Esk Cl URM M41 123 H4
Eskdale CHD/CHDH SK8 169 H5
Eskdale Av BOLE BL2 35 G4
BRAM/HZG SK7 193 F2
DID/WITH M20 142 C4
MPL/ROM SK6 162 A1
OLDS OL8 91 E3
ROCH OL11 42 A2
ROY/SHW OL2 59 E2
UPML OL3 95 E2
Eskdale Cl BURY BL9 69 H1
Eskdale Dr HALE/TIMP WA15 166 D2
MDTN M24 72 C1
Eskdale Gv FWTH BL4 65 E4
Eskdale Ms UPML OL3 * 95 E2
Eskrick St BOL BL1 33 G4
Eskrigge Cl BRO M7 102 A2
Esmond Rd CHH M8 102 B3
Esmont Dr MDTN M24 72 B1
The Esplanade MILN OL16 10 B7
Essex Av BURY BL9 39 H5
DID/WITH M20 157 G2
DROY M43 117 H2
EDGY/DAV SK3 171 E1
Essex Cl FAIL M35 105 E5
ROY/SHW OL2 59 G2
Essex Dr BURY BL9 53 G1
Essex Gdns IRL M44 150 B2
Essex Rd GTN M18 131 E5
RDSH SK5 160 D1
Essex St CMANW M2 6 E5
ROCH OL11 30 A5
Essex Wy OLDTF/WHR M16 127 G3
Essingdon St BOLS/LL BL3 48 C5
Essington Dr
NEWH/MOS M40 103 E4
Estate St OLDS OL8 91 G3
Estate St South OLDS OL8 91 G3
Est Bank Rd RAMS BL0 16 B5
Esther St OLDE OL4 76 B5
Estonfield Dr URM M41 139 F1
Eston St BRUN/LGST M13 129 E4
Eswick St OP/CLY M11 116 D4
Etchells Rd CHD/CHDH SK8 182 A3
Etchells St STKP SK1 13 G3
Etchell St
NEWH/MOS M40 * 102 D5
Ethel Av BKLY M9 88 A3
SWIN M27 99 G2
Ethel Ct MILN OL16 * 30 C5
Ethel St BOLS/LL BL3 2 A7
OLDS OL8 91 G4
WHIT OL12 14 C3
Ethel Ter BNG/LEV M19 144 A2
Etherley Cl IRL M44 136 C1
Etherow Av
MPL/ROM SK6 162 D4
NEWH/MOS M40 * 90 A5
Etherstone St CHH M8 102 D2
Eton Av OLDS OL8 91 F4
Eton Cl OLDTF/WHR M16 127 G3
ROCH OL11 29 E5
Eton Ct OLDTF/WHR M16 * 127 G3
Eton Dr CHD/CHDH SK8 181 H2
Eton Hill Rd RAD M26 52 D4
Eton Wy North RAD M26 52 D4
Eton Wy South RAD M26 52 D4
Etruria Cl BRUN/LGST M13 129 F3
Ettington Cl
TOT/BURYW BL8 37 F3
Ettrick Cl OP/CLY M11 130 C1
Euclid Cl OP/CLY M11 115 H4
Europa Ga TRPK M17 126 A3
Europa Wy EDGY/DAV SK3 171 F3
RAD M26 66 D5
TRPK M17 126 A3
Eustace St BOLS/LL BL3 65 F1
CHAD OL9 74 C3
Euston Av BKLY M9 88 D4
Euxton Cl TOT/BURYW BL8 37 F5
Evan Cl DID/WITH M20 157 F3
Evans Cl DID/WITH M20 157 F3
Evans Rd ECC M30 110 B4
Evans St AUL OL6 120 A1
CSLFD M3 6 C1
MDTN M24 73 E4
OLD OL1 9 G1
Evan St NEWH/MOS M40 103 F5
Eva Rd EDGY/DAV SK3 170 D2
Eva St RUSH/FAL M14 128 D5
WHIT OL12 10 E1
Evelyn St OLD OL1 76 A3
RUSH/FAL M14 143 F3
Evening St FAIL M35 105 E2
Evenley Cl OP/CLY M11 * 130 D2
Everard Cl WALK M28 96 C2
Everard St ORD M5 127 F1
Everbrom Rd BOLS/LL BL3 63 H2
Everest Av AULW OL7 107 E5
Everest Cl HYDE SK14 134 B4
Everest Rd HYDE SK14 134 B4
Everest St ROCH OL11 43 F4
Everett Rd DID/WITH M20 142 D5
Everglade OLDS OL8 106 D1
Everleigh Cl BOLE BL2 35 F1
Everleigh Dr BRO M7 102 A4
Eversden Ct BRO M7 * 114 B1
Everside Dr CHH M8 101 H4
Eversley Rd DID/WITH M20 157 F3
Everton Rd OLDS OL8 91 E4
RDSH SK5 145 F1
Everton St SWIN M27 98 D2
Every St ANC M4 115 G4
BURY BL9 4 E1
RAMS BL0 * 17 E2
Evesham Av HTNM SK4 159 E3
NTHM/RTH M23 167 E2
Evesham Cl BOLS/LL BL3 2 B7
MDTN M24 89 E2
Evesham Dr FWTH BL4 * 65 G2
Evesham Drive WILM/AE SK9 191 H5
Evesham Gdns MDTN M24 * 88 D2
Evesham Gv AUL OL6 107 F3
SALE M33 155 F2
Evesham Rd BKLY M9 88 D5
CHD/CHDH SK8 170 D5
MDTN M24 88 D2
Evesham Wk BOLS/LL BL3 * 48 C4
MDTN M24 89 E2
OLDS OL8 9 F7
Eveside Cl CHD/CHDH SK8 * 171 E5
Eve St OLDS OL8 91 G5
Ewan St GTN M18 130 C2
Ewart Av ORD M5 113 F4
Ewart St BOL BL1 33 H4
Ewhurst Av SWIN M27 98 C4
Ewing Cl CHH M8 102 B1
Ewood OLDS OL8 106 D2
Ewood Dr TOT/BURYW BL8 52 B1
Exbourne Rd WYTH/NTH M22 180 B3
Exbury WHIT OL12 10 B4
Exbury St RUSH/FAL M14 143 F4
Excalibur Wy IRL M44 136 B4
Excelsior Gdns HEY OL10 56 C1
Excelsior Ter LIT OL15 20 C5
Exchange Quay ORD M5 126 D2
Exchange Sq CSLFD M3 6 E3
Exchange St BOL BL1 * 2 E5
CSLFD M3 * 6 E4
EDGY/DAV SK3 12 E4
Exeter Av BOLE BL2 34 C4
DTN/ASHW M34 146 D2
ECC M30 111 H1
FWTH BL4 65 E3
RAD M26 51 G4
Exeter Cl CHD/CHDH SK8 182 C4
DUK SK16 133 G2
Exeter Dr AUL OL6 107 G3
IRL M44 136 D1
Exeter Gv ROCH OL11 43 E1
Exeter Rd RDSH SK5 160 D1
URM M41 124 C4
Exeter St ROCH OL11 43 E1
SLFD M6 112 D3
Exford Cl NEWH/MOS M40 115 G2
RDSH SK5 145 F5
Exford Dr BOLE BL2 50 D3
Exit Rd West MANAIR M90 180 A5
Exmoor Cl AUL OL6 107 F3
Exmouth Av RDSH SK5 160 D1
Exmouth Pl MILN OL16 43 F3
Exmouth Rd SALE M33 153 G1
Exmouth Sq MILN OL16 * 43 F2
Exmouth St MILN OL16 43 F3
Exmouth Wk
OLDTF/WHR M16 127 H5
Eyam Gv OFTN SK2 173 E5
Eyam Rd BRAM/HZG SK7 185 F4
Eycott Dr MDTN M24 72 A3
Eyebrook Rd ALT WA14 176 D3
Eynford Av RDSH SK5 160 C1
Eyre St HULME M15 128 B3

F

Faber St ANC M4 114 D2
Factory Brow MDTN M24 71 H5
Factory La BKLY M9 103 E1
CSLFD M3 * 114 A4
Factory St MDTN M24 72 C4
RAD M26 68 C1
RAMS BL0 16 D1
Failsworth Rd FAIL M35 105 G3
Fair Acres BOLE BL2 35 F3
Fairacres Rd MPL/ROM SK6 186 D4
Fairbank Dr MDTN M24 72 A2
Fairbottom St OLD OL1 9 H3
Fairbourne Av WILM/AE SK9 200 C1
WILM/AE SK9 201 E2
Fairbourne Cl WILM/AE SK9 200 C1
Fairbourne Dr
HALE/TIMP WA15 154 C5
WILM/AE SK9 200 C1
Fairbourne Rd BNG/LEV M19 144 C2
DTN/ASHW M34 146 C1
Fairbrook Dr SLFD M6 112 D3
Fairbrother St ORD M5 127 F1
Fairburn Cl URM M41 123 H4
Fairclough St BOLS/LL BL3 49 E5
OP/CLY M11 116 B3
Fairfax Av DID/WITH M20 157 G2
HALE/TIMP WA15 166 B3
Fairfax Cl MPL/ROM SK6 174 C2
Fairfax Dr LIT OL15 20 C5
WILM/AE SK9 200 C1
Fairfax Rd PWCH M25 85 H2
Fairfield Av CHD/CHDH SK8 182 C2
DROY M43 131 F1
MPL/ROM SK6 161 H2
Fairfield Dr BURY BL9 39 G3
Fairfield Rd DROY M43 117 H5
FWTH BL4 65 H5
HALE/TIMP WA15 166 D4
IRL M44 150 B1
MDTN M24 72 B3
OP/CLY M11 130 D1
Fairfields EDGW/EG BL7 23 E3
OLDS OL8 91 F5
Fairfield Sq DROY M43 117 H5
Fairfield St CMANE M1 7 J7
SLFD M6 100 A5
Fairford Cl RDSH SK5 160 A1
Fairford Dr BOLS/LL BL3 48 D4
Fairford Wy RDSH SK5 160 A1
WILM/AE SK9 199 G3
Fairhaven Av CCHDY M21 141 F4
WHTF M45 69 E5
WHTN BL5 62 C4
Fairhaven Cl BRAM/HZG SK7 184 A5
Fairhaven St WGTN/LGST M12 129 G2
Fairhills Rd IRL M44 136 C3
Fairholme Av URM M41 138 C1
Fairholme Rd DID/WITH M20 143 E5
HTNM SK4 159 F3
Fairhope Av SLFD M6 112 A1
Fairhurst Dr WALK M28 81 E5
Fairisle Cl OP/CLY M11 116 A4
Fairlands Rd BURY BL9 27 G4
SALE M33 154 A4
Fairlands St ROCH OL11 43 G4
Fairlawn HTNM SK4 159 G3
Fairlawn Cl RUSH/FAL M14 128 B4
Fairlea DTN/ASHW M34 147 E1
Fairlea Av DID/WITH M20 157 H4
Fairlee Av DTN/ASHW M34 118 B4
Fairleigh Av SLFD M6 112 B2
Fairless Rd ECC M30 111 E4
Fairlie Av BOLS/LL BL3 47 G4
Fairlie Dr HALE/TIMP WA15 166 C1
Fairlyn Cl WHTN BL5 63 H5
Fairlyn Dr WHTN BL5 63 H5
Fairman St OLDTF/WHR M16 128 A5
Fairmead Rd
NTHM/RTH M23 156 B5
Fairmile Dr DID/WITH M20 169 H1
Fairmount Av BOLE BL2 50 B1
Fairmount Rd SWIN M27 98 A4
Fairoak Ct BOLS/LL BL3 48 C4
Fair Oak Rd BNG/LEV M19 158 C1
Fairstead Wk OP/CLY M11 * 131 E1
Fair St BOLS/LL BL3 * 64 B2
CMANE M1 7 K5
SWIN M27 99 F1
Fairview Av BNG/LEV M19 143 H1
DTN/ASHW M34 145 G2
Fairview Cl CHAD OL9 73 H4
MPL/ROM SK6 175 E2
Fairview Dr MPL/ROM SK6 175 E2
Fairview Rd DTN/ASHW M34 145 G2
HALE/TIMP WA15 166 D4
Fairway BRAM/HZG SK7 193 G1
CHD/CHDH SK8 169 G5
DROY M43 117 H5
PWCH M25 86 C5
ROCH OL11 42 A5
SWIN M27 99 H3
WHIT OL12 18 B1
Fairway Av BOLE BL2 35 H2
NTHM/RTH M23 167 E2
Fairway Crs ROY/SHW OL2 59 E3
Fairway Dr SALE M33 153 H4
Fairway Rd BURY BL9 69 H1
OLDE OL4 92 D3
The Fairways WHTF M45 85 G1
The Fairway NEWH/MOS M40 104 C2
OFTN SK2 173 E2
Fairwood Rd NTHM/RTH M23 167 E2
Fairy La CHH M8 101 H5
SALE M33 155 G2
SALE M33 156 A3
Fairy St TOT/BURYW BL8 37 H4
Fairywell Cl WILM/AE SK9 199 G1
Fairywell Dr SALE M33 154 B5
Fairywell Rd
HALE/TIMP WA15 166 C2
Faith St BOL BL1 32 D5
Falcon Av URM M41 139 E1
Falcon Cl BURY BL9 5 H1
WHIT OL12 28 A1
Falcon Crs SWIN M27 84 C5
Falcon Dr CHAD OL9 8 A1
IRL M44 122 C5
LHULT M38 81 F2
MDTN M24 72 B1
Falcon St OLDS OL8 9 F6
Falconwood Cha WALK M28 96 C4
Falfield Dr CHH M8 102 C5
Falinge Fold WHIT OL12 29 G2
Falinge Ms WHIT OL12 10 A5
Falinge Rd WHIT OL12 10 B4
Falkirk Dr BOLE BL2 50 C3
Falkirk St OLDE OL4 76 B5
Falkland Av NEWH/MOS M40 115 G1
ROCH OL11 29 F3
Falkland Cl OLDE OL4 60 D5
Falkland Rd BOLE BL2 50 D2
Fall Birch Rd HOR/BR BL6 46 A1
Fallons Rd WALK M28 98 B1
Fallow Av GTN M18 144 D1
Fallowfield Av ORD M5 113 G5
Fallowfield Dr WHIT OL12 29 G1
Fallow Fields Dr RDSH SK5 145 G2
The Fallows CHAD OL9 90 B2
Falls Gv CHD/CHDH SK8 181 F1
Falmer Cl GTN M18 131 E2
TOT/BURYW BL8 26 D5
Falmer Dr WYTH/NTH M22 180 C3
Falmouth Av SALE M33 153 G1
URM M41 123 F5
Falmouth Crs RDSH SK5 160 D1
Falmouth Rd IRL M44 136 D1
Falmouth St NEWH/MOS M40 116 A1
OLDS OL8 91 G3
ROCH OL11 43 F1
Falsgrave Cl NEWH/MOS M40 103 H5
Falshaw Dr BURY BL9 27 F3
Falstaff Ms MPL/ROM SK6 161 H3
Falston Av NEWH/MOS M40 89 G5
Falstone Av RAMS BL0 16 D4
Falterley Rd NTHM/RTH M23 167 F1
Fancroft Rd WYTH/NTH M22 168 B4
Faraday Av CHH M8 102 B4
SWIN M27 85 E5
Faraday Dr BOL BL1 33 H5
Faraday Ri WHIT OL12 29 E2
Faraday St CMANE M1 7 H4
Farcroft Av RAD M26 52 D4
Farcroft Cl NTHM/RTH M23 167 G1
OFTN SK2 173 F2
Far Cromwell Rd
MPL/ROM SK6 146 B5
Fardale ROY/SHW OL2 60 A3
Farden Dr NTHM/RTH M23 167 E1
Farewell Cl ROCH OL11 42 B4
Far Hey Cl RAD M26 67 H1
Farholme ROY/SHW OL2 74 D2
Faringdon ROCH OL11 * 29 H5
Faringdon Wk BOLS/LL BL3 * 48 D4
Farland Pl BOLS/LL BL3 47 G4
Farlands Dr DID/WITH M20 169 G2
Farlands Ri MILN OL16 43 H3
Far La GTN M18 130 C4
Farley Av GTN M18 131 F4
Farley Ct CHD/CHDH SK8 170 C5
Farley Rd SALE M33 154 D4
Farley Wy RDSH SK5 145 E2
Farliegh Cl WHTN BL5 62 B2
Farman St BOLS/LL BL3 * 64 C1
Farm Av STRET M32 125 F4
Farm Cl HTNM SK4 144 C5
TOT/BURYW BL8 26 A5
Farmers Cl SALE M33 155 H4
Farmer St HTNM SK4 159 G3
Farmfield SALE M33 139 E5
Farm Hl PWCH M25 * 85 H2
Farmlands Wk OLD OL1 60 B5
Farm La HYDE SK14 147 H3
POY/DIS SK12 197 F1
PWCH M25 70 D4
WALK M28 97 G5
Farm Rd OLDS OL8 105 H2
Farmside Av IRL M44 122 B5
Farmstead Cl FAIL M35 105 H4
Farm St FAIL M35 104 C4
HEY OL10 56 B1
OLD OL1 74 C3
Farm Wk ALT WA14 176 B2
LIT OL15 20 C3
MILN OL16 11 J2
Farmway MDTN M24 72 C5
Farm Yd BNG/LEV M19 144 A2
Farn Av RDSH SK5 145 E1
Farnborough Av OLDE OL4 92 C1
Farnborough Rd BOL BL1 22 D5
NEWH/MOS M40 115 G2
Farndale Sq LHULT M38 81 H4
Farndon Av BRAM/HZG SK7 173 G5
Farndon Cl SALE M33 155 F3
Farndon Dr HALE/TIMP WA15 166 B3
Farndon Rd RDSH SK5 145 E1
Farnham Av BKLY M9 88 A2
Farnham Cl BOL BL1 * 2 C1
CHD/CHDH SK8 182 D5
Farnham Dr IRL M44 136 C2
Farnley Cl WHIT OL12 28 C1
Farnley St WGTN/LGST M12 * 129 H2
Farnsworth Cl AULW OL7 107 E5
Farnworth Dr RUSH/FAL M14 143 E1
Farnworth St BOLS/LL BL3 * 48 B5
HEY OL10 40 D4
Farrand Rd OLDS OL8 90 C5
Farrant Rd WGTN/LGST M12 129 H5
Farrar Rd DROY M43 117 G5
Farrell St BRO M7 114 B2
Farrer Rd BRUN/LGST M13 143 H1
Far Ridings MPL/ROM SK6 162 C3
Farrier Cl SALE M33 155 G3
Farriers La ROCH OL11 42 A2
Farringdon St SLFD M6 * 112 D2
Farrowdale Av ROY/SHW OL2 60 A3
Farrow St ROY/SHW OL2 60 A3
Farrow St East ROY/SHW OL2 60 A3
Farr St EDGY/DAV SK3 12 C5
Farwood Cl OLDTF/WHR M16 127 F3
Far Woodseats La GLSP SK13 149 H5
Fastnet St OP/CLY M11 116 B5
Faulkenhurst Ms OLD OL1 74 D3
Faulkenhurst St OLD OL1 74 D3
Faulkner Dr HALE/TIMP WA15 166 C5
Faulkner Rd STRET M32 140 C2
Faulkner St BOLS/LL BL3 48 D4
CMANE M1 7 F6
MILN OL16 10 D6
Faversham Brow OLD OL1 * 75 F4
Faversham St
NEWH/MOS M40 104 A3
Fawborough Rd
NTHM/RTH M23 155 G5
Fawcett St BOLE BL2 3 K4
Fawley Av HYDE SK14 147 H2
Fawley Gv WYTH/NTH M22 168 C5
Fawns Keep STLY SK15 135 F2
WILM/AE SK9 199 G3
Fay Av BKLY M9 89 E5
Faywood Dr MPL/ROM SK6 175 F3
Fearney Side BOLS/LL BL3 66 C1
Fearnhead Cl FWTH BL4 66 B4
Fearnhead St BOLS/LL BL3 48 B5
Fearn St HEY OL10 40 D4
Featherstall Brook Vie
LIT OL15 20 D3
Featherstall Rd LIT OL15 20 C3
Featherstall Rd North
CHAD OL9 8 C3
Featherstall Rd South
CHAD OL9 8 C5
Federation St ANC M4 7 F2
PWCH M25 85 G2
Feldom Rd NTHM/RTH M23 155 G4
Fellbridge Cl WHTN BL5 62 B3
Fellbrigg Cl GTN M18 130 B5
Fellfoot Cl WALK M28 96 A5
Fellpark Rd NTHM/RTH M23 155 H4
Fells Gv WALK M28 97 G1
Fellside BOLE BL2 35 H3
Fellside Cl TOT/BURYW BL8 * 26 A2
Fellside Gdns LIT OL15 20 C1
Fellside Gn STLY SK15 120 D2
Fell St TOT/BURYW BL8 37 H4
Felltop Dr RDSH SK5 145 G3
Felskirk Rd WYTH/NTH M22 180 B4
Felsted BOL BL1 47 F1
Felt Ct DTN/ASHW M34 146 A1
Felthorpe Dr CHH M8 102 A4
Felton Av WYTH/NTH M22 180 B1
Felton Cl BURY BL9 53 H4
Felton Wk BOL BL1 33 H4
Fencegate Av HTNM SK4 159 G1
Fence St OFTN SK2 173 E5
Fenchurch Av
NEWH/MOS M40 116 D1
Fencot Dr WGTN/LGST M12 129 H4
Fenella St BRUN/LGST M13 129 F4
Fenham Cl NEWH/MOS M40 * 102 D5
Fenmore Av GTN M18 130 A5
Fennel St ANC M4 6 E2
Fenners Cl BOLS/LL BL3 64 C1
Fenney St BRO M7 101 G5
Fenney St East BRO M7 101 H4
Fenn St HULME M15 127 H2
Fenside Rd WYTH/NTH M22 168 D4
Fenton Av OFTN SK2 172 D5
Fenton Ms ROCH OL11 * 42 D1
Fenton St OLDE OL4 92 A1
ROCH OL11 42 D1
ROY/SHW OL2 60 A4
TOT/BURYW BL8 37 H3
WGTN/LGST M12 129 H3
Fenwick Dr HTNM SK4 158 B3
MDTN M24 72 A3
Fenwick St HULME M15 128 B2
ROCH OL11 10 A7
Ferdinand St
NEWH/MOS M40 * 115 G1
Fereday St WALK M28 81 H3
Ferguson Gdns WHIT OL12 19 E5
Ferguson Wy OLDE OL4 76 C3
Fernacre SALE M33 154 D1
Fernally St HYDE SK14 133 H5
Fern Av URM M41 138 A1
Fern Bank
NEWH/MOS M40 * 104 B3
Fernbank RAD M26 * 68 B4
Fern Bank STLY SK15 121 F5
Fern Bank Cl STLY SK15 121 F5
Fern Bank Dr
NTHM/RTH M23 167 F1
Fern Bank St HYDE SK14 148 A3
Fernbray Av BNG/LEV M19 158 A2
Fernbrook Cl
BRUN/LGST M13 129 E3
Fern Cl MDTN M24 73 G4
MPL/ROM SK6 175 E3
OLDE OL4 93 E1
Fern Clough BOL BL1 47 G2
Ferncl ough Rd BKLY M9 103 E4
Fern Crs STLY SK15 121 F5
Ferndale HYDE SK14 134 B3
Ferndale Av MILN OL16 43 H5
OFTN SK2 172 C5

WHTF M45 68 D5
Ferndale Cl OLDE OL4 92 C3
Ferndale Gdns BNG/LEV M19 143 G5
Ferndale Rd SALE M33 154 C4
Fern Dene WHIT OL12 29 E1
Ferndene Rd DID/WITH M20 157 G1
WHTF M45 70 B5
Ferndown Av BRAM/HZG SK7 184 D3
CHAD OL9 73 G5
Ferndown Dr IRL M44 122 B5
Ferndown Rd BOLE BL2 35 F3
NTHM/RTH M23 167 E1
Ferney Field Rd MDTN M24 89 H1
Ferngate Dr DID/WITH M20 142 D5
Ferngrove BURY BL9 39 E2
Fernhill MPL/ROM SK6 175 G3
Fernhill Av BOLS/LL BL3 47 H5
Fernhill Dr GTN M18 130 A4
Fernhills EDGW/EG BL7 22 D1
Fernhill St BURY BL9 4 E2
Fernholme Ct OLDS OL8 90 D3
Fernhurst Rd DID/WITH M20 157 H1
Fernhurst St OLD OL1 74 D3
Fernie St ANC M4 * 114 D2
Fern Isle Cl WHIT OL12 18 A2
Fern Lea CHD/CHDH SK8 181 G3
Fernlea HALE/TIMP WA15 178 A3
Fernlea Av OLD OL1 74 D3
Fernlea Cl WHIT OL12 29 E1
Fernlea Crs SWIN M27 98 D3
Fern Lea Gv LHULT M38 81 E3
Fernleigh Av BNG/LEV M19 144 C2
Fernleigh Dr
OLDTF/WHR M16 * 127 F3
Fernley Av DTN/ASHW M34 147 E1
Fernley Rd OFTN SK2 172 C3
Fern Lodge Dr AUL OL6 107 G5
Fernone WILM/AE SK9 192 A4
Ferns Gv BOL BL1 48 A2
Fernside RAD M26 83 E1
Fernside Av DID/WITH M20 158 A1
Fernside Gv WALK M28 * 82 B3
Fernside Wy WHIT OL12 28 D2
Fernstead BOLS/LL BL3 48 B3
Fern St BOLS/LL BL3 48 B3
BURY BL9 4 E2
CHAD OL9 74 B4
CHH M8 114 D1
FWTH BL4 66 B3
OLDS OL8 8 D6
RAMS BL0 17 E2
ROCH OL11 29 G5
WHIT OL12 19 H2
Fernthorpe Av UPML OL3 79 F3
Fern Vw HALE/TIMP WA15 167 F4
Fernview Dr RAMS BL0 26 C2
Fernwood MPL/ROM SK6 175 H2
Fernwood Av GTN M18 130 C5
Fernwood Gv WILM/AE SK9 199 F2
Ferrand Ldg LIT OL15 21 F1
Ferrand Rd LIT OL15 21 E2
Ferring Wk CHAD OL9 * 90 C1
Ferris St OP/CLY M11 117 E5
Ferrous Wy IRL M44 136 B5
Ferryhill Rd IRL M44 136 C1
Ferrymasters Wy IRL M44 136 C2
Ferry Rd IRL M44 136 D1
Ferry St OP/CLY M11 115 H5
Fettler Cl SWIN M27 98 D4
Feversham Cl ECC M30 111 G1
Fewston Cl BOL BL1 33 H1
Fiddlers La IRL M44 122 C5
Field Bank Gv BNG/LEV M19 144 B2
Field Cl BRAM/HZG SK7 193 G3
MPL/ROM SK6 174 C4
Fieldcroft ROCH OL11 29 E4
Fielden Av CCHDY M21 141 F2
Fielden Ct CCHDY M21 156 C1
Fielden Rd DID/WITH M20 157 E1
Fielders Wy SWIN M27 83 H3
Fieldfare Av NEWH/MOS M40 116 C1
Fieldfare Wy AULW OL7 106 D3
Fieldhead Av ROCH OL11 28 D4
TOT/BURYW BL8 37 F5
Fieldhead Ms WILM/AE SK9 199 H2
Fieldhead Rd WILM/AE SK9 199 H2
Field House La MPL/ROM SK6 175 F4
Fieldhouse Rd WHIT OL12 10 D1
Fielding Av POY/DIS SK12 195 F5
Fielding St ECC M30 110 D4
MDTN M24 72 D2
Field La AUL OL6 107 G5
Field Pl DID/WITH M20 157 G3
Field Rd MILN OL16 31 E4
SALE M33 139 E5
Fieldsend Cl STLY SK15 121 G5
Fields End Fold ECC M30 122 D4
Fields Farm Cl HYDE SK14 149 F2
Fields Farm Rd HYDE SK14 149 G1
Fieldside Cl BRAM/HZG SK7 193 G3
Fields New Rd CHAD OL9 90 B2
Field St DROY M43 117 G5
FAIL M35 104 D3
GTN M18 130 D2
HYDE SK14 133 G3
MPL/ROM SK6 161 G3
ROCH OL11 43 F2
SLFD M6 113 E3
Fieldsway OLDS OL8 91 F5
Field Vale Dr RDSH SK5 145 G2
Fieldvale Rd SALE M33 153 H5
Field View Wk
OLDTF/WHR M16 142 B1
Field Wk HALE/TIMP WA15 * 178 C1
Fieldway MILN OL16 43 G3
Fife Av CHAD OL9 90 A3
Fifield Cl OLDS OL8 91 H4
Fifth Av BOL BL1 48 A2
BOLS/LL BL3 50 C5
BURY BL9 39 G2
DUK SK16 133 E1
OLDS OL8 90 D5
OP/CLY M11 116 D3
TRPK M17 125 H3
Fifth St BOL BL1 32 C2
TRPK M17 125 H3
Filbert St OLD OL1 76 B3
Filby Wk NEWH/MOS M40 115 H1
Fildes St MDTN M24 73 G5
Filey Av OLDTF/WHR M16 141 H1
URM M41 123 H4
Filey Dr SLFD M6 100 A4
Filey Rd OFTN SK2 172 D2
RUSH/FAL M14 143 F3
Filey St MILN OL16 30 D1
Filton Av BOLS/LL BL3 48 C4
Finance St LIT OL15 20 B3
Finborough Cl
OLDTF/WHR M16 127 H4
Finchale Dr HALE/TIMP WA15 178 C3
Finchley Av NEWH/MOS M40 116 D1
Finchley Cl TOT/BURYW BL8 37 G5
Finchley Gv NEWH/MOS M40 103 H1
Finchley Rd HALE/TIMP WA15 177 H1
RUSH/FAL M14 142 D3
Finchwood Rd
WYTH/NTH M22 168 D4
Findon Rd NTHM/RTH M23 167 H3
Finger Post BOLS/LL BL3 50 D5
Finghall Rd URM M41 138 B1
Finishing Wk ANC M4 * 115 F4
Finland Rd EDGY/DAV SK3 171 G2
Finian Rd MDTN M24 57 H4
Finlay St FWTH BL4 * 66 A4
Finney Cl WILM/AE SK9 191 H5
Finney Dr CCHDY M21 141 E4
WILM/AE SK9 191 H5
Finney La CHD/CHDH SK8 181 F4
Finney St BOLS/LL BL3 * 49 E5
Finningley Rd BKLY M9 87 G1
Finny Bank Rd SALE M33 139 G5
Finsbury Av NEWH/MOS M40 116 D1
Finsbury Cl OLDS OL8 92 A3
Finsbury Rd RDSH SK5 145 E3
Finsbury St ROCH OL11 42 C1
Finsbury Wy WILM/AE SK9 192 B5
Finstock Cl ECC M30 110 C4
Fintry Gv ECC M30 111 E4
Fir Av BRAM/HZG SK7 183 H4
Firbank Cl AULW OL7 119 E3
Firbank Rd NTHM/RTH M23 179 H1
Fir Bank Rd ROY/SHW OL2 59 E3
Firbarn Cl MILN OL16 31 E4
Firbeck Dr ANC M4 115 G3
Fir Cl POY/DIS SK12 195 F4
Fircroft Rd OLDS OL8 91 H5
Firdale Av NEWH/MOS M40 104 D1
Firdale Wk CHAD OL9 8 A2
Firecrest Cl WALK M28 96 C2
Firefly Cl CSLFD M3 114 A4
Fire Station Sq ORD M5 * 113 H3
Fire Station Yd ROCH OL11 30 A5
Firethorn Av BNG/LEV M19 143 H5
Firethorn Cl WHTN BL5 62 A2
Firethorn Dr HYDE SK14 148 C1
Firfield Gv WALK M28 82 C4
Fir Gv BNG/LEV M19 144 A2
CHAD OL9 74 C4
Firgrove Av MILN OL16 31 E3
Firgrove Gdns MILN OL16 31 E3
Fir La ROY/SHW OL2 59 E3
Fir Rd BRAM/HZG SK7 183 H4
DTN/ASHW M34 132 D5
FWTH BL4 65 G4
MPL/ROM SK6 174 D5
SWIN M27 98 D4
Firs Av AUL OL6 119 G1
FAIL M35 104 D3
OLDTF/WHR M16 141 F1
Firsby Av MPL/ROM SK6 161 G2
Firsby St BNG/LEV M19 144 A2
Firs Gv CHD/CHDH SK8 169 F5
Firs Rd CHD/CHDH SK8 181 F1
SALE M33 153 H1
First Av BOLS/LL BL3 50 C5
OLDS OL8 91 E5
OP/CLY M11 117 E3
STLY SK15 109 F5
SWIN M27 98 C5
TOT/BURYW BL8 26 A5
TRPK M17 126 A3
The Firs ALT WA14 177 E2
Fir St BOL BL1 34 A4
BURY BL9 5 H4
ECC M30 111 E4
FAIL M35 104 D3
HEY OL10 41 F5
HTNM SK4 12 E2
NEWH/MOS M40 115 G1
OLDTF/WHR M16 * 127 F4
RAD M26 68 C2
RAMS BL0 17 E1
ROY/SHW OL2 59 E4
SLFD M6 113 E3
First St BOL BL1 32 C2
Firs Wy SALE M33 153 F3
Firswood Dr HYDE SK14 134 B5
ROY/SHW OL2 58 D4
SWIN M27 98 D4
Firswood Mt CHD/CHDH SK8 169 F5
Firth St OLD OL1 9 H4
Fir Tree Av OLDS OL8 91 H5
SALE M33 153 F2
WALK M28 96 C4
Fir Tree Cl DUK SK16 120 C5
Fir Tree Crs DUK SK16 120 C5
Fir Tree Dr HYDE SK14 133 H3
Fir Tree La DUK SK16 134 A1
Firvale Av CHD/CHDH SK8 181 G3
Firwood Av FWTH BL4 81 H1
URM M41 139 G2
Firwood Cl OFTN SK2 172 D1
Firwood Crs RAD M26 68 C3
Firwood Gv BOLE BL2 34 C4
Firwood La BOLE BL2 34 D3
Firwood Pk CHAD OL9 73 H5
Fishbourne Sq
RUSH/FAL M14 * 128 D5
Fisherfield WHIT OL12 28 C2
Fishermore Rd
URM M41 137 G1
Fisher St OLD OL1 9 H1
Fishwick St MILN OL16 30 B5
Fistral Av CHD/CHDH SK8 181 H4
Fistral Crs STLY SK15 121 G2
Fitton Av CCHDY M21 141 F5
Fitton Crs SWIN M27 84 A4
Fitton Hill Rd OLDS OL8 91 H4
Fitton St MILN OL16 11 F4
ROY/SHW OL2 59 G2
Fitzgeorge St
NEWH/MOS M40 102 D5
Fitzgerald Cl PWCH M25 85 G5
Fitzgerald Wy SLFD M6 * 113 E2
Fitzhugh St BOL BL1 * 34 B1
Fitzroy St AULW OL7 119 E4
DROY M43 118 A5
STLY SK15 121 G2
Fitzwarren St SLFD M6 113 E3
Fitzwilliam St BRO M7 114 A1
Five Quarters RAD M26 51 H4
Flagcroft Dr NTHM/RTH M23 168 A4
Flagg Wood Av
MPL/ROM SK6 174 C2
Flag Rw ANC M4 * 115 E2
Flagship Av ORD M5 * 113 G5
Flake La ROY/SHW OL2 59 E5
Flamborough Wk
RUSH/FAL M14 * 128 C5
Flamingo Cl WGTN/LGST M12 129 H2
Flamstead Av
NTHM/RTH M23 167 F3
Flannel St WHIT OL12 10 E4
Flashfields PWCH M25 100 C1
Flash St NEWH/MOS M40 104 B4
Flatley Cl HULME M15 128 B2
Flavian Wk OP/CLY M11 * 116 C5
Flaxcroft Rd WYTH/NTH M22 180 A2
Flaxfield Av STLY SK15 121 G3
Flaxman Ri OLD OL1 60 B5
Flaxpool Cl OLDTF/WHR M16 127 H4
Flax St CSLFD M3 6 A1
RAMS BL0 16 B4
Fleece St MILN OL16 10 C6
OLDE OL4 * 76 A5
Fleeson St RUSH/FAL M14 128 D5
Fleet St AUL OL6 119 G3
GTN M18 131 E2
HYDE SK14 133 H4
OLDE OL4 76 B5
Fleetwood Rd WALK M28 81 F4
Fleming Cl WHIT OL12 20 A3
Fleming Pl CHAD OL9 8 D4
Fleming Rd WYTH/NTH M22 180 C2
Flemish Rd DTN/ASHW M34 147 F1
Fletcher Av SWIN M27 84 B4
Fletcher Cl CHAD OL9 8 C4
HEY OL10 41 E4
Fletcher Dr ALT WA14 177 F3
POY/DIS SK12 197 E1
Fletcher Fold Rd BURY BL9 53 G3
Fletcher Sq CMANE M1 * 7 K5
Fletcher's Rd LIT OL15 20 B5
Fletcher St AUL OL6 119 H2
BOLS/LL BL3 48 D4
BOLS/LL BL3 67 E1
BURY BL9 5 G4
FWTH BL4 66 A4
NEWH/MOS M40 103 G5
RAD M26 52 D5
ROCH OL11 43 F1
STKP SK1 13 G3
Fletsand Rd WILM/AE SK9 199 F4
Fletton Cl WHIT OL12 29 H1
Fletton Ms WHIT OL12 29 F1
Flint Cl BRAM/HZG SK7 184 D3
OP/CLY M11 * 116 C3
Flint St DROY M43 118 A3
EDGY/DAV SK3 13 F7
OLD OL1 76 B4
Flitcroft Ct BOLS/LL BL3 * 49 E5
Flitcroft St OLDE OL4 92 B3
Flixton Rd URM M41 137 H2
Floatshall Rd NTHM/RTH M23 167 G3
Floats Rd NTHM/RTH M23 167 F4
Flora St BKLY M9 87 H4
OLD OL1 9 F2
Florence Av BOL BL1 34 A2
Florence Ct EDGY/DAV SK3 * 171 E2
Florence Park Ct
DID/WITH M20 157 H2
Florence St BOLS/LL BL3 * 48 C5
DROY M43 118 A5
ECC M30 110 C4
FAIL M35 105 E2
HTNM SK4 13 F1
MILN OL16 30 C5
SALE M33 139 H5
Florida St OLDS OL8 8 E6
Florin Gdns SLFD M6 113 E2
Florist St EDGY/DAV SK3 171 H2
Flowery Bank OLDS OL8 92 A3
Flowery Fld OFTN SK2 184 B1
Flowery Field Gn HYDE SK14 133 F4
Floyd Av CCHDY M21 141 G5
Floyer Rd BKLY M9 88 B3
Foden La BRAM/HZG SK7 193 G4
Foggbrook Cl OFTN SK2 173 G3
Fogg La BOLS/LL BL3 66 B1
Fog La BNG/LEV M19 158 A2
DID/WITH M20 157 G2
Fold Av DROY M43 118 A3
Fold Crs STLY SK15 109 G4
Fold Gdns WHIT OL12 18 A5
Fold Gn CHAD OL9 90 B1
Fold Ms BRAM/HZG SK7 185 F1
Fold Rd RAD M26 67 F5
Folds Rd BOL BL1 3 G3
Fold St BOL BL1 * 3 F5
BURY BL9 4 B4
HEY OL10 41 F4
NEWH/MOS M40 103 H2
The Fold BKLY M9 88 A4
ROY/SHW OL2 59 H5
URM M41 123 H5
Fold Vw EDGW/EG BL7 22 D2
OLDS OL8 91 H5
Foleshill Av BKLY M9 103 E3
Foley Gdns HEY OL10 56 B2
Foliage Crs RDSH SK5 160 C1
Foliage Gdns RDSH SK5 160 D1
Foliage Rd RDSH SK5 160 C2
Folkestone Rd OP/CLY M11 117 E3
Folkestone Rd East
OP/CLY M11 117 E3
Folkestone Rd West
OP/CLY M11 116 D3
Follows St GTN M18 130 C2
Folly La SWIN M27 98 C5
Folly Wk WHIT OL12 10 D3
Fonthill Gv SALE M33 154 A5
Fontwell Cl OLDTF/WHR M16 127 F5
Fontwell La OLD OL1 75 H3
Fontwell Rd BOLS/LL BL3 66 D2
Fooley Cl DROY M43 117 F5
Foot Mill Crs WHIT OL12 29 G1
Foot Wood Crs WHIT OL12 29 G1
Forber Crs GTN M18 130 B5
Forbes Cl SALE M33 155 E4
STKP SK1 172 C1
Forbes Pk BRAM/HZG SK7 183 G5
Forbes Rd STKP SK1 160 C5
Forbes St MPL/ROM SK6 161 G2
Fordbank Rd DID/WITH M20 157 F4
Ford Gdns ROCH OL11 29 E5
Ford Gv HYDE SK14 135 H4
Fordham Gv BOL BL1 48 B1
Ford La DID/WITH M20 157 F4
SLFD M6 113 F1
WYTH/NTH M22 156 D5
Ford Ldg DID/WITH M20 157 G4
Ford's La BRAM/HZG SK7 193 G1
Ford St CSLFD M3 6 A3
DUK SK16 133 F2
EDGY/DAV SK3 12 C4
RAD M26 66 D4
WGTN/LGST M12 129 E2
Foreland Cl NEWH/MOS M40 103 E5
Forest Cl DUK SK16 133 F2
Forest Ct URM M41 123 E5
Forest Dr HALE/TIMP WA15 166 A3
SALE M33 153 H4
WHTN BL5 62 B4
Forester Dr STLY SK15 121 H1
Forester Hill Av BOLS/LL BL3 65 E1
Forester Hill Cl BOLS/LL BL3 65 E1
Forest Gdns PART M31 150 C3
Forest Range BNG/LEV M19 144 A2
Forest Rd BOL BL1 33 E3
Forest St AUL OL6 119 H1
ECC M30 110 B1
OLDS OL8 91 G5
Forest Vw WHIT OL12 29 G1
Forest Wy EDGW/EG BL7 23 H5
Forfar St BOL BL1 33 H1
Forge St OLDE OL4 76 A5
Formby Av CCHDY M21 141 H4
Formby Dr CHD/CHDH SK8 181 G4
Formby Rd SLFD M6 100 B5
Forrester Dr ROY/SHW OL2 60 C1
STLY SK15 120 D4
Forresters Gn TRPK M17 126 B2
Forrester St WALK M28 97 H2
Forrest Rd DTN/ASHW M34 147 F2
Forshaw Av GTN M18 131 E3
Forsyth St WHIT OL12 28 B1
Fortescue Rd OFTN SK2 173 E2
Forth Pl RAD M26 52 A4
Forth Rd RAD M26 52 A4
Forton Av BOLE BL2 50 B2
Fortran Cl ORD M5 113 F4
Fort Rd PWCH M25 86 C5
Fortrose Av BKLY M9 87 G4
Fortuna Gv BNG/LEV M19 143 H5
Fortune St BOLS/LL BL3 49 G4
Fortyacre Dr MPL/ROM SK6 161 F3
Forum Gv BRO M7 101 H5
Fosbrook Av DID/WITH M20 157 H2
Foscarn Dr NTHM/RTH M23 168 A4
Fossgill Av BOLE BL2 34 D1
Foster Ct BURY BL9 39 G2
Foster La BOLE BL2 35 G5
Foster St DTN/ASHW M34 132 C5
OLDE OL4 92 B1
RAD M26 68 A1
Fotherby Dr BKLY M9 88 A4
Foulds Av TOT/BURYW BL8 37 F4
Foundry La ANC M4 7 H3
Foundry St BOLS/LL BL3 49 E4
BOLS/LL BL3 66 D1
BURY BL9 5 F5
DUK SK16 119 H5
HEY OL10 40 D4
OLDS OL8 8 E5
RAD M26 68 B1
Fountain Av
HALE/TIMP WA15 178 C2
Fountain Gdns OLD OL1 * 75 E3
Fountain Pl WHTF M45 69 G5
Fountains Av BOLE BL2 34 D5
Fountains Rd CHD/CHDH SK8 193 F1
STRET M32 125 E5
Fountain St AUL OL6 120 B2
BURY BL9 5 H5
CMANW M2 7 F5
ECC M30 111 E5
HYDE SK14 134 A5
MDTN M24 72 C4
OLD OL1 9 F3
TOT/BURYW BL8 37 H4
Fountain St North BURY BL9 5 G4
Fountains Wk CHAD OL9 * 90 B2
DUK SK16 133 F2
Fouracres Rd
NTHM/RTH M23 167 G4
Four Lane Ends URM M41 137 G3
Four Lanes HYDE SK14 135 H4
Four Stalls End LIT OL15 20 D4
Fourth Av BOL BL1 48 A2
BOLS/LL BL3 50 C5
BURY BL9 39 F2
CHAD OL9 90 B2
OLDS OL8 90 D5
OP/CLY M11 116 D2
STLY SK15 109 F4
SWIN M27 98 C5
Fourth St BOL BL1 32 C2
TRPK M17 125 H3
Fourways TRPK M17 125 F2
Four Yards CMANW M2 6 E5
Fovant Crs RDSH SK5 145 E2
Fowler Av GTN M18 131 E1
Fowler St OLDS OL8 90 D4
Fownhope Av SALE M33 154 A3
Fownhope Rd SALE M33 154 A3
Foxall Cl MDTN M24 71 H5
Foxall St MDTN M24 71 H5
Foxbank St BRUN/LGST M13 129 F4
Fox Bench Cl BRAM/HZG SK7 193 F1
Foxbench Wk CCHDY M21 141 H5
Fox Cl HALE/TIMP WA15 166 A3
Foxcroft St LIT OL15 20 C3
Foxdale St OP/CLY M11 116 D4
Foxdenton Dr STRET M32 125 E5
Foxdenton La MDTN M24 89 H1
Foxendale Wk BOLS/LL BL3 * 48 D4
Foxfield Cl TOT/BURYW BL8 37 G1
Foxfield Dr OLDS OL8 105 H1
Foxfield Rd NTHM/RTH M23 179 H1
Foxfold Cl WALK M28 96 A3
Foxglove Ct WHIT OL12 18 C5
Foxglove Dr ALT WA14 165 F1
BURY BL9 39 G3
Foxglove La STLY SK15 120 C2
Foxhall Rd DTN/ASHW M34 132 A4
HALE/TIMP WA15 165 H3
Foxham Dr BRO M7 101 H4
Foxhill ALT WA14 164 D4
Fox Hl ROY/SHW OL2 59 F1
Foxhill Cha OFTN SK2 173 H4
Foxhill Dr STLY SK15 121 F5
Foxhill Rd ECC M30 110 A4
Fox Hill Rd ROCH OL11 57 G1
Foxholes Cl WHIT OL12 10 E2
Foxholes La WHIT OL12 11 G1
Foxholes Rd HYDE SK14 147 H3
WHIT OL12 10 E2
Foxlair Rd WYTH/NTH M22 180 A1
Foxland Rd CHD/CHDH SK8 169 G5
Foxley Gv BOLS/LL BL3 2 B6
Fox Park Rd OLDS OL8 105 H1
Fox Platt Rd MOSL OL5 * 108 C1
Fox Platt Ter MOSL OL5 108 D2
Fox St BURY BL9 5 F2
ECC M30 111 G3
EDGY/DAV SK3 12 C6
HEY OL10 40 D4
MILN OL16 11 G4
MILN OL16 31 F5
OLDS OL8 90 D5
Foxton St MDTN M24 71 H5
Foxwood Dr HYDE SK14 133 H4
MOSL OL5 94 A5
Foxwood Gdns BNG/LEV M19 158 B1
Foynes Cl NEWH/MOS M40 * 103 E5
Framingham Rd SALE M33 154 C4
Frampton Cl MDTN M24 73 E5
Fram St BKLY M9 103 G2
SLFD M6 * 112 D3
Frances Av CHD/CHDH SK8 169 F3
Frances St BOL BL1 33 G4
BRUN/LGST M13 128 C2
CHD/CHDH SK8 170 B3
EDGY/DAV SK3 13 F5
HYDE SK14 133 F5
IRL M44 150 D1
MILN OL16 20 A5
OLD OL1 75 H3
Frances St West HYDE SK14 133 F5
Francis Av ECC M30 111 F3
WALK M28 82 C5
Francis Rd DID/WITH M20 157 H1
IRL M44 136 B3
Francis St CSLFD M3 114 C2
DTN/ASHW M34 147 F3
ECC M30 111 E2
FAIL M35 105 E3
FWTH BL4 65 H3
Frankby Cl SWIN M27 * 99 H3
Frank Fold HEY OL10 40 B4
Frankford Av BOL BL1 33 F4
Frankford Sq BOL BL1 * 33 F4
Frankland Cl OP/CLY M11 116 C3
Franklin Cl OLD OL1 9 F1
Franklin Rd DROY M43 117 H4
Franklin St ECC M30 111 E3
MILN OL16 43 G1
OLD OL1 9 F1
Franklyn Av URM M41 137 G1
Franklyn Rd GTN M18 130 D2
Frank Perkins Wy IRL M44 136 B4
Frank St BOL BL1 33 G5
BURY BL9 5 F6
FAIL M35 104 D3
HYDE SK14 148 A1
SLFD M6 113 F1
Frankton Rd WHTF M45 69 G5
Franton Rd OP/CLY M11 116 C3
Fraser Av SALE M33 155 F3
Fraser Pl TRPK M17 126 A3
Fraser Rd CHH M8 102 A1
Fraser St AUL OL6 119 H2
MILN OL16 43 G2
ROY/SHW OL2 59 H1
SWIN M27 99 F1
Frecheville Ct BURY BL9 4 C7
Freckleton Av CCHDY M21 156 B2
Freckleton Dr TOT/BURYW BL8 52 A1
Frederick Av ROY/SHW OL2 * 59 H4
Frederick Rd SLFD M6 113 G2
Frederick St AUL OL6 120 B3
CHAD OL9 74 C4
CSLFD M3 6 B3
DTN/ASHW M34 132 C3
FWTH BL4 66 A4
LIT OL15 20 D2
OLDS OL8 8 C7
RAMS BL0 16 C3
Frederick Ter BKLY M9 * 103 E1
Fred Tilson Cl RUSH/FAL M14 128 B5
Freehold St ROCH OL11 42 D1
Freeman Av AUL OL6 120 A2
Freeman Rd DUK SK16 133 F2
Freeman Sq HULME M15 * 128 B2
Freemantle St EDGY/DAV SK3 12 B5
Freesia Av WALK M28 81 E4
Freestone Cl
TOT/BURYW BL8 4 B2
Freetown Cl RUSH/FAL M14 128 B4
Freetrade St ROCH OL11 42 D1
Fremantle Av GTN M18 130 C5
French Av OLD OL1 76 B3
STLY SK15 121 F4
French Barn La BKLY M9 87 H4
French Gv BOLS/LL BL3 50 A4
French St AUL OL6 120 A1
STLY SK15 121 F4
Fresca Rd OLD OL1 60 C5
Freshfield CHD/CHDH SK8 181 G3
Freshfield Av BOLS/LL BL3 64 C2
HYDE SK14 147 H2

PWCH M25 86 B1
Freshfield Cl FAIL M35 105 F4
MPL/ROM SK6 163 G5
Freshfield Gv BOLS/LL BL3 65 E2
Freshfield Rd HTNM SK4 158 C4
Freshfields RAD M26 51 G4
Freshpool Wy
WYTH/NTH M22 168 D3
Freshville St CMANE M1 * 7 J6
Freshwater Dr AUL OL6 107 H5
DTN/ASHW M34 147 F3
Freshwater St GTN M18 130 D2
Freshwinds Ct OLDE OL4 92 C3
Fresnel Cl HYDE SK14 134 C2
Frewland Av EDGY/DAV SK3 172 A5
Freya Gv ORD M5 113 H5
Friars Cl ALT WA14 177 E3
WILM/AE SK9 198 B2
Friars Crs ROCH OL11 43 E4
Friar's Rd SALE M33 154 C2
Friendship Av GTN M18 * 130 D4
Frieston WHIT OL12 10 B4
Frieston Rd ALT WA14 153 H5
Friezland Cl STLY SK15 109 F5
Friezland La UPML OL3 94 D3
Frimley Gdns WYTH/NTH M22 180 C1
Frinton Av NEWH/MOS M40 * 89 G4
Frinton Cl SALE M33 154 A5
Frinton Rd BOLS/LL BL3 64 A1
Frith Rd DID/WITH M20 157 H1
Frobisher Cl BRUN/LGST M13 129 E3
Frobisher Pl RDSH SK5 159 H2
Frodesley Wk
WGTN/LGST M12 * 129 G2
Frodsham Av HTNM SK4 159 F3
Frodsham Rd SALE M33 155 F4
Frodsham St RUSH/FAL M14 * 128 C5
Frogley St BOLE BL2 * 34 C3
Frogmore Av HYDE SK14 148 A4
Frome Av OFTN SK2 172 D4
URM M41 138 B3
Frome Dr CHH M8 102 C3
Frome St OLDE OL4 92 B1
Frostlands St
OLDTF/WHR M16 127 H5
Frost St ANC M4 * 115 G4
OLDS OL8 91 F3
Froxmer St GTN M18 130 B2
Fulbrook Dr CHD/CHDH SK8 192 D1
Fulford St OLDTF/WHR M16 127 F4
Fulham Av NEWH/MOS M40 104 A5
Fulham St OLDE OL4 92 B1
Fullerton Rd HTNM SK4 159 E4
Full Pot La ROCH OL11 28 B3
Fulmar Cl POY/DIS SK12 194 B3
Fulmar Dr OFTN SK2 173 G4
SALE M33 153 F4
Fulmards Cl WILM/AE SK9 199 F3
Fulmar Gdns ROCH OL11 28 C4
Fulmer Dr ANC M4 115 F3
Fulmere Ct SWIN M27 98 C4
Fulneck Sq DROY M43 117 H5
Fulshaw Av WILM/AE SK9 198 D4
Fulshaw Ct WILM/AE SK9 198 D5
Fulshaw Pk WILM/AE SK9 198 D5
Fulshaw Pk South
WILM/AE SK9 200 C1
Fulstone Ms OFTN SK2 172 C3
Fulwood Av BKLY M9 88 C3
Fulwood Cl TOT/BURYW BL8 37 E5
Furbarn La ROCH OL11 28 A3
Furbarn Rd ROCH OL11 28 A3
Furlong Rd WYTH/NTH M22 180 A2
Furnace St DUK SK16 119 G4
HYDE SK14 133 F4
Furness Av AULW OL7 106 C5
BOLE BL2 34 C4
HEY OL10 40 D3
LIT OL15 20 D2
OLDS OL8 92 B3
WHTF M45 69 H4
Furness Cl MILN OL16 31 F5
POY/DIS SK12 194 D3
Furness Gv HTNM SK4 158 D5
Furness Quay SALQ M50 126 D1
Furness Rd BOL BL1 48 A2
CHD/CHDH SK8 193 F1
MDTN M24 72 C1
RUSH/FAL M14 143 E2
URM M41 124 C5
Furness Sq BOLE BL2 34 C4
Furnival Rd GTN M18 130 B2
Furnival St RDSH SK5 145 E1
Furrow Dr ECC M30 110 C1
Further Fld ROCH OL11 28 A2
Further Heights Rd WHIT OL12 10 B1
Further Hey Cl OLDE OL4 76 D5
Further La HYDE SK14 135 F5
Further Pits ROCH OL11 29 F4
Furze Av WHTN BL5 62 A5
Furzegate MILN OL16 43 H3
Furze La OLDE OL4 76 C3
Fushia Gv BRO M7 * 101 G4
Fylde Av BOLE BL2 50 B2
CHD/CHDH SK8 181 H4
Fylde Rd HTNM SK4 158 D4
Fylde St BOLS/LL BL3 66 A2
Fylde St East BOLS/LL BL3 66 A2

G

Gable Av WILM/AE SK9 198 D3
Gable Dr MDTN M24 72 B3
The Gables SALE M33 * 154 C3
Gable St BOLE BL2 * 35 E1
OP/CLY M11 116 A5
Gabriel's Ter MDTN M24 73 F5
The Gabriels ROY/SHW OL2 59 G2
Gaddum Rd ALT WA14 176 D3
DID/WITH M20 157 H3
Gadwall Cl WALK M28 97 E2
Gail Av HTNM SK4 12 C1
Gail Cl FAIL M35 104 D5
WILM/AE SK9 201 E3
Gainford Av CHD/CHDH SK8 169 G5
Gainford Gdns
NEWH/MOS M40 104 A1
Gainford Rd RDSH SK5 145 F2
Gainford Wk BOLS/LL BL3 * 48 D5
Gainsborough Av BOLS/LL BL3 64 B1
DID/WITH M20 * 157 H1
MPL/ROM SK6 175 G1
OLDS OL8 91 F3
STRET M32 * 126 C5
Gainsborough Cl
WILM/AE SK9 199 G2
Gainsborough Dr
CHD/CHDH SK8 170 C3
ROCH OL11 42 D3
Gainsborough Rd CHAD OL9 73 H4
DTN/ASHW M34 118 C4
RAMS BL0 26 B2
Gainsborough St BRO M7 101 H3
Gairloch Av STRET M32 139 H1
Gair Rd RDSH SK5 160 A2
Gair St HYDE SK14 133 G4
Gaitskell Cl WGTN/LGST M12 115 H4
Galbraith Rd DID/WITH M20 157 H3
Galbraith St CMANE M1 * 7 G7
Galbraith Wy ROCH OL11 28 B3
Gale Cl LIT OL15 21 F1
Gale Dr MDTN M24 72 A2
Gale Rd PWCH M25 85 G4
Gales Ter ROCH OL11 42 D1
Gale St HEY OL10 40 C4
WHIT OL12 19 E5
Galgate Cl HULME M15 127 H1
TOT/BURYW BL8 37 E5
Galindo St BOLE BL2 34 D2
Galland St OLDE OL4 76 C5
Galloway Cl BOLS/LL BL3 47 F4
HEY OL10 40 A5
Galloway Dr SWIN M27 84 A3
Galloway Rd SWIN M27 * 98 C4
Gallowsclough Rd STLY SK15 135 F2
Galston St OP/CLY M11 116 B5
Galsworthy Av CHH M8 102 B5
Galvin Rd BKLY M9 87 G4
Galway St OLD OL1 9 G4
Gambleside Cl WALK M28 96 C2
Gambrel Bank Rd AUL OL6 107 E4
Gambrel Gv AUL OL6 107 E4
Game St OLDE OL4 92 B2
Gamma Wk OP/CLY M11 116 C3
Gandy La WHIT OL12 18 B4
Gantock Wk RUSH/FAL M14 128 D5
Ganton Av WHTF M45 69 E5
Garbrook Av BKLY M9 87 H2
Garden Av DROY M43 118 A3
STRET M32 140 B1
SWIN M27 98 C3
Garden City RAMS BL0 26 B1
Garden Cl LIT OL15 31 G1
Gardenfold Wy DROY M43 118 A3
Garden La ALT WA14 165 G4
CSLFD M3 6 C2
CSLFD M3 6 D4
MILN OL16 10 E5
WALK M28 96 B4
Garden Ms AUL OL6 * 120 A3
Garden Rw HEY OL10 40 C2
The Gardens BOL BL1 23 E5
Garden St DTN/ASHW M34 132 C2
ECC M30 111 F4
FWTH BL4 66 B4
HEY OL10 40 D3
HYDE SK14 133 H4
MILN OL16 45 E2
OFTN SK2 * 172 D4
OLD OL1 9 K2
RAMS BL0 16 D2
TOT/BURYW BL8 26 A4
Garden Ter ROY/SHW OL2 58 D2
Garden Wk AUL OL6 119 H1
Garden Wall Cl ORD M5 113 H5
Garden Wy LIT OL15 31 G1
Gardner Rd PWCH M25 85 G3
Gardner St SLFD M6 113 F2
WGTN/LGST M12 130 A2
Garfield Av BNG/LEV M19 144 B2
Garfield Cl ROCH OL11 28 B3
Garfield Gv BOLS/LL BL3 2 B7
Garfield St BOLS/LL BL3 64 B1
STKP SK1 * 13 J1
Garforth Av ANC M4 115 F3
Garforth Crs DROY M43 118 B2
Garforth Ri BOL BL1 47 H2
Garforth St CHAD OL9 8 A2
Gargrave Av BOL BL1 32 C4
Gargrave St BRO M7 100 C2
OLDE OL4 92 A1
Garland Rd WYTH/NTH M22 180 D1
Garlick St CHAD OL9 8 E4
GTN M18 130 C3
HYDE SK14 * 134 A5
Garnant Cl BKLY M9 103 G2
Garner Av HALE/TIMP WA15 154 B5
Garner Cl ALT WA14 177 G2
Garner Dr ECC M30 * 110 D2
ORD M5 112 C2
Garner's La EDGY/DAV SK3 171 G5
EDGY/DAV SK3 172 A4
Garnet St OLD OL1 76 A4
Garnett Cl HYDE SK14 135 G5
Garnett Rd HYDE SK14 135 G5
Garnett St BOL BL1 33 H3
RAMS BL0 16 C3
STKP SK1 13 G4
Garratt Wy GTN M18 130 B3
Garret Gv ROY/SHW OL2 60 B2
Garrett Wk EDGY/DAV SK3 12 A5
Garrick Gdns WYTH/NTH M22 168 C5
Garsdale Cl BURY BL9 53 H2
Garsdale La BOL BL1 47 E2
Garside Gv BOL BL1 33 F4
Garside Hey Rd
TOT/BURYW BL8 26 D5
Garside St BOL BL1 2 C5
DTN/ASHW M34 * 146 D1
HYDE SK14 148 A2
Garstang Av BOLE BL2 50 B3
Garstang Dr TOT/BURYW BL8 37 E5
Garston Cl HTNM SK4 159 F3
Garston St BURY BL9 38 D2
Garswood Dr TOT/BURYW BL8 26 C5
Garswood Rd BOLS/LL BL3 64 D2
RUSH/FAL M14 142 C1
Garth Av HALE/TIMP WA15 165 H3
Garthland Rd BRAM/HZG SK7 185 G1
Garthorne Cl
OLDTF/WHR M16 127 H4
Garthorp Rd NTHM/RTH M23 155 F5
Garth Rd MPL/ROM SK6 175 F3
OFTN SK2 172 D2
WYTH/NTH M22 168 C5
The Garth ORD M5 112 C3
Garthwaite Av OLDS OL8 91 F4
Gartside St AULW OL7 * 118 D4
CSLFD M3 6 C5
OLDE OL4 92 A2
Garwick Rd BOL BL1 33 E3
Gascoyne St RUSH/FAL M14 128 C5
Gaskell Cl LIT OL15 * 20 D2
Gaskell Ri OLD OL1 60 D4
Gaskell Rd ALT WA14 165 G3
ECC M30 111 F4
Gaskell St BOL BL1 2 C2
DUK SK16 * 119 G4
NEWH/MOS M40 104 B5
SWIN M27 84 A5
Gaskill St HEY OL10 40 B4
Gas St AUL OL6 119 G2
BOL BL1 2 C5
FWTH BL4 66 A3
HEY OL10 41 E4
HTNM SK4 12 E3
ROCH OL11 10 A7
Gatcombe Sq RUSH/FAL M14 128 D5
Gateacre Wk NTHM/RTH M23 167 F2
Gate Field Cl RAD M26 67 H1
Gatehead Cft UPML OL3 78 C1
Gatehead Ms UPML OL3 78 C1
Gatehead Rd UPML OL3 78 C1
Gatehouse LIT OL15 * 21 G2
Gatehouse Rd WALK M28 81 F3
Gate Keeper Fold AULW OL7 106 D3
Gatemere Cl WALK M28 96 C2
Gatesgarth Rd MDTN M24 71 H2
Gateshead Cl RUSH/FAL M14 128 C4
Gate St DUK SK16 132 D2
OP/CLY M11 116 D5
ROCH OL11 43 E1
Gateway Crs CHAD OL9 89 H3
Gateway Rd GTN M18 * 130 B2
The Gateways SWIN M27 99 E1
The Gateway
NEWH/MOS M40 103 G4
Gathill Cl CHD/CHDH SK8 182 C3
Gathurst St GTN M18 130 D2
Gatley Av RUSH/FAL M14 142 C2
Gatley Brow OLD OL1 * 75 F4
Gatley Gn CHD/CHDH SK8 169 F4
Gatley Rd CHD/CHDH SK8 169 H4
SALE M33 155 F3
Gatling Av WGTN/LGST M12 144 A1
Gatwick Av NTHM/RTH M23 168 A3
Gavin Av ORD M5 113 F4
Gawsworth Av
DID/WITH M20 157 H5
Gawsworth Cl BRAM/HZG SK7 193 H2
EDGY/DAV SK3 171 G4
HALE/TIMP WA15 167 E3
POY/DIS SK12 195 G5
ROY/SHW OL2 59 G2
Gawsworth Ms
CHD/CHDH SK8 169 G4
Gawsworth Rd SALE M33 155 F4
Gawthorne Cl BRAM/HZG SK7 184 D2
Gawthorpe Cl BURY BL9 53 H4
Gaydon Rd SALE M33 153 G2
Gaythorne St BOL BL1 34 A3
Gaythorn St ORD M5 113 H4
Geddington Rd ALT WA14 165 F1
Gee Cross Fold HYDE SK14 148 A4
Gee La ECC M30 110 C2
Gee St EDGY/DAV SK3 12 D7
Gellfield La UPML OL3 79 G3
Gemini Rd SLFD M6 113 H1
Gencoyne Dr BOL BL1 22 C5
Gendre Rd EDGW/EG BL7 22 D3
Geneva Rd BRAM/HZG SK7 183 G1
Geneva Ter ROCH OL11 29 F3
Geneva Wk CHAD OL9 8 A4
Genista Gv BRO M7 * 101 G4
Geoffrey St BURY BL9 5 G1
RAMS BL0 16 B4
WHTN BL5 63 G4
George Barton St BOLE BL2 3 J1
George La MPL/ROM SK6 161 H2
George Leigh St ANC M4 7 H3
George Mann Cl
WYTH/NTH M22 180 B3
George Richards Wy
ALT WA14 165 E2
George Rd RAMS BL0 16 C3
George's Cl POY/DIS SK12 195 F4
George Sq OLD OL1 9 F4
George's Rd HTNM SK4 12 D2
SALE M33 154 C3
George's Rd West
POY/DIS SK12 195 F4
George St AUL OL6 119 H2
BURY BL9 5 F5
CHAD OL9 74 B5
CMANE M1 7 F6
DTN/ASHW M34 132 D5
ECC M30 110 D4
FAIL M35 105 E2
FWTH BL4 65 G5
HEY OL10 40 C3
IRL M44 122 C5
LIT OL15 * 21 E3
MILN OL16 10 E4
MILN OL16 20 A5
MILN OL16 31 F4
MOSL OL5 108 D1
MPL/ROM SK6 163 G4
OLD OL1 9 F4
PWCH M25 101 E1
RAD M26 68 A1
ROY/SHW OL2 45 F5
STKP SK1 13 J3
STLY SK15 120 D3
URM M41 139 E1
WHIT OL12 14 B5
WHTF M45 69 F3
WHTN BL5 62 A4
WILM/AE SK9 200 D4
George St East STKP SK1 172 C1
George St North BRO M7 102 A2
George St South BRO M7 101 H2
George St West STKP SK1 172 C1
Georgette Dr CSLFD M3 6 C1
Georgia Av DID/WITH M20 142 B5
Georgiana St FWTH BL4 65 G3
Georgina Ct BOLS/LL BL3 64 A2
Georgina St BOLS/LL BL3 64 A2
Gerald Av CHH M8 102 B2
Gerald Rd SLFD M6 100 D5
Germain Cl BKLY M9 87 H2
Gerrard Av HALE/TIMP WA15 166 B1
Gerrards Cl IRL M44 136 C1
Gerrards Gdns HYDE SK14 148 A4
Gerrards Hollow HYDE SK14 147 H4
The Gerrards HYDE SK14 147 H4
Gerrard St FWTH BL4 66 B4
ROCH OL11 43 F5
SLFD M6 113 F2
STLY SK15 121 E4
Gerrards Wd HYDE SK14 147 H4
Gertrude Cl ORD M5 113 F5
Gervis Cl NEWH/MOS M40 * 103 E5
Ghyll Gv WALK M28 82 B5
Giants Seat Gv SWIN M27 100 A2
Gibbon Av WYTH/NTH M22 180 C2
Gibbon St BOLS/LL BL3 48 C4
OP/CLY M11 116 B3
Gibb Rd WALK M28 98 A3
Gibbs St ORD M5 114 A4
Gib La NTHM/RTH M23 168 B1
Gibraltar La DTN/ASHW M34 147 F3
Gibraltar St BOLS/LL BL3 2 A7
OLDE OL4 92 C2
Gibsmere Cl
HALE/TIMP WA15 167 E3
Gibson Av GTN M18 131 E1
Gibson Gv WALK M28 81 F4
Gibson La WALK M28 81 F4
Gibson Pl ANC M4 114 D2
Gibsons Rd HTNM SK4 159 E2
Gibson St BOLE BL2 34 D5
MILN OL16 11 K4
OLDE OL4 * 92 B1
Gibson Wy ALT WA14 165 F1
Gibwood Rd WYTH/NTH M22 168 B1
Gidlow St GTN M18 130 D2
Gifford Av BKLY M9 88 C3
Gigg La BURY BL9 53 H1
Gilbertbank MPL/ROM SK6 161 H2
Gilbert Rd HALE/TIMP WA15 177 H3
Gilbert St ECC M30 110 C5
HULME M15 127 H1
SLFD M6 * 113 E4
WALK M28 96 D1
Gilbrook Wy MILN OL16 43 G4
Gilchrist Rd IRL M44 136 A5
Gilda Brook Rd ECC M30 111 H4
Gilda Crs ECC M30 111 H2
Gildenhall FAIL M35 105 F3
Gilderdale Cl ROY/SHW OL2 60 A1
Gilderdale St BOLS/LL BL3 49 F4
Gildersdale Dr BKLY M9 87 G1
Gildridge Rd
OLDTF/WHR M16 142 A2
Gilesgate RUSH/FAL M14 128 C5
Giles St WGTN/LGST M12 129 H4
Gillbent Rd CHD/CHDH SK8 192 D1
Gillbrook Rd DID/WITH M20 157 G4
Gillemere Gv
ROY/SHW OL2 60 B2
Gillers Gn WALK M28 81 H5
Gillford Av BKLY M9 103 G2
Gillingham Rd ECC M30 110 C3
Gillingham Sq OP/CLY M11 116 A5
Gill St BKLY M9 103 G1
STKP SK1 160 C3
Gillwood Dr MPL/ROM SK6 161 G5
Gilman Cl BKLY M9 * 87 H5
Gilman St BKLY M9 87 H5
Gilmerton Dr
NEWH/MOS M40 * 104 B5
Gilmore Dr PWCH M25 86 A2
Gilmore St EDGY/DAV SK3 13 F7
Gilmour St MDTN M24 72 D4
Gilmour Ter BKLY M9 103 G1
Gilnow Gdns BOL BL1 48 B3
Gilnow Gv BOL BL1 2 A6
Gilnow La BOLS/LL BL3 48 B3
Gilnow Rd BOL BL1 48 B3
Gilpin Rd URM M41 139 F2
Giltbrook Av
NEWH/MOS M40 115 H1
Gilwell Dr NTHM/RTH M23 167 G5
Gilwood Gv MDTN M24 56 C5
Gingham Pk RAD M26 51 H4
Gipsy La OFTN SK2 172 D3
ROCH OL11 42 B3
Girton St BRO M7 114 B1
Girvan Av NEWH/MOS M40 89 G5
Girvan Cl BOLS/LL BL3 64 B1
Gisborn Dr SLFD M6 100 C5
Gisburn Av BOL BL1 32 B4
Gisburn Dr TOT/BURYW BL8 36 D3
Gisburne Av NEWH/MOS M40 89 G5
Gisburn Rd ROCH OL11 43 F3
Givendale Dr CHH M8 87 F5
Givvons Fold OLDE OL4 76 C3
Glabyn Av HOR/BR BL6 46 A1
Glade Brow OLDE OL4 * 93 F1
Gladeside Rd WYTH/NTH M22 168 B5
Glade St BOL BL1 48 B2
The Glade BOL BL1 2 A1
HTNM SK4 158 D5
Gladewood Cl
WILM/AE SK9 199 F2
Gladstone Cl BOL BL1 * 33 H4
Gladstone Ct HULME M15 127 H4
Gladstone Crs ROCH OL11 43 F3
Gladstone Gv HTNM SK4 158 D3
Gladstone Ms HTNM SK4 * 159 H3
Gladstone Pl FWTH BL4 65 H3
Gladstone Rd ALT WA14 165 G3
ECC M30 111 F3
FWTH BL4 65 H3
URM M41 139 E1
Gladstone St BOL BL1 33 H4
BURY BL9 5 J3
OFTN SK2 172 D5
OLDE OL4 92 A1
SWIN M27 99 F2
Gladstone Terrace Rd
UPML OL3 94 D3
Gladwyn Av DID/WITH M20 156 D2
Gladys St BOLS/LL BL3 66 A2
Glaisdale OLDE OL4 92 C1
Glaisdale Cl BOLE BL2 34 D4
Glaisdale St BOLE BL2 34 C4
Glaister La BOLE BL2 35 E5
Glamis Av HEY OL10 56 B2
OP/CLY M11 116 D2
STRET M32 139 G1
Glamorgan Pl CHAD OL9 8 A6
Glandon Dr CHD/CHDH SK8 183 F5
Glanford Av BKLY M9 87 F4
Glanvor Rd EDGY/DAV SK3 12 A6
Glasshouse St ANC M4 7 K1
Glasson Wk CHAD OL9 90 B1
Glass St FWTH BL4 * 66 B5
Glastonbury WHIT OL12 10 B4
Glastonbury Av
CHD/CHDH SK8 193 F1
HALE/TIMP WA15 178 C2
Glastonbury Dr POY/DIS SK12 195 E2
Glastonbury Rd STRET M32 125 E5
Glaswen Gv RDSH SK5 160 A2
Glazebrook Cl HEY OL10 40 D5
Glazebury Dr NTHM/RTH M23 168 A4
WHTN BL5 62 A2
Glazedale Av ROY/SHW OL2 58 D5
Glaze Wk WHTF M45 70 B2
Gleaves Av BOLE BL2 35 H2
Gleaves Rd ECC M30 111 F4
Gleave St BOL BL1 * 3 F3
SALE M33 139 H5
Glebeland Rd BOLS/LL BL3 47 H4
Glebelands Rd
NTHM/RTH M23 167 G3
PWCH M25 85 H2
SALE M33 139 G5
Glebe La OLD OL1 76 D1
Glebe Rd URM M41 138 D1
Glebe St BOLE BL2 3 G6
CHAD OL9 90 B4
RAD M26 68 C1
ROY/SHW OL2 60 A2
STKP SK1 13 K4
Gleden St NEWH/MOS M40 115 H3
Gledhall St STLY SK15 120 D3
Gledhill Av ORD M5 126 D1
Gledhill Cl ROY/SHW OL2 44 D5
Gledhill St DID/WITH M20 142 D4
Gledhill Wy EDGW/EG BL7 23 F3
Glemsford Cl
NEWH/MOS M40 * 104 A4
Glenacre Gdns GTN M18 130 D5
Glenart ECC M30 111 F2
Glen Av BKLY M9 103 F1
BOLS/LL BL3 48 A4
FWTH BL4 83 E1
SALE M33 139 G5
SWIN M27 98 C2
WALK M28 97 H2
Glenavon Dr ROY/SHW OL2 59 G1
WHIT OL12 18 C5
Glenbarry Cl BRUN/LGST M13 128 C2
Glenbarry St WGTN/LGST M12 115 G5
Glenbeck Rd WHTF M45 69 F3
Glenboro Av TOT/BURYW BL8 37 G4
Glen Bott St BOL BL1 33 G4
Glenbourne Pk
BRAM/HZG SK7 193 G2
Glenbrook Gdns FWTH BL4 66 A2
Glenbrook Rd BKLY M9 87 F2
Glenburn St BOLS/LL BL3 64 C1
Glenby Av WYTH/NTH M22 181 E1
Glencastle Rd GTN M18 130 B3
Glen Cl GOL/RIS/CUL WA3 150 A4
Glencoe Cl HEY OL10 39 H5
Glencoe Dr BOLE BL2 50 C3
SALE M33 153 F4
Glencoe Pl ROCH OL11 29 G4
Glencoe St OLDS OL8 * 90 D5
Glen Cottages BOL BL1 * 32 B4
Glencross Av
OLDTF/WHR M16 141 E1
Glendale SWIN M27 99 G1
Glendale Av BNG/LEV M19 143 H5
BURY BL9 69 G1
Glendale Ct OLDS OL8 91 G3
Glendale Dr BOLS/LL BL3 47 G3
Glendale Rd ECC M30 111 H2
GTN M18 130 B4
WALK M28 96 A3
Glendene Av BRAM/HZG SK7 193 G2
DROY M43 118 B2
Glenden Foot WHIT OL12 29 G1
Glendevon Cl BOLS/LL BL3 47 G5
Glendevon Pl WHTF M45 70 A5
Glendinning St SLFD M6 112 D3
Glendon Ct OLD OL1 60 D5
Glendon Crs AUL OL6 107 E3
Glendore ORD M5 112 B3
Glendower Dr
NEWH/MOS M40 102 D5
Gleneagles BOLS/LL BL3 63 G1
Gleneagles Av HEY OL10 56 A1
Gleneagles Cl BRAM/HZG SK7 184 B5
WILM/AE SK9 199 G2
Gleneagles Rd
CHD/CHDH SK8 181 H3
URM M41 123 F4
Gleneagles Wy RAMS BL0 16 C3
Glenfield ALT WA14 165 E5
Glenfield Cl OLDE OL4 92 C1
Glenfield Dr POY/DIS SK12 195 E4
Glenfield Rd HTNM SK4 159 G2
Glenfield Sq FWTH BL4 65 G2
Glenfyne Rd SLFD M6 100 A5
Glen Gdns WHIT OL12 19 E5
Glengarth UPML OL3 79 E5
Glengarth Dr HOR/BR BL6 46 D3
Glen Gv MDTN M24 89 F1
ROY/SHW OL2 59 E4
Glenhaven Av URM M41 138 C1
Glenholme Rd BRAM/HZG SK7 183 G5
Glenhurst Rd BNG/LEV M19 * 158 B1
Glenilla Av WALK M28 97 F3

Glenlea Dr DID/WITH M20 169 G1
Glenmere Cl PWCH M25 85 G1
Glenmere Rd DID/WITH M20 169 H1
Glenmoor Rd STKP SK1 13 J4
Glenmore Av DID/WITH M20 156 D2
FWTH BL4 65 F2
Glenmore Cl BOLS/LL BL3 47 F4
ROCH OL11 41 F1
Glenmore Dr CHH M8 102 C3
FAIL M35 105 G2
Glenmore Gv DUK SK16 119 H5
Glenmore Rd TOT/BURYW BL8 26 A1
Glenmore St BURY BL9 4 C6
Glenmuir Cl IRL M44 136 C1
Glenolden St OP/CLY M11 117 E3
Glenridding Cl OLD OL1 75 H3
Glenridge Cl BOL BL1 34 A4
Glen Ri HALE/TIMP WA15 166 B4
Glen Rd OLDE OL4 92 B1
Glen Royd WHIT OL12 29 F2
Glensdale Dr NEWH/MOS M40 104 D1
Glenshee Dr BOLS/LL BL3 47 G4
Glenside Av GTN M18 130 C5
Glenside Dr BOLS/LL BL3 65 E2
MPL/ROM SK6 162 A1
WILM/AE SK9 199 F4
Glenside Gdns FAIL M35 105 F3
Glenside Gv WALK M28 82 B4
Glen St RAMS BL0 16 C1
SALQ M50 126 D1
The Glen BOL BL1 47 F2
MDTN M24 89 E1
Glenthorn Av BKLY M9 88 A1
Glenthorne St BOL BL1 33 H5
Glenthorn Gv SALE M33 154 C3
Glentrool Ms BOL BL1 47 H2
Glent Vw STLY SK15 120 D1
Glentwood ALT WA14 177 G3
Glenvale Cl RAD M26 68 C1
Glen Vw ROY/SHW OL2 59 E4
Glenville Rd CHH M8 102 A5
Glenville Wy DTN/ASHW M34 147 E1
Glenwood Av HYDE SK14 133 G3
Glenwood Cl RAD M26 68 C2
Glenwood Dr BKLY M9 103 F3
MDTN M24 73 G2
Glenwood Gv OFTN SK2 184 C1
Glenwyn Av BKLY M9 88 B3
Globe Cl OLDTF/WHR M16 127 G3
Globe La DUK SK16 133 E1
Globe Sq DUK SK16 132 D1
Globe St OLDE OL4 76 A5
Glodwick Rd OLDE OL4 92 A2
Gloster St BOLE BL2 3 H5
Gloucester Av BNG/LEV M19 144 B3
HEY OL10 55 H2
MPL/ROM SK6 175 E3
WHIT OL12 20 A4
WHTF M45 69 G4
Gloucester Cl AUL OL6 107 G2
Gloucester Dr SALE M33 153 G2
Gloucester Pl SLFD M6 113 F2
Gloucester Ri DUK SK16 134 B1
Gloucester Rd CHD/CHDH SK8 181 H5
DROY M43 117 H2
DTN/ASHW M34 145 G1
HYDE SK14 148 A3
MDTN M24 88 D1
POY/DIS SK12 195 E4
SLFD M6 112 B1
URM M41 138 D2
Gloucester St CMANE M1 * 128 A1
ORD M5 113 H5
SLFD M6 113 F1
Gloucester St North CHAD OL9 8 A7
Glover Dr HYDE SK14 148 A1
Glyn Av HALE/TIMP WA15 178 B2
Glynne St FWTH BL4 65 H4
Glynrene Dr SWIN M27 83 F5
Glynwood Pk FWTH BL4 65 H3
Goadsby St ANC M4 7 G2
Goats Gate Ter WHTF M45 * 69 E2
Godbert Av CCHDY M21 156 B1
Goddard St OLDS OL8 91 G3
Godfrey Av DROY M43 117 E2
Godfrey Range GTN M18 131 E4
Godfrey Rd SLFD M6 99 H5
Godlee Dr SWIN M27 98 D3
Godley Cl OP/CLY M11 130 B1
Godley Hill Rd HYDE SK14 134 C5
Godley St HYDE SK14 133 H4
Godmond Hall Dr WALK M28 96 A5
Godolphin Cl ECC M30 111 F1
Godson St OLD OL1 75 F3
Godwin St GTN M18 130 D2
Golborne Av DID/WITH M20 142 B4
Goldbourne Dr ROY/SHW OL2 60 A1
Goldbrook Cl HEY OL10 41 F5
Goldcrest Cl WALK M28 96 C3
WYTH/NTH M22 169 E4
Goldenhill Av OP/CLY M11 116 D2
Golden St ECC M30 111 E4
ROY/SHW OL2 60 D1
Goldfinch Dr BURY BL9 39 F1
Goldfinch Wy DROY M43 118 B2
Goldie Av WYTH/NTH M22 181 E3
Goldrill Av BOLE BL2 50 C1
Goldrill Gdns BOLE BL2 50 C1
Goldsmith Av OLD OL1 60 D5
ORD M5 112 C3
Goldsmith Rd RDSH SK5 144 D2
Goldsmith St BOLS/LL BL3 48 C5
Gold St CMANE M1 * 7 G5
Goldswcrthy Rd URM M41 137 G1
Goldsworth Rd OLD OL1 76 C1
Goldsworthy Rd URM M41 123 F5
Golf Rd HALE/TIMP WA15 178 A1
SALE M33 155 G2
Golfview Dr ECC M30 111 E1
Goodacre HYDE SK14 134 C2
Gooden St HEY OL10 41 F5
Goodiers Dr ORD M5 113 F5
Goodier St
NEWH/MOS M40 103 F5
SALE M33 154 B2
Goodier Vw HYDE SK14 134 A3
Goodison Cl BURY BL9 70 A1
Goodlad St TOT/BURYW BL8 37 G2
Goodman St BKLY M9 103 F1
Goodrich ROCH OL11 * 29 H5
Goodridge Av
WYTH/NTH M22 180 B2
Goodrington Rd
WILM/AE SK9 192 B5
Goodshaw Rd WALK M28 96 D2
Good Shepherd Cl MILN OL16 11 F5
Goodwill Cl SWIN M27 99 E3
Goodwin Sq BKLY M9 * 103 E3
Goodwin St BOL BL1 3 G3
Goodwood Av
NTHM/RTH M23 167 E1
SALE M33 153 F2
Goodwood Cl BOLS/LL BL3 66 C1
Goodwood Crs
HALE/TIMP WA15 166 D3
Goodwood Dr EDGY/DAV SK3 171 H5
OLD OL1 75 H3
SWIN M27 99 G3
Goodwood Rd MPL/ROM SK6 174 D4
Goole St OP/CLY M11 116 B5
Goose Cote Hl EDGW/EG BL7 22 D2
Goose Gn ALT WA14 165 G5
Goose La WHIT OL12 10 C4
Goosetrey Cl WILM/AE SK9 199 H1
Goostrey Av DID/WITH M20 142 B3
Gordon Av BNG/LEV M19 144 B2
BOLS/LL BL3 48 B4
BRAM/HZG SK7 185 E1
CHAD OL9 90 B4
OLDE OL4 92 B1
Gordon Ct LIT OL15 21 E2
Gordon Pl DID/WITH M20 157 G1
Gordon Rd ECC M30 111 E2
SALE M33 139 H5
SWIN M27 98 B4
Gordon St AUL OL6 * 120 A1
BRO M7 114 A1
BURY BL9 4 C1
CHAD OL9 90 A3
GTN M18 130 D2
HTNM SK4 13 F1
HYDE SK14 148 A1
MILN OL16 45 E3
OLDE OL4 93 F1
OLDTF/WHR M16 127 G4
ROCH OL11 43 F1
ROY/SHW OL2 60 B2
STLY SK15 121 E4
Gordon Ter BKLY M9 * 103 F2
Gordon Wy HEY OL10 40 A5
Gore Av FAIL M35 105 G3
ORD M5 112 C3
Gorebrook Ct
WGTN/LGST M12 129 H4
Gore Cl BURY BL9 39 F5
Gore Crs ORD M5 112 C2
Goredale Av GTN M18 130 D5
Gore Dr ORD M5 112 C3
Gorelan Rd GTN M18 * 130 C3
Gore St CMANE M1 7 H5
CSLFD M3 6 B4
SLFD M6 113 F2
Goring Av GTN M18 130 C2
Gorrells Wy ROCH OL11 42 C3
Gorrels Cl ROCH OL11 42 C3
Gorrel St ROCH OL11 43 F1
Gorse Av DROY M43 118 B3
MOSL OL5 109 F1
MPL/ROM SK6 174 D3
OLDS OL8 92 B4
STRET M32 126 C5
Gorse Bank BURY BL9 39 F3
Gorse Bank Rd
HALE/TIMP WA15 178 D5
Gorse Crs STRET M32 126 C5
Gorse Dr LHULT M38 81 E1
STRET M32 126 C5
Gorsefield Cl RAD M26 52 B5
Gorsefield Dr SWIN M27 99 E3
Gorsefield Hey WILM/AE SK9 199 H2
Gorse Hall Cl DUK SK16 * 134 A1
Gorse Hall Dr STLY SK15 120 D5
Gorse Hall Rd DUK SK16 133 H1
Gorselands CHD/CHDH SK8 193 E2
Gorse La STRET M32 126 C5
Gorse Rd MILN OL16 31 G5
SWIN M27 98 D4
WALK M28 82 B5
Gorses Mt BOLE BL2 49 H4
Gorse Sq PART M31 150 C3
Gorses Rd BOLS/LL BL3 50 A4
Gorse St CHAD OL9 90 A3
STRET M32 126 B5
The Gorse ALT WA14 177 E4
Gorseway RDSH SK5 160 C2
Gorsey Av WYTH/NTH M22 168 B5
Gorsey Bank Rd
EDGY/DAV SK3 171 E1
Gorsey Brow MPL/ROM SK6 161 H4
Gorsey Clough Wk
TOT/BURYW BL8 37 E1
Gorsey Dr WYTH/NTH M22 168 B5
Gorseyfields DROY M43 117 H5
Gorsey Hill St HEY OL10 41 E5
Gorsey La ALT WA14 165 E4
AUL OL6 108 A4
Gorsey Mount St STKP SK1 13 H4
Gorsey Rd WILM/AE SK9 198 C3
WYTH/NTH M22 168 B5
Gorsey Wy AUL OL6 107 H4
Gorsley Bank LIT OL15 21 F1
Gorston Wk WYTH/NTH M22 180 B4
Gort Cl BURY BL9 69 H3
Gorton Crs DTN/ASHW M34 131 H5
Gorton Gv WALK M28 81 H2
Gorton La WGTN/LGST M12 129 H2
Gorton Rd OP/CLY M11 129 G1
RDSH SK5 145 F3
Gorton St AULW OL7 119 E4
BOLE BL2 3 G6
CHAD OL9 90 C1
CSLFD M3 * 6 D2
ECC M30 110 B4
FWTH BL4 65 G5
HEY OL10 41 F4
Gortonvilla Wk
WGTN/LGST M12 129 G2
Gosforth Cl OLD OL1 75 H3
TOT/BURYW BL8 37 H1
Goshen La BURY BL9 53 G3
Gosport Sq BRO M7 101 G5
Goss Hall St OLDE OL4 * 92 B1
Gotha Wk BRUN/LGST M13 * 128 D2
Gotherage Cl MPL/ROM SK6 162 D4
Gotherage La MPL/ROM SK6 162 D4
Gothic Cl MPL/ROM SK6 163 E4
Gough St EDGY/DAV SK3 12 D4
HEY OL10 * 41 F4
Goulden Rd DID/WITH M20 157 F1
Goulden St ANC M4 7 H2
SLFD M6 112 D3
Goulder Rd GTN M18 130 D5
Gould St DTN/ASHW M34 132 B5
OLD OL1 76 A4
Gourham Dr CHD/CHDH SK8 182 C2
Govan St WYTH/NTH M22 156 D5
Gowan Dr MDTN M24 72 A3
Gowanlock's St BOL BL1 33 H4
Gowan Rd OLDTF/WHR M16 142 A2
Gower Av BRAM/HZG SK7 184 D1
Gowerdale Rd RDSH SK5 160 D1
Gower Hey Gdns HYDE SK14 148 A2
Gower Rd HTNM SK4 159 G2
HYDE SK14 147 H2
Gowers St MILN OL16 11 G4
Gower St AUL OL6 * 119 H2
BOL BL1 2 A3
FWTH BL4 65 H3
OLD OL1 9 J2
SWIN M27 99 F1
Gowran Pk OLDE OL4 92 C1
Gowy Cl WILM/AE SK9 199 H1
Goyt Av MPL/ROM SK6 175 E5
Goyt Crs MPL/ROM SK6 161 G3
STKP SK1 160 C3
Goyt Rd MPL/ROM SK6 175 E5
STKP SK1 160 C3
Goyt Valley Rd MPL/ROM SK6 161 G4
Goyt Wy MPL/ROM SK6 163 E5
Grace St WHIT OL12 11 F1
Grace Wk ANC M4 115 G4
Gracie Av OLD OL1 76 A3
Gradwell St EDGY/DAV SK3 12 D5
Grafton Av ECC M30 111 H1
Grafton Ct MILN OL16 * 30 C5
The Graftons ALT WA14 * 165 G5
Grafton St ALT WA14 165 G5
AUL OL6 120 A3
BOL BL1 2 A1
BRUN/LGST M13 128 C3
BURY BL9 53 G1
FAIL M35 105 E2
HTNM SK4 159 H3
MILN OL16 30 C5
OLD OL1 60 D5
STLY SK15 121 G2
Graham Crs IRL M44 150 B2
Graham Dr POY/DIS SK12 187 H5
Graham Rd SLFD M6 112 B1
STKP SK1 172 C1
Graham St AULW OL7 119 E4
BOL BL1 * 2 E2
OP/CLY M11 116 B5
Grainger Av WGTN/LGST M12 129 H5
Grains Rd ROY/SHW OL2 60 B2
UPML OL3 61 G4
Grain Vw ORD M5 * 113 F5
Gralam Cl SALE M33 155 F5
Grammar School Rd OLDS OL8 90 C5
Grampian Cl CHAD OL9 90 B2
Grampian Wy ROY/SHW OL2 59 H1
Granada Ms
OLDTF/WHR M16 * 142 A2
Granada Rd DTN/ASHW M34 131 F5
Granary La WALK M28 110 A1
Granary Wy SALE M33 154 A4
Granby Rd CHD/CHDH SK8 183 E4
HALE/TIMP WA15 154 B5
OFTN SK2 172 C4
STRET M32 140 C2
SWIN M27 98 B3
Granby Rw CMANE M1 7 H7
Granby St CHAD OL9 90 B5
TOT/BURYW BL8 37 E2
Grandale St RUSH/FAL M14 * 128 D5
Grand Central Sq STKP SK1 * 13 F5
Grandidge St ROCH OL11 42 D1
Grand Union Wy ECC M30 111 E5
Granford Cl ALT WA14 * 165 G2
Grange Av BNG/LEV M19 143 H3
BOLS/LL BL3 67 F1
CHD/CHDH SK8 182 C1
ECC M30 111 E1
HALE/TIMP WA15 166 C2
HALE/TIMP WA15 178 B2
HTNM SK4 159 F1
MILN OL16 44 C2
OLDS OL8 90 D3
STRET M32 140 B1
SWIN M27 83 G5
URM M41 137 G1
Grange Cl HYDE SK14 148 B2
Grange Ct OLDS OL8 * 90 D3
Grange Crs URM M41 138 C2
Grange Dr BKLY M9 88 C4
ECC M30 111 E1
Grangeforth Rd CHH M8 102 A2
Grange Gv WHTF M45 69 G4
Grange La DID/WITH M20 157 G4
Grange Park Av AUL OL6 108 A4
CHD/CHDH SK8 170 A4
WILM/AE SK9 198 D2
Grangepark Rd BKLY M9 88 C4
Grange Park Rd
CHD/CHDH SK8 170 A4
EDGW/EG BL7 23 H5
Grange Pl IRL M44 150 C1
Grange Rd ALT WA14 177 F3
BOLS/LL BL3 48 A4
BRAM/HZG SK7 184 B2
CCHDY M21 141 E1
ECC M30 110 A1
EDGW/EG BL7 23 H4
FWTH BL4 65 F3
HALE/TIMP WA15 166 C2
MDTN M24 57 G3
SALE M33 154 A2
TOT/BURYW BL8 37 G4
URM M41 138 C2
WHIT OL12 14 C3
Grange Rd North HYDE SK14 148 B1
Grange Rd South HYDE SK14 148 B2
Grange St CHAD OL9 8 E2
FAIL M35 104 C4
SLFD M6 112 D3
The Grange HYDE SK14 148 B2
OLD OL1 * 76 A4
RUSH/FAL M14 128 D5
Grangethorpe Dr
BNG/LEV M19 143 G4
Grangethorpe Rd
RUSH/FAL M14 143 E1
URM M41 138 C2
Grangeway WILM/AE SK9 192 A3
Grangewood EDGW/EG BL7 23 H4
Grangewood Dr BKLY M9 103 E3
Granite St OLD OL1 76 A4
Gransden Dr CHH M8 102 D4
Granshaw St
NEWH/MOS M40 115 H2
Gransmoor Av OP/CLY M11 131 E1
Gransmoor Rd OP/CLY M11 131 E1
Grantchester Pl FWTH BL4 65 E3
Grantchester Wy BOLE BL2 35 F5
Grant Cl BKLY M9 88 A5
Grantham Cl BOL BL1 * 33 H5
Grantham Dr TOT/BURYW BL8 38 A1
Grantham Rd HTNM SK4 12 B2
Grantham St OLDE OL4 9 K6
Grants La RAMS BL0 16 D2
Grant St FWTH BL4 65 G2
ROCH OL11 42 C4
Granville Av BRO M7 101 H2
Granville Cl CHAD OL9 8 A2
Granville Ct MILN OL16 45 E3
Granville Gdns DID/WITH M20 157 F4
Granville Rd BOLS/LL BL3 64 B1
CHD/CHDH SK8 171 F4
DTN/ASHW M34 118 A4
HALE/TIMP WA15 166 D3
RUSH/FAL M14 143 E3
URM M41 138 D2
WILM/AE SK9 198 C5
Granville St AUL OL6 120 A3
CHAD OL9 8 A1
ECC M30 111 E2
FWTH BL4 66 A3
OLD OL1 75 F3
WALK M28 81 H4
Granville Wk CHAD OL9 8 A1
Grasmere Av BOLS/LL BL3 50 D5
FWTH BL4 65 E5
HEY OL10 56 A1
HTNM SK4 145 E5
SWIN M27 83 F5
URM M41 137 G2
WHTF M45 68 D5
Grasmere Cl STLY SK15 120 D1
Grasmere Crs BRAM/HZG SK7 183 H4
ECC M30 110 C1
MPL/ROM SK6 186 D3
Grasmere Dr BURY BL9 53 H2
Grasmere Gv AULW OL7 119 E1
Grasmere Rd CHD/CHDH SK8 181 G1
HALE/TIMP WA15 166 D3
OLDE OL4 92 B1
PART M31 150 D3
ROY/SHW OL2 59 E3
SALE M33 154 D4
STRET M32 126 A5
SWIN M27 99 E4
WILM/AE SK9 200 D4
Grasmere St BOL BL1 34 A4
WGTN/LGST M12 130 A5
WHIT OL12 10 C2
Grasmere Wk MDTN M24 72 C2
Grason Av WILM/AE SK9 199 F1
Grasscroft RDSH SK5 146 A5
Grasscroft Cl RUSH/FAL M14 142 B1
Grasscroft Rd STLY SK15 120 D4
Grassfield Av BRO M7 101 F4
Grassholme Dr OFTN SK2 173 H4
Grassingham Gdns SLFD M6 113 E2
Grassington Av
NEWH/MOS M40 103 H1
Grassington Ct
TOT/BURYW BL8 36 D2
Grassington Dr BURY BL9 39 H5
Grassington Pl BOLE BL2 34 B5
Grass Md DTN/ASHW M34 147 E3
Gratrix Av ORD M5 127 E1
Gratrix La SALE M33 155 G3
Gratrix St GTN M18 130 D4
Gratten Ct WALK M28 81 H3
Gravel Bank Rd
MPL/ROM SK6 147 F5
Gravel La CSLFD M3 6 D2
WILM/AE SK9 198 C5
Gravel Wks OLDE OL4 76 A5
Gravenmoor Dr BRO M7 101 H4
Graver La NEWH/MOS M40 104 C5
Gray Cl HYDE SK14 135 G5
Graymar Rd LHULT M38 81 F3
Graymarsh Dr POY/DIS SK12 195 F5
Graysands Rd
HALE/TIMP WA15 178 A1
Grayson Av WHTF M45 69 H5
Grayson Rd LHULT M38 81 G3
Grayson Wy UPML OL3 95 E1
Gray St BOL BL1 2 D2
Gray St North BOL BL1 2 E2
Graythorpe Wk ORD M5 * 113 F4
Graythorp Wk RUSH/FAL M14 128 C5
Graythwaite Rd BOL BL1 32 C4
Grazing Dr IRL M44 122 D5
Greame St OLDTF/WHR M16 128 A5
Great Ancoats St ANC M4 7 H3
CMANE M1 115 G5
Great Bent Cl WHIT OL12 20 A4
Great Bridgewater St
CMANE M1 6 D7
Great Cheetham St East
BRO M7 101 H4
Great Cheetham St West
BRO M7 101 F5
Great Clowes St BRO M7 101 G3
Great Ducie St CHH M8 114 C1
CSLFD M3 6 E1
Great Eaves Rd RAMS BL0 16 D1
Great Egerton St STKP SK1 13 F2
Greatfield Rd WYTH/NTH M22 168 A5
Great Flatt WHIT OL12 29 E2
Great Gable Cl OLD OL1 75 H4
Great Gates Cl ROCH OL11 43 F2
Great Gates Rd ROCH OL11 43 F4
Great George St CSLFD M3 114 A3
MILN OL16 10 D7
Great Hall Cl RAD M26 52 B5
Great Heaton Cl MDTN M24 * 71 H5
Great Holme BOLS/LL BL3 65 E1
Great Howarth WHIT OL12 19 G4
Great Jackson St HULME M15 127 H1
Great John St CSLFD M3 6 B6
Great Jones St
WGTN/LGST M12 129 H2
Great Lee WHIT OL12 18 C5
Great Lee Wk WHIT OL12 29 G1
Great Marlborough St
CMANE M1 6 E7
Great Marld Cl BOL BL1 32 C4
Great Meadow ROY/SHW OL2 44 C5
Great Moor St BOL BL1 2 E6
OFTN SK2 172 C4
Great Newton St
NEWH/MOS M40 104 B5
Great Norbury St HYDE SK14 147 H1
Great Portwood St STKP SK1 13 H1
Great Southern St
RUSH/FAL M14 128 C5
Great Stone Cl RAD M26 * 67 G1
Great Stone Rd STRET M32 126 C4
Great Stones Cl EDGW/EG BL7 22 D1
Great St CMANE M1 115 F5
Great Underbank STKP SK1 13 G3
Great Western St
OLDTF/WHR M16 127 H4
Greave MPL/ROM SK6 162 C2
Greave Av ROCH OL11 29 E3
Greave Fold MPL/ROM SK6 162 C2
Greave Rd STKP SK1 172 D1
Greaves Av FAIL M35 104 D4
Greaves Rd WILM/AE SK9 198 B2
Greaves St MOSL OL5 93 H5
OLD OL1 9 H4
OLDE OL4 93 E1
ROY/SHW OL2 * 60 B2
Greave St ROY/SHW OL2 60 B2
Grebe Cl POY/DIS SK12 194 C3
Grecian Crs BOLS/LL BL3 49 E5
Grecian St BRO M7 101 F5
Grecian St North BRO M7 101 F5
Grecian Ter BRO M7 * 101 F5
Gredle Cl URM M41 139 F1
Greeba Rd NTHM/RTH M23 167 F3
Greek St CMANE M1 * 128 C1
EDGY/DAV SK3 13 F6
Green Acre WHTN BL5 62 A5
Greenacre Cl RAMS BL0 17 F1
Greenacre La WALK M28 110 A1
Green Acre Pk BOL BL1 * 34 A5
Greenacres Dr BNG/LEV M19 158 B2
Greenacres Rd OLDE OL4 76 B5
Green Av BOLS/LL BL3 65 G1
LHULT M38 80 D2
SWIN M27 99 E3
Green Bank BOLE BL2 35 F3
Greenbank FWTH BL4 65 H3
Greenbank Av CHD/CHDH SK8 169 F4
HTNM SK4 158 B4
SWIN M27 * 98 C4
UPML OL3 79 F3
Greenbank Crs MPL/ROM SK6 175 E5
Greenbank Dr LIT OL15 20 C5
Greenbank Rd BOLS/LL BL3 * 48 A5
CHD/CHDH SK8 169 F3
MPL/ROM SK6 163 G5
RAD M26 52 A4
SALE M33 153 H1
SLFD M6 112 D2
WHIT OL12 10 E1
Green Bank Ter HTNM SK4 13 F1
Green Bank Ter MDTN M24 73 F3
Greenbeech Cl MPL/ROM SK6 174 D2
Green Booth Cl DUK SK16 134 A1
Green Bridge Cl ROCH OL11 * 43 E2
Greenbridge La UPML OL3 94 D2
Green Brook Cl BURY BL9 38 D2
Greenbrook St BURY BL9 38 D2
Greenbrow Rd
NTHM/RTH M23 179 G1
Greenburn Dr BOLE BL2 35 F4
Green Cl CHD/CHDH SK8 169 F3
Greencourt Dr LHULT M38 81 E3
Green Cts ALT WA14 177 E1
Green Cft MPL/ROM SK6 162 C3
Greencroft Meadow
ROY/SHW OL2 59 G4
Greencroft Rd ECC M30 110 C1
Greencroft Wy MILN OL16 20 A5
Greendale Dr BKLY M9 88 B4
RAD M26 68 C3
Greendale Gv DTN/ASHW M34 147 F3
Green Dr BNG/LEV M19 143 H2
HALE/TIMP WA15 166 B2
HOR/BR BL6 46 D2
WILM/AE SK9 192 A5
Green End BNG/LEV M19 158 B1
DTN/ASHW M34 147 F3
Green End Rd BNG/LEV M19 158 B1
Greenfield Av ECC M30 123 H1
URM M41 138 D1
Greenfield Cl EDGY/DAV SK3 171 H3
HALE/TIMP WA15 166 D3
TOT/BURYW BL8 37 F5
WHTN BL5 62 B3
Greenfield Ct HEY OL10 41 E5
Greenfield La MILN OL16 20 A5
ROCH OL11 43 F2
ROY/SHW OL2 60 A3
Greenfield St DTN/ASHW M34 132 A1
HYDE SK14 147 H1
ROCH OL11 43 F2
Green Fold GTN M18 131 E2
Greenfold Av FWTH BL4 65 G5
Greenford Cl
CHD/CHDH SK8 171 E5
Greenford Rd CHH M8 102 B3
Green Gables Cl
CHD/CHDH SK8 181 G3
Greengate CSLFD M3 6 D2

HALE/TIMP WA15 179 E5
HYDE SK14 147 H3
MDTN M24 89 F2
NEWH/MOS M40 89 F4
Greengate Cl WHIT OL12 20 A4
Greengate East
NEWH/MOS M40 89 F4
Greengate La BOLE BL2 50 C1
PWCH M25 85 H3
Greengate Rd
DTN/ASHW M34 132 D4
Greengate St OLDE OL4 9 J6
Greengate West CSLFD M3 6 B1
Greengrove Bank MILN OL16 19 H5
Greenhalgh Moss La
TOT/BURYW BL8 37 G1
Greenhalgh St FAIL M35 104 B4
HTNM SK4 13 F1
Greenhalgh Wk ANC M4 7 K3
Green Hall Ms WILM/AE SK9 199 E4
Greenham Rd
NTHM/RTH M23 155 G5
Greenhaven Cl WALK M28 82 C4
Greenheys BOLE BL2 35 F3
DROY M43 117 H3
Greenheys Crs
TOT/BURYW BL8 25 H2
Greenheys La HULME M15 128 A3
Greenheys La West
HULME M15 128 A3
Greenheys Rd LHULT M38 80 D1
Greenhill OLD OL1 9 J4
PWCH M25 85 H3
Greenhill Av BOLS/LL BL3 48 A4
FWTH BL4 81 H1
ROY/SHW OL2 44 B5
SALE M33 139 G5
WHIT OL12 10 A4
Greenhill La BOLS/LL BL3 47 G5
Greenhill Pas OLD OL1 9 J4
Green Hill Rd HYDE SK14 134 B5
Greenhill Rd CHH M8 102 B3
HALE/TIMP WA15 166 D3
MDTN M24 73 F5
TOT/BURYW BL8 37 F5
Green Hill St EDGY/DAV SK3 12 C7
Green Hill Ter EDGY/DAV SK3 12 C7
Greenhill Ter OLDE OL4 9 J5
Green Hollow Fold STLY SK15 121 G1
Greenholm Cl
NEWH/MOS M40 104 C1
Greenhow St DROY M43 117 G5
Greenhurst Crs OLDS OL8 91 H5
Greenhurst La AUL OL6 107 H4
Greenhurst Rd AUL OL6 107 G3
Greenhythe Rd
CHD/CHDH SK8 191 H1
Greening Rd BNG/LEV M19 144 B1
Greenland Rd BOLS/LL BL3 65 E2
Greenlands Cl CHD/CHDH SK8 182 B4
Greenland St CHH M8 102 A3
SLFD M6 * 112 D3
Green La AUL OL6 107 E5
BOLS/LL BL3 65 E1
BRAM/HZG SK7 185 E1
ECC M30 110 D3
FAIL M35 117 F1
FWTH BL4 66 D5
GTN M18 130 C2
HALE/TIMP WA15 166 C5
HEY OL10 41 F4
HEY OL10 * 56 B1
HTNM SK4 12 C2
HYDE SK14 148 C2
IRL M44 150 C1
MDTN M24 73 E3
MDTN M24 73 G5
MPL/ROM SK6 162 A5
OLDE OL4 77 F2
OLDS OL8 91 F5
POY/DIS SK12 196 B3
SALE M33 139 E5
WHIT OL12 * 10 B4
WHTF M45 69 G3
WILM/AE SK9 199 E3
WILM/AE SK9 200 C5
Green La North
HALE/TIMP WA15 166 C5
Greenlea Av GTN M18 130 C5
Greenleach La WALK M28 97 G2
Greenleaf Cl WALK M28 96 A4
Greenleas HOR/BR BL6 46 D3
Greenlees St WHIT OL12 10 C4
Greenleigh Cl BOL BL1 33 G1
Greenmans La UPML OL3 94 D4
Green Meadow WHIT OL12 20 A4
Green Mdw MPL/ROM SK6 175 E2
Green Meadows Dr
MPL/ROM SK6 175 E2
Green Meadows Wk
WYTH/NTH M22 180 D3
Greenmount Cl
TOT/BURYW BL8 26 A1
Greenmount Ct BOL BL1 47 H1
Greenmount Dr HEY OL10 56 C2
TOT/BURYW BL8 16 A5
Greenmount La BOL BL1 47 G1
Greenmount Pk FWTH BL4 82 D1
Greenoak RAD M26 67 F5
Greenoak Dr SALE M33 154 D5
WALK M28 81 H2
Greenock Cl BOLS/LL BL3 47 F4
Greenpark Cl TOT/BURYW BL8 25 H2
Greenpark Rd
WYTH/NTH M22 156 C5
Green Park Vw OLD OL1 76 C2
Green Pastures HTNM SK4 158 B5
Green Rd PART M31 150 D3
Greenroyd Av BOLE BL2 35 F4
Greenroyde ROCH OL11 * 42 D3
Greensbridge Gdns WHTN BL5 62 A3
Greenshank Cl ROCH OL11 * 28 C4
Greenside BOLE BL2 36 B5
HTNM SK4 158 D5
WALK M28 97 H5
Greenside Av FWTH BL4 82 C1
OLDE OL4 76 C2
Greenside Cl DUK SK16 120 D5
Greenside Crs DROY M43 117 G2
Greenside Dr ALT WA14 177 H3
IRL M44 136 B2
TOT/BURYW BL8 26 A3
Greenside La DROY M43 117 F2
Greenside Pl DTN/ASHW M34 147 E3
Greenside St OP/CLY M11 116 C4
Greenside Vw HYDE SK14 134 A3
Greenside Wy MDTN M24 89 F2
Greenson Dr MDTN M24 72 B5
Greenstead Av CHH M8 102 B2
The Greens WHIT OL12 14 B4
Greenstone Dr SLFD M6 100 C5
Green St BOL BL1 3 F4
ECC M30 110 C5
EDGY/DAV SK3 172 A3
FWTH BL4 65 H3
HYDE SK14 148 A2
MDTN M24 73 F3
OLDS OL8 8 D5
RAD M26 68 B1
RUSH/FAL M14 143 G4
STRET M32 140 A3
TOT/BURYW BL8 37 E2
WILM/AE SK9 200 D4
The Green CHD/CHDH SK8 182 C4
HTNM SK4 12 A1
MPL/ROM SK6 187 F1
OLDS OL8 91 H4
ROCH OL11 42 B3
SWIN M27 84 C5
TOT/BURYW BL8 26 A2
WALK M28 97 G5
WILM/AE SK9 192 B4
Greenthorne Av HTNM SK4 144 D4
Green Tree Gdns
MPL/ROM SK6 162 A4
Greenvale ROCH OL11 28 A3
Greenvale Dr CHD/CHDH SK8 169 H3
Greenview Cha OLDE OL4 93 G2
Greenview Dr DID/WITH M20 169 H1
ROCH OL11 28 C3
Green Villa Pk WILM/AE SK9 200 B1
Green Wk ALT WA14 176 D1
CHD/CHDH SK8 169 F3
HALE/TIMP WA15 166 A2
OLDTF/WHR M16 141 G1
STRET M32 139 H1
Green Wks PWCH M25 86 B4
Greenwatch Cl ECC M30 110 D4
Green Wy BOL BL1 34 C3
ROCH OL11 42 A5
Greenway ALT WA14 164 D4
BRAM/HZG SK7 193 G1
HYDE SK14 147 H2
MDTN M24 88 B2
MPL/ROM SK6 162 D5
ROY/SHW OL2 44 C5
WILM/AE SK9 198 D4
WYTH/NTH M22 168 D1
Greenway Av BNG/LEV M19 144 B3
Green Way Cl BOL BL1 34 C2
Greenway Cl SALE M33 153 G3
TOT/BURYW BL8 37 G3
Greenway Dr MOSL OL5 93 H5
Greenway Rd CHD/CHDH SK8 191 H1
HALE/TIMP WA15 154 B5
Greenways AULW OL7 106 C4
NEWH/MOS M40 104 C1
Greenwich Cl
NEWH/MOS M40 117 E1
ROCH OL11 28 C5
Greenwood Av AUL OL6 107 F5
OFTN SK2 172 D3
SWIN M27 99 G1
WALK M28 81 H4
Greenwood Cl
HALE/TIMP WA15 167 E4
Greenwood Dr WILM/AE SK9 199 G2
Greenwood Rd
WYTH/NTH M22 168 B4
Greenwoods La BOLE BL2 35 G2
Greenwood St ALT WA14 165 G5
FWTH BL4 66 A4
LIT OL15 21 E3
MILN OL16 10 D7
OLDE OL4 76 B4
OLDS OL8 * 106 C1
SLFD M6 113 E1
Greenwood V BOL BL1 33 H3
Greenwood V South BOL BL1 * 34 A3
Greer St OP/CLY M11 116 D5
Greetland Dr BKLY M9 88 C3
Gregge St HEY OL10 41 F5
Greg Ms WILM/AE SK9 191 G5
Gregory Av BOLE BL2 50 B1
MPL/ROM SK6 162 A5
Gregory St HYDE SK14 133 H3
OLDS OL8 90 D4
WGTN/LGST M12 129 G2
Gregory Wy RDSH SK5 145 F5
Gregson Fld BOLS/LL BL3 48 D5
Gregson Rd RDSH SK5 145 E5
Gregson St OLD OL1 9 H4
Greg St RDSH SK5 145 E5
Greiley Wk RUSH/FAL M14 128 C5
Grendale Av BRAM/HZG SK7 185 F3
STKP SK1 160 C5
Grendon Av OLDS OL8 91 F4
Grendon St BOLS/LL BL3 64 B1
Grendon Wk WGTN/LGST M12 129 H2
Grenfell Rd DID/WITH M20 157 F3
Grenham Av HULME M15 127 G2
Grenville Rd BRAM/HZG SK7 184 D1
Grenville St DUK SK16 119 H5
EDGY/DAV SK3 12 C5
STLY SK15 121 G1
Gresford Cl CCHDY M21 141 E3
Gresham Cl WHTF M45 69 E5
Gresham Dr CHAD OL9 8 B3
Gresham St BOL BL1 34 A3
DTN/ASHW M34 132 C4
Gresham Wk HTNM SK4 159 H3
Gresham Wy SALE M33 154 B5
Gresty Av WYTH/NTH M22 181 E3
Greswell St DTN/ASHW M34 132 B4
Greta Av CHD/CHDH SK8 191 H1
Greton Cl BRUN/LGST M13 129 F4
Gretton Cl ROY/SHW OL2 59 G5
Greville St BRUN/LGST M13 129 F5
Grey Cl MPL/ROM SK6 161 H2
Greyfriars Rd WYTH/NTH M22 180 A2
Greyhound Dr SLFD M6 101 E5
Grey Knotts WALK M28 96 B5
Greylag Crs WALK M28 97 E2
Greylands Cl SALE M33 153 H2
Greylands Rd DID/WITH M20 169 H1
Grey Mare La OP/CLY M11 116 B5
Greymont Rd BURY BL9 27 G5
Grey Rd ALT WA14 165 F4
Greystoke Av BNG/LEV M19 144 C2
HALE/TIMP WA15 167 E3
SALE M33 154 C3
Greystoke Crs WHTF M45 69 F2
Greystoke Dr BOL BL1 22 C5
MDTN M24 72 A2
WILM/AE SK9 200 D3
Greystoke La FAIL M35 104 C4
Greystoke St STKP SK1 13 K4
Greystone Av CCHDY M21 142 B3
Grey St AUL OL6 119 H2
DTN/ASHW M34 132 A5
MDTN M24 72 C3
PWCH M25 86 B3
STLY SK15 121 F4
WGTN/LGST M12 129 F2
Greyswood Av CHH M8 102 A4
Greytown Cl SLFD M6 100 C5
Greywood Av BURY BL9 5 K4
Grierson St BOL BL1 33 H3
OLDTF/WHR M16 127 H4
Griffe La BURY BL9 70 B1
Griffin Cl BURY BL9 5 J1
Griffin Ct CSLFD M3 * 6 B3
Griffin Gv BNG/LEV M19 144 A3
Griffin La CHD/CHDH SK8 182 A5
Griffin Rd FAIL M35 104 C3
Griffin St BRO M7 101 F4
Griffiths Cl BRO M7 * 114 A1
Griffiths St NEWH/MOS M40 104 B5
Grimes St WHIT OL12 28 C2
Grime St RAMS BL0 16 B4
Grimscott Cl BKLY M9 * 103 G1
Grimshaw Av FAIL M35 105 F2
Grimshaw Cl MPL/ROM SK6 161 H2
Grimshaw La MDTN M24 73 E5
NEWH/MOS M40 103 G5
Grimshaw St FAIL M35 * 104 D2
STKP SK1 13 K3
Grimstead Cl NTHM/RTH M23 167 F3
Grindall Av NEWH/MOS M40 89 E5
Grindley Av CCHDY M21 156 C1
Grindlow St BRUN/LGST M13 129 F3
Grindon Av BRO M7 100 D3
Grindrod St RAD M26 52 B5
Grindsbrook Rd RAD M26 52 A2
Grinton Av BRUN/LGST M13 143 G1
Grisdale Dr MDTN M24 72 B2
Grisdale Rd BOLS/LL BL3 48 B4
Grisebeck Wy OLD OL1 9 F2
Grisedale Av ROY/SHW OL2 58 D1
Grisedale Cl GTN M18 130 B4
MDTN M24 72 A1
Grisedale Rd ROCH OL11 42 A2
Gristlehurst La BURY BL9 40 A1
Grizebeck Cl GTN M18 130 B2
Grizedale Cl BOL BL1 32 C4
STLY SK15 109 F3
Grizedale Rd MPL/ROM SK6 162 A2
Groby Pl ALT WA14 165 F4
Groby Rd ALT WA14 165 F5
CCHDY M21 141 F3
DTN/ASHW M34 132 B1
Groby Rd North
DTN/ASHW M34 118 C5
Groby St OLDS OL8 91 H4
STLY SK15 121 F4
Groom St CMANE M1 128 C1
Grosvenor Av WHTF M45 69 F4
Grosvenor Cl WALK M28 81 H2
WILM/AE SK9 200 D1
Grosvenor Ct AULW OL7 119 F4
CHD/CHDH SK8 170 A3
Grosvenor Crs HYDE SK14 147 G2
Grosvenor Dr POY/DIS SK12 194 D4
WALK M28 81 H2
Grosvenor Gdns BRO M7 114 A1
STLY SK15 * 120 D4
WYTH/NTH M22 168 D3
Grosvenor House Sq
STLY SK15 120 D4
Grosvenor Pl AULW OL7 * 119 F4
Grosvenor Rd ALT WA14 165 H3
CHD/CHDH SK8 171 F5
ECC M30 110 B2
HTNM SK4 158 D3
HYDE SK14 147 H2
MPL/ROM SK6 175 E2
OLDTF/WHR M16 141 H1
SALE M33 154 A1
SWIN M27 99 G3
URM M41 138 C1
WALK M28 81 H2
WHTF M45 69 F3
Grosvenor Sq SALE M33 154 B2
Grosvenor St AULW OL7 119 F4
BOLE BL2 3 G7
BOLS/LL BL3 50 D5
BRAM/HZG SK7 185 E1
BRUN/LGST M13 128 C1
BURY BL9 53 G1
DTN/ASHW M34 132 A4
EDGY/DAV SK3 13 G6
FWTH BL4 66 C4
HEY OL10 40 D5
PWCH M25 86 B3
RAD M26 68 A1
ROCH OL11 42 B5
STLY SK15 120 D4
STRET M32 140 B1
SWIN M27 84 A5
Grosvenor Wy ROY/SHW OL2 75 E2
Grotton Hollow OLDE OL4 93 G1
Grotton Mdw OLDE OL4 93 G2
Grouse St WHIT OL12 10 C2
Grove Av FAIL M35 104 D5
WILM/AE SK9 198 D3
Grove Bank OLDE OL4 94 B2
Grove Cl RUSH/FAL M14 128 D5
Grove Ct BRAM/HZG SK7 * 185 F1
SALE M33 155 E2
Grove Hl WALK M28 96 A4
Grovehurst SWIN M27 98 A4
Grove La CHD/CHDH SK8 193 E2
DID/WITH M20 157 G4
HALE/TIMP WA15 166 B3
HALE/TIMP WA15 178 B1
Grove Ms WALK M28 * 82 A4
Grove Rd HALE/TIMP WA15 177 H1
MDTN M24 73 E2
STLY SK15 121 G1
UPML OL3 79 E5
Grove St AULW OL7 106 B5
BOL BL1 33 G4
BRAM/HZG SK7 * 185 F1
BRO M7 101 H5
DROY M43 117 G5
DUK SK16 120 A4
FWTH BL4 66 B4
HEY OL10 41 F4
OLD OL1 9 K2
ROCH OL11 42 D1
UPML OL3 95 E2
WILM/AE SK9 * 199 E3
The Grove ALT WA14 * 165 G4
BOLE BL2 49 G4
BOLS/LL BL3 67 E1
CHD/CHDH SK8 192 D1
DID/WITH M20 157 G5
ECC M30 111 G4
OFTN SK2 171 H2
ROY/SHW OL2 59 H3
SALE M33 154 C3
UPML OL3 78 C3
URM M41 137 H2
Grove Wy WILM/AE SK9 199 E3
Grovewood Cl AULW OL7 106 B5
Grundey St BRAM/HZG SK7 185 F2
Grundy Av PWCH M25 85 F5
Grundy Cl BURY BL9 5 G7
Grundy La BURY BL9 * 53 F1
Grundy Rd FWTH BL4 66 B5
Grundy St BOLS/LL BL3 48 C5
HEY OL10 56 B1
HTNM SK4 158 B4
WALK M28 82 C4
Guardian Cl WHIT OL12 20 A3
Guardian Ms
NTHM/RTH M23 * 154 D5
Guernsey Cl BNG/LEV M19 * 144 A5
Guest Rd PWCH M25 85 H1
Guide La AULW OL7 118 D5
Guide Post Sq
BRUN/LGST M13 * 129 E2
Guide Post St BRUN/LGST M13 129 E2
Guide St SALQ M50 112 B4
Guido St BOL BL1 33 G4
FAIL M35 104 D3
Guild Av WALK M28 82 A5
Guildford Av CHD/CHDH SK8 192 D1
Guildford Cl STKP SK1 172 C2
Guildford Dr AUL OL6 107 F3
Guildford Gv MDTN M24 73 F1
Guildford Rd BNG/LEV M19 144 B1
BOL BL1 33 E4
DUK SK16 134 B1
SLFD M6 112 A1
URM M41 124 D4
Guildford St MILN OL16 * 10 E7
Guildhall Cl HULME M15 128 B3
Guild St EDGW/EG BL7 23 G5
Guilford Rd ECC M30 110 C4
Guinness Rd TRPK M17 111 H5
Guiseley Cl BURY BL9 27 F3
Gullane Cl NEWH/MOS M40 104 B3
Gull Cl POY/DIS SK12 194 C4
Gulvain Pl CHAD OL9 74 A4
Gunson St NEWH/MOS M40 115 F2
Gun St ANC M4 7 J3
Gurner Av ORD M5 127 E1
Gurney St ANC M4 115 G4
Gutter La RAMS BL0 16 C1
Guy Fawkes St ORD M5 127 E1
Guywood La MPL/ROM SK6 162 B3
Gwelo St OP/CLY M11 116 B3
Gwenbury Av STKP SK1 160 C5
Gwendor Av CHH M8 87 E4
Gwladys St STLY SK15 109 F4
Gylden Cl HYDE SK14 134 C3
Gypsy La ROCH OL11 42 B3

H

Habergham Cl WALK M28 96 D3
Hackberry Cl ALT WA14 165 E1
Hacken Bridge Rd BOLS/LL BL3 50 A5
Hacken La BOLS/LL BL3 49 H5
Hackford Cl BOL BL1 48 B1
TOT/BURYW BL8 38 A1
Hacking St BRO M7 101 H4
BURY BL9 5 G5
PWCH M25 85 H3
Hackle St OP/CLY M11 116 D3
Hackleton Cl ANC M4 115 G4
Hackness Rd CCHDY M21 141 E3
Hackney Av NEWH/MOS M40 116 D1
Hackney Cl RAD M26 52 B4
Haddington Dr BKLY M9 88 B4
Haddon Av NEWH/MOS M40 104 D1
Haddon Cl BURY BL9 53 H4
MPL/ROM SK6 196 D1
WILM/AE SK9 200 C3
Haddon Gv HALE/TIMP WA15 166 A2
RDSH SK5 145 E4
SALE M33 154 B3
Haddon Hall Rd DROY M43 117 F3
Haddon Rd BRAM/HZG SK7 185 F3
CCHDY M21 156 C1
CHD/CHDH SK8 181 H5
ECC M30 110 D5
WALK M28 98 B5
Haddon St ROCH OL11 42 D1
SLFD M6 101 E5
STRET M32 126 A4
Haddon Wy ROY/SHW OL2 60 B1
Hadfield Av CHAD OL9 90 C2
Hadfield Cl RUSH/FAL M14 129 E5
Hadfield Crs AUL OL6 107 H5
Hadfield St BRO M7 101 H4
DUK SK16 132 D1
OLDS OL8 91 F4
OLDTF/WHR M16 127 F2
Hadleigh Cl BOL BL1 23 F5
Hadley Av BRUN/LGST M13 143 G1
Hadley Cl CHD/CHDH SK8 182 C3
Hadley St SLFD M6 101 E5
Hadlow Gn RDSH SK5 145 H5
Hadlow Wk
NEWH/MOS M40 * 115 H2
Hadwin St BOL BL1 2 E1
Hafton Rd BRO M7 101 E4
Haggate ROY/SHW OL2 74 D1
Haggate Crs ROY/SHW OL2 74 D1
Hagley Rd ORD M5 126 D2
The Hags BURY BL9 53 H4
Hague Rd DID/WITH M20 157 F1
Hague St AUL OL6 119 H1
NEWH/MOS M40 103 G5
OLDE OL4 76 D4
Haig Av IRL M44 150 B2
Haig Ct TOT/BURYW BL8 37 G5
Haigh Av HTNM SK4 159 H1
Haigh Hall Cl RAMS BL0 16 C4
Haigh La CHAD OL9 73 H3
Haigh Pk HTNM SK4 159 H1
Haigh St BOL BL1 2 E2
ROCH OL11 30 B5
Haig Rd STRET M32 126 A5
TOT/BURYW BL8 37 G4
Haile Dr WALK M28 96 A4
Hailsham Cl TOT/BURYW BL8 26 D4
Hail St RAMS BL0 * 16 B4
Halbury Wk BOL BL1 * 34 A4
Halcyon Cl WHIT OL12 29 E1
Haldon Rd DID/WITH M20 158 A1
Hale Av POY/DIS SK12 195 E5
Hale Bank WHTN BL5 62 A2
Hale La FAIL M35 104 D2
Hale Low Rd
HALE/TIMP WA15 178 A1
Hale Rd HALE/TIMP WA15 177 H1
HALE/TIMP WA15 178 D4
HTNM SK4 159 F3
Hales Cl DROY M43 117 G2
Halesden Rd HTNM SK4 159 G1
Halesworth Wk
NEWH/MOS M40 * 115 F1
Hale Vw ALT WA14 * 177 G2
Haley Cl RDSH SK5 145 F3
Haley St CHH M8 102 B3
Half Acre RAD M26 52 A3
Half Acre Dr ROCH OL11 29 F5
Half Acre La ROCH OL11 29 E5
Half Acre Ms ROCH OL11 29 E5
Half Acre Rd ROCH OL11 29 E5
Halfacre Rd WYTH/NTH M22 168 C5
Half Edge La ECC M30 111 G2
Half Moon La OFTN SK2 173 F3
Halford Dr NEWH/MOS M40 104 A2
Half St CSLFD M3 * 6 C1
Halifax Rd MILN OL16 11 G2
Halifax St AUL OL6 119 G1
Haliwell St LIT OL15 21 F3
Hallacres La CHD/CHDH SK8 182 B4
Hallam Rd NEWH/MOS M40 104 A5
Hallam St OFTN SK2 172 B3
RAD M26 53 E5
Hallas Gv NTHM/RTH M23 156 A5
Hall Av HALE/TIMP WA15 166 A2
RUSH/FAL M14 129 E5
SALE M33 139 E5
STLY SK15 108 D5
Hall Bank ECC M30 110 D3
Hallbottom St HYDE SK14 134 A3
Hallbridge Gdns BOL BL1 34 B3
Hall Cl HYDE SK14 135 H3
The Hall Coppice
EDGW/EG BL7 22 C2
Hallcroft PART M31 151 E2
Hallcroft Gdns MILN OL16 31 F5
Hall Dr HYDE SK14 135 H3
MDTN M24 88 C1
Hall Farm Av URM M41 124 A5
Hall Farm Cl BRAM/HZG SK7 185 H1
Hall Fold WHIT OL12 14 B5
Hall Gdns WHIT OL12 29 F1
Hallgate Dr CHD/CHDH SK8 181 F2
Hallgate Rd STKP SK1 172 C1
Hall Green Cl DUK SK16 * 119 H4
Hall Green Rd DUK SK16 119 H4
Hall Gv RUSH/FAL M14 129 E5
Halliday Rd NEWH/MOS M40 116 C1
Halliford Rd NEWH/MOS M40 103 H4
Hallington Cl BOLS/LL BL3 49 E5
Hall i' th' Wood La BOL BL1 34 B2
Halliwell Av OLDS OL8 91 F4
Halliwell La CHH M8 102 A3
Halliwell Rd BOL BL1 33 G4
PWCH M25 100 C1
Halliwell St BOL BL1 * 33 G4
CHAD OL9 * 105 F1
MILN OL16 31 F4
WHIT OL12 10 A5
Halliwell St West CHH M8 * 102 A3
Hall La FWTH BL4 66 B1
MPL/ROM SK6 147 F5
NTHM/RTH M23 168 A3
PART M31 151 E2
Hall Lee Dr WHTN BL5 62 B3
Hall Meadow CHD/CHDH SK8 182 B3
Hall Moss La BRAM/HZG SK7 193 F3
Hall Moss Rd BKLY M9 88 D4
Hallows Av CCHDY M21 156 B1
Hallows Farm Av WHIT OL12 29 G1
Hall Pool Dr OFTN SK2 173 F2
Hall Rd ALT WA14 177 F3
AUL OL6 107 F5
BRAM/HZG SK7 183 G3
RUSH/FAL M14 129 E5
WILM/AE SK9 192 B4
WILM/AE SK9 198 D3
Hallroyd Brow OLD OL1 * 75 F4
Hallstead Av LHULT M38 80 D3
Hallstead Gv LHULT M38 80 D3
Hall St AUL OL6 120 B3
BOLS/LL BL3 66 A2
BURY BL9 26 D2
CHD/CHDH SK8 170 A3
CMANW M2 6 E6

FAIL M35 104 C4
HEY OL10 41 E5
HYDE SK14 133 E5
MDTN M24 * 72 D4
OLDE OL4 76 A5
RAD M26 52 A3
ROY/SHW OL2 59 E5
STKP SK1 172 C1
SWIN M27 84 A5
TOT/BURYW BL8 36 D1
TOT/BURYW BL8 37 H2
WHIT OL12 14 B5
Hallsville Rd BNG/LEV M19 144 C2
Halls Wy UPML OL3 94 D1
Hallsworth Rd ECC M30 110 B4
Hallview Wy WALK M28 81 E4
Hallwood Av SLFD M6 112 B1
Hallwood Rd NTHM/RTH M23 167 H3
WILM/AE SK9 192 B4
Hall Wood Rd WILM/AE SK9 192 B5
Hallworth Av DTN/ASHW M34 118 A4
Hallworth Rd CHH M8 102 C2
Halmore Rd NEWH/MOS M40 115 G3
Halsall Cl BURY BL9 27 G5
Halsall Dr BOLS/LL BL3 64 D2
Halsbury Cl WGTN/LGST M12 129 F2
Halsey Cl CHAD OL9 89 H4
Halshaw La FWTH BL4 66 C5
Halsmere Dr BKLY M9 88 B4
Halstead Av CCHDY M21 141 E4
SLFD M6 100 B5
Halstead Dr IRL M44 136 D1
Halstead Gv CHD/CHDH SK8 169 E4
Halstead St BOLE BL2 3 H5
BURY BL9 38 D1
Halstead Wk BURY BL9 * 38 D1
Halstock Wk NEWH/MOS M40 103 E5
Halstone Av WILM/AE SK9 200 B1
Halston St HULME M15 127 H2
Halter Cl RAD M26 52 B4
Halton Bank SLFD M6 113 E1
Halton Dr HALE/TIMP WA15 154 C5
Halton Rd OP/CLY M11 116 D3
Halton St BOLE BL2 3 K5
HYDE SK14 134 A5
Halvard Av BURY BL9 27 G5
Halvard Ct BURY BL9 27 G5
Halvis Gv OLDTF/WHR M16 141 F1
Hambleden Cl BOLS/LL BL3 47 G4
Hambleton Cl TOT/BURYW BL8 37 E5
Hambleton Dr SALE M33 153 G1
Hambleton Rd
CHD/CHDH SK8 181 H4
Hambridge Cl CHH M8 102 B3
Hamel St BOLS/LL BL3 64 C1
HYDE SK14 134 A3
Hamer Dr OLDTF/WHR M16 127 G3
Hamer Hall Crs WHIT OL12 11 G2
Hamer Hl BKLY M9 87 H4
Hamer La MILN OL16 11 G3
Hamer St BOLE BL2 34 C5
HEY OL10 40 C4
RAD M26 52 D5
RAMS BL0 26 C1
Hamerton Rd
NEWH/MOS M40 115 F1
Hamilcar Av ECC M30 111 F3
Hamilton Av ECC M30 111 F4
IRL M44 150 C2
ROY/SHW OL2 74 C1
Hamilton Cl PWCH M25 85 H4
TOT/BURYW BL8 37 G3
Hamilton Crs HTNM SK4 159 E5
Hamilton Gv
OLDTF/WHR M16 127 G3
Hamilton Ms ECC M30 * 110 C2
PWCH M25 * 85 H4
Hamilton Rd BRUN/LGST M13 129 G5
PWCH M25 85 H4
WHTF M45 69 F4
Hamilton Sq HTNM SK4 159 H3
Hamilton St AULW OL7 119 E4
BOL BL1 33 H2
BRO M7 * 101 G3
BURY BL9 38 C2
CHAD OL9 74 B5
ECC M30 110 C2
OLDE OL4 9 K4
OLDTF/WHR M16 127 G3
STLY SK15 120 C3
SWIN M27 98 C1
Hamilton Wy HEY OL10 39 H5
Hamlet Dr SALE M33 139 E5
The Hamlet HOR/BR BL6 46 C1
Hammerstone Rd GTN M18 130 B2
Hammett Rd CCHDY M21 141 E3
Hammond Av HTNM SK4 159 H1
Hamnet Cl BOL BL1 34 B1
Hamnett St HYDE SK14 * 147 H1
OP/CLY M11 117 E4
Hamon Rd HALE/TIMP WA15 165 H5
Hampden Crs GTN M18 130 B3
Hampden Gv ECC M30 111 E3
Hampden Rd PWCH M25 86 A3
ROY/SHW OL2 60 C3
SALE M33 154 B3
Hampden St HEY OL10 41 E5
ROCH OL11 30 A5
Hampshire Cl BURY BL9 53 H1
Hampshire Rd CHAD OL9 90 C2
DROY M43 117 H2
PART M31 150 C4
RDSH SK5 160 D1
Hampson Cl ECC M30 110 C4
Hampson Crs WILM/AE SK9 191 H3
Hampson Fold RAD M26 52 A5
Hampson Mill La BURY BL9 53 G4
Hampson Rd AUL OL6 107 H4
STRET M32 140 A1
Hampson St CSLFD M3 6 A6
DROY M43 117 H3
ECC M30 110 C4
NEWH/MOS M40 * 115 G1
ORD M5 114 A4
RAD M26 68 B1
SALE M33 155 E2
STKP SK1 * 172 C1
SWIN M27 99 F1
Hampstead Av URM M41 137 G2
Hampstead Dr OFTN SK2 172 D4
WHTF M45 69 F3
Hampstead La OFTN SK2 172 D4
Hampton Gv ALT WA14 153 H5
BURY BL9 27 G5
CHD/CHDH SK8 182 B2
Hampton Rd BOLS/LL BL3 65 F1
CCHDY M21 140 D2
FAIL M35 105 F2
IRL M44 150 C2
URM M41 138 D2
Hampton St OLDS OL8 91 E3
Hamsell Rd BRUN/LGST M13 128 D1
Hancock Cl RUSH/FAL M14 128 C5
Hancock St STRET M32 140 B3
Handel Av URM M41 138 A1
Handel Ms SALE M33 154 D2
Handel St BOL BL1 33 G3
Handforth Gv
BRUN/LGST M13 143 G1
Handforth Rd RDSH SK5 160 A1
WILM/AE SK9 199 H1
Handley Av RUSH/FAL M14 142 D2
Handley Cl EDGY/DAV SK3 171 F4
Handley Gdns BOL BL1 48 A2
Handley Rd BRAM/HZG SK7 183 H1
Handley St BURY BL9 53 G1
WHIT OL12 29 G3
Hands La ROCH OL11 28 D4
Handsworth St
WGTN/LGST M12 129 E1
Hanging Chadder La
ROY/SHW OL2 58 D2
Hankinson Cl PART M31 151 E4
Hankinson Wy SLFD M6 113 F2
Hanley Cl MDTN M24 88 D2
Hanlith Ms BNG/LEV M19 143 H3
Hanlon St CHH M8 102 A1
Hannah Baldwin Cl
OP/CLY M11 116 A5
Hannah St WGTN/LGST M12 144 A1
Hannerton Rd ROY/SHW OL2 60 C1
Hannesburg Gdns
NTHM/RTH M23 * 167 G5
Hannet Rd WYTH/NTH M22 180 C3
Hanover Ct BRO M7 101 G3
WALK M28 * 98 A4
Hanover Crs RUSH/FAL M14 129 E4
Hanover Gdns BRO M7 101 H2
Hanover Rd ALT WA14 165 E2
Hanover St ANC M4 7 F2
BOL BL1 2 C5
LIT OL15 20 D3
MOSL OL5 93 H5
ROCH OL11 42 B4
STLY SK15 120 C3
Hanover St North
DTN/ASHW M34 118 D5
Hanover St South
DTN/ASHW M34 * 118 D5
Hansby Cl OLD OL1 75 F3
Hansdon Cl CHH M8 102 B4
Hanson Cl MDTN M24 72 D3
Hanson Ms STKP SK1 160 C4
Hanson Pk MDTN M24 * 73 F4
Hanson Rd NEWH/MOS M40 103 H3
Hanson St BURY BL9 38 C2
MDTN M24 72 D4
OLDE OL4 76 B5
Hanworth Cl BRUN/LGST M13 128 C1
Hapton Av STRET M32 140 B2
Hapton Pl HTNM SK4 * 159 H3
Hapton St BNG/LEV M19 144 A2
Harbern Cl ECC M30 111 E1
Harbord St MDTN M24 72 D4
Harboro Gv SALE M33 154 A2
Harboro Rd SALE M33 153 H2
Harboro Wy SALE M33 154 A2
Harbour Farm Rd HYDE SK14 133 H3
Harbour La MILN OL16 44 C1
Harbour La North MILN OL16 31 G5
Harbourne Av WALK M28 96 D2
Harbourne Cl WALK M28 96 D2
Harbury Cl BOLS/LL BL3 63 H1
Harbury Crs WYTH/NTH M22 168 B4
Harcles Dr RAMS BL0 26 C1
Harcombe Rd DID/WITH M20 143 E5
Harcourt Av URM M41 139 F2
Harcourt Cl URM M41 139 F2
Harcourt Rd ALT WA14 165 G3
SALE M33 139 G5
Harcourt St OLD OL1 76 A4
RDSH SK5 145 F3
STRET M32 126 B5
WALK M28 82 A2
Hardberry Pl OFTN SK2 173 F3
Hardcastle Av CCHDY M21 141 G5
Hardcastle Cl BOLE BL2 23 H5
Hardcastle Gdns BOLE BL2 23 H5
Hardcastle Rd EDGY/DAV SK3 171 G2
Hardcastle St BOL BL1 34 A4
Harden Dr BOLE BL2 35 E4
Harden Hills ROY/SHW OL2 60 C1
Harden Pk WILM/AE SK9 200 D2
Hardfield Rd MDTN M24 88 D2
Hardfield St HEY OL10 41 E4
Hardicker St HTNM SK4 144 B4
Hardie Av FWTH BL4 65 G5
Harding St ANC M4 115 G4
CSLFD M3 6 D2
HYDE SK14 133 G3
SLFD M6 113 F1
STKP SK1 160 C5
Hard La WHIT OL12 15 F5
Hardman Av MPL/ROM SK6 161 H3
PWCH M25 86 C5
Hardman Cl RAD M26 52 A3
Hardman La FAIL M35 104 D2
Hardman Rd RDSH SK5 145 F3
Hardmans EDGW/EG BL7 23 E4
Hardmans La EDGW/EG BL7 23 E3
Hardman's Ms WHTF M45 85 G1
Hardman's Rd WHTF M45 85 H1
Hardman St BURY BL9 4 E1
CHAD OL9 90 C4
CSLFD M3 6 C5
EDGY/DAV SK3 12 D5
FAIL M35 104 C3
FWTH BL4 66 B5
HEY OL10 41 E4
RAD M26 52 A3
Hardon Gv BRUN/LGST M13 143 H1
Hardrush Fold FAIL M35 105 F4
Hardshaw Cl
BRUN/LGST M13 * 128 C2
Hardwick Cl MPL/ROM SK6 197 E1
RAD M26 51 E4
Hardwicke Rd POY/DIS SK12 195 G3
Hardwicke St ROCH OL11 42 D2
Hardwick Rd PART M31 151 F3
Hardwick St AULW OL7 119 E3
Hardwood Cl CHH M8 102 B3
Hardy Av CCHDY M21 141 E3
Hardy Cl ROCH OL11 43 E3
Hardy Dr BRAM/HZG SK7 183 G5
HALE/TIMP WA15 166 A2
Hardy Gv SWIN M27 98 C5
WALK M28 97 G2
Hardy La CCHDY M21 141 G5
Hardy Mill Rd BOLE BL2 35 G3
Hardy St AUL OL6 107 H4
ECC M30 110 C4
OLDE OL4 9 K6
Hardywood Rd
DTN/ASHW M34 147 E4
Harebell Av WALK M28 * 81 E4
Harebell Cl WHIT OL12 18 C5
Harecastle Av ECC M30 111 F5
Haredale Dr CHH M8 102 C4
Hare Dr BURY BL9 54 A5
Harefield Av ROCH OL11 43 E1
Harefield Dr DID/WITH M20 157 F4
HEY OL10 41 G4
WILM/AE SK9 198 D5
Harefield Rd WILM/AE SK9 192 B3
Harehill Cl BRUN/LGST M13 128 C1
Hare Hill Rd HYDE SK14 134 D5
LIT OL15 20 D2
Hareshill Rd HEY OL10 55 H2
Hare St ANC M4 * 7 G3
ROCH OL11 30 B5
Harewood Av ROCH OL11 28 A1
SALE M33 153 G2
Harewood Cl ROCH OL11 28 A2
Harewood Dr ROY/SHW OL2 58 D4
Harewood Gv RDSH SK5 145 E3
Harewood Rd IRL M44 136 D1
ROY/SHW OL2 60 B1
Harewood Wy SWIN M27 84 A5
Harford Cl BRAM/HZG SK7 184 B3
Hargate Av WHIT OL12 28 D1
Hargate Cl BURY BL9 26 D1
Hargate Dr HALE/TIMP WA15 178 B3
IRL M44 122 B5
Hargrave Cl BKLY M9 87 H1
Hargreaves Rd
HALE/TIMP WA15 166 D3
Hargreave's St ANC M4 114 D2
BOL BL1 * 33 H4
CHAD OL9 8 B4
OLD OL1 9 F2
ROCH OL11 42 B2
Harkerside Cl CCHDY M21 141 G3
Harkness St WGTN/LGST M12 128 D1
Harland Dr CHH M8 102 C3
Harland Wy WHIT OL12 28 D1
Harlech Av WHTF M45 86 A1
Harlech Dr BRAM/HZG SK7 184 D3
Harleen Gv OFTN SK2 173 E2
Harlesden Crs BOLS/LL BL3 * 48 A4
Harley Av BOLE BL2 35 F3
BOLE BL2 36 C5
RUSH/FAL M14 129 F5
Harley Ct MDTN M24 72 C3
Harley Rd MDTN M24 72 C3
SALE M33 154 D1
Harley St AUL OL6 * 119 G2
OP/CLY M11 117 E5
Harling Rd WYTH/NTH M22 168 C2
Harlow Dr GTN M18 130 C5
Harlyn Av BRAM/HZG SK7 184 A5
Harmer Cl NEWH/MOS M40 103 H5
Harmol Gv AULW OL7 106 C4
Harmony St OLDE OL4 9 J6
Harmsworth Dr HTNM SK4 159 E1
Harmsworth St SLFD M6 112 D3
Harold Av DUK SK16 120 A4
GTN M18 131 E4
Haroldene St BOLE BL2 34 C4
Harold Lees Rd HEY OL10 41 G3
Harold Priestnall Cl
NEWH/MOS M40 104 A5
Harold St BOL BL1 33 G4
CHAD OL9 8 C3
FAIL M35 * 104 D3
MDTN M24 72 B4
MILN OL16 31 E4
OLDTF/WHR M16 127 F2
PWCH M25 85 G3
STKP SK1 172 D1
Harper Ct EDGY/DAV SK3 13 F7
Harper Fold Rd RAD M26 67 H1
Harper Green Rd FWTH BL4 65 G3
Harper Pl AUL OL6 119 H2
Harper Rd WYTH/NTH M22 168 D2
Harpers La BOL BL1 33 E4
Harper Sq ROY/SHW OL2 60 B2
Harper St EDGY/DAV SK3 12 E7
FWTH BL4 65 G2
OLDS OL8 91 F3
ROCH OL11 42 D1
Harpford Cl BOLE BL2 50 D4
Harpford Dr BOLE BL2 50 D4
Harp Rd TRPK M17 111 H5
Harp St OP/CLY M11 130 C1
Harpurhey Rd CHH M8 102 D2
Harridge Av STLY SK15 121 G3
WHIT OL12 18 B5
Harridge St WHIT OL12 18 B5
The Harridge WHIT OL12 18 B5
Harrier Cl WALK M28 97 E2
WYTH/NTH M22 168 D4
Harriet St IRL M44 150 D1
WALK M28 82 A4
Harriett St ANC M4 115 F3
MILN OL16 10 E7
Harringay Rd
NEWH/MOS M40 104 A5
Harrington Cl BURY BL9 53 H2
Harrington Rd ALT WA14 165 E4
Harrington St GTN M18 130 D3
Harris Av DTN/ASHW M34 131 G5
URM M41 124 C3
Harris Cl DTN/ASHW M34 131 G5
HEY OL10 39 H5
Harris Dr BURY BL9 70 A2
HYDE SK14 134 B4
Harrison Av BNG/LEV M19 144 B1
Harrison Cl WHIT OL12 28 C2
Harrisons Dr MPL/ROM SK6 162 B1
Harrison St ANC M4 115 G4
BRO M7 114 A1
ECC M30 110 B5
HYDE SK14 148 B3
LHULT M38 81 F3
OFTN SK2 172 A2
OLD OL1 9 G4
RAMS BL0 16 D1
STLY SK15 120 D3
Harris St BOLS/LL BL3 2 C7
BRO M7 114 B1
Harrogate Av PWCH M25 86 C5
Harrogate Cl OP/CLY M11 130 D1
Harrogate Dr RDSH SK5 145 E3
Harrogate Rd RDSH SK5 145 E2
Harrop Edge Rd HYDE SK14 135 F5
Harrop Fold OLDS OL8 106 D1
Harrop Rd HALE/TIMP WA15 178 A2
Harrop St BOLS/LL BL3 47 H5
GTN M18 131 E2
STKP SK1 13 J7
STLY SK15 120 C3
WALK M28 81 G4
Harrow Av BNG/LEV M19 144 A5
OLDS OL8 91 E4
ROCH OL11 28 D5
Harrowby Dr
NEWH/MOS M40 103 E5
Harrowby Fold FWTH BL4 65 H4
Harrowby La FWTH BL4 65 H4
Harrowby Rd BOL BL1 32 C4
BOLS/LL BL3 * 63 H1
SWIN M27 98 D4
Harrowby St FWTH BL4 65 G4
Harrow Cl BURY BL9 53 G4
WILM/AE SK9 199 G2
Harrow Dr SALE M33 154 B4
Harrow Ms ROY/SHW OL2 60 A2
Harrow Rd BOL BL1 48 A2
SALE M33 154 B4
Harrow St CHH M8 102 C1
ROCH OL11 * 43 G4
Harrycroft Rd MPL/ROM SK6 162 A1
Harry Hall Gdns BRO M7 * 113 H1
Harry Rd RDSH SK5 145 F3
Harry Rowley Cl
WYTH/NTH M22 * 180 B2
Harry St CHAD OL9 8 B5
ROCH OL11 42 A3
ROY/SHW OL2 75 F2
Harry Thorneycroft Wk
OP/CLY M11 115 H5
Harrytown MPL/ROM SK6 161 H4
Hart Av DROY M43 118 A4
SALE M33 155 G3
Hart Ct MOSL OL5 93 G5
Hart Dr BURY BL9 54 A5
Harter St CMANE M1 7 F6
Hartfield Cl BRUN/LGST M13 128 D2
Hartford Av HEY OL10 40 C4
HTNM SK4 144 D5
WILM/AE SK9 198 C5
Hartford Cl HEY OL10 40 C3
Hartford Gdns
HALE/TIMP WA15 167 E4
Hartford Rd SALE M33 153 G5
URM M41 124 D4
Hartford Sq CHAD OL9 * 8 E5
Hartford St DTN/ASHW M34 * 132 B3
Hart Hill Dr ORD M5 112 C2
Harthill St CHH M8 102 A5
Hartington Cl URM M41 139 E1
Hartington Ct ROY/SHW OL2 60 A2
Hartington Dr BRAM/HZG SK7 185 F4
OP/CLY M11 116 C2
Hartington Rd ALT WA14 165 G2
BOL BL1 48 B1
BRAM/HZG SK7 193 H1
CCHDY M21 141 F3
CHD/CHDH SK8 181 G2
ECC M30 110 B2
MPL/ROM SK6 196 D1
OFTN SK2 173 E5
Hartington St
RUSH/FAL M14 128 A5
Hartis Av BRO M7 101 H4
Hartland Cl OFTN SK2 172 D1
POY/DIS SK12 195 E2
Hartland St HEY OL10 41 E4
Hartlebury ROCH OL11 * 29 H5
Hartlepool Cl RUSH/FAL M14 128 C5
Hartley Av PWCH M25 86 B4
Hartley Gv IRL M44 122 C4
Hartley Hall Gdns
OLDTF/WHR M16 142 A2
Hartley La ROCH OL11 42 D3
Hartley Rd ALT WA14 165 F4
CCHDY M21 141 E2
Hartley St EDGY/DAV SK3 12 C6
HEY OL10 41 E4
LIT OL15 20 D3
MILN OL16 * 31 E4
NEWH/MOS M40 103 G2
STLY SK15 121 G2
WHIT OL12 19 H2
WHIT OL12 29 E2
Hart Mill Cl MOSL OL5 93 G5
Harton Av GTN M18 130 B5
Harton Cl ROY/SHW OL2 59 H3
Hart Rd RUSH/FAL M14 142 D2
Hartshead Av AUL OL6 107 F4
STLY SK15 120 D2
Hartshead Cl AUL OL6 120 B1
OP/CLY M11 131 F1
Hartshead Crs FAIL M35 105 H4
Hartshead Rd AUL OL6 * 107 F4
Hartshead St OLDE OL4 93 E2
Hartshead Vw HYDE SK14 148 B2
Hartsop Dr MDTN M24 71 H2
Hartspring Av SWIN M27 99 F3
Hart St ALT WA14 165 H4
CMANE M1 7 G6
DROY M43 117 H3
Hartswood Cl
DTN/ASHW M34 132 D4
Hartswood Rd
DID/WITH M20 143 F5
Hartwell Cl BOLE BL2 34 D4
OP/CLY M11 116 A5
Harvard Cl MPL/ROM SK6 162 B1
Harvard Gv SLFD M6 112 B2
Harvard Rd GTN M18 130 A3
Harvard St ROCH OL11 43 F2
Harvest Cl SALE M33 155 H3
SLFD M6 100 B5
Harvest Pk BOL BL1 48 B1
Harvey St BOL BL1 33 G3
STKP SK1 13 G3
TOT/BURYW BL8 37 H3
WHIT OL12 11 G1
Harvin Gv DTN/ASHW M34 147 E1
Harwich Cl BNG/LEV M19 * 144 A2
RDSH SK5 146 A5
Harwin Cl WHIT OL12 18 C5
Harwood Ct SLFD M6 113 G1
Harwood Crs TOT/BURYW BL8 25 H4
Harwood Dr TOT/BURYW BL8 37 F5
Harwood Gv BOLE BL2 * 34 C5
Harwood Meadow BOLE BL2 35 G3
Harwood Rd BNG/LEV M19 143 G5
BOLE BL2 36 A2
HTNM SK4 158 B4
Harwood St HTNM SK4 159 H3
LIT OL15 20 C3
Harwood V BOLE BL2 35 F3
Haseley Cl POY/DIS SK12 195 F2
RAD M26 51 E4
Haselhurst Wk
NTHM/RTH M23 155 G4
Hasguard Cl BOL BL1 47 G2
Haslam Brow BURY BL9 53 F1
Haslam Hall Ms BOL BL1 47 F2
Haslam Hey Cl BOLE BL2 * 36 B5
TOT/BURYW BL8 37 E4
Haslam Rd EDGY/DAV SK3 171 H3
Haslam St BOLS/LL BL3 48 C4
BURY BL9 38 D2
MDTN M24 * 73 F5
WHIT OL12 29 G3
Haslemere Av
HALE/TIMP WA15 188 D1
Haslemere Dr CHD/CHDH SK8 182 D3
Haslemere Rd DID/WITH M20 143 F5
URM M41 138 B2
Haslington Rd
WYTH/NTH M22 180 D2
Hasper Av DID/WITH M20 142 C4
Hassall Av DID/WITH M20 142 B3
Hassall St RAD M26 53 F4
STLY SK15 * 121 E4
Hassop Av BRO M7 100 D3
Hassop Cl OP/CLY M11 115 H4
Hassop Rd RDSH SK5 145 G2
Hastings Av CCHDY M21 141 E3
WHTF M45 70 A5
Hastings Cl CHD/CHDH SK8 183 F2
STKP SK1 172 C2
WHTF M45 70 A5
Hastings Dr URM M41 123 F5
Hastings Rd BOL BL1 48 A1
ECC M30 110 B1
PWCH M25 86 B2
Hastings St ROCH OL11 43 E1
Haston Cl RDSH SK5 160 A2
Hasty La HALE/TIMP WA15 179 G5
Hatchett Rd WYTH/NTH M22 180 D3
Hatchmere Cl CHD/CHDH SK8 170 C5
HALE/TIMP WA15 167 E3
Hatfield Av BNG/LEV M19 143 H5
Hatfield Rd BOL BL1 33 F5
Hathaway Dr BOL BL1 34 B1
Hathaway Gdns
MPL/ROM SK6 161 G3
Hathaway Rd BURY BL9 69 H1
Hatherley Rd DID/WITH M20 143 F5
Hatherlow MPL/ROM SK6 161 H4
Hatherlow La BRAM/HZG SK7 185 E2
Hatherop Cl ECC M30 110 C4
Hathersage Rd
BRUN/LGST M13 128 D4
Hathersage St CHAD OL9 8 A5
Hathershaw La OLDS OL8 91 G4
Hatro Ct URM M41 139 G2
Hatters Ct STKP SK1 13 H6
Hattersley Rd East
HYDE SK14 149 G1
Hattersley Rd West
HYDE SK14 149 F2
Hatter St ANC M4 7 H2
Hatton Gv BOL BL1 34 B1
Hattons Ct STRET M32 125 H5
Hattons Rd TRPK M17 125 G2
Hatton St STKP SK1 13 F2
WGTN/LGST M12 129 H5
Haugh Hill Rd OLDE OL4 76 D1
Haugh La MILN OL16 45 F2
Haughton Cl MPL/ROM SK6 147 E5
Haughton Dr WYTH/NTH M22 156 C5
Haughton Green Rd
DTN/ASHW M34 147 F3
Haughton Hall Rd
DTN/ASHW M34 132 D5
Haughton St
DTN/ASHW M34 132 C3
HYDE SK14 148 A2
Havana Cl OP/CLY M11 116 A4
Haveley Rd WYTH/NTH M22 168 B4
Havelock Dr BRO M7 114 A1
Havelock St OLDS OL8 9 G7
Havenbrook Gv RAMS BL0 * 16 B5
Haven Cl BRAM/HZG SK7 184 D3
OLDE OL4 94 A1
RAD M26 51 G4
Haven Dr DROY M43 117 F3
Haven La OLDE OL4 76 D1
Havenscroft Av ECC M30 111 E5
Havenside Cl OLDE OL4 76 D1
Haven St SLFD M6 112 D4
The Haven
HALE/TIMP WA15 178 A1
Haverfield Rd BKLY M9 88 B4

Haverford St
WGTN/LGST M12 129 G2
Haverhill Gv BOLE BL2 34 C4
Haversham Rd CHH M8 86 D5
Havers Rd GTN M18 130 D3
Havisham Cl HOR/BR BL6 46 C5
Hawarden Av
OLDTF/WHR M16 141 G1
Hawarden Rd ALT WA14 165 G3
Hawarden St BOL BL1 33 H2
Haw Clough La UPML OL3 95 G1
Hawdraw Gn OFTN SK2 173 F3
Hawes Av FWTH BL4 64 D5
RUSH/FAL M14 143 G4
SWIN M27 * 99 E4
Hawes Cl OFTN SK2 172 B3
TOT/BURYW BL8 37 G1
Haweswater Cl
DTN/ASHW M34 145 G1
Haweswater Crs BURY BL9 54 A4
Haweswater Dr MDTN M24 72 B2
Hawfinch Gv WALK M28 97 E2
Hawk Cl BURY BL9 5 J1
Hawker Av BOLS/LL BL3 64 C1
Hawkeshead Rd CHH M8 102 C4
Hawke St STLY SK15 121 F4
Hawk Green Rd
MPL/ROM SK6 187 E1
Hawkhurst Rd
BRUN/LGST M13 129 G5
Hawkins St RDSH SK5 159 H2
Hawkridge Dr
NTHM/RTH M23 155 G4
Hawk Rd IRL M44 122 B5
Hawkshaw Ct ORD M5 113 F4
Hawkshead Dr BOLS/LL BL3 63 H1
MDTN M24 72 B3
ROY/SHW OL2 59 E3
Hawkshead Rd ROY/SHW OL2 59 H1
Hawksheath Cl EDGW/EG BL7 23 E2
Hawksley St OLDS OL8 90 D4
Hawksmoor Dr ROY/SHW OL2 60 A1
Hawkstone Av DROY M43 117 F2
WHTF M45 69 E5
Hawkstone Cl BOLE BL2 35 F3
Hawkswick Dr
NTHM/RTH M23 155 H4
Hawk Yard La UPML OL3 95 G2
Hawley Dr HALE/TIMP WA15 178 C4
Hawley Gn WHIT OL12 29 G1
Hawley La HALE/TIMP WA15 178 C4
Hawley St BNG/LEV M19 144 B3
Haworth Av RAMS BL0 26 C1
Haworth Cl BURY BL9 53 G3
Haworth Dr STRET M32 125 F5
Haworth Rd GTN M18 130 B4
Haworth St OLD OL1 75 G3
RAD M26 68 C1
TOT/BURYW BL8 37 E2
Hawthorn Av ECC M30 111 E2
HALE/TIMP WA15 166 A2
MPL/ROM SK6 174 C3
RAD M26 68 C3
RAMS BL0 26 B1
TOT/BURYW BL8 37 H2
URM M41 139 F2
WALK M28 97 F1
WILM/AE SK9 198 D3
Hawthorn Cl
HALE/TIMP WA15 166 A2
Hawthorn Crs OLDS OL8 91 G5
ROY/SHW OL2 * 60 A3
TOT/BURYW BL8 26 A4
Hawthorn Dr BNG/LEV M19 143 H4
IRL M44 150 C1
SLFD M6 111 H1
STLY SK15 120 C5
SWIN M27 99 H3
Hawthorne Av FWTH BL4 65 G4
Hawthorne Dr WALK M28 98 A3
Hawthorne Gv AULW OL7 119 E4
CHAD OL9 74 C4
MPL/ROM SK6 161 F2
POY/DIS SK12 196 B3
Hawthorne Rd BOLS/LL BL3 48 A5
Hawthorne St BOLS/LL BL3 48 A4
Hawthorn Gv BRAM/HZG SK7 193 F1
HTNM SK4 159 E3
HYDE SK14 147 H2
WILM/AE SK9 199 E3
Hawthorn La CCHDY M21 * 140 D3
SALE M33 138 D5
WILM/AE SK9 198 D3
Hawthorn Pk WILM/AE SK9 198 D3
Hawthorn Rd CHD/CHDH SK8 169 F4
DROY M43 118 B3
DTN/ASHW M34 131 G4
FWTH BL4 83 E2
HALE/TIMP WA15 177 H1
HTNM SK4 158 B4
NEWH/MOS M40 104 D1
OLDS OL8 105 G1
ROCH OL11 28 B5
STRET M32 140 C3
WHTN BL5 62 A5
Hawthorn Rd South
DROY M43 118 B3
The Hawthorns
DTN/ASHW M34 132 A2
Hawthorn St DTN/ASHW M34 132 B2
GTN M18 130 C2
WILM/AE SK9 198 D4
Hawthorn Ter HTNM SK4 * 159 E3
Hawthorn Vw WILM/AE SK9 198 D3
Hawthorn Wk LIT OL15 20 C3
WILM/AE SK9 * 198 D3
Hawthorpe Gv UPML OL3 79 E4
Haxby Rd GTN M18 130 C5
Haybarn Rd NTHM/RTH M23 168 A2
Hayburn Rd OFTN SK2 172 D1
Haycock Cl STLY SK15 135 F1
Hay Cft CHD/CHDH SK8 182 B4
Haydn Av RUSH/FAL M14 128 C4
Haydock Av SALE M33 153 F4
Haydock Cl STRET M32 126 C4
Haydock Dr BRAM/HZG SK7 185 G2
HALE/TIMP WA15 166 C4
WALK M28 96 C4
Haydock La EDGW/EG BL7 23 G3
Haydock St BOL BL1 2 E2
Haye's Rd IRL M44 150 D1
Hayeswater Rd URM M41 124 B5
Hayfield Av MPL/ROM SK6 161 H2
Hayfield Cl MDTN M24 73 F1
OLDE OL4 61 E5
TOT/BURYW BL8 26 A2
WGTN/LGST M12 129 F2
Hayfield Rd MPL/ROM SK6 161 H2
SLFD M6 112 A1
Hayfield St SALE M33 154 B2
Hayfield Wk
HALE/TIMP WA15 166 D3
Hayle Rd OLD OL1 60 C5
Hayley St WGTN/LGST M12 * 129 F4
Hayling Cl TOT/BURYW BL8 26 D5
Hayling Rd SALE M33 153 H1
Haymaker Ri WHIT OL12 19 H2
Haymans Wk
BRUN/LGST M13 128 C1
Haymarket St BURY BL9 4 D5
The Haymarket BURY BL9 4 E4
Haymill Av LHULT M38 81 F1
Haymond Cl SLFD M6 100 D4
Haynes St BOLS/LL BL3 64 A1
WHIT OL12 10 D4
Haysbrook Av LHULT M38 81 E3
Haysbrook Cl AULW OL7 106 D3
Haythorp Av WYTH/NTH M22 180 D1
Hayward Av BOLS/LL BL3 67 F1
Hayward St TOT/BURYW BL8 37 H3
Hazel Av AUL OL6 107 H4
BURY BL9 5 K4
CHD/CHDH SK8 170 B4
LHULT M38 80 D2
MILN OL16 44 D3
MPL/ROM SK6 162 C4
OLDTF/WHR M16 141 H1
RAD M26 66 D4
RAMS BL0 26 C2
SALE M33 154 C3
SWIN M27 99 F3
TOT/BURYW BL8 37 E1
WHTN BL5 62 A5
Hazelbadge Cl POY/DIS SK12 194 D3
Hazelbadge Rd POY/DIS SK12 194 D3
Hazelbank Av DID/WITH M20 142 D4
Hazelbottom Rd CHH M8 102 C3
Hazel Cl DROY M43 118 B3
MPL/ROM SK6 174 D5
Hazelcroft WILM/AE SK9 200 D5
Hazel-dene Cl BURY BL9 53 G2
Hazeldene Rd
NEWH/MOS M40 104 D1
Hazel Dr OFTN SK2 173 E3
POY/DIS SK12 195 G4
WYTH/NTH M22 181 F4
Hazelfields WALK M28 98 A3
Hazel Gv CHAD OL9 74 C4
FWTH BL4 65 G4
ORD M5 112 B3
RAD M26 68 A4
URM M41 139 E1
Hazel Hall La TOT/BURYW BL8 26 C2
Hazelhurst Cl BOL BL1 33 H4
RAMS BL0 16 C4
Hazelhurst Dr MDTN M24 56 C5
Hazelhurst Fold WALK M28 98 B3
Hazelhurst Rd AUL OL6 108 A4
STLY SK15 120 D1
WALK M28 98 A3
Hazel La OLDS OL8 91 E5
Hazelmere Av ECC M30 110 C1
Hazel Mt EDGW/EG BL7 22 D1
Hazel Rd ALT WA14 165 G4
CHD/CHDH SK8 183 E3
MDTN M24 73 E2
STLY SK15 121 F2
WHTF M45 70 A4
Hazel St BRAM/HZG SK7 * 185 F1
DTN/ASHW M34 132 B2
RAMS BL0 16 B4
Hazel Ter BKLY M9 * 88 A3
Hazelwell SALE M33 154 C3
Hazelwood CHAD OL9 73 H5
Hazelwood Av BOLE BL2 35 F3
Hazelwood Cl HYDE SK14 148 C1
Hazelwood Dr BURY BL9 27 G4
DTN/ASHW M34 132 B2
Hazelwood Rd BOL BL1 33 E4
BRAM/HZG SK7 185 F2
HALE/TIMP WA15 177 H2
OFTN SK2 172 B5
WILM/AE SK9 199 G2
WYTH/NTH M22 180 C4
Hazlemere FWTH BL4 66 D5
Headingley Dr
OLDTF/WHR M16 126 D5
Headingley Rd
RUSH/FAL M14 143 F4
Headingley Wy BOLS/LL BL3 64 C1
Headlands Dr PWCH M25 85 H5
Headlands Rd BRAM/HZG SK7 184 A3
Headlands St WHIT OL12 10 A2
Heady Hill Cl HEY OL10 40 B5
Heady Hill Rd HEY OL10 40 B4
Heald Av RUSH/FAL M14 128 C5
Heald Cl ALT WA14 177 F2
LIT OL15 20 D5
WHIT OL12 18 B5
Heald Dr ALT WA14 177 F2
WHIT OL12 18 B5
Heald Gv CHD/CHDH SK8 181 F3
RUSH/FAL M14 128 C5
Heald La LIT OL15 20 D5
Heald Pl RUSH/FAL M14 128 C5
Heald Rd ALT WA14 177 F2
Healds Gn OLD OL1 74 A1
Heald St STKP SK1 13 J1
Healdwood Rd MPL/ROM SK6 162 B2
Healey Av HEY OL10 41 F3
WHIT OL12 18 C4
Healey Cl BRO M7 101 F2
NTHM/RTH M23 155 G4
Healey Gv WHIT OL12 18 B3
Healey La WHIT OL12 18 D4
Healey St MILN OL16 29 H5
Healing St ROCH OL11 43 F1
Heanor Av DTN/ASHW M34 147 E3
Heap Br BURY BL9 39 F4
Heap Brow BURY BL9 39 G5
Heape St ROCH OL11 42 B5
Heaplands TOT/BURYW BL8 26 A2
Heap Rd WHIT OL12 28 A1
Heaps Farm Ct STLY SK15 121 G5
Heap St BOLS/LL BL3 48 D5
BURY BL9 39 G5
OLDE OL4 76 B5
RAD M26 68 C1
WHTF M45 * 69 G5
Heapworth Av RAMS BL0 16 C2
Heapy Cl TOT/BURYW BL8 37 E4
Heath Av BRO M7 113 H1
RAMS BL0 26 C2
Heathbank Rd BKLY M9 87 H2
CHD/CHDH SK8 182 C4
EDGY/DAV SK3 171 E2
Heathcliffe Wk
BRUN/LGST M13 128 D3
Heath Cl BOLS/LL BL3 64 A2
Heathcote Av HTNM SK4 159 F3
Heathcote Rd GTN M18 130 B4
Heath Crs OFTN SK2 172 A4
Heather Av DROY M43 118 B3
ROY/SHW OL2 60 C1
Heather Bank LIT OL15 * 21 G2
TOT/BURYW BL8 * 25 H4
Heather Brow STLY SK15 135 F1
Heather Cl OLDE OL4 76 D3
Heatherdale Dr CHH M8 102 B4
Heatherfield BOL BL1 33 G1
Heatherfield Ct WILM/AE SK9 199 H2
Heather Gv DROY M43 118 A5
Heatherlands WHIT OL12 14 C1
Heather Lea DTN/ASHW M34 147 E1
Heather Rd ALT WA14 177 H3
Heatherside RDSH SK5 145 G2
STLY SK15 121 G3
Heatherside Av MOSL OL5 109 F1
Heatherside Rd RAMS BL0 16 C1
The Heathers OFTN SK2 172 C5
Heather St OP/CLY M11 116 C3
Heather Wy MPL/ROM SK6 174 D4
Heatherway SALE M33 153 G1
Heath Farm La PART M31 151 G3
Heathfield BOLE BL2 35 G2
FWTH BL4 66 B3
WALK M28 97 G5
WILM/AE SK9 198 D5
Heathfield Av CHD/CHDH SK8 169 G4
DTN/ASHW M34 146 B1
HTNM SK4 159 F1
Heathfield Cl SALE M33 155 G3
Heathfield Dr BOLS/LL BL3 64 A2
SWIN M27 99 F4
Heathfield Rd BURY BL9 69 G1
OFTN SK2 172 A3
Heathfields UPML OL3 79 F4
Heathfield St
NEWH/MOS M40 104 B5
Heathland Rd BRO M7 101 E1
Heathlands Dr PWCH M25 100 D1
Heathland Ter EDGY/DAV SK3 171 H2
Heathlea Cl BOL BL1 22 D5
Heath Pl BRO M7 113 H1
Heath Rd ALT WA14 177 G2
HALE/TIMP WA15 166 A1
OFTN SK2 172 A3
WHIT OL12 19 H2
Heathside Gv WALK M28 82 A4
Heathside Park Rd
EDGY/DAV SK3 170 C2
Heathside Rd DID/WITH M20 157 H1
EDGY/DAV SK3 170 D2
Heath St CHH M8 102 A3
ROCH OL11 29 G5
The Heath AULW OL7 106 D3
MDTN M24 89 E1
Heathwood UPML OL3 79 F4
Heathwood Rd BNG/LEV M19 158 B2
Heatley Rd MILN OL16 31 E5
Heaton Av BOL BL1 32 C5
BOLE BL2 35 F1
BOLS/LL BL3 50 D5
BRAM/HZG SK7 183 G1
FWTH BL4 65 H4
Heaton Cl BURY BL9 53 H4
HTNM SK4 158 D3
Heaton Ct BURY BL9 53 F2
Heaton Dr BURY BL9 53 H4
Heaton Fold BURY BL9 53 F1
Heaton Grange Dr BOL BL1 47 H2
Heaton Gv BURY BL9 53 F2
Heaton La HTNM SK4 12 E3
Heaton Moor Rd HTNM SK4 159 E3
Heaton Mt BOL BL1 32 C5
Heaton Park Rd BKLY M9 87 F2
Heaton Park Rd West BKLY M9 87 F2
Heaton Rd BOLE BL2 51 E4
DID/WITH M20 143 E4
HOR/BR BL6 47 E3
HTNM SK4 159 G3
Heatons Gv WHTN BL5 62 B2
Heaton St BRO M7 101 H3
DTN/ASHW M34 132 A5
MDTN M24 71 G5
MILN OL16 44 D1
PWCH M25 86 B3
Heaviley Gv OFTN SK2 172 B3
Hebble Butt Cl MILN OL16 * 31 F5
Hebble Cl BOLE BL2 34 C1
Hebburn Dr TOT/BURYW BL8 37 H1
Hebburn Wk RUSH/FAL M14 128 C4
Hebden Av MPL/ROM SK6 161 H2
SLFD M6 112 B2
Hebden Wk HULME M15 128 A3
Heber Pl LIT OL15 21 E3
Heber St RAD M26 68 B1
Hebron St ROY/SHW OL2 75 H1
Hector Av MILN OL16 11 G4
Hector Rd BRUN/LGST M13 129 G5
Heddon Cl HTNM SK4 158 B3
Hedge Rows WHIT OL12 14 B3
The Hedgerows HYDE SK14 134 B5
Hedges St FAIL M35 105 F2
Hedley St BOL BL1 33 F4
Heginbottom Crs AUL OL6 107 F5
Heights Av WHIT OL12 10 A2
Heights Cl WHIT OL12 10 A1
Heights La OLD OL1 74 A2
WHIT OL12 10 A1
Helena St SLFD M6 99 H5
Helen St BRO M7 101 F5
ECC M30 110 C5
FWTH BL4 66 A4
Helensville Av SLFD M6 100 C5
Helga St NEWH/MOS M40 115 G1
Helias Cl WALK M28 81 E4
Helmclough Wy WALK M28 96 D2
Helmet St CMANE M1 115 F5
Helmsdale WALK M28 81 H5
Helmsdale Av BOLS/LL BL3 47 G3
Helmsdale Cl RAMS BL0 16 B5
Helmshore Av OLDE OL4 76 C1
Helmshore Wk
BRUN/LGST M13 * 128 C1
Helmshore Wy ROY/SHW OL2 60 A1
Helsby Cl OLDE OL4 93 F1
Helsby Gdns BOL BL1 34 A2
Helsby Rd SALE M33 155 F4
Helsby Wk WGTN/LGST M12 115 H5
Helston Cl BRAM/HZG SK7 184 A5
IRL M44 136 D1
Helston Dr ROY/SHW OL2 59 G5
Helston Gv CHD/CHDH SK8 181 H4
Helvellyn Dr MDTN M24 72 A2
Helvellyn Wk OLD OL1 * 75 G3
Hembury Av BNG/LEV M19 143 H5
Hembury Cl MDTN M24 73 E2
Hemlock Av OLDS OL8 91 F4
Hemming Dr ECC M30 111 F4
Hemmington Dr BKLY M9 103 E3
Hemmons Rd
WGTN/LGST M12 144 B1
Hempcroft Rd
HALE/TIMP WA15 166 D4
Hempshaw La STKP SK1 13 H7
Hemsley St BKLY M9 103 F1
Hemsley St South BKLY M9 103 F2
Hemswell Cl SLFD M6 112 D1
Hemsworth Rd BOL BL1 2 B2
GTN M18 130 C5
Henbury Dr MPL/ROM SK6 147 F5
Henbury La CHD/CHDH SK8 192 C1
Henbury Rd WILM/AE SK9 * 192 A3
Henbury St OFTN SK2 172 D5
RUSH/FAL M14 128 B5
Henderson Av SWIN M27 99 E1
Henderson St BNG/LEV M19 144 B3
LIT OL15 20 D3
WHIT OL12 11 G1
Henderville St LIT OL15 20 D2
Hendham Cl BRAM/HZG SK7 184 B2
Hendham Dr ALT WA14 165 E4
Hendham V BKLY M9 102 D3
Hendon Dr BURY BL9 53 G4
EDGY/DAV SK3 170 D2
Hendon Rd BKLY M9 87 H3
Hendriff Pl WHIT OL12 * 10 B2
Hengist St BOLE BL2 49 H2
GTN M18 130 C4
Henley Av CHD/CHDH SK8 182 C2
IRL M44 136 A5
OLDTF/WHR M16 127 E5
Henley Cl TOT/BURYW BL8 52 C1
Henley Dr AULW OL7 119 E1
HALE/TIMP WA15 166 A2
Henley Gv BOLS/LL BL3 64 B1
Henley Pl BNG/LEV M19 144 A5
Henley St CHAD OL9 90 B4
OLD OL1 75 E4
WHIT OL12 10 B3
Henley Ter ROCH OL11 42 D1
Henniker Rd BOLS/LL BL3 63 H2
Henniker St SWIN M27 98 D4
WALK M28 97 E1
Hennon St BOL BL1 33 G5
Henrietta St AUL OL6 119 G1
BOLS/LL BL3 48 A5
OLDTF/WHR M16 127 F3
Henry Herman St
BOLS/LL BL3 63 H1
Henry Lee St BOLS/LL BL3 * 64 B1
Henry St ANC M4 7 H3
BOLE BL2 3 G7
DROY M43 117 H4
DTN/ASHW M34 * 147 F3
ECC M30 110 D4
FAIL M35 105 E3
HYDE SK14 147 H1
LIT OL15 20 C5
MDTN M24 72 C4
MILN OL16 30 A5
OLDTF/WHR M16 127 F3
PWCH M25 86 B2
RAMS BL0 17 E1
STKP SK1 172 C1
WHIT OL12 19 H1
Henshaw Ct
OLDTF/WHR M16 127 E4
Henshaw La CHAD OL9 90 A5
Henshaw St OLD OL1 9 F3
STRET M32 140 B1
Henshaw Wk BOL BL1 33 H4
Henson Gv HALE/TIMP WA15 166 B5
Henthorn St ROY/SHW OL2 60 A3
Henton Wk NEWH/MOS M40 115 F1
Henty Cl ECC M30 110 C4
Henwick Hall Av RAMS BL0 16 C4
Henwood Rd
DID/WITH M20 157 H1
Hepley Rd POY/DIS SK12 195 H4
Hepple Cl HTNM SK4 158 C3
Heppleton Rd
NEWH/MOS M40 89 G5
Hepple Wk AULW OL7 * 106 B5
Hepton St OLD OL1 8 E1
Hepworth St HYDE SK14 148 A4
Herbert St BOLS/LL BL3 67 E1
CHAD OL9 74 C5
CHH M8 * 102 A5
DROY M43 117 G4
DTN/ASHW M34 132 D4
EDGY/DAV SK3 12 D7
OLDE OL4 76 C3
PWCH M25 85 G3
RAD M26 52 A4
STRET M32 140 B1
Hereford Cl AUL OL6 107 G3
ROY/SHW OL2 59 G2
Hereford Crs BOLS/LL BL3 51 E5
Hereford Dr BURY BL9 53 G1
PWCH M25 86 B5
SWIN M27 99 E4
WILM/AE SK9 192 B4
Hereford Gv URM M41 138 C1
Hereford Rd BOL BL1 48 A1
CHD/CHDH SK8 170 D5
ECC M30 99 F5
RDSH SK5 160 D1
Hereford St BOL BL1 34 A4
CHAD OL9 8 A6
ROCH OL11 43 F1
SALE M33 154 C2
Hereford Wy MDTN M24 73 F3
STLY SK15 135 E1
Herevale Gra WALK M28 96 C3
Herevale Hall Dr RAMS BL0 16 C4
Heriston Av DTN/ASHW M34 132 B5
Heritage Gdns DID/WITH M20 157 G4
Herle Dr WYTH/NTH M22 180 B3
Hermitage Av MPL/ROM SK6 163 E4
Hermitage Gdns
MPL/ROM SK6 163 E4
Hermitage Rd CHH M8 102 B1
HALE/TIMP WA15 178 B1
Hermon Av OLDS OL8 91 F4
Herne St OP/CLY M11 116 B5
Heron Av DUK SK16 133 H1
Heron Ct SLFD M6 112 A2
Herondale Cl
NEWH/MOS M40 104 A5
Heron Dr DTN/ASHW M34 118 B4
IRL M44 122 B5
POY/DIS SK12 194 B4
Heron Ml OLDS OL8 * 91 E4
Heron St EDGY/DAV SK3 12 D6
HULME M15 127 H3
OLDS OL8 90 D4
SWIN M27 99 F1
Herries St AUL OL6 120 A1
Herristone Rd CHH M8 87 F5
Herrod Av HTNM SK4 159 H1
Herschel St NEWH/MOS M40 103 H2
Hersey St SLFD M6 * 112 D3
Hertford Rd BKLY M9 103 E1
Hertfordshire Park Cl
ROY/SHW OL2 * 60 A1
Hertford St AULW OL7 119 F4
Hesford Av BKLY M9 103 G3
Hesketh Av BOL BL1 34 A1
DID/WITH M20 157 F3
ROY/SHW OL2 59 H4
Hesketh Rd MILN OL16 11 J6
SALE M33 154 A3
Hesketh St HTNM SK4 159 H3
Hessel St SALQ M50 112 C4
Hester Wk HULME M15 * 128 A2
Heston Av BRUN/LGST M13 143 G1
Heston Dr URM M41 124 B5
Heswall Av DID/WITH M20 142 D4
Heswall Dr TOT/BURYW BL8 36 D1
Heswall Rd RDSH SK5 145 F2
Hetherington Wk
WGTN/LGST M12 129 G4
Hethorn St NEWH/MOS M40 104 B5
Hetton Av BRUN/LGST M13 143 G1
Heversham Av ROY/SHW OL2 60 C2
Hewart Cl NEWH/MOS M40 115 F1
Hewart Dr BURY BL9 39 F4
Hewitt Av DTN/ASHW M34 131 E5
Hewitt St HULME M15 128 A1
Hewlett Rd CCHDY M21 141 E2
Hewlett St BOLE BL2 3 G5
Hexham Av BOL BL1 32 C5
Hexham Cl CHAD OL9 8 A2
OFTN SK2 173 F4
Hexham Rd GTN M18 130 A4
Hexon Cl SLFD M6 112 D2
Hey Bottom La WHIT OL12 19 F2
Heybrook Cl WHTF M45 70 B4
Heybrook Rd NTHM/RTH M23 168 A4
Heybrook St MILN OL16 * 11 G3
Heybury Cl OP/CLY M11 116 A5
Hey Crs OLDE OL4 77 E5
Hey Cft WHTF M45 68 D5
Heyes Av HALE/TIMP WA15 166 C2
Heyes Dr HALE/TIMP WA15 166 C2
Heyes La HALE/TIMP WA15 166 C1
WILM/AE SK9 201 E3
Heyes Leigh
HALE/TIMP WA15 * 166 C2
Heyes Ter HALE/TIMP WA15 * 166 C1
Heyford Av NEWH/MOS M40 89 G5
Heyheads New Rd STLY SK15 109 F3
Hey Hill Cl ROY/SHW OL2 59 H4
Heyland Rd NTHM/RTH M23 167 H3
Heyridge Dr WYTH/NTH M22 156 C5
Heyrod St CMANE M1 7 K6
STLY SK15 109 E5
Heyrose Wk HULME M15 127 G2
Heys Av MPL/ROM SK6 162 D3
NTHM/RTH M23 155 H5
SWIN M27 83 G5
Heys Cl North SWIN M27 83 F5
Heyscroft Rd DID/WITH M20 143 E5
HTNM SK4 158 D4
Heysham Av DID/WITH M20 142 B4
Heyside ROY/SHW OL2 59 H5
Heyside Av ROY/SHW OL2 75 H1
Heyside Cl STLY SK15 109 F4
Heyside Wy BURY BL9 5 F6
Heys La HEY OL10 40 B4
MPL/ROM SK6 162 D3
Heys Rd AUL OL6 120 A2
PWCH M25 86 A2
Heys St TOT/BURYW BL8 4 A4
The Heys AUL OL6 120 A2
PWCH M25 86 A2
RDSH SK5 145 G2
Hey St MILN OL16 11 G5
Heys Vw PWCH M25 86 A3
The Hey ROY/SHW OL2 * 45 H5
Heythrop Cl WHTF M45 69 F3
Heywood Av OLDE OL4 77 F4
SWIN M27 84 C5
Heywood Cl WILM/AE SK9 201 E3
Heywood Fold Rd OLDE OL4 77 E5
Heywood Gdns BOLS/LL BL3 48 D5
PWCH M25 86 A3
Heywood Gv SALE M33 139 G5

Heywood Hall Rd HEY OL10 41 E3
Heywood La OLDE OL4 77 F5
Heywood Old Rd HEY OL10 55 H5
MDTN M24 71 F4
Heywood Park Vw
BOLS/LL BL3 48 D4
Heywood Rd PWCH M25 86 A4
ROCH OL11 42 A4
SALE M33 154 C3
WILM/AE SK9 201 E3
Heywoods Hollow BOL BL1 34 A3
Heywood St BOL BL1 2 E2
BOLS/LL BL3 67 E1
BURY BL9 5 G6
CHH M8 102 B4
FAIL M35 104 C3
OLDE OL4 76 D4
SWIN M27 98 D2
Heywood Wy SLFD M6 113 E2
Heyworth Av MPL/ROM SK6 162 C3
Heyworth St ORD M5 * 112 D4
Hibbert Av DTN/ASHW M34 132 A3
HYDE SK14 148 A2
Hibbert Crs FAIL M35 105 F3
Hibbert La MPL/ROM SK6 175 E4
Hibbert St BOL BL1 34 A4
HTNM SK4 159 H1
OLDE OL4 77 E5
RUSH/FAL M14 128 D5
Hibernia St BOLS/LL BL3 48 B4
Hibernia Wy STRET M32 125 F3
Hibson Av WHIT OL12 28 B1
Hibson Cl WHIT OL12 19 H2
Hickenfield Rd HYDE SK14 134 A3
Hicken Pl HYDE SK14 134 A3
Hickton Dr ALT WA14 165 E4
Higginshaw La OLD OL1 75 H2
Higginshaw Rd OLD OL1 75 G3
Higginson Rd RDSH SK5 145 E4
Higgs Cl OLDE OL4 76 C5
Higham Cl ROY/SHW OL2 59 H4
Higham La HYDE SK14 148 B3
Higham St CHD/CHDH SK8 182 D4
Higham Vw SLFD M6 113 F2
High Ash Gv DTN/ASHW M34 132 A1
High Av BOLE BL2 * 50 B2
High Bank ALT WA14 165 G4
EDGW/EG BL7 23 E4
GTN M18 130 D3
High Bank Av STLY SK15 135 E1
Highbank Crs OLDE OL4 94 B2
High Bank Crs PWCH M25 86 B4
Highbank Dr DID/WITH M20 169 G1
Highbank Gra HOR/BR BL6 46 C1
High Bank Gv PWCH M25 86 B4
High Bank La HOR/BR BL6 46 C2
High Bank Rd DROY M43 117 G5
HYDE SK14 134 A5
SWIN M27 99 G2
Highbank Rd BURY BL9 69 G1
MILN OL16 45 F3
High Bank Side STKP SK1 13 G3
High Bank St BOLE BL2 49 H2
High Barn Cl ROCH OL11 42 D1
High Barn La WHIT OL12 14 B2
High Barn Rd MDTN M24 72 D5
ROY/SHW OL2 59 G5
High Barn St ROY/SHW OL2 59 F5
High Beeches BOLE BL2 51 E4
High Bent Av CHD/CHDH SK8 192 D1
Highbridge Cl BOLE BL2 50 D3
Highbury Av IRL M44 136 C2
URM M41 137 G1
Highbury Rd HTNM SK4 144 C5
OLDTF/WHR M16 142 A2
Highbury Wy ROY/SHW OL2 59 E3
Highclere Av CHH M8 102 A4
Highclere Rd CHH M8 87 E5
Highcliffe Rd BKLY M9 87 F4
Highclove La WALK M28 96 A5
High Crest Av CHD/CHDH SK8 169 E4
Highcroft BOL BL1 34 B3
HYDE SK14 148 A4
Highcroft Av DID/WITH M20 156 D2
High Croft Cl DUK SK16 120 D5
Highcroft Rd MPL/ROM SK6 162 B3
Highcroft Wy WHIT OL12 19 E4
Highdales Rd NTHM/RTH M23 168 A4
High Elm Dr HALE/TIMP WA15 178 D4
High Elm Rd
HALE/TIMP WA15 178 D5
High Elms CHD/CHDH SK8 193 E2
Higher Ainsworth Rd RAD M26 51 H2
Higher Ardwick
WGTN/LGST M12 128 D1
Higher Arthurs UPML OL3 95 E1
Higher Bank Rd LIT OL15 20 D5
Higher Barlow Rw STKP SK1 13 H5
Higher Bents La
MPL/ROM SK6 161 G3
Higher Bridge St BOL BL1 2 E2
Higher Bury St HTNM SK4 12 C2
Higher Cambridge St
HULME M15 128 B3
Higher Carr La UPML OL3 79 E5
Higher Chatham St
HULME M15 * 128 B2
Higher Cleggswood Av
LIT OL15 20 D5
Higher Cft ECC M30 110 D5
WHTF M45 84 D1
Higher Crossbank OLDE OL4 77 E5
Higher Cross La UPML OL3 79 F5
Higher Damshead WHTN BL5 62 A4
Higher Darcy St BOLE BL2 49 H4
Higher Dean St RAD M26 67 H1
Higher Downs ALT WA14 177 F1
Higher Dunscar EDGW/EG BL7 22 D2
Higher Fold Farm
MPL/ROM SK6 * 186 D3
Higher Fold La RAMS BL0 17 F1
Higher Fullwood OLD OL1 60 C5
Higher Gn AUL OL6 119 H1
Higher Henry St HYDE SK14 147 H2
Higher Hillgate STKP SK1 13 H5
Higher House Cl CHAD OL9 90 B3
Higher La WHTF M45 69 F4
Higher Lime Rd OLDS OL8 105 H2
Higher Lomax La HEY OL10 40 C3
Higher Lydgate Pk OLDE OL4 93 H1
Higher Market St FWTH BL4 66 B4
Higher Mdw BNG/LEV M19 144 C2
Higher Ormond St
HULME M15 * 128 B2
Higher Oswald St ANC M4 7 G2
Higher Pk ROY/SHW OL2 45 F5
Higher Pit La BOLE BL2 51 H1
Higher Ridings EDGW/EG BL7 23 E4
Higher Ri ROY/SHW OL2 44 D5
Higher Rd URM M41 139 E1
Higher Rw BURY BL9 5 J2
Higher Shady La EDGW/EG BL7 23 H4
Higher Shore Rd LIT OL15 20 B1
Higher Summerseat RAMS BL0 26 C2
Higher Swan La BOLS/LL BL3 48 C5
Higher Tame St STLY SK15 121 E3
Higher Turf La OLDE OL4 77 G4
Higher Turf Pk ROY/SHW OL2 75 F1
Higher Wharf St AULW OL7 119 G3
Higher Wheat La MILN OL16 11 J5
Higher Wood St MDTN M24 72 C2
Highfield CHD/CHDH SK8 181 H1
SALE M33 154 D3
Highfield Av BOLE BL2 35 H3
HEY OL10 40 B4
MPL/ROM SK6 161 G4
RAD M26 68 D3
Highfield Cl EDGY/DAV SK3 172 A5
HYDE SK14 134 A2
STRET M32 140 A3
Highfield Crs WILM/AE SK9 199 F1
Highfield Dr ECC M30 111 E2
FWTH BL4 65 F5
MDTN M24 72 C5
MOSL OL5 108 D2
ROY/SHW OL2 75 F2
SWIN M27 99 H3
URM M41 124 B5
Highfield Est WILM/AE SK9 199 F1
Highfield Gdns HYDE SK14 134 A5
Highfield Gln AUL OL6 108 A5
Highfield La BURY BL9 69 G1
Highfield Pk HTNM SK4 158 C4
Highfield Park Rd
MPL/ROM SK6 161 F2
Highfield Pkwy
BRAM/HZG SK7 193 G3
Highfield Pl GTN M18 * 131 E4
PWCH M25 85 H2
Highfield Range GTN M18 * 131 E4
Highfield Rd BNG/LEV M19 144 C2
BOL BL1 33 E4
BRAM/HZG SK7 184 A1
BRAM/HZG SK7 185 H2
CHD/CHDH SK8 182 C3
ECC M30 111 E1
FWTH BL4 64 D4
HALE/TIMP WA15 166 C4
HALE/TIMP WA15 178 B2
LHULT M38 81 E2
MILN OL16 31 H5
MPL/ROM SK6 175 E4
POY/DIS SK12 * 194 B3
PWCH M25 85 H1
ROCH OL11 28 B2
SLFD M6 113 E2
STRET M32 140 A3
Highfield St BRO M7 102 A3
CHAD OL9 8 D3
DTN/ASHW M34 132 C2
DUK SK16 119 G4
EDGY/DAV SK3 12 A5
FWTH BL4 82 D1
MDTN M24 73 E4
Highfield Ter BKLY M9 103 E2
OLDE OL4 76 C2
Highgate BOLS/LL BL3 62 D2
Highgate Av URM M41 123 H4
Highgate Crs GTN M18 130 C4
Highgate Dr LHULT M38 80 D2
ROY/SHW OL2 58 D2
Highgate La LHULT M38 80 D2
WHIT OL12 18 B2
Highgate Rd ALT WA14 165 E5
High Gates SALE M33 155 F1
Highgrove HALE/TIMP WA15 154 B5
Highgrove Cl BOL BL1 34 A3
High Grove Rd
CHD/CHDH SK8 169 H4
OLDE OL4 94 B2
The Highgrove BOL BL1 32 A5
High Houses BOL BL1 * 22 C5
High Hurst Cl MDTN M24 * 71 H5
Highland Rd EDGW/EG BL7 23 H3
Highlands LIT OL15 20 D5
ROY/SHW OL2 74 D1
Highlands Dr OFTN SK2 173 G3
Highlands Rd OFTN SK2 173 G3
ROCH OL11 41 E1
ROY/SHW OL2 59 G1
ROY/SHW OL2 74 D1
The Highlands MOSL OL5 * 108 C1
High La CCHDY M21 141 F3
MPL/ROM SK6 162 A2
High Lea CHD/CHDH SK8 169 H4
High Lee La OLDE OL4 61 G5
High Legh Rd OP/CLY M11 117 E5
High Level Rd ROCH OL11 30 B5
High Meadow
CHD/CHDH SK8 * 182 B4
Highmeadow RAD M26 68 A3
High Mdw EDGW/EG BL7 23 G3
MPL/ROM SK6 162 B3
Highmead St GTN M18 130 C3
Highmead Wk
OLDTF/WHR M16 127 G3
High Moor Crs OLDE OL4 76 D3
Highmore Dr BKLY M9 88 B4
High Mt BOLE BL2 35 F3
High Peak Rd AUL OL6 108 B4
WHIT OL12 18 B2
High Peak St
NEWH/MOS M40 104 A4
Highshore Dr CHH M8 102 A3
High Stile La UPML OL3 79 G2
High Stile St FWTH BL4 66 B5
Highstone Dr CHH M8 102 D4
High St ALT WA14 165 G5
ANC M4 7 G3
BOLS/LL BL3 48 D5
BOLS/LL BL3 67 E1
BRAM/HZG SK7 185 G2
CHD/CHDH SK8 170 A3
DROY M43 117 H4
HEY OL10 40 C4
HYDE SK14 134 A5
LIT OL15 20 C3
MDTN M24 72 D3
MOSL OL5 94 A5
OLD OL1 9 G3
OLDE OL4 92 D1
ROY/SHW OL2 * 59 E5
ROY/SHW OL2 60 A3
STKP SK1 13 G3
STLY SK15 120 D4
TOT/BURYW BL8 37 E3
UPML OL3 79 E4
WALK M28 81 H4
WHIT OL12 10 C5
Highthorne Gn ROY/SHW OL2 58 D1
High View St BOL BL1 33 H1
BOLS/LL BL3 * 48 B5
Highwood ROCH OL11 28 B2
Highwood Cl BOLE BL2 * 35 G5
High Wood Fold
MPL/ROM SK6 175 H1
Highworth Cl BOLS/LL BL3 * 48 D4
Highworth Dr
NEWH/MOS M40 89 G5
Higifield Av SALE M33 154 D3
Higson Av CCHDY M21 141 F4
ECC M30 110 D5
MPL/ROM SK6 161 G4
Hilary Av CHD/CHDH SK8 182 A4
OLDS OL8 106 C1
Hilary Cl HTNM SK4 12 C1
Hilary Gv FWTH BL4 65 H5
Hilary Rd WYTH/NTH M22 180 A3
Hilary St ROCH OL11 * 42 C5
Hilbre Av ROY/SHW OL2 75 E2
Hilbury Av BKLY M9 103 E1
Hilda Av CHD/CHDH SK8 170 B4
TOT/BURYW BL8 26 A5
Hilda Gv RDSH SK5 160 A2
Hilda Rd HYDE SK14 147 H4
Hilda St BOLS/LL BL3 49 F5
CHAD OL9 8 D2
HEY OL10 41 E4
Hilden Ct OLDTF/WHR M16 127 G4
Hilden St BOLE BL2 3 H6
Hilditch Cl NTHM/RTH M23 168 A3
Hiley Rd ECC M30 110 A5
Hillam Cl URM M41 139 F2
Hillary Av AULW OL7 107 E5
Hillary Rd HYDE SK14 134 B3
Hillbank Cl BOL BL1 33 F3
Hill Bank Cl STLY SK15 109 E5
Hillbank St MDTN M24 57 G3
Hillbre Wy WILM/AE SK9 192 A3
Hillbrook Av NEWH/MOS M40 * 89 E5
Hillbrook Rd BRAM/HZG SK7 193 G1
STKP SK1 172 D1
Hillbury Rd BRAM/HZG SK7 184 A3
Hill Cl OLDE OL4 92 B2
Hillcote Wk GTN M18 * 130 A2
Hill Cot Rd BOL BL1 34 A1
Hill Court Ms MPL/ROM SK6 162 A4
Hillcourt Rd MPL/ROM SK6 162 B2
MPL/ROM SK6 186 D5
Hillcourt St CMANE M1 128 B1
Hill Crs BKLY M9 87 F4
Hillcrest HYDE SK14 148 B4
MDTN M24 72 C1
SLFD M6 * 111 H2
Hillcrest Av HEY OL10 40 B3
Hill Crest Av HTNM SK4 158 D4
Hillcrest Crs HEY OL10 40 B3
Hillcrest Dr BNG/LEV M19 144 C4
DTN/ASHW M34 147 F2
Hillcrest Rd BRAM/HZG SK7 184 A3
OFTN SK2 172 D3
PWCH M25 85 G5
ROCH OL11 42 C4
Hillcroft OFTN SK2 173 F3
OLDS OL8 106 D2
Hillcroft Cl CHH M8 102 B2
Hillcroft Rd ALT WA14 164 D4
Hilldale Av BKLY M9 88 A3
Hill Dr WILM/AE SK9 192 B4
Hill End MPL/ROM SK6 * 162 C2
Hillend La HYDE SK14 149 H2
Hillend Pl NTHM/RTH M23 155 H4
Hillend Rd NTHM/RTH M23 155 H4
Hill Farm Cl OLDS OL8 92 A4
Hillfield ORD M5 112 C3
Hillfield Cl BRUN/LGST M13 129 E3
Hillfield Dr BOLE BL2 34 C5
WALK M28 96 B3
Hillfield Wk BOLE BL2 34 C5
Hillfoot Wk HULME M15 * 127 G2
Hillgate Av ORD M5 127 E1
Hillgate St AUL OL6 119 H1
Hillier St BKLY M9 103 F2
Hillier St North BKLY M9 103 F2
Hillingdon Cl OLDS OL8 105 G1
Hillingdon Dr NEWH/MOS M40 89 E5
Hillingdon Rd STRET M32 140 C2
WHTF M45 68 D5
Hillington Rd EDGY/DAV SK3 12 A6
SALE M33 153 H2
Hillkirk Dr WHIT OL12 18 B5
Hillkirk St OP/CLY M11 115 H4
Hill La BKLY M9 88 A4
BOLE BL2 3 H2
Hillman Cl NEWH/MOS M40 103 E5
Hill Mt DUK SK16 120 D5
Hill Ri ALT WA14 164 D4
MPL/ROM SK6 162 A4
RAMS BL0 16 B4
Hillsborough Dr BURY BL9 70 A2
Hill's Ct TOT/BURYW BL8 37 G2
Hillsdale Gv BOLE BL2 35 F3
Hill Side BOL BL1 47 G2
Hillside Av BRO M7 100 D2
EDGW/EG BL7 23 G4
FWTH BL4 65 H5
HYDE SK14 148 B5
OLDE OL4 76 B5
OLDE OL4 93 G2
ROY/SHW OL2 59 F4
ROY/SHW OL2 60 C2
STLY SK15 109 G4
UPML OL3 79 F1
WALK M28 81 H3
WHTF M45 69 F2
Hillside Cl BOLE BL2 35 F1
BOLS/LL BL3 63 E2
BRAM/HZG SK7 184 B5
NEWH/MOS M40 103 H1
Hillside Crs AUL OL6 108 A5
BURY BL9 27 G5
Hillside Dr MDTN M24 72 D3
SWIN M27 100 A4
Hillside Gv MPL/ROM SK6 163 G5
Hillside Rd HALE/TIMP WA15 178 B1
MPL/ROM SK6 162 B1
OFTN SK2 173 E2
RAMS BL0 16 B3
Hillside St BOLS/LL BL3 48 C4
Hillside Vw DTN/ASHW M34 147 E4
Hillside Wk WHIT OL12 18 C4
Hillside Wy WHIT OL12 14 B4
Hills La BURY BL9 70 B2
Hillspring Rd OLDE OL4 93 F1
Hillstone Av WHIT OL12 18 B4
Hillstone Cl TOT/BURYW BL8 26 A1
Hill St AULW OL7 119 F3
BRO M7 101 G4
BURY BL9 16 D5
DID/WITH M20 142 D4
HEY OL10 40 D4
MDTN M24 72 D1
MILN OL16 10 E7
MPL/ROM SK6 162 A4
OLDE OL4 76 A5
RAD M26 52 A5
ROY/SHW OL2 60 B3
TOT/BURYW BL8 37 E2
Hill Top BOLS/LL BL3 50 D5
HALE/TIMP WA15 178 B3
MPL/ROM SK6 162 A3
Hill Top Av CHD/CHDH SK8 183 E4
PWCH M25 86 A3
WILM/AE SK9 199 E2
Hilltop Av BKLY M9 88 A4
WHTF M45 70 A4
Hill Top Ct CHD/CHDH SK8 183 E3
Hill Top Dr HALE/TIMP WA15 178 B2
ROCH OL11 43 F4
Hilltop Dr MPL/ROM SK6 174 B2
ROY/SHW OL2 75 F2
TOT/BURYW BL8 25 H5
Hilltop Gv WHTF M45 70 A4
Hill Top Rd WALK M28 82 A3
Hill Vw STLY SK15 135 E2
Hill View Cl OLD OL1 76 B2
Hillview Rd BOL BL1 * 33 H2
DTN/ASHW M34 145 G2
Hillwood Av CHH M8 87 E4
Hillyard St TOT/BURYW BL8 37 H3
Hilly Cft EDGW/EG BL7 23 E3
Hilmarton Cl BOLE BL2 35 F1
Hilrose Av URM M41 139 F1
Hilton Av URM M41 138 D1
Hilton Ct EDGY/DAV SK3 * 12 E5
Hilton Crs AUL OL6 107 F5
PWCH M25 86 A5
WALK M28 96 C4
Hilton Dr AULW OL7 106 C5
IRL M44 150 B1
PWCH M25 86 A5
Hilton Fold La MDTN M24 73 E3
Hilton Gv POY/DIS SK12 195 E3
WALK M28 81 G4
Hilton La PWCH M25 85 H5
WALK M28 81 G5
Hilton Rd BRAM/HZG SK7 184 A2
BURY BL9 4 E5
POY/DIS SK12 187 G5
POY/DIS SK12 196 B2
WYTH/NTH M22 168 D4
Hiltons Cl OLDS OL8 8 E7
Hiltons Farm Cl
DTN/ASHW M34 132 B3
Hilton Sq SWIN M27 99 F1
Hilton St ANC M4 7 G3
BOLE BL2 49 H2
BRO M7 101 H5
BURY BL9 5 F1
EDGY/DAV SK3 12 D5
HYDE SK14 * 134 A3
LHULT M38 81 F3
Hilton St North BRO M7 101 G4
Hilton Wk MDTN M24 71 H4
Himley Rd OP/CLY M11 116 D2
Hinchcombe Cl LHULT M38 * 81 F1
Hinchley Rd BKLY M9 89 E4
Hinchley Wy SWIN M27 84 A5
Hinckley St OP/CLY M11 116 A5
Hindburn Cl WHTF M45 70 A4
Hindburn Dr WALK M28 96 B2
Hinde St NEWH/MOS M40 103 H2
Hind Hill St HEY OL10 41 E5
Hindle Dr ROY/SHW OL2 74 D1
Hindle St RAD M26 68 B1
Hindley Av WYTH/NTH M22 180 A2
Hindley St AULW OL7 119 E4
STKP SK1 13 H6
Hindsford Cl NTHM/RTH M23 155 E5
Hinds La BURY BL9 52 D2
TOT/BURYW BL8 37 H5
Hind St BOLE BL2 50 A2
Hinkler Av BOLS/LL BL3 64 D1
Hinton WHIT OL12 10 B4
Hinton Cl ROCH OL11 28 B5
Hinton Gv HYDE SK14 148 C3
Hinton St ANC M4 * 7 J1
OLDS OL8 9 H6
Hipley Cl MPL/ROM SK6 161 H1
Hirons La OLDE OL4 93 F2
Hirst Av WALK M28 82 A2
Hitchen Cl DUK SK16 134 A1
Hitchen Dr DUK SK16 134 A1
Hitchin Wk BRUN/LGST M13 128 D3
Hive St OLDS OL8 90 C5
Hobart Cl BRAM/HZG SK7 194 A3
Hobart St BOL BL1 33 G4
GTN M18 130 C3
Hob Hl STLY SK15 120 C4
Hob Mill Ri MOSL OL5 94 B3
Hobson Ct DTN/ASHW M34 132 B2
Hobson Crs DTN/ASHW M34 132 B2
Hobson Moor Rd HYDE SK14 135 H2
Hobson St FAIL M35 104 C4
OLD OL1 9 G5
OP/CLY M11 131 F1
RDSH SK5 145 F1
Hockenhull Cl
WYTH/NTH M22 180 D2
Hockerley Cl SALE M33 153 G1
Hockley Cl POY/DIS SK12 195 G4
Hockley Paddock
POY/DIS SK12 195 G4
Hockley Rd NTHM/RTH M23 167 G4
POY/DIS SK12 195 G4
Hodder Av LIT OL15 20 C2
Hodder Bank OFTN SK2 173 F4
Hodder Wy WHTF M45 70 B4
Hoddesdon St CHH M8 102 C3
Hodge Clough Rd OLD OL1 60 C5
Hodge La HYDE SK14 149 H3
SLFD M6 113 E4
Hodge Rd OLD OL1 76 C1
WALK M28 82 A5
Hodge St BKLY M9 103 G1
Hodgson Dr HALE/TIMP WA15 166 B1
Hodgson St AUL OL6 119 F3
CHH M8 102 A5
Hodnett Av URM M41 137 G2
Hodson Fold OLDS OL8 106 D1
Hodson Rd SWIN M27 83 H5
Hogarth Ri OLD OL1 60 C5
Hogarth Rd MPL/ROM SK6 175 G1
ROCH OL11 43 E4
Holbeach Cl TOT/BURYW BL8 38 A1
Holbeck Av WHIT OL12 18 C4
Holbeck Gv RUSH/FAL M14 129 F4
Holbeton Cl CHH M8 101 H5
Holborn Av FAIL M35 105 G3
RAD M26 51 H5
Holborn Dr CHH M8 102 C5
Holborn Gdns ROCH OL11 42 C1
Holborn Sq ROCH OL11 42 C1
Holborn St ROCH OL11 42 C1
STKP SK1 13 G4
Holbrook Av LHULT M38 81 F1
Holbrook St CMANE M1 * 7 G7
Holcombe Av TOT/BURYW BL8 37 G4
Holcombe Cl ALT WA14 165 E3
FWTH BL4 82 D2
OLDE OL4 77 F5
SLFD M6 113 F3
Holcombe Ct RAMS BL0 26 A1
Holcombe Crs FWTH BL4 82 D1
Holcombe Lee RAMS BL0 16 B5
Holcombe Old Rd
TOT/BURYW BL8 16 A5
Holcombe Rd BOLS/LL BL3 66 C1
RUSH/FAL M14 143 G4
TOT/BURYW BL8 26 A1
Holcombe View Cl OLDE OL4 76 C2
Holden Av BOL BL1 22 D5
BURY BL9 39 H2
OLDTF/WHR M16 142 A2
RAMS BL0 16 B3
Holden Clough Dr AULW OL7 106 D3
Holden Fold La ROY/SHW OL2 74 D2
Holden Rd BRO M7 101 G1
Holden St AUL OL6 119 H1
OLDS OL8 91 G4
WHIT OL12 11 F1
Holder Av BOLS/LL BL3 51 E4
Holderness Dr ROY/SHW OL2 74 D2
Holdgate Cl HULME M15 127 H3
Holdsworth St SWIN M27 98 C3
Holebottom AUL OL6 107 F4
Hole House Fold
MPL/ROM SK6 162 A4
Holford Av RUSH/FAL M14 142 D1
Holford Wk MILN OL16 31 E4
Holgate St OLDE OL4 76 D3
Holhouse La TOT/BURYW BL8 26 A1
Holiday La OFTN SK2 173 G3
Holkar Mdw EDGW/EG BL7 23 G3
Holker Cl BRUN/LGST M13 129 E4
POY/DIS SK12 195 G3
Holkham Cl ANC M4 * 115 F3
Holland Av STLY SK15 120 D3
Holland Ct POY/DIS SK12 195 F4
RAD M26 52 D5
Holland Gv AUL OL6 107 E4
Holland Ri WHIT OL12 10 B5
Holland Rd BRAM/HZG SK7 183 H5
CHH M8 87 E5
HYDE SK14 134 A3
Holland St BOL BL1 34 A2
DTN/ASHW M34 132 A4
HEY OL10 41 E4
MILN OL16 20 A4
NEWH/MOS M40 115 G3
RAD M26 52 D5
SLFD M6 100 C5
WHIT OL12 10 A6
Holland St East
DTN/ASHW M34 132 A4
Holland St West
DTN/ASHW M34 131 H4
Hollies Dr MPL/ROM SK6 175 F4
The Hollies CHD/CHDH SK8 * 169 G4
DID/WITH M20 157 E3
Hollin Acre WHTN BL5 62 A4
Hollin Bank HTNM SK4 144 D4
Hollin Crs UPML OL3 94 B3
Hollin Dr MDTN M24 56 B5
Holliney Av WYTH/NTH M22 181 E3
Holliney Rd
WYTH/NTH M22 181 E3
Holling Gn MDTN M24 72 D1
Hollingworth Av
NEWH/MOS M40 90 A5
Hollingworth Cl STKP SK1 * 13 G5
Hollingworth Dr
MPL/ROM SK6 187 E1
Hollingworth Rd LIT OL15 21 E4
MPL/ROM SK6 161 F2
Hollingworth St CHAD OL9 90 C4
Hollinhall St OLDE OL4 76 C5
Hollin Hey Rd BOL BL1 32 B3
Hollinhurst Dr HOR/BR BL6 46 D2
Hollinhurst Rd RAD M26 68 D2

Hollin La MDTN M24 56 C5
ROCH OL11 28 B5
WILM/AE SK9 191 E2
Hollins FWTH BL4 * 64 C4
Hollins Av HYDE SK14 148 A4
OLDE OL4 77 E4
Hollins Brook Cl BURY BL9 * 54 A4
Hollins Brook Wy BURY BL9 54 A3
Hollins Brow BURY BL9 53 G5
Hollins Cl BURY BL9 54 A5
Hollinsclough Cl
WYTH/NTH M22 168 D4
Hollinscroft Av
HALE/TIMP WA15 167 E4
Hollins Green Rd
MPL/ROM SK6 175 E3
Hollins Gv SALE M33 154 B2
WGTN/LGST M12 129 H5
Hollins La BURY BL9 53 H4
MOSL OL5 109 E1
MPL/ROM SK6 175 E3
MPL/ROM SK6 175 H1
UPML OL3 95 G2
Hollins Ms BURY BL9 54 B5
Hollins Mt MPL/ROM SK6 175 G1
Hollins Rd OLDE OL4 77 E4
OLDS OL8 90 D5
OLDS OL8 91 G4
Hollins St BOLE BL2 3 J7
OLDE OL4 93 E1
STLY SK15 120 C5
Hollinswood Rd BOLE BL2 3 K6
WALK M28 96 C4
Hollinwell Cl MDTN M24 56 C5
Hollinwood Av CHAD OL9 90 B5
NEWH/MOS M40 89 G5
Hollinwood La MPL/ROM SK6 187 G2
Holloway Dr WALK M28 98 B1
Hollowbrook Wy WHIT OL12 29 G1
Hollow End RDSH SK5 145 H4
Hollowfield ROCH OL11 28 A2
Hollow Mdw RAD M26 83 F1
Hollowspell WHIT OL12 19 H5
The Hollows
CHD/CHDH SK8 * 181 H3
Hollow Vale Dr RDSH SK5 145 G3
Holly Av CHD/CHDH SK8 170 A4
URM M41 138 B1
WALK M28 82 B5
Holly Bank DROY M43 118 B2
NEWH/MOS M40 * 104 B3
ROY/SHW OL2 59 E4
SALE M33 154 D3
Hollybank Ri DUK SK16 120 C5
Holly Bank Rd WILM/AE SK9 199 E1
Hollybank St RAD M26 68 A1
Hollybrook Dene
MPL/ROM SK6 162 D4
Hollybush St GTN M18 130 D2
Holly Cl HALE/TIMP WA15 166 B3
Holly Ct HYDE SK14 148 C1
Hollycroft Av BOLE BL2 50 B4
WYTH/NTH M22 168 C3
Holly Dene Dr HOR/BR BL6 46 C2
Holly Dr SALE M33 154 B2
Hollyedge Dr PWCH M25 85 H5
Holly Fold WHTF M45 69 G3
Holly Gra ALT WA14 177 G2
BRAM/HZG SK7 184 A1
Holly Gv BOL BL1 33 F5
CHAD OL9 74 C4
DTN/ASHW M34 132 D5
FWTH BL4 65 F4
HOR/BR BL6 46 C2
OLDE OL4 76 D4
SALE M33 155 E2
STLY SK15 120 B5
Hollyhedge Av
WYTH/NTH M22 168 C4
Hollyhedge Court Rd
WYTH/NTH M22 168 D4
Hollyhedge Rd
NTHM/RTH M23 168 A4
Hollyhey Dr NTHM/RTH M23 156 A5
Hollyhouse Dr MPL/ROM SK6 161 H1
Holly House Dr URM M41 137 H1
Hollyhurst WALK M28 98 A4
Holly La OLDS OL8 90 D5
WILM/AE SK9 190 D2
Holly Mill Crs BOL BL1 34 A2
Hollymount Av OFTN SK2 172 D4
Hollymount Dr OFTN SK2 172 D4
OLDE OL4 76 D1
Hollymount Gdns OFTN SK2 173 E4
Hollymount Rd OFTN SK2 172 D4
Holly Oak Gdns HEY OL10 40 D5
Holly Rd BRAM/HZG SK7 193 H2
HTNM SK4 159 F1
MPL/ROM SK6 186 D5
POY/DIS SK12 195 F4
SWIN M27 98 C4
Holly Rd North WILM/AE SK9 198 D4
Holly Rd South WILM/AE SK9 198 D5
Holly Royde Cl DID/WITH M20 142 C5
Holly St BOL BL1 34 A2
BURY BL9 5 H4
BURY BL9 16 D5
DROY M43 117 E3
MILN OL16 43 G4
STKP SK1 13 K4
TOT/BURYW BL8 26 K5
WGTN/LGST M12 115 H5
WHIT OL12 19 H2
Hollythorn Av CHD/CHDH SK8 183 F5
Hollyway WYTH/NTH M22 168 D1
Hollywood Rd BOL BL1 33 E4
Hollywood Wy HTNM SK4 12 C4
Holmbrook Wk CHH M8 102 B4
Holm Ct SLFD M6 * 113 F2
Holmcroft Rd GTN M18 144 D1
Holmdale Av BNG/LEV M19 158 B1
Holme Av TOT/BURYW BL8 37 H1
Holme Beech Gv OFTN SK2 * 172 D1
Holme Crs ROY/SHW OL2 74 D2
Holmefield SALE M33 154 C2
Holme Park Gdns WALK M28 96 B5
Holme Park Wy FAIL M35 105 G3
Holme Rd DID/WITH M20 157 E3
Holmes Cottages BOL BL1 * 33 F3
Holmes Rd WHIT OL12 29 G4
Holmes St BOLS/LL BL3 49 E5
CHD/CHDH SK8 170 B3
OFTN SK2 13 F7
WHIT OL12 19 H5
WHIT OL12 29 G3
Holme St HYDE SK14 147 H1
Holmeswood Cl WILM/AE SK9 199 F2
Holmeswood Rd BOLS/LL BL3 64 C2
Holmfield Av BKLY M9 103 G3
PWCH M25 86 B4
Holmfield Av West BKLY M9 103 G4
Holmfield Cl HTNM SK4 159 G3
Holmfield Dr CHD/CHDH SK8 183 E4
Holmfield Gn BOLS/LL BL3 63 G1
Holmfirth Rd UPML OL3 95 G3
Holmfirth St BRUN/LGST M13 129 G4
Holmlea Rd DROY M43 117 F3
Holmleigh Av BKLY M9 103 F1
Holmpark Rd OP/CLY M11 131 E1
Holmside Gdns BNG/LEV M19 158 A2
Holmwood ALT WA14 176 D1
Holmwood Rd DID/WITH M20 157 G1
Holroyd St MILN OL16 10 E7
OP/CLY M11 * 116 B5
Holset Dr ALT WA14 165 E4
Holst Av CHH M8 102 B4
Holstein Av WHIT OL12 18 C4
Holtby St BKLY M9 103 F1
Holthouse Rd TOT/BURYW BL8 36 D1
Holt La FAIL M35 105 G3
Holt Lane Ms FAIL M35 105 F3
Holts La OLDE OL4 92 C3
WILM/AE SK9 191 E4
Holts Ter WHIT OL12 10 B1
Holt St ALT WA14 165 F2
BOLS/LL BL3 48 C4
DTN/ASHW M34 118 D5
ECC M30 110 D5
MILN OL16 * 44 D1
NEWH/MOS M40 103 G5
OLDE OL4 76 B4
RAMS BL0 17 E2
STKP SK1 13 H6
SWIN M27 84 A5
WHIT OL12 14 B4
Holt St West RAMS BL0 16 C3
Holt Town NEWH/MOS M40 115 H3
Holwick Rd NTHM/RTH M23 155 G5
Holwood Dr OLDTF/WHR M16 142 A3
Holy Harbour St BOL BL1 * 33 F4
Holyhurst Wk BOL BL1 * 33 H4
Holyoake Rd WALK M28 82 A5
Holyoake St DROY M43 118 B3
Holyoake St NEWH/MOS M40 104 B4
Holyrood Cl PWCH M25 86 B1
Holyrood Dr PWCH M25 86 B1
SWIN M27 98 B3
Holyrood Gv PWCH M25 86 B1
Holyrood Rd PWCH M25 86 B2
Holyrood St
NEWH/MOS M40 117 E1
OLD OL1 75 H3
Holywood St RUSH/FAL M14 128 C5
Homebury Dr OP/CLY M11 * 116 C3
Home Dr MDTN M24 88 C1
Home Farm Av HYDE SK14 149 H2
Homelands Cl SALE M33 154 A4
Homelands Rd SALE M33 154 A4
Homer Dr MPL/ROM SK6 175 G1
Homerton Rd
NEWH/MOS M40 116 C1
Homestead Cl PART M31 151 F2
Homestead Crs BNG/LEV M19 158 A3
Homestead Gdns WHIT OL12 20 A3
Homestead Rd POY/DIS SK12 197 H1
Hometel RUSH/FAL M14 143 E2
Homewood Av
WYTH/NTH M22 156 C5
Homewood Rd
WYTH/NTH M22 156 B5
Honduras St OLDE OL4 9 K3
Hondwith Cl BOLE BL2 34 C1
Honeycombe Cottages
CHD/CHDH SK8 * 170 B4
Honey St CHH M8 114 D1
Honeysuckle Cl
MPL/ROM SK6 161 H1
NTHM/RTH M23 155 E5
Honeysuckle Dr STLY SK15 121 E3
Honeysuckle Wy WHIT OL12 18 C5
Honeywell La OLDS OL8 91 G4
Honeywood Cl RAMS BL0 16 B5
Honford Rd WYTH/NTH M22 168 A5
Hong Kong Av
HALE/TIMP WA15 179 H4
Honister Dr MDTN M24 72 C2
Honister Rd BKLY M9 103 G3
Honister Wy ROCH OL11 42 A2
Honiton Av HYDE SK14 149 E1
Honiton Cl CHAD OL9 73 H3
HEY OL10 55 H1
Honiton Dr BOLE BL2 50 D3
Honiton Gv RAD M26 51 G4
Honiton Wy ALT WA14 164 D3
Honor St BRUN/LGST M13 129 F5
Hood Sq OLDE OL4 93 F2
Hood St ANC M4 7 J3
Hoole Cl CHD/CHDH SK8 170 D4
Hooley Range HTNM SK4 159 E3
Hooper St EDGY/DAV SK3 13 F4
OLDE OL4 9 K5
WGTN/LGST M12 115 G5
Hooton St BOLS/LL BL3 64 B1
NEWH/MOS M40 115 H2
Hopcroft Cl BKLY M9 87 G1
Hope Av BOLE BL2 3 K7
BOLE BL2 35 F1
LHULT M38 81 G3
STRET M32 125 G5
WILM/AE SK9 192 A4
Hopecourt Cl SLFD M6 112 A1
Hopedale Rd RDSH SK5 145 F5
Hopefield St BOLS/LL BL3 48 C5
Hopefold Dr WALK M28 82 B5
Hope Green Wy POY/DIS SK12 195 E5
Hope Hey La LHULT M38 81 E2
Hopelea St DID/WITH M20 142 D4
Hope Park Cl PWCH M25 86 A4
Hope Park Rd PWCH M25 86 A4
Hope Pl ROCH OL11 * 42 B5
Hope Rd PWCH M25 85 H5
RUSH/FAL M14 129 E4
SALE M33 154 C3
Hopes Carr STKP SK1 13 H4
Hope St AUL OL6 107 G5
BRAM/HZG SK7 185 E2
BRO M7 101 G3
CMANE M1 7 H5
DTN/ASHW M34 132 B3
DUK SK16 119 H5
HEY OL10 56 C1
HTNM SK4 12 D3
LHULT M38 81 F3
OLD OL1 76 A5
ORD M5 113 H4
RAMS BL0 16 C3
ROY/SHW OL2 60 A2
SWIN M27 99 F2
WHIT OL12 10 C4
Hope Ter DUK SK16 * 119 G5
EDGY/DAV SK3 * 13 F6
Hopkin Av OLD OL1 76 A4
Hopkin Fld ALT WA14 177 E3
Hopkinson Av
DTN/ASHW M34 132 B3
Hopkinson Cl UPML OL3 79 E4
Hopkinson Rd BKLY M9 88 A2
Hopkins St HYDE SK14 133 H4
Hopkin St OLD OL1 9 H3
WGTN/LGST M12 129 H5
Hoppet La DROY M43 118 B3
Hopton Av WYTH/NTH M22 180 D1
Hopwood Av ECC M30 111 E2
HEY OL10 56 A1
Hopwood Cl BURY BL9 69 G1
Hopwood Rd MDTN M24 56 D5
Hopwood St CSLFD M3 * 6 C2
NEWH/MOS M40 104 A4
SWIN M27 99 F2
Horace Barnes Cl
RUSH/FAL M14 128 B5
Horace Gv HTNM SK4 159 H2
Horace St BOL BL1 33 G4
Horatio St GTN M18 * 131 E2
Horbury Av GTN M18 130 C5
Horbury Dr TOT/BURYW BL8 37 H4
Horeb St BOLS/LL BL3 48 C4
Horest La UPML OL3 61 G1
Horley Cl TOT/BURYW BL8 26 D4
Hornbeam Cl
HALE/TIMP WA15 167 F4
SALE M33 153 F1
Hornbeam Ct SLFD M6 113 F2
Hornbeam Rd BNG/LEV M19 144 B1
Hornby Av BKLY M9 88 B2
Hornby Dr BOLS/LL BL3 63 E2
Hornby Rd STRET M32 126 C4
Hornby St BURY BL9 38 C1
CHH M8 114 C1
HEY OL10 41 E5
MDTN M24 72 D4
OLDS OL8 8 D6
Horncastle Cl TOT/BURYW BL8 38 A1
Horncastle Rd
NEWH/MOS M40 104 A1
Hornchurch Ct HEY OL10 56 B2
Hornchurch St HULME M15 127 H2
Horne Dr ANC M4 115 F3
Horne St BURY BL9 53 G1
Hornsea Cl CHAD OL9 74 A3
TOT/BURYW BL8 37 E4
Hornsea Rd OFTN SK2 173 H4
Hornsea Wk OP/CLY M11 * 116 B4
Horridge Fold Av WHTN BL5 63 G2
Horridge St TOT/BURYW BL8 37 G2
Horrobin Fold EDGW/EG BL7 * 23 H1
Horrobin La EDGW/EG BL7 23 H1
Horrocks Fold Av BOL BL1 22 C5
Horrocks St BOLS/LL BL3 47 H4
RAD M26 * 52 D5
Horsa St BOLE BL2 3 J1
Horsedge St OLD OL1 9 H1
Horsefield Av WHIT OL12 18 B2
Horsefield Cl CCHDY M21 142 A4
Horseforth La UPML OL3 94 D3
Horseshoe La EDGW/EG BL7 23 F3
MDTN M24 90 A1
WILM/AE SK9 200 D3
Horsfield St BOLS/LL BL3 47 H5
Horsfield Wy MPL/ROM SK6 146 D5
Horsham Av BRAM/HZG SK7 184 D3
Horsham Cl TOT/BURYW BL8 26 D4
Horsham St SLFD M6 112 D3
Horstead Wk BNG/LEV M19 144 A1
Horton Av BOL BL1 22 D5
Horton Rd RUSH/FAL M14 142 C1
Horton St STKP SK1 172 A2
Hortree Rd STRET M32 140 C1
Horwood Crs DID/WITH M20 158 A1
Hoscar Dr BNG/LEV M19 143 G4
Hoskins Cl WGTN/LGST M12 129 H3
Hospital Rd EDGW/EG BL7 23 F3
SWIN M27 99 G3
Hotel Rd MANAIR M90 180 B5
Hotel St BOL BL1 2 E5
Hothersall Rd RDSH SK5 145 F4
Hotspur Cl RUSH/FAL M14 142 C3
Hough Cl OLDS OL8 91 H5
Hough End Av CCHDY M21 141 G5
Houghend Crs CCHDY M21 142 A4
Hough Fold Wy BOLE BL2 35 E2
Hough Hall Rd
NEWH/MOS M40 103 G2
Hough Hill Rd STLY SK15 120 D4
Hough La EDGW/EG BL7 23 E4
HYDE SK14 134 A3
MDTN M24 58 A4
WILM/AE SK9 199 G4
Hough St BOLS/LL BL3 47 H5
Houghton Av OLDS OL8 91 E5
Houghton Cl MILN OL16 30 D5
Houghton La SWIN M27 98 C5
Houghton Rd CHH M8 102 B1
Houghton St BOLS/LL BL3 48 D4
BURY BL9 4 C7
ROY/SHW OL2 75 F2
SWIN M27 100 A4
Hough Wk BRO M7 113 H2
Houldsworth Av ALT WA14 165 H2
Houldsworth Ml RDSH SK5 * 145 E4
Houldsworth St CMANE M1 7 H3
RAD M26 52 A4
RDSH SK5 145 E4
Houseley Av CHAD OL9 90 B4
Houson St OLDS OL8 9 G6
Houston Pk SALQ M50 113 E4
Hove Cl TOT/BURYW BL8 26 A2
Hoveden St CHH M8 114 C1
Hove Dr RUSH/FAL M14 143 G4
Hove St BOLS/LL BL3 48 B4
Hove St North BOLS/LL BL3 * 48 B4
Hovey Cl CHH M8 * 102 A3
Hovingham St MILN OL16 11 G5
Hovis St OP/CLY M11 116 D5
Howard Av BOLS/LL BL3 47 H5
CHD/CHDH SK8 182 D3
ECC M30 111 E2
FWTH BL4 66 C5
HTNM SK4 144 C5
Howard Cl MPL/ROM SK6 161 H4
Howard Ct AUL OL6 119 G2
HALE/TIMP WA15 * 166 C3
Howard Dr HALE/TIMP WA15 178 B3
Howard Hl BURY BL9 53 H5
Howardian Cl OLDS OL8 91 F5
Howard La DTN/ASHW M34 132 C4
Howard Pl MILN OL16 10 C5
Howard Rd WYTH/NTH M22 156 C5
Howards La MOSL OL5 109 F1
Howard St AULW OL7 119 F2
BOL BL1 34 A5
CHH M8 114 B1
DTN/ASHW M34 132 B3
OLDE OL4 76 D4
ORD M5 113 F5
RAD M26 68 C1
ROY/SHW OL2 59 H2
STKP SK1 13 G1
STLY SK15 121 G1
STRET M32 140 B1
WHIT OL12 10 B4
Howarth Av WALK M28 98 B3
Howarth Cross St MILN OL16 30 C1
Howarth Dr IRL M44 136 B2
Howarth Farm Wy
WHIT OL12 19 H5
Howarth Sq MILN OL16 11 F5
Howarth St FWTH BL4 66 A5
LIT OL15 21 E2
OLDTF/WHR M16 127 F4
WHTN BL5 62 A4
Howbridge Cl WALK M28 96 D2
Howbro Dr AULW OL7 106 B5
How Clough Cl WALK M28 82 C5
How Clough Dr WALK M28 82 C5
Howcroft Cl BOL BL1 2 C3
Howcroft St BOLS/LL BL3 48 C4
Howden Cl RDSH SK5 145 E1
Howden Rd BKLY M9 87 H2
Howe Dr RAMS BL0 26 C1
Howell Cft North BOL BL1 2 E4
Howell Cft South BOL BL1 * 2 E5
Howells Av SALE M33 154 B1
Howe St AULW OL7 118 D5
BRO M7 101 F5
Howgill Crs OLDS OL8 91 F4
Howgill St OP/CLY M11 117 E4
How Lea Dr BURY BL9 27 G5
Howsin Av BOLE BL2 34 C2
Howton Cl WGTN/LGST M12 129 H4
Howty Cl WILM/AE SK9 199 G1
Hoxton Cl MPL/ROM SK6 161 H2
Hoy Dr URM M41 124 C3
Hoylake Cl NEWH/MOS M40 104 C2
Hoylake Rd EDGY/DAV SK3 170 D1
SALE M33 155 G4
Hoyland Cl WGTN/LGST M12 129 G2
Hoyle Av OLDS OL8 8 E6
Hoyles Ct RAD M26 * 52 D5
Hoyle's Ter MILN OL16 * 31 F5
Hoyle St RAD M26 68 C3
WHIT OL12 14 C2
Hoyle Wk BRUN/LGST M13 * 128 C2
Hucclecote Av
WYTH/NTH M22 180 B2
Hucklow Av NTHM/RTH M23 179 H2
Hudcar La BURY BL9 5 G1
Huddart Cl ORD M5 113 G5
Huddersfield Rd OLDE OL4 76 B4
OLDE OL4 77 F4
STLY SK15 121 F3
UPML OL3 79 F1
Hudson Rd BOLS/LL BL3 64 A1
HYDE SK14 148 A4
Hudson St CHAD OL9 90 B5
Hudsons Wk ROCH OL11 29 E4
Hudswell Cl WHTF M45 69 F4
Hughenden Ct
TOT/BURYW BL8 * 26 A4
Hughes Cl BURY BL9 5 G3
FAIL M35 104 D2
Hughes St BOL BL1 33 G4
OP/CLY M11 115 H5
Hughley Cl ROY/SHW OL2 59 G4
Hugh Lupus St BOL BL1 34 B1
Hugh Oldham Dr BRO M7 101 F4
Hugh St MILN OL16 10 E5
Hughtrede St MILN OL16 * 43 G3
Hugo St FWTH BL4 65 G2
NEWH/MOS M40 103 H3
ROCH OL11 42 C4
Hulbert St MDTN M24 73 E3
TOT/BURYW BL8 37 H5
Hull Sq CSLFD M3 114 A3
Hully St STLY SK15 120 C3
Hulme Dr HALE/TIMP WA15 166 D2
Hulme Hall Av CHD/CHDH SK8 182 D4
Hulme Hall Cl CHD/CHDH SK8 182 D3
Hulme Hall Crs CHD/CHDH SK8 182 D4
Hulme Hall La
NEWH/MOS M40 115 H1
Hulme Hall Rd CHD/CHDH SK8 182 D3
HULME M15 127 G1
Hulme Pl ORD M5 * 113 H4
Hulme Rd BOLE BL2 24 B5
DTN/ASHW M34 131 G5
HTNM SK4 159 G1
RAD M26 83 F1
SALE M33 155 E3
Hulmes Rd NEWH/MOS M40 104
Hulme St AUL OL6 120 A1
BOL BL1 3 F3
HULME M15 127 H1
OLDS OL8 91 F3
ORD M5 113 H4
STKP SK1 172 C2
TOT/BURYW BL8 4 A2
Hulton Av WALK M28 81 G4
Hulton Cl BOLS/LL BL3 47 H5
Hulton Dr BOLS/LL BL3 63 H1
OLDTF/WHR M16 127 H4
Hulton La BOLS/LL BL3 63 H1
Hulton St DTN/ASHW M34 132 B4
FAIL M35 104 C3
ORD M5 126 D1
Humber Dr BURY BL9 27 G3
Humber Rd MILN OL16 31 H5
Humberstone Av HULME M15 127 H1
Humber St CHH M8 102 B3
SALQ M50 112 C4
Hume St BNG/LEV M19 * 144 B3
MILN OL16 43 F1
Humphrey Crs URM M41 139 G1
Humphrey La URM M41 139 G1
Humphrey Pk URM M41 139 G2
Humphrey Rd
OLDTF/WHR M16 127 E3
Humphrey St CHH M8 102 A2
Huncoat Av HTNM SK4 159 G1
Huncote Dr BKLY M9 103 F1
Hunger Hill Av BOLS/LL BL3 63 F2
Hunstanton Dr
TOT/BURYW BL8 38 A1
Hunston Rd SALE M33 154 A3
Hunt Av AULW OL7 107 E5
Hunter Dr RAD M26 52 B4
Hunters Cl MPL/ROM SK6 161 G3
Hunters Ct STLY SK15 121 G5
Hunters Gn RAMS BL0 16 A5
Hunters Hl BURY BL9 54 A5
Hunters La MILN OL16 10 C5
OLD OL1 9 H3
Hunters Ms SALE M33 154 B2
WILM/AE SK9 199 F3
Hunterston Av ECC M30 111 H3
Hunt Fold Dr TOT/BURYW BL8 26 A2
Huntingdon Av CHAD OL9 90 C2
Huntingdon Crs RDSH SK5 * 160 D1
Huntingdon Wk BOL BL1 33 H4
Huntington Av
DID/WITH M20 142 C4
Hunt La CHAD OL9 74 B5
Huntley Mount Rd BURY BL9 5 J1
Huntley Rd CHH M8 86 D5
EDGY/DAV SK3 171 E2
Huntley St BURY BL9 5 K2
Huntly Cha WILM/AE SK9 199 G4
Hunt Rd HYDE SK14 134 B3
Huntroyde Av BOLE BL2 3 K1
Hunts Bank CSLFD M3 6 E2
Huntsham Cl ALT WA14 165 E3
Huntsman Dr IRL M44 136 B4
Huntspill Rd ALT WA14 165 G1
Hunts Rd SLFD M6 100 A5
Hunt St BKLY M9 103 E1
Hurdlow Av BRO M7 100 D3
Hurdsfield Rd OFTN SK2 172 D5
Hurford Av GTN M18 130 C2
Hurlbote Cl WILM/AE SK9 192 A2
Hurley Dr CHD/CHDH SK8 182 B2
Hurlston Rd BOLS/LL BL3 64 C2
Hurst Av CHD/CHDH SK8 193 F1
SALE M33 153 F3
Hurstbank Av BNG/LEV M19 * 158 A2
Hurst Bank Rd AUL OL6 120 B1
Hurstbourne Av OP/CLY M11 116 C2
Hurst Brook Cl AUL OL6 119 H1
Hurstbrook Dr STRET M32 139 F1
Hurst Cl WHTN BL5 63 G5
Hurstead Gn WHIT OL12 * 20 A4
Hurstead Rd MILN OL16 31 G5
Hurstfield Rd WALK M28 96 C2
Hurstfold Av BNG/LEV M19 158 A3
Hurst Green Cl RAD M26 52 A1
Hurst Gv AUL OL6 107 H5
Hurst Hall Dr AUL OL6 107 H5
Hursthead Rd CHD/CHDH SK8 183 E5
Hursthead Wk
BRUN/LGST M13 128 C1
Hurst Hill Crs AUL OL6 120 A1
Hurst Lea Ct WILM/AE SK9 200 D2
Hurst Meadow MILN OL16 43 G4
Hurst St BOLS/LL BL3 64 B1
BURY BL9 5 H6
CHAD OL9 8 C3
DUK SK16 132 D2
RDSH SK5 145 E4
ROCH OL11 43 F1
WALK M28 81 H1
Hurstvale Av CHD/CHDH SK8 181 G3
Hurstville Rd CCHDY M21 141 F5
Hurstway Dr BKLY M9 88 B4
Hurstwood AUL OL6 108 A4
BOL BL1 33 G1
Hurstwood Cl OLDS OL8 92 B3
Hurstwood Ct BOLS/LL BL3 49 H5
Hurstwood Gv OFTN SK2 173 G3
Hus St DROY M43 117 G5
Husteads La UPML OL3 78 B3
Hutchins La OLDE OL4 76 C3
Hutchinson Rd ROCH OL11 28 A2
Hutchinson St ROCH OL11 29 E5
Hutchinson Wy RAD M26 68 B2
Hutton Av AUL OL6 120 B3
WALK M28 96 A4
Huxley Av CHH M8 102 B4
Huxley Cl BRAM/HZG SK7 183 H5
Huxley Dr BRAM/HZG SK7 183 H5
Huxley St ALT WA14 165 G2
BOL BL1 33 F4
OLDE OL4 92
Huxley Ter ALT WA14 *
Huxton Gn BRAM/HZG SK7
Hyacinth Cl EDGY/DAV
Hyacinth Wk PA
Hyde Dr WA
Hyde

Hyde Pl *BRUN/LGST* M13 128 D3
Hyde Rd *DTN/ASHW* M34 132 C5
GTN M18 131 E4
HYDE SK14 135 G5
MDTN M24 89 H1
MPL/ROM SK6 162 A1
WALK M28 81 H5
WGTN/LGST M12 129 E2
Hyde Sq *MDTN* M24 72 B4
Hyde St *BOLS/LL* BL3 * 64 B1
DROY M43 118 B1
DUK SK16 120 A5
Hydon Brook Wk *ROCH* OL11 42 B2
Hydra Cl *BRO* M7 113 H2
Hydrangea Cl *SALE* M33 153 F1
Hyldavale Av *CHD/CHDH* SK8 169 G3
Hylton Dr *CHD/CHDH* SK8 183 F4
Hypatia St *BOLE* BL2 3 K4
Hythe Cl *RUSH/FAL* M14 128 D5
Hythe Rd *EDGY/DAV* SK3 171 E1
Hythe St *BOLS/LL* BL3 * 47 H5
Hythe Wk *CHAD* OL9 * 90 C1

I

Ibsley *WHIT* OL12 10 B4
Ice House Cl *WALK* M28 81 E4
Iceland St *SLFD* M6 112 D3
Idonia St *BOL* BL1 33 G3
Ilex Gv *BRO* M7 101 G4
Ilford St *OP/CLY* M11 116 C3
Ilfracombe Rd *OFTN* SK2 173 E1
Ilfracombe St
NEWH/MOS M40 104 C4
Ilkley Cl *CHAD* OL9 90 C1
Ilkley Crs *RDSH* SK5 145 E3
Ilkley Dr *URM* M41 123 H4
Ilkley St *NEWH/MOS* M40 103 H1
Ilk St *OP/CLY* M11 116 C3
Illingworth Av *STLY* SK15 121 F4
Illona Dr *BRO* M7 100 D2
Ilminster *ROCH* OL11 * 29 H5
Imperial Ter *SALE* M33 * 139 G5
Ina Av *BOL* BL1 32 C5
Ince Cl *DID/WITH* M20 142 D4
HTNM SK4 159 H3
Ince St *HTNM* SK4 159 H3
Inchcape Dr *BKLY* M9 87 G3
Inchfield Cl *ROCH* OL11 28 B3
Inchfield Rd *NEWH/MOS* M40 103 H1
Inchley Rd *BRUN/LGST* M13 128 C2
Inchwood Ms *OLDE* OL4 60 D5
Incline Rd *OLDS* OL8 90 C5
Independent St *BOLS/LL* BL3 66 D1
Indigo St *SLFD* M6 100 C5
Indus Pl *BRO* M7 113 H1
Industrial St *WHTN* BL5 62 A5
Industry Rd *WHIT* OL12 10 C3
Industry St *CHAD* OL9 90 B3
LIT OL15 21 E3
ROCH OL11 28 B2
WHIT OL12 14 C3
Infant St *PWCH* M25 * 86 B3
Infirmary St *BOL* BL1 3 F5
Ingham Rd *ALT* WA14 153 G5
Inghams La *LIT* OL15 21 E3
Ingham St *BURY* BL9 5 G6
NEWH/MOS M40 * 117 F1
OLD OL1 9 J3
Inghamwood Cl *BRO* M7 102 A3
Ingleby Av *BKLY* M9 88 C3
Ingleby Cl *ROY/SHW* OL2 59 H1
WHTN BL5 62 A2
Ingleby Ct *STRET* M32 140 C2
Ingleby Wy *ROY/SHW* OL2 59 H1
Ingledene Av *BRO* M7 101 H1
Ingledene Gv *BOL* BL1 * 32 D4
Ingle Dr *OFTN* SK2 172 D2
Inglefield *ROCH* OL11 28 B2
Inglehead Cl *DTN/ASHW* M34 147 E1
Inglenook Cl *PART* M31 137 H4
Ingle Rd *CHD/CHDH* SK8 170 D3
Ingles Fold *WALK* M28 96 C2
Inglesham Cl *NTHM/RTH* M23 168 A3
Ingleton Av *CHH* M8 102 C1
Ingleton Cl *BOLE* BL2 35 E2
CHD/CHDH SK8 169 H3
ROY/SHW OL2 59 E4
Ingleton Ms *TOT/BURYW* BL8 37 G2
Ingleton Rd *EDGY/DAV* SK3 12 A6
Inglewhite Cl *BURY* BL9 53 E2
Inglewood Cl *AULW* OL7 106 C5
BURY BL9 39 F2
PART M31 150 D2
Inglewood Hollow *STLY* SK15 121 F5
Inglewood Rd *CHAD* OL9 73 H3
Inglewood Wk
BRUN/LGST M13 * 128 D2
Inglis St *LIT* OL15 21 E2
Ingoe Cl *HEY* OL10 41 G3
Ingoldsby Av *BRUN/LGST* M13 129 E4
Ingram Dr *HTNM* SK4 158 B3
Ings Av *WHIT* OL12 29 E1
Ings La *WHIT* OL12 29 F2
Inkerman St *HYDE* SK14 133 F4
NEWH/MOS M40 103 E5
WHIT OL… 10 C3
Ink St M… 10 D6
Inmar… 53 F1
… 132 C5
Ir… 130 A5
… 104 B5
… 3 G5
… 129 E3
… 74 A3
… D4

Ipswich St *ROCH* OL11 43 E1
Iqbal Cl *WGTN/LGST* M12 129 H3
Ireby Cl *MDTN* M24 71 H2
Iredine St *OP/CLY* M11 116 D4
Irene Av *HYDE* SK14 133 H4
Iris Av *FWTH* BL4 65 F3
FWTH BL4 82 C2
Iris St *OLDS* OL8 91 G5
RAMS BL0 16 C2
Irkdale St *CHH* M8 102 D4
Irk Vale Dr *OLD* OL1 73 H3
Irlam Av *ECC* M30 111 E4
Irlam Rd *IRL* M44 136 D2
SALE M33 154 D1
URM M41 137 E2
Irlam Sq *SLFD* M6 100 A5
Irlam St *BOL* BL1 33 H3
NEWH/MOS M40 103 F5
Irlam Wharf Rd *IRL* M44 136 C5
Irma St *BOL* BL1 34 A3
Iron St *DTN/ASHW* M34 * 132 C5
NEWH/MOS M40 115 H2
Irvin Dr *WYTH/NTH* M22 181 F4
Irvine Av *WALK* M28 96 B4
Irving Cl *OFTN* SK2 184 B1
Irving St *BOL* BL1 33 H4
OLDS OL8 90 C5
Irvin St *NEWH/MOS* M40 104 B4
Irwell Av *ECC* M30 111 G4
LHULT M38 81 G3
Irwell Gv *ECC* M30 111 G4
Irwell Pl *ECC* M30 111 G4
ORD M5 113 H4
RAD M26 67 E4
Irwell Sculpture Trail *BRO* M7 101 F4
Irwell St *BURY* BL9 4 C5
CSLFD M3 6 B4
CSLFD M3 114 B1
RAD M26 66 D5
RAD M26 68 C2
RAMS BL0 16 D2
Irwell Valley Wy *BURY* BL9 27 E2
RAMS BL0 16 D4
Irwin Dr *WILM/AE* SK9 191 H2
Irwin Rd *ALT* WA14 165 F1
Irwin St *DTN/ASHW* M34 132 B5
Isaac Cl *ORD* M5 113 F5
Isaac St *BOL* BL1 48 B1
Isabella Cl *OLDTF/WHR* M16 127 F4
Isabella St *WHIT* OL12 10 D1
Isabel Wk *BOLS/LL* BL3 48 C4
Isaiah St *OLDS* OL8 * 91 G3
Isa St *RAMS* BL0 16 B4
Isca St *OP/CLY* M11 116 A4
Isherwood Dr *MPL/ROM* SK6 174 C3
Isherwood Rd *PART* M31 137 H5
Isherwood St *HEY* OL10 41 F5
ROCH OL11 43 F1
Isis Cl *BRO* M7 100 D2
Islington Rd *OFTN* SK2 172 D5
Islington St *CSLFD* M3 6 A3
Islington Wy *CSLFD* M3 114 A4
Isobel Cl *ECC* M30 110 C4
OLDTF/WHR M16 128 A4
Ivanhoe Ct *BOLS/LL* BL3 65 H2
Ivanhoe St *BOLS/LL* BL3 65 H2
OLD OL1 76 B3
Iveagh Ct *MILN* OL16 * 30 C5
Ivor St *ROCH* OL11 42 A3
Ivy Bank Cl *BOL* BL1 33 H1
Ivy Bank Rd *BOL* BL1 33 H1
Ivybridge Cl *BRUN/LGST* M13 129 E3
Ivy Cl *DROY* M43 117 G2
ROY/SHW OL2 60 A2
Ivy Cottages *WHIT* OL12 * 29 F2
Ivy Dr *MDTN* M24 88 C1
Ivygreen Dr *OLDE* OL4 93 E1
Ivygreen Rd *CCHDY* M21 140 D3
Ivy Gv *FWTH* BL4 65 G4
FWTH BL4 * 66 C5
LHULT M38 81 E3
Ivyleaf Sq *BRO* M7 101 H4
Ivylea Rd *BNG/LEV* M19 158 B2
Ivy Rd *BOL* BL1 33 F5
POY/DIS SK12 195 F4
TOT/BURYW BL8 37 G4
WHTN BL5 62 A5
Ivy St *BOLS/LL* BL3 48 B5
ECC M30 111 E4
NEWH/MOS M40 103 H2

J

Jack Brady Cl *NTHM/RTH* M23 167 F5
Jackdaw Rd *TOT/BURYW* BL8 26 A1
Jack La *DROY* M43 118 B3
URM M41 139 E1
Jackman Av *HEY* OL10 56 A2
Jackroom Dr *ANC* M4 * 7 K4
Jackson Av *DUK* SK16 120 A5
Jackson Cl *HALE/TIMP* WA15 166 D2
OLDS OL8 8 E6
Jackson Ct *URM* M41 123 H5
Jackson Crs *HULME* M15 127 H2
Jackson Gdns *DTN/ASHW* M34 146 B1
Jackson Ms *OLDE* OL4 76 C3
Jacksons Edge Rd
POY/DIS SK12 187 F5
Jacksons La *BRAM/HZG* SK7 184 C4
Jacksons Rw *CMANW* M2 6 D5
Jackson St *AUL* OL6 119 G1
CHD/CHDH SK8 170 B3
FAIL M35 104 C4
FWTH BL4 66 A4
FWTH BL4 66 C5
HYDE SK14 147 H1
MDTN M24 73 E3
MILN OL16 30 C5
OLDE OL4 76 A5
RAD M26 68 C2
SALE M33 155 E1
STRET M32 140 A2
…K M28 81 H3
…OL12 19 H2
…45 69 G5
… BL2 34 D5
… *WHIT* OL12 * 11 G3

Jacob Bright Ms *WHIT* OL12 10 C1
Jacobite Cl *BRO* M7 101 F1
Jacobsen Av *HYDE* SK14 134 A4
James Andrew St *MDTN* M24 * 73 E3
James Brindley Basin
CMANE M1 7 K5
James Butterworth Ct
MILN OL16 * 30 C5
James Butterworth St
MILN OL16 30 C5
James Cl *DUK* SK16 120 B5
James Corbett Rd *SALQ* M50 112 B4
James Dr *HYDE* SK14 148 A1
James Henry Av *ORD* M5 113 G5
James Hill St *LIT* OL15 21 E3
James Leech St *STKP* SK1 13 F5
James Leigh St *CMANE* M1 7 F7
Jameson St *ROCH* OL11 42 A4
James Rd *ROY/SHW* OL2 60 A1
James's St *OLDE* OL4 76 C3
James St *BOLS/LL* BL3 67 E1
BURY BL9 5 H6
DROY M43 118 A3
DTN/ASHW M34 118 D5
DTN/ASHW M34 * 132 D5
DUK SK16 * 120 B5
EDGY/DAV SK3 12 E7
FAIL M35 105 F2
FWTH BL4 66 C4
HEY OL10 * 41 E4
LIT OL15 20 C3
MPL/ROM SK6 161 H1
NEWH/MOS M40 115 G2
ORD M5 114 A4
PWCH M25 85 H2
RAD M26 68 C2
ROY/SHW OL2 59 H4
SALE M33 155 E2
WHIT OL12 * 10 E3
WHIT OL12 14 C3
James St North *RAD* M26 68 C2
James St South *CHAD* OL9 * 74 B5
Jamieson Cl *CHH* M8 101 H5
Jammy St *CHAD* OL9 8 A5
Jane St *CHAD* OL9 90 C1
WHIT OL12 10 A4
Janus Dr *OLD* OL1 75 E3
Japan St *BRO* M7 102 A3
Jardine Wy *CHAD* OL9 90 A3
Jarvis St *OLDE* OL4 9 K5
WHIT OL12 10 D2
Jasmine Av *DROY* M43 118 B3
Jasmine Cl *NTHM/RTH* M23 155 F5
Jasmine Ct *BOLS/LL* BL3 64 D1
Jason St *ANC* M4 115 E2
Jauncey St *BOLS/LL* BL3 48 B4
Jayton Av *DID/WITH* M20 169 G2
Jean Cl *BNG/LEV* M19 144 A1
Jedburgh Av *BOL* BL1 48 A1
Jefferson Wy *WHIT* OL12 19 E5
Jeffreys Dr *DUK* SK16 120 A5
Jehlum Cl *CHH* M8 102 C3
Jellicoe Av *IRL* M44 136 A5
Jenkinson St *HULME* M15 128 B2
Jennaby Wk *BOL* BL1 33 H4
Jennings Av *ORD* M5 113 F5
Jennings Cl *HYDE* SK14 134 C3
ORD M5 113 F5
Jennings St *EDGY/DAV* SK3 171 G2
Jennison Cl *WGTN/LGST* M12 130 A2
Jenny La *BRAM/HZG* SK7 193 H4
Jenny Lind Cl *BOLS/LL* BL3 65 H2
Jenny St *OLDS* OL8 90 D5
Jepheys Pl *WHIT* OL12 * 10 C2
Jepheys St *WHIT* OL12 10 D2
Jepson St *OFTN* SK2 172 B3
Jericho Rd *BURY* BL9 39 H3
Jermyn St *WHIT* OL12 10 E4
Jerrold St *LIT* OL15 21 E3
Jersey Rd *RDSH* SK5 160 A2
Jersey St *ANC* M4 7 J3
AUL OL6 119 G1
Jerusalem Pl *CMANW* M2 * 6 D6
Jesmond Av *PWCH* M25 86 A5
Jesmond Dr *TOT/BURYW* BL8 37 H1
Jesmond Gv *CHD/CHDH* SK8 183 E4
Jesmond Rd *BOL* BL1 33 E2
Jespersen St *OLD* OL1 9 G2
Jessamine Av *BRO* M7 114 A1
Jessel Cl *BRUN/LGST* M13 128 D2
Jessie St *BOLS/LL* BL3 48 B4
NEWH/MOS M40 103 H4
Jessop Dr *MPL/ROM* SK6 175 E1
Jessop Forge *BOLS/LL* BL3 66 D1
Jessop St *GTN* M18 130 C3
Jethro St *BOLE* BL2 34 D2
BOLE BL2 49 H1
Jetson St *GTN* M18 131 E2
Jimmy McMullen Wk
RUSH/FAL M14 * 128 B5
Jinnah Cl *OLDE* OL4 92 B2
OP/CLY M11 116 D5
J J Thomson Ms
RUSH/FAL M14 * 143 E2
Joan St *NEWH/MOS* M40 103 H3
Jobling St *OP/CLY* M11 116 A5
Jocelyn St *NEWH/MOS* M40 103 F4
Joddrell St *CSLFD* M3 6 C5
Joel La *HYDE* SK14 148 B4
Johannesburg Gdns
NTHM/RTH M23 167 G5
John Ashworth St *WHIT* OL12 11 G3
John Atkinson Ct *ORD* M5 * 112 C3
John Av *CHD/CHDH* SK8 170 B4
John Beeley Av *OP/CLY* M11 117 E5
John Booth St *OLDE* OL4 93 E2
John Brown St *BOL* BL1 * 2 C3
John Clynes Av
NEWH/MOS M40 * 115 F2
John Cross St *BOLS/LL* BL3 48 D5
John Dalton St *CMANW* M2 6 D5
John Foran Cl
NEWH/MOS M40 104 A4
John Gilbert Wy *TRPK* M17 126 B3
John Heywood St
OP/CLY M11 116 C3
John Kennedy Gdn
HYDE SK14 135 H5
John Kennedy Rd *HYDE* SK14 135 G5
John Knott St *OLDE* OL4 93 E1

John Lee Fold *MDTN* M24 72 D3
John Nash Crs *HULME* M15 127 H2
Johnny King Cl
NEWH/MOS M40 103 E5
John Roberts Cl *ROCH* OL11 42 D1
Johns Cl *CCHDY* M21 141 F3
John Shepley St *HYDE* SK14 148 A1
John Smeaton Ct *CMANE* M1 7 K5
Johnsonbrook Rd *HYDE* SK14 133 G3
Johnson Fold Av *BOL* BL1 32 B4
Johnson Gv *MDTN* M24 72 B4
Johnson's Sq
NEWH/MOS M40 115 G1
Johnson St *BOL* BL1 3 F6
CSLFD M3 6 C3
HULME M15 127 G2
RAD M26 68 C2
SWIN M27 100 A4
Johns Pl *MPL/ROM* SK6 162 B4
Johnston *WHIT* OL12 10 B4
Johnston Av *LIT* OL15 * 20 C5
John St *ALT* WA14 165 G5
ANC M4 7 G3
BOLS/LL BL3 * 67 E1
BRAM/HZG SK7 185 E1
BRO M7 114 A1
BURY BL9 4 E3
CSLFD M3 6 C2
DROY M43 117 G5
DTN/ASHW M34 * 132 C4
ECC M30 110 C4
EDGW/EG BL7 23 F4
FAIL M35 105 E1
FWTH BL4 66 B4
HEY OL10 41 E4
HYDE SK14 133 G5
IRL M44 150 D1
LIT OL15 20 D3
MILN OL16 10 E5
MILN OL16 19 H5
MPL/ROM SK6 161 H1
MPL/ROM SK6 163 G4
MPL/ROM SK6 175 F4
OLDS OL8 8 E4
PWCH M25 70 D4
ROY/SHW OL2 59 E5
ROY/SHW OL2 59 H4
SALE M33 154 C1
STKP SK1 13 G5
STLY SK15 108 D5
SWIN M27 99 F2
WALK M28 82 A3
WHIT OL12 14 C3
John St East *AULW* OL7 119 F4
John St West *AULW* OL7 119 E5
John William St *ECC* M30 111 G3
OP/CLY M11 * 116 D4
Joiner St *ANC* M4 7 G4
ORD M5 113 H4
Join Rd *SALE* M33 155 E2
Jolly Brows *BOLE* BL2 35 E3
Jonas St *BKLY* M9 103 F2
CSLFD M3 114 B2
Jones Sq *STKP* SK1 13 H7
Jones St *BOL* BL1 2 E2
MILN OL16 30 B5
OLD OL1 9 K1
RAD M26 52 C5
ROY/SHW OL2 75 F2
SLFD M6 113 E2
Jonquil Dr *WALK* M28 81 E5
Jopson St *MDTN* M24 73 E3
Jordan Av *ROY/SHW* OL2 60 C1
Jordan St *HULME* M15 127 H1
Josephine Dr *SWIN* M27 99 F3
Joseph Johnson Ms
WYTH/NTH M22 * 156 D5
Joseph St *ECC* M30 110 C4
FAIL M35 105 F2
FWTH BL4 66 A3
LIT OL15 21 E2
MDTN M24 72 C3
MPL/ROM SK6 * 175 F3
RAD M26 68 C2
WHIT OL12 29 G1
Joshua La *MDTN* M24 73 G5
Josslyn Rd *ORD* M5 112 C2
Jo St *ORD* M5 113 F4
Joule Cl *ORD* M5 113 E5
Joules Ct *STKP* SK1 13 H4
Joule St *BKLY* M9 103 F1
Jowett St *OLD* OL1 76 B3
RDSH SK5 160 A2
Jowett's Wk *AULW* OL7 119 F3
Jowkin La *ROCH* OL11 28 A4
Joyce St *NEWH/MOS* M40 104 A3
Joynson Av *BRO* M7 114 A1
Joynson St *SALE* M33 154 C1
Joy St *RAMS* BL0 16 C2
WHIT OL12 30 A1
Jubilee Av *DUK* SK16 120 B4
RAD M26 68 D3
Jubilee Houses *WALK* M28 * 81 H4
Jubilee Rd *MDTN* M24 73 E3
Jubilee St *AULW* OL7 119 E4
ROY/SHW OL2 60 B2
SLFD M6 113 E3
Jubilee Ter *MDTN* M24 73 E2
Jubilee Wy *BURY* BL9 4 B5
Judith St *WHIT* OL12 18 B5
Judson Av *CCHDY* M21 156 B1
Julia St *CSLFD* M3 114 C2
WHIT OL12 10 B5
Julius St *BNG/LEV* M19 144 B3
Junction Aly *MILN* OL16 10 D7
Junction Rd *BOLS/LL* BL3 47 G4
OFTN SK2 13 G7
Junction Rd West *HOR/BR* BL6 47 E4
Junction St *HYDE* SK14 133 F3
MDTN M24 89 G1
OLDS OL8 * 91 F3
June Av *HTNM* SK4 * 159 E4
Juniper Bank *RDSH* SK5 145 G3
Juniper Cl *BOL* BL1 33 H5
OLDE OL4 61 E5
SALE M33 139 G5
Juniper Dr *MILN* OL16 31 E5
Juno St *OLD* OL1 75 H3
Jura Cl *DUK* SK16 120 A5
Jura Dr *URM* M41 124 D3

Jura Gv *HEY* OL10 40 C5
Jurby Av *BKLY* M9 87 H3
Jury St *CHH* M8 114 C1
Justin Cl *BRUN/LGST* M13 128 C1
Jutland Av *ROCH* OL11 29 F3
Jutland St *CMANE* M1 7 J5

K

Kale St *BRUN/LGST* M13 128 C1
Kalima Gv *BRO* M7 101 G4
Kansas Av *SALQ* M50 112 D5
Kara St *SLFD* M6 112 D3
Kate St *RAMS* BL0 * 16 C2
Kathan Cl *MILN* OL16 11 H7
Katherine Rd *OFTN* SK2 172 D4
Katherine St *AULW* OL7 119 E3
Kathleen Gv *RUSH/FAL* M14 143 E1
Kathleen St *WHIT* OL12 29 G3
Kay Av *MPL/ROM* SK6 161 E3
Kay Brow *HEY* OL10 40 D4
RAMS BL0 16 D2
Kayfields *BOLE* BL2 35 F2
Kay's Av *STKP* SK1 160 C5
Kays Gdns *CSLFD* M3 6 A2
Kay St *BOL* BL1 2 E1
BOL BL1 3 F3
BOLS/LL BL3 66 D1
BURY BL9 5 H2
BURY BL9 16 D5
HEY OL10 40 D4
OP/CLY M11 129 G1
ROCH OL11 42 D1
SLFD M6 100 C4
STLY SK15 120 D4
Kays Wood Rd *MPL/ROM* SK6 174 C3
Keadby Cl *ECC* M30 111 E5
Keal Dr *IRL* M44 122 C4
Kearsley Dr *BOLS/LL* BL3 65 G1
Kearsley Hall Rd *RAD* M26 67 F5
Kearsley Rd *CHH* M8 87 F5
RAD M26 67 F4
Kearsley St *ECC* M30 110 C3
Kearsley V *RAD* M26 67 E4
Kearton Dr *ECC* M30 111 H4
Keary Cl *GTN* M18 130 C2
Keaton Cl *SLFD* M6 112 D1
Keats Av *DROY* M43 117 H3
DTN/ASHW M34 147 E3
WHIT OL12 28 D2
Keats Crs *RAD* M26 51 H5
Keats Fold *DUK* SK16 134 C1
Keats Ms *NTHM/RTH* M23 166 D1
Keats Rd *ECC* M30 111 E4
OLD OL1 * 76 A3
TOT/BURYW BL8 26 A1
Keb La *OLDS* OL8 106 D2
Keble Av *OLDS* OL8 91 F4
Kedleston Av *RUSH/FAL* M14 129 F4
Kedleston Gn *OFTN* SK2 173 E2
Keele Cl *NEWH/MOS* M40 115 F2
Keele Wk *NEWH/MOS* M40 115 F2
Keepers Dr *WHIT* OL12 28 B1
The Keep *BOL* BL1 47 F2
Keighley Av *DROY* M43 117 H2
Keighley Cl *TOT/BURYW* BL8 37 E4
Keighley St *BOL* BL1 33 F4
Keilder Ms *BOL* BL1 47 H1
Keith Dr *EDGY/DAV* SK3 171 E2
Keith Wk *NEWH/MOS* M40 115 G2
Kelboro Av *DTN/ASHW* M34 132 A1
Kelbrook Ct *OFTN* SK2 173 F4
Kelbrook Rd *OP/CLY* M11 116 C5
Kelby Av *NTHM/RTH* M23 168 A2
Keld Cl *TOT/BURYW* BL8 37 G1
Kelfield Av *SALE* M33 155 H4
Kellbrook Crs *BRO* M7 * 100 D2
Kellets Rw *WALK* M28 * 82 A2
Kellett St *BOL* BL1 23 E5
MILN OL16 11 G5
Kelling Wk *HULME* M15 * 127 G1
Kelmarsh Cl *OP/CLY* M11 * 130 C1
Kelsall Crs *EDGY/DAV* SK3 171 G3
Kelsall Dr *DROY* M43 117 G2
HALE/TIMP WA15 166 D3
Kelsall Rd *CHD/CHDH* SK8 170 D4
Kelsall St *CHAD* OL9 8 C4
MILN OL16 10 E6
SALE M33 154 B2
WGTN/LGST M12 129 G2
Kelso Cl *OLDS* OL8 106 C1
Kelson Av *AULW* OL7 106 D5
Kelstern Av *BRUN/LGST* M13 129 F5
Kelstern Sq *BRUN/LGST* M13 129 F5
Kelton Cl *RDSH* SK5 160 A1
Kelverlow St *OLDE* OL4 92 B1
Kelvin Av *MDTN* M24 71 G5
SALE M33 154 C2
Kelvindale Dr
HALE/TIMP WA15 166 D2
Kelvin Gv *CHH* M8 102 B4
Kelvington Dr *BKLY* M9 103 E4
Kelvin St *ANC* M4 7 G3
AULW OL7 119 E5
Kemble Av *NTHM/RTH* M23 156 B5
Kemmel Av *WYTH/NTH* M22 168 D4
Kemp Av *ROCH* OL11 42 C1
Kempnough Hall Rd
WALK M28 97 G3
Kemp Rd *MPL/ROM* SK6 175 H1
Kempsey Ct *CHAD* OL9 74 B5
Kempsford Cl
NTHM/RTH M23 168 A3
Kempster St *BRO* M7 114 A1
Kempston Gdns *BOL* BL1 33 H4
Kemp St *HYDE* SK14 133 H4
MDTN M24 72 C4
Kempton Av *BOLS/LL* BL3 66 D2
SALE M33 153 G3
Kempton Cl *BRAM/HZG* SK7 185 H2
DROY M43 118 B3
Kempton Wy *CHAD* OL9 8 A3
Kemsing Wk *ORD* M5 * 113 F3
Kenchester Av *OP/CLY* M11 117 E5
Kendal Av *AULW* OL7 119 E1
DTN/ASHW M34 147 E2
HYDE SK14 133 F3

SALE M33 ....154 D3
URM M41 ....125 F4
HEY OL10 ....56 B1
WHIT OL12 ....39 E2
Kendal Cl HALE/TIMP WA15 ..167 E4
Kendal Dr BRAM/HZG SK7 ..193 F2
BURY BL9 ....53 E2
CHD/CHDH SK8 ....169 H5
ROY/SHW OL2 ....60 C3
Kendal Gdns MPL/ROM SK6 ..162 A2
WHTF M45 ....69 G4
Kendal Gv WALK M28 ....82 C5
Kendal Rd BOL BL1 ....48 B4
RAMS BL0 ....26 A1
SLFD M6 ....99 H5
STRET M32 ....126 A5
Kendal Rd West RAMS BL0 ....26 A1
Kendon Gv DTN/ASHW M34 ..132 D5
Kendrew Rd BOLS/LL BL3 ......47 H5
Kenilworth Av CHAD OL9 ......73 H3
CHD/CHDH SK8 ....182 D1
DID/WITH M20 ....157 E1
SWIN M27 ....84 C4
WHTF M45 ....85 H1
WILM/AE SK9 ....198 C3
Kenilworth Cl MPL/ROM SK6 ..175 E1
OLDE OL4 ....93 E3
RAD M26 ....52 A5
Kenilworth Dr
BRAM/HZG SK7 ....185 E4
Kenilworth Gv
DTN/ASHW M34 ....118 B5
Kenilworth Rd EDGY/DAV SK3 ..170 C2
MILN OL16 ....58 D1
SALE M33 ....153 H2
URM M41 ....137 E2
Kenilworth Sq BOL BL1 ....33 E5
Kenion Rd ROCH OL11 ....28 D5
Kenion St MILN OL16 ....10 D7
Kenley Dr HEY OL10 ....56 B3
Kenley Ldg BRAM/HZG SK7 * ..185 G5
Kenley Wk CHH M8 * 102 D4
Kenmay Av BOLS/LL BL3 ......47 G3
Kenmore Av NEWH/MOS M40 ..104 A1
Kenmor Av TOT/BURYW BL8 ....52 B1
Kenmore Dr
HALE/TIMP WA15 ....178 D1
Kenmore Rd SALE M33 ....155 F5
WHTF M45 ....70 A4
WYTH/NTH M22 ....168 C2
Kenmore Wy WHTF M45 ......70 A4
Kennard Cl BKLY M9 ....103 G1
Kennedy Dr BOLS/LL BL3 ......47 F1
BURY BL9 ....70 A2
Kennedy Rd ORD M5 ....112 B5
Kennedy Sq HYDE SK14 ......149 H1
Kennedy St CMANW M2 ......6 E5
OLDS OL8 ....9 F7
Kennedy Wy DTN/ASHW M34 ..146 B1
HTNM SK4 ....12 B2
Kennerley Rd OFTN SK2 ......172 B4
Kennerys La WILM/AE SK9 ..198 D3
Kennet Cl WHTN BL5 ....62 A3
WILM/AE SK9 ....192 A5
Kenneth Av STKP SK1 ....101 H4
Kenneth Dr MPL/ROM SK6 ....161 C2
Kennett Rd NTHM/RTH M23 ..179 H1
Kenninghall Rd
WYTH/NTH M22 ....180 C1
Kennington Av
NEWH/MOS M40 ....116 C1
Kennington Fold
BOLS/LL BL3 ....64 C1
Kenny Cl OLDE OL4 ....92 D2
Kensington Av AUL OL6 ......120 B1
CHAD OL9 ....73 H4
HYDE SK14 ....148 A2
ROY/SHW OL2 ....58 D3
RUSH/FAL M14 ....129 E4
Kensington Cl MILN OL16 ......31 H5
TOT/BURYW BL8 ....26 B2
Kensington Ct BOL BL1 * 2 B3
HYDE SK14 ....148 A2
WILM/AE SK9 ....198 D4
Kensington Dr ORD M5 ......112 C2
TOT/BURYW BL8 ....52 B1
Kensington Gdns
HALE/TIMP WA15 ....178 A3
Kensington Gv ALT WA14 ..165 H1
DTN/ASHW M34 ....131 C4
STLY SK15 ....120 D3
Kensington Rd
CCHDY M21 ....141 E1
EDGY/DAV SK3 ....171 E2
FAIL M35 ....105 G2
OLDS OL8 ....91 E3
Kensington St BOL BL1 ....33 E4
HYDE SK14 ....148 A2
ROCH OL11 ....42 D2
RUSH/FAL M14 ....128 D5
Kenslow Av CHH M8 ....87 E5
Kensworth Cl BOL BL1 * 33 G5
Kensworth Dr BOL BL1 ......33 G5
Kent Av CHAD OL9 ....90 B1
CHD/CHDH SK8 ....171 F5
DROY M43 ....117 F4
Kent Cl WALK M28 ....81 F5
Kent Ct BOL BL1 ....2 D3
Kent Dr BURY BL9 ....53 G1
FWTH BL4 ....83 E1
Kentford Dr
NEWH/MOS M40 ....115 F1
Kentford Rd BOL BL1 ....2 D1
Kentmere Av ROCH OL11 ....29 H3
Kentmere Cl CHD/CHDH SK8 ..181 G1
Kentmere Dr MDTN M24 ......72 B1
Kentmere Gv FWTH BL4 ......65 E5
Kentmere Rd BOLE BL2 ......35 G5
HALE/TIMP WA15 ....177 E2
Kentmore Ct HTNM SK4 ......158 B4
WGTN/LGST M12 ....129 H1
Kenton Av GTN M18 ....130 D5
Kenton Cl BOL BL1 ....33 G5
DTN/ASHW M34 ....132 A1
Kenton Rd ROY/SHW OL2 ....59 H2
Kenton St OLDS OL8 ....92 A2

Kent Rd DTN/ASHW M34 ......145 G1
EDGY/DAV SK3 ....171 E1
IRL M44 ....150 B1
PART M31 ....150 D4
Kent Rd East RUSH/FAL M14 ..129 E5
Kent Rd West RUSH/FAL M14 ..128 D5
Kentsford Dr RAD M26 ......53 H4
Kentstone Av BNG/LEV M19 ..158 A3
Kent St BOL BL1 ....2 D2
BRO M7 ....114 A1
CMANW M2 * 6 E4
OLDS OL8 ....91 G3
ROCH OL11 ....30 A5
SWIN M27 ....84 A5
Kentucky St OLDE OL4 ......92 B1
Kentwell Cl DUK SK16 ......133 F1
Kenwick Dr NEWH/MOS M40 ..89 H5
Kenwood Av BNG/LEV M19 ..143 H5
BRAM/HZG SK7 ....193 G2
CHD/CHDH SK8 ....169 F3
HALE/TIMP WA15 ....178 B2
Kenwood Cl STRET M32 ......140 C1
Kenwood La WALK M28 ......97 C5
Kenwood Rd BOL BL1 ......33 E5
OLD OL1 ....74 D3
RDSH SK5 ....145 E4
STRET M32 ....140 C2
Kenworthy Av AUL OL6 ......107 G1
Kenworthy Cl HYDE SK14 ..149 G1
Kenworthy Gdns UPML OL3 ..79 E4
Kenworthy La
WYTH/NTH M22 ....156 C4
Kenworthy St MILN OL16 ......11 J6
STLY SK15 ....120 D4
Kenwright St ANC M4 ....7 G2
Kenwyn St NEWH/MOS M40 ..115 H2
OLDS OL8 ....9 G6
SALE M33 ....155 F4
Kenyon Cl HYDE SK14 ......134 A3
Kenyon Crs BURY BL9 ......27 G5
Kenyon Fold ROCH OL11 ......41 F1
Kenyon Gv LHULT M38 ......80 D5
Kenyon La MDTN M24 ......103 H2
PWCH M25 ....86 B3
Kenyon Rd BOLE BL2 ....51 E4
Kenyon St AUL OL6 ....119 E2
BURY BL9 ....5 G2
DUK SK16 ....119 G5
GTN M18 ....130 D2
HEY OL10 ....40 D4
OLDS OL8 ....16 D1
Kenyon Ter LHULT M38 ......80 D4
Kenyon Wy LHULT M38 ......37 E1
TOT/BURYW BL8 ....37 E1
Keppel Rd CCHDY M21 ......141 E2
Keppel St AUL OL6 ....119 H2
Kepplecove Meadow
WALK M28 ....96 A5
Kepwick Dr WYTH/NTH M22 ..180 D3
Kerenhappuch St RAMS BL0 ..16 C3
Kerfoot Cl WYTH/NTH M22 ..168 D1
Kermoor Av BOL BL1 ....2 D3
Kerne Gv NTHM/RTH M23 ..155 H5
Kerrera Dr ORD M5 ....112 C4
Kerridge Dr MPL/ROM SK6 ..161 C2
Kerris Cl WYTH/NTH M22 ..180 A1
Kerr St BKLY M9 ....88 A4
Kerry Gv BOLE BL2 ....3 K2
Kersal Av LHULT M38 ......81 G3
SWIN M27 ....99 H2
Kersal Bank BRO M7 ....100 D1
Kersal Cl BOLS/LL BL3 ......47 H5
Kersal Crag BRO M7 ....100 D1
Kersal Dr HALE/TIMP WA15 ..166 D2
Kersal Hall Av BRO M7 ......100 D1
Kersal Rd PWCH M25 ......100 D1
Kersal Vale Rd PWCH M25 ..100 C1
Kersal Wy BRO M7 ....100 D1
Kerscort Rd NTHM/RTH M23 ..155 G4
Kersh Av BNG/LEV M19 ......144 B3
PWCH M25 ....50 D5
Kershaw Av BOLS/LL BL3 ......48 C4
BURY BL9 ....5 C5
DROY M43 ....117 G4
HEY OL10 ....40 C4
ROY/SHW OL2 ....59 E4
WHIT OL12 * 14 B2
Kershaw Dr CHAD OL9 ......89 G3
Kershaw La DTN/ASHW M34 ..118 A5
Kershaw Rd FAIL M35 ......105 E2
Kershaw St AULW OL7 ......119 E5
BOLE BL2 ....34 D1
BOLS/LL BL3 ....48 C4
BURY BL9 ....5 C5
DROY M43 ....117 C4
HEY OL10 ....40 C4
ROY/SHW OL2 ....59 E4
WHIT OL12 * 14 B2
Kershaw St East ROY/SHW OL2 ..60 A2
Kershaw Wk WGTN/LGST M12 ..129 E2
Kershope Gv ORD M5 ......113 F5
Kersley St OLDE OL4 ......92 A1
Kerwin Wk OP/CLY M11 * ..116 B5
Kerwood Dr ROY/SHW OL2 ..75 F1
Kesteven Rd BKLY M9 ......103 E3
Keston Av BKLY M9 ....103 H4
DROY M43 ....117 F4
Keston Crs RDSH SK5 ......145 H5
Keston Rd OLD OL1 ....76 B3
Kestor St BOLE BL2 ....3 J4
Kestrel Av DTN/ASHW M34 ..118 B4
FWTH BL4 * 65 E5
LHULT M38 ....81 F2
OLDE OL4 ....92 B2
SWIN M27 ....98 D1
Kestrel Cl HYDE SK14 ......133 H4
MPL/ROM SK6 ....187 F1
PWCH M25 ....85 H1
Kestrel Dr BURY BL9 ....5 J1
IRL M44 ....150 A5
Kestrel Rd TRPK M17 ......111 G5
Kestrel St BOLE BL2 ....3 G5
Kestrel Wk WGTN/LGST M12 ..129 H2
Keswick Av AULW OL7 ......106 C5
CHAD OL9 ....74 B5
CHD/CHDH SK8 ....181 G1
DTN/ASHW M34 ....133 F4
HYDE SK14 ....133 F4
OLDS OL8 ....91 H3

URM M41 ....137 G2
Keswick Cl BRUN/LGST M13 ..129 E4
IRL M44 ....150 C2
MDTN M24 ....72 C1
STLY SK15 ....120 D3
Keswick Dr BRAM/HZG SK7 ..193 F2
BURY BL9 ....53 E2
Keswick Gv SLFD M6 ......113 E2
Keswick Rd HALE/TIMP WA15 ..167 E3
HTNM SK4 ....158 D4
MPL/ROM SK6 ....186 D4
STRET M32 ....125 H5
URM M41 ....137 F1
Keswick St BOL BL1 ....34 A4
ROCH OL11 ....42 B1
Kettering Rd BNG/LEV M19 ..144 B3
Kettleshulme Wy
POY/DIS SK12 ....195 H5
Ketton Cl OP/CLY M11 ......130 D1
Kevin Av ROY/SHW OL2 ......75 F2
Kevin Dr CHD/CHDH SK8 ......182 B2
Kevin St BNG/LEV M19 ......144 A4
Kew Av HYDE SK14 ....148 A2
Kew Dr CHD/CHDH SK8 ......182 B2
Kew Gdns NEWH/MOS M40 ..115 H3
Kew Rd FAIL M35 ....105 F2
OLDS OL8 ....92 A1
ROCH OL11 ....43 F3
Keyhaven Wk
NEWH/MOS M40 ....115 H1
Keymer St OP/CLY M11 ......116 C2
Keynsham Rd OP/CLY M11 ..116 C2
Keystone Cl SLFD M6 ......112 D1
Key West Cl OP/CLY M11 ..116 A4
Keyworth Wk
NEWH/MOS M40 ....115 H1
Khartoum St
OLDTF/WHR M16 ....127 C4
OP/CLY M11 ....117 E5
Kibbles Brow EDGW/EG BL7 ..23 G3
Kibboth Crew RAMS BL0 ......16 C1
Kibworth Cl WHTF M45 ......69 E4
Kidderminster Wy CHAD OL9 ..74 A3
Kid St MDTN M24 ....72 C3
Kiel Cl ECC M30 ....111 F5
Kielder Hl MDTN M24 ......56 C5
Kilbride Av BOLE BL2 ......50 C5
Kilburn Av BKLY M9 ....88 A2
Kilburn Cl CHD/CHDH SK8 ..181 H5
Kilburn Rd EDGY/DAV SK3 ..12 B7
RAD M26 ....51 G5
Kilburn St OLD OL1 ....76 B3
Kilcoby Av SWIN M27 ......100 B2
Kildale Cl BOLS/LL BL3 ......47 F5
Kildare Crs ROCH OL11 ......43 F4
Kildare Rd CCHDY M21 ......141 H5
SWIN M27 ....98 D3
Kildare St FWTH BL4 ......65 E3
Kildonan Dr BOLS/LL BL3 ..47 C3
Killer St RAMS BL0 * 16 D2
Killon St BURY BL9 ....5 G7
Kilmaine Av BKLY M9 ......89 E4
Kilmaine Dr BOLS/LL BL3 ..47 E4
Kilmington Dr CHH M8 ......102 A4
Kilmory Dr BOLE BL2 ......50 C3
Kiln Bank La WHIT OL12 ....14 B8
Kilnbrook Cl OLDE OL4 ......93 G3
Kiln Brow EDGW/EG BL7 ....23 H3
Kiln Cft MPL/ROM SK6 ......161 G5
Kiln Croft La WILM/AE SK9 ..192 B3
Kiln Fld BURY BL9 ....54 A5
Kilner Cl BURY BL9 ....54 A5
Kilnerdeyne Ter MILN OL16 * ..29 H1
Kilner Wk NEWH/MOS M40 ..115 H1
Kiln Fld EDGW/EG BL7 ......23 E3
Kilnhurst Wk BOL BL1 * 2 B5
Kiln La MILN OL16 ....31 H4
Kilnside Dr BKLY M9 ......103 E3
Kiln St RAMS BL0 ....16 C3
Kiln Wk WHIT OL12 ....29 H1
Kilnwick Cl GTN M18 ......130 A5
The Kilphin HOR/BR BL6 ......46 A1
Kilrush Av ECC M30 ....111 E5
Kilsby Cl FWTH BL4 ....65 G2
HOR/BR BL6 ....46 B5
Kilsby Wk NEWH/MOS M40 * ..115 G1
Kilton Wk NEWH/MOS M40 * ..115 F1
Kilvert Dr SALE M33 ......154 A1
Kilvert St TRPK M17 ......124 A1
Kilworth Av SALE M33 ......154 A3
Kilworth Dr HOR/BR BL6 ....47 E1
Kilworth St ROCH OL11 ......42 C1
Kimberley Av MPL/ROM SK6 ..162 A4
Kimberley St BRO M7 * 101 H3
DTN/ASHW M34 ....131 F3
IRL M44 ....136 A5
MPL/ROM SK6 ....161 H3
OLDS OL8 ....9 H6
OLDTF/WHR M16 ....126 D5
PWCH M25 ....86 B5
ROY/SHW OL2 ....59 F2
SALE M33 ....154 A2
STRET M32 ....140 C1
WILM/AE SK9 ....198 B2
Kings St WHTN BL5 ....62 A3
Kingston Av BOLE BL2 ......34 D5
CHAD OL9 ....90 B3
DID/WITH M20 ....157 G5
OLD OL1 ....76 A3
Kingston Cl BRO M7 ......101 G4
HYDE SK14 ....149 G1
ROY/SHW OL2 ....60 A2
SALE M33 ....153 C4
TOT/BURYW BL8 ....52 C1
Kingston Dr ROY/SHW OL2 ..60 A2
SALE M33 ....155 F1
URM M41 ....138 B3
Kingston Gdns HYDE SK14 ..133 E5
Kingston Gv BKLY M9 ......88 C3
Kingston Hl CHD/CHDH SK8 ..170 A5
Kingston Ms HYDE SK14 ....133 E5
Kingston Rd DID/WITH M20 ..157 G5
FAIL M35 ....105 G3
RAD M26 ....52 D5
WILM/AE SK9 ....191 H5
Kingston St EDGY/DAV SK3 ..12 D4

King St BOL BL1 ....2 D4
BOLE BL2 ....35 E1
BRO M7 ....101 H5
CMANW M2 ....6 E4
CSLFD M3 ....5 H3
DROY M43 ....117 H5
DTN/ASHW M34 ....132 C2
DUK SK16 ....119 G5
ECC M30 ....111 G4
EDGW/EG BL7 ....23 E3
FAIL M35 ....104 C4
FWTH BL4 ....66 A4
HEY OL10 ....40 D4
HYDE SK14 ....133 C5
MDTN M24 ....72 D3
MILN OL16 ....10 C6
MOSL OL5 ....109 E1
OLDS OL8 ....9 F4
RAD M26 ....68 C2
RAMS BL0 ....16 C2
SLFD M6 ....100 A5
STLY SK15 ....120 D3
WHIT OL12 ....14 C3
King St East ROCH OL11 ......13 C1
STKP SK1 ....13 C1
King St South ROCH OL11 ......42 D1
King St West CSLFD M3 ......6 D4
HTNM SK4 ....12 E3
Kings Vw HTNM SK4 * 12 B3
Kingsway ALT WA14 ......165 G4
BNG/LEV M19 ....143 C4
BRAM/HZG SK7 ....184 A2
CHD/CHDH SK8 ....169 H5
DID/WITH M20 ....133 H1
DUK SK16 ....133 H1
FWTH BL4 ....88 C1
MDTN M24 ....88 C1
MILN OL16 ....30 D5
MPL/ROM SK6 ....161 F5
STRET M32 ....140 A2
SWIN M27 ....98 B2
WALK M28 ....97 E2
Kingsway Av BNG/LEV M19 ..143 H2
Kingsway Cl OLDS OL8 ......8 E7
Kingsway Crs BNG/LEV M19 ..158 B1
Kingsway Pk URM M41 ......124 C4
Kingswear Dr BOL BL1 ......33 F5
Kingswood Gv RDSH SK5 ..145 F2
Kingswood Rd ECC M30 ......110 C4
MDTN M24 ....72 C1
PWCH M25 ....85 C2
RUSH/FAL M14 ....143 G4
Kingthorpe Gdns
BOLS/LL BL3 ....48 D5
King William St ECC M30 ....110 B2
SALF M50 ....113 F5
Kingwood Av BOL BL1 ......47 G1
Kinlay Rd FWTH BL4 ....65 E5
Kinley Cl WGTN/LGST M12 ..130 A1
Kinloch Dr BOL BL1 ....48 A2
Kinloch Gdns OLDS OL8 ......91 G3
Kinloch St OLDS OL8 ......91 H3
OP/CLY M11 ....116 B3
Kinmel Av RDSH SK5 ......160 D2
Kinnaird Crs STKP SK1 ......172 C1
Kinnaird Rd DID/WITH M20 ..157 H1
Kinnerly Gv WALK M28 ......96 B1
Kinross Av OFTN SK2 ......184 B1
Kinross Cl RAMS BL0 ....26 B1
Kinross Dr BOLS/LL BL3 ......47 F2
Kinross Rd RUSH/FAL M14 ..143 G4
Kinsey Av NTHM/RTH M23 ..167 G2
Kinsley Dr WALK M28 ......81 H5
Kintore Av BRAM/HZG SK7 ..185 G2
Kintra Gv OP/CLY M11 ......116 D4
Kintyre Cl OP/CLY M11 ......116 D4
Kintyre Dr BOLS/LL BL3 ......47 F2
Kinver Rd NEWH/MOS M40 ..89 F5
Kipling Av DROY M43 ......117 H2
DTN/ASHW M34 ....132 A3
Kipling Cl OFTN SK2 ......173 F2
Kipling Rd OLD OL1 ....76 A2
Kipling St BRO M7 ....101 G4
Kippax St RUSH/FAL M14 ..128 C5
Kirby Av CHAD OL9 ....90 A3
SWIN M27 ....98 C5
Kirkbank St OLD OL1 ....8 D1
Kirkburn Vw TOT/BURYW BL8 ..37 H1
Kirkby Av NEWH/MOS M40 ..104 A3
Kirkby Cl BURY BL9 ....53 F1
Kirkby Dr SALE M33 ......155 E4
Kirkby Rd BOL BL1 ....48 A1
Kirkdale Av NEWH/MOS M40 ..89 G5
Kirkdale Dr ROY/SHW OL2 ..60 B3
Kirkebrok Rd BOLS/LL BL3 ..47 H5
Kirkfell Dr MPL/ROM SK6 ..186 D4
Kirkfell Wk OLD OL1 * 76 A1
Kirkgate Cl NEWH/MOS M40 * ..115 F2
Kirkhall La BOL BL1 ....48 B1
Kirkham Av GTN M18 ......130 C2
Kirkham Cl DTN/ASHW M34 ..132 C5
Kirkham Rd CHD/CHDH SK8 ..181 H4
Kirkham St BOLE BL2 ......34 D5
CHAD OL9 ....8 B2
LHULT M38 ....81 F2
SALF M50 ....112 D4
Kirkhaven Sq
NEWH/MOS M40 ....115 H1
Kirkhill Gra WHTN BL5 ......62 B2
Kirkhope Dr BOL BL1 ....2 B1
Kirklands BOLE BL2 ....35 E4
SALE M33 ....154 B4
Kirklee Av CHAD OL9 ......74 B3
Kirklee Rd ROCH OL11 ......43 F4
Kirklees St TOT/BURYW BL8 ..26 B4
Kirkley St HYDE SK14 ......147 H2
Kirklinton Dr BKLY M9 ......103 E4
Kirkman Av ECC M30 ......110 C3
Kirkman Cl GTN M18 ......130 C4
Kirkmanshulme La
GTN M18 ....129 H4
WGTN/LGST M12 ....129 H4
Kirkman St BURY BL9 ......69 G1
Kirk Rd BNG/LEV M19 ......144 B4
Kirkstall Av HEY OL10 ......40 B3
LIT OL15 ....20 D2

Kirkstall Cl POY/DIS SK12 195 E3
Kirkstall Rd MDTN M24 72 C1
URM M41 124 D5
Kirkstall Sq BRUN/LGST M13 128 D2
Kirkstead Cl OP/CLY M11 116 B5
Kirkstead Rd CHD/CHDH SK8 183 F5
Kirkstile Pl SWIN M27 83 H3
Kirkstone Av WALK M28 97 G1
Kirkstone Cl OLD OL1 75 G3
Kirkstone Dr MDTN M24 72 B2
ROY/SHW OL2 58 D3
Kirkstone Rd HYDE SK14 133 F3
NEWH/MOS M40 89 F5
Kirk St GTN M18 130 C3
Kirkwall Dr BOLE BL2 49 G4
Kirkway BKLY M9 88 D3
MDTN M24 88 D1
ROCH OL11 43 E4
Kirkwood Dr
NEWH/MOS M40 115 F1
Kirtley Av ECC M30 111 E2
Kirtlington Cl ROY/SHW OL2 59 H4
Kitchener Av IRL M44 150 B2
Kitchener St BOLS/LL BL3 65 G1
TOT/BURYW BL8 37 H5
Kitchener Wy FWTH BL4 65 E3
Kitchen St MILN OL16 10 E5
Kitepool St ECC M30 * 110 B2
Kitter St WHIT OL12 19 H5
Kitt's Moss La BRAM/HZG SK7 193 G1
Kitty Wheeldon Gdns
SALE M33 * 154 B1
Kiveton Cl WALK M28 81 H5
Kiwi St SLFD M6 113 G3
Knaresborough Cl RDSH SK5 145 E2
Knarr Barn La UPML OL3 78 A1
Knarr La UPML OL3 78 B2
Knight Crs MDTN M24 72 A1
Knightley Wk
NEWH/MOS M40 103 E5
Knightsbridge STKP SK1 13 G1
Knightsbridge Cl BRO M7 101 G2
WILM/AE SK9 199 G1
Knight's Cl PWCH M25 86 A2
Knight St AULW OL7 119 E3
BOL BL1 2 E2
DID/WITH M20 157 G4
HYDE SK14 148 B2
TOT/BURYW BL8 * 37 H4
Knightswood BOLS/LL BL3 63 G1
Knightswood Rd CHH M8 102 B3
Kniveton Cl WGTN/LGST M12 129 G2
Kniveton Rd WGTN/LGST M12 129 G2
Knivton St HYDE SK14 * 134 A5
Knole Av POY/DIS SK12 195 G3
Knoll St BRO M7 101 G3
ROCH OL11 42 A3
The Knoll MOSL OL5 108 C1
ROY/SHW OL2 * 60 B3
Knott Fold HYDE SK14 147 H3
Knott Hill La UPML OL3 78 B1
Knott La BOL BL1 32 C4
HYDE SK14 147 H3
Knott Lanes OLDS OL8 106 B2
Knott St ORD M5 112 C4
Knowe Av WYTH/NTH M22 180 C3
Knowl Cl
DTN/ASHW M34 145 G1
RAMS BL0 16 D4
Knowldale Wy
WGTN/LGST M12 129 F3
Knowle Av AULW OL7 119 F1
Knowle Dr PWCH M25 85 H5
Knowle Pk WILM/AE SK9 191 H4
Knowle Rd
MPL/ROM SK6 175 H3
Knowles Edge St BOL BL1 33 F4
Knowles St
RAD M26 52 B5
The Knowles OLDS OL8 105 G1
Knowl Hill Dr WHIT OL12 28 B1
Knowl Rd MILN OL16 31 E5
ROY/SHW OL2 60 B3
Knowls La OLDE OL4 93 E2
Knowl St OLDS OL8 90 D5
STLY SK15 121 E3
Knowl Syke St WHIT OL12 19 H1
Knowl Top La UPML OL3 79 G5
Knowl Vw LIT OL15 31 G1
TOT/BURYW BL8 26 B5
Knowsley Av OLDE OL4 77 F5
ORD M5 113 G5
URM M41 124 B4
Knowsley Crs STKP SK1 172 C1
Knowsley Dr OLDE OL4 77 F5
SWIN M27 98 C4
Knowsley Gra BOL BL1 47 E2
Knowsley Gn OLDE OL4 77 F5
ORD M5 * 113 G5
Knowsley Rd BOL BL1 33 E4
BOLE BL2 36 B5
BRAM/HZG SK7 185 G4
STKP SK1 172 C1
WHTF M45 69 G4
Knowsley St BOL BL1 2 E3
BURY BL9 4 C7
CHH M8 114 D1
WHIT OL12 10 B4
Knowsley Ter OLDE OL4 * 77 F5
STKP SK1 * 172 C1
Knutsford Av HTNM SK4 144 D4
SALE M33 155 F2
Knutsford Rd GTN M18 130 B4
WILM/AE SK9 198 C5
Knutsford St SLFD M6 112 D3
Knutshaw Crs BOLS/LL BL3 63 E2
Knypersley Av OFTN SK2 172 D2
Krokus Sq CHAD OL9 * 74 B5
Kylemore Av BOLS/LL BL3 48 A4
Kyle Rd BRAM/HZG SK7 * 185 G3
Kynder St
DTN/ASHW M34 132 C5

L

Labrador Quay SALQ M50 126 C1
Labtec St SWIN M27 99 G1
Laburnum Av AUL OL6 107 F4
CHAD OL9 74 C3
DTN/ASHW M34 118 B4
ECC M30 110 B5
FAIL M35 105 E4
HYDE SK14 147 H3
ROY/SHW OL2 60 A3
STLY SK15 120 C5
SWIN M27 98 D4
TOT/BURYW BL8 26 A4
WHTF M45 * 85 G1
Laburnum Cl
HALE/TIMP WA15 166 C4
Laburnum Dr WHTF M45 69 H3
Laburnum Gv PWCH M25 85 H2
Laburnum La
HALE/TIMP WA15 177 H4
MILN OL16 44 D3
Laburnum Pk BOLE BL2 34 D1
Laburnum Rd
DTN/ASHW M34 131 E5
FWTH BL4 65 G4
GTN M18 130 C4
IRL M44 150 C1
MDTN M24 73 F4
OLDS OL8 105 H2
URM M41 124 A4
WALK M28 82 B5
Laburnum St BOL BL1 2 A3
SLFD M6 113 E3
Laburnum Ter ROCH OL11 42 D2
Laburnum Wy EDGY/DAV SK3 171 E1
LIT OL15 20 C3
Lacerta Ms BRO M7 113 H2
Lacey Av WILM/AE SK9 199 E2
Lacey Gn WILM/AE SK9 199 E1
Lacey Gv WILM/AE SK9 199 F1
Lackford Dr NEWH/MOS M40 115 F1
Lacrosse Av OLDS OL8 90 D3
Lacy Gv STRET M32 140 B2
Lacy St STKP SK1 13 G5
STRET M32 140 B2
Lacy Wk WGTN/LGST M12 115 G5
Ladbrooke Cl AUL OL6 119 H1
Ladbrooke Rd AUL OL6 107 F5
Ladcastle Rd UPML OL3 78 D3
UPML OL3 94 D1
Ladhill La UPML OL3 95 E2
Ladybarn Crs BRAM/HZG SK7 194 A1
RUSH/FAL M14 143 F4
Ladybarn La RUSH/FAL M14 143 F3
Ladybarn Rd RUSH/FAL M14 143 F3
Ladybower CHD/CHDH SK8 183 F1
Ladybridge Av WALK M28 96 D2
Lady Bridge La BOL BL1 47 G2
Ladybridge Ri CHD/CHDH SK8 183 F1
Ladybridge Rd
CHD/CHDH SK8 183 F1
Ladybrook Av
HALE/TIMP WA15 166 C2
Ladybrook Rd BRAM/HZG SK7 183 F3
Ladyfield St WILM/AE SK9 199 E3
Ladyfield Ter WILM/AE SK9 199 F3
Ladyhill Vw WALK M28 96 D2
Ladyhouse Cl MILN OL16 44 D2
Ladyhouse La MILN OL16 44 D1
Lady Kelvin Rd ALT WA14 165 F3
Ladymere Dr WALK M28 96 C2
Lady Rd OLDE OL4 92 D1
Ladys Cl POY/DIS SK12 195 F3
Ladyshore Cl ORD M5 113 E4
Ladyshore Rd BOLS/LL BL3 67 F2
Ladysmith Av BURY BL9 38 D1
Ladysmith Dr AUL OL6 108 A5
Ladysmith Rd AUL OL6 108 A5
DID/WITH M20 157 H4
STLY SK15 120 D1
Ladysmith St EDGY/DAV SK3 171 H2
OLDS OL8 90 D4
The Ladysmith AUL OL6 108 A5
Ladythorn Av MPL/ROM SK6 175 F4
Ladythorn Ct PWCH M25 85 H5
Ladythorn Crs
BRAM/HZG SK7 194 A1
Ladythorne Av PWCH M25 85 H5
Ladythorne Dr PWCH M25 85 H5
Ladythorn Gv BRAM/HZG SK7 194 A1
Ladythorn Rd BRAM/HZG SK7 193 H1
Ladywell Av LHULT M38 81 F3
Ladywell Cl BRAM/HZG SK7 184 B2
Ladywell Gv LHULT M38 81 F2
Lagos Cl RUSH/FAL M14 128 B4
Laindon Rd RUSH/FAL M14 129 F5
Lake Bank LIT OL15 20 D5
Lake Dr MDTN M24 72 C5
Lakeland Crs BURY BL9 53 F3
Lakeland Dr ROY/SHW OL2 * 58 D1
Lakelands Dr BOLS/LL BL3 47 G4
Lakenheath Cl BOL BL1 23 E5
Lakenheath Dr BOL BL1 23 E5
Lake Rd DTN/ASHW M34 132 C4
STLY SK15 120 C1
TRPK M17 125 H1
Lake Side BURY BL9 53 G3
LIT OL15 31 H1
Lakeside CHD/CHDH SK8 181 H2
Lakeside Av AULW OL7 119 E1
BOLS/LL BL3 65 F2
WALK M28 82 A2
Lakeside Cl GTN M18 131 E2
Lakeside Dr POY/DIS SK12 195 F2
Lakeside Gn OFTN SK2 172 D3
Lakeside Ri BKLY M9 87 F4
Lakeside Wy BURY BL9 4 E6
Lakes Rd DUK SK16 119 H5
MPL/ROM SK6 175 G4
Lake St BOLS/LL BL3 * 49 E4
OFTN SK2 172 C4
Lakeswood DUK SK16 * 119 G5
Lake Vw BKLY M9 88 D5
Lakin St NEWH/MOS M40 103 H3
Laleham Gn BRAM/HZG SK7 183 G1
Lamb Cl WGTN/LGST M12 * 129 G3
Lamb Ct CSLFD M3 * 6 B3
Lambert Dr SALE M33 138 D5
Lamberton Dr
NTHM/RTH M23 167 F3
Lambert St AULW OL7 119 E4
Lambeth Av FAIL M35 105 F2
Lambeth Gv MPL/ROM SK6 161 H1
Lambeth Rd NEWH/MOS M40 116 D1
RDSH SK5 145 F4
Lambeth Ter ROCH OL11 42 C1
Lamb La CSLFD M3 6 B3
Lambourn Cl BOLS/LL BL3 48 D4
POY/DIS SK12 195 E3
Lambourne Cl
WYTH/NTH M22 180 C4
Lambourne Gv MILN OL16 44 C1
Lambourn Rd URM M41 123 E4
Lambton Rd CCHDY M21 141 H3
WALK M28 98 B4
Lambton St BOLS/LL BL3 64 B2
ECC M30 110 C1
Lamburn Av NEWH/MOS M40 * 89 G5
Lamerton Wy WILM/AE SK9 192 B5
Lamorna Cl BRO M7 101 E2
Lamphey Cl BOL BL1 47 E1
Lamplight Wy SWIN M27 100 B3
Lamport Cl CMANE M1 128 C1
Lamport Ct CMANE M1 128 C1
Lampson St CHH M8 114 B1
Lampton Cl ALT WA14 165 G2
Lamsholme Cl BNG/LEV M19 144 A1
Lanark Av WYTH/NTH M22 168 C1
Lanark Cl BRAM/HZG SK7 185 H2
HEY OL10 40 A5
Lanbury Dr CHH M8 102 A3
Lancashire Ct CHAD OL9 8 A6
Lancashire Hl HTNM SK4 159 H3
Lancashire Rd PART M31 150 D4
Lancashire St
NEWH/MOS M40 103 G5
Lancaster Av FAIL M35 104 D3
FWTH BL4 65 E4
MDTN M24 73 F5
RAMS BL0 16 B4
STLY SK15 120 D2
URM M41 124 D5
WHTF M45 69 H5
Lancaster Cl BOL BL1 3 G5
BRAM/HZG SK7 185 E4
MPL/ROM SK6 161 H5
Lancaster Dr BOLS/LL BL3 51 E5
BURY BL9 27 G3
PWCH M25 86 B5
Lancaster Rd DID/WITH M20 157 F3
DROY M43 117 G2
DTN/ASHW M34 146 D2
IRL M44 150 B1
SLFD M6 112 D1
WILM/AE SK9 199 H1
Lancaster St CHAD OL9 90 B4
MOSL OL5 * 108 C1
RAD M26 67 H1
STKP SK1 13 J1
Lancaster Wk BOL BL1 * 33 H4
Lancelot Rd WYTH/NTH M22 181 E2
Lancelyn Dr WILM/AE SK9 199 G2
Lanchester Dr BOLS/LL BL3 48 C4
Lanchester St
NEWH/MOS M40 115 H2
Lancing Av DID/WITH M20 158 A3
Lancing Wk CHAD OL9 * 90 B1
Landau Dr WALK M28 81 E4
Landcross Rd RUSH/FAL M14 143 E2
Landedmans WHTN BL5 62 A5
Lander Gv BKLY M9 88 C4
Landkey Cl NTHM/RTH M23 155 G4
Land La WILM/AE SK9 199 F4
Landmark Ct BOL BL1 32 C5
Landos Rd NEWH/MOS M40 115 F2
Landrace Dr WALK M28 96 C4
Landsberg Rd FAIL M35 105 G2
Landseer Dr MPL/ROM SK6 175 G2
Landseer St OLDE OL4 9 J6
Lands End Rd MDTN M24 71 G5
Lane Brow OLDE OL4 93 G2
Lane Dr OLDE OL4 93 G2
Lane End ECC M30 111 G4
HEY OL10 56 C1
Lane End Cl FAIL M35 105 F4
Lane End Rd BNG/LEV M19 158 A2
Lane Ends MPL/ROM SK6 162 C3
Lanegate HYDE SK14 147 H3
Lane Head Rd OLDE OL4 93 F4
Lane Meadow ROY/SHW OL2 59 H3
Lane North BOLS/LL BL3 * 48 A5
Laneside Av ROY/SHW OL2 60 C2
Laneside Cl LIT OL15 20 D2
Laneside Dr BRAM/HZG SK7 184 B3
Laneside Rd DID/WITH M20 169 H1
The Lane BOL BL1 47 E2
Lanfield Dr CHH M8 102 A3
Langcroft Dr
NEWH/MOS M40 104 B5
Langdale Av BNG/LEV M19 144 B3
MILN OL16 58 D1
OLDS OL8 91 E3
Langdale Cl CHD/CHDH SK8 181 H1
DTN/ASHW M34 146 C2
HALE/TIMP WA15 166 B4
MPL/ROM SK6 186 D4
Langdale Dr BURY BL9 69 H1
MDTN M24 72 C1
WALK M28 97 G1
Langdale Rd BRAM/HZG SK7 193 F2
HTNM SK4 144 C5
MPL/ROM SK6 162 A1
PART M31 150 D3
RUSH/FAL M14 129 E4
SALE M33 153 H5
STRET M32 * 125 H5
Langdale St BOLS/LL BL3 64 D1
FWTH BL4 65 H5
Langden Cl ROY/SHW OL2 59 H1
Langdon Cl BOL BL1 2 B2
Langfield Av
OLDTF/WHR M16 127 G5
Langfield Crs DROY M43 * 118 B3
Langford Dr IRL M44 136 C2
Langford Gdns BOLS/LL BL3 48 D5
Langford Rd DID/WITH M20 142 C5
HTNM SK4 159 F2
Langford St
DTN/ASHW M34 * 132 C5
Langham Cl BOL BL1 23 F5
Langham Ct STRET M32 125 F4
Langham Gv
HALE/TIMP WA15 166 C1
Langham Rd ALT WA14 177 F2
HTNM SK4 159 E5
OLDS OL8 91 F3
SLFD M6 113 E3
Langham St AULW OL7 106 D5
Langholm Dr BOLE BL2 50 C3
Langholme Cl HULME M15 * 127 G1
Langholme Pl ECC M30 110 C3
Langholme Wy HEY OL10 40 A5
Langland Cl BNG/LEV M19 144 D1
Langland Dr ECC M30 124 B1
Langley Av BRAM/HZG SK7 184 C3
MDTN M24 56 B5
OLDE OL4 93 G2
PWCH M25 86 A2
Langley Cl URM M41 139 E1
Langley Dr WILM/AE SK9 192 B4
Langley Gdns PWCH M25 86 A1
Langley Hall Rd PWCH M25 86 A1
Langley La HEY OL10 55 H5
Langley Rd PWCH M25 85 H2
RUSH/FAL M14 143 E2
SALE M33 153 H2
SWIN M27 100 C2
Langley Rd South SLFD M6 100 D5
Langness St OP/CLY M11 116 D4
Lango St OLDTF/WHR M16 * 127 F4
Langport Av WGTN/LGST M12 129 F3
Langsett Av SLFD M6 112 D1
Langshaw Rd BOLS/LL BL3 48 B4
Langshaw St
OLDTF/WHR M16 127 F4
SLFD M6 113 E2
Langshaw Wk BOLS/LL BL3 * 48 B4
Langside Av BKLY M9 88 B3
Langside Dr BOLS/LL BL3 47 F5
Langston Gn BRAM/HZG SK7 184 B3
Langston St CSLFD M3 * 114 C2
Langthorne St BNG/LEV M19 144 B3
Langthorne Wk BOLS/LL BL3 2 A7
Langton Cl FAIL M35 105 G2
Langton St HEY OL10 40 D3
MDTN M24 72 D4
SLFD M6 112 D3
Langton Ter ROCH OL11 42 D2
Langtree Cl WALK M28 96 C2
Langworthy Av LHULT M38 81 G3
Langworthy Rd
NEWH/MOS M40 103 H3
SLFD M6 113 E2
Lanhill Dr CHH M8 102 D4
Lankro Wy TRPK M17 111 G4
Lansdale Gdns BNG/LEV M19 158 B1
Lansdale St ECC M30 110 B5
Lansdown Cl CHD/CHDH SK8 183 F5
Lansdowne Av
DTN/ASHW M34 118 B4
MPL/ROM SK6 162 C4
Lansdowne Cl BOLE BL2 * 34 C5
RAMS BL0 16 C3
Lansdowne Ct CHAD OL9 90 C1
Lansdowne Dr WALK M28 96 D2
Lansdowne Rd ALT WA14 165 G3
BOLE BL2 34 C5
CHAD OL9 8 A4
CHH M8 102 B2
ECC M30 111 E2
SALE M33 139 G5
URM M41 137 G3
Lansdowne Rd North
URM M41 137 G2
Lansdowne St ROCH OL11 29 F4
Lanstead Dr NEWH/MOS M40 115 H3
Lapwing Cl ROCH OL11 28 B4
STLY SK15 120 D1
Lapwing La DID/WITH M20 157 F1
RDSH SK5 146 A5
Larch Av CHD/CHDH SK8 182 D3
RAD M26 68 C3
STRET M32 140 B2
SWIN M27 98 B4
Larch Cl FAIL M35 105 E4
MPL/ROM SK6 174 D4
NTHM/RTH M23 166 D1
POY/DIS SK12 195 G4
The Larches MOSL OL5 109 E1
Larch Gv CHAD OL9 74 C4
SWIN M27 83 E5
Larch Rd DTN/ASHW M34 132 D5
ECC M30 110 B1
PART M31 150 D3
Larch St BURY BL9 5 K4
OLDS OL8 8 D5
Larchview Rd MDTN M24 73 F4
Larchway BRAM/HZG SK7 183 F5
MILN OL16 31 E4
MPL/ROM SK6 187 E5
Larchwood CHAD OL9 73 H5
Larchwood Av BKLY M9 103 G3
Larchwood Cl SALE M33 153 F2
Larchwood Dr WILM/AE SK9 199 H2
Larchwood St BOL BL1 34 A4
Larke Ri DID/WITH M20 157 E3
Larkfield Av LHULT M38 81 E2
Larkfield Cl AULW OL7 107 E3
TOT/BURYW BL8 25 H1
Larkfield Gv BOLE BL2 3 K2
Larkfield Ms LHULT M38 81 E2
Larkhall Ri WYTH/NTH M22 168 D4
Lark Hl FWTH BL4 66 A5
STLY SK15 120 D1
Larkhill Cl HALE/TIMP WA15 166 C3
Lark Hill La UPML OL3 78 D1
Larkhill Pl WHIT OL12 10 B2
Larkhill Rd CHD/CHDH SK8 171 F4
Lark Hill Rd EDGY/DAV SK3 12 B5
UPML OL3 78 C2
Larkhill Vw CHD/CHDH SK8 171 F4
Larkhill Wk CHH M8 102 C4
Larkside Av WALK M28 82 B4
Larkspur Cl BOL BL1 34 B3
Larks Ri DROY M43 118 C2
Lark St BOL BL1 3 F3
FWTH BL4 * 66 A5
OLD OL1 * 76 C1
Larkswood Dr OFTN SK2 173 G4
Larkwood Cl STLY SK15 109 F3
Larmuth Av CCHDY M21 141 G5
Larne Av EDGY/DAV SK3 171 E2
STRET M32 140 A1
Larne St OP/CLY M11 116 B5
Larwood Av HTNM SK4 158 D5
Lascar Av ORD M5 113 F5
Lashbrook Cl
NEWH/MOS M40 115 G1
Lassell Fold HYDE SK14 134 C2
Lassell St OP/CLY M11 * 131 E1
Lastingham St
NEWH/MOS M40 104 B4
Latchford St AULW OL7 119 F1
Latchmere Rd RUSH/FAL M14 143 E3
Latham Cl MPL/ROM SK6 161 G1
Latham St BOL BL1 34 A4
OP/CLY M11 131 E1
Lathbury Rd BKLY M9 103 E4
Lathom Gv SALE M33 155 F3
Lathom Hall Av OLDE OL4 * 77 F5
Lathom Rd DID/WITH M20 143 F4
IRL M44 136 B3
Lathom St BURY BL9 5 F1
Latimer St OLDE OL4 9 K5
Latin St MILN OL16 * 29 H5
Latrigg Crs MDTN M24 71 H2
Latrobe St DROY M43 117 H5
Lauderdale Crs
BRUN/LGST M13 128 D2
Launceston Cl BRAM/HZG SK7 184 A5
OLDS OL8 92 B3
Launceston Rd RAD M26 51 G4
Laundry St SLFD M6 113 E1
Laura St BURY BL9 26 D1
Laureate Wy DTN/ASHW M34 147 E4
Laurel Av BOLS/LL BL3 50 B4
CHAD OL9 73 G4
CHD/CHDH SK8 170 A4
RUSH/FAL M14 142 C1
Laurel Bank HYDE SK14 147 G3
STLY SK15 121 E5
Laurel Bank Gdns BKLY M9 88 A3
Laurel Ct BOL BL1 2 E2
MILN OL16 * 30 C5
Laurel Dr HALE/TIMP WA15 166 C5
LHULT M38 81 F3
Laurel End La HTNM SK4 158 D3
Laurel Gn DTN/ASHW M34 147 E1
Laurel Gv SLFD M6 * 112 B3
Laurel Rd HTNM SK4 159 E2
Laurels Dr LIT OL15 31 G1
The Laurels MOSL OL5 109 E1
Laurel St BOL BL1 48 B2
BURY BL9 5 J4
HTNM SK4 12 E2
MDTN M24 73 G4
OLDE OL4 92 A1
TOT/BURYW BL8 26 A5
Laurel Wk PART M31 150 D4
Laurel Wy BRAM/HZG SK7 183 F4
Laurence Cl WGTN/LGST M12 129 H2
Lauren Cl OLDE OL4 93 E1
Lauria Ter BOLE BL2 36 C5
Laurie Pl WHIT OL12 10 C2
Lausanne Rd BRAM/HZG SK7 183 H1
DID/WITH M20 142 D4
Lavender Cl NTHM/RTH M23 155 F5
SALE M33 153 F1
Lavender Rd FWTH BL4 65 F3
OLDE OL4 92 D3
Lavenders Brow STKP SK1 13 H3
Lavender St RAD M26 67 G1
Lavenham Av OP/CLY M11 117 E4
Lavenham Cl BRAM/HZG SK7 185 F4
BURY BL9 69 G1
Laverton Cl BURY BL9 39 H5
Lavington Av CHD/CHDH SK8 170 D4
Lavington Gv GTN M18 130 C4
Lavinia St ECC M30 110 C3
Lavister Av BNG/LEV M19 158 A3
Lawefield Crs SWIN M27 83 G2
Lawers Av CHAD OL9 74 B4
Lawflat WHIT OL12 19 H3
Lawler Av ORD M5 127 E2
Lawnbank Cl MDTN M24 72 B3
Lawn Cl OLDS OL8 92 B4
Lawndale Cl RAD M26 68 C2
Lawn Dr HALE/TIMP WA15 165 H3
SWIN M27 98 D3
Lawngreen Av CCHDY M21 141 E4
Lawnside Ms DID/WITH M20 157 F1
The Lawns ALT WA14 177 F1
Lawn St BOL BL1 2 A1
Lawnswood ROCH OL11 42 B2
Lawnswood Dr SWIN M27 99 F4
Lawnswood Park Rd
SWIN M27 99 F4
Lawrence Cl WHIT OL12 28 D2
Lawrence Pl POY/DIS SK12 195 E5
Lawrence Rd ALT WA14 165 F3
BRAM/HZG SK7 185 F1
URM M41 123 F5
Lawrence St BURY BL9 53 G5
EDGY/DAV SK3 13 F4
Lawrie Av RAMS BL0 16 C3
Lawson Av CHD/CHDH SK8 169 G4
Lawson Cl MDTN M24 56 D5
WALK M28 98 B3
Lawson Gv SALE M33 139 G5
Lawson Rd BOL BL1 33 F4
Lawson St BKLY M9 87 H5
BOL BL1 33 H2
Law St ROCH OL11 42 B1
Lawton Av BRAM/HZG SK7 183 H4
Lawton Cl MPL/ROM SK6 161 G5
Lawton Moor Rd
NTHM/RTH M23 155 H5
Lawton Rd HTNM SK4 159 F2
Lawton St DROY M43 118 A3
OP/CLY M11 130 C1
STLY SK15 121 E4
WHIT OL12 10 E3
Laxey St NEWH/MOS M40 * 104 A3
Laxfield Dr URM M41 123 E4
Laxford Gv BOLS/LL BL3 47 F3
Laxley Cl CHAD OL9 90 C2
Layard St AUL OL6 119 F2
Laycock Av BOLE BL2 34 C3
STLY SK15 121 H1
Laycock Crs FAIL M35 105 E4
Laycock Dr DUK SK16 134 B1
Laycock Gv FAIL M35 105 E3
Laycock St MILN OL16 20 A5

Layfield Cl TOT/BURYW BL8 25 G3
Laystall St CMANE M1 7 J4
Laythe Barn Cl MILN OL16 31 F5
Layton Av HYDE SK14 133 E5
Layton Cl STKP SK1 13 J5
Layton Dr FWTH BL4 82 C1
MPL/ROM SK6 162 B3
Layton St NEWH/MOS M40 115 G3
Leabank St BNG/LEV M19 144 A2
Leabrook Dr NEWH/MOS M40 104 D2
Leaburn Dr BNG/LEV M19 158 B2
Leach Cl MILN OL16 30 D1
Leach St BOLS/LL BL3 48 D4
FWTH BL4 66 B3
GTN M18 130 A3
MILN OL16 30 C5
PWCH M25 85 G3
ROY/SHW OL2 60 B3
Leach Wk OLDE OL4 76 D4
Leaconfield Dr WALK M28 97 G3
Lea Ct FAIL M35 104 D3
Leacroft Av BOLE BL2 50 A4
Leacroft Rd CCHDY M21 156 C1
Leadale Ri OLDE OL4 * 93 F1
Leader Williams Rd IRL M44 136 B2
Lea Dr BKLY M9 88 C4
Leafield Av DID/WITH M20 158 A2
Leafield Cl RAD M26 67 H1
Leafield Dr CHD/CHDH SK8 192 C1
WALK M28 96 B4
Leafield Rd POY/DIS SK12 197 H1
Leaford Av DTN/ASHW M34 132 A4
Leaford Cl DTN/ASHW M34 132 A4
Leaf St BOLE BL2 49 G4
HULME M15 128 A2
RDSH SK5 145 E4
Leagate URM M41 139 E2
Lea Gate Cl BOLE BL2 35 E1
League St MILN OL16 43 F1
Leaholme Cl NEWH/MOS M40 104 C5
Leah St LIT OL15 * 21 E3
Leak St OLDTF/WHR M16 127 F2
Leamington Av BURY BL9 27 F3
DID/WITH M20 157 E2
Leamington Rd ECC M30 110 C2
RDSH SK5 145 E4
URM M41 124 A5
Leamington St OLDE OL4 76 B4
OP/CLY M11 130 C1
WHIT OL12 10 B4
Lea Mount Dr BURY BL9 39 G2
Leam St AUL OL6 120 A1
Leander Cl BKLY M9 88 B5
Leander Dr ROCH OL11 42 C5
Lea Rd CHD/CHDH SK8 181 G3
HTNM SK4 159 E2
Leaside Av OLD OL1 74 B2
Leaside Cl WHIT OL12 29 G1
Leaside Dr DID/WITH M20 158 A1
Leaside Gv WALK M28 82 B4
Leaside Wy WILM/AE SK9 199 F4
The Leas HALE/TIMP WA15 178 C1
Leaton Av NTHM/RTH M23 167 H3
Leavale Cl LHULT M38 81 E3
Lea Vw ROY/SHW OL2 74 D1
Leaway WHIT OL12 19 H2
Lecester Rd CHH M8 102 C4
Leckenby Cl WALK M28 96 B4
Leconfield Dr BKLY M9 88 B4
Leconfield Rd ECC M30 110 A1
Lecturers Cl BOLS/LL BL3 49 E4
Ledbrooke Cl ORD M5 127 E1
Ledburn Cl HULME M15 127 G2
Ledbury Av URM M41 124 B5
Ledbury Cl MDTN M24 88 D1
Ledbury Rd FAIL M35 * 117 F1
Ledge Ley CHD/CHDH SK8 182 C4
Ledsham Av BKLY M9 87 F2
Ledson Rd NTHM/RTH M23 167 G4
Ledward La ALT WA14 177 E2
Lee Av ALT WA14 165 F2
BOLS/LL BL3 64 C1
Lee Bank WHTN BL5 62 B4
Leech Av AUL OL6 107 H5
Leech Brook Av
DTN/ASHW M34 132 B3
Leech Brook Cl
DTN/ASHW M34 132 B2
Leech St HYDE SK14 148 B1
STLY SK15 120 D4
Lee Cl IRL M44 136 B2
Lee Ct WYTH/NTH M22 * 168 D1
Lee Crs STRET M32 140 C1
Lee Dale Cl
DTN/ASHW M34 147 E1
Leeds Cl BURY BL9 70 A2
Leefields Cl UPML OL3 79 E4
Lee Ga BOLE BL2 35 E1
Leegate Cl HTNM SK4 158 C2
Leegate Dr BKLY M9 88 C3
Leegate Gdns HTNM SK4 158 C2
Leegate Rd HTNM SK4 158 D2
Leegrange Rd BKLY M9 103 F1
Lee Gv FWTH BL4 65 E4
Leek St RAD M26 67 H1
Leemans Hill St
TOT/BURYW BL8 37 F1
Lees Av DTN/ASHW M34 146 C1
Lees Brook Pk OLDE OL4 92 C1
Lees Gv OLDE OL4 92 C2
Lees Hall Crs RUSH/FAL M14 143 F3
Leeside HTNM SK4 158 D5
Lees New Rd AUL OL6 107 G1
OLDE OL4 93 E3
Lees Park Av DROY M43 118 B3
Lees Rd AUL OL6 107 G3
BRAM/HZG SK7 193 G2
MOSL OL5 93 G4
OLDE OL4 9 K3
OLDE OL4 92 B1
Lees St AUL OL6 119 G1
DROY M43 118 A3
GTN M18 130 D2
MDTN M24 73 G5
MOSL OL5 * 93 H5
OLDS OL8 106 C2
STLY SK15 120 D3
SWIN M27 99 E1
Lees St East ROY/SHW OL2 60 A2
Leestone Rd WYTH/NTH M22 168 D3
Lee St BURY BL9 27 G3
LIT OL15 21 E2
MDTN M24 72 C1
OLDS OL8 8 E6
STKP SK1 13 G4
UPML OL3 79 E4
Leesway OLDE OL4 92 D2
Leesway Dr DTN/ASHW M34 147 E1
Leeswood Av CCHDY M21 141 G5
Leewood SWIN M27 83 G3
Left Bank CSLFD M3 6 C4
Le Gendre St BOLE BL2 34 D5
Legh Cl POY/DIS SK12 195 F4
Legh Dr DTN/ASHW M34 118 A4
MPL/ROM SK6 147 F5
Legh Rd BRO M7 101 G2
POY/DIS SK12 197 F1
SALE M33 155 F3
Legh St BRO M7 101 G2
ECC M30 110 D4
Legion Gv BRO M7 101 H4
Legwood Ct URM M41 138 C1
Leicester Av BRO M7 * 102 A2
DROY M43 117 G2
DTN/ASHW M34 146 D2
HALE/TIMP WA15 166 B1
Leicester Rd BRO M7 101 H3
FAIL M35 105 F5
HALE/TIMP WA15 177 H2
SALE M33 154 C1
WHTF M45 69 E3
Leicester St AULW OL7 119 G1
OLDE OL4 92 A1
RDSH SK5 145 E1
ROCH OL11 43 F1
Leigh Av MPL/ROM SK6 174 D3
SWIN M27 98 C5
Leighbrook Rd
RUSH/FAL M14 142 D3
Leigh Cl TOT/BURYW BL8 25 H4
Leigh Fold HYDE SK14 133 H3
Leigh La TOT/BURYW BL8 37 F3
Leigh Rd HALE/TIMP WA15 177 H2
WALK M28 96 B4
WHTN BL5 62 A5
WILM/AE SK9 198 A5
Leigh St FWTH BL4 66 A4
HEY OL10 40 D4
HYDE SK14 148 A1
MILN OL16 31 E4
TOT/BURYW BL8 37 E2
Leighton Av BOL BL1 48 A1
LIT OL15 31 G1
Leighton Dr MPL/ROM SK6 175 H1
Leighton Rd OLDTF/WHR M16 127 F4
Leighton St NEWH/MOS M40 103 H2
Leinster Rd SWIN M27 98 D3
Leinster St FWTH BL4 65 H4
Leith Av SALE M33 155 F2
Leith Pl OLDS OL8 91 F5
Leith Rd SALE M33 155 F3
Le Mans Crs BOL BL1 2 E5
Lemnos St OLD OL1 9 J2
Lena St BOL BL1 34 A4
CMANE M1 7 H5
Len Cox Wk ANC M4 * 7 H3
Lenfield La OLD OL1 75 F3
Leng Rd NEWH/MOS M40 104 C5
Lenham Cl RDSH SK5 145 H5
Lenham Gdns BOLE BL2 50 B3
Lennox Gdns BOLS/LL BL3 47 G4
Lennox St AUL OL6 119 H2
Lenora St BOLS/LL BL3 48 A5
Lenten Gv HEY OL10 56 B2
Lentmead Dr BKLY M9 103 H1
Lenton Gdns WYTH/NTH M22 168 D4
Lentworth Dr WALK M28 81 H2
Leominster Dr
WYTH/NTH M22 180 D1
Leominster Rd MDTN M24 * 89 E1
Leonardin Cl ROY/SHW OL2 59 G1
Leonard St BOLS/LL BL3 64 D1
ROCH OL11 42 B5
Leopold Av DID/WITH M20 157 F1
Leopold St ROCH OL11 29 G4
Lepp Crs TOT/BURYW BL8 26 D5
Leroy Dr BKLY M9 88 A5
Lerryn Dr BRAM/HZG SK7 183 G3
Lesley Rd URM M41 139 G2
Leslie Av BURY BL9 69 G1
CHAD OL9 90 C4
Leslie Gv HALE/TIMP WA15 166 B3
Leslie Hough Wy SLFD M6 113 G2
Leslie St BOLE BL2 3 J1
RUSH/FAL M14 128 C5
Lester Rd LHULT M38 80 D2
Lester St STRET M32 140 B1
Letchworth Av ROCH OL11 43 F1
Letchworth St RUSH/FAL M14 128 C5
Letham St OLDS OL8 91 G5
Levedale Rd BKLY M9 88 B3
Leven Cl FWTH BL4 83 E2
Levenhurst Rd CHH M8 102 A3
Levens Cl CHD/CHDH SK8 169 G5
Levens Dr BOLE BL2 35 F5
Levenshulme Rd GTN M18 130 C4
Levenshulme Ter
BNG/LEV M19 * 144 A2
Levens Rd BRAM/HZG SK7 184 D2
Levens St NEWH/MOS M40 103 H3
SLFD M6 101 E5
Levens Wk CHAD OL9 90 B2
Lever Av SWIN M27 84 C5
Lever Bridge Pl BOLS/LL BL3 49 H4
Lever Dr BOLS/LL BL3 48 D4
Lever Edge La BOLS/LL BL3 64 B2
Leverett Cl ALT WA14 164 D4
Lever Gv BOLE BL2 49 F4
Lever Hall Rd BOLE BL2 50 A2
Leverhulme Av BOLS/LL BL3 65 F1
Lever St BOLS/LL BL3 49 E5
BOLS/LL BL3 50 D5
BRAM/HZG SK7 185 E2
CMANE M1 7 H4
HEY OL10 41 E3
MDTN M24 72 D3
RAD M26 52 A4
RAMS BL0 16 D2
Lever Wk MDTN M24 72 C5
Levington Dr OLDS OL8 106 D2
Levi St BOL BL1 32 C5
Lewes Av DTN/ASHW M34 146 D2
Lewis Av BKLY M9 103 F1
URM M41 124 C3
Lewis Dr HEY OL10 40 A5
Lewisham Av
NEWH/MOS M40 116 C1
Lewisham Cl ROY/SHW OL2 * 58 D3
Lewis Rd DROY M43 117 F3
RDSH SK5 145 F2
Lewis St ECC M30 111 E4
HEY OL10 * 41 F3
NEWH/MOS M40 115 G2
ROY/SHW OL2 60 A4
Lewtas St ECC M30 111 F4
Lexton Av CHH M8 87 G5
Leybourne Av BNG/LEV M19 144 B1
Leybourne St BOL BL1 33 H4
Leybrook Rd WYTH/NTH M22 180 B1
Leyburn Av ROY/SHW OL2 59 E5
STRET M32 140 A1
URM M41 138 A2
Leyburn Cl WHTF M45 69 F4
Leyburne Rd OFTN SK2 172 D3
Leyburn Gv MPL/ROM SK6 162 B4
Leyburn Rd NEWH/MOS M40 89 F5
Leycett Dr NTHM/RTH M23 155 H5
Leycroft St CMANE M1 7 J6
Ley Dr HEY OL10 56 B2
Leyfield Av MPL/ROM SK6 162 B4
Leyfield Rd MILN OL16 31 E5
Ley Hey Av MPL/ROM SK6 175 E2
Ley Hey Rd MPL/ROM SK6 175 E2
Leyland Av CHD/CHDH SK8 169 G3
DID/WITH M20 158 A3
IRL M44 122 C4
Leylands La HYDE SK14 149 G5
Leyland St BURY BL9 53 G5
HTNM SK4 12 E3
Ley La MPL/ROM SK6 175 H1
Leys Rd ALT WA14 165 H1
Leyton Av NEWH/MOS M40 104 A3
Leyton Cl FWTH BL4 65 E3
Leyton Dr BURY BL9 53 G4
Leyton St WHIT OL12 30 A1
Leywell Dr OLD OL1 76 C1
Leywell Rd BKLY M9 103 G2
Library La CHAD OL9 8 D1
Library St WHTN BL5 62 A4
Libra St BOL BL1 33 G4
Lichens Crs OLDS OL8 91 H4
Lichfield Av AUL OL6 107 G3
BOLE BL2 34 C4
HALE/TIMP WA15 178 D2
RDSH SK5 145 E4
Lichfield Cl FWTH BL4 65 F4
Lichfield Dr CHAD OL9 74 B3
CHH M8 102 C3
PWCH M25 86 B5
SWIN M27 99 E4
TOT/BURYW BL8 4 B1
Lichfield Rd ECC M30 111 G1
RAD M26 51 G4
URM M41 124 C4
Lichfield St SLFD M6 100 D5
Lichfield Ter MILN OL16 43 H2
Lichfield Wk MPL/ROM SK6 161 H5
Lidbrook Wk WGTN/LGST M12 129 F2
Liddington Hall Dr RAMS BL0 16 C4
Lidgett Cl LHULT M38 81 H2
Lidiard St CHH M8 102 B1
Liffey Av WYTH/NTH M22 180 D1
Lifton Av NEWH/MOS M40 115 H1
Light Alders La POY/DIS SK12 187 F5
Lightbourne Rd SALE M33 153 G2
Lightbounds Rd BOL BL1 32 C3
Lightbourne Av SWIN M27 99 E3
Lightbowne Rd
NEWH/MOS M40 103 H4
Lightburn Av LIT OL15 20 C4
Lightburne Av BOL BL1 48 A2
Lighthorne Av EDGY/DAV SK3 170 C2
Lighthorne Gv EDGY/DAV SK3 170 C2
Lighthorne Rd EDGY/DAV SK3 170 C2
Light Oaks Rd SLFD M6 112 A1
Lightowlers La LIT OL15 21 G1
Lightwood WALK M28 96 C2
Lightwood Cl FWTH BL4 66 B3
Lignum Av CHAD OL9 74 C4
Lilac Av BURY BL9 53 E2
HYDE SK14 147 H3
MILN OL16 44 D3
SWIN M27 99 F2
Lilac Ct SLFD M6 113 F3
Lilac Gv CHAD OL9 74 C4
NEWH/MOS M40 103 H1
PWCH M25 85 H1
Lilac La OLDS OL8 91 E5
Lilac Rd HALE/TIMP WA15 178 B1
ROCH OL11 43 E4
Lilac St OFTN SK2 172 A3
Lilac View Cl ROY/SHW OL2 60 C3
Lilac View Rd ROY/SHW OL2 60 B3
Lila St BKLY M9 103 G3
Lilburn Cl RAMS BL0 16 D4
Liley St MILN OL16 11 F7
Lilford Cl WGTN/LGST M12 129 H2
Lillian Gv RDSH SK5 145 F3
Lillian St OLDTF/WHR M16 127 F4
Lilly St BOL BL1 2 A2
HYDE SK14 148 B3
Lilmore Av CHH M8 102 D4
NEWH/MOS M40 104 B4
Lily Av FWTH BL4 65 G3
Lily Cl EDGY/DAV SK3 171 G4
Lily Hill St WHTF M45 69 F2
Lily La BKLY M9 103 G3
Lily Lanes AUL OL6 107 H2
Lily St ECC M30 110 C4
MDTN M24 73 F4
MILN OL16 31 G5
OLD OL1 75 F3
ROY/SHW OL2 59 G5
Lima St BURY BL9 5 K2
Limbert Cir CHH M8 102 D1
Lime Av SWIN M27 98 B4
URM M41 138 B1
WHTF M45 69 G5
Lime Bank St WGTN/LGST M12 115 G5
Limebrook Cl OP/CLY M11 130 D1
Lime Cl DUK SK16 133 G2
SLFD M6 113 F2
Lime Ct SLFD M6 * 113 F2
Lime Crs OLDTF/WHR M16 127 E4
Limeditch Rd FAIL M35 105 G2
Lime Fld MILN OL16 31 F4
Limefield MDTN M24 72 B5
MOSL OL5 93 G5
Limefield Av FWTH BL4 66 A3
Limefield Brow BURY BL9 27 G4
Limefield Cl BOL BL1 32 D2
Limefield Rd BOL BL1 33 E2
BRO M7 101 G1
BURY BL9 27 G4
RAD M26 67 G1
Limefield Ter BNG/LEV M19 144 A2
Lime Gdns DUK SK16 119 G5
MDTN M24 72 B4
Lime Ga OLDS OL8 90 D5
Lime Gn OLDS OL8 106 A1
Lime Green Rd OLDS OL8 105 H2
Lime Gv AUL OL6 107 F5
BURY BL9 27 G4
CHD/CHDH SK8 170 A3
DTN/ASHW M34 132 C4
HALE/TIMP WA15 166 C3
HEY OL10 40 D3
LIT OL15 20 C3
OLDTF/WHR M16 127 E4
PWCH M25 85 H1
RAMS BL0 17 E1
ROY/SHW OL2 59 E3
STLY SK15 120 B5
WALK M28 97 E1
Limehurst Av AULW OL7 106 D4
RUSH/FAL M14 142 B3
Limehurst Ct OLDS OL8 106 A1
Limehurst Rd AULW OL7 106 D4
Lime Kiln La MPL/ROM SK6 175 F4
Limekiln La WGTN/LGST M12 115 G5
Lime La OLDS OL8 105 H1
Lime Rd STRET M32 140 B2
Limers Ga WHIT OL12 19 E3
Limerston Dr NEWH/MOS M40 103 G5
Limesdale Cl BOLE BL2 51 E4
Limeside Rd OLDS OL8 90 D5
Limestead Av CHH M8 102 B2
The Limes MOSL OL5 108 C1
MOSL OL5 109 F1
Lime St BURY BL9 27 G5
DUK SK16 119 G5
ECC M30 111 E4
FWTH BL4 66 B4
MPL/ROM SK6 161 F2
NEWH/MOS M40 115 G2
OLD OL1 74 D3
ROCH OL11 42 B2
Lime Tree Cl URM M41 139 E2
Lime Tree Gv FAIL M35 105 G3
Limetrees Rd MDTN M24 72 C4
Limley Gv CCHDY M21 141 G4
Linacre Av BOLS/LL BL3 64 D2
Linby St HULME M15 127 H1
Lincoln Av BNG/LEV M19 144 B2
BOLS/LL BL3 66 D1
CHD/CHDH SK8 181 G5
DROY M43 117 H2
DTN/ASHW M34 146 D2
IRL M44 150 B2
STRET M32 125 E5
Lincoln Cl AUL OL6 107 G2
ROCH OL11 30 B5
Lincoln Dr BURY BL9 * 53 G1
HALE/TIMP WA15 166 C4
LIT OL15 20 D5
Lincoln Gv BOLE BL2 35 G2
BRUN/LGST M13 128 D3
SALE M33 155 F2
Lincoln Leach Ct ROCH OL11 * 43 E1
Lincoln Ri MPL/ROM SK6 161 H5
Lincoln Rd BOL BL1 48 A1
FAIL M35 105 F4
MDTN M24 89 F2
WILM/AE SK9 199 H1
Lincoln St BRUN/LGST M13 129 G4
CHAD OL9 90 C2
ECC M30 110 D4
ROCH OL11 30 B5
Lincombe Rd WYTH/NTH M22 180 B4
Linda Dr BRAM/HZG SK7 185 E3
Lindale HYDE SK14 133 F3
Lindale Av BOL BL1 47 G1
BURY BL9 69 H1
CHAD OL9 90 B1
NEWH/MOS M40 89 G5
ROY/SHW OL2 58 D2
URM M41 123 G5
Lindale Dr MDTN M24 72 B1
Lindale Ri ROY/SHW OL2 60 C2
Lindbury Av OFTN SK2 172 D2
Linden Av BOLS/LL BL3 50 D4
DTN/ASHW M34 132 A1
HALE/TIMP WA15 165 H4
OLDE OL4 76 C4
RAMS BL0 17 E2
SALE M33 154 A2
SLFD M6 100 B4
SWIN M27 98 C3
Linden Cl DTN/ASHW M34 132 D5
Linden Crs TOT/BURYW BL8 37 E1
Linden Dr ORD M5 113 F5
Linden Gv BRAM/HZG SK7 193 G3
OFTN SK2 172 A2
RUSH/FAL M14 143 F3
Linden Ms WALK M28 96 A4
Linden Pk BNG/LEV M19 144 A3
Linden Rd CHD/CHDH SK8 182 D1
DID/WITH M20 157 F2
DTN/ASHW M34 132 D5
STLY SK15 135 E1
WALK M28 96 A4
Linden Wk BOLE BL2 34 C1
Linden Wy MPL/ROM SK6 187 F5
Lindenwood CHAD OL9 73 H4
Lindeth Av GTN M18 130 C4
Lindfield Dr BOL BL1 33 H5
Lindfield Est North
WILM/AE SK9 198 D4
Lindfield Est South
WILM/AE SK9 198 D4
Lindfield Rd RDSH SK5 145 F2
Lindinis Av ORD M5 113 F3
Lindisfarne WHIT OL12 10 B5
Lindisfarne Cl SALE M33 154 C5
Lindisfarne Dr POY/DIS SK12 195 E3
Lindisfarne Pl BOLE BL2 34 D4
Lindisfarne Rd AULW OL7 106 B5
Lindley Gv EDGY/DAV SK3 171 G4
Lindley St BOLS/LL BL3 * 67 E1
FWTH BL4 83 E1
Lindleywood Rd
RUSH/FAL M14 143 G3
Lindon Wy DROY M43 117 F5
Lindop Rd HALE/TIMP WA15 178 A3
Lindow Cl TOT/BURYW BL8 26 D5
Lindow Ct MPL/ROM SK6 * 161 E3
Lindow Fold Dr WILM/AE SK9 200 A1
Lindow La WILM/AE SK9 198 B4
Lindow Rd OLDTF/WHR M16 141 F1
Lindow St SALE M33 155 G3
Lindrick Av WHTF M45 85 E1
Lindrick Cl NEWH/MOS M40 104 B3
Lindrick Ter BOLS/LL BL3 48 C4
Lindsay Av BNG/LEV M19 143 H2
CHD/CHDH SK8 183 E3
SWIN M27 98 D3
Lindsay Cl OLDE OL4 * 76 C2
Lindsay Rd BNG/LEV M19 143 H3
Lindsay St STLY SK15 121 E3
Lindsell Rd ALT WA14 165 F1
Lindsgate Dr
HALE/TIMP WA15 166 C2
Lind St NEWH/MOS M40 115 G3
Lindum Av OLDTF/WHR M16 127 F4
Lindum St RUSH/FAL M14 128 C5
Lindwall Cl NTHM/RTH M23 156 A4
Linehan Cl HTNM SK4 158 A4
Lineholme ROY/SHW OL2 74 D2
Linen Ct CSLFD M3 114 A2
Lines Rd DROY M43 118 A4
IRL M44 136 B3
Linfield Cl BOLE BL2 35 E2
Linfield St OP/CLY M11 116 C4
Linford Av NEWH/MOS M40 89 F5
Lingard La MPL/ROM SK6 161 E1
Lingard Rd WYTH/NTH M22 156 C5
Lingard St RDSH SK5 145 F3
Lingcrest Rd HTNM SK4 144 C4
Lingdale Rd CHD/CHDH SK8 182 C2
Lingfield Av BRAM/HZG SK7 185 G2
SALE M33 153 E4
Lingfield Cl FWTH BL4 65 H5
TOT/BURYW BL8 26 D4
Lingfield Rd OP/CLY M11 116 D3
Lingholme Dr MDTN M24 71 H2
Lingmell Cl BOL BL1 47 G1
MDTN M24 72 A2
URM M41 123 G4
Lingmoor Cl MDTN M24 71 H2
Lingmoor Rd BOL BL1 32 C5
Lingmoor Wk HULME M15 * 128 A3
Lings Wk WYTH/NTH M22 180 D3
Linhope Cl HTNM SK4 158 B3
Link Av URM M41 139 G2
Linkfield Dr WALK M28 96 A4
Link La OLDS OL8 91 F5
Link Rd OLDE OL4 77 E5
SALE M33 153 G4
Links Av FAIL M35 105 E5
Links Crs PWCH M25 86 D5
Links Dr HOR/BR BL6 46 C2
Linksfield DTN/ASHW M34 132 C3
Linkside Av ROY/SHW OL2 59 E4
Links Pl AUL OL6 107 H4
Links Ri URM M41 123 H4
Links Rd BOLE BL2 35 H3
HEY OL10 56 A1
HOR/BR BL6 46 C2
MPL/ROM SK6 162 C3
MPL/ROM SK6 175 E5
WILM/AE SK9 200 B2
The Links NEWH/MOS M40 104 B3
Links Vw PWCH M25 100 D1
ROCH OL11 29 E5
Links Wy CHAD OL9 8 A1
Linksway CHD/CHDH SK8 169 F5
PWCH M25 86 C5
SWIN M27 99 F4
Linksway Cl HTNM SK4 158 D1
Linksway Dr BURY BL9 69 H1
The Link RDSH SK5 146 A5
ROY/SHW OL2 44 C5
WILM/AE SK9 192 A4
Linley Av RAD M26 53 F4
Linley Dr OLDE OL4 92 C3
Linley Gv RAMS BL0 26 B1
Linley Rd CHD/CHDH SK8 183 E4
SALE M33 154 C1
Linnell Dr ROCH OL11 28 B3
Linnet Cl DTN/ASHW M34 118 B3
OFTN SK2 173 G4
WGTN/LGST M12 129 G4
Linnet Dr BURY BL9 5 K1
IRL M44 122 B5
Linnet Hl ROCH OL11 29 F5
Linnet's Wood Ms WALK M28 82 B4
Linney La ROY/SHW OL2 60 B2
Linney Rd BRAM/HZG SK7 183 G2
Linn St CHH M8 102 B1
Linslade Gdns BOLS/LL BL3 48 D4
Linsley St CSLFD M3 * 6 C2
Linstead Dr CHH M8 * 102 A4
Linthorpe Wk BOLS/LL BL3 48 A5
Linton Av BURY BL9 38 C1
DTN/ASHW M34 131 F5
Linton Cl ANC M4 115 G5
Linton Rd SALE M33 140 A5
Linton Wk BRO M7 100 C2
Linwood Gv WGTN/LGST M12 144 A1
Linwood St NEWH/MOS M40 104 B4
Lion Brow BKLY M9 88 A5
Lion Fold La BKLY M9 88 A4
Lions Dr SWIN M27 99 F3
Lion St BKLY M9 88 A5
Lisbon St ROCH OL11 29 E3
Lisburn Av OLDTF/WHR M16 141 G2
SALE M33 154 B3
Lisburne Av OFTN SK2 173 E3
Lisburne Cl OFTN SK2 * 173 E3
Lisburne La OFTN SK2 172 D4

Lisburn Rd NEWH/MOS M40 103 H2
Liscard Av RUSH/FAL M14 142 D2
Lisetta Av OLDE OL4 * 92 A2
Liskeard Av ROY/SHW OL2 59 H5
Liskeard Cl MILN OL16 11 J3
Liskeard Dr BRAM/HZG SK7 184 A5
Lisle St WHIT OL12 10 E4
Lismore Av BOLS/LL BL3 47 G4
EDGY/DAV SK3 171 E2
Lismore Rd DUK SK16 133 G1
Lismore Wy URM M41 124 C3
Lissadel St SLFD M6 113 F1
Lisson Gv HALE/TIMP WA15 177 H2
Lister Rd MDTN M24 87 G1
Lister St BOLS/LL BL3 64 A1
Liston St DUK SK16 120 C5
Litcham Cl CMANE M1 128 C1
Litchfield Gv WALK M28 98 A3
Litherland Av WYTH/NTH M22 180 D2
Litherland Rd BOLS/LL BL3 64 D2
SALE M33 155 F3
Little 66 BURY BL9 54 A3
Little Ancoats St CMANE M1 7 H3
Little Bank St OLDE OL4 92 A1
Littlebourne Wk BOL BL1 23 F5
Littlebrook Cl CHD/CHDH SK8 171 F5
Little Brook Rd SALE M33 153 F5
Little Brow EDGW/EG BL7 23 F4
Little Clegg Rd LIT OL15 20 C5
Littledale St WHIT OL12 10 A5
Little David St CMANE M1 7 H6
Little Ees La SALE M33 139 F4
Little Egerton St STKP SK1 13 F2
Littlefields HYDE SK14 135 H4
Little Flatt WHIT OL12 29 E2
Little Gn MDTN M24 * 73 E3
Littlegreen Gdns SLFD M6 113 E2
Little Harwood Lee BOLE BL2 35 E3
Littlehaven Cl WGTN/LGST M12 129 F3
Little Heath La ALT WA14 164 A4
Little Hey St ROY/SHW OL2 60 A5
Littlehills Cl MDTN M24 72 B3
Little Holme St ANC M4 115 G4
Little Holme Wk BOLS/LL BL3 * 49 E5
Little Howarth Wy
WHIT OL12 * 19 H4
Little John St CSLFD M3 6 B6
Little Lever St CMANE M1 7 H4
Little Meadow Rd ALT WA14 177 E3
Little Mdw EDGW/EG BL7 * 23 E4
Little Moor Clough
EDGW/EG BL7 22 D1
Little Moor Cottages
STKP SK1 172 C1
Little Moor La OLDE OL4 76 B4
Little Moss La SWIN M27 84 A5
Littlemoss Rd DROY M43 118 B2
Little Nelson St ANC M4 * 7 G1
Little Oak Cl OLDE OL4 92 D1
Little Peter St HULME M15 128 A1
Little Pitt St CMANE M1 * 7 J4
Little Quay St CSLFD M3 6 D5
Little Stones Rd EDGW/EG BL7 22 D1
Littleton Rd BRO M7 100 D2
Little Underbank STKP SK1 13 G3
Littlewood Av BURY BL9 38 C1
Littlewood Rd
WYTH/NTH M22 168 C5
Littlewood St SLFD M6 112 D3
Littondale Cl ROY/SHW OL2 59 F4
Liverpool Cl RDSH SK5 145 E4
Liverpool Rd CSLFD M3 6 A6
ECC M30 110 C4
ECC M30 123 E2
ECC M30 123 E4
IRL M44 150 B3
Liverpool St RDSH SK5 145 E4
SLFD M6 112 D3
Liverstudd Av RDSH SK5 145 F3
Livesey St ANC M4 115 F2
BNG/LEV M19 144 A3
OLD OL1 76 B4
Livingston Av
WYTH/NTH M22 180 A2
Livingstone Av MOSL OL5 108 C1
Livingstone St OLDE OL4 92 D2
Livsey Ct BOL BL1 2 E2
Livsey La HEY OL10 40 B4
Livsey St MILN OL16 10 E7
WHTF M45 69 G4
Lizmar Ter BKLY M9 103 G2
Llanberis Rd CHD/CHDH SK8 182 B3
Llanfair Rd EDGY/DAV SK3 12 B6
Lloyd Av CHD/CHDH SK8 169 F3
Lloyd Gdns ALT WA14 177 G1
Lloyd Rd BNG/LEV M19 144 B4
Lloyd Sq ALT WA14 165 G5
Lloyd St ALT WA14 165 G5
CMANW M2 6 E5
HEY OL10 41 E5
HTNM SK4 12 D1
ROCH OL11 42 C2
WHIT OL12 14 B4
Lloyd St South
RUSH/FAL M14 142 C2
Lobden Crs WHIT OL12 18 C1
Lobelia Av FWTH BL4 65 F3
Lobley Cl WHIT OL12 30 C1
Lochawe Cl HEY OL10 40 B5
Lochinver Gv HEY OL10 40 B5
Lochmaddy Cl
BRAM/HZG SK7 185 G3
Lock Cl HEY OL10 56 B1
Lockett Gdns CSLFD M3 6 A2
Lockett St CHH M8 114 B1
SLFD M6 100 D5
Lockhart Cl WGTN/LGST M12 129 H3
Lockhart St MILN OL16 43 G1
Lockingate St AUL OL6 107 F4
Locking Gate Ri OLDE OL4 76 D3
Lock Keepers Ms SWIN M27 100 A2
Locklands La IRL M44 136 C1
Lock La HOR/BR BL6 46 D5
PART M31 150 B3
Lock Rd ALT WA14 165 F3
Lockside MPL/ROM SK6 175 F3
Lockside Vw MOSL OL5 94 B4
Locksley Cl HTNM SK4 12 B1
Lockton Cl RDSH SK5 145 E5
Lockton Ct CMANE M1 128 C1
Lockwood St
WGTN/LGST M12 130 A5
Lodge Av URM M41 139 E1
Lodge Bank Rd LIT OL15 20 C5
Lodge Brow RAD M26 68 C2
Lodge Cl DUK SK16 133 H1
Lodge Ct HTNM SK4 158 C4
HYDE SK14 135 H4
Lodge Farm Cl
BRAM/HZG SK7 183 H2
Lodge Fold DROY M43 118 A3
Lodge Gn DUK SK16 133 H1
Lodge La DUK SK16 120 A5
HYDE SK14 133 G4
Lodgepole Cl ECC M30 110 A5
Lodge Rd RAD M26 68 C2
Lodgeside Cl DROY M43 118 A3
Lodge St AULW OL7 119 E4
HYDE SK14 133 H3
LIT OL15 21 E3
MDTN M24 72 D3
NEWH/MOS M40 103 F5
RAMS BL0 16 D2
WHIT OL12 19 H2
Lodge Vw DROY M43 118 A3
Loen Crs BOL BL1 33 F3
Loganberry Av SLFD M6 113 F2
Logan St BOL BL1 33 H1
Logwood Av TOT/BURYW BL8 4 B2
Loisine Cl ROCH OL11 41 H3
Lokfu Gdns CHH M8 101 H5
Lomas Cl BNG/LEV M19 158 A3
Lomas St EDGY/DAV SK3 12 D7
FAIL M35 105 F1
MDTN M24 73 E3
Lomax's Buildings BOLE BL2 3 F6
Lomax St BOL BL1 33 H4
BURY BL9 5 G3
CMANE M1 7 K4
RAD M26 68 B2
WHIT OL12 10 D4
WHTF M45 * 69 F2
Lombard Cl MPL/ROM SK6 161 G2
Lombard Gv RUSH/FAL M14 143 E3
Lombard St OLD OL1 9 F2
WHIT OL12 29 G3
Lombardy Ct SLFD M6 * 113 F2
Lomond Av HALE/TIMP WA15 178 B1
STRET M32 126 A5
Lomond Cl OFTN SK2 184 B1
Lomond Dr TOT/BURYW BL8 37 G2
Lomond Pl BOLS/LL BL3 47 F3
Lomond Rd WYTH/NTH M22 181 E2
Lomond Ter MILN OL16 43 H2
London Pl STKP SK1 13 G4
London Rd BRAM/HZG SK7 173 E5
CMANE M1 7 J7
OLD OL1 76 A3
WILM/AE SK9 200 D4
London Rd North
POY/DIS SK12 195 E3
London Rd South
POY/DIS SK12 195 E5
London Sq STKP SK1 13 G4
London St BOLS/LL BL3 48 D5
SLFD M6 113 G1
WHTF M45 69 G5
Long Acres Dr WHIT OL12 14 C4
Longacres La WHIT OL12 14 C3
Longacres Rd
HALE/TIMP WA15 178 D5
Longacre St CMANE M1 7 K6
Longbow Ct BRO M7 * 114 A1
Longbridge Rd TRPK M17 125 F2
Long Cswy FWTH BL4 66 A5
Longcliffe Wk BOL BL1 * 34 A4
Long Clough ROY/SHW OL2 74 D2
Longcrag Wk HULME M15 * 128 A3
Longcroft Dr ALT WA14 165 E5
Longcroft Gv DTN/ASHW M34 118 A5
NTHM/RTH M23 167 H2
Long Croft La CHD/CHDH SK8 182 C4
Longdale Cl ROY/SHW OL2 58 D5
Longdale Dr HYDE SK14 135 H5
Longden Av OLDE OL4 76 D1
Longden Rd WGTN/LGST M12 144 A1
Longden St BOL BL1 48 B1
Longfellow Av BOLS/LL BL3 64 A1
Longfellow Crs OLD OL1 60 C5
Longfield BURY BL9 * 38 D2
Longfield Av CHD/CHDH SK8 181 H5
HALE/TIMP WA15 166 D3
URM M41 138 B1
Longfield Cl HYDE SK14 133 H2
Longfield Crs OLDE OL4 76 B3
Longfield Dr URM M41 138 B1
Longfield La OLDE OL4 76 C3
Longfield Pk ROY/SHW OL2 59 H4
Longfield Rd BOLS/LL BL3 64 A2
NTHM/RTH M23 167 G1
ROCH OL11 29 F3
ROY/SHW OL2 59 H3
Longford Av BOL BL1 33 F4
STRET M32 140 C1
Longford Cl STRET M32 126 B5
Longford Pk STRET M32 140 D1
Longford Pl RUSH/FAL M14 129 F4
Longford Rd CCHDY M21 141 E2
RDSH SK5 145 F2
STRET M32 126 B5
Longford Rd West
BNG/LEV M19 144 D2
Longford St GTN M18 130 C2
HEY OL10 40 D4
Long Grain Pl OFTN SK2 173 E4
Longham Cl BRAM/HZG SK7 183 F3
OP/CLY M11 115 H4
Long Hey HALE/TIMP WA15 178 B1
Longhey Rd WYTH/NTH M22 168 C4
Long Hl ROCH OL11 42 C2
Longhirst Cl BOL BL1 33 E3
Longhope Rd WYTH/NTH M22 180 B2
Longhurst La MPL/ROM SK6 175 G2
Longhurst Rd BKLY M9 87 G3
Longlands Av HYDE SK14 134 C5
Longlands Dr HYDE SK14 134 C5
Long La BOLE BL2 50 A4
BURY BL9 27 G4
CHAD OL9 90 A4
UPML OL3 78 D2
Longlevens Rd
WYTH/NTH M22 180 B2
Longley Dr WALK M28 98 A4
Longley La WYTH/NTH M22 168 D2
Longley St OLD OL1 9 G5
ROY/SHW OL2 60 A4
WALK M28 82 A5
Long Marl Dr WILM/AE SK9 192 C3
Longmead Av BRAM/HZG SK7 185 E3
Longmeade Gdns
WILM/AE SK9 199 F4
Longmeadow CHD/CHDH SK8 183 F5
Long Meadow EDGW/EG BL7 23 H4
HYDE SK14 134 A2
Longmeadow Gv
DTN/ASHW M34 146 C1
Longmeadow Pas HYDE SK14 133 G5
Longmead Rd SLFD M6 100 A5
Longmead Wy MDTN M24 72 D3
Longmere Av WYTH/NTH M22 180 C1
Long Millgate CSLFD M3 6 E2
Longnor Rd BRAM/HZG SK7 185 F5
CHD/CHDH SK8 182 A5
Longport Av DID/WITH M20 142 C4
Longridge EDGW/EG BL7 23 H3
Longridge Av STLY SK15 120 D1
Longridge Crs BOL BL1 32 C4
Longridge Dr HEY OL10 40 A4
TOT/BURYW BL8 52 B1
Long Rw STLY SK15 109 G3
Long Rushes ROY/SHW OL2 59 G1
Longshaw Av SWIN M27 99 E1
Longshaw Dr LHULT M38 81 F3
Longshaw Ford Rd BOL BL1 32 C1
Longshut La OFTN SK2 13 G7
Longshut La West OFTN SK2 13 G7
Longsides Rd
HALE/TIMP WA15 178 D5
Longsight BOLE BL2 35 E1
Longsight La BOLE BL2 35 E2
CHD/CHDH SK8 192 C2
Longsight Rd BOLE BL2 35 E3
GTN M18 130 A5
RAMS BL0 26 B1
Longsight St HTNM SK4 12 C2
Longson St BOL BL1 3 G1
Long St GTN M18 130 D2
MDTN M24 72 D3
SWIN M27 99 E3
Longton Av DID/WITH M20 157 F1
Longton Rd BKLY M9 87 H3
SLFD M6 99 H5
Longton St BURY BL9 53 G5
Longtown Gdns BOL BL1 * 33 H4
Longview Dr SWIN M27 98 B1
Longwall Av WALK M28 96 D2
Longwood Av OFTN SK2 172 C3
Longwood Cl MPL/ROM SK6 162 D3
Longwood Rd TRPK M17 125 G2
WYTH/NTH M22 180 D1
Longworth Cl URM M41 137 F2
Longworth Clough
EDGW/EG BL7 22 C1
Longworth La EDGW/EG BL7 22 C3
Longworth St BOLE BL2 49 H2
CSLFD M3 6 C6
Lonsdale Av MILN OL16 43 G1
RDSH SK5 131 E5
SWIN M27 98 C5
URM M41 124 A4
Lonsdale Rd BNG/LEV M19 144 B1
BOL BL1 48 A1
OLDS OL8 90 C5
Lonsdale St
NEWH/MOS M40 104 B4
TOT/BURYW BL8 37 H4
Loom St ANC M4 7 J3
Loonies Ct STKP SK1 * 13 G5
Lord Byron Sq SALQ M50 113 E5
Lord Derby Rd HYDE SK14 148 A5
Lord La FAIL M35 117 F1
Lord Napier Dr ORD M5 126 D1
Lord North St
NEWH/MOS M40 115 H1
Lord's Av ORD M5 * 112 C3
Lordsfields Av AULW OL7 119 G1
Lords Fold BOL BL1 * 32 C4
Lord Sheldon Wy AULW OL7 118 D3
Lordship Cl BKLY M9 103 G1
Lordsmead St HULME M15 127 G1
Lord Sq MILN OL16 10 C6
Lord's Stile La EDGW/EG BL7 23 G4
Lord's St IRL M44 150 B1
Lord St ANC M4 114 D2
AUL OL6 119 G1
BURY BL9 5 F5
BURY BL9 39 F5
DTN/ASHW M34 131 F4
DUK SK16 120 C5
FWTH BL4 66 B4
MDTN M24 72 D3
OLD OL1 9 G2
RAD M26 68 B1
STKP SK1 13 G4
Loretto Rd URM M41 139 F2
Lorgill Cl EDGY/DAV SK3 172 A5
Loring St NEWH/MOS M40 104 B5
Lorland Rd EDGY/DAV SK3 171 E2
Lorna Gv CHD/CHDH SK8 169 E3
Lorna Rd CHD/CHDH SK8 183 E2
Lorna Wy IRL M44 136 D3
Lorne Av ROY/SHW OL2 74 C1
Lorne Gv EDGY/DAV SK3 171 H3
URM M41 139 E1
Lorne Rd RUSH/FAL M14 143 E3
Lorne St BOL BL1 2 E4
BRUN/LGST M13 128 D3
ECC M30 110 C5
FWTH BL4 65 H2
HEY OL10 41 E5
MOSL OL5 108 D1
OLDS OL8 91 F3
WHIT OL12 19 G5
Lorne Wy HEY OL10 40 A5
Lorraine Cl HEY OL10 56 B1
Lorraine Rd
HALE/TIMP WA15 166 B4
Lorton Cl MDTN M24 71 H2
WALK M28 96 A4
Lorton Gv BOLE BL2 50 C1
Lostock Av BNG/LEV M19 144 B2
BRAM/HZG SK7 184 C3
POY/DIS SK12 194 C3
SALE M33 155 F2
URM M41 124 A5
Lostock Cl HEY OL10 40 C3
Lostock Dr BURY BL9 27 G5
Lostock Gv STRET M32 125 G5
Lostock Hall Rd POY/DIS SK12 194 C4
Lostock Junction La
HOR/BR BL6 46 D3
Lostock Park Dr HOR/BR BL6 46 B2
Lostock Rd ORD M5 112 D3
POY/DIS SK12 194 D5
URM M41 124 C4
Lostock St NEWH/MOS M40 115 G2
Lostock Wy WILM/AE SK9 192 A3
Lothian Av ECC M30 110 C2
Lottery Rw BOL BL1 3 F5
Lottery St EDGY/DAV SK3 12 D4
Lottie St SWIN M27 99 F2
Loughborough Cl SALE M33 153 G3
Loughfield URM M41 138 A1
Loughrigg Av ROY/SHW OL2 58 D1
Louisa St BOL BL1 33 G4
OP/CLY M11 117 E5
WALK M28 82 A3
Louis Av BURY BL9 38 C2
Louise Cl WHIT OL12 19 H5
Louise Gdns WHIT OL12 19 G5
Louise St WHIT OL12 19 G5
Louvaine Av BOL BL1 32 C2
Louvain St FAIL M35 104 D3
Lovalle St BOL BL1 33 F5
Lovat Rd BOLE BL2 50 C2
Love La HTNM SK4 12 E1
Lovell Dr HYDE SK14 134 A4
Lovers La OLDE OL4 93 H1
Lowbrook Av BKLY M9 89 E4
Lowcroft Crs CHAD OL9 74 A4
Low Crompton Rd
ROY/SHW OL2 59 F3
Lowcross Rd
NEWH/MOS M40 103 H4
Lowe Gn ROY/SHW OL2 59 F4
Lower Albion St CMANE M1 7 H7
Lower Alma St DUK SK16 119 G4
Lowerbank DTN/ASHW M34 132 C3
Lower Bank St BURY BL9 4 C5
Lower Beechwood ROCH OL11 42 C1
Lower Bennett St HYDE SK14 133 F4
Lower Bents La
MPL/ROM SK6 161 G2
Lower Birches OLDE OL4 93 E3
Lower Bridgeman St BOLE BL2 3 G7
Lower Broadacre STLY SK15 135 F2
Lower Brook La WALK M28 * 97 H5
Lower Brook St CMANE M1 * 7 H6
Lower Broughton Rd
BRO M7 101 F5
Lower Bury St HTNM SK4 12 C3
Lower Byrom St CSLFD M3 6 B6
Lower Carr La UPML OL3 95 E1
Lower Carrs AUL OL6 107 G5
STKP SK1 13 H4
Lower Chatham St
CMANE M1 128 A1
Lower Cft WHTF M45 84 D1
Lowercroft Rd
TOT/BURYW BL8 37 E4
Lower Crossbank OLDE OL4 77 E4
Lower Darcy St BOLE BL2 49 H4
Lower Dingle OLD OL1 60 B5
Lower Faling WHIT OL12 10 C4
Lowerfield Dr OFTN SK2 173 G4
Lowerfields OLDS OL8 92 A3
Lower Flds UPML OL3 78 D3
Lowerfields Ri ROY/SHW OL2 60 A1
Lower Fold DTN/ASHW M34 147 E1
MPL/ROM SK6 175 G1
Lower Fold Av ROY/SHW OL2 59 H5
Lowerfold Cl WHIT OL12 18 B4
Lowerfold Crs WHIT OL12 18 B4
Lowerfold Dr WHIT OL12 18 B4
Lowerfold Wy WHIT OL12 18 B4
Lower Frenches Dr UPML OL3 94 D1
Lower Goodwin Cl BOLE BL2 35 F3
Lower Gn AUL OL6 119 H1
MDTN M24 88 C2
WHIT OL12 29 F2
Lower Hardman St CSLFD M3 6 B5
Lower Hey La MOSL OL5 94 B4
Lower Hillgate STKP SK1 13 H4
Lower House Dr HOR/BR BL6 46 D2
Lower House La WHIT OL12 19 G1
Lower House St OLD OL1 76 A4
Lower House Wk
EDGW/EG BL7 23 F3
Lower Jowkin La ROCH OL11 28 A4
Lower Landedmans WHTN BL5 62 A5
Lower La MILN OL16 43 H3
Lowerlea POY/DIS SK12 197 H1
Lower Lime Rd OLDS OL8 105 H3
Lower Marlands EDGW/EG BL7 23 E3
Lower Md EDGW/EG BL7 23 E2
Lower Meadow Rd
WILM/AE SK9 192 B3
Lower Moat Cl HTNM SK4 159 H3
Lower Monton Rd ECC M30 111 F3
Lower Mosley St CMANE M1 6 D7
Lower Moss La HULME M15 127 G1
WHTF M45 69 G4
Lower New Rw WALK M28 96 B1
Lower Ormond St CMANE M1 128 B1
Lower Park Crs POY/DIS SK12 194 C1
Lower Park Rd POY/DIS SK12 194 C2
RUSH/FAL M14 128 D4
Lower Rawson St FWTH BL4 66 B3
Lower Seedley Rd SLFD M6 112 D2
Lower Sheriff St WHIT OL12 10 A5
Lower St FWTH BL4 65 H5
MILN OL16 43 F2
Lower Strines Rd
MPL/ROM SK6 175 F4
Lower Sutherland St
SWIN M27 98 D2
Lower Tenterfield ROCH OL11 28 A1
Lower Tong EDGW/EG BL7 23 E4
Lower Turf La OLDE OL4 77 G4
Lower Tweedale St ROCH OL11 30 A5
Lower Victoria St CHAD OL9 74 C5
Lower Wharf St AUL OL6 119 G3
Lower Wheat End MILN OL16 11 H5
Lower Woodhill Rd
TOT/BURYW BL8 4 B3
Lowerwood La BOLE BL2 34 C5
Lowes Rd BURY BL9 27 G5
Lowestead Rd OP/CLY M11 116 D3
The Lowes ALT WA14 177 E3
Lowestoft St RUSH/FAL M14 142 D1
Lowe St DTN/ASHW M34 133 E5
RAD M26 52 A5
STKP SK1 13 G4
Loweswater Rd
CHD/CHDH SK8 181 G1
FWTH BL4 65 E5
Lowfield Av AUL OL6 108 A5
DROY M43 117 G2
Lowfield Gv OFTN SK2 172 A2
Lowfield Rd EDGY/DAV SK3 171 H3
Low Grove La UPML OL3 * 94 B2
Low Hl WHIT OL12 19 H5
Lowhouse Cl MILN OL16 31 H4
Lowick Av BOLS/LL BL3 65 F1
Lowick Cl BRAM/HZG SK7 185 E2
Lowick Gn MPL/ROM SK6 161 G1
Lowland Gv AULW OL7 106 D4
Lowland Rd OFTN SK2 172 C5
Lowlands Cl MDTN M24 89 F3
Low Lea Rd MPL/ROM SK6 175 G3
Low Mdw ROY/SHW OL2 59 E3
Lowndes Cl OFTN SK2 172 C2
Lowndes La OFTN SK2 172 C2
Lowndes St BOL BL1 48 A1
Lowndes Wk
BRUN/LGST M13 * 128 D2
Lownorth Rd WYTH/NTH M22 180 D4
Lowood Av URM M41 123 G4
Lowry Ct WHTF M45 * 69 E2
Lowry Dr MPL/ROM SK6 175 G1
SWIN M27 99 E1
Lowry Gv HYDE SK14 135 G5
Lowry Houses ECC M30 * 111 F3
Lowry Wk BOL BL1 33 G5
Lowside Av BOL BL1 46 D3
MPL/ROM SK6 147 G5
Lowside Dr OLDE OL4 92 A2
Low's Pl WHIT OL12 10 D1
Lowstern Cl EDGW/EG BL7 23 E2
The Lows OLDE OL4 92 A2
Lowther Av GTN M18 130 A5
HALE/TIMP WA15 166 B3
ROY/SHW OL2 58 D1
Lowther Cl PWCH M25 85 H4
Lowther Crs MDTN M24 72 B3
Lowther Gdns URM M41 123 E5
Lowther Rd CHH M8 102 B1
PWCH M25 85 G4
ROCH OL11 42 D2
Lowther St BOLS/LL BL3 65 F2
Lowthorpe St RUSH/FAL M14 142 C1
Lowton Av BKLY M9 103 G3
Lowton Rd SALE M33 153 G4
Lowton St RAD M26 52 B5
Low Wood Cl BRAM/HZG SK7 183 F3
Low Wood Rd
DTN/ASHW M34 131 F4
Loxford Ct HULME M15 128 A1
Loxford St HULME M15 128 B1
Loxham St BOLS/LL BL3 66 A2
Lttn Cl CMANE M1 128 C1
Lubeck St BKLY M9 103 F2
Lucas Rd FWTH BL4 65 F4
Lucas St BURY BL9 5 H2
OLDE OL4 76 A5
Lucas Wk OP/CLY M11 116 A5
Lucerne Cl CHAD OL9 8 A5
Lucerne Rd BRAM/HZG SK7 183 H1
Lucien Cl WGTN/LGST M12 129 F3
Lucknow St ROCH OL11 43 E1
Lucy St BOL BL1 32 D5
BRO M7 101 G5
EDGY/DAV SK3 12 E6
HULME M15 127 G2
Ludford Gv SALE M33 154 A4
Ludgate Hl ANC M4 7 H1
Ludgate Rd NEWH/MOS M40 116 D1
ROCH OL11 43 F4
Ludgate St ANC M4 7 G1
Ludlow Av SWIN M27 84 B5
WHTF M45 86 A1
Ludlow Pk OLDE OL4 92 C1
Ludlow Rd OFTN SK2 172 D1
Lugano Rd BRAM/HZG SK7 183 H1
Luke Rd DROY M43 118 A4
Lullington Cl WYTH/NTH M22 180 B3
Lullington Rd SLFD M6 112 C1
Lulworth Av URM M41 137 H1
Lulworth Cl TOT/BURYW BL8 26 D5
Lulworth Crs FAIL M35 105 G2
Lulworth Gdns
NTHM/RTH M23 167 G1
Lulworth Rd BOLS/LL BL3 63 H1
ECC M30 110 D3
MDTN M24 73 E2
Lumb Carr Av RAMS BL0 16 B4
Lumb Carr Rd RAMS BL0 16 B5
Lumb Cl BRAM/HZG SK7 193 H1
Lumber La WALK M28 97 F2
Lumb La BRAM/HZG SK7 193 H1
DROY M43 106 A5
DTN/ASHW M34 118 B4
Lumley Cl RUSH/FAL M14 128 C4
Lumn Hollow HYDE SK14 148 A1
Lumn Rd HYDE SK14 148 A1
Lumn's La SWIN M27 84 D5
Lumn St BURY BL9 27 G3
Lumsdale Rd STRET M32 125 F4
Lumsden St BOLS/LL BL3 48 D4
Lum St BOL BL1 3 G3
Lumwood BOL BL1 33 E3
Luna St ANC M4 7 H3
Lund Av RAD M26 68 C4
Lund St OLDTF/WHR M16 127 F2
Lundy Av CCHDY M21 156 B1
Lune Cl WHTF M45 69 H4
Lunedale Gn OFTN SK2 173 F3
Lune Dr WHTF M45 69 H4
Lune Gv HEY OL10 40 B3
Lune St OLDS OL8 91 F3

Lune Wy RDSH SK5 160 A1
Lunn Av GTN M18 131 E2
Lupin Av FWTH BL4 65 F3
Lupin Cl OLD OL1 76 D1
Lupton St CSLFD M3 * 6 A3
DTN/ASHW M34 132 C4
Lurden Wk CHAD OL9 * 90 B3
Lurgan Av SALE M33 154 D3
Lutener Av ALT WA14 165 F1
Luton Dr NTHM/RTH M23 167 H5
Luton Rd RDSH SK5 145 F3
Luton St BOLS/LL BL3 49 F5
TOT/BURYW BL8 37 G5
Luxhall Wk NEWH/MOS M40 104 A5
Luxor Gv DTN/ASHW M34 131 E5
Luzley Brook Rd ROY/SHW OL2 59 H4
Luzley Rd AUL OL6 108 C5
Lyceum Pas MILN OL16 10 C6
Lyceum Pl HULME M15 128 B1
Lychgate Ct OLDE OL4 92 D4
Lychgate Ms HTNM SK4 * 158 B4
Lydbrook Cl BOL BL1 2 C6
Lydden Av OP/CLY M11 * 117 E2
Lydford ROCH OL11 * 29 H5
Lydford Gdns BOLE BL2 50 C4
Lydford St SLFD M6 113 G1
Lydford Wk
BRUN/LGST M13 * 128 D2
Lydgate Av BOLE BL2 50 B1
Lydgate Cl DTN/ASHW M34 147 F2
STLY SK15 109 F4
WHTF M45 69 H4
Lydgate Dr OLDE OL4 92 B2
Lydgate Rd DROY M43 117 F2
SALE M33 154 D4
Lydiate Cl BOLS/LL BL3 65 E2
Lydiat La WILM/AE SK9 200 D5
Lydney Av CHD/CHDH SK8 181 H5
Lydney Rd URM M41 123 E5
Lyefield Wk MILN OL16 30 C5
Lyme Av WILM/AE SK9 199 E1
Lyme Clough Wy MDTN M24 56 C5
Lymefield Dr WALK M28 96 B3
Lymefield Gv OFTN SK2 172 C3
Lyme Gv ALT WA14 165 F5
DROY M43 117 G5
MPL/ROM SK6 162 C4
MPL/ROM SK6 175 E4
OFTN SK2 13 G7
Lyme Rd BRAM/HZG SK7 185 F3
POY/DIS SK12 187 F5
POY/DIS SK12 196 B4
Lymes ALT WA14 177 F3
Lyme St BRAM/HZG SK7 * 185 E1
HTNM SK4 158 B4
Lymewood Dr POY/DIS SK12 197 G1
WILM/AE SK9 * 199 H2
Lymington Cl MDTN M24 89 E2
Lymington Dr
NTHM/RTH M23 167 E1
Lymm Cl EDGY/DAV SK3 171 G3
WALK M28 81 F4
Lyncombe Cl CHD/CHDH SK8 193 E1
Lyndale Av RDSH SK5 131 E5
SWIN M27 98 C4
Lyndale Dr LIT OL15 20 D2
Lyndene Av WALK M28 97 H2
Lyndene Gdns CHD/CHDH SK8 169 G3
Lyndene Rd WYTH/NTH M22 168 C4
Lyndhurst Av AUL OL6 107 E5
BRAM/HZG SK7 184 D3
CHAD OL9 90 A2
DTN/ASHW M34 * 132 B5
IRL M44 122 C5
MPL/ROM SK6 161 G2
PWCH M25 86 D4
ROCH OL11 57 G1
SALE M33 154 A3
URM M41 124 B4
Lyndhurst Cl WILM/AE SK9 198 A5
Lyndhurst Dr
HALE/TIMP WA15 178 B2
Lyndhurst Rd DID/WITH M20 157 F2
OLDS OL8 91 E4
RDSH SK5 * 145 E1
STRET M32 139 H1
Lyndhurst St SLFD M6 112 D3
Lyndhurst Vw DUK SK16 * 119 H4
Lyndon Cl OLDE OL4 77 G4
TOT/BURYW BL8 26 A5
Lyndon Rd IRL M44 136 B2
Lyne Edge Crs DUK SK16 134 A1
Lyne Edge Rd DUK SK16 134 B1
Lyne Vw HYDE SK14 134 B2
Lyngard Cl WILM/AE SK9 199 G1
Lyngate Cl STKP SK1 13 J5
Lyn Gv HEY OL10 40 B3
Lynham Dr HEY OL10 56 A1
Lynmouth Av DID/WITH M20 142 C5
OLDS OL8 91 G4
RDSH SK5 145 E4
ROY/SHW OL2 74 D1
URM M41 138 B3
Lynmouth Cl CHAD OL9 73 H3
RAD M26 52 D5
Lynmouth Gv PWCH M25 85 G4
Lynn Av SALE M33 140 A5
Lynndene Ct HEY OL10 * 40 D3
Lynn Dr DROY M43 117 F3
Lynn St CHAD OL9 90 D3
Lynnwood Dr ROCH OL11 29 E3
Lynnwood Rd BNG/LEV M19 158 A4
Lynroyle Wy ROCH OL11 42 C3
Lynsted Av BOLS/LL BL3 65 F1
Lynthorpe Rd NEWH/MOS M40 89 G5
Lynton Av HYDE SK14 149 E1
IRL M44 136 A5
OLDS OL8 90 D5
ROCH OL11 42 A3
SWIN M27 99 E1
URM M41 137 E1
Lynton Cl CHAD OL9 74 A3
Lynton Crs WALK M28 97 E2
Lynton Dr BNG/LEV M19 143 H4
MPL/ROM SK6 186 D4
PWCH M25 86 B1
Lynton Gv HALE/TIMP WA15 166 B4
Lynton La WILM/AE SK9 200 D3
Lynton Lea RAD M26 52 D5
Lynton Ms WILM/AE SK9 200 D3
Lynton Park Rd
CHD/CHDH SK8 182 C4
Lynton Rd BOLS/LL BL3 64 B2
CCHDY M21 141 E2
CHD/CHDH SK8 169 H4
HTNM SK4 159 E1
SWIN M27 99 E1
Lynton St RUSH/FAL M14 * 142 D1
Lyntonvale Av
CHD/CHDH SK8 169 F3
Lynway Dr DID/WITH M20 157 G1
Lynway Gv MDTN M24 73 E2
Lynwell Rd ECC M30 111 E3
Lynwood HALE/TIMP WA15 178 B4
Lynwood Av BOLS/LL BL3 65 G2
ECC M30 111 E3
OLDTF/WHR M16 141 G1
Lynwood Cl AULW OL7 106 D3
Lynwood Dr OLDE OL4 76 D5
Lynwood Gv BOLE BL2 35 E2
DTN/ASHW M34 118 B4
HTNM SK4 144 C5
SALE M33 154 D1
Lyon Gv WALK M28 97 H2
Lyon Rd ALT WA14 165 F2
FWTH BL4 82 B2
Lyons Dr TOT/BURYW BL8 37 F5
Lyons Fold SALE M33 139 H5
Lyons Rd TRPK M17 125 F1
Lyon St ROY/SHW OL2 60 A2
SWIN M27 98 D3
Lyra Pl BRO M7 113 H2
Lysander Cl RUSH/FAL M14 142 C3
Lytham Av CCHDY M21 141 G4
Lytham Cl AUL OL6 107 H4
Lytham Dr BRAM/HZG SK7 184 B5
HEY OL10 40 D5
Lytham Rd CHD/CHDH SK8 181 G3
RUSH/FAL M14 143 H2
URM M41 137 F1
Lytham St EDGY/DAV SK3 172 A3
WHIT OL12 18 D5
Lytherton Av IRL M44 150 C2
Lyth St RUSH/FAL M14 143 F4
Lytton Av CHH M8 102 B4
Lytton Rd DROY M43 117 H3
Lytton St BOL BL1 33 G4

M

Mabel Av BOLS/LL BL3 65 F1
WALK M28 97 H3
Mabel Rd FAIL M35 105 F1
Mabel's Brow FWTH BL4 66 B5
Mabel St BOL BL1 48 B1
NEWH/MOS M40 104 C5
WHIT OL12 29 G1
Mabfield Rd RUSH/FAL M14 143 E2
Mableden Cl CHD/CHDH SK8 182 A4
Mabs Ct AUL OL6 120 A3
Macaulay St ROCH OL11 42 B5
ROY/SHW OL2 59 F5
Macauley Cl DUK SK16 134 B1
Macauley Rd
OLDTF/WHR M16 141 F1
RDSH SK5 144 D2
Macclesfield Rd
BRAM/HZG SK7 185 G4
WILM/AE SK9 199 F4
WILM/AE SK9 201 F5
Macdonald Av FWTH BL4 65 F5
Macdonald Rd IRL M44 136 A4
Macdonald St OLDS OL8 91 G3
Macefin Av CCHDY M21 156 C2
Macfarren St
WGTN/LGST M12 129 H5
Mackenzie Gv BOL BL1 33 G2
Mackenzie Rd BRO M7 101 E4
Mackenzie St BOL BL1 33 G2
WGTN/LGST M12 129 H5
Mackenzie Wk OLD OL1 60 D4
Mackeson Dr AUL OL6 120 B1
Mackeson Rd AUL OL6 120 B1
Mackintosh Wy OLD OL1 9 G2
Mackworth St HULME M15 127 G3
Maclaren Dr CHH M8 101 H1
Maclure Rd ROCH OL11 30 A5
Macnair Ct MPL/ROM SK6 175 F4
Macnair Ms MPL/ROM SK6 * 175 E3
MPL/ROM SK6 175 F5
Madams Wood Rd WALK M28 81 E4
Maddison Rd DROY M43 117 G5
Madeley Cl ALT WA14 177 H4
Madeley Dr CHAD OL9 90 C1
Madeley Gdns BOL BL1 33 H4
WHIT OL12 29 G2
Maden's Sq LIT OL15 21 E3
Maden Wk CHAD OL9 * 74 C4
Madison Av CHD/CHDH SK8 182 D2
DTN/ASHW M34 118 B5
Madison Gdns WHTN BL5 62 B2
Madison Pk WHTN BL5 62 A2
Madison St GTN M18 130 D2
Madras Rd EDGY/DAV SK3 * 171 F2
Mafeking Av BURY BL9 38 D1
Mafeking Rd BOLE BL2 * 50 B2
Mafeking St OLDS OL8 90 D4
Magdala St HEY OL10 * 56 B1
OLD OL1 75 F4
Magda Rd OFTN SK2 172 D4
Magenta Av IRL M44 136 A5
Magnolia Cl SALE M33 138 C5
Magnolia Dr CHH M8 * 102 B4
Magpie Cl DROY M43 118 B2
Magpie La OLDE OL4 92 D3
Magpie Wk OP/CLY M11 * 116 A4
Maher Gdns HULME M15 127 H4
Mahood St EDGY/DAV SK3 12 D7
Maida St BNG/LEV M19 144 B1
Maiden Cl AULW OL7 106 D4
Maidford Cl ANC M4 * 115 G4
STRET M32 140 C1
Maidstone Av CCHDY M21 141 E2
Maidstone Ms CCHDY M21 141 E2
Maidstone Rd BNG/LEV M19 158 A4
Main Av BNG/LEV M19 143 H4
TRPK M17 125 H4
Main Dr ALT WA14 176 B1
OLD OL1 75 E3
Maine Rd RUSH/FAL M14 142 C1
Mainprice Cl SLFD M6 113 E1
Main Rd CHAD OL9 8 B2
SWIN M27 85 E4
Main St FAIL M35 105 E2
HYDE SK14 133 G4
Mainwaring Dr WILM/AE SK9 199 G2
Mainwaring Ter
NTHM/RTH M23 155 H4
Mainway MDTN M24 88 C1
Mainway East MDTN M24 89 F1
Mainwood Rd
HALE/TIMP WA15 166 D4
Maismore Rd WYTH/NTH M22 179 H3
Maitland Av CCHDY M21 156 B2
Maitland Cl WHIT OL12 19 H5
Maitland St STKP SK1 172 C2
Maitland Wk CHAD OL9 * 74 C4
Major St CMANE M1 7 G6
MILN OL16 31 G5
RAMS BL0 16 C2
Makin St CMANE M1 * 7 G7
Makkah Cl NEWH/MOS M40 103 H5
Malaga Av MANAIR M90 180 A5
Malakoff St STLY SK15 120 B5
Malbrook Wk
BRUN/LGST M13 * 128 D2
Malby St OLD OL1 9 G1
Malcolm Av SWIN M27 84 B5
Malcolm Dr SWIN M27 84 B5
Malcolm St ROCH OL11 42 C3
Malden Gv NTHM/RTH M23 167 H2
Maldon Cl BOLS/LL BL3 66 D1
OFTN SK2 173 H4
Maldon Crs SWIN M27 99 E4
Maldon Dr ECC M30 111 F1
Maldon St ROCH OL11 43 E1
Maldwyn Av BOLS/LL BL3 64 A2
CHH M8 87 F5
Maleham St BRO M7 * 101 H4
Malgam Dr DID/WITH M20 169 G1
Malham Cl ROY/SHW OL2 59 E5
Malham Ct OFTN SK2 173 E3
Malham Dr WHTF M45 69 H4
Mallard Cl DUK SK16 133 H1
OFTN SK2 173 H4
OLDS OL8 91 E5
Mallard Crs POY/DIS SK12 194 B3
Mallard Gn ALT WA14 165 E1
Mallards Reach
MPL/ROM SK6 162 A4
Mallard St CMANE M1 128 B1
Mallet Crs BOL BL1 32 C4
Malling Rd NTHM/RTH M23 167 H5
Mallison St BOL BL1 34 A3
Mallory Av AULW OL7 107 E5
Mallory Rd HYDE SK14 134 B4
Mallow Cft MILN OL16 43 H2
Mallowdale WALK M28 96 C2
Mallowdale Av
RUSH/FAL M14 142 D3
Mallowdale Cl BOL BL1 47 E3
Mallowdale Rd OFTN SK2 173 F4
Mallow St HULME M15 127 H2
The Mall BURY BL9 4 E5
STLY SK15 135 F2
Mally Gdns MOSL OL5 109 E2
Malmesbury Cl POY/DIS SK12 195 E3
Malmesbury Rd
CHD/CHDH SK8 193 E1
Malpas Cl CHD/CHDH SK8 170 D4
WILM/AE SK9 199 H1
Malpas Dr ALT WA14 153 H5
Malpas St OLD OL1 9 H2
WGTN/LGST M12 129 H2
Malpas Wk
OLDTF/WHR M16 * 127 G3
Malrae HALE/TIMP WA15 * 177 H3
Malsham Rd NTHM/RTH M23 155 G4
Malta Cl MDTN M24 73 G5
Malta St ANC M4 115 G4
OLDE OL4 92 C1
Maltby Ct OLDE OL4 93 E2
Maltby Dr BOLS/LL BL3 64 B2
Maltby Rd NTHM/RTH M23 167 G3
Maltings La ROCH OL11 42 B5
Malton Av BOLS/LL BL3 47 H5
CCHDY M21 141 F4
WHTF M45 69 G2
Malton Cl CHAD OL9 74 A3
Malton Dr ALT WA14 164 D3
BRAM/HZG SK7 185 E5
Malton Rd HTNM SK4 158 D2
Malton St OLDS OL8 8 D6
Malt St HULME M15 127 G2
Malus Ct SLFD M6 113 F2
Malvern Av AUL OL6 107 F3
BOL BL1 32 D5
BURY BL9 38 C1
CHD/CHDH SK8 169 E4
DROY M43 118 B3
URM M41 138 B1
Malvern Cl FWTH BL4 65 E3
HTNM SK4 159 G3
MILN OL16 31 H4
PWCH M25 86 B2
ROY/SHW OL2 59 G1
ROY/SHW OL2 74 D1
SWIN M27 100 A4
Malvern Dr ALT WA14 165 E4
SWIN M27 100 A4
Malvern Gv DID/WITH M20 142 C5
SLFD M6 112 B2
WALK M28 82 A4
Malvern Rd MDTN M24 88 D2
Malvern Rw HULME M15 * 127 F2
Malvern St OLDS OL8 8 D6
Malvern St East ROCH OL11 29 F4
Malvern St West ROCH OL11 29 F4
Manby Rd GTN M18 130 A4
Manby Sq GTN M18 130 A4
Manchester Chambers
OLD OL1 9 F3
Manchester New Rd
MDTN M24 88 C1
PART M31 151 E3
Manchester Old Rd BURY BL9 4 C7
MDTN M24 71 H5
Manchester Rd ALT WA14 165 G3
BOLE BL2 49 F4
BOLS/LL BL3 65 H1
BURY BL9 4 D5
BURY BL9 17 F3
BURY BL9 53 F3
CCHDY M21 141 F2
DID/WITH M20 170 A1
DROY M43 117 F4
DTN/ASHW M34 131 F4
DTN/ASHW M34 131 G1
DTN/ASHW M34 132 B5
GOL/RIS/CUL WA3 150 A4
HEY OL10 56 A3
HTNM SK4 159 G1
HYDE SK14 133 E5
MDTN M24 57 G2
MOSL OL5 108 D3
OLDS OL8 90 D3
PART M31 151 F2
RAMS BL0 17 F2
ROCH OL11 29 H5
ROY/SHW OL2 59 H4
SWIN M27 84 A4
SWIN M27 98 C1
WALK M28 82 C5
WHTN BL5 62 A2
WILM/AE SK9 199 F2
Manchester Rd East
LHULT M38 81 F3
Manchester Rd North
DTN/ASHW M34 131 H4
Manchester Rd South
DTN/ASHW M34 131 H5
Manchester Rd West
LHULT M38 80 D2
Manchester St CHAD OL9 8 C6
HEY OL10 41 E4
OLDTF/WHR M16 127 F3
Manchet St ROCH OL11 42 A5
Mancroft Av BOLS/LL BL3 48 C5
Mancroft Ter BOLS/LL BL3 * 48 C5
Mancroft Wk CMANE M1 128 C1
Mancunian Rd
DTN/ASHW M34 147 E3
Mancunian Wy
WGTN/LGST M12 128 D1
Mandalay Gdns
MPL/ROM SK6 174 C2
Mandarin Gn ALT WA14 165 E1
Mandarin Wk SLFD M6 * 113 F2
Mandeville St BNG/LEV M19 144 B3
Mandley Av NEWH/MOS M40 * 89 G5
Mandley Cl BOLS/LL BL3 51 E4
Mandley Park Av BRO M7 101 H3
Mandon Cl RAD M26 51 H4
Manesty Cl MDTN M24 71 H2
Manet Cl BRO M7 101 E2
Mangle St CMANE M1 7 H4
Mango Pl SLFD M6 113 F3
Manifold Dr MPL/ROM SK6 197 E1
Manifold St SLFD M6 101 E5
Manilla Wk OP/CLY M11 116 A4
Manipur St OP/CLY M11 115 H5
Manley Av SWIN M27 84 A3
Manley Cl BURY BL9 26 D1
Manley Crs WHTN BL5 62 C3
Manley Gv BRAM/HZG SK7 193 H1
HYDE SK14 135 G5
Manley Rd CCHDY M21 141 G2
OLDS OL8 91 F3
OLDTF/WHR M16 142 A1
ROCH OL11 42 B3
SALE M33 153 H5
Manley St BRO M7 101 G4
Manley Ter BOL BL1 * 33 H2
Manningham Rd BOLS/LL BL3 48 A4
Mannington Dr BKLY M9 102 D4
Mannock St OLDS OL8 8 D6
The Manns UPML OL3 94 C2
Manor Av BOLS/LL BL3 67 F1
OLDTF/WHR M16 141 H1
SALE M33 153 G2
URM M41 138 D2
Manor Cl CHAD OL9 8 A1
CHD/CHDH SK8 183 F4
DTN/ASHW M34 147 F1
OLDE OL4 94 B2
WILM/AE SK9 198 B2
Manor Ct STRET M32 139 H2
Manor Dr CCHDY M21 156 C2
ROY/SHW OL2 75 F1
Manor Farm Cl AULW OL7 106 C5
Manor Farm Ri OLDE OL4 76 C5
Manorfield Cl BOL BL1 32 D5
Manor Gdns WILM/AE SK9 199 G3
Manor Gate Rd BOLE BL2 50 D1
Manor Hill Rd MPL/ROM SK6 175 E3
Manorial Dr LHULT M38 80 D2
Manor Ml CHAD OL9 * 74 D4
Manor Mill Cl MILN OL16 20 A5
Manor Pk URM M41 * 138 D2
Manor Rd BNG/LEV M19 144 B1
CHD/CHDH SK8 183 F3
DROY M43 117 F4
DTN/ASHW M34 131 G1
DTN/ASHW M34 147 F2
HALE/TIMP WA15 165 H5
HYDE SK14 134 A3
MDTN M24 88 C1
MPL/ROM SK6 162 A1
MPL/ROM SK6 175 E2
OLDE OL4 92 B3
RDSH SK5 160 C1
ROY/SHW OL2 59 H2
SALE M33 154 C1
SLFD M6 112 C1
STRET M32 139 H2
SWIN M27 99 E4
WILM/AE SK9 198 B2
Manor St BOL BL1 3 F4
BURY BL9 5 G4
DTN/ASHW M34 132 C1
FWTH BL4 65 H5
FWTH BL4 83 E2
MDTN M24 72 D2
MOSL OL5 93 H5
RAMS BL0 16 C1
ROY/SHW OL2 75 H2
WGTN/LGST M12 128 D1
Manor Vw MPL/ROM SK6 147 F5
The Manse MOSL OL5 108 D2
Mansfield Av BKLY M9 88 A3
DTN/ASHW M34 132 A3
RAMS BL0 26 C2
Mansfield Cl AULW OL7 119 E4
DTN/ASHW M34 132 A3
Mansfield Crs
DTN/ASHW M34 132 A4
Mansfield Dr BKLY M9 88 B3
Mansfield Gra ROCH OL11 29 F5
Mansfield Gv BOL BL1 33 E5
Mansfield Rd BKLY M9 88 B3
HYDE SK14 148 A2
MOSL OL5 109 F1
OLDS OL8 92 A2
ROCH OL11 28 B4
URM M41 138 A2
Mansfield St AULW OL7 118 D5
Mansford Dr NEWH/MOS M40 103 G5
Manshaw Crs DTN/ASHW M34 131 F1
Manshaw Rd OP/CLY M11 131 F1
Mansion Av WHTF M45 69 F1
Manson Av HULME M15 127 G2
Manstead Wk
NEWH/MOS M40 * 115 H3
Manston Dr CHD/CHDH SK8 182 D2
Manswood Dr CHH M8 102 B3
Manthorpe Av WALK M28 97 H3
Mantley La UPML OL3 61 F2
Manton Av BKLY M9 89 E4
DTN/ASHW M34 131 F5
Manton Cl BRO M7 102 A4
Manvers St RDSH SK5 159 H3
Manwaring St FAIL M35 104 D2
Maple Av BOL BL1 * 33 E5
BURY BL9 5 K4
CCHDY M21 141 F3
CHD/CHDH SK8 182 C2
DTN/ASHW M34 118 A4
DTN/ASHW M34 132 B5
ECC M30 110 B1
HALE/TIMP WA15 167 F4
MPL/ROM SK6 175 E5
POY/DIS SK12 195 G4
STLY SK15 120 C5
STRET M32 140 B2
WHTF M45 69 G5
Maple Cl FWTH BL4 82 C2
MDTN M24 73 G4
OFTN SK2 172 C3
ROY/SHW OL2 * 59 G1
SLFD M6 113 E2
Maplecroft STKP SK1 172 C1
Mapledon Rd BKLY M9 103 G2
Maplefield Dr WALK M28 96 C3
Maple Gv FAIL M35 104 D5
NEWH/MOS M40 89 H5
PWCH M25 85 H1
RAMS BL0 17 E3
TOT/BURYW BL8 37 F1
WALK M28 97 E2
Maple Rd BRAM/HZG SK7 193 H2
CHAD OL9 74 C3
FWTH BL4 65 F4
NTHM/RTH M23 166 D1
PART M31 150 D3
SWIN M27 98 D4
WILM/AE SK9 201 E3
Maple Rd West
NTHM/RTH M23 166 D1
Maple St BOLE BL2 34 D1
BOLS/LL BL3 48 C4
OLDS OL8 90 D4
ROCH OL11 29 G5
Maple Wk NTHM/RTH M23 166 D1
Maplewood Cl BKLY M9 87 H5
ROY/SHW OL2 74 D2
Maplewood Ct BRO M7 101 G3
Maplewood Gdns BOL BL1 * 33 H4
Maplewood Gv STLY SK15 121 G2
Maplewood House BOL BL1 33 H5
Maplewood Rd WILM/AE SK9 199 H2
Mapley Av WYTH/NTH M22 168 C1
Maplin Cl BRUN/LGST M13 128 D1
Maplin Dr OFTN SK2 173 H4
Marble St CMANW M2 7 F4
OLD OL1 * 76 A4
Marbury Av RUSH/FAL M14 142 D2
Marbury Cl EDGY/DAV SK3 170 D2
URM M41 123 E5
Marbury Rd HTNM SK4 144 D4
WILM/AE SK9 * 198 D1
Marcer Rd NEWH/MOS M40 115 G3
March Av HTNM SK4 159 E4
Marchbank Dr
CHD/CHDH SK8 169 H3
March Dr TOT/BURYW BL8 38 A1
Marchers Ms ECC M30 110 C4
Marchioness St GTN M18 * 131 E2
Marchmont Cl
BRUN/LGST M13 129 E2
March St MILN OL16 11 F6
Marchwood Av CCHDY M21 141 H2
Marcliffe Dr BNG/LEV M19 144 C2
ROCH OL11 29 E5
Marcliff Gv HTNM SK4 159 E4
Marcroft Pl ROCH OL11 43 F2
Marcus Gv RUSH/FAL M14 143 E1
Marcus St BOL BL1 33 E5
Mardale Av DID/WITH M20 157 H1
ROY/SHW OL2 58 D1
SWIN M27 83 F5
URM M41 123 G5
Mardale Cl BOLE BL2 35 G5
OLDE OL4 76 C5
PWCH M25 70 B5
STLY SK15 120 D2
Mardale Dr BOLE BL2 35 G5
CHD/CHDH SK8 169 G3
MDTN M24 72 B3
Mardale Rd SWIN M27 98 C4
Marden Rd NTHM/RTH M23 167 H4
Mardyke WHIT OL12 10 B5
Marfield BKLY M9 * 103 F1
Marfield Av CHAD OL9 90 B2
Marford Cl WYTH/NTH M22 168 C3
Marford Crs SALE M33 154 A4
Margaret Ashton Cl BKLY M9 103 G3
Margaret Av MILN OL16 11 J7

Margaret Rd DROY M43 * 117 F3
DTN/ASHW M34 132 D4
Margaret Sands St
HULME M15 127 G2
Margaret St AUL OL6 119 F3
BURY BL9 5 F6
HEY OL10 40 C4
OLDS OL8 90 C5
RDSH SK5 145 E4
ROY/SHW OL2 * 60 A3
Margate Av NEWH/MOS M40 104 A5
Margate Rd RDSH SK5 145 F4
Margrove Cha HOR/BR BL6 46 D4
Margrove Cl FAIL M35 105 H3
Margrove Rd SLFD M6 112 B1
Margroy Cl WHIT OL12 11 F1
Marguerita Rd
NEWH/MOS M40 117 E1
Marham Cl CCHDY M21 * 142 A5
HYDE SK14 133 G2
Maria St BOL BL1 33 H4
Marie Cl DTN/ASHW M34 146 D1
Marie St BRO M7 * 101 H3
Marigold St ROCH OL11 43 E1
Mariman Dr CHH M8 87 F5
Marina Av DTN/ASHW M34 147 E2
Marina Cl WILM/AE SK9 192 A2
Marina Crs OP/CLY M11 116 C2
Marina Dr MPL/ROM SK6 174 B2
Marina Rd DROY M43 118 A3
MPL/ROM SK6 161 F2
Marine Av PART M31 150 C3
Marion St BOLS/LL BL3 65 H2
OLDS OL8 91 G4
Marjorie Cl GTN M18 130 A2
Mark Av SLFD M6 113 G1
Markenfield Dr ROY/SHW OL2 59 G2
Market Pde BURY BL9 4 E5
Market Pl AUL OL6 119 G2
BURY BL9 4 D4
HYDE SK14 * 135 H5
MDTN M24 72 D3
OLD OL1 * 9 F3
RAMS BL0 16 D1
STKP SK1 13 G2
Market St ALT WA14 165 G5
BOL BL1 2 E4
BOLS/LL BL3 66 D1
BURY BL9 4 D5
CMANE M1 7 F4
DROY M43 118 A3
DTN/ASHW M34 132 C5
FWTH BL4 66 A3
HEY OL10 40 D4
HYDE SK14 133 G5
HYDE SK14 135 H4
HYDE SK14 148 A2
MDTN M24 72 C3
MOSL OL5 108 D1
RAD M26 67 E4
ROY/SHW OL2 60 A3
STLY SK15 120 D3
SWIN M27 99 F1
TOT/BURYW BL8 26 A5
WHIT OL12 18 B2
Market Wk SALE M33 * 154 C2
Market Wy SLFD M6 113 E2
Markfield Av BRUN/LGST M13 129 E3
Markham Cl WGTN/LGST M12 115 H5
Markham St HYDE SK14 133 G2
Markington St RUSH/FAL M14 128 B5
Markland Hl BOL BL1 47 F1
Markland Hill Cl BOL BL1 32 C5
Markland Hill La BOL BL1 32 C5
Markland St BOL BL1 2 E6
HYDE SK14 148 A2
RAMS BL0 * 16 D2
Mark La ROY/SHW OL2 60 C3
Marks St RAD M26 68 B1
Mark St CHAD OL9 8 D2
WALK M28 96 A3
WHIT OL12 11 F3
Marland Av CHD/CHDH SK8 182 C2
OLDS OL8 106 D1
ROCH OL11 42 A2
Marland Cl ROCH OL11 42 A1
Marland Crs RDSH SK5 145 F3
Marland Fold ROCH OL11 42 A2
Marland Fold La OLDS OL8 106 C1
Marland Gn ROCH OL11 42 A2
Marland Hill Rd ROCH OL11 42 B1
Marland Old Rd ROCH OL11 42 A2
Marland St CHAD OL9 90 B4
Marland Wy STRET M32 126 A5
Marlborough Av
CHD/CHDH SK8 183 E3
OLDTF/WHR M16 141 G2
WILM/AE SK9 201 E3
Marlborough Cl AULW OL7 118 D5
DTN/ASHW M34 132 C5
MPL/ROM SK6 174 C2
RAMS BL0 16 D5
Marlborough Dr FAIL M35 104 D4
HTNM SK4 * 159 G2
Marlborough Gdns FWTH BL4 65 E4
Marlborough Rd ALT WA14 177 G2
BRO M7 102 A4
ECC M30 111 H1
HYDE SK14 148 A3
IRL M44 122 C5
ROY/SHW OL2 75 F2
SALE M33 154 C2
STRET M32 125 H5
URM M41 123 G5
Marlborough St AULW OL7 119 E4
BOL BL1 2 A3
HEY OL10 56 B1
OLDE OL4 9 J5
WHIT OL12 29 F2
Marlbrook Wk BOLS/LL BL3 49 E5
Marlcroft Av HTNM SK4 159 E4
Marlcroft Cl NTHM/RTH M23 167 H2
Marld Crs BOL BL1 32 C4
Marle Av MOSL OL5 109 F1
Marle Cft WHTF M45 84 D1
Marle Ri MOSL OL5 109 F1
Marler Rd HYDE SK14 133 H4
Marley Cl HALE/TIMP WA15 166 A2
Marley Dr SALE M33 139 G5
Marleyer Cl NEWH/MOS M40 104 B3
Marleyer Ri MPL/ROM SK6 173 H1
Marley Rd BNG/LEV M19 144 B3
POY/DIS SK12 195 F5
Marlfield Rd
HALE/TIMP WA15 179 E5
ROY/SHW OL2 59 F1
Marlfield St BKLY M9 103 F1
Marlhill Cl OFTN SK2 173 F4
Marlinford Dr
NEWH/MOS M40 104 B5
Marlor St DTN/ASHW M34 132 B4
Marlow Cl BOLE BL2 35 G5
CHD/CHDH SK8 182 C2
URM M41 124 A4
Marlow Dr ALT WA14 176 C2
IRL M44 122 B5
SWIN M27 98 D4
WILM/AE SK9 191 H2
Marlowe Dr DID/WITH M20 157 G2
Marlowe Wks MPL/ROM SK6 161 F4
Marlow Rd BKLY M9 103 G1
Marlwood Rd BOL BL1 32 C4
Marmion Dr CCHDY M21 141 E3
Marne Av AUL OL6 108 A5
WYTH/NTH M22 168 D4
Marne Crs ROCH OL11 29 F4
Marnland Gv BOLS/LL BL3 47 F5
Maroon Rd WYTH/NTH M22 181 E5
Marple Av BOL BL1 34 B2
Marple Cl OLDS OL8 91 E5
Marple Gv STRET M32 125 H5
Marple Hall Dr MPL/ROM SK6 174 C3
Marple Old Rd OFTN SK2 173 H3
Marple Rd OFTN SK2 173 E2
OFTN SK2 173 H3
Marple St HULME M15 127 G3
Marquis Av BURY BL9 38 B2
Marquis Dr CHD/CHDH SK8 182 A5
Marquis St BNG/LEV M19 144 D2
Marrick Av CHD/CHDH SK8 169 H4
Marriotts Ct CMANW M2 7 F4
Marriott St DID/WITH M20 142 D5
STKP SK1 13 H6
Marron Pl CMANW M2 * 6 D6
Mars Av BOLS/LL BL3 64 B1
Marsden Cl AULW OL7 106 B5
MILN OL16 58 D1
Marsden Dr HALE/TIMP WA15 166 D3
Marsden Rd BOL BL1 2 D4
MPL/ROM SK6 162 B3
Marsden St BURY BL9 4 E2
CMANW M2 6 E4
ECC M30 110 D2
MDTN M24 73 F5
WALK M28 96 A4
Marsett Cl WHIT OL12 28 C2
Marshall Ct AUL OL6 120 A3
OLD OL1 * 75 F4
Marshall Rd BNG/LEV M19 144 A2
Marshall Stevens Wy
TRPK M17 125 G3
Marshall St ANC M4 7 H2
MILN OL16 11 H7
WGTN/LGST M12 128 D2
Marsham Cl BRUN/LGST M13 129 F4
OLDE OL4 93 G2
Marsham Dr MPL/ROM SK6 175 F4
Marsham Rd BRAM/HZG SK7 184 C3
Marshbrook Dr BKLY M9 102 D1
Marshbrook Rd URM M41 124 B5
Marsh Cl EDGY/DAV SK3 171 G3
Marshdale Rd BOL BL1 47 G1
Marshfield Rd
HALE/TIMP WA15 166 D4
Marshfield Wk
BRUN/LGST M13 128 D2
Marsh Fold La BOL BL1 48 B1
Marsh Hey Cl LHULT M38 81 E1
Marsh La FWTH BL4 65 F4
Marsh Rd BOLS/LL BL3 50 D5
LHULT M38 81 G3
Marsh St WALK M28 82 C4
Marsland Av
HALE/TIMP WA15 166 C1
Marsland Cl
DTN/ASHW M34 131 G5
Marsland Rd
HALE/TIMP WA15 166 C3
MPL/ROM SK6 174 D2
SALE M33 154 B3
Marslands UPML OL3 79 E1
Marsland St
BRAM/HZG SK7 * 185 E2
Marsland St North BRO M7 101 H3
Marsland St South BRO M7 102 A3
Marsland Ter STKP SK1 172 C1
Mars St CHAD OL9 8 B2
Marston Cl FAIL M35 105 G4
HOR/BR BL6 46 A1
WHTF M45 70 B4
Marston Dr IRL M44 136 D1
Marston Rd BRO M7 101 H2
STRET M32 140 C1
Marston Wy South
CMANE M1 * 6 E4
Marsworth Dr ANC M4 115 F3
Martens Rd IRL M44 150 D1
Marthall Dr SALE M33 155 F4
Martham Dr OFTN SK2 173 H4
Martha's Ter MILN OL16 19 H5
Martha St BOLS/LL BL3 * 48 C5
OLD OL1 8 D1
Martin Av BOLS/LL BL3 67 F1
OLDE OL4 92 B2
Martin Cl DTN/ASHW M34 132 C3
OFTN SK2 173 G4
Martindale Cl ROY/SHW OL2 59 F4
Martindale Crs MDTN M24 72 A1
WGTN/LGST M12 129 F2
Martindale Gdns BOL BL1 33 H4
Martin Dr IRL M44 122 B4
Martingale Cl RAD M26 52 B4
Martingale Wy DROY M43 118 C2
Martin Gv FWTH BL4 66 C5
Martin La WHIT OL12 29 E2
Martin Rd SWIN M27 84 C5
Martinsclough HOR/BR BL6 46 D3
Martinscroft Rd
NTHM/RTH M23 167 H4
Martins Fld WHIT OL12 28 C2
Martin St BURY BL9 39 G3
DTN/ASHW M34 132 C1
HYDE SK14 148 A1
ORD M5 112 C3
Martlesham Wk ANC M4 * 7 G3
Martlet Av POY/DIS SK12 197 H1
ROCH OL11 28 B4
Martlet Cl RUSH/FAL M14 142 C2
Martock Av WYTH/NTH M22 180 D1
Marton Av BOLE BL2 49 H1
DID/WITH M20 157 H4
Marton Gra PWCH M25 86 D5
Marton Gn EDGY/DAV SK3 171 G3
Marton Gv HTNM SK4 145 E5
Marton Pl SALE M33 154 B2
Marwood Cl ALT WA14 165 E3
RAD M26 66 D4
Marwood Dr NTHM/RTH M23 179 G1
Maryfield Ct
OLDTF/WHR M16 * 142 A3
Mary France St HULME M15 127 H2
Mary Hulton Ct WHTN BL5 62 B4
Maryland Av BOLE BL2 50 A2
Marylon Dr WYTH/NTH M22 168 D1
Maryport Dr
HALE/TIMP WA15 167 E2
Mary St CHD/CHDH SK8 170 A3
CSLFD M3 114 C2
DROY M43 118 A4
DTN/ASHW M34 * 132 C4
DUK SK16 119 G5
FWTH BL4 66 A5
HEY OL10 40 D4
HYDE SK14 133 F5
MILN OL16 20 A4
RAMS BL0 16 C3
STKP SK1 13 J2
Masboro St CHH M8 102 A3
Masbury Cl BOL BL1 22 D4
Masefield Av PWCH M25 85 G4
RAD M26 51 H5
Masefield Cl DUK SK16 134 C1
Masefield Crs DROY M43 117 H4
Masefield Dr FWTH BL4 65 G5
HTNM SK4 158 D4
Masefield Gv RDSH SK5 145 E2
Masefield Rd BOLS/LL BL3 51 E5
DROY M43 117 H4
OLD OL1 76 A2
Mason Gdns BOLS/LL BL3 2 C7
Mason St ANC M4 7 H2
AULW OL7 119 E4
BURY BL9 5 G5
EDGW/EG BL7 * 22 D2
HEY OL10 40 C4
MILN OL16 10 D7
Massey Av AUL OL6 107 F4
FAIL M35 105 G2
Massey Cft WHIT OL12 18 B1
Massey Rd HALE/TIMP WA15 165 H5
SALE M33 155 F2
Massey St BURY BL9 5 J2
STKP SK1 13 G4
WILM/AE SK9 200 D4
Massey Wk WYTH/NTH M22 181 E3
Massie St CHD/CHDH SK8 170 A3
Matham Wk HULME M15 * 128 A1
Mather Av ECC M30 111 F3
PWCH M25 101 F1
WHTF M45 69 G2
Mather Cl WHTF M45 69 G3
Mather Fold Rd WALK M28 96 C1
Mather Rd BURY BL9 27 G4
ECC M30 111 F3
Mather St BOLS/LL BL3 * 2 D7
FAIL M35 104 C3
FWTH BL4 66 B4
RAD M26 68 B1
Mather Wy SLFD M6 * 113 F2
Matisse Wy BRO M7 101 E2
Matley Cl HYDE SK14 134 C3
Matley Gn RDSH SK5 146 A5
Matley La STLY SK15 134 D2
Matlock Av AUL OL6 108 A4
BRO M7 100 D3
DID/WITH M20 142 B5
DTN/ASHW M34 147 E3
URM M41 138 B3
Matlock Cl FWTH BL4 66 B3
SALE M33 154 D2
Matlock Dr BRAM/HZG SK7 185 F4
Matlock Rd CHD/CHDH SK8 181 H5
RDSH SK5 145 G2
STRET M32 125 F5
Matlock St ECC M30 110 D5
Matt Busby Cl SWIN M27 99 G3
Matthew Cl OLDS OL8 92 B3
Matthew Moss La ROCH OL11 42 A2
Matthews Av FWTH BL4 66 C5
Matthews La BNG/LEV M19 144 B1
Matthew's St
WGTN/LGST M12 129 G1
Matthew St MPL/ROM SK6 175 F3
Mattison St OP/CLY M11 130 D1
Maudsley St BURY BL9 4 C6
Maud St BOLE BL2 34 D1
WHIT OL12 10 E1
Mauldeth Cl HTNM SK4 158 D3
Mauldeth Rd BNG/LEV M19 143 G5
BNG/LEV M19 158 C2
DID/WITH M20 143 E4
Mauldeth Rd West
CCHDY M21 142 A3
Maunby Gdns LHULT M38 81 H4
Maureen Av CHH M8 102 B2
Maureen St WHIT OL12 11 F1
Maurice Cl DUK SK16 120 B5
Maurice Dr SLFD M6 113 E1
Maurice St SLFD M6 113 E1
Maveen Gv OFTN SK2 172 B5
Mavis Gv MILN OL16 31 H5
Mavis St ROCH OL11 42 B5
Mawdsley Dr CHH M8 102 D2
Mawdsley St BOL BL1 2 E5
Maxwell Av OFTN SK2 172 D4
Maxwell St BOL BL1 33 H2
BURY BL9 5 J3
Max Woosnam Wk
RUSH/FAL M14 128 B5
Mayall St MOSL OL5 108 D1
Mayall St East OLDE OL4 * 76 B5
May Av CHD/CHDH SK8 193 E1
HTNM SK4 * 12 A2
Maybank St BOLS/LL BL3 48 C5
Mayberth Av CHH M8 87 F5
Maybreck Cl BOLS/LL BL3 48 B4
Mayburn Cl MDTN M24 89 F2
Maybury Cl RAMS BL0 16 C3
Maybury St GTN M18 130 D2
Maycroft Av DID/WITH M20 157 H1
May Dr BNG/LEV M19 143 H5
Mayer St OFTN SK2 * 172 D2
Mayes Gdns ANC M4 115 G4
Mayes St ANC M4 7 G2
Mayfair Av RAD M26 51 G5
SLFD M6 112 A2
URM M41 138 B1
WHTF M45 * 69 G5
Mayfair Cl DUK SK16 120 C5
POY/DIS SK12 195 F2
Mayfair Ct HALE/TIMP WA15 * 166 C2
Mayfair Crs FAIL M35 105 G2
Mayfair Dr IRL M44 136 C1
ROY/SHW OL2 75 E2
SALE M33 153 H4
Mayfair Gdns ROCH OL11 42 C1
Mayfair Ms DID/WITH M20 * 157 E2
Mayfair Pk DID/WITH M20 * 157 E2
Mayfair Rd WYTH/NTH M22 168 D5
Mayfield BOLE BL2 35 E1
Mayfield Av BOLS/LL BL3 65 G1
DTN/ASHW M34 147 E4
FWTH BL4 65 H5
OLDE OL4 77 F5
RDSH SK5 160 A1
SALE M33 155 F2
STRET M32 139 H2
WALK M28 82 A4
WALK M28 98 B4
Mayfield Cl HALE/TIMP WA15 166 C3
RAMS BL0 26 B1
Mayfield Gv GTN M18 131 E5
RDSH SK5 160 A1
WILM/AE SK9 198 B5
Mayfield Houses RAD M26 * 67 H2
Mayfield Rd BRAM/HZG SK7 193 H3
BRO M7 112 D1
HALE/TIMP WA15 166 C3
MPL/ROM SK6 163 G5
OLD OL1 76 A3
OLDTF/WHR M16 127 H5
RAMS BL0 26 B1
Mayfield St DTN/ASHW M34 132 B3
MILN OL16 11 H3
Mayfield Ter MILN OL16 11 H2
Mayflower Av ORD M5 113 F5
Mayford Rd BNG/LEV M19 144 A1
Maygate CHAD OL9 75 E4
May Gv BNG/LEV M19 144 B3
Mayhill Dr SLFD M6 111 H1
WALK M28 97 H2
Mayhurst Av CCHDY M21 156 C3
Mayorlowe Av RDSH SK5 160 D2
Mayor's Rd HALE/TIMP WA15 165 H5
Mayor St BOL BL1 2 B6
TOT/BURYW BL8 37 H3
Mayo St WGTN/LGST M12 115 G5
Maypool Dr RDSH SK5 145 F5
May Rd CHD/CHDH SK8 192 D1
OLDTF/WHR M16 127 G5
SWIN M27 99 G4
May St BOLE BL2 3 H5
ECC M30 110 D1
HEY OL10 * 56 B1
NEWH/MOS M40 104 B5
OLDS OL8 90 D3
RAD M26 68 B1
Mayton St OP/CLY M11 116 B5
Mayville Dr DID/WITH M20 157 G1
Maywood Av DID/WITH M20 169 G1
Maze St BOLS/LL BL3 50 A4
McConnell Rd
NEWH/MOS M40 103 H3
McCready Dr ORD M5 * 113 G5
McDonna St BOL BL1 33 F3
McDonough Cl OLDS OL8 91 H4
McEvoy St BOL BL1 34 A4
McKean St BOLS/LL BL3 49 F5
McKie Cl OLDS OL8 91 H4
McLaren Ct CCHDY M21 141 E2
McLean Dr IRL M44 122 B4
McNaught St MILN OL16 30 C5
Meachin Av CCHDY M21 156 B1
Meade Cl URM M41 138 C1
Meade Gv BRUN/LGST M13 129 G5
Meade Hill Rd CHH M8 87 E4
PWCH M25 86 D4
The Meade BOLS/LL BL3 64 D2
WILM/AE SK9 199 E2
Meadfoot Av PWCH M25 86 B4
Meadfoot Rd GTN M18 130 C2
Meadland Gv BOL BL1 34 A2
Meadow Av HALE/TIMP WA15 178 C1
SWIN M27 99 G1
Meadowbank AULW OL7 106 D4
Meadow Bank CCHDY M21 141 E4
HALE/TIMP WA15 166 B2
HTNM SK4 159 E4
MPL/ROM SK6 161 G3
Meadowbank Cl FAIL M35 105 F4
Meadow Bank Cl OLDE OL4 * 92 D3
Meadow Bank Ct STRET M32 139 H2
Meadowbank Rd BOLS/LL BL3 64 A2
Meadowbrook Cl BURY BL9 39 F2
HOR/BR BL6 62 D1
Meadow Brook Wy
CHD/CHDH SK8 171 E5
Meadow Brow WILM/AE SK9 200 D3
Meadow Cl BOLS/LL BL3 67 E2
DTN/ASHW M34 147 E4
HALE/TIMP WA15 178 C1
HEY OL10 40 D4
MOSL OL5 94 B4
MPL/ROM SK6 161 H1
MPL/ROM SK6 187 E4
STRET M32 140 C2
WILM/AE SK9 200 B1
Meadow Ct CCHDY M21 140 D3
Meadow Cft BRAM/HZG SK7 185 F1
WHTF M45 84 D1
Meadowcroft HYDE SK14 135 G4
RAD M26 52 A4
WHTN BL5 62 A5
Meadowcroft La OLD OL1 75 H3
ROCH OL11 28 C5
Meadowfield HOR/BR BL6 46 C2
MILN OL16 43 G3
Meadowfield Ct HYDE SK14 133 G4
Meadowfield Dr WALK M28 96 C4
Meadow Fold UPML OL3 79 F4
Meadowgate URM M41 138 D2
WALK M28 97 G2
Meadowgate Rd SLFD M6 112 B3
Meadow Head Av WHIT OL12 18 C2
Meadow La BOLE BL2 50 D2
DTN/ASHW M34 147 E4
DUK SK16 120 A5
OLDS OL8 91 F5
WALK M28 97 G5
Meadow Ri ROY/SHW OL2 44 D5
Meadow Rd BRO M7 113 H3
MDTN M24 88 B1
URM M41 138 D2
Meadows Cl BRAM/HZG SK7 185 F1
Meadowside BRAM/HZG SK7 183 F2
MILN OL16 45 F2
Meadowside Av BOLE BL2 49 H1
IRL M44 136 C1
WALK M28 82 B3
WYTH/NTH M22 168 C5
Meadowside Cl RAD M26 52 B4
Meadowside Gv WALK M28 82 B4
Meadows La BOLE BL2 35 G3
Meadows Rd CHD/CHDH SK8 181 G3
CHD/CHDH SK8 182 C4
HTNM SK4 144 C5
SALE M33 140 A5
The Meadows MDTN M24 89 E1
MPL/ROM SK6 162 A2
OLDE OL4 93 F1
PWCH M25 86 A3
RAD M26 51 H4
UPML OL3 79 E5
WHIT OL12 14 B4
Meadow St HYDE SK14 148 A2
OFTN SK2 172 D4
The Meadow BOL BL1 47 E2
Meadow Vw WHIT OL12 28 D2
Meadow Wk FWTH BL4 65 F5
LIT OL15 * 20 C3
Meadow Wy
HALE/TIMP WA15 178 C1
NEWH/MOS M40 103 H1
TOT/BURYW BL8 25 H5
WILM/AE SK9 200 B1
Meadscroft Dr WILM/AE SK9 200 C4
Meads Gv FWTH BL4 64 C4
The Meads CHAD OL9 90 B1
The Mead CCHDY M21 * 141 F4
ORD M5 112 D3
Meadway BRAM/HZG SK7 193 H2
BURY BL9 53 G3
CHAD OL9 89 H5
DUK SK16 133 H1
MPL/ROM SK6 187 E4
POY/DIS SK12 194 C2
ROCH OL11 42 A2
SALE M33 153 H4
STLY SK15 135 F2
Meadway Cl SALE M33 153 H3
Meadway Rd CHD/CHDH SK8 183 E1
Mealhouse Brow STKP SK1 13 G3
Mealhouse La BOL BL1 2 E4
Meal St HTNM SK4 159 H3
Meanwood Fold ROCH OL11 29 F3
Measham Ms CMANE M1 128 B1
Meddings Cl WILM/AE SK9 200 D5
Medina Cl CHD/CHDH SK8 171 E5
Medley St WHIT OL12 10 C2
Medlock Cl FWTH BL4 65 G4
Medlock Dr OLDS OL8 106 D1
Medlock Rd FAIL M35 105 F5
Medlock St DROY M43 117 H3
HULME M15 128 A1
OLD OL1 9 K2
Medlock Valley Wy OLDE OL4 61 F4
Medlock Wy OLDE OL4 92 D1
WHTF M45 70 B4
Medway Cl OLDS OL8 90 D4
ORD M5 112 C2
WILM/AE SK9 192 A5
Medway Crs ALT WA14 165 F3
Medway Dr FWTH BL4 83 E2
Medway Rd OLDS OL8 90 D4
ROY/SHW OL2 59 H1
WALK M28 96 C2
The Medway HEY OL10 40 C3
Medway Wk NEWH/MOS M40 115 G2
Meech St OP/CLY M11 116 D5
Meek St ROY/SHW OL2 75 H2
Meerbrook Rd EDGY/DAV SK3 170 D1
Mee's Sq ECC M30 111 E5
Megna Cl CHAD OL9 8 B2
Melandra Crs HYDE SK14 149 G1
Melanie Dr RDSH SK5 145 F3
Melba St OP/CLY M11 117 F5
Melbecks Wk NTHM/RTH M23 155 G4
Melbourne Av CHAD OL9 74 B5
MANAIR M90 179 H4
STRET M32 140 B1
Melbourne Cl ROCH OL11 43 F4
Melbourne Rd BOLS/LL BL3 48 A4
BRAM/HZG SK7 193 H1
ROCH OL11 43 G4
Melbourne St BKLY M9 103 F2
BRO M7 101 G5
CHAD OL9 74 C5
DTN/ASHW M34 146 C1
RDSH SK5 145 F3
STLY SK15 120 D4
SWIN M27 99 G2
Melbourne St North AUL OL6 119 H1
Melbourne St South AUL OL6 119 H2
Melbury Av DID/WITH M20 158 A2
Melbury Dr HOR/BR BL6 46 A1
Melbury Rd CHD/CHDH SK8 193 E1
Meldon Rd BRUN/LGST M13 143 G1
Meldrum St OLDS OL8 91 G3
Melford Av NEWH/MOS M40 104 D1
Melford Gv OLDE OL4 92 C1

Melford Rd *BRAM/HZG* SK7 .....185 G3
Melfort Av *STRET* M32 .....140 C2
Meliden Crs *BOL* BL1 * 33 E5
  WYTH/NTH M22 .....180 D2
Melksham Cl *ORD* M5 .....113 G3
Mellalieu St *MDTN* M24 .....72 B3
  ROY/SHW OL2 .....75 F2
Melland Av *CCHDY* M21 .....156 B1
Melland Rd *GTN* M18 .....130 D5
Meller Rd *BRUN/LGST* M13 .....143 H1
  HTNM SK4 .....75 H3
Melling Av *CHAD* OL9 .....73 H3
Melling Cl *SWIN* M27 .....99 E3
Melling St *WGTN/LGST* M12 .....129 H4
Mellington Av *DID/WITH* M20 .....169 H1
Mellodew Dr *OLD* OL1 .....76 C1
Mellor Brow *HEY* OL10 .....40 C4
Mellor Cl *AUL* OL6 .....120 B3
Mellor Ct *OFTN* SK2 .....173 F2
Mellor Dr *BURY* BL9 .....
  WALK M28 .....96 D1
Mellor Gv *BOL* BL1 .....33 E5
Mellor Rd *AUL* OL6 .....120 C1
  CHD/CHDH SK8 .....183 E3
Mellors Rd *TRPK* M17 .....117 G4
Mellor St *DROY* M43 .....117 G4
  ECC M30 .....111 E4
  FAIL M35 .....104 C3
  NEWH/MOS M40 .....115 G2
  OLDE OL4 .....92 D1
  OLDS OL8 .....90 D5
  PWCH M25 .....85 G3
  RAD M26 .....68 C2
  ROY/SHW OL2 .....59 E4
  STRET M32 .....126 A4
Mellor Wy *OLD* OL1 .....90 B3
Mellowstone Dr *CCHDY* M21 .....142 B3
Melly Pl *CHH* M8 .....114 D1
Melon Pl *SLFD* M6 .....113 G3
Melrose *WHIT* OL12 .....10 B5
Melrose Av *BOL* BL1 .....32 D5
  DID/WITH M20 .....157 H3
  ECC M30 .....110 B1
  EDGY/DAV SK3 * 170 C2
  HEY OL10 .....40 C5
  LIT OL15 .....20 D1
  SALE M33 .....154 C3
  TOT/BURYW BL8 .....37 H5
Melrose Cl *WHTF* M45 .....69 G2
Melrose Crs *EDGY/DAV* SK3 .....171 G5
  HALE/TIMP WA15 .....178 C3
  POY/DIS SK12 .....196 C2
Melrose Gdns *RAD* M26 .....67 H4
Melrose Rd *BOLS/LL* BL3 .....66 C1
  RAD M26 .....
Melrose St *NEWH/MOS* M40 .....104 B5
  OLD OL1 .....76 A3
  RAMS BL0 .....26 C1
  ROCH OL11 .....29 G4
Melsomby Rd *NTHM/RTH* M23 .....155 H4
Meltham Av *DID/WITH* M20 .....142 C5
Meltham Cl *HTNM* SK4 .....158 B3
Meltham Pl *BOLS/LL* BL3 * 48 B5
Meltham Rd *HTNM* SK4 .....158 B5
Melton Av *DTN/ASHW* M34 .....131 F5
  URM M41 .....122 D5
Melton Cl *HEY* OL10 .....40 C5
  WALK M28 .....81 H5
Melton Dr *BURY* BL9 .....53 H4
Melton Rd *CHH* M8 .....101 H1
Melton St *BKLY* M9 .....103 G1
  HEY OL10 .....40 C5
  RAD M26 .....52 A5
  RDSH SK5 .....160 A2
Melverley Rd *BKLY* M9 .....87 F2
Melville Cl *OP/CLY* M11 .....130 D1
Melville Rd *FWTH* BL4 .....82 C1
  IRL M44 .....150 B1
  STRET M32 .....125 G5
Melville St *AUL* OL6 .....119 G1
  BOLS/LL BL3 .....49 F5
  CSLFD M3 .....6 A3
  OLD OL1 .....75 H3
  ROCH OL11 .....42 C5
Melvin Av *WYTH/NTH* M22 .....168 D5
Melyncourt Rd *HYDE* SK14 * 135 F1
Memorial Cottages
  SWIN M27 * .....
Memorial Rd *WALK* M28 .....84 A4
Menai Gv *CHD/CHDH* SK8 .....170 D3
Menai Rd *EDGY/DAV* SK3 .....171 H3
Menai St *BOLS/LL* BL3 .....48 A5
Mendip Av *WYTH/NTH* M22 .....169 G5
Mendip Cl *BOLE* BL2 .....50 D2
  CHAD OL9 .....
  CHD/CHDH SK8 .....181 G5
  HTNM SK4 .....159 H3
  ROY/SHW OL2 .....
Mendip Crs *TOT/BURYW* BL8 .....37 F3
Mendip Dr *BOLE* BL2 .....50 D3
  MILN OL16 .....
Mendip Rd *OLDS* OL8 .....91 E4
Mendips Cl *ROY/SHW* OL2 .....59 G1
Menston Av *NEWH/MOS* M40 .....104 D1
Mentmore Rd *MILN* OL16 .....31 E4
Mentone Crs *WYTH/NTH* M22 .....168 C5
Mentone Rd *HTNM* SK4 .....159 E3
Mentor St *BRUN/LGST* M13 .....144 H1
Mercer La *ROCH* OL11 .....28 B3
Mercer Rd *GTN* M18 .....130 C3
  HEY OL10 .....56 A2
Mercer St *BNG/LEV* M19 .....144 B2
  DROY M43 .....118 A3
Merchants Quay *SALO* M50 .....126 C2
Mercian Mt *AUL* OL6 * 119 G2
Mercian Wy *EDGY/DAV* SK3 .....
Mercia St *BOLS/LL* BL3 .....48 B4
Mercury Pk *URM* M41 .....125 E2
Mercury Wy *URM* M41 .....125 E3
Mere Av *DROY* M43 .....117 F5
  MDTN M24 .....88 D1
  SLFD M6 .....112 D3
Merebank Cl *ROCH* OL11 .....28 B3
Mere Bank Cl *WALK* M28 .....81 H4
Mere Cl *BURY* BL9 .....54 A4
  DTN/ASHW M34 .....145 H1
  SALE M33 .....155 C3

Mereclough Av *WALK* M28 .....97 C1
Meredew Av *SWIN* M27 .....98 D4
Meredith St *BOLS/LL* BL3 .....65 E1
  RUSH/FAL M14 .....143 F4
Mere Dr *DID/WITH* M20 .....157 G2
  SWIN M27 .....84 B5
Merefield Av *ROCH* OL11 .....42 D1
Merefield Rd
  HALE/TIMP WA15 .....166 D4
Merefield St *ROCH* OL11 .....42 D1
Merefield Ter *ROCH* OL11 * 42 D1
Mere Fold *WALK* M28 .....81 G4
Mere Gdns *BOL* BL1 .....2 C2
Merehall Cl *BOL* BL1 .....2 C2
Merehall Dr *BOL* BL1 .....2 C2
Merehall St *BOL* BL1 .....2 C2
Mereland Av *DID/WITH* M20 .....157 H2
Mere La *ROCH* OL11 .....43 E1
Meremanor *WALK* M28 .....97 G1
Merepool Cl *MPL/ROM* SK6 .....174 B2
Mere Side *STLY* SK15 .....120 C1
Mereside Cl *CHD/CHDH* SK8 .....170 C5
Mereside Gv *WALK* M28 .....82 B4
Mere St *ROCH* OL11 .....30 A5
The Mere *AUL* OL6 .....107 H4
  CHD/CHDH SK8 .....170 C5
Mere Wk *BOL* BL1 * 2 C2
Merewood Av
  HALE/TIMP WA15 .....
Meriden Cl *RAD* M26 .....52 A5
Meriden Gv *HOR/BR* BL6 .....47 E3
Meridian Pl *DID/WITH* M20 .....157 F2
Merinall Cl *MILN* OL16 .....11 K7
Meriton Rd *WILM/AE* SK9 .....191 H5
Merlewood Av *BNC/LEV* M19 .....144 C4
  DTN/ASHW M34 * 118 A4
  UPML OL3 .....79 E4
Merlewood Dr *SWIN* M27 .....98 B4
Merlin Cl *LIT* OL15 .....31 H1
  OFTN SK2 .....173 H5
  OLDS OL8 .....106 D2
Merlin Dr *SWIN* M27 .....84 C5
Merlin Gv *BOL* BL1 .....33 E5
Merlin Rd *IRL* M44 .....122 B4
  MILN OL16 .....31 G5
Merlyn Av *DID/WITH* M20 .....157 H2
  DTN/ASHW M34 .....146 C1
  SALE M33 .....154 D1
Merrick Av *WYTH/NTH* M22 .....168 D5
Merrick St *HEY* OL10 .....41 F5
Merridale Rd
  NEWH/MOS M40 .....104 B1
The Merridale
  HALE/TIMP WA15 .....178 B4
Merrill St *ANC* M4 .....115 G4
Merriman St *OLDTF/WHR* M16 .....127 H4
Merrion St *FWTH* BL4 .....65 H2
Merrow Wk *CMANE* M1 * 128 C1
Merrybent Cl *OFTN* SK2 .....173 E5
Merrybower Rd *BRO* M7 .....101 H2
Merrydale Av *ECC* M30 .....111 F1
Merryman Hall *HALE/TIMP* WA15 * 30 C1
Merseybank Av *CCHDY* M21 .....156 C2
Mersey Crs *DID/WITH* M20 .....156 C3
Mersey Dr *PART* M31 .....151 F2
  WHTF M45 .....69 G4
Mersey Mdw *DID/WITH* M20 .....157 E3
  DID/WITH M20 .....157 E3
  HTNM SK4 .....158 C4
  SALE M33 .....154 C1
Mersey Rd North *FAIL* M35 .....105 F1
Mersey Sq *STKP* SK1 .....12 E3
Mersey St *DROY* M43 .....117 F5
  STKP SK1 .....13 K1
Merseyw *URM* M41 .....137 G3
Merseyway *STKP* SK1 .....12 E3
Merston Dr *DID/WITH* M20 .....169 H2
Merton Av *BRAM/HZG* SK7 .....185 G4
  MPL/ROM SK6 .....161 H2
  OLDS OL8 .....
Merton Cl *BOLS/LL* BL3 * 48 B4
Merton Dr *DROY* M43 .....117 F4
Merton Gv *CHAD* OL9 .....89 G4
  HALE/TIMP WA15 .....166 C3
Merton Rd *EDGY/DAV* SK3 * 171 E2
  POY/DIS SK12 .....197 G3
  PWCH M25 .....86 B2
  SALE M33 .....154 B1
Merville Av *NEWH/MOS* M40 .....103 C1
Mervyn Rd *BRO* M7 .....100 D4
Merwood Av *CHD/CHDH* SK8 .....182 A4
Merwood Gv *RUSH/FAL* M14 .....129 F4
Meshaw Cl *NTHM/RTH* M23 .....155 F5
Mesnefield Rd *BRO* M7 .....100 D2
Mesne Lea Gv *WALK* M28 * 97 F2
Mesne Lea Rd *WALK* M28 .....97 F2
Metcalfe Ct *LHULT* M38 .....81 E3
Metcalfe Dr *MPL/ROM* SK6 .....162 A4
Metcalf Gdns *UPML* OL3 .....79 E4
Metfield Pl *BOL* BL1 .....
Methuen St *WGTN/LGST* M12 .....130 A5
Methwold St *BOLS/LL* BL3 * 48 B5
The Mews *CHD/CHDH* SK8 .....
  CHD/CHDH SK8 .....169 G4
  NEWH/MOS M40 .....115 H2
  PWCH M25 .....85 E3
  SALE M33 * 154 D3
  WHTF M45 * 69 E4
Mexborough St *OLDE* OL4 .....76 C4
Meyer St *EDGY/DAV* SK3 .....171 F3
Meyrick Rd *SLFD* M6 .....113 F2
Miall St *ROCH* OL11 .....30 B5
Micawber Rd *POY/DIS* SK12 .....195 F5
Michael St *MDTN* M24 .....72 C4
Michigan Av *SALQ* M50 .....126 C3
Micklebury Wk *NTHM/RTH* M20 .....156 D2
Micklehurst Av *DID/WITH* M20 .....156 D2
Micklehurst Gn *OFTN* SK2 .....173 F4
Micklehurst Rd *MOSL* OL5 .....109 F1
Middlebourne St *SLFD* M6 .....112 D3
Middlebrook Dr *HOR/BR* BL6 .....46 D5
Middlefield *OLDS* OL8 .....106 D2
Middlefields *CHD/CHDH* SK8 .....171 G5
Middlegate *NEWH/MOS* M40 .....89 G4
Middle Ga *OLDS* OL8 .....91 F5
Middle Gn *AUL* OL6 .....119 H1

Middleham St *RUSH/FAL* M14 .....142 C1
Middle Hi *WHIT* OL12 .....19 E4
Middle Hillgate *STKP* SK1 .....13 H4
Middlesex Dr *BURY* BL9 .....53 C1
Middlesex Rd *BKLY* M9 .....88 A5
  RDSH SK5 .....146 A5
Middlesex Wk *CHAD* OL9 .....8 D4
Middlestone Dr *BKLY* M9 .....103 E5
Middle St *WHIT* OL12 .....14 B4
Middleton Av *FAIL* M35 .....105 E3
Middleton Gdns *BURY* BL9 .....69 C1
Middleton Old Rd *BKLY* M9 .....88 A5
Middleton Rd *BKLY* M9 .....87 E5
  CHAD OL9 .....8 D3
  CHH M8 .....73 H3
  CHH M8 .....87 E5
  HEY OL10 .....56 B4
  RDSH SK5 .....145 F1
  ROY/SHW OL2 .....74 C1
Middleton Wy *MDTN* M24 .....72 C4
Middle Wood Cl *OLDE* OL4 .....93 C2
Middlewood *OLDE* OL4 .....93 C2
Middlewood Ct *ORD* M5 .....113 H4
Middlewood Dr *HTNM* SK4 .....158 B5
Middlewood Gn *CHAD* OL9 .....74 B5
Middle Wood La *LIT* OL15 .....20 B2
Middlewood Rd
  MPL/ROM SK6 .....186 C5
  POY/DIS SK12 .....195 H5
Middlewood St *ORD* M5 .....113 H4
Midford Av *ECC* M30 .....110 C5
Midford Dr *BOL* BL1 .....22 D4
Midge Hall Dr *ROCH* OL11 .....28 D5
Midgley Av *GTN* M18 .....130 D2
Midgley Crs *AUL* OL6 .....120 B1
Midgley Dr *MILN* OL16 .....43 C4
Midgley St *SWIN* M27 .....98 C4
Midgrove La *UPML* OL3 .....78 C1
Midhurst Av
  NEWH/MOS M40 * 116 C1
Midhurst Cl *CHD/CHDH* SK8 .....182 C4
Midhurst St *ROCH* OL11 .....43 E1
Midland Rd *BRAM/HZG* SK7 .....183 H1
  RDSH SK5 .....145 F1
Midland St *WGTN/LGST* M12 .....129 E1
Midland Ter *ALT* WA14 * 177 G2
Midland Wk *BRAM/HZG* SK7 .....183 H1
Midlothian St *OP/CLY* M11 .....116 C3
Midville Rd *OP/CLY* M11 .....116 D2
Midway *CHD/CHDH* SK8 .....193 E2
Midway Dr *POY/DIS* SK12 .....195 E5
Midway St *WGTN/LGST* M12 .....144 A1
Milan St *BRO* M7 .....101 H4
Milbourne Rd *BURY* BL9 .....27 G5
Milburn Av *NTHM/RTH* M23 .....156 A4
Milburn Dr *BOLE* BL2 .....34 D4
Milbury Dr *LIT* OL15 .....31 H1
Milden Cl *DID/WITH* M20 .....157 H2
Mildred Av *ROY/SHW* OL2 .....59 F2
  PWCH M25 .....86 B5
  ROY/SHW OL2 .....75 F2
Mildred St *BRO* M7 .....101 F3
Mile End La *OFTN* SK2 .....172 D5
Mile La *TOT/BURYW* BL8 .....37 E5
Miles St *BOL* BL1 * 34 C4
  HYDE SK14 .....148 B1
  OLD OL1 .....76 A4
  WGTN/LGST M12 .....129 H1
Milford Av *OLDS* OL8 .....90 D5
Milford Brow *OLDE* OL4 .....76 D5
Milford Crs *LIT* OL15 .....21 F2
Milford Dr *BNG/LEV* M19 .....144 C3
Milford Gv *OFTN* SK2 .....172 C2
Milford Rd *BOLE* BL2 .....35 C2
  BOLS/LL BL3 .....64 D1
Milford St *BKLY* M9 .....87 G4
  MILN OL16 .....
  SLFD M6 .....112 D4
Milkstone Pl *ROCH* OL11 * 30 A5
Milkstone Rd *ROCH* OL11 .....30 A5
Milk St *CMANW* M2 .....7 F4
  HYDE SK14 .....147 H1
  OLDE OL4 76
  RAMS BL0 .....16 C3
  ROCH OL11 .....30 A5
Milkwood Gv *GTN* M18 .....130 C4
Millais St *NEWH/MOS* M40 .....103 H2
Millard St *CHAD* OL9 .....74 B5
Millbank Gdns *BOL* BL1 * 33 F5
Millbank Rd *RAD* M26 .....
Millbank St *CMANE* M1 .....7 K5
  HEY OL10 .....40 C4
Millbeck Gv *BOLS/LL* BL3 * 48 D5
Millbeck Rd *MDTN* M24 .....72 C3
Millbeck St *HULME* M15 .....128 B2
Millbrae Gdns *ROY/SHW* OL2 .....59 C2
Millbrook Av *DTN/ASHW* M34 .....146 B2
Millbrook Bank *ROCH* OL11 .....28 D5
Millbrook Ct *ROY/SHW* OL2 .....
Millbrook Fold *BRAM/HZG* SK7 .....185 H5
Millbrook Rd *NTHM/RTH* M23 .....167 H5
Millbrook St *STKP* SK1 .....13 G5
Mill Brow *AUL* OL6 .....107 F1
  CHH M8 * 86 D1
  OLD OL1 .....74 B2
  WALK M28 .....97 G4
Mill Court Dr *RAD* M26 .....67 E4
Millcrest Cl *WALK* M28 .....96 A5
Mill Cft *BOL* BL1 .....2 D2
  ROY/SHW OL2 .....60 B3
Milldale Cl *HOR/BR* BL6 .....46 D2
Miller Rd *OLDS* OL8 .....91 F4
Millers Brook Cl *HEY* OL10 * 41 E3
Millers Cl *SALE* M33 .....155 H5
Millers Ct *ORD* M5 .....111 H5
Millers St *ECC* M30 .....110 D4
Miller St *ANC* M4 .....7 G2
  AUL OL6 .....119 G1
  BOL BL1 .....33 H2
  HEY OL10 .....41 E4
  RAD M26 .....52 A3
  RAMS BL0 .....
Millett St *BURY* BL9 .....
  RAMS BL0 .....17 E1
Mill Fld *ROCH* OL11 * 28 B2
Millfield *CHD/CHDH* SK8 .....171 E5
Millfield Dr *WALK* M28 .....96 C4
Millfield Gv *MILN* OL16 .....30 C5
Millfield Rd *BOLE* BL2 .....50 D2
Millfold *WHIT* OL12 .....14 C3
Mill Fold Gdns *LIT* OL15 .....20 D4
Mill Fold Rd *MDTN* M24 .....72 C5
Millford Av *URM* M41 .....137 G2

Mill Ga *MILN* OL16 .....30 C1
  OLDS OL8 .....91 E4
Millgate ANC M4 * 7 G3
  EDGW/EG BL7 .....22 C1
  STKP SK1 .....13 H2
Millgate La *DID/WITH* M20 .....157 G5
Mill Green St
  WGTN/LGST M12 .....115 G5
Millhall Cl *HULME* M15 .....127 H3
Millhead Av *NEWH/MOS* M40 .....115 H3
Mill Hl *BOLE* BL2 .....3 H3
  LHULT M38 .....80 D1
Mill Hill Av *POY/DIS* SK12 .....185 E5
Mill Hill Caravan Pk *BOLE* BL2 .....3 H3
Mill Hill Gv *HYDE* SK14 * 149 H1
Mill Hill Hollow *POY/DIS* SK12 .....185 E5
Mill Hill St *BOLE* BL2 .....3 H3
Millhouse Av *NTHM/RTH* M23 .....167 H5
Mill House Cl *WHIT* OL12 .....20 A4
Milliner Ct *OFTN* SK2 * 172 C2
Millington Wk *HULME* M15 .....127 G2
Mill La *AUL* OL6 .....90 D5
  BRAM/HZG SK7 .....185 G4
  CHAD OL9 .....90 D5
  CHD/CHDH SK8 .....180 A1
  CHD/CHDH SK8 .....183 H1
  DTN/ASHW M34 .....147 F2
  FAIL M35 .....104 B3
  HALE/TIMP WA15 .....189 F3
  MOSL OL5 .....93 H5
  MPL/ROM SK6 .....161 H1
  RDSH SK5 .....145 G4
  ROY/SHW OL2 .....58 D5
  TOT/BURYW BL8 .....37 G2
  UPML OL3 .....78 A3
  WYTH/NTH M22 .....156 D5
Mill Nook *WHIT* OL12 .....18 A2
Millom Av *NTHM/RTH* M23 .....156 A5
Millom Cl *MILN* OL16 .....11 J3
Millom Ct *HALE/TIMP* WA15 * 167 E3
Millom Dr *BURY* BL9 .....69 H2
Millom Pl *CHD/CHDH* SK8 .....181 G1
Mill St *ANC* M4 .....7 F1
Millpond Av *BOLS/LL* BL3 .....48 D5
Mill Pond Cl *ROY/SHW* OL2 .....60 A3
Mill Rd *BURY* BL9 .....27 G3
  WILM/AE SK9 .....199 E3
Mills Farm Cl *OLDS* OL8 .....106 D1
Millshaw Dr *MDTN* M24 .....73 G3
Mills Hill Rd *MDTN* M24 .....73 C4
  WHIT OL12 .....14 C4
Millstone Cl *MPL/ROM* SK6 .....161 H3
  POY/DIS SK12 .....195 G2
Millstone Rd *BOL* BL1 .....32 B2
Millstream La
  NEWH/MOS M40 .....117 F2
Mill St *ALT* WA14 .....165 H4
  BOL BL1 .....33 G4
  BRAM/HZG SK7 .....185 E1
  EDGW/EG BL7 .....23 E3
  FAIL M35 .....104 C3
  FWTH BL4 .....65 H1
  HYDE SK14 .....133 H3
  MOSL OL5 .....108 D2
  OP/CLY M11 .....116 B3
  RAD M26 .....68 C2
  RAMS BL0 .....16 D4
  ROY/SHW OL2 .....59 E5
  SLFD M6 .....113 F1
  STLY SK15 .....121 F4
  TOT/BURYW BL8 .....26 A3
  UPML OL3 .....79 E4
  WALK M28 .....96 B5
  WHTN BL5 .....62 A4
  WILM/AE SK9 .....199 E3
Milltown St *RAD* M26 .....68 C2
Millwall Cl *GTN* M18 .....130 C3
Millway *HALE/TIMP* WA15 .....178 D5
Millwell La *BOL* BL1 .....2 E4
Millwood Cl
  BURY BL9 .....53 C3
Millwood Ter *HYDE* SK14 .....147 H1
Millwright St
  NEWH/MOS M40 .....104 A5
Mill Yd *BURY* BL9 .....5 C3
Milne Cl *WGTN/LGST* M12 .....129 H2
Milner Av *ALT* WA14 .....165 F4
  BURY BL9 .....53 H2
Milner St *OLDTF/WHR* M16 .....127 C4
  RAD M26 .....52 B3
  SWIN M27 .....99 F2
  WHTN BL5 .....14 B5
Milne St *CHAD* OL9 .....74 C5
  CHAD OL9 .....8 D6
  OLD OL1 .....75 H2
  ROCH OL11 .....42 B4
  ROY/SHW OL2 .....59 G4
Milngate Cl *MILN* OL16 .....43 H5
Milnholme *BOL* BL1 .....33 E4
Milnrow Cl *BRUN/LGST* M13 .....128 C1
Milnrow Rd *LIT* OL15 .....31 G1
  MILN OL16 .....11 G6
  ROY/SHW OL2 .....45 F5
Milnthorpe Rd *BOLE* BL2 .....50 B1
Milnthorpe St *SLFD* M6 .....100 D5
Milnthorpe Wy
  WGTN/LGST M12 .....129 F2
Milo St *BKLY* M9 .....88 A4
Milsom Av *BOLS/LL* BL3 .....64 B1
Milstead Wk
  NEWH/MOS M40 * 115 H1
Milton Av *BOLS/LL* BL3 .....64 A1
  DROY M43 .....117 H4
  IRL M44 .....136 A5
  ORD M5 .....112 C3
  STLY SK15 .....121 H1
Milton Cl *DUK* SK16 .....133 C2
  STRET M32 .....126 A5
Milton Crs *BNG/LEV* M19 .....158 B2
  CHD/CHDH SK8 .....169 H4
Milton Dr *CHD/CHDH* SK8 .....181 C1
  HALE/TIMP WA15 .....154 B5
  POY/DIS SK12 .....194 D3
  SALE M33 .....139 C5
Milton Gv *OLDTF/WHR* M16 .....141 C1
  SALE M33 .....139 C5
Milton Pl *SLFD* M6 .....113 F2

Milton Rd *BRAM/HZG* SK7 .....183 H5
  DTN/ASHW M34 .....118 C4
  PWCH M25 .....86 B2
  RAD M26 .....51 G5
  STRET M32 .....126 B5
  SWIN M27 .....98 C1
Milton St *BRO* M7 .....114 B1
  ECC M30 .....111 E5
  HYDE SK14 .....133 C4
  MDTN M24 .....72 C5
  MILN OL16 .....10 D6
  MOSL OL5 .....93 H5
  RAMS BL0 .....16 C2
  ROY/SHW OL2 .....
  WHIT OL12 .....14 C5
Milverton Av *HYDE* SK14 .....149 E1
Milverton Cl *HOR/BR* BL6 .....47 E4
Milverton Dr *BRAM/HZG* SK7 .....193 C2
Milverton Rd *RUSH/FAL* M14 .....129 C5
Milverton Wk *HYDE* SK14 .....149 E1
Milwain Dr *HTNM* SK4 .....144 C5
Milwain Rd *BNG/LEV* M19 .....143 H3
  STRET M32 .....140 A2
Mimosa Dr *SWIN* M27 .....84 A5
Mincing St *ANC* M4 * 7 H3
Minden Cl *DID/WITH* M20 .....157 H2
  TOT/BURYW BL8 .....37 G4
Minden Pde *BURY* BL9 .....4 E5
Minehead Av *DID/WITH* M20 .....142 B4
  URM M41 .....138 B3
Minerva Rd *DUK* SK16 .....119 H3
  FWTH BL4 .....65 E3
Minnie St *BOLS/LL* BL3 * 48 A5
  WHIT OL12 * 14 C5
Minoan Gdns *BRO* M7 .....101 F5
Minorca Cl *ROCH* OL11 .....28 B3
Minorca St *BOLS/LL* BL3 .....48 B5
Minor St *FAIL* M35 .....105 F2
  OLDS OL8 .....9 F6
  ROCH OL11 .....42 B5
Minshull St *CMANE* M1 .....7 G5
Minshull St South *CMANE* M1 * 7 H6
Minstead Cl *HYDE* SK14 .....148 C2
Minster Cl *BOLE* BL2 .....34 D4
  DUK SK16 .....133 C2
Minster Dr *ALT* WA14 .....176 D3
  CHD/CHDH SK8 .....170 D4
Minsterley Pde
  WYTH/NTH M22 * 180 B3
Minster Rd *BKLY* M9 .....103 C2
  BOLE BL2 .....34 D4
Minster Wy *CHAD* OL9 .....74 B3
Minstrel Cl *SWIN* M27 .....98 C5
Minton St *NEWH/MOS* M40 .....104 B2
  OLDE OL4 .....9 J6
Minto St *AULW* OL7 .....119 F1
Mirabel St *CSLFD* M3 .....6 D1
Mirfield Av *BKLY* M9 .....88 A3
  HTNM SK4 .....159 E4
  OLDS OL8 .....91 F3
Mirfield Dr *ECC* M30 .....111 E1
  MDTN M24 .....72 C3
  URM M41 .....124 D4
Mirfield Rd *BKLY* M9 .....88 A3
Miriam St *BOLS/LL* BL3 * 48 A5
  FAIL M35 .....104 D5
Mission St *HEY* OL10 .....40 D4
Missouri Av *SALQ* M50 .....112 D4
Mistletoe Gv *CSLFD* M3 * 6 A1
Mitcham Av *BKLY* M9 .....88 D4
Mitchell Cl *CHD/CHDH* SK8 * 169 E3
Mitchell Hey *WHIT* OL12 .....10 A6
Mitchells Quay *FAIL* M35 .....104 D5
Mitchell St *BKLY* M9 .....
  MILN OL16 .....19 H5
  NEWH/MOS M40 .....104 A5
  OLD OL1 * 75 E4
  OP/CLY M11 .....129 C1
  TOT/BURYW BL8 * .....
  WHIT OL12 .....29 G3
Mitcheson Gdns *SLFD* M6 .....113 E2
Mitford Rd *RUSH/FAL* M14 .....143 E4
Mitford St *STRET* M32 .....140 A2
Mitre Rd *BRUN/LGST* M13 .....129 C4
Mitre St *BOL* BL1 .....33 H2
  FAIL M35 .....105 E2
Mitton Cl *HEY* OL10 .....40 A4
  TOT/BURYW BL8 .....37 E4
Mizpah Gv *TOT/BURYW* BL8 .....37 G4
Moadlock *MPL/ROM* SK6 .....162 B2
Moat Av *WYTH/NTH* M22 .....168 B5
Moatfield Gdns *BOL* BL1 .....2 A2
Moat Gdns *WYTH/NTH* M22 .....168 B5
Moat Hall Av *ECC* M30 .....110 B5
Moat Rd *WYTH/NTH* M22 .....168 B5
Mobberley Cl *BNG/LEV* M19 .....158 B2
Mobberley Rd *BOLE* BL2 .....50 A1
Mocha Pde *BRO* M7 .....114 A2
Modbury Cl *BRAM/HZG* SK7 .....184 B3
Mode Hill La *WHTF* M45 .....70 B4
Model Cottages
  HALE/TIMP WA15 * 167 G5
Mode Wheel Rd South
  SALQ M50 .....112 C4
Modwen Rd *ORD* M5 .....127 C2
Moelfre Dr *CHD/CHDH* SK8 .....183 F5
Moffat Cl *BOLE* BL2 .....50 C3
Moisant St *BOLS/LL* BL3 .....64 C1
Molesey Av *SWIN* M27 .....99 C3
  OLD OL1 .....75 F4
Molesworth St *MILN* OL16 .....10 E7
Mollets Wd
  DTN/ASHW M34 .....132 D3
Mollington Rd
  WYTH/NTH M22 .....180 D4
Mollis Gv *OLD* OL1 .....76 D1
Molyneux Rd *BNG/LEV* M19 .....144 C2
  WHTN BL5 .....62 C3
Mona Av *CHD/CHDH* SK8 .....183 A3
  STRET M32 .....125 H5
Monaco Dr *WYTH/NTH* M22 .....156 C4
Monarch Cl *IRL* M44 .....
  ROY/SHW OL2 .....75 F2
Mona Rd *CHAD* OL9 .....90 C2
Monart Rd *BKLY* M9 .....103 F1

Mona St HYDE SK14 148 A1
SLFD M6 113 F1
Mona Wy IRL M44 136 D3
Mond Rd IRL M44 122 C4
Money Ash Rd
HALE/TIMP WA15 177 G1
Monfa Av OFTN SK2 172 B5
Monica Av CHH M8 87 E5
Monica Gv BNG/LEV M19 143 H3
Monks Cl MILN OL16 31 F5
Monksdale Av URM M41 138 B1
Monks Hall Gv ECC M30 111 G3
Monks La BOLE BL2 35 E4
Monkton Av GTN M18 130 B5
Monkwood Dr BKLY M9 * 103 F2
Monmouth Av BURY BL9 38 C1
SALE M33 154 A1
Monmouth Rd
CHD/CHDH SK8 183 E3
Monmouth St CHAD OL9 8 A7
GTN M18 130 D2
MDTN M24 73 F4
ROCH OL11 30 A5
Monroe Cl SLFD M6 112 D1
Monsal Av BRO M7 100 D3
OFTN SK2 173 E2
Monsall Cl BURY BL9 69 H2
Monsall Rd NEWH/MOS M40 103 F4
Monsall St NEWH/MOS M40 103 E5
OLDS OL8 91 F4
Mons Av ROCH OL11 29 F3
Montague Rd AUL OL6 120 A2
OLDTF/WHR M16 126 D3
SALE M33 154 C2
Montague St BOLS/LL BL3 * 64 A1
Montague Wy STLY SK15 120 D3
Montagu Rd OFTN SK2 173 E2
Montagu St MPL/ROM SK6 163 G4
Montana Sq OP/CLY M11 130 D1
Montcliffe Crs
OLDTF/WHR M16 142 B2
Monteagle St BKLY M9 87 G3
Montford St SALQ M50 113 E5
Montgomery ROCH OL11 * 29 H5
Montgomery Dr BURY BL9 70 A2
Montgomery Rd
BRUN/LGST M13 143 H1
Montgomery St OLDS OL8 90 C5
ROCH OL11 42 C2
Montgomery Wy RAD M26 51 F4
Monton Av ECC M30 111 F2
Montondale ECC M30 110 D2
Montonfields Rd ECC M30 110 D2
Monton Gn ECC M30 111 E1
Monton La ECC M30 111 F3
Monton Mill Gdns ECC M30 110 D2
Monton Rd ECC M30 111 E2
RDSH SK5 160 D2
Monton St BOLS/LL BL3 64 D1
RAD M26 68 A1
RUSH/FAL M14 128 B4
Montpellior Rd
WYTH/NTH M22 180 C2
Montreal St BNG/LEV M19 144 B2
OLDS OL8 91 G3
Montrose Av BOLE BL2 34 D5
DID/WITH M20 157 E1
DUK SK16 133 F1
OFTN SK2 184 B1
RAMS BL0 26 B1
STRET M32 139 H1
Montrose Crs BNG/LEV M19 144 A2
Montrose Dr EDGW/EG BL7 23 H4
Montrose St ROCH OL11 57 F1
Montserrat Rd BOL BL1 32 B4
Moon Gv RUSH/FAL M14 143 F1
Moon St CHAD OL9 8 B2
Moor Bank La MILN OL16 44 A2
Moorbank La MILN OL16 44 B3
Moorby Av BNG/LEV M19 158 B2
Moorby St OLD OL1 9 J1
Moorby Wk BOLS/LL BL3 * 48 D4
Moor Cl RAD M26 51 H4
Moorclose St MDTN M24 73 F4
Moorcock Av SWIN M27 99 G2
Moor Crs UPML OL3 79 E1
Moorcroft ROCH OL11 43 E3
Moorcroft Dr BNG/LEV M19 158 C2
Moorcroft Rd
NTHM/RTH M23 155 G5
Moorcroft St DROY M43 * 117 H4
OLDS OL8 90 D5
Moordale Av OLDE OL4 76 D3
Moordale St DID/WITH M20 157 F1
Moordown Cl CHH M8 102 C4
Moor Edge Rd MOSL OL5 109 G1
Mooredge Ter ROY/SHW OL2 75 F2
Moor End WYTH/NTH M22 168 C1
Moor End Av BRO M7 101 F2
Moore's Ct BOL BL1 48 B1
Moore St MILN OL16 10 D7
Moorfield WALK M28 96 A3
WALK M28 97 G2
Moorfield Av DID/WITH M20 143 E4
DTN/ASHW M34 147 E2
LIT OL15 20 D1
STLY SK15 135 E1
Moorfield Cha FWTH BL4 66 A5
Moorfield Cl IRL M44 * 122 C5
SWIN M27 98 C4
Moorfield Dr HYDE SK14 * 133 H3
WILM/AE SK9 198 B5
Moorfield Gv BOLE BL2 34 C5
HTNM SK4 159 E2
SALE M33 155 E3
Moorfield Hts STLY SK15 109 F3
STLY SK15 109 H4
Moorfield Ms ROY/SHW OL2 * 60 A2
Moorfield Pl WHIT OL12 * 10 B2
Moorfield Rd DID/WITH M20 157 E2
IRL M44 122 C5
OLDS OL8 90 C5
SLFD M6 100 A5
SWIN M27 98 B4
Moorfield St DID/WITH M20 142 D4
Moor Ga BOLE BL2 35 E1
Moorgate BURY BL9 5 F3
Moorgate Av DID/WITH M20 142 B5
ROCH OL11 28 D4
Moorgate Ct BOLE BL2 3 K1
Moorgate Dr STLY SK15 109 F4
Moorgate La LIT OL15 20 B1
Moorgate Ms STLY SK15 * 109 F3
Moorgate Rd RAD M26 51 H1
STLY SK15 109 F3
Moorgate St UPML OL3 79 E4
Moorhead St ANC M4 7 J1
Moorhey Rd LHULT M38 81 E1
Moorhey St OLDE OL4 92 A1
Moor Hl ROCH OL11 28 C2
Moorhouse Farm MILN OL16 31 F5
Moor House Fold MILN OL16 31 F5
Moorings Rd TRPK M17 112 A5
The Moorings MOSL OL5 94 B4
WALK M28 97 H5
Moorland Av CHH M8 87 E5
DROY M43 117 F4
MILN OL16 31 H5
ROCH OL11 28 C2
SALE M33 154 D3
UPML OL3 78 C1
WHIT OL12 18 B2
Moorland Crs WHIT OL12 18 C1
Moorland Dr CHD/CHDH SK8 182 C4
LHULT M38 81 F1
Moorland Gv BOL BL1 32 D4
Moorland Rd DID/WITH M20 157 G3
OFTN SK2 172 B5
STLY SK15 109 F5
Moorlands Av URM M41 * 124 A5
Moorlands Crs MOSL OL5 109 E1
Moorlands Dr MOSL OL5 94 B4
Moorlands St ROY/SHW OL2 60 B2
Moorland St WHIT OL12 10 B2
Moorlands Vw BOLS/LL BL3 63 H2
Moorland Ter WHIT OL12 28 D2
Moor La BOL BL1 2 D5
BRAM/HZG SK7 193 G4
BRO M7 100 D2
NTHM/RTH M23 155 H4
UPML OL3 79 F2
URM M41 123 H5
WILM/AE SK9 198 B5
Moor Nook SALE M33 155 E3
Moor Park Av ROCH OL11 42 A4
Moor Park Rd
DID/WITH M20 * 157 H5
Moor Rd NTHM/RTH M23 167 F1
TOT/BURYW BL8 16 B2
Moorsholme Av
NEWH/MOS M40 103 H3
Moorside HALE/TIMP WA15 * 166 D2
ROCH OL11 43 E3
SWIN M27 98 C3
Moorside Av BOL BL1 32 D4
BOLE BL2 36 C5
DROY M43 118 B2
FWTH BL4 65 G5
OLDE OL4 61 E5
Moorside Ct DTN/ASHW M34 132 C4
Moorside Crs DROY M43 118 B3
Moorside La DTN/ASHW M34 132 D4
Moor Side La RAMS BL0 17 H1
Moorside Rd BRO M7 101 F1
CHH M8 * 102 B1
HTNM SK4 158 D4
MOSL OL5 109 F1
SWIN M27 98 C2
TOT/BURYW BL8 36 D1
URM M41 123 F5
Moorside St DROY M43 118 A3
Moorside Vw TOT/BURYW BL8 26 A5
Moorsley Dr BKLY M9 88 C3
Moor St BURY BL9 5 F3
ECC M30 110 C4
HEY OL10 40 C4
OLD OL1 * 76 A5
ROY/SHW OL2 59 H3
SWIN M27 99 E3
Moorsview RAMS BL0 16 C2
Moorton Av BNG/LEV M19 143 H4
Moorton Pk BNG/LEV M19 143 H4
Moortop Cl BKLY M9 87 H2
Moor Top Pl HTNM SK4 159 E3
Moor View Cl WHIT OL12 28 C2
Moorville Rd SLFD M6 99 H5
Moorway Dr BKLY M9 88 D3
Moorwood Dr OLDS OL8 92 B3
SALE M33 153 H3
Mora Av CHAD OL9 74 C3
Moran Cl WILM/AE SK9 192 A5
Moran Wk HULME M15 128 A2
Morar Dr BOLE BL2 50 D2
Morar Rd DUK SK16 133 G1
Mora St BKLY M9 103 G3
Moravian Cl DUK SK16 119 H4
Moravian Fld DROY M43 * 117 H5
Moray Cl RAMS BL0 16 B4
Moray Rd CHAD OL9 90 B3
Morbourne Cl
WGTN/LGST M12 129 F2
Morecambe Cl
NEWH/MOS M40 104 A4
Morely St OLDE OL4 76 D3
Moresby Dr DID/WITH M20 169 G1
Moreton Av BRAM/HZG SK7 193 H2
SALE M33 153 H3
STRET M32 140 B1
WHTF M45 69 G3
Moreton Cl DUK SK16 133 G2
Moreton Dr POY/DIS SK12 195 G3
TOT/BURYW BL8 37 G3
WILM/AE SK9 192 B4
Moreton La OFTN SK2 172 D2
Moreton St CHAD OL9 74 A4
Morgan Pl RDSH SK5 160 A2
Morgan St LIT OL15 21 E3
Morillon Rd IRL M44 122 B4
Morland Rd OLDTF/WHR M16 127 F4
Morley Av RUSH/FAL M14 142 C2
SWIN M27 98 D4
Morley Green Rd
WILM/AE SK9 190 B5
Morley Rd RAD M26 51 G5
Morley St BOLS/LL BL3 2 B6
BURY BL9 53 G1
MILN OL16 11 G3
WHTF M45 69 G4
Morley Wy UPML OL3 95 E2
Morna Wk WGTN/LGST M12 115 G5
Morningside Cl MILN OL16 * 30 C5
OP/CLY M11 131 E1
Morningside Dr
DID/WITH M20 169 H1
Mornington Av
CHD/CHDH SK8 170 A5
Mornington Crs
RUSH/FAL M14 142 C3
Mornington Rd BOL BL1 48 A1
CHD/CHDH SK8 170 A5
ROCH OL11 43 F3
SALE M33 155 E1
Morpeth Cl AULW OL7 118 D1
WGTN/LGST M12 129 F3
Morpeth St SWIN M27 98 D4
Morrell Rd WYTH/NTH M22 168 D1
Morris Fold Dr HOR/BR BL6 46 D3
Morris Gn BOLS/LL BL3 64 B2
Morris Green La BOLS/LL BL3 64 B1
Morris Green St BOLS/LL BL3 * 64 B2
Morris Gv URM M41 137 G3
Morrison St BOLS/LL BL3 64 D1
Morris St BOL BL1 3 G4
DID/WITH M20 142 D4
OLDE OL4 9 K6
RAD M26 53 F4
Morrowfield Av CHH M8 102 A3
Morse Rd NEWH/MOS M40 104 A5
Mortar St OLDE OL4 76 B5
Mortfield Gdns BOL BL1 2 A2
Mortfield La BOL BL1 2 A2
Mortimer Av BKLY M9 88 B3
Mortimer St OLD OL1 75 H3
Mortlake Cl WALK M28 81 E4
Mortlake Dr NEWH/MOS M40 104 A5
Mort La TYLD M29 80 D5
Morton St FAIL M35 104 B3
HTNM SK4 159 H2
MDTN M24 72 D3
RAD M26 68 C2
Mort St FWTH BL4 65 G4
Morven Av BRAM/HZG SK7 185 G1
Morven Dr NTHM/RTH M23 167 H4
Morven Gv BOLE BL2 50 C2
Morville Rd CCHDY M21 141 H2
Morville St CMANE M1 * 7 K6
Moscow Rd EDGY/DAV SK3 171 G2
Moscow Rd East
EDGY/DAV SK3 171 H2
Mosedale Cl NTHM/RTH M23 167 F3
Mosedale Rd MDTN M24 72 A2
Moseldene Rd OFTN SK2 173 E4
Moseley Rd BNG/LEV M19 143 H3
CHD/CHDH SK8 182 C1
RUSH/FAL M14 143 G3
Moseley St EDGY/DAV SK3 12 E6
Mosley Av BURY BL9 38 C1
RAMS BL0 26 C1
Mosley Cl HALE/TIMP WA15 166 A2
Mosley Rd HALE/TIMP WA15 166 C3
TRPK M17 125 H4
Mosley Rd North TRPK M17 112 B5
Mosley St CMANE M1 7 F5
CMANW M2 * 6 E5
RAD M26 52 A5
Mossack Av WYTH/NTH M22 180 C3
Moss Av MILN OL16 30 D5
Moss Bank BRAM/HZG SK7 193 F2
CHH M8 102 B2
Moss Bank Av DROY M43 118 B3
Moss Bank Cl BOL BL1 33 G2
Moss Bank Ct DROY M43 * 118 B3
Mossbank Gv HEY OL10 40 D3
Moss Bank Gv SWIN M27 83 F5
Moss Bank Pk BOL BL1 * 32 C3
Moss Bank Rd SWIN M27 83 G5
Moss Bank Wy BOL BL1 32 B5
Mossbray Av BNG/LEV M19 158 A2
Moss Bridge Rd MILN OL16 30 C5
Mossbrook Dr LHULT M38 80 D1
Moss Brook Rd BKLY M9 103 F3
Moss Cl RAD M26 51 G4
Mossclough Ct BKLY M9 103 F3
Moss Colliery Rd SWIN M27 83 H4
Mosscot Wk BRUN/LGST M13 128 C1
Moss Croft Cl URM M41 123 F5
Mossdale Av BOL BL1 47 E2
Mossdale Rd NTHM/RTH M23 155 G5
SALE M33 153 H5
Mossdown Rd ROY/SHW OL2 75 H1
Moss Farm Cl MDTN M24 89 E1
Mossfield Cl BURY BL9 5 K2
HTNM SK4 159 E4
Mossfield Ct BOL BL1 2 C2
Mossfield Dr BKLY M9 88 D3
Mossfield Rd FWTH BL4 65 G4
FWTH BL4 82 C2
HALE/TIMP WA15 167 E3
SWIN M27 83 H5
Mossgate Rd ROY/SHW OL2 44 C5
Moss Grange Av
OLDTF/WHR M16 * 127 G5
Moss Gn PART M31 137 H5
Moss Gv ROY/SHW OL2 44 B5
Mossgrove Rd
HALE/TIMP WA15 166 A3
Mosshall Cl HULME M15 127 G2
Moss Hall Rd BURY BL9 39 G5
Moss Hey Dr NTHM/RTH M23 156 B5
Moss Hey St ROY/SHW OL2 60 B3
Moss House La WALK M28 96 B5
Moss House Ter BKLY M9 * 102 D1
Mossland Cl HEY OL10 56 A1
Mossland Gv BOLS/LL BL3 63 E2
Moss La AULW OL7 118 D3
BOL BL1 32 D3
BRAM/HZG SK7 193 F2
FWTH BL4 83 E2
HALE/TIMP WA15 165 H5
HALE/TIMP WA15 166 A2
HYDE SK14 149 H3
IRL M44 150 C1
LYMM WA13 150 D5
MDTN M24 88 C2
MILN OL16 30 B5
PART M31 151 F3
ROY/SHW OL2 75 H1
SALE M33 153 E3
SALE M33 153 G3
SWIN M27 98 C1
URM M41 124 D3
WALK M28 82 C4
WHIT OL12 18 A1
WHTF M45 69 G4
WILM/AE SK9 190 D1
WILM/AE SK9 201 E4
Moss La East
OLDTF/WHR M16 127 H4
Moss La West HULME M15 127 H4
RUSH/FAL M14 128 B4
Moss Lea BOL BL1 33 G2
Mosslee Av CHH M8 87 E4
Mossley Rd AUL OL6 119 H2
MOSL OL5 94 A3
Moss Meadow Rd SLFD M6 * 112 B1
Mossmere Rd CHD/CHDH SK8 170 D5
Moss Mill St MILN OL16 43 G1
Moss Park Rd STRET M32 139 G1
Moss Pl BURY BL9 * 53 F1
Moss Rd SALE M33 153 E2
STRET M32 125 H5
WILM/AE SK9 201 F3
Moss Rose WILM/AE SK9 201 E3
Moss Rw BURY BL9 4 E6
Moss Shaw Wy RAD M26 51 H4
Moss Side La MILN OL16 43 H1
Moss St BRO M7 101 G5
BURY BL9 4 D5
BURY BL9 27 E1
DROY M43 118 A3
FWTH BL4 66 B3
HEY OL10 40 D4
MILN OL16 30 C5
OLDE OL4 76 D4
Moss St West AULW OL7 119 E3
Moss Ter MILN OL16 30 B5
The Moss MDTN M24 89 E1
Moss Vale Crs STRET M32 125 E4
Moss Vale Rd STRET M32 125 E5
URM M41 139 E1
Moss View Rd BOLE BL2 50 B1
PART M31 151 F3
Mossway MDTN M24 88 C2
Moss Wy SALE M33 153 H2
Mosswood Pk DID/WITH M20 169 G1
Mosswood Rd WILM/AE SK9 199 H1
Mossylea Cl MDTN M24 89 E2
Moston Bank Av BKLY M9 103 F3
Moston La BKLY M9 103 F2
NEWH/MOS M40 103 H2
Moston La East
NEWH/MOS M40 104 D1
Moston Rd MDTN M24 89 G1
RDSH SK5 145 F4
Moston St BRO M7 102 A3
Mostyn Av BURY BL9 38 C1
CHD/CHDH SK8 182 B3
RUSH/FAL M14 143 G3
Mostyn Rd BRAM/HZG SK7 184 D3
Mostyn St DUK SK16 120 C5
Motcombe Farm Rd
CHD/CHDH SK8 181 G3
Motcombe Gv CHD/CHDH SK8 181 F1
Motcombe Rd CHD/CHDH SK8 181 F2
Motherwell Av BNG/LEV M19 144 A2
Mottershead Av BOLS/LL BL3 50 D5
Mottershead Rd
WYTH/NTH M22 168 A5
Mottram Av CCHDY M21 156 B1
Mottram Cl CHD/CHDH SK8 170 D4
Mottram Dr HALE/TIMP WA15 166 B4
Mottram Fold STKP SK1 13 G5
Mottram Old Rd HYDE SK14 148 C3
STLY SK15 135 E1
Mottram Rd HYDE SK14 148 B1
SALE M33 155 F3
STLY SK15 121 F4
WILM/AE SK9 201 E4
Mottram St STKP SK1 13 G5
Mough La CHAD OL9 89 G4
Mouldsworth Av
DID/WITH M20 142 C4
HTNM SK4 144 D5
Moulton St CHH M8 114 B1
Mouncey St CMANE M1 * 128 B1
Mountain Ash WHIT OL12 18 A5
Mountain Ash Cl SALE M33 153 F1
WHIT OL12 18 A5
Mountain Gv WALK M28 81 H3
Mountain St MOSL OL5 108 D1
NEWH/MOS M40 117 E1
STKP SK1 13 K2
WALK M28 81 H3
Mount Av LIT OL15 20 D1
WHIT OL12 20 B4
Mountbatten Av DUK SK16 134 A2
Mountbatten Cl BURY BL9 70 A2
Mountbatten St GTN M18 130 B3
Mount Carmel Crs ORD M5 * 127 F1
Mount Dr MPL/ROM SK6 175 E4
URM M41 139 F1
Mountfield PWCH M25 86 A3
Mountfield Rd
BRAM/HZG SK7 193 H2
EDGY/DAV SK3 171 F2
Mountfield Wk OP/CLY M11 116 A4
Mount Fold MDTN M24 72 D5
Mountford Av CHH M8 * 87 E5
Mount Gv CHD/CHDH SK8 169 E4
Mount La UPML OL3 78 B3
Mountmorres Cl WHTN BL5 63 G5
Mount Pleasant BOLS/LL BL3 * 49 H4
BRAM/HZG SK7 185 E1
BURY BL9 17 G5
MDTN M24 71 H4
PWCH M25 70 D4
WILM/AE SK9 199 E1
Mount Pleasant Rd
DTN/ASHW M34 146 D1
FWTH BL4 65 E4
Mount Pleasant St AUL OL6 119 H2
DTN/ASHW M34 132 C2
OLDE OL4 * 76 A5
Mount Pleasant Wk RAD M26 52 B5
Mount Rd GTN M18 * 130 A3
HTNM SK4 12 B1
HYDE SK14 148 C5
MDTN M24 72 D5
PWCH M25 70 B5
Mountroyal Cl HYDE SK14 134 A3
Mount St Joseph's Rd
BOLS/LL BL3 48 A4
Mountside Cl WHIT OL12 10 C1
Mountside Crs PWCH M25 85 G3
Mount Sion Houses RAD M26 * 67 G2
Mount Sion Rd RAD M26 67 H2
Mount Skip La LHULT M38 81 F3
Mount St BOL BL1 33 H5
CMANW M2 6 E6
CSLFD M3 6 A2
ECC M30 110 D5
HEY OL10 41 E5
HYDE SK14 148 A1
RAMS BL0 16 C1
ROCH OL11 42 B5
ROY/SHW OL2 75 F1
SWIN M27 99 E3
WHIT OL12 10 A5
The Mount ALT WA14 165 G4
HALE/TIMP WA15 178 D4
Mount View Rd ROY/SHW OL2 60 C3
Mount Zion Rd BURY BL9 53 G4
Mousell St CHH M8 114 D1
Mowbray Av PWCH M25 86 B5
SALE M33 154 D3
Mowbray St AULW OL7 119 E3
BOL BL1 * 33 E5
OLD OL1 9 H4
ROCH OL11 42 A3
STKP SK1 13 H5
Mow Halls La UPML OL3 78 D3
Moxley Rd CHH M8 101 H1
Moyse Av TOT/BURYW BL8 37 E1
Mozart Cl ANC M4 115 F3
Muirfield Av MPL/ROM SK6 161 H2
Muirfield Cl BOLS/LL BL3 63 G1
HEY OL10 41 E5
NEWH/MOS M40 104 B3
WILM/AE SK9 199 G2
Mulberry Cl CHD/CHDH SK8 181 H5
RAD M26 68 B2
ROCH OL11 42 D1
Mulberry Ct SLFD M6 * 113 F2
Mulberry Ms HTNM SK4 12 E1
Mulberry Mount St
EDGY/DAV SK3 13 F6
Mulberry Rd SLFD M6 113 F3
Mulberry St AUL OL6 * 119 H2
CMANW M2 6 D5
Mulberry Wk DROY M43 117 F5
SALE M33 138 D5
Mule St BOLE BL2 3 H3
Mulgrave Rd WALK M28 97 H2
Mulgrave St BOLS/LL BL3 64 B2
SWIN M27 98 C1
Mullacre Rd WYTH/NTH M22 168 C3
Mull Av WGTN/LGST M12 129 F3
Mulliner St BOL BL1 * 34 A5
Mullion Cl BNG/LEV M19 144 D1
Mullion Dr HALE/TIMP WA15 165 H2
Mullion Wk CHH M8 102 C4
Mulmount Cl OLDS OL8 90 D4
Mumps Rbt OLD OL1 9 K3
Munday St ANC M4 115 G4
Municipal Cl HEY OL10 * 41 E4
Munn Rd BKLY M9 87 G2
Munro Av WYTH/NTH M22 181 E2
Munster St ANC M4 * 7 F1
Muriel St BRO M7 101 G5
HEY OL10 41 F4
MILN OL16 43 G1
Murieston Rd
HALE/TIMP WA15 177 H2
Murrayfield ROCH OL11 28 B5
Murray Rd BURY BL9 4 E5
Murray St ANC M4 7 K3
BRO M7 101 G4
Musabbir Sq MILN OL16 * 10 E4
Musbury Av CHD/CHDH SK8 183 E2
Museum St CMANW M2 6 E6
Musgrave Gdns BOL BL1 48 B1
Musgrave Rd BOL BL1 48 B1
WYTH/NTH M22 180 C1
Muslin St ORD M5 113 H4
Muter Av WYTH/NTH M22 181 E2
Mutual St HEY OL10 41 F3
Myerscroft Cl
NEWH/MOS M40 104 C2
Myrrh St BOL BL1 33 H3
Myrtle Bank PWCH M25 100 D1
Myrtle Cl OLDS OL8 9 F7
Myrtle Gdns BURY BL9 5 J4
Myrtle Gv DROY M43 118 B3
DTN/ASHW M34 131 E5
PWCH M25 86 A5
WHTF M45 69 E2
Myrtleleaf Gv ORD M5 * 112 C3
Myrtle Pl BRO M7 113 H1
Myrtle Rd MDTN M24 73 F3
PART M31 150 C4
Myrtle St BOL BL1 2 B3
EDGY/DAV SK3 171 E1
OLDTF/WHR M16 * 127 F4
OP/CLY M11 115 H5
Myrtle St North BURY BL9 5 J4
Myrtle St South BURY BL9 5 J5
My St ORD M5 112 D4
Mytham Rd BOLS/LL BL3 67 E1
Mythholme Av IRL M44 150 B3
Mytton Rd BOL BL1 33 E3
Mytton St HULME M15 127 H3

N

Nabbs Fold TOT/BURYW BL8 16 A5
Nabbs Wy TOT/BURYW BL8 26 B2
Naburn Cl RDSH SK5 146 A5
Naburn St BRUN/LGST M13 129 E4
Nada Rd CHH M8 102 A1
Nadine St SLFD M6 112 D2
Nadin St OLDS OL8 91 F4
Nairn Cl NEWH/MOS M40 * 115 H2
Nailgate MILN OL16 43 H4
Nall St BNG/LEV M19 144 B4
MILN OL16 31 F5
Nameplate Cl ECC M30 110 C3
Nancy St HULME M15 127 G2

Nandywell BOLS/LL BL3 67 E1
Nangreave Rd OFTN SK2 172 C3
Nan Nook Rd NTHM/RTH M23 155 G5
Nansen Av ECC M30 110 D2
Nansen Cl STRET M32 126 B4
Nansen Rd CHD/CHDH SK8 169 F5
Nansen St OP/CLY M11 115 H5
SLFD M6 112 D3
STRET M32 126 B4
Nansmoss La WILM/AE SK9 198 A1
Nantwich Av WHIT OL12 19 E5
Nantwich Rd RUSH/FAL M14 142 C2
Nantwich Wk BOLS/LL BL3 * 48 D5
Napier Ct HULME M15 * 127 F2
Napier Gn ORD M5 127 E1
Napier Rd CCHDY M21 141 F3
ECC M30 110 D2
HTNM SK4 159 E3
Napier St BRAM/HZG SK7 185 E1
HYDE SK14 148 A2
ROY/SHW OL2 60 A1
SWIN M27 98 C3
Napier St East OLDS OL8 8 D6
Napier St West OLDS OL8 8 B7
Naples Rd EDGY/DAV SK3 171 E3
Naples St ANC M4 7 H1
Narbonne Av ECC M30 111 H1
Narbuth Dr CHH M8 102 A3
Narrowgate Brow
ROY/SHW OL2 59 E2
The Narrows ALT WA14 165 F5
Naseby Av BKLY M9 88 C3
Naseby Pl PWCH M25 86 B2
Naseby Rd RDSH SK5 145 E3
Naseby Wk WHTF M45 70 B4
Nash Rd TRPK M17 111 F5
Nash St HULME M15 127 H2
Nasmyth Av DTN/ASHW M34 132 D4
Nasmyth Rd ECC M30 110 D5
Nasmyth St CHH M8 102 D5
Nately Rd OLDTF/WHR M16 * 141 E1
Nathan Dr CSLFD M3 6 B2
Nathans Rd WYTH/NTH M22 168 B5
National Dr ORD M5 113 F5
Naunton Rd MDTN M24 73 E5
Naval St ANC M4 7 K3
Nave Ct SLFD M6 113 E1
Navenby Av OLDTF/WHR M16 127 F4
Navigation Rd ALT WA14 165 G2
Naylor St NEWH/MOS M40 115 G2
OLD OL1 9 F2
Nazeby Wk CHAD OL9 8 B7
Naze Ct OLD OL1 * 75 F4
Neal Av AUL OL6 120 A2
CHD/CHDH SK8 181 F4
Neale Av UPML OL3 95 F2
Neale Rd CCHDY M21 141 E4
Near Birches Pde OLDE OL4 92 D3
Nearbrook Rd
WYTH/NTH M22 168 B5
Nearcroft Rd NTHM/RTH M23 167 H2
Near Hey Cl RAD M26 67 H1
Nearmaker Av
WYTH/NTH M22 168 B5
Nearmaker Rd
WYTH/NTH M22 168 B5
Neary Wy URM M41 124 B3
Neasden Gv BOLS/LL BL3 * 48 B4
Neath Av WYTH/NTH M22 168 C2
Neath Cl POY/DIS SK12 195 E2
WHTF M45 70 B5
Neath Fold BOLS/LL BL3 64 C1
Neath St CHAD OL9 8 D3
Nebo St BOLS/LL BL3 48 C5
Nebraska St BOL BL1 * 33 H5
Neden Cl OP/CLY M11 116 C5
Needham Av CCHDY M21 141 F3
Needwood Cl
NEWH/MOS M40 103 E5
Needwood Rd MPL/ROM SK6 162 B1
Neenton Sq WGTN/LGST M12 129 H1
Neild St CMANE M1 7 J7
OLDS OL8 91 F3
Neill St BRO M7 114 B1
Neilson Cl MDTN M24 73 F5
Nell Carrs RAMS BL0 17 F1
Nellie St HEY OL10 40 C4
Nell La CCHDY M21 142 A5
Nell St BOL BL1 34 A2
Nelson Av ECC M30 111 E2
POY/DIS SK12 195 H4
Nelson Cl POY/DIS SK12 195 H4
Nelson Dr DROY M43 117 E3
IRL M44 136 A5
Nelson Fold SWIN M27 99 F1
Nelson Rd BKLY M9 88 A2
Nelson Sq BOL BL1 3 F5
Nelson St BOLS/LL BL3 49 F4
BOLS/LL BL3 * 67 E1
BRAM/HZG SK7 173 G5
BRO M7 101 G5
BRUN/LGST M13 128 C3
BURY BL9 53 G1
DTN/ASHW M34 132 C2
DTN/ASHW M34 * 132 C4
ECC M30 111 E3
FWTH BL4 66 B4
HEY OL10 41 E5
HYDE SK14 148 A1
LIT OL15 21 E3
MDTN M24 73 F5
MILN OL16 10 D7
NEWH/MOS M40 115 G1
OLDE OL4 * 92 D2
ORD M5 112 D4
STRET M32 140 B2
Nelson Wy CHAD OL9 * 90 B3
Nelstrop Crs HTNM SK4 144 D5
Nelstrop Rd HTNM SK4 144 C5
Nelstrop Rd North
BNG/LEV M19 144 D3
Nepaul Rd BKLY M9 103 F1
Neptune Gdns BRO M7 113 H1
Nesbit St BOLE BL2 * 34 C3
Nesfield Rd NTHM/RTH M23 155 G4
Neston Av BOL BL1 34 A1
DID/WITH M20 142 C5
SALE M33 155 F4
Neston Cl ROY/SHW OL2 60 C2
Neston Gv EDGY/DAV SK3 171 G4
Neston Rd MILN OL16 43 H2
TOT/BURYW BL8 37 E2
Neston St OP/CLY M11 131 E1
Neston Wy WILM/AE SK9 192 A4
Netherbury Cl GTN M18 130 B5
Nethercote Av
NTHM/RTH M23 168 A3
Nethercroft ROCH OL11 28 B3
Nethercroft Rd
HALE/TIMP WA15 166 D4
Netherfield Cl OLDS OL8 90 D3
Netherfield Rd BOLS/LL BL3 64 D2
Netherfields WILM/AE SK9 200 D5
Netherhey La ROY/SHW OL2 74 D2
Nether Hey St OLDS OL8 92 A3
Netherhouse Rd
ROY/SHW OL2 59 H2
Netherland St SALQ M50 113 E4
Netherlees OLDE OL4 92 C2
Nether St HYDE SK14 148 B3
WGTN/LGST M12 * 7 K7
Netherton Rd RUSH/FAL M14 142 C2
Nethervale Dr BKLY M9 103 F3
Netherwood FAIL M35 105 G2
Netherwood Rd
WYTH/NTH M22 168 B2
Netherwood Wy WHTN BL5 62 B2
Netley Av WHIT OL12 19 E5
Netley Gv OLDS OL8 * 92 B3
Netley Rd NTHM/RTH M23 167 H5
Nettlebarn Rd
WYTH/NTH M22 168 B4
Nettleford Rd CCHDY M21 142 A3
Nettleton Gv BKLY M9 103 G1
Nevada St BOL BL1 * 33 H5
Nevendon Dr NTHM/RTH M23 167 G5
Nevern Cl BOL BL1 47 G1
Nevile Rd BRO M7 101 E2
Neville Cardus Wk
RUSH/FAL M14 143 E1
Neville Cl BOL BL1 2 D3
Neville Dr IRL M44 122 B4
Neville St BRAM/HZG SK7 185 E1
CHAD OL9 8 B2
Nevill Rd BRAM/HZG SK7 183 H2
Nevin Av CHD/CHDH SK8 182 B3
Nevin Cl BRAM/HZG SK7 184 B5
Nevin Rd NEWH/MOS M40 104 C1
Nevis Gv BOL BL1 33 G1
Nevis St ROCH OL11 43 F4
New Allen St NEWH/MOS M40 115 F2
Newall Rd NTHM/RTH M23 179 G1
Newall St CHAD OL9 90 C5
LIT OL15 21 E2
Newark Av RAD M26 51 F4
RUSH/FAL M14 128 C5
Newark Park Wy
ROY/SHW OL2 58 D3
Newark Rd RDSH SK5 160 A1
SWIN M27 84 C5
WHIT OL12 19 E5
Newark Sq WHIT OL12 19 E5
New Bailey St CSLFD M3 6 B4
Newbank Cha CHAD OL9 74 B4
Newbank Cl MDTN M24 73 E5
UPML OL3 78 C3
New Bank St WGTN/LGST M12 129 F3
New Barn Cl ROY/SHW OL2 59 H2
New Barn La ROCH OL11 42 D1
New Barns Av CCHDY M21 141 G5
New Barn St BOL BL1 33 E5
MILN OL16 43 F1
ROY/SHW OL2 59 H2
New Barton St SLFD M6 99 H5
Newbeck St ANC M4 * 7 G2
New Beech Rd HTNM SK4 158 B4
New Beech St HYDE SK14 133 G5
Newberry Gv EDGY/DAV SK3 171 G4
Newbold Hall Dr MILN OL16 11 J6
Newbold Moss MILN OL16 11 H6
Newbold St MILN OL16 11 K6
TOT/BURYW BL8 37 H4
Newboult Rd CHD/CHDH SK8 170 B3
Newbourne Cl
BRAM/HZG SK7 185 E1
Newbreak Cl OLDE OL4 76 C4
Newbridge Gdns BOLE BL2 35 F2
New Bridge Gdns BURY BL9 53 F4
Newbridge La STKP SK1 13 J3
New Bridge St CSLFD M3 6 E1
Newbridge Vw MOSL OL5 * 109 E2
New Briggs Fold
EDGW/EG BL7 22 D1
New Broad La MILN OL16 43 H3
Newbrook Av CCHDY M21 156 C3
New Buildings Pl MILN OL16 10 C5
Newburn Av BKLY M9 88 C3
Newbury Av SALE M33 153 F2
Newbury Cl CHD/CHDH SK8 192 D1
Newbury Ct
HALE/TIMP WA15 * 166 A3
Newbury Dr ECC M30 110 C2
URM M41 124 B3
Newbury Gv HEY OL10 55 H1
Newbury Rd BOLS/LL BL3 66 C1
CHD/CHDH SK8 181 H5
Newbury Wk BOL BL1 * 2 C2
CHAD OL9 8 A2
Newby Cl BURY BL9 53 H2
Newby Dr ALT WA14 * 165 G3
CHD/CHDH SK8 169 F4
MDTN M24 72 C1
SALE M33 155 E3
Newby Rd BOLE BL2 35 F5
BRAM/HZG SK7 184 D2
HTNM SK4 12 A2
Newcastle St HULME M15 128 A1
Newchurch OLDS OL8 106 D2
New Church Ct WHTF M45 * 69 G5
Newchurch Pl ROCH OL11 * 42 B5
New Church Rd BOL BL1 32 C4
New Church St RAD M26 68 C1
Newchurch St OP/CLY M11 116 A5
ROCH OL11 42 B5
New City Rd WALK M28 96 B2
Newcliffe Rd BKLY M9 88 C3
New Coin St ROY/SHW OL2 60 A1
New Colliers Rw BOL BL1 * 32 B1
Newcombe Cl OP/CLY M11 116 A4
Newcombe Dr LHULT M38 81 E1
Newcombe Rd RAMS BL0 26 B2
Newcombe St CSLFD M3 * 114 C2
New Copper Moss
HALE/TIMP WA15 166 A5
Newcroft FAIL M35 105 G4
Newcroft Crs URM M41 139 F2
Newcroft Dr BKLY M9 102 D1
EDGY/DAV SK3 171 G3
URM M41 139 F2
Newcroft Rd URM M41 139 F2
New Cross St ORD M5 112 B3
SWIN M27 99 F3
Newdale Rd WGTN/LGST M12 144 B1
Newearth Rd WALK M28 96 C2
New Earth St MOSL OL5 94 A5
OLDE OL4 92 B2
New Ellesmere Ap WALK M28 81 H3
New Elm Rd CSLFD M3 6 A7
New Field Cl MILN OL16 11 J5
RAD M26 67 H1
Newfield Head La MILN OL16 45 E1
Newfield Vw MILN OL16 31 H5
New Forest Rd
NTHM/RTH M23 166 D1
Newgate MILN OL16 10 C6
Newgate Cottages
WHTN BL5 * 63 H3
Newgate Dr LHULT M38 81 E1
Newgate Rd SALE M33 153 E5
WILM/AE SK9 198 A3
New George St
TOT/BURYW BL8 37 H3
New Hall Av BRO M7 101 G2
CHD/CHDH SK8 181 G5
Newhall Av BOLE BL2 51 E3
ECC M30 123 H1
New Hall Cl SALE M33 155 G2
Newhall Dr NTHM/RTH M23 155 H4
New Hall La BOL BL1 47 H1
New Hall Ms BOL BL1 32 A5
New Hall Pl BOL BL1 47 H1
New Hall Rd BRO M7 101 G3
BURY BL9 39 H2
SALE M33 * 155 G3
Newhall Rd RDSH SK5 145 G1
Newham Av OP/CLY M11 116 C3
Newham Dr TOT/BURYW BL8 37 G5
Newhart Gv WALK M28 81 H5
Newhaven Av OP/CLY M11 131 E1
Newhaven Cl CHD/CHDH SK8 183 F2
TOT/BURYW BL8 26 D4
New Herbert St SLFD M6 99 H5
Newhey Av WYTH/NTH M22 168 C4
New Hey Rd CHD/CHDH SK8 170 B4
Newhey Rd MILN OL16 44 D2
WYTH/NTH M22 168 C5
New Heys Wy BOLE BL2 24 A5
New Holder St BOL BL1 2 C5
Newholme Gdns WALK M28 81 H4
Newholme Rd DID/WITH M20 156 D1
Newhouse Cl WHIT OL12 19 H2
Newhouse Crs ROCH OL11 28 B3
Newhouse Rd HEY OL10 56 A1
New Houses OLDE OL4 77 H4
Newington Av CHH M8 87 E4
Newington Ct ALT WA14 177 E1
Newington Dr BOL BL1 * 2 E1
TOT/BURYW BL8 52 B1
Newington Wk BOL BL1 * 2 D1
New Islington ANC M4 115 F3
New Kings Head Yd CSLFD M3 * 6 D2
Newland Dr WHTN BL5 63 G5
Newlands FAIL M35 117 F1
Newlands Av BOLE BL2 35 G5
BRAM/HZG SK7 183 H4
CHD/CHDH SK8 182 D5
ECC M30 110 A5
IRL M44 122 A5
WHIT OL12 19 E5
WHTF M45 * 69 F3
Newlands Cl CHD/CHDH SK8 182 D5
WHIT OL12 19 E5
Newlands Dr DID/WITH M20 169 H1
PWCH M25 85 H2
SWIN M27 99 H4
WILM/AE SK9 198 B5
Newlands Rd CHD/CHDH SK8 170 B3
NTHM/RTH M23 167 G1
Newland St CHH M8 102 C1
New La BOLE BL2 35 E5
ECC M30 110 C3
MDTN M24 72 D3
ROY/SHW OL2 59 E5
New Lane Ct BOLE BL2 35 F4
New Lawns RDSH SK5 145 G2
Newlea Cl BOL BL1 33 F4
New Lees St AUL OL6 107 G5
New Lester Wy LHULT M38 80 D3
Newlyn Av STLY SK15 121 G2
Newlyn Cl BRAM/HZG SK7 185 E3
Newlyn Dr MPL/ROM SK6 161 H3
SALE M33 154 D5
Newlyn St RUSH/FAL M14 142 D1
Newman St AUL OL6 119 F2
HYDE SK14 133 H5
MILN OL16 19 H5
New Market CMANW M2 6 E4
Newmarket Cl SALE M33 153 E4
Newmarket Gv AULW OL7 106 B5
New Market La CMANW M2 6 E4
Newmarket Rd AULW OL7 106 B5
BOLS/LL BL3 66 D2
New Meadow HOR/BR BL6 46 D2
New Mill St LIT OL15 20 D3
New Moor La BRAM/HZG SK7 185 E1
New Mount St ANC M4 * 7 G1
Newnham St BOL BL1 34 A3
New Park Rd ORD M5 127 E1
Newpark Wk CHH M8 102 B4
Newport Av RDSH SK5 145 E4
Newport Rd BOLS/LL BL3 65 F1
CCHDY M21 141 E2
DTN/ASHW M34 147 F3
Newport St BOL BL1 2 E6
BOLS/LL BL3 3 F6
FWTH BL4 66 A5
MDTN M24 73 F3
OLDS OL8 8 C6
RUSH/FAL M14 128 C5
SLFD M6 112 D3
TOT/BURYW BL8 37 F1
Newquay Av BOLE BL2 36 C5
RDSH SK5 145 E4
Newquay Dr BRAM/HZG SK7 184 A5
New Quay St CSLFD M3 6 B4
New Radcliffe St OLD OL1 8 E3
New Raven Ct BOLS/LL BL3 * 66 D1
New Ridd Ri HYDE SK14 147 H3
New Riven Ct BOLS/LL BL3 66 D1
New Rd LIT OL15 20 B4
OLDS OL8 91 F3
RAD M26 68 C2
WHIT OL12 14 A5
New Royd Av OLDE OL4 77 E3
Newry Rd ECC M30 111 F5
Newry St BOL BL1 33 G3
Newsham Cl BOLS/LL BL3 2 A7
Newsham Rd EDGY/DAV SK3 171 H3
Newsham Wk
WGTN/LGST M12 * 130 A5
Newsholme St CHH M8 102 A3
New Springs BOL BL1 * 33 E3
Newstead WHIT OL12 10 B5
Newstead Av AUL OL6 107 F3
DID/WITH M20 158 A1
Newstead Cl POY/DIS SK12 195 E2
Newstead Dr BOLS/LL BL3 63 H2
Newstead Gv MPL/ROM SK6 161 G3
Newstead Rd URM M41 124 D5
Newstead Ter
HALE/TIMP WA15 166 A2
New St ALT WA14 165 F5
BOLS/LL BL3 2 D6
DROY M43 117 H5
ECC M30 110 D4
LIT OL15 20 C4
MILN OL16 44 D1
NEWH/MOS M40 115 H1
OLDE OL4 92 D1
RAD M26 68 C2
STLY SK15 120 D5
SWIN M27 99 F1
TOT/BURYW BL8 26 A5
UPML OL3 79 E4
WHIT OL12 29 H1
New Tempest Rd HOR/BR BL6 46 D5
New Ter HYDE SK14 * 148 A2
New Thomas St SLFD M6 * 113 F1
Newton Av DID/WITH M20 142 C5
WGTN/LGST M12 129 G4
Newton Crs MDTN M24 72 A1
Newton Dr TOT/BURYW BL8 26 B2
New Tong Fld EDGW/EG BL7 23 E4
Newton Hall Rd HYDE SK14 133 F3
Newton Rd ALT WA14 165 H2
FAIL M35 104 D5
MDTN M24 71 G5
URM M41 138 C1
WILM/AE SK9 198 D1
Newton St AUL OL6 * 119 H2
BOL BL1 33 H4
BURY BL9 27 G5
CMANE M1 7 H4
DROY M43 118 B2
EDGY/DAV SK3 12 E6
FAIL M35 * 104 B4
HYDE SK14 133 G4
MILN OL16 43 G1
STLY SK15 * 120 C3
STRET M32 140 B2
Newton Ter BOL BL1 * 33 H4
Newton Wk BOL BL1 33 H4
Newton Wood Rd DUK SK16 133 F2
Newtown Av DTN/ASHW M34 146 D1
Newtown Cl OP/CLY M11 116 C5
SWIN M27 84 A5
Newtown St PWCH M25 86 B3
ROY/SHW OL2 60 A3
New Union St ANC M4 7 K3
New Vernon St BURY BL9 5 F1
New Viaduct St
NEWH/MOS M40 115 H3
Newville Dr DID/WITH M20 158 A1
New Vine St HULME M15 * 128 A2
New Wakefield St CMANE M1 128 B1
New Wy WHIT OL12 14 B4
New York BOLS/LL BL3 47 G5
New York St HEY OL10 40 C4
New Zealand Rd STKP SK1 13 K2
Neyland Cl BOL BL1 47 G2
Ney St AULW OL7 106 C4
Niagara St OFTN SK2 172 B3
Nicholas Cft ANC M4 7 F3
Nicholas Owen Cl
OP/CLY M11 116 D5
Nicholas Rd OLDS OL8 91 F3
Nicholas St BOLE BL2 3 H3
CMANW M2 7 F5
Nicholls St SLFD M6 * 113 F2
Nicholson Rd HYDE SK14 133 F3
Nicholson Sq DUK SK16 * 119 G5
Nicholson St HTNM SK4 13 F1
OLDE OL4 92 D1
ROCH OL11 43 E1
Nichols St SLFD M6 113 G2
Nickleby Rd POY/DIS SK12 195 F4
Nicolas Rd CCHDY M21 141 E2
Nield Rd DTN/ASHW M34 132 C5
Nield's Brow ALT WA14 * 177 F2
Nield St MOSL OL5 93 G5
Nigel Rd BKLY M9 103 G3
Nigher Moss Av MILN OL16 11 K7
Nightingale Cl WILM/AE SK9 199 E1
Nightingale Dr
DTN/ASHW M34 118 B3
Nightingale Gdns
NTHM/RTH M23 155 H5
Nile St AULW OL7 119 E5
BOLS/LL BL3 49 E4
MILN OL16 11 F5
OLD OL1 9 F1
Nile Ter BRO M7 101 G5
Nimble Nook CHAD OL9 90 B2
Nina Dr NEWH/MOS M40 89 F4
Nine Acre Dr ORD M5 127 E1
Ninehouse La BOLS/LL BL3 49 E5
Ninfield Rd NTHM/RTH M23 168 A5
Ninth Av OLDS OL8 106 A1
Nipper La WHTF M45 69 F3
Nisbet Av WYTH/NTH M22 180 D1
Niven St WGTN/LGST M12 128 D1
Nixon Rd BOLS/LL BL3 64 B1
Nixon Rd South BOLS/LL BL3 64 B1
Nixon St EDGY/DAV SK3 13 F6
FAIL M35 104 D3
ROCH OL11 42 A3
No 11 Pas DID/WITH M20 * 157 E1
Noble Meadow WHIT OL12 * 20 A4
Noble St BOLS/LL BL3 48 D4
OLDS OL8 91 G3
Noel Dr SALE M33 155 E2
Noel St BOL BL1 2 D4
Nolan St BKLY M9 103 F3
Nona St SLFD M6 112 D3
Nook Farm Av WHIT OL12 19 E5
Nook Flds BOLE BL2 35 F4
Nook La AUL OL6 107 G4
The Nook ECC M30 110 B2
URM M41 138 D2
WALK M28 97 G2
Noon Sun Cl UPML OL3 94 D3
Noon Sun St WHIT OL12 10 C2
Norbet Wk BKLY M9 * 103 F3
Norbreck Av CCHDY M21 141 F4
CHD/CHDH SK8 170 D3
Norbreck St BOLE BL2 49 H1
Norburn Rd BRUN/LGST M13 143 H1
Norbury Av MPL/ROM SK6 174 D3
OLDE OL4 93 H1
SALE M33 154 A2
SLFD M6 100 A5
Norbury Cl NEWH/MOS M40 * 115 G1
Norbury Crs BRAM/HZG SK7 185 E2
Norbury Dr MPL/ROM SK6 175 E3
Norbury Gv BOL BL1 34 A2
BRAM/HZG SK7 185 E2
SWIN M27 99 E1
Norbury Hollow Rd
BRAM/HZG SK7 186 A4
Norbury La OLDS OL8 92 C4
Norbury Ms MPL/ROM SK6 * 174 D3
Norbury St BRO M7 101 H4
MILN OL16 * 43 G2
STKP SK1 13 G4
Norcot Wk HULME M15 * 127 G2
Norcross Cl OFTN SK2 173 E4
Nordale Pk WHIT OL12 28 A1
Nordek Cl ROY/SHW OL2 59 E4
Nordek Dr ROY/SHW OL2 58 D4
Norden Av DID/WITH M20 142 C5
Norden Ct BOLS/LL BL3 48 D5
Norden Rd ROCH OL11 41 E1
Nordens Dr CHAD OL9 74 A3
Nordens Rd CHAD OL9 74 A4
Nordens St CHAD OL9 74 B4
Noreen Av PWCH M25 86 B2
Norfield Cl DUK SK16 119 H5
Norfolk Av DROY M43 117 G2
DTN/ASHW M34 131 F5
GTN M18 * 130 B4
HEY OL10 40 A4
HTNM SK4 144 C5
WHTF M45 69 H4
Norfolk Cl BOLS/LL BL3 51 E5
IRL M44 150 B1
ROY/SHW OL2 59 G2
Norfolk Crs FAIL M35 104 D4
Norfolk Dr FWTH BL4 66 A3
Norfolk Gdns URM M41 123 E5
Norfolk Rd GTN M18 130 B4
Norfolk St CHAD OL9 90 D3
CMANW M2 6 E4
HYDE SK14 147 H1
ROCH OL11 29 H5
SLFD M6 100 D5
WALK M28 82 A1
Norfolk Wy ROY/SHW OL2 75 E2
Norford Wy ROCH OL11 28 B4
Norgate St DID/WITH M20 157 G3
Norlan Av DTN/ASHW M34 132 B1
Norleigh Rd WYTH/NTH M22 168 C1
Norley Av STRET M32 126 C5
Norley Cl OLD OL1 74 C2
Norley Dr BNG/LEV M19 144 C1
SALE M33 155 F3
Norman Av BRAM/HZG SK7 184 D1
Normanby Cha ALT WA14 165 E5
Normanby Gv SWIN M27 98 D1
Normanby Rd WALK M28 96 D1
Normanby St BOLS/LL BL3 64 A2
RUSH/FAL M14 128 B4
SWIN M27 98 D1
Norman Cl MDTN M24 * 73 F3
Normandale Av BOL BL1 32 D5
Normandy Crs RAD M26 68 A1
Norman Gv RDSH SK5 145 E4
WGTN/LGST M12 * 129 H4
Norman Rd ALT WA14 165 F3
AUL OL6 107 F4
BRO M7 * 101 H3
HTNM SK4 159 E3
ROCH OL11 29 G5
RUSH/FAL M14 143 F1
SALE M33 154 C2
STLY SK15 120 C3
Norman Rd West BKLY M9 * 103 G3
Norman's Pl ALT WA14 165 G5
Norman St BURY BL9 5 J1
FAIL M35 105 F1
HYDE SK14 148 A1
MDTN M24 73 E3
OLD OL1 8 D1
WGTN/LGST M12 130 A3
Normanton Av SLFD M6 112 B2
Normanton Dr BKLY M9 88 B3
Normanton Rd
EDGY/DAV SK3 170 D2
Norman Weall Ct
MDTN M24 * 72 D2
Normington St OLDE OL4 * 76 A5
Norreys Av URM M41 123 F5
Norreys St MILN OL16 10 E5
Norris Av HTNM SK4 12 A2
Norris Bank Ter HTNM SK4 12 A3
Norris Hill Dr HTNM SK4 12 A1
Norris Rd SALE M33 154 D4
Norris St BOLS/LL BL3 48 D4
BOLS/LL BL3 66 D1
FWTH BL4 65 H5
Northallerton Rd BRO M7 101 E4

Northampton Rd
NEWH/MOS M40.....103 F4
North Av BNG/LEV M19.....143 H4
BURY BL9.....54 A5
FWTH BL4.....65 F4
STLY SK15.....120 D2
TOT/BURYW BL8.....26 A1
UPML OL3.....95 F2
URM M41.....124 D1
North Back Rock BURY BL9.....4 E4
Northbank Gdns
BNG/LEV M19.....143 G5
North Blackfield La BRO M7.....101 F2
Northbourne St SLFD M6.....112 D3
Northbrook Av CHH M8.....87 E3
North Cir WHTF M45.....85 H1
North Clifden La BRO M7.....101 H4
Northcliffe Rd OFTN SK2.....172 D1
Northcombe Rd
EDGY/DAV SK3.....171 H4
Northcote Av WYTH/NTH M22.....180 C1
Northcote Rd BRAM/HZG SK7.....184 A5
North Crs NEWH/MOS M40.....89 G4
OP/CLY M11.....117 E2
North Cft OLDS OL8.....91 H4
Northdale Rd BKLY M9.....87 G2
North Dean St SWIN M27.....99 F1
Northdene Dr ROCH OL11.....28 C5
Northdown Av HULME M15.....127 G2
MPL/ROM SK6.....162 B1
North Downs Rd
CHD/CHDH SK8.....182 C1
Northdowns Rd ROY/SHW OL2.....59 G1
North Dr DTN/ASHW M34.....118 B4
SWIN M27.....99 G3
Northenden Rd
CHD/CHDH SK8.....169 F4
SALE M33.....154 D2
Northend Rd STLY SK15.....121 F2
Northen Gv DID/WITH M20.....157 E2
Northern Av SWIN M27.....84 D4
Northern Gv BOL BL1.....33 F5
Northern Service Rd
NTHM/RTH M23 *.....167 G4
Northfield Av NEWH/MOS M40.....90 A5
Northfield Dr WILM/AE SK9.....199 G2
Northfield Rd BURY BL9.....27 G5
NEWH/MOS M40.....90 A5
Northfield St BOLS/LL BL3.....48 B4
Northfleet Rd ECC M30.....110 A5
North Ga OLDS OL8.....91 F4
Northgate WHIT OL12.....18 B1
Northgate La OLD OL1.....60 D5
Northgate Rd EDGY/DAV SK3.....12 A5
North George St CSLFD M3.....114 A2
North Gv BRUN/LGST M13.....129 E3
URM M41.....138 C2
WALK M28.....81 H4
North Hill St CSLFD M3.....6 A1
Northland Rd BKLY M9.....88 D4
BOL BL1.....23 E5
Northlands RAD M26.....51 H4
North La WHIT OL12.....10 D4
Northleach Cl TOT/BURYW BL8.....37 F3
Northleigh Dr PWCH M25 *.....86 C4
Northleigh Rd
OLDTF/WHR M16.....127 E5
North Lonsdale St STRET M32 *.....126 B5
North Md CCHDY M21.....141 F4
Northmoor Rd
WGTN/LGST M12.....129 H4
North Nook OLDE OL4.....77 E4
Northolme Gdns
BNG/LEV M19.....158 B2
Northolt Ct OP/CLY M11 *.....117 E3
Northolt Dr BOLS/LL BL3.....49 E5
Northolt Fold HEY OL10.....56 B2
Northolt Rd NTHM/RTH M23.....155 H5
North Pde CSLFD M3.....6 D4
MILN OL16.....45 F2
SALE M33.....155 E4
North Park Rd
BRAM/HZG SK7.....183 H2
North Phoebe St ORD M5.....113 G5
North Pl STKP SK1.....13 G3
Northridge Rd BKLY M9.....88 A1
North Ri UPML OL3.....95 E2
North Rd DTN/ASHW M34.....118 C4
HALE/TIMP WA15.....178 B4
MANAIR M90.....190 B1
OP/CLY M11.....116 D3
PART M31.....152 A2
PWCH M25.....85 G2
STRET M32.....125 G4
Northside Av URM M41.....137 H2
North Star Dr CSLFD M3.....6 A4
Northstead Av
DTN/ASHW M34.....147 F1
North St AUL OL6.....119 F3
CHH M8.....114 D1
HEY OL10.....40 C4
MDTN M24.....72 D2
MILN OL16.....10 E4
RAD M26.....52 D5
ROY/SHW OL2.....75 E1
WHIT OL12.....14 B4
Northumberland Av
AULW OL7.....119 G1
Northumberland Cl
OLDTF/WHR M16.....127 F3
Northumberland Crs
OLDTF/WHR M16 *.....127 F3
Northumberland Rd
OLDTF/WHR M16.....127 F4
PART M31.....150 D4
RDSH SK5.....145 H5
Northumberland St BRO M7.....101 G3
Northumberland Wy
WYTH/NTH M22.....168 D3
Northumbria St BOLS/LL BL3.....48 B4
Northurst Dr CHH M8.....87 E4
North Vale Rd
HALE/TIMP WA15.....166 A3
North Veiw WHTF M45.....69 F2
North View Cl OLDE OL4.....93 H2
Northward Rd WILM/AE SK9.....198 C4
North Wy BOL BL1.....34 C2
HYDE SK14.....148 A1
RDSH SK5.....146 A5
Northway DROY M43.....117 H5
North Western St
BNG/LEV M19.....144 A3
CMANE M1.....7 K6
Northwold Dr BKLY M9.....89 E4
BOL BL1.....47 F1
Northwood BOLE BL2.....35 E2
Northwood Crs BOLS/LL BL3 *.....48 B4
Northwood Gv SALE M33.....154 C2
Norton Av DTN/ASHW M34.....131 F5
SALE M33.....153 G1
URM M41.....124 C4
WGTN/LGST M12.....130 A5
Norton Gra PWCH M25.....86 C4
Norton Gv HTNM SK4.....159 E5
Norton Rd WHIT OL12.....19 E5
Norton St BOL BL1.....34 A3
BRO M7.....101 H3
CMANE M1.....115 F5
CSLFD M3.....6 D2
NEWH/MOS M40.....115 H1
Norview Dr DID/WITH M20.....169 G2
Norville Av NEWH/MOS M40.....89 G4
Norway Gv RDSH SK5 *.....160 A2
Norway St BOL BL1 *.....33 G4
SLFD M6.....112 D3
STRET M32.....126 B5
Norwell Rd WYTH/NTH M22.....168 D4
Norwich Av CHAD OL9.....74 B3
DTN/ASHW M34.....146 D2
ROCH OL11.....28 D4
Norwich Cl AUL OL6.....107 G2
DUK SK16.....134 B1
Norwich Dr TOT/BURYW BL8.....4 A2
Norwich Rd STRET M32.....125 E5
Norwich St ROCH OL11.....43 F1
Norwick Cl BOLS/LL BL3.....47 F5
Norwood PWCH M25.....86 A5
Norwood Av BRAM/HZG SK7.....193 F2
BRO M7.....101 E2
CHD/CHDH SK8.....182 D1
DID/WITH M20.....158 A2
MPL/ROM SK6.....186 C5
Norwood Cl ROY/SHW OL2.....59 H1
WALK M28.....97 F2
Norwood Crs ROY/SHW OL2.....75 F2
Norwood Dr
HALE/TIMP WA15.....167 E4
SWIN M27.....98 C3
Norwood Gv BOL BL1 *.....48 B1
Norwood Rd CHD/CHDH SK8.....169 G3
OFTN SK2.....172 C5
STRET M32.....140 C2
Nottingham Av RDSH SK5.....160 D1
Nottingham Cl RDSH SK5.....146 A5
Nottingham Dr AUL OL6.....107 E3
BOL BL1.....2 C1
FAIL M35.....105 F5
RDSH SK5.....146 A5
Nowell Rd MDTN M24.....72 D1
Nudger Cl UPML OL3.....78 C2
Nudger Gn UPML OL3.....78 D2
Nuffield Cl BOL BL1.....33 E5
Nuffield Rd WYTH/NTH M22.....168 D5
Nugent Rd BOLS/LL BL3.....64 D1
Nugget St OLDE OL4 *.....92 A1
Nuneaton Dr
NEWH/MOS M40.....115 G2
Nuneham Av DID/WITH M20.....143 E4
Nunfield Cl NEWH/MOS M40.....89 E5
Nunnery Rd BOLS/LL BL3.....48 A5
Nunthorpe Dr CHH M8.....102 D2
Nursery Av HALE/TIMP WA15.....177 H4
Nursery Cl OFTN SK2.....173 E2
SALE M33.....155 E2
Nursery Dr POY/DIS SK12.....195 E3
Nursery Gdns MILN OL16.....11 K5
Nursery Gv PART M31.....151 E2
Nursery La EDGY/DAV SK3.....170 D2
WILM/AE SK9.....198 C4
Nursery Rd CHD/CHDH SK8.....182 C3
FAIL M35.....105 F4
HTNM SK4.....12 A1
PWCH M25.....85 H1
URM M41.....124 A4
Nursery St OLDTF/WHR M16.....128 A5
SLFD M6.....113 E2
Nuthatch Av WALK M28.....97 E2
Nuthurst Rd NEWH/MOS M40.....104 B1
Nutsford V WGTN/LGST M12.....129 H4
Nut St BOL BL1 *.....33 G4
Nuttall Av BOLS/LL BL3.....67 F1
WHTF M45.....69 G4
Nuttall Cl RAMS BL0.....16 D3
Nuttall Hall Rd RAMS BL0.....17 E4
Nuttall La RAMS BL0.....16 D4
Nuttall Ms WHTF M45.....69 G4
Nuttall Rd RAMS BL0.....17 E4
Nuttall Sq BURY BL9.....53 G4
Nuttall St BURY BL9.....5 G6
IRL M44.....136 A5
MILN OL16.....10 E7
OLDS OL8 *.....92 A3
OLDTF/WHR M16.....127 F3
OP/CLY M11.....129 H1
Nutt La PWCH M25.....70 D4

O

Oadby Cl WGTN/LGST M12.....129 H4
Oadby Pl RDSH SK5.....131 E5
Oak Av BOLS/LL BL3.....67 E1
CCHDY M21.....141 F3
CHD/CHDH SK8.....182 C2
HTNM SK4.....159 E2
IRL M44.....150 C1
MDTN M24.....72 D5
MPL/ROM SK6.....162 B4
RAMS BL0.....26 B1
ROY/SHW OL2.....59 E3
WHTF M45.....69 G5
WILM/AE SK9.....198 C5
Oak Bank BKLY M9.....103 E2
PWCH M25.....100 C1
Oak Bank Av BKLY M9.....103 G1
Oakbank Av CHAD OL9.....73 H4
Oak Bank Cl WHTF M45.....70 A4
Oakbank Dr BOL BL1.....22 C5
Oakbarton HOR/BR BL6.....46 D5
Oakcliffe Rd NTHM/RTH M23.....167 H2
WHIT OL12.....19 H4
Oak Cl HYDE SK14.....135 H4
WHIT OL12.....14 C1
WILM/AE SK9.....198 C4
Oak Coppice BOL BL1.....47 H2
Oakcroft STLY SK15.....135 F1
Oakcroft Wy WYTH/NTH M22.....168 D3
Oakdale BOLE BL2.....35 E2
Oakdale Cl WHTF M45.....69 E4
Oakdale Ct UPML OL3.....78 B1
Oakdale Dr CHD/CHDH SK8.....181 G2
DID/WITH M20.....157 H5
Oak Dene UPML OL3.....94 D3
Oakdene WALK M28.....98 A4
Oakdene Av CHD/CHDH SK8.....181 G5
HTNM SK4.....159 G1
Oakdene Crs MPL/ROM SK6.....175 E2
Oakdene Gdns MPL/ROM SK6.....175 E2
Oakdene Rd HALE/TIMP WA15.....166 C1
MDTN M24.....73 F4
MPL/ROM SK6.....175 E2
Oakdene St BKLY M9.....103 G2
Oak Dr BRAM/HZG SK7.....183 F5
DTN/ASHW M34.....131 F4
MPL/ROM SK6.....174 C3
RUSH/FAL M14.....143 F2
Oaken Bank Rd HEY OL10.....56 C3
Oakenbottom Rd BOLE BL2.....50 A3
Oaken Clough AULW OL7.....106 C4
Oakenclough Cl WILM/AE SK9.....192 A5
Oaken Clough Dr AULW OL7.....106 C4
Oakenclough Dr BOL BL1.....32 C4
Oakenrod Hl ROCH OL11.....29 F4
Oakenshaw Av WHIT OL12.....18 B2
Oakenshaw Vw WHIT OL12.....18 B2
Oaker Av DID/WITH M20.....156 D2
Oakes St FWTH BL4.....66 C5
Oakfield DUK SK16.....133 H2
PWCH M25.....86 C4
SALE M33.....154 B1
Oakfield Av CHD/CHDH SK8.....170 B3
DROY M43.....117 G4
OLDTF/WHR M16.....126 D5
OLDTF/WHR M16.....127 G5
STLY SK15.....109 F4
Oakfield Cl BRAM/HZG SK7.....193 H3
WILM/AE SK9.....201 E2
Oakfield Dr LHULT M38.....80 D2
Oakfield Gv FWTH BL4.....81 H1
GTN M18.....130 C4
Oakfield Rd DID/WITH M20.....157 F3
EDGY/DAV SK3.....172 A4
HALE/TIMP WA15.....165 H4
HYDE SK14.....133 H3
POY/DIS SK12.....195 G3
WILM/AE SK9.....201 E3
Oakfield St CHH M8.....102 B4
HALE/TIMP WA15.....165 H4
Oakfield Ter ROCH OL11.....29 F3
Oakfold Av AUL OL6.....107 G4
Oakford Av NEWH/MOS M40.....115 F2
Oakford Wk BOLS/LL BL3.....48 B5
Oak Gates EDGW/EG BL7.....22 D2
Oak Gv AUL OL6.....107 G4
CHD/CHDH SK8.....170 B4
ECC M30.....110 C4
POY/DIS SK12.....195 E3
URM M41.....139 E1
Oakham Av DID/WITH M20.....142 C3
Oakham Cl TOT/BURYW BL8.....38 B1
Oakham Ms BRO M7.....101 F1
Oakham Rd DTN/ASHW M34 *.....147 E2
Oak Hl LIT OL15.....20 C3
Oakhill Cl BOLE BL2.....50 D2
Oakhill Wy CHH M8.....102 A3
Oakhouse Dr CCHDY M21.....141 F4
Oakhurst Cha WILM/AE SK9.....200 D3
Oakhurst Dr EDGY/DAV SK3.....171 E4
Oakhurst Gdns PWCH M25.....85 H3
Oakington Av
RUSH/FAL M14 *.....128 C5
Oakland Av BNG/LEV M19.....158 B2
OFTN SK2.....172 D3
SLFD M6.....111 H1
Oakland Gv BOL BL1 *.....32 D4
Oaklands BOL BL1.....47 G2
Oaklands Av CHD/CHDH SK8.....182 D2
MPL/ROM SK6.....175 E1
Oaklands Cl WILM/AE SK9.....199 H1
Oaklands Dene HYDE SK14.....148 C1
Oaklands Dr BRAM/HZG SK7.....185 F3
HYDE SK14.....148 C1
PWCH M25.....86 A2
SALE M33.....154 B1
Oaklands Pk OLDE OL4.....94 B2
Oaklands Rd BRO M7.....100 D3
ROY/SHW OL2.....75 F2
SWIN M27.....98 C4
UPML OL3.....94 C2
Oak La WHTF M45.....70 A4
WILM/AE SK9.....198 C4
Oak Lea Av WILM/AE SK9.....198 D5
Oaklea Rd SALE M33.....139 E5
Oakleigh Av BNG/LEV M19.....143 H4
BOLS/LL BL3.....65 F2
HALE/TIMP WA15.....166 B2
Oakleigh Cl HEY OL10.....56 B2
Oakleigh Rd CHD/CHDH SK8.....182 B4
Oakley Cl NEWH/MOS M40.....104 B5
RAD M26.....68 B4
Oakley Dr OLD OL1.....60 C5
Oakley Pk BOL BL1.....47 G2
Oakley St ORD M5.....112 C4
Oakley Vls HTNM SK4.....159 E3
Oak Ldg BRAM/HZG SK7 *.....184 A5
Oakmere Av ECC M30.....110 D1
Oakmere Cl WYTH/NTH M22.....168 C5
Oakmere Rd CHD/CHDH SK8.....170 C5
WILM/AE SK9.....192 A2
Oak Ms WILM/AE SK9.....199 F1
Oakmoor Dr BRO M7.....100 D2
Oakmoor Rd NTHM/RTH M23.....167 H3
Oak Mt DID/WITH M20 *.....157 G4
Oak Rd BRO M7.....101 F4
CHD/CHDH SK8.....170 B3
DID/WITH M20.....157 G1
FAIL M35.....105 E4
HALE/TIMP WA15.....177 H1
OLDS OL8.....90 D5
PART M31.....150 C4
SALE M33.....155 E2
Oaks Av BOLE BL2.....34 D2
Oak Shaw Cl BKLY M9.....88 A5
Oakshaw Dr WHIT OL12.....28 D2
Oaks La BOLE BL2.....34 C1
The Oaks CHD/CHDH SK8.....181 F2
HYDE SK14.....134 B5
Oak St ANC M4.....7 H3
BRAM/HZG SK7.....185 E1
DTN/ASHW M34.....132 C2
ECC M30.....111 E4
EDGY/DAV SK3.....171 E1
HEY OL10.....40 C3
HYDE SK14.....133 H4
LIT OL15.....21 F3
MDTN M24 *.....73 G5
MILN OL16.....10 C7
MILN OL16.....44 D3
RAMS BL0 *.....16 C3
ROY/SHW OL2.....60 B2
SWIN M27.....99 F1
WHIT OL12.....14 C1
Oak Tree Cl OFTN SK2.....173 E1
Oak Tree Ct CHD/CHDH SK8.....170 B4
Oak Tree Crs STLY SK15.....120 D5
Oak Tree Dr DUK SK16.....134 A1
Oak Vw OLD OL1.....75 E3
Oak View Rd UPML OL3.....95 E2
Oakville Dr SLFD M6.....111 H1
Oakville Ter NEWH/MOS M40.....103 G1
Oakway DID/WITH M20.....169 H1
MDTN M24.....56 C5
Oakwell Dr BRO M7.....101 H1
BURY BL9.....70 A1
Oakwell Man BRO M7.....101 H1
Oakwood CHAD OL9.....73 H5
SALE M33.....153 F2
Oakwood Av CHD/CHDH SK8.....169 G4
DTN/ASHW M34.....132 B1
NEWH/MOS M40.....104 C1
SWIN M27.....83 H3
WALK M28.....82 C5
WILM/AE SK9.....198 B4
Oakwood Cl TOT/BURYW BL8.....37 G3
Oakwood Ct ALT WA14.....177 E4
Oakwood Dr BOL BL1.....47 G1
SLFD M6.....99 G5
WALK M28.....82 C5
Oakwood La ALT WA14.....176 D3
Oakwood Rd MPL/ROM SK6.....162 C5
Oakworth Cft OLDE OL4.....61 E5
Oakworth Dr BOL BL1.....33 G1
Oakworth St BKLY M9.....87 H4
Oatlands WILM/AE SK9.....201 E5
Oatlands Rd WYTH/NTH M22.....180 B2
Oat St STKP SK1.....13 J7
Oban Av NEWH/MOS M40.....116 C1
OLD OL1.....76 A3
Oban Crs EDGY/DAV SK3.....171 G5
Oban Dr SALE M33.....155 F3
Oban Gv BOL BL1.....33 H1
Oban St BOL BL1 *.....33 G3
Oberlin St OLDE OL4.....76 C5
ROCH OL11.....42 C1
Occlestone Cl SALE M33.....155 F5
Occupiers La
BRAM/HZG SK7 *.....186 A3
Ocean St ALT WA14.....165 E3
Ockendon Dr BKLY M9.....103 F3
Octagon Ct BOL BL1 *.....2 E5
Octavia Dr NEWH/MOS M40.....116 D1
Odell St OP/CLY M11 *.....130 A1
Odessa Av SLFD M6.....112 A1
Odette St GTN M18.....130 B4
Offerton Dr OFTN SK2.....173 E2
Offerton Fold OFTN SK2.....172 D2
Offerton Gn OFTN SK2.....173 H3
Offerton La OFTN SK2.....172 D1
Offerton Rd BRAM/HZG SK7.....185 H1
OFTN SK2.....173 H5
Offerton St STKP SK1.....160 C4
Off Grove Rd STLY SK15.....121 G1
Off Ridge Hill La STLY SK15 *.....120 C3
Off Stamford St STLY SK15 *.....121 G1
Ogbourne Wk
BRUN/LGST M13.....128 D2
Ogden Cl HEY OL10.....40 B4
WHTF M45.....69 H3
Ogden Gv CHD/CHDH SK8 *.....169 E5
Ogden La MILN OL16.....45 G1
OP/CLY M11.....130 C1
Ogden Rd BRAM/HZG SK7.....193 G2
FAIL M35.....105 E4
Ogden Sq DUK SK16.....119 G5
Ogden St CHAD OL9.....74 C4
DID/WITH M20.....157 G3
MDTN M24.....72 D4
OLDE OL4 *.....92 C1
PWCH M25.....86 B3
ROCH OL11.....42 B4
SWIN M27.....99 E3
Ogwen Dr PWCH M25.....86 A2
Ohio Av SALQ M50.....113 E5
Okehampton Cl RAD M26.....51 F4
Okehampton Crs SALE M33.....153 G1
Okeover Rd BRO M7.....101 G2
Olaf St BOLE BL2.....3 J1
Olanyian Dr CHH M8.....101 H5
Old Bank Cl MPL/ROM SK6.....161 H3
Old Bank St CMANW M2.....6 E4
Old Bank Vw OLD OL1.....60 B5
Old Barn Pl EDGW/EG BL7.....23 F3
Old Barton Rd ECC M30.....124 B1
Old Bent La WHIT OL12.....19 F1
Old Birley St HULME M15.....128 A3
Old Broadway
DID/WITH M20.....157 H1
Old Brook Cl ROY/SHW OL2.....60 C1
Oldbrook Fold
HALE/TIMP WA15.....166 C5
Old Brow MOSL OL5.....108 D2
Old Brow La MILN OL16.....19 H5
Old Brown Ct MOSL OL5.....108 D2
Oldbury Cl HEY OL10.....56 A2
NEWH/MOS M40.....115 G2
Oldcastle Av DID/WITH M20.....142 C4
Old Chapel St EDGY/DAV SK3.....12 B7
Old Church Ms DUK SK16.....120 B5
Old Church St
NEWH/MOS M40.....104 A4
OLD OL1.....9 H3
Old Clay Dr WHIT OL12.....20 A4
Old Clough La WALK M28.....97 G2
Old Colliers Rw BOL BL1 *.....32 B1
Oldcott Cl WALK M28.....96 A5
Old Court St HYDE SK14.....147 H1
The Old Ctyd
WYTH/NTH M22 *.....169 E4
Old Cft OLDE OL4.....93 F1
Old Croft Ms STKP SK1.....172 C2
Old Crofts Bank URM M41.....124 B5
Old Cross St AUL OL6 *.....119 H2
Old Dairy Ms HYDE SK14.....133 F3
Old Delph Rd ROCH OL11.....28 C2
Old Doctors St
TOT/BURYW BL8.....26 A4
Old Eagley Ms BOL BL1.....23 E5
Old Edge La ROY/SHW OL2.....75 F2
Old Elm St BRUN/LGST M13 *.....128 D2
Oldershaw Dr BKLY M9.....103 E4
Old Farm Crs DROY M43.....117 G5
Old Farm Dr OFTN SK2.....173 G3
Oldfield Cl WHTN BL5.....62 A4
Oldfield Dr HALE/TIMP WA15.....166 A3
Oldfield Gv SALE M33.....154 D1
Oldfield Ms ALT WA14.....165 F4
Oldfield Rd ALT WA14.....164 D4
ORD M5.....127 F1
PWCH M25.....70 B5
SALE M33.....154 D1
Oldfield St OP/CLY M11.....116 C4
Old Gardens St STKP SK1.....13 H5
The Old Gdn
HALE/TIMP WA15.....166 C2
Oldgate Wk HULME M15 *.....127 G2
Old Gn BOLE BL2.....24 B5
Old Ground St RAMS BL0 *.....16 D2
Old Hall Cl TOT/BURYW BL8.....26 C4
Old Hall Clough HOR/BR BL6.....46 D2
Old Hall Crs WILM/AE SK9.....192 B4
Old Hall Dr GTN M18.....130 C4
OFTN SK2.....173 F3
Old Hall La BRUN/LGST M13.....143 G1
HYDE SK14.....135 H3
MPL/ROM SK6.....175 H4
PWCH M25.....71 E5
WALK M28.....97 F3
WHTF M45.....84 D1
Old Hall Rd BRO M7.....101 G2
CHD/CHDH SK8.....169 F3
NEWH/MOS M40.....104 A3
SALE M33.....155 F2
STRET M32.....125 F4
WHTF M45.....68 D5
Old Hall St DUK SK16.....132 D1
FWTH BL4.....66 B5
MDTN M24.....72 D4
OP/CLY M11 *.....130 D1
Old Hall St North BOL BL1.....2 E5
Oldham Av STKP SK1.....160 C5
Oldham Dr MPL/ROM SK6.....161 H2
Oldham Rd ANC M4.....7 J2
AULW OL7.....119 F1
FAIL M35.....105 F1
MDTN M24.....72 C4
MILN OL16.....10 D7
NEWH/MOS M40.....115 G2
OLDE OL4.....93 F1
OLDS OL8.....106 C3
ROCH OL11.....58 C1
ROY/SHW OL2.....60 A5
ROY/SHW OL2.....75 F2
UPML OL3.....61 F3
UPML OL3.....78 A3
Oldhams La BOL BL1.....33 G1
Oldham St CMANE M1.....7 G4
DROY M43.....118 A3
DTN/ASHW M34.....146 A1
HYDE SK14.....147 H1
ORD M5.....114 A4
RDSH SK5 *.....145 E4
Oldham Wy CHAD OL9.....8 D2
MILN OL16.....44 C5
OLD OL1.....9 J4
OLDE OL4.....94 A2
Old Kiln La BOL BL1.....32 A4
OLDE OL4.....93 G3
Oldknow Rd MPL/ROM SK6.....175 F3
Old La BURY BL9.....27 G3
CHAD OL9.....90 C3
LHULT M38.....81 E2
OLDE OL4.....77 E4
OLDE OL4.....94 B1
OP/CLY M11.....130 C1
Old Lansdowne Rd
DID/WITH M20.....157 E2
Old Lees St AUL OL6.....107 G5
Old Malt La DID/WITH M20.....142 C4
Old Market Pl ALT WA14.....165 G4
Old Market St BKLY M9.....87 H5
Old Meadow Dr
DTN/ASHW M34.....132 C3
Old Meadow La
HALE/TIMP WA15.....178 D1
Old Medlock St CSLFD M3 *.....6 A6
Old Mill Cl SWIN M27.....99 G2
Old Mill La BRAM/HZG SK7.....185 H4
OLDE OL4.....93 F2
Old Mills Hl MDTN M24.....73 G3
Old Mill St ANC M4.....115 F4
Oldmill St WHIT OL12.....10 C2
Old Moat La DID/WITH M20.....142 D5
Oldmoor Rd MPL/ROM SK6.....161 F1
Old Mount St ANC M4.....7 G1
Old Nans La BOLE BL2.....35 G4
Old Nursery Fold BOLE BL2.....35 F2
Old Oak Cl BOLE BL2.....51 E4
Old Oak Dr DTN/ASHW M34.....132 D5
Old Oake Cl WALK M28 *.....82 B5
Old Oak St DID/WITH M20.....157 G3
Old Orch WILM/AE SK9.....198 D3
The Old Orch
HALE/TIMP WA15.....166 C1
Old Park La TRPK M17.....124 B2
Old Parrin La ECC M30.....110 C2
Old Pasture Cl OFTN SK2.....173 F2
Old Quarry La
EDGW/EG BL7.....23 E2

Old Rectory Gdns
CHD/CHDH SK8 170 A4
Old River Cl IRL M44 136 C1
Old Rd AUL OL6 108 A5
BKLY M9 88 A5
BOL BL1 33 H3
CHD/CHDH SK8 170 C3
DUK SK16 119 H5
FAIL M35 104 D3
HTNM SK4 159 H3
HYDE SK14 133 G4
HYDE SK14 135 G3
MILN OL16 20 B4
STLY SK15 121 F5
WILM/AE SK9 192 A4
WILM/AE SK9 199 E2
Old School Dr BKLY M9 * 87 H5
Old School La CHD/CHDH SK8 182 D4
Old School Ms DUK SK16 * 120 B5
Old Shaw St ORD M5 * 113 F5
The Old Stables
DTN/ASHW M34 132 C2
Old Station St ECC M30 110 D4
Oldstead Gv BOLS/LL BL3 47 G5
Old St AUL OL6 119 G3
OLDE OL4 92 C2
STLY SK15 120 D4
Old Swan Cl EDGW/EG BL7 * 22 D1
Old Thorn La UPML OL3 95 G1
Old Towns Cl TOT/BURYW BL8 26 A4
Old Vicarage Gdns WALK M28 82 A4
Old Wellington Rd ECC M30 111 F3
Old Wells Cl LHULT M38 81 F1
Oldwood Rd NTHM/RTH M23 179 H1
Old Wool La CHD/CHDH SK8 170 C5
Old York St HULME M15 127 H2
Olebrook Cl WGTN/LGST M12 129 E2
Oleo Ter IRL M44 122 D5
Olga St BOL BL1 33 G4
Olga Ter BKLY M9 * 88 A5
Olivant St BURY BL9 53 F1
Olive Bank TOT/BURYW BL8 37 G2
Oliver Cl LIT OL15 20 C3
Olive Rd HALE/TIMP WA15 166 B1
Oliver St EDGY/DAV SK3 13 G6
OP/CLY M11 * 116 A5
Olive Shapley Av
DID/WITH M20 157 G3
Olive St BOLS/LL BL3 48 C5
FAIL M35 104 D2
HEY OL10 41 F4
RAD M26 68 D1
ROCH OL11 * 42 B5
TOT/BURYW BL8 4 A4
Olivia Gv RUSH/FAL M14 129 E5
Ollerbarrow Rd
HALE/TIMP WA15 177 H2
Ollerbrook Ct BOL BL1 34 A4
Ollerton WHIT OL12 10 B5
Ollerton Av SALE M33 153 G1
Ollerton Dr FAIL M35 105 E1
Ollerton Rd WILM/AE SK9 192 A2
Ollerton St BOL BL1 23 E5
Ollier Av WGTN/LGST M12 144 A1
Olney ROCH OL11 * 29 H5
Olney Av WYTH/NTH M22 168 C3
Olney St BRUN/LGST M13 129 E4
Olsberg Cl RAD M26 52 D5
Olwen Crs RDSH SK5 145 F3
Olympic Ct SALQ M50 113 E5
Omer Av BRUN/LGST M13 143 H1
Omer Dr BNG/LEV M19 143 G4
Onchan Av OLDE OL4 92 A1
One Ash Cl WHIT OL12 10 C1
Onslow Av NEWH/MOS M40 104 D1
Onslow Cl OLD OL1 8 E1
Onslow Rd EDGY/DAV SK3 12 A6
Onslow St ROCH OL11 42 B2
Onward St HYDE SK14 147 H1
Oozewood Rd MDTN M24 58 B4
Opal Ct RUSH/FAL M14 * 143 F3
Opal St BNG/LEV M19 144 B3
Openshaw Fold Rd BURY BL9 53 E2
Openshaw La IRL M44 136 A5
Openshaw Pl FWTH BL4 65 G4
Openshaw St BURY BL9 5 G6
Orama Av SLFD M6 111 H1
Orama Ml WHIT OL12 * 14 B5
Oram St BURY BL9 38 D2
Orange Hill Rd PWCH M25 86 B2
Orange St SLFD M6 113 F2
Orbital Wy DTN/ASHW M34 132 A5
Orchard Av BOL BL1 34 A3
GTN M18 130 D4
PART M31 151 E2
WALK M28 96 C3
Orchard Cl CHD/CHDH SK8 183 F5
POY/DIS SK12 195 F4
WILM/AE SK9 198 C5
Orchard Ct OFTN SK2 * 173 E3
Orchard Dr HALE/TIMP WA15 178 B1
WILM/AE SK9 192 B5
Orchard Gdns BOLE BL2 35 G3
Orchard Gn WILM/AE SK9 201 E4
Orchard Gv DID/WITH M20 157 E1
ROY/SHW OL2 59 H2
Orchard Pl HALE/TIMP WA15 166 C2
POY/DIS SK12 * 195 E3
SALE M33 154 C1
Orchard Ri HYDE SK14 148 B3
Orchard Rd FAIL M35 105 E3
HALE/TIMP WA15 165 H4
MPL/ROM SK6 163 G4
Orchard Rd East
WYTH/NTH M22 156 C4
Orchard Rd West
WYTH/NTH M22 156 C4
Orchard St DID/WITH M20 157 E1
HEY OL10 41 F3
HYDE SK14 148 A1
SLFD M6 113 F1
STKP SK1 13 H3
Orchard V EDGY/DAV SK3 171 F3
Orchid Av FWTH BL4 65 G3
Orchid Cl IRL M44 136 A3
OLD OL1 75 E3
Orchid Dr BURY BL9 53 H2
Orchid Gdns CHD/CHDH SK8 169 E3
Orchid St BKLY M9 103 E3
Ordsall Av LHULT M38 81 G3
Ordsall Dr ORD M5 127 E1
Ordsall La ORD M5 114 A5
ORD M5 126 D2
Oregon Av OLD OL1 75 F3
Oregon Cl BRUN/LGST M13 128 D2
Orford Cl MPL/ROM SK6 186 B5
Orford Rd NEWH/MOS M40 104 B5
PWCH M25 85 H2
Oriel Av OLDS OL8 91 F4
Oriel Cl CHAD OL9 90 B3
OFTN SK2 172 C3
Oriel Rd DID/WITH M20 157 F2
Oriel St BOLS/LL BL3 48 B4
ROCH OL11 43 E1
Orient Rd SLFD M6 111 H1
Orient St BRO M7 102 A3
Oriole Cl WALK M28 96 C3
Oriole Dr WALK M28 96 C2
Orion Pl BRO M7 * 113 H1
Orkney Cl NTHM/RTH M23 167 H5
RAD M26 52 C5
Orkney Dr URM M41 124 C3
Orlanda Av SLFD M6 111 H1
Orlanda Dr BRO M7 102 A4
Orlando St BOLE BL2 49 F4
Orleans Wy OLD OL1 9 F2
Orley Wk OLD OL1 60 C5
Orme Av MDTN M24 72 D5
SLFD M6 112 A1
Orme Cl OP/CLY M11 115 H4
URM M41 139 F1
Ormerod Av ROY/SHW OL2 75 F1
Ormerod Cl MPL/ROM SK6 161 G5
Ormerod St HEY OL10 41 F5
Orme St OLDE OL4 9 J6
STKP SK1 * 160 C4
WILM/AE SK9 200 D4
Ormonde Av SLFD M6 112 A1
Ormonde Ct AUL OL6 119 H1
Ormond St BOLS/LL BL3 50 A4
BURY BL9 5 G3
Ormrod St BOLE BL2 34 D1
BOLS/LL BL3 2 D6
BURY BL9 5 H5
FWTH BL4 65 H4
Ormsby Av GTN M18 130 A4
Ormsby Cl EDGY/DAV SK3 171 H5
Ormsgill Cl HULME M15 128 A2
Orms Gill Pl OFTN SK2 * 173 F3
Ormsgill St HULME M15 128 A2
Ormskirk Av DID/WITH M20 142 B5
Ormskirk Cl TOT/BURYW BL8 52 A1
Ormskirk Rd RDSH SK5 145 F5
Ornatus St BOL BL1 * 34 A1
Orphanage St HTNM SK4 159 H3
Orpington Dr TOT/BURYW BL8 37 G5
Orpington Rd BKLY M9 103 F3
Orrell St OP/CLY M11 * 117 E5
TOT/BURYW BL8 4 A3
Orrel St SLFD M6 112 D3
Orrishmere Rd CHD/CHDH SK8 182 C1
Orron St LIT OL15 20 D3
Orsett Cl NEWH/MOS M40 115 F2
Orthes Gv HTNM SK4 159 G1
Orton Av NTHM/RTH M23 155 H5
Orton Rd NTHM/RTH M23 155 H5
Orvietto Av SLFD M6 111 H1
Orville Dr BNG/LEV M19 143 H4
Orwell Av DTN/ASHW M34 131 F5
WYTH/NTH M22 168 C3
Orwell Cl TOT/BURYW BL8 4 B2
WILM/AE SK9 192 A5
Orwell Rd BOL BL1 33 E4
Osborne Cl TOT/BURYW BL8 52 C1
Osborne Dr SWIN M27 99 H3
Osborne Gv BOL BL1 33 F5
CHD/CHDH SK8 181 F1
Osborne Rd BKLY M9 * 103 F3
BNG/LEV M19 143 H2
DTN/ASHW M34 132 C4
HALE/TIMP WA15 165 H4
HYDE SK14 148 A2
OFTN SK2 172 A2
OLDS OL8 8 C7
SLFD M6 * 111 H2
Osborne St CHAD OL9 8 B1
HEY OL10 41 E5
MPL/ROM SK6 160 D3
NEWH/MOS M40 115 F1
ROCH OL11 42 D1
ROY/SHW OL2 60 A3
SLFD M6 113 E2
Osborne Ter SALE M33 154 C2
Osbourne Cl FWTH BL4 66 A3
WILM/AE SK9 199 G4
Osbourne Pl ALT WA14 165 G5
Osbourne St DID/WITH M20 157 F3
Oscar St BOL BL1 * 33 F4
NEWH/MOS M40 103 H3
Oscott Av LHULT M38 81 F2
Oscroft Cl CHH M8 102 A4
Osmond St OLDE OL4 76 B5
Osmund Av BOLE BL2 50 A2
Osprey Cl DUK SK16 133 H1
HULME M15 127 H3
Osprey Dr DROY M43 118 B2
IRL M44 122 B5
WILM/AE SK9 199 F2
Osprey Wk BRUN/LGST M13 * 128 D2
Ossory St RUSH/FAL M14 128 C5
Osterley Rd BKLY M9 88 D4
Ostlers Ga DROY M43 118 C3
Ostrich La PWCH M25 86 B4
Oswald Cl SLFD M6 100 D5
Oswald La CCHDY M21 141 F2
Oswald Rd CCHDY M21 141 F1
Oswald St ANC M4 7 F1
BOLS/LL BL3 48 B5
CHAD OL9 75 E4
MILN OL16 11 F4
RDSH SK5 145 E5
ROY/SHW OL2 60 B1
Oswestry Cl TOT/BURYW BL8 25 H3
Otago Rd OLDE OL4 76 B3
Otago St OLDE OL4 * 76 B3
Othello Dr ECC M30 111 E3
Otley Av SLFD M6 112 B2
Otley Cl CHAD OL9 90 C1
Otley Gv EDGY/DAV SK3 171 G5
Otmoor Wy ROY/SHW OL2 59 H5
Otranto Av SLFD M6 112 A1
Ottawa Cl NTHM/RTH M23 167 G5
Ott Cl HULME M15 128 A2
Otterburn Pl OFTN SK2 173 E3
Otterbury Cl TOT/BURYW BL8 37 E4
Otter Dr BURY BL9 54 A5
CHH M8 101 H5
Otterspool Rd MPL/ROM SK6 162 A5
Oulder Hl ROCH OL11 28 D4
Oulder Hill Dr ROCH OL11 29 E4
Oulder Mt ROCH OL11 * 29 E4
Ouldfield Cl MILN OL16 * 30 C5
Oulton Av SALE M33 155 F1
Oulton St BOL BL1 34 B1
Oulton Wk NEWH/MOS M40 115 G3
Oundle Cl RUSH/FAL M14 128 D5
Ouse St SALQ M50 112 B4
Outram Cl MPL/ROM SK6 * 175 E5
Outram Rd DUK SK16 133 E2
Outram Sq DROY M43 * 117 H5
Outrington Dr OP/CLY M11 116 B5
Outwood Av SWIN M27 83 G3
Outwood Dr CHD/CHDH SK8 181 F4
Outwood Gv BOL BL1 33 H1
Outwood La MANAIR M90 180 B4
Outwood La West
MANAIR M90 180 A4
Outwood Rd CHD/CHDH SK8 181 G4
RAD M26 68 B3
Oval Dr DUK SK16 133 E1
The Oval CHD/CHDH SK8 181 G4
Overbridge Rd BRO M7 114 B1
Overbrook Av
NEWH/MOS M40 103 E5
Overbrook Dr PWCH M25 86 A4
Overdale SWIN M27 99 F4
Overdale Cl OLD OL1 75 F3
Overdale Crs URM M41 137 H1
Overdale Dr BOL BL1 47 H2
Overdale Rd MPL/ROM SK6 161 H5
WYTH/NTH M22 168 C4
Overdell Dr WHIT OL12 18 B5
Overdene Cl HOR/BR BL6 46 C3
Overens St OLDE OL4 76 A5
Overfield Wy WHIT OL12 30 A1
Overgreen BOLE BL2 35 F3
Overhill Dr WILM/AE SK9 199 H3
Overhill La WILM/AE SK9 199 H3
Overhill Rd CHAD OL9 74 A4
WILM/AE SK9 199 G3
Overlea Dr BNG/LEV M19 158 B1
Overlinks Dr SLFD M6 99 G5
Overstone Dr CHH M8 102 A3
Overton Av WYTH/NTH M22 168 C4
Overton Cl RAD M26 68 C3
Overton Crs BRAM/HZG SK7 173 F5
SALE M33 153 G4
Overton Rd WYTH/NTH M22 168 C4
Overt St ROCH OL11 43 E1
Overwood Rd
WYTH/NTH M22 168 C1
Owenington Gv LHULT M38 81 F2
Owens Cl CHAD OL9 73 H4
Owens Farm Dr OFTN SK2 173 F2
Owens Pk RUSH/FAL M14 * 143 F2
Owen St ECC M30 110 C4
EDGY/DAV SK3 12 D4
OLD OL1 76 D1
SLFD M6 100 D5
Owlerbarrow Rd
TOT/BURYW BL8 37 F3
Owler La CHAD OL9 89 G4
Owlwood Cl LHULT M38 80 D4
Owlwood Dr LHULT M38 80 D4
Oxbridge Cl SALE M33 153 G3
Oxbrow Wy WHTF M45 69 H4
Oxendale Dr MDTN M24 71 H3
Oxenhurst Gn OFTN SK2 173 F4
Oxford Av DROY M43 117 G2
ROCH OL11 28 D5
SALE M33 153 G2
WHTF M45 69 H4
Oxford Cl FWTH BL4 65 E4
Oxford Ct CMANW M2 * 6 E7
OLDTF/WHR M16 * 127 G3
Oxford Dr MDTN M24 73 F2
MPL/ROM SK6 162 B2
Oxford Gv BOL BL1 2 A2
Oxford Ml AULW OL7 * 119 E5
Oxford Pl MILN OL16 43 F1
RUSH/FAL M14 128 D4
Oxford Rd ALT WA14 177 G1
BOLS/LL BL3 66 C1
BRUN/LGST M13 128 C3
DUK SK16 120 A5
HOR/BR BL6 46 A1
SLFD M6 111 H1
Oxford St BOL BL1 2 E5
BURY BL9 5 G6
CHAD OL9 8 A7
CMANE M1 6 E6
ECC M30 111 F4
ROY/SHW OL2 60 A2
STLY SK15 121 F4
STLY SK15 121 G1
Oxford St East AULW OL7 119 E5
Oxford St West AULW OL7 119 E5
Oxford Wy HTNM SK4 159 G3
WHIT OL12 29 H1
Ox Ga BOLE BL2 35 E1
Ox Hey Cl RAMS BL0 16 D1
Ox Hey La HOR/BR BL6 46 A2
Oxney Rd RUSH/FAL M14 128 D4
Ox St RAMS BL0 16 C3
Oxton Av WYTH/NTH M22 168 B5
Oxton St OP/CLY M11 131 E1

P

Pacific Rd ALT WA14 164 D3
Pacific Wy SALQ M50 112 B5
Packer St BOL BL1 33 F4
MILN OL16 10 C6
Packwood Cha CHAD OL9 74 A4
Padbury Cl URM M41 123 E5
Padbury Wy BOLE BL2 35 F4
Padden Brook MPL/ROM SK6 162 A4
Paddington Av
NEWH/MOS M40 * 104 A5
Paddington Cl SLFD M6 113 F3
Paddison St SWIN M27 98 D3
Paddock Cha POY/DIS SK12 195 G1
Paddock La FAIL M35 105 E5
Paddock Rd HYDE SK14 * 147 H3
The Paddocks EDGY/DAV SK3 172 B4
Paddock St WGTN/LGST M12 128 D1
The Paddock BRAM/HZG SK7 183 G3
CHD/CHDH SK8 170 B4
HALE/TIMP WA15 166 C5
RAMS BL0 16 C1
UPML OL3 94 C3
WALK M28 97 F3
Paderborn Ct BOL BL1 2 C6
Padiham Cl BURY BL9 53 E2
Padstow Cl HYDE SK14 135 E5
Padstow Dr BRAM/HZG SK7 184 A5
Padstow St
NEWH/MOS M40 * 115 H2
Padstow Wk HYDE SK14 135 E5
Pagan St MILN OL16 10 D5
Paget St NEWH/MOS M40 103 E5
Pagnall Ct CHAD OL9 * 90 C2
Paignton Av BNG/LEV M19 143 H3
HYDE SK14 149 E1
Paignton Dr SALE M33 153 G1
Paignton Gv RDSH SK5 145 E4
Pailin Dr DROY M43 118 B3
Pailton Cl HOR/BR BL6 47 E3
Painswick Rd WYTH/NTH M22 180 A3
Paisley Pk FWTH BL4 66 A3
Paiton St BOL BL1 48 B2
Palace Gdns ROY/SHW OL2 75 E2
Palace Rd AUL OL6 107 H5
SALE M33 154 B1
Palace St BOL BL1 2 E3
BURY BL9 5 H5
CHAD OL9 8 B3
Palatine Av DID/WITH M20 142 D5
Palatine Cl IRL M44 136 B2
Palatine Crs DID/WITH M20 157 G1
Palatine Dr BURY BL9 27 G3
Palatine Rd DID/WITH M20 157 E3
ROCH OL11 28 D3
WYTH/NTH M22 156 D4
Palatine St BOL BL1 2 E4
DTN/ASHW M34 132 B3
MILN OL16 11 J7
RAMS BL0 16 D2
Paley St BOL BL1 3 F4
Palfrey Pl WGTN/LGST M12 128 D1
Palgrave Av NEWH/MOS M40 103 E5
Pall Ml CMANW M2 6 E5
Palma Av HALE/TIMP WA15 179 H4
Palm Cl SALE M33 153 F1
Palmer Av CHD/CHDH SK8 170 C3
Palmer Cl OLDS OL8 91 G3
Palmerston Av
OLDTF/WHR M16 141 H1
Palmerston Cl
DTN/ASHW M34 131 G5
RAMS BL0 16 C5
Palmerston Rd
DTN/ASHW M34 131 G5
OFTN SK2 184 C1
Palmerston St
WGTN/LGST M12 115 G5
Palmer St BRO M7 101 F5
DUK SK16 119 G4
SALE M33 154 B2
Palm Gv CHAD OL9 74 C4
Palm St BOL BL1 34 A3
BRUN/LGST M13 129 G5
DROY M43 117 E3
OLDE OL4 76 B4
Pandora St DID/WITH M20 157 F1
Panfield Rd WYTH/NTH M22 168 B5
Pangbourne Av URM M41 124 D5
Pangbourne Cl
EDGY/DAV SK3 171 F3
Pankhurst Wk
RUSH/FAL M14 128 C5
Panmure St OLDS OL8 91 G3
Pansy Rd FWTH BL4 65 F4
Paper Mill Rd EDGW/EG BL7 23 E4
Paprika Cl OP/CLY M11 130 C1
Parade Rd MANAIR M90 180 B5
Paradise St DTN/ASHW M34 132 C1
RAMS BL0 16 D2
Paramel Av BOLS/LL BL3 51 E4
Parbold Av DID/WITH M20 142 C4
Pargate Cha ROCH OL11 28 D3
Paris Av ORD M5 127 E1
Parish Vw ORD M5 113 G5
Paris St BOLS/LL BL3 48 A5
Park 66 BURY BL9 * 54 A3
Park Av ALT WA14 165 H1
BNG/LEV M19 143 H2
BOL BL1 * 33 H2
BRAM/HZG SK7 193 F2
BRO M7 102 A2
CHAD OL9 74 C3
CHD/CHDH SK8 182 C3
EDGY/DAV SK3 170 C2
FAIL M35 104 C2
HALE/TIMP WA15 178 A3
HYDE SK14 133 G4
MPL/ROM SK6 162 B4
OLDTF/WHR M16 127 F3
POY/DIS SK12 195 F3
PWCH M25 86 A3
RAD M26 53 E5
RAMS BL0 17 E2
SALE M33 139 G5
URM M41 138 C1
WHTF M45 85 E1
WILM/AE SK9 199 F2
Park Bridge Rd AULW OL7 106 D3
Parkbrook Rd
NTHM/RTH M23 168 A2
Park Brow Cl CCHDY M21 141 G4
Park Cl ALT WA14 166 A1
STLY SK15 120 C2
WHTF M45 85 G1
Park Cottages BOL BL1 * 33 F3
ROY/SHW OL2 59 G1
Park Court Ms
CHD/CHDH SK8 * 170 B5
Park Crs AUL OL6 120 B3
CHAD OL9 74 A3
RUSH/FAL M14 128 D5
WILM/AE SK9 199 E1
Parkdale CHAD OL9 74 C3
Parkdale Av DTN/ASHW M34 132 A1
GTN M18 130 B3
Parkdale Rd BOLE BL2 34 D5
Parkdene Cl BOLE BL2 35 E2
Park Dr ECC M30 111 E1
HALE/TIMP WA15 166 B2
HALE/TIMP WA15 178 A3
HTNM SK4 159 E4
HYDE SK14 133 G4
OLDTF/WHR M16 141 G1
WILM/AE SK9 199 E1
Park Edge WHTN BL5 62 B5
Parkend Rd NTHM/RTH M23 167 H4
Parker St BURY BL9 5 G5
CMANE M1 7 G5
Parkfield CHAD OL9 74 B3
DROY M43 117 H3
ECC M30 * 122 D4
ORD M5 112 C3
Parkfield Av FWTH BL4 65 H5
MPL/ROM SK6 175 E3
OLDS OL8 90 C5
PWCH M25 86 C4
RUSH/FAL M14 128 C5
URM M41 138 B2
Parkfield Dr MDTN M24 72 B4
Parkfield Rd ALT WA14 165 F5
BOLS/LL BL3 65 E1
CHD/CHDH SK8 182 C3
OLDE OL4 94 B1
Parkfield Rd North
NEWH/MOS M40 89 H5
Parkfield Rd South
DID/WITH M20 157 F2
Parkfields STLY SK15 121 G2
Parkfield St MILN OL16 43 G4
RUSH/FAL M14 128 C5
Parkgate CHAD OL9 74 C3
TOT/BURYW BL8 36 D1
Park Gate Av DID/WITH M20 142 D5
Park Gate Cl MPL/ROM SK6 161 F1
Parkgate Dr BOL BL1 34 A1
OFTN SK2 172 C5
SWIN M27 99 G3
Parkgate Rd ALT WA14 165 F1
Park Gates Av CHD/CHDH SK8 183 F3
Park Gates Dr CHD/CHDH SK8 183 F3
Park Gv BNG/LEV M19 144 A1
HTNM SK4 159 E2
RAD M26 52 A5
WALK M28 97 E2
Park Hl PWCH M25 * 86 C5
Parkhill Av CHH M8 87 G5
Park Hill Dr WHTF M45 69 F4
Park Hill Rd HALE/TIMP WA15 178 B3
Parkhills Cl BURY BL9 53 G1
Parkhills Rd BURY BL9 5 F7
BURY BL9 53 F1
Park Hill St BOL BL1 2 A3
Park House Bridge Est
SLFD M6 * 100 C3
Park House Bridge Rd
SLFD M6 100 C4
Parkhouse St OP/CLY M11 116 D5
Parkhurst Av
NEWH/MOS M40 104 D1
Parkin Cl DUK SK16 119 H5
Parkinson St BOLS/LL BL3 48 B4
BURY BL9 38 C1
Parkin St WGTN/LGST M12 129 H5
Parklake Av BRO M7 101 H2
Parklands ROY/SHW OL2 58 D3
ROY/SHW OL2 60 C1
WHTF M45 69 F4
Parklands Dr SALE M33 153 G4
Parklands Rd NTHM/RTH M23 167 G2
The Parklands HTNM SK4 159 H2
RAD M26 67 E4
Parklands Wy POY/DIS SK12 195 F3
Park La BRO M7 101 G2
DUK SK16 119 H5
HALE/TIMP WA15 178 B3
OLDS OL8 91 G5
POY/DIS SK12 195 F3
ROY/SHW OL2 59 F4
SLFD M6 99 H5
STKP SK1 172 C1
UPML OL3 95 F2
WHIT OL12 10 C5
WHTF M45 69 F5
Park Lane Ct WHTF M45 * 69 E5
Park La West SWIN M27 100 A3
Parkleigh Dr NEWH/MOS M40 89 H5
Park Ldg BNG/LEV M19 144 A2
Park Lodge Cl CHD/CHDH SK8 170 B5
Park Meadow WHTN BL5 62 B4
Park Ms OLDTF/WHR M16 141 G1
Parkmount Rd BKLY M9 103 F1
Park Pde AUL OL6 119 F3
ROY/SHW OL2 45 F5
Park Pl ANC M4 114 D2
HTNM SK4 158 C4
PWCH M25 86 B2
SLFD M6 111 H2
Park Range RUSH/FAL M14 129 E5
Park Ri MPL/ROM SK6 162 B3
Park Rd ALT WA14 176 D2
BOL BL1 2 A5
BOLS/LL BL3 50 C5
BURY BL9 4 D1
CHD/CHDH SK8 169 E3
CHD/CHDH SK8 170 B3
CHD/CHDH SK8 183 F3
DTN/ASHW M34 118 C5
DTN/ASHW M34 132 B5
DUK SK16 120 A4
ECC M30 111 E1
HALE/TIMP WA15 166 A1
HALE/TIMP WA15 178 A3
HTNM SK4 159 E1
HYDE SK14 133 G4
MDTN M24 72 C4
MPL/ROM SK6 162 B3
OLDS OL8 9 G6
PART M31 151 F3

POY/DIS SK12 197 E1
PWCH M25 86 C4
RAMS BL0 16 A5
SALE M33 139 G5
SLFD M6 111 H1
STRET M32 140 A1
WALK M28 96 D1
WHIT OL12 11 F2
WHTN BL5 62 A4
WHTN BL5 62 C3
WILM/AE SK9 198 C3
Park Rd North URM M41 124 B5
Park Rd South URM M41 138 C1
Park Rw BOL BL1 23 E5
HTNM SK4 158 C5
Park Seventeen WHTF M45 69 G4
Parkside MDTN M24 88 B1
Park Side Av ROY/SHW OL2 60 B1
Parkside Av BRO M7 101 H2
ECC M30 110 D4
FAIL M35 104 D5
WALK M28 97 E1
Parkside Cl MPL/ROM SK6 186 C4
RAD M26 53 F5
RAD M26 68 C1
Parkside La MPL/ROM SK6 175 H3
Parkside Ms WHTF M45 69 G3
Parkside Rd RUSH/FAL M14 142 B1
SALE M33 155 E3
Parkside St BOLE BL2 * 34 D5
Parkside Wk BRAM/HZG SK7 183 H1
BURY BL9 4 E7
Parks Nook FWTH BL4 65 H5
Park Sq AUL OL6 120 B1
OLDTF/WHR M16 141 E1
Parkstead Dr BKLY M9 103 E4
Parkstone Av GTN M18 131 E2
WHTF M45 85 E1
Parkstone Cl TOT/BURYW BL8 37 E4
Parkstone Dr SWIN M27 99 G4
Parkstone La WALK M28 110 A1
Parkstone Rd IRL M44 122 B5
Park St AUL OL6 119 G3
BOL BL1 2 A3
BRO M7 101 F2
CSLFD M3 114 A4
CSLFD M3 114 C2
DROY M43 118 B3
DTN/ASHW M34 132 A5
FWTH BL4 66 A3
HEY OL10 56 B1
MILN OL16 30 A5
MOSL OL5 108 D2
MPL/ROM SK6 161 G3
OLDS OL8 8 E6
PWCH M25 86 B3
RAD M26 52 D5
ROY/SHW OL2 59 F5
ROY/SHW OL2 60 A3
STKP SK1 13 G2
STLY SK15 121 E4
SWIN M27 99 F3
Parksway BKLY M9 87 G1
PWCH M25 86 B5
SWIN M27 99 H4
Parks Yd BURY BL9 4 D4
Park Ter HEY OL10 41 E3
MOSL OL5 * 108 D2
The Park OLDE OL4 94 A2
UPML OL3 95 F2
Park Vw BKLY M9 102 D4
CHAD OL9 74 B3
DTN/ASHW M34 * 118 C5
EDGY/DAV SK3 170 C2
FWTH BL4 66 A3
FWTH BL4 66 C5
LIT OL15 21 E2
RUSH/FAL M14 * 143 G4
STKP SK1 172 C2
Park View Ct PWCH M25 * 86 A4
Park View Rd BOLS/LL BL3 * 48 B5
PWCH M25 86 A4
Parkville Rd DID/WITH M20 157 H1
WHTF M45 70 B5
Park Wy STRET M32 125 E4
Parkway BRAM/HZG SK7 183 H2
CHAD OL9 74 B3
DTN/ASHW M34 131 H5
EDGY/DAV SK3 170 C2
LHULT M38 80 D4
ROCH OL11 29 E3
WILM/AE SK9 199 E4
Parkway Gv LHULT M38 80 D3
Parkwood Dr WHTN BL5 63 G5
Parkwood Rd
NTHM/RTH M23 168 B2
Parliament Pl BURY BL9 4 C7
Parliament St BURY BL9 4 D7
Parndon Dr OFTN SK2 172 D2
Parnell Av WYTH/NTH M22 168 C1
Parnham Cl RAD M26 51 E4
Parrbrook Cl BURY BL9 69 H3
Parr Cl FWTH BL4 65 G4
Parrenthorn Rd PWCH M25 70 B5
Parrfield Rd WALK M28 97 H3
Parr Fold BURY BL9 70 A2
Parr Fold Av WALK M28 96 D1
Parrin La ECC M30 110 D2
Parr La BURY BL9 69 H3
Parrot St BOLS/LL BL3 48 D4
OP/CLY M11 116 D4
Parrs Mount Ms HTNM SK4 158 C4
Parr St ECC M30 111 E4
OP/CLY M11 * 130 D1
Parrs Wood Av
DID/WITH M20 157 H5
Parrs Wood La
DID/WITH M20 158 A5
Parrs Wood Rd
DID/WITH M20 157 H5
Parry Md MPL/ROM SK6 161 H2
Parry Rd WGTN/LGST M12 129 H4
Parslow Av CHH M8 102 B2
Parsonage Cl BURY BL9 5 H4
ORD M5 113 H5
Parsonage Dr WALK M28 81 H5
Parsonage Gdns CSLFD M3 * 6 D4
MPL/ROM SK6 175 F5
Parsonage La
CSLFD M3 * 6 D3
Parsonage Rd DID/WITH M20 143 E4
HTNM SK4 159 E2
RAD M26 * 67 F5
URM M41 137 G2
WALK M28 81 H5
Parsonage St BURY BL9 5 H4
CHH M8 102 A1
HTNM SK4 12 E2
HULME M15 127 H3
HYDE SK14 * 147 H1
Parsonage Wk MILN OL16 * 31 G4
Parsonage Wy
CHD/CHDH SK8 170 D4
Parsons Dr MDTN M24 72 C2
Parsons Fld SLFD M6 * 100 D5
Parson's La BURY BL9 4 E3
Parsons Wy BKLY M9 103 F3
Parth St BURY BL9 39 G5
Partington Ct FWTH BL4 65 H3
Partington La SWIN M27 98 D3
Partington Pk ROCH OL11 57 F1
Partington Pl SALE M33 154 C1
Partington St BOLS/LL BL3 64 B2
ECC M30 111 E2
FAIL M35 105 E3
HEY OL10 40 B4
NEWH/MOS M40 103 G5
OLD OL1 * 9 J3
ROCH OL11 42 A4
WALK M28 98 B2
Partridge Av NTHM/RTH M23 168 A3
Partridge Cl ROCH OL11 28 C4
Partridge Ct OFTN SK2 * 172 C5
Partridge Ri DROY M43 118 C2
Partridge Rd FAIL M35 105 H4
Partridge St STRET M32 126 C3
Partridge Wy CHAD OL9 73 G4
Parvet Av DROY M43 117 G2
Pascal St BNG/LEV M19 144 A3
Passmonds Crs ROCH OL11 29 E3
Passmonds Wy ROCH OL11 29 E3
Pass St CHAD OL9 8 C5
The Pass MILN OL16 11 F5
Paston Rd WYTH/NTH M22 168 C2
Pasture Cl HEY OL10 40 C5
Pasturefield Cl SALE M33 155 G3
Pasture Field Rd
WYTH/NTH M22 181 E3
Pasturegreen Wy IRL M44 122 C5
Pastures La OLDE OL4 77 G4
Patch Croft Rd
WYTH/NTH M22 181 E3
Patchett St WGTN/LGST M12 129 G2
Patch La BRAM/HZG SK7 193 H2
Patey St WGTN/LGST M12 129 H5
Patience St WHIT OL12 29 F2
Patmos St RAMS BL0 17 E2
Paton Av BOLS/LL BL3 65 F1
Paton Ct BRO M7 113 H1
Paton St CMANE M1 7 H5
WHIT OL12 18 C5
Patricia Dr WALK M28 82 B5
Patten St DID/WITH M20 142 D5
Patterdale Av AULW OL7 106 C5
URM M41 124 A4
Patterdale Cl OLD OL1 75 H3
ROCH OL11 42 A3
Patterdale Dr BURY BL9 53 F2
MDTN M24 72 B2
Patterdale Rd AULW OL7 106 C5
BOLE BL2 35 F2
MPL/ROM SK6 162 A2
PART M31 150 D3
STKP SK1 172 C3
WYTH/NTH M22 168 D1
Patterson Av CCHDY M21 141 E2
Patterson St BOLS/LL BL3 47 H5
DTN/ASHW M34 132 C4
Patting Cl IRL M44 122 D5
Pattishall Cl ANC M4 115 G4
Pattison Cl WHIT OL12 18 B5
Patton Cl BURY BL9 70 A2
Paulden Av NTHM/RTH M23 168 A3
OLDE OL4 76 D3
Paulden Dr FAIL M35 105 F3
Paulette St BOL BL1 33 H4
Paulhan Rd DID/WITH M20 158 A2
Paulhan St BOLS/LL BL3 64 D1
Pavilion Cl WHIT OL12 30 A1
Pavilion Dr AUL OL6 107 G5
The Pavilions CHD/CHDH SK8 170 A5
Pavilion Wk RAD M26 52 A5
Paxford Pl WILM/AE SK9 198 D5
Paythorne Gn OFTN SK2 173 F4
Peabody St BOLS/LL BL3 48 D5
Peacefield MPL/ROM SK6 174 D4
Peace St BOLS/LL BL3 48 C4
FAIL M35 * 105 F1
Peaceville Rd BNG/LEV M19 143 H2
Peach Bank MDTN M24 72 D4
Peach Rd OLDE OL4 76 C4
Peach St PWCH M25 86 B2
Peach Tree Cl BRO M7 * 102 A4
Peach Tree Ct SLFD M6 * 113 F3
Peacock Av SLFD M6 100 B5
Peacock Cl GTN M18 130 B2
Peacock Dr CHD/CHDH SK8 191 G1
Peacock Gv GTN M18 130 C4
Peak Bank MPL/ROM SK6 161 H4
Peak Cl OLDE OL4 61 E5
Peakdale Av CHD/CHDH SK8 181 F3
Peakdale Rd DROY M43 117 F2
MPL/ROM SK6 175 F5
Peaknaze Cl SWIN M27 99 G2
Peak St BOL BL1 33 G4
CHAD OL9 8 A5
CMANE M1 7 J5
STKP SK1 13 J3
Pear Av BURY BL9 39 F3
Pear Cl MDTN M24 89 E1
Peardale Cl ECC M30 110 D5
Pearl Av BRO M7 101 H1
Pearl Mill Cl OLDS OL8 92 A3
Pearl St BRAM/HZG SK7 173 F5
DTN/ASHW M34 132 B5
ROCH OL11 29 F3
Pearly Bank OLD OL1 60 C5
Pearn Rd BNG/LEV M19 158 C1
Pearson Cl MILN OL16 31 G4
PART M31 151 F3
Pearson Gv OLDE OL4 92 D1
Pearson St BURY BL9 5 J2
DUK SK16 133 F2
MILN OL16 11 K4
RDSH SK5 160 A3
Peart Av MPL/ROM SK6 147 G5
Pear Tree Cl MPL/ROM SK6 175 G1
SLFD M6 113 F3
Pear Tree Ct SLFD M6 113 F3
Pear Tree Dr FWTH BL4 65 F5
STLY SK15 121 E3
Peart St DTN/ASHW M34 132 B5
Peary St ANC M4 115 E2
Peaslake Cl MPL/ROM SK6 162 C4
Peatfield Av SWIN M27 83 G5
Peatfield Wk HULME M15 * 128 A3
Pebble Cl STLY SK15 120 D1
Pebworth Cl MDTN M24 88 C2
Peckford Dr NEWH/MOS M40 103 H5
Peckforton Cl CHD/CHDH SK8 169 F4
Peckmill Cl WILM/AE SK9 192 B5
Pedder St BOL BL1 33 F5
Pedler Brow La WHIT OL12 20 B2
Pedley Wk BRUN/LGST M13 * 128 C1
Peebles Dr NEWH/MOS M40 117 E1
Peel Av ALT WA14 177 G2
Peel Brow RAMS BL0 17 E2
Peel Cir URM M41 124 D2
Peel Cross Rd ORD M5 113 F4
Peel Dr LHULT M38 81 E3
SALE M33 155 F2
Peelgate Dr CHD/CHDH SK8 181 F2
Peel Green Rd ECC M30 110 D5
Peel Gv WALK M28 97 F2
WGTN/LGST M12 129 H4
Peel Hall Rd RAMS BL0 26 C1
WYTH/NTH M22 181 E1
Peel La CHH M8 114 D1
HEY OL10 40 C3
LHULT M38 81 E3
Peel Moat Rd HTNM SK4 159 E1
Peel Mt RAMS BL0 16 B4
SLFD M6 113 G2
Peel Park Crs LHULT M38 81 E3
Peel Rd HALE/TIMP WA15 177 H1
Peels Av OLDE OL4 77 F5
Peel St AUL OL6 119 G2
CHAD OL9 74 C5
DROY M43 117 G5
DTN/ASHW M34 132 B2
DTN/ASHW M34 132 B4
DUK SK16 119 H4
ECC M30 111 G3
FAIL M35 104 C4
FWTH BL4 66 B4
HEY OL10 40 C4
HYDE SK14 148 B2
LIT OL15 21 E3
OFTN SK2 172 A3
RAD M26 68 C2
STLY SK15 120 C4
WHIT OL12 10 A4
Peel Vw TOT/BURYW BL8 26 B5
Peel Wk BURY BL9 27 F3
TOT/BURYW BL8 4 C1
TOT/BURYW BL8 16 A3
Peel Wy BURY BL9 4 D4
Peelwood Av LHULT M38 81 F3
Peers Cl URM M41 123 E4
Peers St TOT/BURYW BL8 37 H4
Pegamoid St BOLE BL2 34 C5
Pegasus Ct ROCH OL11 * 29 F5
Pegasus Sq BRO M7 113 H2
Pegwell Dr BRO M7 101 H5
Pekin St AUL OL6 119 H1
Pelham Pl CHH M8 87 G5
Pelham St AULW OL7 118 D5
BOLS/LL BL3 64 B1
OLDS OL8 91 G5
Pellowe Rd OLDS OL8 91 F4
Pelton Av SWIN M27 83 G5
Pemberton St BOL BL1 * 33 H2
LHULT M38 81 G3
ROCH OL11 42 B4
Pemberton Wy ROY/SHW OL2 60 A1
Pembridge Fold MDTN M24 73 F4
Pembridge Rd BKLY M9 88 C3
Pembroke Av ECC M30 111 E3
SALE M33 154 A1
Pembroke Cl BRUN/LGST M13 129 E2
Pembroke Ct
BRAM/HZG SK7 * 185 F2
WHIT OL12 10 C3
Pembroke Dr BURY BL9 53 F2
OLDE OL4 60 D5
Pembroke St BOL BL1 2 B3
BRO M7 101 H4
LIT OL15 21 E2
OLDS OL8 * 8 D5
SLFD M6 112 D4
Pembry Cl RDSH SK5 160 C1
Pembury Cl WYTH/NTH M22 180 B1
Penarth Rd BOLS/LL BL3 48 A5
WYTH/NTH M22 168 C1
Pencarrow Cl DID/WITH M20 157 E3
Pencombe Cl
WGTN/LGST M12 129 H4
Pencroft Wy HULME M15 128 B3
Pendale Av CHH M8 102 C2
Pendeen Cl WYTH/NTH M22 180 D3
Pendennis ROCH OL11 * 29 H5
Pendennis Av HOR/BR BL6 47 E4
Pendennis Cl RAD M26 51 F4
Pendennis Rd HTNM SK4 159 F3
Pendle Av BOL BL1 22 D5
Pendlebury Cl PWCH M25 85 G5
Pendlebury Fold BOLS/LL BL3 63 E2
Pendlebury Rd
CHD/CHDH SK8 169 F3
SWIN M27 99 F2
Pendlebury St BOL BL1 34 A3
Pendle Cl OLDE OL4 92 C2
TOT/BURYW BL8 37 G3
Pendle Ct BOL BL1 33 G3
Pendlecroft Av SWIN M27 99 H3
Pendlegreen Cl OP/CLY M11 116 A5
Pendle Gv ROY/SHW OL2 74 D1
Pendle Rd DTN/ASHW M34 146 D2
Pendleton Gn SLFD M6 * 113 E2
Pendleton Wy SLFD M6 113 F2
Pendleway SWIN M27 99 F1
Pendragon Pl FAIL M35 105 F3
Penelope Rd SLFD M6 100 A5
Penerly Dr BKLY M9 103 E4
Penfield Cl CMANE M1 128 C1
Penfold Wk
WGTN/LGST M12 * 129 G2
Pengwern Av BOLS/LL BL3 48 A4
Penhale Ms BRAM/HZG SK7 184 A5
Penistone Av BKLY M9 88 D4
MILN OL16 30 D5
SLFD M6 112 B2
Penketh Av GTN M18 130 A4
Penmere Gv SALE M33 153 H5
Penmoor Cha BRAM/HZG SK7 184 C3
Penmore Cl ROY/SHW OL2 60 B2
Pennant Dr PWCH M25 85 H2
Pennant St OLD OL1 76 A4
Pennell St OP/CLY M11 117 E4
Penn Gn CHD/CHDH SK8 183 E3
Penn House Cl
BRAM/HZG SK7 183 H5
Pennine Av CHAD OL9 90 B2
Pennine Bridleway WHIT OL12 18 C2
Pennine Cl BKLY M9 88 C3
TOT/BURYW BL8 37 F3
Pennine Ct STLY SK15 121 G2
Pennine Dr ALT WA14 165 E4
AUL OL6 120 B1
MILN OL16 31 H5
WHIT OL12 19 H2
Pennine Gv AUL OL6 107 H4
Pennine Rd BRAM/HZG SK7 184 C3
MPL/ROM SK6 147 G5
Pennine V ROY/SHW OL2 60 B1
Pennine Vw DTN/ASHW M34 132 B3
MOSL OL5 109 E1
ROY/SHW OL2 59 F5
STLY SK15 108 D5
Pennington Cl LHULT M38 80 D3
Pennington Rd BOLS/LL BL3 65 E1
Pennington St CHAD OL9 90 C4
TOT/BURYW BL8 36 D2
WALK M28 82 B5
WGTN/LGST M12 144 A1
Pennon Cl BRO M7 101 H4
Penn St FWTH BL4 65 H4
HEY OL10 41 E5
MILN OL16 10 D5
NEWH/MOS M40 103 G2
OLDS OL8 8 C6
Penny Bridge La URM M41 138 A1
Penny Meadow AUL OL6 119 H2
Pennymoor Dr ALT WA14 165 E3
Penrhos Av CHD/CHDH SK8 183 E5
Penrhyn Av CHD/CHDH SK8 182 B3
MDTN M24 72 D5
Penrhyn Crs BRAM/HZG SK7 184 D4
Penrhyn Dr BRAM/HZG SK7 184 D3
PWCH M25 86 A3
Penrhyn Rd EDGY/DAV SK3 12 A6
Penrice Cl RAD M26 51 G4
Penrice Fold WALK M28 96 C3
Penrith Av AULW OL7 106 C5
BOL BL1 32 D5
OLDS OL8 90 D4
RDSH SK5 145 F2
SALE M33 154 D4
WALK M28 82 C5
WHTF M45 70 A5
Penrith Cl PART M31 150 D2
Penrith St ROCH OL11 43 E1
Penrod Pl SLFD M6 113 G1
Penrose Cl CHH M8 102 B4
Penrose Gdns MDTN M24 73 E3
Penrose Wk MDTN M24 56 C5
Penroy Av DID/WITH M20 156 C3
Penruddock Wk
BRUN/LGST M13 * 129 G4
Penry Av IRL M44 136 A5
Penryn Av ROY/SHW OL2 75 G1
SALE M33 154 D5
Pensarn Av RUSH/FAL M14 143 G3
Pensarn Gv RDSH SK5 160 A2
Pensby Cl SWIN M27 99 H3
Pensford Ct BOLE BL2 24 B5
Pensford Rd NTHM/RTH M23 179 G1
Penshurst Rd RDSH SK5 145 H5
Penthorpe Dr ROY/SHW OL2 75 F1
Pentland Av NEWH/MOS M40 89 F5
Pentland Cl BRAM/HZG SK7 184 C3
Pentlands Av BRO M7 101 G4
The Pentlands ROY/SHW OL2 59 G1
Pentland Ter BOL BL1 * 33 H5
Pentland Wy HYDE SK14 134 C2
Pentwyn Gv NTHM/RTH M23 168 A2
Penwell Fold OLD OL1 75 F3
Penwortham St
NEWH/MOS M40 116 A1
Penydarren Vw BOLS/LL BL3 65 H2
Penzance St NEWH/MOS M40 115 H2
Penznance St
NEWH/MOS M40 * 115 H2
Peover Av SALE M33 155 F2
Peover Rd WILM/AE SK9 192 B2
Pepler Av NTHM/RTH M23 156 A4
Pepperhill Rd
OLDTF/WHR M16 128 A4
Peppermint Cl MILN OL16 45 F2
Pepper Rd BRAM/HZG SK7 184 C2
Percival Cl CHH M8 * 102 A4
Percival Rd DROY M43 118 A4
Percy Dr ORD M5 127 E1
Percy Rd DTN/ASHW M34 146 C1
Percy St BOL BL1 * 34 A4
BURY BL9 5 H2
FWTH BL4 * 66 B5
HULME M15 127 G2
MILN OL16 43 G1
OLDE OL4 76 B5
RAMS BL0 16 C3
STKP SK1 13 G2
STLY SK15 * 121 E4
Peregrine Crs DROY M43 118 B2
Peregrine Dr IRL M44 122 B5
Peregrine Rd OFTN SK2 173 H5
Peregrine St HULME M15 128 A3
Perendale Ri BOL BL1 33 H2
Perivale Dr OLDS OL8 92 A3
Pernham St OLDE OL4 76 B5
Perrin St HYDE SK14 147 H1
Perry Av HYDE SK14 134 B4
Perry Cl ROCH OL11 42 C1
Perrygate Av DID/WITH M20 142 C5
Perrymead PWCH M25 86 A1
Perry Rd HALE/TIMP WA15 166 C3
Pershore WHIT OL12 10 B5
Pershore Rd MDTN M24 72 D1
Perth Av CHAD OL9 90 B3
Perth Cl BRAM/HZG SK7 193 H2
Perth Rd ROCH OL11 43 G4
Perth St BOLS/LL BL3 64 B1
ROY/SHW OL2 59 H5
SWIN M27 98 C3
Peru St CSLFD M3 114 A3
Peterborough Cl AUL OL6 107 E4
Peterborough Dr BOL BL1 2 D1
Peterborough St GTN M18 131 E2
Peterborough Wk BOL BL1 2 D1
Peterhead Cl BOL BL1 2 B1
Peterhead Wk ORD M5 * 113 F4
Peterhouse Gdns
MPL/ROM SK6 162 B2
Peterloo Ct SLFD M6 * 112 D3
Peter Moss Wy BNG/LEV M19 144 C2
Petersburg Rd EDGY/DAV SK3 171 F3
Petersfield Dr
NTHM/RTH M23 167 E2
Petersfield Wk BOL BL1 2 C1
Peter St ALT WA14 177 G1
BRAM/HZG SK7 185 E1
BURY BL9 5 F2
CMANE M1 6 E6
DTN/ASHW M34 132 D5
ECC M30 111 E4
OLD OL1 9 G4
STKP SK1 13 J1
Peterswood Cl
WYTH/NTH M22 180 A1
Peterwood Gdns STRET M32 139 G2
Petheridge Dr
WYTH/NTH M22 180 A3
Petrel Av POY/DIS SK12 194 B3
Petrel Cl DROY M43 118 B2
EDGY/DAV SK3 171 G3
ROCH OL11 28 C4
Petrie St WHIT OL12 10 C3
Petts Crs LIT OL15 20 D2
Petworth Cl WYTH/NTH M22 168 D4
Petworth Rd CHAD OL9 90 C1
Pevensey Rd SLFD M6 100 B5
Pevensey Wk CHAD OL9 * 90 C1
Peveril Cl WHTF M45 70 B5
Peveril Crs CCHDY M21 141 E1
Peveril Dr BRAM/HZG SK7 185 G4
Peveril Rd ALT WA14 165 F2
OLD OL1 76 B3
ORD M5 112 C3
Peveril St BOLS/LL BL3 64 A1
Peveril Ter HYDE SK14 148 B3
Pewsey Rd WYTH/NTH M22 181 E1
Pexwood OLD OL1 73 H3
Pheasant Cl WALK M28 96 C4
Pheasant Dr CCHDY M21 141 H4
Pheasant Ri ALT WA14 177 G3
Phelan Cl NEWH/MOS M40 102 D5
Phethean St BOLE BL2 3 H4
FWTH BL4 65 H3
Philip Av DTN/ASHW M34 132 A3
Philip Dr SALE M33 154 C4
Philips Av FWTH BL4 66 A5
Philips Park Rd OP/CLY M11 115 H3
WHTF M45 84 D2
Philip St BOLS/LL BL3 48 C4
ECC M30 111 E4
OLDE OL4 76 B4
ROCH OL11 43 E1
Phillimore St OLDE OL4 92 D2
Phillips Park Rd WHTF M45 85 G1
Phipps St WALK M28 81 H3
Phoebe St BOLS/LL BL3 * 48 B5
ORD M5 113 F5
Phoenix Cl HEY OL10 41 G5
Phoenix St BOL BL1 3 G2
BURY BL9 4 B4
CMANW M2 * 7 F4
FWTH BL4 66 A5
LIT OL15 21 E2
OLD OL1 9 G5
WHIT OL12 29 F2
Phoenix Wy HULME M15 128 A3
RAD M26 68 B2
URM M41 124 D2
Phyllis St MDTN M24 73 F5
WHIT OL12 29 E2
Piccadilly CMANE M1 7 H5
STKP SK1 13 G4
Piccadilly Plaza CMANE M1 7 G5
Piccadilly South CMANE M1 7 H6
Piccard Cl ANC M4 7 K1
Pickering Cl HALE/TIMP WA15 166 B2
RAD M26 * 66 D4
TOT/BURYW BL8 37 G1
URM M41 138 B1
Pickering St HULME M15 127 H3
Pickford Av BOLS/LL BL3 67 F1
Pickford Ct DUK SK16 * 119 H5
Pickford La DUK SK16 119 H5
Pickford Ms DUK SK16 * 119 H5
Pickford's Brow STKP SK1 13 G3
Pickford St ANC M4 7 J3
Pickhill La UPML OL3 79 E4
Pickhill Ms UPML OL3 79 E4
Pickmere Av DID/WITH M20 142 D3
Pickmere Cl DROY M43 118 A4
EDGY/DAV SK3 171 F3
SALE M33 155 G4
Pickmere Gdns
CHD/CHDH SK8 170 C4
Pickmere Ms UPML OL3 79 E4
Pickmere Rd WILM/AE SK9 192 A2
Pickup St MILN OL16 10 E7
Pickwick Rd POY/DIS SK12 195 E4
Picton Cl CSLFD M3 6 B2
Picton Dr WILM/AE SK9 199 H1
Picton Sq OLDE OL4 9 J5
Picton St AULW OL7 106 D4
BRO M7 114 A2
Picton Wk OLDTF/WHR M16 128 A5
Pierce St OLD OL1 76 B3

Piercy St ANC M4 115 G4
FAIL M35 * 104 D3
Piethorne Cl MILN OL16 45 F2
Pigeon St CMANE M1 7 J4
Pigginshaw WILM/AE SK9 198 B2
Piggott St FWTH BL4 65 H5
Pike Av FAIL M35 105 H4
Pike Fold La BKLY M9 87 H4
Pike Rd BOLS/LL BL3 48 C5
Pike St ROCH OL11 43 E1
Pike View Cl OLDE OL4 92 A2
Pilgrim Dr OP/CLY M11 116 A4
Pilgrim Wy OLD OL1 76 C1
Pilkington Dr WHTF M45 70 A2
Pilkington Rd BKLY M9 88 D5
FWTH BL4 82 C1
RAD M26 52 A4
Pilkington St BOLS/LL BL3 48 D4
MDTN M24 73 F3
RAMS BL0 16 C3
Pilkington Wy RAD M26 68 B2
Pilling Fld EDGW/EG BL7 22 D2
Pilling St DTN/ASHW M34 132 C5
NEWH/MOS M40 103 G5
TOT/BURYW BL8 37 H3
WHIT OL12 29 G3
Pilning St BOLS/LL BL3 49 F5
Pilot St BURY BL9 5 F7
Pilsworth Rd BURY BL9 53 H3
Pilsworth Wy BURY BL9 53 H3
Pimblett St CSLFD M3 114 C2
Pimhole Fold BURY BL9 5 H6
Pimhole Rd BURY BL9 5 H5
Pimlico Cl BRO M7 * 101 G4
Pimlott Gv HYDE SK14 133 G3
PWCH M25 85 F5
Pimlott Rd BOL BL1 34 C3
Pimmcroft Wy SALE M33 155 G3
Pine Av WHTF M45 69 G5
Pine Cl DTN/ASHW M34 132 B2
MPL/ROM SK6 174 D5
Pine Gv DTN/ASHW M34 132 D5
DUK SK16 120 C5
ECC M30 111 F1
FWTH BL4 65 G4
PWCH M25 85 H1
ROY/SHW OL2 59 E3
RUSH/FAL M14 129 F4
SALE M33 138 D5
SWIN M27 98 C3
WALK M28 97 F2
Pinehurst Rd
NEWH/MOS M40 103 F5
Pine Ldg BRAM/HZG SK7 * 184 A5
Pine Meadow RAD M26 83 F1
Pine Rd BRAM/HZG SK7 184 A4
DID/WITH M20 157 F2
DUK SK16 120 B5
POY/DIS SK12 195 G4
Pine St AUL OL6 119 G1
BOL BL1 34 A4
BURY BL9 5 J4
CHAD OL9 74 B4
CMANE M1 7 F5
HEY OL10 41 E4
HYDE SK14 133 G3
LIT OL15 21 E2
MDTN M24 73 F5
MILN OL16 * 11 G7
MILN OL16 45 E3
MPL/ROM SK6 162 A1
Pine St North BURY BL9 5 J3
Pine St South BURY BL9 5 J5
Pinetop Cl CCHDY M21 141 H4
Pine Tree Rd OLDS OL8 106 A1
Pinetree St GTN M18 130 B3
Pineway OLDE OL4 93 E1
Pinewood ALT WA14 176 D2
CHAD OL9 73 H5
SALE M33 153 G2
Pinewood Cl BOL BL1 33 H4
DUK SK16 119 H4
HTNM SK4 158 D3
Pinewood Ct ALT WA14 177 H3
SALE M33 155 E1
Pinewood Rd CCHDY M21 * 141 E4
WILM/AE SK9 199 H2
The Pinewoods
MPL/ROM SK6 162 A1
Pinfold Av BKLY M9 88 D5
Pinfold Cl HALE/TIMP WA15 179 E5
Pinfold Dr CHD/CHDH SK8 182 D3
Pinfold La HALE/TIMP WA15 189 G1
MPL/ROM SK6 162 D2
WHTF M45 69 F4
Pinfold Rd WALK M28 96 D1
Pingate Dr CHD/CHDH SK8 192 D1
Pingate La CHD/CHDH SK8 192 D1
Pingate La South
CHD/CHDH SK8 192 D1
Pingot Av NTHM/RTH M23 156 A5
The Pingot IRL M44 122 C5
Pink Bank La
WGTN/LGST M12 129 H4
Pinnacle Dr EDGW/EG BL7 22 C1
Pinner Pl BNG/LEV M19 158 D1
Pinners Cl RAMS BL0 16 D1
Pinnington La STRET M32 * 140 B2
Pinnington Rd GTN M18 130 C2
Pintail Av EDGY/DAV SK3 171 G3
Pintail Cl WHIT OL12 29 E1
Pioneer Rd SWIN M27 85 E5
Pioneer St LIT OL15 21 E3
OP/CLY M11 116 C2
ROCH OL11 30 B5
Pioneer Vls MILN OL16 * 45 H1
Piperhill Av WYTH/NTH M22 156 C5
Pipers Cl ROCH OL11 28 A3
Pipers Ct IRL M44 122 D5
Pipewell Av GTN M18 130 B3
Pipit Cl DTN/ASHW M34 118 B3
Pitchcombe Rd
WYTH/NTH M22 180 A2
Pitcombe Cl BOL BL1 22 C4
Pitfield Gdns NTHM/RTH M23 167 G2
Pitfield La BOLE BL2 35 G3
Pitfield St BOLE BL2 3 J5
Pit La ROY/SHW OL2 44 A5
Pitman Cl OP/CLY M11 116 B5
Pits Farm Av ROCH OL11 29 F4
Pitsford Rd NEWH/MOS M40 103 F5
Pitshouse La WHIT OL12 * 28 B1
Pit St CHAD OL9 90 C3
DTN/ASHW M34 132 C5
Pittbrook St WGTN/LGST M12 129 E1
Pitt St EDGY/DAV SK3 12 D6
HEY OL10 40 D4
HYDE SK14 133 G5
OLDE OL4 9 K5
RAD M26 67 H1
WHIT OL12 10 D4
Pitt St East OLDE OL4 92 A2
Pixmore Av BOL BL1 34 C2
Place Rd ALT WA14 165 F3
Plain Pit St HYDE SK14 133 F3
Plainsfield Cl
OLDTF/WHR M16 128 A4
Plainsfield St
OLDTF/WHR M16 127 H4
Plane Ct SLFD M6 * 113 F3
Plane Rd FAIL M35 105 E5
Plane St OLDE OL4 76 A5
Plane Tree Cl MPL/ROM SK6 174 C4
Planetree Rd
HALE/TIMP WA15 178 B2
Plane Tree Rd PART M31 150 C3
Planet Wy DTN/ASHW M34 132 B3
Plantation Av WALK M28 81 H3
Plantation St AUL OL6 120 A4
GTN M18 130 D3
Plant Cl SALE M33 154 B1
Plant Hill Rd BKLY M9 87 H2
Plant St CMANE M1 * 7 H5
Plant Ter BKLY M9 * 88 A2
Plate St OLD OL1 9 H3
Plato St CHAD OL9 8 C3
Platt Av AUL OL6 107 F4
Plattbrook Cl RUSH/FAL M14 142 D2
Platt Cl MILN OL16 44 D1
Platt Hill Av BOLS/LL BL3 47 H5
Platting Gv AULW OL7 106 C5
Platting La ROCH OL11 43 F2
Platting Rd OLDE OL4 77 H5
Platt La RUSH/FAL M14 142 B2
UPML OL3 78 C2
Platts Dr IRL M44 136 C1
Platt St CHD/CHDH SK8 170 B3
DUK SK16 132 D1
OLDE OL4 93 E1
Plattwood Wk HULME M15 * 127 G2
Playfair Cl HEY OL10 56 B2
Playfair St BOL BL1 23 E5
RUSH/FAL M14 128 C4
Pleachway HTNM SK4 158 C4
Pleasant Gdns BOL BL1 2 C2
Pleasant Rd ECC M30 111 F4
Pleasant St BKLY M9 103 E3
HEY OL10 40 D2
ROCH OL11 42 B4
TOT/BURYW BL8 37 E2
Pleasant Wy CHD/CHDH SK8 193 F1
Pleasington Dr
NEWH/MOS M40 89 F5
TOT/BURYW BL8 36 D4
Plevna St BOLE BL2 3 H4
Plodder La FWTH BL4 64 C4
WHTN BL5 63 H4
Ploughbank Dr CCHDY M21 142 A4
Plough Cl URM M41 137 E2
Plough Flds WALK M28 96 A5
Plough St DUK SK16 120 A5
Plover Cl ROCH OL11 28 B4
Plover Dr ALT WA14 165 E1
BURY BL9 39 E2
IRL M44 122 B4
Plowden Av BOLS/LL BL3 64 B1
Plowden Rd WYTH/NTH M22 180 A2
Plowley Cl DID/WITH M20 157 G4
Plucksbridge Rd
MPL/ROM SK6 187 F1
Plumbley Dr OLDTF/WHR M16 127 F5
Plumbley St OP/CLY M11 * 130 D1
Plumley Cl EDGY/DAV SK3 172 A4
Plumley Rd WILM/AE SK9 192 A2
Plummer Av CCHDY M21 141 F5
Plumpton Cl ROY/SHW OL2 75 F3
Plumpton Dr BURY BL9 27 F5
Plumpton Rd ROCH OL11 58 C1
Plumpton Wk
BRUN/LGST M13 * 129 G4
Plum St OLDS OL8 8 C6
Plum Tree Ct SLFD M6 113 F3
Pluto Cl SLFD M6 * 113 H1
Plymouth Av BRUN/LGST M13 129 F3
Plymouth Cl AUL OL6 107 F3
Plymouth Dr BRAM/HZG SK7 184 A5
FWTH BL4 65 E4
Plymouth Gv
BRUN/LGST M13 129 E3
EDGY/DAV SK3 171 E2
RAD M26 51 G4
Plymouth Gv West
BRUN/LGST M13 129 F3
Plymouth Rd SALE M33 153 G1
Plymouth St OLDS OL8 91 G3
Plymouth Vw
BRUN/LGST M13 128 D2
Plymtree Cl CHH M8 86 D5
Pobgreen La UPML OL3 79 G3
Pochard Dr ALT WA14 165 E2
POY/DIS SK12 194 B3
Pochin St NEWH/MOS M40 115 H2
Pocket Nook Rd HOR/BR BL6 62 C1
Pocklington Dr
NTHM/RTH M23 167 G2
Podsmead Rd
WYTH/NTH M22 180 A2
Poise Brook Dr OFTN SK2 173 G4
Poise Brook Rd OFTN SK2 173 G4
Poise Cl BRAM/HZG SK7 185 H1
Poland St ANC M4 7 K2
DTN/ASHW M34 118 D5
Polden Cl OLDS OL8 91 F4
Poleacre La MPL/ROM SK6 147 G5
Polebrook Cl
WGTN/LGST M12 129 E2
Pole Ct BURY BL9 * 70 B1
Polefield Ap PWCH M25 86 A1
Polefield Cir PWCH M25 86 A1
Polefield Gdns PWCH M25 86 A1
Polefield Gra PWCH M25 86 A1
Polefield Gv PWCH M25 86 A1
Polefield Hall Rd PWCH M25 86 A1
Polefield Rd BKLY M9 88 A5
PWCH M25 70 A5
Pole La BURY BL9 70 B2
FAIL M35 105 E2
Pole St BOLE BL2 3 J1
Polesworth Cl
WGTN/LGST M12 129 H2
Police St ALT WA14 165 G4
CMANW M2 6 D4
ECC M30 110 D3
Pollard Ct OLD OL1 * 75 F4
Pollards La BURY BL9 26 D1
Pollard Sq PART M31 151 F3
Pollard St ANC M4 115 G4
Pollard St East ANC M4 115 G3
Pollen Cl SALE M33 154 D4
Pollen Rd ALT WA14 165 F3
Polletts Av RDSH SK5 146 A5
Pollitt Cft MPL/ROM SK6 161 G5
Pollitt Av AUL OL6 107 F5
Pollitt Cl WGTN/LGST M12 * 129 G2
Pollitts Cl ECC M30 110 C3
Polonia Ct OLDS OL8 90 D4
Polperro Cl ROY/SHW OL2 59 H5
Polruan Rd CCHDY M21 141 E1
Polworth Rd BKLY M9 103 F1
Polygon Av BRUN/LGST M13 128 D2
Polygon Rd CHH M8 102 A1
Polygon St BRUN/LGST M13 128 D1
The Polygon BRO M7 101 F4
ECC M30 111 H3
Pomfret St SLFD M6 * 99 H5
WGTN/LGST M12 129 H2
Pomona Crs ORD M5 127 E1
Pomona Strd HULME M15 127 F2
ORD M5 126 D3
Pomona St ROCH OL11 43 E1
Ponds Cl CCHDY M21 * 141 F2
Pondwater Cl WALK M28 81 E4
Ponsford Av BKLY M9 88 D4
Ponsonby Rd STRET M32 126 A5
Pontefract Cl SWIN M27 99 G3
Pool Bank St MDTN M24 71 H5
Poolcroft SALE M33 155 G3
Poole Cl BRAM/HZG SK7 183 G3
Pooley Cl MDTN M24 71 G3
Poolfield Cl RAD M26 67 H1
Pool Fold FAIL M35 105 F4
Pool House Rd POY/DIS SK12 196 B2
Pool Rd GOL/RIS/CUL WA3 150 A3
Pool St BOL BL1 2 D4
OLDS OL8 91 G3
Pool Ter BOL BL1 32 D4
Poolton Rd BKLY M9 87 G3
Poorfield St OLDS OL8 9 F6
Poplar Av ALT WA14 165 G3
BNG/LEV M19 144 B4
BOL BL1 34 A2
BOLE BL2 23 H5
BURY BL9 5 K3
OLDE OL4 93 H3
OLDS OL8 91 E5
WILM/AE SK9 198 B5
Poplar Cl CHD/CHDH SK8 169 G4
Poplar Ct DTN/ASHW M34 * 132 C2
EDGY/DAV SK3 * 172 A4
Poplar Dr PWCH M25 85 H5
Poplar Gv AUL OL6 107 F5
GTN M18 130 C4
OFTN SK2 172 D5
RAMS BL0 17 E1
SALE M33 154 C3
URM M41 139 E1
Poplar Rd BNG/LEV M19 158 A3
DUK SK16 134 A1
ECC M30 111 F1
STRET M32 140 A3
SWIN M27 98 C3
WALK M28 82 B5
Poplars Rd STLY SK15 121 G2
The Poplars MOSL OL5 109 F1
Poplar St DTN/ASHW M34 132 C2
FAIL M35 104 C4
HTNM SK4 158 B4
Poplar Wk CHAD OL9 * 74 C4
Poplar Wy MPL/ROM SK6 187 F5
Poplin Dr CSLFD M3 6 C1
Poppy Cl CHAD OL9 73 G5
NTHM/RTH M23 155 F5
Poppyfield Vw ROCH OL11 28 B3
Poppythorn La PWCH M25 85 H2
Porchester Dr RAD M26 51 F4
Porchfield Sq CSLFD M3 6 C6
Porlock Av DTN/ASHW M34 118 B5
HYDE SK14 149 E1
Porlock Cl STKP SK1 172 D1
Porlock Rd NTHM/RTH M23 168 A3
URM M41 138 B3
Porritt Cl ROCH OL11 28 B5
Porritt St BURY BL9 5 J1
Porritt Wy RAMS BL0 16 D1
Portal Gv DTN/ASHW M34 147 F2
Porter Dr NEWH/MOS M40 103 E4
Porter St BURY BL9 38 C2
Portfield Cl BOL BL1 47 G1
Porthleven Dr
NTHM/RTH M23 167 F3
Portinscale Cl
TOT/BURYW BL8 37 G3
Portland Cl BRAM/HZG SK7 184 C3
Portland Crs BRUN/LGST M13 129 E4
Portland Gv HTNM SK4 159 E2
Portland Houses
MPL/ROM SK6 * 174 D4
Portland Pl AULW OL7 119 F4
Portland Rd ALT WA14 177 G1
BRUN/LGST M13 129 G5
ECC M30 111 G2
STRET M32 126 B5
SWIN M27 99 F3
WALK M28 81 H2
Portland St BOL BL1 33 H4
BURY BL9 5 G1
CMANE M1 7 F6
MILN OL16 10 D5
Portland St North AUL OL6 119 F2
Portland St South AUL OL6 119 F3
Portloe Rd CHD/CHDH SK8 181 G5
Portman Rd
OLDTF/WHR M16 127 H5
Portrea Cl EDGY/DAV SK3 171 H4
Portree Cl ECC M30 110 C3
Portrush Rd WYTH/NTH M22 180 D2
Portside Cl WALK M28 96 C5
Portsmouth Cl BRO M7 101 G5
Portsmouth St
BRUN/LGST M13 128 C3
Port Soderick Av ORD M5 113 F4
Portstone Cl
OLDTF/WHR M16 127 H4
Portstone St
OLDTF/WHR M16 * 127 H4
Port St CMANE M1 7 H4
OLDS OL8 91 G3
STKP SK1 12 E2
Portugal Rd PWCH M25 86 A5
Portugal St ANC M4 115 F2
AULW OL7 119 E5
BOLE BL2 3 J5
Portugal St East CMANE M1 7 K6
Portville Rd BNG/LEV M19 144 A2
Portway WYTH/NTH M22 180 B3
Portwood Pl RDSH SK5 13 G1
Posnett St EDGY/DAV SK3 12 A5
Postal St CMANE M1 * 7 H4
Postbridge Cl
BRUN/LGST M13 128 D2
Post Office St ALT WA14 165 G5
Potato Whf CSLFD M3 6 A7
Pot Hl AUL OL6 119 H1
Pot Hill Sq AUL OL6 * 119 H1
Potters La BKLY M9 103 F3
Potter St BURY BL9 5 H2
RAD M26 53 E5
Pottery La OP/CLY M11 116 B5
Pottinger St AULW OL7 119 E5
Pott St SWIN M27 84 A5
Poulton Av BOLE BL2 50 B2
Poulton St OP/CLY M11 130 D1
Poundswick La
WYTH/NTH M22 180 C1
Powder Mill Cl IRL M44 136 C2
Powell Av HYDE SK14 133 H5
Powell St OLDTF/WHR M16 127 F4
OP/CLY M11 117 E3
TOT/BURYW BL8 37 G5
Powicke Dr MPL/ROM SK6 161 G5
Powicke Wk MPL/ROM SK6 161 H5
Powis Rd URM M41 137 E2
Pownall Av BRAM/HZG SK7 194 A1
DID/WITH M20 142 C3
Pownall Rd ALT WA14 177 G1
CHD/CHDH SK8 182 D3
WILM/AE SK9 198 C2
Pownall St BRAM/HZG SK7 185 E1
Poynings Dr WYTH/NTH M22 180 B3
Poynt Cha WALK M28 96 C5
Poynter St NEWH/MOS M40 104 B1
Poynton St BURY BL9 5 G7
HULME M15 128 A2
Praed Rd TRPK M17 125 H3
The Precinct EDGY/DAV SK3 * 12 E7
OFTN SK2 * 173 E3
Preece Cl HYDE SK14 134 B4
Preesall Av CHD/CHDH SK8 181 G4
Preesall Cl TOT/BURYW BL8 52 A1
Premier Rd CHH M8 114 C1
Premier St OLDTF/WHR M16 127 G4
Prenton St OP/CLY M11 117 F5
Prenton Wy TOT/BURYW BL8 37 E1
Presall St BOLE BL2 * 49 H1
Prescot Cl BURY BL9 5 G7
Prescot Rd BKLY M9 103 E3
HALE/TIMP WA15 178 A2
Prescott Rd WILM/AE SK9 199 E1
Prescott St BOLS/LL BL3 * 48 B5
MILN OL16 30 D1
WALK M28 81 G4
Press St OP/CLY M11 130 C1
Presswood Ct SLFD M6 * 99 H4
Prestage St OLDTF/WHR M16 127 G4
WGTN/LGST M12 144 B1
Prestbury Av
HALE/TIMP WA15 165 H3
RUSH/FAL M14 142 B2
Prestbury Cl BURY BL9 5 G7
OFTN SK2 173 E5
Prestbury Dr MPL/ROM SK6 161 F3
OLD OL1 75 E3
Prestbury Rd BOL BL1 34 B1
WILM/AE SK9 199 H5
Prestfield Rd WHTF M45 69 H5
Presto Gdns BOLS/LL BL3 * 48 A5
Prestolee Rd BOLS/LL BL3 66 D3
RAD M26 67 F3
Preston Av ECC M30 111 H2
IRL M44 136 B4
Preston Cl ECC M30 * 111 H2
Preston Rd BNG/LEV M19 144 A3
Preston St BOLS/LL BL3 * 49 G5
GTN M18 130 B2
MDTN M24 72 D4
OLDE OL4 9 J5
WHIT OL12 29 F3
Presto St BOLS/LL BL3 48 A5
FWTH BL4 66 B3
Prestwich Cl OFTN SK2 172 C2
Prestwich Hills PWCH M25 85 H5
Prestwich Park Rd South
PWCH M25 85 H4
Prestwood Cl BOL BL1 33 F5
Prestwood Dr BOL BL1 33 G5
Prestwood Rd FWTH BL4 65 F3
SLFD M6 112 B1
Pretoria Rd BOLE BL2 50 B2
OLDS OL8 90 D4
Pretoria St WHIT OL12 * 29 F2
Prettywood BURY BL9 39 G4
Price St ANC M4 * 115 G4
BURY BL9 5 G7
DUK SK16 * 119 H5
FWTH BL4 66 A3
Prichard St STRET M32 140 B1
Prickshaw La WHIT OL12 18 A2
Pridmouth Rd DID/WITH M20 143 E5
Priest Av CHD/CHDH SK8 169 F5
Priestley Rd WALK M28 98 B2
Priestley Wy ROY/SHW OL2 60 C2
Priestnall Rd HTNM SK4 158 C3
Priest St STKP SK1 13 H7
Priestwood Av OLDE OL4 61 E5
Primrose Av FWTH BL4 65 F3
HYDE SK14 147 H4
MPL/ROM SK6 174 D3
UPML OL3 79 F3
URM M41 * 138 D1
WALK M28 81 G5
Primrose Bank ALT WA14 177 F3
OLDS OL8 8 E7
TOT/BURYW BL8 25 H4
WALK M28 81 G5
Primrose Cl BOLE BL2 35 H2
ORD M5 113 E3
Primrose Cottages
ALT WA14 * 177 F3
Primrose Crs HYDE SK14 147 H3
Primrose Dr BURY BL9 39 G3
DROY M43 118 B2
Primrose St ANC M4 7 J2
BOL BL1 * 34 A2
FWTH BL4 66 B5
OLDS OL8 9 F6
WHIT OL12 29 G3
Primrose Wk OLDS OL8 9 F6
Primula St BOL BL1 34 A2
Prince Albert Av
BNG/LEV M19 * 144 A1
Prince Charlie St OLD OL1 76 A4
Princedom St BKLY M9 103 F2
Prince Edward Av
DTN/ASHW M34 146 D1
OLDE OL4 76 B5
Prince George St OLD OL1 76 B3
Prince Mead Pl TRPK M17 125 G3
Prince Rd POY/DIS SK12 196 B2
Prince's Av BOLS/LL BL3 51 E5
DID/WITH M20 157 H2
IRL M44 122 D5
MPL/ROM SK6 161 H3
Princes Ct ECC M30 * 111 E2
Prince's Dr MPL/ROM SK6 174 D2
SALE M33 155 E3
Princes Rd ALT WA14 165 G3
HTNM SK4 158 D2
MPL/ROM SK6 161 H3
SALE M33 154 D3
Princess Av CHD/CHDH SK8 182 D1
DTN/ASHW M34 132 B5
FWTH BL4 82 C2
PWCH M25 86 B5
WHIT OL12 19 H4
Princess Cl DUK SK16 120 A5
HEY OL10 41 E5
MOSL OL5 109 F2
Princess Dr MDTN M24 72 B4
Princess Gv FWTH BL4 66 A4
Princess Pde BURY BL9 4 E5
RUSH/FAL M14 142 B2
Princess Pkwy
WYTH/NTH M22 156 B5
Princess Rd CHAD OL9 89 H4
DID/WITH M20 156 C3
HOR/BR BL6 46 C2
HULME M15 128 A3
MILN OL16 31 E4
PWCH M25 * 86 B3
ROY/SHW OL2 59 H3
URM M41 138 B1
WILM/AE SK9 198 C5
Princess St ALT WA14 165 F1
AUL OL6 120 A1
BOL BL1 3 F5
CMANW M2 6 E5
ECC M30 110 D3
FAIL M35 104 D3
HYDE SK14 148 A1
OLDE OL4 92 D1
RAD M26 67 H1
SLFD M6 113 F1
SWIN M27 99 F3
WHIT OL12 10 D3
Prince's St STKP SK1 13 F3
Prince St BOL BL1 2 D2
HEY OL10 41 E4
MILN OL16 43 G1
OLD OL1 9 J3
RAMS BL0 16 D2
Princes Wk BRAM/HZG SK7 184 B5
Princethorpe Cl HOR/BR BL6 47 E3
Princeton Cl SLFD M6 112 B2
Prinknash Rd
WYTH/NTH M22 180 C3
Printers Cl BNG/LEV M19 158 A4
Printers Dr STLY SK15 109 H3
Printers La EDGW/EG BL7 23 H5
Printer St OLD OL1 9 G4
OP/CLY M11 * 117 E5
Printon Av BKLY M9 87 G4
Printworks La BNG/LEV M19 144 C2
Printworks Rd STLY SK15 121 E2
Prior St OLDS OL8 92 A3
Priory Av BRO M7 101 F4
CCHDY M21 141 F3
Priory Cl DUK SK16 133 G2
OLDS OL8 91 E4
SALE M33 140 B5
Priory Ct RDSH SK5 145 E3
Priory Gv BRO M7 101 F4
CHAD OL9 90 B3
Priory La RDSH SK5 145 E3
Priory Pl BOLE BL2 34 D4
Priory Rd ALT WA14 177 E4
CHD/CHDH SK8 170 D4
SALE M33 155 E1
SWIN M27 98 D2
WILM/AE SK9 198 B2
Priory St ALT WA14 177 F4
The Priory BRO M7 101 F4
Pritchard St CMANE M1 * 7 G7
Privet St OLDE OL4 76 C3
Proctor St TOT/BURYW BL8 37 H5
Progress Av DTN/ASHW M34 132 C3
Progress St AUL OL6 119 F2
BOL BL1 34 A5
ROCH OL11 42 B5
Promenade St HEY OL10 41 F4
Propps Hall Dr FAIL M35 104 D4

Prospect Av FWTH BL4 66 A5
IRL M44 136 A5
Prospect Ct TOT/BURYW BL8 26 A4
Prospect Dr FAIL M35 105 E5
HALE/TIMP WA15 179 E5
Prospect Hl BOLE BL2 35 G2
Prospect Pl AUL OL6 107 G5
FWTH BL4 65 H5
HEY OL10 41 E3
Prospect Rd AUL OL6 107 H5
CHAD OL9 8 A2
DUK SK16 120 A5
IRL M44 136 A5
Prospect St BOL BL1 34 A5
HEY OL10 56 B1
LIT OL15 * 21 E2
ROCH OL11 42 D2
Prospect Ter TOT/BURYW BL8 4 A1
Prospect V CHD/CHDH SK8 181 G3
Prospect Vw SWIN M27 99 F3
Prout St WGTN/LGST M12 129 H5
Provender Cl ALT WA14 165 G1
Providence St ANC M4 115 G4
AUL OL6 * 119 H1
BOLS/LL BL3 49 E4
DTN/ASHW M34 132 C1
Provident Av BNG/LEV M19 144 C2
Provident St ROY/SHW OL2 * 60 A2
Provident Wy
HALE/TIMP WA15 166 B2
Provis Rd CCHDY M21 141 F4
Prubella Av DTN/ASHW M34 132 B3
Pryce St BOL BL1 2 B1
Pryme St HULME M15 127 H1
Pudding La HYDE SK14 134 D5
Puffin Av POY/DIS SK12 194 B4
Puffingate Cl STLY SK15 109 F3
Pulborough Cl
TOT/BURYW BL8 26 C4
Pulford Av CCHDY M21 156 C2
Pulford Rd SALE M33 154 D4
Pullman Cl BNG/LEV M19 144 B3
Pullman Dr STRET M32 139 F1
Pullman St ROCH OL11 43 E1
Punch La BOLS/LL BL3 63 E2
Punch St BOLS/LL BL3 2 B7
Purbeck Cl WYTH/NTH M22 180 B3
Purbeck Dr HOR/BR BL6 46 A1
TOT/BURYW BL8 26 D5
Purcell Cl BOL BL1 33 G5
Purcell St WGTN/LGST M12 129 H5
Purdon St BURY BL9 27 G5
Purley Av NTHM/RTH M23 156 A5
Purley Dr IRL M44 150 B1
Purple St BOL BL1 3 F4
Purslow Cl WGTN/LGST M12 115 H4
Putney Cl OLD OL1 75 F3
Pymgate Dr CHD/CHDH SK8 181 F2
Pymgate La CHD/CHDH SK8 181 F2
Pym St ECC M30 111 E3
HEY OL10 41 E5
NEWH/MOS M40 * 103 G2
Pyramid Ct BRO M7 101 G4
Pyrus Cl ECC M30 110 A5
Pytha Fold Rd
DID/WITH M20 158 A1

Q

The Quadrant BKLY M9 88 D4
DROY M43 117 G4
MPL/ROM SK6 161 H4
STKP SK1 160 C5
Quail Dr IRL M44 122 B5
Quail St OLDE OL4 92 B2
Quakers Fld
TOT/BURYW BL8 26 A3
Quantock Cl HTNM SK4 12 E1
Quantock Dr OLDS OL8 91 G4
Quantock St
OLDTF/WHR M16 * 127 H4
Quarmby Rd GTN M18 131 E4
Quarry Bank Rd
WILM/AE SK9 191 E4
Quarry Clough STLY SK15 121 G5
Quarry Hts STLY SK15 120 C5
Quarry La UPML OL3 78 A3
Quarry Pond Rd WALK M28 81 E4
Quarry Ri MPL/ROM SK6 162 A4
STLY SK15 120 C5
Quarry Rd FWTH BL4 66 D5
MPL/ROM SK6 162 A4
Quarry St MPL/ROM SK6 * 162 A1
RAD M26 68 C1
RAMS BL0 17 E2
STLY SK15 120 C4
WHIT OL12 10 B3
Quarry Wk OP/CLY M11 * 116 A4
Quayside Cl WALK M28 96 C5
The Quays SALQ M50 126 C1
Quay St CSLFD M3 6 B5
CSLFD M3 6 C3
HEY OL10 * 41 F5
Quay Vw ORD M5 113 F5
Quebec Pl BOLS/LL BL3 48 B4
Quebec St BOLS/LL BL3 48 C4
CHAD OL9 8 B1
DTN/ASHW M34 132 B4
Queen Alexandra Cl
ORD M5 * 113 H5
Queen Ann Dr WALK M28 96 C3
Queenhill Dr HYDE SK14 134 A3
Queenhill Rd
WYTH/NTH M22 156 D5
Queen's Av EDGW/EG BL7 23 F4
MPL/ROM SK6 161 H3
WHIT OL12 19 H4
Queensbrook BOL BL1 2 C4
Queensbury Cl BOL BL1 33 G1
WILM/AE SK9 199 G2
Queensbury Pde
NEWH/MOS M40 * 115 H2
Queens Cl HTNM SK4 158 D4
HYDE SK14 * 148 A4
WALK M28 96 A3
Queens Ct
NEWH/MOS M40 103 E5
Queens Dr CHD/CHDH SK8 182 D1
HTNM SK4 158 D4
HYDE SK14 148 B4
PWCH M25 86 B5
ROCH OL11 42 D3
Queensferry St
NEWH/MOS M40 104 B4
Queensgate BOL BL1 48 A1
BRAM/HZG SK7 193 H2
Queensgate Dr ROY/SHW OL2 58 D3
Queen's Gv WGTN/LGST M12 129 H4
Queensland Rd GTN M18 130 A3
Queensmere Dr SWIN M27 84 B5
Queens Pk BOL BL1 * 2 A5
Queen's Park Rd HEY OL10 41 E3
Queens Pl BURY BL9 26 D1
Queen's Rd AUL OL6 107 G5
BOLS/LL BL3 48 A5
BRAM/HZG SK7 185 F1
CHAD OL9 74 B5
CHD/CHDH SK8 170 C5
CHH M8 102 C5
HALE/TIMP WA15 177 H1
LIT OL15 * 21 E3
MPL/ROM SK6 161 H3
NEWH/MOS M40 103 E5
OLDS OL8 9 J6
SALE M33 154 A2
URM M41 138 D2
WILM/AE SK9 198 D4
Queenston Rd
DID/WITH M20 157 F2
Queen St AUL OL6 120 A2
BOL BL1 2 D5
BURY BL9 5 G4
CHD/CHDH SK8 170 B3
CSLFD M3 6 C2
CSLFD M3 6 D5
DTN/ASHW M34 132 B4
DTN/ASHW M34 132 C2
DUK SK16 119 G4
ECC M30 * 111 G3
FAIL M35 104 D3
FWTH BL4 66 A4
HEY OL10 41 E4
HYDE SK14 148 A2
LHULT M38 81 G4
LIT OL15 21 E3
MDTN M24 73 F4
MOSL OL5 108 D1
MPL/ROM SK6 175 E3
OLD OL1 9 H3
RAD M26 68 D2
RAMS BL0 16 C3
ROY/SHW OL2 59 E5
ROY/SHW OL2 60 A3
SLFD M6 100 A5
STLY SK15 * 120 D3
TOT/BURYW BL8 37 F1
WHIT OL12 10 D4
Queen St West
DID/WITH M20 142 D4
Queens Vw LIT OL15 20 D5
Queensway BNG/LEV M19 158 A4
CHD/CHDH SK8 181 H4
DUK SK16 134 A1
FWTH BL4 82 C1
IRL M44 136 B1
MOSL OL5 109 E3
PART M31 151 E2
POY/DIS SK12 195 E4
ROCH OL11 42 C3
SWIN M27 84 B5
UPML OL3 95 E1
URM M41 124 D4
WALK M28 96 C2
Queen Victoria St ECC M30 110 D3
ROCH OL11 43 F3
Queenby St HULME M15 127 G2
Quendon Av BRO M7 114 B1
Quickedge La OLDE OL4 93 G3
Quickedge Rd MOSL OL5 93 H5
Quick Rd MOSL OL5 93 H3
Quick Vw MOSL OL5 94 B4
Quill Ct IRL M44 136 A5
Quilter Gv BKLY M9 87 H5
Quinney Crs
OLDTF/WHR M16 128 A5
Quinn St OP/CLY M11 116 B4
Quinton WHIT OL12 10 B5
Quinton Wk BRUN/LGST M13 128 C2

R

Rabbit La HYDE SK14 135 H2
Raby St OLDTF/WHR M16 127 H4
RUSH/FAL M14 128 A4
Racecourse Pk WILM/AE SK9 198 C4
Racecourse Rd WILM/AE SK9 198 B4
Racefield Rd ALT WA14 165 F5
The Race WILM/AE SK9 192 A5
Rachel St WGTN/LGST M12 115 F5
Rackhouse Rd
NTHM/RTH M23 156 A5
Radbourne Cl
WGTN/LGST M12 129 H2
Radbourne Gv BOLS/LL BL3 47 G5
Radcliffe Moor Rd BOLE BL2 51 E4
Radcliffe New Rd RAD M26 68 D2
Radcliffe Park Crs SLFD M6 99 H5
Radcliffe Park Rd SLFD M6 99 H5
Radcliffe Rd BOLE BL2 3 J5
BOLS/LL BL3 50 D5
BURY BL9 53 F2
OLDE OL4 76 C2
Radcliffe St OLD OL1 9 G2
OLDE OL4 93 F1
ROY/SHW OL2 59 F5
Radclyffe St CHAD OL9 74 C4
MDTN M24 72 D2
Radelan Gv RAD M26 51 G5
Radford Cl OFTN SK2 173 E2
Radford Dr BKLY M9 103 F2
IRL M44 122 B5
Radford St BRO M7 101 F2
Radium St ANC M4 7 J2
Radlet Dr HALE/TIMP WA15 166 B1
Radlett Wk BRUN/LGST M13 * 128 D3
Radley Cl BOL BL1 32 D5
SALE M33 153 G3
Radley St DROY M43 117 F5
OLDTF/WHR M16 128 A5
Radnor Av DTN/ASHW M34 131 G5
Radnormere Dr
CHD/CHDH SK8 170 C5
Radnor St CHAD OL9 8 A6
GTN M18 130 B4
HULME M15 128 A3
STRET M32 140 B2
Radstock Cl BOL BL1 22 D4
RUSH/FAL M14 142 D2
Radstock Rd STRET M32 140 A1
Raeburn Dr MPL/ROM SK6 175 G1
Rae St EDGY/DAV SK3 12 B5
Raglan Av SWIN M27 84 C5
WHTF M45 70 A5
Raglan Dr ALT WA14 165 H1
Raglan Rd SALE M33 154 A3
STRET M32 125 G5
Raglan St BOL BL1 33 G4
HYDE SK14 147 G1
ROCH OL11 42 B5
Raglan Wk HULME M15 * 128 A2
Ragley Cl POY/DIS SK12 195 G3
Raikes La BOLS/LL BL3 49 G5
Raikes Rd BOLS/LL BL3 50 A4
Raikes Wy BOLS/LL BL3 50 A4
Railton Av OLDTF/WHR M16 127 G5
Railton Ter BKLY M9 * 103 G3
Railway Ap ROCH OL11 42 B4
Railway Rd CHAD OL9 8 C5
CHAD OL9 90 B5
STKP SK1 13 F5
STRET M32 126 C3
URM M41 138 D1
Railway St ALT WA14 165 G5
BURY BL9 26 C1
DUK SK16 119 G5
FWTH BL4 66 B3
GTN M18 130 B2
HEY OL10 41 F5
HTNM SK4 12 E3
LIT OL15 21 E3
MILN OL16 30 B5
MILN OL16 45 F2
RAD M26 68 B2
RAMS BL0 16 D2
Railway Ter TOT/BURYW BL8 37 H5
Railway Vw OLDE OL4 93 E1
ROY/SHW OL2 60 B1
Raimond St BOL BL1 33 F3
Rainbow Cl CCHDY M21 141 F4
Raincliff Av BRUN/LGST M13 143 H1
Raines Crest MILN OL16 31 H5
Rainford Av DID/WITH M20 142 C3
HALE/TIMP WA15 166 B4
Rainford St BOLE BL2 23 H5
Rainforth St BRUN/LGST M13 129 G5
Rainham Dr CHH M8 102 B3
Rainham Wy CHAD OL9 90 C1
RDSH SK5 145 H5
Rainow Av DROY M43 117 F5
Rainow Dr POY/DIS SK12 195 H5
Rainow Rd EDGY/DAV SK3 * 171 F3
Rainshaw St BOL BL1 34 A2
OLDE OL4 * 76 C4
Rainsough Av PWCH M25 100 C1
Rainsough Brow PWCH M25 100 C1
Rainsough Cl PWCH M25 100 D1
Rainwood CHAD OL9 73 H4
Raja Cl CHH M8 102 C3
Rake ROCH OL11 28 A4
Rake La SWIN M27 84 A4
Rake St BURY BL9 38 C2
Rake Ter LIT OL15 21 F3
Rakewood Dr OLDE OL4 60 D5
Rakewood Rd LIT OL15 21 E5
Raleigh Cl DID/WITH M20 157 F1
OLD OL1 75 G4
Raleigh St RDSH SK5 159 H2
STRET M32 140 B1
Ralli Cts CSLFD M3 6 B4
Ralph Av HYDE SK14 148 A4
Ralph Green St CHAD OL9 90 C5
Ralphs La DUK SK16 133 F1
Ralph St BOL BL1 33 G4
OP/CLY M11 117 E4
WHIT OL12 10 E3
Ralston Cl BRO M7 102 A2
Ralstone Av OLDS OL8 91 G3
Ramage Wk WGTN/LGST M12 115 H4
Ramillies Av CHD/CHDH SK8 183 E3
Ramp Rd East MANAIR M90 180 B5
Ramp Rd South MANAIR M90 180 A5
Ramp Rd West MANAIR M90 180 A5
Ramsay Av FWTH BL4 65 G5
Ramsay Pl MILN OL16 10 E5
Ramsay St BOL BL1 33 H2
MILN OL16 10 E5
Ramsay Ter MILN OL16 * 10 E5
Ramsbottom La RAMS BL0 16 D1
Ramsbottom Rd
TOT/BURYW BL8 24 D1
Ramsbury Dr NEWH/MOS M40 89 G5
Ramsdale Rd BRAM/HZG SK7 183 H4
Ramsdale St CHAD OL9 74 B5
Ramsden Cl OLD OL1 8 E2
Ramsden Crs OLD OL1 8 E2
Ramsden Fold SWIN M27 84 A5
Ramsden Rd WHIT OL12 15 H5
Ramsden St AUL OL6 119 G1
BOLS/LL BL3 50 A4
OLD OL1 8 E2
Ramsey Av BNG/LEV M19 144 D2
Ramsey Gv TOT/BURYW BL8 37 G4
Ramsey St CHAD OL9 90 C2
NEWH/MOS M40 104 A3
OLD OL1 76 A4
Ramsgate Rd
NEWH/MOS M40 116 D1
RDSH SK5 145 F4
Ramsgate St BRO M7 101 H5
Ramsgill Cl NTHM/RTH M23 155 F5
Ramsgreave Cl BURY BL9 53 E2
Ram St LHULT M38 81 E3
Ramwell Gdns BOLS/LL BL3 * 48 C4
Ramwells Brow EDGW/EG BL7 23 E3
Ramwells Ct EDGW/EG BL7 * 23 G3
Ramwells Ms EDGW/EG BL7 * 23 G3
Ranby Av BKLY M9 88 C3
Randale Dr BURY BL9 69 H2
Randal St BOLS/LL BL3 48 B5
Randerson St
WGTN/LGST M12 128 D1
Randlesham St PWCH M25 86 B3
Randolph Pl EDGY/DAV SK3 13 F7
Randolph Rd FWTH BL4 66 C5
Randolph St BNG/LEV M19 144 A1
BOLS/LL BL3 2 A6
OLDS OL8 90 D5
Rands Clough Dr WALK M28 96 C4
Rand St OLD OL1 76 C3
Ranelagh Rd SWIN M27 99 H3
Ranelagh St OP/CLY M11 116 C3
Raneley Gv ROCH OL11 43 F4
Ranford Rd BNG/LEV M19 144 A3
Range Dr MPL/ROM SK6 147 G5
Rangemore Av
WYTH/NTH M22 * 168 C1
Range Rd DUK SK16 134 C2
EDGY/DAV SK3 171 H3
OLDTF/WHR M16 127 H5
STLY SK15 121 E5
Range St BOLS/LL BL3 48 C5
OP/CLY M11 116 D5
Rankine Ter BOLS/LL BL3 * 48 C4
Rannoch Rd BOLE BL2 50 C2
Ransfield Rd CCHDY M21 141 E1
Ranulph Ct SLFD M6 * 100 A5
Ranworth Av HTNM SK4 158 C4
Ranworth Cl BOL BL1 23 F5
Raper St OLDE OL4 76 B4
Raphael St BOL BL1 33 G4
Rappax Rd HALE/TIMP WA15 178 B4
Rasbottom St BOLS/LL BL3 2 B7
Raspberry La IRL M44 122 A4
Rassbottom Brow STLY SK15 * 120 C3
Rassbottom St STLY SK15 120 C3
Ratcliffe Av IRL M44 136 C1
Ratcliffe St BNG/LEV M19 144 B2
STKP SK1 13 G6
Rathan Rd URM M41 124 B4
Rathbone St MILN OL16 11 J7
Rathbourne Av BKLY M9 88 A4
Rathen Rd DID/WITH M20 157 G1
Rathmel Rd NTHM/RTH M23 155 G4
Rathmore Av
NEWH/MOS M40 103 F5
Rathvale Dr WYTH/NTH M22 180 B4
Rathybank Cl BOL BL1 33 F5
Rattenbury Ct SLFD M6 99 H5
Raveden Cl BOL BL1 33 F3
Raveley Av RUSH/FAL M14 143 F3
Ravelston Dr BKLY M9 103 E4
Raven Av CHAD OL9 90 B2
Raven Cl DROY M43 118 B2
HALE/TIMP WA15 154 C5
Ravendale Cl WHIT OL12 28 D2
Raven Dr IRL M44 122 B5
Ravenfield Gv BOL BL1 * 2 B2
Ravenhead Cl RUSH/FAL M14 143 F3
Ravenhead Sq STLY SK15 109 F5
Ravenhurst Dr BOL BL1 47 E3
Ravenna Av NTHM/RTH M23 167 E2
Ravenoak Av BNG/LEV M19 144 B3
Ravenoak Dr FAIL M35 105 F2
Ravenoak Park Rd
CHD/CHDH SK8 183 E4
Ravenoak Rd CHD/CHDH SK8 183 E4
OFTN SK2 172 B5
Raven Rd BOLS/LL BL3 * 47 H5
Ravensbury St OP/CLY M11 116 C3
Ravenscar Crs
WYTH/NTH M22 180 C4
Ravens Cl PWCH M25 86 D5
Ravenscraig Rd LHULT M38 81 G1
Ravensdale Gdns ECC M30 111 F2
Ravensdale Rd BOL BL1 47 E2
Ravensdale St RUSH/FAL M14 128 D5
Ravens Holme BOL BL1 47 F2
Ravenside Pk CHAD OL9 90 B2
Ravenstonedale Dr
ROY/SHW OL2 59 F4
Ravenstone Dr SALE M33 155 F1
UPML OL3 79 F1
Raven St BURY BL9 5 F1
ROCH OL11 28 A2
WGTN/LGST M12 115 F5
Ravensway PWCH M25 86 C5
Ravens Wd BOL BL1 47 F2
Ravenswood Av HTNM SK4 158 D5
Ravenswood Dr BKLY M9 88 B4
BOL BL1 47 F2
CHD/CHDH SK8 183 E4
Ravenswood Rd STRET M32 126 C3
WILM/AE SK9 200 C1
Raven Wy SLFD M6 113 E2
Ravenwood CHAD OL9 73 G5
Ravenwood Dr
DTN/ASHW M34 132 B2
HALE/TIMP WA15 179 E5
Ravine Av BKLY M9 103 F3
Rawcliffe Av BOLE BL2 50 C2
Rawcliffe St RUSH/FAL M14 128 C5
Rawdon Cl BNG/LEV M19 144 B2
Rawkin Cl HULME M15 127 H3
Rawlyn Rd BOL BL1 32 C5
Rawpool Gdns
NTHM/RTH M23 167 H2
Rawson Av FWTH BL4 66 B3
Rawson Rd BOL BL1 33 F5
Rawsons Rake
TOT/BURYW BL8 16 B2
Rawson St FWTH BL4 66 A3
Rawsthorne Av GTN M18 144 D1
Rawsthorne St BOL BL1 33 H4
Rawstron St WHIT OL12 14 B4
Raycroft Av BKLY M9 88 D5
Raydon Av NEWH/MOS M40 * 103 E5
Rayleigh Av OP/CLY M11 131 E1
Raymond Av BURY BL9 38 C1
CHAD OL9 90 C4
Raymond Rd NTHM/RTH M23 156 A4
Raymond St SWIN M27 99 E1
Rayner La AULW OL7 118 C4
Rayners Cl STLY SK15 120 C4
Rayner St STKP SK1 172 C1
Raynham Av DID/WITH M20 157 G3
Raynham St AUL OL6 119 H2
Rayson Hill Dr BKLY M9 87 H5
Reabrook Av
WGTN/LGST M12 129 G2
The Reach WALK M28 82 B5
Read Cl BURY BL9 53 E2
ROY/SHW OL2 60 A3
Reade Av URM M41 137 G2
Reading Cl OP/CLY M11 116 D5
Reading Dr SALE M33 153 G2
Reading St SLFD M6 101 E5
Readitt Wk OP/CLY M11 116 C3
Read St HYDE SK14 133 F5
Read St West HYDE SK14 133 F5
Reaney Wk
WGTN/LGST M12 * 129 H2
Reather Wk NEWH/MOS M40 115 F2
Rebecca St CHH M8 102 B2
Recreation Rd FAIL M35 105 F1
Recreation St BOLE BL2 35 F1
BOLS/LL BL3 48 D5
PWCH M25 86 B3
Rectory Av CHH M8 102 B1
PWCH M25 86 A3
Rectory Cl DTN/ASHW M34 147 E1
RAD M26 53 E5
Rectory Flds STKP SK1 13 J3
Rectory Gdns PWCH M25 86 A3
Rectory Gn PWCH M25 85 H3
STKP SK1 13 J3
Rectory Gv PWCH M25 86 A4
Rectory Hl BURY BL9 39 G3
Rectory La BURY BL9 39 G2
PWCH M25 85 H3
RAD M26 68 D1
Rectory Rd CHH M8 102 A1
Rectory St MDTN M24 72 C3
The Rectory BURY BL9 70 A1
Redacre POY/DIS SK12 195 G1
Redacre Rd GTN M18 130 D3
Red Bank ANC M4 114 D2
Red Bank Rd RAD M26 52 A4
Redbarn Cl MPL/ROM SK6 161 G2
Redbourne Dr URM M41 123 G4
Redbrick Ct AULW OL7 119 F4
Redbrook Av
NEWH/MOS M40 103 F5
Redbrook Cl FWTH BL4 * 66 B3
Redbrook Rd
HALE/TIMP WA15 167 E3
PART M31 150 D4
Red Brook St ROCH OL11 29 G4
Redbrow Hollow
MPL/ROM SK6 163 F4
Redburn Rd NTHM/RTH M23 168 A2
Redby St OP/CLY M11 * 130 A1
Redcar Av DID/WITH M20 142 D5
URM M41 123 H4
Redcar Cl BRAM/HZG SK7 185 H3
OLD OL1 76 A3
Redcar Rd BOL BL1 33 E2
BOLS/LL BL3 66 D1
SWIN M27 99 H3
Redcar St WHIT OL12 10 B4
Red Cedar Pk BOLE BL2 50 A4
Redclyffe Av RUSH/FAL M14 128 D5
Redclyffe Rd DID/WITH M20 157 F1
ECC M30 111 E5
Redcot BOL BL1 * 48 A2
Redcote St NEWH/MOS M40 103 H2
Redcourt Av DID/WITH M20 157 G2
Redcroft Gdns BNG/LEV M19 158 B2
Redcroft Rd SALE M33 139 E5
Redcross St WHIT OL12 10 C4
Redcross St North WHIT OL12 10 C3
Reddaway Cl SLFD M6 100 D5
Reddish Cl BOLE BL2 35 F1
Reddish La GTN M18 130 D5
Reddish Rd RDSH SK5 145 F5
Reddish Vale Rd RDSH SK5 145 G4
Redesmere Cl DROY M43 118 A4
HALE/TIMP WA15 167 E3
Redesmere Dr
CHD/CHDH SK8 170 C5
WILM/AE SK9 200 C4
Redesmere Pk URM M41 138 B3
Redesmere Rd WILM/AE SK9 192 A2
Redfearn Wd WHIT OL12 29 E1
Redfern Av SALE M33 155 F3
Redfern St ANC M4 7 F2
Redfern Wy ROCH OL11 28 A2
Redfield Cl OP/CLY M11 116 A4
Redford Dr BRAM/HZG SK7 184 B2
Redford Rd CHH M8 87 E3
Redford St TOT/BURYW BL8 37 H3
Redgate HYDE SK14 147 H3
Redgate La WGTN/LGST M12 129 H3
Redgates Wk CCHDY M21 * 141 F2
Redgate Wy FWTH BL4 65 E3
Redgrave Pas OLDE OL4 76 C4
Redgrave St OLDE OL4 76 C4
Red Hall St OLDE OL4 92 B1
Redhill Dr MPL/ROM SK6 161 E3
Redhill Gv BOL BL1 2 C1
Redhill St ANC M4 7 J4
Redhouse La MPL/ROM SK6 161 G2
Redington Cl WALK M28 96 B5
Redisher Cl RAMS BL0 16 A5
Redisher Cft RAMS BL0 16 A5
Redland Av RDSH SK5 160 A1
Redland Cl LIT OL15 21 E2
Redland Crs CCHDY M21 141 F5
Red La BOLE BL2 35 E5
POY/DIS SK12 197 G2
WHIT OL12 11 G1
Red Lion St ANC M4 * 7 G3
Redmans Cl ECC M30 110 C4
Redmere Dr BURY BL9 53 H1
Redmere Gv RUSH/FAL M14 143 E3
Redmire Ms DUK SK16 134 A1
Redmond Cl DTN/ASHW M34 132 B1
Redmoor Sq BRUN/LGST M13 128 C1
Redmoss Rw SWIN M27 100 A2
Red Pike Wk OLD OL1 * 75 H4
Redpoll Cl WALK M28 96 C3
Red Rock La RAD M26 83 G1
Red Rose Crs BNG/LEV M19 144 C4
Redruth St RUSH/FAL M14 142 D1
Redshaw Av BOLE BL2 23 H5

Redshaw Cl RUSH/FAL M14 143 F2
Redstart Gv WALK M28 97 E2
Redstock Cl WHTN BL5 62 B3
Redstone Rd BNG/LEV M19 158 A3
Redthorn Av BNG/LEV M19 143 H4
Redthorpe Cl BOLE BL2 34 C5
Redvale Rd BRO M7 101 H4
Redvales Rd BURY BL9 53 F2
Redvers St OLD OL1 8 D1
Redwater Cl WALK M28 96 B4
Redwing Rd TOT/BURYW BL8 26 A1
Redwood CHAD OL9 73 G5
SALE M33 153 F2
Redwood Cl EDGY/DAV SK3 171 E2
WHIT OL12 18 A5
Redwood Dr CHH M8 102 C5
DTN/ASHW M34 132 B2
MPL/ROM SK6 161 G3
Redwood La OLDE OL4 76 D5
Redwood Park Gv MILN OL16 31 E4
Redwood Rd UPML OL3 79 F5
Redwood St SLFD M6 113 F1
Reeceton Gdns BOL BL1 47 H2
Reedbank RAD M26 68 B4
Reed Ct OLD OL1 * 75 F4
Reedham Cl BOL BL1 48 B1
Reedham Wk CHAD OL9 * 90 D3
NEWH/MOS M40 * 115 G1
Reed Hl MILN OL16 10 C5
Reedley Dr WALK M28 96 D2
Reedmace Cl WALK M28 97 F1
Reedshaw Bank OFTN SK2 173 E4
Reedshaw Rd BKLY M9 102 D4
Reed St GTN M18 130 C2
OLD OL1 * 9 J3
Reeman Cl MPL/ROM SK6 161 H2
Reeve Cl OFTN SK2 173 G4
Reeves Rd CCHDY M21 141 F4
Reevey Av BRAM/HZG SK7 184 D2
Reform St WHIT OL12 10 C4
Reform Wk OP/CLY M11 116 C5
Regal Cl WHTF M45 70 A4
Regal Fold WHIT OL12 19 G4
Regan Av CCHDY M21 141 H4
Regan St BOL BL1 33 G3
RAD M26 68 C2
Regatta Cl CHAD OL9 90 B4
Regatta St SLFD M6 100 C4
Regency Cl NEWH/MOS M40 103 E5
OLDS OL8 91 E3
Regency Ct
HALE/TIMP WA15 * 178 C3
ROCH OL11 28 C4
Regency Gdns
CHD/CHDH SK8 182 B4
HYDE SK14 134 A4
Regency Ldg PWCH M25 * 85 H4
Regency Pk WILM/AE SK9 198 C5
Regent Av LHULT M38 81 H3
RUSH/FAL M14 142 B1
Regent Cl BRAM/HZG SK7 193 H3
CHD/CHDH SK8 171 F5
HEY OL10 40 C5
WILM/AE SK9 198 C5
Regent Ct HTNM SK4 159 F1
Regent Crs FAIL M35 104 D4
ROY/SHW OL2 75 E2
Regent Dr DTN/ASHW M34 146 B2
HOR/BR BL6 46 C2
Regent Pl RUSH/FAL M14 128 D4
Regent Rd ALT WA14 165 G5
HOR/BR BL6 46 C3
OFTN SK2 172 B3
ORD M5 113 G5
Regents Dr MOSL OL5 109 E3
Regents Hl HOR/BR BL6 46 D3
Regents Pk ORD M5 * 113 H5
Regent Sq ORD M5 113 G5
The Regents WILM/AE SK9 199 F2
Regent St BURY BL9 4 E1
ECC M30 111 H3
HEY OL10 40 C5
LIT OL15 21 E3
MDTN M24 72 C2
NEWH/MOS M40 104 C5
OLD OL1 9 J3
RAMS BL0 16 B4
WHIT OL12 10 D2
Regent Wk FWTH BL4 * 66 A4
Regina Av STLY SK15 120 D3
Reginald St BOLS/LL BL3 * 63 H2
ECC M30 110 B5
OP/CLY M11 131 E1
SWIN M27 98 C1
Reid Cl DTN/ASHW M34 147 E3
Reigate Cl TOT/BURYW BL8 * 37 G5
Reigate Rd URM M41 137 G3
Reilly St HULME M15 * 127 H2
Reins Lee Av OLDS OL8 91 H5
Reins Lee Rd AULW OL7 106 D4
Reliance St NEWH/MOS M40 104 B4
Rembrandt Wk OLD OL1 60 C4
Rena Cl HTNM SK4 159 G3
Rendel Cl STRET M32 140 B1
Renfrew Dr BOLS/LL BL3 63 G1
Rennie Cl STRET M32 140 B1
Renshaw Av ECC M30 111 E4
Renshaw Dr BURY BL9 39 F3
Renshaw St ECC M30 111 E4
Renton Rd BOLS/LL BL3 64 A1
STRET M32 140 C1
WYTH/NTH M22 168 C5
Repton Av DROY M43 117 E2
DTN/ASHW M34 131 F5
HYDE SK14 133 H5
NEWH/MOS M40 104 D1
OLDS OL8 91 E4
URM M41 137 F1
Repton Cl SALE M33 153 G3
Reservoir Rd EDGY/DAV SK3 171 G2
Reservoir St CSLFD M3 6 C1
MILN OL16 11 J4
SLFD M6 113 E3
The Residences PWCH M25 86 B4
Retford Av MILN OL16 43 G3
Retford Cl TOT/BURYW BL8 38 B1
Retford St OLDE OL4 * 92 A2
Retiro St OLD OL1 9 H3
The Retreat MPL/ROM SK6 162 A5
Reuben St HTNM SK4 159 H2
Revers St TOT/BURYW BL8 4 A3
Reveton Gn BRAM/HZG SK7 184 B2
Rexcine Wy HYDE SK14 134 B3
Reynard Rd CCHDY M21 141 F4
Reynard St HYDE SK14 * 133 G5
Reynell Rd BRUN/LGST M13 143 H1
Reyner St AUL OL6 120 B3
CMANE M1 7 F6
Reynolds Dr GTN M18 130 C2
MPL/ROM SK6 175 G1
WHTN BL5 63 G5
Reynolds Ms WILM/AE SK9 199 H2
Reynolds Rd
OLDTF/WHR M16 127 F4
Reynold St HYDE SK14 147 H1
Rhine Cl TOT/BURYW BL8 26 A4
Rhine Dr CHH M8 101 H5
Rhiwlas Dr BURY BL9 53 G1
Rhodes Av OLDE OL4 93 E2
UPML OL3 79 F3
Rhodes Bank OLD OL1 9 J4
Rhodes Crs ROCH OL11 43 E3
Rhodes Dr BURY BL9 69 H2
Rhodes Hl OLDE OL4 93 E2
Rhodes St HYDE SK14 133 F5
NEWH/MOS M40 115 H1
OLD OL1 9 J3
OLDE OL4 77 E5
WHIT OL12 19 G5
Rhodes St North HYDE SK14 133 F5
Rhode St TOT/BURYW BL8 26 A5
Rhos Av CHD/CHDH SK8 182 C3
MDTN M24 72 D5
RUSH/FAL M14 143 G3
Rhos Dr BRAM/HZG SK7 185 E3
Rhosleigh Av BOL BL1 33 H2
Rialto Gdns BRO M7 * 101 H4
Ribble Av BOLE BL2 50 B2
CHAD OL9 74 A3
LIT OL15 20 C2
Ribble Dr BURY BL9 27 G3
FWTH BL4 83 E2
WALK M28 96 A4
WHTF M45 69 H3
Ribble Rd OLDS OL8 90 D4
Ribblesdale Cl HEY OL10 * 56 B2
Ribblesdale Dr
NEWH/MOS M40 102 D5
Ribblesdale Rd BOLS/LL BL3 48 C5
Ribble St ROCH OL11 42 D2
Ribbleton Cl TOT/BURYW BL8 37 E5
Ribchester Dr BURY BL9 53 E2
Ribchester Gv BOLE BL2 35 F5
Ribston St HULME M15 127 H2
Rice St CSLFD M3 6 B7
Richard Burch St BURY BL9 5 F2
Richards Cl DTN/ASHW M34 132 B1
Richardson Cl WHTF M45 69 G3
Richardson Rd ECC M30 111 F3
Richardson St OP/CLY M11 130 D1
STKP SK1 172 B2
Richard St FAIL M35 105 E3
RAD M26 68 A1
RAMS BL0 17 F1
ROCH OL11 30 B5
STKP SK1 13 H1
Richbell Cl IRL M44 136 B4
Richborough Cl BRO M7 101 H5
Richelieu St BOLS/LL BL3 49 F5
Richmond Av CHAD OL9 90 B3
PWCH M25 101 F1
ROY/SHW OL2 59 E5
URM M41 139 E1
WILM/AE SK9 192 A2
Richmond Cl DUK SK16 133 G2
MILN OL16 43 H3
MOSL OL5 109 F2
ROY/SHW OL2 60 A4
SALE M33 155 G3
STLY SK15 120 D4
TOT/BURYW BL8 26 A5
WHTF M45 69 E5
Richmond Crs MOSL OL5 109 F2
Richmond Dr WALK M28 98 B2
Richmond Gdns BOLS/LL BL3 65 G1
Richmond Gn ALT WA14 177 E2
BRAM/HZG SK7 * 194 A1
Richmond Gv
BRUN/LGST M13 129 F4
CHD/CHDH SK8 182 C3
FWTH BL4 * 65 F3
Richmond Gv East
WGTN/LGST M12 129 F3
Richmond Hill Rd
CHD/CHDH SK8 169 H4
Richmond Rd ALT WA14 165 G4
ALT WA14 177 E2
DTN/ASHW M34 * 131 F5
DUK SK16 133 G2
FAIL M35 105 F2
HTNM SK4 158 C4
MPL/ROM SK6 162 B3
RUSH/FAL M14 143 F3
TRPK M17 125 F1
Richmond St AULW OL7 119 E1
BURY BL9 53 F1
CMANE M1 7 G6
CSLFD M3 6 B1
DROY M43 * 118 B3
DTN/ASHW M34 132 B2
HYDE SK14 148 A1
STLY SK15 121 E3
Richmond Wk CHAD OL9 8 C4
Ricroft Rd MPL/ROM SK6 163 G3
Ridding Av WYTH/NTH M22 180 D1
Ridding Cl OFTN SK2 173 E3
Riddings Ct HALE/TIMP WA15 166 A1
Riddings Rd HALE/TIMP WA15 166 B1
HALE/TIMP WA15 178 A3
Ridge Av HALE/TIMP WA15 188 D1
MPL/ROM SK6 175 F5
Ridge Cl MPL/ROM SK6 162 D4
Ridge Crs MPL/ROM SK6 187 E1
WHTF M45 70 A4
Ridgecroft AULW OL7 107 E4
The Ridgedales OLD OL1 60 D5
Ridge End Fold
MPL/ROM SK6 187 F3
Ridgefield CMANW M2 6 D5
Ridgefield St FAIL M35 104 D4
Ridgegreen WALK M28 * 96 B5
Ridge Gv WHTF M45 70 A4
Ridge Hill La STLY SK15 120 D2
Ridgemont Av HTNM SK4 159 E4
Ridge Pk BRAM/HZG SK7 193 G1
Ridge Rd MPL/ROM SK6 175 F5
Ridgeway BOL BL1 * 2 E4
SWIN M27 99 G1
Ridgeway Gates BOL BL1 2 E4
Ridgeway Rd
HALE/TIMP WA15 166 D4
Ridgeway St NEWH/MOS M40 115 G3
The Ridgeway POY/DIS SK12 187 H5
Ridgewood Av CHAD OL9 73 H4
NEWH/MOS M40 103 F5
Ridgmont Dr WALK M28 96 A4
Ridgmont Rd BRAM/HZG SK7 193 H3
The Ridgway MPL/ROM SK6 161 H5
Riding Cl SALE M33 155 G2
Riding Fold DROY M43 118 B2
Riding Fold La WALK M28 97 H5
Riding Ga BOLE BL2 24 B5
Riding Gate Ms BOLE BL2 24 B5
Ridings Ct UPML OL3 78 D2
Ridings St NEWH/MOS M40 103 G5
OP/CLY M11 116 C5
Riding St CSLFD M3 6 B4
Ridley Dr ALT WA14 153 H5
Ridley Gv SALE M33 155 G3
Ridley St OLDE OL4 9 K5
Ridley Wk HULME M15 * 128 A3
Ridling La HYDE SK14 148 A1
Ridsdale Av DID/WITH M20 142 C5
Ridyard St LHULT M38 81 H3
Riefield BOL BL1 33 E3
Rifle Rd SALE M33 155 G1
Rifle St OLD OL1 9 G1
Riga Rd RUSH/FAL M14 143 E2
Riga St ANC M4 7 G2
Rigby Av RAD M26 52 D4
Rigby Ct BOLS/LL BL3 49 E5
Rigby Gv LHULT M38 80 D3
Rigby La BOLE BL2 35 E1
Rigby St ALT WA14 177 G1
BOLS/LL BL3 49 E5
BRO M7 101 G3
Rigel St ANC M4 115 F2
Rigton Cl WGTN/LGST M12 129 H3
Rildene Wk ROCH OL11 28 A3
Riley Cl SALE M33 153 E5
Riley Ct BOL BL1 34 A5
Riley Wood Cl MPL/ROM SK6 * 161 G5
Rimington Fold MDTN M24 56 A5
Rimmer Cl OP/CLY M11 115 H5
Rimmington Cl BKLY M9 88 D5
Rimsdale Cl CHD/CHDH SK8 181 F1
Rimworth Dr
NEWH/MOS M40 115 F1
Ringcroft Gdns
NEWH/MOS M40 104 A1
Ringley Cha WHTF M45 69 F4
Ringley Cl WHTF M45 69 E4
Ringley Dr WHTF M45 69 E5
Ringley Gv BOL BL1 33 H1
Ringley Hey WHTF M45 69 E4
Ringley Mdw RAD M26 67 F5
Ringley Old Brow RAD M26 67 F5
Ringley Pk WHTF M45 69 E4
Ringley Rd RAD M26 67 E4
RAD M26 67 G5
RAD M26 68 C4
Ringley Rd West RAD M26 67 H4
Ringley St BKLY M9 * 103 E2
Ringlow Av SWIN M27 98 B3
Ringlow Park Rd SWIN M27 98 B4
Ring Lows La WHIT OL12 19 F4
Ringmer Dr WYTH/NTH M22 180 B3
Ringmere Ct OLD OL1 * 75 F4
Ringmore Rd BRAM/HZG SK7 184 B2
Rings Cl FAIL M35 105 E4
Ringstead Cl WILM/AE SK9 199 G1
Ringstead Dr
NEWH/MOS M40 115 F2
WILM/AE SK9 199 G1
Ringstone PWCH M25 85 H4
Ringway Gv SALE M33 155 F4
Ringway Rd MANAIR M90 180 B5
Ringway Rd West
WYTH/NTH M22 180 B4
Ringwood Av BRAM/HZG SK7 184 C3
DTN/ASHW M34 118 B4
HYDE SK14 148 C2
RAD M26 68 C3
RAMS BL0 16 B4
WGTN/LGST M12 144 B1
Ringwood Wy CHAD OL9 8 A1
Rink St RUSH/FAL M14 143 F4
Ripley Av CHD/CHDH SK8 193 E2
OFTN SK2 172 C5
Ripley Cl ANC M4 * 115 G5
BRAM/HZG SK7 185 F4
Ripley Crs URM M41 123 G3
Ripley St BOLE BL2 34 C2
Ripon Av BOL BL1 32 C5
WHTF M45 69 G2
Ripon Cl BOLS/LL BL3 66 C1
CHAD OL9 90 C1
HALE/TIMP WA15 178 D3
RAD M26 53 E4
STKP SK1 13 G6
WHTF M45 69 G2
Ripon Crs STRET M32 125 E5
Ripon Dr BOL BL1 32 C5
Ripon Gv SALE M33 139 F5
Ripon Hall Av RAMS BL0 16 C4
Ripon Rd STRET M32 125 F5
Ripon St AUL OL6 * 119 H2
OLD OL1 75 E4
Rippenden Av CCHDY M21 141 E1
Rippingham Rd
DID/WITH M20 142 D4
Rippleton Rd WYTH/NTH M22 168 D5
Ripponden Rd OLDE OL4 76 C3
Ripponden St OLD OL1 76 B3
The Rise OLDE OL4 77 E5
Rishton Av BOLS/LL BL3 65 E2
Rishton La BOLS/LL BL3 65 E1
Rishworth Cl OFTN SK2 173 E4
Rishworth Dr
NEWH/MOS M40 104 D2
Rishworth Ri ROY/SHW OL2 44 C5
Rising La OLDS OL8 91 F5
Risley Av BKLY M9 103 E2
Risley St OLD OL1 75 G4
Rissington Av
NTHM/RTH M23 168 A3
Rita Av RUSH/FAL M14 * 128 C5
Ritson Cl GTN M18 130 A2
Riva Rd BNG/LEV M19 158 A4
Riverbank UPML OL3 78 C3
Riverbank Dr TOT/BURYW BL8 4 B1
Riverbanks BOLS/LL BL3 49 H4
The Riverbank RAD M26 66 D4
Riverbrook Rd ALT WA14 153 F5
Riverdale Rd BKLY M9 87 F4
River La PART M31 151 E2
Rivermead MILN OL16 45 E3
Rivermead Av
HALE/TIMP WA15 188 C1
Rivermead Cl DTN/ASHW M34 147 E4
Rivermead Rd
DTN/ASHW M34 147 F4
Rivermead Wy WHTF M45 69 H4
Riverpark Rd
NEWH/MOS M40 116 B2
River Pl HULME M15 127 H1
MILN OL16 * 31 G5
Riversdale Dr OLDS OL8 106 D1
Riversdale Rd CHD/CHDH SK8 169 H4
Riversdale Vw MPL/ROM SK6 161 H1
The Rivers Edge WHIT OL12 14 B5
Rivershill SALE M33 139 G5
Rivershill Dr HEY OL10 40 C5
Rivershill Gdns
HALE/TIMP WA15 188 D1
Riverside BOL BL1 34 A4
BRO M7 113 H2
DUK SK16 119 H3
OLD OL1 73 H3
Riverside Av IRL M44 136 C2
Riverside Ct MPL/ROM SK6 * 175 F1
Riverside Dr BURY BL9 16 C5
MILN OL16 11 J1
RAD M26 67 E4
URM M41 138 B3
Riverside Gdns SALE M33 139 G5
Riverside Rd RAD M26 53 E5
Rivers La URM M41 124 B3
Riversleigh Cl BOL BL1 32 C3
Riversmeade EDGW/EG BL7 23 H4
Riverstone Br LIT OL15 20 D3
Riverstone Dr
NTHM/RTH M23 167 E2
River St BOLE BL2 3 G5
HEY OL10 41 E2
HULME M15 128 A1
MILN OL16 10 D6
RAD M26 68 C1
RAMS BL0 16 D2
STKP SK1 160 C3
WGTN/LGST M12 * 115 F5
WILM/AE SK9 199 E2
Riverton Rd DID/WITH M20 169 G2
River Vw RDSH SK5 145 G4
River View Cl PWCH M25 85 G5
Riverview Wk BOL BL1 * 2 A6
Rivington Av SWIN M27 99 H3
Rivington Dr ROY/SHW OL2 60 C2
TOT/BURYW BL8 37 F5
Rivington Gv DTN/ASHW M34 118 B5
Rivington Rd
HALE/TIMP WA15 178 A2
OLDE OL4 77 F5
SLFD M6 112 B1
Rivington St OLD OL1 75 G4
WHIT OL12 10 D3
Rivington Wk
WGTN/LGST M12 * 129 F3
Rixon St OLDE OL4 76 C3
Rixson St OLDE OL4 * 76 C3
Rix St BOL BL1 33 H4
Rixtonleys Dr IRL M44 136 D3
Roach Bank Rd BURY BL9 54 B2
Roaches Ms MOSL OL5 94 A4
Roaches Wy MOSL OL5 94 B4
Roachill Cl ALT WA14 165 E4
Roach Pl MILN OL16 10 E5
Roach St BURY BL9 39 F5
BURY BL9 53 G5
Roach V MILN OL16 30 D1
Roachwood Cl CHAD OL9 73 H5
Roading Brook Rd BOLE BL2 36 A3
Road La WHIT OL12 18 C4
Roads Ford Av MILN OL16 31 G4
Roan Wy WILM/AE SK9 201 E5
Roaring Gate La
HALE/TIMP WA15 179 F1
Robert Hall St ORD M5 127 E1
Robert Lawrence Ct
URM M41 * 138 A2
Robert Malcolm Cl
NEWH/MOS M40 103 E5
Robert Owen Gdns
WYTH/NTH M22 * 168 C1
Robert Salt Ct ALT WA14 165 H3
Robertscroft Cl
WYTH/NTH M22 168 B5
Robertshaw Av CCHDY M21 141 F5
Robertson St RAD M26 52 B5
Roberts St ECC M30 111 E4
Robert St BOLE BL2 * 35 F1
CSLFD M3 114 C2
DUK SK16 119 G5
FAIL M35 105 F1
HEY OL10 56 B1
HYDE SK14 147 G1
MILN OL16 10 E5
NEWH/MOS M40 103 G5
OLDS OL8 90 C5
PWCH M25 86 B3
SALE M33 155 F2
TOT/BURYW BL8 37 H3
Robeson Wy
WYTH/NTH M22 169 E3
Robin Cft MPL/ROM SK6 161 E3
Robin Dr IRL M44 122 B5
Robin Hood St CHH M8 102 A2
Robinia Cl ECC M30 110 A5
Robin Rd ALT WA14 153 F5
BURY BL9 16 C5
Robinsbay Rd
WYTH/NTH M22 180 D5
Robins Cl BRAM/HZG SK7 183 H5
DROY M43 118 B2
Robin's La BRAM/HZG SK7 183 H5
Robinson La AULW OL7 119 E2
Robinson Pk STLY SK15 120 B4
Robinson St CHAD OL9 90 C1
EDGY/DAV SK3 12 D7
HYDE SK14 * 134 A5
MILN OL16 10 E6
OLDS OL8 91 G4
STLY SK15 120 C4
Robin St OLD OL1 * 75 F4
Robinsway ALT WA14 177 F3
Robinswood Rd
WYTH/NTH M22 180 C3
Robson Av URM M41 124 D1
Robson St OLD OL1 9 H4
Roby Rd ECC M30 110 D5
Roby St CMANE M1 7 H5
Roch Av HEY OL10 40 B4
Roch Bank BKLY M9 87 E4
Rochbury Cl ROCH OL11 28 C5
Roch Cl WHTF M45 70 A3
Roch Crs WHTF M45 70 A3
Rochdale La HEY OL10 41 E4
ROY/SHW OL2 59 E4
Rochdale Old Rd BURY BL9 39 F3
Rochdale Rd BKLY M9 103 E3
BURY BL9 4 E4
HEY OL10 41 E4
MDTN M24 57 G3
MDTN M24 73 E1
MILN OL16 31 E4
NEWH/MOS M40 115 F1
OLD OL1 8 E1
ROY/SHW OL2 44 B5
ROY/SHW OL2 58 D3
Rochdale Rd East HEY OL10 41 G3
Rochdale Wy MILN OL16 44 B4
Roche Gdns CHD/CHDH SK8 193 E1
Rochester Av BOLE BL2 35 F5
CCHDY M21 141 H5
PWCH M25 86 B5
WALK M28 96 D1
Rochester Cl AUL OL6 107 F3
DUK SK16 134 B1
Rochester Dr ALT WA14 153 H5
Rochester Gv BRAM/HZG SK7 185 F1
Rochester Rd URM M41 124 C4
Rochester Wy CHAD OL9 90 C1
Rochford Av WHTF M45 69 E5
Rochford Cl WHTF M45 69 E5
Rochford Rd ECC M30 110 A5
Roch Mills Crs ROCH OL11 42 B1
Roch Mills Gdns ROCH OL11 42 B1
Roch St MILN OL16 11 H2
Roch Valley Wy ROCH OL11 29 F5
Roch Wy WHTF M45 70 A3
Rockall Wk OP/CLY M11 * 116 A4
Rock Av BOL BL1 33 F4
Rock Bank BRO M7 * 101 F4
MOSL OL5 * 108 D1
Rockdove Av HULME M15 128 A1
Rocket Wy CSLFD M3 6 A4
Rockfield Dr BKLY M9 * 103 F2
Rock Fold EDGW/EG BL7 * 23 F2
Rockhampton St GTN M18 130 D3
Rockhouse Cl ECC M30 111 E5
Rockingham Cl ROY/SHW OL2 59 F1
WGTN/LGST M12 129 E2
Rockley Gdns SLFD M6 113 G1
Rocklyn Av NEWH/MOS M40 89 F5
Rocklynes MPL/ROM SK6 162 A4
Rockmead Dr BKLY M9 88 B4
Rock Rd URM M41 139 F1
Rock St AULW OL7 106 D5
BRO M7 101 G4
HEY OL10 41 F5
HYDE SK14 148 A4
OLD OL1 9 G3
OP/CLY M11 130 D1
RAD M26 68 C2
RAMS BL0 17 F1
Rock Ter EDGW/EG BL7 23 E2
MOSL OL5 94 A4
The Rock BURY BL9 4 D4
Rocky La ECC M30 111 E1
Roda St BKLY M9 103 G3
Rodborough Rd
NTHM/RTH M23 179 H1
Rodeheath Cl WILM/AE SK9 199 G3
Rodenhurst Dr
NEWH/MOS M40 103 H4
Rodepool Cl WILM/AE SK9 192 A5
Rodmell Av NEWH/MOS M40 * 103 E5
Rodmell Cl EDGW/EG BL7 23 E4
Rodmill Ct RUSH/FAL M14 143 E2
Rodmill Dr CHD/CHDH SK8 169 F5
Rodney Ct ANC M4 7 K1
Rodney Dr MPL/ROM SK6 161 H1
Rodney St ANC M4 115 F3
AUL OL6 120 A1
CSLFD M3 114 A4
ROCH OL11 42 A4
Roeacre St HEY OL10 41 F4
Roebuck Gdns SALE M33 * 154 B2
Roebuck La OLDE OL4 77 F1
SALE M33 154 B2
Roe Cross Gn HYDE SK14 135 G3
Roe Cross Rd HYDE SK14 135 G3
Roedean Gdns URM M41 137 F1
Roefield Ter WHIT OL12 29 F3
Roe Gn WALK M28 97 H2
Roe Green Av WALK M28 97 H2
Roe La OLDE OL4 92 C2
Roe St ANC M4 7 K1
WHIT OL12 29 F2
Rogate Dr NTHM/RTH M23 167 H4
Roger Cl MPL/ROM SK6 161 G5
Rogerson Cl
HALE/TIMP WA15 166 D2
Rogerstead BOLS/LL BL3 * 48 B3
Roger St ANC M4 114 D2
Roger Wy CHD/CHDH SK8 182 D2
Rokeby Av STRET M32 140 B2
Roker Av BRUN/LGST M13 143 H1
Roker Park Av
DTN/ASHW M34 132 B1

Roland Rd BOLS/LL BL3 48 B4
RDSH SK5 145 F4
Rolla St CSLFD M3 6 C2
Rollesby Cl TOT/BURYW BL8 38 A1
Rolleston Av ANC M4 115 G3
Rollins La MPL/ROM SK6 163 F5
Rolls Crs HULME M15 127 H2
Rollswood Dr
NEWH/MOS M40 103 H4
Romana Sq ALT WA14 165 H1
Roman Rd FAIL M35 105 F2
HTNM SK4 13 F2
PWCH M25 100 C1
ROY/SHW OL2 75 E1
Roman St RAD M26 67 H1
Romer Av NEWH/MOS M40 * 104 D1
Rome Rd NEWH/MOS M40 7 K1
Romer St BOLE BL2 49 H2
Romford Av DTN/ASHW M34 132 D4
Romford Cl OLDS OL8 9 F7
Romford Rd SALE M33 139 E5
Romiley Crs BOLE BL2 50 A1
Romiley Dr BOLE BL2 50 A1
Romiley St SLFD M6 100 A5
STKP SK1 160 C4
Romley Rd URM M41 124 C4
Romney Av ROCH OL11 42 D4
Romney Cha BOL BL1 33 H2
Romney Rd BOL BL1 32 B4
Romney St AUL OL6 119 H2
NEWH/MOS M40 103 H2
SLFD M6 100 D5
Romney Wk CHAD OL9 90 C1
Romney Wy RDSH SK5 145 H5
Romsey WHIT OL12 10 B5
Romsey Av MDTN M24 72 C1
Romsey Dr CHD/CHDH SK8 193 E1
Romsley Cl WGTN/LGST M12 129 H2
Romsley Dr BOLS/LL BL3 64 B1
Rona Cl WGTN/LGST M12 129 G3
Ronaldsay Gdns ORD M5 112 D4
Ronald St OLDE OL4 76 B5
OP/CLY M11 117 E4
ROCH OL11 42 B5
Rondin Cl WGTN/LGST M12 129 F1
Rondin Rd WGTN/LGST M12 129 F1
Roocroft Ct BOL BL1 2 B1
Rookery Av GTN M18 131 E2
Rookery Cl STLY SK15 135 F1
Rookerypool Cl WILM/AE SK9 192 A5
Rooke St ECC M30 110 B5
Rookfield Av SALE M33 154 D1
Rookley Wk RUSH/FAL M14 * 128 D5
Rook St HULME M15 127 H3
OLDE OL4 92 B2
RAMS BL0 16 D2
Rookswood Dr ROCH OL11 42 A3
Rookway MDTN M24 72 C5
Rookwood OLD OL1 73 H3
Rookwood Av
NTHM/RTH M23 167 G2
Rookwood Hl BRAM/HZG SK7 183 H3
Rooley Moor Rd WHIT OL12 29 E1
Rooley St WHIT OL12 29 F2
Roosevelt Rd FWTH BL4 66 C5
Rooth St HTNM SK4 12 C2
Ropefield Wy WHIT OL12 18 D5
Rope St WHIT OL12 10 C4
Rope Wk CSLFD M3 6 C1
Rosa Gv BRO M7 101 G4
Rosamond Dr CSLFD M3 6 A3
Rosamond St BOLS/LL BL3 48 B5
HULME M15 128 B2
Rosamond St West
HULME M15 128 B2
Rosary Cl OLDS OL8 106 C1
Rosary Rd OLDS OL8 106 D1
Roscoe Ct WHTN BL5 62 A5
Roscoe Rd IRL M44 136 A2
Roscoe St EDGY/DAV SK3 12 D5
OLD OL1 9 J4
Roscow Av BOLE BL2 50 B1
Roscow Rd FWTH BL4 82 D1
Rose Acre WALK M28 96 C3
Roseacre Dr CHD/CHDH SK8 181 H3
Rose Av IRL M44 136 B2
LIT OL15 20 C5
ROCH OL11 28 A1
Rosebank HOR/BR BL6 46 D2
Rosebank Cl BOLE BL2 36 B5
Rosebank Rd IRL M44 150 B3
NEWH/MOS M40 116 C1
Rosebay Cl ROY/SHW OL2 59 G5
Roseberry Cl RAMS BL0 16 D5
Roseberry St BOLS/LL BL3 48 B5
OLDS OL8 * 8 D5
Rosebery St OFTN SK2 173 E5
RUSH/FAL M14 128 A5
WHTN BL5 62 A4
Rosebury Av OLD OL1 76 A3
Rose Cottage Rd
DID/WITH M20 142 D4
Rose Crs IRL M44 136 B2
Rosecroft Cl EDGY/DAV SK3 171 H5
Rosedale Av BOL BL1 33 H1
Rosedale Cl OLD OL1 76 A3
Rosedale Ct DTN/ASHW M34 * 132 B5
Rosedale Rd HTNM SK4 159 G1
RUSH/FAL M14 142 C1
Rosedale Wy DUK SK16 133 F2
Rosefield Cl EDGY/DAV SK3 171 H4
Rosefield Crs MILN OL16 11 H7
Rosegarth Av DID/WITH M20 156 C2
Rose Gv FWTH BL4 66 C5
TOT/BURYW BL8 37 F4
Rosehay Av DTN/ASHW M34 146 D1
Rose Hey La FAIL M35 117 F1
Rose Hl BOLE BL2 49 F4
DTN/ASHW M34 132 A5
STLY SK15 120 C5
UPML OL3 78 C1
Rose Hill Av
NEWH/MOS M40 * 116 C1
Rose Hill Cl EDGW/EG BL7 23 F4
Rosehill Cl SLFD M6 113 E3
Rose Hill Rd AUL OL6 108 A5
Rosehill Rd SWIN M27 84 A5
Rose Hill St HEY OL10 40 C4
Roseland Av DID/WITH M20 157 G2
Roseland Dr PWCH M25 86 B1
Roselands Av SALE M33 154 A4
Rose La MPL/ROM SK6 174 D4
Rose Lea BOLE BL2 35 F2
Rosemary Dr HYDE SK14 147 H4
LIT OL15 20 C2
Rosemary Gv BRO M7 101 F5
Rosemary La STKP SK1 13 J4
WHTN BL5 80 A1
Rosemary Rd CHAD OL9 73 H4
Rosemount HYDE SK14 133 G3
Rose Mt MDTN M24 72 C2
Rosemount Crs HYDE SK14 133 G3
Roseneath BRAM/HZG SK7 183 G3
Roseneath Av BNG/LEV M19 144 C2
Roseneath Gv BOLS/LL BL3 64 C1
Roseneath Rd BOLS/LL BL3 64 C1
URM M41 124 B5
Rosen Sq CHAD OL9 * 74 C5
Rose St BOLE BL2 49 F4
CHAD OL9 90 B4
MDTN M24 73 F4
RDSH SK5 160 A3
Rose Ter STLY SK15 120 D4
Rosethorns Cl MDTN M24 56 C5
Rose V CHD/CHDH SK8 181 G3
Rosevale Av BNG/LEV M19 158 B1
Roseway BRAM/HZG SK7 184 A2
Rosewell Cl NEWH/MOS M40 115 G1
Rose Wd DTN/ASHW M34 132 A5
Rosewood ROCH OL11 28 B2
Rosewood Av DROY M43 118 B2
HTNM SK4 158 D5
TOT/BURYW BL8 26 B5
Rosewood Cl DUK SK16 133 G2
Rosewood Crs CHAD OL9 74 C3
Rosewood Gdns
CHD/CHDH SK8 169 E3
Rosford Av RUSH/FAL M14 142 D1
Rosgill Cl HTNM SK4 158 B4
Rosgill Dr MDTN M24 72 A3
Rosina St OP/CLY M11 131 E1
Roslin St OP/CLY M11 117 E3
Roslyn Av URM M41 137 G3
Roslyn Rd EDGY/DAV SK3 171 H4
Rossall Av RAD M26 68 D4
STRET M32 125 H5
Rossall Cl BOLE BL2 49 H1
Rossall Dr BRAM/HZG SK7 194 A1
Rossall Rd BOLE BL2 49 H1
WHIT OL12 10 E1
Rossall St BOLE BL2 49 H1
Rossall Wy SLFD M6 113 F2
Ross Av CHAD OL9 90 A4
EDGY/DAV SK3 171 H4
WHTF M45 85 G1
Ross Dr SWIN M27 83 H3
Rossenclough Rd
WILM/AE SK9 199 G1
Rossendale Av BKLY M9 103 G1
Rossendale Cl ROY/SHW OL2 60 C2
Rossendale Rd
CHD/CHDH SK8 181 H4
Rossendale Wy WHIT OL12 15 F2
Rossett Av HALE/TIMP WA15 166 B1
WYTH/NTH M22 180 C3
Rossett Dr URM M41 123 G4
Ross Gv URM M41 138 C1
Rosshill Wk HULME M15 * 127 G2
Rossington St
NEWH/MOS M40 104 C5
Rossini St BOL BL1 33 G3
Rosslare Rd WYTH/NTH M22 180 D2
Ross Lave La DTN/ASHW M34 146 B2
Rosslyn Gv HALE/TIMP WA15 166 B3
Rosslyn Rd CHD/CHDH SK8 182 A3
NEWH/MOS M40 103 H1
OLDTF/WHR M16 141 E1
Rossmere Av ROCH OL11 29 F5
Rossmill La HALE/TIMP WA15 178 D5
Ross St OLDS OL8 8 D6
Rostherne Av MPL/ROM SK6 186 D4
RUSH/FAL M14 142 C2
Rostherne Gdns BOLS/LL BL3 48 A5
Rostherne Rd EDGY/DAV SK3 171 H4
SALE M33 155 G3
WILM/AE SK9 198 B5
Rostherne St ALT WA14 177 G1
SLFD M6 * 112 D4
Rosthernmere Rd
CHD/CHDH SK8 170 C5
Rosthwaite Cl MDTN M24 71 H3
Roston Rd BRO M7 101 H2
Rostrevor Rd EDGY/DAV SK3 171 H4
Rostron Av WGTN/LGST M12 129 F2
Rostron Rd RAMS BL0 16 C2
Rostron St BNG/LEV M19 144 B2
Rothay Cl BOLE BL2 35 G5
WHTF M45 70 B4
Rothay Dr MDTN M24 72 B1
RDSH SK5 145 F3
Rothbury Av AULW OL7 106 B5
Rothbury Cl TOT/BURYW BL8 37 E4
Rothbury Ct BOLS/LL BL3 64 A1
Rotherby Rd WYTH/NTH M22 168 D5
Rotherdale Av
HALE/TIMP WA15 167 E4
Rotherwood Av STRET M32 126 B5
Rotherwood Rd WILM/AE SK9 198 A5
Rothesay Av DUK SK16 133 F1
Rothesay Crs SALE M33 153 F4
Rothesay Rd BOLS/LL BL3 * 64 A1
CHH M8 86 D5
OLD OL1 76 B3
Rothesay Ter MILN OL16 43 H2
Rothiemay Rd URM M41 137 G2
Rothley Av WYTH/NTH M22 168 C4
Rothman Cl NEWH/MOS M40 104 B4
Rothwell Crs LHULT M38 80 D1
Rothwell La LHULT M38 80 D2
Rothwell St BOLS/LL BL3 48 D4
FAIL M35 104 D4
NEWH/MOS M40 104 B4
RAMS BL0 16 C2
ROY/SHW OL2 74 D1
WALK M28 82 C4
WHIT OL12 11 G2
Rottingdene Dr
WYTH/NTH M22 180 B3
Roughey Gdns
WYTH/NTH M22 168 B5
Rough Hey Wk MILN OL16 30 C5
Rough Hill La BURY BL9 39 H2
Roughlee Av SWIN M27 98 C3
Roughtown Ct MOSL OL5 94 A5
Roughtown Rd MOSL OL5 94 A5
Roundcroft MPL/ROM SK6 162 C3
Roundhey CHD/CHDH SK8 181 G4
Round Hey MOSL OL5 108 D2
Round Hill Wy BOL BL1 3 F2
Roundhill Wy OLDE OL4 76 D3
Round Thorn Rd MDTN M24 73 E5
Roundthorn Rd
NTHM/RTH M23 167 G3
OLDE OL4 92 B2
Roundway BRAM/HZG SK7 193 G1
Roundwood Rd
WYTH/NTH M22 168 C2
Rousdon Cl NEWH/MOS M40 * 103 E5
Rouse St ROCH OL11 42 B2
Roving Bridge Ri SWIN M27 100 A2
Rowan Av OLDTF/WHR M16 127 F5
SALE M33 154 D4
URM M41 124 C5
Rowan Cl FAIL M35 105 E5
Rowan Crs DUK SK16 134 A1
Rowan Dr BURY BL9 5 K3
CHD/CHDH SK8 183 F4
Rowanlea PWCH M25 * 86 B3
Rowan Pl PWCH M25 86 A4
Rowans Cl STLY SK15 121 F2
Rowanside Dr WILM/AE SK9 199 H2
Rowans St TOT/BURYW BL8 37 H2
The Rowans BOL BL1 47 F2
MOSL OL5 109 E1
Rowan St HYDE SK14 148 B2
Rowanswood Dr HYDE SK14 134 B5
Rowan Tree Dr SALE M33 154 C5
Rowan Tree Rd OLDS OL8 106 A1
Rowanwood CHAD OL9 73 H5
Rowany Cl PWCH M25 85 H5
Rowarth Av DTN/ASHW M34 147 E3
Rowarth Rd NTHM/RTH M23 179 G2
Rowbottom Wk OLDS OL8 9 F7
Rowcon Cl DTN/ASHW M34 132 B3
Rowden Rd OLDE OL4 92 D3
Rowe Gn DTN/ASHW M34 132 C5
Rowena St BOLS/LL BL3 65 H2
Rowendale St HULME M15 * 6 D7
Rowfield Dr NTHM/RTH M23 179 G1
Rowland Av URM M41 124 D5
Rowland Ct MILN OL16 * 30 C5
Rowlands Rd BURY BL9 27 F2
Rowland St MILN OL16 30 C5
ORD M5 113 F5
Rowlandsway
WYTH/NTH M22 180 C2
Rowland Wy OLDE OL4 76 D5
Rowley Rd BRAM/HZG SK7 185 F4
Rowley St AUL OL6 107 G4
Rowood Av CHH M8 102 C4
RDSH SK5 145 F1
Rowrah Crs MDTN M24 71 G3
Rowsley Av BOL BL1 32 D5
DID/WITH M20 156 D2
Rowsley Gv RDSH SK5 145 E4
Rowsley Rd ECC M30 110 D5
STRET M32 125 F5
Rowsley St OP/CLY M11 115 H3
SLFD M6 101 E5
Rowson Ct SALE M33 * 155 E2
Rowton St BOLE BL2 34 C3
Roxalina St BOLS/LL BL3 48 D5
Roxburgh St GTN M18 130 C3
Roxbury Av OLDE OL4 92 C2
Roxby Cl WALK M28 81 G4
Roxholme Wk
WYTH/NTH M22 180 B4
Roxton Rd HTNM SK4 144 C5
Royal Av BURY BL9 38 C1
CCHDY M21 141 E4
DROY M43 118 A3
HEY OL10 41 E5
URM M41 138 D1
Royal Court Dr BOL BL1 2 B3
Royal Crs CHD/CHDH SK8 181 H2
Royal Ex CMANW M2 * 6 E4
Royal Exchange Ar
CMANW M2 * 6 E4
Royal Gdns ALT WA14 176 C2
Royal George St
EDGY/DAV SK3 13 F6
Royal Oak Rd NTHM/RTH M23 167 H2
Royal Pde OLD OL1 75 F3
Royal St MILN OL16 30 D1
Royalthorn Dr
WYTH/NTH M22 168 B3
Royalthorn Rd
WYTH/NTH M22 168 C3
Royce Av HALE/TIMP WA15 165 H4
Royce Rd HULME M15 127 H2
Roydale St NEWH/MOS M40 115 H2
Royden Av BKLY M9 88 A2
IRL M44 136 B3
Roydes St MDTN M24 73 E2
Royds Cl BRUN/LGST M13 129 E3
TOT/BURYW BL8 37 F1
Royds Pl MILN OL16 43 F1
Royds St BURY BL9 39 G2
LIT OL15 21 F3
MILN OL16 43 G1
MILN OL16 44 D1
TOT/BURYW BL8 26 A4
Royds St West MILN OL16 43 F1
Royd St OLDS OL8 90 D3
Royland Av BOLS/LL BL3 65 F1
Royle Barn Rd ROCH OL11 42 B4
Royle Cl OFTN SK2 172 B4
OLDS OL8 91 G4
Royle Green Rd
WYTH/NTH M22 168 D1
Royle Rd ROCH OL11 42 C3
Royle St DTN/ASHW M34 132 C3
OFTN SK2 13 H7
RUSH/FAL M14 143 F4
SLFD M6 * 113 E4
WALK M28 82 A5
Royley ROY/SHW OL2 74 D1
Royley Crs ROY/SHW OL2 74 D1
Royley Rd OLDS OL8 91 F3
Royon Dr EDGY/DAV SK3 171 E3
Royston Av BOLE BL2 3 K2
DTN/ASHW M34 131 E5
OLDTF/WHR M16 127 G5
Royston Cl TOT/BURYW BL8 26 A2
Royston Rd OLDTF/WHR M16 127 E5
URM M41 124 D5
Roy St BOLS/LL BL3 48 A5
ROY/SHW OL2 59 E5
Royton Av SALE M33 155 F4
Rozel Sq CSLFD M3 6 C6
Ruabon Rd DID/WITH M20 157 H4
Rubens Cl MPL/ROM SK6 175 H1
Ruby St BOL BL1 34 A3
BURY BL9 16 D5
DTN/ASHW M34 132 B5
HULME M15 128 B2
Rudcroft Cl BRUN/LGST M13 128 C2
Rudding St ROY/SHW OL2 75 H2
Ruddpark Rd WYTH/NTH M22 180 C3
Rudd St NEWH/MOS M40 103 H3
Rudford Gdns BOLS/LL BL3 49 E5
Rudgwick Dr TOT/BURYW BL8 26 D4
Rudheath Av DID/WITH M20 142 C4
Rudman Dr ORD M5 113 H5
Rudman St ROCH OL11 29 F5
Rudman St AULW OL7 119 F4
WHIT OL12 10 A1
Rudolph St BOLS/LL BL3 65 E1
Rudston Av NEWH/MOS M40 89 E5
Rudyard Av MDTN M24 73 F1
Rudyard Gv HTNM SK4 144 D5
ROCH OL11 43 E4
SALE M33 153 H4
Rudyard Rd SLFD M6 99 H5
Rudyard St BRO M7 101 G4
Rufford Av HYDE SK14 148 B1
ROCH OL11 42 C2
Rufford Cl AUL OL6 107 F3
ROY/SHW OL2 59 G2
WHTF M45 69 H2
Rufford Dr BOLS/LL BL3 64 C2
WHTF M45 69 G2
Rufford Gv BOLS/LL BL3 64 C2
Rufford Pl GTN M18 * 131 E4
Rufford Rd OLDTF/WHR M16 127 G5
Rufus St RUSH/FAL M14 143 G4
Rugby Dr SALE M33 154 B4
Rugby Rd SLFD M6 111 H2
WHIT OL12 10 E3
Rugby St CHH M8 114 B1
Rugeley St SLFD M6 101 E5
Ruins La BOLE BL2 35 F2
Ruislip Av NEWH/MOS M40 103 F5
Ruislip Cl OLDS OL8 92 A3
Rumworth Rd HOR/BR BL6 46 D3
Rumworth St BOLS/LL BL3 48 C5
Runcorn St HULME M15 127 F1
Runger La HALE/TIMP WA15 179 G4
Runhall Cl WGTN/LGST M12 129 H2
Running Hill Ga UPML OL3 79 H3
Running Hill La UPML OL3 79 H2
Runnymeade SWIN M27 99 F4
Runnymede Cl EDGY/DAV SK3 171 F3
Runnymede Ct BOLS/LL BL3 48 C4
ROY/SHW OL2 59 F5
Rupert St BOLS/LL BL3 65 E1
NEWH/MOS M40 117 F1
RAD M26 68 C3
RDSH SK5 145 E4
WHIT OL12 29 F2
Ruscombe Fold MDTN M24 72 A1
Rush Acre Cl RAD M26 67 H1
Rush Bank ROY/SHW OL2 59 G1
Rushbrooke Av OP/CLY M11 116 D2
Rushbury Dr ROY/SHW OL2 59 H5
Rushcroft Rd ROY/SHW OL2 59 G1
Rushden Rd BNG/LEV M19 144 B1
Rushen St OP/CLY M11 116 D4
Rushey Cl HALE/TIMP WA15 179 E5
Rushey Fld EDGW/EG BL7 23 E3
Rushey Fold La BOL BL1 33 G4
Rusheylea Cl BOL BL1 33 G4
Rushey Rd WYTH/NTH M22 168 B4
Rushfield Dr BRUN/LGST M13 129 F5
Rushfield Rd CHD/CHDH SK8 192 D1
Rushford Av BNG/LEV M19 144 A1
Rushford Gv BOL BL1 34 A2
Rushford St WGTN/LGST M12 129 H4
Rush Gv UPML OL3 79 E5
Rush Hill Rd UPML OL3 79 E5
Rush Hill Ter UPML OL3 79 E5
Rushlake Gdns ROCH OL11 28 B3
Rushley Av BRO M7 101 E4
Rushmere AUL OL6 107 H4
Rushmere Av BNG/LEV M19 144 B2
Rushmere Dr TOT/BURYW BL8 37 H1
Rushmere Wk
OLDTF/WHR M16 127 G3
Rushmoor Cl IRL M44 136 C1
Rush Mt ROY/SHW OL2 44 C5
Rusholme Gv RUSH/FAL M14 128 D5
Rusholme Pl RUSH/FAL M14 128 D4
Rushside Rd CHD/CHDH SK8 192 C1
Rush St DUK SK16 120 C5
Rushton Cl MPL/ROM SK6 * 175 F4
Rushton Dr BRAM/HZG SK7 183 G1
MPL/ROM SK6 162 B3
MPL/ROM SK6 175 E5
Rushton Gv OLDE OL4 76 D1
OP/CLY M11 130 D1
Rushton Rd BOL BL1 33 E5
CHD/CHDH SK8 192 D1
EDGY/DAV SK3 171 E2
Rushton St DID/WITH M20 157 G4
WALK M28 82 A5
Rushway Av BKLY M9 89 E5
Rushwick Av
NEWH/MOS M40 103 F5
Rushworth Ct HTNM SK4 159 F1
Rushycroft HYDE SK14 135 H4
Rushyfield Crs MPL/ROM SK6 162 C3
Rushy Hill Vw WHIT OL12 * 29 E2
Ruskin Av CHAD OL9 90 A4
DTN/ASHW M34 131 H1
DTN/ASHW M34 146 C2
FWTH BL4 66 C3
RUSH/FAL M14 128 C4
Ruskin Crs PWCH M25 85 G4
Ruskin Dr SALE M33 153 F2
Ruskin Gdns MPL/ROM SK6 161 H3
Ruskin Gv MPL/ROM SK6 161 H3
Ruskington Dr BKLY M9 103 E3
Ruskin Rd BOLS/LL BL3 51 E5
DROY M43 117 H3
OLDTF/WHR M16 127 F5
PWCH M25 85 F4
RDSH SK5 145 E2
ROCH OL11 42 D4
Ruskin St OLD OL1 8 D1
RAD M26 52 D5
Rusland Ct OFTN SK2 * 172 C2
Rusland Dr BOLE BL2 35 F4
Russell Av MPL/ROM SK6 186 D5
OLDTF/WHR M16 141 H1
SALE M33 155 E1
Russell Cl BOL BL1 48 B1
Russell Ct FWTH BL4 * 66 B4
LHULT M38 81 H4
Russell Dr IRL M44 136 C1
Russell Gdns HTNM SK4 159 E5
Russell Rd OLDTF/WHR M16 127 G5
PART M31 151 F3
SLFD M6 99 G5
Russell St AUL OL6 120 A1
BURY BL9 5 F1
CHAD OL9 * 74 C5
CHH M8 114 C1
DUK SK16 119 H5
ECC M30 111 F3
FWTH BL4 66 A5
HEY OL10 41 F5
LHULT M38 81 H4
MOSL OL5 108 D1
OFTN SK2 172 B3
OLDTF/WHR M16 128 A5
PWCH M25 86 B3
Russet Rd BKLY M9 103 E1
Russet Wy WILM/AE SK9 200 B2
Ruth Av NEWH/MOS M40 104 D1
Ruthen La OLDTF/WHR M16 127 E4
Rutherford Av RUSH/FAL M14 128 C5
Rutherford Cl HYDE SK14 147 H1
Rutherford Dr WHTN BL5 63 G5
Rutherglade Cl
NEWH/MOS M40 102 D4
Rutherglen Dr BOLS/LL BL3 47 G3
Rutherglen Wk
NEWH/MOS M40 103 F5
Ruthin Av BKLY M9 87 H2
CHD/CHDH SK8 182 B2
MDTN M24 88 D1
Ruthin Cl OLDS OL8 90 C5
Ruth St BOL BL1 2 C3
BURY BL9 5 F1
GTN M18 130 C5
OLD OL1 9 H1
WHIT OL12 14 C4
Rutland ROCH OL11 * 29 H5
Rutland Av DID/WITH M20 157 F1
OLDTF/WHR M16 126 D5
SWIN M27 84 A5
URM M41 139 E1
Rutland Cl AUL OL6 120 A3
BOLS/LL BL3 51 E5
CHD/CHDH SK8 169 G3
Rutland Crs RDSH SK5 161 E1
Rutland Dr BRO M7 101 F2
BURY BL9 53 H1
Rutland Gv BOL BL1 33 F5
FWTH BL4 * 65 H5
Rutland La SALE M33 155 H1
Rutland Rd ALT WA14 165 G3
BRAM/HZG SK7 185 F4
DROY M43 117 F3
ECC M30 111 G2
IRL M44 150 C1
PART M31 150 D4
WALK M28 97 E1
Rutland St AUL OL6 120 A3
BOLS/LL BL3 48 C5
CHAD OL9 8 A7
FAIL M35 * 105 E2
GTN M18 130 D2
HEY OL10 41 E3
HYDE SK14 133 G3
SWIN M27 98 D1
Rutland Wy ROY/SHW OL2 60 B1
Rutter's La
BRAM/HZG SK7 184 D2
Ryall Av ORD M5 113 G5
Ryall Av South ORD M5 113 G5
Ryan St OP/CLY M11 130 D1
Rydal Av BRAM/HZG SK7 184 D1
CHAD OL9 73 H3
DROY M43 117 F4
ECC M30 110 C1
HYDE SK14 133 F3
MDTN M24 88 C1
MPL/ROM SK6 186 D4
ROY/SHW OL2 58 D1
SALE M33 154 A1
URM M41 138 A3
Rydal Cl BURY BL9 53 F2
CHD/CHDH SK8 181 G1
DTN/ASHW M34 145 H1
Rydal Ct BOL BL1 * 32 C5
Rydal Crs SWIN M27 99 E4
WALK M28 97 F1
Rydal Dr HALE/TIMP WA15 179 E4
Rydal Gv AULW OL7 119 E1
FWTH BL4 65 E5
HEY OL10 56 A1
WHTF M45 69 G4
Rydal Rd BOL BL1 47 H1
BOLS/LL BL3 66 D1
STRET M32 126 A5
Ryde Av DTN/ASHW M34 147 F3
HTNM SK4 159 E4
Ryder Av ALT WA14 165 H2
Ryder Brow GTN M18 130 C4
Ryderbrow Rd GTN M18 130 C4
Ryder St BOL BL1 33 F4
HEY OL10 * 41 E4
NEWH/MOS M40 115 G1
Ryde St BOLS/LL BL3 * 47 H5
Rydings La WHIT OL12 19 F2
Rydings Rd WHIT OL12 19 G3
Rydley St BOLE BL2 3 J6
Ryebank Gv AUL OL6 107 G5
Ryebank Ms CCHDY M21 * 140 D2
Ryebank Rd CCHDY M21 140 D2

Rye Bank Rd
OLDTF/WHR M16 141 E1
Ryeburn Av WYTH/NTH M22 180 C1
Ryeburn Dr BOLE BL2 34 C1
Ryeburne St OLDE OL4 76 B5
Ryeburn Wk URM M41 123 G4
Rye Cft WHTF M45 68 D5
Rye Croft Av SLFD M6 112 B2
Ryecroft Av HEY OL10 41 F4
TOT/BURYW BL8 26 A5
Ryecroft Cl CHAD OL9 90 A4
Ryecroft Gv NTHM/RTH M23 167 H2
Ryecroft La DTN/ASHW M34 132 B1
WALK M28 110 A1
Ryecroft Rd STRET M32 140 A2
Ryecroft St AULW OL7 119 E4
Ryecroft Vw DTN/ASHW M34 118 B5
Ryedale Av NEWH/MOS M40 103 E5
Ryedale Cl HTNM SK4 159 E3
Ryefield Cl HALE/TIMP WA15 166 D4
Ryefield Rd SALE M33 153 F4
Ryefields ROCH OL11 28 D5
Ryefields Dr UPML OL3 79 F3
Ryefield St BOL BL1 3 G1
Rye Hl WHTN BL5 * 62 A4
Ryeland Cl MILN OL16 43 G2
Ryelands WHTN BL5 62 A4
Ryelands Ct WHTN BL5 * 62 A4
Rye St HEY OL10 41 F3
Rylance St OP/CLY M11 115 H4
Rylands St GTN M18 * 130 D2
Rylane Wk NEWH/MOS M40 103 E5
Ryley Av BOLS/LL BL3 48 A4
Ryleys La WILM/AE SK9 200 C4
Ryley St BOLS/LL BL3 * 2 A7
Rylstone Av CCHDY M21 156 C3
Ryther Gv BKLY M9 87 G2
Ryton Av GTN M18 130 B5

S

Sabden Cl BURY BL9 27 G4
HEY OL10 40 B4
NEWH/MOS M40 115 H2
Sabden Rd BOL BL1 32 B4
Sabrina St CHH M8 101 H5
Sackville Cl ROY/SHW OL2 44 D5
Sackville St AUL OL6 119 G2
BOLE BL2 * 49 H2
CMANE M1 7 G7
CSLFD M3 6 B3
ROCH OL11 42 B5
Saddleback Cl WALK M28 96 C4
Saddlecote WALK M28 110 B1
Saddlecote Cl CHH M8 102 C2
Saddle Gv DROY M43 118 C2
Saddle St BOLE BL2 34 C4
Saddlewood Av
BNG/LEV M19 158 A4
Sadie Av STRET M32 125 F4
Sadler Ct HULME M15 127 H3
Sadler St BOLS/LL BL3 49 F5
MDTN M24 72 C3
Saffron Dr OLDE OL4 76 C2
Sagars Rd WILM/AE SK9 191 H3
Sagar St CHH M8 114 C1
St Agnes Rd BRUN/LGST M13 143 H1
St Agnes St RDSH SK5 131 E5
St Aidan's Cl ROCH OL11 42 C1
St Aidan's Gv BRO M7 101 E4
St Albans Av AUL OL6 107 E4
HTNM SK4 159 F1
NEWH/MOS M40 104 A5
St Albans Cl OLDS OL8 91 G3
St Albans Crs ALT WA14 165 F1
St Alban's St MILN OL16 29 H5
St Alban's Ter CHH M8 102 A5
ROCH OL11 * 29 H5
St Aldates MPL/ROM SK6 161 G4
St Aldwyn's Rd
DID/WITH M20 157 G1
St Ambrose Gdns SLFD M6 * 113 E3
St Ambrose Rd OLD OL1 76 B3
St Andrew's Av DROY M43 117 F4
ECC M30 111 F4
HALE/TIMP WA15 165 H2
St Andrews Cl HTNM SK4 159 E2
LIT OL15 20 B4
MPL/ROM SK6 162 A5
RAMS BL0 16 D3
SALE M33 153 F5
St Andrews Ct BOL BL1 * 2 E5
St Andrew's Dr HEY OL10 41 E5
St Andrews Rd
CHD/CHDH SK8 181 H3
HOR/BR BL6 46 B2
HTNM SK4 159 E2
RAD M26 52 A3
STRET M32 139 H1
St Andrew's Sq CMANE M1 115 F5
St Andrew's St CMANE M1 7 K6
St Andrew's Vw RAD M26 52 A3
St Anne's Av ROY/SHW OL2 75 F1
SLFD M6 112 D2
St Anne's Ct DTN/ASHW M34 * 132 C2
SALE M33 154 D2
SLFD M6 * 113 E1
St Anne's Crs OLDE OL4 93 H2
St Anne's Dr DTN/ASHW M34 132 D4
St Anne's Gdns HEY OL10 41 G4
St Annes Meadow
TOT/BURYW BL8 26 A4
St Annes Rd CCHDY M21 141 F4
DTN/ASHW M34 132 C2
DTN/ASHW M34 132 D4
St Annes St BURY BL9 * 38 C2
St Anns Cl PWCH M25 85 H4
St Anns Pas CMANW M2 6 E4
St Ann's Rd BRAM/HZG SK7 184 D3
MILN OL16 11 K5
PWCH M25 85 G4
St Ann's Rd North
CHD/CHDH SK8 181 G3
St Ann's Rd South
CHD/CHDH SK8 181 H3
St Ann's Sq CHD/CHDH SK8 181 H4
CMANW M2 6 E4
St Ann's St CMANW M2 6 D4
SALE M33 155 G3
SWIN M27 98 D2
St Ann St BOL BL1 33 H5
St Anthonys Dr MOSL OL5 94 A5
St Asaphs Dr AUL OL6 107 E4
St Aubin's Rd BOLE BL2 3 J7
St Augustine's Rd
EDGY/DAV SK3 171 E1
St Augustine St BOL BL1 33 G4
NEWH/MOS M40 103 F5
St Austell Dr CHD/CHDH SK8 181 G4
TOT/BURYW BL8 26 A1
St Austell Rd
OLDTF/WHR M16 142 A3
St Austells Dr PWCH M25 86 A2
SWIN M27 99 H4
St Barnabas's Dr LIT OL15 20 D2
St Barnabas Sq OP/CLY M11 116 C5
St Bartholomew's Dr ORD M5 113 H5
St Bartholomew St
BOLS/LL BL3 49 F5
St Bede's Av BOLS/LL BL3 64 A2
St Bees Cl CHD/CHDH SK8 181 G1
RUSH/FAL M14 128 B4
St Bees Rd BOLE BL2 34 D4
St Benedicts Av
WGTN/LGST M12 * 129 G2
St Benedict's Sq
WGTN/LGST M12 129 G2
St Bernard's Av SLFD M6 101 F5
St Boniface Rd BRO M7 113 H1
St Brannocks Rd CCHDY M21 141 E5
CHD/CHDH SK8 183 E5
St Brelades Dr BRO M7 102 A2
St Brendans Rd
DID/WITH M20 142 D4
St Brendans Rd North
DID/WITH M20 142 D4
St Brides Wy
OLDTF/WHR M16 127 G3
St Catherines Dr FWTH BL4 65 E4
St Catherine's Rd
DID/WITH M20 142 D4
St Chads Av MPL/ROM SK6 162 B4
St Chads Ct MILN OL16 10 D7
St Chads Crs OLDS OL8 106 A1
UPML OL3 79 F4
St Chads Gv MPL/ROM SK6 162 B4
St Chad's Rd DID/WITH M20 143 F4
St Chad's St CHH M8 * 114 D1
St Christopher's Av AUL OL6 107 H4
St Christophers Cl
DID/WITH M20 142 B5
St Christophers Dr
MPL/ROM SK6 161 H4
St Christopher's Rd AUL OL6 107 G4
St Clair Rd TOT/BURYW BL8 * 16 A5
St Clare Ter HOR/BR BL6 * 46 A1
St Clements Ct OLDS OL8 9 G6
St Clement's Dr ORD M5 127 E1
St Clements Fold URM M41 * 139 E1
St Clements Rd CCHDY M21 141 E4
St Cuthberts Fold OLDS OL8 106 D1
St Davids Av MPL/ROM SK6 162 A4
St David's Cl AUL OL6 107 G3
St David's Rd BRAM/HZG SK7 184 D3
CHD/CHDH SK8 170 D4
St Domingo Pl OLD OL1 * 9 F3
St Dominics Ms BOLS/LL BL3 64 B1
St Dominics Wy MDTN M24 72 D5
St Edmund Hall Cl RAMS BL0 16 D4
St Edmund's Rd
NEWH/MOS M40 103 F4
St Edmund St BOL BL1 2 D4
St Elisabeth's Wy RDSH SK5 145 E4
St Elmo Av OFTN SK2 173 E2
St Elmo Pk POY/DIS SK12 196 B3
St Ethelbert's Av BOLS/LL BL3 48 A4
St Gabriel's Cl ROCH OL11 42 C5
St George's Av
HALE/TIMP WA15 166 B1
HULME M15 * 127 G1
St George's Ct ALT WA14 165 E2
BOL BL1 2 E3
HYDE SK14 * 147 H1
STRET M32 * 140 A2
St George's Crs
HALE/TIMP WA15 166 B1
SLFD M6 * 111 H2
WALK M28 82 A5
St Georges Dr HYDE SK14 147 H2
NEWH/MOS M40 104 A3
St Georges Gdns
DTN/ASHW M34 147 E2
St George's Rd BOL BL1 2 B3
BURY BL9 54 B5
DROY M43 117 G2
PART M31 137 F5
ROCH OL11 28 C3
RUSH/FAL M14 143 G4
STRET M32 139 H1
St Georges Sq BOL BL1 3 F3
CHAD OL9 89 H4
St George's St BOL BL1 2 E3
STLY SK15 120 D2
St George's Wy SLFD M6 113 F1
St Germain St FWTH BL4 65 H4
St Giles Dr HYDE SK14 148 B1
St Gregorys Cl FWTH BL4 65 H5
St Gregorys Rd
WGTN/LGST M12 128 D1
St Helena Rd BOL BL1 2 C4
St Helens Cl
GOL/RIS/CUL WA3 150 A3
St Helens Rd BOLS/LL BL3 48 B5
WHTN BL5 63 H3
St Helier's Dr BRO M7 102 A2
St Heliers St BOLS/LL BL3 48 C5
St Hilarys Pk WILM/AE SK9 200 D4
St Hilda's Dr OLD OL1 75 E4
St Hilda's Rd DTN/ASHW M34 132 B2
OLDTF/WHR M16 127 F3
WYTH/NTH M22 156 C5
St Hilda's Vw DTN/ASHW M34 132 B3
St Hugh's Cl ALT WA14 165 H1
St Ignatius Wk ORD M5 * 113 G5
St Ives Av CHD/CHDH SK8 170 D3
St Ives Crs SALE M33 154 B5
St Ives Rd RUSH/FAL M14 142 D1
St James Av BOLE BL2 50 B1
TOT/BURYW BL8 37 G3
St James Cl MILN OL16 58 D1
St James Ct HALE/TIMP WA15 165 H5
SLFD M6 * 112 A2
St James Dr SALE M33 154 B3
WILM/AE SK9 198 D4
St James Rd HTNM SK4 159 E1
St James's Gv ALT WA14 154 A5
St James's Rd BRO M7 101 H4
St James's Sq CMANW M2 6 E5
St James's St OLD OL1 76 A5
St James's Ter HEY OL10 40 D4
St James St AUL OL6 120 A3
CMANE M1 7 F6
ECC M30 * 111 F3
FWTH BL4 65 G5
HEY OL10 40 D4
MILN OL16 31 G5
ROY/SHW OL2 60 A2
St James' Wy CHD/CHDH SK8 192 C1
St John's Av DROY M43 118 A3
St John's Cl BRO M7 101 G4
DUK SK16 120 B5
MPL/ROM SK6 162 A4
St Johns Ct BRO M7 * 101 G4
HOR/BR BL6 46 C5
HYDE SK14 134 A5
MILN OL16 * 30 C5
OLDE OL4 77 E5
RAD M26 68 C2
St John's Dr HYDE SK14 134 A5
MILN OL16 30 C5
St John's Gdns MOSL OL5 93 H5
St John's Rd ALT WA14 177 F1
BRAM/HZG SK7 184 C3
BRUN/LGST M13 129 G4
DTN/ASHW M34 132 C3
HOR/BR BL6 62 C1
HTNM SK4 158 B4
OLDTF/WHR M16 127 F4
WALK M28 96 A3
WILM/AE SK9 200 B2
St John's St BRO M7 101 G4
CHAD OL9 8 B6
FWTH BL4 66 B4
RAD M26 68 C2
St John St CSLFD M3 6 C6
DUK SK16 * 120 B5
ECC M30 111 E4
IRL M44 136 C1
OLDE OL4 92 D1
SWIN M27 100 A4
WALK M28 81 H3
St John's Wk CHAD OL9 8 B5
EDGY/DAV SK3 * 171 E1
St Johns Wd HOR/BR BL6 46 C5
St Josephs Av WHTF M45 70 B5
St Josephs Cl ROY/SHW OL2 60 B1
St Joseph's Dr MILN OL16 43 G2
ORD M5 113 G5
St Joseph St BOL BL1 33 G4
St Kilda Av FWTH BL4 82 C1
St Kildas Av DROY M43 117 G2
St Kilda's Dr BRO M7 102 A2
St Lawrence Quay SALQ M50 126 C1
St Lawrence Rd
DTN/ASHW M34 132 C5
St Leonard's Ct SALE M33 154 A2
St Leonards Dr
HALE/TIMP WA15 166 A3
St Leonard's Rd HTNM SK4 159 G1
St Leonard's St MDTN M24 72 D3
St Lesmo Rd EDGY/DAV SK3 12 A7
St Lukes Ct CHAD OL9 74 B5
St Luke's Rd SLFD M6 112 C3
St Luke St ROCH OL11 * 43 E1
St Margaret's Av
BNG/LEV M19 143 H5
St Margaret's Cl ALT WA14 165 F5
BOL BL1 * 48 A1
PWCH M25 86 B1
St Margarets Gdns OLDS OL8 * 90 D4
St Margaret's Rd ALT WA14 165 F5
BOL BL1 48 A1
CHD/CHDH SK8 170 D3
NEWH/MOS M40 89 G4
PWCH M25 86 B2
St Mark's Av ALT WA14 164 D4
ROY/SHW OL2 59 H5
St Mark's Cl ROY/SHW OL2 59 H5
St Mark's Crs WALK M28 97 E1
St Mark's La BRO M7 102 A2
St Mark's Sq BURY BL9 5 F1
St Mark's St BNG/LEV M19 144 C2
BOLS/LL BL3 49 E4
MPL/ROM SK6 161 H2
St Mark St DUK SK16 119 G4
St Mark's Vw BOLS/LL BL3 * 49 E4
St Marks Wk BOLS/LL BL3 48 D5
St Martin's Av HTNM SK4 12 A2
St Martins Cl DROY M43 117 G2
HYDE SK14 * 148 B1
St Martin's Dr BRO M7 102 A2
St Martin's Rd
MPL/ROM SK6 175 F3
OLDS OL8 91 H5
SALE M33 138 D5
St Martin's St ROCH OL11 42 B5
St Mary's Av BOLS/LL BL3 48 A4
DTN/ASHW M34 147 E3
St Mary's Cl MILN OL16 43 G2
PWCH M25 85 H3
STKP SK1 13 J3
St Marys Ct
NEWH/MOS M40 104 A2
OLD OL1 * 9 F2
St Mary's Crest UPML OL3 95 F2
St Mary's Dr CHD/CHDH SK8 * 170 C3
RDSH SK5 160 A1
UPML OL3 95 F2
St Marys Est OLD OL1 9 G2
St Mary's Ga CMANE M1 6 E3
MILN OL16 10 B5
ROY/SHW OL2 * 60 A2
UPML OL3 * 79 E4
St Mary's Hall Rd CHH M8 102 A1
St Mary's Parsonage
CSLFD M3 6 D4
St Mary's Pl BURY BL9 4 C5
St Mary's Rd ALT WA14 177 E2
ECC M30 111 G3
HYDE SK14 133 H3
NEWH/MOS M40 104 A3
PWCH M25 85 H3
SALE M33 154 B1
WALK M28 81 H3
St Mary's St CSLFD M3 6 D4
HULME M15 127 H3
OLD OL1 9 G1
OLDTF/WHR M16 128 A4
St Mary's Wy OLD OL1 9 F2
STKP SK1 13 J6
St Matthews Ct STRET M32 * 140 A2
St Matthew's Dr OLD OL1 74 B2
St Matthews Gra BOL BL1 * 33 H5
St Matthew's Rd
EDGY/DAV SK3 12 D6
St Matthews Ter
EDGY/DAV SK3 * 12 D6
St Matthews Wk BOL BL1 * 33 H5
St Mawes Ct RAD M26 * 51 F4
St Michael's Av BOLS/LL BL3 65 G2
BRAM/HZG SK7 183 H5
St Michaels Cl TOT/BURYW BL8 52 B1
St Michaels Ct SALE M33 139 E5
St Michaels Gdns WHTF M45 70 A3
St Michael's Rd HYDE SK14 148 B1
St Michael's Sq ANC M4 * 7 G1
St Modwen Rd STRET M32 125 E3
St Nicholas Rd HULME M15 127 H1
St Osmund's Dr BOLE BL2 50 B2
St Osmund's Gv BOLE BL2 50 B2
St Oswald's Rd BNG/LEV M19 144 B1
St Pauls Cl STLY SK15 121 F3
St Paul's Ct RAD M26 68 B3
WALK M28 82 A5
St Paul's Hill Rd HYDE SK14 148 B1
St Paul's Rd BRO M7 101 F1
DID/WITH M20 143 E5
HTNM SK4 159 E2
WALK M28 * 82 B5
St Paul's St BURY BL9 5 H3
HYDE SK14 133 H5
RAMS BL0 * 16 D2
STKP SK1 160 B3
STLY SK15 121 F3
St Pauls Vls BURY BL9 5 H3
St Peter's Av BOL BL1 32 D4
St Peters Cl AULW OL7 119 E3
St Peters Ct STRET M32 * 126 B5
St Peter's Dr HYDE SK14 * 148 B1
St Petersgate STKP SK1 13 G3
St Peter's Rd BURY BL9 53 G3
SWIN M27 98 D3
St Peter's Sq CMANW M2 6 E6
STKP SK1 13 F3
St Peter's St AUL OL6 119 F3
MILN OL16 30 C5
St Peter's Ter FWTH BL4 66 A5
St Peter's Wy BOL BL1 3 F3
BOLE BL2 3 H7
BOLS/LL BL3 65 H1
St Philip's Av BOLS/LL BL3 48 C5
St Philip's Pl CSLFD M3 * 114 A3
St Philip's Rd GTN M18 130 C4
St Phillip's Dr ROY/SHW OL2 75 F3
St Saviour's Rd OFTN SK2 172 D4
Saintsbridge Rd
WYTH/NTH M22 180 B2
St Simons Cl OFTN SK2 172 D1
St Simon St CSLFD M3 6 B1
St Stephen's Av
DTN/ASHW M34 118 D5
St Stephen's Cl BOLE BL2 49 H4
BRUN/LGST M13 129 E3
St Stephens Ct BKLY M9 * 103 E3
St Stephens St OLD OL1 9 J1
St Stephen St CSLFD M3 6 B3
OLD OL1 9 J1
St Stephens Vw DROY M43 117 H3
St Teresa's Rd
OLDTF/WHR M16 126 D5
St Thomas Ct BURY BL9 5 H4
St Thomas' Pl CHH M8 114 D1
St Thomas's Cir OLDS OL8 8 D7
St Thomas's Pl STKP SK1 13 G6
St Thomas St BOL BL1 * 33 G4
St Thomas St North OLDS OL8 8 D6
St Thomas St South OLDS OL8 8 D7
St Vincent St ANC M4 115 F3
St Werburghs Rd CCHDY M21 141 G3
St Wilfred's Dr WHIT OL12 * 18 C4
St Wilfrids St HULME M15 127 H2
St Williams Av BOLS/LL BL3 64 D1
Salcombe Av BOLE BL2 36 C5
Salcombe Cl SALE M33 153 H1
Salcombe Gv BOLE BL2 50 C3
Salcombe Rd OFTN SK2 172 D1
OP/CLY M11 117 E5
Salcot Wk NEWH/MOS M40 * 115 F2
Sale Heys Rd SALE M33 154 A3
Sale La WALK M28 96 A2
Salem Gv OLDE OL4 92 C1
Sale Rd NTHM/RTH M23 155 H4
Sale St LIT OL15 21 E2
Salford Rd WHTN BL5 63 H4
Salford St BURY BL9 38 D2
OLDE OL4 92 B2
Salik Gdns ROCH OL11 43 E1
Salisbury Av HEY OL10 55 H1
Salisbury Crs AUL OL6 107 G3
Salisbury Dr DUK SK16 134 B1
PWCH M25 86 B5
Salisbury Rd CCHDY M21 141 F2
ECC M30 111 G1
OLDE OL4 92 A1
RAD M26 51 H4
SWIN M27 98 D3
URM M41 124 C4
WHTF M45 69 G4
Salisbury St BOLS/LL BL3 2 B6
MDTN M24 73 E3
RDSH SK5 145 F3
ROY/SHW OL2 59 G1
RUSH/FAL M14 128 B4
Salisbury Ter BOLS/LL BL3 67 F1
Salkeld St ROCH OL11 43 E1
Salmon Flds ROY/SHW OL2 75 G1
Salmon St ANC M4 7 G3
Salmsbury Hall Cl RAMS BL0 16 C4
Salop St BOLE BL2 3 G6
SLFD M6 113 F1
Saltash Cl WYTH/NTH M22 180 C3
Saltdene Rd WYTH/NTH M22 180 B3
Saltergate BOLS/LL BL3 47 G5
Saltergate Ms ORD M5 * 113 F3
Salterton Dr BOLS/LL BL3 63 G2
Salteye Rd ECC M30 110 B4
Saltford Av ANC M4 115 F3
Saltford Ct ANC M4 115 F3
Salthill Av HEY OL10 56 B2
Salthill Dr WYTH/NTH M22 180 D2
Salthouse Cl TOT/BURYW BL8 26 D5
Saltire Gdns BRO M7 101 H2
Saltney Av DID/WITH M20 142 B4
Saltram Cl RAD M26 51 F4
Saltrush Rd WYTH/NTH M22 180 C2
Salts Dr LIT OL15 20 D2
Salts St ROY/SHW OL2 60 A2
Saltwood Gv BOL BL1 2 E1
Salutation St HULME M15 128 A2
Sam Cowan Cl RUSH/FAL M14 128 B5
Samian Gdns BRO M7 101 F5
Samlesbury Cl DID/WITH M20 157 E3
ROY/SHW OL2 59 G2
Samouth Cl NEWH/MOS M40 115 G2
Sampson Sq RUSH/FAL M14 128 B4
Samson St MILN OL16 11 K4
Sam Swire St HULME M15 127 H3
Samuel La ROY/SHW OL2 59 F1
Samuel Ogden St CMANE M1 7 G7
Samuel St BNG/LEV M19 144 B3
BURY BL9 5 G2
FAIL M35 105 E2
HTNM SK4 159 G3
ROCH OL11 42 B4
Sanby Av GTN M18 130 B4
Sanby Rd GTN M18 130 B4
Sanctuary Cl HULME M15 128 C3
The Sanctuary HULME M15 127 H2
Sandacre Rd NTHM/RTH M23 168 A2
Sandal St NEWH/MOS M40 115 H2
Sandbach Av RUSH/FAL M14 142 B3
Sandbach Rd RDSH SK5 * 145 E1
SALE M33 155 G3
Sandbank Gdns WHIT OL12 14 B3
Sand Banks BOL BL1 23 E5
Sandbed La MOSL OL5 93 H5
Sandbrook Pk ROCH OL11 * 42 D2
Sandbrook Wy
DTN/ASHW M34 132 C3
ROCH OL11 42 D2
Sandby Dr MPL/ROM SK6 175 G1
Sanderling Rd OFTN SK2 173 H4
Sanderson Cl WALK M28 98 A2
Sanderson St BURY BL9 5 H3
NEWH/MOS M40 103 F5
Sanderstead Dr BKLY M9 88 B4
Sandfield Dr HOR/BR BL6 46 D3
Sandfield Rd MILN OL16 43 G1
Sandfold La BNG/LEV M19 144 C1
Sandford Av GTN M18 * 130 C2
Sandford Cl BOLE BL2 35 F3
Sandford Rd SALE M33 155 G3
Sandford Station La
RDSH SK5 144 D1
Sandford St RAD M26 53 E5
Sandgate Av OP/CLY M11 117 E3
RAD M26 67 E5
Sandgate Dr URM M41 124 C4
Sandgate Rd CHAD OL9 90 C1
WHTF M45 70 A5
Sandham St BOLS/LL BL3 49 E5
Sandham Wk BOLS/LL BL3 * 49 E5
Sandheys DTN/ASHW M34 132 C3
Sandheys Gv GTN M18 130 D4
Sandhill Cl BOLS/LL BL3 49 E5
Sandhill St HYDE SK14 134 A5
Sandhill Wk WYTH/NTH M22 180 A2
Sandhole La ROCH OL11 41 F1
Sand Hole La ROCH OL11 43 E5
Sand Hole Rd FWTH BL4 83 E1
Sandhurst Av DID/WITH M20 142 C5
Sandhurst Cl TOT/BURYW BL8 37 G3
Sandhurst Ct BOLE BL2 50 B3
Sandhurst Dr BOLE BL2 50 B3
WILM/AE SK9 199 F2
Sandhurst Rd DID/WITH M20 157 G4
OFTN SK2 172 C4
Sandhurst St OLDE OL4 92 B3
Sandhutton Rd BKLY M9 103 E1
Sandilands Rd
NTHM/RTH M23 167 E1
Sandileigh Av CHD/CHDH SK8 170 D3
DID/WITH M20 157 G1
HALE/TIMP WA15 178 A1
RDSH SK5 160 C2
Sandileigh Dr BOL BL1 34 C3
HALE/TIMP WA15 178 A1
Sandiway BRAM/HZG SK7 183 H2
HEY OL10 41 F4
IRL M44 136 C1
MPL/ROM SK6 161 G3
Sandiway Cl MPL/ROM SK6 175 E1
Sandiway Dr DID/WITH M20 157 F3
Sandiway Pl ALT WA14 165 G4
Sandiway Rd ALT WA14 165 G3
SALE M33 154 A2
WILM/AE SK9 192 A2
Sandon St BOLS/LL BL3 48 C5
Sandown Av SLFD M6 112 D3
Sandown Cl OLD OL1 75 H3
WILM/AE SK9 199 G2
Sandown Crs BOLS/LL BL3 66 D2
GTN M18 130 C5
Sandown Dr DTN/ASHW M34 147 F3
HALE/TIMP WA15 188 D1
SALE M33 153 H3
Sandown Gdns URM M41 138 A1
Sandown Rd BOLE BL2 35 G3
BRAM/HZG SK7 185 H3
BURY BL9 69 H2
EDGY/DAV SK3 171 E1
Sandown St GTN M18 130 D2
Sandpiper Cl DUK SK16 133 H1
FWTH BL4 65 E5
ROCH OL11 28 C4
Sandpiper Dr EDGY/DAV SK3 171 G3
Sandray Cl BOLS/LL BL3 47 G4

Sandray Gv ORD M5 112 D4
Sandridge Cl FWTH BL4 66 B4
Sandridge Wk
WGTN/LGST M12 129 F2
Sandringham Av
DTN/ASHW M34 131 F5
DTN/ASHW M34 132 A2
STLY SK15 120 D2
Sandringham Cl ALT WA14 176 C3
Sandringham Dr DUK SK16 134 A2
HTNM SK4 158 D5
MILN OL16 31 H5
POY/DIS SK12 195 E4
TOT/BURYW BL8 26 B2
Sandringham Gra PWCH M25 86 D4
Sandringham Rd
BRAM/HZG SK7 185 G2
CHD/CHDH SK8 182 D1
HYDE SK14 148 A4
MPL/ROM SK6 160 D3
WALK M28 96 B4
Sandringham St GTN M18 130 B4
Sandringham Wy
ROY/SHW OL2 58 D3
WILM/AE SK9 198 D4
Sands Av CHAD OL9 73 H4
Sands Cl HYDE SK14 149 F2
Sandsend Cl CHH M8 101 H5
Sandsend Rd URM M41 124 B5
Sandstone Rd MILN OL16 31 G4
Sandstone Wy CCHDY M21 141 H5
Sand St NEWH/MOS M40 115 F1
STLY SK15 120 C5
Sandwell Dr SALE M33 139 H5
Sandwich Rd ECC M30 111 G2
Sandwich St WALK M28 82 A5
Sandwick Crs BOLS/LL BL3 48 C4
Sandwood Av BOLS/LL BL3 47 F4
Sandy Acre MOSL OL5 108 D2
Sandy Bank ROY/SHW OL2 59 G1
Sandy Bank Av HYDE SK14 149 F2
Sandy Bank Rd CHH M8 102 A2
Sandy Bank Wk HYDE SK14 * 149 F2
Sandybrook Cl
TOT/BURYW BL8 26 A5
Sandybrook Dr BKLY M9 87 H5
Sandy Brow BKLY M9 88 A5
Sandy Cl BURY BL9 53 G5
Sandycroft Av
WYTH/NTH M22 180 C1
Sandygate Cl SWIN M27 98 D3
Sandy Gv DUK SK16 120 A5
SLFD M6 112 D2
SWIN M27 99 E2
Sandy Haven Cl HYDE SK14 149 F2
Sandyhill Rd BKLY M9 87 F4
Sandyhills BOLS/LL BL3 48 D5
Sandylands Dr PWCH M25 100 C1
Sandy La CCHDY M21 141 F3
DROY M43 118 B2
DUK SK16 120 A5
IRL M44 122 B5
MDTN M24 73 E5
MPL/ROM SK6 162 B3
NTHM/RTH M23 167 E2
OLDS OL8 * 8 D5
PWCH M25 85 H5
RDSH SK5 159 H3
ROCH OL11 29 F4
ROY/SHW OL2 59 E5
SLFD M6 112 D2
STRET M32 139 H2
UPML OL3 79 E2
WILM/AE SK9 198 A2
Sandy Meade PWCH M25 85 H4
Sandywarps IRL M44 136 C3
Sandyway PWCH M25 * 85 H4
Sandywell Cl OP/CLY M11 130 C1
Sandywell St OP/CLY M11 117 E5
Sandy Wd SLFD M6 112 D2
Sangster Ct ORD M5 113 F5
Sankey Gv BKLY M9 87 G4
Sankey St BURY BL9 4 B4
Santiago St RUSH/FAL M14 128 C5
Santley St WGTN/LGST M12 129 H5
Santon Av RUSH/FAL M14 143 G3
Sapling Gv SALE M33 153 G4
Sapling Rd BOLS/LL BL3 64 B2
SWIN M27 98 C5
Sarah Butterworth Ct
MILN OL16 11 H7
Sarah Butterworth St
MILN OL16 30 C5
Sarah St ECC M30 110 C4
MDTN M24 72 C4
OP/CLY M11 116 A5
ROCH OL11 30 A5
ROY/SHW OL2 60 A4
Sargent Dr OLDTF/WHR M16 127 H4
Sargent Rd MPL/ROM SK6 161 E4
Sark Rd CCHDY M21 141 E1
Sarn Av WYTH/NTH M22 168 C5
Saturn Gv SLFD M6 113 H1
Saunton Av BOLE BL2 35 G4
Saunton Rd OP/CLY M11 117 E5
Sautridge Cl MDTN M24 57 G2
Savernake Rd MPL/ROM SK6 162 B1
Savick Av BOLE BL2 50 B2
Saville Rd CHD/CHDH SK8 169 G3
RAD M26 52 A2
Saville St BOLE BL2 3 G5
MDTN M24 73 G5
Saviours Ter BOLS/LL BL3 * 48 B4
Savio Wy MDTN M24 72 D5
Savoy Ct WHTF M45 * 69 F3
Savoy Dr ROY/SHW OL2 75 E2
Savoy St OLDE OL4 92 A2
ROCH OL11 29 F3
Sawley Av LIT OL15 20 D1
OLDE OL4 92 C3
WHTF M45 69 G2
Sawley Dr CHD/CHDH SK8 193 E1
Sawley Rd NEWH/MOS M40 115 G1
Sawmill Wy LIT OL15 20 D4
Saw St BOL BL1 33 H4
Sawyer Brow HYDE SK14 134 A4
Sawyer St TOT/BURYW BL8 37 G2
WHIT OL12 10 C3
Saxby Av EDGW/EG BL7 23 E3
Saxby St SLFD M6 99 H5
Saxelby Dr CHH M8 102 C4
Saxfield Dr NTHM/RTH M23 168 B3
Saxon Av CHH M8 87 F5
DUK SK16 119 H5
Saxon Cl TOT/BURYW BL8 37 G4
Saxon Dr CHAD OL9 73 H4
DROY M43 117 H3
DTN/ASHW M34 132 B1
Saxonholme Rd ROCH OL11 57 F2
Saxon St DROY M43 118 A3
DTN/ASHW M34 132 C5
MDTN M24 73 E4
NEWH/MOS M40 115 H2
OLDE OL4 76 B5
RAD M26 68 A1
Saxthorpe Cl SALE M33 153 G1
Saxthorpe Wk
WGTN/LGST M12 129 F3
Saxwood Av BKLY M9 103 E1
Saxwood Cl WHIT OL12 28 C2
Scafell Av AULW OL7 119 E1
Scafell Cl MPL/ROM SK6 186 D4
OLD OL1 75 G3
Scale St ORD M5 113 G4
Scarborough St
NEWH/MOS M40 103 H2
Scarcroft Rd WGTN/LGST M12 129 H3
Scardale Av BOL BL1 32 D5
Scarfield Dr ROCH OL11 28 B2
Scargill Cl RUSH/FAL M14 * 143 E3
Scargill Rd BOLS/LL BL3 47 H5
Scarisbrick Av DID/WITH M20 158 A3
Scarisbrick Rd BNG/LEV M19 143 H3
Scarr Av RAD M26 68 D3
Scarr Dr WHIT OL12 30 A1
Scarr La ROY/SHW OL2 60 B2
Scarsdale Rd RUSH/FAL M14 129 F4
Scarsdale St SLFD M6 113 G2
Scarthwood Cl BOLE BL2 35 F1
Scawfell Av BOLE BL2 34 C4
Schofield Rd DROY M43 118 A4
ECC M30 110 B4
Schofield St FAIL M35 * 105 E2
HEY OL10 41 E5
LIT OL15 21 F2
MILN OL16 44 D1
OLDS OL8 91 F4
OP/CLY M11 116 D3
ROCH OL11 43 F2
ROY/SHW OL2 59 E4
Scholar Green Rd STRET M32 125 F3
Scholars Dr DID/WITH M20 142 C4
Scholars Wy MDTN M24 72 C4
Scholes Dr NEWH/MOS M40 89 H5
Scholes La PWCH M25 86 B4
Scholes St CHAD OL9 90 B3
FAIL M35 105 F1
OLD OL1 9 J3
ROCH OL11 42 B5
SWIN M27 99 F2
TOT/BURYW BL8 37 H3
Scholes Wk PWCH M25 86 B4
Scholey St BOLE BL2 49 F4
Scholfield Av URM M41 139 F2
School Av AUL OL6 107 G4
STRET M32 * 126 C5
School Brow BURY BL9 4 E4
MPL/ROM SK6 161 H4
WALK M28 97 G4
School Cl POY/DIS SK12 195 G4
School Ct ANC M4 7 K3
EDGY/DAV SK3 172 A3
School Crs STLY SK15 120 D2
School Gv DID/WITH M20 143 E5
PWCH M25 85 H5
School Gv West
DID/WITH M20 * 143 E5
School Hl BOL BL1 2 D2
School House Flats OLDS OL8 * 90 D5
School La ALT WA14 164 A5
BKLY M9 87 H5
BURY BL9 27 F3
DID/WITH M20 157 H3
HTNM SK4 159 F1
HYDE SK14 148 A4
IRL M44 136 B1
IRL M44 150 C1
MILN OL16 10 C7
MPL/ROM SK6 163 G1
MPL/ROM SK6 163 G3
PART M31 137 G5
POY/DIS SK12 195 G4
STLY SK15 109 F3
School Ms MILN OL16 * 45 E2
School Rd ECC M30 110 D5
FAIL M35 105 E3
HALE/TIMP WA15 178 A1
OLDS OL8 90 C5
SALE M33 154 B1
STRET M32 140 A1
WILM/AE SK9 192 A3
Schools Hl CHD/CHDH SK8 182 A1
Schoolside Cl CHH M8 102 C4
Schoolside La MDTN M24 71 H5
Schools Rd GTN M18 130 D3
School St ANC M4 7 G1
BOLS/LL BL3 67 E1
BRAM/HZG SK7 185 F2
BURY BL9 5 J6
ECC M30 110 C2
EDGW/EG BL7 23 E4
HEY OL10 40 D4
LIT OL15 20 B3
OLDE OL4 93 F1
OLDS OL8 8 D6
RAD M26 68 A1
RAMS BL0 16 C3
UPML OL3 79 E4
WHIT OL12 10 C5
School Wk OLDTF/WHR M16 127 G3
Schuter Rd RUSH/FAL M14 129 E5
Schwabe St MDTN M24 71 H4
Scobell St TOT/BURYW BL8 37 E1
Scoltock Wy OLD OL1 9 G2
Score St OP/CLY M11 116 B4
Scorton Av BOLE BL2 50 C2
Scorton St BOL BL1 * 48 B1
Scotforth Cl HULME M15 127 H1
Scotland Hall Rd
NEWH/MOS M40 116 C1
Scotland St AUL OL6 119 H3
NEWH/MOS M40 104 B5
Scott Av CCHDY M21 141 F1
ECC M30 110 D2
Scott Cl RDSH SK5 160 A2
Scott Dr HALE/TIMP WA15 166 A5
MPL/ROM SK6 175 G1
Scottfield OLDS OL8 9 F7
Scottfield Rd OLDS OL8 9 G7
Scott Ga DTN/ASHW M34 132 B1
Scottia Rd ECC M30 110 C5
Scott Rd DROY M43 117 H4
DTN/ASHW M34 146 C2
PWCH M25 85 G4
Scott St OLDS OL8 9 G7
RAD M26 67 G5
Scout Dr NTHM/RTH M23 167 G5
Scout Gn MDTN M24 72 D1
Scout Vw TOT/BURYW BL8 26 B5
Scovell St BRO M7 101 G4
Scowcroft La ROY/SHW OL2 59 H3
Scowcroft St BOLE BL2 3 J1
Scroggins La PART M31 151 E2
Scropton St NEWH/MOS M40 103 E5
Seabright Wk OP/CLY M11 * 116 A4
Seabrook Crs URM M41 124 C4
Seabrook Rd NEWH/MOS M40 116 D1
Seacombe Av RUSH/FAL M14 142 C2
Seacombe Gv EDGY/DAV SK3 171 E1
Seaford Rd BOLE BL2 24 B5
SLFD M6 101 E5
Seaford Wk CHAD OL9 * 90 C1
Seaforth Rd BOL BL1 33 H1
Seaham Dr TOT/BURYW BL8 37 H1
Seaham Wk RUSH/FAL M14 128 C5
Sealand Cl SALE M33 155 F4
Sealand Dr ECC M30 110 B5
Sealand Rd NTHM/RTH M23 155 G4
Seale Av DTN/ASHW M34 132 A1
Sealey Wk NEWH/MOS M40 * 115 H1
Seal Rd BRAM/HZG SK7 184 B5
Seamon's Dr ALT WA14 164 D4
Seamon's Rd ALT WA14 164 D3
Searby Rd GTN M18 130 A4
Searness Rd MDTN M24 71 H2
Seascale Av OP/CLY M11 116 C2
Seathwaite Cl MDTN M24 72 A2
Seathwaite Rd FWTH BL4 65 E5
Seatoller Dr MDTN M24 71 H3
Seaton Cl BRAM/HZG SK7 185 E3
Seaton Ms AULW OL7 118 D1
Seaton Rd BOL BL1 33 F4
Sebastian Cl MPL/ROM SK6 175 G2
Sebastopol Wk ANC M4 7 K3
Second Av BOL BL1 48 A2
BOLS/LL BL3 50 C5
BURY BL9 39 G2
OLDS OL8 90 D5
OP/CLY M11 117 E3
STLY SK15 109 F5
SWIN M27 98 C5
TRPK M17 126 A3
Second St BOL BL1 32 C2
Section St BOL BL1 2 E6
Sedan Cl ORD M5 113 F4
Sedburgh Cl SALE M33 153 G3
Sedbury Cl NTHM/RTH M23 155 G5
Seddon Av GTN M18 130 C2
RAD M26 53 F4
Seddon Cl RAD M26 52 B5
Seddon Gdns RAD M26 66 D4
Seddon La RAD M26 66 D4
Seddon Rd ALT WA14 177 G2
Seddons Av TOT/BURYW BL8 52 B1
Seddon St BNG/LEV M19 144 B1
BOLS/LL BL3 * 67 E1
LHULT M38 81 E2
RAD M26 68 B1
Sedgeborough Rd
OLDTF/WHR M16 127 H5
Sedge Cl RDSH SK5 145 G3
Sedgefield Cl ORD M5 113 F3
Sedgefield Dr BOL BL1 33 E3
Sedgefield Pk OLDE OL4 92 C1
Sedgefield Rd RAD M26 68 A4
Sedgeford Cl WILM/AE SK9 199 F1
Sedgeford Rd
NEWH/MOS M40 103 E5
Sedgemoor Cl
CHD/CHDH SK8 183 E2
Sedgemoor V BOLE BL2 35 G4
Sedgemoor Wy OLD OL1 9 F2
Sedgley Av MILN OL16 43 G2
PWCH M25 86 B5
Sedgley Cl MDTN M24 73 F5
Sedgley Park Rd PWCH M25 86 B5
Sedgley Rd CHH M8 102 B2
Sedgley St MDTN M24 73 F5
Seedfield Rd BURY BL9 38 C1
Seedley Av LHULT M38 81 G3
Seedley Park Rd SLFD M6 112 D3
Seedley Rd SLFD M6 112 D2
Seedley St RUSH/FAL M14 128 C5
Seedley Ter SLFD M6 112 D2
Seedley View Rd ORD M5 112 D2
Seed St BOL BL1 48 B2
Seel St MOSL OL5 108 C1
Sefton Cl BRUN/LGST M13 128 C2
MDTN M24 72 B4
OLD OL1 60 C5
Sefton Crs SALE M33 139 H5
Sefton Dr BURY BL9 27 H5
SWIN M27 98 C5
WALK M28 97 H4
WILM/AE SK9 191 H5
Sefton Rd BOL BL1 33 E4
CCHDY M21 141 F3
MDTN M24 72 B4
SALE M33 154 C1
SWIN M27 99 E1
Sefton St BURY BL9 27 G5
CHAD OL9 90 B5
CHH M8 102 B2
HEY OL10 41 F5
RAD M26 68 D3
ROCH OL11 42 D1
WHTF M45 69 G5
Segal Cl BRO M7 101 G3
Selborne Rd CCHDY M21 141 F2
Selbourne Cl WHTN BL5 62 B3
Selby Av CHAD OL9 74 A3
WHTF M45 69 G2
Selby Cl MILN OL16 31 F5
POY/DIS SK12 * 195 E2
RAD M26 53 E4
STRET M32 125 E5
Selby Dr SLFD M6 112 A2
URM M41 123 G3
Selby Gdns CHD/CHDH SK8 193 F1
Selby Rd MDTN M24 72 C1
STRET M32 125 F5
Selby St HTNM SK4 159 H2
MILN OL16 11 G4
OP/CLY M11 116 B5
Selham Wk BRUN/LGST M13 * 128 D1
Selhurst Av OP/CLY M11 116 D3
Selkirk Av OLDS OL8 91 E3
Selkirk Dr BKLY M9 88 C4
Selkirk Rd BOL BL1 33 G1
CHAD OL9 90 A3
Sellars Sq DROY M43 117 H5
Sellers Wy CHAD OL9 90 B4
Selsby Av ECC M30 110 C3
Selsey Av EDGY/DAV SK3 170 C2
SALE M33 154 A3
Selsey Dr DID/WITH M20 169 H1
Selside Wk RUSH/FAL M14 143 E3
Selstead Rd WYTH/NTH M22 180 B3
Selston Rd BKLY M9 87 G3
Selworth Av SALE M33 155 F2
Selworth Cl HALE/TIMP WA15 165 H3
Selworthy Rd
OLDTF/WHR M16 127 H4
Selwyn Av BKLY M9 103 E2
Selwyn Cl OLDS OL8 * 8 E6
Selwyn Dr CHD/CHDH SK8 183 F5
Selwyn St BOLE BL2 3 H6
OLDS OL8 8 E6
Senior Av RUSH/FAL M14 143 G4
Senior Rd ECC M30 110 A5
Senior St CSLFD M3 6 C1
Senior Vw HYDE SK14 * 133 H3
Sepal Cl RDSH SK5 145 G2
Sepia Gv MDTN M24 72 G3
Sequoia St BKLY M9 103 F2
Sergeants La WHTF M45 68 D5
Serin Cl OFTN SK2 173 G5
Service St HTNM SK4 171 E1
Sesame Gdns IRL M44 122 D5
Set St STLY SK15 120 C4
Settle Cl TOT/BURYW BL8 37 E4
Settle St BOLS/LL BL3 64 D1
BOLS/LL BL3 67 F2
Seven Acres La WHIT OL12 28 B1
Seven Acres Rd WHIT OL12 28 B1
Sevenoaks Av HTNM SK4 158 D1
URM M41 124 C4
Sevenoaks Dr BOLS/LL BL3 64 D1
SWIN M27 99 F4
Sevenoaks Rd CHD/CHDH SK8 169 G3
Sevenoaks Wk
BRUN/LGST M13 * 128 D3
Seven Stiles Dr MPL/ROM SK6 174 D2
Seventh Av OLDS OL8 105 H1
Severn Cl ALT WA14 165 F3
BURY BL9 27 G4
Severn Dr BRAM/HZG SK7 193 F1
MILN OL16 31 H5
Severn Rd CHAD OL9 74 A4
HEY OL10 40 B3
OLDS OL8 105 G1
Severn Wy FWTH BL4 83 E2
RDSH SK5 160 A1
Seville St ROY/SHW OL2 59 H4
ROY/SHW OL2 75 F2
Sewell Wy LHULT M38 81 E4
Sewerby Cl OLDTF/WHR M16 128 A4
Sewerby St OLDTF/WHR M16 127 H4
Sexa St OP/CLY M11 117 E5
Sexton St HEY OL10 40 D4
Seymour Av OP/CLY M11 117 E3
Seymour Cl OLDTF/WHR M16 127 F3
Seymour Dr BOLE BL2 23 H5
Seymour Gv FWTH BL4 * 65 F3
HALE/TIMP WA15 166 B4
MILN OL16 43 G3
MPL/ROM SK6 174 D3
OLDTF/WHR M16 127 E4
SALE M33 154 C2
Seymour Pl
OLDTF/WHR M16 * 127 E3
Seymour Rd BOL BL1 34 A3
CHD/CHDH SK8 182 D4
CHH M8 102 A1
OFTN SK2 172 C3
Seymour Rd South
OP/CLY M11 117 E3
Seymour St BOLE BL2 23 H5
DTN/ASHW M34 132 A5
GTN M18 130 C2
HEY OL10 40 D5
RAD M26 68 C1
Shackleton Gv BOL BL1 32 C4
Shackleton St ECC M30 110 D2
Shackliffe Rd NEWH/MOS M40 89 E5
Shaddock Av WHIT OL12 28 C2
Shade Av OLDE OL4 93 E2
Shadowbrook Av
NTHM/RTH M23 167 H5
Shadowbrook Cl OLD OL1 75 F3
Shadowmoss Rd
WYTH/NTH M22 180 D4
Shadows La MOSL OL5 94 B3
Shadwell St East HEY OL10 41 F3
Shadwell St West HEY OL10 41 E3
Shadworth Cl MOSL OL5 94 B3
Shady La EDGW/EG BL7 23 G5
NTHM/RTH M23 167 E3
Shady Oak Rd OFTN SK2 173 G3
Shaftesbury Av
CHD/CHDH SK8 183 F3
ECC M30 110 D5
HALE/TIMP WA15 166 C4
HOR/BR BL6 46 A1
LIT OL15 31 H1
Shaftesbury Dr WHIT OL12 20 A2
Shaftesbury Gdns URM M41 137 E1
Shaftesbury Rd CHH M8 102 B3
EDGY/DAV SK3 170 D3
SWIN M27 99 E3
Shaftsbury Dr HEY OL10 55 H1
Shakespeare Av BURY BL9 53 G3
DTN/ASHW M34 146 D3
RAD M26 51 H5
STLY SK15 121 H2
Shakespeare Crs DROY M43 117 H3
ECC M30 111 E3
Shakespeare Dr
CHD/CHDH SK8 170 C3
Shakespeare Rd DROY M43 117 H3
MPL/ROM SK6 161 F3
OLD OL1 76 A2
PWCH M25 85 G4
SWIN M27 98 C2
Shakespeare Wk
BRUN/LGST M13 128 D3
Shakleton Av BKLY M9 88 D4
Shalbourne Rd WALK M28 81 H4
Shaldon Dr NEWH/MOS M40 117 F1
Shalfleet Cl BOLE BL2 35 F1
Shambles Sq CMANE M1 6 E3
Shandon Av WYTH/NTH M22 156 C5
Shanklin Av URM M41 138 C1
Shanklin Cl CCHDY M21 141 E2
DTN/ASHW M34 * 147 F3
Shanklin Wk BOLS/LL BL3 49 H4
Shanley Ct CHAD OL9 74 C4
Shannon Cl HEY OL10 40 B3
Shannon Rd WYTH/NTH M22 168 D5
Shap Av HALE/TIMP WA15 167 E4
Shap Dr WALK M28 82 C5
Sharcott Cl OLDTF/WHR M16 128 A4
Shardlow Cl NEWH/MOS M40 115 G1
Shargate Cl WILM/AE SK9 199 F1
Sharman St BOLS/LL BL3 49 G4
Sharnford Cl BOLE BL2 3 J7
Sharnford Sq
WGTN/LGST M12 129 H2
Sharon Av OLDE OL4 94 A1
Sharon Cl AULW OL7 118 D4
Sharples Av BOL BL1 22 D5
Sharples Dr TOT/BURYW BL8 37 E2
Sharples Hall Dr BOL BL1 23 E5
Sharples Hall Fold BOL BL1 34 A1
Sharples Hall Ms BOL BL1 23 E5
Sharples Hall St OLDE OL4 76 C3
Sharples Pk BOL BL1 33 G2
Sharples St HTNM SK4 159 H3
Sharp St ANC M4 7 H1
MDTN M24 72 D4
PWCH M25 * 85 H3
TOT/BURYW BL8 37 G2
WALK M28 82 B4
Sharrington Dr
NTHM/RTH M23 167 F3
Sharston Rd WYTH/NTH M22 168 D2
Shaving La WALK M28 97 E1
Shaw Av HYDE SK14 148 B3
Shawbrook Av WALK M28 96 C2
Shawbrook Rd BNG/LEV M19 158 D1
Shawbury Gv SALE M33 154 A4
Shawbury Rd
NTHM/RTH M23 168 A5
Shawbury St MDTN M24 73 F5
Shawclough Cl WHIT OL12 18 C5
Shawclough Dr WHIT OL12 18 B5
Shawclough Ri WHIT OL12 * 29 G1
Shawclough Rd WHIT OL12 18 B5
Shawclough Wy WHIT OL12 18 B5
Shawcroft Cl ROY/SHW OL2 59 H4
Shawcross Fold STKP SK1 13 G2
Shawcross La
WYTH/NTH M22 169 E1
Shawcross St HYDE SK14 148 B3
SLFD M6 113 E4
STKP SK1 13 H6
Shawdene Rd
WYTH/NTH M22 168 B1
Shawe Hall Av URM M41 138 A3
Shawe Hall Crs URM M41 138 A3
Shawe Rd URM M41 138 A1
Shawe Vw URM M41 138 A1
Shawfield Cl RUSH/FAL M14 142 C3
Shawfield La WHIT OL12 28 D1
Shawfields STLY SK15 121 G2
Shawford Rd NEWH/MOS M40 89 F5
Shawgreen Cl HULME M15 127 G2
Shaw Hall Av HYDE SK14 134 C3
Shaw Hall Bank Rd UPML OL3 94 C2
Shaw Hall Cl UPML OL3 94 C2
Shaw Head Dr FAIL M35 105 E4
Shaw Heath EDGY/DAV SK3 12 E6
OFTN SK2 172 A2
Shawheath Cl HULME M15 127 G2
Shawhill Wk NEWH/MOS M40 115 H3
Shaw La MILN OL16 31 G3
Shawlea Av BNG/LEV M19 143 G5
Shaw Moor Av STLY SK15 121 F4
Shaw Rd HTNM SK4 159 E1
MILN OL16 43 G5
MILN OL16 45 E3
OLD OL1 75 H3
ROY/SHW OL2 59 G5
Shaw Rd South
EDGY/DAV SK3 171 H3
Shaws Fold OLDE OL4 * 77 F5
Shaws La UPML OL3 79 F5
Shaw's Rd ALT WA14 165 G5
Shaw St AUL OL6 120 A2
BOLS/LL BL3 48 D4
BURY BL9 5 J3
CSLFD M3 6 E1
FWTH BL4 * 65 H2
HYDE SK14 135 H4
OLD OL1 9 H2
OLDE OL4 93 F1
ROY/SHW OL2 59 F5
UPML OL3 94 D2
WHIT OL12 11 G1
Shay Av HALE/TIMP WA15 179 F3
Shayfield Av CHAD OL9 73 H5
WYTH/NTH M22 168 C4
Shayfield Dr WYTH/NTH M22 168 C4
Shayfield Rd WYTH/NTH M22 168 C4
Shay La HALE/TIMP WA15 179 F3
Sheader Dr ORD M5 112 B3
Sheaf Field Wk RAD M26 52 B5
Sheard Av AUL OL6 107 G4
Shearer Wy SWIN M27 100 A3
Shearing Av WHIT OL12 28 C2

Shearsby Cl HULME M15 127 H2
Shearwater Dr WALK M28 81 H4
Shearwater Gdns ECC M30 110 B5
Shearwater Rd OFTN SK2 173 G4
The Sheddings BOLS/LL BL3 49 F5
Shed St WHIT OL12 14 C4
Sheepfoot La OLD OL1 75 E3
PWCH M25 86 C4
Sheepfoot Wk OLD OL1 75 E3
Sheep Gap WHIT OL12 29 E2
Sheep Gate Dr
TOT/BURYW BL8 36 D1
Sheerness St GTN M18 130 C3
Sheffield Rd HYDE SK14 134 A5
Sheffield St CMANE M1 7 J6
HTNM SK4 159 H3
Shefford Cl OP/CLY M11 116 A5
Sheiling Ct ALT WA14 165 F5
Shelbourne Av BOL BL1 33 E4
Shelderton Cl
NEWH/MOS M40 103 H3
Sheldon Cl PART M31 151 E3
Sheldon Ct AULW OL7 107 E5
Sheldon Rd BRAM/HZG SK7 185 F5
POY/DIS SK12 196 B5
Sheldon St OP/CLY M11 116 C3
Sheldrake Cl DUK SK16 133 H1
Sheldrake Rd ALT WA14 165 E1
Shelfield Cl ROCH OL11 28 C2
Shelfield La ROCH OL11 28 C2
Shelford Av GTN M18 130 A4
Shelley Av MDTN M24 73 E2
Shelley Gv DROY M43 117 H4
HYDE SK14 133 G4
STLY SK15 121 H1
Shelley Ri DUK SK16 134 C1
Shelley Rd CHAD OL9 90 A4
LHULT M38 * 81 F2
OLD OL1 76 B3
PWCH M25 85 G4
RDSH SK5 144 D2
SWIN M27 98 C2
Shelley St NEWH/MOS M40 104 B2
Shelley Wk BOL BL1 33 G5
Shelton Av SALE M33 153 G2
Shenfield Wk
NEWH/MOS M40 115 G2
Shenhurst Cl WILM/AE SK9 200 B1
Shentonfield Rd
WYTH/NTH M22 168 D3
Shenton Park Av SALE M33 153 F5
Shenton St HYDE SK14 133 F4
Shepherd Cross St BOL BL1 33 F5
Shepherds Cl TOT/BURYW BL8 26 A2
Shepherd St BKLY M9 * 103 E1
BURY BL9 5 F6
HEY OL10 * 40 D4
ROCH OL11 28 A2
ROY/SHW OL2 59 F5
TOT/BURYW BL8 26 A3
WHIT OL12 * 10 C4
Shepherds Wy MILN OL16 44 B1
Shepley Av BOLS/LL BL3 48 B4
Shepley Cl BRAM/HZG SK7 185 E4
DUK SK16 120 A5
Shepley Dr BRAM/HZG SK7 185 E3
Shepley La MPL/ROM SK6 175 E5
Shepley Rd DTN/ASHW M34 132 C2
Shepley St DTN/ASHW M34 132 C1
FAIL M35 105 F1
HYDE SK14 148 A1
OLDE OL4 * 92 D1
Shepton Cl BOL BL1 22 C4
Shepton Dr NTHM/RTH M23 179 H2
Sheraton Rd OLDS OL8 91 F3
Sherborne Rd EDGY/DAV SK3 170 D2
URM M41 124 D5
Sherborne St CHH M8 114 C1
Sherborne St West CSLFD M3 114 B2
Sherbourne Cl
CHD/CHDH SK8 193 E1
OLDS OL8 92 B3
RAD M26 51 G4
Sherbourne Dr HEY OL10 40 B3
Sherbourne Rd BOL BL1 32 D5
MDTN M24 72 C1
Sherbourne St PWCH M25 * 85 H3
Sherbrook Cl SALE M33 154 A3
Sherbrooke Av UPML OL3 79 F3
Sherbrook Ri WILM/AE SK9 199 F4
Sherdley Ct CHH M8 102 B1
Sherdley Rd CHH M8 102 B1
Sherford Cl BRAM/HZG SK7 184 B2
Sheridan Wy CHAD OL9 * 73 H4
Sheriff St BOLE BL2 34 C5
MILN OL16 44 D1
WHIT OL12 10 A5
Sheringham Dr HYDE SK14 134 B5
SWIN M27 99 E4
TOT/BURYW BL8 37 H1
Sheringham Pl BOLS/LL BL3 48 C4
Sheringham Rd
DID/WITH M20 143 F4
Sherlock St RUSH/FAL M14 143 F4
Sherratt St ANC M4 7 J2
Sherrington St
WGTN/LGST M12 129 H5
Sherway Dr HALE/TIMP WA15 166 D3
Sherwell Rd BKLY M9 87 G4
Sherwin Wy ROCH OL11 42 C5
Sherwood Av BRO M7 101 E3
DROY M43 118 B3
HTNM SK4 158 D5
RAD M26 52 A1
RUSH/FAL M14 143 E3
SALE M33 154 D1
Sherwood Cl AUL OL6 107 F3
MPL/ROM SK6 175 E5
ORD M5 112 C2
TOT/BURYW BL8 26 A4
Sherwood Dr SWIN M27 99 G3
Sherwood Rd
DTN/ASHW M34 131 G5
MPL/ROM SK6 162 A1
Sherwood St BOL BL1 34 A3
OLD OL1 75 E4
ROCH OL11 42 C4
RUSH/FAL M14 143 E3
Sherwood Wy ROY/SHW OL2 59 F1
Shetland Rd NEWH/MOS M40 115 G2
Shetland Wy RAD M26 52 B4
URM M41 124 C3
Shevington Gdns
NTHM/RTH M23 156 A5
Shieldborn Dr BKLY M9 103 E3
Shield Cl OLDS OL8 8 E5
Shield Dr WALK M28 98 B2
Shield St EDGY/DAV SK3 12 E5
Shiel St WALK M28 82 A4
Shiers Dr CHD/CHDH SK8 170 B5
Shiffnall St BOLE BL2 3 G6
Shilford Dr ANC M4 7 J1
Shillingford Rd FWTH BL4 65 H4
Shillingstone Cl BOLE BL2 35 H3
Shillingten Cl WALK M28 81 E4
Shiloh La OLDE OL4 77 G2
Shilton Gdns BOLS/LL BL3 * 48 D4
Shilton St RAMS BL0 16 C3
Shipgate BOL BL1 3 F4
Shipla Cl CHAD OL9 8 E2
Ship La OLDE OL4 61 G4
Shipley Av SLFD M6 112 B2
Shipley Vw URM M41 123 G3
Shipper Bottom La RAMS BL0 17 F2
Shippey St RUSH/FAL M14 143 F4
Shipston Cl TOT/BURYW BL8 37 G3
Shipton St BOL BL1 33 E5
Shirburn ROCH OL11 * 29 H5
Shirebrook Dr RAD M26 52 C5
Shireburn Av BOLE BL2 49 H1
Shiredale Cl CHD/CHDH SK8 171 E5
Shiredale Dr BKLY M9 103 E3
Shiregreen Av
NEWH/MOS M40 102 D5
Shirehills PWCH M25 85 H4
Shireoak Rd DID/WITH M20 143 F4
The Shires DROY M43 118 C2
RAD M26 52 B4
Shirley Av BRO M7 100 D3
CHAD OL9 89 H5
CHD/CHDH SK8 191 H1
DTN/ASHW M34 118 B5
DTN/ASHW M34 131 E5
ECC M30 110 D5
HYDE SK14 133 G3
MPL/ROM SK6 174 D3
STRET M32 126 C5
SWIN M27 99 H3
Shirley Cl BRAM/HZG SK7 184 D2
Shirley Gv EDGY/DAV SK3 171 H4
Shirley Rd CHH M8 102 B3
Shirley St ROCH OL11 42 B4
Shoecroft Av DTN/ASHW M34 146 C1
Sholver Hill Cl OLD OL1 60 D5
Sholver La OLD OL1 60 C5
Shone Av WYTH/NTH M22 181 E2
Shore Av ROY/SHW OL2 45 F5
Shoreditch Cl HTNM SK4 159 E1
Shorefield Cl MILN OL16 31 G4
Shorefield Mt EDGW/EG BL7 22 D3
Shore Fold LIT OL15 20 C2
Shoreham Wk CHAD OL9 * 90 B1
Shore Hl LIT OL15 21 F2
Shore Lea LIT OL15 20 C2
Shore Mt LIT OL15 20 C2
Shore Rd LIT OL15 20 C1
Shore St MILN OL16 31 G5
OLD OL1 9 K2
Shoreswood BOL BL1 33 G1
Shorland St SWIN M27 98 B3
Shorrocks St TOT/BURYW BL8 37 E3
Short Av DROY M43 117 G5
Shortcroft St HULME M15 * 128 A1
Shortland Crs BNG/LEV M19 158 A3
Shortlands Av BURY BL9 5 F7
Short St BRAM/HZG SK7 185 E1
BRO M7 114 B2
CMANE M1 7 G4
HEY OL10 40 C5
HTNM SK4 159 H3
Short St East HTNM SK4 159 H3
Shotton Wk RUSH/FAL M14 * 128 C5
Shrewsbury Ct
OLDTF/WHR M16 * 127 G3
Shrewsbury Gdns
CHD/CHDH SK8 193 F1
Shrewsbury Rd BOL BL1 48 A1
DROY M43 117 H3
PWCH M25 85 H4
SALE M33 154 B4
Shrewsbury St OLDE OL4 76 B4
OLDTF/WHR M16 127 G3
Shrigley Cl WILM/AE SK9 199 G1
Shrigley Rd POY/DIS SK12 196 B5
Shrigley Rd North
POY/DIS SK12 196 B4
Shropshire Av RDSH SK5 146 A5
Shropshire Rd FAIL M35 105 F4
Shropshire Sq
WGTN/LGST M12 * 129 F2
Shrowbridge Wk
WGTN/LGST M12 129 H2
Shudehill ANC M4 7 G2
Shudehill Rd WALK M28 96 B1
Shurmer St BOLS/LL BL3 48 B5
Shutt La UPML OL3 78 C2
Shuttle St ECC M30 * 111 G3
RAD M26 68 D3
Shuttleworth Cl
OLDTF/WHR M16 142 A3
Shutts La STLY SK15 121 G5
Siam St OP/CLY M11 116 A5
Sibley Rd HTNM SK4 159 E3
Sibley St GTN M18 130 C3
Sibson Rd CCHDY M21 141 E2
SALE M33 154 B2
Sickle St CMANW M2 7 F4
OLDE OL4 9 J6
Sidbury Rd CCHDY M21 141 G3
Sidcup Rd NTHM/RTH M23 167 G4
Siddall St HEY OL10 56 B1
OLD OL1 9 G1
RAD M26 52 B5
ROY/SHW OL2 60 A2
WGTN/LGST M12 144 A1
Siddington Av DID/WITH M20 142 C4
EDGY/DAV SK3 171 F3
Siddington Rd POY/DIS SK12 195 G5
WILM/AE SK9 * 192 A2
Side Av ALT WA14 177 F3
Sidebotham St MPL/ROM SK6 161 G2
Sidebottom St DROY M43 * 117 G4
OLDE OL4 76 D4
STLY SK15 120 D3
Side St OLDS OL8 90 D5
OP/CLY M11 116 C4
Sidford Cl BOLS/LL BL3 50 A4
The Sidings WALK M28 97 H5
Sidlaw Cl OLDS OL8 91 G5
Sidley Av BKLY M9 88 C3
Sidley St HYDE SK14 134 A5
Sidmouth Av URM M41 123 F5
Sidmouth Dr BKLY M9 88 A5
Sidmouth Gv CHD/CHDH SK8 182 C5
Sidmouth Rd SALE M33 153 G1
Sidmouth St CHAD OL9 90 C2
DTN/ASHW M34 132 A1
Sidney Rd BKLY M9 103 E1
Sidney St BOLS/LL BL3 49 E4
CMANE M1 128 B1
CSLFD M3 6 A3
CSLFD M3 * 6 D5
OLD OL1 75 H3
Sidwell Wk ANC M4 * 115 G4
Siebers Bank WHIT OL12 * 29 G1
Siemens Rd IRL M44 150 D1
Sienna Cl IRL M44 136 A5
Signal Cl ECC M30 110 C3
Signal Dr NEWH/MOS M40 103 E4
Signet Wk CHH M8 102 C5
Silas St AUL OL6 * 107 G5
Silburn Wy MDTN M24 71 H5
Silchester Dr
NEWH/MOS M40 103 E4
Silchester Wy BOLE BL2 35 F5
Silfield Cl OP/CLY M11 115 H4
Silkhey Gv WALK M28 97 E1
Silkin Cl BRUN/LGST M13 * 128 C1
Silkstone St OP/CLY M11 130 B1
Silk St ANC M4 7 J2
CSLFD M3 114 A2
MDTN M24 72 C4
NEWH/MOS M40 104 B4
ROCH OL11 42 C2
Sillavan Wy CSLFD M3 6 B3
Silsden Av BKLY M9 87 G2
Silton St BKLY M9 103 G3
Silverbirch Cl SALE M33 153 G4
Silver Birches DTN/ASHW M34 147 F2
Silver Birch Gv SWIN M27 99 G4
Silver Birch Ms DUK SK16 133 H1
Silverbirch Wy FAIL M35 105 E3
Silver Cl DUK SK16 133 E1
Silvercroft St HULME M15 127 H1
Silverdale SWIN M27 84 B5
Silverdale Av CHAD OL9 90 B2
DTN/ASHW M34 147 E1
IRL M44 122 C4
PWCH M25 86 D5
Silverdale Cl BURY BL9 53 H1
MPL/ROM SK6 186 D4
Silverdale Dr OLDE OL4 93 E1
WILM/AE SK9 200 D1
Silverdale Rd BOL BL1 48 B2
CCHDY M21 141 G2
CHD/CHDH SK8 169 G5
FWTH BL4 65 F3
HTNM SK4 159 F2
Silverdale St OP/CLY M11 131 E1
Silver Hl MILN OL16 31 G5
Silver Hill Rd HYDE SK14 148 A2
Silver Jubilee Wk ANC M4 7 H3
Silverlea Dr BKLY M9 87 H5
Silvermere AUL OL6 107 H4
Silver Spring HYDE SK14 148 B3
Silverstone Dr
NEWH/MOS M40 117 E1
Silver St BURY BL9 4 D5
CMANE M1 7 G5
IRL M44 122 C4
OLD OL1 9 F4
RAMS BL0 16 D2
WHIT OL12 * 29 G3
WHTF M45 * 69 F3
Silverthorne Cl STLY SK15 120 D4
Silverton Cl HYDE SK14 149 F1
Silverton Gv BOL BL1 34 A2
MDTN M24 56 A5
Silverwell La BOL BL1 3 F5
Silverwell St BOL BL1 3 F5
NEWH/MOS M40 104 C5
Silverwell Yd BOL BL1 3 F5
Silverwood CHAD OL9 73 H5
Silverwood Av CCHDY M21 141 F3
Simeon St ANC M4 * 7 H1
MILN OL16 31 G5
Simister Dr BURY BL9 69 H2
Simister Gn PWCH M25 70 D4
Simister La MDTN M24 71 F3
PWCH M25 70 C4
Simister Rd FAIL M35 105 E3
Simister St BKLY M9 103 F2
Simkin Wy OLDS OL8 106 D1
Simms Cl CSLFD M3 114 A3
Simonbury Cl TOT/BURYW BL8 37 E4
Simon Freeman Cl
BNG/LEV M19 144 C5
Simon La MDTN M24 71 F2
Simons Cl SALE M33 154 B3
Simonsway NTHM/RTH M23 179 H1
WYTH/NTH M22 180 B2
Simpson Av SWIN M27 84 D5
Simpson Gv WALK M28 96 B4
Simpson Hill Cl HEY OL10 41 G3
Simpson Rd WALK M28 96 C4
Simpson St ANC M4 7 H1
CHAD OL9 90 C3
EDGY/DAV SK3 * 13 F6
HYDE SK14 133 F5
OP/CLY M11 116 B4
WILM/AE SK9 * 198 D4
Sinclair St ROCH OL11 42 C3
Sinderland La ALT WA14 151 H5
Sinderland Rd ALT WA14 151 H5
ALT WA14 165 E1
Sindsley Gv BOLS/LL BL3 64 D1
Sindsley Rd SWIN M27 83 G5
Singapore Av MANAIR M90 179 H4
Singleton Av BOLE BL2 50 C2
Singleton Cl BRO M7 101 F1
Singleton Gv WHTN BL5 62 C4
Singleton Rd BRO M7 101 F1
HTNM SK4 159 E2
Singleton St RAD M26 51 G5
Sion St RAD M26 68 A2
Sirdar St OP/CLY M11 * 117 G5
Sirius Pl BRO M7 114 A2
Sir Matt Busby Wy
TRPK M17 126 C3
Sir Richard Fairey Rd
HTNM SK4 144 A4
Sir Robert Thomas Ct
BKLY M9 * 103 E2
Siskin Rd OFTN SK2 173 G4
Sisley Cl BRO M7 101 E2
Sisson St FAIL M35 104 D3
Sisters' St DROY M43 117 H5
Sixpools Gv WALK M28 96 D2
Sixth Av BOL BL1 48 A2
BOLS/LL BL3 50 C5
BURY BL9 39 G2
OLDS OL8 105 H1
Sixth St TRPK M17 126 A3
Size St WHIT OL12 14 C4
Skagen Ct BOL BL1 2 D1
Skaife Rd SALE M33 155 F2
Skarratt Cl WGTN/LGST M12 129 G2
Skegness Cl TOT/BURYW BL8 38 A1
Skelton Gv BOLE BL2 50 C1
BRUN/LGST M13 143 H1
Skelton Rd ALT WA14 165 H2
STRET M32 126 A5
Skelwith Av BOLS/LL BL3 65 E2
Skelwith Cl URM M41 123 H4
Skerry Cl BRUN/LGST M13 128 C1
Skerton Rd OLDTF/WHR M16 127 E4
Skiddaw Cl MDTN M24 72 A1
Skip Pl ANC M4 114 D2
Skipton Av CHAD OL9 74 A3
NEWH/MOS M40 104 C1
Skipton Cl BRAM/HZG SK7 184 D4
RDSH SK5 145 E3
TOT/BURYW BL8 37 E4
Skipton Dr URM M41 123 G3
Skipton St BOLE BL2 49 H2
OLDS OL8 92 A3
Skipton Wk BOLE BL2 49 H2
Skye Cl HEY OL10 40 A5
Skye Cft MPL/ROM SK6 162 C3
Skye Rd URM M41 124 C3
Slackcote La UPML OL3 61 H2
Slackey Brow FWTH BL4 83 F2
Slack Fold La FWTH BL4 64 C3
Slack Ga WHIT OL12 14 D5
Slack Hall OLDE OL4 77 E4
Slack La BOLE BL2 24 B4
SWIN M27 99 F1
WHTN BL5 62 A2
Slack Rd BKLY M9 102 D1
Slack St HYDE SK14 134 A4
MILN OL16 10 D6
Slade Gv BRUN/LGST M13 129 G5
Slade Hall Rd WGTN/LGST M12 144 A1
Slade La BNG/LEV M19 143 H3
Slade Mt BNG/LEV M19 * 143 H3
Sladen St WHIT OL12 10 C3
Slade St BOLS/LL BL3 66 D1
Slaidburn Av BOLE BL2 50 C3
Slaidburn Cl MILN OL16 44 C1
Slaidburn Dr TOT/BURYW BL8 36 D3
Slaithwaite Dr OP/CLY M11 116 D3
Slateacre Rd HYDE SK14 148 B4
Slate Av ANC M4 115 F4
Slate La AULW OL7 118 D5
DTN/ASHW M34 118 B5
Slaterfield BOLS/LL BL3 48 D4
Slater La BOL BL1 3 G2
Slater St BOL BL1 2 D2
CHAD OL9 8 E4
ECC M30 110 C3
FAIL M35 105 E1
FWTH BL4 66 A4
Slate Whf HULME M15 * 6 A7
Slawson Wy HEY OL10 41 G3
Sleaford Cl NEWH/MOS M40 115 G2
TOT/BURYW BL8 38 A1
Sleddale Cl OFTN SK2 173 E4
Sledmere Cl BOL BL1 34 A4
OP/CLY M11 116 B4
Sledmoor Rd NTHM/RTH M23 155 G5
Slimbridge Cl BOLE BL2 35 H5
Sloane Av OLDE OL4 76 D4
Sloane St AUL OL6 120 A2
BOLS/LL BL3 64 B1
OP/CLY M11 * 116 B3
Smallbridge Cl WALK M28 96 D2
Smallbrook Rd ROY/SHW OL2 45 F4
Smalldale Av
OLDTF/WHR M16 128 A5
Smalley St ROCH OL11 42 B4
Smallfield Dr BKLY M9 103 E2
Smallridge Cl
NEWH/MOS M40 115 G2
Smallshaw La AUL OL6 107 F5
Smallwood St
NEWH/MOS M40 104 B4
Smart St WGTN/LGST M12 129 H5
Smeaton Cl STRET M32 140 C1
Smeaton St CHH M8 102 C4
Smedley Av BOLS/LL BL3 65 F1
Smedley La CHH M8 102 C4
Smedley Rd CHH M8 102 B4
Smedley St CHH M8 102 B4
Smethurst Hall Rd BURY BL9 39 H2
Smethurst La BOLS/LL BL3 64 A2
Smethurst St BKLY M9 103 E1
HEY OL10 40 C4
MDTN M24 73 G5
TOT/BURYW BL8 37 G2
Smithfold La WALK M28 81 F4
Smith Hl MILN OL16 31 G5
Smithies Av MDTN M24 72 D2
Smithies St HEY OL10 41 F4
Smithills Croft Rd BOL BL1 33 E3
Smithills Dean Rd BOL BL1 32 D1
Smithills Dr BOL BL1 32 C4
Smithills Hall Cl RAMS BL0 16 C4
Smith La EDGW/EG BL7 23 E3
Smiths Lawn WILM/AE SK9 198 D5
Smith's Rd BOLS/LL BL3 66 A1
Smith St AULW OL7 119 E4
BURY BL9 5 G2
CHD/CHDH SK8 * 170 C3
DTN/ASHW M34 146 D1
HEY OL10 41 E4
HYDE SK14 133 G3
LIT OL15 21 E3
MILN OL16 10 D6
MOSL OL5 93 G5
OLDE OL4 76 D4
OLDTF/WHR M16 127 F2
RAMS BL0 16 C3
WALK M28 82 A4
Smithybridge Rd LIT OL15 20 C5
Smithy Bridge Rd LIT OL15 31 H1
Smithy Cft EDGW/EG BL7 23 E3
Smithy Dr ALT WA14 176 A1
Smithy Fold WHIT OL12 29 F2
Smithy Fold Rd HYDE SK14 148 A3
Smithy Gn CHD/CHDH SK8 * 182 D4
MPL/ROM SK6 162 A1
Smithy Gv AUL OL6 119 H1
Smithy Hl BOLS/LL BL3 47 H5
Smithy La ALT WA14 176 B1
CSLFD M3 * 6 D4
HYDE SK14 148 A2
PART M31 151 E3
UPML OL3 79 E4
Smithy St BRAM/HZG SK7 185 E1
RAMS BL0 * 16 D2
Smyrna St HEY OL10 40 D5
OLDE OL4 * 92 B2
ORD M5 112 D4
RAD M26 52 A5
Snape St RAD M26 52 A4
Snell St ANC M4 115 G4
Snipe Av ROCH OL11 28 C4
Snipe Cl POY/DIS SK12 194 B4
Snipe Rd OLDS OL8 92 A5
Snipe St BOLS/LL BL3 49 E4
Snipe Wy AULW OL7 118 C4
Snowden Av URM M41 138 B3
Snowden St BOL BL1 2 C3
HEY OL10 56 B1
OLDS OL8 91 G3
Snowdon Rd ECC M30 111 H2
Snowdon St ROCH OL11 43 F4
Snow Hill Rd BOLS/LL BL3 50 A4
Snydale Cl WHTN BL5 62 B2
Snydale Wy BOLS/LL BL3 63 E2
Soapstone Wy IRL M44 136 C3
Soap St ANC M4 7 G3
Society St ROY/SHW OL2 60 A2
Sofa St BOL BL1 33 E5
Soho St BOL BL1 2 E6
OLDE OL4 76 A5
Solent Av CHH M8 87 F5
Solent Dr BOLS/LL BL3 49 H4
Solness St BURY BL9 27 G5
Soloman Rd ALT WA14 153 F5
Solway Cl BOLS/LL BL3 64 C1
OLDS OL8 9 F7
SWIN M27 83 H3
Solway Rd WYTH/NTH M22 168 D5
Somerby Dr WYTH/NTH M22 180 B3
Somerdale Av BOL BL1 47 H2
Somerfield Rd BKLY M9 103 E1
Somerford Av DID/WITH M20 142 C3
Somerford Rd RDSH SK5 145 G1
Somersby Dr EDGW/EG BL7 23 E3
Somersby Wk BOLS/LL BL3 * 48 D4
Somerset Av ROY/SHW OL2 59 G2
Somerset Cl RDSH SK5 160 D2
Somerset Dr BURY BL9 53 G1
Somerset Gv ROCH OL11 28 D3
Somerset Pl SALE M33 139 H5
Somerset Rd ALT WA14 165 G3
BOL BL1 48 A1
DROY M43 117 H2
ECC M30 111 H1
FAIL M35 104 D4
Somerset St OLDE OL4 92 B1
Somers Rd RDSH SK5 145 F2
Somerton Av SALE M33 154 D3
WYTH/NTH M22 * 180 B1
Somerton Rd BOLE BL2 50 C4
Somerville Gdns
HALE/TIMP WA15 166 A2
Somerville Sq BOL BL1 33 F3
Somerville St BOL BL1 33 F3
Somerwood Wk
WGTN/LGST M12 * 129 G2
Sonning Dr BOLS/LL BL3 63 H2
Sopwith Dr RUSH/FAL M14 142 C2
Sorby Rd IRL M44 136 C4
Sorrel Bank SLFD M6 113 E1
Sorrel Dr LIT OL15 20 C2
Sorrell Bank RDSH SK5 145 G3
Sorrel St HULME M15 127 H2
Sorrel Wy OLDE OL4 76 D2
Soudan Rd OFTN SK2 172 B3
Soudan St MDTN M24 73 F3
Souracre Fold STLY SK15 121 E2
South Acre Dr WILM/AE SK9 192 A4
Southall St CSLFD M3 114 C2
Southampton Cl BRO M7 101 G5
Southam St BRO M7 102 A3
South Av BNG/LEV M19 143 H4
FWTH BL4 82 C2
HEY OL10 40 C4
SWIN M27 98 C5
UPML OL3 95 E1
URM M41 124 D2
WHTF M45 69 F3
South Back Rock BURY BL9 4 E4
South Bank Cl WILM/AE SK9 * 201 E3
Southbank Rd BNG/LEV M19 158 A1
South Bank Rd BURY BL9 4 C7
Southbourne Av URM M41 139 F1
Southbourne St SLFD M6 112 D3
Southbrook Av CHH M8 87 E4
Southbrook Gv BOLS/LL BL3 65 E1
Southcliffe Rd RDSH SK5 145 F5
South Cliffe St OP/CLY M11 131 E1
South Cl BURY BL9 69 H1
WILM/AE SK9 198 C4
South Crs NEWH/MOS M40 89 G4
OP/CLY M11 117 E3
South Cft OLDS OL8 92 A4
Southcross Rd GTN M18 130 C5

South Cross St BURY BL9 ... 5 F5
South Croston St
OLDTF/WHR M16 ... 127 G4
Southdene Av DID/WITH M20 ... 156 D2
Southdown Cl HTNM SK4 ... 12 D1
ROCH OL11 ... 42 B2
Southdown Crs BKLY M9 ... 88 D5
CHD/CHDH SK8 ... 182 C4
Southdown Dr WALK M28 ... 96 A4
Southdowns Cl ROY/SHW OL2 ... 59 G1
South Downs Dr ALT WA14 ... 177 G4
South Downs Rd ALT WA14 ... 177 F3
South Dr BOLE BL2 ... 35 F3
CCHDY M21 ... 141 F5
CHD/CHDH SK8 ... 169 F5
HALE/TIMP WA15 ... 166 B2
WILM/AE SK9 ... 199 E4
Southend Av HULME M15 ... 127 G2
Southend St BOLS/LL BL3 ... 64 B1
Southern Ap SWIN M27 ... 84 D5
Southernby Cl
BRUN/LGST M13 * ... 129 G4
Southern Cl BRAM/HZG SK7 ... 184 A3
DTN/ASHW M34 ... 146 C3
Southern Crs BRAM/HZG SK7 ... 184 A3
Southern Rd SALE M33 ... 139 G5
Southern St CSLFD M3 ... 6 C7
SLFD M6 ... 112 D3
WALK M28 ... 82 A2
Southey Cl LIT OL15 ... 31 G1
Southfield Av BURY BL9 ... 27 F5
Southfield Cl DUK SK16 ... 133 G2
Southfield Dr WHTN BL5 ... 62 A5
Southfield Rd RAMS BL0 ... 26 B1
Southfields Av OP/CLY M11 ... 116 D3
Southfields Dr
HALE/TIMP WA15 ... 166 C2
Southfield St BOLS/LL BL3 ... 49 G5
Southgarth Rd SLFD M6 ... 112 D2
Southgate BOLE BL2 ... 35 F2
CCHDY M21 ... 141 F4
HTNM SK4 ... 159 F1
UPML OL3 ... 78 D2
URM M41 ... 138 B3
WHIT OL12 ... 18 A1
Southgate Av
NEWH/MOS M40 * ... 116 B1
Southgate College Land
CSLFD M3 ... 6 D4
Southgate Rd BURY BL9 ... 69 G1
CHAD OL9 ... 89 H4
Southgate St OLD OL1 ... 9 H4
South Gv BRUN/LGST M13 ... 129 E3
SALE M33 ... 154 C3
WALK M28 ... 81 H5
WILM/AE SK9 ... 200 D4
Southgrove Av BOL BL1 ... 22 D5
South Hl OLDE OL4 ... 93 E2
South Hill St OLDE OL4 ... 9 K5
South King St CSLFD M3 ... 6 D4
ECC M30 ... 110 C3
Southlands Av ECC M30 ... 110 A5
South Langworthy Rd
ORD M5 ... 113 E4
Southlea Rd DID/WITH M20 ... 158 A1
Southleigh Dr BOLE BL2 ... 50 D3
Southlink OLDE OL4 * ... 9 K4
South Lonsdale St STRET M32 ... 126 B5
South Md POY/DIS SK12 ... 194 C2
South Meade CCHDY M21 ... 141 F4
HALE/TIMP WA15 ... 166 B2
PWCH M25 ... 86 C5
South Meadway
MPL/ROM SK6 ... 187 E5
Southmere Cl BKLY M9 ... 89 F5
South Mesnefield Rd BRO M7 ... 100 D3
Southmill St CMANW M2 ... 6 D6
Southmoor Rd
NTHM/RTH M23 ... 167 F4
Southmoor Wk
BOLS/LL BL3 * ... 48 D4
South Oak La WILM/AE SK9 ... 198 C4
South Pde BRAM/HZG SK7 ... 184 A2
MILN OL16 ... 10 C6
South Park Dr POY/DIS SK12 ... 195 F3
South Park Rd
CHD/CHDH SK8 ... 169 G3
Southpool Cl BRAM/HZG SK7 ... 184 B2
South Pump St CMANE M1 * ... 7 H6
South Radford St BRO M7 ... 100 D3
South Rdg DTN/ASHW M34 ... 132 C3
South Rd ALT WA14 ... 177 F2
ALT WA14 ... 177 G4
DID/WITH M20 ... 157 G4
STRET M32 ... 125 F4
SWIN M27 ... 85 E5
South Rw PWCH M25 ... 100 C1
South Royd St
TOT/BURYW BL8 ... 26 A4
Southsea St OP/CLY M11 ... 130 C1
Southside MPL/ROM SK6 ... 146 C5
WILM/AE SK9 * ... 190 A3
South St AULW OL7 ... 118 D5
BOLS/LL BL3 ... 64 D1
MILN OL16 ... 10 E5
OLDS OL8 ... 90 C5
OP/CLY M11 ... 130 B1
RAMS BL0 ... 17 E2
WGTN/LGST M12 ... 129 F3
WILM/AE SK9 ... 200 D4
South Ter BURY BL9 ... 53 E2
South Terrace Ct MILN OL16 ... 43 F1
South Vale Crs
HALE/TIMP WA15 ... 166 A4
South Vw MPL/ROM SK6 ... 147 G5
RDSH SK5 ... 131 E5
ROCH OL11 ... 28 B5
STLY SK15 ... 109 G4
South View Gdns
CHD/CHDH SK8 ... 181 H1
South View Rd MILN OL16 ... 20 B5
South View St BOLE BL2 ... 49 H2
South View Ter MILN OL16 ... 20 B4
Southview Wk OLDE OL4 * ... 76 D3
Southwark Dr DUK SK16 ... 133 G2
Southway ALT WA14 ... 165 H3
AULW OL7 ... 106 D4
DROY M43 ... 117 H5
NEWH/MOS M40 ... 90 A5
South Wy OLDS OL8 ... 91 F5
Southwell Cl BOL BL1 ... 2 C2
MPL/ROM SK6 ... 161 H5
Southwell Ct STRET M32 * ... 140 A2
Southwell Gdns AUL OL6 ... 107 E3
Southwell St BKLY M9 ... 103 F3
Southwick Rd
NTHM/RTH M23 ... 155 H4
South William St CSLFD M3 * ... 114 A4
Southwood Cl BOLS/LL BL3 ... 65 E1
Southwood Dr BKLY M9 ... 87 F2
South Woodley Gdns RAD M26 ... 68 D4
Southwood Rd OFTN SK2 ... 172 C5
Southyard St BNG/LEV M19 * ... 144 B3
Sovereign St SLFD M6 ... 113 F1
Sowerby Cl TOT/BURYW BL8 ... 37 E4
Spa Cl RDSH SK5 ... 145 E3
Spa Crs LHULT M38 ... 81 F1
Spa Gv LHULT M38 ... 81 F1
Spa La LHULT M38 ... 81 F1
OLDE OL4 ... 92 C2
Spalding Dr NTHM/RTH M23 ... 179 H2
Sparkford Av NTHM/RTH M23 ... 155 E5
Sparkle St CMANE M1 ... 7 J5
Spark Rd NTHM/RTH M23 ... 167 G2
Spa Rd BOL BL1 ... 2 B6
Sparrow Cl RDSH SK5 ... 145 E1
Sparrowfield Cl STLY SK15 ... 109 F3
Sparrow Hl MILN OL16 ... 10 B7
Sparrow St ROY/SHW OL2 ... 75 F2
Sparta Av WALK M28 ... 81 H5
Sparta Wk OP/CLY M11 ... 116 B5
Sparth Bottoms Rd
ROCH OL11 ... 29 G5
Sparthfield Av ROCH OL11 ... 42 D1
Sparthfield Rd HTNM SK4 ... 159 G3
Sparth La HTNM SK4 ... 159 G3
Sparth Rd NEWH/MOS M40 ... 104 C5
Spa St HULME M15 ... 128 C3
Spath La WILM/AE SK9 ... 192 A2
Spath La East CHD/CHDH SK8 ... 193 E2
Spath Rd DID/WITH M20 ... 157 F3
Spath Wk CHD/CHDH SK8 ... 193 E2
Spaw St CSLFD M3 ... 6 B3
Spear St CMANE M1 ... 7 H4
Spectator St ANC M4 ... 115 G3
Spencer Av BOLS/LL BL3 ... 67 F1
HYDE SK14 ... 133 G3
OLDTF/WHR M16 ... 141 G1
WHTF M45 ... 69 F2
Spencer La ROCH OL11 ... 41 F1
Spencer St CHAD OL9 ... 90 C3
DUK SK16 ... 119 H5
ECC M30 ... 110 D4
MOSL OL5 ... 108 C1
OLD OL1 ... 9 K1
RAD M26 * ... 52 D5
RAMS BL0 ... 16 C3
RDSH SK5 ... 145 F3
TOT/BURYW BL8 ... 37 H3
Spender Av CHH M8 ... 102 B4
Spen Fold LIT OL15 ... 20 D4
TOT/BURYW BL8 ... 52 B1
Spennithorne Rd URM M41 ... 138 B1
Spenser Av DTN/ASHW M34 ... 147 E3
RAD M26 ... 51 H5
Spenwood Rd LIT OL15 ... 20 C3
Spey Cl ALT WA14 ... 165 F3
Speyside Cl WHTF M45 * ... 69 H4
Spindle Av STLY SK15 ... 121 F2
Spindle Cft FWTH BL4 ... 66 A5
Spindlepoint Dr WALK M28 ... 96 D2
The Spindles MOSL OL5 ... 109 E2
Spindle Wk WHTN BL5 ... 62 A2
Spindlewood Cl STLY SK15 ... 121 G3
Spingfield St BOLS/LL BL3 ... 49 F5
Spiningdale LHULT M38 ... 80 C1
Spinks St OLDE OL4 ... 92 A2
Spinners Gdns WHIT OL12 ... 19 H4
Spinners Gn WHIT OL12 ... 30 A1
Spinners La POY/DIS SK12 ... 194 D3
Spinners Ms BOL BL1 ... 2 D2
Spinners Wy OLDE OL4 ... 61 E5
Spinney Dr BURY BL9 ... 27 G5
SALE M33 ... 153 G3
Spinney Gv DTN/ASHW M34 ... 132 C3
Spinney Nook BOLE BL2 ... 35 E4
Spinney Rd NTHM/RTH M23 ... 168 A2
The Spinney CHD/CHDH SK8 ... 182 B1
EDGW/EG BL7 ... 23 H1
OLDE OL4 ... 77 F4
URM M41 * ... 138 A1
WALK M28 * ... 98 B4
WHIT OL12 ... 18 C5
WHTF M45 ... 68 D5
Spinningfields BOL BL1 * ... 2 A2
Spinningfield Wy HEY OL10 ... 56 A2
Spinning Jenny Wk ANC M4 * ... 115 F3
Spinning Meadow BOL BL1 ... 2 B2
Spinning Mdw BOL BL1 ... 2 B2
The Spinnings BURY BL9 * ... 16 D5
Spire Wk WGTN/LGST M12 * ... 115 G5
Spirewood Gdns
MPL/ROM SK6 ... 161 H4
Spodden Fold WHIT OL12 ... 14 B5
Spodden St WHIT OL12 ... 29 G3
Spod Rd WHIT OL12 ... 29 F2
Spokeshave Wy MILN OL16 ... 30 D1
Sportside Av WALK M28 ... 82 A4
Sportside Cl WALK M28 ... 82 A4
Sportside Gv WALK M28 ... 82 A3
Sportsmans Dr OLDS OL8 ... 91 H4
Spotland Rd WHIT OL12 ... 29 G3
Spotland Tops WHIT OL12 ... 28 D2
Spreadbury St
NEWH/MOS M40 ... 103 H3
Spring Av HYDE SK14 ... 148 B3
WHTF M45 ... 69 F2
Springbank CHAD OL9 * ... 74 B5
Spring Bank STLY SK15 ... 121 E5
Spring Bank Av AUL OL6 ... 107 E5
DTN/ASHW M34 ... 132 A1
Springbank Cl MPL/ROM SK6 ... 147 G5
Spring Bank La ROCH OL11 ... 28 B3
STLY SK15 ... 108 D5
Spring Bank Pl STKP SK1 * ... 13 F5
Springbank Rd MPL/ROM SK6 ... 147 G5
Spring Bank St OLDS OL8 ... 90 D3
Spring Bridge Rd
OLDTF/WHR M16 ... 142 B1
Springburn Cl WALK M28 ... 96 B4
Spring Cl AULW OL7 ... 106 D4
OLDE OL4 ... 92 C2
RAMS BL0 ... 16 C2
TOT/BURYW BL8 ... 25 H5
Spring Clough WALK M28 ... 98 A5
Spring Clough Av WALK M28 ... 82 C5
Spring Clough Dr OLDS OL8 ... 92 B3
WALK M28 ... 82 C5
Springdale Gdns
DID/WITH M20 ... 157 F3
Springfield RAD M26 ... 83 F1
URM M41 ... 138 C1
Springfield Av BRAM/HZG SK7 ... 185 E1
CHH M8 ... 102 C2
HTNM SK4 ... 145 E4
LIT OL15 ... 20 D1
MPL/ROM SK6 * ... 175 E3
Springfield Cl FAIL M35 ... 104 D2
Springfield Dr WILM/AE SK9 ... 198 A5
Springfield Gdns FWTH BL4 ... 82 D1
Springfield La CSLFD M3 ... 6 C1
IRL M44 ... 136 B1
MILN OL16 ... 20 A5
ROY/SHW OL2 ... 58 D2
Springfield Rd ALT WA14 ... 165 G4
BOL BL1 ... 22 D4
CHD/CHDH SK8 ... 169 G4
DROY M43 ... 117 G2
FWTH BL4 ... 65 F3
FWTH BL4 ... 82 C1
MDTN M24 ... 72 C2
RAMS BL0 ... 26 B1
SALE M33 ... 154 C2
Springfield St AUL OL6 * ... 107 H5
DTN/ASHW M34 ... 132 C2
HEY OL10 ... 40 B4
Spring Gdns BOLE BL2 ... 35 G2
BRAM/HZG SK7 ... 185 E1
CMANW M2 ... 7 F4
HALE/TIMP WA15 ... 166 D4
HYDE SK14 ... 133 G4
MDTN M24 ... 72 D2
SLFD M6 ... 113 E2
STKP SK1 ... 13 K4
Spring Garden St
ROY/SHW OL2 ... 59 E5
Spring Gv UPML OL3 ... 95 E2
WHTF M45 ... 69 F2
Spring Hall Ri OLDE OL4 ... 61 E5
Springhead Av DID/WITH M20 ... 142 C4
OLDE OL4 ... 93 E2
Springhill ROY/SHW OL2 ... 59 E5
Spring La OLDE OL4 ... 92 D2
RAD M26 ... 68 C1
Springlawn BOL BL1 ... 47 G1
Springlawns BOL BL1 * ... 47 G1
Spring Meadow La UPML OL3 ... 79 F4
Spring Mill Wk MILN OL16 ... 30 D1
Spring Pl WHIT OL12 ... 14 C3
Spring Ri ROY/SHW OL2 ... 44 D5
Spring Rd ALT WA14 ... 177 G2
POY/DIS SK12 ... 195 G5
Springside HTNM SK4 ... 144 D4
Spring Side WHIT OL12 ... 14 C1
Springside Av WALK M28 ... 82 B4
Springside Cl WALK M28 * ... 82 B4
Springside Gv WALK M28 ... 82 B4
Springside Rd BURY BL9 ... 27 F3
Springside Vw
TOT/BURYW BL8 ... 26 D4
Springside Wk HULME M15 * ... 127 G2
Springs La STLY SK15 ... 120 C1
Springs Rd MDTN M24 ... 89 H1
The Springs ALT WA14 ... 177 E2
ROCH OL11 ... 28 B4
Spring St BOLS/LL BL3 ... 49 E4
BURY BL9 ... 5 F6
FWTH BL4 ... 66 A3
MOSL OL5 ... 93 H5
OLDE OL4 ... 76 B4
RAMS BL0 ... 16 C2
RAMS BL0 ... 17 E1
STLY SK15 ... 120 D3
TOT/BURYW BL8 ... 25 H4
TOT/BURYW BL8 ... 37 E2
UPML OL3 * ... 79 E4
WGTN/LGST M12 ... 144 A1
WILM/AE SK9 ... 198 D3
Spring Ter CHAD OL9 ... 74 B5
MILN OL16 * ... 45 E3
Spring Thyme Fold LIT OL15 ... 20 D3
Spring V BRAM/HZG SK7 * ... 185 F2
MDTN M24 ... 72 D4
PWCH M25 ... 85 H5
Springvale Cl AULW OL7 ... 106 C5
Spring Vale Dr TOT/BURYW BL8 ... 25 H5
Spring Vale St TOT/BURYW BL8 ... 26 A5
Spring Vale Ter LIT OL15 ... 21 E3
Spring Vale Wy ROY/SHW OL2 ... 59 H4
Spring Vw BURY BL9 * ... 39 G1
Springville Av BKLY M9 ... 103 G3
Springwater Av RAMS BL0 ... 16 B5
Springwater Cl BOLE BL2 ... 35 F3
Springwater La WHTF M45 ... 69 F2
Springwell Cl SLFD M6 * ... 112 D3
Springwell Gdns HYDE SK14 ... 149 G2
Springwood Av CHAD OL9 ... 73 H4
SWIN M27 ... 99 G4
Springwood Crs
MPL/ROM SK6 ... 162 D4
Springwood Hall Rd OLDS OL8 ... 91 H5
Springwood La MPL/ROM SK6 ... 163 E4
Spring Wood St RAMS BL0 ... 16 C1
Spruce Av BURY BL9 ... 5 K4
Spruce Ct SLFD M6 ... 113 G3
Spruce Crs BURY BL9 ... 27 G4
Spruce St HULME M15 ... 127 H2
MILN OL16 * ... 11 F7
RAMS BL0 ... 16 B4
Sprucewood CHAD OL9 ... 73 G4
Spurn La UPML OL3 ... 79 E1
The Spur OLDS OL8 ... 91 H5
Square St RAMS BL0 ... 16 D2
The Square DUK SK16 * ... 134 A1
HALE/TIMP WA15 ... 178 D4
SWIN M27 ... 98 D5
UPML OL3 ... 78 D2
WHTF M45 ... 69 F4
Squire Rd CHH M8 ... 102 A3
Squirrel Dr ALT WA14 ... 165 F1
Squirrel's Jump WILM/AE SK9 ... 201 E4
Stablefold MOSL OL5 ... 108 D2
Stable Fold RAD M26 ... 52 B5
Stablefold WALK M28 ... 97 H5
Stableford Av ECC M30 ... 110 D1
The Stables DROY M43 ... 118 C2
WHIT OL12 ... 14 B4
Stable St CHAD OL9 ... 90 B5
The Stablings WILM/AE SK9 ... 198 D5
Stafford Rd ECC M30 ... 111 F2
FAIL M35 ... 105 F5
SWIN M27 ... 99 E2
WALK M28 ... 96 D1
Stafford St CHAD OL9 ... 90 D3
TOT/BURYW BL8 ... 38 A2
Stag Pasture Rd OLDS OL8 ... 106 A1
Stainburne Rd OFTN SK2 ... 172 D3
Stainburn Rd OP/CLY M11 ... 116 C5
Staindale OLDE OL4 ... 92 C1
Stainer St WGTN/LGST M12 ... 129 H5
Stainforth Cl TOT/BURYW BL8 ... 37 E3
Stainforth St OP/CLY M11 ... 129 G1
Stainmoor Ct OFTN SK2 ... 173 E3
Stainmore Av AUL OL6 ... 107 F3
Stainton Av GTN M18 ... 130 D4
Stainton Cl RAD M26 ... 52 A5
Stainton Dr MDTN M24 ... 72 A1
Stainton Rd RAD M26 ... 51 H4
Staithes Rd WYTH/NTH M22 ... 180 C4
Stakeford Dr CHH M8 ... 102 D2
Stakehill La MDTN M24 ... 57 H4
Staley Cl STLY SK15 * ... 121 F3
Staley Hall Crs STLY SK15 ... 121 F2
Staley Hall Rd STLY SK15 ... 121 F3
Staley St OLDE OL4 * ... 92 B1
OLDE OL4 ... 93 E1
Stalham Cl
NEWH/MOS M40 ... 115 G2
Stalmine Av CHD/CHDH SK8 ... 181 G4
Stalybridge Rd HYDE SK14 ... 135 H4
Stalyhill Dr STLY SK15 ... 135 F1
Stamford Av ALT WA14 ... 164 D3
STLY SK15 ... 120 B3
Stamford Cl STLY SK15 ... 120 B3
Stamford Dr FAIL M35 ... 105 G5
STLY SK15 ... 120 B3
Stamford Gv STLY SK15 ... 120 C3
Stamford New Rd ALT WA14 ... 165 G5
Stamford Park Rd
HALE/TIMP WA15 ... 177 H1
Stamford Pl SALE M33 ... 154 D2
Stamford Rd ALT WA14 ... 177 F2
BRO M7 ... 101 E4
BRUN/LGST M13 ... 129 G5
DTN/ASHW M34 ... 132 A1
MOSL OL5 ... 93 H5
OLDE OL4 ... 77 E4
PART M31 ... 137 F4
URM M41 ... 138 B1
WILM/AE SK9 ... 198 D1
WILM/AE SK9 ... 200 D4
Stamford Sq AUL OL6 ... 120 A3
Stamford St ALT WA14 ... 165 G4
HEY OL10 ... 41 F5
MILN OL16 ... 30 C5
MOSL OL5 ... 108 C1
OLDE OL4 * ... 92 D1
OLDTF/WHR M16 ... 127 G5
SALE M33 ... 139 G5
STLY SK15 ... 120 D3
STLY SK15 ... 121 G1
SWIN M27 ... 99 F1
Stamford St Central AUL OL6 ... 119 H2
Stamford St East AUL OL6 ... 119 H3
Stamford St West AUL OL6 ... 119 G3
Stamford Wy ALT WA14 ... 165 G4
Stampstone St OLD OL1 ... 76 A5
Stanage Av BKLY M9 * ... 88 C3
Stanbank St HTNM SK4 ... 159 H2
Stanbourne Dr BOL BL1 ... 34 A2
Stanbrook St BNG/LEV M19 ... 144 C3
Stanbury Cl BURY BL9 * ... 39 G5
Stanbury Dr DUK SK16 ... 120 A5
Stanbury Wk
NEWH/MOS M40 * ... 115 G2
Stancliffe Rd WYTH/NTH M22 ... 168 D4
Stancross Rd NTHM/RTH M23 ... 154 D5
Stand Av WHTF M45 ... 69 F3
Stand Cl WHTF M45 ... 68 D4
Standedge Rd UPML OL3 ... 79 E1
Standfield Dr WALK M28 ... 96 B4
Standish Rd RUSH/FAL M14 ... 143 F3
Stand La RAD M26 ... 68 C2
Standmoor Ct WHTF M45 * ... 69 E5
Standmoor Rd WHTF M45 ... 69 E5
Standrick Hill Ri STLY SK15 ... 109 E5
Standring Av TOT/BURYW BL8 ... 52 B1
Stand Ri RAD M26 ... 68 C4
Stanedge Cl RAMS BL0 ... 16 D4
Stanford Cl RAD M26 * ... 67 F5
Stanford Hall Crs RAMS BL0 ... 16 C4
Stanhope Av DTN/ASHW M34 ... 132 B3
PWCH M25 ... 85 H2
Stanhope Cl DTN/ASHW M34 ... 132 B3
WILM/AE SK9 ... 199 G2
Stanhope Ct PWCH M25 ... 85 H1
Stanhope Rd ALT WA14 ... 176 D2
SLFD M6 ... 100 B5
Stanhope St AUL OL6 * ... 120 A1
BNG/LEV M19 ... 144 B2
DTN/ASHW M34 ... 132 B3
MOSL OL5 ... 108 D2
RDSH SK5 * ... 145 E4
ROCH OL11 ... 43 E1
Stanhope Wy FAIL M35 ... 104 D2
Stanhorne Av CHH M8 ... 87 F5
Stanier Av ECC M30 ... 111 E2
Stanier St BKLY M9 ... 103 F2
Stanion Gv DUK SK16 ... 119 H5
Stan Jolly Wk OP/CLY M11 ... 116 D5
Stanley Av BRAM/HZG SK7 ... 185 E1
HYDE SK14 ... 133 H4
MPL/ROM SK6 ... 174 C2
RUSH/FAL M14 ... 128 D5
Stanley Av North PWCH M25 ... 85 H1
Stanley Av South PWCH M25 ... 85 H1
Stanley Cl WHTF M45 ... 69 G3
WHTN BL5 ... 62 B5
Stanley Ct BURY BL9 ... 5 F3
OLDTF/WHR M16 ... 127 F3
Stanley Dr CHD/CHDH SK8 ... 192 A1
HALE/TIMP WA15 ... 166 B4
WHTF M45 ... 85 G1
Stanley Gv GTN M18 ... 130 A4
HTNM SK4 ... 159 E2
URM M41 ... 138 D1
WGTN/LGST M12 ... 129 H4
Stanley Hall La POY/DIS SK12 ... 187 H5
Stanley Ms BOLE BL2 ... 50 A2
Stanley Mt SALE M33 ... 154 B3
Stanley Park Wk BOLE BL2 ... 49 H1
Stanley Pl WHIT OL12 ... 10 B4
Stanley Rd BOL BL1 ... 33 E5
BRO M7 ... 101 H2
CHAD OL9 ... 90 D4
CHD/CHDH SK8 ... 192 A1
DTN/ASHW M34 ... 131 G5
ECC M30 ... 110 D4
FWTH BL4 ... 64 D4
HTNM SK4 ... 159 E2
OLDTF/WHR M16 ... 127 F3
OLDTF/WHR M16 ... 142 A1
RAD M26 ... 51 H3
SWIN M27 ... 99 F2
WALK M28 ... 82 A5
WHTF M45 ... 69 G3
Stanley St BKLY M9 * ... 103 F2
CHAD OL9 ... 74 C5
CHH M8 ... 114 D1
CSLFD M3 ... 6 B4
HEY OL10 ... 41 E5
NEWH/MOS M40 ... 103 G5
OLDE OL4 ... 92 D2
OLDE OL4 * ... 93 F1
OP/CLY M11 ... 130 D1
PWCH M25 ... 86 B3
RAMS BL0 ... 16 C3
STKP SK1 ... 13 J2
STLY SK15 * ... 120 C4
WHIT OL12 ... 10 B3
WHTF M45 * ... 69 G3
Stanley St South BOLS/LL BL3 ... 2 C6
Stanmore Av STRET M32 ... 139 H1
Stanmore Dr BOLS/LL BL3 ... 48 B4
Stannard Rd ECC M30 ... 110 A4
Stanneybrook Cl MILN OL16 ... 11 H5
Stanney Cl MILN OL16 ... 44 B1
Stanneylands Cl
WILM/AE SK9 ... 191 H5
Stanneylands Dr
WILM/AE SK9 ... 191 G5
Stanneylands Rd
WILM/AE SK9 ... 191 G3
Stannybrook Rd FAIL M35 ... 106 A4
Stanrose Cl EDGW/EG BL7 ... 22 D2
Stansbury Pl OFTN SK2 ... 173 F3
Stansby Gdns
WGTN/LGST M12 ... 129 F2
Stansfield Cl BOLE BL2 * ... 49 H2
Stansfield Dr ROCH OL11 ... 28 B2
Stansfield Rd BOLE BL2 ... 3 J3
FAIL M35 ... 105 F1
HYDE SK14 ... 133 H4
Stansfield St CHAD OL9 ... 90 C2
NEWH/MOS M40 ... 117 E1
OLD OL1 ... 75 F4
OP/CLY M11 ... 117 E5
Stanthorne Av DID/WITH M20 ... 142 C4
Stanton Av BRO M7 ... 101 E4
DID/WITH M20 ... 156 D2
Stanton Gdns HTNM SK4 ... 159 E5
Stanton St CHAD OL9 ... 90 C4
OP/CLY M11 ... 116 D3
STRET M32 ... 126 A4
Stanway Av BOLS/LL BL3 * ... 2 B7
Stanway Cl BOLS/LL BL3 * ... 2 B7
MDTN M24 ... 89 E1
Stanway Dr HALE/TIMP WA15 ... 178 A1
Stanway Rd WHTF M45 ... 70 A4
Stanway St BKLY M9 ... 103 F2
STRET M32 ... 126 A5
Stanwell Rd NEWH/MOS M40 ... 104 B1
SWIN M27 ... 98 D3
Stanwick Av BKLY M9 ... 87 F3
Stanworth Av BOLE BL2 ... 50 B2
Stanworth Cl
OLDTF/WHR M16 ... 127 H5
Stanyard Ct ORD M5 ... 113 F5
Stanycliffe La MDTN M24 ... 73 E1
Stapleford Cl NTHM/RTH M23 ... 167 G5
SALE M33 ... 155 F1
TOT/BURYW BL8 ... 37 F4
Staplehurst Rd
NEWH/MOS M40 ... 116 B1
Stapleton Av BOL BL1 ... 47 F1
Stapleton St SLFD M6 ... 99 H5
Starbeck Cl TOT/BURYW BL8 ... 37 E4
Starcliffe St BOLS/LL BL3 ... 66 A2
Starfield Av LIT OL15 ... 31 G1
Star Gv BRO M7 ... 101 H4
Starkey St HEY OL10 ... 41 E3
Starkie Rd BOLE BL2 ... 3 K4
The Starkies BURY BL9 * ... 53 F2
Starkie St WALK M28 ... 97 H2
Starling Cl DROY M43 ... 118 C2
WYTH/NTH M22 ... 168 D3
Starling Dr FWTH BL4 ... 65 E5
Starling Rd RAD M26 ... 51 H1
Starmoor Dr CHH M8 ... 102 B4
Starmount Cl BOLE BL2 ... 50 D3
Starring La LIT OL15 ... 20 C3
Starring Rd LIT OL15 ... 20 B3
Starring Wy LIT OL15 ... 20 C3
Stash Gv NTHM/RTH M23 ... 168 A2
Statford Av ECC M30 ... 110 D5
Statham Cl DTN/ASHW M34 ... 132 D5
Statham Fold HYDE SK14 ... 134 B4
Statham St SLFD M6 ... 113 G3
Station Ap CMANE M1 ... 7 F7
CMANE M1 ... 7 H5
UPML OL3 ... 78 C1
Station Cl HYDE SK14 ... 147 G1
Stationers Entry MILN OL16 ... 10 C6
Station La OLDE OL4 ... 93 G2
Station Rd CHD/CHDH SK8 ... 183 E3
CHH M8 ... 102 B1
ECC M30 ... 110 D4
EDGY/DAV SK3 ... 12 E5
FWTH BL4 ... 66 C5
HTNM SK4 ... 158 B5

HYDE SK14 .....148 D1
IRL M44 .....136 A4
LIT OL15 .....21 E3
MILN OL16 .....44 C1
MOSL OL5 .....109 E1
MPL/ROM SK6 .....162 A1
MPL/ROM SK6 .....175 E3
MPL/ROM SK6 .....187 H3
OLDE OL4 .....93 F2
RDSH SK5 .....145 E1
ROCH OL11 .....30 A5
STRET M32 .....126 A5
SWIN M27 .....99 E1
TOT/BURYW BL8 .....26 A2
UPML OL3 .....79 E4
URM M41 .....138 D2
WHIT OL12 .....14 C2
WILM/AE SK9 .....191 H4
WILM/AE SK9 .....199 E3
Station St AUL OL6 .....119 G4
BOLS/LL BL3 .....3 F7
BRAM/HZG SK7 .....185 G5
OLDE OL4 .....93 E1
Station to Station Wk LIT OL15 .....21 E3
Station Vw BNG/LEV M19 .....144 A2
Staton Av BOL BL2 .....49 H1
Staton St OP/CLY M11 .....116 D5
Statter St BURY BL9 .....53 H5
Staveleigh Ml AUL OL6 * 119 G2
Staveley Av BOL BL1 .....22 D5
STLY SK15 .....120 D2
Staveley Cl MDTN M24 .....72 B3
ROY/SHW OL2 .....60 C5
Staverton Cl BRUN/LGST M13 .....128 C1
Staveton Cl BRAM/HZG SK7 .....184 A1
Stavordale WHIT OL12 .....14 B5
Staycott St OLDTF/WHR M16 .....128 A4
Stayley Dr STLY SK15 .....121 F3
Stayley Rd MOSL OL5 .....109 E2
Stead St RAMS BL0 .....16 D2
Steadway UPML OL3 .....95 F2
Stedman Cl OP/CLY M11 .....115 H4
Steeles Gdns BOLE BL2 .....50 A5
Steeles Av HYDE SK14 .....133 H5
Steeple Cl CHH M8 .....102 A5
Steeple Dr ORD M5 .....113 F5
Steeple Vw ROY/SHW OL2 .....59 E5
Stelfox Av WALK M28 .....146 C2
Stelfox La DTN/ASHW M34 .....132 C1
Stelfox St ECC M30 .....110 C5
Stella St BKLY M9 .....87 G3
Stelling St GTN M18 .....130 C3
Stenbury Cl RUSH/FAL M14 .....142 D3
Stenner La DID/WITH M20 .....157 F4
Stephen Cl TOT/BURYW BL8 * 37 H4
Stephenson Av DROY M43 .....117 H4
Stephenson Rd STRET M32 .....140 C1
Stephenson St FAIL M35 .....105 F3
OLDE OL4 .....76 C4
Stephens Cl DID/WITH M20 .....157 H1
STLY SK15 .....120 D1
Stephens St BOLE BL2 .....50 B1
Stephen St CSLFD M3 .....114 C1
STKP SK1 .....7 H4
TOT/BURYW BL8 .....37 H4
URM M41 .....139 E1
Stephen St South
BRAM/HZG SK7 .....37 H5
Stephen Wk STKP SK1 * 172 C1
Steps Meadow WHIT OL12 .....19 H4
Steptoe Dr OL4 .....75 E3
Stern Av ORD M5 * 113 F5
Sterndale Rd EDGY/DAV SK3 .....171 H4
MPL/ROM SK6 .....162 A5
WALK M28 .....96 B5
Sterratt St BOL BL1 .....2 A5
Stetchworth Dr WALK M28 .....96 C3
Steuber Dr IRL M44 .....151 E1
Stevenson Dr OL12 .....60 D5
Stevenson Pl CMANE M1 .....7 H4
Stevenson Rd SWIN M27 .....98 D2
WHIT OL12 .....19 G5
Stevenson St CSLFD M3 .....114 A4
WALK M28 .....81 G4
Stevens St WILM/AE SK9 .....200 D4
Stewart Av FWTH BL4 .....65 G5
Stewart St AULW OL7 .....119 E3
BOL BL1 .....33 H5
MILN OL16 .....10 E5
TOT/BURYW BL8 .....37 H2
Steynton Cl BOL BL1 .....47 G1
Stile Cl URM M41 .....137 E1
Stiles Av MPL/ROM SK6 .....174 D2
Stillwater Dr OP/CLY M11 .....116 B3
Stilton Dr OP/CLY M11 * 116 B5

Stockport Rd AULW OL7 .....119 E5
BNG/LEV M19 .....144 A3
BRUN/LGST M13 .....129 E2
DTN/ASHW M34 .....146 C2
EDGY/DAV SK3 .....170 D2
HALE/TIMP WA15 .....166 A4
HYDE SK14 .....148 A2
HYDE SK14 .....149 C2
MOSL OL5 .....93 H5
MPL/ROM SK6 .....162 A4
MPL/ROM SK6 .....174 C5
OLDE OL4 .....93 H2
MPL/ROM SK6 .....129 F4
Stockport Rd East
MPL/ROM SK6 .....161 G2
Stockport Rd West
MPL/ROM SK6 .....160 D3
Stockport Village STKP SK1 * 13 F5
Stocksfield Dr BKLY M9 .....88 B4
LHULT M38 .....81 E2
Stocks Gdns STLY SK15 .....121 F4
Stocksgate WHIT OL12 .....29 E1
Stocks La STLY SK15 .....121 E4
Stocks St CHH M8 .....114 D1
Stocks St East CHH M8 .....114 D1
Stockton Av EDGY/DAV SK3 .....171 E1
Stockton Dr TOT/BURYW BL8 .....37 C1
FWTH BL4 .....65 H2
Stockton Rd CCHDY M21 .....141 E3
FWTH BL4 .....65 H2
WILM/AE SK9 .....200 C1
Stockton St LIT OL15 .....20 D3
OLDTF/WHR M16 .....127 H4
SWIN M27 .....98 D3
Stoke Abbott Cl
BRAM/HZG SK7 .....183 H5
Stokesay Cl BURY BL9 .....53 C4
ROY/SHW OL2 .....59 H5
Stokesay Dr BRAM/HZG SK7 .....184 D5
Stokesay Rd SALE M33 .....153 H1
Stokes St OP/CLY M11 .....117 E4
Stoke St OLDE OL4 .....30 C5
Stokoe Av ALT WA14 .....164 D3
Stonall Av HULME M15 .....127 C2
Stoneacre HOR/BR BL6 .....46 A1
Stoneacre Ct WHIT M22 .....99 E3
Stoneacre Rd
WYTH/NTH M22 .....180 B2
Stonebeck Rd
NTHM/RTH M23 .....167 G4
Stone Breaks Rd OLDE OL4 .....77 G5
Stonebridge Cl HOR/BR BL6 .....46 D3
Stonechat Cl DROY M43 .....118 B2
WALK M28 .....96 C2
Stonecliffe Av STLY SK15 .....120 D3
Stone Cl RAMS BL0 .....16 B4
Stoneclough Rd RAD M26 .....67 E4
Stoneclough Rd FWTH BL4 .....66 C5
Stonedelph Cl BOLE BL2 .....36 C5
Stonefield Dr CHH M8 .....114 B1
Stonehaven BOLS/LL BL3 .....63 C1
Stonehead St BKLY M9 * 103 G3
Stonehewer St RAD M26 .....68 C2
Stone Hill La WHIT OL12 .....28 D1
Stone Hill Rd FWTH BL4 .....82 A1
Stonehouse EDGW/EG BL7 .....23 C4
Stonehurst Cl
WGTN/LGST M12 .....129 H2
Stonelands Wy OLDE OL4 .....93 F3
Stoneleigh Av SALE M33 .....153 H1
Stoneleigh Dr RAD M26 .....67 E5
Stoneleigh Rd OLDE OL4 .....77 F5
Stoneleigh St OL1 .....76 A3
Stonelow Cl HULME M15 .....128 A2
Stone Md MPL/ROM SK6 .....162 D3
Stone Mead Av
HALE/TIMP WA15 .....178 D5
Stonemead Cl BOLS/LL BL3 .....49 E5
Stonemead Cl BKLY M9 .....88 A3
Stonepail Cl CHD/CHDH SK8 .....169 E4
Stonepail Cottages
CHD/CHDH SK8 * 169 F4
Stonepail Rd CHD/CHDH SK8 .....169 F4
Stone Pale WHIT M45 .....69 G5
Stone Pl RUSH/FAL M14 .....142 D5
Stone Rw MPL/ROM SK6 .....175 F5
Stonesby Cl OLDTF/WHR M16 .....127 H4
Stonesdale Dr ROY/SHW OL2 .....59 F4
Stonesteads Dr EDGW/EG BL7 .....23 F3
Stonesteads Wy
EDGW/EG BL7 .....23 F3
Stone St BOLE BL2 .....3 J1
CSLFD M3 .....6 C7
Stoneswood Dr MOSL OL5 .....94 A5
Stoneswood Rd UPML OL3 .....78 B1
Stoney Bank RAD M26 .....67 F5
Stoney Bridge La
HALE/TIMP WA15 .....166 B2
Stoneyfield STLY SK15 .....120 D1
Stoneyfield Cl
OLDTF/WHR M16 .....142 B1
Stoneygate Wk OP/CLY M11 .....130 C1
Stoneyhurst HULME M15 .....128 A2
Stoney La WILM/AE SK9 .....198 C5
Stoneyroyd WHIT OL12 .....14 C5
Stoneyside Av WALK M28 .....82 B3
Stoneyside Gv WALK M28 .....82 B4
Stonie Heyes Av WHIT OL12 .....19 G5
Stonyford Rd SALE M33 .....155 E2
Stonyhurst Av BOL BL1 .....33 H1
Stopes Rd BOLS/LL BL3 .....67 E1
Stopford Av LIT OL15 .....20 B4
Stopford St EDGY/DAV SK3 .....12 D6
OP/CLY M11 .....116 D5
Stores Cottages OLDE OL4 * 94 B1
Stores St PWCH M25 .....86 B3
Store St AULW OL7 .....106 D4
CMANE M1 .....7 K5
OFTN SK2 .....172 D5
OP/CLY M11 * 130 A1
RAD M26 .....53 E5
ROCH OL11 .....28 B2
ROY/SHW OL2 .....60 B1
Storeton Cl WYTH/NTH M22 .....180 D2
Stortford Dr NTHM/RTH M23 .....156 A4
Stothard Rd STRET M32 .....139 H2
Stott Dr URM M41 .....137 F2
Stottfield ROY/SHW OL2 .....74 C1

Stott La BOLE BL2 .....34 C5
MDTN M24 .....56 C4
SLFD M6 .....112 A2
Stott Milne St CHAD OL9 .....90 B2
Stott Rd CHAD OL9 .....89 H4
SWIN M27 .....98 C4
Stott's La NEWH/MOS M40 .....104 C4
Stott St FAIL M35 .....104 C4
MDTN M24 .....20 A4
MILN OL16 .....44 C2
WHIT OL12 .....10 D3
Stourbridge Av LHULT M38 .....81 F1
Stour Cl ALT WA14 .....165 F3
Stourport St MPL/ROM SK6 .....161 H5
Stourport St OLD OL1 .....9 K1
Stovell Av WGTN/LGST M12 .....144 A1
Stovell Rd NEWH/MOS M40 .....103 H2
Stow Cl TOT/BURYW BL8 .....38 A1
Stowell Ct BOL BL1 .....2 C1
Stowell St BOL BL1 .....33 H5
ORD M5 .....112 D4
Stowfield Cl BKLY M9 .....87 G3
Stow Gdns DID/WITH M20 .....142 C5
Stracey St NEWH/MOS M40 * 115 H2
Stradbroke Cl GTN M18 .....130 A3
Strain Av BKLY M9 .....88 A3
Strand Cl STRET M32 .....140 A3
The Strand ROCH OL11 .....43 E4
Strand Ct ROY/SHW OL2 .....75 E2
Strangford St RAD M26 .....51 C5
Strang St RAMS BL0 .....16 D2
Stranton Dr WALK M28 .....98 B2
Stratfield Av NTHM/RTH M23 .....155 E5
Stratford Av BOL BL1 .....33 E5
DID/WITH M20 .....157 E1
OLDS OL8 .....91 H4
ROCH OL11 .....42 D1
Stratford Cl FWTH BL4 .....65 E3
Stratford Gdns MPL/ROM SK6 .....161 G5
Stratford Rd MDTN M24 .....89 C2
Strathblane Cl DID/WITH M20 .....142 D4
Strathdale Dr OP/CLY M11 .....116 C3
Strathmere Av STRET M32 .....126 A5
Strathmore Av CCHDY M21 .....141 H1
DTN/ASHW M34 .....147 F1
Strathmore Cl RAMS BL0 .....16 D5
Strathmore Rd BOLE BL2 .....35 F5
Stratton Rd OFTN SK2 .....172 D1
OLDTF/WHR M16 .....141 F1
SWIN M27 .....99 E1
Strawberry Bank SLFD M6 * 113 G2
Strawberry Cl ALT WA14 .....165 E2
Strawberry Hl BOLE BL2 .....113 G2
Strawberry Hill Rd BOLE BL2 .....33 H4
Strawberry La MOSL OL5 .....94 A3
WILM/AE SK9 .....198 D4
Strawberry Rd SLFD M6 .....113 F2
Stray St OP/CLY M11 .....117 E5
The Stray BOL BL1 .....34 C2
Streamside Cl
HALE/TIMP WA15 .....166 C5
Stream Ter STKP SK1 .....160 C5
Streetbridge OLD OL1 .....74 B2
Street Bridge Rd OLD OL1 .....74 B2
Street Elmfield BOL BL1 .....34 A4
Streetgate LHULT M38 .....81 F2
Streethouse La UPML OL3 .....78 C3
Street Kirklees
TOT/BURYW BL8 .....26 A4
Street La RAD M26 .....51 H1
Stretford Rd HULME M15 .....128 A2
OLDTF/WHR M16 .....127 F3
URM M41 .....138 D2
Stretton Av DID/WITH M20 .....157 H3
SALE M33 .....153 H2
STRET M32 .....125 F5
Stretton Cl NEWH/MOS M40 .....103 E5
Stretton Rd BOLS/LL BL3 .....48 A5
RAMS BL0 .....26 B1
Striding Edge Wk OLD OL1 * 75 H5
Strines Rd MPL/ROM SK6 .....175 F4
Stringer Av HYDE SK14 .....149 H1
Stringer Cl HYDE SK14 .....149 H1
Stringer St STKP SK1 .....13 K2
Stroma Gdns URM M41 .....124 B3
Strong St BRO M7 .....114 B1
Stroud Av ECC M30 .....110 C2
Stroud Cl MDTN M24 .....88 D2
Stuart Av IRL M44 .....136 B1
MPL/ROM SK6 .....174 B2
Stuart Rd ALT WA14 .....146 B5
STRET M32 .....126 A5
Stuart St MDTN M24 .....73 F4
MILN OL16 .....30 C5
OLDS OL8 .....8 E7
OP/CLY M11 .....116 B3
Stuart St East OP/CLY M11 .....116 B3
Stuart Wk MDTN M24 .....72 C5
Stubbins Cl NTHM/RTH M23 .....167 E3
Stubbins St TOT/BURYW BL8 .....26 D1
Stubbins Vale Rd RAMS BL0 .....17 E1
Stubley Gdns LIT OL15 .....20 D3
Stubley La LIT OL15 .....20 C4
Stubley Mill Rd LIT OL15 .....20 B4
Studforth Wk HULME M15 * 128 A3
Studland Rd WYTH/NTH M22 .....181 E1
Studley Cl ROY/SHW OL2 .....59 H5
Styal Av RDSH SK5 .....160 A1
STRET M32 .....125 F5
Styal Cl CHD/CHDH SK8 .....181 F1
Styal Rd WILM/AE SK9 .....198 D1
Styal Vw WILM/AE SK9 .....191 G5
Styhead Dr MDTN M24 .....72 A1
Style St ANC M4 .....7 C1
Styperson Wy POY/DIS SK12 .....195 F4
Sudbury Dr CHD/CHDH SK8 .....181 H5
HOR/BR BL6 .....46 A2
Sudbury Rd BRAM/HZG SK7 .....185 F4
Sudden St ROCH OL11 .....42 B2
Sudell St ANC M4 .....7 H1
Sudley Rd ROCH OL11 .....42 B1
Sudlow St MILN OL16 .....10 D4
Sudren St TOT/BURYW BL8 .....37 E3
Suffield St MDTN M24 .....72 C4
Suffolk Av DROY M43 .....117 H2
Suffolk Cl BOLS/LL BL3 .....51 E4
Suffolk Dr RDSH SK5 .....146 A5
WILM/AE SK9 .....199 F1
Suffolk Rd ALT WA14 .....165 E5

Suffolk St CHAD OL9 .....90 C3
ROCH OL11 .....30 A5
SLFD M6 .....100 D5
Sugar La UPML OL3 .....78 D2
Sugar Mill Sq ORD M5 * 112 C3
Sugden St AUL OL6 .....120 A2
Sulby Av STRET M32 .....140 C1
Sulby St NEWH/MOS M40 .....103 H2
RAD M26 .....67 E4
Sulgrave Av POY/DIS SK12 .....195 C3
Sullivan St WGTN/LGST M12 .....129 H5
Sultan St BURY BL9 .....53 C1
Sulway Cl SWIN M27 * 99 F5
Sumac St OP/CLY M11 .....117 E5
Sumner Av URM M41 .....139 E1
Summer Castle MILN OL16 .....10 D7
Summercroft CHAD OL9 .....89 H5
Summerdale Dr RAMS BL0 .....26 C1
Summerfield Av DROY M43 .....117 F2
Summerfield Dr MDTN M24 .....72 A3
Summerfield Pl WILM/AE SK9 * 198 D4
Summerfield Rd BOLS/LL BL3 .....48 A5
WALK M28 .....97 H5
WYTH/NTH M22 .....180 B2
Summerfields Vw OLDS OL8 .....92 B4
Summer Hl MOSL OL5 * 94 A5
Summerlea CHD/CHDH SK8 * 183 E4
Summer Pl RUSH/FAL M14 .....143 E1
Summers Av STLY SK15 .....121 F3
Summerseat Cl OLDE OL4 .....93 F5
ORD M5 * 113 F5
Summerseat La RAMS BL0 .....26 B1
Summershades La OLDE OL4 .....94 A1
Summershades Ri OLDE OL4 .....94 A1
Summers St CHAD OL9 .....8 A3
Summer St MILN OL16 .....10 E7
Summerville Av BKLY M9 .....103 G3
Summerville Rd SLFD M6 .....100 B5
Summit Cl BURY BL9 .....40 A2
Summit St HEY OL10 .....40 B4
Sumner Av BOLE BL2 .....36 C5
Sumner Rd SLFD M6 .....100 A5
Sumner St ROY/SHW OL2 .....60 A4
Sumner Wy URM M41 .....138 D1
Sunadale Cl BOLS/LL BL3 .....48 A4
Sunbank Cl
HALE/TIMP WA15 .....189 E1
Sunbank La WILM/AE SK9 .....189 E5
WILM/AE SK9 .....192 B5
Sunbury Dr NEWH/MOS M40 .....117 E1
Sunderland Av AUL OL6 .....107 H3
Sundew Pl MDTN M24 .....73 C5
Sundial Cl HYDE SK14 .....135 E5
Sundial Rd OFTN SK2 .....173 E3
Sundridge Cl BOLS/LL BL3 .....63 H1
Sunfield MPL/ROM SK6 .....162 A3
Sunfield Av OLDE OL4 .....60 D5
Sunfield Crs ROY/SHW OL2 .....75 G1
Sunfield Dr ROY/SHW OL2 .....75 G1
Sunfield Rd OLDE OL4 .....60 D5
Sunfield Wy OLDE OL4 .....116 A3
Sunflower Meadow IRL M44 .....136 D1
Sunhill Cl MILN OL16 .....43 G4
Sunk La MDTN M24 .....72 D5
Sunlight Rd BOL BL1 .....34 A4
Sunningdale Av OP/CLY M11 .....116 C3
RAD M26 .....51 G4
SALE M33 .....155 F3
WHTF M45 .....68 D5
Sunningdale Cl HYDE SK14 .....133 H3
BURY BL9 .....52 B1
Sunningdale Dr
BRAM/HZG SK7 .....184 B5
HEY OL10 .....56 A1
IRL M44 .....122 A5
PWCH M25 .....85 H2
SLFD M6 .....99 F5
Sunningdale Rd
CHD/CHDH SK8 .....182 D5
DTN/ASHW M34 .....147 F2
URM M41 .....138 B2
Sunningdale Wk BOLS/LL BL3 * 48 B4
Sunning Hill St BOLS/LL BL3 .....48 B5
Sunny Av BURY BL9 .....38 C1
Sunny Bank OLDE OL4 .....92 D2
RAD M26 .....67 H3
WILM/AE SK9 .....200 A1
Sunny Bank Av ALT WA14 .....117 G4
HTNM SK4 .....158 C2
Sunny Bank Rd ALT WA14 .....177 F4
BRUN/LGST M13 .....129 G5
BURY BL9 .....69 H1
Sunnybank Rd BOL BL1 .....33 F4
DROY M43 .....117 G4

Surrey St AUL OL6 .....107 G5
BKLY M9 * 87 H1
CHAD OL9 .....8 A7
Surrey Wy RDSH SK5 .....160 B2
Surtees Rd NTHM/RTH M23 .....155 H4
Sussex Cl CHAD OL9 .....90 C1
DID/WITH M20 .....157 G2
Sussex Cl CHAD OL9 .....90 C1
DROY M43 .....84 B5
Sussex Dr BURY BL9 .....39 H5
DROY M43 .....117 H2
Sussex Pl HYDE SK14 .....134 A3
Sussex Rd EDGY/DAV SK3 .....171 E1
PART M31 .....150 D4
Sussex St BRO M7 .....114 A2
CMANW M2 .....6 E4
ROCH OL11 * 30 A5
Sutcliffe Av WGTN/LGST M12 .....144 A1
Sutcliffe St AULW OL7 .....119 E4
BOL BL1 .....33 H4
LIT OL15 .....21 E2
MDTN M24 .....73 F4
OLDS OL8 .....9 F7
ROY/SHW OL2 .....75 H1
Sutherland Cl OLDS OL8 .....106 C1
Sutherland Gv FWTH BL4 .....65 H4
Sutherland Rd BOL BL1 .....47 H1
HEY OL10 .....40 A5
OLDTF/WHR M16 .....126 D5
Sutherland St AUL OL6 .....120 C2
ECC M30 .....110 C2
FWTH BL4 .....65 H4
SWIN M27 .....98 D1
Suthers St ROY/SHW OL2 .....60 B3
RAD M26 .....68 D3
Sutton Cl TOT/BURYW BL8 .....52 C1
Sutton Dr DROY M43 .....117 F2
Sutton Dwellings SLFD M6 .....113 C2
Sutton Rd BOLS/LL BL3 .....47 G5
HTNM SK4 .....130 B5
POY/DIS SK12 .....195 H5
WILM/AE SK9 .....200 C4
Suttons La MPL/ROM SK6 .....175 F4
Swailes St OLDE OL4 .....92 A1
Swaindrod La LIT OL15 .....21 H1
Swaine St EDGY/DAV SK3 .....12 E4
Swainsthorpe Dr BKLY M9 .....103 F2
Swain St WHIT OL12 .....10 B2
Swalecliff Av NTHM/RTH M23 .....155 E5
Swale Cl WILM/AE SK9 .....192 B5
Swaledale Cl ROY/SHW OL2 .....59 F4
Swale Dr ALT WA14 .....165 F3
Swallow Bank Dr ROCH OL11 * 42 A3
Swallow Cl STLY SK15 .....109 G5
Swallow Dr BURY BL9 .....39 E2
IRL M44 .....122 B5
ROCH OL11 .....28 C4
Swallow La OLDE OL4 .....109 G3
Swallow St OLDS OL8 .....91 E5
OP/CLY M11 .....116 A4
STKP SK1 .....13 H7
WGTN/LGST M12 * 144 A1
Swanage Av NTHM/RTH M23 .....155 E5
OFTN SK2 .....173 E3
Swanage Cl TOT/BURYW BL8 .....26 D5
Swanage Rd ECC M30 .....110 C2
Swanbourne Gdns
EDGY/DAV SK3 .....171 F3
Swan Cl POY/DIS SK12 .....194 C5
Swan Ct ROY/SHW OL2 * 60 A3
Swanhill Cl GTN M18 .....131 E3
Swanley Av NEWH/MOS M40 .....103 F5
Swann Gv CHD/CHDH SK8 .....183 E4
Swann La CHD/CHDH SK8 .....183 E4
Swan Rd HALE/TIMP WA15 .....154 B5
TOT/BURYW BL8 .....26 B5
Swansea St OLDS OL8 .....92 A3
Swan St ANC M4 .....7 G2
AUL OL6 .....119 H2
WILM/AE SK9 .....199 E3
Swarbrick Dr PWCH M25 .....85 G5
Swayfield Av BRUN/LGST M13 .....129 G5
Swaylands Dr SALE M33 .....154 C5
Sweetbriar Cl ROY/SHW OL2 .....60 A2
Sweet Briar Cl WHIT OL12 .....29 H1
Sweet Briar La WHIT OL12 .....33 H1
Sweetlove's Gv BOL BL1 .....33 H1
Sweetlove's La BOL BL1 .....33 H1
Sweetnam Dr WILM/AE SK9 .....192 A2
Swettenham Rd WILM/AE SK9 .....192 A2
Swift Cl MPL/ROM SK6 .....162 B1
ROCH OL11 .....28 C4
Swift St AUL OL6 .....107 G5
Swinbourne Gv
DID/WITH M20 .....143 E4
Swinburne Av DROY M43 .....117 H2
Swinburne Gn RDSH SK5 .....144 D2
Swinburn St BKLY M9 .....133 H3
Swindells St HYDE SK14 .....133 H3
OP/CLY M11 .....130 D1
Swindon Cl GTN M18 .....130 C3
Swinfield Av CCHDY M21 .....140 D3
Swinford Gv ROY/SHW OL2 .....59 H4
Swinside Cl BURY BL9 .....71 H2
Swinside Rd BOLE BL2 .....50 C1
Swinstead Av
NEWH/MOS M40 .....103 F5
Swinton Crs BURY BL9 .....53 H5
Swinton Gv BRUN/LGST M13 .....128 D3
Swinton Hall Rd SWIN M27 .....99 F2
Swinton Park Rd SLFD M6 .....99 H5
Swinton St BOLE BL2 .....50 B2
OLDE OL4 .....92 B2
Swiss Hl WILM/AE SK9 .....201 E4
Swithin Rd WYTH/NTH M22 .....180 D4
Swithland Rd ALT WA14 * 153 F1
Swythamley Ct
Swythamley Rd
EDGY/DAV SK3 .....170 D1
Sybil St LIT OL15 .....20 D2
Sycamore Av ALT WA14 .....164 D4
BURY BL9 .....90 A4
DTN/ASHW M34 .....146 D1
HEY OL10 .....56 B1
MILN OL16 .....44 C2
OLDE OL4 .....76 C4
RAD M26 .....68 A4

Sycamore Cl AUL OL6 120 B3
DID/WITH M20 * 143 E4
DUK SK16 120 C5
LIT OL15 20 C3
WILM/AE SK9 199 E1
Sycamore Ct SLFD M6 113 F2
Sycamore Crs AUL OL6 107 F5
Sycamore Dr BURY BL9 27 G5
RAD M26 52 B4
Sycamore Gv FAIL M35 105 G3
Sycamore Ldg
BRAM/HZG SK7 * 184 A5
Sycamore Pl WHTF M45 85 G1
Sycamore Rd ECC M30 110 B1
MPL/ROM SK6 161 H2
PART M31 150 C3
TOT/BURYW BL8 37 E1
The Sycamores MOSL OL5 109 F1
OLDE OL4 76 D4
RAD M26 83 E1
STLY SK15 121 E5
Sycamore St EDGY/DAV SK3 171 E1
SALE M33 155 F2
Sycamore Wk CHD/CHDH SK8 170 A3
Sydall St DTN/ASHW M34 132 C5
Syddal Cl BRAM/HZG SK7 193 G2
Syddal Crs BRAM/HZG SK7 193 G3
Syddal Gn BRAM/HZG SK7 193 G2
Syddall Av CHD/CHDH SK8 182 A4
Syddall St HYDE SK14 147 H1
Syddal Rd BRAM/HZG SK7 193 G2
Sydenham St OLD OL1 76 A3
Sydney Av ECC M30 111 E3
MANAIR M90 179 H4
Sydney Barnes Cl ROCH OL11 42 A4
Sydney Jones Ct
NEWH/MOS M40 104 B1
Sydney Rd BRAM/HZG SK7 194 A2
Sydney St FAIL M35 104 D3
MOSL OL5 109 E2
OFTN SK2 172 D2
SLFD M6 112 D3
STRET M32 140 B1
SWIN M27 98 C2
Syke La WHIT OL12 19 E4
Syke Rd WHIT OL12 19 F5
Sykes Av BURY BL9 54 A5
Sykes Cl UPML OL3 95 E2
Sykes Ct MILN OL16 * 30 C5
Sykes Meadow
EDGY/DAV SK3 171 G3
Sykes St BURY BL9 5 G2
MILN OL16 30 C5
MILN OL16 44 D2
RDSH SK5 145 F3
Sylvan Av FAIL M35 104 D5
HALE/TIMP WA15 166 A1
SALE M33 154 D3
URM M41 124 C5
WILM/AE SK9 198 C5
Sylvan Cl MDTN M24 72 A2
Sylvandale Av BNG/LEV M19 144 A2
Sylvan Gv ALT WA14 165 G4
Sylvan St CHAD OL9 8 B2
Sylvester Av OFTN SK2 172 C3
Sylvester Cl HYDE SK14 149 G1
Sylvia Gv RDSH SK5 145 E4
Symms St SLFD M6 113 G1
Symond Rd BKLY M9 88 B2
Symons Rd SALE M33 154 C1
Symons St BRO M7 101 H3
Syndall Av WGTN/LGST M12 129 E2
Syndall St WGTN/LGST M12 129 E2

T

Tabley Av RUSH/FAL M14 142 D1
Tabley Gdns MPL/ROM SK6 175 F5
Tabley Gv BRUN/LGST M13 143 H1
HALE/TIMP WA15 166 B1
RDSH SK5 145 E4
Tabley Mere Gdns
CHD/CHDH SK8 182 C1
Tabley Ms ALT WA14 165 G4
Tabley Rd BOLS/LL BL3 48 A5
SALE M33 * 155 F4
WILM/AE SK9 192 A2
Tabley St DUK SK16 120 B5
MOSL OL5 109 E2
SLFD M6 101 E5
Tabor St MDTN M24 72 C2
Tackler Cl SWIN M27 99 E3
Tadcaster Dr NEWH/MOS M40 103 E4
Tadman Gv ALT WA14 164 D3
Tadmor Cl LHULT M38 81 E3
Tagore Cl BRUN/LGST M13 129 F4
Tag Wood Vw RAMS BL0 16 B4
Tahir Cl CHH M8 102 C3
Tait Ms HTNM SK4 158 C4
Talavera St BRO M7 101 G5
Talbenny Cl BOL BL1 47 G1
Talbot Av BOLS/LL BL3 50 D5
Talbot Cl OLDE OL4 76 B4
Talbot Ct BOL BL1 34 A2
Talbot Gv BURY BL9 27 H5
Talbot Pl OLDTF/WHR M16 127 E3
Talbot Rd ALT WA14 177 E2
HYDE SK14 133 H3
RUSH/FAL M14 143 G4
SALE M33 * 155 F2
STRET M32 126 C4
WILM/AE SK9 201 E4
Talbot St AUL OL6 119 F2
BRAM/HZG SK7 173 E5
ECC M30 111 F4
MDTN M24 72 D2
ROCH OL11 30 A5
Talford Gv DID/WITH M20 157 F1
Talgarth Rd NEWH/MOS M40 115 F1
Talkin Dr MDTN M24 72 B1
Talland Wk BRUN/LGST M13 129 E3
Tallarn Cl DID/WITH M20 143 E4
Tallis St WGTN/LGST M12 129 H5
Tallow Wy IRL M44 136 C3
Tall Trees Cl ROY/SHW OL2 58 D5
Tall Trees Pl OFTN SK2 172 D3
Tallyman Wy SWIN M27 100 B3
Tamar Cl FWTH BL4 83 E2
WHTF M45 69 H4
Tamar Ct HULME M15 127 G2
Tamar Dr NTHM/RTH M23 167 H5
Tamarin Cl SWIN M27 98 B1
Tamebank MOSL OL5 94 A4
Tame Barn Cl MILN OL16 31 H5
Tame Cl STLY SK15 121 F2
Tame La UPML OL3 61 H2
Tamerton Dr CHH M8 102 B4
Tameside Ct DUK SK16 * 133 E1
Tame St ANC M4 115 G4
DTN/ASHW M34 132 C1
DTN/ASHW M34 132 C4
MOSL OL5 94 B4
STLY SK15 120 B4
UPML OL3 79 E4
Tame Valley Cl MOSL OL5 94 B4
Tamworth Av ORD M5 113 G5
WHTF M45 70 A5
Tamworth Av West ORD M5 * 113 F5
Tamworth Cl BRAM/HZG SK7 * 184 D4
HULME M15 127 H3
Tamworth Dr TOT/BURYW BL8 37 H1
Tamworth Gn STKP SK1 160 C4
Tamworth St CHAD OL9 8 A6
STKP SK1 160 C4
Tamworth Wk ORD M5 113 F5
Tandis Ct SLFD M6 * 111 H2
Tandle Hill Rd ROY/SHW OL2 58 C3
Tandlewood Ms
NEWH/MOS M40 104 B5
Tandlewood Pk ROY/SHW OL2 58 C3
Tanfield Dr RAD M26 67 E5
Tanfield Rd DID/WITH M20 169 G2
Tangmere Av HEY OL10 56 C2
Tangmere Cl NEWH/MOS M40 * 89 F4
Tanhill Cl OFTN SK2 173 F3
Tanhill La OLDS OL8 91 H5
Tanhouse Rd URM M41 123 E5
Tanners Cft RAMS BL0 16 C2
Tanners Fold OLDS OL8 91 H5
Tanners Gn SLFD M6 113 E2
Tanners St RAMS BL0 16 C2
Tanner St HYDE SK14 * 133 G5
Tannery Wy ALT WA14 165 H2
Tannock Rd BRAM/HZG SK7 185 G3
Tanpits Rd BURY BL9 4 C3
Tansey Gv BRO M7 102 A4
Tansley Rd CHH M8 87 F5
Tanworth Wk BOL BL1 33 H4
Tan Yard Brow GTN M18 130 D4
Tanyard Dr HALE/TIMP WA15 188 D1
Tanyard Gn RDSH SK5 160 A1
Tanyard La HALE/TIMP WA15 188 A2
Taper St RAMS BL0 16 C2
Tapley Av POY/DIS SK12 195 F5
Taplin Dr GTN M18 130 B3
Taplow Gv CHD/CHDH SK8 182 C2
Taplow Wk RUSH/FAL M14 129 F5
Tarbet Dr BOLE BL2 50 C3
Tarbet Rd DUK SK16 133 F1
Tarbolton Crs
HALE/TIMP WA15 178 D1
Tariff St CMANE M1 7 J4
Tarleton Cl TOT/BURYW BL8 37 E5
Tarleton Pl BOLS/LL BL3 63 H1
Tarleton Wk
BRUN/LGST M13 * 128 D2
Tarnbrook Cl WHTF M45 70 B4
Tarnbrook Wk HULME M15 * 128 A3
Tarn Dr BURY BL9 53 F3
Tarn Gv WALK M28 97 G1
Tarnside Cl MILN OL16 19 H5
OFTN SK2 173 G3
The Tarns CHD/CHDH SK8 181 G1
Tarporley Av RUSH/FAL M14 142 C3
Tarporley Cl EDGY/DAV SK3 171 F4
Tarran Gv DTN/ASHW M34 147 F2
Tarran Pl ALT WA14 165 H3
Tarrington Cl WGTN/LGST M12 129 H3
Tartan St OP/CLY M11 116 C3
Tarvin Av DID/WITH M20 142 C4
HTNM SK4 144 D4
Tarvin Dr MPL/ROM SK6 161 F2
Tarvington Cl
NEWH/MOS M40 * 102 D4
Tarvin Rd CHD/CHDH SK8 170 D5
Tarvin Wk BOL BL1 33 H4
Tasle Aly CMANW M2 6 E5
Tatchbury Rd FAIL M35 105 F3
Tate St OLDS OL8 92 A3
Tatham Cl BRUN/LGST M13 129 G5
Tatham St MILN OL16 10 E7
Tatland Dr WYTH/NTH M22 181 E1
Tattersall Av BOL BL1 32 B4
Tattersall St CHAD OL9 8 C5
Tatton Cl BRAM/HZG SK7 173 G5
CHD/CHDH SK8 170 D5
Tatton Gdns MPL/ROM SK6 162 C1
Tatton Gv DID/WITH M20 142 D5
Tatton Mere Dr DROY M43 118 A4
Tattonmere Gdns
CHD/CHDH SK8 170 D5
Tatton Pl SALE M33 154 C1
Tatton Rd DTN/ASHW M34 147 E2
SALE M33 154 C1
WILM/AE SK9 192 B2
Tatton Rd North HTNM SK4 159 F1
Tatton Rd South HTNM SK4 159 F2
Tatton St HULME M15 127 G2
HYDE SK14 148 A4
ORD M5 113 G5
STKP SK1 13 G3
STLY SK15 121 E3
Taunton Av AULW OL7 119 F1
ECC M30 110 C2
RDSH SK5 160 D1
URM M41 138 B3
Taunton Brook La
AULW OL7 106 C5
Taunton Cl BOL BL1 * 33 F5
BRAM/HZG SK7 185 H2
Taunton Dr FWTH BL4 65 E3
Taunton Gn AULW OL7 106 C5
Taunton Gv WHTF M45 85 H1
Taunton Hall Cl AULW OL7 106 C5
Taunton Lawns AULW OL7 119 F1
Taunton Pl AULW OL7 * 106 C5
Taunton Platting AULW OL7 * 106 C4
Taunton Rd AULW OL7 106 D5
CHAD OL9 74 B3
SALE M33 153 G2
Taunton St ANC M4 115 G4
Taurus St OLDE OL4 76 B4
Tavern Court Av FAIL M35 105 F3
Tavery Cl ANC M4 115 F3
Tavistock Cl HYDE SK14 149 G1
Tavistock Dr CHAD OL9 74 A3
Tavistock Rd BOL BL1 2 A6
ROCH OL11 43 E3
SALE M33 153 G1
Tawton Av HYDE SK14 135 F5
Tay Cl OLDS OL8 8 E7
Tayfield Rd WYTH/NTH M22 180 B2
Taylor Av ROCH OL11 28 C3
Taylor Green Wy OLDE OL4 77 E5
Taylor La DTN/ASHW M34 132 A4
Taylor Rd ALT WA14 164 D4
URM M41 124 D1
Taylor's La BOLE BL2 51 E2
Taylorson St ORD M5 127 E1
Taylorson St South ORD M5 126 D2
Taylors Pl WHIT OL12 * 10 C3
Taylor's Rd STRET M32 126 B4
Taylor St BOLS/LL BL3 * 3 F6
BURY BL9 5 G2
CHAD OL9 74 B5
DROY M43 117 H4
DTN/ASHW M34 132 C4
GTN M18 130 B2
HEY OL10 40 D3
HYDE SK14 134 A5
MDTN M24 72 D4
OLD OL1 76 B4
OLDE OL4 92 D1
PWCH M25 86 B3
RAD M26 68 B1
ROY/SHW OL2 * 59 E4
RUSH/FAL M14 128 D5
STLY SK15 121 E4
WHIT OL12 10 D2
WHIT OL12 14 C5
Taywood Rd BOLS/LL BL3 63 E2
Teak Dr FWTH BL4 83 G3
Teak St BURY BL9 5 J4
Teal Av POY/DIS SK12 194 B3
Tealby Av OLDTF/WHR M16 127 F4
Tealby Rd GTN M18 130 A4
Teal Cl ALT WA14 165 E1
OFTN SK2 173 G4
Teal Ct ROCH OL11 28 C4
Teal St BOLS/LL BL3 49 E5
Teasdale Cl CHAD OL9 89 H4
Tebbutt St ANC M4 7 J1
Tedder Cl BURY BL9 70 A2
Tedder Dr WYTH/NTH M22 181 E5
Teddington Rd
NEWH/MOS M40 104 B1
Ted Jackson Wk
OP/CLY M11 * 116 A5
Teer St ANC M4 115 G3
Teesdale Av URM M41 123 H4
Teesdale Cl OFTN SK2 173 F3
Tees St MILN OL16 * 30 C5
Teignmouth Av
NEWH/MOS M40 * 115 F1
Teignmouth St
NEWH/MOS M40 115 F1
Telfer Av BRUN/LGST M13 143 G1
Telfer Rd BRUN/LGST M13 143 G1
Telford Cl DTN/ASHW M34 132 B1
Telford Ms UPML OL3 79 E3
Telford Rd MPL/ROM SK6 175 F5
Telford St CHH M8 102 D5
Telford Wk OLDTF/WHR M16 127 G4
Telford Wy ROCH OL11 43 F4
Tellson Cl SLFD M6 100 A4
Tellson Crs SLFD M6 100 A4
Tell St WHIT OL12 29 G4
Temperance St BOLS/LL BL3 48 C4
WGTN/LGST M12 128 D1
Tempest Cha HOR/BR BL6 46 C5
Tempest Ct HOR/BR BL6 * 46 D5
Tempest Rd HOR/BR BL6 62 D1
WILM/AE SK9 201 F4
Tempest St BOLS/LL BL3 48 A5
Temple Cl OLDE OL4 76 D4
Templecombe Dr BOL BL1 22 C5
Temple Dr BOL BL1 33 F3
SWIN M27 99 G3
Temple Rd BOL BL1 33 F3
SALE M33 155 E2
Temple Sq CHH M8 102 B5
Temple St HEY OL10 41 E4
MDTN M24 73 E3
OLD OL1 76 A5
Templeton Cl ALT WA14 165 E3
Ten Acre Ct WHTF M45 * 69 E5
Ten Acre Dr WHTF M45 69 E5
Ten Acres La NEWH/MOS M40 116 B1
Tenax Rd TRPK M17 125 G1
Tenbury Cl SLFD M6 * 113 E2
Tenbury Dr MDTN M24 88 D2
Tenby Av BOL BL1 32 D5
DID/WITH M20 142 D5
STRET M32 126 B4
Tenby Ct OLDTF/WHR M16 * 127 F2
Tenby Dr CHD/CHDH SK8 183 E3
SLFD M6 100 B5
Tenby Gv WHIT OL12 29 F2
Tenby Rd EDGY/DAV SK3 171 E2
OLDS OL8 90 C5
Tenby St WHIT OL12 29 F2
Tenement La BRAM/HZG SK7 183 G2
Teneriffe St BRO M7 101 G5
Tennis St BOL BL1 33 G4
OLDTF/WHR M16 127 E4
Tennyson Av BURY BL9 53 G3
DTN/ASHW M34 * 147 E4
DUK SK16 134 B1
RAD M26 51 H5
Tennyson Cl HTNM SK4 158 D5
Tennyson Gdns PWCH M25 85 G4
Tennyson Rd CHD/CHDH SK8 170 C3
DROY M43 117 H3
FWTH BL4 81 G1
MDTN M24 73 E2
RDSH SK5 144 D2
SWIN M27 98 C2
Tennyson St BOL BL1 33 H5
BRUN/LGST M13 128 D3
OLD OL1 76 B3
ROCH OL11 43 F1
Tensing Av AULW OL7 107 E5
Tensing St OLDS OL8 106 D2
Tentercroft WHIT OL12 10 A6
Tenterden St BURY BL9 4 B5
Tenterhill La ROCH OL11 28 A1
Tenters St BURY BL9 4 B5
Tenth St TRPK M17 126 A2
Terence St NEWH/MOS M40 104 C5
Terminal Rd East
MANAIR M90 180 A5
Terminal Rd North
MANAIR M90 180 B5
Terminal Rd South
MANAIR M90 180 A5
Tern Cl ALT WA14 165 E1
DUK SK16 133 H1
ROCH OL11 28 C4
Tern Dr POY/DIS SK12 194 C3
Ternhill Ct FWTH BL4 65 H4
Terrace St OLDE OL4 76 A5
The Terrace PWCH M25 86 A4
Terrington Cl CCHDY M21 142 A4
Tetbury Dr BOLE BL2 50 C1
Tetbury Rd WYTH/NTH M22 180 A3
Tetlow Gv ECC M30 110 D4
Tetlow La BRO M7 101 H2
Tetlow St CHAD OL9 * 8 D5
HYDE SK14 * 133 H3
MDTN M24 72 D4
NEWH/MOS M40 104 B5
Teviot St BRUN/LGST M13 129 F4
Tewkesbury Av AUL OL6 107 F3
DROY M43 117 H2
HALE/TIMP WA15 178 D1
MDTN M24 72 C1
URM M41 124 C4
Tewkesbury Cl
CHD/CHDH SK8 193 E1
POY/DIS SK12 195 E3
Tewkesbury Dr PWCH M25 86 B5
Tewkesbury Rd
EDGY/DAV SK3 171 E3
NEWH/MOS M40 115 G2
Texas St AUL OL6 119 H3
Textile St WGTN/LGST M12 129 H1
Textilose Rd TRPK M17 125 G3
Thackeray Cl CHH M8 102 B4
Thackeray Gv DROY M43 117 H3
Thackeray Rd OLD OL1 76 B3
Thames Cl BURY BL9 27 G4
OP/CLY M11 116 C5
Thames Ct HULME M15 127 G2
Thames Rd MILN OL16 31 H5
Thames St MILN OL16 30 C5
OLD OL1 9 J1
Thanet Cl BRO M7 101 H5
Thankerton Av
DTN/ASHW M34 118 C4
Thatcher Cl ALT WA14 177 F4
Thatcher St OLDS OL8 91 H4
Thatch Leach CHAD OL9 90 A2
Thatch Leach La WHTF M45 69 H5
Thaxmead Dr
NEWH/MOS M40 117 E1
Thaxted Dr OFTN SK2 173 H4
Thaxted Pl BOL BL1 48 B1
Theatre St OLD OL1 9 H3
Thekla St CHAD OL9 8 D1
Thelma St RAMS BL0 16 C2
Thelwall Av BOLE BL2 50 A1
RUSH/FAL M14 142 B3
Thelwall Cl HALE/TIMP WA15 165 H3
Thelwall Rd SALE M33 155 F3
Theobald Rd ALT WA14 177 G3
Theta Cl OP/CLY M11 116 C3
Thetford WHIT OL12 10 A5
Thetford Cl TOT/BURYW BL8 38 A1
Thetford Dr CHH M8 102 C3
Thicketford Brow BOLE BL2 35 E5
Thicketford Cl BOLE BL2 34 D4
Thicketford Rd BOLE BL2 34 D5
Thimble Cl WHIT OL12 20 A4
The Thimbles WHIT OL12 20 A4
Third Av BOL BL1 48 A2
BOLS/LL BL3 50 C5
BURY BL9 39 G2
OLDS OL8 90 D5
OP/CLY M11 116 D3
STLY SK15 109 F5
SWIN M27 98 D5
TRPK M17 126 A3
Third St BOL BL1 32 C2
Thirlby Dr WYTH/NTH M22 180 C3
Thirlmere Rd STKP SK1 172 C2
Thirlmere Av AULW OL7 119 E1
STRET M32 125 H5
SWIN M27 99 F3
Thirlmere Cl WILM/AE SK9 200 C4
Thirlmere Dr BURY BL9 * 53 F2
LHULT M38 81 F2
MDTN M24 72 B2
Thirlmere Gv FWTH BL4 64 D4
ROY/SHW OL2 59 E3
Thirlmere Rd PART M31 150 D2
ROCH OL11 42 A2
URM M41 123 F5
WHTN BL5 63 G5
WYTH/NTH M22 180 A3
Thirlspot Cl BOL BL1 22 D5
Thirlstone Av OLDE OL4 * 61 E5
Thirsfield Dr OP/CLY M11 116 D3
Thirsk Av CHAD OL9 74 A3
SALE M33 153 F3
Thirsk Cl TOT/BURYW BL8 37 G1
Thirsk Rd BOLS/LL BL3 66 D2
Thirsk St WGTN/LGST M12 128 D1
Thistle Bank Cl BKLY M9 102 D1
Thistle Cl STLY SK15 135 F1
Thistledown Cl ECC M30 110 D5
Thistle Gn MILN OL16 31 F4
Thistle Sq PART M31 150 D4
Thistleton Rd BOLS/LL BL3 63 G1
Thistle Wy OLDE OL4 76 C2
Thistlewood Dr WILM/AE SK9 199 G3
Thistleyfields MILN OL16 * 31 F4
Thomas Cl DTN/ASHW M34 132 D4
Thomas Dr BOLS/LL BL3 48 C4
Thomas Gibbon Cl
STRET M32 * 140 A2
Thomas Henshaw Ct
ROCH OL11 42 B2
Thomas Holden St BOL BL1 2 C3
Thomas Johnson Cl ECC M30 * 110 D4
Thomas More Cl FWTH BL4 82 C1
Thomasson Cl BOL BL1 33 H5
Thomas St ANC M4 7 G3
BOLS/LL BL3 48 C4
CHH M8 102 A2
FWTH BL4 66 B4
HALE/TIMP WA15 165 H5
MILN OL16 10 E4
MPL/ROM SK6 161 H3
MPL/ROM SK6 163 G4
OFTN SK2 13 G7
OLDE OL4 92 D2
RAD M26 68 C1
ROY/SHW OL2 60 B3
ROY/SHW OL2 75 G1
STRET M32 126 A5
Thomas St West OFTN SK2 13 G7
Thomas Telford Basin
CMANE M1 7 J5
Thompson Av BOLE BL2 36 C5
WHTF M45 69 H5
Thompson Cl DTN/ASHW M34 131 G5
Thompson Ct DTN/ASHW M34 131 G5
Thompson Dr BURY BL9 39 F3
Thompson Fold STLY SK15 120 C3
Thompson La CHAD OL9 90 B3
Thompson Rd BOL BL1 33 E5
DTN/ASHW M34 131 G5
TRPK M17 111 F5
Thompson St ANC M4 7 H2
BOLS/LL BL3 49 E4
CSLFD M3 * 114 B2
NEWH/MOS M40 103 G5
Thomson Rd GTN M18 130 B4
Thomson St BRUN/LGST M13 128 D2
EDGY/DAV SK3 13 F6
Thoralby Cl WGTN/LGST M12 129 H3
Thorburn Dr WHIT OL12 18 A1
Thoresby Cl RAD M26 51 F4
Thoresway Rd
BRUN/LGST M13 129 F5
WILM/AE SK9 198 C5
Thor Gv ORD M5 113 H5
Thorley Cl CHAD OL9 89 H5
Thorley Dr HALE/TIMP WA15 166 C4
URM M41 138 D1
Thorley La HALE/TIMP WA15 166 C3
HALE/TIMP WA15 179 G3
Thorley Ms BRAM/HZG SK7 184 A5
Thorley St FAIL M35 105 E2
Thornage Dr NEWH/MOS M40 115 F1
Thorn Av FAIL M35 105 E4
Thornbank BOLS/LL BL3 48 B3
Thorn Bank DROY M43 * 117 G2
Thornbank Cl HEY OL10 56 B2
Thornbeck Dr BOL BL1 32 C5
Thornbeck Rd BOL BL1 32 C5
Thornbridge Av CCHDY M21 141 F3
Thornbury ROCH OL11 * 29 H5
Thornbury Av HYDE SK14 135 F5
Thornbury Cl CHD/CHDH SK8 183 F3
Thornbury Rd STRET M32 126 B4
Thornbury Wy GTN M18 130 B3
Thornbush Wy MILN OL16 11 J5
Thorncliff Av OLDS OL8 91 F4
Thorncliffe Av DUK SK16 133 F1
ROY/SHW OL2 58 D3
Thorncliffe Gv BNG/LEV M19 144 C2
Thorncliffe Pk ROY/SHW OL2 58 D3
Thorncliffe Rd BOL BL1 34 A1
Thorn Cl HEY OL10 40 C3
Thorncombe Rd
OLDTF/WHR M16 127 H5
Thorn Ct SLFD M6 113 G3
Thorncross Cl HULME M15 127 F1
Thorndale Cl ROY/SHW OL2 59 F4
Thorndale Gv
HALE/TIMP WA15 166 B4
Thorn Dr WYTH/NTH M22 181 F4
Thorne Av URM M41 123 H5
Thorneside DTN/ASHW M34 132 C3
Thorne St FWTH BL4 65 H3
Thorneycroft Av CCHDY M21 156 B1
Thorneycroft Rd
HALE/TIMP WA15 166 C4
Thorney Dr CHD/CHDH SK8 193 F1
Thorney Hill Cl OLDE OL4 * 9 K5
Thorneyholme Cl HOR/BR BL6 46 D3
Thorneylea WHIT OL12 14 C4
Thornfield Av AUL OL6 120 B2
Thornfield Crs LHULT M38 81 E2
Thornfield Dr SWIN M27 98 D3
Thornfield Gv CHD/CHDH SK8 182 D2
LHULT M38 81 E2
Thornfield Hey WILM/AE SK9 199 H2
Thornfield Houses
CHD/CHDH SK8 * 182 D2
Thornfield Rd BNG/LEV M19 158 B1
HTNM SK4 158 D3
TOT/BURYW BL8 25 G4
Thornfield St ORD M5 112 C4
Thorngate Rd CHH M8 102 B5
Thorn Gv CHD/CHDH SK8 183 E5
HALE/TIMP WA15 177 H1
RUSH/FAL M14 143 F3
SALE M33 154 C2
Thorngrove Av
NTHM/RTH M23 167 E2
Thorngrove Dr WILM/AE SK9 199 F4
Thorngrove Hl WILM/AE SK9 199 F4
Thorngrove Rd WILM/AE SK9 199 F4
Thornham Cl
TOT/BURYW BL8 26 D5
Thornham Ct ROY/SHW OL2 58 D1
Thornham Dr BOL BL1 23 E5
Thornham La MDTN M24 57 H3
MDTN M24 58 B2
ROY/SHW OL2 58 D1
Thornham New Rd
ROCH OL11 57 H1
Thornham Rd ROY/SHW OL2 59 E2
SALE M33 153 H4
Thornhill Dr WALK M28 97 F2

Thornhill Rd DROY M43 118 A3
HTNM SK4 158 C4
RAMS BL0 26 B2
Thornholme Cl GTN M18 130 A5
Thornholme Rd
MPL/ROM SK6 175 F5
Thorniley Brow ANC M4 7 F3
Thorn Lea BOLE BL2 35 E2
Thornlea DROY M43 117 F4
HALE/TIMP WA15 166 A5
Thornlea Av OLDS OL8 105 H1
SWIN M27 98 C4
Thorn Lea Cl BOL BL1 47 G2
Thornlea Dr WHIT OL12 29 E1
Thornleigh Rd RUSH/FAL M14 142 D2
Thornley Av BOL BL1 33 F4
Thornley Cl OLDE OL4 93 F2
Thornley Crs MPL/ROM SK6 161 H2
OLDE OL4 93 F2
Thornley La OLDE OL4 93 F2
Thornley La North RDSH SK5 131 E5
Thornley La South RDSH SK5 145 G2
Thornley Ms BOL BL1 * 33 F4
Thornley Park Rd OLDE OL4 93 F2
Thornley Rd DTN/ASHW M34 132 D4
PWCH M25 70 B5
Thornley St HYDE SK14 148 A2
MDTN M24 73 E3
RAD M26 68 C2
Thornmere Cl SWIN M27 83 F5
Thorn Rd BRAM/HZG SK7 193 H2
OLDS OL8 92 B4
SWIN M27 98 D4
Thorns Av BOL BL1 33 G3
Thorns Cl BOL BL1 33 G3
Thornsett Cl BKLY M9 * 103 F2
Thornsgreen Rd
WYTH/NTH M22 180 C4
Thorns Rd BOL BL1 33 G3
The Thorns CCHDY M21 141 F4
Thorn St BOL BL1 34 A4
BURY BL9 16 D5
Thorns Villa Gdns WALK M28 96 B5
Thornton Av BOL BL1 32 C5
DTN/ASHW M34 118 B5
URM M41 138 A1
Thornton Cl BOLS/LL BL3 67 F2
FWTH BL4 65 G5
Thornton Crs PWCH M25 85 G2
Thornton Dr WILM/AE SK9 192 A4
Thornton Ga CHD/CHDH SK8 169 F3
Thornton Pl HTNM SK4 159 E2
Thornton Rd CHD/CHDH SK8 181 H3
RUSH/FAL M14 142 C1
Thornton St BOLE BL2 3 H4
NEWH/MOS M40 115 F1
OLDE OL4 9 H6
ROCH OL11 * 43 E1
Thornton St North
NEWH/MOS M40 115 G1
Thorntree Cl BKLY M9 103 F3
Thorntree Pl WHIT OL12 29 G3
Thorn Vw BURY BL9 39 F3
Thornway BRAM/HZG SK7 183 F4
MPL/ROM SK6 187 E5
WALK M28 96 B3
Thornway Dr AULW OL7 119 E3
Thornwood Av GTN M18 130 D4
Thornydyke Av BOL BL1 34 A1
Thorold Gv SALE M33 155 F2
Thorpe Av RAD M26 53 E4
SWIN M27 98 D1
Thorpebrook Rd
NEWH/MOS M40 103 H4
Thorpe Cl DTN/ASHW M34 132 C4
OLDE OL4 77 F4
Thorpe Gv HTNM SK4 144 D5
Thorpe Hall Gv HYDE SK14 134 A2
Thorpe La OLDE OL4 77 F4
Thorpeness Sq GTN M18 130 C2
Thorpe St BOL BL1 33 G4
MDTN M24 71 H5
OLDTF/WHR M16 127 F4
RAMS BL0 * 16 C3
WALK M28 82 A3
Thorp Rd NEWH/MOS M40 103 H4
ROY/SHW OL2 59 E5
Thorp St ECC M30 110 C5
WHTF M45 69 F2
Thorp Vw ROY/SHW OL2 58 D4
Thorsby Av HYDE SK14 148 B1
Thorsby Cl EDGW/EG BL7 23 E3
Thorsby Rd HALE/TIMP WA15 165 H4
Thrapston Av DTN/ASHW M34 118 C4
Threadfold Wy EDGW/EG BL7 23 E4
Threaphurst La
BRAM/HZG SK7 186 B3
Threapwood Rd
WYTH/NTH M22 180 D3
Three Acre Av ROY/SHW OL2 59 H5
Three Acres La
CHD/CHDH SK8 182 B5
Threlkeld Cl MDTN M24 71 H3
Threlkeld Rd BOL BL1 22 C4
MDTN M24 71 H3
Thresher Cl SALE M33 155 G3
Threshfield Cl BURY BL9 27 G4
Threshfield Dr
HALE/TIMP WA15 166 D2
Throstle Bank St HYDE SK14 133 F4
Throstle Gv MPL/ROM SK6 174 D4
TOT/BURYW BL8 37 H1
Throstle Hall Ct MDTN M24 * 72 C3
Throstles Cl DROY M43 118 B2
Thrum Fold WHIT OL12 18 C4
Thrum Hall La WHIT OL12 18 D5
Thrush Dr BURY BL9 5 J1
Thrush St WHIT OL12 29 F2
Thruxton Cl OLDTF/WHR M16 127 H5
Thurcaston Rd ALT WA14 * 153 F5
Thurland Rd OLDE OL4 92 B1
Thurland St CHAD OL9 73 H4
Thurlby Av BKLY M9 88 B2
Thurlby St BRUN/LGST M13 129 E4
Thurleigh Rd DID/WITH M20 157 G2
Thurlestone Av BOLE BL2 36 C5
Thurlestone Dr
BRAM/HZG SK7 184 C2
URM M41 124 B5
Thurlestone Rd ALT WA14 165 E3
Thurloe St RUSH/FAL M14 128 D5
Thurlow St SALQ M50 113 E5
Thurlston Crs CHH M8 102 C3
Thurlwood Av DID/WITH M20 142 C4
Thurnham St BOLS/LL BL3 64 B1
Thursfield St SLFD M6 101 E5
Thurstane St BOL BL1 33 F4
Thurston Cl BURY BL9 69 H2
Thurston Clough Rd OLDE OL4 78 A3
Thurston Gn WILM/AE SK9 200 D4
Thynne St BOLS/LL BL3 49 E4
FWTH BL4 65 H3
Tiber Av OLDS OL8 105 H1
Tib La CMANW M2 6 E5
Tib St CMANE M1 7 G4
DTN/ASHW M34 146 D1
RAMS BL0 * 16 C3
Tideswell Av NEWH/MOS M40 115 G2
Tideswell Cl CHD/CHDH SK8 182 A4
Tideswell Rd BRAM/HZG SK7 185 F4
DROY M43 117 F2
Tideway Cl BRO M7 100 C2
Tidworth Av ANC M4 115 G3
Tiflis St WHIT OL12 10 B4
Tig Fold Rd FWTH BL4 64 D4
Tilbury St OLD OL1 75 F4
Tilby Cl URM M41 137 G1
Tildsley St BOLS/LL BL3 48 D5
Tile St BURY BL9 4 E2
Tillard Av EDGY/DAV SK3 171 E1
Tillerman Cl SWIN M27 100 A2
Tillhey Rd WYTH/NTH M22 180 C2
Tilney Av STRET M32 140 C2
Tilshead Wk
BRUN/LGST M13 * 128 D2
Tilside Gv HOR/BR BL6 46 C3
Tilson Rd NTHM/RTH M23 167 G4
Tilton St OLD OL1 76 B2
Timberbottom BOLE BL2 34 D2
Timberhurst BURY BL9 39 G4
Times St MDTN M24 73 E4
Timothy Cl SLFD M6 112 A2
Timperley Cl OLDS OL8 91 H5
Timperley Fold AUL OL6 107 F4
Timperley Rd AUL OL6 107 E4
Timperley St OP/CLY M11 * 116 D5
Timpson Rd NTHM/RTH M23 167 F2
Timsbury Cl BOLE BL2 50 C4
Timson St FAIL M35 105 E3
Tindall St ECC M30 110 C5
RDSH SK5 131 E5
Tindle St WALK M28 82 C4
Tinline St BURY BL9 5 H5
Tinningham Cl OP/CLY M11 130 D1
Tinshill Cl WGTN/LGST M12 129 H3
Tinsley Cl NEWH/MOS M40 115 H3
Tinsley Gv BOLE BL2 3 K2
Tin St BOLS/LL BL3 * 48 D4
Tintagel Ct RAD M26 51 F4
STLY SK15 120 C3
Tintern Av BOLE BL2 34 C4
DID/WITH M20 157 E1
HEY OL10 40 D2
LIT OL15 20 D1
URM M41 138 A3
WHIT OL12 29 H1
WHTF M45 69 G3
Tintern Cl POY/DIS SK12 195 E2
Tintern Dr HALE/TIMP WA15 178 D2
Tintern Gv STKP SK1 160 C5
Tintern Pl HEY OL10 40 D2
Tintern Rd CHD/CHDH SK8 193 E1
MDTN M24 72 C1
Tintern St RUSH/FAL M14 142 D1
Tipperary St STLY SK15 109 F5
Tipping St ALT WA14 177 G1
Tipton Cl CHD/CHDH SK8 171 E5
RAD M26 51 G4
Tipton Dr NTHM/RTH M23 155 H4
Tiree Cl BRAM/HZG SK7 185 G3
Tirza Av BNG/LEV M19 143 H4
Titanian Ri OLD OL1 60 C4
Titchfield Rd OLDS OL8 92 B3
Tithe Barn Cl WHIT OL12 * 20 A4
Tithe Barn Crs BOL BL1 34 C2
Tithebarn Rd
HALE/TIMP WA15 178 D4
Tithe Barn Rd HTNM SK4 158 C2
Tithebarn St BURY BL9 4 E4
Titherington Cl
BNG/LEV M19 * 144 D2
Titterington Av CCHDY M21 141 F1
Tiverton Av SALE M33 154 A3
Tiverton Cl RAD M26 51 G4
Tiverton Dr SALE M33 154 A3
WILM/AE SK9 199 G1
Tiverton Pl AULW OL7 106 D5
Tiverton Rd URM M41 124 D4
Tiverton Wk BOL BL1 * 33 F5
Tiviot Dl STKP SK1 13 G2
Tiviot Wy RDSH SK5 160 A3
Tivoli St CSLFD M3 6 D5
Toad La WHIT OL12 10 B5
Tobermory Cl
OP/CLY M11 117 E4
Tobermory Rd
CHD/CHDH SK8 181 H2
Todd St BRO M7 101 G4
BURY BL9 4 E1
CSLFD M3 7 F2
HEY OL10 40 B4
MILN OL16 10 E7
Todmorden Rd LIT OL15 21 F2
Toft Rd GTN M18 130 B4
Toledo St OP/CLY M11 117 E4
Tolland La HALE/TIMP WA15 178 A4
Tollard Av NEWH/MOS M40 103 E5
Tollard Cl CHD/CHDH SK8 183 E5
Toll Bar St STKP SK1 13 H5
WGTN/LGST M12 129 F2
Tollemache Cl HYDE SK14 135 H3
Tollemache Rd HYDE SK14 135 H3
Tollesbury Cl
NEWH/MOS M40 115 G1
Toll Gate Cl BRUN/LGST M13 129 F4
Tollgate Wy MILN OL16 11 J5
Toll St RAD M26 51 G5
Tolworth Dr CHH M8 102 C3
Tomcroft La DTN/ASHW M34 146 B1
Tomlinson Cl OLDS OL8 9 F7
Tomlinson St HULME M15 127 H2
NEWH/MOS M40 89 F4
ROCH OL11 42 B2
Tomlin Sq BOLE BL2 49 H2
Tommy Browell Cl
RUSH/FAL M14 128 B5
Tommy Johnson Wk
RUSH/FAL M14 128 B5
Tommy La BOLE BL2 36 B5
Tommy Taylor Cl
NEWH/MOS M40 * 104 B5
Tom Shepley St HYDE SK14 148 A1
Tonacliffe Rd WHIT OL12 18 B3
Tonacliffe Ter WHIT OL12 18 B1
Tonacliffe Wy WHIT OL12 18 B2
Tonbridge Cl TOT/BURYW BL8 26 D4
Tonbridge Rd BNG/LEV M19 144 B3
RDSH SK5 145 F3
Tonge Bridge Wy BOLE BL2 3 J4
Tonge Cl WHTF M45 70 A3
Tonge Fold Rd BOLE BL2 49 H2
Tonge Gn STLY SK15 * 135 F2
Tonge Hall Cl MDTN M24 73 E4
Tonge Meadow MDTN M24 73 E4
Tonge Moor Rd BOLE BL2 3 K1
Tong End WHIT OL12 14 B3
Tonge Old Rd BOLE BL2 49 H2
Tonge Park Av BOLE BL2 34 D5
Tonge Roughs MDTN M24 73 G4
Tonge St HEY OL10 41 E4
MILN OL16 * 30 B5
WGTN/LGST M12 * 129 E1
Tongfields EDGW/EG BL7 23 E3
Tong Head Av BOL BL1 34 C2
Tong La WHIT OL12 14 B4
Tong Rd BOLS/LL BL3 50 D5
Tong St FWTH BL4 83 E2
Tonman St CSLFD M3 6 C6
Toon Crs TOT/BURYW BL8 26 D5
Tootal Dr SLFD M6 112 B2
Tootal Gv SLFD M6 112 B3
Tootal Rd ORD M5 112 B3
Topcroft Cl WYTH/NTH M22 168 D1
Topfield Rd WYTH/NTH M22 180 B1
Topgate Brow SWIN M27 100 A2
Topham St BURY BL9 53 H1
Topley St BKLY M9 102 D4
Top o th Brow BOLE BL2 * 24 B5
Top o' th' Gn CHAD OL9 90 D3
Top o' th' La BOLS/LL BL3 * 50 A4
Top o' th' Meadows La
OLDE OL4 77 F3
Topping Fold Rd BURY BL9 39 F3
Toppings Gn EDGW/EG BL7 23 F4
The Toppings MPL/ROM SK6 161 H3
Topping St BOL BL1 33 H5
BURY BL9 5 F2
Topp St FWTH BL4 66 B5
Topp Wy BOL BL1 2 D3
Top Schwabe St MDTN M24 71 H4
Topside OLD OL1 75 F3
Top St MDTN M24 72 B3
OLDE OL4 76 C4
Torah St CHH M8 114 D1
Tor Av TOT/BURYW BL8 26 A2
Torbay Dr OFTN SK2 172 C2
Torbay Rd CCHDY M21 141 G3
URM M41 139 E2
Torcross Rd BKLY M9 87 G2
Tor Heg Ms TOT/BURYW BL8 26 A1
Torkington Av SWIN M27 99 E1
Torkington La BRAM/HZG SK7 186 C1
Torkington Rd BRAM/HZG SK7 185 H2
CHD/CHDH SK8 169 G4
WILM/AE SK9 199 F4
Torkington St EDGY/DAV SK3 12 C7
Torness Wk OP/CLY M11 116 C4
Toronto Av MANAIR M90 180 A5
Toronto Rd OFTN SK2 172 B3
Toronto St BOLE BL2 50 B1
Torquay Cl BRUN/LGST M13 129 E3
Torquay Gv OFTN SK2 172 C5
Torra Barn Cl EDGW/EG BL7 22 D1
Torrax Cl SLFD M6 99 G4
Torre Cl MDTN M24 72 D1
Torrens St SLFD M6 100 A5
Torridon Rd BOLE BL2 50 C2
Torrin Cl EDGY/DAV SK3 172 A4
Torrington Av BKLY M9 88 D5
BOL BL1 33 H4
Torrington Dr HYDE SK14 149 F1
Torrington Rd SWIN M27 99 G4
Torrington St HEY OL10 56 B1
Torrisdale Cl BOLS/LL BL3 48 A4
Torside Wy SWIN M27 84 A5
Torver Dr BOLE BL2 50 C1
MDTN M24 72 A2
Torwood Rd CHAD OL9 73 H3
Totland Cl WGTN/LGST M12 129 H5
Totnes Av BRAM/HZG SK7 184 B2
CHAD OL9 74 A3
Totnes Rd CCHDY M21 141 G3
SALE M33 153 G1
Totridge Cl OFTN SK2 173 E4
Tottenham Dr
NTHM/RTH M23 167 E2
Tottington Av OLDE OL4 77 E5
Tottington La PWCH M25 85 F2
Tottington Rd BOLE BL2 35 F1
EDGW/EG BL7 24 C1
TOT/BURYW BL8 37 G2
Tottington St OP/CLY M11 116 D3
Totton Rd FAIL M35 105 E3
Touchet Hall Rd MDTN M24 73 G1
Tours Av NTHM/RTH M23 155 H4
Towcester Cl ANC M4 115 G4
Tower Av RAMS BL0 16 B3
Tower Ct TOT/BURYW BL8 * 26 A3
Towers Av BOLS/LL BL3 47 H5
Towers Cl POY/DIS SK12 195 G2
Tower Sq BRUN/LGST M13 * 128 D2
Towers Rd POY/DIS SK12 195 G2
Towers St OLDE OL4 76 C3
Tower St DUK SK16 120 A4
HEY OL10 40 D4
HYDE SK14 147 H2
RAD M26 53 E5
Towey Cl GTN M18 130 C2
Towncliffe Wk HULME M15 * 127 G2
Towncroft DTN/ASHW M34 132 C4
Towncroft Av MDTN M24 72 C2
Towncroft La BOL BL1 47 F1
Townend St HYDE SK14 148 A1
Townfield URM M41 138 B2
Townfield Gdns ALT WA14 165 G4
Townfield Rd ALT WA14 * 165 G4
Town Fields Cl BURY BL9 4 E6
Townfield St OLDE OL4 * 76 A5
Townfield Wk HULME M15 * 127 G2
Town Fold MPL/ROM SK6 175 G2
Town Gate Dr URM M41 137 E1
Towngate Wy IRL M44 136 D2
Town Hall La CMANW M2 * 6 E5
Town House Rd LIT OL15 21 E2
Town La DTN/ASHW M34 146 B2
DUK SK16 119 H5
Townley Fold HYDE SK14 134 C2
Townley Rd MILN OL16 31 H5
Townley St CHH M8 102 A5
MDTN M24 72 D3
OP/CLY M11 * 116 A5
Townley Ter MPL/ROM SK6 * 175 F3
Town Mdw MILN OL16 10 B7
Town Mill Brow WHIT OL12 10 B5
Townrow St HEY OL10 * 41 F4
Townscliffe La MPL/ROM SK6 175 G3
Townsend Rd SWIN M27 99 E1
Townside Rw BURY BL9 4 E6
Townsley Gv AUL OL6 107 H5
Town St MPL/ROM SK6 175 G2
Towton St BKLY M9 103 F2
Towyn Av ORD M5 113 F3
Toxteth St OP/CLY M11 130 D1
Tracey St CHH M8 102 B1
Traders Av URM M41 124 D1
Trafalgar Av DTN/ASHW M34 131 H1
POY/DIS SK12 195 H4
Trafalgar Cl POY/DIS SK12 195 H4
Trafalgar Gv BRO M7 * 101 G5
Trafalgar Pl DID/WITH M20 157 F2
Trafalgar Rd SALE M33 140 A5
SLFD M6 111 H2
Trafalgar Sq AULW OL7 119 E4
Trafalgar St AULW OL7 119 E4
BRO M7 101 H5
MILN OL16 11 F5
Trafford Av URM M41 124 D5
Trafford Bank Rd
OLDTF/WHR M16 * 127 F3
Trafford Bvd URM M41 124 B2
Trafford Dr HALE/TIMP WA15 166 C1
LHULT M38 81 G2
Trafford Gv FWTH BL4 66 B3
STRET M32 140 B2
Trafford Park Rd TRPK M17 125 H1
Trafford Pl OLDTF/WHR M16 127 G2
WILM/AE SK9 * 199 G4
Trafford Rd ECC M30 111 E5
SALQ M50 126 D2
WILM/AE SK9 198 D1
WILM/AE SK9 200 D4
Trafford St CSLFD M3 6 C7
FWTH BL4 66 A3
OLDS OL8 9 F6
ROCH OL11 42 D1
Trafford Wharf Rd TRPK M17 125 H1
Tragan Cl OFTN SK2 173 E3
Tragan Dr OFTN SK2 173 E3
Trail St SLFD M6 112 D3
Tram St OP/CLY M11 130 B1
Tramway Rd AUL OL6 119 H2
IRL M44 136 B4
Tranby Cl WYTH/NTH M22 169 E5
Tranmere Cl GTN M18 130 A3
Tranmere Dr WILM/AE SK9 192 B5
Tranmere Rd EDGY/DAV SK3 171 E1
Transvaal St OP/CLY M11 117 E4
Travis Brow HTNM SK4 12 C3
Travis St CMANE M1 7 K6
HYDE SK14 148 A1
MILN OL16 45 E2
ROY/SHW OL2 60 B2
Trawden Av BOL BL1 33 F4
Trawden Dr BURY BL9 27 F3
Trawden Gn OFTN SK2 173 E5
Traylen Wy WHIT OL12 28 D2
Traynor Cl MDTN M24 72 C3
Tree Av DROY M43 117 H2
Tree House Av AULW OL7 106 C4
Treelands Wk ORD M5 127 E2
Tree Tops EDGW/EG BL7 23 H5
Treetops Av RAMS BL0 16 B5
Treetops Cl UPML OL3 * 78 C3
Trefoil Wy LIT OL15 20 C2
Tregaer Fold MDTN M24 73 F4
Trenam Pl ORD M5 113 G3
Trenant Rd SLFD M6 112 C1
Trenchard Dr WYTH/NTH M22 181 E5
Trencherbone RAD M26 51 H4
Trengrove St WHIT OL12 * 29 F2
Trent Av CHAD OL9 73 H4
HEY OL10 40 B3
MILN OL16 31 H5
Trent Bridge Wk
OLDTF/WHR M16 126 D5
Trent Cl BRAM/HZG SK7 193 F1
RDSH SK5 160 D1
Trent Ct HULME M15 * 127 G2
Trent Dr BURY BL9 27 G3
WALK M28 81 G5
Trentham Av FWTH BL4 65 H3
HTNM SK4 158 C3
Trentham Cl FWTH BL4 65 H3
Trentham Gv
NEWH/MOS M40 103 H1
Trentham Lawns SLFD M6 113 F1
Trentham Rd
OLDTF/WHR M16 126 D5
Trentham St FWTH BL4 65 H3
HULME M15 127 F1
SWIN M27 * 98 D1
Trent Rd ROY/SHW OL2 59 H1
Trent St MILN OL16 30 C5
Trent Wk DROY M43 118 A5
Trent Wy FWTH BL4 83 E2
Tresco Av STRET M32 140 C2
Trevelyan St ECC M30 111 H3
Trevor Av SALE M33 154 A4
Trevor Dr NEWH/MOS M40 89 H5
Trevor Gv STKP SK1 13 K5
Trevor Rd ECC M30 110 C2
SWIN M27 98 D4
URM M41 123 G5
Trevor St OP/CLY M11 130 D1
ROCH OL11 42 A3
The Triangle
HALE/TIMP WA15 166 C2
Tribune Av ALT WA14 165 E2
Trident Rd ECC M30 123 G1
Trillo Av BOLE BL2 3 K7
Trimdon Cl OP/CLY M11 116 C3
Trimingham Dr
TOT/BURYW BL8 27 E5
Trimley Av NEWH/MOS M40 103 E5
Trinity Av SALE M33 155 E2
Trinity Buildings MOSL OL5 * 94 A5
Trinity Cl DUK SK16 120 B5
Trinity Ct AUL OL6 119 F2
Trinity Crs WALK M28 82 B5
Trinity Gdns EDGY/DAV SK3 184 A1
Trinity Gn RAMS BL0 26 C1
Trinity Rd SALE M33 154 D2
Trinity St BOLS/LL BL3 2 D7
BURY BL9 4 E6
MDTN M24 * 72 C4
MPL/ROM SK6 * 175 E3
OLD OL1 75 F4
STLY SK15 120 D4
Trinity Wy CSLFD M3 6 A5
Trippier Rd ECC M30 110 A5
Tripps Ms DID/WITH M20 157 E2
Triscombe Wy
OLDTF/WHR M16 127 H5
Tristam Cl BRUN/LGST M13 128 D2
Trojan Gdns BRO M7 101 F5
Troon Cl BOLS/LL BL3 63 G1
BRAM/HZG SK7 184 B5
Troon Dr CHD/CHDH SK8 181 H3
Troon Rd NTHM/RTH M23 167 G3
Trough Ga OLDS OL8 91 E5
Troutbeck Av ANC M4 115 F3
Troutbeck Cl TOT/BURYW BL8 25 E1
Troutbeck Dr RAMS BL0 16 D1
Troutbeck Rd CHD/CHDH SK8 181 G1
HALE/TIMP WA15 167 E4
Troutbeck Wy ROCH OL11 42 A2
Trowbridge Dr
NEWH/MOS M40 104 B1
Trowbridge Rd
DTN/ASHW M34 147 E2
Trows La ROCH OL11 42 C5
Trowtree Av WGTN/LGST M12 129 F2
Troydale Dr NEWH/MOS M40 103 H4
Troy Wk ORD M5 * 127 E1
Trumpet St CMANE M1 6 D7
Truro Av AUL OL6 107 G3
RDSH SK5 160 D1
STRET M32 140 C1
Truro Cl BRAM/HZG SK7 184 A5
TOT/BURYW BL8 4 B2
Truro Dr SALE M33 153 G2
Truro Rd CHAD OL9 74 B3
Trust Rd GTN M18 130 B5
Tucana Av BRO M7 113 H2
Tudbury Wy CSLFD M3 6 A2
Tudor Av BKLY M9 103 F1
BOL BL1 48 A2
CHAD OL9 89 G4
FWTH BL4 65 G5
STLY SK15 121 G2
Tudor Cl MOSL OL5 109 F1
RDSH SK5 145 E4
Tudor Ct PWCH M25 86 B4
WHIT OL12 11 G2
Tudor Gn WILM/AE SK9 199 H1
Tudor Gv MDTN M24 72 A1
Tudor Hall St ROCH OL11 42 B4
Tudor Rd ALT WA14 165 E2
WILM/AE SK9 199 H1
Tudor St BOLS/LL BL3 * 48 B5
MDTN M24 73 E4
OLDS OL8 8 E7
ROY/SHW OL2 60 A2
Tuffley Rd NTHM/RTH M23 167 H5
Tugford Cl OLDTF/WHR M16 127 H5
Tuley St OP/CLY M11 129 G1
Tulip Av FWTH BL4 65 F3
FWTH BL4 82 C2
Tulip Cl CHAD OL9 73 H5
EDGY/DAV SK3 171 G4
SALE M33 153 F2
Tulip Dr HALE/TIMP WA15 166 A3
Tulip Gv WHIT OL12 18 D5
Tulip Rd PART M31 150 D4
Tully Pl BRO M7 114 B1
Tully St BRO M7 101 H3
Tully St South BRO M7 101 H4
Tulpen Sq CHAD OL9 74 C5
Tulworth Rd POY/DIS SK12 195 E3
Tumblewood Dr
CHD/CHDH SK8 170 B5
Tunbridge Sq ORD M5 113 F3
Tunshill Rd NTHM/RTH M23 155 F5
Tuns Rd OLDS OL8 92 A5
Tunstall Cl BURY BL9 53 H2
Tunstall Rd OLDE OL4 92 B1
Tunstall St HTNM SK4 13 F1
OP/CLY M11 * 130 D1
Tunstead Av DID/WITH M20 142 B5
Tunstead La UPML OL3 95 G2
Turbary Wk MILN OL16 31 E5
Turf Cl ROY/SHW OL2 75 F1
Turf Hill Rd MILN OL16 43 H2
Turf House Cl LIT OL15 20 C1
Turfland Av ROY/SHW OL2 75 F1
Turf La CHAD OL9 90 B4
ROY/SHW OL2 75 G1
Turf Lea Rd MPL/ROM SK6 187 G3
Turf Park Rd ROY/SHW OL2 75 G1
Turf Pit La OLDE OL4 61 E5
Turf St RAD M26 68 A1
Turf Ter LIT OL15 20 D2
Turfton Rd ROY/SHW OL2 75 G1
Turks Rd RAD M26 51 G4
Turk St BOL BL1 48 B1
Turley St CHH M8 102 C4
Turnberry BOLS/LL BL3 63 G1
Turnberry Dr WILM/AE SK9 199 G2
Turnberry Rd CHD/CHDH SK8 181 H3
Turnbull Av PWCH M25 70 B5

Turnbull Rd ALT WA14 165 E1
BRUN/LGST M13 143 H1
GTN M18 131 E5
Turnbury Cl SALE M33 139 H5
Turnbury Rd WYTH/NTH M22 168 D4
Turncliff Crs MPL/ROM SK6 174 C2
Turncroft La STKP SK1 13 K4
STKP SK1 172 C1
Turncroft Wy WALK M28 96 A3
Turnell Wy WALK M28 97 H5
Turner Av FAIL M35 104 D4
IRL M44 122 B5
Turner Bridge Rd BOLE BL2 49 H1
Turner Dr URM M41 139 F1
Turnerford Cl EDGW/EG BL7 22 D2
Turner Gdns HYDE SK14 133 H4
Turner La AUL OL6 119 G1
HYDE SK14 134 A4
MPL/ROM SK6 146 D5
Turner Rd MPL/ROM SK6 175 E4
Turner's Pl WHIT OL12 18 D5
Turner St ANC M4 7 G3
AUL OL6 119 G1
BOL BL1 3 H2
BRO M7 101 H3
DTN/ASHW M34 132 C3
GTN M18 130 C3
OLDE OL4 76 D4
OLDTF/WHR M16 127 F2
OP/CLY M11 116 D4
STKP SK1 13 G2
WHIT OL12 10 B2
Turnfield Cl MILN OL16 20 A5
Turnfield Rd CHD/CHDH SK8 181 H1
Turnhill Rd MILN OL16 43 G3
Turn Moss Rd STRET M32 140 D3
Turnough Rd MILN OL16 31 G4
Turnpike Gn SLFD M6 * 113 E2
The Turnpike MPL/ROM SK6 174 C2
Turnpike Wk OP/CLY M11 116 A4
Turnstone Rd BOLE BL2 3 G7
OFTN SK2 173 H4
Turn St AUL OL6 120 A1
Turton Cl HEY OL10 40 B4
TOT/BURYW BL8 52 B1
Turton Ct BOL BL1 3 G2
Turton Hts BOLE BL2 23 G5
Turton La PWCH M25 85 G2
Turton Rd BOLE BL2 23 H5
TOT/BURYW BL8 25 H3
Turton St BOL BL1 3 F2
OP/CLY M11 * 130 C1
Turves Rd CHD/CHDH SK8 182 C3
Tuscan Rd DID/WITH M20 169 G1
Tuscany Vw BRO M7 101 E2
Tutbury St ANC M4 115 G4
Tuxford Wk NEWH/MOS M40 103 E5
Tweedale Av BKLY M9 87 H2
Tweedale St ROCH OL11 42 D1
Tweedale Wy CHAD OL9 90 A5
Tweed Cl ALT WA14 165 F3
OLDS OL8 9 F6
Tweedle Hill Rd BKLY M9 87 H3
Tweenbrook Av
NTHM/RTH M23 179 H1
Tweesdale Cl WHTF M45 70 A3
Twelve Yards Rd ECC M30 123 E1
Twigworth Rd
WYTH/NTH M22 180 B2
Twillbrook Dr CSLFD M3 * 6 C1
Twinegate WHIT OL12 18 D5
Twingates Cl ROY/SHW OL2 60 A4
Twining Brook Rd
CHD/CHDH SK8 183 E1
Twining Rd ECC M30 111 E5
Twinnies Rd WILM/AE SK9 199 E1
Twin St HEY OL10 41 F5
Twirl Hill Rd AUL OL6 107 H2
Twisse Rd BOLE BL2 50 C2
Twoacre Av WYTH/NTH M22 168 B4
Two Acre Dr ROY/SHW OL2 59 G1
Two Acre La OLDE OL4 77 G2
Two Bridges Rd MILN OL16 45 E3
Two Brooks La
TOT/BURYW BL8 25 E1
Two Trees La DTN/ASHW M34 147 E2
Twyford Cl DID/WITH M20 157 E3
Tybyrne Cl WALK M28 96 A3
Tydden St OLDS OL8 91 G4
Tydeman Wk MILN OL16 * 44 D1
Tyldesley St RUSH/FAL M14 128 B5
Tyler St WILM/AE SK9 200 D4
Tymm St NEWH/MOS M40 104 B2
Tyndall Av NEWH/MOS M40 103 H1
Tyndall St OLDE OL4 92 B2
Tyne Ct WALK M28 81 H4
Tynedale Cl RDSH SK5 159 H1
Tynesbank WALK M28 81 H5
Tynesbank Cottages
WALK M28 * 81 H4
Tyne St OLDE OL4 76 B5
Tynwald St OLDE OL4 76 B5
Tyrol Wk OP/CLY M11 116 A5
Tyrone Cl NTHM/RTH M23 167 E1
Tyrone Dr ROCH OL11 41 G1
Tyro St OLDS OL8 * 91 G4
Tyrrell Gv HYDE SK14 148 C2
Tyrrel Rd RDSH SK5 145 F2
Tysoe Gdns CSLFD M3 6 A2
Tyson St CHH M8 102 A2
Tytherington Dr BNG/LEV M19 144 D2

U

Uganda St BOLS/LL BL3 64 B2
Ukraine Rd BRO M7 100 D4
Uldale Dr MDTN M24 72 B3
Ullesthorpe WHIT OL12 10 B5
Ulleswater Cl BOLS/LL BL3 66 C1
Ulleswater St BOL BL1 34 A4
Ullswater Av AULW OL7 119 F1
ROY/SHW OL2 59 E3
WHIT OL12 29 F2
Ullswater Dr BURY BL9 * 53 F2
FWTH BL4 64 D5
MDTN M24 72 C1
Ullswater Gv HEY OL10 56 A1
Ullswater Rd STKP SK1 172 C2
URM M41 123 F5
WILM/AE SK9 191 H3
WYTH/NTH M22 180 A2
Ullswater Ter STLY SK15 120 D1
Ulster Av ROCH OL11 42 D1
Ulundi St RAD M26 68 B1
Ulverston Av CHAD OL9 90 B1
DID/WITH M20 142 B4
Umberton Rd WHTN BL5 63 G5
Uncouth Rd MILN OL16 31 F4
Underhill MPL/ROM SK6 162 B4
Underhill Rd OLD OL1 75 F3
Underhill Wk
NEWH/MOS M40 116 C1
Under La CHAD OL9 90 C4
OLDE OL4 93 G3
Underwood WHIT OL12 10 B6
Underwood Cl GTN M18 131 E2
Underwood Rd HYDE SK14 135 E5
WILM/AE SK9 201 F4
Underwood St DUK SK16 119 G5
Underwood Wy ROY/SHW OL2 60 C1
Undsworth Ct HEY OL10 * 41 E4
Unicorn St ECC M30 110 C5
Union Ar BURY BL9 4 E4
Union Buildings BOLE BL2 3 F6
Union Ct BOLE BL2 * 34 B4
Union Rd AUL OL6 119 H1
BOLE BL2 3 H1
MPL/ROM SK6 * 175 E3
WHIT OL12 20 B4
Union St ANC M4 7 G3
AUL OL6 119 G1
BURY BL9 4 E4
CHAD OL9 90 C3
EDGW/EG BL7 22 C1
GTN M18 130 D2
HYDE SK14 148 A1
MDTN M24 72 D3
OLD OL1 9 G4
OLDE OL4 92 D1
RAMS BL0 16 D2
ROY/SHW OL2 59 E5
RUSH/FAL M14 * 128 C5
SLFD M6 113 F1
STKP SK1 13 G6
SWIN M27 98 D2
SWIN M27 99 F2
WGTN/LGST M12 128 D1
WHIT OL12 10 C4
WHIT OL12 14 B5
Union St West OLDS OL8 8 E6
Union Ter BRO M7 * 102 A2
United Rd OLDTF/WHR M16 126 B3
Unity Cl HEY OL10 40 C5
Unity Crs HEY OL10 40 C5
Unity Dr BRO M7 101 H4
Unity St HEY OL10 40 C5
Unity Wy STKP SK1 13 J6
University Rd ORD M5 113 G3
University Rd West ORD M5 * 113 G3
Unsworth St RAD M26 52 A5
Unsworth Wy OLD OL1 9 F1
Unwin Av GTN M18 130 C4
Upavon Rd WYTH/NTH M22 181 E1
Upcast La WILM/AE SK9 200 A2
Upland Dr LHULT M38 81 E1
Upland Rd OLDS OL8 91 F3
Uplands MDTN M24 72 D5
Uplands Av RAD M26 68 D2
Uplands Rd HYDE SK14 148 C5
URM M41 137 G3
The Uplands MOSL OL5 109 E1
Upper Brook St
BRUN/LGST M13 128 D3
STKP SK1 13 H4
Upper Camp St BRO M7 101 G5
Upper Chorlton Rd
OLDTF/WHR M16 127 F5
Upper Cleminson St
CSLFD M3 114 A3
Upper Cliff Hl ROY/SHW OL2 45 F5
Upper Conran St BKLY M9 103 F2
Upper Downs ALT WA14 177 F1
Upper George St WHIT OL12 10 D3
Upper Gloucester St SLFD M6 113 F2
Upper Hayes Cl MILN OL16 11 J5
Upper Helena St
NEWH/MOS M40 115 H3
Upper Hibbert La
MPL/ROM SK6 175 E5
Upper Kent Rd
RUSH/FAL M14 129 E5
Upper Kirby St ANC M4 115 F4
Upper Lees Dr WHTN BL5 62 B3
Upper Lloyd St
RUSH/FAL M14 128 B5
Upper Md EDGW/EG BL7 23 E2
Upper Medlock St
HULME M15 128 A2
Uppermill Dr BNG/LEV M19 158 A3
Upper Monsall St
NEWH/MOS M40 103 F4
Upper Moss La HULME M15 127 H2
Upper Park Rd BRO M7 101 H1
RUSH/FAL M14 128 D4
Upper Passmonds Gv
ROCH OL11 29 E3
Upper Stone Dr MILN OL16 31 E5
Upper West Gv
BRUN/LGST M13 129 E3
Upper Wharf St ORD M5 113 H4
Upper Wilton St PWCH M25 86 B3
Uppingham Dr RAMS BL0 16 C1
Upton ROCH OL11 29 H5
Upton Av CHD/CHDH SK8 182 D4
HTNM SK4 158 B2
Upton Cl MDTN M24 88 D2
Upton Dr ALT WA14 165 H1
Upton Wy TOT/BURYW BL8 37 E1
Urban Dr HALE/TIMP WA15 165 H5
Urban Rd
HALE/TIMP WA15 165 H5
SALE M33 154 B2
Urmson St OLDS OL8 91 G4
Urmston La STRET M32 139 G2
Urmston Pk URM M41 139 E1
Urwick Rd MPL/ROM SK6 162 A5
Usk Cl WHTF M45 70 B5
Uttley St BOL BL1 33 G4
ROCH OL11 42 B2
Uxbridge Av OP/CLY M11 116 D3
Uxbridge St AUL OL6 119 F2

V

Vaal St OLDS OL8 90 D4
Valance Cl WGTN/LGST M12 129 H2
Valdene Cl FWTH BL4 66 A5
Valdene Dr FWTH BL4 66 A5
WALK M28 97 E2
Vale Av BURY BL9 53 E2
HYDE SK14 134 B5
RAD M26 67 F5
SALE M33 155 F1
SWIN M27 99 F1
URM M41 137 G2
Vale Cl BRAM/HZG SK7 173 F5
HTNM SK4 158 C4
MPL/ROM SK6 162 D4
Vale Coppice RAMS BL0 16 D5
Vale Cottages LIT OL15 20 D3
Vale Crs CHD/CHDH SK8 182 C2
Vale Dr CHAD OL9 8 C5
PWCH M25 85 H5
Vale Edge RAD M26 52 B4
Vale Head WILM/AE SK9 192 A5
Vale La FAIL M35 117 H1
Valencia Rd BRO M7 101 E4
Valentia Rd BKLY M9 88 A3
Valentine St FAIL M35 104 D3
OLDE OL4 92 B1
Vale Park Wy CHH M8 102 D3
Valerie Wk HULME M15 128 A1
Vale Rd ALT WA14 177 E3
DROY M43 118 A2
HALE/TIMP WA15 166 B4
HTNM SK4 158 C5
MPL/ROM SK6 174 A1
ROY/SHW OL2 60 C3
STLY SK15 109 F4
WILM/AE SK9 198 B2
Vale Side MOSL OL5 108 D2
Vale St AULW OL7 106 D4
BOLE BL2 50 D2
HEY OL10 41 F4
MDTN M24 73 E4
OP/CLY M11 116 D3
The Vale MOSL OL5 108 C1
Vale Top Av BKLY M9 103 F3
Valetta Cl RUSH/FAL M14 142 D3
Vale Vw ALT WA14 * 177 F3
Valewood Av HTNM SK4 158 D5
Valletts La BOL BL1 33 F5
Valley Av TOT/BURYW BL8 37 G2
Valley Cl CHD/CHDH SK8 182 B1
MOSL OL5 93 G5
Valley Dr WILM/AE SK9 191 H4
Valley Gv DTN/ASHW M34 147 F1
Valley Ms UPML OL3 95 F3
Valley Ml EDGW/EG BL7 * 23 E3
Valley Mill La BURY BL9 5 G7
Valley New Rd ROY/SHW OL2 75 F1
Valley Park Rd PWCH M25 85 G2
Valley Ri ROY/SHW OL2 44 D5
Valley Rd BRAM/HZG SK7 184 A3
CHD/CHDH SK8 182 B1
HYDE SK14 149 G3
MDTN M24 73 E2
MPL/ROM SK6 161 E2
ROY/SHW OL2 75 F1
URM M41 123 E4
Valley Rd South URM M41 137 F1
Valley Vw HYDE SK14 134 B4
WHIT OL12 14 C1
Valley Wk OP/CLY M11 116 A4
Valley Wy STLY SK15 121 F4
Valpy Av BOLE BL2 34 C3
Vancouver Quay SALQ M50 126 C1
Vandyke Av SLFD M6 112 A2
Vandyke St WHIT OL12 28 C2
Vane St ECC M30 110 D3
Vannes Gv HYDE SK14 135 G5
Vantomme St BOL BL1 33 H2
Vant St OLDE OL4 92 B3
Varden Gv EDGY/DAV SK3 171 G4
Varden Rd POY/DIS SK12 195 F4
Vardon Dr WILM/AE SK9 199 G4
Varey St GTN M18 130 C3
Varley Rd BOLS/LL BL3 47 H5
Varley St NEWH/MOS M40 115 G1
Varna St OP/CLY M11 130 C1
Vauban Dr SLFD M6 112 A2
Vaudrey Dr BRAM/HZG SK7 185 F2
CHD/CHDH SK8 182 D2
HALE/TIMP WA15 166 B1
Vaudrey La DTN/ASHW M34 147 E2
Vaudrey Rd MPL/ROM SK6 161 H1
Vaudrey St STLY SK15 120 D4
Vaughan Av NEWH/MOS M40 103 H2
Vaughan Gv OLDE OL4 93 E5
Vaughan Rd ALT WA14 153 F5
CCHDY M21 141 H3
HTNM SK4 159 G3
Vaughan St ECC M30 110 C2
ROY/SHW OL2 75 F1
WGTN/LGST M12 129 G1
Vauxhall St NEWH/MOS M40 115 E1
Vavasour Ct MILN OL16 * 30 C5
Vawdrey Dr NTHM/RTH M23 155 G4
Vaynor WHIT OL12 10 B4
Vega St CHH M8 114 B1
Vela Wk BRO M7 113 H2
Velmere Av BKLY M9 87 F2
Velour Cl CSLFD M3 114 A2
Vendale Av SWIN M27 98 C4
Venetia St
NEWH/MOS M40 * 104 B5
Venice St BOLS/LL BL3 48 B5
CMANE M1 * 7 G7
Venlow Gdns CHD/CHDH SK8 183 E3
Ventnor Av BNG/LEV M19 144 C3
BOL BL1 34 A3
BURY BL9 69 G1
SALE M33 139 H5
Ventnor Cl DTN/ASHW M34 147 F3
Ventnor Rd DID/WITH M20 157 H3
HTNM SK4 158 D4
Ventnor St ROCH OL11 43 E1
SLFD M6 101 E5
Ventor St BKLY M9 103 E2
Ventura Cl RUSH/FAL M14 142 C2
Venture Scout Wy CHH M8 102 A4
Venture Wy POY/DIS SK12 195 G4
Venwood Ct PWCH M25 * 85 G5
Venwood Rd PWCH M25 85 G5
Verbena Av FWTH BL4 65 F3
Verbena Cl PART M31 151 E3
Verdant La ECC M30 110 A5
Verdant Wy MILN OL16 43 H3
Verdun Av SLFD M6 112 A2
Verdun Crs ROCH OL11 29 F3
Verdun Rd ECC M30 110 C1
Verdure Av BOL BL1 47 F1
SALE M33 154 D5
Verdure Cl FAIL M35 105 G2
Vere St SALQ M50 113 E4
Verity Cl DID/WITH M20 142 D5
ROY/SHW OL2 75 E1
Vermont St BOL BL1 2 A2
Verne Av SWIN M27 98 D2
Verne Dr OLD OL1 60 D4
Verney Rd ROY/SHW OL2 75 F2
Vernham Wk BOLS/LL BL3 48 D5
Vernon Av ECC M30 * 111 G3
STKP SK1 160 C4
STRET M32 140 B2
Vernon Cl CHD/CHDH SK8 182 B3
POY/DIS SK12 195 F5
Vernon Dr MPL/ROM SK6 174 B2
PWCH M25 85 H5
Vernon Gv SALE M33 155 F3
Vernon Pk HALE/TIMP WA15 166 B2
Vernon Rd BRO M7 101 F1
DROY M43 117 F3
MPL/ROM SK6 161 G3
POY/DIS SK12 195 F5
TOT/BURYW BL8 26 A2
Vernon St AUL OL6 119 H1
BKLY M9 103 F3
BOL BL1 2 C3
BRAM/HZG SK7 185 E1
BRO M7 101 G5
BURY BL9 4 E1
FWTH BL4 66 B4
HYDE SK14 148 A1
MOSL OL5 * 93 H5
OLDTF/WHR M16 127 F3
STKP SK1 * 13 G2
Vernon Wk BOL BL1 2 D2
Verona Dr NEWH/MOS M40 116 D1
Veronica Rd DID/WITH M20 157 H3
Verrill Av NTHM/RTH M23 156 B5
Vesper St FAIL M35 105 F2
Vesta St ANC M4 115 F4
RAMS BL0 16 C2
Vestris Dr SLFD M6 112 A2
Vetch Cl GOL/RIS/CUL WA3 150 A1
Viaduct Rd ALT WA14 165 G2
Viaduct St CSLFD M3 6 C2
EDGY/DAV SK3 12 E4
WGTN/LGST M12 115 H5
Vicarage Av CHD/CHDH SK8 183 E4
Vicarage Cl BURY BL9 27 F3
DUK SK16 120 B5
OLDE OL4 77 E5
SLFD M6 112 A2
Vicarage Crs AUL OL6 107 G5
Vicarage Dr DUK SK16 120 B5
MILN OL16 19 H5
Vicarage Gdns
EDGY/DAV SK3 * 12 E6
HYDE SK14 148 A1
Vicarage Gv ECC M30 111 G3
Vicarage La ALT WA14 177 F3
MDTN M24 73 G5
POY/DIS SK12 195 F2
Vicarage Rd AULW OL7 107 E5
EDGY/DAV SK3 171 H3
IRL M44 136 C1
SWIN M27 98 D2
URM M41 124 A5
WALK M28 81 H3
Vicarage Rd North ROCH OL11 42 C5
Vicarage Rd South
ROCH OL11 42 B5
Vicarage St BOLS/LL BL3 48 C4
OLDS OL8 90 D5
RAD M26 68 B1
ROY/SHW OL2 60 A2
Vicarage Vw ROCH OL11 42 C5
Vicar's Dr MILN OL16 10 C7
Vicar's Ga MILN OL16 10 C7
Vicars Hall Gdns WALK M28 96 A5
Vicars Hall La WALK M28 96 A5
Vicars Rd CCHDY M21 141 E3
Vicars St ECC M30 111 G3
Vicker Cl SWIN M27 84 A5
Vicker Gv DID/WITH M20 157 E1
Vickerman St BOL BL1 33 G4
Vickers Rw FWTH BL4 65 G4
Vickers St BOLS/LL BL3 48 C4
NEWH/MOS M40 115 H2
Victor Av BURY BL9 38 B2
Victoria Av BKLY M9 87 H2
BNG/LEV M19 144 A3
BRAM/HZG SK7 * 185 F1
CHD/CHDH SK8 182 D2
DID/WITH M20 157 F3
ECC M30 111 G2
HALE/TIMP WA15 165 H2
MPL/ROM SK6 161 G3
SWIN M27 99 F2
WHTF M45 69 H4
Victoria Av East BKLY M9 88 C3
Victoria Bridge St
CSLFD M3 6 D2
Victoria Cl BRAM/HZG SK7 193 G1
EDGY/DAV SK3 13 F7
WALK M28 * 96 B4
Victoria Ct AULW OL7 119 F4
FWTH BL4 65 H2
Victoria Crs ECC M30 111 G2
Victoria Dr SALE M33 155 E3
Victoria Gdns HYDE SK14 134 A4
ROY/SHW OL2 * 60 A2
Victoria Gv BOL BL1 33 F5
HTNM SK4 159 F1
RUSH/FAL M14 143 E4
Victoria La SWIN M27 98 C2
WHTF M45 69 G5
Victoria Ldg BRO M7 * 101 F5
Victoria Ms BURY BL9 70 A2
Victoria Pk STKP SK1 * 172 C1
Victoria Pl TRPK M17 126 C3
Victoria Rd ALT WA14 177 G2
BOL BL1 47 E2
ECC M30 111 F2
FWTH BL4 82 D1
HALE/TIMP WA15 166 B3
IRL M44 136 B2
OLDTF/WHR M16 141 H1
RUSH/FAL M14 142 D3
SALE M33 155 E3
SLFD M6 111 H1
STKP SK1 160 C5
STRET M32 140 B1
URM M41 138 B1
WILM/AE SK9 198 D4
WYTH/NTH M22 168 C1
Victoria Sq ANC M4 * 7 J2
BOL BL1 2 E5
Victoria Station Ap CSLFD M3 6 E2
Victoria St ALT WA14 165 G4
AULW OL7 119 F4
BOLE BL2 36 B5
CHAD OL9 8 A1
CSLFD M3 6 E2
DTN/ASHW M34 132 B5
DUK SK16 120 A5
FAIL M35 104 C4
FWTH BL4 65 G3
HEY OL10 41 F5
HYDE SK14 134 A4
HYDE SK14 134 C3
LIT OL15 21 E3
MDTN M24 72 D4
OLDE OL4 9 K4
OLDE OL4 92 D1
OLDS OL8 * 106 C2
OP/CLY M11 116 D5
RAD M26 68 B1
RAMS BL0 16 C2
ROY/SHW OL2 60 A2
STLY SK15 120 C3
STLY SK15 121 G1
TOT/BURYW BL8 4 A4
TOT/BURYW BL8 25 H4
WALK M28 96 B4
WHIT OL12 * 10 C3
WHIT OL12 * 14 B5
WHTN BL5 62 A4
Victoria St East AULW OL7 119 F4
Victoria Ter ROY/SHW OL2 * 59 E4
WGTN/LGST M12 129 G4
Victoria Wk CHAD OL9 74 D3
Victoria Wy BRAM/HZG SK7 193 G1
Victor Mann St OP/CLY M11 131 F1
Victor St CSLFD M3 6 A3
HEY OL10 56 B1
NEWH/MOS M40 115 F1
OLDS OL8 105 G1
Victory Gv DTN/ASHW M34 131 H1
Victory Rd BOLS/LL BL3 50 D5
IRL M44 150 B2
Victory St BOL BL1 * 48 B1
RUSH/FAL M14 128 D5
Vienna Rd EDGY/DAV SK3 171 G3
Vienna Rd East EDGY/DAV SK3 171 G3
Viewlands Dr WILM/AE SK9 192 A5
View St BOLS/LL BL3 48 C5
Vigo Av BOLS/LL BL3 64 A1
Vigo St HEY OL10 41 F5
OLDE OL4 92 C2
Viking Cl OP/CLY M11 116 A4
Viking St BOLS/LL BL3 49 F5
ROCH OL11 29 F3
Village Ct TRPK M17 125 H2
Village Mnr UPML OL3 79 E4
Village St BRO M7 101 F5
The Village URM M41 137 H3
Village Wy WILM/AE SK9 199 G1
Village Wy (Ashburton Rd East)
TRPK M17 125 H2
Villa Rd OLDS OL8 91 G3
Villdale Av OFTN SK2 172 D2
Villiers Ct WHTF M45 * 85 H1
Villiers Dr OLDS OL8 8 E6
Villiers St AUL OL6 120 A3
BURY BL9 5 H2
HYDE SK14 134 A5
Vinca Gv BRO M7 101 G4
Vincent Av CCHDY M21 141 E2
OLDE OL4 76 B4
Vincent St BOL BL1 2 A6
BRO M7 101 H3
HYDE SK14 148 B2
LIT OL15 20 D2
MDTN M24 72 D2
MILN OL16 * 43 F1
OP/CLY M11 116 D5
Vine Av SWIN M27 99 G2
Vine Cl ROY/SHW OL2 60 A2
SALE M33 153 F1
Vine Ct MILN OL16 30 C5
STRET M32 140 B2
Vine Fold NEWH/MOS M40 105 E1
Vine Gv OFTN SK2 172 D3
Vine Pl ROCH OL11 43 E1
Vinery Gv DTN/ASHW M34 132 B5
Vine St BRAM/HZG SK7 185 F1
BRO M7 101 E2
CHAD OL9 90 C4
ECC M30 110 D4
OP/CLY M11 130 D1
PWCH M25 86 B2
RAMS BL0 16 B4
Vineyard Cl WHIT OL12 19 H1
Vineyard St OLDE OL4 76 A5
Viola St OP/CLY M11 117 E3
Violet Av FWTH BL4 65 F3
Violet St GTN M18 131 E2
OFTN SK2 172 A3
Violet Wy MDTN M24 73 G5
Virgil St OLDTF/WHR M16 127 F2
Virginia Cha CHD/CHDH SK8 182 C4

Virginia Cl NTHM/RTH M23 167 E2
Virginia St BOLS/LL BL3 48 A5
ROCH OL11 * 42 D2
Viscount Dr CHD/CHDH SK8 182 A5
MANAIR M90 * 179 G5
Viscount St RUSH/FAL M14 128 D5
The Vista IRL M44 150 B2
Vivian St ROCH OL11 42 D1
Vixen Cl CCHDY M21 142 A4
Voltaire Av SLFD M6 112 A2
Vorlich Dr CHAD OL9 74 A4
Vulcan St OLD OL1 76 B4
Vyner Gv SALE M33 139 F5

W

Waddicor Av AUL OL6 107 H4
Waddington Cl
TOT/BURYW BL8 36 D4
Waddington Fold MILN OL16 43 H4
Waddington Rd BOL BL1 32 D5
Waddington St CHAD OL9 8 B1
Wade Bank WHTN BL5 62 A4
Wadebridge Av
NTHM/RTH M23 167 E2
Wadebridge Dr
TOT/BURYW BL8 37 E4
Wadeford Cl ANC M4 * 115 F3
Wade Hill La UPML OL3 78 B4
Wade Rw UPML OL3 79 E4
Wadesmill Wk
BRUN/LGST M13 * 128 C1
Wadeson Rd BRUN/LGST M13 128 C1
Wade St BOLS/LL BL3 65 E1
MDTN M24 89 G1
Wade Wk OP/CLY M11 116 B5
Wadham Gdns MPL/ROM SK6 162 B1
Wadham Wy
HALE/TIMP WA15 178 A3
Wadhurst Wk
BRUN/LGST M13 * 128 D3
Wadlow Cl CSLFD M3 * 6 B1
Wadsley St BOL BL1 2 C2
Wadsworth Cl WILM/AE SK9 192 B4
Wadsworth Ms DROY M43 117 G4
Waggoners Ct SWIN M27 99 E3
Waggon Rd AULW OL7 107 E2
BOLE BL2 50 A1
MOSL OL5 108 D2
Wagner St BOL BL1 33 G3
Wagstaffe Dr FAIL M35 105 E3
Wagstaffe St MDTN M24 72 D3
Wagtail Cl WALK M28 97 E2
Waincliffe Av CCHDY M21 156 C2
Waingap Crs WHIT OL12 14 C5
Waingap Ri WHIT OL12 19 E4
Waingap Vw WHIT OL12 18 C1
Wainman St SLFD M6 101 E5
Wainwright Av
DTN/ASHW M34 131 E5
Wainwright Cl OFTN SK2 172 B2
OLDE OL4 77 F5
Wainwright Rd ALT WA14 165 E4
Wainwright St DUK SK16 120 B4
OLDS OL8 9 F6
Waithlands Rd MILN OL16 30 C5
Wakefield Crs MPL/ROM SK6 161 H5
Wakefield Dr OLD OL1 74 D3
SWIN M27 83 G3
Wakefield Ms EDGW/EG BL7 23 E4
Wakefield Rd STLY SK15 121 E3
Wakeling Rd DTN/ASHW M34 146 C3
Walcott Cl BRUN/LGST M13 129 E3
Wald Av RUSH/FAL M14 143 G4
Waldeck St BOL BL1 48 B1
Walden Av OLDE OL4 76 C2
Walden Cl RUSH/FAL M14 142 C3
Walden Crs BRAM/HZG SK7 184 D1
Walderton Av
NEWH/MOS M40 103 H4
Waldon Av CHD/CHDH SK8 170 A4
Waldon Cl BOLS/LL BL3 48 B5
Wales St OLD OL1 76 B3
Walkdene Dr WALK M28 81 G4
Walkden Market Pl
WALK M28 * 82 A4
Walkden Rd WALK M28 97 E1
Walkden St WHIT OL12 10 C3
Walker Av BOLS/LL BL3 65 E1
FAIL M35 * 105 G4
STLY SK15 121 F3
WHTF M45 85 H1
Walker Cl FWTH BL4 82 D1
HYDE SK14 148 B1
Walker Fold Rd BOL BL1 32 A2
Walker La HYDE SK14 148 B1
Walker Rd BKLY M9 88 B3
CHAD OL9 90 A5
ECC M30 110 B1
IRL M44 * 136 B2
Walkers Cl UPML OL3 79 E4
Walkers Ct FWTH BL4 66 A4
Walker's Cft CSLFD M3 6 E2
Walker's La OLDE OL4 93 F1
Walker's Rd OLDS OL8 90 D5
Walker St BOL BL1 2 B6
BURY BL9 53 F1
DTN/ASHW M34 132 B4
HEY OL10 40 D5
MDTN M24 71 H5
MILN OL16 11 F7
OLDS OL8 8 C5
RAD M26 68 D3
STKP SK1 13 F3
Walkerwood Dr STLY SK15 121 G3
Walkmill UPML OL3 78 C3
Walk Mill Cl WHIT OL12 20 A4
The Walk MILN OL16 10 C6
The Walkway BOLS/LL BL3 47 G4
Wallace Av RUSH/FAL M14 143 F1
Wallace St OLDS OL8 91 G3
Wallasey Av RUSH/FAL M14 142 C2
Wallbank Dr WHIT OL12 18 A1
Wallbank Rd BRAM/HZG SK7 184 B3
Wallbrook Crs LHULT M38 81 F1
Wallbrook Dr BKLY M9 87 H5
The Walled Gdn SWIN M27 98 C4
Waller Av RUSH/FAL M14 143 E3
Walley St BOL BL1 33 H3
Wallhead Rd MILN OL16 31 E4
Wall Hill Rd UPML OL3 78 C3
Wallingford Rd URM M41 124 D5
WILM/AE SK9 191 H2
Wallis St CHAD OL9 90 B3
NEWH/MOS M40 * 104 B5
Wallness La SLFD M6 113 H2
Wallshaw Pl OLD OL1 9 K3
Wallshaw St OLD OL1 9 J3
Wall St OLDS OL8 9 G6
SLFD M6 113 E3
Wall Wy GTN M18 130 D4
Wallwork Cl ROCH OL11 28 B2
Wallwork St OP/CLY M11 117 F5
RAD M26 52 B5
RDSH SK5 * 145 F1
Wallworth Av GTN M18 130 C3
Wally Sq BRO M7 101 H4
Walmer Dr BRAM/HZG SK7 184 B3
Walmersley Ct
MPL/ROM SK6 * 175 E3
Walmersley Old Rd BURY BL9 27 G1
Walmersley Rd BURY BL9 5 F2
BURY BL9 25 F2
NEWH/MOS M40 104 D1
Walmer St GTN M18 130 D2
RUSH/FAL M14 128 C5
Walmer St East
RUSH/FAL M14 128 D5
Walmley Gv BOLS/LL BL3 64 B1
Walmsley Av LIT OL15 20 C5
Walmsley Gv URM M41 138 D1
Walmsley St RDSH SK5 * 159 H3
STLY SK15 120 D5
TOT/BURYW BL8 37 G2
Walney Rd WYTH/NTH M22 168 C5
Walnut Av BURY BL9 5 K3
OLDE OL4 76 C4
Walnut Cl HYDE SK14 148 C1
SWIN M27 83 G3
WILM/AE SK9 199 H2
Walnut Rd ECC M30 110 B1
PART M31 150 C3
Walnut St BOL BL1 34 A3
GTN M18 130 C2
Walnut Tree Rd
EDGY/DAV SK3 170 D2
Walnut Wk STRET M32 140 A3
Walpole St MILN OL16 11 F7
Walsall St SLFD M6 100 D5
Walsden St OP/CLY M11 116 D3
Walsh Av BKLY M9 87 H5
Walshaw Brook Cl
TOT/BURYW BL8 37 E2
Walshaw Dr SWIN M27 99 E3
Walshaw La TOT/BURYW BL8 37 E2
Walshaw Rd TOT/BURYW BL8 37 E2
Walshe St BURY BL9 4 B5
Walsh St CHAD OL9 90 C1
Walsingham Av
DID/WITH M20 157 E2
MDTN M24 88 D2
Walter Scott St OLD OL1 76 A4
Walters Dr OLDS OL8 91 H4
Walter St BKLY M9 103 E2
GTN M18 130 D2
OLD OL1 9 H4
OLDTF/WHR M16 127 F4
PWCH M25 85 G3
RAD M26 52 A3
WALK M28 82 A5
Waltham Dr CHD/CHDH SK8 193 E1
Waltham Rd OLDTF/WHR M16 142 A2
Waltham St OLDE OL4 92 C3
Walton Cl MDTN M24 71 H3
Walton Ct BOLS/LL BL3 49 E5
Walton Dr BURY BL9 27 F3
MPL/ROM SK6 174 C2
Walton Hall Dr BNG/LEV M19 144 D2
Walton Houses FAIL M35 * 105 E2
Walton Pl FWTH BL4 66 B5
Walton Rd ALT WA14 165 E4
BKLY M9 88 A2
SALE M33 154 A5
Walton St AULW OL7 106 C5
HEY OL10 56 A1
MDTN M24 * 72 D2
STKP SK1 * 13 H7
Walwyn Cl STRET M32 140 C2
Wandsworth Av OP/CLY M11 117 E3
Wansbeck Cl STRET M32 140 C2
Wansfell Wk ANC M4 115 G3
Wansford St RUSH/FAL M14 128 B5
Wanstead Av BKLY M9 88 D4
Wapping St BOL BL1 33 G4
Warbeck Cl RDSH SK5 145 G1
Warbeck Rd NEWH/MOS M40 89 G5
Warbreck Cl BOLE BL2 50 C2
Warbreck Dr URM M41 138 C2
Warbreck Gv SALE M33 155 E3
Warburton Bridge Rd
GOL/RIS/CUL WA3 150 A5
Warburton Cl
HALE/TIMP WA15 189 E1
MPL/ROM SK6 161 H5
Warburton Dr
HALE/TIMP WA15 189 E1
Warburton La PART M31 151 E3
Warburton Rd WILM/AE SK9 192 A3
Warburton St BOL BL1 34 A4
DID/WITH M20 157 G3
ECC M30 111 F4
ORD M5 127 E2
Warburton Wy
HALE/TIMP WA15 166 D2
Warcock Rd OLDE OL4 76 B5
Wardend Cl LHULT M38 * 81 F1
Warden St NEWH/MOS M40 104 A4
Warde St HULME M15 127 H2
Wardle Brook Av
HYDE SK14 135 E5
Wardle Cl RAD M26 51 H4
STRET M32 140 C1
Wardle Edge WHIT OL12 19 G5
Wardle Fold WHIT OL12 19 H1
Wardle Gdns WHIT OL12 19 H5
Wardle Rd SALE M33 154 C3
WHIT OL12 19 H3
Wardle St BOLE BL2 49 G4
LIT OL15 20 D2
NEWH/MOS M40 115 H2
OLDE OL4 92 A1
Wardley Av CCHDY M21 142 A3
WALK M28 81 G5
Wardley Hall La WALK M28 97 H2
Wardley Hall Rd WALK M28 98 A1
Wardley St SWIN M27 99 E2
Wardlow St BOLS/LL BL3 48 A5
Ward Rd DID/WITH M20 157 G3
DROY M43 118 A4
Wardsend Wk HULME M15 * 127 G2
Ward St BKLY M9 87 H5
CHAD OL9 8 A3
FAIL M35 104 D2
HYDE SK14 148 A1
MPL/ROM SK6 161 G3
NEWH/MOS M40 103 G2
OLD OL1 75 E4
STKP SK1 13 J7
Wareham Gv ECC M30 110 D2
Wareham St CHH M8 * 102 C1
Wareings Yd ROCH OL11 43 F2
Wareing Wy BOLS/LL BL3 2 C6
Warford Av POY/DIS SK12 195 H5
Warford St ANC M4 115 E1
Warham St WILM/AE SK9 199 E3
The Warke WALK M28 97 G4
Warley Cl CHD/CHDH SK8 170 B3
Warley Gv DUK SK16 119 H5
Warley Rd OLDTF/WHR M16 126 D5
Warley St LIT OL15 21 E2
Warlingham Cl
TOT/BURYW BL8 37 G5
Warlow Crest UPML OL3 94 D3
Warlow Dr UPML OL3 94 D3
Warmington Dr
WGTN/LGST M12 129 F2
Warmley Rd NTHM/RTH M23 167 E1
Warne Av DROY M43 118 B3
Warnford Cl NEWH/MOS M40 117 E1
War Office Rd ROCH OL11 28 B5
Warren Av CHD/CHDH SK8 170 A4
Warren Bank BKLY M9 87 H4
Warren Bruce Rd TRPK M17 126 A2
Warren Cl BRAM/HZG SK7 183 G2
DTN/ASHW M34 146 B1
POY/DIS SK12 194 C3
Warren Dr HALE/TIMP WA15 179 E5
SWIN M27 98 C5
Warrener St SALE M33 155 E3
Warren Hey WILM/AE SK9 199 H2
Warren La OLDS OL8 92 A3
Warren Lea MPL/ROM SK6 163 G4
POY/DIS SK12 195 F2
Warren Rd CHD/CHDH SK8 182 D2
EDGY/DAV SK3 171 H3
TRPK M17 125 G2
WALK M28 82 B4
Warren St BKLY M9 87 H5
BRO M7 102 A2
STKP SK1 13 G2
TOT/BURYW BL8 37 G5
Warre St AUL OL6 119 G2
Warrington Rd BKLY M9 87 H3
Warrington St AUL OL6 119 G3
OLDE OL4 92 D2
STLY SK15 121 E4
Warsall Rd WYTH/NTH M22 168 D2
Warslow Dr SALE M33 155 F5
Warsop Av WYTH/NTH M22 168 D4
Warstead Wk
BRUN/LGST M13 * 128 D3
Warth Fold Rd RAD M26 52 D3
Warth Rd BURY BL9 52 D2
Warton Cl BRAM/HZG SK7 184 B5
TOT/BURYW BL8 37 E5
Warton Dr NTHM/RTH M23 167 H4
Warwick Av DID/WITH M20 157 E2
DTN/ASHW M34 146 D2
SWIN M27 83 G5
WHTF M45 70 A5
Warwick Cl CHD/CHDH SK8 170 D5
DUK SK16 133 F2
HTNM SK4 159 F2
MDTN M24 88 D2
ROY/SHW OL2 59 G2
TOT/BURYW BL8 26 B2
TOT/BURYW BL8 37 G2
WHTF M45 69 H5
Warwick Ct MDTN M24 * 72 D4
OLDTF/WHR M16 126 D5
Warwick Dr BRAM/HZG SK7 185 E4
HALE/TIMP WA15 177 H3
SALE M33 155 E2
URM M41 124 A4
Warwick Gdns BOLS/LL BL3 64 A2
Warwick Gv DTN/ASHW M34 118 B5
Warwick Rd AUL OL6 107 F5
CCHDY M21 141 F2
FAIL M35 105 E5
HALE/TIMP WA15 177 F3
HTNM SK4 159 F3
IRL M44 150 C1
MDTN M24 89 E2
MPL/ROM SK6 161 H4
OLDTF/WHR M16 126 D4
RAD M26 52 A3
STRET M32 126 C3
WALK M28 96 D1
Warwick Rd South
OLDTF/WHR M16 126 D5
Warwick St ANC M4 7 H3
BOL BL1 33 H2
CHAD OL9 8 A7
HULME M15 127 H2
PWCH M25 85 H3
SWIN M27 99 E1
WHIT OL12 11 G1
Wasdale Av BOLE BL2 35 G5
URM M41 124 A5
Wasdale Dr CHD/CHDH SK8 181 G1
MDTN M24 72 B2
Wasdale St ROCH OL11 42 B5
Wasdale Ter STLY SK15 120 D1
Wasdale Wk OLD OL1 9 J1
Washacre WHTN BL5 62 A5
Washacre Cl WHTN BL5 62 A5
Washbrook CHAD OL9 90 C3
Washbrook Av WALK M28 96 C1
Washbrook Dr STRET M32 139 H2
Wash Ford TOT/BURYW BL8 37 G2
Washford Dr NTHM/RTH M23 167 E1
Washington Cl
CHD/CHDH SK8 182 C4
Washington Ct BURY BL9 5 F2
Washington St BOLS/LL BL3 48 B3
CHAD OL9 8 B3
Wash La BURY BL9 5 H3
BURY BL9 5 K5
Wash Lane Ter BURY BL9 5 K4
Wash Ter TOT/BURYW BL8 37 G1
Washway Rd SALE M33 153 H5
Washwood Cl LHULT M38 * 81 G1
Wasnidge Wk HULME M15 * 128 A3
Wasp Av ROCH OL11 43 F3
Wasp Mill Dr WHIT OL12 19 H2
Wastdale Av BURY BL9 69 H1
Wastdale Rd NTHM/RTH M23 167 G5
Waste St OLD OL1 * 9 K2
Wastwater St OLD OL1 75 H3
Watchgate BRAM/HZG SK7 184 D2
Watchgate Cl MDTN M24 72 A1
Waterbridge WALK M28 97 H5
Watercroft ROCH OL11 28 A2
Waterdale Cl WALK M28 96 C5
Waterdale Dr WHTF M45 69 H4
Waterfield Cl BURY BL9 27 G4
Waterfield Wy FAIL M35 105 F4
Waterfold La BURY BL9 5 K7
Waterfoot Cottages
HYDE SK14 135 H4
Waterford Av DID/WITH M20 156 C3
MPL/ROM SK6 162 D4
Waterfront Quay SALQ M50 126 C1
Watergate DTN/ASHW M34 118 B5
Water Ga UPML OL3 79 E4
Watergate Dr WHTN BL5 64 B5
Watergate La WHTN BL5 64 B5
Water Grove Rd DUK SK16 134 A1
Waterhead OLDE OL4 76 D4
Waterhouse Cl WHIT OL12 19 H3
Waterhouse Rd GTN M18 130 D4
Waterhouse St WHIT OL12 10 C5
Waterhouse Wy RDSH SK5 145 E4
Water La DROY M43 117 F4
FWTH BL4 66 B5
MILN OL16 44 D1
RAD M26 68 A1
WILM/AE SK9 198 D3
Water Lane St RAD M26 68 A1
Waterloo Ct BURY BL9 * 53 F1
Waterloo Gdns AUL OL6 107 H5
Waterloo Pl STKP SK1 * 13 H4
Waterloo Rd AUL OL6 107 E5
BKLY M9 103 E1
BRAM/HZG SK7 184 A3
CHH M8 114 B1
MPL/ROM SK6 162 D4
POY/DIS SK12 195 H5
STKP SK1 13 H4
STLY SK15 120 D3
Waterloo St AUL OL6 120 A1
BOL BL1 3 F1
CHH M8 102 D2
CMANE M1 7 F6
OLD OL1 9 H4
TOT/BURYW BL8 4 A4
Watermans Cl BKLY M9 103 G2
Waterman Vw MILN OL16 11 J4
Watermead SALE M33 154 B5
Watermead Cl EDGY/DAV SK3 171 H5
Watermeetings La
MPL/ROM SK6 162 D4
Watermill Cl MILN OL16 31 E5
Water Mill Clough
ROY/SHW OL2 74 D2
Watermill Ct AULW OL7 106 D5
Watermillock Gdns BOL BL1 34 A3
Waterpark Rd BRO M7 101 H2
Waters Edge AUL OL6 107 H5
FWTH BL4 65 F2
MPL/ROM SK6 175 F1
WALK M28 82 C5
Watersedge Cl
CHD/CHDH SK8 183 E1
Waters Edge Fold OLD OL1 60 B5
Watersfield Cl CHD/CHDH SK8 182 C4
Watersheddings St OLDE OL4 76 C3
Waterside HYDE SK14 149 F1
MPL/ROM SK6 175 E5
SALE M33 154 D1
TRPK M17 126 C2
UPML OL3 95 F3
Waterside Av MPL/ROM SK6 175 E4
Waterside Cl CCHDY M21 156 C2
HYDE SK14 149 F1
OLD OL1 60 B5
RAD M26 53 E5
Waterside Ct URM M41 * 137 F1
Waterside La MILN OL16 11 H5
Waterside Rd BURY BL9 26 D1
Waterside Vw DROY M43 117 F5
Waterslea ECC M30 110 D3
Waterslea Dr BOL BL1 47 G2
Watersmead Cl BOL BL1 34 A4
Watersmead St BOL BL1 34 A4
Watersmeet STRET M32 125 H4
Waters Meeting Rd BOL BL1 34 A3
Water's Nook Rd WHTN BL5 62 B4
Waterson Av NEWH/MOS M40 103 H3
Waters Reach MOSL OL5 94 B3
POY/DIS SK12 195 G3
TRPK M17 126 C2
Water Sreet RAD M26 68 B1
Water St AUL OL6 119 G2
BKLY M9 103 E2
BOL BL1 3 F4
CSLFD M3 6 A7
DTN/ASHW M34 132 C1
EDGW/EG BL7 22 C1
HYDE SK14 133 G5
MDTN M24 72 C4
MILN OL16 10 D6
ROY/SHW OL2 59 H5
STKP SK1 160 B3
STLY SK15 * 120 D3
WHIT OL12 14 A5
Waterton Av MOSL OL5 93 G5
Waterton La MOSL OL5 93 G5
Waterview Cl MILN OL16 45 E3
Waterworks Rd OLDE OL4 76 D3
Watford Av RUSH/FAL M14 142 D1
Watkin Cl BRUN/LGST M13 128 C2
Watkins Dr PWCH M25 86 D4
Watkin St CSLFD M3 * 114 A2
HYDE SK14 134 B3
Watling St LIT OL15 20 C3
TOT/BURYW BL8 24 C1
TOT/BURYW BL8 52 A1
Watlington Cl OLD OL1 76 C1
Watson Gdns WHIT OL12 18 C5
Watson Rd FWTH BL4 65 E4
Watson Sq STKP SK1 13 H4
Watson St CSLFD M3 6 D7
DTN/ASHW M34 133 E5
ECC M30 110 D3
OLDE OL4 76 B4
RAD M26 52 B5
SWIN M27 99 E1
Watton Cl SWIN M27 * 84 A5
Watts St BNG/LEV M19 144 B3
CHAD OL9 74 C5
OLDS OL8 91 E5
WHIT OL12 10 D4
Waugh Av FAIL M35 105 E4
Wavell Dr BURY BL9 69 H3
Wavell Rd WYTH/NTH M22 180 C2
Waveney Dr ALT WA14 165 F3
WILM/AE SK9 192 A5
Waveney Rd ROY/SHW OL2 59 H1
WYTH/NTH M22 168 D5
Waverley WHIT OL12 10 B4
Waverley Av FWTH BL4 82 C1
STRET M32 126 B5
Waverley Crs DROY M43 117 H2
Waverley Dr CHD/CHDH SK8 193 E1
Waverley Rd BKLY M9 103 G3
BOL BL1 33 H3
EDGY/DAV SK3 12 B7
HYDE SK14 147 H3
MDTN M24 72 D1
SALE M33 140 A5
SWIN M27 99 H3
WALK M28 96 C1
Waverley Rd West BKLY M9 103 G4
Waverley St OLD OL1 76 A4
ROCH OL11 42 B5
Waverton Av HTNM SK4 144 D4
Waverton Rd RUSH/FAL M14 142 C2
Wavertree Rd BKLY M9 87 H3
Wayfarers Wy SWIN M27 98 D3
Wayfaring WHTN BL5 62 A2
Wayland Rd GTN M18 130 C5
Wayland Rd South GTN M18 130 C5
Wayne Cl DROY M43 118 B1
Wayne St OP/CLY M11 117 F5
Wayside Dr POY/DIS SK12 194 D3
Wayside Gdns BRAM/HZG SK7 185 H2
Wayside Gv WALK M28 82 B3
Weald Cl BRUN/LGST M13 128 D2
Wealdstone Gv BOLE BL2 * 34 C4
Weardale Rd BKLY M9 87 G2
Weaste Av LHULT M38 81 G3
Weaste Dr ORD M5 112 C2
Weaste La ORD M5 112 C2
Weaste Rd ORD M5 112 C4
Weatherall St North BRO M7 102 A3
Weatherley Cl OLDS OL8 106 C1
Weatherley Dr MPL/ROM SK6 174 C3
Weaver Av WALK M28 81 F5
Weaver Cl ALT WA14 177 F3
Weaver Ct HULME M15 * 127 G2
Weaver Dr BURY BL9 27 G3
Weaverham Cl
BRUN/LGST M13 129 G5
Weavers Ct BOLS/LL BL3 48 D4
MDTN M24 72 C3
Weavers Gn FWTH BL4 66 A5
Weavers La BRAM/HZG SK7 193 G1
Weavers Rd MDTN M24 72 C3
Webb Gv HYDE SK14 149 G2
Webb La STKP SK1 13 K4
Webb St TOT/BURYW BL8 4 A3
Webdale Dr NEWH/MOS M40 103 H3
Weber Dr BOLS/LL BL3 48 C4
Webster Gv PWCH M25 85 G5
Webster St BOLS/LL BL3 49 G4
MOSL OL5 93 H5
OLDS OL8 9 G6
Wedgewood St
NEWH/MOS M40 116 A1
Wedgwood Rd SWIN M27 84 D5
Wedhurst St OLDE OL4 76 B5
Weedall Av ORD M5 126 D2
Weedon St MILN OL16 11 G5
Weeton Av BOLE BL2 50 C2
Weighbridge Ct IRL M44 122 C5
Weir Rd MILN OL16 31 F4
Weir St FAIL M35 104 D3
Welbeck Av CHAD OL9 89 G4
LIT OL15 20 D2
URM M41 124 D5
Welbeck Cl MILN OL16 31 F5
WHTF M45 69 G2
Welbeck Gv BRO M7 101 H3
Welbeck Rd BOL BL1 47 H1
ECC M30 111 F1
HYDE SK14 148 B1
MILN OL16 43 G2
RDSH SK5 145 F3
WALK M28 98 A4
Welbeck St GTN M18 130 C2
Welbeck St South AUL OL6 119 F3
Welburn Av WYTH/NTH M22 180 D1
Welburn St ROCH OL11 43 E1
Welbury Rd NTHM/RTH M23 155 G5
Welby St BRUN/LGST M13 129 E4
Welch Rd HYDE SK14 134 A4
Welcomb Cl MPL/ROM SK6 161 G2
Welcomb St OP/CLY M11 130 A1
Welcome Pde OLDS OL8 92 C4
Welcroft St STKP SK1 13 H5
Weldon Av BOLS/LL BL3 63 H2
Weldon Crs EDGY/DAV SK3 171 H5
Weldon Dr BKLY M9 88 A2
Weldon Rd ALT WA14 165 F3
Weld Rd DID/WITH M20 143 F4
Welford Cl WILM/AE SK9 199 H2

Welford Gn RDSH SK5 160 A1
Welford Rd CHH M8 87 E3
Welford St SLFD M6 113 G1
Welkin Rd MPL/ROM SK6 160 D3
Wellacre Av URM M41 137 F1
Welland Av HEY OL10 40 A3
Welland Cl HULME M15 * 127 G2
Welland Ct HULME M15 127 G2
Welland Rd ROY/SHW OL2 59 H1
WILM/AE SK9 192 A5
Welland St OP/CLY M11 117 E5
RDSH SK5 145 F2
Wellbank PWCH M25 * 85 G4
STLY SK15 121 F5
Wellbank Av AUL OL6 107 H4
Wellbank Cl BOLS/LL BL3 67 E1
OLDS OL8 91 H3
Wellbank St TOT/BURYW BL8 26 A5
Wellbank Vw WHIT OL12 28 C2
Wellbrow Ter WHIT OL12 29 G2
Wellens Wy MDTN M24 71 H5
Weller Av CCHDY M21 141 H4
POY/DIS SK12 195 E5
Weller Cl POY/DIS SK12 195 E5
Wellesbourne Dr
NTHM/RTH M23 167 G2
Wellesley Av GTN M18 130 C2
Wellfield Cl BURY BL9 53 F3
Wellfield La HALE/TIMP WA15 166 D5
Wellfield Pl ROCH OL11 43 F1
Wellfield Rd BOLS/LL BL3 48 B4
CHH M8 102 B2
NTHM/RTH M23 167 H2
OFTN SK2 172 D3
Wellfield St ROCH OL11 43 F1
Wellgate Av BNG/LEV M19 144 B3
Wellgreen Cl
HALE/TIMP WA15 178 D1
Well Green Ldg
HALE/TIMP WA15 * 178 D1
Well Gv WHTF M45 69 F1
Wellhead Cl HULME M15 128 A3
Wellhouse Dr NEWH/MOS M40 89 F4
Well-i-hole Rd UPML OL3 94 C3
Welling Rd NEWH/MOS M40 104 D2
Welling St BOLE BL2 3 J1
Wellington Av
OLDTF/WHR M16 141 H1
Wellington Cl SALE M33 140 A5
Wellington Clough AULW OL7 106 C4
Wellington Ct OLDS OL8 * 91 E3
Wellington Crs
OLDTF/WHR M16 127 F5
Wellington Gv HULME M15 127 G2
OFTN SK2 172 A2
Wellington Pl ALT WA14 177 G1
MILN OL16 11 F5
Wellington Rd AUL OL6 119 G2
BRAM/HZG SK7 186 A4
BURY BL9 4 E7
BURY BL9 53 F1
CHH M8 102 C2
ECC M30 111 F3
HALE/TIMP WA15 166 A3
OLDS OL8 90 D3
OLDTF/WHR M16 142 A1
RUSH/FAL M14 143 E4
SWIN M27 99 E2
UPML OL3 94 D1
Wellington Rd North
BNG/LEV M19 144 B4
Wellington Rd South
OFTN SK2 13 G7
Wellington Sq TOT/BURYW BL8 37 G5
Wellington St AUL OL6 119 G3
BOLS/LL BL3 2 B6
BRAM/HZG SK7 185 G1
CHAD OL9 74 C4
CSLFD M3 6 A2
DTN/ASHW M34 132 C2
FAIL M35 * 105 F1
FWTH BL4 66 A4
GTN M18 130 C3
HYDE SK14 133 F5
LIT OL15 21 E3
MILN OL16 31 H5
OLD OL1 9 H4
RAD M26 52 D5
STKP SK1 13 G4
STRET M32 140 A2
TOT/BURYW BL8 4 A6
WHIT OL12 10 D3
Wellington St East BRO M7 101 G3
Wellington St West BRO M7 101 G4
Wellington Ter ORD M5 112 C3
Wellington Vls
TOT/BURYW BL8 37 H5
Wellington Wk BOLS/LL BL3 2 C6
Well I' Th' La ROCH OL11 43 F1
Well La WHTF M45 69 G2
Well Md MPL/ROM SK6 161 F3
Wellmead Cl CHH M8 102 A5
Well Meadow HYDE SK14 133 G4
Well Meadow La UPML OL3 79 F4
Wells Av CHAD OL9 74 B3
PWCH M25 86 B5
Wells Cl CHD/CHDH SK8 181 H5
DROY M43 117 G5
MDTN M24 71 H5
Wells Ct DUK SK16 133 F2
Wells Dr DUK SK16 133 F2
HTNM SK4 158 B4
Wells Rd OLD OL1 60 D4
Wells St BURY BL9 4 C7
Wellstock La LHULT M38 81 E1
Well St BOL BL1 3 F4
BOLE BL2 36 B5
HEY OL10 41 F5
ROCH OL11 43 F1
Well St West RAMS BL0 16 C3
Wellwood Dr NEWH/MOS M40 103 H3
Wellyhole St OLDE OL4 92 C1
Welman Wy HALE/TIMP WA15 166 A5
Welney Rd OLDTF/WHR M16 127 E5
Welshpool Cl NTHM/RTH M23 156 A4
Weltdown Gdns ROY/SHW OL2 59 G1
Welton Av DID/WITH M20 157 H4
Welton Cl WILM/AE SK9 200 C1
Welton Dr WILM/AE SK9 200 B1
Welton Gv WILM/AE SK9 200 B1
Welwyn Cl URM M41 124 B3
Welwyn Dr SLFD M6 99 F5
Welwyn Wk NEWH/MOS M40 115 G3
Wembley Cl EDGY/DAV SK3 171 G4
Wembley Gv RUSH/FAL M14 143 E3
Wembley Rd GTN M18 130 B5
Wembury St BKLY M9 * 103 F3
Wembury St North BKLY M9 103 F2
Wemsley Gv BOLE BL2 34 C5
Wem St CHAD OL9 90 B3
Wemyss Av RDSH SK5 145 F2
Wendlebury Gn ROY/SHW OL2 59 H4
Wendon Rd NTHM/RTH M23 168 A4
Wendover Dr BOLS/LL BL3 47 F4
Wendover Rd NTHM/RTH M23 166 D2
URM M41 138 C2
Wenfield Dr BKLY M9 88 D4
Wenlock Av AULW OL7 107 E5
Wenlock Cl OFTN SK2 173 H3
Wenlock Rd SALE M33 154 B4
Wenlock St SWIN M27 98 C2
Wenlock Wy WGTN/LGST M12 129 H2
Wenning Cl WHTF M45 70 B3
Wensleydale Av
CHD/CHDH SK8 169 H3
Wensleydale Cl BURY BL9 69 H1
NTHM/RTH M23 179 G1
ROY/SHW OL2 58 D4
Wensley Dr BRAM/HZG SK7 185 E5
DID/WITH M20 157 G1
Wensley Rd BRO M7 100 D1
CHD/CHDH SK8 169 H3
RDSH SK5 160 A2
Wensley Wy MILN OL16 30 C5
Wentbridge Rd BOL BL1 2 B3
Wentworth Av FWTH BL4 65 H5
GTN M18 130 D3
HALE/TIMP WA15 166 B3
HEY OL10 56 A1
IRL M44 * 122 B5
SLFD M6 112 B2
TOT/BURYW BL8 37 G2
WHTF M45 69 E5
Wentworth Cl MDTN M24 72 B4
MPL/ROM SK6 175 E1
RAD M26 51 G5
Wentworth Dr
BRAM/HZG SK7 184 B5
SALE M33 154 A1
Wentworth Rd ECC M30 111 G1
RDSH SK5 145 F2
SWIN M27 98 C4
Wenworth Av URM M41 138 B2
Werneth Av HYDE SK14 148 B3
RUSH/FAL M14 142 D1
Werneth Cl BRAM/HZG SK7 * 173 F5
DTN/ASHW M34 146 D1
Werneth Crs OLDS OL8 90 D3
Werneth Hall Rd OLDS OL8 8 C7
Werneth Hollow
MPL/ROM SK6 147 F5
Werneth Low Rd HYDE SK14 148 D4
MPL/ROM SK6 162 C2
Werneth Ri HYDE SK14 148 B4
Werneth Rd HYDE SK14 148 B1
MPL/ROM SK6 162 B1
Werneth St DTN/ASHW M34 132 C3
STKP SK1 160 C3
Wesley Cl WHIT OL12 30 C1
Wesley Ct WALK M28 * 82 A3
Wesley Dr AUL OL6 107 G4
WALK M28 97 G2
Wesley Gn ORD M5 113 G5
Wesley Ms BOLE BL2 * 3 J5
Wesley Sq URM M41 138 A1
The Wesleys FWTH BL4 65 E4
Wesley St BOLS/LL BL3 * 48 D4
BRAM/HZG SK7 185 F1
ECC M30 110 D3
EDGW/EG BL7 23 F3
FAIL M35 105 F1
FWTH BL4 66 B5
HEY OL10 40 D4
MILN OL16 31 F5
OP/CLY M11 116 B5
ROY/SHW OL2 75 F1
STKP SK1 13 H4
STRET M32 126 B5
SWIN M27 99 E2
TOT/BURYW BL8 25 H4
WHIT OL12 * 19 G5
Wessenden Bank East
OFTN SK2 173 E4
Wessenden Bank West
OFTN SK2 173 E4
Wessex Park Cl ROY/SHW OL2 60 A1
Westage Gdns
NTHM/RTH M23 167 H2
West Ashton St SALQ M50 113 E5
West Av ALT WA14 164 D4
BNG/LEV M19 143 H4
CHD/CHDH SK8 181 H3
FWTH BL4 65 G4
GTN M18 * 130 D3
NEWH/MOS M40 104 C1
STLY SK15 120 D3
WALK M28 81 H4
WHTF M45 69 F2
West Bank OP/CLY M11 131 F1
WILM/AE SK9 200 D5
Westbank Rd DID/WITH M20 158 B1
HOR/BR BL6 47 E3
West Bank St ORD M5 113 H5
Westbourne Av BOLS/LL BL3 65 F1
SWIN M27 83 G2
WHTF M45 69 E3
Westbourne Dr WILM/AE SK9 199 G2
Westbourne Gv BKLY M9 103 E2
DID/WITH M20 142 C5
RDSH SK5 145 F3
SALE M33 154 B2
Westbourne Pk URM M41 124 C5
Westbourne Range
GTN M18 131 E5
Westbourne Rd
DTN/ASHW M34 146 C1
ECC M30 110 C1
RUSH/FAL M14 143 F3
URM M41 138 D1
Westbourne St CHAD OL9 8 D3
Westbrook Cl BOLE BL2 3 G7
ROCH OL11 57 G1
Westbrook Ct BOLE BL2 * 3 G7
Westbrook Rd SWIN M27 98 D3
TRPK M17 125 H1
Westbrook Sq
WGTN/LGST M12 129 H2
Westbrook St BOLE BL2 3 H7
Westbury Av SALE M33 153 F5
Westbury Cl TOT/BURYW BL8 37 F5
WHTN BL5 62 B3
Westbury Dr MPL/ROM SK6 174 D4
Westbury Rd CHH M8 102 B1
Westbury St AUL OL6 119 H2
HYDE SK14 133 F3
Westbury Wy ROY/SHW OL2 75 E2
Westby Cl BRAM/HZG SK7 184 B5
Westby Gv BOLE BL2 3 K3
West Canteen Rd TRPK M17 125 H4
West Central Dr SWIN M27 99 G3
West Charles St ORD M5 113 G4
West Church St HEY OL10 40 D4
Westcliffe Rd BOL BL1 23 E5
Westcombe Dr
TOT/BURYW BL8 37 H2
Westcott Av DID/WITH M20 142 C5
Westcott Cl BOLE BL2 35 F1
Westcott Gv ROY/SHW OL2 59 H4
Westcourt Rd BOLS/LL BL3 64 C1
SALE M33 154 B1
Westcraig Av NEWH/MOS M40 89 F4
West Craven St ORD M5 127 E1
West Crs MDTN M24 72 C5
Westcroft Rd DID/WITH M20 158 A2
West Crown Av ORD M5 113 G5
Westdale Gdns BNG/LEV M19 158 D1
Westdean Crs BNG/LEV M19 158 C1
West Dean St ORD M5 113 H4
West Downs Rd
CHD/CHDH SK8 182 C1
West Dr BURY BL9 38 B1
CHD/CHDH SK8 169 F5
DROY M43 117 G4
SLFD M6 100 B4
SWIN M27 99 G3
West Duke St ORD M5 114 A4
West Egerton St ORD M5 113 G4
West End Av CHD/CHDH SK8 169 F3
West End St CHAD OL9 8 D3
Westend St FWTH BL4 65 G4
Westerdale OLDE OL4 92 B1
Westerdale Dr BOLS/LL BL3 47 H4
ROY/SHW OL2 58 D4
Westerham Av ORD M5 113 F4
Westerham Cl TOT/BURYW BL8 26 C4
Wester Hill Rd OLDS OL8 106 D1
Westerling Wy
OLDTF/WHR M16 127 H5
Western Access TRPK M17 * 111 G5
Western Av SWIN M27 85 E5
Western Cir BNG/LEV M19 143 H5
Western Rd URM M41 137 G2
Western St GTN M18 130 D2
SLFD M6 112 D2
Westerton Ct BOLS/LL BL3 48 C4
Westfield SLFD M6 112 D1
Westfield Av MDTN M24 72 D5
Westfield Cl ROCH OL11 28 C2
Westfield Dr MPL/ROM SK6 162 B1
Westfield Gv DTN/ASHW M34 132 B3
Westfield Rd BOLS/LL BL3 64 A2
CCHDY M21 141 F2
CHD/CHDH SK8 182 C4
DROY M43 117 F3
Westfields HALE/TIMP WA15 178 A4
Westfield St BRO M7 101 G1
CHAD OL9 74 D4
Westgate HALE/TIMP WA15 177 H2
SALE M33 154 B2
URM M41 138 B2
WHIT OL12 18 A1
WILM/AE SK9 198 D5
Westgate Av BKLY M9 * 87 H5
BOL BL1 48 B2
BURY BL9 4 C7
RAMS BL0 26 A1
Westgate Cl WHIT OL12 18 A1
Westgate Dr SWIN M27 99 E4
Westgate Rd SLFD M6 112 A1
Westgate St AULW OL7 119 F4
West Gn MDTN M24 71 G5
West Gv BRUN/LGST M13 129 E3
MOSL OL5 108 D2
SALE M33 154 C3
Westgrove Av BOL BL1 * 22 D5
West High St ORD M5 113 F3
West Hl ROCH OL11 * 29 H5
Westholm Av HTNM SK4 144 B4
Westholme Ct WILM/AE SK9 200 D3
Westholme Rd DID/WITH M20 157 G2
PWCH M25 70 B5
West Hope St ORD M5 113 G4
Westhulme Av OLD OL1 75 E3
Westhulme St OLD OL1 75 E3
Westhulme Wy OLD OL1 74 D3
Westinghouse Rd TRPK M17 125 H3
West King St CSLFD M3 6 B2
Westland Av BOL BL1 32 D5
FWTH BL4 81 H1
STKP SK1 * 160 C5
Westland Dr BKLY M9 88 A3
Westlands WHTF M45 85 G1
The Westlands SWIN M27 99 G4
West Lea DTN/ASHW M34 132 D5
Westlea Dr GTN M18 130 C5
Westleigh Dr PWCH M25 86 C4
Westleigh St BKLY M9 103 F1
West Malling Cl HEY OL10 56 C2
Westmarsh Cl BOL BL1 2 D1
West Marwood St BRO M7 101 H4
Westmead Dr
HALE/TIMP WA15 166 C2
West Meade BOLS/LL BL3 64 D2
CCHDY M21 141 E4
PWCH M25 * 86 C5
SWIN M27 98 D4
Westmeade Rd WALK M28 81 H2
West Meadow RDSH SK5 145 G2
Westmere Dr BKLY M9 102 D4
Westminister Cl ROY/SHW OL2 60 A1
Westminster Av AUL OL6 107 G3
FWTH BL4 65 H4
OLDTF/WHR M16 141 G1
RAD M26 51 G5
RDSH SK5 145 E4
ROY/SHW OL2 58 D3
WHTF M45 69 G4
Westminster Cl
MPL/ROM SK6 174 C2
SALE M33 153 G3
Westminster Dr
CHD/CHDH SK8 193 E1
WILM/AE SK9 200 C1
Westminster Rd BOL BL1 33 H1
ECC M30 111 F2
FAIL M35 105 G2
HALE/TIMP WA15 178 B1
URM M41 124 C4
WALK M28 82 A5
Westminster St
BNG/LEV M19 * 144 B2
BURY BL9 4 D7
FWTH BL4 65 H4
OLD OL1 76 A4
ROCH OL11 42 C1
SWIN M27 98 C1
Westminster Wy DUK SK16 133 G2
Westmoreland Cl ALT WA14 177 E4
BURY BL9 53 F3
Westmorland Av AULW OL7 119 G1
DUK SK16 120 B5
Westmorland Cl RDSH SK5 * 146 A5
Westmorland Dr RDSH SK5 145 H5
WHIT OL12 20 A2
Westmorland Rd
DID/WITH M20 157 F4
ECC M30 99 F5
PART M31 150 D4
SALE M33 154 D4
URM M41 138 C2
West Mosley St CMANW M2 7 F5
Westmount Cl
NEWH/MOS M40 102 D4
West Oak Pl CHD/CHDH SK8 * 182 C3
Weston Av MILN OL16 43 G2
NEWH/MOS M40 104 D1
SWIN M27 84 A3
URM M41 138 B2
Weston Dr CHD/CHDH SK8 171 G5
DTN/ASHW M34 132 D5
Weston Gv HTNM SK4 144 C5
WYTH/NTH M22 168 D1
Weston Rd IRL M44 136 C1
WILM/AE SK9 199 G4
Weston St BOLS/LL BL3 49 E5
MILN OL16 31 G5
NEWH/MOS M40 * 115 G3
OLDE OL4 92 B3
RDSH SK5 * 159 H2
Westover MPL/ROM SK6 173 H1
Westover Rd URM M41 124 B5
Westover St SWIN M27 98 D1
West Pk HYDE SK14 148 A4
West Park Av
DTN/ASHW M34 147 F1
POY/DIS SK12 194 B3
West Park Rd BRAM/HZG SK7 183 G2
STKP SK1 160 C4
West Park St ORD M5 127 E1
West Pl BNG/LEV M19 143 H4
Westray Crs ORD M5 * 112 D4
Westray Rd BRUN/LGST M13 143 G1
Westridge Cha
ROY/SHW OL2 59 E4
West Rd ALT WA14 177 F2
PWCH M25 85 G2
STRET M32 125 F4
West Rw PWCH M25 100 C1
West Starkey St HEY OL10 40 D3
West St AUL OL6 119 G2
BOL BL1 48 B2
CHAD OL9 8 C4
DUK SK16 119 G4
EDGY/DAV SK3 12 C4
FAIL M35 104 D3
FWTH BL4 66 B3
HEY OL10 41 E4
HYDE SK14 * 133 G3
LIT OL15 21 E3
MDTN M24 72 D2
MILN OL16 10 E4
MILN OL16 31 E4
OLD OL1 9 F3
OLDE OL4 92 D2
OP/CLY M11 116 C3
RAMS BL0 16 C3
STLY SK15 120 C3
WILM/AE SK9 200 D4
West Towers Ms
MPL/ROM SK6 175 F5
West Towers St SLFD M6 113 E4
West V RAD M26 52 B4
West Vale Rd
HALE/TIMP WA15 166 A4
West Vw LIT OL15 21 F3
WILM/AE SK9 * 198 B3
West View Gv WHTF M45 69 E3
West View Rd
WYTH/NTH M22 168 D1
Westville Gdns BNG/LEV M19 158 B1
West Wk EDGW/EG BL7 22 C1
Westward Ho MILN OL16 31 G5
Westward Rd WILM/AE SK9 198 C4
West Wy BOL BL1 34 C3
LHULT M38 81 F2
Westway BKLY M9 87 F1
DROY M43 131 F1
OLDE OL4 92 D2
ROY/SHW OL2 60 A3
Westwood Av BRO M7 101 H2
HALE/TIMP WA15 166 A2
HYDE SK14 134 C5
NEWH/MOS M40 * 104 D1
URM M41 139 F2
WALK M28 81 F5
Westwood Cl FWTH BL4 66 A4
Westwood Crs ECC M30 110 C1
Westwood Dr CHAD OL9 8 C3
SALE M33 154 C4
SWIN M27 99 H4
Westwood Rd BOL BL1 48 B1
CHD/CHDH SK8 181 G4
OFTN SK2 172 C5
STRET M32 139 H1
Westwood St RUSH/FAL M14 128 A4
Westwood Wy OLD OL1 75 E3
West Works Rd TRPK M17 125 H4
Westworth Cl BOL BL1 2 B2
Wetheral Dr BOLS/LL BL3 64 D1
Wetherall St BNG/LEV M19 144 B2
Wetherby Dr BRAM/HZG SK7 * 185 H2
ROY/SHW OL2 58 D4
Wetherby St OP/CLY M11 130 D1
Weybourne Av BKLY M9 88 D5
Weybourne Dr MPL/ROM SK6 161 G2
Weybourne Gv BOLE BL2 34 C2
Weybridge Rd ANC M4 115 F3
Weybrook Rd BNG/LEV M19 144 C4
Weycroft Cl BOLE BL2 50 D3
Weygates Dr
HALE/TIMP WA15 188 D1
Weyhill Rd NTHM/RTH M23 167 H5
Weylands Gv SLFD M6 99 G5
Weymouth Rd AUL OL6 107 H4
ECC M30 110 C2
Weymouth St BOL BL1 33 H4
Weythorne Dr BOL BL1 34 A2
BURY BL9 40 A1
Whalley Av BNG/LEV M19 144 B1
BOL BL1 32 C3
CCHDY M21 141 G4
LIT OL15 20 D2
OLDTF/WHR M16 127 G5
SALE M33 154 D1
URM M41 124 D5
Whalley Cl HALE/TIMP WA15 166 A1
MILN OL16 * 31 F5
WHTF M45 69 G3
Whalley Dr TOT/BURYW BL8 37 E4
Whalley Gdns WHIT OL12 29 E2
Whalley Gv AUL OL6 107 F3
OLDTF/WHR M16 141 H1
Whalley Rd HALE/TIMP WA15 178 B2
HEY OL10 40 B4
MDTN M24 72 C1
OFTN SK2 172 D2
OLDTF/WHR M16 127 G5
WHIT OL12 29 E2
WHTF M45 69 G3
Whalley St NEWH/MOS M40 115 G3
Wham Bar Dr HEY OL10 40 B4
Wham Bottom La WHIT OL12 18 C4
Wham St HEY OL10 40 C4
Wharf Cl CMANE M1 7 J5
Wharfedale WHTN BL5 62 A2
Wharfedale Av
NEWH/MOS M40 103 H1
Wharfedale Rd RDSH SK5 145 E3
Wharf End TRPK M17 126 D2
Wharf Rd ALT WA14 165 G2
SALE M33 154 D1
Wharfside Av ECC M30 111 E5
Wharf St CHAD OL9 90 C4
DUK SK16 119 H4
HTNM SK4 159 H3
Wharmton Ri OLDE OL4 94 A1
Wharmton Vw MOSL OL5 94 B4
UPML OL3 94 D1
Wharton Av CCHDY M21 141 H4
Wharton La LHULT M38 80 D2
Wharton Ldg ECC M30 111 F2
Wheat Cl BRUN/LGST M13 128 D3
Wheat Cft EDGY/DAV SK3 172 A4
Wheaters St BRO M7 * 113 H1
Wheaters Ter BRO M7 114 A1
Wheatfield STLY SK15 135 F1
Wheatfield Cl BURY BL9 27 G4
MPL/ROM SK6 161 H2
Wheatfield Crs ROY/SHW OL2 74 D1
Wheatfield St BOLE BL2 49 G4
Wheathill St MILN OL16 43 F2
Wheatley Rd SWIN M27 83 G5
Wheatley Wk
WGTN/LGST M12 129 G2
Wheeldale OLDE OL4 92 C1
Wheeldale Cl BOL BL1 33 H4
Wheelock Cl WILM/AE SK9 199 G1
Wheelton Cl TOT/BURYW BL8 37 F5
Wheelwright Cl
MPL/ROM SK6 175 E1
ROCH OL11 * 42 A2
Wheelwright Dr MILN OL16 19 H5
Whelan Av BURY BL9 53 F2
Whelan Cl BURY BL9 53 F2
Wheler St OP/CLY M11 117 E5
Whernside Av AUL OL6 107 F3
NEWH/MOS M40 103 H1
Whernside Cl HTNM SK4 13 F1
Whetstone Hill Cl OLD OL1 76 B2
Whetstone Hill La OLD OL1 76 B3
Whetstone Hill Rd OLD OL1 76 A2
Whewell Av RAD M26 53 E4
Whickham Cl RUSH/FAL M14 128 C5
Whiley St BRUN/LGST M13 129 G4
Whimberry Cl ORD M5 127 F1
Whimberry Dr STLY SK15 109 E5
Whimberry Wy
DID/WITH M20 143 F5
Whimbrel Rd OFTN SK2 173 H4
Whimbury Dr STLY SK15 121 H1
Whinberry Rd ALT WA14 165 E2
Whinberry Wy OLDE OL4 60 D5
Whinchat Cl OFTN SK2 173 H5
Whinfell Dr MDTN M24 71 G3
Whins Av FWTH BL4 64 D4
Whins Crest HOR/BR BL6 46 D2
Whinslee Dr HOR/BR BL6 46 D2
Whinstone Wy OLD OL1 73 H3
Whipp St HEY OL10 40 C3
Whirley Cl HTNM SK4 159 G1
Whiston Dr BOLE BL2 49 H3
Whiston Rd CHH M8 102 C2
Whitaker St MDTN M24 72 C4
Whitbrook Wy MDTN M24 57 F4
Whitburn Av BRUN/LGST M13 143 G1
Whitburn Cl BOLS/LL BL3 47 F5
Whitburn Dr
TOT/BURYW BL8 37 H1
Whitburn Rd
NTHM/RTH M23 167 H5

Whitby Av HEY OL10 40 D3
OLDTF/WHR M16 141 H1
RUSH/FAL M14 143 G3
SLFD M6 112 B2
URM M41 139 E1
Whitby Cl CHD/CHDH SK8 169 H3
POY/DIS SK12 194 D3
TOT/BURYW BL8 37 E4
Whitby Rd OLDS OL8 92 B4
RUSH/FAL M14 143 F3
Whitby St MDTN M24 73 F3
ROCH OL11 43 F1
Whitchurch Dr
OLDTF/WHR M16 127 G3
Whitchurch Gdns BOL BL1 33 H4
Whitchurch Rd
DID/WITH M20 142 B4
Whitchurch St BRO M7 114 B2
Whiteacre Rd AUL OL6 120 A1
Whiteacres SWIN M27 98 B3
White Bank Av RDSH SK5 160 D2
White Bank Rd OLDS OL8 106 A2
Whitebarn Rd WILM/AE SK9 201 E5
Whitebeam Cl
HALE/TIMP WA15 167 F4
MILN OL16 44 D3
SLFD M6 113 F2
Whitebeam Ct SLFD M6 * 113 F2
Whitebeam Wk WHTN BL5 62 A2
White Birk Cl TOT/BURYW BL8 26 A1
White Brook La UPML OL3 79 F4
Whitebrook Rd
RUSH/FAL M14 142 D2
Whitecar Av NEWH/MOS M40 104 D1
White Carr La BURY BL9 27 H2
Whitecarr La
HALE/TIMP WA15 179 F1
Whitechapel Cl BOLE BL2 50 B2
Whitechapel St
DID/WITH M20 157 G3
White City Wy
OLDTF/WHR M16 126 D3
Whitecliff Cl RUSH/FAL M14 128 D5
Whitecroft Av ROY/SHW OL2 62 C2
Whitecroft Dr TOT/BURYW BL8 37 E4
Whitecroft Gdns
BNG/LEV M19 158 B2
Whitecroft Rd BOL BL1 32 D5
MPL/ROM SK6 187 H2
Whitecroft St OLD OL1 76 B3
Whitefield HTNM SK4 159 G3
Whitefield Av ROCH OL11 28 C3
Whitefield Rd BURY BL9 53 F3
MPL/ROM SK6 161 F2
SALE M33 154 A1
Whitegate BOLS/LL BL3 62 D2
LIT OL15 20 B4
Whitegate Av CHAD OL9 90 A3
Whitegate Cl
NEWH/MOS M40 104 D1
Whitegate Dr BOL BL1 34 A1
ORD M5 112 C2
SWIN M27 84 C5
Whitegate La CHAD OL9 90 B3
Whitegate Pk URM M41 137 G1
Whitegate Rd CHAD OL9 89 G4
Whitegates Cl
HALE/TIMP WA15 166 C4
Whitegates La OLDE OL4 77 G2
Whitegates Rd
CHD/CHDH SK8 170 A4
MDTN M24 57 F5
Whitehall Cl WILM/AE SK9 198 D5
Whitehall La BOL BL1 22 C5
OLDE OL4 61 E5
Whitehall Rd DID/WITH M20 157 H3
SALE M33 154 C4
Whitehall St OLD OL1 9 H1
WHIT OL12 10 C3
White Hart Meadow
MDTN M24 72 D2
White Hart St HYDE SK14 133 G4
Whitehaven Gdns
DID/WITH M20 157 F4
Whitehaven Rd
BRAM/HZG SK7 193 F2
Whitehead Crs RAD M26 67 E5
TOT/BURYW BL8 37 H1
Whitehead Rd CCHDY M21 140 D3
SWIN M27 84 C5
Whitehead St
DTN/ASHW M34 132 C1
MILN OL16 * 31 F5
MILN OL16 45 G2
ROY/SHW OL2 59 G1
WALK M28 82 A3
White Hill Cl WHIT OL12 18 C4
Whitehill Dr
NEWH/MOS M40 103 H3
Whitehill St HTNM SK4 159 H2
RDSH SK5 160 A1
Whitehill St West HTNM SK4 159 G2
Whiteholme Av CCHDY M21 156 C2
White Horse Gdns SWIN M27 * 98 B4
White Horse Gv WHTN BL5 62 B2
White Horse Mdw MILN OL16 * 43 H4
Whitehouse Av OLDE OL4 92 B2
White House Av PWCH M25 86 D4
White House Cl HEY OL10 56 A2
Whitehouse Dr
HALE/TIMP WA15 178 C4
NTHM/RTH M23 167 H4
Whitehouse La ALT WA14 164 A2
Whitehurst Rd HTNM SK4 158 C2
Whitekirk Cl BRUN/LGST M13 128 C2
White Lady Cl WALK M28 81 E4
Whitelake Av URM M41 123 G5
Whitelake Vw URM M41 123 F5
Whiteland Av BOLS/LL BL3 48 A4
Whitelands DUK SK16 119 H3
Whitelands Rd AUL OL6 119 H3
Whitelea Dr EDGY/DAV SK3 171 G4
Whitelees Rd LIT OL15 20 D3
Whitelegge St
TOT/BURYW BL8 37 G2
Whiteley Dr MDTN M24 73 F5
Whiteley Pl ALT WA14 165 G3
Whiteley St CHAD OL9 90 C3
OP/CLY M11 116 C3
White Lion Brow BOL BL1 2 C5
Whitelow Rd BURY BL9 17 F3
CCHDY M21 141 E3
HTNM SK4 158 D3
Whitemoss WHIT OL12 * 29 E1
White Moss Av CCHDY M21 141 G3
White Moss Rd BKLY M9 88 B4
Whitemoss Rd East BKLY M9 88 C3
Whiteoak Cl MPL/ROM SK6 174 D2
Whiteoak Rd RUSH/FAL M14 143 E3
Whiteoak Vw BOLS/LL BL3 50 A4
Whites Cft SWIN M27 99 E2
Whiteside Cl ORD M5 112 C3
Whiteside Fold WHIT OL12 28 D2
Whitestone Cl HOR/BR BL6 47 E3
Whitestone Wk
BRUN/LGST M13 * 129 E3
White St HULME M15 127 G2
SLFD M6 112 D4
TOT/BURYW BL8 37 H5
White Swallows Rd SWIN M27 99 F4
Whitethorn Av BNG/LEV M19 144 A4
OLDTF/WHR M16 127 G5
Whitethorn Cl MPL/ROM SK6 174 D2
Whitewater Dr BRO M7 100 C3
Whiteway St BKLY M9 103 F3
Whitewell Cl BURY BL9 53 E2
MILN OL16 11 J4
Whitewillow Cl FAIL M35 105 F4
Whitfield Crs MILN OL16 45 E3
Whitfield Dr MILN OL16 44 B1
Whitfield Ri ROY/SHW OL2 44 D5
Whitfield St CSLFD M3 114 D2
Whiting Gv BOLS/LL BL3 47 F3
Whitland Av BOL BL1 47 G1
Whitland Dr OLDS OL8 90 C5
Whit La SLFD M6 100 D5
Whitley Gdns
HALE/TIMP WA15 166 D2
Whitley Pl HALE/TIMP WA15 166 C2
Whitley Rd HTNM SK4 159 E3
NEWH/MOS M40 115 F1
Whitley St BOLS/LL BL3 66 A2
Whitlow Av ALT WA14 165 E1
Whitman St BKLY M9 103 G2
Whitmore Rd RUSH/FAL M14 142 D2
Whitnall Cl OLDTF/WHR M16 127 H5
Whitnall St HYDE SK14 * 133 G3
Whitsand Rd WYTH/NTH M22 168 D4
Whitsbury Av GTN M18 130 C5
Whitstable Cl CHAD OL9 90 C1
Whitstable Rd
NEWH/MOS M40 * 104 B1
Whitsters Hollow BOL BL1 33 E3
Whitsundale WHTN BL5 62 A2
Whittaker Dr LIT OL15 31 G1
Whittaker Fold LIT OL15 * 21 H3
Whittaker La LIT OL15 21 G4
PWCH M25 86 B3
ROCH OL11 28 A2
Whittaker St AUL OL6 107 G5
CHAD OL9 74 C5
NEWH/MOS M40 103 H2
RAD M26 52 C5
ROCH OL11 * 28 B2
WGTN/LGST M12 115 G5
Whittingham Dr RAMS BL0 16 D5
Whittingham Gv OLD OL1 75 E4
Whittington St AULW OL7 119 F4
Whittlebrook Gv HEY OL10 56 B2
Whittle Dr ROY/SHW OL2 60 C1
WALK M28 82 A2
Whittle Gv BOL BL1 33 E5
WALK M28 82 B4
Whittle La HEY OL10 55 F4
Whittles Av DTN/ASHW M34 132 D5
Whittle's Cft CMANE M1 * 7 J5
Whittles St WHIT OL12 14 C1
Whittle St ANC M4 * 7 H3
LIT OL15 20 C3
SWIN M27 98 D3
TOT/BURYW BL8 * 37 H3
WALK M28 82 B4
Whitwell Wy GTN M18 130 B3
Whitworth Cl AUL OL6 119 H1
Whitworth La RUSH/FAL M14 143 F2
Whitworth Rake WHIT OL12 14 C5
Whitworth Rd WHIT OL12 10 C1
Whitworth Sq WHIT OL12 14 C5
Whitworth St CMANE M1 7 H6
MILN OL16 * 30 D1
MILN OL16 31 G5
OP/CLY M11 130 A1
Whitworth St East
OP/CLY M11 130 B1
Whitworth St West CMANE M1 6 E7
Whixhall Av WGTN/LGST M12 129 F2
Whoolden St FWTH BL4 65 H3
Whowell Fold BOL BL1 33 F3
Whowell St BOLS/LL BL3 2 C7
Wibbersley Pk URM M41 * 137 H1
Wichbrook Rd WALK M28 81 E4
Wicheaves Crs WALK M28 81 E5
The Wicheries WALK M28 81 E4
Wicken Bank HEY OL10 56 B2
Wickenby Dr SALE M33 154 B2
Wicken St OFTN SK2 172 D2
Wickentree Holt WHIT OL12 28 D1
Wickentree La FAIL M35 105 F1
Wicker La HALE/TIMP WA15 178 C4
Wicket Gv SWIN M27 83 H3
Wickliffe Pl ROCH OL11 30 A5
Wickliffe St BOL BL1 2 D3
Wicklow Av EDGY/DAV SK3 171 E2
Wicklow Dr WYTH/NTH M22 180 D2
Wicklow Gv OLDS OL8 91 F4
Widcombe Dr BOLE BL2 50 C4
Widdop St CHAD OL9 8 C3
Widecombe Cl URM M41 * 124 A4
Widgeon Cl POY/DIS SK12 194 C3
RUSH/FAL M14 142 D3
Widgeon Rd ALT WA14 165 E2
Widnes St OP/CLY M11 * 130 B1
Wigan Rd BOLS/LL BL3 63 F1
Wiggins Wk RUSH/FAL M14 * 128 D5
Wigley St WGTN/LGST M12 129 F1
Wigmore Rd CHH M8 102 A3
Wigmore St AUL OL6 120 A1
Wigsby Av NEWH/MOS M40 104 B1
Wigwam Cl POY/DIS SK12 194 D3
Wike St TOT/BURYW BL8 4 A3
Wilbraham Rd CCHDY M21 141 F3
OLDTF/WHR M16 142 A2
RUSH/FAL M14 142 D2
WALK M28 82 A4
Wilburn St ORD M5 114 A5
Wilby Av BOLS/LL BL3 50 D4
Wilby Cl TOT/BURYW BL8 * 38 A1
Wilby St CHH M8 102 C4
Wilcock Cl OLDTF/WHR M16 127 H4
Wilcott Dr SALE M33 153 H1
WILM/AE SK9 200 C1
Wilcott Rd CHD/CHDH SK8 169 F4
Wildbank Cha STLY SK15 135 F1
Wildbrook Cl LHULT M38 80 D4
Wildbrook Crs OLDS OL8 91 H4
Wildbrook Gv LHULT M38 80 D4
Wildbrook Rd LHULT M38 80 D3
Wildbrook Ter OLDS OL8 * 91 H4
Wild Clough HYDE SK14 148 B2
Wildcroft Av NEWH/MOS M40 103 H1
Wilders Moor Cl WALK M28 96 D2
Wilderswood Cl
DID/WITH M20 157 H1
Wilde St DTN/ASHW M34 132 C5
Wildhouse La LIT OL15 31 G2
Wildman La FWTH BL4 65 E4
Wildmoor Av OLDE OL4 92 D4
Wild Moor Wood Cl STLY SK15 109 E5
Wilds Pl RAMS BL0 * 16 C3
Wild St BRAM/HZG SK7 * 185 E2
DUK SK16 120 A5
HEY OL10 41 F4
MPL/ROM SK6 161 G4
OLD OL1 9 K2
OLDE OL4 92 D1
RAD M26 53 E5
ROY/SHW OL2 60 B3
Wildwood Cl OFTN SK2 172 B4
RAMS BL0 16 B4
Wilford Av SALE M33 154 B4
Wilfred Dr BURY BL9 5 J1
Wilfred Rd ECC M30 110 B5
WALK M28 82 A5
Wilfred St BRO M7 114 B1
EDGW/EG BL7 * 23 F4
NEWH/MOS M40 103 H2
Wilfrid St SWIN M27 99 E2
Wilkes St OLD OL1 76 C1
Wilkin Cft CHD/CHDH SK8 182 B4
Wilkins La WILM/AE SK9 190 D2
Wilkinson Av BOLS/LL BL3 50 D5
Wilkinson Rd BOL BL1 33 G1
HTNM SK4 12 E1
Wilkinson St AUL OL6 119 F2
HTNM SK4 12 D1
MDTN M24 72 C4
SALE M33 155 E2
Wilks Av WYTH/NTH M22 181 E2
Willand Cl BOLE BL2 50 D3
Willand Dr BOLE BL2 50 D4
Willan Rd BKLY M9 87 H3
ECC M30 111 F3
Willard St BRAM/HZG SK7 * 185 E1
Willaston Cl CCHDY M21 141 E4
Willbutts La ROCH OL11 29 F3
Willdale Cl OP/CLY M11 116 B3
Willdor Gv EDGY/DAV SK3 171 E3
Willenhall Rd NTHM/RTH M23 156 B4
Willerby Rd BRO M7 101 H5
Willesden Av BRUN/LGST M13 129 F5
Will Griffith Wk OP/CLY M11 115 H5
William Chadwick Cl
NEWH/MOS M40 115 F2
William Cl URM M41 138 C2
William Greenwood Cl
HEY OL10 40 D4
William Henry St ROCH OL11 43 F2
William Jessop Ct CMANE M1 7 K5
William Kay Cl
OLDTF/WHR M16 127 H4
William Lister Cl
NEWH/MOS M40 * 117 E1
Williams Crs CHAD OL9 90 A4
Williamson Av MPL/ROM SK6 161 H2
RAD M26 52 A3
Williamson La DROY M43 118 A5
Williamson St ANC M4 115 E2
AUL OL6 119 G3
RDSH SK5 145 E4
Williams Rd GTN M18 130 B3
NEWH/MOS M40 104 A3
Williams St BOLS/LL BL3 67 E1
GTN M18 130 B4
William St AULW OL7 119 F4
CSLFD M3 6 B3
DID/WITH M20 157 G3
FAIL M35 105 F1
LIT OL15 20 D3
MDTN M24 73 E4
MILN OL16 20 A4
RAD M26 52 C5
ROCH OL11 30 A5
STKP SK1 172 C2
WGTN/LGST M12 115 G5
WHIT OL12 14 B4
Willingdon Cl TOT/BURYW BL8 26 D4
Willingdon Dr PWCH M25 86 A2
Willis Rd EDGY/DAV SK3 171 H3
Willis St BOLS/LL BL3 48 B5
Willock St BRO M7 101 H4
Willoughby Av DID/WITH M20 157 H2
Willoughby Cl SALE M33 154 B1
Willow Av CHD/CHDH SK8 182 C2
MDTN M24 73 F5
RDSH SK5 160 A2
URM M41 139 E1
Willow Bank CHD/CHDH SK8 192 D1
OLDE OL4 76 D4
RUSH/FAL M14 143 E3
Willowbank RAD M26 68 B4
Willowbank Av BOLE BL2 3 K7
Willow Bank Cl OFTN SK2 173 E2
Willowbrook Av
NEWH/MOS M40 103 H3
Willow Cl BOLS/LL BL3 48 A5
BURY BL9 70 A2
DUK SK16 134 A1
POY/DIS SK12 195 F4
Willow Ct MPL/ROM SK6 175 E4
SALE M33 155 F1
Willowdale Av
CHD/CHDH SK8 181 G2
Willowdene Cl EDGW/EG BL7 23 E3
NEWH/MOS M40 102 D5
Willow Dr BURY BL9 70 A2
SALE M33 153 H4
WILM/AE SK9 192 A4
Willowfield Rd OLDE OL4 76 C2
Willow Fold DROY M43 118 A5
Willow Gv CHAD OL9 * 74 C4
DTN/ASHW M34 132 B5
GTN M18 * 130 D4
MPL/ROM SK6 175 E4
Willow Hey EDGW/EG BL7 23 H5
Willow Hill Rd CHH M8 102 B1
Willow Lawn CHD/CHDH SK8 * 182 D2
Willowmead Wy WHIT OL12 28 D1
Willowmoss Cl WALK M28 97 F1
Willow Ri LIT OL15 20 C5
Willow Rd ECC M30 110 B1
MPL/ROM SK6 187 E5
PART M31 150 D4
PWCH M25 85 H1
UPML OL3 79 F5
Willows Dr FAIL M35 117 G1
Willows End STLY SK15 121 G2
Willows La BOLS/LL BL3 48 B5
MILN OL16 31 F4
Willows Rd ORD M5 * 112 C3
The Willows BOLS/LL BL3 50 D4
CCHDY M21 141 E4
MOSL OL5 109 F1
PART M31 151 E3
Willow St BURY BL9 5 K4
CHH M8 114 B1
HEY OL10 41 E4
OLD OL1 9 K2
OP/CLY M11 116 B4
SWIN M27 98 C5
WALK M28 98 B3
Willow Tree Ms
CHD/CHDH SK8 181 G3
Willow Tree Rd ALT WA14 177 G2
Willow Wy BRAM/HZG SK7 183 F5
DID/WITH M20 157 H3
Willow Wood Cl AUL OL6 120 B2
Wilma Av BKLY M9 87 H3
Wilmcote Cl HOR/BR BL6 47 E3
Wilmcote Rd
NEWH/MOS M40 115 F1
Wilmington Rd STRET M32 * 139 H1
Wilmot St BOL BL1 33 F3
Wilmott St HULME M15 128 B2
Wilmslow Av BOL BL1 33 H1
Wilmslow Old Rd
HALE/TIMP WA15 189 G1
Wilmslow Park Rd
WILM/AE SK9 199 G3
Wilmslow Rd CHD/CHDH SK8 170 A5
CHD/CHDH SK8 182 A1
CHD/CHDH SK8 182 A4
DID/WITH M20 157 H5
HALE/TIMP WA15 189 G2
RUSH/FAL M14 143 E1
WILM/AE SK9 192 A2
WILM/AE SK9 200 D3
Wilmur Av BRO M7 101 H4
WHTF M45 69 H5
Wilpshire Av WGTN/LGST M12 130 A5
Wilshaw Gv AULW OL7 107 E4
Wilshaw La AULW OL7 106 D5
Wilson Av HEY OL10 40 B4
SWIN M27 99 G1
Wilson Crs AUL OL6 120 B1
Wilson Rd BKLY M9 103 E1
HTNM SK4 159 E2
Wilsons Pk NEWH/MOS M40 * 103 F5
Wilson St BOLS/LL BL3 * 2 E6
BRUN/LGST M13 128 D2
BURY BL9 5 G6
FWTH BL4 66 B4
HYDE SK14 148 A1
OLDS OL8 91 F3
OP/CLY M11 116 B5
RAD M26 52 A5
STRET M32 126 B4
UPML OL3 94 D2
WHIT OL12 10 C4
Wilson Wy OLD OL1 9 G2
Wilsthorpe Cl BNG/LEV M19 144 C5
Wilton Av CHD/CHDH SK8 181 H5
OLDTF/WHR M16 126 D5
PWCH M25 86 C5
SWIN M27 99 H3
Wilton Ct GTN M18 131 F4
Wilton Crs WILM/AE SK9 200 C3
Wilton Dr BURY BL9 53 H4
HALE/TIMP WA15 178 D4
Wilton Gdns RAD M26 52 D4
Wilton Gv DTN/ASHW M34 131 F4
HEY OL10 41 E5
Wilton Paddock
DTN/ASHW M34 131 F4
Wilton Pl CSLFD M3 * 114 A3
Wilton Rd BOL BL1 33 H1
CCHDY M21 141 F3
CHH M8 87 F5
SLFD M6 112 A1
Wilton St BOL BL1 34 A3
CHAD OL9 90 C4
DTN/ASHW M34 132 B4
HEY OL10 40 D4
MDTN M24 71 G5
PWCH M25 86 B3
RDSH SK5 145 F1
WHTF M45 69 G5
Wilton Ter WHIT OL12 10 A4
Wiltshire Av RDSH SK5 160 D2
Wiltshire Cl BURY BL9 53 H1
Wiltshire Rd CHAD OL9 90 C2
FAIL M35 105 E4
PART M31 150 D4
Wiltshire St BRO M7 101 H4
Wimberry Cl UPML OL3 95 E2
Wimbledon Dr EDGY/DAV SK3 171 F3
ROCH OL11 42 C1
Wimbledon Rd FAIL M35 105 G2
Wimborne Av URM M41 124 C4
Wimborne Cl CHD/CHDH SK8 171 F5
Wimbourne Av CHAD OL9 74 B3
Wimpole St AUL OL6 119 H2
OLD OL1 75 H4
Wimpory St OP/CLY M11 130 C1
Winbolt St OFTN SK2 172 D5
Wincanton Av
NTHM/RTH M23 167 E1
Wincanton Dr BOL BL1 22 C4
Wincanton Pk OLDE OL4 92 C1
Wince Cl MDTN M24 89 F1
Wincham Cl HULME M15 127 G2
Wincham Rd SALE M33 153 H4
Winchester Av AUL OL6 107 G3
CHAD OL9 74 A3
DTN/ASHW M34 146 D2
HEY OL10 55 H1
PWCH M25 86 B5
Winchester Cl ROCH OL11 28 C4
TOT/BURYW BL8 26 D4
WILM/AE SK9 198 B5
Winchester Dr HTNM SK4 159 E4
SALE M33 153 G2
Winchester Pk DID/WITH M20 157 E3
Winchester Rd DUK SK16 134 B1
ECC M30 111 H1
HALE/TIMP WA15 178 D3
RAD M26 51 G4
SLFD M6 112 B1
URM M41 124 C5
Winchester Wy BOLE BL2 35 E5
Wincle Av POY/DIS SK12 195 G5
Wincombe St RUSH/FAL M14 142 D1
Windale WALK M28 81 G4
Windcroft Cl OP/CLY M11 116 A5
Winder Dr ANC M4 115 F4
Windermere Av BOLS/LL BL3 50 D5
DTN/ASHW M34 145 G1
SALE M33 155 E3
SWIN M27 99 F3
Windermere Cl OP/CLY M11 116 B5
PWCH M25 85 F2
STRET M32 125 H5
Windermere Crs AULW OL7 * 119 E1
Windermere Dr BURY BL9 53 F2
RAMS BL0 16 D1
WILM/AE SK9 200 C4
Windermere Rd DUK SK16 119 H5
FWTH BL4 64 D5
HYDE SK14 133 F3
MDTN M24 71 H2
MPL/ROM SK6 186 C3
ROY/SHW OL2 59 E3
STKP SK1 172 C2
STLY SK15 120 D2
URM M41 * 138 C2
WILM/AE SK9 191 H3
Windermere St BOL BL1 34 A3
Winder St BOL BL1 2 E2
Winders Wy SLFD M6 113 G1
Windfields Cl CHD/CHDH SK8 183 E1
Wind Gate Ri STLY SK15 109 E5
Windham St MILN OL16 19 H5
Windle Av CHH M8 87 E4
Windle Ct OFTN SK2 173 F4
Windlehurst Dr WALK M28 96 C3
Windlehurst Old Rd
MPL/ROM SK6 187 E2
Windlehurst Rd
MPL/ROM SK6 186 C4
Windley St BOLE BL2 3 H2
Windmill Av ORD M5 127 E1
Windmill Cl DTN/ASHW M34 145 H1
Windmill Ct MILN OL16 * 30 C5
Windmill La DTN/ASHW M34 145 G1
Windmill Rd SALE M33 155 G3
WALK M28 81 H2
Windmill St CMANW M2 6 D6
MILN OL16 30 C5
Windover Cl WHTN BL5 63 H5
Windover St BOLS/LL BL3 47 H5
Windrush Av RAMS BL0 26 B1
Windrush Dr BKLY M9 103 E3
WHTN BL5 62 A3
The Windrush WHIT OL12 18 B4
Windsor Av BOLS/LL BL3 66 D1
CHAD OL9 90 B3
CHD/CHDH SK8 169 E4
FAIL M35 105 G2
HEY OL10 40 C4
HTNM SK4 158 D3
IRL M44 122 C5
LHULT M38 81 G2
SALE M33 139 H5
SWIN M27 84 B5
URM M41 137 H1
WHTF M45 69 H5
WILM/AE SK9 198 C4
Windsor Cl POY/DIS SK12 195 E3
TOT/BURYW BL8 26 B2
Windsor Crs PWCH M25 86 D4
Windsor Dr ALT WA14 166 A1
ALT WA14 176 C3
AULW OL7 119 E1
DTN/ASHW M34 118 C4
DUK SK16 134 A1
MPL/ROM SK6 174 D4
STLY SK15 120 D2
TOT/BURYW BL8 52 C1
Windsor Gv AUL OL6 107 F3
BOL BL1 33 F5
CHD/CHDH SK8 182 C4
MPL/ROM SK6 162 D4
RAD M26 67 E5
Windsor Rd BKLY M9 103 F3
BNG/LEV M19 143 H2
BRAM/HZG SK7 185 G2
DROY M43 117 E3
DTN/ASHW M34 131 F5
EDGW/EG BL7 23 F4
HYDE SK14 147 H4
MPL/ROM SK6 160 D3
NEWH/MOS M40 117 F1
OLDS OL8 8 C6
PWCH M25 86 D4
Windsor St FAIL M35 105 F3
GTN M18 130 B4
NEWH/MOS M40 117 F1
OFTN SK2 172 B3
OLD OL1 75 H3
ORD M5 113 G4
ROCH OL11 43 F1

Windsor Ter *MILN* OL16 11 K6
MILN OL16 31 F5
Windybank *BKLY* M9 87 H2
Windy Harbour La
EDGW/EG BL7 23 G3
Windyhill Dr *BOLS/LL* BL3 63 H1
Winfell Dr *NEWH/MOS* M40 115 G2
Winfield Av *DID/WITH* M20 158 A1
Winfield Dr *GTN* M18 130 C2
Winfield Gv *MPL/ROM* SK6 163 G5
Winfield St *HYDE* SK14 148 B1
Winford St *BKLY* M9 103 F2
Wingate Av *TOT/BURYW* BL8 37 G4
Wingate Dr *DID/WITH* M20 157 H4
HALE/TIMP WA15 166 C4
WHTF M45 69 F3
Wingate Rd *HTNM* SK4 159 F2
LHULT M38 81 G3
Wingate St *ROCH* OL11 28 A2
Wingfield Av *WILM/AE* SK9 198 B4
Wingfield Dr *SWIN* M27 99 F4
WILM/AE SK9 198 B4
Wingfield St *STRET* M32 126 A4
Wings Gv *HEY* OL10 56 A2
Winifred Av *BURY* BL9 40 A2
Winifred Rd *DID/WITH* M20 157 G3
FWTH BL4 65 F3
NEWH/MOS M40 104 A3
OFTN SK2 172 B4
URM M41 124 B5
Winifred St *ECC* M30 110 C4
HYDE SK14 148 A4
RAMS BL0 16 C3
WHIT OL12 29 E2
Winmarith Dr
HALE/TIMP WA15 179 E5
Winmarleigh Cl
TOT/BURYW BL8 37 E5
Winnie St *NEWH/MOS* M40 103 H2
Winning Hill Cl *GTN* M18 130 C4
Winnington Gn *OFTN* SK2 173 E4
Winnington Rd
MPL/ROM SK6 175 E1
Winnipeg Quay *SALQ* M50 126 C1
The Winnows
DTN/ASHW M34 132 A5
Winscombe Dr
NEWH/MOS M40 115 F1
Winser St *CMANE* M1 7 F7
Winsfield Rd *BRAM/HZG* SK7 185 E4
Winsford Dr *ROCH* OL11 41 G1
Winsford Gv *BOLS/LL* BL3 47 H4
Winsford Rd *RUSH/FAL* M14 142 C2
Winskill Rd *IRL* M44 136 C3
Winslade Cl *BRAM/HZG* SK7 184 B2
OLDE OL4 76 C3
Winslade Ms *FWTH* BL4 66 A3
Winsley Rd *NTHM/RTH* M23 155 G4
Winslow Av *HYDE* SK14 149 H1
Winslow Pl *BNG/LEV* M19 143 H5
Winslow Rd *BOLS/LL* BL3 62 D2
Winslow St *OP/CLY* M11 116 B5
Winstanley Rd
NEWH/MOS M40 115 G2
SALE M33 154 D1
Winster Av *BRO* M7 101 E4
DID/WITH M20 156 D2
STRET M32 125 F5
Winster Cl *BOLE* BL2 35 G5
WHTF M45 70 A4
Winster Dr *BOLE* BL2 35 F5
MDTN M24 72 B2
Winster Gv *OFTN* SK2 172 B3
Winster Rd *ECC* M30 110 C5
Winston Av *BOLS/LL* BL3 67 F1
ROCH OL11 28 B5
Winston Cl *MPL/ROM* SK6 174 C2
RAD M26 51 H4
Winston Rd *BKLY* M9 103 G1
SALE M33 154 A1
Winswell Cl *OP/CLY* M11 116 C3
Winterbottom Gv *HYDE* SK14 149 H1
Winterbottom St *CHAD* OL9 8 D3
Winterburn Av *BOLE* BL2 23 G5
CCHDY M21 156 B2
Winterburn Gn *OFTN* SK2 173 F4
Winterdyne St *BKLY* M9 103 F3
Winterfield Dr *BOLS/LL* BL3 63 H1
Winterford Av
BRUN/LGST M13 129 E3
Winterford Rd *BRO* M7 102 A3
MOSL OL5 109 F1
Wintermans Rd *CCHDY* M21 141 H5
Winterslow Av
NTHM/RTH M23 155 E5
Winter St *BOL* BL1 33 G3
Winterton Cl *WHTN* BL5 62 B3
Winterton Rd *RDSH* SK5 145 G2
Winthrop Av *NEWH/MOS* M40 103 E5
Winton Av *DTN/ASHW* M34 132 A1
NEWH/MOS M40 104 C1
Winton Cl *BRAM/HZG* SK7 183 G3
Winton Gn *HOR/BR* BL6 46 A1
Winton Gv *BOLS/LL* BL3 47 F5
Winton Rd *ALT* WA14 177 F2
SLFD M6 100 A4
Winton St *AUL* OL6 119 G2
LIT OL15 21 E3
STLY SK15 121 E4
Winward St *BOLS/LL* BL3 * 47 H5
Winwood Dr *MDTN* M24 73 E2
Winwood Rd *DID/WITH* M20 169 H1
Wirral Cl *SWIN* M27 * 84 B5
Wirral Crs *EDGY/DAV* SK3 170 D1
Wisbech Dr *NTHM/RTH* M23 155 G5
Wisbeck Rd *BOLE* BL2 49 H1
Wiseley St *OP/CLY* M11 115 H5
Wiseman Ter *PWCH* M25 86 B3
Wishaw Sq *CCHDY* M21 142 A5
Wisley Cl *RDSH* SK5 145 F3
Wistaria Rd *GTN* M18 130 C3
Witham Av *WYTH/NTH* M22 168 D4
Witham Cl *HEY* OL10 40 B3
Witham St *AUL* OL6 120 B1
Withenfield Rd
NTHM/RTH M23 167 G1
Withens Gn *OFTN* SK2 173 F3
Withington Gn *MDTN* M24 56 D5
Withington Rd *CCHDY* M21 141 H3
OLDTF/WHR M16 127 G5
Withington St *HEY* OL10 * 56 B1
Withinlea Cl *WHTN* BL5 62 B2
Withins Av *RAD* M26 52 D4
Withins Cl *BOLE* BL2 50 B1
Withins Dr *BOLE* BL2 50 B1
Withins Gv *BOLE* BL2 50 B1
Withins Hall Rd *FAIL* M35 105 G4
Withins La *BOLE* BL2 50 B1
RAD M26 52 D4
Withins Rd *OLDS* OL8 90 C5
Withins St *RAD* M26 52 D5
Withnell Dr *TOT/BURYW* BL8 37 F5
Withnell Rd *BNG/LEV* M19 158 A3
Withycombe Pl *SLFD* M6 100 D5
Withy Gv *ANC* M4 7 F3
Withypool Dr *OFTN* SK2 172 D4
Withy Tree Gv
DTN/ASHW M34 * 147 E1
Witley Dr *SALE* M33 138 D5
Witley Rd *MILN* OL16 11 H7
Wittenbury Rd *HTNM* SK4 159 E4
Witterage Cl
WGTN/LGST M12 * 129 G2
Woburn Abbey *UPML* OL3 * 78 D3
Woburn Av *BOLE* BL2 34 D3
Woburn Cl *MILN* OL16 31 F5
Woburn Dr *BURY* BL9 53 G4
HALE/TIMP WA15 178 C2
Woburn Rd *OLDTF/WHR* M16 141 E1
Woburn St *OLDTF/WHR* M16 128 A5
Wodens Av *ORD* M5 127 F1
Woden St *ORD* M5 127 F1
Woking Back Gdns *BOL* BL1 33 H5
Woking Rd *CHD/CHDH* SK8 192 D1
Woking Ter *BOL* BL1 * 33 H5
Wolfenden St *BOL* BL1 33 H4
Wolfenden Ter *BOL* BL1 * 33 H4
Wolfreton Crs *SWIN* M27 84 B4
Wolseley Pl *DID/WITH* M20 157 G1
Wolseley Rd *SALE* M33 139 H5
Wolseley St *MILN* OL16 45 E2
TOT/BURYW BL8 37 G5
Wolsey Dr *ALT* WA14 176 D3
Wolsey St *HEY* OL10 40 D5
RAD M26 68 B1
Wolstenholme Av *BURY* BL9 27 G5
Wolstenvale Cl *MDTN* M24 73 E3
Wolver Cl *LHULT* M38 * 81 G1
Wolverton Av *OLDS* OL8 91 E4
Wolverton Dr *WILM/AE* SK9 199 F1
Wolvesey *ROCH* OL11 * 29 H5
Wolveton St *OP/CLY* M11 129 G1
Woodacre *OLDTF/WHR* M16 142 A2
Woodacres Ct *WILM/AE* SK9 198 C4
Woodall Cl *SALE* M33 155 E2
Woodark Cl *OLDE* OL4 93 E2
Woodbank *BOLE* BL2 35 E4
Woodbank Av *MPL/ROM* SK6 161 F3
STKP SK1 172 C1
Woodbank Ct *URM* M41 * 124 A5
Woodbank Dr *TOT/BURYW* BL8 37 H2
Wood Bank Rd *LIT* OL15 20 D5
Woodbine Av *IRL* M44 150 C2
Woodbine Crs *OFTN* SK2 172 A2
Woodbine Rd *BOLS/LL* BL3 64 B1
Woodbine St *MILN* OL16 43 F1
Woodbine St East *MILN* OL16 43 G1
Woodbourne Rd *HTNM* SK4 144 C5
SALE M33 154 B4
Woodbray Av *BNG/LEV* M19 158 B1
Woodbridge Av
DTN/ASHW M34 132 A1
Woodbridge Gdns *WHIT* OL12 29 F1
Woodbridge Gv
NTHM/RTH M23 155 H5
Woodbridge Rd *URM* M41 123 E5
Woodbrook Av *OLDE* OL4 77 G5
Wood Brook La *OLDE* OL4 77 G5
Wood Brook Rd *OLDE* OL4 77 G5
Woodbrook Rd *WILM/AE* SK9 201 E4
Woodburn Dr *BOL* BL1 33 E3
Woodburn Rd
WYTH/NTH M22 168 C1
Woodbury Crs *DUK* SK16 * 133 E1
Woodbury Rd *EDGY/DAV* SK3 171 E2
Woodchurch Wk *CHAD* OL9 * 90 C1
Woodcock Cl *DROY* M43 118 B2
ROCH OL11 28 C4
Woodcote Av *BRAM/HZG* SK7 183 F3
Woodcote Rd *ALT* WA14 153 G5
PART M31 152 D2
Wood Cottage Cl *WALK* M28 81 E4
Woodcott Bank *BOL* BL1 33 G2
Wood Crs *OLDE* OL4 92 D4
Woodcroft *OFTN* SK2 173 E3
Woodcroft Av *BNG/LEV* M19 158 B2
Woodeaton Cl *ROY/SHW* OL2 59 H5
Wooded Cl *BURY* BL9 38 C1
Wood Edge Cl *BOLS/LL* BL3 * 65 H1
Wood End *BRAM/HZG* SK7 183 G2
Woodend *ROY/SHW* OL2 45 F5
Woodend Dr *STLY* SK15 135 E2
Woodend La *HYDE* SK14 147 G2
STLY SK15 135 E1
WHIT OL12 20 A2
Woodend Rd *EDGY/DAV* SK3 172 A5
WYTH/NTH M22 168 C5
Woodend St *OLD* OL1 75 F3
OLDE OL4 93 E2
Woodfield *WYTH/NTH* M22 180 C1
Woodfield Av *HYDE* SK14 147 H3
MPL/ROM SK6 161 H2
WHIT OL12 10 A1
Woodfield Cl *OLDS* OL8 90 D3
Woodfield Ct *OFTN* SK2 * 172 B5
Woodfield Crs *MPL/ROM* SK6 161 G4
Woodfield Dr *WALK* M28 96 C4
Woodfield Gv *ECC* M30 110 D4
FWTH BL4 81 H1
SALE M33 139 G5
Woodfield Ms *HYDE* SK14 * 147 H3
Woodfield Rd *ALT* WA14 165 F3
CHD/CHDH SK8 183 E5
CHH M8 102 B1
MDTN M24 88 B1
SLFD M6 112 C1
Woodfield St *BOLS/LL* BL3 65 F1
Wood Fold *EDGW/EG* BL7 23 H5
Woodfold Av *BNG/LEV* M19 144 A1
Woodfold Rd *FAIL* M35 105 F2
Woodford Av *DTN/ASHW* M34 132 D4
ECC M30 110 C3
ROY/SHW OL2 60 C2
Woodford Dr *SWIN* M27 83 H5
Woodford Gdns
DID/WITH M20 157 F4
Woodford Gv *BOLS/LL* BL3 48 B5
Woodford Rd *BRAM/HZG* SK7 193 H2
POY/DIS SK12 194 C2
Woodgarth Av
NEWH/MOS M40 104 C5
Woodgarth Dr *SWIN* M27 98 D4
Woodgarth La *WALK* M28 97 G5
Woodgate Av *BURY* BL9 39 G2
ROCH OL11 28 D5
Woodgate Cl *MPL/ROM* SK6 161 G3
Woodgate Dr *PWCH* M25 86 B1
Woodgate Hill Rd *BURY* BL9 39 G2
Woodgate Rd
OLDTF/WHR M16 142 A2
Woodgate St *BOLS/LL* BL3 65 F1
Woodgrange Cl *SLFD* M6 112 D3
Woodgreen Dr *RAD* M26 68 B4
Wood Gv *DTN/ASHW* M34 132 C4
MPL/ROM SK6 161 H1
WHTF M45 69 F1
Woodhall Av *DID/WITH* M20 142 C4
WHTF M45 85 E1
Woodhall Cl *BOLE* BL2 34 D3
BRAM/HZG SK7 193 G4
TOT/BURYW BL8 * 38 A1
Woodhall Crs *RDSH* SK5 160 B2
Woodhall Rd *RDSH* SK5 160 B2
Woodhall St *FAIL* M35 105 E2
Woodhalt Rd *CHH* M8 102 B2
Woodham Rd
NTHM/RTH M23 155 G5
Woodham Wk *BOLS/LL* BL3 48 C4
Woodhead Cl *OLDE* OL4 76 D5
RAMS BL0 16 D4
Woodhead Dr
HALE/TIMP WA15 178 A3
Woodhead Rd
HALE/TIMP WA15 178 A3
Woodhead St
OLDTF/WHR M16 127 H4
Wood Hey Cl *RAD* M26 67 G1
Wood Hey Gv
DTN/ASHW M34 * 147 E1
WHIT OL12 19 E4
Woodhey Rd *RAMS* BL0 16 B5
Woodheys *HTNM* SK4 158 C3
Woodheys Dr *SALE* M33 153 G5
Woodheys Rd *LIT* OL15 31 H1
Woodhill Cl *MDTN* M24 72 C2
WGTN/LGST M12 130 A4
Woodhill Dr *PWCH* M25 86 A5
Woodhill Fold *TOT/BURYW* BL8 4 B2
Woodhill Gv *PWCH* M25 86 A4
Woodhill Rd *TOT/BURYW* BL8 4 B1
TOT/BURYW BL8 27 E5
TOT/BURYW BL8 38 B2
Woodhill St *TOT/BURYW* BL8 4 A1
Woodhill V *TOT/BURYW* BL8 4 A2
Woodhouse La *SALE* M33 153 E5
WYTH/NTH M22 180 C5
Woodhouse La East
HALE/TIMP WA15 154 C5
Woodhouse Rd *ROY/SHW* OL2 45 F5
URM M41 123 G4
WYTH/NTH M22 180 C4
Woodhouse St *GTN* M18 130 D3
Wooding Cl *PART* M31 151 F2
Woodlake Av *CCHDY* M21 156 B2
Woodland Av *BOLS/LL* BL3 65 G2
BRAM/HZG SK7 185 F3
GTN M18 130 D4
Woodland Crs *PWCH* M25 86 A5
Woodland Gv *EDGW/EG* BL7 22 C1
Woodland Pk *ROY/SHW* OL2 58 D5
Woodland Rd *BNG/LEV* M19 144 A3
GTN M18 130 D4
HEY OL10 41 F3
WHIT OL12 29 F1
Woodlands *FAIL* M35 117 F1
URM M41 124 B5
Woodlands Av *CHD/CHDH* SK8 182 B2
ECC M30 110 A5
IRL M44 122 B5
MPL/ROM SK6 161 H1
ROCH OL11 28 D4
STRET M32 126 A4
URM M41 137 E1
WALK M28 98 B4
WHTF M45 69 F3
Woodlands Cl *CHD/CHDH* SK8 182 D4
HYDE SK14 149 H2
STLY SK15 135 E1
WALK M28 97 F3
Woodlands Dr *MPL/ROM* SK6 162 A1
OFTN SK2 172 D1
SALE M33 154 D5
Woodlands Gv *HYDE* SK14 149 H2
TOT/BURYW BL8 37 G3
Woodlands La
HALE/TIMP WA15 165 H4
Woodlands Park Rd
OFTN SK2 173 E1
Woodlands Pkwy
HALE/TIMP WA15 165 H4
Woodlands Rd *ALT* WA14 165 H4
AUL OL6 107 H4
CHH M8 102 B2
HTNM SK4 158 A4
MILN OL16 44 B1
OLDTF/WHR M16 142 A2
POY/DIS SK12 197 F1
SALE M33 154 D2
STLY SK15 135 E1
WALK M28 97 G3
WILM/AE SK9 192 B4
WILM/AE SK9 198 B1
Woodlands St *CHH* M8 102 A2
The Woodlands *DROY* M43 * 117 F2
HEY OL10 56 B1
HOR/BR BL6 46 D1
TOT/BURYW BL8 38 A1
Woodland St *HEY* OL10 41 E4
WGTN/LGST M12 130 A3
WHIT OL12 30 B1
Woodlands Vw *MILN* OL16 11 J5
Woodland Vw *EDGW/EG* BL7 23 G3
HYDE SK14 134 A5
Woodland Wy *MDTN* M24 88 C1
Wood La *AULW* OL7 107 E5
HALE/TIMP WA15 166 B4
MDTN M24 73 E5
MPL/ROM SK6 174 C4
PART M31 150 D3
Woodlark Cl *CSLFD* M3 * 6 A4
Woodlawn Ct
OLDTF/WHR M16 127 F5
Woodlea *CHAD* OL9 73 G5
WALK M28 97 F2
Woodlea Av *BNG/LEV* M19 158 B1
Woodlea Cha *SWIN* M27 83 G2
Woodleigh Ct *TOT/BURYW* BL8 37 G1
Woodleigh Dr *DROY* M43 118 B1
Woodleigh Rd *OLDE* OL4 77 F5
Woodleigh St *BKLY* M9 103 G1
Woodley Av *RAD* M26 68 C3
Woodley Cl *OFTN* SK2 173 E2
Woodley St *BURY* BL9 53 G1
Woodman Dr *BURY* BL9 27 F5
Woodman St *STKP* SK1 13 F2
Woodmeadow Ct *MOSL* OL5 93 H5
Woodmere Dr *BKLY* M9 88 B4
Wood Mt *HALE/TIMP* WA15 166 C4
Woodmount Cl *MPL/ROM* SK6 162 D4
Woodnewton Cl *GTN* M18 130 B4
Woodpark Cl *OLDS* OL8 91 H4
Woodpecker Pl *WALK* M28 * 97 E2
Woodridge Dr *BOLE* BL2 34 C5
Wood Rd *HALE/TIMP* WA15 154 B5
OLDTF/WHR M16 127 F5
Wood Road La *BURY* BL9 26 D3
Wood Rd North
OLDTF/WHR M16 127 F5
Woodrow Wk
WGTN/LGST M12 129 G2
Woodrow Wy *IRL* M44 136 B3
Woodroyd Cl *BRAM/HZG* SK7 183 G3
Woodroyd Dr *BURY* BL9 39 F3
Woodruffe Gdns
MPL/ROM SK6 173 H1
Woods Ct *BOL* BL1 3 F4
Woodseaves Cl *IRL* M44 136 D2
Woodsend Cir *URM* M41 123 E5
Woodsend Crescent Rd
URM M41 123 E5
Woodsend Rd *URM* M41 123 F5
Woodsend Rd South
URM M41 137 G2
Woods Gv *CHD/CHDH* SK8 183 E5
Woodshaw Gv *WALK* M28 96 D2
Woodside *HTNM* SK4 158 C5
MILN OL16 45 F1
ROY/SHW OL2 60 C1
Woodside Av *BNG/LEV* M19 158 C1
WALK M28 82 C5
Woodside Cl *OLDE* OL4 92 D1
Woodside Dr *HYDE* SK14 148 A2
MPL/ROM SK6 186 D5
RAMS BL0 16 B3
SLFD M6 112 B2
Woodside La *POY/DIS* SK12 195 F3
Woodside Rd
OLDTF/WHR M16 141 F1
Woodside St *STLY* SK15 109 F4
Woods La *CHD/CHDH* SK8 183 E5
UPML OL3 78 D3
Woods Lea *BOL* BL1 47 G2
Woodsley Rd *BOL* BL1 32 C4
Woodsmoor La
EDGY/DAV SK3 172 B5
Woodsmoor Rd *SWIN* M27 98 C3
Wood Sq *DROY* M43 117 H5
UPML OL3 95 E1
Woods Rd *IRL* M44 136 B3
The Woods *ALT* WA14 165 H3
OLDE OL4 93 G1
ROCH OL11 42 B3
Woodstock Av
CHD/CHDH SK8 182 D5
RDSH SK5 160 A1
Woodstock Cl *HEY* OL10 41 F4
Woodstock Crs
MPL/ROM SK6 161 H1
Woodstock Dr *BOL* BL1 32 D5
SWIN M27 99 F4
TOT/BURYW BL8 25 G4
WALK M28 97 H4
Woodstock Gn *RDSH* SK5 160 B1
Woodstock Rd *ALT* WA14 165 F1
MPL/ROM SK6 161 H1
NEWH/MOS M40 104 B1
OLDTF/WHR M16 127 E5
Woodstock St *OLDE* OL4 9 H6
WHIT OL12 29 F2
Wood St *ALT* WA14 165 G5
AUL OL6 119 G3
BOL BL1 3 F5
CHD/CHDH SK8 170 A3
CSLFD M3 6 C3
CSLFD M3 6 C5
DTN/ASHW M34 132 C4
DUK SK16 133 F2
EDGY/DAV SK3 12 C5
HYDE SK14 148 A1
LIT OL15 21 E3
MDTN M24 72 A2
MDTN M24 72 C3
MILN OL16 30 B5
MILN OL16 45 F2
OLD OL1 76 A4
OP/CLY M11 130 A1
RAD M26 67 H4
RAMS BL0 16 C3
ROY/SHW OL2 59 F2
STLY SK15 120 C3
TOT/BURYW BL8 37 H3
Wood Ter *BOLE* BL2 36 C5
Woodthorpe Ct *PWCH* M25 86 C5
Woodthorpe Dr
CHD/CHDH SK8 182 D2
Woodthorpe Gra *PWCH* M25 86 C5
Woodtop Av *ROCH* OL11 41 G1
Wood Top Cl *OFTN* SK2 173 F2
Woodvale *ALT* WA14 177 F2
MDTN M24 56 D5
Woodvale Av *BOLS/LL* BL3 64 C2
Woodvale Dr *BOLS/LL* BL3 64 C2
Woodvale Gdns *BOLS/LL* BL3 64 C2
Woodvale Gv *BOLS/LL* BL3 64 C2
Woodvale Rd *RAD* M26 68 C3
Woodvale Wk *OP/CLY* M11 * 116 A4
Wood Vw *HEY* OL10 40 D2
WYTH/NTH M22 156 C5
Woodview Av *BNG/LEV* M19 158 C1
Woodville Dr *MPL/ROM* SK6 174 D5
SALE M33 154 B1
STLY SK15 121 G2
Woodville Gv *RDSH* SK5 145 F5
Woodville Rd *ALT* WA14 165 F5
SALE M33 154 B1
Woodville Ter
NEWH/MOS M40 103 G1
Woodward Cl *BURY* BL9 38 C1
Woodward Ct *ANC* M4 * 115 F3
Woodward Pl *ANC* M4 115 F3
Woodward Rd *PWCH* M25 85 G5
Woodward St *ANC* M4 115 F3
Woodwise La
NTHM/RTH M23 155 F5
Woolden St *ECC* M30 110 C2
Woollacot St *OLD* OL1 * 9 H4
Woollam Pl *CSLFD* M3 6 A6
Woolley Av *POY/DIS* SK12 195 E5
Woolley St *CHH* M8 114 C1
Woolmore Av *OLD* OL1 75 F3
Woolpack Gn *SLFD* M6 * 113 E2
Wool Rd *UPML* OL3 79 E2
Wootton St *HYDE* SK14 133 G4
Worcester Av *DTN/ASHW* M34 147 E2
RDSH SK5 160 D2
Worcester Cl *AUL* OL6 107 G2
BURY BL9 53 H1
MPL/ROM SK6 161 H5
Worcester Rd *BOLS/LL* BL3 66 C1
CHD/CHDH SK8 170 D5
MDTN M24 88 C2
SALE M33 153 G3
SLFD M6 112 B1
SWIN M27 83 G5
Worcester St *BOL* BL1 * 33 H5
BRO M7 101 H4
CHAD OL9 90 C2
ROCH OL11 42 D2
TOT/BURYW BL8 38 A2
Wordsworth Av *BURY* BL9 * 53 G3
CHH M8 102 B4
DROY M43 117 G3
FWTH BL4 65 G5
RAD M26 67 H1
Wordsworth Cl *DUK* SK16 134 B1
Wordsworth Crs *AULW* OL7 106 B5
LIT OL15 31 G1
Wordsworth Gdns *PWCH* M25 85 G4
Wordsworth Rd
DTN/ASHW M34 147 E4
LHULT M38 81 F2
MDTN M24 73 E2
OLD OL1 76 A3
OLDTF/WHR M16 127 E5
RDSH SK5 144 D2
SWIN M27 98 C1
Wordsworth St *BOL* BL1 * 33 G4
Wordsworth Wy *ROCH* OL11 28 B5
Workesleigh St
NEWH/MOS M40 104 B5
World Wy *MANAIR* M90 180 A4
Worrall St *EDGY/DAV* SK3 12 E7
NEWH/MOS M40 103 H4
ORD M5 127 F1
WHIT OL12 29 G1
Worsbrough Av *WALK* M28 81 H5
Worsefold St
NEWH/MOS M40 * 103 H2
Worseley Av *NEWH/MOS* M40 103 G1
Worsel St *BOLS/LL* BL3 48 B5
Worsley Av *WALK* M28 81 F5
Worsley Brow *WALK* M28 97 F4
Worsley Ct *WALK* M28 82 A4
Worsley Crs *OFTN* SK2 172 C2
Worsley Gv *BNG/LEV* M19 144 A2
WALK M28 81 F5
Worsley Pl *ROY/SHW* OL2 59 H3
Worsley Rd *BOLS/LL* BL3 47 H5
ECC M30 110 C3
FWTH BL4 82 A1
WALK M28 97 H5
Worsley Rd North *WALK* M28 82 A2
Worsley St *BOLS/LL* BL3 * 48 D4
CSLFD M3 6 C4
CSLFD M3 * 6 C7
HULME M15 127 G1
MILN OL16 11 G7
OLDS OL8 92 A2
SWIN M27 84 A5
SWIN M27 99 F3
TOT/BURYW BL8 25 H4
Worston Av *BOL* BL1 32 C4
Worth Ct *POY/DIS* SK12 195 E5
Worthenbury Wk
BRUN/LGST M13 129 F5
Worthing Cl *OFTN* SK2 173 E3
Worthing St *RUSH/FAL* M14 142 D1
Worthington Av *HEY* OL10 56 B2
PART M31 151 E3
Worthington Cl *HYDE* SK14 * 149 G1
Worthington Dr *BRO* M7 101 G1
Worthington Rd
DTN/ASHW M34 147 F2
SALE M33 155 F2
Worthington St *AULW* OL7 106 D5
BOLS/LL BL3 64 B1
NEWH/MOS M40 104 B2
STLY SK15 120 C4
Worthington Wy
DTN/ASHW M34 132 B4
Worths La *DTN/ASHW* M34 147 E4
Wortley Av *SLFD* M6 112 B2
Wortley Gv *NEWH/MOS* M40 89 E5
Wragby Cl *TOT/BURYW* BL8 38 A1
Wrath Cl *BOLE* BL2 34 C1
Wray Cl *WYTH/NTH* M22 180 C1
Wray Gdns *BNG/LEV* M19 144 C3
Wray Pl *MILN* OL16 30 D5
Wrekin Av *NTHM/RTH* M23 179 H1
Wren Av *SWIN* M27 84 C4

Wrenbury Av DID/WITH M20 142 B4
Wrenbury Crs EDGY/DAV SK3 171 F4
Wrenbury Dr BOL BL1 23 E5
CHD/CHDH SK8 170 B3
MILN OL16 43 H2
Wren Cl DTN/ASHW M34 118 B3
FWTH BL4 65 E4
OFTN SK2 173 G4
Wren Dr BURY BL9 39 E2
IRL M44 122 B4
Wren Gdns MDTN M24 72 C3
Wren Gn MILN OL16 30 C5
Wren's Nest Av ROY/SHW OL2 60 B1
Wren St OLDE OL4 92 B1
Wrenswood Dr WALK M28 96 D2
Wren Wy OP/CLY M11 115 H5
Wrexham Cl OLDS OL8 90 C5
Wrigglesworth Cl
TOT/BURYW BL8 37 E3
Wright Robinson Cl
OP/CLY M11 115 H5
Wrights Bank North
OFTN SK2 173 F4
Wrights Bank South
OFTN SK2 173 E4
Wright St AUL OL6 120 A1
CHAD OL9 90 B2
DTN/ASHW M34 118 D5
FAIL M35 105 E2
OLD OL1 9 J3
OLDTF/WHR M16 127 F3
RAD M26 68 A1
Wrigley Crs FAIL M35 105 E3
Wrigley Fold MDTN M24 55 H5
Wrigley Head FAIL M35 105 E2
Wrigley Head Crs FAIL M35 * 105 E2
Wrigley Pl LIT OL15 * 20 C5
Wrigley St AUL OL6 119 G1
OLDE OL4 76 A5
OLDE OL4 77 G4
OLDE OL4 93 E1
Wroe St CSLFD M3 114 A4
OLDE OL4 93 E1
SWIN M27 84 A4
Wroe Ter SWIN M27 * 84 A4
Wrotham Cl ORD M5 113 F4
Wroxham Av DTN/ASHW M34 131 F5
URM M41 124 A5
Wroxham Cl TOT/BURYW BL8 * 38 A1
Wroxham Rd BKLY M9 87 H4
Wuerdle Cl MILN OL16 20 B5
Wuerdle Farm Wy MILN OL16 20 B4
Wuerdle Pl MILN OL16 20 B4
Wuerdle St MILN OL16 20 B4
Wyatt Av ORD M5 * 127 F1
Wyatt St DUK SK16 119 H5
HTNM SK4 12 E2
Wybersley Rd MPL/ROM SK6 187 F3
Wychbury St ORD M5 112 D3
Wychelm Rd PART M31 151 E3
Wycherley Rd WHIT OL12 29 E1
Wych Fold HYDE SK14 148 A4
Wych St AUL OL6 * 119 G3
Wychwood ALT WA14 177 E3
Wychwood Cl MDTN M24 73 E5
Wycliffe Av WILM/AE SK9 198 D4
Wycliffe Rd URM M41 138 C1
Wycliffe St ECC M30 110 D3
HTNM SK4 12 D2
Wycombe Av GTN M18 130 D2
Wycombe Cl URM M41 124 B3
Wye Av FAIL M35 * 105 E3
Wyecroft Cl MPL/ROM SK6 162 A1
Wye St OLDS OL8 8 D6
Wykeham Gv WHIT OL12 29 E2
Wykeham Ms BOL BL1 47 H2
Wykeham St RUSH/FAL M14 128 B5
Wyke Pk OLDE OL4 92 C1
Wylam Wk WGTN/LGST M12 130 A5
The Wylde BURY BL9 4 D4
Wynchgate Rd
BRAM/HZG SK7 185 H1
Wyndale Dr FAIL M35 105 E5
Wyndale Rd OLDS OL8 91 G4
Wyndcliff Dr URM M41 137 G2
Wyndham Av BOLS/LL BL3 63 H2
SWIN M27 84 A5
Wyndham Cl BRAM/HZG SK7 183 H5
Wyne Cl BRAM/HZG SK7 185 H1
Wynfield Av WYTH/NTH M22 181 E5
Wynford Sq SALQ M50 113 E4
Wyngate Rd CHD/CHDH SK8 182 C3
HALE/TIMP WA15 178 A4
Wynne Av SWIN M27 84 A4
Wynne Cl DTN/ASHW M34 146 D2
OP/CLY M11 116 A5
Wynne Gv DTN/ASHW M34 146 D2
Wynne St BOL BL1 33 H4
LHULT M38 81 F3
SLFD M6 113 G1
Wynnstay Gv RUSH/FAL M14 143 E3
Wynnstay Rd SALE M33 154 C1
Wynyard Cl SALE M33 155 E4
Wynyard Rd WYTH/NTH M22 180 B1
Wyre Dr WALK M28 96 C3
Wyresdale Rd BOL BL1 48 B1
Wyre St CMANE M1 7 J7
MOSL OL5 108 C1
Wythall Av LHULT M38 81 G1
Wythburn Av BOL BL1 32 D5
CHH M8 102 D4
URM M41 124 A5
Wythburn Rd MDTN M24 72 B1
STKP SK1 172 C2
Wythburn St ORD M5 112 D3
Wythenshawe Pk
NTHM/RTH M23 * 167 H1
Wythenshawe Rd
NTHM/RTH M23 167 F1
SALE M33 155 F2
Wythens Rd CHD/CHDH SK8 181 G4
Wythop Gdns ORD M5 113 F4
Wyvern Av HTNM SK4 159 H1
Wyverne Rd CCHDY M21 141 H3
Wyville Cl BRAM/HZG SK7 185 H2
Wyville Dr BKLY M9 87 G1
SLFD M6 113 E2
SWIN M27 98 D4

Y

Yale Rd GTN M18 130 A3
Yarburgh St OLDTF/WHR M16 127 H5
Yardley Av STRET M32 139 G2
Yardley Cl STRET M32 139 G1
Yarmouth Dr NTHM/RTH M23 156 A5
Yarnton Cl ROY/SHW OL2 59 H4
Yarn Wk ANC M4 * 115 F4
Yarrow Cl ROCH OL11 43 E1
Yarrow Pl BOL BL1 2 B1
Yarwell WHIT OL12 10 B4
Yarwood Av NTHM/RTH M23 167 G2
Yarwood Cl HEY OL10 41 F3
Yarwoodheath La ALT WA14 176 B4
Yarwood St ALT WA14 177 G1
BURY BL9 5 G4
Yasmin Gdns OLD OL1 75 E4
Yates Dr WALK M28 81 F4
Yates St BOLE BL2 3 H1
MDTN M24 71 H5
OLD OL1 75 H4
STKP SK1 160 C3
Yates Ter TOT/BURYW BL8 38 A1
Yattendon Av
NTHM/RTH M23 167 E1
Yeadon Rd GTN M18 130 C5
Yea Fold LIT OL15 20 B5
Yealand Av HTNM SK4 159 G3
Yealand Cl ROCH OL11 29 E5
Yeardsley Cl BRAM/HZG SK7 183 H1
Yeb Fold NEWH/MOS M40 * 104 A1
Yellow Lodge Dr WHTN BL5 62 C3
Yeoford Dr ALT WA14 165 E3
Yeoman Cl
BRAM/HZG SK7 * 185 E1
Yeoman's Cl MILN OL16 31 G4
Yeoman Wk OP/CLY M11 116 A4
Yeovil St OLDTF/WHR M16 128 A5
Yewbarrow Rd OLD OL1 75 H4
Yew Cl BOLS/LL BL3 48 A5
Yew Crs OLDE OL4 76 C4
Yewdale SWIN M27 84 C5
Yewdale Av BOLE BL2 35 G4
Yewdale Dr FAIL M35 105 G2
MDTN M24 72 B3
Yewdale Gdns BOLE BL2 35 G4
Yew Dale Gdns ROCH OL11 42 A2
Yewdale Rd STKP SK1 172 C3
Yewlands Av BKLY M9 88 A2
Yew St BRO M7 101 F4
DTN/ASHW M34 132 C3
HEY OL10 40 C4
HULME M15 127 H3
Yew Tree Av BNG/LEV M19 144 A2
BRAM/HZG SK7 185 G4
RUSH/FAL M14 128 B5
WYTH/NTH M22 156 C5
Yew Tree Cl AULW OL7 106 D4
MPL/ROM SK6 174 D4
WILM/AE SK9 199 G3
Yew Tree Crs RUSH/FAL M14 142 D2
Yew Tree Dr HOR/BR BL6 46 C3
MDTN M24 73 G5
MPL/ROM SK6 161 E3
PWCH M25 86 A3
SALE M33 155 F2
URM M41 123 G4
WYTH/NTH M22 156 C5
Yew Tree Gv CHD/CHDH SK8 181 F1
Yew Tree La BOL BL1 34 B2
DUK SK16 134 B1
Yewtree La NTHM/RTH M23 156 A4
POY/DIS SK12 195 G4
WYTH/NTH M22 156 C5
Yew Tree Park Rd
CHD/CHDH SK8 193 E1
Yew Tree Rd
DTN/ASHW M34 146 C2
EDGY/DAV SK3 184 A1
RUSH/FAL M14 142 D1
York Av BOLS/LL BL3 66 D1
OLDS OL8 91 E3
OLDTF/WHR M16 141 G1
PWCH M25 86 C5
ROCH OL11 28 D5
SALE M33 154 C1
SWIN M27 83 G5
York Cl CHD/CHDH SK8 170 D4
York Crs WILM/AE SK9 199 G3
Yorkdale Rd OLDE OL4 76 C5
York Dr ALT WA14 177 G3
BRAM/HZG SK7 185 H2
MANAIR M90 179 G5
RAMS BL0 16 B5
York Pl AULW OL7 119 F3
York Rd ALT WA14 177 F3
CCHDY M21 141 F3
CHAD OL9 74 A4
DROY M43 117 G2
DTN/ASHW M34 132 C4
HTNM SK4 159 E1
HYDE SK14 148 A3
IRL M44 150 C1
SALE M33 154 B1
York Rd East MDTN M24 89 F2
York Rd West MDTN M24 89 F2
Yorkshire Rd PART M31 150 D4
Yorkshire St AULW OL7 119 G1
CSLFD M3 6 C3
MILN OL16 10 D5
OLD OL1 9 H3
WHIT OL12 11 F4
York St AULW OL7 118 D5
BNG/LEV M19 144 A3
BURY BL9 5 G4
CHAD OL9 8 E4
CMANE M1 7 F7
CMANE M1 128 B1
CMANW M2 7 F4
DID/WITH M20 157 G3
EDGY/DAV SK3 12 E5
FWTH BL4 66 B4
HALE/TIMP WA15 177 H1
HEY OL10 41 E4
HULME M15 127 H1
MILN OL16 30 C5
RAD M26 53 F4
WHTF M45 69 G4
York Ter SALE M33 * 139 G5
Young St CSLFD M3 6 C5
FWTH BL4 66 A5
RAMS BL0 16 C2
Yulan Dr SALE M33 153 F2
Yule St EDGY/DAV SK3 12 C5

Z

Zama St RAMS BL0 * 16 B4
Zealand St OLDE OL4 76 B4
Zedburgh WHIT OL12 10 B4
Zeta St BKLY M9 103 G3
Zetland Av BOLS/LL BL3 64 A2
Zetland Av North BOLS/LL BL3 64 A2
Zetland Rd CCHDY M21 141 F3
Zetland St DUK SK16 119 H4
Zinnia Dr IRL M44 136 A3
Zion Ter WHIT OL12 28 B1
Zulu St BOLE BL2 3 K4
Zurich Gdns BRAM/HZG SK7 183 H1
Zyburn Ct SLFD M6 * 111 H2

Index - featured places

AA Office CHD/CHDH SK8 170 B3
Abbey College Manchester
CMANW M2 6 E5
Abbey Hey Primary School
GTN M18 130 D3
Abbey Tutorial College
CMANE M1 7 F4
Abbotsford Preparatory
School URM M41 138 A1
Abbott Primary School
NEWH/MOS M40 115 F2
Abingdon Primary School
RDSH SK5 145 F4
Abraham Moss High School
CHH M8 102 C2
Acacias CP School
BNG/LEV M19 143 H4
Acorn Business Park
EDGY/DAV SK3 12 D4
Acorns School MPL/ROM SK6 175 E4
Acre Hall Primary School
URM M41 137 F1
Adlow Industrial Park
WGTN/LGST M12 115 F5
Adswood Clinic
EDGY/DAV SK3 171 H4
Adswood Industrial Estate
EDGY/DAV SK3 171 G4
Adswood Primary School
EDGY/DAV SK3 171 G4
Adult Learning Centre
RUSH/FAL M14 128 B4
Agecroft Crematorium
SWIN M27 100 C2
Air & Space Museum CSLFD M3 6 C6
Al-Afifah High School for
Girls OLDTF/WHR M16 127 F4
Albany Trading Estate
CCHDY M21 141 F2
Albert Close Trading Estate
WHTF M45 69 H4
Albion Drive Clinic DROY M43 117 H2
The Albion High School
BRO M7 101 G5
Albion Road Industrial Estate
ROCH OL11 29 G5
Albion Trading Estate
AUL OL6 120 A2
SLFD M6 113 F1
Alder Community High
School HYDE SK14 149 F1
Alderley Edge CC
WILM/AE SK9 201 E4
Alderley Edge Golf Club
WILM/AE SK9 200 B2
Alderley Edge Hotel
WILM/AE SK9 201 E5
Alderley Edge Primary School
WILM/AE SK9 200 C3
Alderley Edge School for Girls
WILM/AE SK9 200 D3
Alderman Kay Special School
MDTN M24 72 D1
Alder Park CP School
ECC M30 110 C1
Aldwyn CP School
DTN/ASHW M34 118 B4
Alexandra Business Centre
UPML OL3 79 E5
The Alexandra Hospital
CHD/CHDH SK8 170 A3
Alexandra Industrial Estate
DTN/ASHW M34 132 D4
Alexandra Park Junior School
EDGY/DAV SK3 171 F2
OLDS OL8 91 H3
Alexandra Retail Park OLDE OL4 9 H5
Alice Ingham RC Primary
School MILN OL16 30 D1
Al-jamiyah-islamiyah-
darul-Uloom Islamic College
EDGW/EG BL7 23 F3
Alkrington Clinic Centre
MDTN M24 88 D2
Alkrington Moss Primary
School MDTN M24 89 E2
Alkrington Primary School
MDTN M24 88 D1
All Hallows RC High School
ORD M5 112 C2
Alliance Francaise CMANE M1 7 F7
Alliston House Medical Centre
URM M41 138 D1
All Saints Catholic College
DUK SK16 133 G1
All Saints CE Primary School
FWTH BL4 66 A3
HTNM SK4 159 G2
MPL/ROM SK6 175 F4
NEWH/MOS M40 104 B5
WHIT OL12 10 E1
WHTF M45 69 H2
All Saints Primary School
GTN M18 130 A2
All Souls CE Primary School
HEY OL10 41 G3
All Souls RC Primary School
ORD M5 112 C4
Alma Industrial Estate
WHIT OL12 10 E3
Alma Lodge Hotel OFTN SK2 172 B3
Alma Park Primary School
BNG/LEV M19 144 A3
Alpha Court Industrial Estate
DTN/ASHW M34 131 H5
Alt Primary School OLDS OL8 92 C4
Altrincham CE Primary School
ALT WA14 165 F4
Altrincham College of Arts
HALE/TIMP WA15 166 B5
Altrincham Crematorium
ALT WA14 164 A1
Altrincham FC
HALE/TIMP WA15 178 A1
Altrincham General Hospital
ALT WA14 165 F5
Altrincham Golf Club
HALE/TIMP WA15 166 A4
Altrincham Grammar School
for Boys ALT WA14 177 G2
Altrincham Grammar School
for Girls ALT WA14 177 F1
Altrincham Ice Rink ALT WA14 165 G3
Altrincham Industrial Centre
ALT WA14 164 D3
Altrincham (Kersal) RFC
HALE/TIMP WA15 166 D2
Altrincham Leisure Centre
HALE/TIMP WA15 165 H4
Altrincham Preparatory
School ALT WA14 177 F2
Altrincham Priory Hospital
HALE/TIMP WA15 178 B4
Altrincham Retail Park
ALT WA14 165 F2
Alvanley Industrial Estate
MPL/ROM SK6 161 G2
Amalgamated Sports Club
POY/DIS SK12 197 G1
Amblehurst Hotel SALE M33 154 B2
AMC Cinema CSLFD M3 6 D7
Ancoats Hospital ANC M4 115 F4
Angel Trading Estate ANC M4 7 G1
Angouleme Way Retail Park
BURY BL9 5 F5
Ann Street Health Centre
DTN/ASHW M34 132 B5
Anson Medical Centre
RUSH/FAL M14 129 E4
Apollo Theatre
WGTN/LGST M12 128 D1
Aquinas College OFTN SK2 172 C3
Arcades Shopping Centre
AUL OL6 119 G2
Arcadia Sports Centre
BNG/LEV M19 144 A2
Arden Business Centre
MPL/ROM SK6 146 C5
Arden Primary School
MPL/ROM SK6 161 E3
Arlies Primary School
STLY SK15 108 B5
Armitage CE Primary School
WGTN/LGST M12 129 F2
Arndale Shopping Centre
STRET M32 140 A2
Arrow Trading Estate
DTN/ASHW M34 132 A3
Arts & Craft College BURY BL9 4 D5
Arundale Primary School
HYDE SK14 135 G5
Ashbury Meadow Primary
School OP/CLY M11 116 A5
Ashdene Independant Pre
School WILM/AE SK9 198 C5
Ashfield Valley Primary School
ROCH OL11 42 D2
Ashgate Specialist Primary
Support School
WYTH/NTH M22 169 E5
Ash Lea School ECC M30 111 F2
Ashton on Mersey School
SALE M33 154 A2
Ashton Retail Park AUL OL6 119 G2
Ashton Swimming Pool
AUL OL6 119 G2
Ashton-under-Lyne Golf Club
AUL OL6 107 H3
Ashton-under-Lyne RFC
AUL OL6 107 E3
Ashton-under-Lyne Sixth
Form College AUL OL6 120 A1
Ashton United FC AUL OL6 107 G4
Ashton upon Mersey Cricket
& Tennis Club SALE M33 139 E4
Ashton upon Mersey
Golf Club
SALE M33 139 E4
Aspinal Primary School
GTN M18 130 D5
Astley Bridge CC BOL BL1 33 G2
Astra Business Park
TRPK M17 111 G5
Astra Industrial Centre
ROCH OL11 42 B3
Atlantic Business Centre
ALT WA14 165 F2
Atlas Trading Estate
RDSH SK5 145 E4
Audenshaw Primary School
DTN/ASHW M34 131 H1
Audenshaw School
DTN/ASHW M34 132 B2
Austerlands CC OLDE OL4 77 F4
Avenue Medical Centre
BKLY M9 88 B2
Aviation Viewing Park
HALE/TIMP WA15 189 H2
Avicenna Grammar School
DID/WITH M20 157 E2
Avondale Health Centre
BOL BL1 33 F5
Avondale High School
EDGY/DAV SK3 12 A7
Avondale Industrial Estate
EDGY/DAV SK3 171 E1
Avondale Recreation Centre
EDGY/DAV SK3 171 E2
Baguley Hall Primary School
NTHM/RTH M23 167 H3
Baillie Street Health Centre
MILN OL16 10 D5
Balderstone Technology
College ROCH OL11 43 F3
Bamford Business Park
RDSH SK5 159 H1
Bamford Primary School
ROCH OL11 28 B5
Band on the Wall ANC M4 7 G2
Bankfield Trading Estate
HTNM SK4 159 H2
Bank Meadow Primary School
WGTN/LGST M12 115 G5
Banks Lane Infant School
STKP SK1 172 C1
Bare Trees J & I School
CHAD OL9 74 C4
Baring Street Industrial Estate
CMANE M1 7 K7
Barlow Hall Primary School
CCHDY M21 156 B1
Barlow Medical Centre
DID/WITH M20 157 F3
The Barlow RC High School
DID/WITH M20 157 H4
Barrack Hill Primary School
MPL/ROM SK6 161 H4
Barrington Medical Centre
ALT WA14 165 G3
Barton Business Park
ECC M30 110 D4
Barton Clough Primary
School
STRET M32 125 E4
Barton Moss Community
Primary School ECC M30 110 A4
Bayley Industrial Estate
STLY SK15 120 C4
BBC North CMANE M1 128 B1
Bealey Community Hospital
RAD M26 53 E5
Bealey Industrial Estate
RAD M26 53 E4
Beal Vale Primary School
ROY/SHW OL2 60 A2
Beaumont Hospital
HOR/BR BL6 46 C1
Beaumont Primary School
BOLS/LL BL3 47 F4
Beaver Road Primary School
DID/WITH M20 157 G3
Beech House School
ROCH OL11 42 D1
Beech Street Primary School
ECC M30 110 C4
Beetham Tower CSLFD M3 6 C7
Beever Primary School OLD OL1 9 J1
Beis Rochel Girls School
CHH M8 102 A1
The Beis Yaakov Jewish High
School BRO M7 101 F2
Belfield Community Primary
School MILN OL16 11 J4
Belfield Trading Estate
MILN OL16 31 E2

Belford College *OLDS* OL8 90 D3
Belfry House Hotel *WILM/AE* SK9 192 A1
Belle Vue Regional Hockey Centre *WGTN/LGST* M12 129 H4
Benchill Primary School *WYTH/NTH* M22 168 B3
Bentinck Street Industrial Estate *HULME* M15 127 G1
Best Western Cresta Court Hotel *ALT* WA14 165 G4
Best Western Hotel Smokies Park *OLDS* OL8 106 C2
Birches Health Centre *PWCH* M25 86 B1
Birchfields Primary School *RUSH/FAL* M14 143 G2
Birch Industrial Estate *HEY* OL10 55 F3
Birchinley Manor Showground *MILN* OL16 31 G3
Birtenshaw Hall School *EDGW/EG* BL7 23 G5
Birtle View Special School *HEY* OL10 40 C4
Bishop Bilsborrow Memorial RC Primary School *OLDTF/WHR* M16 142 B1
Bishop Bridgeman CE Primary School *BOLS/LL* BL3 48 D5
B & J Leisure Centre *WILM/AE* SK9 198 D3
Blackbrook Trading Estate *BNG/LEV* M19 144 B3
Blackley Cemetery *BKLY* M9 87 F3
Blackley Crematorium *BKLY* M9 87 F3
Blackley Golf Club *BKLY* M9 89 E3
Blackshaw Lane CP School *ROY/SHW* OL2 59 H5
Blackshaw Primary School *BOLE* BL2 50 D3
Blessed Thomas Holford RC School *HALE/TIMP* WA15 165 H5
Blue Chip Business Park *ALT* WA14 165 E2
Blue Coat CE School *OLD* OL1 9 H2
Bnos Yisroel Schools *BRO* M7 101 H3
Boarshaw Industrial Estate *MDTN* M24 73 E4
Boarshurst Business Park *UPML* OL3 95 E1
Bodmin Road Clinic *SALE* M33 153 G1
B of the Bang *OP/CLY* M11 116 A4
Boggart Hole Clough Track *BKLY* M9 88 C5
Bolholt Country Park Hotel *TOT/BURYW* BL8 37 F2
Bollin CP School *ALT* WA14 177 E3
Bolshaw Primary School *CHD/CHDH* SK8 181 G5
Bolton Business Centre *BOLE* BL2 3 G6
Bolton CC *BOLS/LL* BL3 65 F2
Bolton Community College *BOLE* BL2 3 G7
Bolton Gates Retail Park *BOL* BL1 3 F2
Bolton Golf Club *HOR/BR* BL6 46 B1
Bolton Institute *BOLS/LL* BL3 2 C7
Bolton Little Theatre *BOL* BL1 2 C5
Bolton Muslim Girls School *BOLS/LL* BL3 48 C5
Bolton Old Links Golf Club *BOL* BL1 32 A3
Bolton Open Golf Club *BOLE* BL2 35 E3
Bolton Parish CE Primary School *BOLE* BL2 3 J4
Bolton Road Industrial Estate *WHTN* BL5 62 A3
Bolton Rugby Union FC *BOL* BL1 2 A2
Bolton School (Beech House, Infant Department) *BOL* BL1 48 A2
Bolton School Girls Division *BOL* BL1 48 A2
Bolton School (Junior Boys Division) *BOL* BL1 48 B2
Bolton School (Senior Boys Division) *BOL* BL1 48 B2
Bolton Sixth Form College North Campus *BOL* BL1 33 E2
Bond Street Industrial Estate *WGTN/LGST* M12 7 K7
Bonholt Industrial Estate *TOT/BURYW* BL8 37 F2
Booth Hall Hospital School *BKLY* M9 88 C4
Booth House Trading Estate *CHAD* OL9 8 B5
Boothstown Methodist Primary School *WALK* M28 96 A4
The Borchardt Medical Centre *DID/WITH* M20 142 B5
Bornmore Industrial Centre *TOT/BURYW* BL8 37 G3
Boundary Industrial Estate *BOLE* BL2 50 D2
Boundary Trading Estate *IRL* M44 122 D4
Bowdon CE Primary School *ALT* WA14 177 F3
Bowdon CC *ALT* WA14 177 F3
Bowdon Preparatory School for Girls *ALT* WA14 177 F2
Bowdon RUFC *HALE/TIMP* WA15 166 D5
Bowdon Vale CC *ALT* WA14 177 F4
Bowker Bank Industrial Park *CHH* M8 87 G5
Bowker Vale Primary School *CHH* M8 87 E3
Bowness Primary School *BOLS/LL* BL3 66 C1
Brabyns Recreation Centre *MPL/ROM* SK6 175 F2
Brabyns School *MPL/ROM* SK6 175 F2
Brackley Municipal Golf Club *LHULT* M38 80 D1
Bradley Fold Trading Estate *BOLE* BL2 51 F3
Bradley Green Primary School *HYDE* SK14 134 A2
Bradshaw CC *BOLE* BL2 34 D1
Bradshaw Hall J & I School *CHD/CHDH* SK8 182 B3
Bradshaw Trading Estate *MDTN* M24 89 G2
Bramall Hall & Park *BRAM/HZG* SK7 183 H3
Bramall Park Golf Club *CHD/CHDH* SK8 183 F3
Bramall Park Lawn Tennis Club *BRAM/HZG* SK7 183 G2
Bramall Park Tennis Club *BRAM/HZG* SK7 183 G4
Bramhall Golf Club *BRAM/HZG* SK7 194 A1
Bramhall Health Centre *BRAM/HZG* SK7 193 H1
Bramhall High School *BRAM/HZG* SK7 184 A4
Bramhall Moor Industrial Estate *BRAM/HZG* SK7 184 C2
Bramhall Park Medical Centre *BRAM/HZG* SK7 183 H2
Bramhall Village Shopping Centre *BRAM/HZG* SK7 193 G1
Brandwood Primary School *BOLS/LL* BL3 48 B5
Branwood Preparatory School *ECC* M30 111 F2
Bredbury Clinic *MPL/ROM* SK6 161 G2
Bredbury Green Primary School *MPL/ROM* SK6 161 G5
Bredbury Hall Hotel & Country Club *MPL/ROM* SK6 161 E4
Breeze Hill Comprehensive School *OLDE* OL4 92 C2
Breightmet FC *BOLE* BL2 50 C2
Breightmet Golf Club *BOLE* BL2 35 H5
Breightmet Industrial Estate *BOLE* BL2 50 C2
Brentnall Primary School *BRO* M7 101 G3
Brentwood Special School *ALT* WA14 165 H2
Bridge College *OFTN* SK2 173 E1
Bridge Hall Primary School *EDGY/DAV* SK3 171 G3
Bridge House Medical Centre *CHD/CHDH* SK8 183 E1
Bridge Mills Business Park *SLFD* M6 100 C5
Bridgeside Business Centre *MPL/ROM* SK6 146 B5
Bridge Trading Estate *TOT/BURYW* BL8 4 A4
Bridgewater Concert Hall *CMANE* M1 6 E7
Bridgewater Primary School *LHULT* M38 81 H3
Bridgewater School *WALK* M28 97 H4
Brighton Road Industrial Estate *HTNM* SK4 159 E5
Brimrod Primary School *ROCH* OL11 42 C1
Brindale Primary School *RDSH* SK5 160 D2
Brindle Heath Industrial Estate *SLFD* M6 113 E1
Brindle House Community Mental Health Centre *HYDE* SK14 147 H1
Brinksway Trading Estate *HTNM* SK4 12 B5
Brinnington Health Centre *RDSH* SK5 160 D1
Briscoe Lane Primary School *NEWH/MOS* M40 104 A5
Britannia Business Park *BOLE* BL2 34 C4
Britannia Mill Industrial Estate *HEY* OL10 40 C4
Broadbent Fold Primary School *DUK* SK16 134 B1
Broadbottom Primary School *HYDE* SK14 149 H3
Broadfield Industrial Estate *HEY* OL10 40 C5
Broadfield Primary School *MILN* OL16 10 C7
OLDS OL8 91 G3
Broadheath Primary School *ALT* WA14 165 F1
Broadhurst Primary School *NEWH/MOS* M40 104 B3
Broadoak Business Park *TRPK* M17 125 E1
Broadoak High School *PART* M31 150 D4
Broadoak Primary School *AUL* OL6 107 F4
SWIN M27 98 B4
Broad Oak Primary School *DID/WITH* M20 169 G1
Broadoak Sports Centre *AUL* OL6 107 F4
Broadstone Hall Primary School *HTNM* SK4 144 D5
Broadwalk Primary School *SLFD* M6 113 F2
Broadway Business Park *CHAD* OL9 89 G3
Broadway Industrial Estate *HYDE* SK14 133 E3
ORD M5 113 F5
Brookburn Primary School *CCHDY* M21 141 E4
Brookdale Golf Club *FAIL* M35 105 G5
Brookfield Business Park *CHD/CHDH* SK8 170 C4
Brookhead Junior School *CHD/CHDH* SK8 170 C4
Brooklands Primary School *SALE* M33 154 B4
Brooks Bar Medical Centre *OLDTF/WHR* M16 127 G4
Brookside Business Park *MDTN* M24 89 G1
Brookside Primary School *MPL/ROM* SK6 196 D1
Brookway High School & Sports College *NTHM/RTH* M23 167 F1
Broomwood CP School *HALE/TIMP* WA15 167 E4
Broughton Baths *BRO* M7 101 G4
Broughton CC *BRO* M7 101 F4
Broughton Jewish Cassel-Fox Primary School *BRO* M7 101 G2
Brownhill Countryside Centre *UPML* OL3 78 D3
Brownhill Special School *WHIT* OL12 10 B3
Brownlow Business Centre *BOL* BL1 33 G5
Brownlow Fold Community Learning Centre *BOL* BL1 33 G5
Brownlow Fold Primary School *BOL* BL1 33 G5
Brunswick Health Centre *BRUN/LGST* M13 128 C2
Bruntwood Primary School *CHD/CHDH* SK8 182 B2
Buckley Road Industrial Estate *WHIT* OL12 30 C1
Buckstones Primary School *ROY/SHW* OL2 60 C1
Buckton Vale Primary School *STLY* SK15 109 G3
Buile Hill High School *SLFD* M6 112 C1
Bullough Moor Primary School *HEY* OL10 40 B4
Burgess Primary School *BKLY* M9 103 F3
Burnage High School For Boys *BNG/LEV* M19 158 C1
Burnage Rugby Club *HTNM* SK4 158 B5
Burnden Industrial Estate *BOLS/LL* BL3 49 G5
Burnley Brow Community School *CHAD* OL9 74 D3
Burrs Country Park *TOT/BURYW* BL8 27 E5
Bury Atheneum *BURY* BL9 4 D5
Bury Business Centre *BURY* BL9 5 H1
Bury Catholic Preparatory School *BURY* BL9 53 F1
Bury CE High School *BURY* BL9 53 F1
Bury Cemetery *BURY* BL9 53 G2
Bury College *BURY* BL9 4 D6
Bury County Court *BURY* BL9 4 B5
Bury FC (Gigg Lane) *BURY* BL9 53 G2
Bury Golf Club *BURY* BL9 53 G5
Bury Grammar School (Boys) *BURY* BL9 4 B5
Bury Industrial Estate *BOLE* BL2 50 C1
Bury Market *BURY* BL9 4 E5
Bury Sports Club *BURY* BL9 53 F1
Bury & Whitefield Jewish Primary School *BURY* BL9 70 A1
Business & Arts Centre *HTNM* SK4 144 D4
Butterstile Primary School *PWCH* M25 85 H5
Button Lane School *NTHM/RTH* M23 155 G4
Byron Street Infant Community School *ROY/SHW* OL2 59 F5
Cadishead Recreation Centre *IRL* M44 150 C1
Caius House School *URM* M41 138 C2
Caldershaw Primary School *WHIT* OL12 28 C2
Cale Green Primary School *EDGY/DAV* SK3 171 H2
Camberwell Park School *BKLY* M9 87 H3
Cambrian Business Park *BOLS/LL* BL3 48 C4
Cambridge Industrial Estate *BRO* M7 114 B1
Campanile Hotel *ORD* M5 113 H5
Cams Lane Primary School *RAD* M26 68 A1
Canalside Industrial Estate *MILN* OL16 43 G1
Canon Burrows CE Primary School *AULW* OL7 106 C5
Canon Johnson CE Primary School *AULW* OL7 119 G1
Canon Slade School *BOLE* BL2 34 C2
Capital Business Centre *BRAM/HZG* SK7 193 G1
Cardinal Langley RC High School *MDTN* M24 57 F5
Cariocca Business Park *NEWH/MOS* M40 115 H2
WGTN/LGST M12 129 E2
Carlton Industrial Centre *BOLE* BL2 3 G6
Carrbrook Industrial Estate *STLY* SK15 109 H4
Carrington Business Park *PART* M31 137 E5
Castlebrook High School *BURY* BL9 70 B1
Castlefield Gallery *CSLFD* M3 6 C7
Castle Hawk Golf Club *ROCH* OL11 41 H5
Castle Hill Primary School *BOLE* BL2 34 C4
Castle Hill School *RDSH* SK5 146 A5
Castle Leisure Centre *BURY* BL9 4 C4
Castle Park Industrial Estate *OLD* OL1 76 A5
Castleton Primary School *ROCH* OL11 42 C4
Castleton Swimming Pool *ROCH* OL11 42 B3
Cathedral Gardens *ANC* M4 6 E2
Cavendish Industrial Estate *AUL* OL6 119 F2
Cavendish Road Primary School *DID/WITH* M20 157 F1
Central Art Gallery *AUL* OL6 119 G3
Central Industrial Estate *BOLS/LL* BL3 49 E4
MDTN M24 72 D4
Central Leisure Centre *MILN* OL16 10 E6
Central Primary School *DTN/ASHW* M34 132 B5
Central Retail Park *ANC* M4 7 K4
Century Mill Industrial Estate *FWTH* BL4 65 G4
CE School of the Resurrection *OP/CLY* M11 116 A4
Chadderton AFC *CHAD* OL9 74 C4
Chadderton Cemetery *CHAD* OL9 74 B4
Chadderton Hall Junior School *CHAD* OL9 74 B2
Chadderton Industrial Estate *MDTN* M24 89 F2
Chadderton Shopping Precinct *CHAD* OL9 74 C4
Chadderton Sports Centre & Public Baths *CHAD* OL9 74 C5
Chadderton Town Health Centre *CHAD* OL9 74 C5
Chadkirk Industrial Estate *MPL/ROM* SK6 174 A1
Chantlers Primary School *TOT/BURYW* BL8 37 F4
Chapelfield Primary School *RAD* M26 68 D3
Chapel Medical Centre *IRL* M44 136 C1
Chapel Street Primary School *BNG/LEV* M19 144 B2
Charleston Industrial Estate *AULW* OL7 119 G1
Charlestown Health Centre *BKLY* M9 88 D5
Charlestown Primary School *BKLY* M9 89 E4
SLFD M6 113 G1
Cheadle Catholic Primary School *CHD/CHDH* SK8 182 B2
Cheadle CC *CHD/CHDH* SK8 169 H4
Cheadle Golf Club *CHD/CHDH* SK8 170 B5
Cheadle Heath Clinic *EDGY/DAV* SK3 170 D1
Cheadle Heath Primary School *EDGY/DAV* SK3 170 D2
Cheadle Heath Sports Centre *CHD/CHDH* SK8 170 D3
Cheadle Hulme High School *CHD/CHDH* SK8 183 E5
Cheadle Hulme Medical Centre *CHD/CHDH* SK8 182 D4
Cheadle Hulme Recreation Centre *CHD/CHDH* SK8 183 E5
Cheadle Hulme School *CHD/CHDH* SK8 182 D4
Cheadle & Marple Sixth Form College *CHD/CHDH* SK8 182 B1
Cheadle Primary School *CHD/CHDH* SK8 170 A3
Cheadle Royal Business Park *CHD/CHDH* SK8 181 H1
Cheadle Royal Hospital *CHD/CHDH* SK8 181 H2
Cheadle Royal Shopping Centre *CHD/CHDH* SK8 182 A2
Cheadle Swimming & Recreation Centre *CHD/CHDH* SK8 170 B5
Cheadle Town FC *CHD/CHDH* SK8 170 B4
Cheetham CE Community School *BRO* M7 102 A3
Cheetham Hill CC *CHH* M8 101 H1
Cheethwood Community & Sports Centre *BRO* M7 102 A4
Cheetwood Primary School *CHH* M8 114 B1
Cherry Manor Primary School *SALE* M33 153 F4
Cherry Tree Hospital *OFTN* SK2 172 D4
Cherry Tree Primary School *FWTH* BL4 64 D4
Chesham Industrial Estate *BURY* BL9 38 D2
Chesham Primary School *BURY* BL9 27 H5
Chester Court Hotel *STRET* M32 126 C4
Chethams Library & Music School *CSLFD* M3 6 E2
Chichester Business Centre *MILN* OL16 11 F7
Child Health Clinic *MDTN* M24 72 C3
Chinese Medical Centre *CSLFD* M3 6 C6
Chorlton CE Primary School *CCHDY* M21 141 E3
Chorlton-cum-Hardy CC *CCHDY* M21 141 F5
Chorlton-cum-Hardy Golf Club *CCHDY* M21 156 B1
Chorlton High School *CCHDY* M21 141 G4
Chorlton Leisure Centre *CCHDY* M21 141 F2
Chorlton Park Primary School *CCHDY* M21 141 G4
Chorlton Shopping Centre *CCHDY* M21 141 E2
Chorlton Water Park *CCHDY* M21 156 B2
Christchurch Ainsworth CE Primary School *BOLE* BL2 36 B5
Christ Church CE Primary School *CHAD* OL9 90 B1
Christchurch CE Primary School *ECC* M30 110 D3
TOT/BURYW BL8 37 E2
Christie Hospital & Holt Radium Institute *DID/WITH* M20 142 D5
Christie Street Industrial Estate *STKP* SK1 13 J7
Christs Church CE Primary School *BOLE* BL2 35 G4
Christ the King RC Primary School *NEWH/MOS* M40 104 B5
WALK M28 82 B5
Christ the King School *SALE* M33 154 A3
Church Road Primary School *BOL* BL1 32 D4
Church Street Industrial Estate *MDTN* M24 72 D2
Cineworld *BOL* BL1 34 B3
DID/WITH M20 158 A5
STKP SK1 13 F5
City Centre Campus *CSLFD* M3 6 B4
City College Manchester *CHH* M8 102 C2
DID/WITH M20 157 E2
NTHM/RTH M23 156 B5
NTHM/RTH M23 167 E1
NTHM/RTH M23 167 G1
City Course Trading Estate *OP/CLY* M11 129 H1
City Court Trading Estate *ANC* M4 7 K2
City Park Business Village *OLDTF/WHR* M16 127 E3
Claremont Primary School *RUSH/FAL* M14 128 B5
Clarendon Cottage School *ECC* M30 111 G2
Clarendon CP School *BOLS/LL* BL3 48 D4
Clarendon Fields Primary School *DUK* SK16 119 G5
Clarendon Industrial Estate *HYDE* SK14 133 H5
Clarendon Road Primary School *ECC* M30 111 G2
Clarendon Square Shopping Centre *HYDE* SK14 147 H1
Clarke Industrial Estate *STRET* M32 125 F4
Clarksfield Primary School *OLDE* OL4 92 B1
Clayton Health Centre *OP/CLY* M11 116 C3
Clayton Industrial Estate *OP/CLY* M11 130 C1
Cleavley Athletics Track *ECC* M30 110 B2
Cleggs Lane Industrial Site *LHULT* M38 81 G1
Clevelands Preparatory School *BOL* BL1 47 H2
Clifton Country Park *SWIN* M27 83 H2
Clifton Industrial Estate *SWIN* M27 84 D4
Clifton Primary School *SWIN* M27 84 A4
Cloughside School *PWCH* M25 85 G2
Cloverlea Primary School *HALE/TIMP* WA15 166 C4
The Club Theatre *ALT* WA14 177 G1
Cobden Mill Industrial Estate *FWTH* BL4 65 G3
Coldhurst Community Centre *OLD* OL1 8 E1
Coldhurst Industrial Estate *OLD* OL1 9 F1
Coliseum Theatre *OLD* OL1 9 J3
Collegiate Medical Centre *CHH* M8 102 B3
Comfort Inn *WGTN/LGST* M12 129 H2
Commonwealth House *MANAIR* M90 180 A4
Community Hall *STLY* SK15 120 D3
Concord Business Park *WYTH/NTH* M22 180 D3
Constellation Trading Estate *RAD* M26 52 A3
Co-operative College *ANC* M4 7 F2
Co-operative Museum *WHIT* OL12 10 B5
Copley High School *STLY* SK15 121 G3
Copper Beeches School *SALE* M33 154 A2
Coppice Industrial Estate *OLDS* OL8 8 C6
Coppice J & I School *OLDS* OL8 91 F3
Copthorne Hotel *SALQ* M50 126 D2
Cornbrook Estate *HULME* M15 127 G1
Cornerhouse Cinema *CMANE* M1 7 F7
Cornishway Industrial Estate *WYTH/NTH* M22 180 C4
Cornwall Street Industrial Estate *OP/CLY* M11 130 C1
Corpus Christi RC Primary School *CHAD* OL9 90 C3
Corpus Christi with St Anne RC Primary School *ANC* M4 115 G4
Corrie Primary School *DTN/ASHW* M34 146 D2
Counthill School *OLDE* OL4 76 C2
County End Business Centre *OLDE* OL4 77 E5
Covenant Christian School *HTNM* SK4 159 F2

Crab Lane Primary School BKLY M9 ..... 87 G3
Cravenwood Primary School CHH M8 ..... 102 A2
Crescent Community High School for Girls RUSH/FAL M14 ..... 129 E5
Croft Industrial Estate BURY BL9 ..... 53 H4
Cromer Industrial Estate MDTN M24 ..... 73 E3
Cromford Business Park OLD OL1 ..... 76 A4
Crompton CC ROY/SHW OL2 ..... 60 A1
Crompton Fold Primary School BOLE BL2 ..... 50 B2
Crompton Health Centre ROY/SHW OL2 ..... 60 A3
Crompton House CE School ROY/SHW OL2 ..... 59 G2
Crompton Place Shopping Centre BOL BL1 ..... 2 E5
Crompton Primary School ROY/SHW OL2 ..... 59 H3
Crompton & Royton Golf Club ROY/SHW OL2 ..... 59 G4
Crompton Swimming Pool ROY/SHW OL2 ..... 60 A3
Cromwell High School DUK SK16 ..... 133 H2
Cromwell House Community Mental Health Centre ECC M30 ..... 111 E3
Cromwell Special School RDSH SK5 ..... 145 F1
Crosland Industrial Estate MPL/ROM SK6 ..... 161 F2
Crossacres Primary School WYTH/NTH M22 ..... 169 E5
Crossgates Primary School MILN OL16 ..... 31 H4
Crosslee Primary School BKLY M9 ..... 88 D3
Crowcroft Park Primary School WGTN/LGST M12 ..... 129 H5
Crown Business Centre FAIL M35 ..... 105 E2
Crown Industrial Estate ALT WA14 ..... 165 H2
ANC M4 ..... 7 K2
Crown Royal Industrial Park STKP SK1 ..... 13 H5
Crumpsall Lane Primary School CHH M8 ..... 102 B1
Culcheth Hall School ALT WA14 ..... 177 F1
Curzon Ashton FC AULW OL7 ..... 119 E3
Curzon Cinema URM M41 ..... 124 A5
Cutgate Shopping Precinct WHIT OL12 ..... 29 E2
Dagenham Road Industrial Estate RUSH/FAL M14 ..... 128 D5
Daisy Nook Country Park OLDS OL8 ..... 106 B3
Dale Grove Primary School (Bankside) HYDE SK14 ..... 148 B2
Dale Grove Special School AULW OL7 ..... 106 D5
The Dale Primary School MPL/ROM SK6 ..... 174 C2
Dale Street Industrial Estate RAD M26 ..... 68 B2
Dancehouse Theatre & Northern Ballet School CMANE M1 ..... 128 B1
Dane Bank Primary School RDSH SK5 ..... 145 G1
Dane Road Industrial Estate SALE M33 ..... 154 D1
Darnhill CP School HEY OL10 ..... 40 A5
Darul Uloom Al Arabiya Al Islamia TOT/BURYW BL8 ..... 16 B4
Davaar Medical Centre DUK SK16 ..... 119 H5
Davenport Golf Club POY/DIS SK12 ..... 196 A3
David Cuthbert Business Centre OP/CLY M11 ..... 130 B1
David Lloyd Fitness Centre BOL BL1 ..... 2 B4
David Medical Centre CCHDY M21 ..... 141 G5
Davyhulme J & I School URM M41 ..... 124 C5
Davyhulme Park Golf Club URM M41 ..... 123 G4
Deakins Business Park EDGW/EG BL7 ..... 22 C1
Deane Golf Club BOLS/LL BL3 ..... 47 H4
Deane Leisure Centre BOLS/LL BL3 ..... 47 G5
Dean Lane Medical Centre BRAM/HZG SK7 ..... 185 E4
Dean Row Community Junior School WILM/AE SK9 ..... 199 H1
The Deans CP School SWIN M27 ..... 98 D2
Deans Road Industrial Estate SWIN M27 ..... 98 C2
Deanway Trading Estate WILM/AE SK9 ..... 192 A4
Deeplish Primary School ROCH OL11 ..... 43 F1
Delamere School URM M41 ..... 137 F1
Delta Business Park DTN/ASHW M34 ..... 132 B1
Denton Cemetery DTN/ASHW M34 ..... 146 D3
Denton Cricket & Sports Club DTN/ASHW M34 ..... 132 B3
Denton Golf Club DTN/ASHW M34 ..... 131 G4
Denton St Lawrence CC DTN/ASHW M34 ..... 146 D1
Denton West End Primary School DTN/ASHW M34 ..... 131 F5
Department of Clinical Psychology ROY/SHW OL2 ..... 75 F2
Derby High School BURY BL9 ..... 53 E1
Derby Shopping Centre BOLS/LL BL3 ..... 48 C4
Derwent Street Trading Estate ORD M5 ..... 127 F1
The Designer Outlet SALQ M50 ..... 126 C1
Devonshire Road Primary School BOL BL1 ..... 47 H1
Devonshire Street Industrial Estate WGTN/LGST M12 ..... 129 E2
Dial Park Primary School OFTN SK2 ..... 173 F3
Diamond Lodge GTN M18 ..... 130 A3
Didsbury CC DID/WITH M20 ..... 157 H5
Didsbury CE Primary School DID/WITH M20 ..... 157 G3
Didsbury Golf Club WYTH/NTH M22 ..... 157 E5
Didsbury Medical Centre DID/WITH M20 ..... 157 F2
Didsbury Road Primary School HTNM SK4 ..... 158 C4
Didsbury School DID/WITH M20 ..... 157 G2
Disley Golf Club POY/DIS SK12 ..... 187 H5
Doffcocker Lodge Nature Reserve BOL BL1 ..... 32 B5
Downing Street Industrial Estate WGTN/LGST M12 ..... 128 C1
Dowry Park Industrial Estate OLDE OL4 ..... 76 D5
Dowson Primary School HYDE SK14 ..... 148 A3
Droylsden AFC DROY M43 ..... 117 H4
Droylsden High School for Girls DROY M43 ..... 117 F3
Droylsden Sports Centre DROY M43 ..... 117 F3
Droylsden Swimming Pool DROY M43 ..... 117 H5
Ducie Athletics Ground Running Track WGTN/LGST M12 ..... 130 A4
Ducie High School RUSH/FAL M14 ..... 128 B4
Ducie Sports Centre HULME M15 ..... 128 C4
Dukesgate Primary School LHULT M38 ..... 81 F2
Dukinfield Crematorium DUK SK16 ..... 120 A4
Dukinfield Golf Club DUK SK16 ..... 134 B1
Dukinfield Joint Cemetery DUK SK16 ..... 120 A4
Dunham Forest Golf & Country Club ALT WA14 ..... 164 C5
Dunham Massey (NT) ALT WA14 ..... 176 A1
Dunscar Golf Club EDGW/EG BL7 ..... 22 C3
Dunscar Industrial Estate EDGW/EG BL7 ..... 22 D4
Durnford Medical Centre MDTN M24 ..... 72 C3
Durn Street Industrial Estate LIT OL15 ..... 21 F2
Eagley Infant School EDGW/EG BL7 ..... 23 F3
Eagley Junior School EDGW/EG BL7 ..... 23 G3
East Crompton St Georges CE Primary School ROY/SHW OL2 ..... 60 B2
East Crompton St James CE Primary School ROY/SHW OL2 ..... 60 A2
East Lancashire Railway BURY BL9 ..... 5 H7
BURY BL9 ..... 27 E3
BURY BL9 ..... 54 D1
RAMS BL0 ..... 16 D3
East Ward Primary School BURY BL9 ..... 5 K4
Eaton Place Business Centre SALE M33 ..... 154 B2
Eccles Crematorium ECC M30 ..... 110 A5
Eccles Health Centre ECC M30 ..... 111 G3
Eccles Recreation Centre ECC M30 ..... 111 G4
Eccles Town Hall ECC M30 ..... 111 G3
Edge Fold Industrial Estate FWTH BL4 ..... 64 B3
Egerton & Dunscar Health Centre EDGW/EG BL7 ..... 23 E3
Egerton High School URM M41 ..... 124 D4
Egerton House Hotel EDGW/EG BL7 ..... 22 D1
Egerton Park Arts College DTN/ASHW M34 ..... 132 B3
Egerton Park Community High School DTN/ASHW M34 ..... 132 A4
Elk Mill Central Retail Park OLD OL1 ..... 74 C1
Ellenbrook Primary School WALK M28 ..... 96 C3
Ellesmere Bowling & Tennis Club WALK M28 ..... 97 E2
Ellesmere Golf Club WALK M28 ..... 97 G1
Ellesmere Retail Park WALK M28 ..... 81 H4
Ellesmere Shopping Centre LHULT M38 ..... 81 H4
Elmridge Primary School HALE/TIMP WA15 ..... 178 D4
Elms Bank Community High School WHTF M45 ..... 69 G1
Elms Medical Centre WHTF M45 ..... 69 F3
Elm Wood Primary School MDTN M24 ..... 73 F4
Elsinore Business Centre OLDTF/WHR M16 ..... 126 D4
The Elton High School TOT/BURYW BL8 ..... 37 F3
Elton Primary School TOT/BURYW BL8 ..... 37 H3
Emmanuel Christian School WHIT OL12 ..... 10 A2
Emmanuel Holcombe Primary School TOT/BURYW BL8 ..... 16 B2
Empress Business Centre OLDTF/WHR M16 ..... 127 F2
English Martyrs RC Primary School URM M41 ..... 138 C1
Enterprise Trading Estate GTN M18 ..... 130 D2
TRPK M17 ..... 111 H5
Esplanade Arts & Heritage Centre ROCH OL11 ..... 10 B7
Estcourt Preparatory School OLDS OL8 ..... 91 E3
Etchells Primary School CHD/CHDH SK8 ..... 181 H3
Eton Hill Industrial Estate RAD M26 ..... 52 D4
Etrop Grange Hotel MANAIR M90 ..... 180 A3
Etz Chaim School CHH M8 ..... 86 D5
Europa Business Park EDGY/DAV SK3 ..... 171 E3
Europa Trading Estate RAD M26 ..... 67 E5
Ewing School DID/WITH M20 ..... 157 F1
Express by Holiday Inn SALQ M50 ..... 126 C1
Express Trading Estate FWTH BL4 ..... 82 A1
The Eye Clinic CMANW M2 ..... 6 E5
Fahay Industrial Estate NEWH/MOS M40 ..... 115 H3
Failsworth Health Centre FAIL M35 ..... 104 D3
Failsworth Industrial Estate FAIL M35 ..... 104 B4
Failsworth Shopping Centre FAIL M35 ..... 105 E2
Fairfield Community Primary School BURY BL9 ..... 39 G3
Fairfield General Hospital BURY BL9 ..... 39 H2
Fairfield Golf & Sailing Club DTN/ASHW M34 ..... 131 G1
Fairfield High School for Girls DROY M43 ..... 117 G5
Fairfield Road Primary School DROY M43 ..... 117 G5
Fairhill Industrial Estate IRL M44 ..... 136 B4
Fairview Medical Centre URM M41 ..... 138 B1
Fairway Primary School OFTN SK2 ..... 173 F2
Fairways Lodge PWCH M25 ..... 101 E1
Faling Park High School WHIT OL12 ..... 29 G2
Fallowfield Medical Centre RUSH/FAL M14 ..... 143 F3
Fallowfield Shopping Centre RUSH/FAL M14 ..... 143 G2
Farjo Medical Centre CMANE M1 ..... 7 G5
Farnworth Cemetery FWTH BL4 ..... 66 B3
Farnworth Leisure Centre FWTH BL4 ..... 66 A4
Farnworth Little Theatre FWTH BL4 ..... 66 A4
Farnworth Park Industrial Estate FWTH BL4 ..... 66 A3
Farnworth Social Circle CC FWTH BL4 ..... 65 H5
Farrowdale House School ROY/SHW OL2 ..... 60 A3
Fiddlers Lane Primary School IRL M44 ..... 122 C5
Fieldhouse CC ROCH OL11 ..... 28 B5
Fieldhouse Industrial Estate WHIT OL12 ..... 10 D1
Firbank Primary School ROY/SHW OL2 ..... 59 E2
Firgrove Business Park MILN OL16 ..... 31 E3
Firs CP School SALE M33 ..... 153 G2
Fir Tree Primary School RDSH SK5 ..... 145 E1
Firwood Industrial Estate BOLE BL2 ..... 34 D4
Firwood Manor Preparatory School CHAD OL9 ..... 74 C3
Firwood Special School BOLE BL2 ..... 34 D4
Fishbrook Industrial Estate FWTH BL4 ..... 66 C5
Fishpool Infant School BURY BL9 ..... 53 G1
Fitton Hill Shopping Precinct OLDS OL8 ..... 91 G4
Five Fold Industrial Park CHAD OL9 ..... 8 D4
Flixton CC URM M41 ..... 123 F5
Flixton FC URM M41 ..... 123 E5
Flixton Girls High School URM M41 ..... 138 A1
Flixton Golf Club URM M41 ..... 138 A3
Flixton Health Clinic URM M41 ..... 137 F1
Flixton J & I School URM M41 ..... 137 H1
Flowery Field Primary School HYDE SK14 ..... 133 G4
Forest Gate Community Primary School PART M31 ..... 150 C3
Forest Park School SALE M33 ..... 154 B2
Forest School HALE/TIMP WA15 ..... 166 A3
Forge Industrial Estate OLDE OL4 ..... 76 A5
Forum Leisure Centre WYTH/NTH M22 ..... 180 B1
Fourways Trading Estate TRPK M17 ..... 125 F2
Freehold Community Primary School CHAD OL9 ..... 8 A6
Freetown Business Park BURY BL9 ..... 5 G1
The Friars Primary School CSLFD M3 ..... 6 A1
Friezland Primary School OLDE OL4 ..... 94 B2
Fulshaw CE Primary School WILM/AE SK9 ..... 198 C4
Furrow Community School MDTN M24 ..... 71 H1
Galleon Leisure Centre DID/WITH M20 ..... 169 H1
Gallery of Costume RUSH/FAL M14 ..... 143 E1
Gallery Oldham, Library & Lifelong Learning Centre OLD OL1 ..... 9 H4
Garrick Playhouse ALT WA14 ..... 165 G3
Garrick Theatre EDGY/DAV SK3 ..... 13 F4
Gaskell Primary School BOL BL1 ..... 2 B2
The Gates Primary School WHTN BL5 ..... 62 A2
The Gates Shopping Centre BOL BL1 ..... 2 E4
Gateway Industrial Estate CMANE M1 ..... 7 J5
Gatley Golf Club CHD/CHDH SK8 ..... 181 G1
Gatley Health Centre CHD/CHDH SK8 ..... 169 F3
Gatley Primary School CHD/CHDH SK8 ..... 169 F4
Gee Cross Holy Trinity CE Primary School HYDE SK14 ..... 148 B3
Gee Cross Social & Sports Club HYDE SK14 ..... 148 A3
George H Carnall Leisure Centre URM M41 ..... 124 D4
George Tomlinson School FWTH BL4 ..... 82 B1
Georgian Health Centre OLD OL1 ..... 9 H3
Gilnow Mill Industrial Estate BOL BL1 ..... 48 B3
Gilnow Primary School BOL BL1 ..... 48 B3
Glebe House School ROCH OL11 ..... 29 H5
Glen Trading Estate OLDE OL4 ..... 92 C1
Globe Industrial Estate RAD M26 ..... 68 C1
Globe Lane Industrial Estate DUK SK16 ..... 133 E1
Globe Lane Primary School DUK SK16 ..... 133 E2
Glodwick Health Centre OLDE OL4 ..... 92 A1
Glodwick Infant School OLDE OL4 ..... 92 A2
Gloucester House Medical Centre URM M41 ..... 138 D1
GMB National College OLDTF/WHR M16 ..... 141 G1
Godfrey Ermen Memorial CE Primary School ECC M30 ..... 110 D5
Godley CP School HYDE SK14 ..... 134 A5
Golden Tulip Hotel TRPK M17 ..... 126 C2
Gorrells Industrial Estate ROCH OL11 ..... 42 D3
Gorsefield Primary School RAD M26 ..... 52 B5
Gorse Hall Primary School STLY SK15 ..... 120 C4
Gorse Hill Health Centre STRET M32 ..... 126 B5
Gorse Hill Primary School STRET M32 ..... 126 B4
Gorsey Bank Primary School WILM/AE SK9 ..... 198 C3
Gorton Brook First School WGTN/LGST M12 ..... 129 H2
Gorton Industrial Estate GTN M18 ..... 130 B2
Gorton Medical Centre GTN M18 ..... 130 C3
Gorton Mount Primary School GTN M18 ..... 130 A5
Gorton Retail Market GTN M18 ..... 130 C3
Goshen Sports Centre BURY BL9 ..... 53 H3
Grafton House Preparatory School AUL OL6 ..... 119 G3
Granada Studios CSLFD M3 ..... 6 B5
Grange Primary School WILM/AE SK9 ..... 191 H3
Grange School CHAD OL9 ..... 8 E2
RUSH/FAL M14 ..... 129 E5
Grasscroft Independent School OLDE OL4 ..... 93 H2
Great Moor Infant School OFTN SK2 ..... 172 C4
Greater Manchester Police Headquarters OLDTF/WHR M16 ..... 126 D3
Great Moor Clinic OFTN SK2 ..... 172 D4
Great Moor Infant School OFTN SK2 ..... 172 C4
Great Northern Shopping & Leisure Centre CSLFD M3 ..... 6 D6
Greave Primary School MPL/ROM SK6 ..... 162 B2
Greenacres Primary School OLDE OL4 ..... 76 B5
Greenbank Primary School WHIT OL12 ..... 10 D2
Greenbank School CHD/CHDH SK8 ..... 182 C3
Greenbrow Infant School NTHM/RTH M23 ..... 179 G1
Greencourts Business Park WYTH/NTH M22 ..... 181 F5
Green End Junior School BNG/LEV M19 ..... 158 B1
Greenfield CC UPML OL3 ..... 95 E2
Greenfield Primary School HYDE SK14 ..... 148 A2
UPML OL3 ..... 95 E1
Green Fold Special School FWTH BL4 ..... 65 E4
Greengate Industrial Estate MDTN M24 ..... 89 F2
Greenheys Business Centre HULME M15 ..... 128 B3
Greenhill Primary School OLDE OL4 ..... 9 H6
TOT/BURYW BL8 ..... 37 E5
Green Lane Industrial Estate HTNM SK4 ..... 12 B2
Greenmount CC TOT/BURYW BL8 ..... 26 A2
Greenmount Primary School TOT/BURYW BL8 ..... 25 H1
Green Room Theatre CMANE M1 ..... 6 E7
Greenside Primary School DROY M43 ..... 117 G3
Greenside Trading Centre DROY M43 ..... 117 H4
Greenwood Business Centre ORD M5 ..... 113 F4
Greenwood Primary School ECC M30 ..... 111 F1
Greswell Primary School DTN/ASHW M34 ..... 146 C1
Greyhound & Speedway Stadium GTN M18 ..... 130 A3
Greyland Medical Centre PWCH M25 ..... 86 A1
Griffin Business Centre SLFD M6 ..... 101 F5
Grosvenor Business Park MPL/ROM SK6 ..... 146 D5
Grosvenor Industrial Estate AULW OL7 ..... 119 F4
Grosvenor Road Primary School SWIN M27 ..... 99 G4
Guardian Angels RC Primary School TOT/BURYW BL8 ..... 37 G3
Guide Bridge Industrial Estate AULW OL7 ..... 118 D5
Guide Bridge Theatre DTN/ASHW M34 ..... 118 D5
Guide Bridge Trading Estate DTN/ASHW M34 ..... 118 D5
Guinness Road Trading Estate TRPK M17 ..... 111 G5
Hale Barns CC HALE/TIMP WA15 ..... 179 F4
Hale Golf Club HALE/TIMP WA15 ..... 178 B5
Hale Preparatory School HALE/TIMP WA15 ..... 177 H1
Halfpenny Bridge Industrial Estate MILN OL16 ..... 30 B5
Hall i' th' Wood Museum BOL BL1 ..... 34 B2
Halliwell Industrial Estate BOL BL1 ..... 33 G3
Hamer CP School MILN OL16 ..... 11 H1
Hampson Street Trading Estate ORD M5 ..... 114 A4
Handforth Dean Shopping Centre WILM/AE SK9 ..... 192 B3
Handforth Health Centre WILM/AE SK9 ..... 192 A4
Hanover Business Park ALT WA14 ..... 165 E2
Harcourt Industrial Centre WALK M28 ..... 82 A2
Hardman Fold Special School FAIL M35 ..... 104 C3
Hardy Mill Primary School BOLE BL2 ..... 35 G2
Harper Green School FWTH BL4 ..... 65 G3
Harp Industrial Estate ROCH OL11 ..... 42 C4
Harp Trading Estate TRPK M17 ..... 111 H5
Harpurhey Business Centre BKLY M9 ..... 103 E1
Harpurhey Health Centre BKLY M9 ..... 103 E2
Harpur Mount Primary School BKLY M9 ..... 103 E2
Harrop Fold School WALK M28 ..... 81 G4
Harrytown Catholic High School MPL/ROM SK6 ..... 161 H4
Hartford Industrial Estate CHAD OL9 ..... 8 B5
Hartshead High School AUL OL6 ..... 107 H3
Harwood Golf Club (Bolton) BOLE BL2 ..... 35 H2
Harwood Health Centre BOLE BL2 ..... 35 E1
Harwood Meadows Primary School BOLE BL2 ..... 35 G3
Harwood Park Primary School HEY OL10 ..... 41 E5
Haslam Park Primary School BOLS/LL BL3 ..... 48 A4
Hathershaw Technology College OLDS OL8 ..... 91 G5
Hattersley Health Clinic HYDE SK14 ..... 149 G1
Hattersley Industrial Estate HYDE SK14 ..... 149 G2
Hat Works Museum EDGY/DAV SK3 ..... 13 F3
Haveley Hey Primary School WYTH/NTH M22 ..... 168 B5
Hawkins Clinic MILN OL16 ..... 10 D7
Hawksley Industrial Estate OLDS OL8 ..... 90 D4
Hawthorns Special School DTN/ASHW M34 ..... 132 A3
Hayward School BOLS/LL BL3 ..... 64 B2
Hayward Sports Centre BOLS/LL BL3 ..... 64 B2
Hazeldene Medical Centre NEWH/MOS M40 ..... 104 D1
Hazel Grove Clinic BRAM/HZG SK7 ..... 185 F1
Hazel Grove Golf Club BRAM/HZG SK7 ..... 186 A3

Hazel Grove High School *BRAM/HZG* SK7 .... 184 D3
Hazel Grove Pools & Fitness Centre *BRAM/HZG* SK7 .... 184 B3
Hazel Grove Primary School *BRAM/HZG* SK7 .... 185 F1
Hazel Grove Recreation Centre *BRAM/HZG* SK7 .... 184 D4
Hazlehurst Community Primary School *RAMS* BL0 .... 16 B4
Heald Green Medical Centre *CHD/CHDH* SK8 .... 181 G4
Heald Place Primary School *RUSH/FAL* M14 .... 128 C5
Healey Dell Nature Reserve *WHIT* OL12 .... 18 A4
Healey Primary School *WHIT* OL12 .... 18 D5
Heap Bridge Primary School *BURY* BL9 .... 39 G5
Heathfield Primary School *BOLS/LL* BL3 .... 63 H2
Heaton CC *BOL* BL1 .... 32 D4
Heaton Cemetery *BOL* BL1 .... 48 A3
Heaton Medical Centre *BOL* BL1 .... 32 C5
Heaton Moor Golf Club *HTNM* SK4 .... 158 D1
Heaton Moor Medical Centre *HTNM* SK4 .... 159 E1
Heaton Moor RUFC *HTNM* SK4 .... 159 E3
Heaton Norris Health Centre *HTNM* SK4 .... 159 G3
Heaton Park *PWCH* M25 .... 86 D2
Heaton Park Golf Centre *PWCH* M25 .... 86 D1
Heaton Park Primary School *WHTF* M45 .... 86 A1
Heaton Special School *HTNM* SK4 .... 159 E1
Helen O'Grady Drama Academy *ALT* WA14 .... 165 F5
Hempshaw Business Centre *STKP* SK1 .... 172 C2
Henshaw Society for the Blind *OLDTF/WHR* M16 .... 126 D4
Hertford Industrial Estate *AULW* OL7 .... 119 F4
Heybrook Primary School *WHIT* OL12 .... 11 F3
Heyes Lane Infant School *HALE/TIMP* WA15 .... 166 C1
The Heys Primary School *AUL* OL6 .... 120 A2
Hey-with-Zion Primary School *OLDE* OL4 .... 76 D5
Heywood Cemetery *ROCH* OL11 .... 41 G2
Heywood Community High School *BURY* BL9 .... 39 H5
HEY OL10 .... 40 A5
Heywood Industrial Park *HEY* OL10 .... 55 F1
Heywood Sports Complex *HEY* OL10 .... 40 C3
Higginshaw Sports Club *OLD* OL1 .... 9 J1
Highbank Trading Estate *OP/CLY* M11 .... 130 C1
Highbarn Junior School *ROY/SHW* OL2 .... 59 F4
High Birch Special School *ROCH* OL11 .... 42 A1
Higher Broughton Health Centre *BRO* M7 .... 101 H4
Higher Failsworth Primary School *FAIL* M35 .... 105 F2
Higher Lane Primary School *WHTF* M45 .... 69 F4
Higher Openshaw Community School *OP/CLY* M11 .... 117 E5
Highfield Cemetery *MPL/ROM* SK6 .... 161 G4
Highfield Hospital *ROCH* OL11 .... 42 C1
Highfield Primary School *FWTH* BL4 .... 65 F4
URM M41 .... 139 F1
High Lane Medical Centre *MPL/ROM* SK6 .... 186 D5
High Lane Primary School *MPL/ROM* SK6 .... 186 D4
High Lawn Primary School *BOL* BL1 .... 22 D5
Highlea Secondary School *WALK* M28 .... 96 A2
Hillcrest Grammar School *EDGY/DAV* SK3 .... 172 A3
Hillgate Business Centre *STKP* SK1 .... 13 H6
Hill Top Community Primary School *ROCH* OL11 .... 43 F5
Hill Top Community Special School *OLDE* OL4 .... 61 F5
Hilton Lane Primary School *WALK* M28 .... 81 F4
HM Prison *CHH* M8 .... 114 C1
Hodge Clough Infant School *OLD* OL1 .... 76 C1
Hodge Clough Junior School *OLD* OL1 .... 76 C1
Holcombe Brook Primary School *RAMS* BL0 .... 26 B1
Holcombe Brook Sports Club *RAMS* BL0 .... 16 B5
Holden Clough Primary School *AUL* OL6 .... 107 G3
Holiday Inn *BOL* BL1 .... 2 E3
NEWH/MOS M40 .... 103 G5
WILM/AE SK9 .... 190 A5
Hollingworth High School *MILN* OL16 .... 31 H5
Hollingworth Lake Activity Centre *LIT* OL15 .... 31 H1
Hollin Primary School *MDTN* M24 .... 72 D1
Hollins Grundy Primary School *BURY* BL9 .... 53 H4
Hollinwood Business Centre *FAIL* M35 .... 105 G2
Hollinwood Cemetery *OLDS* OL8 .... 105 H1
Hollinwood CC *OLDS* OL8 .... 105 H2
Holly Bank Industrial Estate *RAD* M26 .... 68 A1
Holly Mount RC Primary School *TOT/BURYW* BL8 .... 25 G2
Hollywood Bowl *NEWH/MOS* M40 .... 104 C1
Holt Town Industrial Estate *NEWH/MOS* M40 .... 115 H3
Holy Cross & All Saints RC Primary School *ECC* M30 .... 111 E5
Holy Cross College *BURY* BL9 .... 53 F1
Holy Family Catholic Primary School *SALE* M33 .... 155 F2
Holy Family RC Primary School *OLDS* OL8 .... 106 A2
Holy Family VA RC Primary School *ROCH* OL11 .... 43 F4
Holy Infant RC Primary School *BOL* BL1 .... 33 H2
Holy Name RC Primary School *HULME* M15 .... 128 B3
Holy Rosary RC Primary School *OLDS* OL8 .... 91 G5
Holy Trinity CE Dobcross School *UPML* OL3 .... 78 C2
Holy Trinity CE Primary School *AUL* OL6 .... 119 F2
BKLY M9 .... 103 F2
BURY BL9 .... 4 E6
LIT OL15 .... 21 F2
Hong Sing Chinese Medical Centre *BRAM/HZG* SK7 .... 185 F1
Hooley Bridge Industrial Estate *HEY* OL10 .... 40 D2
Hope High School *SLFD* M6 .... 112 B1
Hope Hospital *SLFD* M6 .... 112 A3
Hopwood Hall College *MDTN* M24 .... 57 E4
WHIT OL12 .... 10 B6
Hopwood Medical Centre *HEY* OL10 .... 41 F5
Hopwood Primary School *HEY* OL10 .... 56 B1
Hotel Ibis *CMANE* M1 .... 7 F6
CMANE M1 .... 128 B1
Hotel Rossetti *CMANE* M1 .... 7 H5
Houldsworth Golf Club *RDSH* SK5 .... 145 E3
Houldsworth Medical Centre *RDSH* SK5 .... 145 F4
Hoyle Street Industrial Estate *WGTN/LGST* M12 .... 128 D1
Hubert House Jewish Boys School *BRO* M7 .... 101 G2
Hulme Adult Education Centre *HULME* M15 .... 127 H2
Hulme Arch *HULME* M15 .... 128 A2
The Hulme Court Preparatory School *OLDS* OL8 .... 91 E3
The Hulme Grammar School for Boys *OLDS* OL8 .... 91 E3
Hulme Hall Grammar School *CHD/CHDH* SK8 .... 182 D3
Hulton Hospital *BOLS/LL* BL3 .... 63 H1
Hurstfield Industrial Estate *RDSH* SK5 .... 145 E5
Hursthead Junior School *CHD/CHDH* SK8 .... 193 F1
Hurst Knoll CE Primary School *AUL* OL6 .... 119 H1
Hyde Clarendon Sixth Form College *HYDE* SK14 .... 133 G4
Hyde CC *HYDE* SK14 .... 148 B5
Hyde Leisure Pool *HYDE* SK14 .... 148 A1
Hyde Technology School *HYDE* SK14 .... 133 F4
Hyde United FC *HYDE* SK14 .... 148 B1
IKEA Store Manchester *AUL* OL6 .... 119 F2
IMAX Cinema *ANC* M4 .... 7 F3
IMEX Business Park *BRUN/LGST* M13 .... 129 G5
Imperial War Museum North *TRPK* M17 .... 126 B1
Indoor Tennis Centre *OP/CLY* M11 .... 116 A3
Inland Revenue Office *CSLFD* M3 .... 6 C4
Innes Special School *WHIT* OL12 .... 29 F2
Innkeeper's Lodge *HTNM* SK4 .... 159 F1
OLD OL1 .... 74 C2
WILM/AE SK9 .... 200 D2
Inscape House School *CHD/CHDH* SK8 .... 182 A1
Inscape House Special School *WALK* M28 .... 97 F1
The Instructor College *STKP* SK1 .... 13 G4
International Convention Centre *CSLFD* M3 .... 6 D6
Iranian School of Manchester *WGTN/LGST* M12 .... 130 A5
Irlam & Cadishead Community High School *IRL* M44 .... 136 A4
Irlam CP School *IRL* M44 .... 136 B2
Irlam Endowed Primary School *IRL* M44 .... 136 C1
Irlam Industrial Estate *IRL* M44 .... 136 A4
Irlam Swimming Pool *IRL* M44 .... 136 C2
James Brindley Primary School *WALK* M28 .... 96 D1
The Jeff Joseph Sale Moor Technology College *SALE* M33 .... 155 E4
Jewish Museum *CHH* M8 .... 114 D1
Jewish Senior Boys School *BRO* M7 .... 101 G3
John Rylands Library *CSLFD* M3 .... 6 D5
Johnson Fold Community Primary School *BOL* BL1 .... 32 C3
Joseph Adamson Industrial Estate *HYDE* SK14 .... 147 G1
Joseph Rayner Independent School *OLDS* OL8 .... 106 D2
Jumbles Country Park *BOLE* BL2 .... 24 A2
Jurys Inn *CMANE* M1 .... 6 D7
Kaskenmoor School *OLDS* OL8 .... 105 G1
Kassim Darwish Grammar School for Boys *OLDTF/WHR* M16 .... 142 A2
Kayley Industrial Estate *AULW* OL7 .... 119 E2
Kearsley West Primary School *FWTH* BL4 .... 66 B5
Kenmore Medical Centre *WILM/AE* SK9 .... 198 D4
Kentmere Primary School *WHIT* OL12 .... 19 G5
Kenyon Business Park *BOL/LL* BL3 .... 48 D4
Kiely Business Park *BURY* BL9 .... 5 G1
King David Junior & High School *CHH* M8 .... 102 A1
Kingfisher Community Special School *CHAD* OL9 .... 90 A2
The King of Kings School *ANC* M4 .... 7 G1
Kings Road Primary School *OLDTF/WHR* M16 .... 126 D5
King Street Remedial Clinic *DUK* SK16 .... 119 G4
Kingsway CP School *URM* M41 .... 124 D4
Kingsway Retail Park *MILN* OL16 .... 31 E4
Kingsway School *CHD/CHDH* SK8 .... 169 H5
Kingsway Secondary School *CHD/CHDH* SK8 .... 169 H4
Knoll Street Industrial Park *BRO* M7 .... 101 G3
Knowsley Junior School *OLDE* OL4 .... 77 F5
Kratos Industrial Estate *URM* M41 .... 125 E3
Lacey Green Primary School *WILM/AE* SK9 .... 198 D1
Lady Barn House School *CHD/CHDH* SK8 .... 182 A1
Ladybarn Primary School *DID/WITH* M20 .... 143 F5
Ladybridge High School *BOLS/LL* BL3 .... 47 G5
Ladybridge Primary School *BOLS/LL* BL3 .... 47 G4
CHD/CHDH SK8 .... 171 E4
Ladybrook Primary School *BRAM/HZG* SK7 .... 184 A5
Ladysmith Shopping Centre *AUL* OL6 .... 119 G2
Ladywell Hospital Lodge *SALQ* M50 .... 111 H3
Ladywood School *BOLS/LL* BL3 .... 51 E5
Lancashire CCC (Old Trafford) *STRET* M32 .... 126 C5
Lancasterian School *DID/WITH* M20 .... 156 D1
Lance Burn Health Centre *SLFD* M6 .... 113 F3
Lane End Primary School *CHD/CHDH* SK8 .... 183 F2
Langley Primary School *MDTN* M24 .... 72 B1
Langworthy Clinic *SLFD* M6 .... 113 E3
Langworthy Road Primary School *SLFD* M6 .... 113 E2
Lark Hill Primary School *EDGY/DAV* SK3 .... 12 B5
SLFD M6 .... 113 E3
Last Drop Village Hotel *EDGW/EG* BL7 .... 23 F2
The Last Drop Village *EDGW/EG* BL7 .... 23 F2
Lavenham Business Centre *CHAD* OL9 .... 8 B5
Lawn Cemetery *ALT* WA14 .... 164 A1
Lawnhurst Trading Estate *CHD/CHDH* SK8 .... 171 E4
Leigh Infant & Primary School *HYDE* SK14 .... 148 A1
Leigh Street Primary School *HYDE* SK14 .... 148 B1
Lemon Park Industrial Estate *HEY* OL10 .... 41 F5
Levenshulme Baths *BNG/LEV* M19 .... 144 B2
Levenshulme Health Centre *BNG/LEV* M19 .... 144 B2
Levenshulme High School *BNG/LEV* M19 .... 144 A4
Levenshulme Trading Estate *BNG/LEV* M19 .... 144 C1
Lever Edge Primary School *BOLS/LL* BL3 .... 64 C2
Leverhulme Park Athletics Stadium *BOLS/LL* BL3 .... 50 A3
Light Oaks Junior School *SLFD* M6 .... 112 A1
Lily Lane J & I School *NEWH/MOS* M40 .... 103 H2
Limehurst Primary School *OLDS* OL8 .... 106 A2
Limeside Primary School *OLDS* OL8 .... 105 H1
The Limes School *AULW* OL7 .... 119 F1
Lime Tree Primary School *SALE* M33 .... 155 F3
Linden Road Primary School *DTN/ASHW* M34 .... 132 D5
Lindow Primary School *WILM/AE* SK9 .... 200 A2
Linguard Business Park *MILN* OL16 .... 10 E7
Linkway Industrial Estate *MDTN* M24 .... 73 E1
Linnyshaw Industrial Estate *FWTH* BL4 .... 82 B1
Littleborough CC *LIT* OL15 .... 21 E2
Littleborough Primary School *LIT* OL15 .... 21 E1
Little Heaton VC CE Primary School *MDTN* M24 .... 71 H5
Little Hulton Skills Centre *WALK* M28 .... 81 F3
Little Lever School Specialist Language College *BOLS/LL* BL3 .... 66 B1
Littlemoor Primary School *OLDE* OL4 .... 76 B4
Littlemoss Business Park *DROY* M43 .... 118 B2
Littlemoss High School *DROY* M43 .... 118 B1
Livingstone Primary School *MOSL* OL5 .... 108 C2
L & M Business Park *ALT* WA14 .... 165 E3
Lobden Golf Club *WHIT* OL12 .... 18 D1
Local Studies Library *OLD* OL1 .... 9 H4
Lockside Medical Centre *STLY* SK15 .... 121 E3
Longdendale Recreation Centre *HYDE* SK14 .... 135 G5
Longford Park Special School *STRET* M32 .... 140 D1
Longford Trading Estate *STRET* M32 .... 126 A5
Longsight CC *WGTN/LGST* M12 .... 129 H5
Longsight Health Centre *WGTN/LGST* M12 .... 129 G4
Longsight Industrial Estate *WGTN/LGST* M12 .... 129 G4
Lords College *BOLE* BL2 .... 3 G7
Loreto Grammar School *ALT* WA14 .... 165 F4
Lostock College *STRET* M32 .... 125 F5
Lostock Hall Primary School *POY/DIS* SK12 .... 194 C4
Lostock Primary School *HOR/BR* BL6 .... 46 D3
Lower Broughton Health Centre *BRO* M7 .... 114 A1
Lowercroft Primary School *TOT/BURYW* BL8 .... 36 D4
Lower Kersal Primary School *BRO* M7 .... 101 E4
Lower Park Primary School *POY/DIS* SK12 .... 194 D3
Lowerplace Primary School *MILN* OL16 .... 43 G2
Lowes Park Golf Club *BURY* BL9 .... 27 H5
The Lowry Hotel *CSLFD* M3 .... 6 C3
The Lowry *TRPK* M17 .... 126 B1
Ludworth Primary School *MPL/ROM* SK6 .... 175 F1
Lum Head Primary School *CHD/CHDH* SK8 .... 181 G1
The Lyceum Musical Theatre *OLD* OL1 .... 9 G4
Lyme Park Country Park *POY/DIS* SK12 .... 197 G5
Lyndhurst Primary School *DUK* SK16 .... 119 H4
OLDS OL8 .... 91 E4
Lyntown Trading Estate *ECC* M30 .... 111 E3
Lyon Industrial Estate *ALT* WA14 .... 165 E2
Lyon Road Industrial Estate *FWTH* BL4 .... 82 B2
Macdonald Norton Grange Hotel *ROCH* OL11 .... 57 F2
Macdonald Road Medical Centre *IRL* M44 .... 136 A3
Mackenzie Industrial Estate *CHD/CHDH* SK8 .... 171 E3
Magda House Medical Centre *OFTN* SK2 .... 173 E5
Malbern Industrial Estate *DTN/ASHW* M34 .... 131 H4
The Mall Shopping Centre *ECC* M30 .... 111 G3
Malmaison Hotel *CMANE* M1 .... 7 H5
Mancentral Trading Estate *ORD* M5 .... 6 A4
Manchester Academy *RUSH/FAL* M14 .... 128 B4
Manchester Airport Hotel *MANAIR* M90 .... 180 B5
Manchester Airport World Freight Terminal *MANAIR* M90 .... 189 H1
Manchester Aquatics Centre *BRUN/LGST* M13 .... 128 B1
Manchester Arndale Shopping Centre *CMANE* M1 .... 7 F3
Manchester Art Gallery *CMANE* M1 .... 7 F5
Manchester (Barton) Airfield *ECC* M30 .... 123 F1
Manchester Business Park *MANAIR* M90 .... 180 B4
Manchester Business School *HULME* M15 .... 128 B2
Manchester Cathedral *CSLFD* M3 .... 6 E2
Manchester Cathedral Visitor Centre *CSLFD* M3 .... 6 E3
Manchester Central *CSLFD* M3 .... 6 D7
Manchester Central Library *CMANW* M2 .... 6 E6
Manchester Centre for the Deaf *BRUN/LGST* M13 .... 128 C2
Manchester Centre for Vision *BRUN/LGST* M13 .... 128 C3
Manchester City FC (City of Manchester Stadium) *OP/CLY* M11 .... 116 A4
Manchester City Museum & Tour *OP/CLY* M11 .... 116 A3
Manchester College of Arts & Technology *CMANE* M1 .... 7 H4
CSLFD M3 .... 6 B5
WGTN/LGST M12 .... 129 E1
Manchester Conference Centre & Hotel *CMANE* M1 .... 7 H7
The Manchester Crematorium *CCHDY* M21 .... 141 G5
Manchester Golf Club *MDTN* M24 .... 57 F3
Manchester Grammar School *BRUN/LGST* M13 .... 143 G1
Manchester High School for Girls *RUSH/FAL* M14 .... 143 E2
Manchester Industrial Centre *CSLFD* M3 .... 6 A6
Manchester International Airport *MANAIR* M90 .... 190 A2
Manchester Islamic High School for Girls *CCHDY* M21 .... 141 E3
Manchester Junior Girls School *BRO* M7 .... 101 G1
Manchester Mesivta High School *PWCH* M25 .... 86 A4
Manchester Mesivta School *PWCH* M25 .... 86 A4
Manchester Metropolitan University *BRUN/LGST* M13 .... 128 D4
CMANE M1 .... 7 G6
CMANE M1 .... 128 B1
DID/WITH M20 .... 157 E3
DID/WITH M20 .... 157 G4
OLDTF/WHR M16 .... 142 B1
RUSH/FAL M14 .... 128 D5
Manchester Metropolitan University Institute of Education Didsbury *DID/WITH* M20 .... 157 G4
Manchester Museum *BRUN/LGST* M13 .... 128 C2
Manchester Road Primary School *DROY* M43 .... 117 F4
Manchester Royal Infirmary *BRUN/LGST* M13 .... 128 D3
Manchester RUFC *CHD/CHDH* SK8 .... 192 D1
Manchester School of Management *BRUN/LGST* M13 .... 128 B2
Manchester Southern Cemetery *CCHDY* M21 .... 141 H5
Manchester United FC (Old Trafford) *OLDTF/WHR* M16 .... 126 C3
Manchester United Museum & Tour Centre *TRPK* M17 .... 126 B3
Manchester University *BRUN/LGST* M13 .... 128 D3
Manchester Victoria & Albert Hotel *CSLFD* M3 .... 6 A5
Manchester Youth Theatre *HULME* M15 .... 128 A3
Mandelay Health Centre *BOL* BL1 .... 22 D5
Manley Park Junior School *OLDTF/WHR* M16 .... 141 G1
Manley Park Primary School *OLDTF/WHR* M16 .... 141 G1
Manor Golf Club *FWTH* BL4 .... 83 E3
Manor Green Primary School *DTN/ASHW* M34 .... 147 E3
Manor High School *SALE* M33 .... 153 F1
Manway Business Park *ALT* WA14 .... 165 H2
The Maples Medical Centre *NTHM/RTH* M23 .... 167 G5
Marcliffe Industrial Estate *BRAM/HZG* SK7 .... 185 G3
Marjory Lees Health Centre *OLD* OL1 .... 9 H2
Market Place Shopping Centre *BOL* BL1 .... 2 E4
Market Street Athletics Track *BURY* BL9 .... 4 E7
Markland Hill Primary School *BOL* BL1 .... 47 G1
Marland Hill Primary School *ROCH* OL11 .... 42 B1
Marland Park Golf Club *ROCH* OL11 .... 41 H1
Marlborough Road Primary School *BRO* M7 .... 102 A4
Marple Clinic *MPL/ROM* SK6 .... 175 E3
Marple Golf Club *MPL/ROM* SK6 .... 186 D1
Marple Hall School *MPL/ROM* SK6 .... 174 B2
Marriott Hotel *HALE/TIMP* WA15 .... 179 F5
Marriott Worsley Park Hotel & Country Club *WALK* M28 .... 97 F3
Marsland Street Industrial Centre *BRAM/HZG* SK7 .... 185 E2
Masefield Primary School *BOLS/LL* BL3 .... 51 E5
Mather Street Primary School *FAIL* M35 .... 104 C2
Matthew Moss High School *HEY* OL10 .... 41 H2
Mauldeth Medical Centre *DID/WITH* M20 .... 143 F4
Mauldeth Road Primary School *RUSH/FAL* M14 .... 143 G4
Mayfield Industrial Park *IRL* M44 .... 122 D5
Mayfield Primary School *OLD* OL1 .... 76 A4
Maypole Farm Estate *PART* M31 .... 137 F5
Meade Hill School *CHH* M8 .... 87 E3
Meadowbank Primary School *CHD/CHDH* SK8 .... 170 C4
Meadow Industrial Estate *FAIL* M35 .... 104 C4
STKP SK1 .... 160 A3
The Meadows School *BKLY* M9 .... 88 C3
Meadway Health Centre *SALE* M33 .... 153 H4
Meanwood Primary School *WHIT* OL12 .... 29 F2
Mechinoh School *BRO* M7 .... 101 H1
Medlock Infant School *BRUN/LGST* M13 .... 128 C1

Medlock Leisure Centre *DROY* M43 ... 118 A2
Medlock Primary School *BRUN/LGST* M13 ... 128 D1
Medlock Valley Community School *OLDS* OL8 ... 91 H4
Megabowl *BURY* BL9 ... 54 A3
OLDTF/WHR M16 ... 126 D3
Melland High School *GTN* M18 ... 144 D1
MEN Arena *CSLFD* M3 ... 6 E1
Mental Health Centre *BOLE* BL2 ... 35 G5
Mereside Educational Trust *SALE* M33 ... 155 E3
Meridian Clinic *BURY* BL9 ... 4 C5
Mersey Drive Primary School *BURY* BL9 ... 70 B2
Mersey Road Industrial Estate *FAIL* M35 ... 105 G1
Mersey Trading Estate *HTNM* SK4 ... 158 C5
Mersey Vale Primary School *HTNM* SK4 ... 158 D5
Merseyway Centre *STKP* SK1 ... 13 F2
Mesne Lea Primary School *WALK* M28 ... 97 F1
Methodist Cemetery *BOLE* BL2 ... 35 F2
Metro Cinema *AUL* OL6 ... 119 G3
Micklehurst All Saints Primary School *MOSL* OL5 ... 109 F1
Micklehurst CC *MOSL* OL5 ... 109 F1
Middleton Cemetery *MDTN* M24 ... 73 F2
Middleton Crematorium *MDTN* M24 ... 73 F2
Middleton CC *MDTN* M24 ... 72 C2
Middleton Parish Church School *MDTN* M24 ... 72 C2
Middleton Public Baths *MDTN* M24 ... 72 D4
Middleton Shopping Centre *MDTN* M24 ... 72 C4
Middleton Technology School *MDTN* M24 ... 73 E4
Midland Hotel *CMANW* M2 ... 6 E6
Miles Platting Pool *NEWH/MOS* M40 ... 115 G2
Milking Green Industrial Estate *OLDE* OL4 ... 92 D2
Mill 5 Belgrave Industrial Estate *OLDS* OL8 ... 91 H4
Millbrook Business Centre *NTHM/RTH* M23 ... 167 F3
Millbrook Industrial Estate *NTHM/RTH* M23 ... 167 F3
Millbrook Primary School *STLY* SK15 ... 109 F5
Mill Gate Shopping Centre *BURY* BL9 ... 4 E5
Mills Hill Primary School *CHAD* OL9 ... 73 H4
Mill Street Industrial Estate *BOL* BL1 ... 3 G4
Millwood Primary Special School *BURY* BL9 ... 53 G3
Milnrow CC *MILN* OL16 ... 44 C1
Milnrow CE Aided Primary School *MILN* OL16 ... 31 G5
Milnrow Health Centre *MILN* OL16 ... 44 C1
Milo Industrial Park *DROY* M43 ... 118 A3
Milton St Johns CE Primary School *MOSL* OL5 ... 93 H5
Minden Medical Centre *BURY* BL9 ... 5 F4
Moat House School *HTNM* SK4 ... 159 H3
Monde Trading Estate *TRPK* M17 ... 125 F2
Montague Business Park *OLDTF/WHR* M16 ... 126 D4
Monton Bowling Club *ECC* M30 ... 111 F1
Monton CC *ECC* M30 ... 111 F1
Monton Green Primary School *ECC* M30 ... 111 F1
Monton House Hotel *ECC* M30 ... 111 E2
Monton Medical Centre *ECC* M30 ... 110 D1
Moor Allerton School *DID/WITH* M20 ... 157 E2
Moorfield Community Primary School *IRL* M44 ... 122 B5
Moorfield Primary School *BRAM/HZG* SK7 ... 184 D3
Moorgate Primary School *BOLE* BL2 ... 3 K2
Moorgate Retail Park *BURY* BL9 ... 5 F3
Moorhouse Primary School *MILN* OL16 ... 31 F5
Moorlands Junior School *SALE* M33 ... 155 F1
Moorside High School *SWIN* M27 ... 98 C3
Moorside Leisure Centre *SWIN* M27 ... 98 C3
Moorside Primary School *DROY* M43 ... 118 A4
SWIN M27 ... 98 C3
Moravian College *DROY* M43 ... 117 H5
Morris Green Business Park *BOLS/LL* BL3 ... 48 B5
Moses Gate Country Park *FWTH* BL4 ... 66 B2
Moses Park Country Park *BOLS/LL* BL3 ... 50 A5
Moss Field Community Primary School *HEY* OL10 ... 40 D3
Mossfield CP School *SWIN* M27 ... 99 E1
Moss Hey Primary School *BRAM/HZG* SK7 ... 193 F2
Moss Industrial Estate *MILN* OL16 ... 43 G1
Moss Lane Industrial Estate *ROY/SHW* OL2 ... 75 H1
Mossley AFC *MOSL* OL5 ... 108 D1
Mossley Health Centre *MOSL* OL5 ... 108 D1
Mossley Hollins High School *MOSL* OL5 ... 109 F1
Moss Park Junior & Infant School *STRET* M32 ... 139 H1
Moss Side Health Centre *RUSH/FAL* M14 ... 128 B4
Moss Side Leisure Centre *HULME* M15 ... 128 A3
Moss View Primary School *PART* M31 ... 151 F3
Moston Fields Primary School *NEWH/MOS* M40 ... 103 H1
Moston Indoor Market *NEWH/MOS* M40 ... 103 G2
Moston Lane Primary School *BKLY* M9 ... 103 F2
Mottram CE Primary School *HYDE* SK14 ... 135 H5
Mount Carmel RC Junior School *BKLY* M9 ... 88 A5
Mount Carmel RC Primary School *BKLY* M9 ... 103 E1
Mountheath Industrial Park *PWCH* M25 ... 101 E1
Mount Pleasant Business Centre *OLDE* OL4 ... 76 A5
Mount St Joseph Business & Enterprise College *BOLS/LL* BL3 ... 65 E2
The Museum of Science & Industry in Manchester *CSLFD* M3 ... 6 A6
Museum of the Manchester Regiment *AUL* OL6 ... 119 G2
Museum of Trade Union History *CMANE* M1 ... 7 F6
Museum of Transport *CHH* M8 ... 102 B4
The Music School *CHH* M8 ... 102 B2
Mytham Primary School *BOLS/LL* BL3 ... 67 E1
Nasmyth Business Centre *ECC* M30 ... 110 D3
National Cycling Centre (Velodrome) *OP/CLY* M11 ... 116 B3
National Industrial Estate *AULW* OL7 ... 119 F3
National Squash Centre *OP/CLY* M11 ... 116 A3
National Trading Estate *BRAM/HZG* SK7 ... 184 D1
Natural History Museum *CHAD* OL9 ... 8 B7
Navigation Primary School *ALT* WA14 ... 165 G3
Navigation Trading Estate *NEWH/MOS* M40 ... 103 H5
Nelson Business Centre *DTN/ASHW* M34 ... 132 C4
Neville Street Industrial Estate *CHAD* OL9 ... 8 A3
Nevill Road Infant School *BRAM/HZG* SK7 ... 183 H2
Newall Green High School *NTHM/RTH* M23 ... 167 G5
Newall Green Primary School *NTHM/RTH* M23 ... 168 A5
New Ardwick Sports Centre *WGTN/LGST* M12 ... 129 E2
New Bridge School *OLDS* OL8 ... 105 G2
Newbridge Special School *OLDS* OL8 ... 92 A5
Newbrook School *DID/WITH* M20 ... 156 D1
Newby Road Industrial Estate *BRAM/HZG* SK7 ... 185 E2
New Croft Community High School *SLFD* M6 ... 113 E2
New Harvest Learning Centre *CSLFD* M3 ... 6 A3
Newhaven Business Park *ECC* M30 ... 111 F4
Newhey Community Primary School *MILN* OL16 ... 44 D2
New Kingsway Health Centre *BNG/LEV* M19 ... 158 A2
Newlands Medical Centre *BOL* BL1 ... 47 H2
New Moston Primary School *NEWH/MOS* M40 ... 89 H5
New Museum *OLD* OL1 ... 9 F1
New North Manchester Golf Club *MDTN* M24 ... 72 A4
Newton Business Park *HYDE* SK14 ... 134 B3
Newton Moor Industrial Estate *HYDE* SK14 ... 133 H3
Newton Street Police Museum *CMANE* M1 ... 7 H4
Nicholas Varley Community School *NEWH/MOS* M40 ... 115 H1
Nicholls Sixth Form Centre *WGTN/LGST* M12 ... 129 E2
Norbury Hall Primary School *BRAM/HZG* SK7 ... 185 F3
Norden Community Primary School *WHIT* OL12 ... 28 C1
Norden CC *WHIT* OL12 ... 28 B1
Norris Bank Medical Centre *HTNM* SK4 ... 12 A3
Norris Bank Primary School *HTNM* SK4 ... 159 E3
Nortex Business Centre *BOL* BL1 ... 48 B1
Northbank Industrial Park *IRL* M44 ... 136 A5
IRL M44 ... 151 E1
North Cestrian Grammar School *ALT* WA14 ... 165 F4
North Chadderton School *CHAD* OL9 ... 74 B2
North Cheshire Jewish Primary School *CHD/CHDH* SK8 ... 181 G2
Northenden Golf Club *WYTH/NTH* M22 ... 156 D4
Northenden Primary School *WYTH/NTH* M22 ... 156 C5
Northern A & O Medical Centre *BURY* BL9 ... 4 E4
Northern Cemetery *SWIN* M27 ... 100 C3
Northern Moor Clinic *NTHM/RTH* M23 ... 155 G5
North Grecian Street Primary School *BRO* M7 ... 101 F4
North Heaton Primary School *HTNM* SK4 ... 144 C5
North Manchester General Hospital *CHH* M8 ... 102 D1
North Manchester High School for Boys *BKLY* M9 ... 89 E4
North Manchester High School for Girls *NEWH/MOS* M40 ... 88 D5
North Quays Business Park *ALT* WA14 ... 153 H5
North Reddish Health Centre *RDSH* SK5 ... 145 E2
North Reddish J & I School *RDSH* SK5 ... 145 F2
North Trafford College *STRET* M32 ... 126 C4
North Walkden Primary School *WALK* M28 ... 81 H2
Novotel *CMANE* M1 ... 7 F6
WALK M28 ... 97 F5
Oakdale Special School *DUK* SK16 ... 133 G2
Oakenclough Primary School *WILM/AE* SK9 ... 199 G1
Oakfield Primary School *HYDE* SK14 ... 133 H3
Oakfield Trading Estate *HALE/TIMP* WA15 ... 165 H4
Oakgrove School *CHD/CHDH* SK8 ... 181 H5
Oakhill Trading Estate *WALK* M28 ... 81 G2
Oaklands Infant School *WILM/AE* SK9 ... 199 H1
Oakleigh Medical Centre *CHH* M8 ... 102 C1
The Oaks Business Park *NTHM/RTH* M23 ... 167 E2
The Oaks Primary School *BOL* BL1 ... 23 E5
Oakwood High School *CCHDY* M21 ... 156 A1
SLFD M6 ... 99 H5
Octagon Theatre *BOL* BL1 ... 2 E5
Odeon Cinema *ROCH* OL11 ... 42 D2
Offerton Green Clinic *OFTN* SK2 ... 173 G4
Offerton Health Centre *OFTN* SK2 ... 172 C1
Offerton High School *OFTN* SK2 ... 173 F2
Offerton Industrial Estate *STKP* SK1 ... 172 C2
Oldfield Brow Primary School *ALT* WA14 ... 164 C4
Old Hall Clinic *CHD/CHDH* SK8 ... 169 G3
Old Hall Drive Primary School *GTN* M18 ... 130 C4
Old Hall Primary School *TOT/BURYW* BL8 ... 26 C4
Oldham Athletic FC (Boundary Park) *ROY/SHW* OL2 ... 75 E2
Oldham Broadway Business Park *CHAD* OL9 ... 73 H4
Oldham Business Centre *OLD* OL1 ... 9 F5
Oldham Central Industrial Park *OLD* OL1 ... 9 K1
Oldham College *CHAD* OL9 ... 8 D3
Oldham County Court *OLD* OL1 ... 8 E2
Oldham Crematorium *OLDS* OL8 ... 105 H1
Oldham CC *OLD* OL1 ... 76 B3
Oldham Golf Club *OLDE* OL4 ... 93 E3
Oldham RUFC *OLDS* OL8 ... 106 C2
Oldham Sixth Form College *OLDS* OL8 ... 8 E5
Oldham Sports Centre *OLD* OL1 ... 9 G3
Oldham Theatre Workshop *ROY/SHW* OL2 ... 59 E5
Oldham West Business Centre *CHAD* OL9 ... 74 C5
Old Mill Hotel *RAMS* BL0 ... 16 C1
Old Moat J & I School *DID/WITH* M20 ... 142 C4
Old Rectory Hotel *DTN/ASHW* M34 ... 147 E4
Old Trafford Community School *OLDTF/WHR* M16 ... 127 F2
Oldwood Primary School *WYTH/NTH* M22 ... 180 A2
Olympia Trading Estate *HULME* M15 ... 127 H1
Olympic House *MANAIR* M90 ... 180 B5
Open University *CCHDY* M21 ... 141 F2
Opera House *CSLFD* M3 ... 6 C5
The Operating Theatre *STRET* M32 ... 126 B5
Orchard House Day Hospital *ROY/SHW* OL2 ... 59 F5
Orchard Industrial Estate *SLFD* M6 ... 113 F1
Orchard Trading Estate *SLFD* M6 ... 100 C5
Ordsall Hall Museum *ORD* M5 ... 127 E2
Ordsall Health Centre *ORD* M5 ... 113 G5
Ordsall Recreation Centre *ORD* M5 ... 126 D1
Oriel Bank High School *OFTN* SK2 ... 172 A4
Oriental Arch *CMANE* M1 ... 7 F5
Orion Business Park *EDGY/DAV* SK3 ... 171 F4
Orion Trading Estate *TRPK* M17 ... 111 H5
Orrishmere Primary School *CHD/CHDH* SK8 ... 182 D1
Osborne Trading Estate *CHAD* OL9 ... 8 B1
Oswald Road Primary School *CCHDY* M21 ... 141 E2
Oulder Hill Community School Language College *ROCH* OL11 ... 29 E4
Our Lady of Grace RC Primary School *PWCH* M25 ... 85 H1
Our Lady of Lourdes Catholic Primary School *PART* M31 ... 150 D3
Our Lady of Lourdes RC Primary School *FWTH* BL4 ... 65 F4
TOT/BURYW BL8 ... 26 D5
Our Lady of Mount Carmel RC Primary School *AUL* OL6 ... 120 A1
Our Lady of the Rosary RC Primary School *URM* M41 ... 124 B4
Our Lady & St Anselms RC Primary School *WHIT* OL12 ... 14 C3
Our Lady & St Pauls RC Primary School *HEY* OL10 ... 39 H4
Our Ladys Catholic Primary School *EDGY/DAV* SK3 ... 12 E6
Our Lady's RC High School *BKLY* M9 ... 88 A1
Our Ladys RC High School *ROY/SHW* OL2 ... 75 E1
Our Ladys RC Primary School *OLDE* OL4 ... 76 D1
OLDTF/WHR M16 ... 127 G5
Our Lady & the Lancashire Martyrs RC Primary School *WALK* M28 ... 81 F4
Outwood Primary School *CHD/CHDH* SK8 ... 181 H5
Overdale Crematorium *BOL* BL1 ... 47 H3
Overdale School *MPL/ROM* SK6 ... 161 G5
Owl Business Centre *OLDE* OL4 ... 92 C1
Oxford Grove Primary School *BOL* BL1 ... 33 F5
OYY Lubavitch Girls School *BRO* M7 ... 101 G1
Palace Cinema *STLY* SK15 ... 120 D3
The Palace Hotel *CMANE* M1 ... 7 F7
Palace Theatre *CMANE* M1 ... 7 F7
Palm Business Centre *CHAD* OL9 ... 74 C5
Paragon Industrial Estate *LIT* OL15 ... 20 C5
Parish Church CE Junior School *OLD* OL1 ... 9 G1
Parker International Estate *DUK* SK16 ... 133 E1
Parkfield Industrial Estate *MDTN* M24 ... 72 B4
Parkfield Primary School *MDTN* M24 ... 72 B3
Parklands High School *WYTH/NTH* M22 ... 180 B1
Park Mill Industrial Estate *MOSL* OL5 ... 94 A3
Park Parade Industrial Estate *AUL* OL6 ... 119 F3
Park Road CP School *SALE* M33 ... 139 G5
Park Road Primary School *ALT* WA14 ... 165 H1
Park School *NTHM/RTH* M23 ... 167 G1
Parkside Industrial Estate *ROY/SHW* OL2 ... 59 F5
Parkview Centre *OLDS* OL8 ... 9 H6
Parkway Business Centre *OLDTF/WHR* M16 ... 142 B2
Parkway Four Industrial Estate *TRPK* M17 ... 125 F1
Parkway Trading Estate *STRET* M32 ... 125 F3
Parochial CE Primary School *AUL* OL6 ... 119 H2
Parrenthorn High School *PWCH* M25 ... 86 B1
Parrs Wood Technology College *DID/WITH* M20 ... 158 A5
Partington CP School *PART* M31 ... 151 E3
Partington Health Centre *PART* M31 ... 151 E3
Partington Shopping Centre *PART* M31 ... 151 E3
Partington Sports Centre *PART* M31 ... 151 E4
Peacefield Primary School *MPL/ROM* SK6 ... 174 D4
Peacock CP School *GTN* M18 ... 130 B2
Pear New Mill Industrial Estate *MPL/ROM* SK6 ... 160 D4
Peel Brow Primary School *RAMS* BL0 ... 17 E2
The Peel Centre *STKP* SK1 ... 13 J2
Peel Hall CP School *LHULT* M38 ... 81 E4
Peel Hall Primary School *WYTH/NTH* M22 ... 181 E1
Peel Health Centre *BURY* BL9 ... 4 E6
Peel Moat Recreation Centre *HTNM* SK4 ... 159 E1
Peerglow Industrial Estate *ALT* WA14 ... 165 H1
Pendleton College *SLFD* M6 ... 112 B2
Pendleton Medical Centre *SLFD* M6 ... 113 F3
Pennant Industrial Estate *OLD* OL1 ... 76 A4
Pennine Business Park *HEY* OL10 ... 55 G1
Peterloo Medical Centre *MDTN* M24 ... 72 B4
Philips High School *WHTF* M45 ... 69 F4
Phoenix Industrial Estate *FAIL* M35 ... 105 F2
Phoenix Medical Centre *STKP* SK1 ... 13 H6
Phoenix Park Industrial Estate *HEY* OL10 ... 56 C1
Piccadilly Trading Estate *CMANE* M1 ... 115 F5
Pictor Special School *SALE* M33 ... 154 A2
Pike Fold Primary School *BKLY* M9 ... 87 H4
Pikes Lane Primary School *BOLS/LL* BL3 ... 2 A7
Pilot Industrial Estate *BOLS/LL* BL3 ... 49 G5
Pilsworth Industrial Estate *BURY* BL9 ... 54 A3
Pinfold J & I School *HYDE* SK14 ... 149 G2
Pinnacle Business Centre *HTNM* SK4 ... 159 H3
Piper Hill School *NTHM/RTH* M23 ... 156 A4
Plantation Industrial Estate *AUL* OL6 ... 119 H3
Plant Hill High School *BKLY* M9 ... 87 H3
Plasman Industrial Centre *BNG/LEV* M19 ... 144 A2
BNG/LEV M19 ... 144 D2
Playhouse Theatre *ORD* M5 ... 113 F3
Plodder Lane Primary School *FWTH* BL4 ... 65 G3
Plymouth Court Business Centre *BRUN/LGST* M13 ... 128 D3
Plymouth Grove Primary School *BRUN/LGST* M13 ... 129 F3
The Point Retail Park *MILN* OL16 ... 10 E6
Poland Industrial Estate *ANC* M4 ... 7 K2
Portland Basin Museum *AULW* OL7 ... 119 F4
Portland Industrial Estate *BURY* BL9 ... 38 D2
Portwood Trading Estate *STKP* SK1 ... 13 K1
Potters House School *BURY* BL9 ... 27 G5
Pownall Green Primary School *BRAM/HZG* SK7 ... 183 H5
Pownall Hall School *WILM/AE* SK9 ... 198 C2
Poynton Clinic *POY/DIS* SK12 ... 195 F3
Poynton High School & Performing Arts College *POY/DIS* SK12 ... 195 F5
Poynton Leisure Centre *POY/DIS* SK12 ... 195 G5
Poynton Sports Club *POY/DIS* SK12 ... 195 F3
Premier Travel Inn *ALT* WA14 ... 153 H5
ALT WA14 ... 165 G3
CCHDY M21 ... 156 C1
CHAD OL9 ... 89 H5
CHD/CHDH SK8 ... 181 H2
CHH M8 ... 87 E3
CMANW M2 ... 6 E6
DTN/ASHW M34 ... 131 H5
HOR/BR BL6 ... 46 A1
HULME M15 ... 128 A1
HYDE SK14 ... 135 F5
MDTN M24 ... 71 G5
MILN OL16 ... 44 D2
OFTN SK2 ... 172 B3
PWCH M25 ... 85 H2
SALE M33 ... 138 D5
SALQ M50 ... 126 D1
STKP SK1 ... 13 H3
SWIN M27 ... 98 D4
SWIN M27 ... 99 H3
TRPK M17 ... 124 C2
WILM/AE SK9 ... 192 A4
WILM/AE SK9 ... 198 B3
WILM/AE SK9 ... 200 D5
WYTH/NTH M22 ... 181 F4
Premier Travel Inn (Manchester Trafford Centre) *URM* M41 ... 124 C1
Prestolee Primary School *RAD* M26 ... 67 E4
Prestwich Arts College *PWCH* M25 ... 86 A2
Prestwich Golf Club *PWCH* M25 ... 100 D1
Prestwich Health Centre *PWCH* M25 ... 85 H2
Prestwich Hospital *PWCH* M25 ... 85 G1
Prestwich Preparatory School *PWCH* M25 ... 86 B2
Priestnall School *HTNM* SK4 ... 158 C3
Prince of Wales Business Park *OLD* OL1 ... 76 B4
Princess on Portland *CMANE* M1 ... 7 F6
The Printworks Leisure Complex *ANC* M4 ... 7 F2
Priorsleigh Medical Centre *POY/DIS* SK12 ... 195 F3
Propps Hall Primary School *FAIL* M35 ... 104 D4
Prospect Vale Primary School *CHD/CHDH* SK8 ... 181 G3
Pump House People's History Museum *CSLFD* M3 ... 6 B4
Python Industrial Estate *LIT* OL15 ... 21 F2
Quality Hotel (Altrincham) *ALT* WA14 ... 177 G2
Quarry Bank Mill & Styal Estate (NT) *WILM/AE* SK9 ... 190 D5
Queen Elizabeth Hall *OLD* OL1 ... 9 F3
Queen Elizabeths School *MDTN* M24 ... 56 C5
Queensbridge Primary School *FWTH* BL4 ... 65 H4
Queensgate Primary School *BRAM/HZG* SK7 ... 193 H3
Queens Road Primary School *CHD/CHDH* SK8 ... 182 D1
Rack House Primary School *NTHM/RTH* M23 ... 155 H5
Radcliffe Borough AFC *RAD* M26 ... 51 H5
Radcliffe CC *RAD* M26 ... 51 H5

Radcliffe Hall CE Methodist Primary School *RAD* M26 52 D5
Radcliffe Hall CE Primary School *RAD* M26 51 H5
Radcliffe Riverside School *RAD* M26 68 A1
Radcliffe Tower (Remains of) *RAD* M26 69 E1
Radclyffe Athletics Centre *CHAD* OL9 74 A5
Radclyffe Primary School *ORD* M5 126 D1
The Radclyffe School (Lower) *CHAD* OL9 90 A1
The Radclyffe School (Upper) *CHAD* OL9 74 A5
Radisson SAS Hotel *MANAIR* M90 180 A5
Raikes Lane Industrial Estate *BOLS/LL* BL3 49 G5
Railway Street Industrial Estate *GTN* M18 130 B2
Ralph Williams Clinic *WHIT* OL12 19 H5
Ramillies Hall School *CHD/CHDH* SK8 183 F2
Ramsbottom Cemetery *RAMS* BL0 16 B4
Ramsbottom Cottage Hospital *RAMS* BL0 16 D3
Ramsbottom Health Centre *RAMS* BL0 16 C2
Ramsbottom Swimming Pool *RAMS* BL0 16 D1
Rassbottom Industrial Estate *STLY* SK15 120 C3
Ravensbury Community School *OP/CLY* M11 116 B3
Ravensfield Industrial Estate *DUK* SK16 119 F4
Ravenside Retail Park *BOLE* BL2 3 F7
Reddish Vale Golf Club *RDSH* SK5 145 G5
Reddish Vale Technology College *RDSH* SK5 145 F4
Red Lane Community School *BOLE* BL2 35 G5
Red Rose Retail Centre *ORD* M5 113 G4
Regal Industrial Estate *WGTN/LGST* M12 129 G1
Regent Cinema *MPL/ROM* SK6 175 E3
Regent Park Golf Course *HOR/BR* BL6 46 C2
Regent Trading Estate *ORD* M5 114 A4
The Regimental Museum of the Lancashire Fusiliers *TOT/BURYW* BL8 37 G5
Reliance Trading Estate *NEWH/MOS* M40 104 B3
Renaissance Hotel *CSLFD* M3 6 D3
Ribble Drive Primary School *WHTF* M45 69 H3
Richmond Medical Centre *AUL* OL6 119 H2
Richmond Park Athletics Stadium *AULW* OL7 118 D1
Richmond Park School *WGTN/LGST* M12 129 F3
Richmond Primary School *CHAD* OL9 8 D4
The Ridge College *MPL/ROM* SK6 174 D4
Ridge Danyers College *CHD/CHDH* SK8 182 B1
Ringway Golf Club *HALE/TIMP* WA15 178 D3
Ringway Primary School *WYTH/NTH* M22 180 C4
Ringway Trading Estate *WYTH/NTH* M22 180 D4
River Meadow Dyeworks *STLY* SK15 121 F2
Riverside Business Park *WILM/AE* SK9 199 E3
Roaches Industrial Estate *MOSL* OL5 94 B3
Rochdale AFC (Spotland Stadium) *ROCH* OL11 29 F3
Rochdale Cemetery *ROCH* OL11 29 E4
Rochdale Crematorium *ROCH* OL11 29 E4
Rochdale Cricket, Lacrosse & Squash Club *ROCH* OL11 29 F4
Rochdale Curtain Theatre *ROCH* OL11 29 H5
Rochdale Golf Club *ROCH* OL11 28 D3
Rochdale Healthcare *WHIT* OL12 20 A3
Rochdale Industrial Centre *ROCH* OL11 29 G5
Rochdale Infirmary *WHIT* OL12 10 C3
Rodney House School *BNG/LEV* M19 143 H3
Roe Cross Industrial Park *HYDE* SK14 135 H3
Roker Industrial Estate *OLD* OL1 76 A4
Rolls Crescent Primary School *HULME* M15 127 H3
Roman Fort *CSLFD* M3 6 B7
Romiley Golf Club *MPL/ROM* SK6 162 C3
Romiley Health Centre *MPL/ROM* SK6 162 B4
Romiley Primary School *MPL/ROM* SK6 162 C4
Roscow Fold Primary School *BOLE* BL2 50 B1
Rosedale Shopping Centre *NEWH/MOS* M40 104 B5
Rosehill Methodist Community Primary School *AUL* OL6 108 A4
Rosehill Methodist Community School *AUL* OL6 108 A5
Rose Hill Primary School *MPL/ROM* SK6 174 D3
Rossendale School *RAMS* BL0 17 G1
Roundthorn Industrial Estate *NTHM/RTH* M23 167 F3
Roundthorn Primary School *OLDE* OL4 92 B2
Roundwood School *WYTH/NTH* M22 168 B2
Roxy Cinema *OLDS* OL8 105 F1
Royal Bolton Hospital *FWTH* BL4 65 E3
Royal Exchange Clinic *CMANW* M2 6 E4
Royal Exchange Shopping Centre *CMANE* M1 6 E3
MILN OL16 10 B6
Royal Exchange Theatre *CSLFD* M3 6 E4
Royal Manchester Childrens Hospital *SWIN* M27 99 G3
Royal Northern College of Music *HULME* M15 128 B2
Royal Oak Industrial Estate *STKP* SK1 13 H6
Royal Oak Primary School *NTHM/RTH* M23 167 H2
Royal Oldham Hospital *OLD* OL1 75 E3
Royal Pennine Trading Estate *ROCH* OL11 42 B3
Royce Trading Estate *TRPK* M17 125 E1
Royle Pennine Trading Estate *ROCH* OL11 42 B3
Royton & Crompton School *ROY/SHW* OL2 59 H5
Royton Medical Centre *ROY/SHW* OL2 59 E5
Royton Public Baths *ROY/SHW* OL2 59 F5
Rugby Road Industrial Estate *WHIT* OL12 10 E3
Rumworth School *BOLS/LL* BL3 47 G4
Rushcroft Primary School *ROY/SHW* OL2 60 A1
Russell Scott Primary School *DTN/ASHW* M34 132 B4
Rycroft Park Sports Club *CHD/CHDH* SK8 182 C3
Rydings Special School *WHIT* OL12 19 G4
Ryecroft Business Park *AULW* OL7 119 E4
The Ryleys School *WILM/AE* SK9 200 C4
Sacred Heart RC Infant School *GTN* M18 130 B4
Sacred Heart RC Junior School *GTN* M18 130 B4
Sacred Heart RC Primary School *MILN* OL16 30 D5
NTHM/RTH M23 167 G3
OLD OL1 76 B2
WHTN BL5 62 A3
Saddleworth Golf Club *UPML* OL3 78 D4
Saddleworth Museum & Art Gallery *UPML* OL3 78 D4
Saddleworth Preparatory School *OLDE* OL4 77 H4
Saddleworth School *UPML* OL3 79 E3
Saddleworth Swimming Pool *UPML* OL3 79 E5
St Agnes CE Primary School *BRUN/LGST* M13 129 G5
OLDE OL4 93 F2
St Aidan & Oswalds RC Primary School *ROY/SHW* OL2 75 E1
St Aidans Catholic Primary School *NTHM/RTH* M23 156 A5
St Alphonsus RC Primary School *OLDTF/WHR* M16 127 F3
St Ambrose Barlow RC High School & Salford College *SWIN* M27 99 E3
St Ambrose College *HALE/TIMP* WA15 178 C3
St Ambrose RC Primary School *CCHDY* M21 156 C2
EDGY/DAV SK3 171 G4
St Andrews CE Primary School *BNG/LEV* M19 144 B3
RAD M26 51 H3
RAMS BL0 16 C3
WALK M28 96 B5
St Andrew's CE Primary School *WHIT* OL12 20 B4
St Andrews CE Primary School *WHTN* BL5 63 H4
St Andrews CE School *ECC* M30 111 F4
St Andrews Medical Centre *ECC* M30 111 F3
St Andrews Methodist Primary School *WALK* M28 81 G4
St Annes CE Lydgate Primary School *OLDE* OL4 93 H1
St Annes CE Primary School *ROY/SHW* OL2 75 F1
SALE M33 154 D2
St Annes Ear Nose & Throat Hospital *ALT* WA14 177 F1
St Annes Primary School *DTN/ASHW* M34 132 D4
St Annes RC High School *HTNM* SK4 159 G2
St Annes RC Primary School *CHH* M8 102 B2
DTN/ASHW M34 131 F1
OLDE OL4 76 B5
St Anns RC Primary School *STRET* M32 140 B1
St Anthonys RC Primary School *WYTH/NTH* M22 180 C3
St Antonys Catholic College *STRET* M32 139 F1
St Augustine of Canterbury RC School *OLDS* OL8 91 E4
St Augustines CE Primary School *NEWH/MOS* M40 103 F5
SWIN M27 99 G2
St Barnabas CE Primary School *OP/CLY* M11 116 C5
St Bartholomews CE Primary School *WHIT* OL12 14 B5
St Bede CE Primary School *BOLS/LL* BL3 64 B2
St Bede's Preparatory School *OLDTF/WHR* M16 127 H5
St Benedict's Catholic Primary School *WILM/AE* SK9 192 B4
St Bernadettes RC Primary School *RDSH* SK5 160 C2
WHTF M45 69 G2
St Bernard RC Primary School *BOLS/LL* BL3 47 F4
St Bernard's RC Primary School *BNG/LEV* M19 143 H5
St Boniface RC Primary School *BRO* M7 101 F4
St Brendan RC Primary School *BOLE* BL2 35 F1
St Brigids RC Primary School *OP/CLY* M11 116 B4
St Catherines Preparatory School *MPL/ROM* SK6 175 G2
St Catherines RC Primary School *DID/WITH* M20 157 H3
St Chads CE Primary School *UPML* OL3 79 F3
St Chads RC Primary School *CHH* M8 102 B5
St Charles RC Primary School *SWIN* M27 98 C2
St Christophers RC Primary School *AUL* OL6 107 H4
MPL/ROM SK6 161 H4
St Chrysostoms CE Primary School *BRUN/LGST* M13 128 D3
St Clares RC Primary School *BKLY* M9 87 H2
St Clement (Egerton) CE Primary School *ORD* M5 113 G5
St Clement's CE Primary School *OP/CLY* M11 130 D1
St Columbas RC Primary School *BOLE* BL2 34 D2
St Cuthberts RC High School *MILN* OL16 43 G5
St Cuthberts RC Primary School *DID/WITH* M20 157 H1
St Damians RC High School *AUL* OL6 107 H3
St Dunstans RC Primary School *NEWH/MOS* M40 103 H2
St Edmunds RC Primary School *LHULT* M38 81 G3
NEWH/MOS M40 103 F4
St Edwards CE Primary School *ROCH* OL11 42 A4
St Edwards RC Primary School *OLDE* OL4 76 D5
RUSH/FAL M14 142 D1
St Elisabeths CE Primary School *RDSH* SK5 145 E3
St Elizabeth RC Primary School *WYTH/NTH* M22 180 D2
St Ethelbert RC Primary School *BOLS/LL* BL3 48 A4
St Gabriels CE Primary School *MDTN* M24 73 F5
St Gabriels Medical Centre *PWCH* M25 86 C5
St Gabriels RC High School *TOT/BURYW* BL8 4 A6
St Gabriels RC Primary School *ROCH* OL11 42 C5
St Georges CE Primary School *HYDE* SK14 147 H2
MOSL OL5 108 C1
OFTN SK2 172 A3
SLFD M6 100 D5
St Georges Craft Centre *BOL* BL1 2 E3
St Georges RC High School *WALK* M28 81 H5
St Gilberts RC Primary School *ECC* M30 110 B3
St Gregory RC Primary School *FWTH* BL4 66 B4
St Helens CE Primary School *GOL/RIS/CUL* WA3 150 A4
St Herberts RC Primary School *CHAD* OL9 74 B5
St Hilarys School *WILM/AE* SK9 200 D4
St Hildas CE Primary School *OLD* OL1 8 E1
PWCH M25 86 B3
St Hugh of Lincoln RC Primary School *STRET* M32 125 E5
St Hughs Catholic Primary School *HALE/TIMP* WA15 166 A2
St Hughs CE Primary School *OLDE* OL4 92 C4
St James Catholic High School *CHD/CHDH* SK8 182 C5
St James Catholic Primary School *HYDE* SK14 149 F1
St James CE Primary School *AUL* OL6 119 H2
FWTH BL4 65 G5
GTN M18 130 C2
RUSH/FAL M14 143 F1
WHIT OL12 19 H2
St James CE Secondary School *FWTH* BL4 65 F4
St James School *HTNM* SK4 159 H3
St James's RC School *SLFD* M6 113 E2
St John Bosco RC Primary School *BKLY* M9 88 C3
St John CE Primary School *FWTH* BL4 66 B4
St John Fisher RC Primary School *DTN/ASHW* M34 147 F2
MDTN M24 73 E1
St John Fisher & St Thomas More RC Primary School *WYTH/NTH* M22 168 C5
St John RC Primary School *ROCH* OL11 30 A5
St Johns Cathedral *CSLFD* M3 114 A3
St Johns CE Infant School *FAIL* M35 105 E2
St Johns CE Junior School *FAIL* M35 105 F3
St Johns CE Primary School *BRUN/LGST* M13 129 F4
HTNM SK4 158 B4
MDTN M24 57 H3
RAD M26 68 B3
SLFD M6 99 H4
STLY SK15 120 B5
St Johns Industrial Estate *OLDE* OL4 92 D1
St Johns Medical Centre *ALT* WA14 177 F1
St Johns Mosley Common CE Primary School *WALK* M28 96 A2
St Johns RC Primary School *CCHDY* M21 141 E2
St Johns with St Marks CE Primary School *BURY* BL9 38 B2
St John the Evangelist RC Primary School *EDGW/EG* BL7 23 E4
St John Vianney School *HTNM* SK4 159 E4
St John Vianney Upper School *OLDTF/WHR* M16 141 F1
St Josephs & St Bedes RC Primary School *BURY* BL9 39 E2
St Josephs RC High School *HEY* OL10 55 H1
St Josephs RC Infant School *RDSH* SK5 145 E3
St Josephs RC Junior School *RDSH* SK5 145 E3
St Josephs RC Primary School *BOL* BL1 33 F4
BRUN/LGST M13 129 F4
HEY OL10 40 D5
LHULT M38 81 F2
MOSL OL5 108 D1
ORD M5 113 G5
RAMS BL0 16 C2
ROY/SHW OL2 59 H4
SALE M33 154 C2
STKP SK1 13 G3
St Josephs the Worker RC Primary School *IRL* M44 122 B5
St Judes CE Primary School *ANC* M4 7 K3
St Kentigerns RC Primary School *RUSH/FAL* M14 142 C2
St Lukes CE Primary School *BRUN/LGST* M13 129 F3
BURY BL9 53 G1
CHAD OL9 74 B5
HEY OL10 41 E3
St Lukes RC Primary School *SLFD* M6 99 H5
St Lukes with All Saints CE Primary School *ORD* M5 112 C4
St Malachys RC Primary School *NEWH/MOS* M40 102 D5
St Margaret Marys RC Primary School *NEWH/MOS* M40 89 G4
St Margarets CE Primary School *HEY* OL10 40 B5
OLDS OL8 90 D5
OLDTF/WHR M16 141 H1
PWCH M25 70 C4
St Margaret Ward RC Primary School *SALE* M33 153 F4
St Maries RC Primary School *BURY* BL9 4 E6
St Marks CE Primary School *MPL/ROM* SK6 161 H2
NEWH/MOS M40 115 G2
WALK M28 97 G4
St Marks RC Primary School *SWIN* M27 84 B5
St Martins CE Primary School *OLDS* OL8 92 A5
St Martins School *SALE* M33 153 H1
St Mary CE Primary School *BOLS/LL* BL3 47 G5
St Mary's Catholic Cemetery *WALK* M28 98 A2
St Marys CE Primary School *DROY* M43 117 H4
NEWH/MOS M40 104 B1
OLDTF/WHR M16 127 H4
PWCH M25 85 H2
RDSH SK5 145 G5
ROCH OL11 43 F2
ROY/SHW OL2 59 G1
St Mary's CE Primary School *IRL* M44 150 B1
SALE M33 154 A2
St Marys CE Primary School *TOT/BURYW* BL8 25 E1
UPML OL3 95 F3
URM M41 124 A4
St Mary's Hospital *BRUN/LGST* M13 128 D4
St Marys Medical Centre *OLD* OL1 9 H3
St Marys RC Primary School *BNG/LEV* M19 144 A3
DTN/ASHW M34 132 B5
DUK SK16 133 H2
FAIL M35 104 D4
HTNM SK4 12 E1
MDTN M24 72 B2
MPL/ROM SK6 175 F2
RAD M26 52 B5
SWIN M27 99 E2
St Mary's RC Primary School *ECC* M30 111 F4
LIT OL15 20 D2
St Matthew CE Primary School *BOL* BL1 2 D1
BOLS/LL BL3 66 D1
St Matthews CE Infant School *OLD* OL1 74 A2
St Matthews CE Primary School *EDGY/DAV* SK3 12 E6
STRET M32 140 A3
St Matthews RC High School *NEWH/MOS* M40 89 F5
St Maxentius CE Primary School *BOLE* BL2 35 E1
St Michael CE Primary School *BOLS/LL* BL3 65 G1
St Michaels CE Aided Primary School *URM* M41 137 H2
St Michaels CE Primary School *HEY* OL10 40 D2
MDTN M24 88 D2
St Michaels RC Primary School *WHTF* M45 70 A3
St Monicas RC High School *PWCH* M25 86 B4
St Monicas RC Primary School *URM* M41 137 F2
St Osmunds & St Andrews Primary School *BOLE* BL2 50 A2
St Patrick's Catholic High School *ECC* M30 110 C3
St Patricks RC Primary School *ANC* M4 115 F2
CHAD OL9 8 D5
St Patricks VA RC Primary School *WHIT* OL12 10 E2
St Paul CE Primary School *BOL* BL1 34 A3
St Pauls Catholic High School *NTHM/RTH* M23 168 A5
St Pauls Catholic Primary School *POY/DIS* SK12 195 F5
St Paul's Cemetery *BOL* BL1 33 F4
St Pauls CE Primary School *BRO* M7 101 E2
BURY BL9 5 J1
DID/WITH M20 142 D5
ORD M5 113 G4
RDSH SK5 160 C2
ROY/SHW OL2 74 D1
STLY SK15 121 F3
WALK M28 82 B4
St Pauls Peel CE Primary School *LHULT* M38 81 E2
St Pauls RC Primary School *HYDE* SK14 134 A4
St Pauls Trading Estate *STLY* SK15 121 F3
St Peter CE Primary School *FWTH* BL4 66 A5
St Peter & St John Primary School *CSLFD* M3 6 A2
St Peter & St Paul RC Primary School *BOLS/LL* BL3 48 D4
St Peters Catholic Primary School *BRAM/HZG* SK7 185 E3
NTHM/RTH M23 179 H1
STLY SK15 121 E4
St Peters CE Primary School *AULW* OL7 119 F4
BURY BL9 53 F3
SWIN M27 98 D2
St Peters RC High School Upper School *DROY* M43 117 F5
St Peter's RC Primary School *MDTN* M24 72 D5
St Peters Smithills Dean CE Primary School *BOL* BL1 33 E2
St Peters VC CE Primary School *MILN* OL16 43 G1
St Philips Catholic Primary School *OFTN* SK2 173 F3
St Philips CE Primary School *HULME* M15 128 A2
St Philips RC Primary School *PWCH* M25 101 F1
St Philips School *CSLFD* M3 114 A4
St Raphaels Catholic Primary School *STLY* SK15 109 F5
St Richards RC Primary School *WGTN/LGST* M12 130 A5
St Saviour Primary School Ringley *RAD* M26 67 F5
St Sebastians RC Primary School *SLFD* M6 100 D5
St Simons Catholic Primary School *BRAM/HZG* SK7 185 F1
St Stephen & All Martyrs CE Primary School *BOLE* BL2 49 H4
St Stephens & All Martyrs Infant School *OLD* OL1 9 H1
St Stephens CE Primary School *DTN/ASHW* M34 118 D5
FWTH BL4 82 D1
OFTN SK2 173 G5
TOT/BURYW BL8 37 G5
St Stephens RC School *DROY* M43 117 H3
St Teresa RC Primary School *BOLS/LL* BL3 66 D1
St Teresas RC Primary School *IRL* M44 136 A3
OLDTF/WHR M16 126 D5
St Thomas Aquinas RC High School *CCHDY* M21 141 G4
St Thomas CE Primary School *BOL* BL1 33 G4
BURY BL9 5 J6
HTNM SK4 144 C5
MILN OL16 45 E2
OLDS OL8 8 E6
STKP SK1 13 H5
WHTN BL5 62 C3
St Thomas Leesfield CE Primary School *OLDE* OL4 92 D2
St Thomas Moorside CE (VA) Primary School *OLD* OL1 60 D5

St Thomas More RC College DTN/ASHW M34 146 D1
St Thomas More RC Primary School MDTN M24 88 D2
St Thomas of Canterbury RC Primary School BOL BL1 47 H1
BRO M7 101 H4
St Thomas Primary School CHH M8 102 D2
St Thomas's Hospital EDGY/DAV SK3 13 F7
St Vincent RC Infant School HALE/TIMP WA15 165 H4
St Vincents RC Primary School WHIT OL12 28 D2
St Wilfrids CE Primary School NEWH/MOS M40 104 C5
WYTH/NTH M22 168 D1
St Wilfrids RC Primary School HULME M15 127 H2
St William RC Primary School BOLS/LL BL3 64 D1
St Willibrords RC Primary School OP/CLY M11 116 D2
St Winifreds RC Primary School HTNM SK4 158 D4
SS Simon & Jude CE Primary School BOLS/LL BL3 65 E1
Sale CC SALE M33 155 E1
Sale Golf Club SALE M33 155 G1
Sale Grammar School SALE M33 154 D3
Sale Leisure Centre SALE M33 154 D1
Sale Water Park SALE M33 140 C5
Salford City Academy ECC M30 110 A4
Salford City Reds RLFC (The Willows) ORD M5 112 C3
Salford College ECC M30 110 B3
SALQ M50 126 D1
SLFD M6 113 G1
SWIN M27 83 F5
WALK M28 97 E1
Salford County Court ORD M5 113 F4
Salford Medical Centre SLFD M6 112 D2
Salford Museum & Art Gallery ORD M5 113 H3
Salford Shopping City SLFD M6 113 F2
Salford University Business Park SLFD M6 113 G1
Samuel Laycock Special School AUL OL6 120 C1
Sandbrook Community Primary School ROCH OL11 42 D3
Sandilands Primary School NTHM/RTH M23 166 D1
Saviour CE Primary School NEWH/MOS M40 102 D5
Savoy Cinema HTNM SK4 158 D3
Saxon Hall Leisure Centre MILN OL16 11 J5
School Street Industrial Estate BRAM/HZG SK7 185 F2
Seaford Industrial Estate SLFD M6 113 G1
Sedgley Park Community Primary School PWCH M25 86 B5
Sedgley Park RUFC WHTF M45 85 E1
Sedgley Park Trading Estate PWCH M25 101 E1
Seedley Primary School SLFD M6 112 D3
Severnside Trading Estate TRPK M17 125 G3
Seymour Park Primary School OLDTF/WHR M16 127 E4
Seymour Road Primary School OP/CLY M11 117 E4
Shandon Clinic (Europe) HULME M15 128 B3
Sharples Primary School BOL BL1 34 B1
Shawclough Community Primary School WHIT OL12 18 D5
Shawclough Trading Estate WHIT OL12 18 C5
Shawgrove School DID/WITH M20 142 B5
Shaw Heath Health Centre EDGY/DAV SK3 13 F7
Shay Lane Medical Centre HALE/TIMP WA15 178 D3
Shepherd Cross Industrial Estate BOL BL1 33 F4
Shepley North Industrial Estate DTN/ASHW M34 132 D1
Shepley South Industrial Estate DTN/ASHW M34 132 D2
Sherborne Trading Estate CHH M8 102 A5
Sherwood Business Park ROCH OL11 42 C4
Shiv Lodge Medical Centre BRUN/LGST M13 129 G5
Showcase Cinemas Belle Vue GTN M18 130 A3
Siddal Moor Sports College HEY OL10 56 A2
Skylink Walkway MANAIR M90 179 H5
Slough Industrial Estate ORD M5 113 H5
Smallbridge Health Centre WHIT OL12 19 H5
Smallbridge Industrial Park MILN OL16 11 J1
Smedleylane Junior School CHH M8 102 C4
Smithills Hall Museum BOL BL1 33 E2
Smithills School BOL BL1 33 E3
Smithy Bridge Primary School LIT OL15 20 C5
Snipe Retail Park AULW OL7 118 C5
South Chadderton School CHAD OL9 90 A5
Southern Cross School CCHDY M21 156 B1
South Failsworth Primary School FAIL M35 104 D5
Southfield Industrial Estate TRPK M17 125 H3
Southgate Industrial Estate HEY OL10 41 G5
Southlink Business Park OLDE OL4 9 K4
South Manchester High School WYTH/NTH M22 180 C1
Southmoor Business Park NTHM/RTH M23 167 F2
Southmoor Industrial Estate NTHM/RTH M23 167 F2
South Oldham Business Park CHAD OL9 74 D4
South Reddish Medical Centre RDSH SK5 160 A2
South Trafford College ALT WA14 165 G1
South West Manchester CC CCHDY M21 141 G2
Spa Road Industrial Estate BOL BL1 2 B5
Spindle Point Primary School FWTH BL4 83 E2
The Spindles Shopping Centre OLD OL1 9 F4
Sport City OP/CLY M11 116 A3
Sports Injury Centre MDTN M24 72 D5
Spotland Bridge Industrial Centre ROCH OL11 29 F3
Spotland Primary School WHIT OL12 29 G2
Spring Brook School CHAD OL9 74 A5
Springfield Business Centre CSLFD M3 6 D1
Springfield Hotel MPL/ROM SK6 175 E2
Springfield House Medical Centre OLD OL1 76 B4
Springfield Industrial Estate FAIL M35 104 D2
Springfield Primary School SALE M33 154 C2
Springhead Community Infant & First School OLDE OL4 93 E1
Springhill High School MILN OL16 43 H1
Springside CP School BURY BL9 27 F4
Springwood Primary School MPL/ROM SK6 162 D3
SWIN M27 99 F3
Spurley Hey High School BNG/LEV M19 144 B1
Stag Industrial Estate ALT WA14 165 E3
Stakehill Industrial Estate MDTN M24 57 G5
Stalybridge Celtic AFC STLY SK15 121 F5
Stalybridge CC DUK SK16 120 B5
Stalybridge Millbrook CC STLY SK15 121 G1
Stalybridge St Pauls CC DUK SK16 134 A1
Stalyhill Infant School STLY SK15 135 F1
Stalyhill Junior School STLY SK15 135 E1
Staly Industrial Estate STLY SK15 121 E3
Stamford Golf Club STLY SK15 109 F3
Stamford High School AUL OL6 120 B1
Stamford Park Junior School HALE/TIMP WA15 177 H1
Stanley Green Industrial Estate CHD/CHDH SK8 192 B1
WILM/AE SK9 192 B3
Stanley Green Retail Park CHD/CHDH SK8 192 C1
Stanley Grove Primary School WGTN/LGST M12 129 G4
Stanley Road Primary School CHAD OL9 90 C3
Stanneylands Hotel WILM/AE SK9 191 G5
Star Industrial Estate OLDS OL8 9 G6
Station Approach Business Estate ROCH OL11 30 A5
Staveleigh Medical Centre STLY SK15 120 D3
Stella Maris School HTNM SK4 158 B4
Stepping Hill Hospital OFTN SK2 172 C5
Stockport Air Raid Shelter STKP SK1 13 F3
Stockport Art Gallery EDGY/DAV SK3 13 F5
Stockport Bus Station HTNM SK4 12 E4
Stockport CC EDGY/DAV SK3 172 A3
Stockport College HTNM SK4 144 B5
Stockport College of Further & Higher Education EDGY/DAV SK3 13 F6
Stockport County Court STKP SK1 13 F4
Stockport County FC & Sale Sharks RUFC (Edgeley Park) EDGY/DAV SK3 171 G2
Stockport Crematorium STKP SK1 172 B2
Stockport Golf Club OFTN SK2 174 A4
Stockport Grammar School OFTN SK2 172 C4
Stockport Mega Bowl STKP SK1 13 F5
Stockport RUFC BRAM/HZG SK7 184 A4
Stockport School OFTN SK2 172 C4
Stockport Trading Estate HTNM SK4 171 E1
Stone Hill Industrial Estate FWTH BL4 65 H5
Stoneleigh Primary School OLD OL1 76 A2
The Strand Medical Centre ROCH OL11 43 E4
Stretford Grammar School STRET M32 140 C2
Stretford High School Community Language College STRET M32 126 B4
Stretford Leisure Centre STRET M32 126 C4
Stretford Memorial Hospital OLDTF/WHR M16 127 E5
Student Union Building CMANE M1 128 B1
Styal Country Park (NT) WILM/AE SK9 190 D4
Styal Golf Club WILM/AE SK9 191 F2
Styal Primary School WILM/AE SK9 190 D3
Sudden Health Centre ROCH OL11 42 B2
Sudell Street Trading Estate ANC M4 7 J1
Sugden Sports Centre CMANE M1 128 B1
Summerseat Methodist Primary School BURY BL9 27 E1
Summerville Primary School SLFD M6 100 A5
Sunning Hill Primary School BOLS/LL BL3 48 C5
Sunnybank Clinic BURY BL9 69 H1
Sunny Bank Primary School BURY BL9 69 H1
Sunset Business Centre FWTH BL4 83 F2
Swinton Cemetery SWIN M27 83 H5
The Swinton County High School SWIN M27 98 D1
Swinton Industrial Estate SWIN M27 99 F2
Swinton Leisure Centre SWIN M27 99 E2
Swinton Park Golf Club SWIN M27 99 F4
Talmud Torah Chinuch Norim School BRO M7 101 G3
Tameside Business Development Centre DTN/ASHW M34 132 A5
Tameside Business Park DUK SK16 133 E1
Tameside College AUL OL6 120 A2
HYDE SK14 147 H4
Tameside County Court AUL OL6 119 H3
Tameside General Hospital STLY SK15 120 C1
Tame Valley Primary School RDSH SK5 146 A4
Tandle Hill Country Park ROY/SHW OL2 58 B3
Tashbar School BRO M7 101 H1
Tavistock Industrial Estate OP/CLY M11 130 C2
Taylors Sports Club ECC M30 111 F4
Temple Primary School CHH M8 102 C4
Ten Acres Sports Complex NEWH/MOS M40 103 H5
Thames Industrial Estate WGTN/LGST M12 129 E1
Thames Trading Centre IRL M44 136 B4
Thistle Hotel CMANE M1 7 G5
WILM/AE SK9 192 A2
Thomasson Memorial Special School BOL BL1 48 A2
Thorn Grove Primary School CHD/CHDH SK8 192 D1
Thornham CC MDTN M24 57 G2
Thornham St James CE Primary School ROY/SHW OL2 59 E1
Thornleigh Salesian College BOL BL1 33 G2
Thorp Primary School ROY/SHW OL2 58 D4
Times Retail Park HEY OL10 40 D4
Timperley Health Centre HALE/TIMP WA15 166 B2
Tithe Barn Primary School HTNM SK4 158 D3
Tonacliffe Primary School WHIT OL12 18 B2
Tonge Bridge Industrial Estate BOLE BL2 3 J3
Tonge CC BOLE BL2 34 D3
Tonge Fold Health Centre BOLE BL2 49 H2
Tonge Moor Health Centre BOLE BL2 34 D5
Tonge Moor Primary School BOLE BL2 3 K1
Tootal Drive CP School ORD M5 112 B3
Top o' th' Brow Primary School BOLE BL2 35 F4
Torkington Primary School BRAM/HZG SK7 185 H2
Tottington Health Centre TOT/BURYW BL8 25 H4
Tottington High School TOT/BURYW BL8 26 A5
Tottington Primary School TOT/BURYW BL8 37 E1
Towers Business Park DID/WITH M20 157 G5
Townfield Industrial Estate OLDE OL4 76 A5
Towngate Business Centre LHULT M38 80 D2
Town Hall & Albert Halls BOL BL1 2 E5
Town Square Shopping Centre OLD OL1 9 G3
Trafalgar Business Park CHH M8 114 B1
Trafford Athletics Track CCHDY M21 140 D2
Trafford Centre TRPK M17 124 C2
Trafford Centre Leisure Complex TRPK M17 124 A2
Trafford FC URM M41 138 A2
Trafford General Hospital URM M41 123 H5
Trafford Healthcare SALE M33 155 E3
Trafford Retail Park URM M41 124 B3
Trafford Water Sports Centre SALE M33 140 C5
Trans Pennine Trading Estate ROCH OL11 42 C3
Travelodge ANC M4 7 H3
BURY BL9 54 A2
CHAD OL9 89 H3
CSLFD M3 6 D3
DID/WITH M20 158 A5
HEY OL10 55 G5
Trent Industrial Estate ROY/SHW OL2 60 A1
The Triangle ANC M4 6 E3
Trinity CE High School HULME M15 128 B2
Trinity Retail Park BOLE BL2 3 H7
BOLE BL2 49 F4
Trinity School STLY SK15 120 C4
Tudor Industrial Estate DUK SK16 132 D2
Tulip Inn Hotel URM M41 124 B2
Tulketh Street Industrial Estate BKLY M9 103 G2
Turton Golf Club EDGW/EG BL7 23 F1
Turton High School EDGW/EG BL7 23 G4
Turton Leisure Centre EDGW/EG BL7 23 F1
Two Trees High School DTN/ASHW M34 147 F2
Tyntesfield CP School SALE M33 153 H5
UCI Cinema TRPK M17 124 C2
Union Mill Industrial Estate MOSL OL5 94 A4
United Trading Estate OLDTF/WHR M16 126 C3
University Dental Hospital of Manchester HULME M15 128 B2
University of Bolton BOLS/LL BL3 2 C7
University of Bolton Chadwick Campus BOLE BL2 3 J6
University of Manchester ANC M4 7 J1
BRUN/LGST M13 128 B3
CMANE M1 7 H7
CMANE M1 7 J5
CMANE M1 128 B1
ECC M30 123 E2
RUSH/FAL M14 128 D5
RUSH/FAL M14 143 F1
University of Salford CSLFD M3 114 A3
ECC M30 111 F3
ORD M5 113 H3
SLFD M6 113 G1
Unsworth Medical Centre BURY BL9 70 B1
Unsworth Primary School BURY BL9 69 H2
Urbis CSLFD M3 6 E2
Urmston Grammar School URM M41 124 B5
Urmston J & I School URM M41 138 B1
Urmston Leisure Centre URM M41 138 B1
Urmston Town FC URM M41 137 H2
Vaishali Medical Centre CCHDY M21 141 F2
Vale Park Industrial Estate CHH M8 102 D3
The Valley Community School BOL BL1 34 A4
The Valley Leisure Centre BOL BL1 34 B3
Valley Special School BRAM/HZG SK7 193 F2
Varley Street Clinic NEWH/MOS M40 115 G1
Varna Street Primary School OP/CLY M11 130 C2
Vaughan Street Industrial Estate WGTN/LGST M12 129 G1
Vauxhall Industrial Estate RDSH SK5 145 E5
RDSH SK5 160 A2
Vernon Industrial Estate STKP SK1 13 H2
STKP SK1 13 K1
The Vernon Infant School POY/DIS SK12 195 F4
The Vernon Junior School POY/DIS SK12 195 F4
Vernon Park Museum STKP SK1 160 C4
Vernon Park Primary School STKP SK1 13 J3
Vernon Road Medical Centre TOT/BURYW BL8 26 B2
Victoria Avenue Primary School BKLY M9 88 A2
Victoria Industrial Estate ANC M4 115 G4
Victoria Medical Centre URM M41 138 D1
Victoria Park Infant School STRET M32 140 B1
Victoria Park Junior School STRET M32 140 B1
Victoria Trading Estate CHAD OL9 90 C4
Victory Trading Estate BOLS/LL BL3 49 F4
The Village Hotel & Leisure Club HYDE SK14 133 F2
Village Medical Centre LIT OL15 21 E3
VIP Centre Industrial Estate OLD OL1 76 B3
Vue Cinema BURY BL9 54 A3
SALQ M50 126 C1
Wadsworth Industrial Park BOLS/LL BL3 48 D5
Walkden High School WALK M28 82 B5
Walmsley CE Primary School EDGW/EG BL7 22 D2
Walshaw Sports Club TOT/BURYW BL8 37 E1
Walton Park Leisure Centre SALE M33 154 B4
Wardle High School WHIT OL12 20 A3
Wardley CE Primary School SWIN M27 83 H5
Wardley Industrial Estate WALK M28 98 B1
Warren Wood Primary School OFTN SK2 173 H4
Warth Park Industrial Estate BURY BL9 52 D2
Washacre Primary School WHTN BL5 62 A5
Washway Road Medical Centre SALE M33 154 B2
Waterfold Business Park BURY BL9 5 K6
The Watergate Clinic MILN OL16 10 D6
Waterloo Industrial Park BOL BL1 3 G2
STKP SK1 13 H4
Waterloo Primary School AULW OL7 106 C5
The Water Place BOL BL1 2 E6
Waters Edge Business Park ORD M5 127 E2
Watersheddings Primary School OLD OL1 76 B3
The Waterside Hotel CHD/CHDH SK8 170 A5
Waterside Industrial Park BOLS/LL BL3 65 H1
Watersports Centre SALQ M50 126 C1
Waybridge Industrial Estate SALQ M50 112 C5
Weaste Trading Estate ORD M5 112 C3
Welfare Clinic MDTN M24 72 A2
Welkin Road Industrial Estate STKP SK1 160 C3
Wellacre Technology College URM M41 137 F1
Wellfield Infant School SALE M33 139 F5
Wellfield Junior School SALE M33 139 F5
Wellfield Medical Centre CHH M8 102 A2
Well Green Primary School HALE/TIMP WA15 178 C2
Wellington Road Industrial Estate AUL OL6 119 F2
Wellington School HALE/TIMP WA15 166 A3
Wentworth High School ECC M30 111 G1
Werneth Cricket Bowling & Tennis Club OLDS OL8 8 E7
Werneth Golf Club OLDS OL8 106 B1
Werneth J & I School OLDS OL8 91 E3
Werneth Low Country Park HYDE SK14 148 D4
Werneth Low Golf Club HYDE SK14 148 D5
Werneth School MPL/ROM SK6 161 G4
Wesley Methodist Primary School RAD M26 51 H4
Westbrook Trading Estate TRPK M17 126 A1
Westbury Street Industrial Estate HYDE SK14 133 F3
West Croft Industrial Estate MDTN M24 71 H5
West End Medical Centre AULW OL7 119 E4
West End Primary School AULW OL7 119 E3
West End Trading Estate SWIN M27 99 E1
Westernlea Clinic DTN/ASHW M34 132 B3
West Gorton Medical Centre WGTN/LGST M12 129 G2
West Hill School STLY SK15 120 C3
Westhoughton High School & Specialist Technology College WHTN BL5 62 A3
Westhoughton Primary School WHTN BL5 62 A3
Westinghouse Industrial Estate TRPK M17 126 A3
Westmorland Primary School RDSH SK5 146 A5
West One Retail Park SALQ M50 111 H4
Westpoint Medical Centre BNG/LEV M19 143 H2
Westwood Business Centre CHAD OL9 8 C4
Westwood Industrial Estate CHAD OL9 8 B3
Westwood Park Primary School ECC M30 110 C2
Westwood Primary School CHAD OL9 8 C3
Westwood Trading Estate MPL/ROM SK6 174 C4
Whalley Range FC CCHDY M21 141 H2
Whalley Range High School OLDTF/WHR M16 142 B3
Wharfside Business Centre TRPK M17 126 C2

Wharton Primary School
LHULT M38 .... 80 D1
Wheatfield Industrial Estate
ROY/SHW OL2 .... 75 E1
Wheatsheaf Industrial Estate
SWIN M27 .... 99 G1
Wheatsheaf Shopping Centre
MILN OL16 .... 10 D5
White City Retail Park
OLDTF/WHR M16 .... 126 D3
Whitefield Community
Primary School *WHTF* M45 .... 69 H4
Whitefield Golf Club
WHTF M45 .... 69 F5
Whitefield Medical Centre
WHTF M45 .... 69 F4
Whitegate End Primary School
CHAD OL9 .... 89 H4
Whitehill Industrial Estate
HTNM SK4 .... 159 H1
Whitehill Primary School
HTNM SK4 .... 159 H2
White Swan Industrial Estate
OLD OL1 .... 76 B4
Whitley Road Medical Centre
NEWH/MOS M40 .... 115 F1
Whittaker Golf Club *LIT* OL15 .... 21 G4
Whittaker Moss Primary
School *ROCH* OL11 .... 28 A2
The Whitworth Art Gallery
HULME M15 .... 128 C4
Whitworth Community High
School *WHIT* OL12 .... 14 B5

Whitworth Football & CC
WHIT OL12 .... 14 B4
Whitworth Park School
RUSH/FAL M14 .... 128 B4
Whitworth Swimming Pool
WHIT OL12 .... 14 C3
Wilbraham Primary School
RUSH/FAL M14 .... 142 C2
Wild Bank Community School
STLY SK15 .... 121 G3
Willan Industrial Estate
ORD M5 .... 113 E4
William Andrews Swimming
Baths *DUK* SK16 .... 133 G1
William Hulmes
Preparatory School
OLDTF/WHR M16 .... 142 B2
William Wroe Municipal Golf
Course *URM* M41 .... 138 A1
Willow Bank Hotel
RUSH/FAL M14 .... 143 E3
Willow Grove Cemetery
RDSH SK5 .... 160 B1
The Willows Primary School
HALE/TIMP WA15 .... 166 A3
WYTH/NTH M22 .... 180 B2
Wilmslow Albion FC
WILM/AE SK9 .... 191 F4
Wilmslow Grange Community
Primary School
WILM/AE SK9 .... 192 A2
Wilmslow Health Centre
WILM/AE SK9 .... 198 D4

Wilmslow High School
WILM/AE SK9 .... 199 E4
Wilmslow Leisure Centre
WILM/AE SK9 .... 199 E4
Wilmslow Preparatory School
WILM/AE SK9 .... 199 E3
Wilmslow RFC
WILM/AE SK9 .... 198 C1
Wilmslow Road Medical
Centre *RUSH/FAL* M14 ...... 128 D5
WILM/AE SK9 .... 192 A3
Windlehurst School
MPL/ROM SK6 .... 187 E2
Windmill Lane Industrial
Estate *DTN/ASHW* M34 .... 146 A1
Withington Bowling Club
RUSH/FAL M14 .... 143 E4
Withington Girls School
RUSH/FAL M14 .... 142 D3
Withington Golf Club
DID/WITH M20 .... 157 E4
Withington Hospital
DID/WITH M20 .... 142 B5
Withington Swimming Baths
DID/WITH M20 .... 142 D5
Withins High School *BOLE* BL2 ... 35 F4
Wolfenden Primary School
BOL BL1 .... 33 H4
Woodbank CC *TOT/BURYW* BL8 .. 38 A2
Woodbank Park Athletics
Track *OFTN* SK2 .... 160 D5
Woodbank Primary School
TOT/BURYW BL8 .... 38 A2

Woodend Mills Industrial
Estate *OLDE* OL4 .... 93 E2
Woodfields Retail Park
BURY BL9 .... 4 D3
Woodford CC
BRAM/HZG SK7 .... 193 H5
Woodhey High School
RAMS BL0 .... 16 B5
Woodheys Primary School
SALE M33 .... 153 H4
Woodhouse Primary School
URM M41 .... 123 H4
Woodhouses Voluntary
Controlled Primary School
FAIL M35 .... 105 H4
Woodlands Hospital
WALK M28 .... 81 E3
Woodley Health Centre
MPL/ROM SK6 .... 161 H1
Woodley Primary School
MPL/ROM SK6 .... 162 A1
Woodley Sports Centre
MPL/ROM SK6 .... 147 E5
Woodsend Primary School
URM M41 .... 122 D5
Woolfold Industrial Estate
TOT/BURYW BL8 .... 37 G2
Woolworths Sports Club
ROCH OL11 .... 42 B3
Worsley Business Park
TYLD M29 .... 96 A2
Worsley Golf Club
ECC M30 .... 110 D1

Worsley Road Industrial
Estate *FWTH* BL4 .... 81 H1
Worsley Trading Estate
LHULT M38 .... 80 D2
Worthington Primary School
SALE M33 .... 155 G2
Worth Primary School
POY/DIS SK12 .... 195 G4
Wright Robinson Sports
College *GTN* M18 .... 131 E2
The Wycliffe Hotel
EDGY/DAV SK3 .... 12 A7
Wythenshawe Hall Country
Park *NTHM/RTH* M23 ...... 168 A1
Wythenshawe Hospital
NTHM/RTH M23 .... 167 G5
Wythenshawe Park Track
NTHM/RTH M23 .... 167 H1
Xaverian Sixth Form College
RUSH/FAL M14 .... 128 D5
Yeargate Industrial Estate
BURY BL9 .... 39 G4
Yeshivah Ohr Torah School
BRO M7 .... 101 G2
Yesoiday Hatorah School
PWCH M25 .... 86 A5
Yew Tree Community School
CHAD OL9 .... 90 A3
Yew Tree Primary Community
School *DUK* SK16 .... 133 G1
YMCA Leisure Centre
CSLFD M3 .... 6 B6

Acknowledgements

Schools address data provided by Education Direct

Petrol station information supplied by Johnsons

Manchester transport information provided by GMPTE © 2007

Garden centre information provided by:

Garden Centre Association 🌼 Britains best garden centres

Wyevale Garden Centres 🌷

The statement on the front cover of this atlas is sourced, selected and quoted from a reader comment and feedback form received in 2004